ACS INTERNATI CRICKET YEAR BOOK 2011

Edited by Philip Bailey

First published in Great Britain by
Association of Cricket Statisticians and Historians
Cardiff CF11 9XR

British Library Cataloguing-in-Publication Data.
A catalogue record for this book is available from the British Library.

ISBN: 978 1 908165 03 9
Typeset by Limlow Books

INTRODUCTION

This book lists every cricketer who appeared in a First-Class, List A or Twenty20 match in the 2010 English season or in the 2009/10 season in other countries, thus the book includes every current major cricketer in the world.

The following tours are listed as season 2010 outside England - Sri Lanka A in Australia, South Africa A in Bangladesh, India in Sri Lanka, Pakistan A in Sri Lanka, South Africa A in Sri Lanka, Zimbabwe in West Indies, South Africa in West Indies. These tours took place at the same time as the English season and are listed as an 'off season'. Figures are combined with 2009/10 where appropriate.

In all countries players are listed alphabetically with all the teams that they played for in the period under review in brackets after their name, together with details of any tours abroad.

Performances in events that were spread over more than one country are split into the appropriate countries.

The lines of statistics after the players biographical details are as follows:

Test	Appearances in Test Cricket in that country in 2009/10 and 2010
FC	Appearances in First-Class Cricket in that country in 2009/10 and 2010 (including Tests)
Int	Appearances in One-Day Internationals in that country in 2009/10 and 2010
Lim	Appearances in List A Limited-overs matches in that country in 2009/10 and 2010 (including ODIs)
I20T	Appearances in Twenty20 Internationals in that country in 2009/10 and 2010
20T	Appearances in Twenty20 matches in that country 2009/10 and 2010 (including I20T matches)

These are followed by similar lines showing the full career record in the appropriate type of cricket, with the season of debut. If a player made his debut and only appeared in a particular match type in his home country in 2009/10 or 2010, then no career line is printed. In limited overs and Twenty20 matches the 5i column gives instances of exactly 4 wickets in an innings, and the 10m column gives instances of 5 or more wickets in an innings.

There is also a section giving career records for those players who took part in Women's Test matches (WT), Women's One-Day International matches (WInt) and Women's Twenty20 International matches (W20T) during 2009/10 and 2010.

LIST OF MATCHES INCLUDED

First-class matches used to compile the figures for this book are those noted in the ACS first-class match lists, published in five volumes and amended and updated periodically. Limited Overs matches used to compile the figures for this book are those included in List A. The ICC have adopted List A into their Classification of Official Cricket from 2006 but the ACS continues to assist on List A status - for details see http://acscricket.com/ListA/Description.html. The Australia v ICC World XI matches are included as Test and ODIs following the ICC ruling.

SOURCE

The statistics in this book were derived from the CricketArchive database. Scorecards of all matches and more player statistics can be seen on the website at www.cricketarchive.com. Full scores of all matches outside England also appear together with details of points tables in the ACS Overseas First-Class Annual 2010 which can be obtained from ACS Sales, price £35.

ACKNOWLEDGEMENTS

Charlie Wat (Australia), Sohel Awrangzeb (Bangladesh), Dinar Gupte, I.U.Khan, Sudhir Vaidya (India), Francis Payne, Ian Smith (New Zealand), Ghulam Mustafa Khan (Pakistan), Andrew Samson (South Africa), Chaminda de Silva (Sri Lanka), John Ward (Zimbabwe), Robin Abrahams, John Bryant, Marion Collin, Peter Griffiths and Harriet Monkhouse.

CONTENTS

TEST MATCHES

Test Match Table of Results 2009/10 and 2010

	P	*W*	*L*	*D*	*T*	*% wins*
Australia	10	8	1	1	0	80.00
England	12	8	2	2	0	66.67
India	10	6	2	2	0	60.00
South Africa	9	4	2	3	0	44.44
New Zealand	6	2	3	1	0	33.33
Pakistan	12	3	8	1	0	25.00
Sri Lanka	6	1	3	2	0	16.67
Bangladesh	7	0	7	0	0	0.00
West Indies	6	0	4	2	0	0.00

Test Match Table of Results 1876/77 to 2010

	P	*W*	*L*	*D*	*T*	*% wins*
Australia	723	340	187	194	2	47.03
England	903	318	260	325	0	35.22
South Africa	353	124	123	106	0	35.13
West Indies	465	152	154	158	1	32.69
Sri Lanka	195	61	70	64	0	31.28
Pakistan	352	106	99	147	0	30.11
India	440	105	138	196	1	23.86
New Zealand	359	68	145	146	0	18.94
Zimbabwe	83	8	49	26	0	9.64
Bangladesh	68	3	59	6	0	4.41
ICC World XI	1	0	1	0	0	0.00

ONE DAY INTERNATIONAL MATCHES

One Day International Table of Results 2009/10 and 2010

	P	*W*	*L*	*T*	*NR*	*% wins*
Australia	32	23	7	0	2	76.67
Ireland	14	10	4	0	0	71.43
England	24	16	8	0	0	66.67
South Africa	16	10	6	0	0	62.50
Sri Lanka	27	15	10	0	2	60.00
Afghanistan	10	6	4	0	0	60.00
New Zealand	20	11	8	0	1	57.89
India	35	17	16	0	2	51.52
Scotland	10	5	5	0	0	50.00
Netherlands	12	5	7	0	0	41.67
Zimbabwe	22	9	13	0	0	40.91
Canada	11	4	7	0	0	36.36
West Indies	20	6	13	0	1	31.58
Pakistan	20	6	14	0	0	30.00
Bangladesh	24	6	18	0	0	25.00
Kenya	13	2	11	0	0	15.38

The percentage calculations exclude no result games

One Day International Table of Results 1970/71 to 2010

	P	*W*	*L*	*T*	*NR*	*% wins*
Asian Cricket Council XI	7	4	2	0	1	66.67
Australia	747	463	252	8	24	64.04
South Africa	439	273	149	5	12	63.93
Afghanistan	13	8	5	0	0	61.54
West Indies	637	335	274	5	23	54.56
Pakistan	723	385	317	6	15	54.38
Ireland	55	27	24	1	3	51.92
India	753	365	351	3	34	50.77
England	542	263	256	5	18	50.19
Sri Lanka	612	286	299	3	24	48.64

New Zealand	588	256	296	5	31	45.96
Netherlands	57	23	32	0	2	41.82
Scotland	50	15	32	0	3	31.91
Kenya	133	36	92	0	5	28.13
Canada	60	16	43	0	1	27.12
Zimbabwe	377	98	265	5	9	26.63
Bangladesh	230	57	171	0	2	25.00
ICC World XI	4	1	3	0	0	25.00
African XI	6	1	4	0	1	20.00
Bermuda	35	7	28	0	0	20.00
United Arab Emirates	11	1	10	0	0	9.09
East Africa	3	0	3	0	0	0.00
Hong Kong	4	0	4	0	0	0.00
Namibia	6	0	6	0	0	0.00
United States of America	2	0	2	0	0	0.00

The percentage calculations exclude no result games

INTERNATIONAL TWENTY20 MATCHES

Twenty20 International Table of Results 2009/10 and 2010

	P	*W*	*L*	*NR*	*% wins*
England	13	9	3	1	75.00
Kenya	4	3	1	0	75.00
Netherlands	4	3	1	0	75.00
Australia	14	10	4	0	71.43
India	9	5	4	0	55.56
South Africa	9	5	4	0	55.56
Afghanistan	8	4	4	0	50.00
New Zealand	12	6	6	0	50.00
Sri Lanka	10	5	5	0	50.00
Pakistan	15	7	8	0	46.67
Ireland	8	3	4	1	42.86
West Indies	10	3	7	0	30.00
Canada	4	1	3	0	25.00
Zimbabwe	5	1	4	0	20.00
Bangladesh	3	0	3	0	0.00
Scotland	4	0	4	0	0.00

Win and loss totals include tied matches decided by a bowl-out or super over
The percentage calculations exclude no result games

Twenty20 International Table of Results 2004/05 to 2010

	P	*W*	*L*	*NR*	*% wins*
Netherlands	10	6	3	1	66.67
Pakistan	40	26	14	0	65.00
South Africa	33	21	12	0	63.64
India	27	15	11	1	57.69
Sri Lanka	33	19	14	0	57.58
Australia	38	21	16	1	56.76
England	34	17	15	2	53.13
Afghanistan	8	4	4	0	50.00
New Zealand	40	19	21	0	47.50
Ireland	17	7	8	2	46.67
West Indies	28	12	16	0	42.86
Kenya	12	4	8	0	33.33
Zimbabwe	12	4	8	0	33.33
Canada	11	3	8	0	27.27
Bangladesh	16	3	13	0	18.75
Scotland	12	2	9	1	18.18
Bermuda	3	0	3	0	0.00

Win and loss totals include tied matches decided by a bowl-out or super over
The percentage calculations exclude no result games

WOMEN'S TEST MATCHES

Women's Test Match Table of Results 1934/35 to 2010

	P	*W*	*L*	*D*	*T*	*% wins*
Sri Lanka Women	1	1	0	0	0	100.00
Ireland Women	1	1	0	0	0	100.00
Australia Women	68	18	9	41	0	26.47
England Women	88	19	11	58	0	21.59
India Women	33	3	5	25	0	9.09
South Africa Women	11	1	4	6	0	9.09
New Zealand Women	45	2	10	33	0	4.44
West Indies Women	11	0	3	8	0	0.00
Netherlands Women	1	0	1	0	0	0.00
Pakistan Women	3	0	2	1	0	0.00

No Women's Test matches were played in 2009/10 or 2010

WOMEN'S ONE DAY INTERNATIONAL MATCHES

Women's One Day International Table of Results 2009/10 and 2010

	P	*W*	*L*	*T*	*NR*	*% wins*
Australia Women	8	8	0	0	0	100.00
India Women	5	3	2	0	0	60.00
England Women	14	7	7	0	0	50.00
South Africa Women	4	2	1	1	0	50.00
Sri Lanka Women	2	1	1	0	0	50.00
West Indies Women	9	4	4	1	0	44.44
Ireland Women	3	1	2	0	0	33.33
New Zealand Women	14	3	11	0	0	21.43
Netherlands Women	1	0	1	0	0	0.00

The percentage calculations exclude no result games

Women's One Day International Table of Results 1973 to 2010

	P	*W*	*L*	*T*	*NR*	*% wins*
Australia Women	240	185	49	1	5	78.72
England Women	249	137	102	2	8	56.85
India Women	178	93	80	1	4	53.45
New Zealand Women	246	127	112	2	5	52.70
Sri Lanka Women	76	38	37	0	1	50.67
South Africa Women	78	33	40	1	4	44.59
West Indies Women	74	31	40	1	2	43.06
Trinidad and Tobago Women	6	2	4	0	0	33.33
Ireland Women	107	34	70	0	3	32.69
Netherlands Women	88	18	70	0	0	20.45
Jamaica Women	5	1	4	0	0	20.00
Pakistan Women	71	13	57	0	1	18.57
Denmark Women	33	6	27	0	0	18.18
International XI Women	18	3	14	0	1	17.65
Young England Women	6	1	5	0	0	16.67
Scotland Women	8	1	7	0	0	12.50
Japan Women	5	0	5	0	0	0.00

The percentage calculations exclude no result games

WOMEN'S INTERNATIONAL TWENTY20 MATCHES

Twenty20 International Table of Results 2009/10 and 2010

	P	*W*	*L*	*NR*	*% wins*
New Zealand Women	13	11	2	0	84.62
West Indies Women	13	10	3	0	76.92
Australia Women	10	5	5	0	50.00
India Women	7	3	4	0	42.86
England Women	12	5	7	0	41.67
Sri Lanka Women	6	1	5	0	16.67
Pakistan Women	3	0	3	0	0.00
South Africa Women	6	0	6	0	0.00

Win and loss totals include tied matches decided by a bowl-out or super over

Twenty20 International Table of Results 2004 to 2010

	P	*W*	*L*	*NR*	*% wins*
West Indies Women	19	14	5	0	73.68
New Zealand Women	30	20	10	0	66.67
Australia Women	25	16	9	0	64.00
England Women	29	16	13	0	55.17
India Women	13	6	7	0	46.15
Ireland Women	6	2	4	0	33.33
Pakistan Women	9	2	7	0	22.22
Sri Lanka Women	9	2	7	0	22.22
South Africa Women	15	1	14	0	6.67
Netherlands Women	3	0	3	0	0.00

Win and loss totals include tied matches decided by a bowl-out or super over
The percentage calculations exclude no result games

NOTABLE PERFORMANCES IN FIRST-CLASS MATCHES 2009/10 and 2010

Test matches are shown in bold

DOUBLE-HUNDREDS

390	S.C.Cook	Lions v Warriors at East London
319	R.R.Rossouw	Eagles v Titans at Centurion
312	Sunny Singh	Haryana v Madhya Pradesh at Indore
309*	R.G.Sharma	Mumbai v Gujarat at Mumbai
302*	Rafatullah Mohmand	WAPDA v Sui Southern Gas at Sheikhupura
293	**V.Sehwag**	**India v Sri Lanka (3rd Test) at Mumbai**
289	Aamer Sajjad	WAPDA v Sui Southern Gas at Sheikhupura
284	Misbah-ul-Haq	Sui Northern Gas v Lahore Shalimar at Lahore
275	**D.P.M.D.Jayawardene**	**Sri Lanka v India (1st Test) at Ahmedabad**
265*	A.M.Rahane	Mumbai v Hyderabad at Hyderabad
261	R.W.T.Key	Kent v Durham at Canterbury
259	A.M.Nayar	West Zone v North Zone at Rajkot
257	A.Mukund	Tamil Nadu v Hyderabad at Hyderabad
254*	Khalid Latif	Karachi Blues v Peshawar at Rawalpindi
253*	**H.M.Amla**	**South Africa v India (1st Test) at Nagpur**
251*	D.J.Hussey	Nottinghamshire v Yorkshire at Leeds
250	S.Badrinath	Tamil Nadu v Mumbai at Mumbai
248	M.R.Ramprakash	Surrey v Northamptonshire at The Oval
245*	P.J.Ingram	Central Districts v Wellington at Wellington
244	L.D.Chandimal	Sri Lanka A v South Africa A at Colombo
241	Khurram Manzoor	PIA v KRL at Karachi
237*	S.M.Ervine	Hampshire v Somerset at Southampton
230*	Naved Ashraf	Rawalpindi v Hyderabad at Islamabad
228*	J.A.Rudolph	Yorkshire v Durham at Leeds
228*	M.E.Trescothick	Somerset v Essex at Colchester
227*	S.L.Stewart	Canterbury v Central Districts at New Plymouth
226	**I.J.L.Trott**	**England v Bangladesh (1st Test) at Lord's**
225	E.J.M.Cowan	Tasmania v South Australia at Hobart
224	S.Dhawan	Delhi v Baroda at Vadodara
223	M.R.Ramprakash	Surrey v Middlesex at The Oval
222*	Rameez Alam	Multan v Peshawar at Multan
221	Zeeshan Butt	Faisalabad v Abbottabad at Sargodha
220*	L.J.Woodcock	Wellington v Central Districts at Wellington
219	W.G.R.K.Alwis	Saracens v Colombo at Colombo
219	**K.C.Sangakkara**	**Sri Lanka v India (2nd Test) at Colombo**
217	B.R.M.Taylor	Mid West Rhinos v Southern Rocks at Masvingo
215	V.Sibanda	Mid West Rhinos v Mountaineers at Mutare
214*	Mohammad Shahzad	Afghanistan v Canada at Sharjah
214	T.T.Samaraweera	Kandurata v Basnahira North at Colombo
212*	R.N.ten Doeschate	Netherlands v Kenya at Nairobi
211	N.A.N.N.Perera	Burgher v Seeduwa Raddoluwa at Colombo
210*	Y.K.Pathan	West Zone v South Zone at Hyderabad
209*	R.S.Dravid	Karnataka v Uttar Pradesh at Bangalore
209	**R.T.Ponting**	**Australia v Pakistan (3rd Test) at Hobart**
209	V.Sibanda	Zimbabwe XI v Kenya at Kwekwe
208*	C.A.Pujara	India A v West Indies A at Croydon
208	S.M.Ervine	Southern Rocks v Mid West Rhinos at Masvingo
207*	M.Klinger	South Australia v Victoria at Melbourne
206*	J.W.A.Taylor	Leicestershire v Middlesex at Leicester
206	E.Steenkamp	Namibia v Bermuda at Windhoek
205	D.M.G.S.Dissanayake	Bloomfield v Badureliya at Colombo
205	Nazimuddin	Chittagong v Dhaka at Bogra
204*	C.A.Pujara	Saurashtra v Maharashtra at Rajkot
204	S.D.Robson	Middlesex v Oxford MCCU at Oxford
203	**S.R.Tendulkar**	**India v Sri Lanka (2nd Test) at Colombo**
202*	Faisal Khan	Sialkot v Peshawar at Sialkot
202*	M.Kaif	Central Zone v East Zone at Amritsar
202	Ashar Zaidi	Islamabad v Sialkot at Sialkot
201	G.J.Hopkins	Auckland v Central Districts at Auckland
200*	Aamer Sajjad	The Rest v Karachi Blues at Hyderabad
200*	Adnan Raees	Abbottabad v Peshawar at Abbottabad
200	C.J.L.Rogers	Derbyshire v Surrey at The Oval

HUNDRED ON FIRST-CLASS DEBUT

108	Asif Ahmed	Barisal v Chittagong at Khulna
	(he also scored a century in his second first-class match)	
109	C.A.H.Barron	KwaZulu-Natal Inland v Griqualand West at Pietermaritzburg
116*	V.Bhalla	Punjab v Hyderabad at Mohali
101*	U.J.Birkenstock	Boland v Griqualand West at Paarl
119	D.J.Broom	Otago v Northern Districts at Whangarei
112*	D.G.Brownlie	Canterbury v Northern Districts at Rangiora
103	D.Hewitt	Northerns v Gauteng at Pretoria
102	M.D.U.S.Jayasundera	Sri Lanka Navy v Sebastianites at Moratuwa
105	J.Mawudzi	Mountaineers v Mid West Rhinos at Mutare
130 and 100*	Noor Ali Zadran	Afghanistan v Zimbabwe XI at Mutare
106	S.C.Prasad	Jharkhand v Goa at Dhanbad
142*	S.J.Rhodes	Wellington v Otago at Queenstown
135	Sharjeel Khan	Hyderabad v Islamabad at Islamabad
185*	A.S.Sharma	Oxford University v Cambridge University at Oxford

HUNDRED IN EACH INNINGS OF A MATCH

114	**123***	**H.M.Amla**	**South Africa v India (2nd Test) at Kolkata**
142	102	R.S.Bopara	Essex v Yorkshire at Chelmsford
162	107	M.A.Carberry	Hampshire v Durham at Basingstoke
208	160	S.M.Ervine	Southern Rocks v Mid West Rhinos at Masvingo
183	150	K.D.Karthik	South Zone v West Zone at Hyderabad
109	105	W.L.Madsen	Derbyshire v Surrey at Chesterfield
104	134*	D.K.H.Mitchell	Worcestershire v Gloucestershire at Cheltenham
130	100*	Noor Ali Zadran	Afghanistan v Zimbabwe XI at Mutare
104	180	M.H.W.Papps	Canterbury v Auckland at Auckland
108	210*	Y.K.Pathan	West Zone v South Zone at Hyderabad
112	135	J.J.Pienaar	Easterns v South Western Districts at Oudtshoorn
143	101*	A.M.Rahane	Mumbai v Haryana at Rohtak
223	103*	M.R.Ramprakash	Surrey v Middlesex at The Oval
200	140*	C.J.L.Rogers	Derbyshire v Surrey at The Oval
209	116*	V.Sibanda	Zimbabwe XI v Kenya at Kwekwe
107	101*	V.Sibanda	Mid West Rhinos v Southern Rocks at Masvingo
172	120	T.Taibu	Zimbabwe XI v Afghanistan at Mutare

FOUR HUNDREDS IN SUCCESSIVE INNINGS

V.Sibanda	209 and 116* Zimbabwe XI v Kenya at Kwekwe
	107 and 101* Mid West Rhinos v Southern Rocks at Masvingo

THREE HUNDREDS IN SUCCESSIVE INNINGS

H.M.Amla (South Africa)	
	253* v India (1st Test) at Nagpur
	114 and 123* v India (2nd Test) at Kolkata
D.S.Jadhav (Assam)	114 v Tripura at Guwahati
	111 v Vidarbha at Guwahati
	165* v Andhra at Guwahati
D.K.H.Mitchell (Worcestershire)	
	104 and 134* v Gloucestershire at Cheltenham
	165* v Glamorgan at Colwyn Bay
A.N.Petersen (Lions)	129 and 105* v Titans at Johannesburg 2008/09
	128 v Eagles at Kimberley
J.J.Pienaar (Easterns)	154 v Namibia at Windhoek
	112 and 135 v South Western Districts at Oudtshoorn
K.C.Sangakkara (Sri Lanka)	
	137 v India (3rd Test) at Mumbai
	103 v India (1st Test) at Galle
	219 v India (2nd Test) at Colombo

CARRYING BAT THROUGH COMPLETED INNINGS

63*	Bismillah Khan	Quetta (106) v Multan at Okara
117*	S.C.Cook	Gauteng (208) v Boland at Johannesburg
117*	M.J.Di Venuto	Durham (213) v Yorkshire at Chester-le-Street
165*	**C.H.Gayle**	**West Indies (317) v Australia (2nd Test) at Adelaide**
54*	M.V.Hodge	Leeward Islands (201) v Trinidad and Tobago at St Philip
90*	Imran Ali	Faisalabad (188) v Multan at Faisalabad
117*	**Imran Farhat**	**Pakistan (223) v New Zealand (3rd Test) at Napier**
165*	D.S.Jadhav	Assam (327) v Andhra at Guwahati
254*	Khalid Latif	Karachi Blues (458) v Peshawar at Rawalpindi
122*	Saeed Anwar	KRL (241) v Habib Bank at Karachi
98*	Shan Masood	Habib Bank (260) v Sui Northern Gas at Karachi

150*	Taposh Ghosh	Khulna (295) v Rajshahi at Chittagong
100*	Taufeeq Umar	Habib Bank (195) v Karachi Blues at Karachi
82*	I.J.Westwood	Warwickshire (197) v Lancashire at Manchester
114*	Zohaib Khan	ZTBL (270) v Sui Northern Gas at Gujranwala

HUNDRED BEFORE LUNCH

104*	M.H.W.Papps	Canterbury v Auckland at Auckland (1st day)
71* to 177	S.P.D.Smith	New South Wales v Tasmania at Hobart (2nd day)

300 RUNS IN A DAY

319	R.R.Rossouw	Eagles v Titans at Centurion

MOST SIXES IN AN INNINGS

10	Y.K.Pathan (210*)	West Zone v South Zone at Hyderabad
10	A.D.Russell (108*)	Jamaica v Ireland at Spanish Town
9	D.N.A.Athulathmudali (153)	Chilaw Marians v Colts at Colombo
9	K.P.S.P.Karunanayake (172)	Sinhalese v Badureliya at Colombo
8	T.P.Attanayake (97)	Badureliya v Colts at Colombo
8	S.I.de Saram (119*)	Ragama v Saracens at Colombo
8	E.M.G.D.Y.Munaweera (153)	Basnahira North v Ruhuna at Galle
8	N.L.T.C.Perera (113*)	Colts v Moors at Colombo
8	R.R.Rossouw (319)	Eagles v Titans at Centurion
7	H.M.C.M.Bandara (108)	Basnahira South v Ruhuna at Colombo
7	Humayun Farhat (80)	Habib Bank v Sui Northern Gas at Karachi
7	J.R.G.Namal (154)	Burgher v Moratuwa at Colombo
7	U.M.A.Prasad (72)	Badureliya v Bloomfield at Colombo
7	N.J.Reardon (147)	Queensland v West Indians at Brisbane
7	**V.Sehwag (293)**	**India v Sri Lanka (3rd Test) at Mumbai**
7	Sunny Singh (312)	Haryana v Madhya Pradesh at Indore
7	R.N.ten Doeschate (212*)	Netherlands v Kenya at Nairobi
7	M.E.Trescothick (228*)	Somerset v Essex at Colchester
7	K.Weeraratne (78)	Ragama v Saracens at Colombo
7	L.J.Wright (94*)	Sussex v Worcestershire at Worcester

MOST RUNS IN BOUNDARIES

	4s	*6s*		
236	47	8	R.R.Rossouw (319)	Eagles v Titans at Centurion
222	54	1	S.C.Cook (390)	Lions v Warriors at East London
218	44	7	Sunny Singh (312)	Haryana v Madhya Pradesh at Indore
202	**40**	**7**	**V.Sehwag (293)**	**India v Sri Lanka (3rd Test) at Mumbai**

LONG INNINGS

mins		
838	S.C.Cook (390)	Lions v Warriors at East London
712	Khurram Manzoor (241)	PIA v KRL at Karachi
675	**H.M.Amla (253*)**	**South Africa v India (1st Test) at Nagpur**
671	S.Badrinath (250)	Tamil Nadu v Mumbai at Mumbai
647	Rafatullah Mohmand (302*)	WAPDA v Sui Southern Gas at Sheikhupura
638	S.Dhawan (224)	Delhi v Baroda at Vadodara
635	J.H.K.Adams (194)	Hampshire v Lancashire at Liverpool
610	**D.P.M.D.Jayawardene (275)**	**Sri Lanka v India (1st Test) at Ahmedabad**

AN HOUR WITHOUT SCORING

73 min	**B.P.Nash**	**West Indies v Australia (3rd Test) at Perth (on 48*)**

UNUSUAL DISMISSALS

Obstructing the Field		
	Riaz Kail (30)	Abbottabad v Quetta at Abbottabad
Retired Out	Fawad Alam (68)	Pakistanis v Kent at Canterbury
Retired Out	J.M.How (62)	Central Districts v Northern Districts at Napier
Retired Out	Imran Farhat (40)	Pakistanis v Tasmania at Hobart
Retired Out	R.W.T.Key (140)	Kent v Loughborough MCCU at Canterbury
Stumped by a Substitute		
	T.E.Linley (16)	Surrey v Gloucestershire at Bristol

HIGHEST WICKET PARTNERSHIPS

First Wicket

428	P.J.Ingram & J.M.How	Central Districts v Wellington at Wellington
374	R.van Schoor & E.Steenkamp	Namibia v Bermuda at Windhoek
294	E.C.Joyce & C.D.Nash	Sussex v Derbyshire at Horsham
273	C.J.L.Rogers & W.L.Madsen	Derbyshire v Northamptonshire at Northampton
259	D.A.King & S.S.Agarwal	Oxford University v Cambridge University at Oxford
244*	R.Dewan & A.Rawat	Haryana v Madhya Pradesh at Indore
236	Nasir Jamshed & Umar Amin	National Bank v Sui Southern Gas at Faisalabad
233	**G.Gambhir & V.Sehwag**	**India v Sri Lanka (2nd Test) at Kanpur**
228	C.D.Nash & M.A.Thornely	Sussex v Northamptonshire at Hove
227	A.Mukund & M.Vijay	Rest of India v Mumbai at Nagpur
221	**M.Vijay & V.Sehwag**	**India v Sri Lanka (3rd Test) at Mumbai**
216	R.van Schoor & G.J.Rudolph	Namibia v Easterns at Windhoek
207	W.U.Tharanga & K.Y.de Silva	Nondescripts v Colombo at Colombo
206	C.R.Pathak & S.D.Jogiyani	Saurashtra v Bengal at Kolkata
205	W.I.Jefferson, J.K.H.Naik & J.J.Cobb	Leicestershire v Cambridge MCCU at Cambridge
	W.I.Jefferson retired hurt after 151 had been added	
204	A.Mukund & S.Dhawan	India A v Yorkshire at Leeds
201	D.N.A.Athulathmudali & M.L.Udawatte	Chilaw Marians v Colts at Colombo
201	S.E.Avontuur & N.Bredenkamp	South Western Districts v North West at Potchefstroom
200	B.A.Parchment & D.P.Hyatt	Jamaica v Trinidad and Tobago at St Andrew's

Second Wicket

580	Rafatullah Mohmand & Aamer Sajjad	WAPDA v Sui Southern Gas at Sheikhupura
480	D.Elgar & R.R.Rossouw	Eagles v Titans at Centurion
369	F.D.M.Karunaratne & L.D.Chandimal	Sri Lanka A v South Africa A at Colombo
314	M.A.Carberry & M.J.Lumb	Hampshire v Durham at Basingstoke
284	K.B.Pawan & G.Satish	Karnataka v Maharashtra at Poona
272	R.W.T. Key & G.O.Jones	Kent v Loughborough MCCU at Canterbury
271	A.G.Puttick & S.van Zyl	Cape Cobras v Dolphins at Cape Town
258	S.O.Kukreja & A.M.Rahane	Mumbai v Hyderabad at Hyderabad
251	N.R.Parlane & C.J.Merchant	Wellington v Otago at Wellington
247	C.D.Cumming & D.J.Broom	Otago v Northern Districts at Whangarei
246	R.R.Hendricks & R.R.Rossouw	Eagles v Warriors at Bloemfontein
245	K.Y.de Silva & D.H.S.Pradeep	Nondescripts v Moors at Colombo
243	N.J.Kruger & W.J.Townsend	Queensland v West Indians at Brisbane
237	**V.Sehwag & R.S.Dravid**	**India v Sri Lanka (3rd Test) at Mumbai**
235	I.Chikunya & B.R.M.Taylor	Mid West Rhinos v Southern Rocks at Masvingo
230	**G.C.Smith & H.M.Amla**	**South Africa v England (3rd Test) at Cape Town**
221	M.A.Carberry & N.D.McKenzie	Hampshire v Oxford MCCU at Oxford
220	A.P.Agathagelou & M.Akoojee	North West v Free State at Bloemfontein
219	W.T.S.Porterfield & C.D.J.Dent	Gloucestershire v Northamptonshire at Northampton
213	P.A.Jaques & Usman Khawaja	New South Wales v Victoria at Newcastle
212	T.G.McIntosh & R.A.Jones	Auckland v Wellington at Auckland
211	J.A.Rudolph & A.McGrath	Yorkshire v Nottinghamshire at Leeds
210	E.M.G.D.Y.Munaweera & S.C.Serasinghe	Basnahira North v Ruhuna at Galle
209	**A.N.Petersen & H.M.Amla**	**South Africa v India (2nd Test) at Kolkata**
203	D.O.Obuya & C.O.Obuya	Kenya v Netherlands at Nairobi
200	**Tamim Iqbal & Junaid Siddique**	**Bangladesh v India (2nd Test) at Mirpur**
200	B.M.Shafayat & M.A.Wagh	Nottinghamshire v Durham MCCU at Durham

Third Wicket

340	**H.M.Amla & J.H.Kallis**	**South Africa v India (1st Test) at Nagpur**
306	S.B.Haig & N.T.Broom	Otago v Central Districts at Napier
306	F.D.M.Karunaratne & J.K.Silva	Basnahira North v Wayamba at Moratuwa
284*	Faisal Khan & Mohammad Ayub	Sialkot v Peshawar at Sialkot
275	**R.S.Dravid, S.R.Tendulkar & M.Vijay**	**India v Bangladesh (2nd Test) at Mirpur**
	R.S.Dravid retired hurt after 222 had been added	
265	P.J.Hughes & P.J.Forrest	New South Wales v South Australia at Adelaide
264*	D.Elgar & H.H.Dippenaar	Eagles v Lions at Kimberley
259	A.Mukund & S.Badrinath	Tamil Nadu v Hyderabad at Hyderabad
252	Asad Shafiq & Wajihuddin	Karachi Blues v Hyderabad at Mirpur Khas
249	K.B.Pawan & A.A.Verma	Karnataka v Bengal at Mysore
249	**V.Sehwag & S.R.Tendulkar**	**India v South Africa (2nd Test) at Kolkata**
236*	A.M.Rahane & W.Jaffer	Mumbai v Hyderabad at Hyderabad
235	H.Masakadza & T.Taibu	Mountaineers v Mid West Rhinos at Kwekwe
229	V.A.Saxena & N.S.Doru	Rajasthan v Jharkhand at Dhanbad
226	Asad Shafiq & Sheharyar Ghani	Karachi Blues v Islamabad at Islamabad
225	Ali Asad & Khalid Latif	Karachi Blues v Quetta at Karachi

225	L.J.Evans & U.Afzaal	Surrey v Bangladeshis at The Oval
225	A.D.S.Fletcher & D.S.Smith	West Indies A v India A at Croydon
223	V.S.Solanki & M.M.Ali	Worcestershire v Surrey at Croydon
217	Jahurul Islam & Farhad Hossain	Rajshahi v Dhaka at Chittagong
215	J.G.Cameron & M.M.Ali	Worcestershire v Sussex at Worcester
214	C.C.Williams & S.A.Gaekwad	Baroda v Maharashtra at Poona
212	A.J.Finch & D.J.Hussey	Victoria v Tasmania at Melbourne
212	M.J.Di Venuto & D.M.Benkenstein	Durham v Essex at Chester-le-Street
208	H.D.R.L.Thirimanne & L.J.P.Gunaratne	Basnahira South v Ruhuna at Colombo
207	P.Bisht & V.Kohli	Delhi v Uttar Pradesh at Lucknow
206	A.McGrath & J.A.Rudolph	Yorkshire v Durham at Leeds
204	F.Kasteni & B.R.M.Taylor	Mid West Rhinos v Mashonaland Eagles at Kwekwe
202	Zohaib Khan & Shahid Yousuf	ZTBL v Karachi Whites at Karachi
201	A.S.Das & M.K.Tiwary	Bengal v Saurashtra at Kolkata
200	D.J.Harris & C.B.Bailey	South Australia v Victoria at Adelaide

Fourth Wicket

360*	J.W.A.Taylor & A.B.McDonald	Leicestershire v Middlesex at Leicester
352	**R.T.Ponting & M.J.Clarke**	**Australia v Pakistan (3rd Test) at Hobart**
342	S.H.Marathe & R.G.Sharma	Mumbai v Gujarat at Mumbai
280	Rameez Alam & Naved Yasin	Multan v Peshawar at Multan
278	J.H.K.Adams & J.M.Vince	Hampshire v Yorkshire at Scarborough
273	R.S.Dravid & M.K.Pandey	Karnataka v Uttar Pradesh at Meerut
272*	C.A.Pujara & R.A.Jadeja	Saurashtra v Maharashtra at Rajkot
266	P.A.Patel & B.D.Thaker	Gujarat v Mumbai at Mumbai
266	O.A.Shah & N.J.Dexter	Middlesex v Leicestershire at Leicester
263	Imran Javed & Naumanullah	National Bank v KRL at Rawalpindi
256	M.Manhas & R.Bhatia	Delhi v Maharashtra at Delhi
254	M.A.Carberry & N.D.McKenzie	Hampshire v Kent at Southampton
253	A.V.Suppiah & J.C.Hildreth	Somerset v Kent at Canterbury
241*	R.A.Jones & R.A.Young	Auckland v Canterbury at Auckland
240	E.J.M.Cowan & D.J.Marsh	Tasmania v South Australia at Hobart
226	M.L.Price & K.R.Smuts	Eastern Province v Easterns at Port Elizabeth
220	**S.Chanderpaul & B.P.Nash**	**West Indies v South Africa (2nd Test) at Basseterre**
209	G.Satish & M.K.Pandey	Karnataka v Mumbai at Mysore
209*	J.K.Silva & S.H.T.Kandamby	Sri Lanka A v Pakistan A at Galle
202*	B.M.A.J.Mendis & G.A.S.K.Gangodawila	Kandurata v Wayamba at Kandy

Fifth Wicket

479	Misbah-ul-Haq & Usman Arshad	Sui Northern Gas v Lahore Shalimar at Lahore
339	J.C.Mickleburgh & J.S.Foster	Essex v Durham at Chester-le-Street
302	Zeeshan Butt & Ijaz Ahmed	Faisalabad v Abbottabad at Sargodha
274	T.T.Samaraweera & B.M.A.J.Mendis	Kandurata v Basnahira North at Colombo
270*	T.Bavuma & S.Burger	Gauteng v Easterns at Benoni
256	**S.R.Tendulkar & S.K.Raina**	**India v Sri Lanka (2nd Test) at Colombo**
253	**M.J.Clarke & M.J.North**	**Australia v New Zealand (1st Test) at Wellington**
249	S.C.Ganguly & W.P.Saha	Bengal v Delhi at Kolkata
247	K.D.Karthik & C.M.Gautam	South Zone v West Zone at Hyderabad
236*	S.L.Stewart & D.G.Brownlie	Canterbury v Northern Districts at Rangiora
227	D.P.Conway & S.Burger	Gauteng v Northerns at Pretoria
221	S.C.Serasinghe & B.M.A.J.Mendis	Tamil Union v Sri Lanka Army at Colombo
219	**P.D.Collingwood & E.J.G.Morgan**	**England v Pakistan (1st Test) at Nottingham**
218	M.R.Ramprakash & G.C.Wilson	Surrey v Leicestershire at Leicester
211	G.A.Lamb & E.Chigumbura	Mashonaland Eagles v Mid West Rhinos at Harare
210	J.C.Hildreth & J.C.Buttler	Somerset v Nottinghamshire at Taunton
208	Aamer Sajjad & Bilal Khilji	WAPDA v National Bank at Lahore
206	G.J.Hopkins & A.K.Kitchen	Auckland v Central Districts at Auckland

Sixth Wicket

379*	S.L.Stewart & C.F.K.van Wyk	Canterbury v Central Districts at New Plymouth
365	S.C.Cook & T.L.Tsolekile	Lions v Warriors at East London
351	**D.P.M.D.Jayawardene & H.A.P.W.Jayawardene**	**Sri Lanka v India (1st Test) at Ahmedabad**
339	**M.J.Guptill & B.B.McCullum**	**New Zealand v Bangladesh (Only Test) at Hamilton**
329	S.Badrinath & C.Ganapathy	Tamil Nadu v Mumbai at Mumbai
283	H.G.Kuhn & T.L.Tsolekile	South Africa A v Bangladesh A at Mirpur
270	D.I.Stevens & J.C.Tredwell	Kent v Nottinghamshire at Tunbridge Wells
270	A.Rawat, S.Rana & J.Sharma *A.Rawat retired hurt after 234 had been added*	Haryana v Tripura at Rohtak
258	Nazimuddin & Arman Hossain	Chittagong v Dhaka at Bogra
253	Bilal Khilji & Ali Azmat	WAPDA v Customs at Islamabad

241	Ashar Zaidi & Naeem Anjum	Islamabad v Sialkot at Sialkot
234	W.Bossenger & C.Pietersen	Griqualand West v Border at East London
226	D.Bundela & M.D.Mishra	Madhya Pradesh v Jammu and Kashmir at Indore
224	**R.S.Dravid & M.S.Dhoni**	**India v Sri Lanka (1st Test) at Ahmedabad**
224	Arun Lal & Shoaib Khan	Quetta v Karachi Blues at Karachi
222	Kamran Younis & Ahmed Butt	Sialkot v Quetta at Sialkot
221	A.R.White & J.F.Mooney	Ireland v Netherlands at Dublin
219	Usman Salahuddin & Adnan Akmal	Sui Northern Gas v Customs at Islamabad
213	C.Pietersen & A.P.McLaren	Griqualand West v Western Province at Kimberley
208	M.Y.Vallie & V.D.Philander	Western Province v North West at Potchefstroom
204	B.J.Pelser & L.J.Kgamadi	North West v Griqualand West at Potchefstroom
202	N.J.Dexter & G.K.Berg	Middlesex v Derbyshire at Lord's
201	Sajjad Ahmed & Azam Jan	Peshawar v Faisalabad at Sargodha

Seventh Wicket

259*	**V.V.S.Laxman & M.S.Dhoni**	**India v South Africa (2nd Test) at Kolkata**
249	B.J.Pelser & C.H.Morris	North West v Namibia at Potchefstroom
237	A.D.Brown & C.M.W.Read	Nottinghamshire v Durham at Nottingham
232	W.W.Hinds & C.S.Baugh	Jamaica v Guyana at St Philip
225	M.W.Goodwin & R.S.C.Martin-Jenkins	Sussex v Derbyshire at Derby
193	A.K.Perera & W.C.A.Ganegama	Nondescripts v Sri Lanka Army at Colombo
183	M.N.W.Spriegel & S.C.Meaker	Surrey v Bangladeshis at The Oval
175	W.G.R.K.Alwis & M.D.Randika	Saracens v Colombo at Colombo
174	P.Mustard & S.G.Borthwick	Durham v Nottinghamshire at Chester-le-Street
172	L.Ronchi & A.A.Noffke	Western Australia v Tasmania at Hobart
164	**B.B.McCullum & D.L.Vettori**	**New Zealand v Pakistan (1st Test) at Dunedin**
162	Afsar Nawaz & Babar Rehman	Karachi Whites v National Bank at Karachi
154	M.R.Ramprakash & G.J.Batty	Surrey v Northamptonshire at The Oval
153	J.Allenby & R.D.B.Croft	Glamorgan v Gloucestershire at Cardiff
151	C.D.Hartley & C.P.Simpson	Queensland v New South Wales at Brisbane
150*	R.G.Sharma & V.R.Samant	Mumbai v Gujarat at Mumbai

Eighth Wicket

332	**I.J.L.Trott & S.C.J.Broad**	**England v Pakistan (4th Test) at Lord's**
197	A.M.Nayar & R.R.Powar	West Zone v North Zone at Rajkot
181	Saad Nasim & Mohammad Saeed	Lahore Shalimar v Karachi Whites at Lahore
167	Humayun Farhat & Mohammad Aslam	Habib Bank v Customs at Islamabad
164	M.W.Goodwin & Naved-ul-Hasan	Sussex v Leicestershire at Hove
163	O.J.Khanwilkar & R.R.Powar	Mumbai v Punjab at Chandigarh
161	V.Sibanda & R.W.Chakabva	Zimbabwe XI v Kenya at Kwekwe

Ninth Wicket

225	L.J.Woodcock & M.J.Tugaga	Wellington v Central Districts at Wellington
158	Zulqarnain Haider & Rehan Riaz	ZTBL v Customs at Islamabad

Tenth Wicket

123	T.D.Groenewald & P.S.Jones	Derbyshire v Worcestershire at Worcester
122	K.R.N.U.Perera & S.H.M.Silva	Badureliya v Saracens at Panadura
118	A.Nel & J.W.Dernbach	Surrey v Northamptonshire at Northampton
118	A.G.Botha & Imran Tahir	Warwickshire v Kent at Birmingham
114	J.Sharma & S.Badhwar	Haryana v Andhra at Anantapur
110	A.Maregwede & H.Matanga	Southern Rocks v Mountaineers at Mutare
103	C.R.Woakes & Imran Tahir	Warwickshire v Hampshire at Birmingham

FIRST WICKET PARTNERSHIP OF 100 IN EACH INNINGS

149*	103*	Noor Ali Zadran & Ahmed Shah	Afghanistan v Zimbabwe XI at Mutare
207*	100*	W.U.Tharanga & K.Y.de Silva (1st innings) C.G.Wijesinghe & C.K.B.Kulasekara (2nd innings)	Nondescripts v Colombo at Colombo
109*	117*	J.T.Smuts & M.L.Price (1st innings) M.B.A.Smith & M.L.Price (2nd innings)	Eastern Province v Griqualand West at Port Elizabeth
169*	121*	J.A.Raval & T.G.McIntosh	Auckland v Wellington at Auckland
163*	103*	A.J.Strauss & S.A.Newman	Middlesex v Surrey at The Oval

EIGHT OR MORE WICKETS IN AN INNINGS

10-143	Zulfiqar Babar	Multan v Islamabad at Multan
9-37	C.J.August	Boland v Western Province at Cape Town
9-37	S.T.Finn	Middlesex v Worcestershire at Worcester
9-42	Rashid Latif	Rawalpindi v Islamabad at Islamabad
9-47	S.C.D.Boralessa	Colombo v Moors at Colombo
9-109	H.K.S.R.Kaluhalamulla	Bloomfield v Sri Lanka Army at Colombo
8-27	Mohammad Rameez	Rawalpindi v Peshawar at Islamabad
8-27	T.G.Southee	Northern Districts v Wellington at Hamilton
8-31	L.S.Baker	Leeward Islands v Combined Campuses and Colleges at Gros Islet
8-32	R.Vinay Kumar	Karnataka v Delhi at Delhi
8-42	T.L.Lambert	Jamaica v Combined Campuses and Colleges at Providence
8-46	Mohammad Rameez	Rawalpindi v Multan at Multan
8-50	H.K.S.R.Kaluhalamulla	Bloomfield v Chilaw Marians at Katunayake
8-52	S.C.J.Broad	Nottinghamshire v Warwickshire at Birmingham
8-53	Tanvir Ahmed	Karachi Blues v Abbottabad at Abbottabad
8-54	O.V.Brown	Jamaica v Combined Campuses and Colleges at Providence
8-64	S.de Kock	Border v South Western Districts at Oudtshoorn
8-66	D.Hettiarachchi	Chilaw Marians v Bloomfield at Katunayake
8-68	W.R.D.Wimaladarma	Saracens v Sri Lanka Army at Panagoda
8-70	S.M.S.M.Senanayake	Sri Lanka A v Australia A at Brisbane
8-84	P.R.George	South Australia v Tasmania at Hobart
8-92	T.A.Copeland	New South Wales v Queensland at Sydney
8-92	A.G.Cremer	Mid West Rhinos v Mashonaland Eagles at Kwekwe
8-98	S.M.Fallah	Maharashtra v Baroda at Poona
8-107	W.R.D.Wimaladarma	Saracens v Tamil Union at Colombo
8-111	S.C.D.Boralessa	Colombo v Badureliya at Colombo
8-114	Imran Tahir	Warwickshire v Durham at Birmingham
8-117	S.M.S.M.Senanayake	Sinhalese v Nondescripts at Colombo
8-123	S.Prasanna	Sri Lanka Army v Sinhalese at Colombo

TWELVE OR MORE WICKETS IN A MATCH

14-106	S.T.Finn	Middlesex v Worcestershire at Worcester
13-83	L.S.Baker	Leeward Islands v Combined Campuses and Colleges at Gros Islet
13-103	J.D.Unadkat	India A v West Indies A at Leicester
13-106	C.J.August	Boland v Western Province at Cape Town
13-113	Saqlain Sajib	Rajshahi v Sylhet at Fatullah
13-116	Mohammad Rameez	Rawalpindi v Peshawar at Islamabad
13-119	H.K.S.R.Kaluhalamulla	Bloomfield v Chilaw Marians at Katunayake
13-122	S.C.D.Boralessa	Colombo v Moors at Colombo
13-132	Mohammad Rameez	Rawalpindi v Multan at Multan
13-138	D.Hettiarachchi	Chilaw Marians v Bloomfield at Katunayake
13-139	Tanvir Ahmed	Karachi Blues v Abbottabad at Abbottabad
13-154	O.A.C.Banks	Leeward Islands v Windward Islands at Georgetown
13-187	H.K.S.R.Kaluhalamulla	Bloomfield v Sri Lanka Army at Colombo
13-225	T.M.U.S.Karunaratne	Seeduwa Raddoluwa v Singha at Colombo
13-226	D.Hettiarachchi	Chilaw Marians v Badureliya at Katunayake
13-259	W.R.D.Wimaladarma	Saracens v Tamil Union at Colombo
12-84	K.Kantasingh	Combined Campuses and Colleges v Trinidad and Tobago at Montego Bay
12-93	S.de Kock	Border v South Western Districts at Oudtshoorn
12-112	R.M.G.K.Sirisoma	Lankan v Sri Lanka Navy at Welisara
12-146	Kashif Daud	ZTBL v Habib Bank at Islamabad
12-168	Zulfiqar Babar	Multan v Islamabad at Multan
12-196	Imran Tahir	Easterns v Boland at Benoni
12-203	A.G.Cremer	Mid West Rhinos v Mashonaland Eagles at Kwekwe

OUTSTANDING INNINGS ANALYSES

39.4-3-143-10	Zulfiqar Babar	Multan v Islamabad at Multan
14.3-3-37-9	C.J.August	Boland v Western Province at Cape Town
15.4-5-37-9	S.T.Finn	Middlesex v Worcestershire at Worcester
6-3-14-7	J.E.C.Franklin	Gloucestershire v Derbyshire at Bristol
6.3-1-7-5	Mohammad Hussain	Customs v Lahore Shalimar at Muridke
5.2-3-2-4	M.N.R.Cooray	Panadura v Sebastianites at Panadura
4.2-2-7-4	K.Nipper	KwaZulu-Natal Inland v Namibia at Windhoek

FOUR WICKETS IN FOUR BALLS

Kamran Hussain	Habib Bank v Lahore Shalimar at Lahore
Tabish Nawab	Karachi Whites v ZTBL at Karachi

HAT-TRICKS

	Anwar Ali	PIA v National Bank at Faisalabad
	Arun Lal	Quetta v Abbottabad at Abbottabad
	A.C.R.Birch	Eastern Province v Boland at Paarl
	R.D.B.Croft	Glamorgan v Gloucestershire at Cheltenham
	Elias Sunny	Chittagong v Rajshahi at Bogra
	S.M.Fallah	Maharashtra v Baroda at Poona
	A.J.Hall	Northamptonshire v Glamorgan at Northampton
	D.Hettiarachchi	Chilaw Marians v Tamil Union at Colombo
	Kamran Hussain	Habib Bank v Lahore Shalimar at Lahore
	N.C.K.Liyanage	Singha v Sebastianites at Colombo
	A.Mithun	Karnataka v Uttar Pradesh at Meerut
	Tabish Nawab	Karachi Whites v ZTBL at Karachi
	J.C.Tredwell	Kent v Yorkshire at Leeds
	Zohaib Shera	Karachi Whites v National Bank at Karachi

MATCH DOUBLE (100 runs and 10 wickets)

	H.K.S.R.Kaluhalamulla	112, 48*; 4-78, 9-109	Bloomfield v Sri Lanka Army at Colombo

SIX OR MORE WICKET-KEEPING DISMISSALS IN AN INNINGS

8 (8ct)	D.C.de Boorder	Otago v Wellington at Wellington
8 (8ct)	A.Z.M.Dyili	Eastern Province v Free State at Port Elizabeth
7 (7ct)	P.Bisht	Delhi v Baroda at Vadodara
7 (5ct, 2st)	P.M.S.M.Fernando	Sri Lanka Air Force v Seeduwa Raddoluwa at Colombo
6 (6ct)	S.R.Adair	Eastern Province v Western Province at Cape Town
6 (6ct)	Ahmed Said	WAPDA v Lahore Shalimar at Lahore
6 (6ct)	Amin-ur-Rehman	National Bank v Sui Southern Gas at Faisalabad
6 (6ct)	M.S.Bisla	Jammu and Kashmir v Andhra at Anantapur
6 (6ct)	W.Bossenger	Griqualand West v Border at East London
6 (6ct)	S.M.Davies	England Lions v Bangladeshis at Derby
6 (5ct, 1st)	A.Z.M.Dyili	Eastern Province v KwaZulu-Natal Inland at Port Elizabeth
6 (6ct)	Farhan Asghar	Lahore Ravi v Quetta at Lahore
6 (6ct)	C.D.Hartley	Queensland v Tasmania at Hobart
6 (6ct)	C.D.Hartley	Queensland v Western Australia at Brisbane
6 (6ct)	Javed Mansoor	Karachi Blues v Abbottabad at Abbottabad
6 (6ct)	T.P.Ludeman	South Australia v New South Wales at Sydney
6 (6ct)	P.D.McGlashan	Northern Districts v Central Districts at Whangarei
6 (6ct)	P.D.McGlashan	Northern Districts v Central Districts at Whangarei
6 (6ct)	M.Mosehle	Easterns v Border at Benoni
6 (6ct)	P.M.Nevill	New South Wales v Tasmania at Hobart
6 (6ct)	T.Ngulube	Matabeleland Tuskers v Southern Rocks at Masvingo
6 (6ct)	C.M.W.Read	Nottinghamshire v Essex at Chelmsford
6 (6ct)	Sarfraz Ahmed	PIA v WAPDA at Lahore
6 (6ct)	Shahbaz Butt	Lahore Ravi v Hyderabad at Lahore
6 (6ct)	R.van Schoor	Namibia v Eastern Province at Port Elizabeth

NINE OR MORE WICKET-KEEPING DISMISSALS IN A MATCH

12 (12ct)	P.D.McGlashan	Northern Districts v Central Districts at Whangarei
10 (10ct)	Ahmed Said	WAPDA v Lahore Shalimar at Lahore
10 (9ct, 1st)	D.C.de Boorder	Otago v Wellington at Wellington
10 (10ct)	A.Z.M.Dyili	Eastern Province v Free State at Port Elizabeth
10 (10ct)	M.Mosehle	Titans v Eagles at Centurion
10 (10ct)	Sarfraz Ahmed	PIA v WAPDA at Lahore
9 (9ct)	Amin-ur-Rehman	National Bank v Sui Southern Gas at Faisalabad
9 (9ct)	B.G.Barnes	KwaZulu-Natal v KwaZulu-Natal Inland at Pietermaritzburg
9 (9ct)	P.Bisht	Delhi v Baroda at Vadodara
9 (9ct)	W.Bossenger	Griqualand West v Border at East London
9 (9ct)	**B.J.Haddin**	**Australia v Pakistan (2nd Test) at Sydney**
9 (9ct)	Javed Mansoor	Karachi Blues v Abbottabad at Abbottabad
9 (9ct)	R.D.McCann	Ireland v Canada at Toronto
9 (8ct, 1st)	**B.B.McCullum**	**New Zealand v Pakistan (3rd Test) at Napier**
9 (9ct)	D.Murphy	Northamptonshire v Glamorgan at Northampton
9 (9ct)	L.Ronchi	Western Australia v Tasmania at Perth
9 (9ct)	Zulfiqar Jan	KRL v Habib Bank at Karachi

FIVE OR MORE CATCHES IN AN INNINGS IN THE FIELD

5	M.D.Bell	Wellington v Northern Districts at Hamilton
5	S.I.de Saram	Ragama v Moors at Colombo
5	N.J.Edwards	Nottinghamshire v Kent at Nottingham
5	Wajahatullah Wasti	ZTBL v Lahore Shalimar at Lahore

SIX OR MORE CATCHES IN A MATCH IN THE FIELD

7	J.M.Kemp	Cape Cobras v Eagles at Cape Town
7	Wajahatullah Wasti	ZTBL v Lahore Shalimar at Lahore
6	C.J.L.Rogers	Derbyshire v Surrey at Chesterfield

NO BYES CONCEDED IN TOTAL OF 500 OR MORE

M.V.Boucher	**South Africa v England (574-9 dec.) (2nd Test) at Durban**
M.S.Dhoni	Indians v Sri Lanka Board President's XI (514-9 dec.) at Colombo
H.A.P.W.Jayawardene	**Sri Lanka v India (726-9 dec.) (3rd Test) at Mumbai**
Kashif Hayat	Peshawar v Sialkot (522-2 dec.) at Sialkot
Kashif Hayat	Peshawar v Multan (538-6 dec.) at Multan
T.P.Ludeman	South Australia v New South Wales (565-6 dec.) at Adelaide
T.P.Ludeman	South Australia v New South Wales (550-9 dec.) at Sydney
A.Maregwede	Southern Rocks v Mashonaland Eagles (512-8 dec.) at Masvingo
R.H.Motwani	Maharashtra v Karnataka (553-4 dec.) at Poona
Mushfiqur Rahim	**Bangladesh v England (505) (1st Test) at Lord's**
P.Mustard	Durham v Yorkshire (610-6 dec.) at Leeds
D.Ramdin	**West Indies v South Africa (543-6 dec.) (2nd Test) at Basseterre**
V.R.Samant	Mumbai v Tamil Nadu (501) at Mumbai
M.N.van Wyk	Eagles v Cape Cobras (573-8 dec.) at Bloemfontein
D.W.A.N.D.Vitharana	Badureliya v Sinhalese (506) at Colombo

HIGHEST TEAM TOTALS

785	Tamil Nadu v Hyderabad at Hyderabad
769	West Zone v North Zone at Rajkot
760-7 dec.	**Sri Lanka v India (1st Test) at Ahmedabad**
727	Kandurata v Basnahira North at Colombo
726-9 dec.	**India v Sri Lanka (3rd Test) at Mumbai**
726	Northern Districts v Canterbury at Rangiora
720	Basnahira South v Ruhuna at Colombo
707	**India v Sri Lanka (2nd Test) at Colombo**
690-9	Lions v Warriors at East London
676-9 dec.	South Africa A v Bangladesh A at Mirpur
671-2	WAPDA v Sui Southern Gas at Sheikhupura
650-9 dec.	Saurashtra v Bengal at Kolkata
648-6 dec.	Mumbai v Gujarat at Mumbai
643-9 dec.	Victoria v South Australia at Adelaide
643-6 dec.	**India v South Africa (2nd Test) at Kolkata**
642	**India v Sri Lanka (2nd Test) at Kanpur**
642-4 dec.	**Sri Lanka v India (2nd Test) at Colombo**
635-6 dec.	Auckland v Central Districts at Auckland
620-7 dec.	Surrey v Northamptonshire at The Oval
617-7 dec.	Queensland v West Indians at Brisbane
611-5 dec.	Oxford University v Cambridge University at Oxford
610-6 dec.	Yorkshire v Durham at Leeds
609-6 dec.	Sui Northern Gas v Lahore Shalimar at Lahore
609-9 dec.	Eagles v Warriors at Bloemfontein

LOWEST TEAM TOTALS

44	Derbyshire v Gloucestershire at Bristol
56	Bermuda v United Arab Emirates at Hamilton
59	Nottinghamshire v Yorkshire at Nottingham
62†	Quetta v Peshawar at Islamabad
62	Uttar Pradesh v Bengal at Kanpur
65	Sylhet v Barisal at Khulna
65	Combined Campuses and Colleges v Leeward Islands at Gros Islet
66	Peshawar v Karachi Blues at Rawalpindi
66	Habib Bank v Karachi Blues at Karachi
66	Middlesex v Worcestershire at Lord's
68†	Southern Rocks v Mashonaland Eagles at Harare
69	Sebastianites v Sri Lanka Air Force at Moratuwa
69	Badureliya v Chilaw Marians at Katunayake
70	Western Province v Namibia at Cape Town
70	Gloucestershire v Derbyshire at Bristol
71	Leicestershire v Glamorgan at Leicester
72	South Australia v Queensland at Brisbane
72	**Pakistan v England (2nd Test) at Birmingham**
73	KwaZulu-Natal v Northerns at Durban
73	Namibia v Eastern Province at Port Elizabeth
74	**Pakistan v England (4th Test) at Lord's**
77	Peshawar v Rawalpindi at Islamabad

78	Sialkot v Sui Northern Gas at Hyderabad
78	Sri Lanka A v Australia A at Townsville
79	Sebastianites v Singha at Colombo
80	**Pakistan v England (1st Test) at Nottingham**
81	Rawalpindi v Peshawar at Islamabad
81	Peshawar v Abbottabad at Abbottabad
81	Kerala v Jammu and Kashmir at Jammu
81	Abbottabad v Islamabad at Islamabad
82	Himachal Pradesh v Punjab at Mohali
83	Ragama v Sri Lanka Army at Panagoda
85	Customs v Sui Southern Gas at Karachi
86	Gloucestershire v Northamptonshire at Bristol
87	Karachi Whites v KRL at Karachi
87	Gujarat v Himachal Pradesh at Surat
88†	Customs v Karachi Whites at Karachi
88	Otago v Northern Districts at Dunedin
88	Namibia v Northerns at Pretoria
88	Boland v Gauteng at Johannesburg
88	**Australia v Pakistan (2nd Test) at Leeds**
89	Barisal v Dhaka at Khulna
91	Moors v Ragama at Colombo
91	Gujarat v Railways at Valsad
91	Kenya v Scotland at Nairobi
91	Dhaka v Sylhet at Bogra
92	Gauteng v South Western Districts at Oudtshoorn
93	Kerala v Haryana at Rohtak
93	Worcestershire v Northamptonshire at Worcester
94	Sri Lanka Air Force v Sebastianites at Moratuwa
94	Central Districts v Northern Districts at Whangarei
94	Pakistan A v Sri Lanka A at Hambantota
96	Hyderabad v Rawalpindi at Islamabad
97	Sri Lanka A v Pakistan A at Hambantota
98	Sylhet v Dhaka at Bogra
99	New Zealand v Pakistan (2nd Test) at Wellington

† indicates one batsman absent hurt

HIGHEST FOURTH INNINGS TOTALS

541-7	West Zone v South Zone at Hyderabad (set 536)
494-4	Afghanistan v Canada at Sharjah (set 494)
445-1	Central Districts v Wellington at Wellington (set 443)
411-4	Northern Districts v Central Districts at Napier (set 407)
407-6	Quetta v Karachi Blues at Karachi (set 495)

MATCH AGGREGATE OF 1,500 RUNS

1598 for 21	**India (426 and 412-4) v Sri Lanka (760-7 dec.) (1st Test) at Ahmedabad**
1590 for 35	Islamabad (438 and 382-8 dec.) v Hyderabad (466 and 304-7) at Islamabad
1578 for 36	South Zone (400 and 386-9 dec.) v West Zone (251 and 541-7) at Hyderabad
1549 for 34	Central Districts (414 and 361-9) v Canterbury (223 and 551-5 dec.) at New Plymouth
1515 for 28	Canada (566 and 191-4 dec.) v Afghanistan (264 and 494-4) at Sharjah
1505 for 31	Netherlands (385 and 367-6 dec.) v Kenya (433 and 320-5) at Nairobi
1501 for 32	New Zealand (553-7 dec. and 258-5 dec.) v Bangladesh (408 and 282) (Only Test) at Hamilton
1501 for 31	Central Districts (217 and 531-7 dec.) v Northern Districts (342 and 411-4) at Napier

MATCHES DOMINATED BY BATTING (1,200 RUNS AT 70 RUNS PER WICKET)

91.27	1369-15	Canterbury (558-4 dec. and 85-1) v Northern Districts (726) at Rangiora
86.94	**1478-17**	**Sri Lanka (642-4 dec. and 129-3 dec.) v India (707) (2nd Test) at Colombo**
80.00	1200-15	Peshawar (295 and 383-3) v Sialkot (522-2 dec.) at Sialkot
78.35	1332-17	Eagles (391-4 dec. and 273-6 dec.) v Warriors (315-3 dec. and 353-4) at East London
76.10	**1598-21**	**India (426 and 412-4) v Sri Lanka (760-7 dec.) (1st Test) at Ahmedabad**
73.89	1330-18	Mumbai (648-6 dec. and 180-2) v Gujarat (502) at Mumbai

FOUR INDIVIDUAL HUNDREDS IN AN INNINGS

4	**India (643-6 dec.) v South Africa (2nd Test) at Kolkata**
4	Auckland (635-6 dec.) v Central Districts at Auckland
4	Basnahira South (720) v Ruhuna at Colombo
4	Sussex (576-3 dec.) v Derbyshire at Horsham

SEVEN INDIVIDUAL HUNDREDS IN A MATCH

7	**India v Sri Lanka (1st Test) at Ahmedabad**
7	**India v South Africa (2nd Test) at Kolkata**

SIX OR MORE INDIVIDUAL FIFTIES IN AN INNINGS

7	West Zone (769) v North Zone at Rajkot
6	**India (726-9 dec.) v Sri Lanka (3rd Test) at Mumbai**
6	**Pakistan (455) v New Zealand (3rd Test) at Napier**
6	Tamil Nadu (785) v Hyderabad at Hyderabad
6	Eagles (609-9 dec.) v Warriors at Bloemfontein
6	Lions (562-8 dec.) v Titans at Benoni

LARGE MARGIN OF VICTORY

Victoria (305 and 591-8 dec.) v Queensland (257 and 182) at Melbourne by 457 runs
Basnahira South (720 and 168-8 dec.) v Ruhuna (180 and 259) at Colombo by 449 runs
Islamabad (182 and 419) v Abbottabad (100 and 81) at Islamabad by 420 runs

WIN AFTER FOLLOWING ON

Peshawar (263 and 77) lost to Rawalpindi (81 and 334) at Islamabad by 75

ELEVEN BOWLERS IN AN INNINGS

Dolphins v Cape Cobras (329-2) at Durban
Ireland v Jamaica (314-7 dec.) at Spanish Town

MOST EXTRAS IN AN INNINGS

total	*b*	*lb*	*w*	*nb*	
76	6	19	13	38	Gloucestershire (242) v Derbyshire at Derby
69	20	26	15	8	Middlesex (442-8 dec.) v Northamptonshire at Northampton
63	32	3	22	6	KRL (352-5 dec.) v Sui Southern Gas at Rawalpindi
61	18	13	4	26	Karachi Whites (486) v National Bank at Karachi
59	9	17	14	19	Lahore Ravi (348) v Hyderabad at Lahore
59	17	0	7	35	Hampshire (553-7 dec.) v Kent at Southampton
58	26	11	1	20	West Indies A (563) v India A at Croydon
56	14	11	8	23	Karachi Whites (520-8 dec.) v Lahore Shalimar at Lahore
55	27	11	1	16	Sussex (429) v Derbyshire at Derby
54	22	14	1	17	Karachi Blues (552-7 dec.) v Hyderabad at Mirpur Khas
54	8	13	1	32	Lancashire (398) v Hampshire at Liverpool
53	18	22	6	7	Habib Bank (353) v National Bank at Lahore
53	20	18	9	6	Karnataka (488) v Baroda at Vadodara
51	3	12	8	28	Abbottabad (238) v Karachi Blues at Abbottabad
51	9	1	32	9	Mumbai (648-6 dec.) v Gujarat at Mumbai
50	5	8	14	23	Karachi Whites (404) v Sui Northern Gas at Karachi

NOTABLE LISTA PERFORMANCES 2009/10 and 2010

ODI matches shown in bold

HIGHEST INDIVIDUAL SCORES

200*	**S.R.Tendulkar**	**India v South Africa at Gwalior**
178*	**H.Masakadza**	**Zimbabwe v Kenya at Harare**
177	**P.R.Stirling**	**Ireland v Canada at Toronto**
175	**S.R.Tendulkar**	**India v Australia at Hyderabad**
171*	P.A.Jaques	New South Wales v Queensland at Sydney
168*	M.N.van Wyk	Eagles v Lions at Bloemfontein
168	R.S.Bopara	England Lions v West Indies A at Worcester
167	N.V.Ojha	Madhya Pradesh v Railways at Indore
164	N.T.Broom	Otago v Canterbury at Timaru
160	**T.M.Dilshan**	**Sri Lanka v India at Rajkot**
158	I.R.Bell	England Lions v India A at Worcester
157	B.D.Snijman	Northerns v South Western Districts at Oudtshoorn
156	M.J.Guptill	Auckland v Canterbury at Christchurch
156	H.Masakadza	Zimbabwe v Kenya at Harare
155*	S.Dhawan	Delhi v Haryana at Rohtak
154	**A.J.Strauss**	**England v Bangladesh at Birmingham**
150*	**G.Gambhir**	**India v Sri Lanka at Kolkata**
150	M.H.W.Papps	Canterbury v Central Districts at Rangiora

HUNDRED ON LISTA DEBUT

148	M.D.U.S.Jayasundera	Sri Lanka Navy v Sri Lanka Air Force at Colombo
123	P.P.Khanapurkar	Mumbai v Punjab at Ahmedabad

CARRYING BAT THROUGH ALL-OUT INNINGS

34*	T.S.Fray	Bermuda (91) v United Arab Emirates at Hamilton
74*	M.Olivier	KwaZulu-Natal Inland (178) v Eastern Province at Despatch

MOST SIXES IN AN INNINGS

10	Y.K.Pathan (108*)	Baroda v Maharashtra at Ahmedabad
9	Y.K.Pathan (80)	West Zone v North Zone at Vadodara
9	C.G.Williams (114*)	Namibia v Easterns at Windhoek
8	H.S.Bhatia (111*)	Madhya Pradesh v Railways at Indore
8	P.Dogra (109)	Himachal Pradesh v Punjab at Sirsa
8	M.D.Mishra (117)	Madhya Pradesh v Uttar Pradesh at Indore
8	R.N.ten Doeschate (109*)	Essex v Derbyshire at Leek
7	N.T.Broom (164)	Otago v Canterbury at Timaru
7	J.C.Buttler (90*)	Somerset v Glamorgan at Taunton
7	S.P.Goswami (149*)	Bengal v Saurashtra at Vadodara
7	D.A.Miller (115*)	South Africa A v Bangladesh A at Mirpur
7	Riaz Afridi (64)	Peshawar Panthers v Hyderabad Hawks at Karachi
7	**Shahid Afridi (109)**	**Pakistan v Sri Lanka at Dambulla**
7	J.G.Strydom (83)	South Western Districts v Northerns at Oudtshoorn
7	S.B.Styris (55)	Auckland v Otago at Oamaru
7	**S.R.Watson (136*)**	**Australia v England at Centurion**
7	A.R.Yadav (119)	Goa v Hyderabad at Chennai

UNUSUAL DISMISSALS

Retired Out	A.N.Cook (52)	England XI v BCB XI at Fatullah

HIGHEST WICKET PARTNERSHIPS

First Wicket

265	A.Mukund & W.Jaffer	India Blue v India Green at Nagpur
247	B.D.Snijman & P.J.Malan	Northerns v South Western Districts at Oudtshoorn
241	A.M.Hegde & V.A.Jagadeesh	Kerala v Hyderabad at Chennai
233*	A.W.Gale & J.A.Rudolph	Yorkshire v Essex at Chelmsford
215	**W.U.Tharanga & D.P.M.D.Jayawardene**	**Sri Lanka v Bangladesh at Mirpur**

Second Wicket

252*	**S.R.Watson & R.T.Ponting**	**Australia v England at Centurion**
250	**A.J.Strauss & I.J.L.Trott**	**England v Bangladesh at Birmingham**
218*	**Karim Sadiq & Mohammad Shahzad**	**Afghanistan v Scotland at Ayr**
215	S.Dhawan & V.Kohli	Delhi v Haryana at Rohtak
205	**Noor Ali Zadran & Mohammad Shahzad**	**Afghanistan v Canada at Sharjah**

Third Wicket

224	A.G.Puttick & J.P.Duminy	Cape Cobras v Lions at Johannesburg
224	**G.Gambhir & V.Kohli**	**India v Sri Lanka at Kolkata**
210	C.A.Ingram & J.P.Kreusch	Warriors v Lions at Potchefstroom
209	G.S.Fotheringham & K.Zondo	KwaZulu-Natal v Easterns at Benoni

Fourth Wicket

207	J.E.C.Franklin & C.G.Taylor	Gloucestershire v Northamptonshire at Northampton
206	**Shoaib Malik & Mohammad Yousuf**	**Pakistan v India at Centurion**

Fifth Wicket

176	C.L.White & M.E.K.Hussey	Australians v Middlesex at Lord's
169	S.L.Stewart & D.G.Brownlie	Canterbury v Wellington at Christchurch
158	J.C.Hildreth & J.C.Buttler	Somerset v Sussex at Taunton
158	C.G.Taylor & S.D.Snell	Gloucestershire v Middlesex at Cheltenham
150	M.Klinger & D.T.Christian	South Australia v New South Wales at Wollongong

Sixth Wicket

188	**T.Taibu & S.Matsikenyeri**	**Zimbabwe v South Africa at Benoni**
173	H.M.Das & R.R.Das	Orissa v Jharkhand at Cuttack
163	S.D.Jogiyani & P.S.Mehta	Saurashtra v Maharashtra at Ahmedabad
159	R.S.Bopara & P.D.Trego	England Lions v West Indies A at Worcester
151*	B.M.A.J.Mendis & C.U.Jayasinghe	Kandurata v Basnahira North at Colombo

Seventh Wicket

152	B.R.M.Taylor & S.F.Mire	Mid West Rhinos v Matabeleland Tuskers at Kwekwe
126	A.Bagai & Umar Bhatti	Canada v Sri Lanka A at Colombo
123	**N.T.Broom & J.D.P.Oram**	**New Zealand v Bangladesh at Napier**
123	Jahangor Mirza & Ahmed Said	WAPDA v Sui Northern Gas at Multan
116	G.R.Todd & Yasir Arafat	Otago v Auckland at Oamaru
108	D.H.Dahanayake & K.P.C.M.Peiris	Sri Lanka Cricket Combined XI v Wayamba at Colombo
108	K.H.R.K.Fernando & L.J.P.Gunaratne	Basnahira South v Basnahira North at Moratuwa
107	**L.J.Wright & T.T.Bresnan**	**England v Australia at Centurion**
106	C.J.L.Rogers & J.W.Hastings	Victoria v South Australia at Melbourne
105	Y.K.Pathan & Iqbal Abdulla	West Zone v North Zone at Vadodara
102	**K.A.Pollard & D.R.Smith**	**West Indies v Australia at Brisbane**
101*	P.J.Malan & S.von Berg	Northerns v Easterns at Pretoria
101	**Mushfiqur Rahim & Naeem Islam**	**Bangladesh v New Zealand at Dunedin**
101	Mohammad Kashif & Khalid Usman	Abbottabad Rhinos v Rawalpindi Rams at Sargodha
101	S.Rana & Dhruv Singh	Haryana v Karnataka at Vadodara

Eighth Wicket

174	R.D.Berrington & M.M.Iqbal	Scotland v India A at Glasgow
113	C.P.Mapatuna & H.R.M.C.Gunasekera	Panadura v Moratuwa at Panadura
111	T.D.T.Soysa & P.P.M.Peiris	Sri Lanka Army v Saracens at Panagoda
101	K.H.R.K.Fernando & H.M.C.M.Bandara	Basnahira South v Wayamba at Kurunegala
94	R.W.T.Key & R.S.Ferley	Kent v Warwickshire at Birmingham
87*	G.H.Worker & G.R.Napier	Central Districts v Northern Districts at Palmerston North
87*	T.R.Ambrose & C.R.Woakes	Warwickshire v Leicestershire at Birmingham
86	R.S.Bopara & D.R.Tuffey	Auckland v Central Districts at Palmerston North
84	**Harbhajan Singh & P.Kumar**	**India v Australia at Vadodara**
83*	P.Utseya & S.W.Masakadza	Mountaineers v Mid West Rhinos at Mutare
82	K.K.Springer & S.J.Benn	Barbados v Guyana at Albion
77	A.A.Ansari & K.R.Adhav	Maharashtra v Baroda at Ahmedabad
77	**A.B.de Villiers & W.D.Parnell**	**South Africa v India at Gwalior**

Ninth Wicket

110	Abid Ali & Abdur Rauf	Baluchistan Bears v Sind Dolphins at Karachi
108*	S,Matsikenyeri & S.W.Masakadza	Mountaineers v Mid West Rhinos at Kwekwe
93	C.M.Gautam & S.Aravind	Karnataka v Bengal at Vadodara

Tenth Wicket

103	Mohammad Aamer & Saeed Ajmal	Pakistan v New Zealand at Abu Dhabi
82	I.H.Romaine & S.K.W.Kelly	Bermuda v Namibia at Windhoek
71	S.H.S.M.K.Silva & R.M.G.K.Sirisoma	Lankan v Moratuwa at Moratuwa
58	S.F.Mire & M.T.Chinouya	Mid West Rhinos v Mountaineers at Mutare
54*	K.M.Vardhan & M.P.Siboto	North West v Gauteng at Johannesburg
52	L.H.D.Dilhara & U.W.M.B.C.A.Welagedara	Moors v Badureliya at Colombo
51	M.P.Siboto & V.C.M.Mazibuko	North West v Boland at Paarl
51	N.M.Odhiambo & J.O.Ngoche	Kenya v Scotland at Rotterdam

SIX OR MORE WICKETS IN AN INNINGS

8-52	K.A.Stoute	West Indies A v Lancashire at Manchester
7-29	D.A.Payne	Gloucestershire v Essex at Chelmsford
7-46	S.Suresh Kumar	Tamil Nadu v Goa at Chennai
6-10	Zulfiqar Babar	Baluchistan Bears v Punjab Stallions at Karachi
6-18	L.D.I.Perera	Lankan v Moratuwa at Moratuwa
6-20	K.D.J.Nishantha	Burgher v Sri Lanka Navy at Colombo
6-20	E.P.Thompson	Central Districts v Canterbury at New Plymouth
6-21	H.O.von Rauenstein	Free State v North West at Bloemfontein
6-24	J.U.Chaturanga	Moors v Sri Lanka Army at Panagoda
6-25	V.C.M.Mazibuko	North West v Eastern Province at Port Elizabeth
6-29	W.A.White	Leicestershire v Nottinghamshire at Leicester
6-32	S.A.Patterson	Yorkshire v Derbyshire at Leeds
6-33	Danish Kaneria	Sind Dolphins v Punjab Stallions at Karachi
6-42	A.D.Russell	West Indies A v Ireland at Belfast
6-42	**Umar Gul**	**Pakistan v England at The Oval**
6-46	D.J.Bravo	Trinidad and Tobago v Barbados at Providence
6-46	P.P.Chawla	Uttar Pradesh v Railways at Indore
6-46	**A.G.Cremer**	**Zimbabwe v Kenya at Harare**
6-48	J.L.Pattinson	Victoria v New South Wales at Sydney
6-49	M.P.Siboto	North West v KwaZulu-Natal at Potchefstroom
6-52	Shoaib Akhtar	Federal Areas Leopards v Khyber Pakhtunkhwa Panthers at Karachi
6-66	B.M.D.K.Mendis	Sri Lanka Navy v Sri Lanka Air Force at Colombo

FOUR WICKETS IN FOUR BALLS

	D.A.Payne	Gloucestershire v Essex at Chelmsford

HAT-TRICKS

	Aqeel Ahmed	Faisalabad Wolves v Lahore Lions at Sargodha
	M.F.Maharoof	**Sri Lanka v India at Dambulla**
	D.A.Payne	Gloucestershire v Essex at Chelmsford
	N.J.Rimmington	Queensland v Western Australia at Brisbane

EXPENSIVE BOWLING

8-0-103-0	B.L.Fransman	South Western Districts v Northerns at Oudtshoorn
8-0-100-0	D.S.Harrison	Glamorgan v Somerset at Taunton
9-0-97-2	**Shafiul Islam**	**Bangladesh v England at Birmingham**
10-0-95-2	**W.D.Parnell**	**South Africa v India at Gwalior**
10-0-95-3	**Shafiul Islam**	**Bangladesh v Pakistan at Dambulla**
9.5-0-94-0	S.M.Fallah	Maharashtra v Saurashtra at Ahmedabad
8-0-93-1	K.Anureet Singh	Railways v Madhya Pradesh at Indore
10-3-92-1	Yasir Arafat	Otago v Auckland at Oamaru
10-0-91-0	**L.N.Onyango**	**Kenya v Zimbabwe at Harare**
10-0-89-0	**D.W.Steyn**	**South Africa v India at Gwalior**
10-1-88-3	K.Diwan	Himachal Pradesh v Punjab at Sirsa
10-0-88-0	**Z.Khan**	**India v Sri Lanka at Rajkot**
10-0-88-1	Shapoor Zadran	Afghanistan v Sri Lanka A at Colombo
10-2-86-2	R.P.Singh	Central Zone v West Zone at Vadodara
8-0-86-1	W.A.White	Leicestershire v Warwickshire at Birmingham
10-0-85-2	Alauddin Babu	BCB XI v England XI at Fatullah
10-0-85-1	**S.L.Malinga**	**Sri Lanka v New Zealand at Johannesburg**
10-0-85-1	Saqlain Sajib	Bangladesh A v South Africa A at Mirpur
10-0-84-0	G.M.Strydom	Matabeleland Tuskers v Mid West Rhinos at Kwekwe
10-0-83-1	**B.W.Hilfenhaus**	**Australia v India at Nagpur**
10-0-83-2	N.T.Pascal	West Indies A v South Africa A at Mirpur
9-0-83-0	**S.Sreesanth**	**India v South Africa at Ahmedabad**
9-0-82-0	**S.E.Bond**	**New Zealand v Sri Lanka at Johannesburg**
10-0-81-2	R.Ashwin	Tamil Nadu v Karnataka at Chennai
10-0-81-4	S.C.J.Broad	England v Pakistan at Leeds
10-0-81-0	A.C.McDermott	Queensland v Victoria at Brisbane
8-0-81-2	B.E.McGain	Victoria v Queensland at Brisbane
7-0-81-0	V.Malik	India Green v India Blue at Nagpur
10-0-81-1	**A.Nehra**	**India v Sri Lanka at Rajkot**
10-0-81-0	S.Tyagi	India A v West Indies A at Northampton
10-0-80-1	K.R.Adhav	Maharashtra v Baroda at Ahmedabad
8-0-80-0	C.P.Ashling	Glamorgan v Worcestershire at Worcester
10-0-80-2	**J.Botha**	**South Africa v India at Ahmedabad**
8-0-80-1	D.A.Cosker	Glamorgan v Surrey at The Oval
9-0-80-2	B.R.Dorey	Western Australia v Victoria at Melbourne
10-1-80-0	Kashif Raza	WAPDA v Sui Northern Gas at Multan
10-0-80-4	N.Niyas	Kerala v Goa at Chennai
10-1-80-2	**Umar Gul**	**Pakistan v Australia at Adelaide**

MATCH DOUBLE (50 RUNS AND 4 WICKETS)

168 ; 4-43	R.S.Bopara	England Lions v West Indies A at Worcester
69 ; 4-29	D.M.G.S.Dissanayake	Bloomfield v Sinhalese at Colombo
61 ; 5-45	D.D.Ebrahim	Matabeleland Tuskers v Southern Rocks at Masvingo
67 ; 4-28	B.M.A.J.Mendis	Tamil Union v Ragama at Colombo
68 ; 4-29	B.Moses	KwaZulu-Natal Inland v Easterns at Pietermaritzburg
56 ; 4-14	Raza Ali Dar	Sui Northern Gas v PIA at Multan
64 ; 6-42	A.D.Russell	West Indies A v Ireland at Belfast
59*; 4-23	A.R.Swanepoel	Griqualand West v Free State at Kimberley
103*; 4-61	J.W.A.Taylor	Leicestershire v Warwickshire at Leicester
73 ; 5-40	P.D.Trego	England Lions v West Indies A at Worcester
114*; 4-24	C.G.Williams	Namibia v Easterns at Windhoek
69 ; 5-51	K.S.Williamson	Northern Districts v Auckland at Auckland

FIVE OR MORE WICKET-KEEPING DISMISSALS IN AN INNINGS

7 (3ct,4st)	W.A.S.Niroshan	Chilaw Marians v Saracens at Katunayake
6 (5ct,1st)	H.H.R.Kavinga	Singha v Moratuwa at Colombo
6 (6st)	A.Mannu	Himachal Pradesh v Punjab at Sirsa
5 (3ct,2st)	Adnan Akmal	Sui Northern Gas v WAPDA at Multan
5 (4ct,1st)	Ali Raza	Lahore Lions v Abbottabad Rhinos at Lahore
5 (4ct,1st)	**M.V.Boucher**	**South Africa v India at Ahmedabad**

5 (4ct,1st)	G.T.de Silva	Tamil Union v Colombo at Colombo
5 (4ct,1st)	**M.S.Dhoni**	**India v Sri Lanka at Dambulla**
5 (5ct)	R.K.Dutta	Tripura v Jharkhand at Cuttack
5 (5ct)	**B.J.Haddin**	**Australia v Pakistan at Perth**
5 (5ct)	H.G.Kuhn	Titans v Lions at Centurion
5 (4ct,1st)	D.R.Lockhart	Scotland v Durham at Chester-le-Street
5 (5ct)	**B.B.McCullum**	**New Zealand v Bangladesh at Napier**
5 (2ct,3st)	P.Mustard	Durham v Scotland at Chester-le-Street
5 (3ct,2st)	**M.A.Ouma**	**Kenya v Netherlands at Nairobi**
5 (5ct)	**T.D.Paine**	**Australia v England at Centurion**
5 (4ct,1st)	L.Ronchi	Western Australia v New South Wales at Perth
5 (4ct,1st)	N.M.S.M.Sepala	Moratuwa v Lankan at Moratuwa
5 (5ct)	N.M.S.M.Sepala	Moratuwa v Sri Lanka Air Force at Moratuwa

FOUR OR MORE CATCHES IN AN INNINGS IN THE FIELD

4	C.B.Cooke	Western Province v KwaZulu-Natal at Chatsworth
4	B.C.de Wett	South Western Districts v North West at Potchefstroom
4	F.du Plessis	Titans v Eagles at Centurion
4	Z.Swartz	Griqualand West v Namibia at Kimberley
4	**L.R.P.L.Taylor**	**New Zealand v India at Dambulla**
4	S.C.van Schalkwyk	Free State v KwaZulu-Natal at Bloemfontein
4	D.J.van Wyk	Free State v Easterns at Benoni

HIGHEST TEAM TOTALS

414-7 (50 overs)	**India v Sri Lanka at Rajkot**
412-6 (50 overs)	Madhya Pradesh v Railways at Indore
411-8 (50 overs)	**Sri Lanka v India at Rajkot**
410-5 (50 overs)	Canterbury v Otago at Timaru
401-3 (50 overs)	**India v South Africa at Gwalior**
386-3 (38 overs)	Surrey v Glamorgan at The Oval
385-7 (50 overs)	**Pakistan v Bangladesh at Dambulla**
379-6 (50 overs)	Tamil Nadu v Bengal at Ahmedabad
376-6 (40 overs)	Worcestershire v Surrey at The Oval
371-7 (50 overs)	Otago v Canterbury at Timaru
370-7 (50 overs)	England XI v BCB XI at Fatullah
368-9 (50 overs)	South Africa A v Bangladesh A at Mirpur
368-4 (40 overs)	Somerset v Glamorgan at Taunton
365-2 (50 overs)	**South Africa v India at Ahmedabad**
362-5 (50 overs)	Auckland v Otago at Oamaru
358-3 (50 overs)	Kerala v Hyderabad at Chennai
354-7 (50 overs)	**India v Australia at Nagpur**
354-6 (50 overs)	**South Africa v England at Cape Town**
351-2 (50 overs)	India Blue v India Green at Nagpur
350-4 (50 overs)	**Australia v India at Hyderabad**
350-8 (50 overs)	Bengal v Tamil Nadu at Ahmedabad

LOWEST TEAM TOTALS

44 (24.5 overs)	**Zimbabwe v Bangladesh at Chittagong**
49 (29.4 overs)	Uganda v United Arab Emirates at Sharjah
58 (25.1 overs)	Saracens v Tamil Union at Colombo
69 (25.2 overs)	Easterns v Griqualand West at Kimberley
73 (30.3 overs)	Moratuwa v Panadura at Panadura
75 (25.5 overs)	Singha v Sebastianites at Gampaha

HIGHEST MATCH AGGREGATES

825 for 15	**India 414-7 (50 overs) v Sri Lanka 411-8 (50 overs) at Rajkot**
781 for 12	Canterbury 410-5 (50 overs) v Otago 371-7 (50 overs) at Timaru
729 for 14	Tamil Nadu 379-6 (50 overs) v Bengal 350-8 (50 overs) at Ahmedabad
697 for 14	**Australia 350-4 (50 overs) v India 347 (49.4 overs) at Hyderabad**
686 for 18	Punjab 344-8 (50 overs) v Himachal Pradesh 342 (50 overs) at Sirsa
686 for 16	England Lions 343-8 (50 overs) v India A 343-8 (50 overs) at Worcester
680 for 13	Delhi 338-9 (50 overs) v Punjab 342-4 (49.1 overs) at Sirsa
662 for 16	Worcestershire 376-6 (40 overs) v Surrey 286 (36.4 overs) at The Oval
661 for 13	Kerala 358-3 (50 overs) v Hyderabad 303 (47.3 overs) at Chennai
655 for 15	Maharashtra 327-9 (50 overs) v Saurashtra 328-6 (49.5 overs) at Ahmedabad
652 for 8	Sussex 325-4 (40 overs) v Unicorns 327-4 (39.3 overs) at Arundel
651 for 13	South Africa A 328-7 (50 overs) v West Indies A 323-6 (50 overs) at Mirpur
649 for 13	**India 401-3 (50 overs) v South Africa 248 (42.5 overs) at Gwalior**
640 for 15	Auckland 362-5 (50 overs) v Otago 278 (46.5 overs) at Oamaru
640 for 16	Madhya Pradesh 412-6 (50 overs) v Railways 228 (39.3 overs) at Indore

640 for 12	**South Africa 365-2 (50 overs) v India 275 (44.3 overs) at Ahmedabad**
632 for 9	**Sri Lanka 315-6 (50 overs) v India 317-3 (48.1 overs) at Kolkata**
632 for 16	Victoria 326-7 (50 overs) v Tasmania 306-9 (50 overs) at Hobart
631 for 12	**Pakistan 385-7 (50 overs) v Bangladesh 246-5 (50 overs) at Dambulla**
630 for 17	Tamil Nadu 316-8 (50 overs) v Karnataka 314-9 (50 overs) at Chennai
629 for 17	South Australia 339-7 (50 overs) v Victoria 290 (43.5 overs) at Melbourne
628 for 16	England XI 370-7 (50 overs) v BCB XI 258-9 (50 overs) at Fatullah
627 for 13	India A 340-6 (50 overs) v West Indies A 287-7 (50 overs) at Leicester
626 for 16	Karachi Zebras 311-8 (50 overs) v National Bank 315-8 (49.4 overs) at Lahore
625 for 14	Victoria 325-4 (50 overs) v Queensland 300 (48.1 overs) at Brisbane
624 for 17	**England 323-8 (50 overs) v South Africa 301-9 (50 overs) at Centurion**
621 for 15	Hyderabad 310-7 (50 overs) v Goa 311-8 (48.5 overs) at Chennai
614 for 11	India Blue 351-2 (50 overs) v India Green 263-9 (50 overs) at Nagpur
610 for 15	Baluchistan Bears 303-8 (50 overs) v Sind Dolphins 307-7 (50 overs) at Karachi
609 for 17	**India 354-7 (50 overs) v Australia 255 (48.3 overs) at Nagpur**
607 for 14	Rajasthan 303-7 (50 overs) v Madhya Pradesh 304-7 (49.2 overs) at Indore
607 for 9	**West Indies 303-6 (50 overs) v South Africa 304-3 (50 overs) at Roseau**
606 for 12	Northern Districts 300-5 (50 overs) v Central Districts 306-7 (47.3 overs) at Palmerston North
605 for 15	PIA 318-5 (50 overs) v WAPDA 287 (47.2 overs) at Bahawalpur
603 for 14	**India 301-7 (50 overs) v Sri Lanka 302-7 (49.1 overs) at Nagpur**
602 for 8	Assam 299-5 (50 overs) v Bengal 303-3 (42.3 overs) at Cuttack
601 for 13	Tasmania 300-7 (50 overs) v Victoria 301-6 (49.2 overs) at Melbourne
601 for 15	Middlesex 299-8 (40 overs) v Gloucestershire 302-7 (39.5 overs) at Cheltenham

LARGEST MARGINS OF VICTORY

249 runs	Somerset 368-4 (40 overs) v Glamorgan 119 (23.3 overs) at Taunton
216 runs	West Zone 335-8 (50 overs) v Central Zone 119 (29.4 overs) at Vadodara
212 runs	**South Africa 331-5 (50 overs) v Zimbabwe 119 (34.3 overs) at Centurion**
208 runs	Haryana 312-4 (50 overs) v Jammu and Kashmir 104 (35.5 overs) at Rohtak
208 runs	West Indies 316-4 (50 overs) v Canada 108 (39.2 overs) at Kingston
207 runs	Sui Northern Gas 335-5 (50 overs) v ZTBL 128 (38.3 overs) at Bahawalpur
203 runs	South Africa A 368-9 (50 overs) v Bangladesh A 165 (32.3 overs) at Mirpur
200 runs	**New Zealand 288 (48.5 overs) v India 88 (29.3 overs) at Dambulla**
10 wickets	Mountaineers 170-0 (36.3 overs) v Mid West Rhinos 169 (43.4 overs) at Mutare
10 wickets	Griqualand West 142-0 (17.3 overs) v Free State 141 (36.3 overs) at Kimberley
10 wickets	Yorkshire 233-0 (35.5 overs) v Essex 232-9 (40 overs) at Chelmsford

TIED MATCHES

Seeduwa Raddoluwa 211-7 (49 overs) v Moratuwa 173-9 (40 overs) at Colombo
Police 249 (49.5 overs) v Lankan 223-7 (46 overs) at Colombo
South Western Districts 159-8 (35 overs) v Eastern Province 159-7 (35 overs) at Port Elizabeth
Namibia 205-5 (40 overs) v Border 205-8 (40 overs) at Windhoek
Canterbury 287-7 (50 overs) v Auckland 287 (50 overs) at Auckland
England Lions 343-8 (50 overs) v India A 343-8 (50 overs) at Worcester
Sri Lanka A 257-8 (50 overs) v Australia A 207-7 (34 overs) at Townsville
Surrey 240 (38.3 overs) v Sussex 240-8 (40 overs) at Hove

NOTABLE PERFORMANCES IN TWENTY20 MATCHES IN 2009/10 and 2010

International Twenty20 matches shown in bold

HIGHEST INDIVIDUAL SCORES

127	M.Vijay	Chennai Super Kings v Rajasthan Royals at Chennai
117	M.J.Prior	Sussex v Glamorgan at Hove
116*	**B.B.McCullum**	**New Zealand v Australia at Christchurch**
111	W.J.Durston	Derbyshire v Nottinghamshire at Nottingham
110*	D.P.M.D.Jayawardene	Kings XI Punjab v Kolkata Knight Riders at Kolkata
108*	B.B.McCullum	Otago v Auckland at Dunedin
108*	S.E.Marsh	Western Australia v New South Wales at Perth
107*	D.A.Warner	Delhi Daredevils v Kolkata Knight Riders at Delhi
106*	S.B.Styris	Essex v Surrey at Chelmsford
106	A.C.Gilchrist	Middlesex v Kent at Canterbury
105*	P.Akshath Reddy	Hyderabad v Mumbai at Indore
105*	R.S.Bopara	Essex v Somerset at Chelmsford
105*	L.Vincent	Auckland v Wellington at Auckland
105	Amjad Ali	United Arab Emirates v Bermuda at Hamilton
104*	H.G.J.M.Kulatunga	Wayamba v Kandurata at Galle
104*	A.G.Puttick	Cape Cobras v Otago at Hyderabad
103*	M.L.Udawatte	Sri Lanka A v Afghanistan at Colombo
103	B.J.Hodge	Leicestershire v Nottinghamshire at Leicester
102	H.Masakadza	Mountaineers v Southern Rocks at Harare
102	R.N.ten Doeschate	Essex v Middlesex at Lord's
101*	J.H.K.Adams	Hampshire v Surrey at Southampton
101*	H.H.Gibbs	Yorkshire v Northamptonshire at Northampton
101*	J.J.Roy	Surrey v Kent at Beckenham
101	**S.K.Raina**	**India v South Africa at Gros Islet**
100*	J.H.K.Adams	Hampshire v Glamorgan at Southampton
100	**D.P.M.D.Jayawardene**	**Sri Lanka v Zimbabwe at Providence**
100	Mohammad Hafeez	Faisalabad Wolves v Lahore Lions at Karachi
100	Y.K.Pathan	Rajasthan Royals v Mumbai Indians at Mumbai

HUNDRED ON TWENTY20 DEBUT

105*	P.Akshath Reddy	Hyderabad v Mumbai at Indore

CARRYING BAT THROUGH ALL-OUT INNINGS

51*	A.S.Kyobe	Uganda (109) v Scotland at Nairobi

MOST SIXES IN AN INNINGS

11	M.Vijay (127)	Chennai Super Kings v Rajasthan Royals at Chennai
10	S.D.Chitnis (89*)	Mumbai v Hyderabad at Indore
9	**L.E.Bosman (94)**	**South Africa v England at Centurion**
9	L.R.P.L.Taylor (80*)	Durham v Leicestershire at Chester-le-Street
8	C.H.Gayle (88)	Kolkata Knight Riders v Kings XI Punjab at Kolkata
8	D.P.Hyatt (89)	Jamaica v Barbados at Port of Spain
8	W.I.Jefferson (83)	Leicestershire v Derbyshire at Chesterfield
8	**B.B.McCullum (116*)**	**New Zealand v Australia at Christchurch**
8	Y.K.Pathan (100)	Rajasthan Royals v Mumbai Indians at Mumbai
8	Y.K.Pathan (73*)	Rajasthan Royals v Deccan Chargers at Ahmedabad
8	S.B.Styris (106*)	Essex v Surrey at Chelmsford
8	L.R.P.L.Taylor (80)	Central Districts v Auckland at New Plymouth
7	P.D.Collingwood (75*)	Delhi Daredevils v Royal Challengers Bangalore at Delhi
7	W.J.Durston (111)	Derbyshire v Nottinghamshire at Nottingham
7	C.H.Gayle (98)	West Indies v India at Bridgetown
7	A.C.Gilchrist (106)	Middlesex v Kent at Canterbury
7	M.L.Hayden (93)	Chennai Super Kings v Delhi Daredevils at Delhi
7	C.O.Obuya (79*)	Kenya v Uganda at Nairobi
7	K.A.Pollard (89*)	Somerset v Middlesex at Lord's
7	K.A.Pollard (53*)	Trinidad and Tobago v Leeward Islands at Bridgetown
7	O.A.Shah (65*)	Wellington v Canterbury at Wellington
7	I.A.Sindhi (88)	Baroda v Gujarat at Poona
7	A.Symonds (62)	Surrey v Kent at The Oval
7	R.N.ten Doeschate (98)	Essex v Kent at Chelmsford
7	R.N.ten Doeschate (102)	Essex v Middlesex at Lord's
7	M.E.Trescothick (78)	Somerset v Hampshire at Taunton
7	**D.A.Warner (67)**	**Australia v West Indies at Sydney**
7	**D.A.Warner (72)**	**Australia v India at Bridgetown**

UNUSUAL DISMISSALS

Retired Out	Shahid Afridi (42)	Pakistanis v Northamptonshire (Northampton) at 2010

HIGHEST WICKET PARTNERSHIPS

First Wicket

170	**G.C.Smith & L.E.Bosman**	**South Africa v England at Centurion**
168	S.E.Marsh & W.M.Robinson	Western Australia v New South Wales at Perth

Second Wicket

179	H.Masakadza & T.Taibu	Mountaineers v Southern Rocks at Harare
166	**D.P.M.D.Jayawardene & K.C.Sangakkara**	**Sri Lanka v West Indies at Bridgetown**

Third Wicket

152	M.Vijay & J.A.Morkel	Chennai Super Kings v Rajasthan Royals at Chennai

Fourth Wicket

133	L.R.P.L.Taylor & K.Noema-Barnett	Central Districts v Auckland at New Plymouth
128	D.A.Warner & P.D.Collingwood	Delhi Daredevils v Kolkata Knight Riders at Delhi
124*	S.B.Styris & G.J.Hopkins	Auckland v Central Districts at Auckland
112*	**K.P.Pietersen & E.J.G.Morgan**	**England v Pakistan at Dubai**
112	N.D.McKenzie & S.M.Ervine	Hampshire v Somerset at Taunton
110	S.S.Tiwary & A.T.Rayudu	Mumbai Indians v Rajasthan Royals at Mumbai
109*	S.Badrinath & M.S.Dhoni	Chennai Super Kings v Kolkata Knight Riders at Kolkata
109	Shuvagoto Hom & Qaiser Abbas	Rajshahi v Khulna at Mirpur
106	Z.de Bruyn & K.A.Pollard	Somerset v Gloucestershire at Taunton

Fifth Wicket

130*	O.A.Shah & A.D.Mathews	Kolkata Knight Riders v Deccan Chargers at Mumbai
113*	A.Maregwede & C.R.Ervine	Southern Rocks v Mid West Rhinos at Harare
107	Y.K.Pathan & P.Dogra	Rajasthan Royals v Mumbai Indians at Mumbai
101	L.Vincent & A.K.Kitchen	Auckland v Wellington at Wellington
101*	Naeemuddin Aslam & Khurram Khan	United Arab Emirates v Netherlands at Dubai

Sixth Wicket

101*	**C.L.White & M.E.K.Hussey**	**Australia v Sri Lanka at Bridgetown**
95*	J.R.Hopes & B.R.Dunk	Queensland v Victoria at Brisbane
90	J.E.C.Franklin & C.J.Nevin	Wellington v Auckland at Wellington
87	D.L.S.van Bunge & P.W.Borren	Netherlands v United Arab Emirates at Dubai
86	B.M.A.J.Mendis & Mehrab Hossain	Dhaka v Sylhet at Savar
84	A.B.Fudadin & I.Khan	West Indies A v Zimbabweans at St Andrew's
80*	D.J.Bravo & K.A.Pollard	Trinidad and Tobago v Leeward Islands at Bridgetown
77	J.C.Hildreth & W.J.Durston	Somerset v Eagles at Hyderabad
75	J.G.Myburgh & D.G.Brownlie	Canterbury v Wellington at Rangiora
75*	K.A.Pollard & J.C.Buttler	Somerset v Nottinghamshire at Southampton

Seventh Wicket

99*	A.Thyagarajan & O.M.Baker	United States of America v Ireland at Abu Dhabi
77	A.K.Kitchen & C.de Grandhomme	Auckland v Otago at Auckland

Eighth Wicket

66	J.A.Morkel & G.R.Breese	Durham v Warwickshire at Chester-le-Street
56*	D.K.Waghmare & K.R.Adhav	Maharashtra v Tamil Nadu at Indore
53	Yashpal Singh & K.G.Chawda	Services v Himachal Pradesh at Delhi
53*	R.McLaren & Harbhajan Singh	Mumbai Indians v Deccan Chargers at Mumbai
53*	**M.E.K.Hussey & M.G.Johnson**	**Australia v Pakistan at Gros Islet**
50	J.C.Hildreth & A.C.Thomas	Somerset v Deccan Chargers at Hyderabad
50*	S.Suresh Kumar & R.Suthesh	Tamil Nadu v Himachal Pradesh at Indore
50	A.S.Raut & A.P.Dole	Rajasthan Royals v Mumbai Indians at Jaipur

Ninh Wicket

52	L.E.Plunkett & B.W.Harmison	Durham v Lancashire at Manchester

FIVE OR MORE WICKETS IN AN INNINGS

6-28	I.G.Butler	Otago v Auckland at Dunedin
5-6	M.S.Diwakar	Jharkhand v Tripura at Dhanbad
5-11	R.L.Jangid	Vidarbha v Uttar Pradesh at Indore
5-12	R.W.Price	Mashonaland Eagles v Mountaineers at Harare
5-13	A.B.McDonald	Leicestershire v Nottinghamshire at Nottingham
5-14	J.D.P.Oram	Central Districts v Otago at New Plymouth
5-17	V.D.Philander	Cape Cobras v Dolphins at Cape Town

5-18	A.Symonds	Surrey v Kent at Beckenham
5-19	**R.McLaren**	**South Africa v West Indies at North Sound**
5-19	D.Wiese	Titans v Warriors at Centurion
5-20	L.Ablash	Punjab v Haryana at Delhi
5-20	N.N.Odhiambo	Kenya v Scotland at Nairobi
5-22	Mukhtar Ali	Rajshahi v Khulna at Savar
5-22	R.J.Nicol	Canterbury v Northern Districts at Christchurch
5-24	Qasim Zubair	United Arab Emirates v Netherlands at Dubai
5-24	K.Santokie	Jamaica v Trinidad and Tobago at Port of Spain
5-24	T.M.J.Smith	Middlesex v Kent at Lord's
5-26	Imran Farhat	Lahore Eagles v Hyderabad Hawks at Karachi
5-26	**D.J.G.Sammy**	**West Indies v Zimbabwe at Port of Spain**
5-27	Asif Afridi	Abbottabad Rhinos v Faisalabad Wolves at Karachi
5-27	G.M.Smith	Mountaineers v Mashonaland Eagles at Harare
5-32	Rubel Hossain	Chittagong v Dhaka at Mirpur
5-35	A.R.Nurse	Barbados v Guyana at Port of Spain
5-41	S.J.Harmison	Durham v Lancashire at Manchester

FOUR WICKETS IN FIVE BALLS

	Asif Afridi	Abbottabad Rhinos v Faisalabad Wolves at Karachi

HAT-TRICKS

	K.H.D.Barker	Warwickshire v Yorkshire at Birmingham
	L.J.Cush	Guyana v Combined Campuses and Colleges at Bridgetown
	B.Geeves	Tasmania v Queensland at Brisbane
	M.S.Gony	Punjab v Services at Delhi
	Imran Tahir	Warwickshire v Durham at Chester-le-Street
	Jannisar Khan	Peshawar Panthers v Quetta Bears at Karachi
	P.Kumar	Royal Challengers Bangalore v Rajasthan Royals at Bangalore
	S.Narwal	Delhi v Haryana at Delhi
	Naved-ul-Hasan	Tasmania v South Australia at Adelaide

ECONOMICAL BOWLING

4-0-5-3	D.R.Briggs	Hampshire v Kent at Canterbury
4-2-5-2	A.C.Thomas	Somerset v Hampshire at Southampton
4-2-6-4	**S.J.Benn**	**West Indies v Zimbabwe at Port of Spain**
4-2-6-2	Mohammad Rafique	Dhaka v Rajshahi at Mirpur
4-1-6-3	**D.L.Vettori**	**New Zealand v Bangladesh at Hamilton**
4-0-8-1	E.Chigumbura	Northamptonshire v Derbyshire at Northampton
4-1-8-1	B.Lee	New South Wales v Sussex at Delhi
4-1-8-0	N.E.Mbhalati	Titans v Eagles at Kimberley
4-1-8-1	D.P.Nannes	Victoria v South Australia at Adelaide
4-2-8-1	**Shapoor Zadran**	**Afghanistan v Scotland at Abu Dhabi**
4-0-9-1	B.J.Arnel	Northern Districts v Canterbury at Christchurch
4-0-9-1	Mohammad Asif	Sialkot Stallions v Faisalabad Wolves at Karachi
4-0-9-3	A.G.Murtaza	Uttar Pradesh v Vidarbha at Indore
4-0-9-3	F.Nsubuga	Uganda v United Arab Emirates at Dubai
4-0-9-2	S.M.S.M.Senanayake	Ruhuna v Kandurata at Moratuwa
4-1-9-2	G.P.Swann	England XI v South Africa A at Bloemfontein
4-1-9-2	H.A.Varaiya	Kenya v Uganda at Nairobi
4-1-9-1	C.R.Woakes	Warwickshire v Derbyshire at Derby
4-0-10-3	N.Boje	Warriors v Cape Cobras at Port Elizabeth
4-0-10-2	S.M.Ervine	Hampshire v Somerset at Southampton
4-0-10-1	G.B.Gaikwad	Maharashtra v Hyderabad at Indore
4-0-10-0	H.M.R.K.B.Herath	Wayamba v Victoria at Delhi
4-0-10-2	D.Mohammed	Trinidad and Tobago v Canada at Bridgetown
4-0-10-2	**S.O.Ngoche**	**Kenya v Scotland at Nairobi**
4-0-10-2	A.B.Sonkar	Haryana v Jammu and Kashmir at Delhi
4-0-10-1	**S.O.Tikolo**	**Kenya v Scotland at Nairobi**
4-0-10-0	**M.H.Yardy**	**England v Pakistan at Cardiff**

EXPENSIVE BOWLING

4-0-67-1	P.K.K.K.Naidu	Hyderabad v Mumbai at Indore
4-0-64-0	Abdul Razzaq	Hampshire v Somerset at Taunton
4-0-61-3	M.D.Bates	Auckland v Central Districts at New Plymouth
4-0-61-0	J.A.R.Harris	Glamorgan v Sussex at Hove
4-0-61-1	**S.I.Mahmood**	**England v South Africa at Centurion**

MATCH DOUBLE (50 RUNS AND 4 WICKETS)

55*; 4-16	Jannisar Khan	Peshawar Panthers v Quetta Bears at Karachi
58*; 5-13	A.B.McDonald	Leicestershire v Nottinghamshire at Nottingham

FIVE WICKET-KEEPING DISMISSALS IN AN INNINGS

5 (4ct,1st)	D.C.de Boorder	Otago v Canterbury at Christchurch

FOUR OR MORE CATCHES IN AN INNINGS IN THE FIELD

4	D.J.Bravo	Trinidad and Tobago v Canada at Bridgetown
4	Hamad-ul-Hasan	Peshawar Panthers v Multan Tigers at Karachi
4	**D.J.G.Sammy**	**West Indies v Ireland at Providence**
4	Shahid Yousuf	Sialkot Stallions v Karachi Dolphins at Karachi
4	M.L.Udawatte	Wayamba v Sri Lanka Cricket Combined XI at Kandy
4	D.A.Warner	Delhi Daredevils v Rajasthan Royals at Delhi

HIGHEST TEAM TOTALS

246-5 (20 overs)	Chennai Super Kings v Rajasthan Royals at Chennai
241-6 (20 overs)	**South Africa v England at Centurion**
239-5 (20 overs)	Sussex v Glamorgan at Hove
229-3 (20 overs)	Auckland v Wellington at Auckland
225-2 (20 overs)	Durham v Leicestershire at Chester-le-Street
223-5 (20 overs)	Rajasthan Royals v Chennai Super Kings at Chennai
222-5 (20 overs)	Derbyshire v Yorkshire at Leeds
220-4 (18 overs)	Somerset v Hampshire at Taunton
219-4 (20 overs)	Bengal v Tripura at Jamadoba
218-7 (20 overs)	Mumbai Indians v Delhi Daredevils at Delhi
217 (19.5 overs)	Kent v Gloucestershire at Gloucester
216-5 (20 overs)	Hampshire v Somerset at Taunton
215-5 (20 overs)	**Sri Lanka v India at Nagpur**
215-6 (20 overs)	Durham v Warwickshire at Birmingham
214-4 (20 overs)	**Australia v New Zealand at Christchurch**
214-6 (20 overs)	**New Zealand v Australia at Christchurch**
213-4 (20 overs)	Trinidad and Tobago v Eagles at Hyderabad
213-4 (20 overs)	Middlesex v Glamorgan at Richmond
213-7 (20 overs)	Yorkshire v Worcestershire at Leeds
212-6 (20 overs)	Mumbai Indians v Rajasthan Royals at Mumbai
212-5 (20 overs)	Leicestershire v Derbyshire at Chesterfield
211-4 (19.1 overs)	**India v Sri Lanka at Mohali**
211-5 (20 overs)	Faisalabad Wolves v Lahore Lions at Karachi
208-5 (20 overs)	Central Districts v Wellington at New Plymouth
208-8 (20 overs)	Wayamba v Ruhuna at Moratuwa
208-7 (20 overs)	Rajasthan Royals v Mumbai Indians at Mumbai
208-7 (20 overs)	Worcestershire v Yorkshire at Worcester
206-7 (20 overs)	**Sri Lanka v India at Mohali**
206-6 (20 overs)	Central Districts v Auckland at New Plymouth
205-3 (20 overs)	Wellington v Central Districts at Wellington
205-5 (20 overs)	Hampshire v Gloucestershire at Southampton
204-2 (18.5 overs)	Royal Challengers Bangalore v Kings XI Punjab at Bangalore
204-2 (18.2 overs)	Kings XI Punjab v Kolkata Knight Riders at Kolkata
204-4 (20 overs)	Pakistanis v Essex at Chelmsford
204-5 (20 overs)	Somerset v Middlesex at Taunton
203-7 (20 overs)	Queensland v Western Australia at Brisbane
203-3 (20 overs)	Kings XI Punjab v Royal Challengers Bangalore at Bangalore
202-6 (20 overs)	**England v South Africa at Johannesburg**
202-7 (20 overs)	South Australia v Victoria at Adelaide
202-4 (20 overs)	Ireland v United States of America at Abu Dhabi
201-2 (20 overs)	Hampshire v Surrey at Southampton
201-4 (20 overs)	Surrey v Kent at Beckenham
200-3 (20 overs)	Kolkata Knight Riders v Kings XI Punjab at Kolkata
200-7 (20 overs)	Warwickshire v Durham at Birmingham
200-6 (20 overs)	Middlesex v Essex at Lord's
200-4 (18.5 overs)	Somerset v Gloucestershire at Taunton
200-8 (20 overs)	Surrey v Hampshire at The Oval

LOWEST TEAM TOTALS

30 (11.1 overs)	Tripura v Jharkhand at Dhanbad
59 (11.5 overs)	Mountaineers v Mashonaland Eagles at Harare
68 (16.4 overs)	**Ireland v West Indies at Providence**
68 (17.5 overs)	Gloucestershire v Hampshire at Bristol
71 (16.2 overs)	New South Wales v Western Australia at Perth

73 (19.2 overs)	Services v Haryana at Delhi
75 (15 overs)	Abbottabad Rhinos v Faisalabad Wolves at Karachi

HIGHEST MATCH AGGREGATES

469 for 10	Chennai Super Kings 246-5 (20 overs) v Rajasthan Royals 223-5 (20 overs) at Chennai
436 for 9	Hampshire 216-5 (20 overs) v Somerset 220-4 (18 overs) at Taunton
428 for 10	**New Zealand 214-6 (20 overs) v Australia 214-4 (20 overs) at Christchurch**
425 for 10	Sussex 239-5 (20 overs) v Glamorgan 186-5 (20 overs) at Hove
420 for 13	Mumbai Indians 212-6 (20 overs) v Rajasthan Royals 208-7 (20 overs) at Mumbai
417 for 11	**Sri Lanka 206-7 (20 overs) v India 211-4 (19.1 overs) at Mohali**
415 for 13	Durham 215-6 (20 overs) v Warwickshire 200-7 (20 overs) at Birmingham
414 for 11	Bengal 219-4 (20 overs) v Tripura 195-7 (20 overs) at Jamadoba
408 for 13	Leicestershire 212-5 (20 overs) v Derbyshire 196-8 (20 overs) at Chesterfield
407 for 5	Kings XI Punjab 203-3 (20 overs) v Royal Challengers Bangalore 204-2 (18.5 overs) at Bangalore
404 for 5	Kolkata Knight Riders 200-3 (20 overs) v Kings XI Punjab 204-2 (18.2 overs) at Kolkata
402 for 9	Trinidad and Tobago 213-4 (20 overs) v Eagles 189-5 (20 overs) at Hyderabad
401 for 14	**Sri Lanka 215-5 (20 overs) v India 186-9 (20 overs) at Nagpur**

LARGEST MARGINS OF VICTORY

127 runs	Western Australia 198-1 (20 overs) v New South Wales 71 (16.2 overs) at Perth
105 runs	Lahore Lions 196-5 (20 overs) v Quetta Bears 91-9 (20 overs) at Karachi
104 runs	Yorkshire 213-7 (20 overs) v Worcestershire 109 (16.5 overs) at Leeds
10 wickets	Jharkhand 32-0 (3.2 overs) v Tripura 30 (11.1 overs) at Dhanbad
10 wickets	**Kenya 110-0 (12.3 overs) v Scotland 109-9 (20 overs) at Nairobi**
10 wickets	**New Zealand 79-0 (8.2 overs) v Bangladesh 78 (17.3 overs) at Hamilton**
10 wickets	**Kenya 126-0 (14.3 overs) v Scotland 123 (19.2 overs) at Nairobi**
10 wickets	Royal Challengers Bangalore 93-0 (10.4 overs) v Rajasthan Royals 92 (19.5 overs) at Bangalore
10 wickets	Gloucestershire 98-0 (9.5 overs) v Surrey 97 (18.1 overs) at The Oval
10 wickets	Trinidad and Tobago 89-0 (10.1 overs) v Jamaica 94-7 (14 overs) at Port of Spain

TIED MATCHES

Sussex 119-7 (20 overs) v Eagles 119-4 (20 overs) at Delhi
(Eagles won in the super over)
Auckland 171-9 (20 overs) v Otago 171-9 (20 overs) at Auckland
(Otago won in the super over)
Scotland 109-8 (20 overs) v Uganda 109 (20 overs) at Nairobi
(Scotland won in the super over)
New Zealand 214-6 (20 overs) v Australia 214-4 (20 overs) at Christchurch
(New Zealand won in the super over)
Kings XI Punjab 136-8 (20 overs) v Chennai Super Kings 136-7 (20 overs) at Chennai
(Kings XI Punjab won in the super over)
Northamptonshire 121-7 (20 overs) v Nottinghamshire 121 (20 overs) at Nottingham
Yorkshire 180-3 (20 overs) v Northamptonshire 180-5 (20 overs) at Northampton
Nottinghamshire 144-7 (20 overs) v Northamptonshire 144-8 (20 overs) at Northampton
Barbados 180-6 (20 overs) v Combined Campuses and Colleges 180-5 (20 overs) at Bridgetown

AFGHANISTAN

CAREER RECORDS FOR AFGHANISTAN PLAYERS

Cmp	Debut	M	I	NO	Runs	HS	Avge	100	50	Balls	Runs	Wkts	Avge	BB	5i	10m	RpO	ct	st
ABDULLAH Mazari (Afghanistan to Scotland) b Mazharsherfa 7.3.1987 LHB SLA																			
FC	2008/09	3	4	0	31	17	7.75	0	0	396	165	3	55.00	2-6	0	0	2.50	0	
AFTAB ALAM (Afghanistan to Netherlands, Afghanistan to United Arab Emirates) b Nangarhar 30.11.1992 RHB RMF																			
Int	2009/10	3	1	1	6	6*		0	0	126	136	2	68.00	1-49	0	0	6.47	0	
Lim	2009/10	3	1	1	6	6*		0	0	126	136	2	68.00	1-49	0	0	6.47	0	
AHMED SHAH (Afghanistan to Zimbabwe) b Paktika 20.10.1983 LHB SLA																			
FC	2009	2	4	0	82	40	20.50	0	0	84	56	0					4.00	1	
Int	2009	1	1	0	2	2	2.00	0	0	6	12	0					12.00	0	
Lim	2009	1	1	0	2	2	2.00	0	0	6	12	0					12.00	0	
ASGHAR STANIKZAI, Mohammad (Afghanistan to Netherlands, Afghanistan to Scotland, Afghanistan to Sri Lanka, Afghanistan to United Arab Emirates, Afghanistan to West Indies, Afghanistan to Zimbabwe) b Kabul 22.2.1987 RHB RMF																			
FC	2009	5	9	1	260	93	32.50	0	1	42	15	0					2.14	2	
Int	2008/09	13	12	1	289	64	26.27	0	1	98	55	2	27.50	1-22	0	0	3.36	2	
Lim	2008/09	21	20	1	494	69	26.00	0	2	146	94	2	47.00	1-22	0	0	3.86	2	
I20T	2009/10	4	3	0	34	30	11.33	0	0									0	
20T	2009/10	5	4	0	60	30	15.00	0	0									0	
DAWLAT Khan AHMADZAI (Afghanistan to Netherlands, Afghanistan to Sri Lanka, Afghanistan to United Arab Emirates, Afghanistan to West Indies, Afghanistan to Zimbabwe) b Loger 5.9.1984 RHB RFM																			
FC	2009/10	2	2	1	13	7*	13.00	0	0	244	138	9	15.33	5-52	1	0	3.39	0	
Int	2008/09	3								112	121	1	121.00	1-40	0	0	6.48	0	
Lim	2008/09	9	5	4	34	11*	34.00	0	0	388	348	2	174.00	1-5	0	0	5.38	0	
I20T	2009/10	2	1	1	2	2*		0	0	24	46	2	23.00	1-21	0	0	11.50	0	
20T	2009/10	2	1	1	2	2*		0	0	24	46	2	23.00	1-21	0	0	11.50	0	
HAMID HASSAN (Afghanistan to Netherlands, Afghanistan to Scotland, Afghanistan to Sri Lanka, Afghanistan to United Arab Emirates, Afghanistan to West Indies, Afghanistan to Zimbabwe) b Negharar 26.8.1986 RHB RFM																			
FC	2007/08	6	9	3	23	7*	3.83	0	0	1300	793	26	30.50	6-40	2	1	3.66	3	
Int	2008/09	11	6	2	33	17	8.25	0	0	576	433	18	24.05	3-32	0	0	4.51	1	
Lim	2007/08	23	11	5	45	17	7.50	0	0	1178	943	38	24.81	5-23	0	1	4.80	5	
I20T	2009/10	8	5	2	33	22	11.00	0	0	175	170	14	12.14	3-21	0	0	5.82	1	
20T	2009/10	11	5	2	33	22	11.00	0	0	247	233	22	10.59	3-14	0	0	5.66	2	
JAVED AHMADI (Afghanistan to Netherlands, Afghanistan to Scotland) b Kunduz 2.1.1992 RHB OB																			
Int	2010	4	3	0	31	25	10.33	0	0									2	
Lim	2010	4	3	0	31	25	10.33	0	0	18	16	0					5.33	2	
KARIM SADIQ Khan (Afghanistan to Netherlands, Afghanistan to Scotland, Afghanistan to Sri Lanka, Afghanistan to United Arab Emirates, Afghanistan to West Indies) b Nangrahar 18.2.1984 RHB OB WK																			
FC	2009/10	3	6	0	201	67	33.50	0	1	180	82	1	82.00	1-31	0	0	2.73	1	
Int	2008/09	11	10	2	212	114*	26.50	1	0	122	82	2	41.00	2-28	0	0	4.03	3	
Lim	2008/09	20	19	2	608	114*	35.76	1	4	475	369	14	26.35	4-27	1	0	4.66	4	
I20T	2009/10	8	8	0	106	42	13.25	0	0	120	128	6	21.33	3-17	0	0	6.40	0	
20T	2009/10	11	11	0	133	42	12.09	0	0	162	180	6	30.00	3-17	0	0	6.66	0	
KHALIQ DAD Noori (Afghanistan to Netherlands) b Baghlan 1.1.1984 RHB RFM																			
Int	2008/09	6	4	1	40	20	13.33	0	0	252	150	9	16.66	3-30	0	0	3.57	0	
Lim	2008/09	10	8	3	57	20	11.40	0	0	396	264	12	22.00	3-30	0	0	4.00	0	
MIRWAIS ASHRAF (Afghanistan to Netherlands, Afghanistan to Scotland, Afghanistan to Sri Lanka, Afghanistan to United Arab Emirates, Afghanistan to West Indies) b Kunduz 30.6.1988 RHB RFM																			
FC	2009	3	4	1	59	31	19.66	0	0	516	251	9	27.88	4-24	0	0	2.91	2	
Int	2009	4	2	0	24	17	12.00	0	0	186	94	4	23.50	2-20	0	0	3.03	0	
Lim	2009	5	3	1	39	17	19.50	0	0	240	128	5	25.60	2-20	0	0	3.20	0	
I20T	2009/10	6	4	1	51	23	17.00	0	0	108	101	1	101.00	1-13	0	0	5.61	2	
20T	2009/10	9	5	2	76	25*	25.33	0	0	174	153	4	38.25	2-15	0	0	5.27	2	
MOHAMMAD NABI Eisakhil (Afghanistan to Netherlands, Afghanistan to Scotland, Afghanistan to Sri Lanka, Afghanistan to United Arab Emirates, Afghanistan to West Indies, Afghanistan to Zimbabwe, Customs) b Loger 7.3.1985 RHB OB																			
FC	2007	14	24	2	637	102	28.95	1	3	1691	818	31	26.38	4-25	0	0	2.90	6	
Int	2008/09	13	11	3	241	62	30.12	0	2	606	421	8	52.62	2-23	0	0	4.16	9	
Lim	2007/08	27	25	4	606	112*	28.85	1	3	1281	893	22	40.59	2-23	0	0	4.18	14	
I20T	2009/10	8	7	1	69	43*	11.50	0	0	168	208	11	18.90	3-23	0	0	7.42	3	
20T	2009/10	11	10	2	98	43*	12.25	0	0	234	274	17	16.11	3-17	0	0	7.02	5	
MOHAMMAD SHAHZAD (Afghanistan to Netherlands, Afghanistan to Scotland, Afghanistan to Sri Lanka, Afghanistan to United Arab Emirates, Afghanistan to West Indies, Afghanistan to Zimbabwe) b Nangarhar 15.7.1991 RHB WK																			
FC	2009	5	10	3	656	214*	93.71	2	3									18	2
Int	2009	12	12	1	605	118	55.00	3	3									12	4
Lim	2008/09	22	22	2	933	118	46.65	3	6									21	8
I20T	2009/10	8	8	1	154	65*	22.00	0	1									4	3
20T	2009/10	11	11	1	219	65*	21.90	0	2									5	4

NAWROZ Khan MANGAL (Afghanistan to Netherlands, Afghanistan to Scotland, Afghanistan to Sri Lanka, Afghanistan to United Arab Emirates, Afghanistan to West Indies, Afghanistan to Zimbabwe) b Khost 28.11.1984 RHB OB

Cmp	Debut	M	I	NO	Runs	HS	Avge	100	50	Balls	Runs	Wkts	Avge	BB	5i	10m	RpO	ct	st
FC	2009	5	9	1	319	84	39.87	0	2	138	96	1	96.00	1-34	0	0	4.17	2	
Int	2008/09	13	12	3	324	70*	36.00	0	2	233	168	6	28.00	3-35	0	0	4.32	4	
Lim	2008/09	23	22	3	699	78	36.78	0	5	341	274	7	39.14	3-35	0	0	4.82	6	
I20T	2009/10	8	8	2	102	27	17.00	0	0	48	61	4	15.25	3-23	0	0	7.62	6	
20T	2009/10	11	11	2	150	30	16.66	0	0	48	61	4	15.25	3-23	0	0	7.62	8	

NOOR ALI ZADRAN (Afghanistan to Netherlands, Afghanistan to Scotland, Afghanistan to Sri Lanka, Afghanistan to United Arab Emirates, Afghanistan to West Indies, Afghanistan to Zimbabwe) b Khost 10.7.1988 RHB RMF

Cmp	Debut	M	I	NO	Runs	HS	Avge	100	50	Balls	Runs	Wkts	Avge	BB	5i	10m	RpO	ct	st
FC	2009	5	10	1	527	130	58.55	2	4	14	25	0					10.71	2	
Int	2008/09	10	10	0	315	114	31.50	1	1									5	
Lim	2008/09	18	18	0	527	122	29.27	2	1	2	6	1	6.00	1-6	0	0	18.00	5	
I20T	2009/10	7	7	0	199	50	28.42	0	1									1	
20T	2009/10	10	10	1	273	50	30.33	0	1									2	

NOOR-UL-HAQ Malekzai (Afghanistan to Scotland) b Laghman 2.4.1992 RHB LB

Cmp	Debut	M	I	NO	Runs	HS	Avge	100	50	Balls	Runs	Wkts	Avge	BB	5i	10m	RpO	ct	st
Int	2010	1	1	0	12	12	12.00	0	0									0	
Lim	2010	1	1	0	12	12	12.00	0	0									0	

RAEES Khan AHMADZAI (Afghanistan to Sri Lanka, Afghanistan to United Arab Emirates, Afghanistan to West Indies, Afghanistan to Zimbabwe) b Loger 3.9.1984 RHB OB

Cmp	Debut	M	I	NO	Runs	HS	Avge	100	50	Balls	Runs	Wkts	Avge	BB	5i	10m	RpO	ct	st
FC	2009	3	5	0	90	27	18.00	0	0	36	35	0					5.83	1	
Int	2008/09	5	4	1	88	39	29.33	0	0	24	16	0					4.00	2	
Lim	2007/08	16	15	4	283	50*	25.72	0	1	150	107	1	107.00	1-37	0	0	4.28	6	
I20T	2009/10	8	6	3	91	33*	30.33	0	0									2	
20T	2009/10	11	9	5	120	33*	30.00	0	0									2	

SAMIULLAH SHENWARI (Afghanistan to Netherlands, Afghanistan to Scotland, Afghanistan to Sri Lanka, Afghanistan to United Arab Emirates, Afghanistan to West Indies, Afghanistan to Zimbabwe) b Nangrahar 31.12.1987 RHB LB

Cmp	Debut	M	I	NO	Runs	HS	Avge	100	50	Balls	Runs	Wkts	Avge	BB	5i	10m	RpO	ct	st
FC	2009	5	7	2	183	102	36.60	1	0	684	402	11	36.54	4-75	0	0	3.52	7	
Int	2008/09	13	8	1	265	82	37.85	0	2	660	465	17	27.35	4-31	1	0	4.22	1	
Lim	2008/09	23	17	3	420	82	30.00	0	2	1104	831	25	33.24	4-28	2	0	4.51	4	
I20T	2009/10	8	7	1	62	19	10.33	0	0	132	126	4	31.50	1-9	0	0	5.72	2	
20T	2009/10	11	9	1	67	19	8.37	0	0	180	198	5	39.60	1-9	0	0	6.60	2	

SHABIR Ahmed NOORI (Afghanistan to Netherlands, Afghanistan to Sri Lanka, Afghanistan to United Arab Emirates) b Nengarhar 23.2.1992 RHB OB

Cmp	Debut	M	I	NO	Runs	HS	Avge	100	50	Balls	Runs	Wkts	Avge	BB	5i	10m	RpO	ct	st
FC	2009/10	2	3	0	166	85	55.33	0	2									0	
Int	2009/10	6	6	0	74	38	12.33	0	0									3	
Lim	2009/10	6	6	0	74	38	12.33	0	0									3	

SHAFIQULLAH, Mohammad (Afghanistan to Sri Lanka, Afghanistan to United Arab Emirates) b Nangrahar 7.8.1989 RHB WK

Cmp	Debut	M	I	NO	Runs	HS	Avge	100	50	Balls	Runs	Wkts	Avge	BB	5i	10m	RpO	ct	st
Int	2009	2	1	0	0	0	0.00	0	0									0	
Lim	2008/09	8	7	0	42	25	6.00	0	0									1	
I20T	2009/10	5	5	0	37	23	7.40	0	0									1	
20T	2009/10	7	6	0	38	23	6.33	0	0									1	

SHAPOOR ZADRAN (Afghanistan to Netherlands, Afghanistan to Scotland, Afghanistan to Sri Lanka, Afghanistan to United Arab Emirates, Afghanistan to West Indies, Afghanistan to Zimbabwe) b Logar 8.7.1987 LHB LFM

Cmp	Debut	M	I	NO	Runs	HS	Avge	100	50	Balls	Runs	Wkts	Avge	BB	5i	10m	RpO	ct	st
FC	2009	5	6	1	9	4	1.80	0	0	786	504	12	42.00	4-28	0	0	3.84	1	
Int	2009	10	6	3	1	1	0.33	0	0	509	400	17	23.52	4-24	1	0	4.71	0	
Lim	2007/08	16	12	5	23	10	3.28	0	0	780	650	24	27.08	4-24	1	0	5.00	0	
I20T	2009/10	8	3	2	1	1*	1.00	0	0	132	153	4	38.25	1-8	0	0	6.95	2	
20T	2009/10	11	3	2	1	1*	1.00	0	0	198	219	6	36.50	1-8	0	0	6.63	2	

AUSTRALIA

Sheffield Shield winners 2009/10 (first-class): Victoria
Ford Ranger Cup winners 2009/19 (limited overs): Tasmania
KFC Twenty20 Big Bash winners 2009/10 (twenty20): Victoria

2009/10 and 2010 AND CAREER RECORDS FOR AUSTRALIAN PLAYERS

Cmp	Debut	M	I	NO	Runs	HS	Avge	100	50	Balls	Runs	Wkts	Avge	BB	5i	10m	RpO	ct	st
BAILEY, Cullen Benjamin (South Australia) b Bedford Park, Adelaide, South Australia 26.2.1985 RHB LBG																			
FC		4	5	1	117	91	29.25	0	1	775	526	9	58.44	4-62	0	0	4.07	0	
FC	2004/05	26	39	9	593	91	19.76	0	2	5261	3296	72	45.77	5-90	2	0	3.75	11	
Lim	2005/06	6	3	2	15	11*	15.00	0	0	282	297	9	33.00	3-33	0	0	6.31	2	
20T	2006	1	1	0	1	1	1.00	0	0	12	21	0					10.50	0	
BAILEY, George John (Australia A, Tasmania, Chennai Super Kings, Scotland to England, Scotland) b Launceston, Tasmania 7.9.1982 RHB RM																			
FC		12	21	2	1002	154*	52.73	3	6	30	22	0					4.40	14	
Lim		14	14	2	587	112*	48.91	1	5									7	
20T		5	5	1	91	35*	22.75	0	0									0	
FC	2004/05	61	112	11	4081	155	40.40	10	22	84	46	0					3.28	47	
Lim	2001/02	105	97	12	2739	123*	32.22	2	17	53	40	1	40.00	1-19	0	0	4.52	50	
20T	2005/06	25	21	3	529	60	29.38	0	4	12	24	0					12.00	8	
BANDY, David Charles (Western Australia) b Subiaco, Perth, Western Australia 19.7.1978 RHB RM																			
FC		3	4	1	99	59*	33.00	0	1	90	59	3	19.66	2-40	0	0	3.93	3	
Lim		4	4	0	61	23	15.25	0	0	54	44	0					4.88	2	
20T		1	1	0	5	5	5.00	0	0									0	
FC	2005/06	24	40	3	1096	88	29.62	0	7	1826	899	33	27.24	7-44	1	0	2.95	16	
Lim	2005/06	17	15	6	264	54	29.33	0	1	330	287	6	47.83	2-21	0	0	5.21	8	
20T	2005/06	13	12	5	145	52*	20.71	0	1	162	240	9	26.66	2-26	0	0	8.88	5	
BATTICCIOTTO, Glen Charles (Queensland) b Redcliffe, Queensland 18.8.1981 LHB RM																			
FC		5	8	0	177	101	22.12	1	0	90	37	1	37.00	1-37	0	0	2.46	4	
Lim		5	5	1	71	38	17.75	0	0									0	
20T		5	3	0	28	13	9.33	0	0									4	
Lim	2008/09	9	9	3	179	54*	29.83	0	1									2	
20T	2008/09	11	9	3	107	38	17.83	0	0									7	
BIRD, Aaron Christopher (New South Wales) b Taree, New South Wales 28.9.1983 RHB RF																			
FC		1	1	0	0	0	0.00	0	0	90	96	1	96.00	1-68	0	0	6.40	0	
20T		3	1	0	5	5	5.00	0	0	55	108	3	36.00	2-26	0	0	11.78	0	
FC	2005/06	6	10	3	101	29	14.42	0	0	857	585	14	41.78	4-80	0	0	4.09	1	
Lim	2005/06	25	18	10	65	12*	8.12	0	0	1122	1051	34	30.91	5-26	2	1	5.62	7	
20T	2005/06	12	4	1	29	17*	9.66	0	0	238	366	21	17.42	3-21	0	0	9.22	5	
BIRT, Travis Rodney (Australia, Australia A, Tasmania, Australia to New Zealand) b Sale, Victoria 9.12.1981 LHB RM																			
FC		1	1	0	8	8	8.00	0	0									0	
Lim		13	13	3	570	97	57.00	0	7									8	1
I20T		2	2	0	14	13	7.00	0	0									1	
20T		8	8	0	125	54	15.62	0	1									2	
FC	2004/05	74	138	8	4676	181	35.96	9	28	190	163	2	81.50	1-24	0	0	5.14	53	
Lim	2003/04	97	95	10	2909	145	34.22	2	20	91	89	5	17.80	2-15	0	0	5.86	35	1
I20T	2009/10	3	2	0	14	13	7.00	0	0									1	
20T	2005/06	31	30	2	547	58	19.53	0	2									12	
BLIZZARD, Aiden Craig (Victoria, Rajshahi, Victoria to India) b Shepparton, Victoria 27.6.1984 LHB LM																			
Lim		3	3	0	34	33	11.33	0	0									1	
20T		1	1	1	42	42*		0	0									0	
FC	2007/08	2	1	0	30	30	30.00	0	0									1	
Lim	2005/06	23	22	1	434	72	20.66	0	1									14	
20T	2006/07	30	30	2	635	89	22.67	0	1	6	10	0					10.00	10	
BOLLINGER, Douglas Erwin (Australia, New South Wales, Australia to England, Australia to India, Australia to Ireland, Australia to New Zealand, Chennai Super Kings, New South Wales to India) b Baulkham Hills, Sydney, New South Wales 24.7.1981 LHB LFM																			
Test		5	4	1	11	9	3.66	0	0	1081	520	25	20.80	5-70	1	0	2.88	2	
FC		7	5	1	20	9	5.00	0	0	1411	695	34	20.44	5-68	2	0	2.95	5	
Int		8	1	1	0	0*		0	0	358	216	15	14.40	4-28	1	0	3.62	0	
Lim		8	1	1	0	0*		0	0	358	216	15	14.40	4-28	1	0	3.62	0	
Test	2008/09	10	10	4	42	21	7.00	0	0	2083	1085	44	24.65	5-28	2	0	3.12	2	
FC	2002/03	64	69	30	301	31*	7.71	0	0	11574	6324	222	28.48	6-47	12	2	3.27	23	
Int	2008/09	26	4	2	4	3	2.00	0	0	1288	930	42	22.14	5-35	1	2	4.33	5	
Lim	2002/03	80	22	11	51	7*	4.63	0	0	3932	3023	113	26.75	5-35	3	2	4.61	15	
20T	2005/06	27	3	2	23	16*	23.00	0	0	571	701	27	25.96	4-13	1	0	7.36	6	

Cmp	Debut	M	I	NO	Runs	HS	Avge	100	50	Balls	Runs	Wkts	Avge	BB	5i	10m	RpO	ct	st
BORGAS, Cameron James (South Australia) b Melrose Park, South Australia 1.9.1983 RHB OB																			
FC		8	14	2	504	164*	42.00	1	2	6	0	0					0.00	1	
Lim		10	9	0	339	90	37.66	0	2	18	18	0					6.00	3	
20T		5	5	1	63	34*	15.75	0	0									2	
FC	2000/01	34	60	4	1773	164*	31.66	4	8	42	9	0					1.28	15	
Lim	2005/06	40	34	4	1108	90	36.93	0	6	90	111	2	55.50	1-2	0	0	7.40	10	
20T	2005/06	11	10	1	96	34*	10.66	0	0									6	
BOYCE, Cameron John (Queensland) b Charleville, Queensland 27.7.1989 RHB LB																			
FC		2	4	1	9	5	3.00	0	0	403	306	8	38.25	6-181	1	0	4.55	0	
BRACKEN, Nathan Wade (New South Wales) b Penrith, New South Wales 12.9.1977 RHB LFM																			
Lim		4	2	0	15	10	7.50	0	0	234	181	8	22.62	3-48	0	0	4.64	2	
Test	2003/04	5	6	2	70	37	17.50	0	0	1110	505	12	42.08	4-48	0	0	2.73	2	
FC	1998/99	67	88	30	1007	63	17.36	0	1	13634	5603	215	26.06	7-4	9	0	2.46	18	
Int	2000/01	116	35	18	198	21*	11.64	0	0	5759	4239	174	24.36	5-47	5	2	4.41	26	
Lim	1998/99	205	72	29	388	21*	9.02	0	0	10339	7520	286	26.29	5-38	8	3	4.36	39	
I20T	2005/06	19	6	3	15	4*	5.00	0	0	377	438	19	23.05	3-11	0	0	6.97	6	
20T	2004/05	28	9	5	22	7*	5.50	0	0	586	705	31	22.74	3-11	0	0	7.21	6	
BRAVO, Dwayne John (Trinidad and Tobago, West Indies, Essex, Mumbai Indians, Trinidad and Tobago to India, Victoria, West Indies to Australia) b Santa Cruz, Trinidad 7.10.1983 RHB RFM																			
Test		3	6	0	176	104	29.33	1	0	565	319	11	29.00	4-42	0	0	3.38	5	
FC		4	8	0	241	104	30.12	1	0	733	405	12	33.75	4-42	0	0	3.31	6	
20T		5	5	2	77	36	25.66	0	0	102	169	4	42.25	3-32	0	0	9.94	3	
Test	2004	37	68	1	2175	113	32.46	3	13	6164	3270	83	39.39	6-55	2	0	3.18	39	
FC	2001/02	94	173	7	5193	197	31.28	8	29	10461	5621	168	33.45	6-11	7	0	3.22	81	
Int	2003/04	107	87	16	1715	112*	24.15	1	5	4260	3721	129	28.84	4-19	4	0	5.24	44	
Lim	2002	144	121	20	2312	112*	22.89	1	7	5489	4677	172	27.19	6-46	6	1	5.11	60	
I20T	2005/06	22	20	5	344	66*	22.93	0	2	338	491	19	25.84	4-38	1	0	8.71	5	
20T	2005/06	74	64	15	1208	70*	24.65	0	8	1315	1811	70	25.87	4-23	2	0	8.26	32	
BROAD, Ryan Andrew (Queensland) b Herston, Brisbane, Queensland 9.3.1982 RHB RM																			
FC		11	17	0	593	129	34.88	2	2	6	0	0					0.00	5	
Lim		7	7	0	129	60	18.42	0	1									2	
FC	2005/06	41	74	3	2525	129	35.56	7	10	30	11	1	11.00	1-5	0	0	2.20	29	
Lim	2005/06	17	17	1	376	81	23.50	0	3									5	
BUTTERWORTH, Luke Rex (Tasmania) b Hobart, Tasmania 28.10.1983 LHB RM																			
FC		6	11	3	228	36	28.50	0	0	1008	510	14	36.42	4-57	0	0	3.03	1	
Lim		7	6	2	149	63*	37.25	0	1	267	252	9	28.00	2-24	0	0	5.66	7	
FC	2006/07	30	53	5	1299	116	27.06	2	4	4479	2317	82	28.25	5-13	2	0	3.10	16	
Lim	2003/04	44	37	8	631	114*	21.75	1	1	1809	1598	47	34.00	3-32	0	0	5.30	14	
20T	2006/07	4	4	1	45	36	15.00	0	0	48	72	1	72.00	1-23	0	0	9.00	0	
CARSELDINE, Lee Andrew (Queensland) b Nambour, Queensland 17.11.1975 LHB LM																			
FC		11	19	1	605	109	33.61	1	3	388	165	2	82.50	1-6	0	0	2.55	17	
Lim		10	10	0	463	105	46.30	1	4	54	46	0					5.11	5	
20T		6	6	0	90	25	15.00	0	0									2	
FC	1998/99	43	70	8	2209	152	35.62	3	12	1377	666	14	47.57	3-25	0	0	2.90	45	
Lim	1999/00	53	51	3	1431	126	29.81	3	7	378	297	11	27.00	4-6	1	0	4.71	17	
20T	2007/08	22	20	4	510	74	31.87	0	4	84	113	7	16.14	2-13	0	0	8.07	9	
CARTERS, Ryan Graham Leslie (Victoria) b Canberra, Australia Capital Territory 25.7.1990 RHB WK																			
20T		1																0	
CASSELL, Robert James (Victoria) b Melbourne, Victoria 28.4.1983 LHB RFM																			
Lim		1	1	1	6	6*		0	0	42	65	0					9.28	0	
FC	2002/03	2	3	1	20	18	10.00	0	0	270	159	7	22.71	4-33	0	0	3.53	0	
Lim	2002/03	4	1	1	6	6*		0	0	180	155	4	38.75	2-32	0	0	5.16	0	
CASSON, Beau (New South Wales) b Subiaco, Perth, Western Australia 7.12.1982 RHB SLC																			
FC		1	1	0	8	8	8.00	0	0	102	69	2	34.50	2-1	0	0	4.05	0	
Test	2008	1	1	0	10	10	10.00	0	0	192	129	3	43.00	3-86	0	0	4.03	2	
FC	2002/03	51	80	14	1491	99	22.59	0	8	8696	5161	119	43.36	6-64	4	1	3.56	22	
Lim	2002/03	21	8	2	47	18	7.83	0	0	624	516	18	28.66	4-31	1	0	4.96	3	
20T	2005/06	5								78	115	1	115.00	1-20	0	0	8.84	1	
CHRISTIAN, Daniel Trevor (Australia, South Australia, Australia to New Zealand, Hampshire) b Camperdown, New South Wales 4.5.1983 RHB RFM																			
FC		9	13	3	277	71	27.70	0	2	1570	818	25	32.72	5-24	1	0	3.12	5	
Lim		9	9	4	288	90*	57.60	0	1	391	401	9	44.55	4-32	1	0	6.15	4	
I20T		1	1	1	4	4*		0	0	24	29	2	14.50	2-29	0	0	7.25	0	
20T		7	7	4	58	17*	19.33	0	0	126	156	8	19.50	2-13	0	0	7.42	5	
FC	2007/08	19	30	3	664	72	24.59	0	4	3020	1786	56	31.89	5-24	2	0	3.54	18	
Lim	2006/07	33	31	9	833	94*	37.86	0	3	850	839	21	39.95	4-32	1	0	5.92	8	
I20T	2009/10	3	1	1	4	4*		0	0	42	69	2	34.50	2-29	0	0	9.85	0	
20T	2005/06	38	31	9	335	54	15.22	0	1	530	717	30	23.90	4-23	1	0	8.11	15	

Cmp	Debut	M	I	NO	Runs	HS	Avge	100	50	Balls	Runs	Wkts	Avge	BB	5i	10m	RpO	ct	st
CLARK, Stuart Rupert (New South Wales, New South Wales to India) b Sutherland, Sydney, New South Wales 28.9.1975 RHB RFM																			
FC		5	4	0	21	11	5.25	0	0	836	402	12	33.50	3-67	0	0	2.88	1	
Lim		5	3	1	45	29	22.50	0	0	276	203	5	40.60	2-47	0	0	4.41	0	
Test	2005/06	24	26	7	248	39	13.05	0	0	5146	2243	94	23.86	5-32	2	0	2.61	4	
FC	1997/98	107	134	37	1335	62	13.76	0	1	21742	10449	381	27.42	8-58	13	1	2.88	28	
Int	2005/06	39	12	7	69	16*	13.80	0	0	1829	1477	53	27.86	4-54	2	0	4.84	10	
Lim	1997/98	139	43	17	241	29	9.26	0	0	7065	5071	187	27.11	6-27	7	1	4.30	29	
I20T	2005/06	9								216	237	13	18.23	4-20	1	0	6.58	4	
20T	2005/06	15	1	1	0	0*		0	0	353	349	22	15.86	4-20	1	0	5.93	5	
CLARKE, Michael John (Australia, New South Wales, Australia to England, Australia to Ireland, Australia to New Zealand, Australia to West Indies) b Liverpool, New South Wales 2.4.1981 RHB SLA																			
Test		6	10	2	464	166	58.00	1	2									9	
FC		7	12	2	588	166	58.80	2	2									9	
Int		8	8	1	311	80	44.42	0	2	42	28	0					4.00	5	
Lim		9	9	1	319	80	39.87	0	2	42	28	0					4.00	5	
I20T		3	2	0	44	32	22.00	0	0	12	19	0					9.50	0	
20T		3	2	0	44	32	22.00	0	0	12	19	0					9.50	0	
Test	2004/05	62	101	12	4514	168	50.71	14	19	1636	782	20	39.10	6-9	1	0	2.86	61	
FC	1999/00	120	204	20	8475	201*	46.05	28	34	2816	1470	31	47.41	6-9	1	0	3.13	118	
Int	2002/03	178	162	34	5509	130	43.03	4	42	2234	1886	52	36.26	5-35	1	1	5.06	69	
Lim	2000/01	243	221	42	7327	130	40.93	5	56	2930	2422	77	31.45	5-35	1	1	4.96	93	
I20T	2004/05	33	27	5	472	67	21.45	0	1	156	225	6	37.50	1-2	0	0	8.65	13	
20T	2004	39	33	5	623	67	22.25	0	1	207	301	7	43.00	1-2	0	0	8.72	17	
CLEARY, Mark Francis (South Australia) b Moorabbin, Melbourne, Victoria 19.7.1980 LHB RFM																			
FC		3	5	1	78	34*	19.50	0	0	384	195	7	27.85	4-82	0	0	3.04	1	
20T		6	3	0	7	3	2.33	0	0	114	171	4	42.75	2-27	0	0	9.00	1	
FC	2002/03	50	75	13	1169	109*	18.85	1	3	8232	4599	148	31.07	7-80	4	1	3.35	17	
Lim	2002/03	71	51	18	524	70	15.87	0	1	3286	2788	86	32.41	4-55	1	0	5.09	17	
20T	2004	22	11	2	76	24*	8.44	0	0	451	623	25	24.92	3-11	0	0	8.28	4	
COCKLEY, Burt Tom (New South Wales) b Waratah, Newcastle, New South Wales 3.4.1986 RHB RFM																			
FC		2								246	194	1	194.00	1-106	0	0	4.73	0	
Lim		2	1	1	6	6*		0	0	73	61	4	15.25	4-39	1	0	5.01	1	
FC	2007/08	10	9	7	19	8*	9.50	0	0	1584	913	30	30.43	5-76	2	0	3.45	0	
Lim	2008/09	5	2	1	6	6*	6.00	0	0	196	219	5	43.80	4-39	1	0	6.70	1	
COETZEE, Justin Petrus (Western Australia) b Durban, Natal, South Africa 12.6.1984 LHB LFM																			
FC		1	2	0	16	15	8.00	0	0	108	55	2	27.50	1-18	0	0	3.05	1	
Lim		2	1	1	2	2*		0	0	60	61	0					6.10	0	
Lim	2008/09	5	4	1	49	39	16.33	0	0	150	135	1	135.00	1-33	0	0	5.40	0	
20T	2008/09	1	1	1	23	23*		0	0									1	
COOPER, Tom Lexley William (Netherlands, Netherlands to England, Netherlands to Ireland, Netherlands to Scotland, South Australia) b Wollongong, New South Wales 26.11.1986 RHB OB																			
FC		4	5	0	121	49	24.20	0	0	6	9	0					9.00	3	
Lim		10	10	1	270	78*	30.00	0	3									3	
20T		6	6	0	55	18	9.16	0	0									4	
FC	2008/09	6	8	0	160	49	20.00	0	0	31	23	0					4.45	4	
Int	2010	10	10	1	589	101	65.44	1	5	171	119	5	23.80	2-19	0	0	4.17	6	
Lim	2008/09	34	33	3	1235	101	41.16	2	10	177	121	5	24.20	2-19	0	0	4.10	15	
20T	2008/09	11	11	0	185	50	16.81	0	1									4	
COPELAND, Trent Aaron (New South Wales) b Gosford, New South Wales 14.3.1986 RHB RFM																			
FC		5	4	0	27	9	6.75	0	0	1405	615	35	17.57	8-92	3	1	2.62	3	
Lim		2								114	113	3	37.66	3-70	0	0	5.94	1	
COSGROVE, Mark James (South Australia, Glamorgan) b Elizabeth, Adelaide, South Australia 14.6.1984 LHB RM																			
FC		8	14	2	511	105	42.58	2	2	264	123	3	41.00	2-20	0	0	2.79	6	
Lim		5	5	0	204	104	40.80	1	0	60	53	2	26.50	2-27	0	0	5.30	0	
20T		6	6	1	154	43*	30.80	0	0									1	
FC	2002/03	90	160	11	6449	233	43.28	19	37	2520	1437	35	41.05	3-3	0	0	3.42	61	
Int	2005/06	3	3	0	112	74	37.33	0	1	30	13	1	13.00	1-1	0	0	2.60	0	
Lim	2002/03	96	93	4	3178	121	35.70	3	25	905	964	17	56.70	2-21	0	0	6.39	28	
20T	2005/06	41	40	2	1020	89	26.84	0	6	153	260	6	43.33	2-11	0	0	10.19	8	
COULTER-NILE, Nathan Mitchell (Western Australia) b Perth, Western Australia 11.10.1987 RHB RF																			
FC		3	6	0	83	31	13.83	0	0	532	296	11	26.90	3-11	0	0	3.33	5	
Lim		5	3	2	30	16*	30.00	0	0	257	203	7	29.00	3-46	0	0	4.73	2	
20T		5	3	2	23	19*	23.00	0	0	102	161	3	53.66	2-44	0	0	9.47	3	
COWAN, Edward James McKenzie (Australia A, Tasmania) b Paddington, Sydney, New South Wales 16.6.1982 LHB LB																			
FC		13	23	1	1127	225	51.22	4	3									7	
Lim		11	11	1	321	61	32.10	0	3									5	
20T		1	1	0	23	23	23.00	0	0									0	
FC	2003	38	69	4	2489	225	38.29	7	8	6	3	0					3.00	25	
Lim	2004/05	38	35	4	922	119	29.74	1	6									12	
20T	2006/07	5	5	0	76	25	15.20	0	0									1	

Cmp	Debut	M	I	NO	Runs	HS	Avge	100	50	Balls	Runs	Wkts	Avge	BB	5i	10m	RpO	ct	st
CRANMER, Michael Robert Craig (South Australia) b Adelaide, South Australia 16.3.1989 RHB RFM																			
Lim		2	1	0	3	3	3.00	0	0									1	
CULLEN, Daniel James (South Australia) b Woodville, Adelaide, South Australia 10.4.1984 RHB OB																			
Lim		1	1	0	22	22	22.00	0	0	36	34	0					5.66	0	
Test	2005/06	1								84	54	1	54.00	1-25	0	0	3.85	0	
FC	2004/05	46	63	27	567	42	15.75	0	0	10538	5757	130	44.28	5-38	4	0	3.27	10	
Int	2005/06	5	1	1	2	2*		0	0	213	147	2	73.50	2-25	0	0	4.14	2	
Lim	2004/05	55	20	8	123	27*	10.25	0	0	2537	1982	56	35.39	3-28	0	0	4.68	10	
20T	2005/06	18	10	4	38	10	6.33	0	0	335	404	16	25.25	3-23	0	0	7.23	6	
CUTTING, Benjamin Colin James (Queensland) b Sunnybank, Brisbane, Queensland 30.1.1987 RHB RF																			
FC		11	18	2	331	57	20.68	0	1	2013	1100	46	23.91	6-37	3	0	3.27	5	
Lim		10	7	2	89	42*	17.80	0	0	546	442	15	29.46	3-30	0	0	4.85	0	
20T		5	3	2	38	20*	38.00	0	0	96	137	4	34.25	2-30	0	0	8.56	1	
FC	2007/08	15	21	3	359	57	19.94	0	1	2783	1630	57	28.59	6-37	3	0	3.51	7	
20T	2008/09	9	4	3	46	20*	46.00	0	0	156	247	7	35.28	2-30	0	0	9.50	1	
DAVIS, Liam Murray (Western Australia) b Perth, Western Australia 2.8.1984 RHB RFM																			
FC		4	8	0	270	67	33.75	0	1									0	
Lim		3	3	0	51	27	17.00	0	0									1	
FC	2007/08	14	28	0	751	116	26.82	1	2	6	6	1	6.00	1-6	0	0	6.00	9	
Lim	2005/06	6	6	0	125	54	20.83	0	1									2	
20T	2007/08	4	4	0	49	24	12.25	0	0									0	
DENTON, Gerard John (Tasmania) b Mount Isa, Queensland 7.8.1975 RHB RFM																			
FC		1	2	1	14	11	14.00	0	0	100	77	1	77.00	1-59	0	0	4.62	1	
Lim		7	1	1	7	7*		0	0	324	269	16	16.81	5-45	0	1	4.98	3	
20T		2	2	2	10	6*		0	0	42	70	2	35.00	2-30	0	0	10.00	1	
FC	1994/95	58	81	30	605	48	11.86	0	0	10318	5663	181	31.28	6-31	5	0	3.29	16	
Lim	1995/96	41	13	7	99	35	16.50	0	0	1933	1552	55	28.21	5-45	0	1	4.81	8	
20T	2005/06	13	5	3	24	10	12.00	0	0	260	355	12	29.58	3-26	0	0	8.19	4	
DIGHTON, Michael Gray (Tasmania, Netherlands to England, Netherlands) b Toowoomba, Queensland 24.4.1976 RHB RM																			
Lim		11	11	0	300	80	27.27	0	3	48	44	1	44.00	1-15	0	0	5.50	3	
20T		2	2	0	24	24	12.00	0	0									1	
FC	1997/98	71	130	6	4208	182*	33.93	8	21	570	322	6	53.66	2-47	0	0	3.38	50	
Lim	1997/98	99	98	3	3190	146*	33.57	4	23	522	462	15	30.80	2-23	0	0	5.31	34	1
20T	2006/07	22	22	3	455	111	23.94	1	0	96	121	9	13.44	6-25	0	1	7.56	6	
DOHERTY, Xavier John (Australia A, Tasmania) b Scottsdale, Tasmania 22.11.1982 LHB SLA																			
FC		3	6	0	90	48	15.00	0	0	572	291	12	24.25	3-41	0	0	3.05	2	
Lim		14	4	3	52	37*	52.00	0	0	667	540	23	23.47	4-28	2	0	4.85	4	
20T		6	2	1	18	10	18.00	0	0	126	154	2	77.00	1-28	0	0	7.33	2	
FC	2001/02	32	52	10	572	53*	13.61	0	2	6354	3752	73	51.39	6-149	2	0	3.54	13	
Lim	2001/02	82	47	19	520	53	18.57	0	1	3727	2891	96	30.11	4-18	6	0	4.65	29	
20T	2005/06	21	9	5	74	33	18.50	0	0	444	609	11	55.36	2-26	0	0	8.23	10	
DOOLAN, Alexander James (Tasmania) b Launceston, Tasmania 29.11.1985 RHB RFM WK																			
FC		10	18	0	642	135	35.66	2	4									7	
20T		3	3	0	16	9	5.33	0	0									2	
FC	2008/09	13	24	0	772	135	32.16	2	4									9	
DORAN, Daniel John (Queensland) b Hobart, Tasmania 18.6.1981 RHB LB																			
FC		4	5	1	76	31*	19.00	0	0	642	471	4	117.75	3-107	0	0	4.40	2	
FC	2005/06	32	49	17	567	61	17.71	0	1	3470	2741	43	63.74	3-33	0	0	4.73	9	
DOREY, Brett Raymond (Western Australia) b East Fremantle, Western Australia 3.10.1977 RHB RFM																			
FC		4	3	1	26	18*	13.00	0	0	649	303	7	43.28	2-54	0	0	2.80	0	
Lim		4	4	1	18	15*	6.00	0	0	204	167	5	33.40	3-29	0	0	4.91	0	
FC	2004/05	40	56	10	796	53	17.30	0	1	8217	3894	151	25.78	7-86	9	1	2.84	15	
Int	2005/06	4	1	0	2	2	2.00	0	0	162	146	2	73.00	1-12	0	0	5.40	0	
Lim	2004/05	43	30	5	224	45	8.96	0	0	2148	1592	46	34.60	5-48	0	1	4.44	14	
20T	2005/06	16	6	2	20	14*	5.00	0	0	372	487	21	23.19	3-19	0	0	7.85	7	
DOROPOULOS, Theo Paul (Western Australia) b Subiaco, Perth, Western Australia 25.4.1985 RHB RFM																			
FC		2	4	1	76	65	25.33	0	1	30	21	2	10.50	2-16	0	0	4.20	2	
Lim		7	7	1	122	63	20.33	0	1	42	57	1	57.00	1-27	0	0	8.14	1	
20T		4	3	1	49	22	24.50	0	0	6	5	0					5.00	5	
FC	2007/08	8	14	2	276	65	23.00	0	2	210	146	4	36.50	2-16	0	0	4.17	6	
Lim	2007/08	20	20	2	473	92	26.27	0	4	180	175	2	87.50	1-14	0	0	5.83	6	
20T	2006/07	14	12	3	197	43	21.88	0	0	12	27	1	27.00	1-22	0	0	13.50	12	
DREW, Brendan Gerard (Australia A, Tasmania) b Lismore, New South Wales 16.12.1983 RHB RFM																			
FC		7	11	1	204	40	20.40	0	0	1243	769	19	40.47	4-81	0	0	3.71	5	
Lim		12	8	4	74	31*	18.50	0	0	496	441	16	27.56	3-56	0	0	5.33	1	
20T		3	2	0	6	6	3.00	0	0	66	89	6	14.83	3-30	0	0	8.09	1	
FC	2005/06	26	37	8	427	40	14.72	0	0	4519	2882	71	40.59	6-94	2	0	3.82	15	
Lim	2005/06	38	27	11	277	33*	17.31	0	0	1760	1653	55	30.05	5-36	0	1	5.63	11	
20T	2006/07	14	9	3	92	25	15.33	0	0	282	390	17	22.94	3-24	0	0	8.29	12	
DUNK, Ben Robert (Queensland) b Innisfail, Queensland 11.3.1987 LHB RSM																			
20T		6	5	1	142	70*	35.50	0	1									4	

Cmp	Debut	M	I	NO	Runs	HS	Avge	100	50	Balls	Runs	Wkts	Avge	BB	5i	10m	RpO	ct	st
DUVAL, Chris John (South Australia) b Elizabethvale, South Australia 3.8.1983 RHB RFM																			
FC		3	2	0	71	53	35.50	0	1	689	284	4	71.00	2-39	0	0	2.47	0	
Lim		1								24	33	1	33.00	1-33	0	0	8.25	1	
FC	2007/08	10	12	2	218	61	21.80	0	2	1889	907	17	53.35	4-29	0	0	2.88	7	
Lim	2004/05	8	5	3	74	32	37.00	0	0	354	386	5	77.20	1-28	0	0	6.54	2	
20T	2008/09	2	2	0	2	2	1.00	0	0	36	44	3	14.66	2-27	0	0	7.33	0	
EDMONDSON, Ben Matthew (Western Australia) b Southport, Queensland 28.9.1978 LHB RFM																			
FC		1	1	0	0	0	0.00	0	0	168	109	3	36.33	3-41	0	0	3.89	0	
Lim		1								60	45	3	15.00	3-45	0	0	4.50	0	
FC	2003/04	51	58	27	135	18	4.35	0	0	8806	5803	177	32.78	7-95	3	1	3.95	15	
Lim	2003	30	16	12	37	16*	9.25	0	0	1547	1307	46	28.41	5-39	1	1	5.06	3	
20T	2005/06	21	6	4	9	2*	4.50	0	0	463	582	30	19.40	4-14	2	0	7.54	3	
FAULKNER, James Peter (Tasmania) b Launceston, Tasmania 29.4.1990 RHB LMF																			
FC		4	5	1	123	59*	30.75	0	1	714	354	8	44.25	2-40	0	0	2.97	2	
Lim		7	3	0	10	8	3.33	0	0	300	265	7	37.85	2-36	0	0	5.30	2	
20T		4	3	2	13	7*	13.00	0	0	71	85	3	28.33	2-11	0	0	7.18	1	
FC	2008/09	5	6	1	148	59*	29.60	0	1	791	380	11	34.54	2-16	0	0	2.88	5	
Lim	2008/09	8	4	0	33	23	8.25	0	0	348	298	7	42.57	2-36	0	0	5.13	3	
FAWCETT, Jake David (Western Australia) b Osborne Park, Perth, Western Australia 22.3.1990 LHB OB																			
Lim		2	2	0	15	15	7.50	0	0	6	7	0					7.00	0	
FELDMAN, Luke William (Australia A, Queensland) b Sunnybank, Brisbane, Queensland 1.8.1984 RHB RFM																			
FC		8	13	8	173	31*	34.60	0	0	1496	791	33	23.96	5-32	1	0	3.17	3	
Lim		2								96	85	4	21.25	3-43	0	0	5.31	0	
FERGUSON, Callum James (Australia to South Africa) b North Adelaide, South Australia 21.11.1984 RHB RM																			
FC	2004/05	47	88	7	2842	132	35.08	4	19	42	38	0					5.42	21	
Int	2008/09	25	22	9	599	71*	46.07	0	5									6	
Lim	2002/03	74	69	14	1908	101	34.69	1	15									16	
I20T	2008/09	3	3	0	16	8	5.33	0	0									1	
20T	2005/06	19	18	0	245	58	13.61	0	1									10	
FINCH, Aaron James (Australia A, Victoria, Rajasthan Royals) b Colac, Victoria 17.11.1986 RHB LM																			
FC		6	11	0	416	102	37.81	1	3	42	21	0					3.00	3	
Lim		13	13	1	395	87*	32.91	0	2									4	
20T		7	6	1	219	58*	43.80	0	1									3	
FC	2007/08	7	11	0	416	102	37.81	1	3	42	21	0					3.00	4	
Lim	2007/08	19	19	2	489	87*	28.76	0	2									6	
20T	2008/09	13	10	1	291	58*	32.33	0	1	7	5	0					4.28	5	
FORREST, Peter James (Australia A, New South Wales) b Windsor, New South Wales 15.11.1985 RHB RM																			
FC		7	11	1	504	141	50.40	1	4									8	
FC	2006/07	26	47	4	1489	177	34.62	3	7									21	
Lim	2007/08	11	10	0	210	57	21.00	0	1									4	
20T	2008/09	2	2	1	21	13*	21.00	0	0									2	
GAYLE, Christopher Henry (Jamaica, West Indies, Kolkata Knight Riders, Western Australia, West Indies to Australia) b Kingston, Jamaica 21.9.1979 LHB OB																			
Test		3	6	1	346	165*	69.20	2	0	126	59	0					2.81	3	
FC		3	6	1	346	165*	69.20	2	0	126	59	0					2.81	3	
Int		5	5	1	55	34	13.75	0	0	66	65	1	65.00	1-32	0	0	5.90	0	
Lim		5	5	1	55	34	13.75	0	0	66	65	1	65.00	1-32	0	0	5.90	0	
I20T		2	2	0	17	12	8.50	0	0	12	15	2	7.50	2-15	0	0	7.50	0	
20T		4	4	0	78	44	19.50	0	0	36	41	3	13.66	2-15	0	0	6.83	1	
Test	1999/00	88	155	6	6007	317	40.31	12	33	6851	2992	72	41.55	5-34	2	0	2.62	84	
FC	1998/99	162	288	21	11761	317	44.04	28	59	12127	5012	129	38.85	5-34	2	0	2.48	142	
Int	1999	220	215	15	7885	153*	39.42	19	42	6816	5395	156	34.58	5-46	3	1	4.74	95	
Lim	1998/99	278	272	22	9957	153*	39.82	21	56	8810	6667	209	31.89	5-46	4	1	4.54	115	
I20T	2005/06	20	20	1	617	117	32.47	1	5	209	254	12	21.16	2-15	0	0	7.29	5	
20T	2005	51	50	5	1357	117	30.15	1	8	634	775	30	25.83	3-13	0	0	7.33	17	
GEEVES, Brett (Tasmania) b Claremont, Tasmania 13.6.1982 RHB RFM																			
FC		6	8	1	140	40	20.00	0	0	1218	571	21	27.19	5-106	1	0	2.81	2	
Lim		8	5	3	97	36	48.50	0	0	434	411	10	41.10	3-42	0	0	5.68	3	
20T		5	5	1	86	22	21.50	0	0	96	151	6	25.16	4-30	1	0	9.43	1	
FC	2004/05	41	65	19	1006	99*	21.86	0	4	8126	4634	140	33.10	6-47	6	0	3.42	11	
Int	2008	2	2	2	10	10*		0	0	90	78	3	26.00	2-11	0	0	5.20	1	
Lim	2000/01	71	41	15	318	37*	12.23	0	0	3485	2937	101	29.07	5-45	0	1	5.05	17	
I20T	2008/09	1								20	35	2	17.50	2-35	0	0	10.50	0	
20T	2007/08	14	7	1	133	28	22.16	0	0	302	461	19	24.26	4-30	1	0	9.15	5	
GEORGE, Peter Robert (Australia A, South Australia) b Woodville, South Australia 16.10.1986 RHB RFM																			
FC		12	12	7	14	6*	2.80	0	0	2522	1264	47	26.89	8-84	2	1	3.00	4	
Lim		4	2	1	4	3	4.00	0	0	216	155	2	77.50	1-45	0	0	4.30	2	
FC	2008/09	18	17	9	18	6*	2.25	0	0	3829	1907	67	28.46	8-84	2	1	2.98	5	
Lim	2008/09	5	2	1	4	3	4.00	0	0	276	193	3	64.33	1-38	0	0	4.19	2	

Cmp	Debut	M	I	NO	Runs	HS	Avge	100	50	Balls	Runs	Wkts	Avge	BB	5i	10m	RpO	ct	st
GILMOUR, Steven Thomas (Victoria) b Numurkah, Victoria 16.10.1986 RHB RFM																			
Lim		1								12	15	1	15.00	1-15	0	0	7.50	0	
FC	2008/09	2	2	0	19	13	9.50	0	0	258	207	4	51.75	2-68	0	0	4.81	0	
GRIFFITH, Adam Richard (Tasmania) b Launceston, Tasmania 11.2.1978 RHB RFM																			
FC		4	7	1	92	40*	15.33	0	0	816	406	13	31.23	5-85	1	0	2.98	1	
FC	2002/03	48	71	16	676	47	12.29	0	0	10432	5683	168	33.82	7-54	8	1	3.26	6	
Lim	2002/03	54	22	9	90	33	6.92	0	0	2798	2206	63	35.01	4-36	1	0	4.73	9	
20T	2005/06	12	3	1	7	6	3.50	0	0	261	289	19	15.21	3-14	0	0	6.64	0	
HABERFIELD, Jake Andy (Australia A, South Australia) b Townsville, Queensland 18.6.1986 RHB RFM																			
FC		7	7	2	10	4	2.00	0	0	1231	794	18	44.11	3-52	0	0	3.87	2	
Lim		12	5	4	13	5*	13.00	0	0	520	455	17	26.76	3-22	0	0	5.25	5	
20T		2								36	53	1	53.00	1-27	0	0	8.83	0	
FC	2008/09	9	8	3	15	5*	3.00	0	0	1537	949	23	41.26	4-60	0	0	3.70	3	
Lim	2008/09	17	6	5	16	5*	16.00	0	0	733	629	27	23.29	3-22	0	0	5.14	8	
HADDIN, Bradley James (Australia, New South Wales, Australia to New Zealand, Australia to West Indies) b Cowra, New South Wales 23.10.1977 RHB WK																			
Test		6	10	2	294	88	36.75	0	2									31	1
FC		8	13	3	370	88	37.00	0	2									33	1
Int		8	7	3	114	32	28.50	0	0									22	2
Lim		10	9	3	154	32	25.66	0	0									26	2
I20T		3	3	1	44	37*	22.00	0	0									1	1
20T		3	3	1	44	37*	22.00	0	0									1	1
Test	2008	27	45	5	1544	169	38.60	2	5									110	2
FC	1999/00	122	201	23	7208	169	40.49	12	37									384	27
Int	2000/01	66	61	6	1796	110	32.65	2	10									90	7
Lim	1997/98	165	157	14	4801	138*	33.57	8	27									229	44
I20T	2005/06	22	20	4	300	47	18.75	0	0									11	3
20T	2004/05	33	31	4	519	54	19.22	0	2									20	10
HARRIS, Daniel Joseph (South Australia) b North Adelaide, South Australia 31.12.1979 RHB RM																			
FC		10	19	1	622	166*	34.55	1	4									11	
Lim		10	10	0	253	68	25.30	0	2									2	
20T		6	6	0	149	48	24.83	0	0									3	
FC	1999/00	43	84	3	2516	166*	31.06	4	15	968	452	11	41.09	3-45	0	0	2.80	48	
Lim	2004/05	34	34	1	924	79	28.00	0	7	98	115	1	115.00	1-24	0	0	7.04	10	
20T	2006/07	18	17	0	531	98	31.23	0	2	24	29	0					7.25	4	
HARRIS, Ryan James (Australia, Queensland, Australia to England, Australia to Ireland, Australia to New Zealand, Australia to West Indies, Deccan Chargers) b Nowra, New South Wales 11.10.1979 RHB RFM																			
FC		1	1	0	84	84	84.00	0	1	240	129	2	64.50	2-30	0	0	3.22	1	
Int		7	5	3	29	21	14.50	0	0	335	220	20	11.00	5-19	0	2	3.94	1	
Lim		8	6	3	33	21	11.00	0	0	371	258	21	12.28	5-19	0	2	4.17	1	
I20T		1								24	27	2	13.50	2-27	0	0	6.75	0	
20T		7	1	0	0	0	0.00	0	0	149	187	10	18.70	3-23	0	0	7.53	0	
Test	2009/10	2	2	1	28	18*	28.00	0	0	423	207	9	23.00	4-77	0	0	2.93	1	
FC	2001/02	40	66	8	1175	94	20.25	0	6	7373	3860	118	32.71	7-108	2	0	3.14	19	
Int	2008/09	17	11	6	43	21	8.60	0	0	845	661	41	16.12	5-19	0	3	4.69	4	
Lim	2000/01	72	45	17	379	39	13.53	0	0	3440	2795	100	27.95	5-19	1	4	4.87	27	
I20T	2009/10	3	1	1	2	2*		0	0	70	95	4	23.75	2-27	0	0	8.14	0	
20T	2006/07	38	22	9	148	31	11.38	0	0	841	1015	50	20.30	3-18	0	0	7.24	12	
HARTLEY, Christopher Desmond (Queensland) b Nambour, Queensland 24.5.1982 LHB WK																			
FC		12	20	2	839	125	46.61	2	4									49	1
Lim		10	10	1	308	70*	34.22	0	3									13	2
FC	2003/04	61	101	15	2745	125	31.91	5	14									267	9
Lim	2003/04	60	50	14	855	70*	23.75	0	3									72	9
20T	2005/06	17	11	4	137	27*	19.57	0	0									13	4
HARWOOD, Shane Michael (Victoria, Victoria to India) b Ballarat, Victoria 1.3.1974 RHB RFM																			
Lim		2								120	145	6	24.16	3-68	0	0	7.25	0	
FC	2002/03	44	56	10	666	68*	14.47	0	1	8761	4488	137	32.75	6-38	4	0	3.07	11	
Int	2008/09	1	1	0	0	0	0.00	0	0	60	57	2	28.50	2-57	0	0	5.70	0	
Lim	2001/02	51	27	9	191	50*	10.61	0	1	2616	1919	78	24.60	5-40	1	3	4.40	8	
I20T	2006/07	3	1	1	0	0*		0	0	72	113	3	37.66	2-21	0	0	9.41	0	
20T	2005/06	29	10	6	81	20*	20.25	0	0	621	769	35	21.97	3-13	0	0	7.43	6	
HASTINGS, John Wayne (Victoria) b Nepean, New South Wales 4.11.1985 RHB RFM																			
FC		11	15	3	446	93	37.16	0	2	2024	941	36	26.13	4-30	0	0	2.79	5	
Lim		11	8	2	155	41*	25.83	0	0	621	565	19	29.73	4-38	1	0	5.45	4	
20T		7	4	0	4	2	1.00	0	0	168	207	10	20.70	3-21	0	0	7.39	2	
FC	2007/08	15	19	3	472	93	29.50	0	2	2694	1255	52	24.13	5-61	1	0	2.79	5	
Lim	2007/08	17	13	3	230	41*	23.00	0	0	867	772	27	28.59	4-38	1	0	5.34	6	
20T	2007/08	12	8	0	38	20	4.75	0	0	225	292	11	26.54	3-21	0	0	7.78	5	

Cmp	Debut	M	I	NO	Runs	HS	Avge	100	50	Balls	Runs	Wkts	Avge	BB	5i	10m	RpO	ct	st
HAURITZ, Nathan Michael (Australia, Australia to England, Australia to India, Australia to Ireland, Australia to New Zealand, Australia to South Africa, New South Wales to India) b Wondai, Queensland 18.10.1981 RHB OB																			
Test		6	9	3	200	75	33.33	0	2	1474	778	29	26.82	5-53	2	0	3.16	2	
FC		6	9	3	200	75	33.33	0	2	1474	778	29	26.82	5-53	2	0	3.16	2	
Int		9	6	4	80	53*	40.00	0	1	408	356	9	39.55	3-28	0	0	5.23	6	
Lim		9	6	4	80	53*	40.00	0	1	408	356	9	39.55	3-28	0	0	5.23	6	
Test	2004/05	15	20	6	370	75	26.42	0	2	3660	1814	57	31.82	5-53	2	0	2.97	3	
FC	2001/02	58	75	19	1053	94	18.80	0	4	11297	5628	133	42.31	5-53	2	0	2.98	28	
Int	2001/02	55	30	17	331	53*	25.46	0	1	2562	2014	62	32.48	4-29	2	0	4.71	24	
Lim	2000/01	147	94	43	1059	53*	20.76	0	1	6983	5418	172	31.50	4-29	6	0	4.65	51	
I20T	2008/09	3	2	0	6	4	3.00	0	0	44	47	2	23.50	1-20	0	0	6.40	1	
20T	2005/06	18	10	6	67	23*	16.75	0	0	326	344	17	20.23	2-21	0	0	6.33	6	
HAZLEWOOD, Josh Reginald (New South Wales, Australia to England) b Tamworth, New South Wales 8.1.1991 LHB RFM																			
FC		5	4	2	21	9*	10.50	0	0	669	371	13	28.53	3-94	0	0	3.32	2	
Lim		8	3	2	8	5*	8.00	0	0	446	337	12	28.08	2-22	0	0	4.53	3	
20T		3	1	1	6	6*		0	0	65	95	1	95.00	1-35	0	0	8.76	0	
FC	2008/09	6	5	3	23	9*	11.50	0	0	844	447	17	26.29	3-94	0	0	3.17	3	
Int	2010	1								42	41	1	41.00	1-41	0	0	5.85	0	
Lim	2009/10	9	3	2	8	5*	8.00	0	0	488	378	13	29.07	2-22	0	0	4.64	3	
HEAL, Aaron Keith (Western Australia) b Armadale, Perth, Western Australia 13.3.1983 LHB SLA																			
FC		3	2	2	81	81*		0	1	528	310	5	62.00	2-55	0	0	3.52	1	
Lim		7	4	1	8	5*	2.66	0	0	384	364	9	40.44	4-58	1	0	5.68	2	
20T		5	2	0	4	3	2.00	0	0	120	117	9	13.00	2-13	0	0	5.85	1	
FC	2003/04	19	24	3	439	81*	20.90	0	4	3393	1789	36	49.69	5-57	2	1	3.16	7	
Lim	2003/04	28	19	4	223	50	14.86	0	1	1470	1182	33	35.81	4-58	1	0	4.82	5	
20T	2006/07	17	8	2	52	13	8.66	0	0	394	458	23	19.91	2-13	0	0	6.97	5	
HENRIQUES, Moises Constantino (Australia A, New South Wales, Australia to India, Delhi Daredevils, New South Wales to India) b Funchal, Portugal 1.2.1987 RHB RFM																			
FC		4	6	0	180	65	30.00	0	2	564	311	10	31.10	3-69	0	0	3.30	2	
Lim		11	11	1	252	59	25.20	0	1	402	383	7	54.71	2-20	0	0	5.71	4	
20T		6	5	1	68	37	17.00	0	0	84	135	2	67.50	1-11	0	0	9.64	3	
FC	2006/07	16	28	2	799	82	30.73	0	5	1931	1011	28	36.10	5-17	2	0	3.14	7	
Int	2009/10	2	2	0	18	12	9.00	0	0	90	84	1	84.00	1-51	0	0	5.60	0	
Lim	2005/06	36	31	5	538	59	20.69	0	1	1391	1278	29	44.06	3-29	0	0	5.51	15	
I20T	2008/09	1	1	0	1	1	1.00	0	0									0	
20T	2005/06	32	28	4	398	51*	16.58	0	1	502	689	25	27.56	3-11	0	0	8.23	17	
HILFENHAUS, Benjamin William (Australia, Australia A, Tasmania, Australia to England, Australia to India) b Ulverstone, Tasmania 15.3.1983 RHB RFM																			
Test		1								138	70	5	14.00	3-20	0	0	3.04	2	
FC		3	2	0	92	50	46.00	0	1	491	224	14	16.00	5-63	1	0	2.73	5	
Lim		1								60	39	1	39.00	1-39	0	0	3.90	0	
Test	2008/09	11	15	6	145	56*	16.11	0	1	2344	1230	42	29.28	4-60	0	0	3.14	3	
FC	2005/06	50	66	22	544	56*	12.36	0	2	11239	5870	204	28.77	7-58	7	1	3.13	17	
Int	2006/07	15	7	4	29	16	9.66	0	0	758	717	18	39.83	2-42	0	0	5.67	7	
Lim	2005/06	53	24	15	92	18*	10.22	0	0	2811	2207	61	36.18	3-29	0	0	4.71	15	
I20T	2006/07	6	2	1	2	2	2.00	0	0	138	143	8	17.87	2-15	0	0	6.21	0	
20T	2005/06	16	7	3	24	7*	6.00	0	0	355	414	22	18.81	3-17	0	0	6.99	2	
HILL, Michael William (Victoria) b Melbourne, Victoria 29.9.1988 LHB RM																			
FC		2	3	1	62	32*	31.00	0	0									3	
Lim		3	2	1	27	15	27.00	0	0									1	
Lim	2008/09	6	4	1	60	19	20.00	0	0									4	
HODGE, Bradley John (Victoria, Kolkata Knight Riders, Leicestershire, Victoria to India) b Sandringham, Victoria 29.12.1974 RHB OB																			
FC		3	4	0	276	195	69.00	1	1	102	48	0					2.82	2	
Lim		11	11	2	622	139	69.11	4	0	174	164	2	82.00	1-31	0	0	5.65	1	
20T		7	7	0	181	90	25.85	0	1									2	
Test	2005/06	6	11	2	503	203*	55.88	1	2	12	8	0					4.00	9	
FC	1993/94	223	388	38	17084	302*	48.81	51	64	5583	3086	74	41.70	4-17	0	0	3.31	127	
Int	2005/06	25	21	2	575	123	30.26	1	3	66	51	1	51.00	1-17	0	0	4.63	16	
Lim	1993/94	234	224	28	8255	164	42.11	25	35	1698	1508	40	37.70	5-28	0	1	5.32	90	
I20T	2007/08	8	5	2	94	36	31.33	0	0	12	20	0					10.00	3	
20T	2003	99	96	11	3077	106	36.20	2	21	720	917	43	21.32	4-17	2	0	7.64	38	
HOGAN, Michael Garry (Western Australia) b Newcastle, New South Wales 31.5.1981 RHB RFM																			
FC		7	11	4	90	25	12.85	0	0	1486	711	23	30.91	5-83	1	0	2.87	4	
Lim		8	3	2	10	9*	10.00	0	0	402	311	6	51.83	2-32	0	0	4.64	3	
20T		3								60	87	2	43.50	1-10	0	0	8.70	1	
HOLLAND, Jonathan Mark (Victoria, Victoria to India) b Sandringham, Victoria 29.5.1987 RHB SLA																			
FC		3	4	2	28	12	14.00	0	0	608	424	6	70.66	3-81	0	0	4.18	1	
Lim		4	4	1	16	14	5.33	0	0	222	170	0					4.59	0	
20T		4	1	1	1	1*		0	0	60	78	4	19.50	2-27	0	0	7.80	0	
FC	2008/09	9	10	5	93	25	18.60	0	0	1831	1016	20	50.80	3-81	0	0	3.32	2	

Cmp	Debut	M	I	NO	Runs	HS	Avge	100	50	Balls	Runs	Wkts	Avge	BB	5i	10m	RpO	ct	st
Lim	2008/09	12	7	4	25	14	8.33	0	0	625	523	6	87.16	2-44	0	0	5.02	1	
20T	2008/09	11	3	1	1	1*	0.50	0	0	180	227	5	45.40	2-27	0	0	7.56	0	
HOPES, James Redfern (Australia, Queensland, Australia to England, Australia to India, Australia to Ireland, Australia to New Zealand, Australia to South Africa) b Townsville, Queensland 24.10.1978 RHB RM																			
FC		3	4	0	70	28	17.50	0	0	606	260	13	20.00	5-66	1	0	2.57	2	
Int		5	5	1	151	57*	37.75	0	1	174	134	2	67.00	1-27	0	0	4.62	0	
Lim		8	8	1	176	57*	25.14	0	1	353	290	4	72.50	1-27	0	0	4.92	1	
20T		6	6	1	185	63	37.00	0	2	120	167	8	20.87	3-33	0	0	8.35	1	
FC	2001/02	61	100	1	2970	146	30.00	5	14	8995	4112	132	31.15	6-70	3	0	2.74	26	
Int	2004/05	83	61	8	1326	63*	25.01	0	3	3115	2328	67	34.74	5-14	0	1	4.48	24	
Lim	2000/01	173	140	16	3311	115	26.70	2	15	7419	5621	193	29.12	5-14	5	2	4.54	48	
I20T	2004/05	12	7	2	105	30	21.00	0	0	222	283	10	28.30	2-26	0	0	7.64	3	
20T	2004/05	44	38	3	782	71	22.34	0	6	765	1109	32	34.65	3-33	0	0	8.69	11	
HUGHES, Phillip Joel (Australia, New South Wales, Australia to New Zealand, Hampshire, New South Wales to India) b Macksville, New South Wales 30.11.1988 LHB OB																			
Test		1	2	0	37	37	18.50	0	0									0	
FC		11	19	0	990	192	52.10	3	5									8	
Lim		9	9	1	221	72*	27.62	0	1									3	
20T		3	3	1	96	71*	48.00	0	1									2	
Test	2008/09	7	13	1	615	160	51.25	2	2									3	
FC	2007/08	43	77	6	3967	198	55.87	13	21	18	9	0					3.00	30	
Lim	2007/08	37	37	4	1117	119	33.84	1	7									12	
20T	2008/09	13	13	3	486	83	48.60	0	4									8	
HUSSEY, David John (Australia, Victoria, Australia to England, Australia to New Zealand, Australia to West Indies, Kolkata Knight Riders, Nottinghamshire, Victoria to India) b Morley, Western Australia 15.7.1977 RHB OB																			
FC		10	17	0	970	174	57.05	3	5	215	123	1	123.00	1-21	0	0	3.43	14	
Lim		9	9	0	298	93	33.11	0	2	114	89	2	44.50	1-10	0	0	4.68	6	
I20T		3	2	1	41	40*	41.00	0	0	6	4	0					4.00	2	
20T		10	8	2	186	60*	31.00	0	1	66	68	2	34.00	2-16	0	0	6.18	4	
FC	2002/03	147	227	22	11417	275	55.69	39	50	2348	1486	21	70.76	4-105	0	0	3.79	180	
Int	2008	23	21	0	598	111	28.47	1	4	257	230	3	76.66	1-6	0	0	5.37	12	
Lim	2001	174	163	23	5636	130	40.25	8	37	1480	1302	30	43.40	3-26	0	0	5.27	86	
I20T	2007/08	25	23	3	579	88*	28.95	0	3	252	267	15	17.80	3-25	0	0	6.35	14	
20T	2004	127	122	23	3219	100*	32.51	1	17	814	990	38	26.05	3-25	0	0	7.29	67	
HUSSEY, Michael Edward Killeen (Australia, Australia to England, Australia to India, Australia to Ireland, Australia to New Zealand, Australia to South Africa, Australia to West Indies, Chennai Super Kings) b Morley, Western Australia 27.5.1975 LHB RM																			
Test		6	11	2	502	134*	55.77	1	3	12	3	1	3.00	1-3	0	0	1.50	8	
FC		6	11	2	502	134*	55.77	1	3	12	3	1	3.00	1-3	0	0	1.50	8	
Int		9	8	2	315	67	52.50	0	1	12	12	0					6.00	3	
Lim		9	8	2	315	67	52.50	0	1	12	12	0					6.00	3	
Test	2005/06	52	90	12	3981	182	51.03	11	21	180	103	2	51.50	1-3	0	0	3.43	50	
FC	1994/95	235	419	43	19906	331*	52.94	52	92	1620	875	22	39.77	3-34	0	0	3.24	255	
Int	2003/04	146	121	38	4287	109*	51.65	2	31	234	227	2	113.50	1-22	0	0	5.82	82	
Lim	1996/97	339	307	65	10933	123	45.17	11	82	780	821	20	41.05	3-52	0	0	6.31	176	
I20T	2004/05	27	20	7	457	60*	35.15	0	2	6	5	0					5.00	18	
20T	2003	42	34	10	1009	116*	42.04	1	5	6	5	0					5.00	26	
IRVINE, Wade George (Tasmania) b Canberra, Australian Capital Territory 11.12.1986 RHB RM,OB																			
Lim		1	1	0	9	9	9.00	0	0									0	
JAQUES, Philip Anthony (New South Wales, Worcestershire) b Wollongong, New South Wales 3.5.1979 LHB SLC																			
FC		10	17	1	636	131	39.75	1	4									3	
Lim		10	10	1	380	171*	42.22	1	2									1	
20T		5	5	1	64	33	16.00	0	0									0	
Test	2005/06	11	19	0	902	150	47.47	3	6									7	
FC	2000/01	147	261	10	12808	244	51.02	36	61	68	87	0					7.67	109	
Int	2005/06	6	6	0	125	94	20.83	0	1									3	
Lim	2000/01	137	134	9	5366	171*	42.92	14	29	18	19	0					6.33	35	
20T	2003	49	48	5	1297	92	30.16	0	8	6	15	0					15.00	14	
JEWELL, Nicholas (Victoria) b Melbourne, Victoria 27.8.1977 RHB LFM																			
FC		11	19	0	682	96	35.89	0	6									6	
FC	2001/02	61	108	4	3920	188	37.69	6	25	216	107	2	53.50	1-7	0	0	2.97	37	
Lim	2001/02	14	14	0	384	60	27.42	0	2	12	11	0					5.50	1	
JOHNSON, Mitchell Guy (Australia, Australia to England, Australia to India, Australia to New Zealand, Australia to South Africa, Australia to West Indies) b Townsville, Queensland 2.11.1981 LHB LFM																			
Test		6	9	0	125	38	13.88	0	0	1328	785	29	27.06	5-103	1	0	3.54	2	
FC		6	9	0	125	38	13.88	0	0	1328	785	29	27.06	5-103	1	0	3.54	2	
Int		5	4	1	43	21	14.33	0	0	210	164	5	32.80	2-42	0	0	4.68	4	
Lim		5	4	1	43	21	14.33	0	0	210	164	5	32.80	2-42	0	0	4.68	4	
I20T		3	2	0	6	4	3.00	0	0	72	74	2	37.00	2-28	0	0	6.16	0	
20T		3	2	0	6	4	3.00	0	0	72	74	2	37.00	2-28	0	0	6.16	0	
Test	2007/08	36	49	8	969	123*	23.63	1	4	8398	4563	158	28.87	8-61	5	2	3.26	9	

Cmp	Debut	M	I	NO	Runs	HS	Avge	100	50	Balls	Runs	Wkts	Avge	BB	5i	10m	RpO	ct	st
FC	2001/02	64	87	19	1649	123*	24.25	1	8	13216	7373	244	30.21	8-61	7	3	3.34	16	
Int	2005/06	82	45	16	467	73*	16.10	0	1	3997	3292	128	25.71	5-26	4	2	4.94	21	
Lim	2003/04	106	55	21	565	73*	16.61	0	1	5317	4354	158	27.55	5-26	6	2	4.91	24	
I20T	2007/08	24	13	4	76	28*	8.44	0	0	512	586	30	19.53	3-15	0	0	6.86	4	
20T	2005/06	27	14	4	81	28*	8.10	0	0	566	640	32	20.00	3-15	0	0	6.78	4	
JOHNSTON, Matt James (Western Australia) b South Perth, Western Australia 15.10.1985 LHB RF																			
FC		1	2	0	44	44	22.00	0	0	48	20	1	20.00	1-17	0	0	2.50	0	
Lim		1	1	0	39	39	39.00	0	0	6	5	0					5.00	0	
Lim	2007/08	8	7	1	186	44	31.00	0	0	6	5	0					5.00	0	
20T	2006/07	2	2	1	24	17	24.00	0	0	6	5	2	2.50	2-5	0	0	5.00	0	
JONES, Brady (Tasmania) b Franklin, Tasmania 16.9.1988 RHB OB WK																			
FC		6	8	4	87	45*	21.75	0	0									14	
Lim		2	1	0	1	1	1.00	0	0									5	
KATICH, Simon Mathew (Australia, New South Wales, Australia to England, Australia to New Zealand, Lancashire, New South Wales to India) b Middle Swan, Western Australia 21.8.1975 LHB SLC																			
Test		5	9	0	513	100	57.00	1	4	90	57	3	19.00	3-34	0	0	3.80	4	
FC		11	18	1	829	108	48.76	2	6	90	57	3	19.00	3-34	0	0	3.80	10	
Lim		6	5	0	113	55	22.60	0	1	30	31	0					6.20	3	
Test	2001	52	91	6	3981	157	46.83	10	24	1009	617	21	29.38	6-65	1	0	3.66	38	
FC	1996/97	223	382	47	18134	306	54.13	50	97	5769	3462	95	36.44	7-130	3	0	3.60	204	
Int	2000/01	45	42	5	1324	107*	35.78	1	9									13	
Lim	1995/96	218	208	22	6900	136*	37.09	7	54	877	818	24	34.08	3-21	0	0	5.59	99	
I20T	2004/05	3	2	0	69	39	34.50	0	0									2	
20T	2003	52	48	9	1239	75	31.76	0	5	12	14	0					7.00	27	
KEEN, Simon John Cobrin (New South Wales) b Wahroonga, New South Wales 4.10.1987 LHB RM																			
Lim		1	1	0	29	29	29.00	0	0	36	38	1	38.00	1-38	0	0	6.33	0	
20T	2008/09	1	1	0	4	4	4.00	0	0									0	
KLINGER, Michael (Australia A, South Australia) b Kew, Melbourne, Victoria 4.7.1980 RHB																			
FC		12	22	5	930	207*	54.70	2	5	6	3	0					3.00	8	
Lim		9	9	0	502	124	55.77	2	3									6	
FC	1998/99	63	110	14	3779	255	39.36	8	17	6	3	0					3.00	60	
Lim	1998/99	76	76	9	2639	133*	39.38	6	18									24	
20T	2005/06	14	13	2	223	42	20.27	0	0									6	
KNOWLES, Bradley Aaron (Western Australia) b Moe, Victoria 29.10.1981 RHB RF																			
FC		7	10	3	118	36	16.85	0	0	1285	750	30	25.00	4-32	0	0	3.50	1	
Lim		8	5	3	27	16*	13.50	0	0	408	342	9	38.00	3-53	0	0	5.02	3	
20T		5	2	1	15	14	15.00	0	0	114	142	9	15.77	3-20	0	0	7.47	1	
FC	2004/05	9	13	5	140	36	17.50	0	0	1579	904	33	27.39	4-32	0	0	3.43	3	
Lim	2003/04	20	11	5	85	23	14.16	0	0	964	758	26	29.15	5-62	0	1	4.71	4	
KREJZA, Jason John (Tasmania) b Newtown, Sydney, New South Wales 14.1.1983 RHB OB																			
FC		8	11	0	81	23	7.36	0	0	1543	945	18	52.50	4-70	0	0	3.67	4	
Lim		11	9	3	118	32*	19.66	0	0	546	396	5	79.20	2-56	0	0	4.35	2	
20T		4	4	1	9	4	3.00	0	0	90	126	2	63.00	1-29	0	0	8.40	0	
Test	2008/09	2	4	1	71	32	23.66	0	0	743	562	13	43.23	8-215	1	1	4.53	4	
FC	2004/05	40	62	12	1047	101*	20.94	1	5	6986	4496	92	48.86	8-215	1	1	3.86	28	
Lim	2004/05	27	24	8	361	52*	22.56	0	1	1283	1060	23	46.08	3-41	0	0	4.95	10	
20T	2007/08	11	10	4	108	33*	18.00	0	0	240	286	10	28.60	3-23	0	0	7.15	1	
KRUGER, Nicholas James (Queensland) b Paddington, Sydney, New South Wales 14.8.1983 LHB RM																			
FC		8	13	0	441	172	33.92	1	1									4	
Lim		2	2	0	82	67	41.00	0	1									1	
FC	2002/03	17	30	1	838	172	28.89	1	3									12	
Lim	2002/03	4	4	0	129	67	32.25	0	1									1	
LAMBERT, Grant Michael (New South Wales) b Parramatta, Sydney, New South Wales 5.8.1977 RHB RFM																			
FC		4	5	1	67	38	16.75	0	0	624	381	10	38.10	3-27	0	0	3.66	2	
Lim		3	3	1	18	7	9.00	0	0	150	151	2	75.50	1-30	0	0	6.04	0	
20T		2								30	51	4	12.75	3-20	0	0	10.20	0	
FC	2001/02	39	58	6	1215	86	23.36	0	6	5105	3166	88	35.97	5-74	2	0	3.72	16	
Lim	2001/02	15	13	5	191	48*	23.87	0	0	696	658	15	43.86	2-33	0	0	5.67	3	
LAUGHLIN, Ben (Queensland) b Box Hill, Victoria 3.10.1982 RHB RFM																			
FC		1	1	0	35	35	35.00	0	0	186	60	0					1.93	1	
Lim		5	4	2	20	14*	10.00	0	0	292	278	9	30.88	3-33	0	0	5.71	0	
FC	2007/08	5	5	1	55	35	13.75	0	0	1044	603	10	60.30	2-55	0	0	3.46	3	
Int	2008/09	5	1	1	1	1*		0	0	224	219	4	54.75	1-28	0	0	5.86	2	
Lim	2008/09	21	10	7	28	14*	9.33	0	0	972	839	36	23.30	6-23	1	1	5.17	5	
I20T	2008/09	1								24	32	1	32.00	1-32	0	0	8.00	0	
20T	2008/09	7								144	176	5	35.20	1-14	0	0	7.33	1	
LEE, Brett (New South Wales, Australia to India, Australia to South Africa, Kings XI Punjab, New South Wales to India) b Wollongong, New South Wales 8.11.1976 RHB RF																			
Lim		1	1	1	19	19*		0	0	54	42	0					4.66	0	
Test	1999/00	76	90	18	1451	64	20.15	0	5	16531	9554	310	30.81	5-30	10	0	3.46	23	
FC	1994/95	116	139	25	2120	97	18.59	0	8	24193	13747	487	28.22	7-114	20	2	3.40	35	

Cmp	Debut	M	I	NO	Runs	HS	Avge	100	50	Balls	Runs	Wkts	Avge	BB	5i	10m	RpO	ct	st
Int	1999/00	186	92	37	897	57	16.30	0	2	9478	7456	324	23.01	5-22	11	9	4.72	44	
Lim	1997/98	219	112	46	1071	57	16.22	0	2	11274	8721	366	23.82	5-22	12	9	4.64	49	
I20T	2004/05	17	9	4	91	43*	18.20	0	0	355	454	17	26.70	3-27	0	0	7.67	5	
20T	2004/05	36	22	11	195	48	17.72	0	0	784	905	34	26.61	3-15	0	0	6.92	13	
LOCKYEAR, Rhett John Gaven (Tasmania) b Mudgee, New South Wales 28.2.1983 RHB RM																			
FC		5	10	0	185	85	18.50	0	1	42	25	1	25.00	1-1	0	0	3.57	2	
Lim		5	5	1	204	111	51.00	1	0									2	
20T		5	5	0	47	25	9.40	0	0									2	
FC	2004/05	15	30	0	570	85	19.00	0	3	126	62	3	20.66	1-1	0	0	2.95	6	
Lim	2005/06	10	10	1	240	111	26.66	1	0	6	12	0					12.00	5	
20T	2005/06	16	16	0	351	64	21.93	0	3	12	11	0					5.50	3	
LUDEMAN, Timothy Paul (South Australia) b Warrnambool, Victoria 23.6.1987 RHB RMF WK																			
FC		6	9	1	203	62	25.37	0	2									22	
Lim		3	3	1	23	13	11.50	0	0									3	
LYNN, Christopher Austin (Queensland) b Herston, Brisbane, Queensland 10.4.1990 RHB SLA																			
FC		3	6	0	220	139	36.66	1	0	24	28	0					7.00	2	
Lim		3	3	0	58	25	19.33	0	0	18	17	0					5.66	1	
20T		2	1	0	5	5	5.00	0	0	6	6	0					6.00	0	
McDERMOTT, Alister Craig (Queensland) b Brisbane, Queensland 7.6.1991 RHB RFM																			
FC		1								180	104	3	34.66	2-53	0	0	3.46	1	
Lim		7	4	4	4	2*		0	0	396	331	10	33.10	3-39	0	0	5.01	1	
20T		1								18	24	1	24.00	1-24	0	0	8.00	0	
20T	2008/09	5								84	98	2	49.00	1-13	0	0	7.00	2	
McDONALD, Andrew Barry (Australia A, Victoria, Delhi Daredevils, Leicestershire, Victoria to India) b Wodonga, Victoria 15.6.1981 RHB RFM																			
FC		12	20	5	470	120	31.33	2	0	2221	950	32	29.68	4-37	0	0	2.56	8	
Lim		12	12	4	340	64	42.50	0	3	661	591	14	42.21	4-50	1	0	5.36	5	
20T		8	7	3	121	32	30.25	0	0	132	166	9	18.44	3-21	0	0	7.54	3	
Test	2008/09	4	6	1	107	68	21.40	0	1	732	300	9	33.33	3-25	0	0	2.45	2	
FC	2001/02	69	112	25	3230	176*	37.12	6	18	9785	4602	159	28.94	6-34	4	0	2.82	51	
Lim	2001/02	77	67	21	1475	67	32.06	0	8	3116	2640	68	38.82	4-50	1	0	5.08	31	
20T	2005/06	39	34	14	678	67	33.90	0	2	678	872	45	19.37	5-13	1	1	7.71	12	
MacDONALD, Timothy Peter (Tasmania) b Subiaco, Perth, Western Australia 7.9.1980 RHB RFM																			
FC		10	14	7	33	11*	4.71	0	0	1796	863	20	43.15	3-65	0	0	2.88	3	
FC	2006/07	21	32	13	120	17	6.31	0	0	3393	1765	50	35.30	6-40	1	0	3.12	8	
Lim	2007/08	1								48	27	0					3.37	1	
20T	2006/07	3	1	1	8	8*		0	0	66	66	3	22.00	1-18	0	0	6.00	0	
McGAIN, Bryce Edward (Victoria, Essex) b Mornington, Victoria 25.3.1972 RHB LBG																			
FC		8	8	4	34	12*	8.50	0	0	1596	845	26	32.50	4-41	0	0	3.17	3	
Lim		7	2	1	1	1	1.00	0	0	372	336	10	33.60	3-37	0	0	5.41	1	
Test	2008/09	1	2	0	2	2	1.00	0	0	108	149	0					8.27	0	
FC	2001/02	32	35	13	242	25	11.00	0	0	6129	3467	100	34.67	6-112	5	0	3.39	11	
Lim	2002	23	11	6	97	51	19.40	0	1	1218	964	34	28.35	3-11	0	0	4.74	7	
20T	2007/08	7	2	2	7	6*		0	0	156	168	9	18.66	2-10	0	0	6.46	4	
McKAY, Clinton James (Australia, Victoria, Australia to England, Australia to India, Australia to Ireland, Australia to New Zealand, Victoria to India, Yorkshire) b Melbourne, Victoria 22.2.1983 RHB RFM																			
Test		1	1	0	10	10	10.00	0	0	168	101	1	101.00	1-56	0	0	3.60	1	
FC		5	6	1	102	55	20.40	0	1	982	469	17	27.58	4-47	0	0	2.86	2	
Int		7	1	1	0	0*		0	0	346	243	17	14.29	4-35	1	0	4.21	0	
Lim		8	2	1	2	2	2.00	0	0	400	295	17	17.35	4-35	1	0	4.42	0	
20T		4	2	1	16	15	16.00	0	0	96	141	5	28.20	2-24	0	0	8.81	2	
FC	2006/07	22	28	2	489	55	18.80	0	2	4508	2015	81	24.87	6-75	2	0	2.68	5	
Int	2009/10	12	3	2	6	4*	6.00	0	0	618	502	22	22.81	4-35	1	0	4.87	0	
Lim	2006/07	36	14	3	143	27	13.00	0	0	1987	1532	59	25.96	4-35	1	0	4.62	5	
20T	2007/08	25	13	6	105	21*	15.00	0	0	561	811	36	22.52	4-33	1	0	8.67	4	
MAGOFFIN, Steven James (Western Australia) b Corinda, Queensland 17.12.1979 LHB RFM																			
FC		10	16	3	260	78	20.00	0	1	2088	853	31	27.51	6-44	2	0	2.45	0	
Lim		1								60	29	2	14.50	2-29	0	0	2.90	0	
FC	2004/05	66	94	26	1252	79	18.41	0	4	13266	6182	222	27.84	8-47	7	1	2.79	17	
Lim	2004/05	48	28	18	216	24*	21.60	0	0	2412	1868	61	30.62	4-58	1	0	4.64	12	
20T	2005/06	8	2	1	12	11*	12.00	0	0	156	228	5	45.60	2-15	0	0	8.76	1	
MAHER, Adam John (Tasmania) b Newcastle, New South Wales 14.11.1981 RHB RFM																			
FC		4	6	2	29	20	7.25	0	0	723	417	12	34.75	3-55	0	0	3.46	2	
MANGAN, Joshua Patrick (Western Australia) b Rutherglen, Victoria 15.1.1986 RHB LBG																			
FC		1	1	1	5	5*		0	0	126	80	1	80.00	1-80	0	0	3.81	2	
FC	2008/09	4	6	1	115	38	23.00	0	0	378	238	3	79.33	2-102	0	0	3.77	2	
MANOU, Graham Allan (South Australia, Australia to India) b Modbury, South Australia 23.4.1979 RHB WK																			
FC		4	5	0	90	40	18.00	0	0									5	
Lim		7	6	0	101	42	16.83	0	0									9	1
20T		6	6	0	75	33	12.50	0	0									2	1
Test	2009	1	2	1	21	13*	21.00	0	0									3	

Cmp	Debut	M	I	NO	Runs	HS	Avge	100	50	Balls	Runs	Wkts	Avge	BB	5i	10m	RpO	ct	st
FC	1998/99	93	158	18	3430	190	24.50	5	16	12	8	0					4.00	288	20
Int	2009/10	4	1	0	7	7	7.00	0	0									5	
Lim	1998/99	110	93	23	1479	63	21.12	0	4									145	15
20T	2005/06	22	21	2	221	43	11.63	0	0									12	3
MARSH, Daniel James (Tasmania) b Subiaco, Perth, Western Australia 14.6.1973 RHB SLA																			
FC		11	20	1	622	134	32.73	1	3	765	430	6	71.66	2-29	0	0	3.37	10	
Lim		3	3	1	34	24	17.00	0	0	78	61	0					4.69	1	
FC	1993/94	150	257	39	8146	157	37.36	16	43	16265	8144	174	46.80	7-57	1	0	3.00	186	
Lim	1993/94	129	117	24	3119	106*	33.53	4	16	3799	3048	61	49.96	4-44	1	0	4.81	59	
20T	2006/07	13	12	1	182	30	16.54	0	0	173	237	9	26.33	3-18	0	0	8.22	5	
MARSH, Mitchell Ross (Western Australia, Deccan Chargers) b Armadale, Perth, Western Australia 20.10.1991 RHB RM																			
FC		6	11	1	219	59*	21.90	0	2									3	
Lim		6	6	1	292	92	58.40	0	3									3	
20T		3	2	0	24	21	12.00	0	0	14	6	4	1.50	4-6	1	0	2.57	5	
Lim	2008/09	8	8	1	309	92	44.14	0	3	186	176	5	35.20	3-37	0	0	5.67	5	
20T	2009/10	6	4	0	52	21	13.00	0	0	74	94	6	15.66	4-6	1	0	7.62	5	
MARSH, Shaun Edward (Australia, Western Australia, Australia to England, Australia to India, Kings XI Punjab) b Narrogin, Western Australia 9.7.1983 LHB SLA																			
FC		5	10	2	477	108*	59.62	1	4	30	11	0					2.20	6	
Int		7	7	0	223	83	31.85	0	1									3	
Lim		11	11	0	413	116	37.54	1	1									6	
20T		5	5	1	175	108*	43.75	1	0	6	2	0					2.00	2	
FC	2000/01	56	104	15	3232	166*	36.31	5	17	174	131	2	65.50	2-20	0	0	4.51	46	
Int	2008	27	27	1	1008	112	38.76	1	7									6	
Lim	2002/03	74	72	3	2487	116	36.04	3	16	36	31	1	31.00	1-14	0	0	5.16	18	
I20T	2008	3	3	0	53	29	17.66	0	0									0	
20T	2005/06	38	38	5	1429	115	43.30	2	10	12	13	0					6.50	12	
MASH, Lloyd Ryan (Victoria) b Melbourne, Victoria 1.12.1981 LHB OB																			
FC		4	8	0	80	40	10.00	0	0									3	
FC	2005/06	27	50	0	1252	94	25.04	0	10	6	0	0					0.00	16	
Lim	2005/06	6	5	0	48	32	9.60	0	0									2	
MAXWELL, Glenn James (Victoria) b 14.10.1988 RHB OB																			
Lim		1	1	0	9	9	9.00	0	0	24	20	0					5.00	1	
20T		2	1	0	10	10	10.00	0	0									3	
MOLLER, Gregory David (Queensland) b Boonah, Queensland 29.1.1983 RHB WK																			
FC		1	2	0	29	15	14.50	0	0									2	
FC	2006/07	11	19	0	417	78	21.94	0	2									9	
Lim	2008/09	4	4	0	48	23	12.00	0	0									1	
NANNES, Dirk Peter (Australia, Victoria, Australia to England, Australia to New Zealand, Australia to West Indies, Delhi Daredevils, Nottinghamshire) b Mount Waverly, Melbourne, Victoria 16.5.1976 RHB LFM																			
FC		1								192	122	4	30.50	3-65	0	0	3.81	1	
Lim		2								120	100	3	33.33	3-40	0	0	5.00	0	
I20T		2	1	0	4	4	4.00	0	0	48	48	4	12.00	3-21	0	0	6.00	0	
20T		9	2	1	4	4	4.00	0	0	204	223	11	20.27	3-21	0	0	6.55	0	
FC	2005/06	23	24	8	108	31*	6.75	0	0	4139	2327	93	25.02	7-50	2	1	3.37	7	
Int	2009	1	1	0	1	1	1.00	0	0	42	20	1	20.00	1-20	0	0	2.85	0	
Lim	2005/06	23	10	5	18	5*	3.60	0	0	1224	965	31	31.12	4-38	1	0	4.73	0	
I20T	2009	16	5	3	22	12*	11.00	0	0	348	431	27	15.96	4-18	1	0	7.43	1	
20T	2007/08	87	12	9	33	12*	11.00	0	0	1947	2307	120	19.22	4-11	5	0	7.10	13	
NAVED-UL-HASAN, Rana (Sialkot Stallions, WAPDA, Pakistan, Pakistan to Australia, Pakistan to South Africa, Sussex, Tasmania) b Sheikhupura, Punjab, Pakistan 28.2.1978 RHB RFM																			
Int		5	5	1	76	33	19.00	0	0	282	290	6	48.33	2-55	0	0	6.17	1	
Lim		5	5	1	76	33	19.00	0	0	282	290	6	48.33	2-55	0	0	6.17	1	
I20T		1	1	0	1	1	1.00	0	0	24	27	1	27.00	1-27	0	0	6.75	0	
20T		6	6	0	80	47	13.33	0	0	137	172	10	17.20	3-15	0	0	7.53	1	
Test	2004/05	9	15	3	239	42*	19.91	0	0	1565	1044	18	58.00	3-30	0	0	4.00	3	
FC	1995/96	122	174	20	3560	139	23.11	5	10	22636	12761	523	24.39	7-49	27	4	3.38	56	
Int	2002/03	74	51	18	524	33	15.87	0	0	3466	3221	110	29.28	6-27	6	1	5.57	16	
Lim	1999/00	170	130	34	2094	74	21.81	0	10	8032	7024	261	26.91	6-27	10	3	5.24	46	
I20T	2006	4	2	1	18	17*	18.00	0	0	85	101	5	20.20	3-19	0	0	7.12	2	
20T	2004/05	47	36	12	545	95	22.70	0	1	978	1122	52	21.57	4-23	1	0	6.88	21	
NEVILL, Peter Michael (New South Wales) b Hawthorne, Melbourne, Victoria 13.10.1985 RHB WK																			
FC		3	2	0	155	105	77.50	1	1									18	
Lim		1	1	1	4	4*		0	0									1	
20T		1																1	
FC	2008/09	4	4	0	173	105	43.25	1	1									19	
Lim	2008/09	4	3	1	13	9	6.50	0	0									5	
NOFFKE, Ashley Allan (Western Australia) b Nambour, Queensland 30.4.1977 RHB RFM																			
FC		6	8	1	233	61	33.28	0	2	1062	522	10	52.20	4-105	0	0	2.94	2	
Lim		7	7	1	92	43	15.33	0	0	380	247	10	24.70	3-43	0	0	3.90	1	
20T		4	3	1	17	13*	8.50	0	0	96	153	4	38.25	2-23	0	0	9.56	1	

Cmp	Debut	M	I	NO	Runs	HS	Avge	100	50	Balls	Runs	Wkts	Avge	BB	5i	10m	RpO	ct	st
FC	1998/99	117	162	24	3741	114*	27.10	2	18	22345	11214	384	29.20	8-24	18	1	3.01	43	
Int	2007/08	1								54	46	1	46.00	1-46	0	0	5.11	0	
Lim	1998/99	120	68	20	801	58	16.68	0	1	5858	4400	138	31.88	4-32	4	0	4.50	28	
I20T	2007/08	2	1	0	0	0	0.00	0	0	45	41	4	10.25	3-18	0	0	5.46	0	
20T	2003	30	23	5	263	34	14.61	0	0	634	789	38	20.76	3-18	0	0	7.46	7	

NORTH, Marcus James (Australia, Western Australia, Australia to England, Australia to New Zealand) b Pakenham, Melbourne, Victoria 28.7.1979 LHB OB

Cmp	Debut	M	I	NO	Runs	HS	Avge	100	50	Balls	Runs	Wkts	Avge	BB	5i	10m	RpO	ct	st
Test		6	9	0	207	79	23.00	0	2	126	62	0					2.95	3	
FC		13	21	0	501	107	23.85	1	2	997	450	12	37.50	4-82	0	0	2.70	10	
Lim		7	7	1	231	85*	38.50	0	2	280	193	8	24.12	3-38	0	0	4.13	1	
Test	2008/09	17	28	2	981	125*	37.73	4	4	934	434	12	36.16	6-55	1	0	2.78	14	
FC	1998/99	153	267	25	10400	239*	42.97	28	55	9762	4953	121	40.93	6-55	2	0	3.04	119	
Int	2008/09	2	2	0	6	5	3.00	0	0	18	16	0					5.33	1	
Lim	1998/99	136	129	16	3866	134*	34.21	6	27	2372	2004	65	30.83	4-26	1	0	5.06	41	
I20T	2008/09	1	1	0	20	20	20.00	0	0									0	
20T	2004	30	29	4	582	59	23.28	0	1	365	420	8	52.50	2-19	0	0	6.90	8	

O'BRIEN, Aaron Warren (South Australia) b St Leonards, New South Wales 2.10.1981 LHB SLA

Cmp	Debut	M	I	NO	Runs	HS	Avge	100	50	Balls	Runs	Wkts	Avge	BB	5i	10m	RpO	ct	st
FC		10	15	1	427	79	30.50	0	1	1750	888	14	63.42	3-49	0	0	3.04	7	
Lim		10	8	2	165	54	27.50	0	1	456	369	12	30.75	4-41	1	0	4.85	4	
20T		5	3	2	28	22*	28.00	0	0	66	64	7	9.14	3-15	0	0	5.81	3	
FC	2001/02	39	62	7	1535	147	27.90	1	6	4068	2030	35	58.00	3-49	0	0	2.99	20	
Lim	2001/02	47	41	12	952	62*	32.82	0	5	1561	1247	28	44.53	4-41	1	0	4.79	15	
20T	2005/06	18	15	6	150	38	16.66	0	0	309	377	19	19.84	3-15	0	0	7.32	6	

O'KEEFE, Stephen Norman John (Australia A, New South Wales, Australia to England) b Malaysia 9.12.1984 RHB SLA

Cmp	Debut	M	I	NO	Runs	HS	Avge	100	50	Balls	Runs	Wkts	Avge	BB	5i	10m	RpO	ct	st
FC		7	7	1	355	91	59.16	0	3	1266	646	24	26.91	7-35	1	0	3.06	6	
Lim		6	2	0	14	12	7.00	0	0	234	181	4	45.25	1-22	0	0	4.64	1	
FC	2005/06	8	8	1	365	91	52.14	0	3	1390	716	26	27.53	7-35	1	0	3.09	7	
Lim	2005/06	16	10	2	136	29	17.00	0	0	582	462	8	57.75	2-34	0	0	4.76	8	
I20T	2010	1	1	0	5	5	5.00	0	0	24	29	3	9.66	3-29	0	0	7.25	1	
20T	2008/09	4	3	0	17	6	5.66	0	0	72	96	4	24.00	3-29	0	0	8.00	2	

PAINE, Timothy David (Australia, Tasmania, Australia to England, Australia to India, Australia to Ireland, Australia to South Africa) b Hobart, Tasmania 8.12.1984 RHB RM WK

Cmp	Debut	M	I	NO	Runs	HS	Avge	100	50	Balls	Runs	Wkts	Avge	BB	5i	10m	RpO	ct	st
FC		6	10	0	309	69	30.90	0	2									14	1
Int		2	2	0	40	24	20.00	0	0									2	
Lim		7	7	0	251	100	35.85	1	1									7	
20T		5	5	0	166	61	33.20	0	1									3	1
Test	2010	2	4	0	104	47	26.00	0	0									11	1
FC	2005/06	39	71	5	2024	215	30.66	1	14	6	3	0					3.00	110	4
Int	2009	23	23	1	716	111	32.54	1	5									33	4
Lim	2005/06	71	69	5	2271	134	35.48	5	11									85	10
I20T	2009	3	2	0	1	1	0.50	0	0									2	
20T	2005/06	20	17	0	274	61	16.11	0	1									16	4

PATTINSON, Darren John (Nottinghamshire, Victoria) b Grimsby, Lincolnshire, England 2.8.1979 RHB RFM

Cmp	Debut	M	I	NO	Runs	HS	Avge	100	50	Balls	Runs	Wkts	Avge	BB	5i	10m	RpO	ct	st
FC		9	10	3	134	25*	19.14	0	0	1370	736	22	33.45	3-15	0	0	3.22	2	
Lim		6	1	1	4	4*		0	0	298	269	10	26.90	3-34	0	0	5.41	1	
Test	2008	1	2	0	21	13	10.50	0	0	181	96	2	48.00	2-95	0	0	3.18	0	
FC	2006/07	51	58	10	561	59	11.68	0	1	8130	4709	133	35.40	6-30	6	0	3.47	5	
Lim	2006/07	43	16	6	69	13*	6.90	0	0	1725	1515	56	27.05	4-29	2	0	5.27	13	
20T	2006/07	32	7	3	19	5	4.75	0	0	609	772	35	22.05	4-19	1	0	7.60	10	

PATTINSON, James Lee (Australia A, Victoria) b Melbourne, Victoria 3.5.1990 LHB RFM

Cmp	Debut	M	I	NO	Runs	HS	Avge	100	50	Balls	Runs	Wkts	Avge	BB	5i	10m	RpO	ct	st
FC		3	2	0	6	5	3.00	0	0	550	231	9	25.66	4-52	0	0	2.52	3	
Lim		8	5	1	37	18	9.25	0	0	400	347	15	23.13	6-48	0	1	5.20	0	
20T		4	2	2	2	1*		0	0	84	119	5	23.80	3-27	0	0	8.50	3	
FC	2008/09	4	3	0	11	5	3.66	0	0	736	328	12	27.33	4-52	0	0	2.67	4	

PHILIPSON, Craig Andrew (Queensland) b Herston, Brisbane, Queensland 18.11.1982 RHB RFM

Cmp	Debut	M	I	NO	Runs	HS	Avge	100	50	Balls	Runs	Wkts	Avge	BB	5i	10m	RpO	ct	st
FC		4	7	0	70	30	10.00	0	0	12	1	1	1.00	1-1	0	0	0.50	9	
Lim		10	10	4	362	100	60.33	1	2	30	25	0					5.00	2	
20T		6	6	3	105	46*	35.00	0	0									2	
FC	2003/04	25	46	5	1023	119	24.95	2	3	132	89	3	29.66	2-18	0	0	4.04	22	
Lim	2003/04	48	45	8	1293	100	34.94	1	7	66	58	2	29.00	1-2	0	0	5.27	18	
20T	2005/06	21	18	3	293	46*	19.53	0	0									5	

POLLARD, Kieron Adrian (Trinidad and Tobago, West Indies, West Indies to Australia, Mumbai Indians, Somerset, South Australia, Trinidad and Tobago to India) b Cacariqua, Trinidad 12.5.1987 RHB RM

Cmp	Debut	M	I	NO	Runs	HS	Avge	100	50	Balls	Runs	Wkts	Avge	BB	5i	10m	RpO	ct	st
Int		5	4	0	170	62	42.50	0	1	234	203	7	29.00	3-45	0	0	5.20	4	
Lim		5	4	0	170	62	42.50	0	1	234	203	7	29.00	3-45	0	0	5.20	4	
I20T		2	2	0	17	12	8.50	0	0	36	35	1	35.00	1-23	0	0	5.83	2	
20T		8	8	0	207	52	25.87	0	1	84	97	6	16.16	2-8	0	0	6.92	5	
FC	2006/07	20	33	1	1199	174	37.46	3	5	571	313	6	52.16	2-29	0	0	3.28	32	
Int	2006/07	30	27	0	538	62	19.92	0	1	936	833	30	27.76	3-27	0	0	5.34	10	
Lim	2006/07	48	43	3	1109	87	27.72	0	7	1410	1214	57	21.29	4-32	1	0	5.16	22	

Cmp	Debut	M	I	NO	Runs	HS	Avge	100	50	Balls	Runs	Wkts	Avge	BB	5i	10m	RpO	ct	st
I20T	2008	20	17	2	190	38	12.66	0	0	258	360	11	32.72	2-22	0	0	8.37	11	
20T	2006	80	69	13	1391	89*	24.83	0	6	1178	1514	81	18.69	4-15	2	0	7.71	35	
POMERSBACH, Luke Anthony (Western Australia) b Bentley, Western Australia 28.9.1984 LHB RM																			
FC		4	8	0	214	74	26.75	0	2	120	41	2	20.50	1-4	0	0	2.05	8	
Lim		3	3	1	127	104*	63.50	1	0	18	16	0					5.33	1	
20T		4	3	0	34	32	11.33	0	0									3	
FC	2006/07	26	48	4	1784	176	40.54	4	13	213	102	4	25.50	1-4	0	0	2.87	30	
Lim	2006/07	25	23	2	524	104*	24.95	1	1	18	16	0					5.33	11	
I20T	2007/08	1	1	0	15	15	15.00	0	0									0	
20T	2005/06	26	25	5	519	79*	25.95	0	2									9	
PONTING, Ricky Thomas (Australia, Australia to England, Australia to India, Australia to Ireland, Australia to New Zealand, Australia to South Africa) b Launceston, Tasmania 19.12.1974 RHB OB,RM																			
Test		6	11	1	514	209	51.40	1	3									5	
FC		6	11	1	514	209	51.40	1	3									5	
Int		10	10	1	420	106	46.66	1	3									3	
Lim		10	10	1	420	106	46.66	1	3									3	
Test	1995/96	146	247	27	12026	257	54.66	39	52	539	242	5	48.40	1-0	0	0	2.69	172	
FC	1992/93	246	418	54	20873	257	57.34	73	90	1434	768	14	54.85	2-10	0	0	3.21	261	
Int	1994/95	351	342	37	13072	164	42.85	29	79	150	104	3	34.66	1-12	0	0	4.16	152	
Lim	1992/93	423	414	50	15428	164	42.38	33	94	349	269	8	33.62	3-34	0	0	4.62	184	
I20T	2004/05	17	16	2	401	98*	28.64	0	2									8	
20T	2004	22	21	2	460	98*	24.21	0	2									10	
PORTER, Drew Nathan (Western Australia) b Attadale, Perth, Western Australia 7.9.1985 RHB RMF																			
Lim		1	1	0	0	0	0.00	0	0	18	17	0					5.66	1	
20T		1	1	0	0	0	0.00	0	0	18	27	2	13.50	2-27	0	0	9.00	0	
FC	2008/09	3	5	1	44	18*	11.00	0	0	414	261	6	43.50	2-27	0	0	3.78	3	
Lim	2008/09	3	3	1	38	36*	19.00	0	0	108	67	1	67.00	1-40	0	0	3.72	2	
PUTLAND, Gary David (South Australia) b Flinders, Adelaide, South Australia 10.2.1986 RHB LFM																			
FC		4	8	1	18	8	2.57	0	0	670	450	11	40.90	4-55	0	0	4.03	1	
Lim		4	3	2	6	3	6.00	0	0	222	195	7	27.85	3-53	0	0	5.27	0	
20T		2	2	2	1	1*		0	0	40	45	2	22.50	1-18	0	0	6.75	1	
Lim	2005/06	12	6	4	19	6*	9.50	0	0	564	493	15	32.86	3-53	0	0	5.24	3	
20T	2005/06	9	7	5	15	4*	7.50	0	0	155	226	7	32.28	2-17	0	0	8.74	4	
QUINEY, Robert John (Victoria, Victoria to India) b Brighton, Victoria 20.8.1982 LHB RM																			
FC		6	9	0	303	153	33.66	1	1	48	17	0					2.12	5	
Lim		6	6	1	72	40	14.40	0	0	36	37	0					6.16	6	
20T		2	2	0	16	12	8.00	0	0									2	
FC	2006/07	29	45	3	1266	153	30.14	2	6	558	257	2	128.50	2-22	0	0	2.76	22	
Lim	2006/07	35	32	2	1045	92	34.83	0	9	90	101	0					6.73	22	
20T	2005/06	31	30	0	442	91	14.73	0	2	6	13	0					13.00	13	
REARDON, Nathan Jon (Queensland) b Chinchilla, Queensland 8.11.1984 LHB RM																			
FC		5	8	0	271	147	33.87	1	1	294	227	5	45.40	2-101	0	0	4.63	1	
Lim		10	10	0	393	83	39.30	0	4	12	16	0					8.00	5	
20T		3	3	0	20	16	6.66	0	0									0	
FC	2007/08	6	10	0	290	147	29.00	1	1	300	232	5	46.40	2-101	0	0	4.64	1	
Lim	2005/06	34	33	2	819	83	26.41	0	6	48	45	1	45.00	1-11	0	0	5.62	13	
20T	2005/06	20	18	1	275	54	16.17	0	2	53	72	3	24.00	2-20	0	0	8.15	5	
RICHARDSON, Kane William (South Australia) b Eudunda, South Australia 12.2.1991 RHB RMF																			
Lim		1	1	0	14	14	14.00	0	0	48	56	0					7.00	0	
Lim	2008/09	3	2	0	14	14	7.00	0	0	114	124	1	124.00	1-42	0	0	6.52	1	
20T	2008/09	1								18	34	0					11.33	0	
RIMMINGTON, Nathan John (Queensland) b Redcliffe, Queensland 11.11.1982 RHB RFM																			
FC		2	2	1	52	32	52.00	0	0	323	137	5	27.40	2-25	0	0	2.54	0	
Lim		10	6	1	35	15*	7.00	0	0	560	407	15	27.13	3-25	0	0	4.36	3	
20T		6	1	1	2	2*		0	0	108	126	8	15.75	3-13	0	0	7.00	2	
FC	2005/06	8	13	6	125	32	17.85	0	0	1083	621	8	77.62	2-25	0	0	3.44	2	
Lim	2006/07	14	9	1	56	15*	7.00	0	0	776	543	25	21.72	4-40	1	0	4.19	3	
20T	2005/06	17	4	2	5	2*	2.50	0	0	328	388	26	14.92	5-27	0	1	7.09	7	
ROBINSON, Wesley Michael (Western Australia) b Duncraig, Perth, Western Australia 26.12.1980 LHB LM																			
FC		10	20	2	582	141	32.33	1	2	24	13	0					3.25	5	
Lim		10	10	0	384	78	38.40	0	3									3	
20T		3	3	0	139	54	46.33	0	2									1	
FC	2008/09	17	34	2	1113	141	34.78	2	5	286	175	5	35.00	2-26	0	0	3.67	8	
ROGERS, Christopher John Llewellyn (Victoria, Derbyshire, Derbyshire to Netherlands) b St George, Sydney, New South Wales 31.8.1977 LHB LBG																			
FC		9	15	2	641	149	49.30	2	2									4	
Lim		10	10	0	342	140	34.20	1	0									5	
Test	2007/08	1	2	0	19	15	9.50	0	0									1	
FC	1998/99	173	305	22	14791	319	52.26	45	68	230	131	1	131.00	1-16	0	0	3.41	173	
Lim	1998/99	128	124	7	4173	140	35.66	4	28	24	26	2	13.00	2-22	0	0	6.50	63	
20T	2005	24	20	1	368	58	19.36	0	3									16	

Cmp	Debut	M	I	NO	Runs	HS	Avge	100	50	Balls	Runs	Wkts	Avge	BB	5i	10m	RpO	ct	st
ROGERS, John William (Tasmania) b Canberra, Australian Capital Territory 11.4.1987 LHB LM																			
FC		1	2	0	1	1	0.50	0	0									1	
20T		3	3	0	45	24	15.00	0	0									0	
ROHRER, Ben James (New South Wales, New South Wales to India) b Bankstown, New South Wales 26.3.1981 LHB																			
FC		6	7	1	235	115*	39.16	1	0	18	16	0					5.33	3	
Lim		6	4	0	175	63	43.75	0	2									2	
20T		3	1	0	0	0	0.00	0	0									1	
FC	2006/07	13	20	3	756	163	44.47	3	2	36	21	0					3.50	8	
Lim	2008/09	9	6	0	188	63	31.33	0	2									5	
20T	2008/09	15	11	2	175	45*	19.44	0	0									2	
RONCHI, Luke (Western Australia) b Dannevirke, Manawatu, New Zealand 23.4.1981 RHB WK																			
FC		10	17	2	716	148	47.73	3	1									42	2
Lim		10	9	2	274	58	39.14	0	3									14	3
20T		5	5	2	121	34*	40.33	0	0									3	1
FC	2002/03	47	76	9	2436	148	36.35	6	10									170	10
Int	2008	4	2	0	76	64	38.00	0	1									5	2
Lim	2001/02	69	65	5	1684	108*	28.06	3	14									89	16
I20T	2008	3	2	0	47	36	23.50	0	0									0	
20T	2005/06	28	27	2	487	76	19.48	0	2									21	8
SHAHID Khan AFRIDI, Sahibzada Mohammad (Karachi Dolphins, Pakistan, Pakistan to Australia, Pakistan to England, Pakistan to South Africa, Pakistan to Sri Lanka, Pakistan to United Arab Emirates, Pakistan to West Indies, South Australia) b Khyber Agency, Pakistan 1.3.1980 RHB LBG																			
Int		5	5	0	127	48	25.40	0	0	300	231	6	38.50	2-31	0	0	4.62	2	
Lim		5	5	0	127	48	25.40	0	0	300	231	6	38.50	2-31	0	0	4.62	2	
20T		5	5	0	48	27	9.60	0	0	108	111	7	15.85	4-19	1	0	6.16	1	
Test	1998/99	27	48	1	1716	156	36.51	5	8	3194	1709	48	35.60	5-52	1	0	3.21	10	
FC	1995/96	111	183	4	5631	164	31.45	12	30	13493	7023	258	27.22	6-101	8	0	3.12	75	
Int	1996/97	301	283	18	6321	124	23.85	6	30	12810	9888	282	35.06	6-38	2	3	4.63	100	
Lim	1995/96	392	371	21	8971	124	25.63	8	49	16905	13046	386	33.79	6-38	3	5	4.63	123	
I20T	2006	37	35	3	602	54*	18.81	0	3	858	884	47	18.80	4-11	2	0	6.18	11	
20T	2004	72	65	5	1049	54*	17.48	0	3	1575	1645	88	18.69	4-11	3	0	6.26	21	
SHERIDAN, William David (Victoria) b Chertsey, Surrey, England 5.7.1987 LHB LB																			
FC		1	1	0	54	54	54.00	0	1	156	142	0					5.46	0	
SIDDLE, Peter Matthew (Australia, Victoria, Australia to India, Australia to South Africa, Victoria to India) b Traralgon, Victoria 25.11.1984 RHB RFM																			
Test		5	4	2	59	38	29.50	0	0	926	474	11	43.09	3-25	0	0	3.07	3	
FC		5	4	2	59	38	29.50	0	0	926	474	11	43.09	3-25	0	0	3.07	3	
Int		3								132	102	3	34.00	2-31	0	0	4.63	0	
Lim		4	1	1	8	8*		0	0	192	142	3	47.33	2-31	0	0	4.43	0	
Test	2008/09	17	22	6	256	38	16.00	0	0	3763	1892	60	31.53	5-21	2	0	3.01	10	
FC	2005/06	32	40	11	433	38	14.93	0	0	6062	3136	109	28.77	6-57	6	0	3.10	15	
Int	2008/09	15	3	1	12	8*	6.00	0	0	660	499	14	35.64	3-55	0	0	4.53	1	
Lim	2005/06	30	11	5	39	12	6.50	0	0	1410	1060	33	32.12	4-27	1	0	4.51	5	
I20T	2008/09	1	1	1	1	1*		0	0	24	24	2	12.00	2-24	0	0	6.00	0	
20T	2005/06	10	2	2	2	1*		0	0	234	266	8	33.25	2-24	0	0	6.82	1	
SIMPSON, Christopher Patrick (Queensland) b Brisbane, Queensland 9.1.1982 RHB OB																			
FC		12	20	1	480	84	25.26	0	3	1580	742	9	82.44	3-40	0	0	2.81	14	
Lim		10	8	1	155	61*	22.14	0	1	477	376	9	41.77	3-39	0	0	4.73	8	
20T		6	5	0	138	76	27.60	0	1	84	112	4	28.00	2-30	0	0	8.00	3	
FC	2002/03	50	86	4	1760	120	21.46	2	10	5911	3192	47	67.91	5-68	1	0	3.24	41	
Lim	2003/04	52	43	7	513	61*	14.25	0	1	2061	1611	48	33.56	4-34	1	0	4.69	21	
20T	2005/06	18	17	1	294	76	18.37	0	1	282	380	16	23.75	3-27	0	0	8.08	5	
SMITH, Daniel Lindsay Richard (New South Wales, New South Wales to India) b Westmead, Sydney, New South Wales 17.3.1982 RHB WK																			
FC		5	9	1	150	58	18.75	0	2									19	
Lim		7	7	3	153	62*	38.25	0	1									6	1
20T		4	3	2	28	20*	28.00	0	0									3	1
FC	2005/06	25	41	7	828	96	24.35	0	6									87	1
Lim	2004/05	23	22	6	453	62*	28.31	0	1									20	2
20T	2005/06	25	23	6	256	28	15.05	0	0									9	5
SMITH, Dwayne Romel (Barbados, West Indies, West Indies to Australia, Deccan Chargers, New South Wales, Sussex, Sussex to India) b Storey Gap, Codrington Hill, St Michael, Barbados 12.4.1983 RHB RM																			
Int		5	4	1	130	59*	43.33	0	1	228	229	7	32.71	3-45	0	0	6.02	2	
Lim		5	4	1	130	59*	43.33	0	1	228	229	7	32.71	3-45	0	0	6.02	2	
I20T		2	2	0	12	8	6.00	0	0	24	47	2	23.50	2-38	0	0	11.75	1	
20T		7	6	0	43	25	7.16	0	0	106	152	8	19.00	2-4	0	0	8.60	4	
Test	2003/04	10	14	1	320	105*	24.61	1	0	651	344	7	49.14	3-71	0	0	3.17	9	
FC	2001/02	81	134	9	3679	155	29.43	7	14	8096	4054	124	32.69	4-22	0	0	3.00	78	
Int	2003/04	77	61	4	925	68	16.22	0	3	2510	2060	56	36.78	5-45	3	1	4.92	26	
Lim	2003/04	133	113	9	2274	96	21.86	0	14	3871	3123	94	33.22	6-29	3	2	4.84	44	

Cmp	Debut	M	I	NO	Runs	HS	Avge	100	50	Balls	Runs	Wkts	Avge	BB	5i	10m	RpO	ct	st
I20T	2005/06	8	8	0	73	29	9.12	0	0	104	155	7	22.14	3-24	0	0	8.94	1	
20T	2005/06	74	70	7	1220	72*	19.36	0	4	1084	1411	55	25.65	4-9	1	0	7.81	28	

SMITH, James David (South Australia) b Murray Bridge, South Australia 11.10.1988 RHB OB

Cmp	Debut	M	I	NO	Runs	HS	Avge	100	50	Balls	Runs	Wkts	Avge	BB	5i	10m	RpO	ct	st
FC		10	19	1	641	116	35.61	1	6	12	13	0					6.50	4	
Lim		3	3	0	25	17	8.33	0	0									2	
FC	2008/09	14	26	2	826	116	34.41	1	7	12	13	0					6.50	9	
Lim	2006/07	5	5	0	58	27	11.60	0	0									3	
20T	2006/07	1	1	0	15	15	15.00	0	0	6	15	1	15.00	1-15	0	0	15.00	0	

SMITH, Steven Peter Devereux (Australia, New South Wales, Australia to England, Australia to New Zealand, Australia to West Indies, New South Wales to India, Worcestershire) b Sydney, New South Wales 2.6.1989 RHB LB

Cmp	Debut	M	I	NO	Runs	HS	Avge	100	50	Balls	Runs	Wkts	Avge	BB	5i	10m	RpO	ct	st
FC		8	13	3	772	177	77.20	4	1	1315	932	21	44.38	7-64	1	0	4.25	17	
Int		1								59	78	2	39.00	2-78	0	0	7.93	2	
Lim		9	8	2	320	92	53.33	0	3	509	464	11	42.18	3-43	0	0	5.47	7	
I20T		3	2	0	16	8	8.00	0	0	48	70	2	35.00	2-34	0	0	8.75	4	
20T		8	6	2	70	35*	17.50	0	0	120	142	9	15.77	4-13	1	0	7.10	7	
Test	2010	2	4	0	100	77	25.00	0	1	186	82	3	27.33	3-51	0	0	2.64	1	
FC	2007/08	15	26	4	1112	177	50.54	4	3	2085	1352	29	46.62	7-64	1	0	3.89	22	
Int	2009/10	5	4	1	94	41	31.33	0	0	275	260	9	28.88	2-34	0	0	5.67	2	
Lim	2007/08	23	20	5	594	92	39.60	0	3	1031	923	24	38.45	3-43	0	0	5.37	11	
I20T	2009/10	13	8	2	62	27	10.33	0	0	240	300	15	20.00	3-20	0	0	7.50	12	
20T	2007/08	38	29	7	355	35*	16.13	0	0	567	686	41	16.73	4-13	2	0	7.25	21	

STARC, Mitchell Aaron (Australia A, New South Wales) b Baulkham Hills, Sydney, New South Wales 13.1.1990 LHB LFM

Cmp	Debut	M	I	NO	Runs	HS	Avge	100	50	Balls	Runs	Wkts	Avge	BB	5i	10m	RpO	ct	st
FC		9	10	6	107	54*	26.75	0	1	1347	792	23	34.43	5-74	1	0	3.52	3	
Lim		5	2	1	33	24*	33.00	0	0	272	229	10	22.90	3-36	0	0	5.05	1	
20T		5	1	0	2	2	2.00	0	0	88	126	4	31.50	1-16	0	0	8.59	0	
FC	2008/09	10	11	7	115	54*	28.75	0	1	1575	884	25	35.36	5-74	1	0	3.36	3	

STOINIS, Marcus Peter (Western Australia) b Perth, Western Australia 16.8.1989 RHB RMF

Cmp	Debut	M	I	NO	Runs	HS	Avge	100	50	Balls	Runs	Wkts	Avge	BB	5i	10m	RpO	ct	st
FC		1	2	0	22	22	11.00	0	0									0	
Lim		1	1	0	12	12	12.00	0	0									1	
FC	2008/09	3	6	0	74	27	12.33	0	0									1	
Lim	2008/09	4	4	0	63	24	15.75	0	0									1	

SULLIVAN, Grant James (Queensland) b Mackay, Queensland 7.3.1984 RHB RFM

Cmp	Debut	M	I	NO	Runs	HS	Avge	100	50	Balls	Runs	Wkts	Avge	BB	5i	10m	RpO	ct	st
FC		1	1	1	13	13*		0	0	78	41	0					3.15	0	
FC	2006/07	10	14	8	68	22	11.33	0	0	1385	1051	16	65.68	3-18	0	0	4.55	6	
Lim	2006/07	7	4	1	21	19	7.00	0	0	206	174	5	34.80	2-43	0	0	5.06	1	
20T	2007/08	2	1	1	0	0*		0	0	42	66	3	22.00	2-36	0	0	9.42	0	

SWAN, Christopher Richard (Queensland) b Southport, Queensland 10.8.1978 RHB RFM

Cmp	Debut	M	I	NO	Runs	HS	Avge	100	50	Balls	Runs	Wkts	Avge	BB	5i	10m	RpO	ct	st
FC		8	13	2	315	82	28.63	0	2	1657	793	31	25.58	5-26	1	0	2.87	4	
Lim		1	1	0	12	12	12.00	0	0	48	36	2	18.00	2-36	0	0	4.50	1	
FC	2006/07	23	35	6	699	82	24.10	0	3	4436	2040	68	30.00	5-26	1	0	2.75	10	
Lim	2007/08	13	9	4	83	30*	16.60	0	0	630	408	22	18.54	4-24	1	0	3.88	2	

SWART, Michael Richard (Western Australia) b Subiaco, Perth, Western Australia 1.10.1982 RHB OB

Cmp	Debut	M	I	NO	Runs	HS	Avge	100	50	Balls	Runs	Wkts	Avge	BB	5i	10m	RpO	ct	st
FC		3	6	0	175	83	29.16	0	2	12	20	0					10.00	1	
Lim		1	1	0	0	0	0.00	0	0	6	9	0					9.00	0	

SYMONDS, Andrew (Queensland, Deccan Chargers, Surrey) b Birmingham, Warwickshire, England 9.6.1975 RHB OB

Cmp	Debut	M	I	NO	Runs	HS	Avge	100	50	Balls	Runs	Wkts	Avge	BB	5i	10m	RpO	ct	st
Lim		1	1	0	4	4	4.00	0	0	60	48	0					4.80	3	
20T		6	6	2	88	38*	22.00	0	0	48	62	2	31.00	1-14	0	0	7.75	4	
Test	2003/04	26	41	5	1462	162*	40.61	2	10	2094	896	24	37.33	3-50	0	0	2.56	22	
FC	1994/95	227	376	33	14477	254*	42.20	40	65	17633	8714	242	36.00	6-105	2	0	2.96	159	
Int	1998/99	198	161	33	5088	156	39.75	6	30	5935	4955	133	37.25	5-18	2	1	5.00	82	
Lim	1993/94	424	377	51	11099	156	34.04	9	64	11713	9379	282	33.25	6-14	2	4	4.80	187	
I20T	2004/05	14	11	4	337	85*	48.14	0	2	185	277	8	34.62	2-14	0	0	8.98	3	
20T	2003	78	72	13	1980	117*	33.55	2	12	1201	1600	51	31.37	5-18	0	1	7.99	37	

TAIT, Shaun William (Australia, South Australia, Australia to England, Australia to New Zealand, Australia to West Indies, Glamorgan, Rajasthan Royals) b Bedford Park, Adelaide, South Australia 22.2.1983 RHB RF

Cmp	Debut	M	I	NO	Runs	HS	Avge	100	50	Balls	Runs	Wkts	Avge	BB	5i	10m	RpO	ct	st
Lim		8	4	1	9	6	3.00	0	0	426	445	10	44.50	3-57	0	0	6.26	1	
I20T		3	1	0	1	1	1.00	0	0	72	70	7	10.00	3-13	0	0	5.83	1	
20T		9	4	0	8	6	2.00	0	0	186	236	15	15.73	3-12	0	0	7.61	3	
Test	2005	3	5	2	20	8	6.66	0	0	414	302	5	60.40	3-97	0	0	4.37	1	
FC	2002/03	50	70	29	509	68	12.41	0	2	9263	5661	198	28.59	7-29	7	1	3.66	15	
Int	2006/07	25	5	3	25	11	12.50	0	0	1233	1060	46	23.04	4-39	2	0	5.15	3	
Lim	2002/03	88	33	17	108	22*	6.75	0	0	4445	3770	162	23.27	8-43	6	3	5.08	18	
I20T	2007/08	17	5	1	10	6	2.50	0	0	382	419	26	16.11	3-13	0	0	6.58	3	
20T	2004/05	50	17	5	77	14*	6.41	0	0	1099	1363	70	19.47	4-14	1	0	7.44	10	

TAYLOR, Luteru Ross Poutoa Lote (Central Districts, New Zealand, Durham, New Zealand to South Africa, New Zealand to Sri Lanka, New Zealand to United Arab Emirates, New Zealand to United States of America, New Zealand to West Indies, Royal Challengers Bangalore, Victoria) b Lower Hutt, Wellington, New Zealand 8.3.1984 RHB OB

Cmp	Debut	M	I	NO	Runs	HS	Avge	100	50	Balls	Runs	Wkts	Avge	BB	5i	10m	RpO	ct	st
20T		2	2	0	62	58	31.00	0	1									2	
Test	2007/08	25	46	1	1941	154*	43.13	5	9	32	14	0					2.62	45	
FC	2002/03	71	120	3	4774	217	40.80	10	26	602	330	4	82.50	2-34	0	0	3.28	89	
Int	2005/06	84	77	11	2376	128*	36.00	3	16	30	32	0					6.40	62	

Cmp	Debut	M	I	NO	Runs	HS	Avge	100	50	Balls	Runs	Wkts	Avge	BB	5i	10m	RpO	ct	st
Lim	2002/03	129	122	15	4028	132*	37.64	7	27	306	240	3	80.00	1-13	0	0	4.70	87	
I20T	2006/07	34	31	2	590	63	20.34	0	3									22	
20T	2005/06	92	87	14	2395	111*	32.80	1	14	180	269	8	33.62	3-28	0	0	8.96	47	
THORNELY, Dominic John (New South Wales) b Albury, New South Wales 1.10.1978 RHB RM																			
FC		3	5	2	96	44	32.00	0	0	432	168	2	84.00	2-39	0	0	2.33	2	
Lim		5	5	1	143	51	35.75	0	1	154	105	2	52.50	1-20	0	0	4.09	0	
20T		4	3	1	21	14*	10.50	0	0	30	35	0					7.00	1	
FC	2003/04	83	140	19	5166	261*	42.69	10	29	4822	2231	56	39.83	3-38	0	0	2.77	51	
Lim	2001/02	99	92	11	2392	108	29.53	2	15	1993	1706	52	32.80	3-17	0	0	5.13	29	
20T	2004/05	39	35	8	631	67*	23.37	0	3	419	536	23	23.30	4-22	1	0	7.67	16	
TOWERS, Luke James Charles (Western Australia) b Subiaco, Perth, Western Australia 18.6.1988 RHB																			
FC		6	12	0	291	124	24.25	1	0									3	
Lim		2	2	0	12	6	6.00	0	0									1	
FC	2008/09	9	18	0	392	124	21.77	1	0									3	
TOWNSEND, Wade James (Queensland) b Herston, Brisbane, Queensland 29.1.1986 LHB OB																			
FC		12	21	2	623	121	32.78	3	2									6	
20T	2008/09	4	4	0	82	35	20.50	0	0									4	
USMAN Tariq KHAWAJA (Australia A, New South Wales) b Islamabad, Punjab, Pakistan 18.12.1986 LHB RM																			
FC		9	15	1	806	132*	57.57	3	4	30	17	0					3.40	8	
Lim		2	2	0	82	56	41.00	0	1									3	
20T		2	2	0	19	13	9.50	0	0									0	
FC	2007/08	20	32	2	1457	172*	48.56	5	6	36	17	0					2.83	13	
Lim	2008/09	4	4	0	136	56	34.00	0	1									3	
VETTORI, Daniel Luca (New Zealand, Northern Districts, Delhi Daredevils, New Zealand to South Africa, New Zealand to United Arab Emirates, New Zealand to United States of America, New Zealand to West Indies, Queensland) b Auckland, New Zealand 27.1.1979 LHB SLA																			
20T		2	1	1	3	3*		0	0	36	31	1	31.00	1-6	0	0	5.16	3	
Test	1996/97	100	152	23	3962	140	30.71	5	22	24997	11007	325	33.86	7-87	18	3	2.64	55	
FC	1996/97	152	220	31	5809	140	30.73	8	32	35722	15920	499	31.90	7-87	28	3	2.67	79	
Int	1996/97	255	160	49	1895	83	17.07	0	4	12111	8367	268	31.22	5-7	7	2	4.14	71	
Lim	1996/97	322	211	57	3149	138	20.44	2	10	15529	10550	347	30.40	5-7	7	2	4.07	102	
I20T	2007/08	28	20	6	187	38	13.35	0	0	649	580	35	16.57	4-20	1	0	5.36	8	
20T	2005/06	57	43	11	669	57	20.90	0	1	1282	1321	67	19.71	4-20	1	0	6.18	22	
VOGES, Adam Charles (Australia, Australia A, Western Australia, Australia to India, Australia to New Zealand, Nottinghamshire, Rajasthan Royals) b Perth, Western Australia 4.10.1979 RHB SLC																			
FC		6	11	3	437	114*	54.62	1	4	239	140	6	23.33	3-38	0	0	3.51	4	
Int		4	4	1	93	45*	31.00	0	0	24	17	0					4.25	0	
Lim		12	12	1	335	81	30.45	0	2	84	64	1	64.00	1-19	0	0	4.57	3	
20T		6	5	0	124	45	24.80	0	0	24	25	0					6.25	2	
FC	2002/03	82	138	18	4867	180	40.55	10	27	2518	1370	40	34.25	4-92	0	0	3.26	100	
Int	2006/07	14	13	4	312	72	34.66	0	1	150	159	1	159.00	1-22	0	0	6.36	2	
Lim	2004/05	103	98	20	3219	104*	41.26	2	25	1244	1092	22	49.63	3-25	0	0	5.26	35	
I20T	2007/08	4	3	1	63	26	31.50	0	0	12	5	2	2.50	2-5	0	0	2.50	2	
20T	2005/06	59	55	11	1489	82*	33.84	0	7	281	405	12	33.75	2-4	0	0	8.64	22	
WADE, Matthew Scott (Australia A, Victoria, Victoria to India) b Hobart, Tasmania 26.12.1987 LHB WK																			
FC		13	19	3	687	96	42.93	0	6									38	2
Lim		14	13	2	444	67	40.36	0	2									18	2
20T		7	6	1	143	80	28.60	0	1									5	
FC	2007/08	34	48	9	1567	100*	40.17	2	11									133	3
Lim	2006/07	19	18	2	516	67	32.25	0	2									20	2
20T	2008/09	14	9	3	192	80	32.00	0	1									6	
WALTER, Scott Hugh (Queensland) b South Brisbane, Queensland 2.5.1989 LHB LMF																			
FC		6	8	4	27	14	6.75	0	0	1046	641	20	32.05	6-121	1	0	3.67	4	
Lim		5	1	1	0	0*		0	0	222	151	7	21.57	4-34	1	0	4.08	3	
FC	2008/09	7	10	6	36	14	9.00	0	0	1094	682	20	34.10	6-121	1	0	3.74	4	
WARNER, David Andrew (Australia, New South Wales, Australia to England, Australia to New Zealand, Australia to West Indies, Delhi Daredevils, Middlesex to England, New South Wales to India) b Paddington, Sydney, New South Wales 27.10.1986 LHB LB																			
FC		3	5	1	89	48*	22.25	0	0	13	12	1	12.00	1-0	0	0	5.53	1	
Lim		8	8	0	195	65	24.37	0	1	24	21	1	21.00	1-11	0	0	5.25	1	
I20T		3	3	0	140	67	46.66	0	1									3	
20T		8	8	0	310	67	38.75	0	3									4	
FC	2008/09	4	6	1	131	48*	26.20	0	0	25	19	1	19.00	1-0	0	0	4.56	3	
Int	2008/09	7	7	0	106	69	15.14	0	1									1	
Lim	2006/07	29	29	2	827	165*	30.62	1	4	90	81	2	40.50	1-11	0	0	5.40	6	
I20T	2008/09	22	22	0	644	89	29.27	0	4									13	
20T	2006/07	79	79	2	2096	107*	27.22	1	11									32	
WATSON, Shane Robert (Australia, Australia to England, Australia to India, Australia to Ireland, Australia to New Zealand, Australia to South Africa, Australia to West Indies, Rajasthan Royals) b Ipswich, Queensland 17.6.1981 RHB RMF																			
Test		6	11	1	609	120*	60.90	1	4	732	336	13	25.84	2-30	0	0	2.75	11	
FC		6	11	1	609	120*	60.90	1	4	732	336	13	25.84	2-30	0	0	2.75	11	

Cmp	Debut	M	I	NO	Runs	HS	Avge	100	50	Balls	Runs	Wkts	Avge	BB	5i	10m	RpO	ct	st
Int		7	7	0	296	69	42.28	0	4	204	167	8	20.87	4-36	1	0	4.91	2	
Lim		7	7	0	296	69	42.28	0	4	204	167	8	20.87	4-36	1	0	4.91	2	
I20T		3	3	1	107	62*	53.50	0	1	54	53	3	17.66	2-24	0	0	5.88	3	
20T		3	3	1	107	62*	53.50	0	1	54	53	3	17.66	2-24	0	0	5.88	3	
Test	2004/05	20	35	1	1247	120*	36.67	1	9	1995	1048	38	27.57	6-33	2	0	3.15	15	
FC	2000/01	84	146	16	5940	203*	45.69	14	32	7872	4478	159	28.16	7-69	5	1	3.41	69	
Int	2001/02	114	96	22	2982	136*	40.29	4	17	4051	3296	118	27.93	4-36	3	0	4.88	33	
Lim	2000/01	179	158	30	4851	136*	37.89	6	28	5937	4976	160	31.10	4-36	3	0	5.02	52	
I20T	2005/06	19	18	2	375	81	23.43	0	3	249	347	10	34.70	2-23	0	0	8.36	7	
20T	2004	52	49	9	1306	97*	32.65	0	12	850	1071	43	24.90	3-10	0	0	7.56	18	
WEEKS, Matthew Craig (South Australia) b Adelaide, South Australia 4.10.1982 RHB RFM																			
Lim		3	3	1	31	21	15.50	0	0	149	136	5	27.20	4-54	1	0	5.47	0	
FC	2005/06	2	3	0	34	14	11.33	0	0	197	143	2	71.50	1-27	0	0	4.35	0	
Lim	2004/05	6	5	2	48	21	16.00	0	0	251	250	6	41.66	4-54	1	0	5.97	1	
20T	2008/09	2	1	0	1	1	1.00	0	0	24	38	1	38.00	1-19	0	0	9.50	2	
WELLS, Jonathan Wayne (Tasmania) b Hobart, Tasmania 13.8.1988 RHB RM																			
FC		8	14	0	214	43	15.28	0	0	72	46	1	46.00	1-28	0	0	3.83	5	
FC	2008/09	14	26	0	530	98	20.38	0	2	84	58	1	58.00	1-28	0	0	4.14	10	
WHITE, Cameron Leon (Australia, Victoria, Australia to England, Australia to India, Australia to Ireland, Australia to New Zealand, Australia to South Africa, Australia to West Indies, Royal Challengers Bangalore, Victoria to India) b Bairnsdale, Victoria 18.8.1983 RHB LBG																			
FC		5	9	2	329	89	47.00	0	3	168	128	2	64.00	1-55	0	0	4.57	4	
Int		10	9	0	369	105	41.00	1	2									6	
Lim		14	13	0	495	105	38.07	1	4	24	16	0					4.00	8	
I20T		3	2	0	19	15	9.50	0	0									2	
20T		9	7	0	100	31	14.28	0	0									4	
Test	2008/09	4	7	2	146	46	29.20	0	0	558	342	5	68.40	2-71	0	0	3.67	1	
FC	2000/01	108	181	23	6680	260*	42.27	15	31	11730	6901	172	40.12	6-66	2	1	3.53	101	
Int	2005/06	68	56	11	1642	105	36.48	2	10	325	345	12	28.75	3-5	0	0	6.36	32	
Lim	2001/02	177	152	22	4586	126*	35.27	6	29	3712	3292	92	35.78	4-15	4	0	5.32	77	
I20T	2006/07	22	21	8	505	85*	38.84	0	3	24	25	1	25.00	1-11	0	0	6.25	11	
20T	2004/05	78	74	20	1816	141*	33.62	2	10	322	477	22	21.68	4-10	1	0	8.88	32	
WRIGHT, Damien Geoffrey (Victoria, Somerset) b Casino, New South Wales 25.7.1975 RHB RFM																			
FC		6	10	0	205	80	20.50	0	1	1311	502	35	14.34	5-37	2	0	2.29	4	
Lim		3	1	0	1	1	1.00	0	0	168	120	1	120.00	1-19	0	0	4.28	0	
FC	1997/98	108	163	22	3500	111	24.82	1	19	22029	9999	349	28.65	8-60	12	0	2.72	53	
Lim	1997/98	104	79	24	929	55	16.89	0	4	5311	3710	128	28.98	5-37	3	1	4.19	23	
20T	2004/05	22	16	3	174	38*	13.38	0	0	412	513	17	30.17	3-17	0	0	7.47	4	

PAKISTAN TO AUSTRALIA 2009/10

Cmp	Debut	M	I	NO	Runs	HS	Avge	100	50	Balls	Runs	Wkts	Avge	BB	5i	10m	RpO	ct	st
ABDUR RAUF																			
Test		1	2	0	8	5	4.00	0	0	198	119	1	119.00	1-86	0	0	3.60	0	
FC		2	4	1	12	5	4.00	0	0	300	162	3	54.00	2-43	0	0	3.24	0	
DANISH KANERIA																			
Test		2	4	0	13	8	3.25	0	0	640	414	9	46.00	5-151	1	0	3.88	1	
FC		2	4	0	13	8	3.25	0	0	640	414	9	46.00	5-151	1	0	3.88	1	
FAISAL IQBAL																			
Test		2	4	0	97	48	24.25	0	0									4	
FC		3	6	1	146	48	29.20	0	0									4	
FAWAD ALAM																			
FC		1	2	0	35	33	17.50	0	0	6	1	0					1.00	0	
Int		3	3	0	117	63	39.00	0	1									1	
Lim		3	3	0	117	63	39.00	0	1									1	
I20T		1	1	0	1	1	1.00	0	0									2	
20T		1	1	0	1	1	1.00	0	0									2	
IFTIKHAR ANJUM																			
Int		2	2	0	21	16	10.50	0	0	116	103	1	103.00	1-39	0	0	5.32	0	
Lim		2	2	0	21	16	10.50	0	0	116	103	1	103.00	1-39	0	0	5.32	0	
IMRAN FARHAT																			
Test		3	6	0	148	53	24.66	0	1	48	26	0					3.25	3	
FC		4	8	0	220	53	27.50	0	1	102	44	2	22.00	2-18	0	0	2.58	4	
I20T		1	1	0	8	8	8.00	0	0									0	
20T		1	1	0	8	8	8.00	0	0									0	
IMRAN NAZIR																			
I20T		1	1	0	0	0	0.00	0	0									1	
20T		1	1	0	0	0	0.00	0	0									1	
KAMRAN AKMAL																			
Test		2	4	0	67	30	16.75	0	0									5	1
FC		3	5	0	176	109	35.20	1	0									6	1

Cmp Debut	*M*	*I*	*NO*	*Runs*	*HS*	*Avge*	*100*	*50*	*Balls*	*Runs*	*Wkts*	*Avge*	*BB*	*5i*	*10m*	*RpO*	*ct*	*st*
Int	4	4	0	68	34	17.00	0	0									3	1
Lim	4	4	0	68	34	17.00	0	0									3	1
I20T	1	1	0	64	64	64.00	0	1									1	1
20T	1	1	0	64	64	64.00	0	1									1	1
KHALID LATIF																		
Int	1	1	0	0	0	0.00	0	0									0	
Lim	1	1	0	0	0	0.00	0	0									0	
I20T	1	1	0	6	6	6.00	0	0									0	
20T	1	1	0	6	6	6.00	0	0									0	
KHURRAM MANZOOR																		
Test	1	2	0	77	77	38.50	0	1									0	
FC	1	2	0	77	77	38.50	0	1									0	
MISBAH-UL-HAQ																		
Test	2	4	1	76	65*	25.33	0	1									4	
FC	3	6	1	120	65*	24.00	0	1									7	
MOHAMMAD AAMER																		
Test	2	4	1	49	30*	16.33	0	0	564	323	8	40.37	5-79	1	0	3.43	0	
FC	3	5	1	49	30*	12.25	0	0	624	341	10	34.10	5-79	1	0	3.27	0	
Int	2	2	0	4	4	2.00	0	0	108	82	4	20.50	3-53	0	0	4.55	0	
Lim	2	2	0	4	4	2.00	0	0	108	82	4	20.50	3-53	0	0	4.55	0	
MOHAMMAD ASIF																		
Test	3	6	3	30	29	10.00	0	0	810	370	13	28.46	6-41	1	0	2.74	0	
FC	3	6	3	30	29	10.00	0	0	810	370	13	28.46	6-41	1	0	2.74	0	
Int	4	4	2	1	1	0.50	0	0	240	177	6	29.50	3-42	0	0	4.42	1	
Lim	4	4	2	1	1	0.50	0	0	240	177	6	29.50	3-42	0	0	4.42	1	
I20T	1	1	1	5	5*		0	0	24	31	1	31.00	1-31	0	0	7.75	0	
20T	1	1	1	5	5*		0	0	24	31	1	31.00	1-31	0	0	7.75	0	
MOHAMMAD SAMI																		
Test	1	2	0	15	13	7.50	0	0	191	101	3	33.66	3-27	0	0	3.17	0	
FC	1	2	0	15	13	7.50	0	0	191	101	3	33.66	3-27	0	0	3.17	0	
MOHAMMAD YOUSUF																		
Test	3	6	0	178	61	29.66	0	1									3	
FC	3	6	0	178	61	29.66	0	1									3	
Int	4	4	0	81	58	20.25	0	1									3	
Lim	4	4	0	81	58	20.25	0	1									3	
NAVED-UL-HASAN																		
Int	5	5	1	76	33	19.00	0	0	282	290	6	48.33	2-55	0	0	6.17	1	
Lim	5	5	1	76	33	19.00	0	0	282	290	6	48.33	2-55	0	0	6.17	1	
I20T	1	1	0	1	1	1.00	0	0	24	27	1	27.00	1-27	0	0	6.75	0	
20T	1	1	0	1	1	1.00	0	0	24	27	1	27.00	1-27	0	0	6.75	0	
SAEED AJMAL																		
Test	1	2	0	14	10	7.00	0	0	415	223	2	111.50	1-73	0	0	3.22	0	
FC	2	3	1	14	10	7.00	0	0	571	307	6	51.16	4-84	0	0	3.22	0	
Int	4	4	1	20	8*	6.66	0	0	237	198	3	66.00	2-55	0	0	5.01	1	
Lim	4	4	1	20	8*	6.66	0	0	237	198	3	66.00	2-55	0	0	5.01	1	
I20T	1	1	1	1	1*		0	0	18	18	0					6.00	0	
20T	1	1	1	1	1*		0	0	18	18	0					6.00	0	
SALMAN BUTT																		
Test	3	6	0	280	102	46.66	1	1									2	
FC	4	7	0	433	153	61.85	2	1									2	
Int	5	5	0	108	72	21.60	0	1									0	
Lim	5	5	0	108	72	21.60	0	1									0	
SARFRAZ AHMED																		
Test	1	2	0	6	5	3.00	0	0									4	
FC	1	2	0	6	5	3.00	0	0									4	
Int	1	1	0	6	6	6.00	0	0									1	
Lim	1	1	0	6	6	6.00	0	0									1	
SHAHID AFRIDI																		
Int	5	5	0	127	48	25.40	0	0	300	231	6	38.50	2-31	0	0	4.62	2	
Lim	5	5	0	127	48	25.40	0	0	300	231	6	38.50	2-31	0	0	4.62	2	
SHOAIB MALIK																		
Test	1	2	0	77	58	38.50	0	1	70	43	2	21.50	2-16	0	0	3.68	1	
FC	1	2	0	77	58	38.50	0	1	70	43	2	21.50	2-16	0	0	3.68	1	
Int	3	3	0	66	36	22.00	0	0	84	65	2	32.50	2-48	0	0	4.64	3	
Lim	3	3	0	66	36	22.00	0	0	84	65	2	32.50	2-48	0	0	4.64	3	
I20T	1	1	0	3	3	3.00	0	0	24	31	2	15.50	2-31	0	0	7.75	0	
20T	1	1	0	3	3	3.00	0	0	24	31	2	15.50	2-31	0	0	7.75	0	
UMAR AKMAL																		
Test	3	6	0	199	51	33.16	0	1									0	
FC	4	8	0	281	55	35.12	0	2									0	
Int	5	5	0	187	67	37.40	0	2									1	

Cmp Debut	M	I	NO	Runs	HS	Avge	100	50	Balls	Runs	Wkts	Avge	BB	5i	10m	RpO	ct	st
Lim	5	5	0	187	67	37.40	0	2									1	
I20T	1	1	0	21	21	21.00	0	0									0	
20T	1	1	0	21	21	21.00	0	0									0	
UMAR GUL																		
Test	2	4	1	56	38*	18.66	0	0	440	264	5	52.80	3-83	0	0	3.60	2	
FC	3	5	1	61	38*	15.25	0	0	470	287	5	57.40	3-83	0	0	3.66	3	
Int	2	2	1	1	1*	1.00	0	0	120	150	3	50.00	2-80	0	0	7.50	1	
Lim	2	2	1	1	1*	1.00	0	0	120	150	3	50.00	2-80	0	0	7.50	1	
I20T	1	1	0	10	10	10.00	0	0	22	20	3	6.66	3-20	0	0	5.45	0	
20T	1	1	0	10	10	10.00	0	0	22	20	3	6.66	3-20	0	0	5.45	0	
YOUNIS KHAN																		
Int	5	5	0	67	46	13.40	0	0									3	
Lim	5	5	0	67	46	13.40	0	0									3	

SRI LANKA A TO AUSTRALIA 2010

Cmp Debut	M	I	NO	Runs	HS	Avge	100	50	Balls	Runs	Wkts	Avge	BB	5i	10m	RpO	ct	st
CHANDIMAL, L.D.																		
FC	2	4	0	92	54	23.00	0	1									1	
Lim	3	3	0	86	59	28.66	0	1									4	
20T	1	1	0	23	23	23.00	0	0									1	
DARSHANAPRIYA, T.D.D.																		
Lim	1								48	42	1	42.00	1-42	0	0	5.25	0	
20T	1								24	43	1	43.00	1-43	0	0	10.75	0	
FERNANDO, A.N.P.R.																		
FC	2	4	1	6	5	2.00	0	0	264	191	3	63.66	2-86	0	0	4.34	2	
Lim	2								78	68	1	68.00	1-29	0	0	5.23	0	
KAPUGEDERA, C.K.																		
Lim	2	2	0	66	38	33.00	0	0									1	
20T	1	1	0	26	26	26.00	0	0									1	
KARUNARATNE, F.D.M.																		
Lim	2	2	0	81	53	40.50	0	1									1	
20T	1	1	0	10	10	10.00	0	0									0	
KULASEKARA, C.K.B.																		
FC	2	4	0	107	56	26.75	0	1	144	71	0					2.95	0	
Lim	3	3	1	79	44*	39.50	0	0	138	99	1	99.00	1-25	0	0	4.30	0	
20T	1	1	0	0	0	0.00	0	0	24	40	1	40.00	1-40	0	0	10.00	0	
MENDIS, B.M.A.J.																		
FC	2	4	0	23	8	5.75	0	0	148	91	2	45.50	2-29	0	0	3.68	0	
Lim	3	3	1	130	81*	65.00	0	1	48	46	2	23.00	2-17	0	0	5.75	1	
MUNAWEERA, E.M.G.D.Y.																		
Lim	1	1	0	10	10	10.00	0	0									0	
20T	1	1	0	6	6	6.00	0	0									0	
NAWELA, N.M.N.P.																		
FC	1	2	0	33	27	16.50	0	0									0	
PARANAVITANA, N.T.																		
FC	2	4	0	67	47	16.75	0	0	48	32	0					4.00	1	
PERERA, N.L.T.C.																		
Lim	3	2	0	15	15	7.50	0	0	132	134	6	22.33	5-37	0	1	6.09	1	
20T	1	1	0	21	21	21.00	0	0	24	31	1	31.00	1-31	0	0	7.75	1	
PRASAD, K.T.G.D.																		
FC	2	4	1	47	25	15.66	0	0	270	157	5	31.40	3-59	0	0	3.48	0	
PRASANNA, S.																		
Lim	2	1	0	0	0	0.00	0	0	102	65	0					3.82	0	
20T	1	1	1	1	1*		0	0	24	27	0					6.75	1	
SENANAYAKE, S.M.S.M.																		
FC	2	4	1	12	8*	4.00	0	0	489	280	13	21.53	8-70	1	1	3.43	3	
Lim	3	2	1	22	17	22.00	0	0	150	113	4	28.25	2-35	0	0	4.52	2	
SILVA, J.K.																		
FC	2	4	0	89	47	22.25	0	0									4	3
SILVA, L.P.C.																		
FC	2	4	0	160	92	40.00	0	2	6	6	0					6.00	0	
Lim	3	3	2	114	104*	114.00	1	0									0	
20T	1	1	1	25	25*		0	0									0	
THIRIMANNE, H.D.R.L.																		
FC	2	4	0	101	47	25.25	0	0	18	19	0					6.33	3	
Lim	1	1	0	0	0	0.00	0	0									1	
UDANA, I.																		
Lim	1	1	1	2	2*		0	0	48	67	3	22.33	3-67	0	0	8.37	2	
20T	1								24	34	1	34.00	1-34	0	0	8.50	0	

Cmp	Debut	M	I	NO	Runs	HS	Avge	100	50	Balls	Runs	Wkts	Avge	BB	5i	10m	RpO	ct	st
UDAWATTE, M.L.																			
Lim		3	3	0	50	36	16.66	0	0									1	
20T		1	1	0	28	28	28.00	0	0									0	
VIDANAPATHIRANA, C.W.																			
FC		1	2	1	6	6	6.00	0	0	108	65	1	65.00	1-45	0	0	3.61	0	

WEST INDIES TO AUSTRALIA 2009/10

Cmp	Debut	M	I	NO	Runs	HS	Avge	100	50	Balls	Runs	Wkts	Avge	BB	5i	10m	RpO	ct	st
BARATH, A.B.																			
Test		2	4	0	139	104	34.75	1	0	6	3	0					3.00	2	
FC		3	6	0	213	104	35.50	1	1	6	3	0					3.00	2	
BENN, S.J.																			
Test		3	6	1	101	33	20.20	0	0	918	408	11	37.09	5-155	1	0	2.66	2	
FC		4	7	1	117	33	19.50	0	0	1122	559	12	46.58	5-155	1	0	2.98	2	
BRAVO, D.J.																			
Test		3	6	0	176	104	29.33	1	0	565	319	11	29.00	4-42	0	0	3.38	5	
FC		4	8	0	241	104	30.12	1	0	733	405	12	33.75	4-42	0	0	3.31	6	
CHANDERPAUL, S.																			
Test		2	4	0	93	62	23.25	0	1									0	
FC		3	6	0	203	69	33.83	0	2									0	
DEONARINE, N.																			
Test		1	2	0	100	82	50.00	0	1	144	75	2	37.50	2-74	0	0	3.12	2	
FC		2	4	0	140	82	35.00	0	1	312	168	3	56.00	2-74	0	0	3.23	2	
Int		5	4	0	99	53	24.75	0	1	57	54	0					5.68	2	
Lim		5	4	0	99	53	24.75	0	1	57	54	0					5.68	2	
I20T		2	2	1	36	36*	36.00	0	0	24	35	0					8.75	0	
20T		2	2	1	36	36*	36.00	0	0	24	35	0					8.75	0	
DOWLIN, T.M.																			
Test		2	4	0	143	62	35.75	0	2									2	
FC		3	6	0	198	62	33.00	0	3									2	
Int		5	5	1	11	8	2.75	0	0									0	
Lim		5	5	1	11	8	2.75	0	0									0	
I20T		1	1	0	31	31	31.00	0	0									0	
20T		1	1	0	31	31	31.00	0	0									0	
GAYLE, C.H.																			
Test		3	6	1	346	165*	69.20	2	0	126	59	0					2.81	3	
FC		3	6	1	346	165*	69.20	2	0	126	59	0					2.81	3	
Int		5	5	1	55	34	13.75	0	0	66	65	1	65.00	1-32	0	0	5.90	0	
Lim		5	5	1	55	34	13.75	0	0	66	65	1	65.00	1-32	0	0	5.90	0	
I20T		2	2	0	17	12	8.50	0	0	12	15	2	7.50	2-15	0	0	7.50	0	
20T		2	2	0	17	12	8.50	0	0	12	15	2	7.50	2-15	0	0	7.50	0	
HINDS, W.W.																			
Int		3	2	0	25	20	12.50	0	0									1	
Lim		3	2	0	25	20	12.50	0	0									1	
I20T		2	2	0	11	11	5.50	0	0									0	
20T		2	2	0	11	11	5.50	0	0									0	
MILLER, N.O.																			
Int		5	4	1	37	22	12.33	0	0	246	214	1	214.00	1-55	0	0	5.22	1	
Lim		5	4	1	37	22	12.33	0	0	246	214	1	214.00	1-55	0	0	5.22	1	
I20T		2	1	1	11	11*		0	0	46	76	4	19.00	2-20	0	0	9.91	1	
20T		2	1	1	11	11*		0	0	46	76	4	19.00	2-20	0	0	9.91	1	
MORTON, R.S.																			
Int		2	2	0	7	4	3.50	0	0									1	
Lim		2	2	0	7	4	3.50	0	0									1	
I20T		2	2	0	40	40	20.00	0	0									1	
20T		2	2	0	40	40	20.00	0	0									1	
NASH, B.P.																			
Test		3	6	0	250	92	41.66	0	2									1	
FC		4	8	1	297	92	42.42	0	2	24	4	0					1.00	1	
POLLARD, K.A.																			
Int		5	4	0	170	62	42.50	0	1	234	203	7	29.00	3-45	0	0	5.20	4	
Lim		5	4	0	170	62	42.50	0	1	234	203	7	29.00	3-45	0	0	5.20	4	
I20T		2	2	0	17	12	8.50	0	0	36	35	1	35.00	1-23	0	0	5.83	2	
20T		2	2	0	17	12	8.50	0	0	36	35	1	35.00	1-23	0	0	5.83	2	
RAMDIN, D.																			
Test		3	6	0	96	54	16.00	0	1									13	
FC		4	8	1	136	54	19.42	0	1									17	
Int		5	4	0	65	30	16.25	0	0									9	
Lim		5	4	0	65	30	16.25	0	0									9	

Cmp Debut	*M*	*I*	*NO*	*Runs*	*HS*	*Avge*	*100*	*50*	*Balls*	*Runs*	*Wkts*	*Avge*	*BB*	*5i*	*10m*	*RpO*	*ct*	*st*
I20T	2	2	0	53	44	26.50	0	0									2	1
20T	2	2	0	53	44	26.50	0	0									2	1
RAMPAUL, R.																		
Test	3	6	2	65	40*	16.25	0	0	462	290	4	72.50	1-21	0	0	3.76	0	
FC	4	7	2	77	40*	15.40	0	0	636	421	5	84.20	1-21	0	0	3.97	1	
Int	5	3	0	25	18	8.33	0	0	263	276	9	30.66	4-61	1	0	6.29	1	
Lim	5	3	0	25	18	8.33	0	0	263	276	9	30.66	4-61	1	0	6.29	1	
ROACH, K.A.J.																		
Test	3	6	1	32	17	6.40	0	0	565	357	7	51.00	3-93	0	0	3.79	1	
FC	4	7	2	32	17	6.40	0	0	757	492	10	49.20	3-93	0	0	3.90	1	
Int	2	2	2	0	0*		0	0	96	85	2	42.50	1-41	0	0	5.31	0	
Lim	2	2	2	0	0*		0	0	96	85	2	42.50	1-41	0	0	5.31	0	
I20T	2								24	63	0					15.75	1	
20T	2								24	63	0					15.75	1	
SAMMY, D.J.G.																		
Test	1	2	0	54	44	27.00	0	0	138	100	2	50.00	1-21	0	0	4.34	0	
FC	1	2	0	54	44	27.00	0	0	138	100	2	50.00	1-21	0	0	4.34	0	
Int	3	2	1	47	47*	47.00	0	0	168	141	5	28.20	2-44	0	0	5.03	1	
Lim	3	2	1	47	47*	47.00	0	0	168	141	5	28.20	2-44	0	0	5.03	1	
I20T	2	2	2	29	26*		0	0	24	50	1	50.00	1-36	0	0	12.50	1	
20T	2	2	2	29	26*		0	0	24	50	1	50.00	1-36	0	0	12.50	1	
SARWAN, R.R.																		
Test	2	4	0	88	42	22.00	0	0									3	
FC	3	6	0	227	73	37.83	0	2									3	
SIMMONS, L.M.P.																		
Int	5	4	0	60	29	15.00	0	0									0	
Lim	5	4	0	60	29	15.00	0	0									0	
I20T	1	1	0	5	5	5.00	0	0									0	
20T	1	1	0	5	5	5.00	0	0									0	
SMITH, D.R.																		
Int	5	4	1	130	59*	43.33	0	1	228	229	7	32.71	3-45	0	0	6.02	2	
Lim	5	4	1	130	59*	43.33	0	1	228	229	7	32.71	3-45	0	0	6.02	2	
I20T	2	2	0	12	8	6.00	0	0	24	47	2	23.50	2-38	0	0	11.75	1	
20T	2	2	0	12	8	6.00	0	0	24	47	2	23.50	2-38	0	0	11.75	1	
TAYLOR, J.E.																		
Test	1	2	0	8	8	4.00	0	0	54	43	1	43.00	1-43	0	0	4.77	0	
FC	1	2	0	8	8	4.00	0	0	54	43	1	43.00	1-43	0	0	4.77	0	
TONGE, G.C.																		
Test	1	2	1	25	23*	25.00	0	0	168	113	1	113.00	1-28	0	0	4.03	0	
FC	1	2	1	25	23*	25.00	0	0	168	113	1	113.00	1-28	0	0	4.03	0	

BANGLADESH

National Cricket League winners 2009/10 (first-class): Rajshahi Division
Destiny Group National Cricket LeagueTwenty20 2009/10 (twenty20): Dhaka Division

2009/10 and 2010 AND CAREER RECORDS FOR BANGLADESH PLAYERS

Cmp	*Debut*	*M*	*I*	*NO*	*Runs*	*HS*	*Avge*	*100*	*50*	*Balls*	*Runs*	*Wkts*	*Avge*	*BB*	*5i*	*10m*	*RpO*	*ct*	*st*
ABDULLAH AL MAMUN (Chittagong)																			
FC		3	5	0	78	43	15.60	0	0	324	113	8	14.12	3-20	0	0	2.09	2	
ABDUR RAZZAK, Khan (Bangladesh, Khulna, Bangladesh to England, Bangladesh to Ireland, Bangladesh to Scotland, Bangladesh to Sri Lanka, Bangladesh to West Indies) b Khulna 15.6.1982 LHB SLA																			
Test		2	4	1	12	8	4.00	0	0	573	409	7	58.42	3-132	0	0	4.28	0	
FC		3	6	2	86	74	21.50	0	1	854	564	14	40.28	4-91	0	0	3.96	0	
Int		12	6	2	24	17*	6.00	0	0	630	489	20	24.45	5-29	0	1	4.65	3	
Lim		12	6	2	24	17*	6.00	0	0	630	489	20	24.45	5-29	0	1	4.65	3	
20T		7	4	1	44	19	14.66	0	0	155	160	10	16.00	3-17	0	0	6.19	1	
Test	2005/06	8	15	5	160	33	16.00	0	0	1881	1079	16	67.43	3-93	0	0	3.44	3	
FC	2001/02	49	81	14	1387	83	20.70	0	7	10889	4987	157	31.76	7-11	5	1	2.74	17	
Int	2004	103	66	28	548	33	14.42	0	0	5421	4092	144	28.41	5-29	3	2	4.52	24	
Lim	2001/02	148	101	35	896	39	13.57	0	0	7634	5468	221	24.74	7-17	4	4	4.29	37	
I20T	2006/07	13	9	5	11	5	2.75	0	0	294	328	20	16.40	4-16	1	0	6.69	2	
20T	2006/07	21	14	7	55	19	7.85	0	0	461	517	30	17.23	4-16	1	0	6.72	3	
ABU JAYED Chowdhury (Sylhet) b 2.8.1993 RHB RMF																			
FC		3	6	2	12	8	3.00	0	0	252	144	4	36.00	2-75	0	0	3.42	0	
ABUL BASHAR Shaikh, Mohammed (Barisal) b 25.12.1986 RHB OB																			
FC		3	5	1	101	33	25.25	0	0	78	51	0					3.92	1	
FC	2004/05	17	30	2	530	82*	18.92	0	2	907	428	16	26.75	6-62	1	0	2.83	16	
Lim	2004/05	34	29	6	475	65	20.65	0	2	1284	1028	18	57.11	5-46	0	1	4.80	11	
ABUL HASAN, Mohammad (Sylhet) b 5.8.1992 LHB RMF																			
FC		1	2	0	32	18	16.00	0	0	118	35	0					1.78	0	
FC	2008/09	2	4	0	49	18	12.25	0	0	187	78	0					2.50	1	
Lim	2008/09	7	7	2	36	13	7.20	0	0	246	193	7	27.57	2-17	0	0	4.70	0	
AFTAB AHMED Chowdhury (Bangladesh, BCB XI, Chittagong, Bangladesh to New Zealand, Bangladesh to West Indies) b Chittagong 10.11.1985 RHB RM																			
Test		1	2	0	27	26	13.50	0	0	6	2	0					2.00	1	
FC		3	6	0	104	42	17.33	0	0	78	40	1	40.00	1-26	0	0	3.07	2	
Int		3	3	0	52	46	17.33	0	0									1	
Lim		4	4	0	64	46	16.00	0	0									1	
20T		5	5	0	44	15	8.80	0	0									0	
Test	2004/05	16	31	3	582	82*	20.78	0	1	344	237	5	47.40	2-31	0	0	4.13	7	
FC	2001/02	39	74	7	1738	129	25.94	1	6	1712	783	24	32.62	7-39	1	0	2.74	23	
Int	2004	85	85	6	1954	92	24.73	0	14	739	656	12	54.66	5-31	0	1	5.32	29	
Lim	2001/02	104	104	6	2383	92	24.31	0	16	1333	1083	20	54.15	5-31	0	1	4.87	33	
I20T	2006/07	11	11	1	228	62*	22.80	0	1	2	8	0					24.00	4	
20T	2006/07	16	16	1	272	62*	18.13	0	1	2	8	0					24.00	4	
ALAUDDIN BABU (BCB XI, Chittagong, Khulna) b 5.12.1991 RHB RMF																			
FC		1	1	0	1	1	1.00	0	0	252	106	1	106.00	1-71	0	0	2.52	0	
Lim		2	2	1	53	43*	53.00	0	0	96	115	3	38.33	2-85	0	0	7.18	0	
20T		7	6	2	47	20*	11.75	0	0	90	136	5	27.20	2-13	0	0	9.06	4	
ALOK KAPALI (Sylhet) b Sylhet, Chittagong 1.1.1984 RHB LB																			
FC		5	10	0	250	66	25.00	0	3	311	194	3	64.66	2-11	0	0	3.74	2	
20T		6	6	1	156	62	31.20	0	1	72	72	1	72.00	1-5	0	0	6.00	3	
Test	2002	17	34	1	584	85	17.69	0	2	1103	709	6	118.16	3-3	0	0	3.85	5	
FC	2000/01	83	148	4	3903	173	27.10	8	15	8522	4032	131	30.77	7-33	5	1	2.83	53	
Int	2002	65	62	3	1170	115	19.83	1	5	1368	1194	24	49.75	3-49	0	0	5.23	25	
Lim	2000/01	122	117	13	2686	115	25.82	4	11	3046	2410	68	35.44	4-23	2	0	4.74	55	
I20T	2007/08	5	5	2	55	19	18.33	0	0	12	23	0					11.50	2	
20T	2007/08	11	11	3	211	62	26.37	0	1	84	95	1	95.00	1-5	0	0	6.78	5	
AMIT MAJUMDER (Khulna) b Khulna 1.1.1991 LHB SLA																			
FC		5	9	0	227	68	25.22	0	2									1	
FC	2008/09	9	17	0	369	68	21.70	0	2									3	
Lim	2008/09	10	10	1	261	58*	29.00	0	2									3	
ANHUR NEWAZ (Barisal)																			
FC		2	4	0	59	27	14.75	0	0									0	

Cmp	Debut	M	I	NO	Runs	HS	Avge	100	50	Balls	Runs	Wkts	Avge	BB	5i	10m	RpO	ct	st
ANISUR RAHMAN, K S (Rajshahi) b Rajshahi 1.1.1977 RHB																			
FC		8	11	1	441	151*	44.10	1	3									4	
20T		1	1	0	6	6	6.00	0	0									0	
FC	2000/01	81	131	10	4105	151*	33.92	8	24	794	471	12	39.25	3-64	0	0	3.55	49	
Lim	2000/01	65	61	9	1652	106*	31.76	2	11	408	290	13	22.30	3-23	0	0	4.26	27	
ARAFAT SALAHUDDIN (Barisal) b Mymensingh 1.3.1984 RHB RFM																			
FC		5	8	0	73	29	9.12	0	0	871	438	21	20.85	6-68	1	0	3.01	1	
FC	2003/04	54	89	11	1771	139	22.70	2	7	8220	3580	148	24.18	6-68	4	0	2.61	24	
Lim	2003/04	42	38	7	914	72	29.48	0	5	2009	1268	40	31.70	3-11	0	0	3.78	8	
ARAFAT SUNNY (Barisal, Dhaka) b 29.9.1986 LHB SLA																			
FC		2	3	2	22	19*	22.00	0	0	761	273	10	27.30	5-87	1	0	2.15	1	
20T		4	2	0	16	11	8.00	0	0	90	100	4	25.00	2-25	0	0	6.66	1	
FC	2001/02	44	69	23	1008	55	21.91	0	2	9180	3693	159	23.22	7-50	12	1	2.41	22	
Lim	2001/02	37	27	8	292	51*	15.36	0	1	1515	901	35	25.74	4-17	1	0	3.56	16	
20T	2008	5	3	1	19	11	9.50	0	0	108	124	5	24.80	2-25	0	0	6.88	1	
ARIFUL HAQUE (Barisal, BCB XI, Sylhet) b 18.11.1992 RHB RMF																			
FC		1	2	0	31	24	15.50	0	0	18	20	0					6.66	0	
Lim		1	1	0	22	22	22.00	0	0									1	
20T		4	3	1	10	10	5.00	0	0									0	
FC	2006/07	7	11	1	329	115	32.90	1	2	576	348	7	49.71	2-65	0	0	3.62	4	
Lim	2006/07	10	10	0	172	51	17.20	0	1	316	304	12	25.33	5-38	0	1	5.77	5	
ARMAN HOSSAIN, Mohammad (Chittagong) b Kalindi 22.6.1983 RHB WK																			
FC		8	15	1	412	97	29.42	0	2									22	2
FC	2006/07	14	26	2	688	97	28.66	0	3									30	4
Lim	2007/08	11	11	0	197	53	17.90	0	1									16	1
ASIF AHMED (Barisal) b 17.12.1992 RHB OB																			
FC		2	4	0	258	121	64.50	2	0									3	
ASLAM ALI Khan (Khulna) RHB																			
FC		3	6	0	92	46	15.33	0	0									0	
FC	2005/06	10	20	1	345	54	18.15	0	1	48	26	0					3.25	9	
Lim	2005/06	7	7	0	206	96	29.42	0	1									4	
AVISHEK MITRA (Rajshahi)																			
FC		1	1	0	0	0	0.00	0	0									1	
BAILEY, Ryan Tyrone (Eagles, Eagles to India, Khulna, South Africa A to Bangladesh, South Africa A to Sri Lanka) b Cape Town, Cape Province, South Africa 8.9.1982 RHB RM																			
Lim		5	5	0	127	37	25.40	0	0	198	177	5	35.40	2-40	0	0	5.36	2	
20T		1	1	0	15	15	15.00	0	0									0	
FC	2003/04	69	121	12	3436	186*	31.52	4	20	2533	1473	26	56.65	3-42	0	0	3.48	33	
Lim	2003/04	77	67	13	1608	105*	29.77	1	8	527	520	12	43.33	2-27	0	0	5.92	18	
20T	2003/04	39	29	8	395	73*	18.80	0	1	162	195	10	19.50	2-25	0	0	7.22	16	
BLIZZARD, Aiden Craig (Victoria to Australia, Rajshahi, Victoria to India) b Shepparton, Victoria, Australia 27.6.1984 LHB LM																			
20T		7	7	0	163	39	23.28	0	0	6	10	0					10.00	3	
FC	2007/08	2	1	0	30	30	30.00	0	0									1	
Lim	2005/06	23	22	1	434	72	20.66	0	1									14	
20T	2006/07	30	30	2	635	89	22.67	0	1	6	10	0					10.00	10	
DELWAR HOSSAIN (Rajshahi) b Rajshahi 1.1.1985 RHB RM																			
FC		7	8	2	80	38	13.33	0	0	840	455	12	37.91	4-106	0	0	3.25	1	
FC	2006/07	15	19	6	266	51*	20.46	0	1	2023	1026	38	27.00	5-33	3	1	3.04	3	
Lim	2006/07	22	15	5	112	13*	11.20	0	0	1099	687	32	21.46	5-34	0	1	3.75	6	
DE SARAM, Samantha Indika (Ragama, Ruhuna, Sylhet) b Matara, Sri Lanka 2.9.1973 RHB OB																			
20T		4	4	1	84	39*	28.00	0	0	12	16	0					8.00	4	
Test	1999/00	4	5	0	117	39	23.40	0	0									1	
FC	1990/91	182	292	21	10585	237	39.05	22	60	913	528	8	66.00	2-92	0	0	3.47	189	8
Int	1999	15	13	2	183	38	16.63	0	0									9	
Lim	1993/94	149	137	9	3704	138	28.93	3	24	436	304	9	33.77	2-5	0	0	4.18	50	1
I20T	2008/09	1																1	
20T	2004/05	30	27	6	631	94	30.04	0	3	30	50	4	12.50	4-34	1	0	10.00	17	2
DHIMAN GHOSH (Bangladesh A, Rajshahi, Sylhet) b Dinajpur 23.11.1987 RHB OB WK																			
FC		7	11	2	306	66*	34.00	0	4	26	14	1	14.00	1-4	0	0	3.23	14	4
Lim		4	4	0	94	27	23.50	0	0									1	2
20T		6	5	0	51	21	10.20	0	0									2	5
FC	2003/04	47	81	9	2126	115	29.52	2	12	315	192	10	19.20	3-7	0	0	3.65	112	15
Int	2007/08	14	12	3	126	30	14.00	0	0									9	4
Lim	2003/04	57	54	7	1368	147	29.10	1	6	6	10	0					10.00	45	21
I20T	2007/08	1	1	0	1	1	1.00	0	0									0	1
20T	2007/08	8	7	0	72	21	10.28	0	0									3	8
DOLAR MAHMUD, Mohammad (Bangladesh, Bangladesh A, Khulna) b Narail, Khulna 30.12.1988 RHB RFM																			
FC		6	9	1	80	29	10.00	0	0	933	495	25	19.80	5-57	1	0	3.18	6	
Int		2	1	0	41	41	41.00	0	0	59	65	1	65.00	1-26	0	0	6.61	0	
Lim		5	4	0	56	41	14.00	0	0	179	185	1	185.00	1-26	0	0	6.20	0	

Cmp	Debut	M	I	NO	Runs	HS	Avge	100	50	Balls	Runs	Wkts	Avge	BB	5i	10m	RpO	ct	st
20T		6	6	3	65	30*	21.66	0	0	74	106	5	21.20	2-31	0	0	8.59	0	
FC	2004/05	31	54	6	639	65	13.31	0	2	4509	2464	98	25.14	7-52	3	0	3.27	15	
Int	2008	7	4	0	61	41	15.25	0	0	210	258	8	32.25	4-28	1	0	7.37	0	
Lim	2004/05	30	22	2	195	41	9.75	0	0	1082	1028	30	34.26	5-47	1	1	5.70	6	
ELIAS SUNNY, Mohammad (Chittagong, Khulna) b Dhaka 2.8.1986 LHB SLA																			
FC		9	16	1	306	51	20.40	0	1	2164	938	42	22.33	6-47	2	0	2.60	3	
20T		7	2	0	7	4	3.50	0	0	126	118	4	29.50	2-20	0	0	5.61	5	
FC	2003/04	48	76	10	1408	176	21.33	1	7	9558	4413	176	25.07	7-79	8	1	2.77	29	
Lim	2003/04	38	29	5	279	46*	11.62	0	0	1889	1257	52	24.17	4-36	1	0	3.99	16	
EMON AHMED (Dhaka)																			
FC		1	1	1	1	1*		0	0	102	61	1	61.00	1-19	0	0	3.58	0	
20T		1	1	1	9	9*		0	0	12	9	0					4.50	0	
FC	2008/09	8	9	4	48	11*	9.60	0	0	1045	543	14	38.78	2-18	0	0	3.11	2	
ENAMUL HAQUE, Mohammad (Bangladesh, Bangladesh A, Chittagong, Sylhet) b Sylhet, Chittagong 5.12.1986 RHB SLA																			
FC		3	6	1	39	12	7.80	0	0	441	277	5	55.40	4-93	0	0	3.76	0	
Int		3	1	0	0	0	0.00	0	0	162	102	6	17.00	3-16	0	0	3.77	2	
Lim		3	1	0	0	0	0.00	0	0	162	102	6	17.00	3-16	0	0	3.77	2	
20T		5	2	1	1	1	1.00	0	0	107	107	8	13.37	3-15	0	0	6.00	0	
Test	2003/04	14	24	15	53	13	5.88	0	0	3189	1609	41	39.24	7-95	3	1	3.02	3	
FC	2001/02	67	108	41	734	42	10.95	0	0	15857	7478	243	30.77	7-47	15	3	2.83	24	
Int	2004/05	10	5	1	12	5	3.00	0	0	576	422	14	30.14	3-16	0	0	4.39	8	
Lim	2002/03	42	27	10	143	37*	8.41	0	0	2172	1424	50	28.48	4-27	3	0	3.93	15	
EZAZ AHMED (Sylhet) b Sylhet 4.10.1984 RHB LB																			
FC		2	4	0	24	8	6.00	0	0									1	
FC	2002/03	37	65	2	1166	120	18.50	1	5	425	293	9	32.55	3-41	0	0	4.13	21	
Lim	2002/03	43	40	3	706	67	19.08	0	3	145	126	5	25.20	4-48	1	0	5.21	8	
FAISAL HOSSAIN (Bangladesh A, BCB XI, Chittagong, Bangladesh to England, Bangladesh to Ireland) b Chittagong 26.10.1978 LHB SLA																			
FC		13	23	1	1147	154	52.13	3	7	1591	960	27	35.55	5-183	1	0	3.62	13	
Lim		6	6	1	236	93	47.20	0	2	144	132	5	26.40	2-35	0	0	5.50	1	
20T		5	4	0	70	43	17.50	0	0	48	70	4	17.50	3-17	0	0	8.75	4	
Test	2004	1	2	0	7	5	3.50	0	0									0	
FC	2001/02	82	138	11	4992	180	39.30	10	27	3550	1973	48	41.10	5-183	1	0	3.33	66	2
Int	2004	6	5	1	43	17	10.75	0	0	73	53	1	53.00	1-27	0	0	4.35	3	
Lim	2000/01	75	73	11	2113	93	34.08	0	18	832	757	22	34.40	4-25	2	0	5.45	33	
FAISAL IQBAL (Karachi Zebras, PIA, Sind Dolphins, Pakistan to Australia, Pakistan to New Zealand, Sylhet) b Karachi, Sind, Pakistan 30.12.1981 RHB RM																			
20T		2	2	0	30	27	15.00	0	0									0	
Test	2000/01	26	44	2	1124	139	26.76	1	8	6	7	0					7.00	22	
FC	1998/99	148	233	24	8247	200*	39.45	15	49	162	126	1	126.00	1-6	0	0	4.66	119	1
Int	1999/00	18	16	2	314	100*	22.42	1	0	18	33	0					11.00	3	
Lim	1997/98	130	118	21	3655	123	37.68	4	27	72	108	1	108.00	1-15	0	0	9.00	41	1
20T	2005/06	16	16	2	322	58	23.00	0	1									3	
FARHAD HOSSAIN (Bangladesh A, Khulna, Rajshahi) b Rajshahi 10.2.1987 OB																			
FC		11	18	1	836	159	49.17	3	3	516	280	4	70.00	2-78	0	0	3.25	16	
20T		7	7	3	128	41*	32.00	0	0	90	95	3	31.66	3-11	0	0	6.33	3	
FC	2004/05	46	82	6	2519	159	33.14	4	13	3376	1538	63	24.41	4-13	0	0	2.73	69	
Lim	2004/05	27	27	1	567	89*	21.80	0	2	574	412	23	17.91	5-16	1	1	4.30	9	
FARHAD REZA (Rajshahi, Sylhet) b Rajshahi 16.6.1986 RHB RFM																			
FC		7	10	3	234	66	33.42	0	3	780	440	8	55.00	2-37	0	0	3.38	4	
20T		6	6	0	104	43	17.33	0	0	101	117	2	58.50	1-22	0	0	6.95	4	
FC	2004/05	37	64	11	1905	177	35.94	1	15	3934	1864	65	28.67	6-54	2	0	2.84	21	
Int	2006	32	29	6	390	50	16.95	0	1	1127	1015	22	46.13	5-42	0	1	5.40	12	
Lim	2004/05	67	63	9	1104	96	20.44	0	5	2386	1933	67	28.85	5-37	1	2	4.86	26	
I20T	2006/07	7	5	0	50	19	10.00	0	0	90	165	4	41.25	2-34	0	0	11.00	3	
20T	2006/07	13	11	0	154	43	14.00	0	0	191	282	6	47.00	2-34	0	0	8.85	7	
FARIDUDDIN, Mohammad (Sylhet) b 7.5.1985 RHB OB																			
20T		4	2	2	2	1*		0	0	84	81	8	10.12	3-16	0	0	5.78	0	
FC	2007/08	7	13	3	316	61	31.60	0	2	450	213	3	71.00	1-15	0	0	2.84	5	
Lim	2006/07	16	12	2	136	45	13.60	0	0	484	391	11	35.54	3-52	0	0	4.84	4	
FAZLE MAHMUD, Mohammad (Barisal) b 30.12.1987 LHB SLA																			
FC		4	8	0	242	95	30.25	0	2	42	16	0					2.28	2	
FC	2003/04	5	10	0	257	95	25.70	0	2	42	16	0					2.28	2	
Lim	2003/04	6	6	1	36	24	7.20	0	0	85	98	1	98.00	1-66	0	0	6.91	1	
GAZI SALAHUDDIN (Chittagong, Sylhet) b Brahmanbaria 8.11.1984 RHB OB																			
FC		9	16	1	565	88	37.66	0	4									10	
20T		2	2	0	50	42	25.00	0	0									1	
FC	2003/04	55	98	1	3293	165	33.94	5	22	131	64	0					2.93	46	
Lim	2003/04	28	28	0	728	90	26.00	0	6									9	
GOLAM KIBRIA, Syed (Barisal) b 28.8.1989 RHB RMF																			
FC		1	2	1	4	4	4.00	0	0	6	22	0					22.00	0	

Cmp	Debut	M	I	NO	Runs	HS	Avge	100	50	Balls	Runs	Wkts	Avge	BB	5i	10m	RpO	ct	st
GOLAM MABUD (Sylhet) b Sylhet 10.10.1984 RHB WK																			
FC		5	10	2	230	48	28.75	0	0	24	23	0					5.75	13	1
FC	2001/02	54	102	7	2695	123	28.36	4	14	462	298	7	42.57	3-46	0	0	3.87	111	10
Lim	2002/03	46	46	2	1080	136	24.54	2	5									43	16
GOLAM RAHMAN (Sylhet) LHB																			
FC		4	8	0	149	42	18.62	0	0	120	91	2	45.50	1-21	0	0	4.55	3	
FC	2003/04	54	98	4	2926	160	31.12	5	15	800	402	11	36.54	2-15	0	0	3.01	23	
Lim	2002/03	38	36	0	826	109	22.94	1	4	192	118	4	29.50	1-22	0	0	3.68	8	
HABIBUL BASHAR, Qazi (Khulna) b Nagakanda, Kushtia 17.8.1972 RHB OB																			
FC		4	7	0	396	103	56.57	1	4									1	
Test	2000/01	50	99	1	3026	113	30.87	3	24	282	217	0					4.61	22	
FC	1997/98	91	170	5	5571	224	33.76	7	41	814	527	8	65.87	2-28	0	0	3.88	40	
Int	1994/95	111	105	5	2168	78	21.68	0	14	175	142	1	142.00	1-31	0	0	4.86	26	
Lim	1994/95	156	149	9	3418	83	24.41	0	24	670	499	8	62.37	2-17	0	0	4.46	33	
HABIBUR RAHMAN (Khulna)																			
FC		2	4	0	62	24	15.50	0	0									0	
FC	2008/09	3	6	0	73	24	12.16	0	0									0	
HAMIDUL ISLAM, Mohammad (Rajshahi) b 12.1.1989 RHB WK																			
FC		2	4	0	20	9	5.00	0	0									5	
FC	2008/09	8	13	1	189	53	15.75	0	1									18	2
Lim	2006/07	12	12	1	267	59	24.27	0	1									13	8
HANNAN SARKAR, Abdul (Barisal, BCB XI, Rajshahi) b Dhaka 1.12.1982 RHB RM																			
FC		3	6	0	175	59	29.16	0	2	42	22	0					3.14	1	
Lim		2	2	0	24	24	12.00	0	0	5	17	0					20.40	1	
20T		7	7	0	104	44	14.85	0	0									4	
Test	2002	17	33	0	662	76	20.06	0	5									7	
FC	2000/01	87	161	1	4120	121	25.75	2	28	2647	1540	36	42.77	5-58	1	0	3.49	42	
Int	2002	20	20	0	383	61	19.15	0	3	3	13	0					26.00	8	
Lim	1997/98	73	73	0	1527	116	20.91	1	11	492	414	8	51.75	4-35	1	0	5.04	25	
IFTEKHAR NAYEM Ahmed (Barisal) b 27.11.1988 RHB RSM																			
FC		1	2	0	52	31	26.00	0	0									0	
FC	2006/07	6	10	0	235	48	23.50	0	0	12	8	0					4.00	3	
Lim	2006/07	6	6	1	200	81	40.00	0	2	18	21	1	21.00	1-21	0	0	7.00	2	
IMRAN AHMED (Barisal) b Mymensingh, Dhaka 1.4.1981 RHB OB																			
FC		2	4	0	7	4	1.75	0	0									0	
FC	2000/01	80	146	4	3719	177	26.19	5	15	738	383	5	76.60	2-37	0	0	3.11	39	
Lim	1998/99	74	74	2	1810	115	25.13	1	9	545	414	12	34.50	2-23	0	0	4.55	25	
IMRAN NAZIR (Khyber Pakhtunkhwa Panthers, Sialkot Stallions, ZTBL, Dhaka, Pakistan to Australia, Pakistan to South Africa, Pakistan to United Arab Emirates) b Gujranwala, Punjab, Pakistan 16.12.1981 RHB LB																			
20T		2	2	0	26	16	13.00	0	0									2	
Test	1998/99	8	13	0	427	131	32.84	2	1									4	
FC	1998/99	106	173	9	5338	164	32.54	7	30	424	339	7	48.42	3-61	0	0	4.79	75	
Int	1998/99	79	79	2	1895	160	24.61	2	9	49	48	1	48.00	1-3	0	0	5.87	26	
Lim	1998/99	148	148	3	3797	160	26.18	7	15	331	306	11	27.81	3-34	0	0	5.54	64	
I20T	2006/07	16	15	1	324	59	23.14	0	2									6	
20T	2004/05	41	39	5	1018	76*	29.94	0	7	8	3	3	1.00	1-0	0	0	2.25	15	
IMRUL KAYES (Bangladesh, BCB XI, Khulna, Bangladesh to England, Bangladesh to Ireland, Bangladesh to New Zealand, Bangladesh to Scotland, Bangladesh to Sri Lanka, Bangladesh to West Indies) b Meherpur, Kushtia 2.2.1987 LHB																			
Test		4	8	0	72	23	9.00	0	0									4	
FC		4	8	0	72	23	9.00	0	0									4	
Int		7	7	0	239	70	34.14	0	2									2	
Lim		9	9	0	252	70	28.00	0	2									3	
20T		7	7	0	228	71	32.57	0	1									1	
Test	2008/09	13	26	0	453	75	17.42	0	1	6	7	0					7.00	12	
FC	2006/07	35	66	1	1667	138	25.64	2	6	12	11	0					5.50	22	
Int	2008/09	22	22	0	671	101	30.50	1	5									3	
Lim	2006/07	44	44	2	1561	133*	37.16	3	10	5	7	0					8.40	9	2
I20T	2010	2	2	0	0	0	0.00	0	0									0	
20T	2008	10	10	0	228	71	22.80	0	1									2	
IMTIAZ HOSSAIN (BCB XI, Khulna, Sylhet) b Sylhet, Chittagong 24.2.1985 RHB OB																			
FC		1	2	0	31	23	15.50	0	0									0	
Lim		1	1	0	0	0	0.00	0	0									0	
20T		1	1	0	1	1	1.00	0	0									0	
FC	2001/02	68	126	3	3592	148	29.20	4	18	2489	1335	42	31.78	3-50	0	0	3.21	49	
Lim	2001/02	63	63	0	1369	124	21.73	1	5	1326	1095	33	33.18	4-22	2	0	4.95	22	
IQBAL HOSSAIN (Chittagong) b Mymensingh, Dhaka 1.9.1971 RHB RMF																			
FC		5	6	3	20	18	6.66	0	0	474	259	6	43.16	2-59	0	0	3.27	1	
FC	2000/01	11	13	5	131	56*	16.37	0	1	1044	472	16	29.50	3-28	0	0	2.71	5	
Lim	2000/01	6	4	2	10	10*	5.00	0	0	282	143	7	20.42	3-28	0	0	3.04	5	
IRFAN SUKKUR (Chittagong)																			
FC		2	3	0	23	13	7.66	0	0									5	

Cmp	Debut	M	I	NO	Runs	HS	Avge	100	50	Balls	Runs	Wkts	Avge	BB	5i	10m	RpO	ct	st
JAHURUL ISLAM, Mohammad (Bangladesh, Dhaka, Rajshahi, Bangladesh to England, Bangladesh to Ireland, Bangladesh to Scotland, Bangladesh to Sri Lanka, Bangladesh to West Indies) b Rajshahi 12.12.1986 RHB OB																			
Test		1	2	0	43	43	21.50	0	0									1	
FC		10	17	1	1008	139	63.00	4	5	6	0	1	0.00	1-0	0	0	0.00	12	
20T		6	5	0	57	36	11.40	0	0									0	1
Test	2009/10	3	6	0	114	46	19.00	0	0									3	
FC	2002/03	66	121	12	3953	158	36.26	8	25	12	7	1	7.00	1-0	0	0	3.50	69	2
Int	2010	6	6	1	156	41	31.20	0	0									6	
Lim	2002/03	42	42	2	1020	89	25.50	0	7	3	1	0					2.00	19	
I20T	2010	1	1	0	18	18	18.00	0	0									1	
20T	2009/10	7	6	0	75	36	12.50	0	0									1	1
JUBAIR AHMED, Mohammad (Rajshahi) b Rajshahi 10.2.1987 RHB RFM																			
FC		2	3	0	100	89	33.33	0	1									1	
FC	2004/05	4	5	0	191	89	38.20	0	2	240	97	5	19.40	2-19	0	0	2.42	1	
Lim	2004/05	6	6	0	42	24	7.00	0	0	143	112	2	56.00	1-30	0	0	4.69	2	
JUNAID SIDDIQUE, Mohammad (Bangladesh, Bangladesh A, BCB XI, Rajshahi, Bangladesh to England, Bangladesh to Ireland, Bangladesh to New Zealand, Bangladesh to Scotland, Bangladesh to Sri Lanka) b Rajshahi 30.10.1987 LHB OB																			
Test		3	6	0	248	106	41.33	1	1	6	9	0					9.00	2	
FC		5	8	0	253	106	31.62	1	1	6	9	0					9.00	2	
Int		6	6	0	55	23	9.16	0	0									5	
Lim		7	7	0	62	23	8.85	0	0									6	
20T		5	5	0	66	23	13.20	0	0									1	
Test	2007/08	18	35	0	942	106	26.91	1	7	18	11	0					3.66	11	
FC	2003/04	42	78	1	1943	114*	25.23	2	11	198	119	1	119.00	1-30	0	0	3.60	28	
Int	2007/08	38	37	0	864	100	23.35	1	4	12	13	0					6.50	15	
Lim	2003/04	65	64	0	1529	120	23.89	3	8	46	40	0					5.21	23	
I20T	2007/08	5	5	0	134	71	26.80	0	1									0	
20T	2007/08	11	11	0	212	71	19.27	0	1									1	
KAMRUL ISLAM (Barisal) b Patuakhali, Barisal 10.12.1991 RHB RMF																			
FC		2	2	0	6	6	3.00	0	0	372	196	9	21.77	3-22	0	0	3.16	1	
FC	2008/09	4	4	0	7	6	1.75	0	0	636	307	15	20.46	3-22	0	0	2.89	4	
KAMRUL ISLAM, Kazi (Chittagong) b 12.10.1987 RHB LMF																			
FC		9	16	3	197	46*	15.15	0	0	1644	887	30	29.56	4-31	0	0	3.23	1	
20T		2	1	0	4	4	4.00	0	0	42	51	6	8.50	4-23	1	0	7.28	2	
FC	2005/06	28	47	10	462	46*	12.48	0	0	4512	2255	77	29.28	5-21	2	0	2.99	13	
Lim	2005/06	16	11	5	71	22	11.83	0	0	815	655	29	22.58	6-47	1	1	4.82	4	
KAMRUL ISLAM, Mohammad (Barisal) b Dhaka 31.7.1986 RHB OB																			
FC		4	8	1	151	93	21.57	0	1									2	
FC	2005/06	23	43	6	937	159	25.32	1	5	144	111	1	111.00	1-12	0	0	4.62	11	
Lim	2005/06	16	13	3	297	78*	29.70	0	1	36	47	0					7.83	6	
KANDAMBY, Sahan Hewa Thilina (Basnahira North, Sinhalese, Sri Lanka to Bangladesh, Sri Lanka A, Sri Lanka Board President's XI, Dhaka, Sri Lanka to India, Sri Lanka to South Africa) b Colombo, Sri Lanka 4.6.1982 LHB LB																			
Int		5	3	0	27	18	9.00	0	0	54	43	0					4.77	1	
Lim		5	3	0	27	18	9.00	0	0	54	43	0					4.77	1	
20T		2	2	1	76	43*	76.00	0	0	6	13	0					13.00	0	
FC	2000/01	107	163	10	5659	202	36.98	12	24	1815	1356	36	37.66	4-36	0	0	4.48	61	
Int	2004	33	31	6	814	93*	32.56	0	5	168	164	2	82.00	2-37	0	0	5.85	5	
Lim	2001/02	148	129	19	3516	128*	31.96	2	24	879	786	23	34.17	4-68	1	0	5.36	37	
I20T	2008/09	4	4	0	13	10	3.25	0	0									3	
20T	2004/05	29	28	3	470	47*	18.80	0	0	93	101	5	20.20	3-21	0	0	6.51	13	
KHALED MASHUD (Rajshahi) b Rajshahi 8.2.1976 RHB WK																			
FC		7	10	1	304	78	33.77	0	4	6	1	0					1.00	5	2
20T		7	3	2	2	1*	2.00	0	0									6	1
Test	2000/01	44	84	10	1409	103*	19.04	1	3									78	9
FC	1997/98	112	191	19	4332	201*	25.18	3	22	56	27	0					2.89	184	20
Int	1994/95	126	110	27	1818	71*	21.90	0	7									91	35
Lim	1994/95	189	165	36	2635	71*	20.42	0	10	7	13	0					11.14	148	49
KHURRAM MANZOOR (Karachi Zebras, PIA, Sind Dolphins, Chittagong, Pakistan to Australia, Pakistan to New Zealand, Pakistan A to Sri Lanka) b Karachi, Sind, Pakistan 10.6.1986 RHB OB																			
20T		3	3	0	29	17	9.66	0	0									1	
Test	2008/09	7	12	1	326	93	29.63	0	3									3	
FC	2002/03	64	110	8	4275	241	41.91	12	16	156	62	1	62.00	1-14	0	0	2.38	45	
Int	2007/08	7	7	0	236	83	33.71	0	3									3	
Lim	2002/03	60	60	6	2430	163*	45.00	4	17	27	28	2	14.00	2-8	0	0	6.22	35	
20T	2004/05	25	25	1	565	100	23.54	1	3	6	17	0					17.00	15	
KULATUNGA, Hettiarachchi Gamage Jeevantha Mahesh (Colts, Wayamba, Barisal, Wayamba to India) b Kurunegala, Sri Lanka 2.11.1973 RHB RM																			
20T		4	4	0	63	26	15.75	0	0									2	
FC	1990/91	186	272	15	8315	234	32.35	13	50	5219	2358	81	29.11	5-67	1	0	2.71	187	
Lim	1993/94	102	92	11	2345	132	28.95	1	14	725	516	22	23.45	5-21	2	1	4.27	54	

Cmp	Debut	M	I	NO	Runs	HS	Avge	100	50	Balls	Runs	Wkts	Avge	BB	5i	10m	RpO	ct	st
I20T	2008/09	2	2	0	19	11	9.50	0	0									2	
20T	2004/05	36	34	5	761	104*	26.24	1	2	210	244	15	16.26	4-28	1	0	6.97	12	
LOKUARACHCHI, Kaushal Samaraweera (Sinhalese, Wayamba, Rajshahi, Wayamba to India) b Colombo, Sri Lanka 20.5.1982 RHB LB																			
20T		2	2	0	17	14	8.50	0	0	37	51	0					8.27	1	
Test	2003	4	5	1	94	28*	23.50	0	0	594	295	5	59.00	2-47	0	0	2.98	1	
FC	2000/01	104	143	13	3405	101*	26.19	2	15	14984	6730	273	24.65	7-17	7	1	2.69	54	
Int	2002/03	21	18	3	210	69	14.00	0	1	1011	725	31	23.38	4-44	1	0	4.30	5	
Lim	2001/02	118	85	14	1529	77*	21.53	0	7	5399	3810	165	23.09	5-27	5	1	4.23	44	
20T	2004/05	25	19	1	255	42	14.16	0	0	380	420	23	18.26	3-16	0	0	6.63	12	
MAHBUBUL ALAM (Bangladesh A, BCB XI, Dhaka, Bangladesh to England) b Faridpur, Dhaka 1.12.1983 RHB RMF																			
FC		5	8	1	34	13	4.85	0	0	732	406	12	33.83	4-55	0	0	3.32	2	
Lim		2	1	0	1	1	1.00	0	0	108	83	3	27.66	2-50	0	0	4.61	0	
20T		2	1	0	4	4	4.00	0	0	42	49	2	24.50	1-21	0	0	7.00	1	
Test	2008/09	4	7	3	5	2	1.25	0	0	587	314	5	62.80	2-62	0	0	3.21	0	
FC	2003/04	32	40	11	178	20	6.13	0	0	5019	2552	91	28.04	5-47	1	0	3.05	12	
Int	2008/09	5	2	0	81	59	40.50	0	1	222	280	7	40.00	2-42	0	0	7.56	1	
Lim	2003/04	28	13	5	143	59	17.87	0	1	1214	1065	32	33.28	4-34	1	0	5.26	8	
20T	2008	3	2	0	9	5	4.50	0	0	66	86	3	28.66	1-21	0	0	7.81	1	
MAHBUBUL KARIM (Chittagong) b Chittagong 10.5.1986 RHB																			
FC		8	15	0	290	85	19.33	0	1	72	54	0					4.50	0	
FC	2003/04	15	28	0	443	85	15.82	0	2	72	54	0					4.50	7	
Lim	2003/04	14	14	0	437	145	31.21	1	1	39	35	2	17.50	2-17	0	0	5.38	3	
MAHMUDUL HASAN, Mohammad (Bangladesh A, Barisal, BCB XI, Chittagong) b 10.12.1990 RHB OB																			
FC		5	8	2	75	59*	12.50	0	1	918	364	7	52.00	2-53	0	0	2.37	7	
Lim		2	2	0	37	22	18.50	0	0	90	118	2	59.00	1-41	0	0	7.86	0	
20T		5	4	0	28	21	7.00	0	0	96	100	4	25.00	3-16	0	0	6.25	4	
FC	2008/09	8	13	2	92	59*	8.36	0	1	1152	456	9	50.66	2-17	0	0	2.37	8	
Lim	2008/09	7	6	1	118	35*	23.60	0	0	276	258	9	28.66	3-15	0	0	5.60	1	
MAHMUDULLAH, Mohammad (Bangladesh, Dhaka, Bangladesh to England, Bangladesh to Ireland, Bangladesh to New Zealand, Bangladesh to Scotland, Bangladesh to Sri Lanka, Bangladesh to West Indies) b Mymensingh 4.2.1986 RHB OB																			
Test		4	8	1	306	96*	43.71	0	4	534	342	6	57.00	2-52	0	0	3.84	3	
FC		4	8	1	306	96*	43.71	0	4	534	342	6	57.00	2-52	0	0	3.84	3	
Int		12	10	3	297	64*	42.42	0	2	325	298	6	49.66	3-52	0	0	5.50	3	
Lim		12	10	3	297	64*	42.42	0	2	325	298	6	49.66	3-52	0	0	5.50	3	
20T		5	5	2	79	25	26.33	0	0	60	68	1	68.00	1-19	0	0	6.80	7	
Test	2009	9	18	2	590	115	36.87	1	4	1367	799	22	36.31	5-51	1	0	3.50	7	
FC	2004/05	51	92	11	2859	152	35.29	5	13	4534	2430	69	35.21	5-51	1	0	3.21	48	
Int	2007	56	47	14	997	64*	30.21	0	4	1687	1489	26	57.26	3-52	0	0	5.29	12	
Lim	2004/05	93	82	19	1813	65*	28.77	0	8	3019	2375	49	48.46	3-27	0	0	4.72	27	
I20T	2007/08	11	11	0	79	21	7.18	0	0	85	101	2	50.50	1-19	0	0	7.12	6	
20T	2007/08	16	16	2	158	25	11.28	0	0	145	169	3	56.33	1-19	0	0	6.99	13	
MAISUQUR RAHMAN (Sylhet)																			
FC		4	8	0	132	60	16.50	0	1	262	83	10	8.30	5-19	1	0	1.90	3	
MARSHALL AYUB, Mohammad (Bangladesh A, Chittagong, Dhaka) b Dhaka 5.12.1988 RHB LB																			
FC		9	17	1	457	72	28.56	0	4	78	63	1	63.00	1-24	0	0	4.84	3	
Lim		4	4	0	140	43	35.00	0	0	6	2	1	2.00	1-2	0	0	2.00	0	
20T		3	3	1	22	20	11.00	0	0									1	
FC	2005/06	38	64	4	1850	181	30.83	3	10	1889	999	33	30.27	6-90	1	0	3.17	20	
Lim	2005/06	22	20	2	564	65*	31.33	0	3	498	418	15	27.86	2-27	0	0	5.03	9	
MASHRAFE Bin MORTAZA (Bangladesh, Bangladesh A, BCB XI, Khulna, Sylhet, Bangladesh to England, Bangladesh to Ireland, Bangladesh to Scotland, Bangladesh to Sri Lanka, Bangladesh to West Indies) b Narail, Khulna 5.10.1983 RHB RFM																			
FC		1	2	0	14	8	7.00	0	0	114	38	2	19.00	1-16	0	0	2.00	5	
Int		1	1	0	4	4	4.00	0	0	36	37	0					6.16	0	
Lim		3	3	0	13	9	4.33	0	0	120	130	1	130.00	1-45	0	0	6.50	0	
20T		6	6	1	93	26	18.60	0	0	130	140	10	14.00	3-24	0	0	6.46	3	
Test	2001/02	36	67	5	797	79	12.85	0	3	5990	3239	78	41.52	4-60	0	0	3.24	9	
FC	2001/02	51	91	7	1341	132*	15.96	1	5	8391	4371	123	35.53	4-27	0	0	3.12	21	
Int	2001/02	113	89	15	1139	51*	15.39	0	1	5710	4410	143	30.83	6-26	5	1	4.63	36	
Lim	2001/02	127	103	18	1392	60*	16.37	0	2	6430	4887	171	28.57	6-26	6	2	4.56	42	
I20T	2006/07	13	12	3	141	36	15.66	0	0	297	435	10	43.50	2-28	0	0	8.78	1	
20T	2006/07	20	19	5	236	36	16.85	0	0	451	633	20	31.65	3-24	0	0	8.42	4	
MEHRAB HOSSAIN (Bangladesh A, BCB XI, Dhaka) b Rajshahi 8.7.1987 LHB SLA																			
FC		8	13	1	314	101	26.16	1	0	460	278	4	69.50	2-96	0	0	3.62	6	
Lim		2	2	0	23	21	11.50	0	0	30	49	0					9.80	0	
20T		6	3	1	78	58*	39.00	0	1	30	23	2	11.50	2-8	0	0	4.60	5	
Test	2007	7	13	1	243	83	20.25	0	1	407	281	4	70.25	2-29	0	0	4.14	2	
FC	2004/05	48	86	9	2398	196	31.14	5	9	3502	2031	45	45.13	6-80	2	1	3.48	26	
Int	2006/07	18	16	0	276	54	17.25	0	1	253	214	4	53.50	2-30	0	0	5.07	7	
Lim	2004/05	52	49	3	1070	65*	23.26	0	6	1495	1123	36	31.19	4-37	1	0	4.50	20	

Cmp	Debut	M	I	NO	Runs	HS	Avge	100	50	Balls	Runs	Wkts	Avge	BB	5i	10m	RpO	ct	st
I20T	2008/09	2	2	1	16	10	16.00	0	0	17	20	0					7.05	0	
20T	2008/09	8	5	2	94	58*	31.33	0	1	47	43	2	21.50	2-8	0	0	5.48	5	
MENDIS, Balapuwaduge Manukulasuriya Amith Jeewan (Kandurata, Sri Lanka A, Tamil Union, Dhaka, Sri Lanka to Zimbabwe, Sri Lanka A to Australia) b Colombo, Sri Lanka 15.1.1983 LHB LB																			
20T		6	5	1	148	44	37.00	0	0	30	29	1	29.00	1-9	0	0	5.80	5	
FC	2000/01	94	150	20	4021	153*	30.93	7	21	4574	2565	85	30.17	5-32	2	0	3.36	89	
Int	2010	4	2	1	42	35*	42.00	0	0	162	119	4	29.75	2-12	0	0	4.40	2	
Lim	2002/03	91	79	11	1700	94	25.00	0	9	1802	1365	51	26.76	5-26	3	1	4.54	37	1
20T	2004/05	31	27	4	553	48	24.04	0	0	114	133	3	44.33	2-20	0	0	7.00	11	
MITHUN ALI, Mohammad (Khulna) b 3.2.1990 RHB WK																			
FC		5	9	0	187	62	20.77	0	1	5	14	0					16.80	6	
20T		7	7	0	81	21	11.57	0	0									5	2
FC	2006/07	18	34	1	730	106	22.12	1	3	5	14	0					16.80	38	6
Lim	2007/08	9	9	1	285	64	35.62	0	3									10	4
MIZANUR RAHMAN (Rajshahi)																			
FC		1	2	0	14	14	7.00	0	0									1	
FC	2008/09	2	4	0	21	14	5.25	0	0									1	
Lim	2007/08	4	4	0	48	22	12.00	0	0									2	
MOBASHIR KHAN (Chittagong)																			
FC		2	4	2	16	6	8.00	0	0	234	164	5	32.80	2-17	0	0	4.20	2	
MOHAMMAD ASHRAFUL (Bangladesh, Dhaka, Bangladesh to England, Bangladesh to New Zealand, Bangladesh to Sri Lanka, Bangladesh to West Indies) b Dhaka 9.9.1984 RHB LB																			
Test		2	4	0	93	39	23.25	0	0	66	52	1	52.00	1-38	0	0	4.72	1	
FC		4	8	0	114	39	14.25	0	0	396	247	7	35.28	4-68	0	0	3.74	6	
Int		9	9	0	212	75	23.55	0	2	96	92	2	46.00	2-28	0	0	5.75	2	
Lim		9	9	0	212	75	23.55	0	2	96	92	2	46.00	2-28	0	0	5.75	2	
20T		6	5	0	38	20	7.60	0	0	96	90	10	9.00	3-13	0	0	5.62	2	
Test	2001/02	55	107	4	2306	158*	22.38	5	7	1591	1188	20	59.40	2-42	0	0	4.48	24	
FC	2000/01	104	196	5	5320	263	27.85	13	22	6448	3940	113	34.86	7-99	5	0	3.66	54	
Int	2000/01	163	156	13	3354	109	23.45	3	20	570	554	15	36.93	3-26	0	0	5.83	33	
Lim	2000/01	199	190	16	3900	109	22.41	3	22	1024	904	29	31.17	4-28	1	0	5.29	46	
I20T	2007/08	15	15	0	265	65	17.66	0	2	138	210	8	26.25	3-42	0	0	9.13	3	
20T	2007/08	22	21	0	305	65	14.52	0	2	234	300	18	16.66	3-13	0	0	7.69	7	
MOHAMMAD AZIM (Barisal)																			
FC		1	2	1	8	8*	8.00	0	0	228	109	3	36.33	2-46	0	0	2.86	0	
FC	2006/07	10	14	8	44	16	7.33	0	0	1508	746	24	31.08	5-54	1	0	2.96	5	
Lim	2006/07	10	6	3	66	39*	22.00	0	0	468	392	13	30.15	2-42	0	0	5.02	2	
MOHAMMAD RAFIQUE (Dhaka) b Dacca (now Dhaka, Bangladesh), Pakistan 5.9.1970 LHB SLA																			
20T		6	3	1	9	7	4.50	0	0	123	92	10	9.20	4-7	1	0	4.48	3	
Test	2000/01	33	63	6	1059	111	18.57	1	4	8744	4076	100	40.76	6-77	7	0	2.79	7	
FC	2000/01	62	108	11	1748	111	18.02	1	9	16304	6640	237	28.01	7-52	12	2	2.44	23	
Int	1994/95	125	106	17	1191	77	13.38	0	2	6414	4739	125	37.91	5-47	3	1	4.43	28	
Lim	1994/95	164	138	20	1551	77	13.14	0	3	8430	5861	184	31.85	5-16	3	2	4.17	43	
I20T	2006/07	1	1	0	13	13	13.00	0	0	24	22	1	22.00	1-22	0	0	5.50	0	
20T	2006/07	7	4	1	22	13	7.33	0	0	147	114	11	10.36	4-7	1	0	4.65	3	
MOHAMMAD SAJIB (Barisal)																			
FC		1	2	0	4	2	2.00	0	0									1	
MOHAMMAD SHAHZADA Hossain (Dhaka, Rajshahi) b Rasai 10.9.1986 RHB RMF																			
FC		6	8	1	101	46*	14.42	0	0	687	365	20	18.25	6-62	1	0	3.18	2	
20T		1								12	14	2	7.00	2-14	0	0	7.00	0	
FC	2003/04	53	71	6	919	109	14.13	1	0	8212	3753	176	21.32	7-95	6	1	2.74	32	
Lim	2003/04	40	27	9	296	41*	16.44	0	0	1762	1311	47	27.89	5-18	0	1	4.46	14	
MOHAMMAD SHARIF (Dhaka, Khulna) b Narayanganj, Dhaka 12.12.1985 RHB RMF																			
FC		8	13	2	203	50	18.45	0	1	1410	813	41	19.82	5-34	3	0	3.46	6	
20T		1	1	0	3	3	3.00	0	0	6	16	0					16.00	0	
Test	2000/01	10	20	3	122	24*	7.17	0	0	1651	1106	14	79.00	4-98	0	0	4.01	5	
FC	2000/01	68	113	22	1425	75*	15.65	0	3	11463	6313	230	27.44	6-31	13	3	3.30	36	
Int	2000/01	9	9	5	53	13*	13.25	0	0	499	424	10	42.40	3-40	0	0	5.09	1	
Lim	2000/01	49	38	7	340	52	10.96	0	1	2410	1843	84	21.94	5-21	3	5	4.58	16	
MOMINUL HAQUE (Chittagong) b 29.9.1991 LHB SLA																			
FC		4	7	0	167	82	23.85	0	1	96	56	1	56.00	1-21	0	0	3.50	5	
FC	2008/09	5	9	1	191	82	23.87	0	1	120	69	1	69.00	1-21	0	0	3.45	5	
Lim	2008/09	1	1	0	5	5	5.00	0	0	30	35	0					7.00	0	
MONIR HOSSAIN Khan (Barisal) b 27.1.1985 LHB SLA																			
FC		4	6	1	61	21	12.20	0	0	669	259	15	17.26	4-50	0	0	2.32	2	
20T		2	2	1	2	1*	2.00	0	0	42	34	2	17.00	1-13	0	0	4.85	0	
FC	2005/06	16	22	2	156	27	7.80	0	0	3361	1434	61	23.50	5-35	3	0	2.56	13	
Lim	2005/06	20	12	4	155	43	19.37	0	0	1021	762	30	25.40	3-23	0	0	4.47	8	

Cmp	Debut	M	I	NO	Runs	HS	Avge	100	50	Balls	Runs	Wkts	Avge	BB	5i	10m	RpO	ct	st
MONIRUL ISLAM (Chittagong) RHB																			
FC		1	2	1	4	4	4.00	0	0	120	93	0					4.65	0	
FC	2005/06	4	8	3	32	15*	6.40	0	0	462	267	8	33.37	6-117	1	0	3.46	3	
Lim	2005/06	5	4	2	22	19	11.00	0	0	276	187	4	46.75	1-27	0	0	4.06	1	
MONOWAR HOSSAIN (Khulna)																			
FC		2	4	1	40	15*	13.33	0	0	186	80	2	40.00	2-56	0	0	2.58	0	
FC	2008/09	4	7	4	86	18*	28.66	0	0	468	213	9	23.66	4-69	0	0	2.73	2	
Lim	2008/09	10	7	2	47	20	9.40	0	0	476	302	14	21.57	4-11	1	0	3.80	4	
MOSHARRAF HOSSAIN, Khondaker (Dhaka, Sylhet) b Dhaka 20.11.1981 LHB SLA																			
FC		6	10	3	137	34	19.57	0	0	1213	442	14	31.57	4-35	0	0	2.18	1	
20T		6	3	0	3	3	1.00	0	0	132	142	6	23.66	3-23	0	0	6.45	1	
FC	2001/02	39	63	9	1048	85	19.40	0	4	9359	3879	136	28.52	9-105	5	1	2.48	16	
Int	2007/08	3	3	0	15	8	5.00	0	0	132	100	1	100.00	1-26	0	0	4.54	0	
Lim	2001/02	35	33	6	663	72	24.55	0	4	1728	1177	37	31.81	4-42	1	0	4.08	10	
MUKHTAR ALI (Rajshahi)																			
20T		7	5	3	36	15*	18.00	0	0	108	147	12	12.25	5-22	0	1	8.16	1	
FC	2006/07	4	5	1	42	40*	10.50	0	0	427	200	3	66.66	2-20	0	0	2.81	2	
Lim	2008/09	5	4	1	49	21	16.33	0	0	203	143	13	11.00	4-22	2	0	4.22	1	
MURAD KHAN, Mohammad (Khulna) b Jessore, Khulna 29.1.1986 LHB SLA																			
FC		5	6	2	16	11	4.00	0	0	1132	528	17	31.05	6-64	1	0	2.79	1	
FC	2006/07	18	24	10	85	21	6.07	0	0	4426	1929	65	29.67	7-53	2	0	2.61	8	
Lim	2006/07	18	15	10	53	12*	10.60	0	0	870	685	26	26.34	5-29	1	2	4.72	9	
MUSHFIQUR RAHIM, Mohammad (Bangladesh, Bangladesh to England, Bangladesh to Ireland, Bangladesh to New Zealand, Bangladesh to Scotland, Bangladesh to Sri Lanka, Bangladesh to West Indies) b Bogra 1.9.1988 RHB WK																			
Test		4	8	1	392	101	56.00	1	2									7	4
FC		4	8	1	392	101	56.00	1	2									7	4
Int		12	11	1	303	76	30.30	0	2									10	3
Lim		12	11	1	303	76	30.30	0	2									10	3
Test	2005	23	45	3	1140	101	27.14	1	6									32	7
FC	2004/05	47	85	10	2190	115*	29.20	3	13									78	11
Int	2006	76	68	11	1319	98	23.14	0	6									50	17
Lim	2004/05	93	83	13	1641	98	23.44	0	8									64	22
I20T	2006/07	15	13	4	85	24	9.44	0	0									7	7
20T	2006/07	15	13	4	85	24	9.44	0	0									7	7
NABIL SAMAD Chowdhury (Bangladesh A, Dhaka, Sylhet) b Dhaka 9.10.1986 LHB SLA																			
FC		5	10	2	53	13	6.62	0	0	857	411	11	37.36	3-66	0	0	2.87	2	
Lim		2	2	0	1	1	0.50	0	0	90	82	1	82.00	1-44	0	0	5.46	1	
20T		6	2	0	0	0	0.00	0	0	96	90	2	45.00	2-28	0	0	5.62	2	
FC	2003/04	54	86	28	512	37	8.82	0	0	12276	4998	191	26.16	8-61	11	2	2.44	19	
Lim	2003/04	43	27	12	112	23	7.46	0	0	1998	1332	53	25.13	5-26	2	2	4.00	15	
NADIF CHOWDHURY (Dhaka, Rajshahi) b Manikganj 21.4.1987 RHB SLA																			
FC		8	13	1	217	48	18.08	0	0	267	176	6	29.33	2-26	0	0	3.95	6	
20T		5	4	0	34	31	8.50	0	0	30	40	3	13.33	2-17	0	0	8.00	4	
FC	2002/03	51	85	12	2145	101*	29.38	1	11	4179	2024	69	29.33	5-34	3	0	2.90	40	1
Lim	2002/03	41	38	4	691	59*	20.32	0	3	747	483	14	34.50	2-24	0	0	3.88	11	
I20T	2006/07	3	3	0	27	12	9.00	0	0									0	
20T	2006/07	9	8	0	63	31	7.87	0	0	30	40	3	13.33	2-17	0	0	8.00	4	
NADIMUDDIN, Mohammad (Dhaka) b Narayangonj 30.8.1990 LHB WK																			
FC		3	6	1	226	147	45.20	1	1									15	2
FC	2006/07	14	25	6	585	147	30.78	1	2									30	3
Lim	2006/07	4	4	0	50	35	12.50	0	0									1	
NAEEM ISLAM, Mohammad (Bangladesh, BCB XI, Rajshahi, Bangladesh to England, Bangladesh to New Zealand, Bangladesh to Sri Lanka, Bangladesh to West Indies) b Gaibandha 31.12.1986 RHB OB																			
Test		2	4	1	136	59*	45.33	0	1	156	104	0					4.00	0	
FC		3	5	2	259	123*	86.33	1	1	236	144	2	72.00	1-7	0	0	3.66	0	
Int		12	11	6	222	73*	44.40	0	1	335	329	9	36.55	3-49	0	0	5.89	3	
Lim		13	12	6	262	73*	43.66	0	1	395	382	9	42.44	3-49	0	0	5.80	3	
20T		7	7	2	132	56*	26.40	0	1	132	147	6	24.50	2-20	0	0	6.68	2	
Test	2008/09	4	8	1	180	59*	25.71	0	1	276	150	1	150.00	1-11	0	0	3.26	1	
FC	2003/04	52	88	10	2790	126	35.76	5	18	2150	1085	21	51.66	3-7	0	0	3.02	35	1
Int	2008/09	36	31	13	512	73*	28.44	0	1	1248	1034	27	38.29	3-32	0	0	4.97	13	
Lim	2004/05	72	67	20	1542	81	32.80	0	9	1614	1340	32	41.87	3-32	0	0	4.98	31	
I20T	2008/09	7	7	1	99	28	16.50	0	0	66	99	2	49.50	2-32	0	0	9.00	0	
20T	2008	15	15	3	251	56*	20.91	0	1	222	279	11	25.36	3-33	0	0	7.54	2	
NAFEES IQBAL Khan, Mohammad (BCB XI, Chittagong) b Chittagong 31.1.1985 RHB RM																			
FC		7	13	0	175	44	13.46	0	0	300	145	6	24.16	3-33	0	0	2.90	4	
Lim		2	2	0	38	27	19.00	0	0									0	
20T		5	4	0	55	25	13.75	0	0									1	
Test	2004/05	11	22	0	518	121	23.54	1	2									2	
FC	2000/01	77	140	7	3869	153	29.09	7	16	361	178	6	29.66	3-33	0	0	2.95	20	

Cmp	Debut	M	I	NO	Runs	HS	Avge	100	50	Balls	Runs	Wkts	Avge	BB	5i	10m	RpO	ct	st
Int	2003/04	16	16	0	309	58	19.31	0	2									2	
Lim	2000/01	66	65	4	1506	137*	24.68	1	14	2	2	0					6.00	14	
NASIR AHMED (Sylhet)																			
FC		1	2	1	16	13	16.00	0	0	114	68	2	34.00	2-68	0	0	3.57	0	
NASIR HOSSAIN, Mohammad (Chittagong, Rajshahi) b 30.11.1991 RHB OB																			
FC		7	11	2	343	122	38.11	1	1	443	186	8	23.25	3-56	0	0	2.51	5	
20T		5	4	1	60	24*	20.00	0	0	98	133	4	33.25	1-11	0	0	8.14	0	
FC	2008/09	17	29	2	850	122	31.48	1	4	1421	606	23	26.34	3-22	0	0	2.55	14	
Lim	2008/09	10	10	2	306	73*	38.25	0	3	462	243	15	16.20	3-19	0	0	3.15	7	
NASIR HOSSAIN (Sylhet)																			
FC		3	6	1	14	7*	2.80	0	0	372	190	12	15.83	5-28	1	0	3.06	0	
FC	2002/03	7	12	3	60	20*	6.66	0	0	888	421	17	24.76	5-28	1	0	2.84	1	
Lim	2002/03	4	2	1	0	0*	0.00	0	0	186	107	10	10.70	5-8	0	1	3.45	0	
NASIRUDDIN FARUQUE (BCB XI) b Dhaka 31.8.1983 LHB RAB																			
Lim		1	1	0	37	37	37.00	0	0									0	
FC	2003/04	44	77	6	2044	141	28.78	4	11	228	159	0					4.18	24	
Lim	2003/04	25	25	2	610	115	26.52	1	3	6	1	0					1.00	5	
NAZIMUDDIN Ahmed, Mohammad (Bangladesh A, Barisal, Chittagong) b Chittagong 1.10.1985 RHB																			
FC		12	22	2	920	205	46.00	2	4	12	6	0					3.00	6	
Lim		3	3	0	156	89	52.00	0	2									0	
20T		5	5	0	88	35	17.60	0	0									0	
FC	2001/02	69	123	10	4278	205	37.85	9	24	168	101	2	50.50	1-9	0	0	3.60	31	
Int	2007/08	7	7	0	90	47	12.85	0	0									0	
Lim	2001/02	58	57	1	1394	108	24.89	1	8	12	14	1	14.00	1-14	0	0	7.00	10	
I20T	2007/08	7	7	0	178	81	25.42	0	1									0	
20T	2007/08	12	12	0	266	81	22.16	0	1									0	
NAZMUL HOSSAIN, Mohammad (Bangladesh, Bangladesh A, Sylhet, Bangladesh to New Zealand, Bangladesh to Scotland) b Hobigonj 5.10.1987 RHB RFM																			
FC		3	5	2	20	8	6.66	0	0	408	184	6	30.66	2-24	0	0	2.70	2	
Int		4	1	1	1	1*		0	0	163	83	5	16.60	3-13	0	0	3.05	1	
Lim		6	3	1	18	15	9.00	0	0	277	186	7	26.57	3-13	0	0	4.02	2	
20T		3	1	1	0	0*		0	0	54	90	2	45.00	1-19	0	0	10.00	0	
Test	2004/05	1	2	1	8	8*	8.00	0	0	155	114	2	57.00	2-114	0	0	4.41	0	
FC	2004/05	31	50	12	384	49	10.10	0	0	4141	1992	65	30.64	5-30	2	0	2.88	16	
Int	2004	33	19	11	35	6*	4.37	0	0	1427	1222	38	32.15	4-40	1	0	5.13	5	
Lim	2004	53	33	17	130	28*	8.12	0	0	2285	1855	59	31.44	4-40	1	0	4.87	8	
I20T	2009	2	2	2	3	3*		0	0	24	33	1	33.00	1-15	0	0	8.25	0	
20T	2008	6	4	3	3	3*	3.00	0	0	102	148	4	37.00	1-15	0	0	8.70	1	
NAZMUL HOSSAIN (Bangladesh A, Sylhet)																			
Lim		2	2	0	31	19	15.50	0	0	24	32	1	32.00	1-22	0	0	8.00	2	
20T		6	6	3	78	28*	26.00	0	0									2	
FC	2006/07	11	17	2	464	95*	30.93	0	4	525	238	16	14.87	4-28	0	0	2.72	8	
Lim	2006/07	25	21	3	547	144	30.38	1	1	215	247	5	49.40	3-58	0	0	6.89	11	
NAZMUL ISLAM, Mohammad (Dhaka) b Dhaka 21.3.1991 LHB SLA																			
FC		1	2	0	12	12	6.00	0	0	216	94	4	23.50	3-58	0	0	2.61	0	
NAZMUS SADAT (Khulna, Sylhet) b Khulna 18.10.1986 LHB SLA																			
FC		7	14	0	280	75	20.00	0	2	384	217	5	43.40	2-12	0	0	3.39	5	
20T		2	2	1	4	4*	4.00	0	0	12	17	0					8.50	0	
FC	2004/05	46	87	1	2491	151	28.96	2	16	2026	1110	21	52.85	2-12	0	0	3.28	23	
Lim	2004/05	35	35	2	1189	110*	36.03	1	9	866	652	35	18.62	4-59	1	0	4.51	8	
I20T	2006/07	1	1	0	4	4	4.00	0	0									0	
20T	2006/07	3	3	1	8	4*	4.00	0	0	12	17	0					8.50	0	
NIZAMUDDIN, S K (Khulna) b 2.2.1986 RHB RAB																			
FC		8	14	1	337	65	25.92	0	1	360	194	3	64.66	1-14	0	0	3.23	3	
FC	2003/04	11	18	1	411	65	24.17	0	1	708	332	7	47.42	2-65	0	0	2.81	4	
Lim	2003/04	3	3	0	47	40	15.66	0	0	84	61	3	20.33	2-51	0	0	4.35	1	
NOOR HOSSAIN, Mohammad (Bangladesh A, Dhaka) b 12.3.1992 RHB LB																			
FC		4	8	0	110	49	13.75	0	0	636	459	8	57.37	4-146	0	0	4.33	2	
Lim		4	4	1	25	18	8.33	0	0	222	193	5	38.60	2-67	0	0	5.21	3	
20T		1								18	31	1	31.00	1-31	0	0	10.33	0	
NURUL HASAN, Qazi (Khulna) b 21.11.1993 RHB WK																			
20T		2	1	0	8	8	8.00	0	0									0	
PETERSEN, Alviro Nathan (Lions, North West to South Africa, South Africa, Khulna, South Africa to India, South Africa to West Indies, South Africa A to Bangladesh) b Port Elizabeth, Cape Province, South Africa 25.11.1980 RHB RM																			
FC		2	3	0	248	116	82.66	1	1									4	
20T		1	1	0	34	34	34.00	0	0									0	
Test	2009/10	4	8	0	272	100	34.00	1	1	42	21	1	21.00	1-2	0	0	3.00	4	
FC	2000/01	97	176	10	6352	152	38.26	19	27	234	125	4	31.25	2-7	0	0	3.20	81	
Int	2006/07	14	12	1	377	80	34.27	0	4	6	7	0					7.00	2	
Lim	2001/02	116	111	7	3316	124	31.88	5	22	161	140	3	46.66	1-13	0	0	5.21	38	

Cmp	Debut	M	I	NO	Runs	HS	Avge	100	50	Balls	Runs	Wkts	Avge	BB	5i	10m	RpO	ct	st
I20T	2010	2	2	0	14	8	7.00	0	0									1	
20T	2003/04	36	32	5	748	78*	27.70	0	7	24	44	0					11.00	19	
QAISER ABBAS (National Bank, Sialkot Stallions, Rajshahi) b Muridke, Punjab, Pakistan 7.5.1982 LHB SLA																			
20T		2	2	1	74	61*	74.00	0	1	36	39	2	19.50	2-24	0	0	6.50	0	
Test	2000/01	1	1	0	2	2	2.00	0	0	96	35	0					2.18	0	
FC	1999/00	109	170	17	5055	168	33.03	5	31	6000	2320	75	30.93	5-20	2	0	2.32	60	
Lim	1999/00	118	107	27	2894	106*	36.17	2	21	4434	3380	105	32.19	4-33	4	0	4.57	48	
20T	2004/05	26	20	5	381	75*	25.40	0	2	222	287	13	22.07	3-17	0	0	7.75	6	
RAIHANUDDIN ARAFAT (BCB XI, Chittagong) LB																			
FC		3	6	1	20	11	4.00	0	0	336	202	5	40.40	2-36	0	0	3.60	1	
Lim		1	1	1	8	8*		0	0	48	54	1	54.00	1-54	0	0	6.75	1	
FC	2003/04	13	21	5	95	24	5.93	0	0	1769	1014	28	36.21	3-35	0	0	3.43	5	
Lim	2005/06	5	3	2	8	8*	8.00	0	0	150	153	3	51.00	1-14	0	0	6.12	6	
RAJAPAKSA, Pramod Bhanuka Bandara (Sinhalese, Sri Lanka Cricket Combined XI, Barisal) b Colombo, Sri Lanka 24.10.1991 LHB RMF																			
20T		3	3	1	39	30*	19.50	0	0									0	
Lim	2009/10	6	6	0	116	59	19.33	0	1									2	
20T	2008/09	11	11	1	242	58	24.20	0	2									2	
RAJIN SALEH Alam, Khondokar Mohammad (Sylhet) b Sylhet, Chittagong 20.11.1983 RHB OB																			
FC		5	10	1	292	112	32.44	1	1	60	49	2	24.50	1-8	0	0	4.90	1	
Test	2003/04	24	46	2	1141	89	25.93	0	7	438	268	2	134.00	1-9	0	0	3.67	15	
FC	2000/01	83	150	13	4852	135	35.41	10	23	1328	773	7	110.42	2-44	0	0	3.49	61	
Int	2003/04	43	43	1	1005	108*	23.92	1	6	539	459	15	30.60	4-16	1	0	5.10	9	
Lim	2000/01	85	84	5	1803	108*	22.82	2	8	909	720	29	24.82	4-16	1	0	4.75	29	
RAQIBUL HASAN, Mohammad (Bangladesh, Bangladesh A, Barisal, BCB XI, Bangladesh to England, Bangladesh to New Zealand) b Jamalpur, Dhaka 8.10.1987 RHB LB																			
Test		2	4	0	39	17	9.75	0	0	6	0	1	0.00	1-0	0	0	0.00	3	
FC		5	9	0	72	19	8.00	0	0	6	0	1	0.00	1-0	0	0	0.00	5	
Int		9	9	2	219	43	31.28	0	0									3	
Lim		15	15	2	401	46	30.84	0	0	3	8	0					16.00	3	
20T		5	5	0	97	43	19.40	0	0									1	
Test	2008/09	7	14	0	268	65	19.14	0	1	18	5	1	5.00	1-0	0	0	1.66	7	
FC	2004/05	35	63	2	1932	313*	31.67	2	10	306	207	5	41.40	1-0	0	0	4.05	26	
Int	2007/08	42	41	5	1103	89	30.63	0	7									12	
Lim	2004/05	74	73	9	2217	133	34.64	2	15	12	21	0					10.50	19	
I20T	2008/09	5	5	0	51	18	10.20	0	0									1	
20T	2008/09	10	10	0	148	43	14.80	0	0									2	
RASHID HANIF (Sylhet) b Karachi, Sind, Pakistan 4.1.1978 LHB SLA																			
20T		2	2	0	12	10	6.00	0	0	48	38	2	19.00	1-11	0	0	4.75	0	
FC	1996/97	12	21	3	452	64*	25.11	0	4	1427	619	20	30.95	7-36	1	0	2.60	6	
Lim	1996/97	16	14	3	194	30	17.63	0	0	703	540	17	31.76	3-28	0	0	4.60	3	
REZAUL HAQUE, Khondokar Mohammad (Sylhet) b Sylhet, Chittagong 20.11.1982 RHB LMF																			
FC		1	2	0	0	0	0.00	0	0	72	42	0					3.50	0	
FC	2000/01	66	115	14	1925	107	19.05	2	7	7550	3132	128	24.46	7-73	5	0	2.48	27	
Lim	2000/01	55	41	10	484	46*	15.61	0	0	2264	1435	61	23.52	4-19	3	0	3.80	8	
REZAUL KARIM (Chittagong) b 8.5.1989 LHB SLA																			
FC		3	6	1	130	65*	26.00	0	1	113	61	1	61.00	1-43	0	0	3.23	0	
FC	2005/06	13	24	3	626	128	29.80	1	4	791	336	8	42.00	2-25	0	0	2.54	0	
Lim	2005/06	21	19	2	420	85	24.70	0	3	683	533	23	23.17	4-25	2	0	4.68	9	
REZWAN KABIR (Khulna)																			
FC		4	7	0	114	43	16.28	0	0	258	94	1	94.00	1-4	0	0	2.18	4	
FC	2004/05	6	11	0	183	43	16.63	0	0	258	94	1	94.00	1-4	0	0	2.18	4	
Lim	2004/05	2	2	0	2	2	1.00	0	0	18	7	0					2.33	2	
RIAZUL KARIM (Khulna)																			
FC		1	2	2	22	22*		0	0	42	28	0					4.00	2	
ROBIUL ISLAM, S K (Bangladesh A, Barisal, Khulna, Bangladesh to England) b Satkhira, Khulna 20.10.1986 RHB RFM																			
FC		6	11	4	35	10*	5.00	0	0	966	644	23	28.00	5-30	2	1	4.00	1	
20T		1								19	35	1	35.00	1-35	0	0	11.05	2	
Test	2010	1	2	2	9	9*		0	0	138	119	0					5.17	0	
FC	2005/06	34	54	21	214	21	6.48	0	0	5701	3400	114	29.82	5-30	6	1	3.57	16	
Lim	2006/07	8	5	1	24	12	6.00	0	0	329	306	9	34.00	4-7	1	0	5.58	1	
RONY TALUKDER (Barisal, Dhaka) b 29.5.1989 RHB RMF																			
FC		5	10	1	158	64	17.55	0	1	458	232	10	23.20	3-11	0	0	3.03	5	
20T		1	1	0	26	26	26.00	0	0									0	
FC	2008/09	13	24	1	630	176	27.39	1	2	464	238	10	23.80	3-11	0	0	3.07	13	
Lim	2008/09	9	9	0	179	29	19.88	0	0	162	81	5	16.20	3-26	0	0	3.00	4	
RUBEL HOSSAIN, Mohammad (Bangladesh, Chittagong, Bangladesh to England, Bangladesh to Ireland, Bangladesh to New Zealand) b Bagerhat, Khulna 1.1.1990 RHB RMF																			
Test		4	8	4	25	17	6.25	0	0	648	488	3	162.66	1-88	0	0	4.51	3	
FC		4	8	4	25	17	6.25	0	0	648	488	3	162.66	1-88	0	0	4.51	3	
Int		6	3	2	2	2*	2.00	0	0	264	317	3	105.66	1-47	0	0	7.20	0	

Cmp	Debut	M	I	NO	Runs	HS	Avge	100	50	Balls	Runs	Wkts	Avge	BB	5i	10m	RpO	ct	st
Lim		6	3	2	2	2*	2.00	0	0	264	317	3	105.66	1-47	0	0	7.20	0	
20T		4	2	2	6	3*		0	0	79	94	8	11.75	5-32	0	1	7.13	2	
Test	2009	8	15	6	43	17	4.77	0	0	1278	997	12	83.08	5-166	1	0	4.68	4	
FC	2007/08	20	31	9	83	17	3.77	0	0	2914	2106	36	58.50	5-60	2	0	4.33	8	
Int	2008/09	18	8	5	8	4	2.66	0	0	786	812	19	42.73	4-33	1	0	6.19	2	
Lim	2007/08	28	14	7	34	14	4.85	0	0	1302	1185	34	34.85	4-33	1	0	5.46	3	
I20T	2009	3	1	1	8	8*		0	0	62	93	2	46.50	1-13	0	0	9.00	1	
20T	2008	8	4	3	14	8*	14.00	0	0	165	206	10	20.60	5-32	0	1	7.49	4	
RUMMAN AHMED (Dhaka, Sylhet) b 5.10.1991 RHB																			
FC		2	4	0	45	20	11.25	0	0									1	
20T		1	1	0	3	3	3.00	0	0									0	
SABBIR RAHMAN, Mohammad (Barisal, Rajshahi) b 20.8.1991 RHB LB																			
FC		4	8	1	341	100*	48.71	1	2	84	52	0					3.71	4	
20T		5	4	0	18	9	4.50	0	0	102	103	4	25.75	3-19	0	0	6.05	0	
FC	2008/09	10	18	3	613	100*	40.86	1	3	362	180	5	36.00	2-1	0	0	2.98	11	
Lim	2008/09	10	10	1	172	44	19.11	0	0	76	46	2	23.00	1-13	0	0	3.63	9	
SADIQUR RAHMAN, Ahmed (Sylhet) b Sylhet 20.12.1987 RHB OB																			
FC		1	2	0	23	23	11.50	0	0	6	7	0					7.00	0	
FC	2003/04	19	35	6	519	59	17.89	0	2	1137	560	17	32.94	4-47	0	0	2.95	6	
Lim	2003/04	15	14	4	311	80	31.10	0	2	306	291	7	41.57	4-70	1	0	5.70	3	
SAGHIR HOSSAIN, Gazi (Bangladesh A, Barisal, BCB XI, Khulna) b Khulna 14.8.1986 RHB WK																			
FC		12	21	1	580	79	29.00	0	3									32	2
Lim		2	2	1	39	35*	39.00	0	0									4	
20T		5	4	0	49	21	12.25	0	0									0	1
FC	2004/05	62	113	4	2764	101	25.35	1	14	94	97	3	32.33	1-9	0	0	6.19	179	15
Lim	2004/05	39	36	5	611	75*	19.70	0	3									42	14
20T	2008	6	5	0	54	21	10.80	0	0									0	1
SAJIDUL ISLAM (Barisal) b Rangpur 18.1.1988 RHB LMF																			
FC		3	6	1	68	23	13.60	0	0	556	319	7	45.57	4-80	0	0	3.44	0	
Test	2007/08	2	4	0	14	6	3.50	0	0	216	175	3	58.33	2-71	0	0	4.86	0	
FC	2005/06	37	59	24	712	75	20.34	0	3	6210	3188	111	28.72	6-51	3	0	3.08	13	
Lim	2005/06	18	13	3	93	40	9.30	0	0	860	684	24	28.50	3-52	0	0	4.77	6	
SAJU DATTA (Sylhet) SLA																			
FC		2	4	1	4	2*	1.33	0	0	174	95	4	23.75	2-17	0	0	3.27	0	
20T		3								54	47	4	11.75	2-20	0	0	5.22	0	
FC	2005/06	19	30	11	86	11*	4.52	0	0	4155	1741	74	23.52	5-58	1	0	2.51	3	
Lim	2005/06	19	11	6	34	13	6.80	0	0	972	692	24	28.83	3-33	0	0	4.27	4	
SANJAMUL ISLAM (Rajshahi)																			
FC		1	2	0	9	9	4.50	0	0	195	121	5	24.20	3-19	0	0	3.72	1	
20T		6	2	1	39	31*	39.00	0	0	132	132	8	16.50	2-15	0	0	6.00	1	
Lim	2008/09	7	7	2	55	18	11.00	0	0	309	167	16	10.43	4-11	1	0	3.24	2	
SAQLAIN SAJIB (Bangladesh A, Chittagong, Rajshahi) b 1.12.1988 LHB SLA																			
FC		9	10	5	46	12*	9.20	0	0	2120	1059	54	19.61	7-29	5	1	2.99	6	
Lim		4	4	3	8	4*	8.00	0	0	210	202	3	67.33	1-41	0	0	5.77	1	
20T		3								66	82	3	27.33	2-38	0	0	7.45	1	
FC	2006/07	20	27	7	168	46	8.40	0	0	4171	1944	97	20.04	7-29	8	1	2.79	12	
Lim	2006/07	24	15	10	73	15*	14.60	0	0	1136	808	35	23.08	4-17	2	0	4.26	8	
SAYEM ALAM Rezvi, Khondakar Mohammad (Sylhet) b 14.4.1993 LHB OB																			
FC		3	6	0	95	27	15.83	0	0	2	4	0					12.00	0	
SAYMON AHMED (Rajshahi)																			
FC		1	2	0	6	6	3.00	0	0	36	20	0					3.33	3	
SHAFAQ AL ZABIR (Barisal, BCB XI) b Rajshahi 10.7.1986 RHB LMF																			
FC		2	2	0	10	10	5.00	0	0	420	207	14	14.78	5-30	1	0	2.95	0	
Lim		1								30	34	0					6.80	2	
FC	2002/03	28	31	9	156	30	7.09	0	0	4368	2069	92	22.48	5-30	3	0	2.84	21	
Lim	2002/03	36	16	8	67	24*	8.37	0	0	1907	1063	73	14.56	5-24	1	2	3.34	6	
SHAFIUL ISLAM (Bangladesh, Rajshahi, Bangladesh to England, Bangladesh to Ireland, Bangladesh to New Zealand, Bangladesh to Scotland, Bangladesh to Sri Lanka, Bangladesh to West Indies) b Bogra 6.10.1989 RHB RFM																			
Test		3	6	0	104	53	17.33	0	1	402	281	4	70.25	3-86	0	0	4.19	0	
FC		3	6	0	104	53	17.33	0	1	402	281	4	70.25	3-86	0	0	4.19	0	
Int		5	2	1	11	11*	11.00	0	0	173	203	4	50.75	1-35	0	0	7.04	0	
Lim		5	2	1	11	11*	11.00	0	0	173	203	4	50.75	1-35	0	0	7.04	0	
20T		6	3	2	5	2*	5.00	0	0	122	173	4	43.25	2-26	0	0	8.50	3	
Test	2009/10	5	10	1	137	53	15.22	0	1	798	502	7	71.71	3-86	0	0	3.77	0	
FC	2007/08	18	28	7	298	53	14.19	0	1	2653	1361	39	34.89	4-38	0	0	3.07	5	
Int	2009/10	16	8	3	43	16	8.60	0	0	715	824	24	34.33	4-59	2	0	6.91	2	
Lim	2006/07	20	9	4	43	16	8.60	0	0	894	978	31	31.54	4-59	2	0	6.56	2	
I20T	2009/10	3	2	0	17	16	8.50	0	0	54	66	1	66.00	1-25	0	0	7.33	1	
20T	2009/10	9	5	2	22	16	7.33	0	0	176	239	5	47.80	2-26	0	0	8.14	4	

Cmp	Debut	M	I	NO	Runs	HS	Avge	100	50	Balls	Runs	Wkts	Avge	BB	5i	10m	RpO	ct	st
SHAHADAT HOSSAIN, Kazi (Bangladesh, Bangladesh A, Dhaka, Bangladesh to England, Bangladesh to New Zealand) b Narayanganj, Dhaka 7.8.1986 RHB RFM																			
Test		3	6	0	109	40	18.16	0	0	474	307	7	43.85	5-71	1	0	3.88	2	
FC		4	8	0	142	40	17.75	0	0	570	387	7	55.28	5-71	1	0	4.07	2	
20T		3	1	1	19	19*		0	0	60	61	4	15.25	2-10	0	0	6.10	0	
Test	2005	29	55	15	394	40	9.85	0	0	4334	2992	66	45.33	6-27	4	0	4.14	7	
FC	2003/04	52	89	28	731	40	11.98	0	0	7662	5162	134	38.52	6-27	7	0	4.04	11	
Int	2005/06	46	25	15	79	16*	7.90	0	0	1928	1824	42	43.42	3-34	0	0	5.67	5	
Lim	2003/04	61	33	16	139	26	8.17	0	0	2625	2358	64	36.84	4-34	1	0	5.39	7	
I20T	2006/07	5	5	3	8	4*	4.00	0	0	96	144	4	36.00	2-22	0	0	9.00	0	
20T	2006/07	8	6	4	27	19*	13.50	0	0	156	205	8	25.62	2-10	0	0	7.88	0	
SHAHIN HOSSAIN, Mohammad (Barisal, BCB XI) b Dhaka 8.8.1984 RHB WK																			
FC		5	9	2	113	65	16.14	0	1									18	1
Lim		2	1	0	4	4	4.00	0	0									0	
FC	2000/01	77	128	13	2407	119*	20.93	2	13	147	126	4	31.50	2-25	0	0	5.14	225	32
Lim	2000/01	67	52	15	628	65	16.97	0	1	6	10	0					10.00	79	17
SHAHRIAR NAFEES Ahmed (Bangladesh, Bangladesh A, Barisal, BCB XI) b Dhaka 25.1.1986 LHB SLA																			
Test		1	2	0	25	21	12.50	0	0									1	
FC		8	15	1	482	133	34.42	1	2	30	15	0					3.00	4	
Lim		2	2	0	20	12	10.00	0	0									0	
20T		5	5	1	73	30	18.25	0	0									3	
Test	2005/06	16	32	0	835	138	26.09	1	4									12	
FC	2003/04	47	92	3	2772	138	31.14	3	19	48	35	0					4.37	28	
Int	2005	60	60	5	1857	123*	33.76	4	10									11	
Lim	2005	75	75	5	2173	147	31.04	5	11									14	
I20T	2006/07	1	1	0	25	25	25.00	0	0									1	
20T	2006/07	6	6	1	98	30	19.60	0	0									4	
SHAKIB AL HASAN (Bangladesh, Khulna, Bangladesh to England, Bangladesh to Ireland, Bangladesh to New Zealand, Bangladesh to Scotland, Bangladesh to Sri Lanka, Bangladesh to West Indies, Worcestershire) b Magura, Khulna 24.3.1987 LHB SLA																			
Test		4	8	0	225	96	28.12	0	1	1297	642	18	35.66	5-62	1	0	2.97	0	
FC		4	8	0	225	96	28.12	0	1	1297	642	18	35.66	5-62	1	0	2.97	0	
Int		12	11	2	340	105*	37.77	1	1	665	434	14	31.00	3-8	0	0	3.91	3	
Lim		12	11	2	340	105*	37.77	1	1	665	434	14	31.00	3-8	0	0	3.91	3	
20T		7	7	0	86	27	12.28	0	0	162	160	8	20.00	2-16	0	0	5.92	4	
Test	2007	21	40	2	1179	100	31.02	1	5	5083	2410	75	32.13	7-36	7	0	2.84	8	
FC	2004/05	54	100	9	2991	129	32.86	4	14	10706	4898	164	29.86	7-32	12	0	2.74	28	
Int	2006	94	90	15	2465	134*	32.86	4	14	4790	3350	109	30.73	4-33	1	0	4.19	24	
Lim	2005/06	117	113	16	3057	134*	31.51	4	19	5725	4010	132	30.37	4-30	4	0	4.20	34	
I20T	2006/07	14	14	0	207	47	14.78	0	0	294	328	17	19.29	4-34	1	0	6.69	4	
20T	2006/07	21	21	0	293	47	13.95	0	0	456	488	25	19.52	4-34	1	0	6.42	8	
SHAMSUR RAHMAN, Mohammad (Bangladesh A, BCB XI, Dhaka) b Comilla, Chittagong 5.6.1988 RHB RM																			
FC		9	17	1	640	134	40.00	1	5	132	75	0					3.40	8	
Lim		6	6	0	86	29	14.33	0	0	216	178	4	44.50	1-26	0	0	4.94	3	
20T		6	6	1	154	51*	30.80	0	1									1	
FC	2004/05	37	66	4	1960	134	31.61	2	15	312	197	2	98.50	1-9	0	0	3.78	30	
Lim	2004/05	33	31	1	735	67	24.50	0	5	246	211	4	52.75	1-26	0	0	5.14	16	1
SHARIFULLAH, Mohammad (BCB XI, Chittagong, Dhaka)																			
FC		6	9	1	194	56	24.25	0	2	156	103	1	103.00	1-22	0	0	3.96	2	
Lim		2	2	0	63	47	31.50	0	0	84	72	3	24.00	2-27	0	0	5.14	0	
20T		2	2	1	12	12*	12.00	0	0	42	52	1	52.00	1-23	0	0	7.42	0	
FC	2006/07	19	30	1	525	74	18.10	0	4	924	426	14	30.42	3-26	0	0	2.76	5	
Lim	2006/07	26	24	1	664	56*	28.86	0	3	604	444	17	26.11	3-25	0	0	4.41	7	
SHOAIB AKHTAR (Federal Areas Leopards, Islamabad Leopards, KRL, Chittagong, Pakistan to England, Pakistan to Sri Lanka, Pakistanis to England) b Rawalpindi, Punjab, Pakistan 13.8.1975 RHB RF																			
20T		3	2	1	8	6	8.00	0	0	66	95	1	95.00	1-35	0	0	8.63	3	
Test	1997/98	46	67	13	544	47	10.07	0	0	8143	4574	178	25.69	6-11	12	2	3.37	12	
FC	1994/95	133	186	50	1670	59*	12.27	0	1	20460	12265	467	26.26	6-11	28	2	3.59	41	
Int	1997/98	152	76	35	383	43	9.34	0	0	7242	5659	235	24.08	6-16	6	4	4.68	18	
Lim	1993/94	210	115	40	866	56	11.54	0	1	10105	8012	326	24.57	6-16	13	7	4.75	33	
I20T	2006	11	3	1	5	4	2.50	0	0	222	287	12	23.91	2-11	0	0	7.75	2	
20T	2003	31	16	3	59	14	4.53	0	0	636	763	31	24.61	5-23	1	1	7.19	7	
SHUVAGOTO HOM Chowdhury (Dhaka, Rajshahi) b Mymensingh, Dhaka 11.11.1986 RHB																			
FC		7	12	2	601	166*	60.10	1	5	126	86	1	86.00	1-16	0	0	4.09	5	
20T		7	7	0	172	62	24.57	0	2	12	17	0					8.50	3	
SIRIWARDENE, Tissa Appuhamilage Milinda (Basnahira South, Chilaw Marians, Sri Lanka A, Dhaka) b Nagoda, Sri Lanka 4.12.1985 LHB SLA																			
20T		2	2	1	11	7	11.00	0	0	42	49	1	49.00	1-29	0	0	7.00	1	
FC	2005/06	45	75	7	2094	151*	30.79	2	14	2457	1616	53	30.49	5-26	2	0	3.94	33	
Lim	2005/06	62	53	10	902	76	20.97	0	2	1302	948	41	23.12	6-40	0	1	4.36	30	
20T	2005/06	28	27	4	340	54*	14.78	0	1	260	324	17	19.05	4-22	1	0	7.47	18	

Cmp	Debut	M	I	NO	Runs	HS	Avge	100	50	Balls	Runs	Wkts	Avge	BB	5i	10m	RpO	ct	st
SOHAG GAZI, Mohammad (Barisal) b 5.8.1991 RHB OB																			
FC		4	7	0	100	34	14.28	0	0	640	307	15	20.46	5-63	1	0	2.87	5	
SUBASHIS ROY (Rajshahi) b 28.11.1988 RHB RFM																			
FC		4	3	0	0	0	0.00	0	0	477	244	7	34.85	3-59	0	0	3.06	2	
FC	2007/08	12	15	6	46	33	5.11	0	0	1748	836	35	23.88	5-18	2	0	2.87	5	
Lim	2007/08	7	3	2	10	8*	10.00	0	0	312	236	9	26.22	2-17	0	0	4.53	2	
SUHRAWADI SHUVO, Mohammad (Bangladesh, Bangladesh A, Rajshahi, Bangladesh to Sri Lanka, Bangladesh to West Indies) b Rajshahi 21.11.1988 RHB SLA																			
FC		8	12	2	381	151	38.10	1	2	1654	871	38	22.92	6-93	5	0	3.16	9	
Int		2	2	1	25	14*	25.00	0	0	78	59	1	59.00	1-45	0	0	4.53	0	
Lim		2	2	1	25	14*	25.00	0	0	78	59	1	59.00	1-45	0	0	4.53	0	
20T		7	6	2	79	33	19.75	0	0	141	159	8	19.87	3-33	0	0	6.76	6	
FC	2004/05	33	51	11	1126	151	28.15	1	6	7806	3417	166	20.58	6-71	14	2	2.62	35	
Int	2009/10	4	3	1	29	14*	14.50	0	0	150	145	1	145.00	1-45	0	0	5.80	1	
Lim	2004/05	26	23	3	264	62	13.20	0	1	1315	824	36	22.88	5-6	1	1	3.76	5	
I20T	2010	1	1	1	1	1*		0	0	6	12	0					12.00	0	
20T	2008	9	8	3	82	33	16.40	0	0	153	188	8	23.50	3-33	0	0	7.37	6	
SYED RASEL (Bangladesh, Bangladesh A, Barisal, Khulna, Bangladesh to Ireland, Bangladesh to Sri Lanka) b Jessore, Khulna 3.7.1984 LHB LFM																			
FC		7	11	1	246	54	24.60	0	1	1158	590	32	18.43	5-59	2	0	3.05	4	
Int		3	1	1	7	7*		0	0	135	132	1	132.00	1-58	0	0	5.86	0	
Lim		3	1	1	7	7*		0	0	135	132	1	132.00	1-58	0	0	5.86	0	
20T		5	4	3	14	6*	14.00	0	0	114	119	7	17.00	3-24	0	0	6.26	0	
Test	2005/06	6	12	4	37	19	4.62	0	0	879	573	12	47.75	4-129	0	0	3.91	0	
FC	2001/02	49	76	23	691	54	13.03	0	1	8241	4053	151	26.84	8-67	5	2	2.95	11	
Int	2005/06	52	27	11	81	15	5.06	0	0	2657	2051	61	33.62	4-22	1	0	4.63	8	
Lim	2001/02	87	50	16	272	41	8.00	0	0	4357	3192	111	28.75	5-35	2	1	4.39	13	
I20T	2007/08	8	3	1	7	6	3.50	0	0	174	202	4	50.50	1-10	0	0	6.96	1	
20T	2007/08	13	7	4	21	6*	7.00	0	0	288	321	11	29.18	3-24	0	0	6.68	1	
TALHA JUBAIR (Bangladesh A, BCB XI, Dhaka) b Faridpur, Dhaka 10.12.1985 RHB RM																			
FC		8	10	2	49	14*	6.12	0	0	1070	656	30	21.86	7-59	1	1	3.67	4	
Lim		3	2	0	9	6	4.50	0	0	156	157	4	39.25	3-45	0	0	6.03	2	
Test	2002	7	14	6	52	31	6.50	0	0	1090	771	14	55.07	3-135	0	0	4.24	1	
FC	2001/02	61	96	21	795	50	10.60	0	1	9390	5301	195	27.18	7-59	5	1	3.38	23	
Int	2002/03	6	5	3	5	4*	2.50	0	0	204	255	6	42.50	4-65	1	0	7.50	1	
Lim	2000/01	21	13	3	27	6	2.70	0	0	889	873	27	32.33	5-38	1	1	5.89	6	
TAMIM IQBAL Khan (Bangladesh, Chittagong, Bangladesh to England, Bangladesh to Ireland, Bangladesh to New Zealand, Bangladesh to Scotland, Bangladesh to Sri Lanka, Bangladesh to West Indies) b Chittagong 20.3.1989 LHB OB																			
Test		4	8	0	471	151	58.87	1	4	12	6	0					3.00	3	
FC		4	8	0	471	151	58.87	1	4	12	6	0					3.00	3	
Int		12	12	0	428	125	35.66	1	2	5	7	0					8.40	1	
Lim		12	12	0	428	125	35.66	1	2	5	7	0					8.40	1	
20T		5	5	1	193	91	48.25	0	2	12	17	0					8.50	2	
Test	2007/08	19	36	0	1445	151	40.13	4	8	24	10	0					2.50	8	
FC	2004/05	40	73	1	2928	151	40.66	6	20	132	77	0					3.50	20	
Int	2006/07	85	85	0	2478	154	29.15	3	15	6	13	0					13.00	25	
Lim	2004/05	99	99	0	2871	154	29.00	4	16	6	13	0					13.00	32	
I20T	2007/08	14	14	0	193	32	13.78	0	0									2	
20T	2007/08	19	19	1	386	91	21.44	0	2	12	17	0					8.50	4	
TANVEER HAIDER Khan (BCB XI, Sylhet) b Rangpur 5.12.1991 RHB LB																			
FC		2	4	1	71	35	23.66	0	0	108	80	0					4.44	3	
Lim		1	1	0	35	35	35.00	0	0	12	17	0					8.50	0	
TAPASH Kumar BAISYA (BCB XI, Dhaka, Sylhet) b Sylhet, Chittagong 25.12.1982 RHB RFM																			
FC		3	6	0	69	29	11.50	0	0	390	174	8	21.75	3-35	0	0	2.67	2	
Lim		2	2	2	7	4*		0	0	78	87	3	29.00	3-72	0	0	6.69	0	
20T		4	1	0	15	15	15.00	0	0	78	98	6	16.33	2-17	0	0	7.53	0	
Test	2002	21	40	6	384	66	11.29	0	2	3376	2137	36	59.36	4-72	0	0	3.79	6	
FC	2000/01	64	108	13	1355	112	14.26	1	4	9522	4959	145	34.20	5-30	1	0	3.12	21	
Int	2002	56	41	13	336	35*	12.00	0	0	2608	2452	59	41.55	4-16	2	0	5.64	8	
Lim	2000/01	94	64	20	696	68	15.81	0	3	4421	3678	110	33.43	4-16	4	0	4.99	13	
TAPOSH GHOSH (Khulna, Rajshahi) b 11.8.1991 LHB SLA																			
FC		6	11	3	381	150*	47.62	1	2	384	237	4	59.25	2-3	0	0	3.70	2	
20T		1								24	26	1	26.00	1-26	0	0	6.50	0	
FC	2006/07	15	28	8	521	150*	26.05	1	2	1854	934	27	34.59	4-88	0	0	3.02	13	
Lim	2007/08	11	9	2	114	37	16.28	0	0	377	360	11	32.72	3-15	0	0	5.72	5	
TAREQ AZIZ Khan, Mohammad (BCB XI, Chittagong, Khulna) b Chittagong 4.9.1983 RHB RMF																			
FC		3	5	2	41	13*	13.66	0	0	566	232	15	15.46	4-47	0	0	2.45	2	
Lim		2	1	0	24	24	24.00	0	0	91	108	3	36.00	3-40	0	0	7.12	0	
20T		1	1	1	4	4*		0	0									0	
Test	2004	3	6	4	22	10*	11.00	0	0	360	261	1	261.00	1-76	0	0	4.35	1	
FC	2001/02	53	84	37	738	39	15.70	0	0	9220	4981	194	25.67	6-46	9	1	3.24	37	

Cmp	Debut	M	I	NO	Runs	HS	Avge	100	50	Balls	Runs	Wkts	Avge	BB	5i	10m	RpO	ct	st
Int	2001/02	10	8	7	26	11*	26.00	0	0	465	424	13	32.61	3-19	0	0	5.47	4	
Lim	2001/02	47	27	14	118	24	9.07	0	0	2135	1756	62	28.32	4-32	1	0	4.93	14	
TARIQUL ISLAM, Mohammad (Barisal) b Rajshahi 2.2.1972 RHB OB																			
FC		2	4	3	5	5*	5.00	0	0	216	119	0					3.30	1	
FC	2000/01	43	62	17	379	55	8.42	0	1	7560	3902	110	35.47	8-88	7	1	3.09	18	
Lim	2000/01	50	29	14	140	35*	9.33	0	0	2323	1740	72	24.16	5-50	3	1	4.49	11	
TUSHAR IMRAN, Sheikh (Khulna) b Kharki, Jessore, Khulna 10.12.1983 RHB RM																			
FC		6	11	1	380	109	38.00	1	1	70	44	2	22.00	1-0	0	0	3.77	3	
20T		5	3	0	27	20	9.00	0	0	12	25	0					12.50	0	
Test	2002	5	10	0	89	28	8.90	0	0	60	48	0					4.80	1	
FC	2000/01	83	151	10	4813	198	34.13	11	23	1823	990	20	49.50	3-22	0	0	3.25	39	
Int	2001/02	41	40	0	574	65	14.35	0	2	126	103	1	103.00	1-24	0	0	4.90	6	
Lim	2000/01	105	102	2	2469	106*	24.69	1	14	690	484	11	44.00	4-26	1	0	4.20	30	
UDAWATTE, Mahela Lakmal (Chilaw Marians, Sri Lanka A, Wayamba, Khulna, Sri Lanka A to Australia, Wayamba to India) b Colombo, Sri Lanka 19.7.1986 LHB OB																			
20T		5	5	0	136	38	27.20	0	0									2	
FC	2005/06	65	116	8	3345	168	30.97	3	22	228	164	5	32.80	2-31	0	0	4.31	36	
Int	2007/08	9	9	0	257	73	28.55	0	2									0	
Lim	2004/05	87	86	2	2607	161	31.03	3	14	42	31	1	31.00	1-24	0	0	4.42	21	
I20T	2008/09	5	5	0	77	25	15.40	0	0									0	
20T	2005	41	39	2	765	103*	20.67	1	2	37	39	2	19.50	2-17	0	0	6.32	14	
UTTAM Kumar SARKAR (Bangladesh A, Chittagong, Dhaka) b 11.11.1986 RHB RM																			
FC		6	12	2	269	73	26.90	0	2	4	4	0					6.00	19	
Lim		2	2	0	6	6	3.00	0	0									1	
20T		5	5	0	77	51	15.40	0	1									3	2
FC	2003/04	28	52	2	1374	93	27.48	0	10	468	198	8	24.75	3-24	0	0	2.53	25	
Lim	2005/06	12	12	0	426	124	35.50	1	3	84	68	1	68.00	1-20	0	0	4.85	5	
WEERARATNE, Kaushalya (Kandurata, Ragama, Sri Lanka to India, Sylhet) b Gampola, Sri Lanka 29.1.1981 LHB RMF																			
20T		4	4	0	110	47	27.50	0	0	18	28	0					9.33	1	
FC	1999/00	89	129	10	3125	135	26.26	2	16	9400	5827	232	25.11	6-47	5	0	3.71	41	
Int	2000	15	9	1	160	41	20.00	0	0	480	385	6	64.16	3-46	0	0	4.81	3	
Lim	1999/00	107	81	21	1497	143	24.95	1	7	3628	2718	110	24.70	5-19	2	2	4.49	31	
I20T	2008/09	5	5	2	49	20*	16.33	0	0	90	126	4	31.50	4-19	1	0	8.40	4	
20T	2005/06	34	31	7	603	76*	25.12	0	2	437	581	15	38.73	4-19	1	0	7.97	11	
ZIAUR RAHMAN, Mohammad (Barisal, Khulna) b Khulna 2.12.1986 RHB RFM																			
FC		4	7	0	78	23	11.14	0	0	534	266	9	29.55	4-77	0	0	2.98	3	
20T		5	4	1	25	12	8.33	0	0	85	112	2	56.00	1-16	0	0	7.90	0	
FC	2004/05	42	70	7	870	65	13.80	0	2	6536	3145	134	23.47	5-36	5	0	2.88	23	
Lim	2004/05	33	28	6	326	65	14.81	0	2	1474	1167	36	32.41	5-24	1	1	4.75	8	
ZOYSA, Demuni Nuwan Tharanga (Basnahira South, Sinhalese, Khulna) b Colombo, Sri Lanka 13.5.1978 LHB LFM																			
20T		5	4	2	39	21	19.50	0	0	102	111	7	15.85	4-26	1	0	6.52	0	
Test	1996/97	30	40	6	288	28*	8.47	0	0	4422	2157	64	33.70	5-20	1	0	2.92	4	
FC	1996/97	118	142	25	2062	114	17.62	1	8	14905	7155	301	23.77	7-58	7	0	2.88	20	
Int	1996/97	95	47	21	343	47*	13.19	0	0	4259	3213	108	29.75	5-26	2	1	4.52	13	
Lim	1996/97	185	108	27	1320	53	16.29	0	3	8311	6004	239	25.12	6-14	5	2	4.33	25	
20T	2004/05	17	14	4	203	41	20.30	0	0	324	376	21	17.90	4-10	2	0	6.96	1	

ENGLAND TO BANGLADESH 2009/10

Cmp	Debut	M	I	NO	Runs	HS	Avge	100	50	Balls	Runs	Wkts	Avge	BB	5i	10m	RpO	ct	st
BELL, I.R.																			
Test		2	3	1	261	138	130.50	1	1									1	
FC		2	3	1	261	138	130.50	1	1									1	
BRESNAN, T.T.																			
Test		2	1	0	91	91	91.00	0	1	498	226	7	32.28	3-63	0	0	2.72	0	
FC		2	1	0	91	91	91.00	0	1	498	226	7	32.28	3-63	0	0	2.72	0	
Int		3	2	1	6	6*	6.00	0	0	168	127	8	15.87	4-28	1	0	4.53	2	
Lim		4	2	1	6	6*	6.00	0	0	216	159	10	15.90	4-28	1	0	4.41	2	
BROAD, S.C.J.																			
Test		2	1	0	3	3	3.00	0	0	474	276	6	46.00	2-70	0	0	3.49	2	
FC		2	1	0	3	3	3.00	0	0	474	276	6	46.00	2-70	0	0	3.49	2	
Int		2								90	80	3	26.66	2-46	0	0	5.33	0	
Lim		2								90	80	3	26.66	2-46	0	0	5.33	0	
CARBERRY, M.A.																			
Test		1	2	0	64	34	32.00	0	0									1	
FC		1	2	0	64	34	32.00	0	0									1	
COLLINGWOOD, P.D.																			
Test		2	3	0	148	145	49.33	1	0	6	8	0					8.00	4	
FC		2	3	0	148	145	49.33	1	0	6	8	0					8.00	4	
Int		3	3	1	118	75*	59.00	0	1	132	116	0					5.27	2	
Lim		4	4	1	227	109	75.66	1	1	150	127	0					5.08	2	

Cmp Debut	M	I	NO	Runs	HS	Avge	100	50	Balls	Runs	Wkts	Avge	BB	5i	10m	RpO	ct	st
COOK, A.N.																		
Test	2	4	1	342	173	114.00	2	0									0	
FC	2	4	1	342	173	114.00	2	0									0	
Int	3	3	0	156	64	52.00	0	2									3	
Lim	5	5	0	264	64	52.80	0	4									4	
FINN, S.T.																		
Test	2	1	1	0	0*		0	0	306	177	4	44.25	1-21	0	0	3.47	1	
FC	2	1	1	0	0*		0	0	306	177	4	44.25	1-21	0	0	3.47	1	
KIESWETTER, C.																		
Int	3	3	0	130	107	43.33	1	0									1	
Lim	5	4	0	273	143	68.25	2	0									3	
MORGAN, E.J.G.																		
Int	3	3	1	179	110*	89.50	1	0									1	
Lim	5	5	1	199	110*	49.75	1	0									2	
PIETERSEN, K.P.																		
Test	2	4	1	250	99	83.33	0	2	48	18	0					2.25	1	
FC	2	4	1	250	99	83.33	0	2	48	18	0					2.25	1	
Int	3	3	0	41	22	13.66	0	0	60	45	1	45.00	1-36	0	0	4.50	0	
Lim	5	5	0	47	22	9.40	0	0	84	61	1	61.00	1-36	0	0	4.35	1	
PLUNKETT, L.E.																		
Int	1								12	12	0					6.00	0	
Lim	3	1	1	14	14*		0	0	102	90	3	30.00	2-57	0	0	5.29	1	
PRIOR, M.J.																		
Test	2	3	1	69	62	34.50	0	1									9	1
FC	2	3	1	69	62	34.50	0	1									9	1
Int	3	2	1	72	42	72.00	0	0									3	
Lim	5	4	2	144	64*	72.00	0	1									3	
SHAHZAD, A.																		
Int	1								54	55	1	55.00	1-55	0	0	6.11	1	
Lim	3								144	123	3	41.00	1-26	0	0	5.12	2	
SIDEBOTTOM, R.J.																		
Int	1								46	46	1	46.00	1-46	0	0	6.00	0	
Lim	2								88	81	3	27.00	2-35	0	0	5.52	0	
SWANN, G.P.																		
Test	2	2	0	38	32	19.00	0	0	868	404	16	25.25	5-90	2	1	2.79	0	
FC	2	2	0	38	32	19.00	0	0	868	404	16	25.25	5-90	2	1	2.79	0	
Int	3	1	0	2	2	2.00	0	0	180	122	7	17.42	3-32	0	0	4.06	1	
Lim	4	2	1	2	2	2.00	0	0	240	166	11	15.09	4-44	1	0	4.15	1	
TREDWELL, J.C.																		
Test	1	1	0	37	37	37.00	0	0	390	181	6	30.16	4-82	0	0	2.78	1	
FC	1	1	0	37	37	37.00	0	0	390	181	6	30.16	4-82	0	0	2.78	1	
Int	1	1	1	2	2*		0	0	60	52	0					5.20	0	
Lim	3	1	1	2	2*		0	0	162	125	3	41.66	2-17	0	0	4.63	1	
TROTT, I.J.L.																		
Test	2	4	0	136	64	34.00	0	1	12	5	0					2.50	1	
FC	2	4	0	136	64	34.00	0	1	12	5	0					2.50	1	
WRIGHT, L.J.																		
Int	3	2	1	39	32*	39.00	0	0	72	58	1	58.00	1-4	0	0	4.83	3	
Lim	5	4	2	84	32*	42.00	0	0	120	100	2	50.00	1-4	0	0	5.00	5	

INDIA TO BANGLADESH 2009/10

Cmp Debut	M	I	NO	Runs	HS	Avge	100	50	Balls	Runs	Wkts	Avge	BB	5i	10m	RpO	ct	st
DHONI, M.S.																		
Test	1	1	0	89	89	89.00	0	1									6	2
FC	1	1	0	89	89	89.00	0	1									6	2
Int	5	4	1	184	101*	61.33	1	0									2	1
Lim	5	4	1	184	101*	61.33	1	0									2	1
DRAVID, R.S.																		
Test	2	3	1	139	111*	69.50	1	0									5	
FC	2	3	1	139	111*	69.50	1	0									5	
GAMBHIR, G.																		
Test	2	4	1	207	116	69.00	1	1									1	
FC	2	4	1	207	116	69.00	1	1									1	
Int	5	5	0	138	71	27.60	0	1									3	
Lim	5	5	0	138	71	27.60	0	1									3	
HARBHAJAN SINGH																		
Test	1	1	0	13	13	13.00	0	0	269	123	2	61.50	1-48	0	0	2.74	0	
FC	1	1	0	13	13	13.00	0	0	269	123	2	61.50	1-48	0	0	2.74	0	
Int	3	2	0	12	11	6.00	0	0	174	144	6	24.00	3-47	0	0	4.96	1	
Lim	3	2	0	12	11	6.00	0	0	174	144	6	24.00	3-47	0	0	4.96	1	

Cmp Debut	M	I	NO	Runs	HS	Avge	100	50	Balls	Runs	Wkts	Avge	BB	5i	10m	RpO	ct	st
JADEJA, R.A.																		
Int	5	2	0	77	39	38.50	0	0	192	149	2	74.50	1-29	0	0	4.65	1	
Lim	5	2	0	77	39	38.50	0	0	192	149	2	74.50	1-29	0	0	4.65	1	
KARTHIK, K.D.																		
Test	1	2	0	27	27	13.50	0	0									4	
FC	1	2	0	27	27	13.50	0	0									4	
Int	2	2	0	82	48	41.00	0	0									1	
Lim	2	2	0	82	48	41.00	0	0									1	
KHAN, Z.																		
Test	2	3	0	31	20	10.33	0	0	477	293	15	19.53	7-87	1	1	3.68	0	
FC	2	3	0	31	20	10.33	0	0	477	293	15	19.53	7-87	1	1	3.68	0	
Int	4	2	0	18	16	9.00	0	0	210	189	3	63.00	3-38	0	0	5.40	0	
Lim	4	2	0	18	16	9.00	0	0	210	189	3	63.00	3-38	0	0	5.40	0	
KOHLI, V.																		
Int	5	5	2	275	102*	91.66	1	2	10	12	0					7.20	4	
Lim	5	5	2	275	102*	91.66	1	2	10	12	0					7.20	4	
LAXMAN, V.V.S.																		
Test	1	2	1	76	69*	76.00	0	1									1	
FC	1	2	1	76	69*	76.00	0	1									1	
MISHRA, A.																		
Test	1	2	0	64	50	32.00	0	1	232	158	7	22.57	4-92	0	0	4.08	1	
FC	1	2	0	64	50	32.00	0	1	232	158	7	22.57	4-92	0	0	4.08	1	
Int	2								115	94	3	31.33	3-40	0	0	4.90	0	
Lim	2								115	94	3	31.33	3-40	0	0	4.90	0	
NEHRA, A.																		
Int	4	2	2	6	4*		0	0	152	159	4	39.75	2-58	0	0	6.27	0	
Lim	4	2	2	6	4*		0	0	152	159	4	39.75	2-58	0	0	6.27	0	
OJHA, P.P.																		
Test	1	1	1	1	1*		0	0	228	126	4	31.50	2-49	0	0	3.31	0	
FC	1	1	1	1	1*		0	0	228	126	4	31.50	2-49	0	0	3.31	0	
RAINA, S.K.																		
Int	5	4	2	210	106	105.00	1	1	18	9	0					3.00	3	
Lim	5	4	2	210	106	105.00	1	1	18	9	0					3.00	3	
SEHWAG, V.																		
Test	2	4	1	153	56	51.00	0	2	66	18	1	18.00	1-7	0	0	1.63	4	
FC	2	4	1	153	56	51.00	0	2	66	18	1	18.00	1-7	0	0	1.63	4	
Int	3	3	0	102	47	34.00	0	0	42	43	0					6.14	1	
Lim	3	3	0	102	47	34.00	0	0	42	43	0					6.14	1	
SHARMA, I.																		
Test	2	3	1	21	13	10.50	0	0	366	211	9	23.44	4-66	0	0	3.45	0	
FC	2	3	1	21	13	10.50	0	0	366	211	9	23.44	4-66	0	0	3.45	0	
SREESANTH, S.																		
Test	1	1	0	1	1	1.00	0	0	140	108	2	54.00	2-55	0	0	4.62	0	
FC	1	1	0	1	1	1.00	0	0	140	108	2	54.00	2-55	0	0	4.62	0	
Int	5	2	1	5	4	5.00	0	0	237	264	4	66.00	1-38	0	0	6.68	1	
Lim	5	2	1	5	4	5.00	0	0	237	264	4	66.00	1-38	0	0	6.68	1	
TENDULKAR, S.R.																		
Test	2	3	1	264	143	132.00	2	0									0	
FC	2	3	1	264	143	132.00	2	0									0	
TYAGI, S.																		
Int	2								78	70	2	35.00	1-24	0	0	5.38	1	
Lim	2								78	70	2	35.00	1-24	0	0	5.38	1	
VIJAY, M.																		
Test	1	1	0	30	30	30.00	0	0									1	
FC	1	1	0	30	30	30.00	0	0									1	
YUVRAJ SINGH																		
Test	2	2	0	37	25	18.50	0	0	52	25	0					2.88	2	
FC	2	2	0	37	25	18.50	0	0	52	25	0					2.88	2	
Int	5	5	1	96	74	24.00	0	1	228	144	4	36.00	1-18	0	0	3.78	2	
Lim	5	5	1	96	74	24.00	0	1	228	144	4	36.00	1-18	0	0	3.78	2	

SOUTH AFRICA A TO BANGLADESH 2010

Cmp Debut	M	I	NO	Runs	HS	Avge	100	50	Balls	Runs	Wkts	Avge	BB	5i	10m	RpO	ct	st
BAILEY, R.T.																		
Lim	5	5	0	127	37	25.40	0	0	198	177	5	35.40	2-40	0	0	5.36	2	
ELGAR, D.																		
FC	2	3	0	69	48	23.00	0	0	304	217	7	31.00	3-68	0	0	4.28	2	
Lim	3	3	1	108	57*	54.00	0	1	138	112	3	37.33	2-39	0	0	4.87	3	

Cmp Debut	M	I	NO	Runs	HS	Avge	100	50	Balls	Runs	Wkts	Avge	BB	5i	10m	RpO	ct	st
FRIEND, Q.																		
FC	1	1	0	11	11	11.00	0	0	90	42	3	14.00	2-23	0	0	2.80	2	
Lim	2	1	0	5	5	5.00	0	0	78	94	4	23.50	2-21	0	0	7.23	0	
HARRIS, P.L.																		
FC	1	1	0	39	39	39.00	0	0	320	175	9	19.44	6-90	1	0	3.28	0	
Lim	4	3	0	22	10	7.33	0	0	216	171	4	42.75	2-44	0	0	4.75	1	
INGRAM, C.A.																		
Lim	5	5	0	220	127	44.00	1	0									2	
KUHN, H.G.																		
FC	2	2	0	239	191	119.50	1	0									4	
MILLER, D.A.																		
Lim	5	4	1	195	115*	65.00	1	0									1	
PETERSEN, A.N.																		
FC	2	3	0	248	116	82.66	1	1									4	
PHILANDER, V.D.																		
FC	2	2	1	59	39*	59.00	0	0	318	162	6	27.00	2-21	0	0	3.05	1	
Lim	3	2	0	8	7	4.00	0	0	108	60	3	20.00	2-32	0	0	3.33	0	
ROSSOUW, R.R.																		
FC	2	3	0	174	81	58.00	0	2									0	
Lim	4	4	0	108	80	27.00	0	1									1	
TSHABALALA, M.S.																		
FC	1	1	1	11	11*		0	0	234	161	2	80.50	2-81	0	0	4.12	0	
Lim	4	2	2	16	9*		0	0	240	186	5	37.20	2-36	0	0	4.65	2	
TSOLEKILE, T.L.																		
FC	2	2	0	251	140	125.50	2	0									11	1
Lim	4	4	1	70	42	23.33	0	0									3	
TSOTSOBE, L.L.																		
FC	2	1	0	4	4	4.00	0	0	319	183	4	45.75	2-29	0	0	3.44	2	
Lim	5	3	1	9	4	4.50	0	0	257	267	9	29.66	3-76	0	0	6.23	2	
VAN DER WATH, J.J.																		
FC	1	1	0	30	30	30.00	0	0	159	102	3	34.00	2-51	0	0	3.84	0	
VANDIAR, J.D.																		
FC	2	2	0	70	51	35.00	0	1									0	
Lim	3	3	0	36	20	12.00	0	0	39	42	3	14.00	3-42	0	0	6.46	1	
VAN WYK, M.N.																		
Lim	5	5	0	180	51	36.00	0	1	6	9	0					9.00	5	
VAN ZYL, S.																		
FC	2	3	1	36	19*	18.00	0	0	108	45	4	11.25	4-37	0	0	2.50	4	
Lim	3	3	1	189	109*	94.50	1	1	108	108	2	54.00	1-19	0	0	6.00	2	

SRI LANKA TO BANGLADESH 2009/10

Cmp Debut	M	I	NO	Runs	HS	Avge	100	50	Balls	Runs	Wkts	Avge	BB	5i	10m	RpO	ct	st
BANDARA, H.M.C.M.																		
Int	1								60	44	0					4.40	1	
Lim	1								60	44	0					4.40	1	
DILSHAN, T.M.																		
Int	3	3	0	186	104	62.00	1	0	48	34	2	17.00	1-16	0	0	4.25	0	
Lim	3	3	0	186	104	62.00	1	0	48	34	2	17.00	1-16	0	0	4.25	0	
JAYAWARDENE, D.P.M.D.																		
Int	3	3	1	184	108	92.00	1	1									0	
Lim	3	3	1	184	108	92.00	1	1									0	
KALUHALAMULLA, H.K.S.R.																		
Int	5	3	0	77	56	25.66	0	1	270	193	5	38.60	2-40	0	0	4.28	1	
Lim	5	3	0	77	56	25.66	0	1	270	193	5	38.60	2-40	0	0	4.28	1	
KANDAMBY, S.H.T.																		
Int	5	3	0	27	18	9.00	0	0	54	43	0					4.77	1	
Lim	5	3	0	27	18	9.00	0	0	54	43	0					4.77	1	
KULASEKARA, K.M.D.N.																		
Int	3								180	142	7	20.28	4-48	1	0	4.73	0	
Lim	3								180	142	7	20.28	4-48	1	0	4.73	0	
LAKMAL, R.A.S.																		
Int	3	1	1	0	0*		0	0	162	186	2	93.00	2-63	0	0	6.88	2	
Lim	3	1	1	0	0*		0	0	162	186	2	93.00	2-63	0	0	6.88	2	
MIRANDO, M.T.T.																		
Int	4	1	0	28	28	28.00	0	0	186	188	4	47.00	2-62	0	0	6.06	0	
Lim	4	1	0	28	28	28.00	0	0	186	188	4	47.00	2-62	0	0	6.06	0	
PERERA, N.L.T.C.																		
Int	4	3	2	53	36*	53.00	0	0	176	140	6	23.33	2-27	0	0	4.77	1	
Lim	4	3	2	53	36*	53.00	0	0	176	140	6	23.33	2-27	0	0	4.77	1	

Cmp Debut	M	I	NO	Runs	HS	Avge	100	50	Balls	Runs	Wkts	Avge	BB	5i	10m	RpO	ct	st
PUSHPAKUMARA, M.																		
Int	2								30	21	0					4.20	0	
Lim	2								30	21	0					4.20	0	
SAMARAWEERA, T.T.																		
Int	5	4	2	173	105*	86.50	1	0	18	29	0					9.66	4	
Lim	5	4	2	173	105*	86.50	1	0	18	29	0					9.66	4	
SANGAKKARA, K.C.																		
Int	5	5	1	274	74	68.50	0	4									7	
Lim	5	5	1	274	74	68.50	0	4									7	
SILVA, L.P.C.																		
Int	1	1	1	4	4*		0	0									0	
Lim	1	1	1	4	4*		0	0									0	
THARANGA, W.U.																		
Int	5	5	1	162	118*	40.50	1	0									1	
Lim	5	5	1	162	118*	40.50	1	0									1	
THIRIMANNE, H.D.R.L.																		
Int	2	1	0	22	22	22.00	0	0									1	
Lim	2	1	0	22	22	22.00	0	0									1	
WELAGEDARA, U.W.M.B.C.A.																		
Int	4	1	0	1	1	1.00	0	0	202	209	8	26.12	5-66	0	1	6.20	2	
Lim	4	1	0	1	1	1.00	0	0	202	209	8	26.12	5-66	0	1	6.20	2	

WEST INDIES A TO BANGLADESH 2010

Cmp Debut	M	I	NO	Runs	HS	Avge	100	50	Balls	Runs	Wkts	Avge	BB	5i	10m	RpO	ct	st
BAKER, L.S.																		
FC	1	1	0	3	3	3.00	0	0	150	97	4	24.25	3-70	0	0	3.88	0	
Lim	4	1	1	18	18*		0	0	192	177	7	25.28	4-32	1	0	5.53	2	
BRAVO, D.M.																		
FC	1	2	0	139	102	69.50	1	0									0	
Lim	5	5	2	309	107*	103.00	1	3									2	
BROWN, O.V.																		
FC	2	2	0	11	8	5.50	0	0	348	163	8	20.37	3-60	0	0	2.81	0	
Lim	1								60	38	1	38.00	1-38	0	0	3.80	1	
DOWLIN, T.M.																		
FC	2	4	0	156	75	39.00	0	1									4	
Lim	5	4	0	94	39	23.50	0	0	204	162	2	81.00	1-32	0	0	4.76	2	
EDWARDS, K.A.																		
FC	2	4	0	113	72	28.25	0	1									1	
Lim	5	5	0	158	50	31.60	0	1									1	
GUILLEN, J.C.																		
FC	1	2	0	19	15	9.50	0	0									0	
Lim	2	2	0	11	11	5.50	0	0									3	
KHAN, I.																		
FC	2	3	0	5	5	1.66	0	0	162	101	1	101.00	1-3	0	0	3.74	1	
Lim	4	4	2	38	31*	19.00	0	0	240	182	4	45.50	2-46	0	0	4.55	0	
NASH, B.P.																		
FC	2	4	3	202	99*	202.00	0	1									1	
Lim	5	4	1	182	71	60.66	0	2	60	54	0					5.40	4	
PASCAL, N.T.																		
FC	1	1	0	0	0	0.00	0	0	48	38	2	19.00	2-38	0	0	4.75	0	
Lim	4	1	0	9	9	9.00	0	0	227	218	12	18.16	4-49	1	0	5.76	0	
PHILLIPS, O.J.																		
FC	1	2	1	47	47*	47.00	0	0									2	
Lim	2	2	0	26	25	13.00	0	0									0	
SHILLINGFORD, S.																		
FC	2	3	1	25	13*	12.50	0	0	455	179	9	19.88	4-30	0	0	2.36	1	
Lim	5	4	3	28	15	28.00	0	0	287	187	11	17.00	4-22	1	0	3.90	2	
SMITH, D.S.																		
FC	1	2	0	92	62	46.00	0	1									2	
Lim	5	5	0	242	115	48.40	1	1									2	
TONGE, G.C.																		
FC	2	2	1	12	9	12.00	0	0	186	107	4	26.75	2-33	0	0	3.45	1	
Lim	3								164	142	7	20.28	4-37	1	0	5.19	0	
WALTON, C.A.K.																		
FC	2	3	0	98	70	32.66	0	1									6	1
Lim	5	4	0	122	64	30.50	0	1									5	1

ZIMBABWE TO BANGLADESH 2009/10

Cmp Debut	*M*	*I*	*NO*	*Runs*	*HS*	*Avge*	*100*	*50*	*Balls*	*Runs*	*Wkts*	*Avge*	*BB*	*5i*	*10m*	*RpO*	*ct*	*st*
CHIBHABHA, C.J.																		
Int	5	5	0	70	39	14.00	0	0	171	158	5	31.60	2-28	0	0	5.54	3	
Lim	7	7	0	100	39	14.28	0	0	255	219	11	19.90	3-29	0	0	5.15	3	
CHIGUMBURA, E.																		
Int	5	5	1	130	60*	32.50	0	1	174	134	5	26.80	3-27	0	0	4.62	1	
Lim	6	6	1	175	60*	35.00	0	1	174	134	5	26.80	3-27	0	0	4.62	3	
COVENTRY, C.K.																		
Int	4	4	0	62	32	15.50	0	0									1	
Lim	6	6	0	85	32	14.16	0	0									2	
CREMER, A.G.																		
Int	5	4	1	28	10	9.33	0	0	201	154	6	25.66	2-11	0	0	4.59	2	
Lim	7	5	1	41	13	10.25	0	0	302	243	9	27.00	2-11	0	0	4.82	4	
JARVIS, K.M.																		
Int	4	3	1	0	0*	0.00	0	0	161	161	5	32.20	3-38	0	0	6.00	0	
Lim	5	4	2	1	1*	0.50	0	0	215	208	6	34.66	3-38	0	0	5.80	0	
MASAKADZA, H.																		
Int	5	5	0	140	84	28.00	0	1									3	
Lim	6	6	0	162	84	27.00	0	1	12	10	0					5.00	3	
MATSIKENYERI, S.																		
Int	5	5	1	85	47*	21.25	0	0	42	34	2	17.00	2-25	0	0	4.85	1	
Lim	7	7	2	97	47*	19.40	0	0	42	34	2	17.00	2-25	0	0	4.85	1	
MPOFU, C.B.																		
Int	1	1	1	0	0*		0	0	60	38	1	38.00	1-38	0	0	3.80	0	
Lim	2	1	1	0	0*		0	0	112	85	3	28.33	2-47	0	0	4.55	0	
MUTIZWA, F.																		
Int	2	2	0	5	5	2.50	0	0									1	
Lim	3	3	0	24	19	8.00	0	0									1	
PRICE, R.W.																		
Int	5	4	1	20	13	6.66	0	0	222	146	4	36.50	2-5	0	0	3.94	1	
Lim	7	5	1	20	13	5.00	0	0	306	191	5	38.20	2-5	0	0	3.74	3	
TAIBU, T.																		
Int	2	2	0	38	38	19.00	0	0									4	
Lim	4	4	0	168	68	42.00	0	2									7	1
TAYLOR, B.R.M.																		
Int	5	5	1	141	118*	35.25	1	0									1	3
Lim	7	7	1	316	139	52.66	2	0									3	3
UTSEYA, P.																		
Int	1								24	15	0					3.75	1	
Lim	3	1	0	2	2	2.00	0	0	126	60	2	30.00	2-10	0	0	2.85	1	
VERMEULEN, M.A.																		
Int	2	2	0	10	7	5.00	0	0									1	
Lim	2	2	0	10	7	5.00	0	0									1	
WALLER, M.N.																		
Int	4	4	0	80	40	20.00	0	0	12	15	0					7.50	1	
Lim	5	5	1	117	40	29.25	0	0	12	15	0					7.50	1	

BERMUDA

2010 AND CAREER RECORDS FOR BERMUDA PLAYERS

Cmp	*Debut*	*M*	*I*	*NO*	*Runs*	*HS*	*Avge*	*100*	*50*	*Balls*	*Runs*	*Wkts*	*Avge*	*BB*	*5i*	*10m*	*RpO*	*ct*	*st*
BURGESS, Christian (Bermuda) b 24.4.1994 LHB WK																			
FC		1	2	2	0	0*		0	0									0	
Lim		2	2	0	25	16	12.50	0	0									2	
20T		2	1	1	4	4*		0	0									0	
CROCKWELL, Fiqre Salassie (Bermuda, Bermuda to Namibia) b 8.7.1985 RHB WK																			
FC		1	2	0	13	12	6.50	0	0									0	
Lim		2	2	0	0	0	0.00	0	0	48	45	0					5.62	1	
20T		1	1	0	25	25	25.00	0	0									0	
FC	2009	3	6	0	45	17	7.50	0	0	42	27	0					3.85	1	
Int	2008/09	2	2	0	68	45	34.00	0	0									0	
Lim	2008/09	10	10	0	177	45	17.70	0	0	48	45	0					5.62	4	
DESILVA, Jordan Anthony (Bermuda, Bermuda to Namibia) b 4.5.1990 LHB LFM																			
FC		1	2	0	22	16	11.00	0	0	153	82	0					3.21	1	
Lim		1	1	0	17	17	17.00	0	0	60	56	1	56.00	1-56	0	0	5.60	0	
20T		2	2	0	28	18	14.00	0	0	48	61	2	30.50	2-33	0	0	7.62	0	
Lim	2009	3	3	0	47	20	15.66	0	0	168	128	5	25.60	4-40	1	0	4.57	1	
DILL, Stafen (Bermuda) b 24.1.1990 RHB RM																			
Lim		1	1	1	0	0*		0	0	30	48	0					9.60	0	
EDNESS, Jekon (Bermuda to Namibia) b 13.9.1983 RHB WK																			
FC	2004	9	18	1	228	46	13.41	0	0									17	4
Int	2007	11	11	2	252	72	28.00	0	1									7	4
Lim	2007	16	16	2	287	72	20.50	0	1									12	6
I20T	2008	3	3	0	13	9	4.33	0	0									0	1
20T	2008	3	3	0	13	9	4.33	0	0									0	1
FOGGO, Christopher Ray (Bermuda, Bermuda to Namibia) b Hamilton 7.5.1982 RHB																			
FC		1	2	0	89	60	44.50	0	1									1	
Lim		2	2	0	23	23	11.50	0	0									1	
20T		1	1	0	12	12	12.00	0	0									0	
FC	2005	6	11	0	250	60	22.72	0	2	55	38	1	38.00	1-38	0	0	4.14	5	
Int	2008	4	4	0	106	60	26.50	0	1	1	2	0					12.00	3	
Lim	2005	13	12	1	244	60	22.18	0	2	31	30	1	30.00	1-28	0	0	5.80	4	
I20T	2008	3	3	0	13	7	4.33	0	0									1	
20T	2008	4	4	0	25	12	6.25	0	0									1	
FRAY, Terryn Sunil (Bermuda) b 30.6.1991 RHB RM																			
Lim		2	2	1	48	34*	48.00	0	0									1	
20T		1	1	0	0	0	0.00	0	0									1	
FC	2009	1	2	0	3	2	1.50	0	0									0	
Lim	2009	3	3	1	51	34*	25.50	0	0									1	
GILBERT, Joshua (Bermuda) b 23.9.1993 RHB OB																			
FC		1	2	0	7	5	3.50	0	0	162	97	3	32.33	3-85	0	0	3.59	0	
Lim		1	1	0	4	4	4.00	0	0	60	47	4	11.75	4-47	1	0	4.70	0	
20T		1	1	1	0	0*		0	0	24	37	1	37.00	1-37	0	0	9.25	0	
HEMP, David Lloyd (Bermuda, Bermuda to Namibia) b Hamilton 8.11.1970 LHB RM																			
FC		1	2	0	87	84	43.50	0	1									1	
Lim		2	2	0	37	37	18.50	0	0									3	
20T		2	2	0	47	46	23.50	0	0									3	
FC	1991	271	462	43	15520	247*	37.04	30	86	1134	821	17	48.29	3-23	0	0	4.34	186	
Int	2006/07	22	22	3	641	102*	33.73	1	4	114	119	1	119.00	1-25	0	0	6.26	7	
Lim	1991	303	272	33	6716	170*	28.10	8	34	303	297	12	24.75	4-32	1	0	5.88	117	
I20T	2008	2	2	0	20	20	10.00	0	0									0	
20T	2003	47	43	7	952	74	26.44	0	4									26	
JONES, Malachi Olin (Bermuda to Namibia) b 26.6.1989 RHB RMF																			
FC	2007	5	10	1	95	24	10.55	0	0	702	462	11	42.00	4-84	0	0	3.94	1	
Int	2006/07	12	12	2	113	27	11.30	0	0	458	482	8	60.25	2-25	0	0	6.31	5	
Lim	2006/07	15	15	2	198	38	15.23	0	0	583	589	10	58.90	2-25	0	0	6.06	7	
KELLY, Stefan Kievon Wayne (Bermuda, Bermuda to Namibia) b 24.8.1988 RHB RFM																			
FC		1	2	0	8	8	4.00	0	0	138	61	0					2.65	0	
FC	2006/07	7	13	3	49	18	4.90	0	0	1049	560	14	40.00	4-53	0	0	3.20	9	
Int	2006/07	10	6	6	14	7*		0	0	389	371	14	26.50	3-36	0	0	5.72	3	
Lim	2006/07	15	9	7	25	8*	12.50	0	0	624	629	17	37.00	3-36	0	0	6.04	4	
I20T	2008	3	2	2	13	11*		0	0	42	50	3	16.66	2-18	0	0	7.14	0	
20T	2008	3	2	2	13	11*		0	0	42	50	3	16.66	2-18	0	0	7.14	0	
OUTERBRIDGE, Steven Davonne (Bermuda, Bermuda to Namibia) b Paget 20.5.1983 LHB OB																			
FC		1	2	0	63	62	31.50	0	1	12	7	0					3.50	0	
20T		2	2	1	69	43*	69.00	0	0	18	32	3	10.66	3-32	0	0	10.66	2	
FC	2004	12	23	0	706	113	30.69	1	6	111	64	2	32.00	1-14	0	0	3.45	4	

Cmp	Debut	M	I	NO	Runs	HS	Avge	100	50	Balls	Runs	Wkts	Avge	BB	5i	10m	RpO	ct	st
Int	2006	23	23	0	338	56	14.69	0	1	120	94	1	94.00	1-11	0	0	4.70	6	
Lim	2006	31	31	1	676	107	22.53	1	3	300	286	4	71.50	1-11	0	0	5.72	10	
I20T	2008	3	3	1	49	37*	24.50	0	0									1	
20T	2008	5	5	2	118	43*	39.33	0	0	18	32	3	10.66	3-32	0	0	10.66	3	
PITCHER, Justin Eugene (Bermuda, Bermuda to Namibia) b 17.2.1987 RHB RMF																			
Lim		1	1	0	1	1	1.00	0	0	60	51	3	17.00	3-51	0	0	5.10	0	
FC	2009/10	1	2	0	18	9	9.00	0	0	83	57	0					4.12	0	
Lim	2009/10	3	3	0	16	13	5.33	0	0	159	133	7	19.00	3-45	0	0	5.01	2	
PITCHER, Oliver Llewellyn (Bermuda) b Paget 27.5.1983 RHB RM																			
Lim		2	2	0	28	21	14.00	0	0	102	122	2	61.00	2-54	0	0	7.17	0	
20T		2	2	0	14	9	7.00	0	0	24	40	2	20.00	2-24	0	0	10.00	0	
FC	2004	2	4	0	36	26	9.00	0	0	24	8	0					2.00	2	
Int	2006/07	5	5	0	72	30	14.40	0	0	15	25	0					10.00	2	
Lim	2005	14	13	0	164	40	12.61	0	0	134	169	3	56.33	2-54	0	0	7.56	4	
I20T	2008	3	3	0	34	15	11.33	0	0	6	7	0					7.00	2	
20T	2006	6	6	0	67	19	11.16	0	0	30	47	2	23.50	2-24	0	0	9.40	2	
RAYNER, Shannon (Bermuda, Bermuda to Namibia) b 26.3.1984 RHB LM																			
FC		1	2	0	12	10	6.00	0	0	54	36	0					4.00	0	
Lim		1	1	0	5	5	5.00	0	0	60	41	0					4.10	1	
20T		1	1	0	0	0	0.00	0	0	12	31	1	31.00	1-31	0	0	15.50	2	
Lim	2009/10	2	2	0	9	5	4.50	0	0	60	41	0					4.10	1	
ROMAINE, Irving Howard (Bermuda, Bermuda to Namibia) b 8.8.1972 LHB RM																			
FC		1	2	0	53	48	26.50	0	0									0	
FC	2004	17	31	1	932	111	31.06	2	4	183	70	1	70.00	1-14	0	0	2.29	9	1
Int	2006	35	34	3	783	101	25.25	1	4	326	355	10	35.50	2-22	0	0	6.53	8	
Lim	1997/98	56	51	3	1240	101	25.83	2	6	462	468	11	42.54	2-22	0	0	6.07	12	
I20T	2008	2	2	0	9	8	4.50	0	0	22	21	2	10.50	2-2	0	0	5.72	1	
20T	2006	4	4	0	18	8	4.50	0	0	34	35	2	17.50	2-2	0	0	6.17	1	
STEEDE, Ryan Devon (Bermuda to Namibia) b 9.11.1975 RHB RFM																			
FC	2004	10	16	6	121	28	12.10	0	0	1037	666	18	37.00	4-127	0	0	3.85	3	
Int	2006	8	7	1	70	20	11.66	0	0	312	257	5	51.40	1-21	0	0	4.94	0	
Lim	2005	13	8	2	71	20	11.83	0	0	504	423	9	47.00	3-40	0	0	5.03	2	
20T	2007/08	1	1	0	0	0	0.00	0	0	14	14	0					6.00	0	
TROTT, Rodney Jamel (Bermuda, Bermuda to Namibia) b 8.9.1987 RHB OB																			
FC		1	2	0	0	0	0.00	0	0	180	96	3	32.00	3-96	0	0	3.20	1	
Lim		1	1	0	0	0	0.00	0	0	60	44	2	22.00	2-44	0	0	4.40	1	
20T		2								48	64	3	21.33	2-28	0	0	8.00	0	
FC	2006/07	10	19	1	213	43	11.83	0	0	1589	862	28	30.78	5-39	1	0	3.25	7	
Int	2007	11	10	4	130	48*	21.66	0	0	537	412	16	25.75	4-46	1	0	4.60	4	
Lim	2007	19	16	4	167	48*	13.91	0	0	993	738	34	21.70	4-30	4	0	4.45	6	
I20T	2008	3	3	1	10	8	5.00	0	0	39	42	0					6.46	0	
20T	2008	5	3	1	10	8	5.00	0	0	87	106	3	35.33	2-28	0	0	7.31	0	
TUCKER, Janeiro J (Bermuda) b 15.3.1975 RHB RM																			
Lim		2	2	0	36	30	18.00	0	0									0	
20T		2	2	0	4	2	2.00	0	0									0	
FC	2005	8	12	0	336	123	28.00	1	1	400	228	5	45.60	3-29	0	0	3.42	7	
Int	2006	26	26	1	496	52	19.84	0	1	819	701	13	53.92	2-23	0	0	5.13	9	
Lim	1996/97	56	52	4	1080	132	22.50	1	4	1912	1600	33	48.48	3-29	0	0	5.02	16	
20T	2006	3	3	0	4	2	1.33	0	0									0	
TUCKER, Kevin (Bermuda) b 20.7.1979 RHB LMF																			
20T		1								24	23	1	23.00	1-23	0	0	5.75	0	
TUCKER, Tamauri Eugene (Bermuda) b 10.12.1988 RHB OB																			
Lim		1	1	0	0	0	0.00	0	0	60	41	1	41.00	1-41	0	0	4.10	0	
20T		1	1	0	1	1	1.00	0	0	24	30	0					7.50	1	
FC	2007	2	4	1	13	13*	4.33	0	0	180	88	2	44.00	1-10	0	0	2.93	1	
Int	2008	5								174	157	7	22.42	4-56	1	0	5.41	2	
Lim	2008	9	2	1	3	3*	3.00	0	0	360	335	9	37.22	4-56	1	0	5.58	4	
I20T	2008	1	1	0	1	1	1.00	0	0	12	5	0					2.50	0	
20T	2008	2	2	0	2	1	1.00	0	0	36	35	0					5.83	1	
WEST, James (Bermuda, Bermuda to Namibia) b 15.9.1982 RHB RMF																			
Lim		1	1	0	0	0	0.00	0	0	60	54	0					5.40	0	
20T		1	1	0	1	1	1.00	0	0	18	37	1	37.00	1-37	0	0	12.33	0	
Lim	2009/10	2	2	1	0	0*	0.00	0	0	85	78	0					5.50	0	

UNITED ARAB EMIRATES TO BERMUDA 2010

Cmp	Debut	M	I	NO	Runs	HS	Avge	100	50	Balls	Runs	Wkts	Avge	BB	5i	10m	RpO	ct	st
ABDUL REHMAN																			
FC		1	2	0	75	65	37.50	0	1									1	
Lim		2	2	1	72	57*	72.00	0	1									0	3
20T		2	2	0	9	9	4.50	0	0									0	1

Cmp	Debut	M	I	NO	Runs	HS	Avge	100	50	Balls	Runs	Wkts	Avge	BB	5i	10m	RpO	ct	st
AHMED RAZA																			
FC		1								237	60	6	10.00	4-55	0	0	1.51	1	
Lim		2	1	1	21	21*		0	0	102	58	8	7.25	5-29	0	1	3.41	0	
20T		2								42	29	2	14.50	2-10	0	0	4.14	1	
AMJAD ALI																			
FC		1	2	2	45	36*		0	0									2	
Lim		2	2	0	47	37	23.50	0	0									2	
20T		2	2	0	158	105	79.00	1	1									2	
AMJAD JAVED																			
FC		1	1	0	7	7	7.00	0	0	96	49	2	24.50	2-10	0	0	3.06	0	
Lim		2	2	1	94	89*	94.00	0	1	54	25	2	12.50	2-11	0	0	2.77	1	
20T		2	2	0	16	9	8.00	0	0	12	16	0					8.00	0	
ARSHAD ALI																			
FC		1	2	1	140	126	140.00	1	0	24	9	1	9.00	1-9	0	0	2.25	0	
Lim		2	2	0	76	66	38.00	0	1									1	
20T		2	2	0	31	16	15.50	0	0	42	34	3	11.33	2-22	0	0	4.85	0	
KHURRAM KHAN																			
FC		1	1	0	28	28	28.00	0	0	150	48	2	24.00	2-48	0	0	1.92	3	
Lim		2	2	0	69	51	34.50	0	1	61	30	3	10.00	3-25	0	0	2.95	0	
20T		1	1	1	6	6*		0	0									0	
MOIZ SHAHID																			
Lim		1	1	1	0	0*		0	0	42	25	2	12.50	2-25	0	0	3.57	0	
20T		2								12	31	1	31.00	1-31	0	0	15.50	1	
PATIL, S.P.																			
FC		1	1	0	37	37	37.00	0	0									1	1
Lim		1	1	0	26	26	26.00	0	0									3	
20T		2	2	0	43	37	21.50	0	0									1	
QASIM ZUBAIR																			
FC		1								102	56	3	18.66	2-48	0	0	3.29	1	
SAQIB ALI																			
FC		1	1	0	34	34	34.00	0	0	84	32	1	32.00	1-32	0	0	2.28	1	
Lim		2	2	0	45	40	22.50	0	0	30	17	0					3.40	1	
20T		2	2	0	26	23	13.00	0	0	36	36	2	18.00	1-9	0	0	6.00	0	
SAQIB SHAH																			
Lim		2	2	0	43	35	21.50	0	0									1	
20T		1	1	0	37	37	37.00	0	0									0	
SHOAIB SARWAR																			
Lim		1								36	16	2	8.00	2-16	0	0	2.66	0	
20T		1	1	0	5	5	5.00	0	0	12	16	1	16.00	1-16	0	0	8.00	0	
SILVA, E.H.S.N.																			
FC		1	1	1	10	10*		0	0	126	20	3	6.66	3-4	0	0	0.95	0	
Lim		2	1	0	9	9	9.00	0	0	90	54	2	27.00	2-37	0	0	3.60	0	
20T		2	2	2	2	2*		0	0	48	49	4	12.25	3-19	0	0	6.12	2	
TAHIR BUTT																			
FC		1								135	88	1	88.00	1-25	0	0	3.91	1	
Lim		1								24	25	0					6.25	0	
20T		1								18	15	0					5.00	0	

CANADA

2010 AND CAREER RECORDS FOR CANADA PLAYERS

Cmp	Debut	M	I	NO	Runs	HS	Avge	100	50	Balls	Runs	Wkts	Avge	BB	5i	10m	RpO	ct	st
ARSALAN QADIR (Canada to United Arab Emirates) b Peshawar, North-West Frontier Province, Pakistan 15.9.1989 RHB RMF																			
I20T	2009/10	1								6	12	0					12.00	0	
20T	2009/10	1								6	12	0					12.00	0	
BAGAI, Ashish (Canada, Canada to Netherlands, Canada to Sri Lanka, Canada to United Arab Emirates, Canada to West Indies, Ragama) b Delhi, India 26.1.1982 RHB WK																			
FC		1	2	0	114	90	57.00	0	1									1	
Int		2	2	0	108	64	54.00	0	1									0	1
Lim		2	2	0	108	64	54.00	0	1									0	1
FC	2004	13	25	1	749	93	31.20	0	6	27	28	0					6.22	29	3
Int	2002/03	54	53	7	1736	137*	37.73	2	14									48	10
Lim	1999/00	86	84	11	2374	137*	32.52	2	18									82	20
I20T	2008	7	7	1	169	53	28.16	0	1									3	4
20T	2008	11	11	2	300	53	33.33	0	2									4	4
BAIDWAN, Harvir Singh (Canada, Canada to Netherlands, Canada to Sri Lanka, Canada to United Arab Emirates, Canada to West Indies, Colts) b Chandigarh, Punjab, India 31.7.1987 RHB RM																			
Int		2	1	1	17	17*		0	0	102	100	5	20.00	3-60	0	0	5.88	2	
Lim		2	1	1	17	17*		0	0	102	100	5	20.00	3-60	0	0	5.88	2	
FC	2009/10	5	1	0	0	0	0.00	0	0	368	147	6	24.50	4-16	0	0	2.39	0	
Int	2008	19	11	5	147	33	24.50	0	0	942	759	24	31.62	3-24	0	0	4.83	4	
Lim	2008	32	18	7	233	38*	21.18	0	0	1401	1144	34	33.64	3-24	0	0	4.89	8	
I20T	2008	11	6	2	6	4*	1.50	0	0	203	245	19	12.89	4-19	1	0	7.24	5	
20T	2008	15	9	2	9	4*	1.28	0	0	276	348	20	17.40	4-19	1	0	7.56	6	
BALAJI RAO, Wandavasi Dorakanti (Canada) b Madras (now Chennai), Tamil Nadu, India 4.3.1978 LHB LBG																			
Int		2	1	0	24	24	24.00	0	0	90	68	1	68.00	1-26	0	0	4.53	0	
Lim		2	1	0	24	24	24.00	0	0	90	68	1	68.00	1-26	0	0	4.53	0	
FC	1994/95	33	39	14	276	27	11.04	0	0	6068	2884	94	30.68	5-47	4	0	2.85	17	
Int	2008	4	3	0	37	24	12.33	0	0	150	149	3	49.66	2-50	0	0	5.96	0	
Lim	1994/95	30	13	3	131	39	13.10	0	0	1314	1035	33	31.36	4-44	1	0	4.72	11	
I20T	2008/09	4	4	1	32	22*	10.66	0	0	84	107	6	17.83	3-21	0	0	7.64	1	
20T	2008/09	4	4	1	32	22*	10.66	0	0	84	107	6	17.83	3-21	0	0	7.64	1	
BARNETT, Geoffrey Edward Fulton (Canada to Netherlands, Canada to United Arab Emirates, Canada to West Indies) b Nelson, New Zealand 3.2.1984 LHB RM																			
FC	2004/05	29	53	3	1190	136	23.80	2	5	130	115	1	115.00	1-10	0	0	5.30	28	
Int	2006	22	22	0	455	77	20.68	0	1									7	
Lim	2004/05	55	55	2	1309	102*	24.69	1	6	12	17	0					8.50	18	
I20T	2008	5	5	1	131	36	32.75	0	0	6	11	0					11.00	2	
20T	2005/06	20	19	1	440	39	24.44	0	0	12	28	0					14.00	6	
BASTIAMPILLAI, Trevin Callistus (Canada, Canada to Netherlands, Canada to Sri Lanka, Canada to United Arab Emirates, Canada to West Indies) b Sri Lanka 26.10.1985 RHB OB																			
FC		1	2	0	37	26	18.50	0	0									0	
FC	2007	10	19	0	478	73	25.15	0	5	66	49	0					4.45	4	
Int	2007	11	11	0	163	49	14.81	0	0	24	31	0					7.75	1	
Lim	2007	14	14	0	219	49	15.64	0	0	24	31	0					7.75	3	
I20T	2009/10	2																0	
20T	2009/10	7	5	1	60	24	15.00	0	0	6	3	1	3.00	1-3	0	0	3.00	0	
BILLCLIFF, Ian Shaw (Canada to United Arab Emirates) b William's Lake, British Columbia 26.10.1972 RHB RM																			
FC	1990/91	46	84	4	1964	126	24.55	2	9	109	61	1	61.00	1-7	0	0	3.35	28	
Int	2002/03	19	19	0	529	93	27.84	0	4									7	
Lim	1991/92	91	89	5	2301	102*	27.39	1	17	30	27	0					5.40	25	
I20T	2009/10	2	2	0	51	37	25.50	0	0									0	
20T	2009/10	3	3	0	51	37	17.00	0	0									0	
CHATTERGOON, Hemnarine (Canada) b New Amsterdam, Guyana 30.7.1977 RHB RSM																			
FC		1	2	0	19	19	9.50	0	0	24	26	0					6.50	1	
FC	2007	2	3	0	29	19	9.66	0	0	24	26	0					6.50	1	
DAVID, Ramesh Randeer (Canada to United Arab Emirates) b Colombo, Sri Lanka 8.2.1975 RHB OB																			
FC	2009/10	1	2	1	55	28*	55.00	0	0	114	78	2	39.00	1-8	0	0	4.10	1	
Int	2008	4	3	0	82	48	27.33	0	0	96	74	2	37.00	2-30	0	0	4.62	0	
Lim	2008	4	3	0	82	48	27.33	0	0	96	74	2	37.00	2-30	0	0	4.62	0	
I20T	2008/09	4	4	0	39	17	9.75	0	0									2	
20T	2008/09	4	4	0	39	17	9.75	0	0									2	
DAVISON, John Michael (Canada to United Arab Emirates) b Campbell River, Vancouver Island, British Columbia 9.5.1970 RHB OB																			
FC	1995/96	51	78	7	1177	165	16.57	1	4	10014	5063	111	45.61	9-76	5	1	3.03	25	
Int	2002/03	27	27	1	766	111	29.46	1	5	1225	870	31	28.06	3-15	0	0	4.26	12	

Cmp	Debut	M	I	NO	Runs	HS	Avge	100	50	Balls	Runs	Wkts	Avge	BB	5i	10m	RpO	ct	st
Lim	1995/96	67	65	4	1700	131	27.86	3	9	2926	2126	71	29.94	5-26	1	1	4.36	24	
I20T	2008	5	5	0	44	19	8.80	0	0	108	91	4	22.75	2-19	0	0	5.05	2	
20T	2008	6	6	0	52	19	8.66	0	0	132	120	5	24.00	2-19	0	0	5.45	2	
DAWOOD, Jawad Jaffar (Canada to United Arab Emirates, Canada to West Indies) b Quetta, Baluchistan, Pakistan 9.5.1982 LHB OB WK																			
Int	2009	2	1	1	25	25*		0	0									0	
Lim	2009	3	2	1	32	25*	32.00	0	0									0	
20T	2009/10	2	2	0	6	6	3.00	0	0									0	
DEAN, Abzal S (Canada) b San Fernando, Trinidad 23.2.1983 LHB OB																			
FC		1	2	0	4	4	2.00	0	0	102	69	2	34.50	2-42	0	0	4.05	0	
I20T	2008/09	1	1	0	7	7	7.00	0	0	12	18	2	9.00	2-18	0	0	9.00	0	
20T	2008/09	1	1	0	7	7	7.00	0	0	12	18	2	9.00	2-18	0	0	9.00	0	
DESAI, Parth Ajaykumar (Canada, Canada to Netherlands, Canada to West Indies) b Navsari, Gujarat, India 11.12.1990 RHB SLA																			
FC		1	2	1	1	1	1.00	0	0	102	39	0					2.29	0	
Int		2	1	0	0	0	0.00	0	0	102	103	3	34.33	2-26	0	0	6.05	1	
Lim		2	1	0	0	0	0.00	0	0	102	103	3	34.33	2-26	0	0	6.05	1	
Int	2009/10	9	5	3	5	2*	2.50	0	0	462	365	10	36.50	3-35	0	0	4.74	2	
Lim	2009/10	10	6	4	5	2*	2.50	0	0	500	384	10	38.40	3-35	0	0	4.60	2	
20T	2009/10	4	1	1	0	0*		0	0	96	73	3	24.33	3-21	0	0	4.56	0	
DHANIRAM, Sunil (Canada, Canada to Netherlands, Canada to Sri Lanka, Canada to United Arab Emirates, Canada to West Indies) b Port Mourant, Berbice, Guyana 17.10.1968 LHB SLA																			
FC		1	2	0	23	17	11.50	0	0	6	4	0					4.00	0	
FC	1992/93	32	53	10	1444	144	33.58	3	6	2674	1060	38	27.89	5-20	1	0	2.37	26	
Int	2006	44	41	4	915	92	24.72	0	6	1775	1252	41	30.53	5-32	1	1	4.23	8	
Lim	2003/04	68	63	8	1456	100*	26.47	1	7	2504	1722	59	29.18	5-32	1	1	4.12	12	
I20T	2008	11	9	0	100	26	11.11	0	0	202	192	6	32.00	2-9	0	0	5.70	4	
20T	2008	14	12	0	103	26	8.58	0	0	262	256	8	32.00	2-9	0	0	5.86	5	
GORDON, Tyson George (Canada to West Indies) b St Mary, Jamaica 31.1.1982 LHB RFM																			
Lim	2004/05	1	1	0	70	70	70.00	0	1	30	33	1	33.00	1-33	0	0	6.60	0	
20T	2010	2	2	0	26	25	13.00	0	0	6	12	0					12.00	0	
GUNASEKERA, Ruvindu (Canada) b Colombo, Sri Lanka 20.7.1991 LHB LBG																			
FC		1	2	0	48	47	24.00	0	0									2	
Int		2	2	0	130	71	65.00	0	2									1	
Lim		2	2	0	130	71	65.00	0	2									1	
FC	2008	2	3	0	48	47	16.00	0	0									2	
Int	2008	3	3	0	134	71	44.66	0	2									2	
Lim	2008	3	3	0	134	71	44.66	0	2									2	
HAMZA TARIQ (Canada, Canada to West Indies) b Karachi, Sind, Pakistan 20.7.1990 RHB WK																			
FC		2	4	1	70	39	23.33	0	0									3	2
20T	2010	2	2	1	16	11*	16.00	0	0									0	
HANSRA, Amarbir Singh (Canada, Canada to Netherlands, Canada to United Arab Emirates) b Ludhiana, Punjab, India 29.12.1984 RHB RS																			
Int		2	2	1	33	32	33.00	0	0	36	41	3	13.66	3-27	0	0	6.83	1	
Lim		2	2	1	33	32	33.00	0	0	36	41	3	13.66	3-27	0	0	6.83	1	
FC	2009	2	3	0	24	17	8.00	0	0	24	18	1	18.00	1-2	0	0	4.50	2	
Int	2010	7	6	3	85	32	28.33	0	0	132	91	4	22.75	3-27	0	0	4.13	2	
Lim	2010	7	6	3	85	32	28.33	0	0	132	91	4	22.75	3-27	0	0	4.13	2	
HOOPER, Calvert Kenroy (Canada to Netherlands) b St Vincent 10.8.1982 RHB RFM																			
Int	2007	5	5	2	49	27	16.33	0	0	169	181	3	60.33	1-17	0	0	6.42	1	
Lim	2002/03	8	8	4	77	27*	19.25	0	0	265	247	4	61.75	1-17	0	0	5.59	2	
JYOTI, Sandeep (Canada, Canada to Sri Lanka, Canada to United Arab Emirates) b Simla, Punjab, India 14.12.1973 RHB OB																			
FC		1	2	0	3	2	1.50	0	0	102	55	2	27.50	2-55	0	0	3.23	0	
FC	2006/07	8	16	1	328	47	21.86	0	0	732	454	11	41.27	3-59	0	0	3.72	4	
Int	2006	14	13	1	264	117	22.00	1	0	120	90	1	90.00	1-26	0	0	4.50	4	
Lim	2003/04	29	25	1	475	117	19.79	1	0	416	346	6	57.66	2-47	0	0	4.99	7	
I20T	2008/09	2	2	1	10	10*	10.00	0	0									0	
20T	2008/09	3	3	1	15	10*	7.50	0	0									0	
KESHVANI, Shaheed (Canada to Sri Lanka, Canada to United Arab Emirates) b 23.5.1984 RHB OB																			
FC	2009	2	4	0	62	34	15.50	0	0	110	69	2	34.50	2-20	0	0	3.76	2	
Int	2009	5	2	0	21	17	10.50	0	0	48	48	0					6.00	1	
Lim	2009	7	4	0	42	18	10.50	0	0	120	102	1	102.00	1-31	0	0	5.10	2	
I20T	2009/10	2	1	1	0	0*		0	0									1	
20T	2009/10	4	3	2	12	11*	12.00	0	0	12	23	0					11.50	1	
KHURRAM Rasheed CHAUHAN (Canada, Canada to Netherlands, Canada to Sri Lanka, Canada to United Arab Emirates, Canada to West Indies) b Lahore, Punjab, Pakistan 22.2.1980 RHB RFM																			
FC		1	2	0	69	59	34.50	0	1	174	124	1	124.00	1-76	0	0	4.27	1	
Int		2	1	0	0	0	0.00	0	0	96	84	4	21.00	3-25	0	0	5.25	0	
Lim		2	1	0	0	0	0.00	0	0	96	84	4	21.00	3-25	0	0	5.25	0	
FC	2002/03	11	18	7	484	59	44.00	0	3	1649	1008	34	29.64	7-70	2	0	3.66	3	
Int	2008/09	15	9	3	92	35*	15.33	0	0	745	594	22	27.00	4-26	3	0	4.78	2	

Cmp	Debut	M	I	NO	Runs	HS	Avge	100	50	Balls	Runs	Wkts	Avge	BB	5i	10m	RpO	ct	st
Lim	2001/02	38	27	12	323	65*	21.53	0	1	1723	1373	52	26.40	4-26	4	0	4.78	7	
I20T	2009/10	4	4	2	18	8	9.00	0	0	73	106	1	106.00	1-24	0	0	8.71	1	
20T	2009/10	8	7	4	28	8*	9.33	0	0	139	183	5	36.60	3-20	0	0	7.89	4	

KUMAR, Nitish Roenik (Canada, Canada to Netherlands, Canada to United Arab Emirates) b Scarborough, Ontario 21.5.1994 RHB OB

Cmp	Debut	M	I	NO	Runs	HS	Avge	100	50	Balls	Runs	Wkts	Avge	BB	5i	10m	RpO	ct	st
FC		2	4	0	31	20	7.75	0	0	12	10	0					5.00	2	
Int		1	1	0	12	12	12.00	0	0									1	
Lim		1	1	0	12	12	12.00	0	0									1	
FC	2009	4	7	0	117	74	16.71	0	1	142	111	3	37.00	3-58	0	0	4.69	3	
Int	2009/10	5	4	0	69	38	17.25	0	0									3	
Lim	2009/10	5	4	0	69	38	17.25	0	0									3	

OSINDE, Henry (Canada, Canada to Sri Lanka, Canada to West Indies, Tamil Union) b Uganda 17.10.1978 RHB RMF

Cmp	Debut	M	I	NO	Runs	HS	Avge	100	50	Balls	Runs	Wkts	Avge	BB	5i	10m	RpO	ct	st
FC		2	4	1	29	12	9.66	0	0	342	190	8	23.75	5-68	1	0	3.33	0	
Int		1								18	22	0					7.33	1	
Lim		1								18	22	0					7.33	1	
FC	2005	20	31	9	231	60*	10.50	0	1	3150	1650	62	26.61	7-53	2	0	3.14	4	
Int	2006	34	22	10	54	21*	4.50	0	0	1359	1133	35	32.37	4-33	1	0	5.00	9	
Lim	2005	48	28	13	66	21*	4.40	0	0	1803	1481	49	30.22	4-33	2	0	4.92	13	
I20T	2008	6	2	1	3	2	3.00	0	0	120	112	6	18.66	2-12	0	0	5.60	6	
20T	2008	9	2	1	3	2	3.00	0	0	156	162	6	27.00	2-12	0	0	6.23	6	

PATEL, Hiral (Canada, Canada to Netherlands, Canada to Sri Lanka, Canada to United Arab Emirates, Canada to West Indies) b Ahmedabad, Gujarat, India 10.8.1991 RHB SLA

Cmp	Debut	M	I	NO	Runs	HS	Avge	100	50	Balls	Runs	Wkts	Avge	BB	5i	10m	RpO	ct	st
FC		1	2	0	39	32	19.50	0	0	19	16	1	16.00	1-16	0	0	5.05	0	
Int		2	2	0	19	10	9.50	0	0	18	15	0					5.00	1	
Lim		2	2	0	19	10	9.50	0	0	18	15	0					5.00	1	
FC	2009/10	2	4	0	94	36	23.50	0	0	97	84	2	42.00	1-16	0	0	5.19	0	
Int	2009	12	12	0	163	43	13.58	0	0	252	192	4	48.00	1-18	0	0	4.57	5	
Lim	2009	13	13	0	168	43	12.92	0	0	252	192	4	48.00	1-18	0	0	4.57	5	
I20T	2009/10	4	4	1	128	88*	42.66	0	1	29	47	0					9.72	0	
20T	2009/10	8	8	1	147	88*	21.00	0	1	101	143	3	47.66	2-11	0	0	8.49	1	

RIZWAN Ahmed CHEEMA (Canada, Canada to Netherlands, Canada to Sri Lanka, Canada to United Arab Emirates, Canada to West Indies) b Pakistan 15.8.1978 RHB RSM

Cmp	Debut	M	I	NO	Runs	HS	Avge	100	50	Balls	Runs	Wkts	Avge	BB	5i	10m	RpO	ct	st
FC		2	4	1	47	46*	15.66	0	0	78	32	1	32.00	1-27	0	0	2.46	4	
Int		1	1	0	0	0	0.00	0	0	24	19	1	19.00	1-19	0	0	4.75	1	
Lim		1	1	0	0	0	0.00	0	0	24	19	1	19.00	1-19	0	0	4.75	1	
FC	2009	6	12	1	176	46*	16.00	0	0	766	380	10	38.00	3-39	0	0	2.97	9	
Int	2008	21	20	1	523	94	27.52	0	5	842	623	19	32.78	3-31	0	0	4.43	9	
Lim	2008	31	30	1	786	94	27.10	0	6	1214	925	28	33.03	3-31	0	0	4.57	13	
I20T	2008/09	8	8	1	210	68	30.00	0	1	144	182	4	45.50	2-19	0	0	7.58	4	
20T	2008/09	14	14	1	252	68	19.38	0	1	216	273	8	34.12	3-19	0	0	7.58	5	

SAAD BIN ZAFAR (Canada to Sri Lanka, Canada to United Arab Emirates) b Gujranwala, Punjab, Pakistan 10.11.1986 LHB SLA

Cmp	Debut	M	I	NO	Runs	HS	Avge	100	50	Balls	Runs	Wkts	Avge	BB	5i	10m	RpO	ct	st
FC	2008	2	4	0	29	14	7.25	0	0	180	73	4	18.25	4-58	0	0	2.43	0	
Lim	2010	2	2	0	32	23	16.00	0	0									1	
20T	2009/10	1	1	0	18	18	18.00	0	0									0	

SAMAD, Abdool Mudassar (Canada to Sri Lanka) b Guyana 3.5.1979 RHB OB

Cmp	Debut	M	I	NO	Runs	HS	Avge	100	50	Balls	Runs	Wkts	Avge	BB	5i	10m	RpO	ct	st
FC	2006	5	9	0	284	119	31.55	1	1	246	164	2	82.00	2-71	0	0	4.00	0	
Int	2002/03	27	27	2	740	130	29.60	1	2	235	281	7	40.14	1-8	0	0	7.17	9	
Lim	2002/03	38	37	2	798	130	22.80	1	2	325	357	8	44.62	1-8	0	0	6.59	14	
I20T	2008	7	6	0	97	29	16.16	0	0	12	36	1	36.00	1-36	0	0	18.00	1	
20T	2008	8	7	0	121	29	17.28	0	0	12	36	1	36.00	1-36	0	0	18.00	2	

SURKARI, Zubin Eruch (Canada, Canada to Netherlands, Canada to West Indies) b Toronto, Ontario 26.2.1980 RHB RM

Cmp	Debut	M	I	NO	Runs	HS	Avge	100	50	Balls	Runs	Wkts	Avge	BB	5i	10m	RpO	ct	st
FC		1	2	0	100	72	50.00	0	1									0	
Int		2	2	1	10	7	10.00	0	0									1	
Lim		2	2	1	10	7	10.00	0	0									1	
FC	2004	7	14	0	314	139	22.42	1	1									6	
Int	2008	15	14	3	210	49	19.09	0	0									3	
Lim	2003/04	30	29	3	441	49	16.96	0	0	6	9	0					9.00	7	
I20T	2008	4	3	0	10	6	3.33	0	0									0	
20T	2008	8	7	0	57	26	8.14	0	0									2	

UMAR BHATTI (Canada, Canada to Netherlands, Canada to Sri Lanka, Canada to United Arab Emirates, Canada to West Indies) b Lahore, Punjab, Pakistan 4.1.1984 LHB LM

Cmp	Debut	M	I	NO	Runs	HS	Avge	100	50	Balls	Runs	Wkts	Avge	BB	5i	10m	RpO	ct	st
FC		2	4	0	20	16	5.00	0	0	295	191	7	27.28	6-98	1	0	3.88	0	
Int		1	1	0	18	18	18.00	0	0	24	31	0					7.75	1	
Lim		1	1	0	18	18	18.00	0	0	24	31	0					7.75	1	
FC	2004	18	31	8	505	83*	21.95	0	3	2946	1604	78	20.56	8-40	7	2	3.26	4	
Int	2006	36	30	8	378	46	17.18	0	0	1630	1149	33	34.81	4-45	1	0	4.22	5	
Lim	2003/04	52	39	11	534	51	19.07	0	1	2243	1599	49	32.63	4-45	1	0	4.27	8	
I20T	2008/09	7	7	3	49	12	12.25	0	0	138	148	8	18.50	3-23	0	0	6.43	0	
20T	2008/09	13	13	5	94	17*	11.75	0	0	216	260	10	26.00	3-23	0	0	7.22	1	

Cmp	Debut	M	I	NO	Runs	HS	Avge	100	50	Balls	Runs	Wkts	Avge	BB	5i	10m	RpO	ct	st
USMAN LIMBADA (Canada, Canada to Sri Lanka, Canada to United Arab Emirates, Canada to West Indies) b 2.10.1989 RHB RM																			
FC		1	2	0	5	5	2.50	0	0	6	5	0					5.00	0	
Int	2009/10	3	3	1	31	14*	15.50	0	0									3	
Lim	2009/10	4	4	1	55	24	18.33	0	0									3	
I20T	2009/10	3																1	
20T	2009/10	6	3	0	21	19	7.00	0	0									1	

IRELAND TO CANADA 2010

Cmp	Debut	M	I	NO	Runs	HS	Avge	100	50	Balls	Runs	Wkts	Avge	BB	5i	10m	RpO	ct	st
BOTHA, A.C.																			
FC		1	2	0	100	61	50.00	0	1	72	25	3	8.33	3-25	0	0	2.08	2	
Int		2	2	0	48	28	24.00	0	0	24	35	0					8.75	0	
Lim		2	2	0	48	28	24.00	0	0	24	35	0					8.75	0	
DOCKRELL, G.H.																			
FC		1	1	0	2	2	2.00	0	0	72	50	0					4.16	1	
Int		2	1	1	2	2*		0	0	102	89	0					5.23	0	
Lim		2	1	1	2	2*		0	0	102	89	0					5.23	0	
EAGLESTONE, P.S.																			
FC		1	1	1	0	0*		0	0	102	66	1	66.00	1-44	0	0	3.88	0	
EASTWOOD, A.W.																			
FC		1	1	0	0	0	0.00	0	0	174	92	4	23.00	3-30	0	0	3.17	0	
JOHNSTON, D.T.																			
FC		1	1	1	5	5*		0	0	54	23	5	4.60	5-23	1	0	2.55	0	
Int		2	2	0	20	13	10.00	0	0	78	47	3	15.66	2-21	0	0	3.61	0	
Lim		2	2	0	20	13	10.00	0	0	78	47	3	15.66	2-21	0	0	3.61	0	
JONES, N.G.																			
Int		2	2	0	30	25	15.00	0	0	33	24	1	24.00	1-11	0	0	4.36	2	
Lim		2	2	0	30	25	15.00	0	0	33	24	1	24.00	1-11	0	0	4.36	2	
McCANN, R.D.																			
FC		1	2	0	4	4	2.00	0	0									9	
Int		2	2	1	20	17	20.00	0	0									2	
Lim		2	2	1	20	17	20.00	0	0									2	
MOONEY, J.F.																			
FC		1	2	1	19	16*	19.00	0	0	12	10	0					5.00	0	
Int		2	2	0	72	47	36.00	0	0	60	42	0					4.20	3	
Lim		2	2	0	72	47	36.00	0	0	60	42	0					4.20	3	
O'BRIEN, K.J.																			
FC		1	2	0	70	57	35.00	0	1	131	54	6	9.00	5-39	1	0	2.47	0	
Int		2	2	0	10	7	5.00	0	0	78	64	3	21.33	2-40	0	0	4.92	0	
Lim		2	2	0	10	7	5.00	0	0	78	64	3	21.33	2-40	0	0	4.92	0	
POYNTER, A.D.																			
Int		2	2	0	40	30	20.00	0	0									2	
Lim		2	2	0	40	30	20.00	0	0									2	
STIRLING, P.R.																			
FC		1	2	0	67	45	33.50	0	0	12	9	0					4.50	1	
Int		2	2	0	212	177	106.00	1	0									0	
Lim		2	2	0	212	177	106.00	1	0									0	
VAN DER MERWE, A.																			
FC		1	1	0	4	4	4.00	0	0	174	80	1	80.00	1-20	0	0	2.75	1	
Int		2	2	2	5	4*		0	0	84	68	5	13.60	5-49	0	1	4.85	0	
Lim		2	2	2	5	4*		0	0	84	68	5	13.60	5-49	0	1	4.85	0	
WHITE, A.R.																			
FC		1	2	1	143	84	143.00	0	2	30	13	0					2.60	0	
Int		2	2	0	17	15	8.50	0	0	18	16	1	16.00	1-11	0	0	5.33	2	
Lim		2	2	0	17	15	8.50	0	0	18	16	1	16.00	1-11	0	0	5.33	2	

ZIMBABWE XI TO CANADA 2010

Cmp	Debut	M	I	NO	Runs	HS	Avge	100	50	Balls	Runs	Wkts	Avge	BB	5i	10m	RpO	ct	st
CHAKABVA, R.W.																			
FC		1	1	0	23	23	23.00	0	0									5	
CHATARA, T.L.																			
FC		1	1	1	5	5*		0	0	140	39	6	6.50	3-18	0	0	1.67	0	
DABENGWA, K.M.																			
FC		1	1	0	24	24	24.00	0	0	72	28	0					2.33	0	
ERVINE, C.R.																			
FC		1	1	0	177	177	177.00	1	0									0	
MARUMA, T.																			
FC		1	1	0	16	16	16.00	0	0	66	39	3	13.00	2-27	0	0	3.54	1	

Cmp	*Debut*	*M*	*I*	*NO*	*Runs*	*HS*	*Avge*	*100*	*50*	*Balls*	*Runs*	*Wkts*	*Avge*	*BB*	*5i*	*10m*	*RpO*	*ct*	*st*
MASAKADZA, S.W.																			
FC		1	1	0	35	35	35.00	0	0	204	80	7	11.42	5-58	1	0	2.35	0	
MATSIKENYERI, S.																			
FC		1	1	0	2	2	2.00	0	0									0	
MUTIZWA, F.																			
FC		1	1	0	11	11	11.00	0	0									2	
RAINSFORD, E.C.																			
FC		1	1	0	0	0	0.00	0	0	185	71	3	23.66	3-45	0	0	2.30	0	
SIBANDA, V.																			
FC		1	1	0	23	23	23.00	0	0									2	
WILLIAMS, S.C.																			
FC		1	1	0	5	5	5.00	0	0									1	

ENGLAND

LV County Championship winners 2010 (first-class): Nottinghamshire
Clydesdale Bank 40 2010 (limited overs): Warwickshire
Friends Provient T20 winners 2010 (twenty20): Hampshire

2010 AND CAREER RECORDS FOR ENGLAND PLAYERS

Cmp	*Debut*	*M*	*I*	*NO*	*Runs*	*HS*	*Avge*	*100*	*50*	*Balls*	*Runs*	*Wkts*	*Avge*	*BB*	*5i*	*10m*	*RpO*	*ct*	*st*
ABDUL RAZZAQ (Sialkot Stallions, ZTBL, Hampshire, Pakistan, Pakistan to England, Pakistan to Sri Lanka, Pakistan to United Arab Emirates, Pakistan to West Indies) b Lahore, Punjab, Pakistan 2.12.1979 RHB RFM																			
Int		3	3	2	86	44*	86.00	0	0	106	106	2	53.00	2-38	0	0	6.00	0	
Lim		4	4	2	88	44*	44.00	0	0	106	106	2	53.00	2-38	0	0	6.00	0	
I20T		4	3	0	21	11	7.00	0	0	24	35	1	35.00	1-15	0	0	8.75	0	
20T		16	15	3	214	44	17.83	0	0	242	313	12	26.08	3-19	0	0	7.76	1	
Test	1999/00	46	77	9	1946	134	28.61	3	7	7008	3694	100	36.94	5-35	1	0	3.16	15	
FC	1996/97	116	182	27	5195	203*	33.51	8	27	18516	10778	340	31.70	7-51	11	2	3.49	32	
Int	1996/97	243	210	53	4726	112	30.10	2	22	10329	8103	258	31.40	6-35	8	3	4.70	33	
Lim	1996/97	303	261	63	6005	112	30.32	2	32	13245	10632	355	29.94	6-35	13	3	4.81	46	
I20T	2006	21	19	8	268	46*	24.36	0	0	261	300	14	21.42	3-20	0	0	6.89	2	
20T	2003	61	57	14	1160	109	26.97	1	3	1097	1331	67	19.86	4-13	2	0	7.28	9	
ABEL, Edward (Oxford MCCU) b Salisbury, Wiltshire 30.1.1988 LHB SLA																			
FC		1	1	0	60	60	60.00	0	1									0	
FC	2008	5	6	1	154	60	30.80	0	1									4	
ACKLAND, Benjamin James (Cambridge MCCU) b Nuneaton, Warwickshire 26.10.1989 RHB OB																			
FC		2	4	1	93	51*	31.00	0	1	6	3	0					3.00	1	
ADAMS, Andre Ryan (Nottinghamshire) b Auckland, New Zealand 17.7.1975 RHB RFM																			
FC		14	20	5	240	37	16.00	0	0	2735	1508	68	22.17	6-79	4	0	3.30	13	
Lim		3	3	1	12	9	6.00	0	0	96	102	2	51.00	2-50	0	0	6.37	1	
Test	2001/02	1	2	0	18	11	9.00	0	0	190	105	6	17.50	3-44	0	0	3.31	1	
FC	1997/98	115	153	16	3158	124	23.05	3	12	22791	11090	463	23.95	6-25	17	2	2.92	81	
Int	2000/01	42	34	10	419	45	17.45	0	0	1885	1643	53	31.00	5-22	2	1	5.23	8	
Lim	1997/98	149	109	28	1437	90*	17.74	0	1	6773	5381	180	29.89	5-7	3	3	4.76	38	
I20T	2004/05	4	2	1	13	7	13.00	0	0	77	105	3	35.00	2-20	0	0	8.18	1	
20T	2004	35	26	6	280	54*	14.00	0	1	726	983	40	24.57	3-35	0	0	8.12	11	
ADAMS, James Henry Kenneth (Hampshire, Hampshire to Scotland) b Winchester, Hampshire 23.9.1980 LHB LM																			
FC		16	29	1	1351	196	48.25	3	8	12	5	0					2.50	17	
Lim		10	10	0	422	131	42.20	1	3									3	
20T		19	19	2	668	101*	39.29	2	2									6	
FC	2002	104	186	16	6423	262*	37.78	10	36	961	662	11	60.18	2-16	0	0	4.13	91	
Lim	2002	47	44	3	1554	131	37.90	1	12	79	105	1	105.00	1-34	0	0	7.97	19	
20T	2005	43	36	6	890	101*	29.66	2	3	36	60	0					10.00	11	
ADKIN, William Anthony (Sussex) b Redhill, Surrey 9.4.1990 LHB RM																			
FC		1	1	0	45	45	45.00	0	0	66	38	1	38.00	1-38	0	0	3.45	0	
Lim		1	1	0	30	30	30.00	0	0	36	16	1	16.00	1-16	0	0	2.66	0	
ADSHEAD, Stephen John (Derbyshire) b Redditch, Worcestershire 29.1.1980 RHB WK																			
FC		4	7	2	125	49	25.00	0	0									13	
Lim		5	4	0	14	8	3.50	0	0									6	1
FC	2000	77	125	20	3304	156*	31.46	3	17									205	15
Lim	1999	104	87	18	1580	87	22.89	0	8									109	31
20T	2003	49	35	9	424	81	16.30	0	1									18	17
AFZAAL, Usman (Surrey) b Rawalpindi, Punjab, Pakistan 9.6.1977 LHB SLA																			
FC		13	22	2	682	159*	34.10	1	4	453	217	8	27.12	2-26	0	0	2.87	4	
Lim		4	4	2	124	51*	62.00	0	1	6	4	0					4.00	4	
20T		2	2	0	14	12	7.00	0	0									0	
Test	2001	3	6	1	83	54	16.60	0	1	54	49	1	49.00	1-49	0	0	5.44	0	
FC	1995	235	406	47	14055	204*	39.15	32	74	9089	5078	98	51.81	4-101	0	0	3.35	104	
Lim	1995	190	179	26	5491	132	35.88	6	34	1602	1567	59	26.55	4-49	1	0	5.86	53	
20T	2003	52	49	7	942	98*	22.42	0	4	195	262	8	32.75	2-15	0	0	8.06	6	
AGA, Ragheb Gul (Kenya to Zimbabwe, Sussex) b Nairobi, Kenya 10.7.1984 RHB RMF																			
FC		2	2	1	66	66*	66.00	0	1	204	99	2	49.50	2-29	0	0	2.91	1	
Lim		4	3	2	46	23*	46.00	0	0	86	75	1	75.00	1-33	0	0	5.23	0	
FC	2003/04	19	29	5	340	66*	14.16	0	1	1782	1024	29	35.31	4-63	0	0	3.44	7	
Int	2004	2	2	0	1	1	0.50	0	0	78	87	2	43.50	2-17	0	0	6.69	0	
Lim	2004	16	13	2	118	23*	10.72	0	0	482	495	15	33.00	4-14	2	0	6.16	3	
I20T	2008	4	4	1	51	28	17.00	0	0	83	83	3	27.66	2-12	0	0	6.00	1	
20T	2008	4	4	1	51	28	17.00	0	0	83	83	3	27.66	2-12	0	0	6.00	1	

Cmp	Debut	M	I	NO	Runs	HS	Avge	100	50	Balls	Runs	Wkts	Avge	BB	5i	10m	RpO	ct	st
AGARWAL, Samridh Sunil (Oxford MCCU, Oxford University) b Agra, Uttar Pradesh, India 13.7.1990 RHB																			
FC		3	4	2	134	117	67.00	1	0	481	249	5	49.80	5-78	1	0	3.10	1	
AHMED, Jahid Sheikh (Unicorns) b Chelmsford, Essex 20.2.1986 RHB RM																			
Lim		2	2	1	5	4*	5.00	0	0	72	104	1	104.00	1-58	0	0	8.66	0	
FC	2005	7	6	4	49	16*	24.50	0	0	733	542	13	41.69	3-42	0	0	4.43	3	
Lim	2006	8	4	3	6	4*	6.00	0	0	312	306	11	27.81	4-32	1	0	5.88	2	
20T	2006	2								36	56	2	28.00	1-25	0	0	9.33	0	
ALI, Kabir (Hampshire) b Moseley, Birmingham, Warwickshire 24.11.1980 RHB RFM																			
FC		4	8	0	64	18	8.00	0	0	824	488	19	25.68	5-33	2	0	3.55	2	
Lim		1	1	1	1	1*		0	0	30	39	1	39.00	1-39	0	0	7.80	2	
Test	2003	1	2	0	10	9	5.00	0	0	216	136	5	27.20	3-80	0	0	3.77	0	
FC	1999	117	164	23	2383	84*	16.90	0	7	20052	12008	448	26.80	8-50	23	4	3.59	32	
Int	2003	14	9	3	93	39*	15.50	0	0	673	682	20	34.10	4-45	1	0	6.08	1	
Lim	2000	157	98	26	1092	92	15.16	0	3	6683	5752	227	25.33	5-36	10	2	5.16	27	
20T	2004	27	20	4	264	49	16.50	0	0	555	738	33	22.36	4-44	1	0	7.97	8	
ALI, Kadeer (Gloucestershire) b Moseley, Birmingham, Warwickshire 7.3.1983 RHB LB																			
FC		6	12	1	240	74	21.81	0	2									5	
Lim		1	1	1	7	7*		0	0									0	
20T		10	8	3	75	24*	15.00	0	0	36	78	3	26.00	2-28	0	0	13.00	3	
FC	2000	99	180	10	4906	161	28.85	6	26	480	304	3	101.33	1-4	0	0	3.80	54	
Lim	1999	63	63	4	1757	114	29.77	3	11	75	68	1	68.00	1-4	0	0	5.44	15	
20T	2003	26	24	6	445	53	24.72	0	1	36	78	3	26.00	2-28	0	0	13.00	6	
ALI, Moeen Munir (England Lions, Worcestershire) b Birmingham, Warwickshire 18.6.1987 LHB OB																			
FC		16	30	3	1270	126	47.03	3	9	1078	626	17	36.82	5-36	1	0	3.48	12	
Lim		12	12	0	383	121	31.91	1	1	360	345	7	49.28	2-29	0	0	5.75	5	
20T		16	15	1	385	72	27.50	0	3	235	285	13	21.92	3-19	0	0	7.27	7	
FC	2005	49	84	7	2697	153	35.02	5	18	2449	1659	27	61.44	5-36	1	0	4.06	21	
Lim	2006	63	59	2	1507	125	26.43	3	8	858	805	19	42.36	3-32	0	0	5.62	17	
20T	2007	37	35	3	727	72	22.71	0	3	283	350	15	23.33	3-19	0	0	7.42	9	
ALLENBY, James (Glamorgan) b Perth, Western Australia, Australia 12.9.1982 RHB RM																			
FC		16	25	4	933	105	44.42	1	10	1981	885	41	21.58	5-59	1	0	2.68	16	
Lim		8	8	0	182	61	22.75	0	1	282	263	3	87.66	2-28	0	0	5.59	1	
20T		15	15	1	317	54	22.64	0	2	271	368	9	40.88	3-23	0	0	8.14	4	
FC	2006	63	96	15	3175	138*	39.19	4	25	6059	2777	99	28.05	5-59	2	0	2.75	60	
Lim	2002	59	54	7	1189	91*	25.29	0	6	1768	1524	49	31.10	5-43	3	1	5.17	18	
20T	2005	55	51	9	1146	110	27.28	1	8	748	986	37	26.64	5-21	0	2	7.90	20	
AMBROSE, Timothy Raymond (Warwickshire) b Newcastle, New South Wales, Australia 1.12.1982 RHB WK																			
FC		11	20	0	267	54	13.35	0	1									33	3
Lim		8	3	1	37	31*	18.50	0	0									7	2
20T		11	7	2	98	31*	19.60	0	0									9	4
Test	2007/08	11	16	1	447	102	29.80	1	3									31	
FC	2001	120	185	15	5533	251*	32.54	9	31	6	1	0					1.00	279	19
Int	2008	5	5	1	10	6	2.50	0	0									3	
Lim	2001	111	94	14	2258	135	28.22	3	8									115	20
I20T	2008	1																1	1
20T	2003	42	33	8	630	77	25.20	0	2									28	14
AMLA, Hashim Mahomed (Dolphins, South Africa, South Africa A, Nottinghamshire, South Africa to India, South Africa to West Indies) b Durban, Natal, South Africa 31.3.1983 RHB RM																			
FC		5	7	1	463	129	77.16	1	5									1	
Lim		3	2	0	86	53	43.00	0	1									0	
Test	2004/05	46	81	6	3383	253*	45.10	10	16	42	28	0					4.00	37	
FC	1999/00	132	219	20	9688	253*	48.68	29	48	315	224	1	224.00	1-10	0	0	4.26	100	
Int	2007/08	29	28	3	1371	140	54.84	3	8									11	
Lim	2001/02	82	80	5	2989	140	39.85	6	19	16	28	0					10.50	31	
I20T	2008/09	2	2	0	52	26	26.00	0	0									0	
20T	2003/04	26	25	0	555	57	22.20	0	2									3	
ANDERSON, James Michael (England, Lancashire, England to South Africa, England to Scotland) b Burnley, Lancashire 30.7.1982 LHB RFM																			
Test		6	8	1	34	13	4.85	0	0	1347	539	32	16.84	6-17	2	1	2.40	3	
FC		10	13	2	69	25*	6.27	0	0	2132	884	48	18.41	6-17	3	1	2.48	3	
Int		12	6	4	12	5*	6.00	0	0	666	566	16	35.37	3-22	0	0	5.09	6	
Lim		13	7	5	14	5*	7.00	0	0	714	604	16	37.75	3-22	0	0	5.07	7	
20T		2	1	1	0	0*		0	0	48	77	2	38.50	2-38	0	0	9.62	2	
Test	2003	52	71	31	502	34	12.55	0	0	10777	5970	188	31.75	7-43	10	1	3.32	21	
FC	2002	111	132	54	792	37*	10.15	0	0	20737	11342	409	27.73	7-43	22	3	3.28	44	
Int	2002/03	133	56	29	159	15	5.88	0	0	6564	5429	179	30.32	5-23	8	1	4.96	36	
Lim	2000	184	77	46	252	15	8.12	0	0	8884	7136	251	28.43	5-23	8	1	4.81	45	
I20T	2006/07	19	4	3	1	1*	1.00	0	0	422	552	18	30.66	3-23	0	0	7.84	3	
20T	2004	39	8	6	22	16	11.00	0	0	831	1136	35	32.45	3-23	0	0	8.20	8	

Cmp	Debut	M	I	NO	Runs	HS	Avge	100	50	Balls	Runs	Wkts	Avge	BB	5i	10m	RpO	ct	st
ANDREW, Gareth Mark (Worcestershire) b Yeovil, Somerset 27.12.1983 LHB RFM																			
FC		9	14	1	425	79	32.69	0	4	1180	656	23	28.52	4-45	0	0	3.33	2	
Lim		11	10	2	249	104	31.12	1	1	293	356	8	44.50	3-30	0	0	7.29	2	
20T		14	11	4	87	27*	12.42	0	0	188	315	9	35.00	2-26	0	0	10.05	2	
FC	2003	42	59	10	1178	92*	24.04	0	7	5495	3654	101	36.17	5-58	2	0	3.99	12	
Lim	2000	83	53	14	640	104	16.41	1	1	2700	2825	83	34.03	5-31	1	1	6.27	25	
20T	2003	63	33	12	199	27*	9.47	0	0	1078	1572	52	30.23	4-22	1	0	8.75	15	
ANSARI, Akbar Shahzaman (Cambridge MCCU, Cambridge University) b Ascot, Berkshire 3.7.1988 RHB LB																			
FC		4	7	1	66	26*	11.00	0	0	36	32	0					5.33	0	
FC	2008	11	17	4	514	193	39.53	2	1	674	461	12	38.41	4-50	0	0	4.10	3	
Lim	2008	1	1	0	0	0	0.00	0	0	24	24	0					6.00	0	
ANSARI, Zafar Shahaan (Surrey) b Ascot, Berkshire 10.12.1991 LHB SLA																			
Lim		1	1	0	6	6	6.00	0	0	30	26	1	26.00	1-26	0	0	5.20	1	
ANYON, James Edward (Sussex) b Lancaster, Lancashire 5.5.1983 LHB RFM																			
FC		11	15	0	174	34	11.60	0	0	1364	767	29	26.44	3-23	0	0	3.37	3	
Lim		1	1	0	12	12	12.00	0	0	42	29	3	9.66	3-29	0	0	4.14	0	
FC	2003	58	74	25	538	37*	10.97	0	0	8727	5276	141	37.41	6-82	2	0	3.62	18	
Lim	2003	38	11	5	34	12	5.66	0	0	1375	1254	41	30.58	3-6	0	0	5.47	8	
20T	2005	21	3	3	16	8*		0	0	333	481	25	19.24	3-6	0	0	8.66	3	
ARFAN AKRAM, Mohammad (Unicorns) b Leytonstone, Essex 17.11.1983 RHB LB																			
Lim		1	1	0	8	8	8.00	0	0									0	
FC	2003	8	14	3	308	110	28.00	1	0	151	132	5	26.40	3-41	0	0	5.24	3	
Lim	2002	3	3	1	18	10*	9.00	0	0									0	
ASHLING, Christopher Paul (Glamorgan) b Manchester, Lancashire 26.11.1988 RHB RMF																			
FC		3	5	2	37	20	12.33	0	0	331	200	6	33.33	3-18	0	0	3.62	0	
Lim		5	4	3	4	3*	4.00	0	0	154	197	1	197.00	1-39	0	0	7.67	0	
20T		4	2	0	6	6	3.00	0	0	66	118	3	39.33	2-39	0	0	10.72	0	
FC	2009	4	6	2	49	20	12.25	0	0	499	316	9	35.11	3-18	0	0	3.80	0	
Lim	2009	8	6	4	11	6*	5.50	0	0	274	304	5	60.80	2-33	0	0	6.65	0	
ASHOK, Anand (Cambridge MCCU, Cambridge University) b Hyderabad, Andhra Pradesh, India 28.11.1988 RHB RM																			
FC		2	4	0	157	93	39.25	0	1	78	67	0					5.15	2	
FC	2009	3	6	1	288	112	57.60	1	1	120	82	1	82.00	1-15	0	0	4.10	2	
ASHRAF, Moin Aqeeb (Yorkshire) b Bradford, Yorkshire 5.1.1992 RHB RFM																			
FC		4	4	0	15	10	3.75	0	0	450	212	11	19.27	5-32	1	0	2.82	1	
ATIQ-UR-REHMAN Chishti (Unicorns) b Lahore, Punjab, Pakistan 8.11.1981 RHB RMF																			
Lim		2	2	0	29	29	14.50	0	0									1	
ATKINSON, James John (Durham MCCU) b Hong Kong 24.8.1990 RHB WK																			
FC		1																1	
FC	2009	3	4	0	21	16	5.25	0	0									3	
Int	2008	2	2	0	41	23	20.50	0	0									1	1
Lim	2008	2	2	0	41	23	20.50	0	0									1	1
AZEEM RAFIQ (Yorkshire) b Karachi, Sind, Pakistan 27.2.1991 RHB OB																			
FC		3	3	1	29	13*	14.50	0	0	528	268	5	53.60	4-92	0	0	3.04	0	
20T		10	3	1	2	1*	1.00	0	0	169	271	7	38.71	3-23	0	0	9.62	3	
FC	2009	7	8	1	146	100	20.85	1	0	1275	755	15	50.33	4-92	0	0	3.55	1	
Lim	2009	2								30	36	1	36.00	1-36	0	0	7.20	1	
20T	2008	15	6	3	20	11*	6.66	0	0	271	388	11	35.27	3-23	0	0	8.59	5	
AZHAR MAHMOOD Sagar (Islamabad Leopards, Kent, Kent to Scotland) b Rawalpindi, Punjab, Pakistan 28.2.1975 RHB RFM																			
FC		8	14	0	317	64	22.64	0	2	1677	847	30	28.23	5-62	2	0	3.03	1	
Lim		6	5	2	109	44	36.33	0	0	198	186	5	37.20	2-7	0	0	5.63	2	
20T		16	15	3	194	34	16.16	0	0	342	394	15	26.26	2-18	0	0	6.91	2	
Test	1997/98	21	34	4	900	136	30.00	3	1	3015	1402	39	35.94	4-50	0	0	2.79	14	
FC	1993/94	163	254	29	6952	204*	30.89	9	35	27559	14277	566	25.22	8-61	24	3	3.10	127	
Int	1996	143	110	26	1521	67	18.10	0	3	6242	4813	123	39.13	6-18	2	3	4.62	37	
Lim	1993/94	291	233	47	3946	101*	21.21	2	15	12836	9919	310	31.99	6-18	11	5	4.63	87	
20T	2003	78	68	20	1219	65*	25.39	0	3	1586	1928	86	22.41	4-20	1	0	7.29	12	
BAIRSTOW, Jonathan Marc (Yorkshire, Yorkshire to Netherlands) b Bradford, Yorkshire 26.9.1989 RHB RAB WK																			
FC		16	29	7	918	81	41.72	0	8									29	5
Lim		8	7	2	107	30	21.40	0	0									6	
20T		15	13	3	219	49*	21.90	0	0									4	1
FC	2009	28	48	13	1510	84*	43.14	0	14									50	5
Lim	2009	17	13	3	179	46*	17.90	0	0									11	
BAKER, Gavin Charles (Loughborough MCCU, Northamptonshire) b Edgware, Middlesex 3.10.1988 RHB RMF																			
FC		3	4	0	53	35	13.25	0	0	379	256	3	85.33	2-35	0	0	4.05	0	
Lim		1	1	0	0	0	0.00	0	0	42	63	1	63.00	1-63	0	0	9.00	0	
FC	2009	5	7	1	196	66	32.66	0	2	543	390	5	78.00	2-35	0	0	4.30	1	
BALCOMBE, David John (Hampshire) b City of London 24.12.1984 RHB RFM																			
FC		8	6	1	56	30	11.20	0	0	1477	812	27	30.07	3-69	0	0	3.29	2	
FC	2005	29	36	7	422	73	14.55	0	1	4558	2832	72	39.33	5-112	1	0	3.72	8	

Cmp	Debut	M	I	NO	Runs	HS	Avge	100	50	Balls	Runs	Wkts	Avge	BB	5i	10m	RpO	ct	st
Lim	2007	9	3	0	4	2	1.33	0	0	384	378	10	37.80	2-39	0	0	5.90	3	
20T	2006	1	1	0	3	3	3.00	0	0	12	15	0					7.50	0	
BALL, Adam James (Kent) b Greenwich, Kent 1.3.1993 RHB LFM																			
Lim		1	1	0	5	5	5.00	0	0	30	16	1	16.00	1-16	0	0	3.20	0	
BALL, Jacob Timothy (Nottinghamshire) b Mansfield, Nottinghamshire 14.3.1991 RHB RM																			
Lim		1	1	0	6	6	6.00	0	0	48	32	3	10.66	3-32	0	0	4.00	0	
Lim	2009	2	2	0	6	6	3.00	0	0	84	65	4	16.25	3-32	0	0	4.64	0	
BALLANCE, Gary Simon (Yorkshire) b Harare, Zimbabwe 22.11.1989 LHB LB																			
FC		3	5	2	84	43	28.00	0	0									1	
20T		3	3	1	60	48*	30.00	0	0									1	
FC	2008	4	7	2	90	43	18.00	0	0	6	3	0					3.00	1	
Lim	2006	5	5	0	162	73	32.40	0	1									1	
BANDARA, Herath Mudiyanselage Charitha Malinga (Basnahira South, Ragama, Kent, Sri Lanka to Bangladesh) b Kalutara, Sri Lanka 31.12.1979 RHB LBG																			
FC		6	10	3	105	29	15.00	0	0	1264	745	18	41.38	4-42	0	0	3.53	5	
Lim		5	1	0	5	5	5.00	0	0	198	143	13	11.00	5-35	0	1	4.33	0	
20T		16	7	1	38	10	6.33	0	0	288	384	17	22.58	3-14	0	0	8.00	5	
Test	1998	8	11	3	124	43	15.50	0	0	1152	633	16	39.56	3-84	0	0	3.29	4	
FC	1996/97	150	214	45	3415	108	20.20	1	14	20992	10943	432	25.33	8-49	14	2	3.12	95	
Int	2005/06	31	17	4	160	31	12.30	0	0	1470	1232	36	34.22	4-31	2	0	5.02	9	
Lim	1998	129	87	28	1005	64	17.03	0	2	5456	4284	181	23.66	5-22	7	4	4.71	38	
I20T	2006/07	4	3	1	12	7	6.00	0	0	84	96	4	24.00	3-32	0	0	6.85	1	
20T	2005/06	36	19	8	126	31*	11.45	0	0	717	903	41	22.02	3-14	0	0	7.55	8	
BANERJEE, Vikram (Gloucestershire) b Bradford, Yorkshire 20.3.1984 LHB SLA																			
FC		7	14	3	108	35	9.81	0	0	1332	793	23	34.47	5-74	2	0	3.57	1	
Lim		2	1	1	1	1*		0	0	78	51	4	12.75	2-20	0	0	3.92	1	
20T		9	3	2	4	2	4.00	0	0	192	262	7	37.42	2-30	0	0	8.18	3	
FC	2004	40	62	20	386	35	9.19	0	0	7311	4184	93	44.98	5-74	2	0	3.43	9	
Lim	2009	12	7	4	12	6	4.00	0	0	570	437	18	24.27	3-47	0	0	4.60	5	
20T	2009	15	5	4	9	5*	9.00	0	0	330	437	13	33.61	2-30	0	0	7.94	5	
BANKS, Omari Ahmed Clemente (Leeward Islands, Somerset to India) b Road Bay, Anguilla 17.7.1982 RHB OB																			
Test	2002/03	10	16	4	318	50*	26.50	0	1	2401	1367	28	48.82	4-87	0	0	3.41	6	
FC	2000/01	78	122	18	2717	108	26.12	2	16	14321	7444	203	36.66	7-41	8	2	3.11	43	
Int	2002/03	5	5	0	83	33	16.60	0	0	270	189	7	27.00	2-24	0	0	4.20	0	
Lim	2001/02	71	58	17	1187	77*	28.95	0	9	3037	2241	81	27.66	4-23	2	0	4.42	16	
20T	2007/08	9	7	2	153	50*	30.60	0	1	144	217	6	36.16	1-14	0	0	9.04	1	
BARKER, Keith Hubert Douglas (Warwickshire, Warwickshire to Scotland) b Manchester, Lancashire 21.10.1986 LHB LM																			
FC		4	5	1	57	22	14.25	0	0	217	135	2	67.50	2-22	0	0	3.73	1	
Lim		10	8	1	124	40	17.71	0	0	364	371	14	26.50	4-33	1	0	6.11	2	
20T		14	9	1	177	46	22.12	0	0	291	350	21	16.66	4-19	1	0	7.21	2	
FC	2009	7	9	1	85	23	10.62	0	0	535	310	3	103.33	2-22	0	0	3.47	1	
Lim	2009	23	15	5	221	40	22.10	0	0	766	725	26	27.88	4-33	1	0	5.67	5	
20T	2009	25	12	2	197	46	19.70	0	0	501	633	37	17.10	4-19	2	0	7.58	3	
BARNARD, Michael Robert (Oxford MCCU) b Shewsbury, Shropshire 8.2.1990 RHB RFM																			
FC		1	1	0	0	0	0.00	0	0	133	64	1	64.00	1-14	0	0	2.88	0	
BATES, Alexander Michael (Hampshire, Hampshire to Scotland) b Portsmouth, Hampshire 10.10.1990 RHB WK																			
FC		8	11	3	92	31	11.50	0	0									28	
Lim		5	3	1	3	2*	1.50	0	0									4	1
20T		4																3	
Lim	2010	6	3	1	3	2*	1.50	0	0									5	2
BATTY, Gareth Jon (Surrey) b Bradford, Yorkshire 13.10.1977 RHB OB																			
FC		15	24	2	550	67	25.00	0	2	2933	1696	42	40.38	5-76	1	0	3.46	12	
Lim		9	6	0	81	29	13.50	0	0	342	339	12	28.25	3-44	0	0	5.94	0	
20T		8	6	1	16	10*	3.20	0	0	120	158	7	22.57	4-23	1	0	7.90	2	
Test	2003/04	7	8	1	144	38	20.57	0	0	1394	733	11	66.63	3-55	0	0	3.15	3	
FC	1997	150	228	38	4852	133	25.53	2	24	28434	14076	410	34.33	7-52	16	1	2.97	103	
Int	2002/03	10	8	2	30	17	5.00	0	0	440	366	5	73.20	2-40	0	0	4.99	4	
Lim	1998	194	153	31	2050	83*	16.80	0	5	7607	5791	172	33.66	5-35	5	1	4.56	66	
I20T	2008/09	1	1	0	4	4	4.00	0	0	18	17	0					5.66	0	
20T	2003	58	49	12	457	87	12.35	0	1	1032	1331	48	27.72	4-23	1	0	7.73	23	
BATTY, Jonathan Neil (Gloucestershire) b Chesterfield, Derbyshire 18.4.1974 RHB WK																			
FC		15	30	2	450	61	16.07	0	1									53	3
Lim		4	4	0	65	54	16.25	0	1									4	1
20T		4	3	3	19	8*		0	0									1	2
FC	1994	206	324	36	9238	168*	32.07	20	39	78	61	1	61.00	1-21	0	0	4.69	553	67
Lim	1994	185	152	26	2808	158*	22.28	1	14									195	34
20T	2003	55	47	18	612	59	21.10	0	2									32	20
BEER, William Andrew Thomas (Sussex) b Crawley, Sussex 8.10.1988 RHB LB																			
FC		2	1	1	37	37*		0	0	196	111	5	22.20	3-31	0	0	3.39	1	
20T		12	5	2	32	22	10.66	0	0	222	268	10	26.80	3-19	0	0	7.24	4	
FC	2008	4	3	2	43	37*	43.00	0	0	292	192	6	32.00	3-31	0	0	3.94	1	

Cmp	Debut	M	I	NO	Runs	HS	Avge	100	50	Balls	Runs	Wkts	Avge	BB	5i	10m	RpO	ct	st
Lim	2009	14	4	0	34	14	8.50	0	0	540	420	8	52.50	2-17	0	0	4.66	4	
20T	2008	27	12	5	74	22	10.57	0	0	498	607	20	30.35	3-19	0	0	7.31	5	
BELL, Ian Ronald (England, England Lions, Warwickshire, England to Bangladesh, England to South Africa, England Lions to United Arab Emirates) b Walsgrave, Coventry, Warwickshire 11.4.1982 RHB RM																			
Test		2	2	0	145	128	72.50	1	0									1	
FC		8	13	1	526	128	43.83	2	2									11	
Int		4	4	2	139	84*	69.50	0	1									1	
Lim		17	17	2	927	158	61.80	2	7									5	
20T		4	4	0	166	85	41.50	0	2									0	
Test	2004	57	100	10	3863	199	42.92	11	23	108	76	1	76.00	1-33	0	0	4.22	50	
FC	1999	171	290	27	11575	262*	44.01	31	60	2809	1564	47	33.27	4-4	0	0	3.34	126	
Int	2004/05	83	80	8	2622	126*	36.41	1	16	88	88	6	14.66	3-9	0	0	6.00	24	
Lim	1999	205	195	20	6811	158	38.92	7	49	1290	1138	33	34.48	5-41	0	1	5.29	70	
I20T	2006	5	5	1	109	60*	27.25	0	1									4	
20T	2003	42	41	6	860	85	24.57	0	4	132	186	3	62.00	1-12	0	0	8.45	16	
BENHAM, Christopher Charles (Hampshire) b Frimley, Surrey 24.3.1983 RHB OB																			
FC		7	13	0	278	45	21.38	0	0									11	
20T		3	3	1	26	16*	13.00	0	0									1	
FC	2004	48	80	3	2103	111	27.31	2	10	30	37	0					7.40	51	
Lim	2001	55	50	6	1564	158	35.54	4	7									25	
20T	2006	37	32	4	447	59	15.96	0	1									20	
BENKENSTEIN, Dale Martin (Dolphins, Durham, Durham to Scotland, Durham to United Arab Emirates) b Salisbury (now Harare), Zimbabwe 9.6.1974 RHB RM,OB																			
FC		16	26	1	799	114	31.96	1	5	486	143	4	35.75	2-17	0	0	1.76	13	
Lim		4	4	0	76	33	19.00	0	0	36	27	3	9.00	3-27	0	0	4.50	3	
20T		15	13	3	249	57*	24.90	0	1	30	48	1	48.00	1-9	0	0	9.60	5	
FC	1993/94	226	343	38	13741	259	45.05	34	72	7037	3375	97	34.79	4-16	0	0	2.87	153	
Int	1998/99	23	20	3	305	69	17.94	0	1	65	44	4	11.00	3-5	0	0	4.06	3	
Lim	1992/93	279	252	58	6826	107*	35.18	1	42	3071	2572	86	29.90	4-16	3	0	5.02	104	
20T	2003/04	74	70	14	1428	57*	25.50	0	4	366	455	16	28.43	3-10	0	0	7.45	25	
BENNING, James Graham Edward (Leicestershire, Leicestershire to Scotland) b Mill Hill, Middlesex 4.5.1983 RHB RM																			
FC		1	2	1	55	29	55.00	0	0	114	59	3	19.66	2-38	0	0	3.10	1	
Lim		6	6	0	186	62	31.00	0	1	198	171	6	28.50	2-29	0	0	5.18	2	
20T		14	14	5	193	45	21.44	0	0	111	155	5	31.00	1-10	0	0	8.37	5	
FC	2003	42	67	7	1938	128	32.30	4	8	2073	1433	24	59.70	3-43	0	0	4.14	17	
Lim	2001	90	89	3	2898	189*	33.69	3	18	1420	1474	43	34.27	4-43	1	0	6.22	28	
20T	2003	64	63	8	1225	88	22.27	0	7	153	212	7	30.28	1-7	0	0	8.31	20	
BERG, Gareth Kyle (Middlesex, Middlesex to Netherlands) b Cape Town, Cape Province, South Africa 18.1.1981 RHB RMF																			
FC		15	26	5	761	125	36.23	1	3	1410	877	24	36.54	4-72	0	0	3.73	7	
Lim		11	11	3	301	53	37.62	0	1	120	92	2	46.00	1-13	0	0	4.60	4	
20T		14	10	4	160	41	26.66	0	0	222	292	6	48.66	2-45	0	0	7.89	7	
FC	2008	31	54	7	1547	125	32.91	1	10	3217	1934	52	37.19	5-55	2	0	3.60	17	
Lim	2008	33	28	5	550	65	23.91	0	2	774	704	24	29.33	4-50	1	0	5.45	9	
20T	2009	21	17	7	297	41	29.70	0	0	327	443	9	49.22	2-31	0	0	8.12	8	
BEST, Tino la Bertram (Barbados, West Indies to South Africa, Yorkshire) b 3rd Avenue, Richmond Gap, St Michael, Barbados 26.8.1981 RHB RF																			
FC		9	9	0	86	40	9.55	0	0	1188	793	18	44.05	4-86	0	0	4.00	4	
Lim		5	1	1	8	8*		0	0	158	166	10	16.60	4-46	1	0	6.30	1	
20T		8	3	2	10	10*	10.00	0	0	176	243	7	34.71	2-26	0	0	8.28	4	
Test	2002/03	14	23	3	196	27	9.80	0	0	2187	1363	28	48.67	4-46	0	0	3.73	1	
FC	2001/02	81	107	19	1102	51	12.52	0	1	10923	6756	239	28.26	7-33	10	2	3.71	23	
Int	2004	12	8	3	52	24	10.40	0	0	545	477	13	36.69	4-35	1	0	5.25	3	
Lim	2002	43	25	13	144	24	12.00	0	0	1753	1507	52	28.98	4-35	2	0	5.15	13	
20T	2007/08	11	4	2	12	10*	6.00	0	0	230	289	7	41.28	2-26	0	0	7.53	4	
BLACKABY, Luke Alexander (Durham MCCU) b Farnborough, Kent 1.2.1991 LHB LM																			
FC		2	1	0	38	38	38.00	0	0	6	11	0					11.00	0	
BLACKWELL, Ian David (Durham, Durham to Scotland, Durham to United Arab Emirates) b Chesterfield, Derbyshire 10.6.1978 LHB SLA																			
FC		15	24	2	794	86	36.09	0	8	2733	1205	43	28.02	5-78	2	0	2.64	2	
Lim		9	9	0	185	35	20.55	0	0	302	240	7	34.28	3-22	0	0	4.76	0	
20T		12	10	0	198	79	19.80	0	1	174	213	8	26.62	2-14	0	0	7.34	2	
Test	2005/06	1	1	0	4	4	4.00	0	0	114	71	0					3.73	0	
FC	1997	181	271	21	9936	247*	39.74	23	55	27354	12431	333	37.33	7-85	12	0	2.72	61	
Int	2002/03	34	29	2	403	82	14.92	0	1	1230	877	24	36.54	3-26	0	0	4.27	8	
Lim	1997	241	222	18	5533	134*	27.12	3	33	8393	6697	194	34.52	5-26	3	1	4.78	60	
20T	2003	52	49	6	823	82	19.13	0	3	913	1090	35	31.14	4-26	1	0	7.16	13	
BLAIN, John Angus Rae (Yorkshire) b Edinburgh, Midlothian, Scotland 4.1.1979 RHB RFM																			
FC		1								84	20	0					1.42	0	
FC	1996	43	47	16	495	93	15.96	0	2	6029	4286	120	35.71	6-42	4	0	4.26	12	
Int	1999	33	25	6	284	41	14.94	0	0	1329	1173	41	28.60	5-22	1	1	5.29	8	
Lim	1996	102	66	25	635	41	15.48	0	0	4388	3679	143	25.72	5-22	3	4	5.03	27	

Cmp	Debut	M	I	NO	Runs	HS	Avge	100	50	Balls	Runs	Wkts	Avge	BB	5i	10m	RpO	ct	st
I20T	2007/08	6	3	1	4	3*	2.00	0	0	120	108	6	18.00	2-23	0	0	5.40	1	
20T	2007/08	6	3	1	4	3*	2.00	0	0	120	108	6	18.00	2-23	0	0	5.40	1	
BLAKE, Alexander James (Kent, Kent to Scotland) b Farnborough, Kent 25.1.1989 LHB RM																			
FC		9	17	1	359	105*	22.43	1	0	114	69	3	23.00	2-9	0	0	3.63	5	
Lim		7	4	3	128	81*	128.00	0	1									1	
20T		15	12	2	122	33	12.20	0	0									9	
FC	2008	14	22	1	484	105*	23.04	1	0	162	101	3	33.66	2-9	0	0	3.74	6	
Lim	2007	18	12	5	285	81*	40.71	0	2	72	61	1	61.00	1-25	0	0	5.08	7	
BOJE, Nico (Warriors, Northamptonshire, Northamptonshire to Netherlands) b Bloemfontein, Orange Free State, South Africa 20.3.1973 LHB SLA																			
FC		9	15	1	471	98	33.64	0	4	1383	796	15	53.06	2-47	0	0	3.45	3	
Lim		5	5	0	108	38	21.60	0	0	152	94	4	23.50	3-10	0	0	3.71	1	
20T		11	10	2	114	54*	14.25	0	1	188	227	11	20.63	3-20	0	0	7.24	4	
Test	1999/00	43	62	10	1312	85	25.23	0	4	8620	4265	100	42.65	5-62	3	0	2.96	18	
FC	1990/91	212	318	55	8975	226*	34.12	8	55	42325	18756	577	32.50	8-93	22	2	2.65	123	
Int	1995/96	115	71	18	1414	129	26.67	2	4	4541	3415	96	35.57	5-21	2	1	4.51	33	
Lim	1993/94	289	207	49	4032	129	25.51	2	16	12064	8742	274	31.90	5-21	9	1	4.34	88	
I20T	2005/06	1								24	27	1	27.00	1-27	0	0	6.75	0	
20T	2003/04	58	41	12	693	58*	23.89	0	3	1062	1225	57	21.49	3-10	0	0	6.92	24	
BOPARA, Ravinder Singh (England, England Lions, Essex, Auckland, England to South Africa, England to West Indies, Kings XI Punjab) b Forest Gate, Essex 4.5.1985 RHB RM																			
FC		9	17	2	590	142	39.33	2	3	211	122	11	11.09	4-14	0	0	3.46	4	
Int		4	4	2	103	45*	51.50	0	0	60	38	4	9.50	4-38	1	0	3.80	1	
Lim		15	15	4	674	168	61.27	1	2	318	248	17	14.58	4-38	2	0	4.67	6	
I20T		2	2	0	23	12	11.50	0	0									2	
20T		18	18	2	496	105*	31.00	1	2	324	397	16	24.81	3-13	0	0	7.35	7	
Test	2007/08	10	15	0	502	143	33.46	3	0	296	199	1	199.00	1-39	0	0	4.03	5	
FC	2002	103	172	22	6332	229	42.21	17	25	6946	4585	107	42.85	5-75	1	0	3.96	67	
Int	2006/07	54	50	10	1140	60	28.50	0	4	391	331	10	33.10	4-38	1	0	5.07	18	
Lim	2001	164	155	32	4607	201*	37.45	6	24	3303	2943	109	27.00	4-38	3	0	5.34	49	
I20T	2008	11	10	0	191	55	19.10	0	1									4	
20T	2003	91	81	9	1807	105*	25.09	1	10	1108	1431	60	23.85	3-13	0	0	7.74	29	
BORRINGTON, Paul Michael (Derbyshire) b Nottingham 24.5.1988 RHB OB																			
FC		7	13	1	246	79*	20.50	0	1									4	
FC	2005	26	42	5	1109	105	29.97	2	5	6	5	0					5.00	16	
Lim	2009	1	1	0	25	25	25.00	0	0									0	
BORTHWICK, Scott George (Durham, Durham to United Arab Emirates) b Sunderland, Co Durham 19.4.1990 LHB LB																			
FC		11	15	3	315	68	26.25	0	2	941	618	15	41.20	2-22	0	0	3.94	8	
Lim		4	4	3	16	10*	16.00	0	0	72	66	1	66.00	1-40	0	0	5.50	0	
20T		2								2	3	0					9.00	1	
FC	2009	13	18	4	341	68	24.35	0	2	1204	797	26	30.65	4-27	0	0	3.97	9	
Lim	2009	10	6	5	21	10*	21.00	0	0	192	244	5	48.80	2-11	0	0	7.62	4	
20T	2008	5								38	58	3	19.33	3-23	0	0	9.15	2	
BOSMAN, Lungile Edgar (Dolphins, KwaZulu-Natal, South Africa, South Africa A, Derbyshire, South Africa to India, South Africa to West Indies) b Kimberley, Cape Province, South Africa 14.4.1977 RHB RM																			
20T		15	14	0	368	94	26.28	0	2									1	
FC	1997/98	94	169	12	4568	140	29.09	5	23	576	343	8	42.87	3-25	0	0	3.57	51	
Int	2006/07	14	12	0	301	88	25.08	0	2									3	
Lim	1997/98	148	143	9	3804	99*	28.38	0	22	85	77	1	77.00	1-36	0	0	5.43	36	
I20T	2005/06	10	10	1	272	94	30.22	0	3									0	
20T	2003/04	57	55	3	1570	104	30.19	1	9									8	
BOTHA, Anthony Greyvensteyn (Warwickshire, Warwickshire to Scotland) b Pretoria, Transvaal, South Africa 17.11.1976 LHB SLA																			
FC		8	14	0	248	76	17.71	0	1	304	175	4	43.75	3-50	0	0	3.45	7	
Lim		7	6	5	52	42	52.00	0	0	204	178	3	59.33	1-34	0	0	5.23	4	
20T		17	9	4	93	26*	18.60	0	0	222	253	12	21.08	3-16	0	0	6.83	11	
FC	1995/96	135	209	27	4311	156*	23.68	4	20	21596	10496	302	34.75	8-53	9	1	2.91	102	
Lim	1996/97	145	109	37	1660	60*	23.05	0	4	5182	4200	142	29.57	5-43	1	2	4.86	66	
20T	2004	64	41	15	465	35*	17.88	0	0	1101	1250	60	20.83	4-14	2	0	6.81	32	
BOYCE, Matthew Andrew Golding (Leicestershire, Leicestershire to Scotland) b Cheltenham, Gloucestershire 13.8.1985 LHB RM																			
FC		15	27	3	761	90	31.70	0	6	6	2	0					2.00	19	
Lim		7	5	0	174	60	34.80	0	1									2	
20T		1	1	1	15	15*		0	0									0	
FC	2006	49	85	6	2188	106	27.69	1	15	42	63	0					9.00	26	
Lim	2007	32	28	3	720	80	28.80	0	4									7	
20T	2008	17	13	2	243	34	22.09	0	0									3	
BRADSHAW, Duncan Phillip (Oxford MCCU) b Harare, Zimbabwe 19.2.1986 RHB RFM																			
FC		2	3	0	116	63	38.66	0	1	192	103	4	25.75	2-41	0	0	3.21	0	
FC	2006	12	17	3	529	127*	37.78	1	2	675	407	6	67.83	2-41	0	0	3.61	2	
Lim	2008	1	1	0	12	12	12.00	0	0									0	

Cmp	Debut	M	I	NO	Runs	HS	Avge	100	50	Balls	Runs	Wkts	Avge	BB	5i	10m	RpO	ct	st
BRAGG, William David (Glamorgan) b Newport, Monmouthshire, Wales 24.10.1986 LHB WK																			
FC		3	6	0	56	44	9.33	0	0									3	1
Lim		6	5	0	52	28	10.40	0	0	6	15	0					15.00	1	
20T		1	1	0	15	15	15.00	0	0									0	
FC	2007	14	22	0	474	92	21.54	0	2	30	23	0					4.60	7	1
Lim	2005	13	12	1	283	78	25.72	0	1	6	15	0					15.00	2	
BRATHWAITE, Ruel Marlon Ricardo (Combined Campuses and Colleges, Durham) b Bridgetown, St Michael, Barbados 6.9.1985 RHB RFM																			
FC		1	2	1	2	2	2.00	0	0	181	118	4	29.50	3-93	0	0	3.91	0	
FC	2006	13	14	4	144	76*	14.40	0	1	2163	1294	30	43.13	5-54	1	0	3.58	0	
Lim	2007	1								18	19	1	19.00	1-19	0	0	6.33	0	
20T	2010	1	1	0	0	0	0.00	0	0	18	33	1	33.00	1-33	0	0	11.00	0	
BRAVO, Dwayne John (Trinidad and Tobago, West Indies, Essex, Mumbai Indians, Trinidad and Tobago to India, Victoria to Australia, West Indies to Australia) b Santa Cruz, Trinidad 7.10.1983 RHB RFM																			
20T		1	1	0	5	5	5.00	0	0	24	46	1	46.00	1-46	0	0	11.50	0	
Test	2004	37	68	1	2175	113	32.46	3	13	6164	3270	83	39.39	6-55	2	0	3.18	39	
FC	2001/02	94	173	7	5193	197	31.28	8	29	10461	5621	168	33.45	6-11	7	0	3.22	81	
Int	2003/04	107	87	16	1715	112*	24.15	1	5	4260	3721	129	28.84	4-19	4	0	5.24	44	
Lim	2002	144	121	20	2312	112*	22.89	1	7	5489	4677	172	27.19	6-46	6	1	5.11	60	
I20T	2005/06	22	20	5	344	66*	22.93	0	2	338	491	19	25.84	4-38	1	0	8.71	5	
20T	2005/06	74	64	15	1208	70*	24.65	0	8	1315	1811	70	25.87	4-23	2	0	8.26	32	
BREESE, Gareth Rohan (Durham, Durham to Scotland) b Montego Bay, St James, Jamaica 9.1.1976 RHB OB																			
FC		2	3	0	27	14	9.00	0	0	18	5	0					1.66	1	
Lim		10	7	0	171	42	24.42	0	0	328	300	9	33.33	2-13	0	0	5.48	5	
20T		15	8	3	75	30*	15.00	0	0	215	242	11	22.00	3-14	0	0	6.75	9	
Test	2002/03	1	2	0	5	5	2.50	0	0	188	135	2	67.50	2-108	0	0	4.30	1	
FC	1995/96	116	185	20	4359	165*	26.41	4	27	18093	8369	280	29.88	7-60	12	3	2.77	96	
Lim	1996/97	149	114	28	1740	68*	20.23	0	3	5704	4414	155	28.47	5-41	2	2	4.64	61	
20T	2004	61	40	9	358	37	11.54	0	0	1032	1156	54	21.40	4-14	2	0	6.72	26	
BRESNAN, Timothy Thomas (England, Yorkshire, England to Bangladesh, England to South Africa, England to United Arab Emirates, England to West Indies, Yorkshire to Netherlands) b Pontefract, Yorkshire 28.2.1985 RHB RMF																			
Test		1	1	0	25	25	25.00	0	0	302	169	4	42.25	3-93	0	0	3.35	1	
FC		7	10	1	228	70	25.33	0	2	1432	707	21	33.66	5-52	1	0	2.96	3	
Int		12	11	4	149	34	21.28	0	0	616	573	11	52.09	3-51	0	0	5.58	3	
Lim		18	16	6	234	58	23.40	0	1	898	837	21	39.85	3-40	0	0	5.59	3	
I20T		2								40	28	4	7.00	3-10	0	0	4.20	0	
20T		3								64	49	5	9.80	3-10	0	0	4.59	0	
Test	2009	5	3	0	125	91	41.66	0	1	986	492	14	35.14	3-45	0	0	2.99	3	
FC	2003	96	127	22	2882	126*	27.44	3	14	15723	8109	250	32.43	5-42	4	0	3.09	41	
Int	2006	33	27	11	408	80	25.50	0	1	1599	1415	36	39.30	4-28	1	0	5.31	8	
Lim	2001	169	119	38	1583	80	19.54	0	4	7235	6090	178	34.21	4-25	4	0	5.05	44	
I20T	2006	14	8	4	50	23*	12.50	0	0	262	334	9	37.11	3-10	0	0	7.64	5	
20T	2003	61	42	16	431	42	16.57	0	0	1197	1461	56	26.08	3-10	0	0	7.32	20	
BRETT, Thomas (Northamptonshire, Northamptonshire to Netherlands) b Kettering, Northamptonshire 13.11.1989 RHB SLA																			
FC		1								102	38	0					2.23	0	
Lim		4	1	1	2	2*		0	0	192	155	2	77.50	1-43	0	0	4.84	1	
Lim	2010	5	1	1	2	2*		0	0	216	179	3	59.66	1-24	0	0	4.97	2	
BRIGGS, Danny Richard (Hampshire, Hampshire to Scotland) b Newport, Isle of Wight 30.4.1991 RHB SLA																			
FC		13	14	3	116	28	10.54	0	0	2264	1294	34	38.05	4-93	0	0	3.42	2	
Lim		6	3	2	13	10*	13.00	0	0	276	236	3	78.66	1-32	0	0	5.13	3	
20T		19	5	3	9	9	4.50	0	0	402	445	31	14.35	3-5	0	0	6.64	4	
FC	2009	16	17	3	153	36	10.92	0	0	2778	1589	42	37.83	4-93	0	0	3.43	3	
Lim	2009	11	4	2	17	10*	8.50	0	0	522	418	6	69.66	2-36	0	0	4.80	5	
BROAD, Stuart Christopher John (England, Nottinghamshire, England to Bangladesh, England to South Africa, England to Scotland, England to United Arab Emirates, England to West Indies) b Nottingham 24.6.1986 LHB RFM																			
Test		4	6	0	250	169	41.66	1	0	683	327	14	23.35	4-38	0	0	2.87	0	
FC		6	9	0	257	169	28.55	1	0	1079	626	33	18.96	8-52	2	1	3.48	0	
Int		13	6	0	34	21	5.66	0	0	720	617	27	22.85	4-44	3	0	5.14	3	
Lim		13	6	0	34	21	5.66	0	0	720	617	27	22.85	4-44	3	0	5.14	3	
I20T		2								48	50	2	25.00	2-18	0	0	6.25	0	
20T		5	1	0	0	0	0.00	0	0	119	140	6	23.33	2-18	0	0	7.05	0	
Test	2007/08	32	45	6	1096	169	28.10	1	5	6274	3328	97	34.30	6-91	3	0	3.18	9	
FC	2005	73	94	18	1905	169	25.06	1	11	13017	7342	253	29.01	8-52	12	1	3.38	21	
Int	2006	73	43	14	372	45*	12.82	0	0	3710	3187	124	25.70	5-23	8	1	5.15	17	
Lim	2005	90	49	15	418	45*	12.29	0	0	4492	3875	149	26.00	5-23	8	1	5.17	19	
I20T	2006	29	11	5	36	10*	6.00	0	0	611	755	35	21.57	3-17	0	0	7.41	13	
20T	2006	44	13	6	45	10*	6.42	0	0	958	1072	55	19.49	3-13	0	0	6.71	14	
BROOKS, Jack Alexander (Northamptonshire) b Oxford 4.6.1984 RHB RMF																			
FC		14	20	3	177	53	10.41	0	1	2241	1260	37	34.05	4-88	0	0	3.37	2	
Lim		6	3	1	4	2*	2.00	0	0	246	203	6	33.83	3-41	0	0	4.95	0	
20T		15	2	2	7	5*		0	0	276	307	12	25.58	3-24	0	0	6.67	4	

Cmp	Debut	M	I	NO	Runs	HS	Avge	100	50	Balls	Runs	Wkts	Avge	BB	5i	10m	RpO	ct	st
FC	2009	17	23	6	197	53	11.58	0	1	2727	1585	46	34.45	4-76	0	0	3.48	3	
Lim	2009	9	4	1	14	10	4.66	0	0	354	302	6	50.33	3-41	0	0	5.11	0	
BROPHY, Gerard Louis (Yorkshire, Yorkshire to Netherlands) b Welkom, Orange Free State, South Africa 26.11.1975 RHB WK																			
FC		9	17	1	472	103	29.50	1	1									20	
Lim		10	9	2	290	93*	41.42	0	3									6	3
20T		12	9	1	97	31*	12.12	0	0									7	2
FC	1996/97	115	184	22	5118	185	31.59	7	26	12	1	0					0.50	286	21
Lim	1997/98	112	92	19	1992	93*	27.28	0	13									110	22
20T	2003	48	41	9	678	57*	21.18	0	2									21	7
BROWN, Alistair Duncan (Nottinghamshire, Nottinghamshire to Scotland) b Beckenham, Kent 11.2.1970 RHB OB																			
FC		17	26	3	863	134	37.52	1	6	54	57	0					6.33	12	
Lim		8	7	0	112	43	16.00	0	0									1	
20T		18	18	1	337	73*	19.82	0	2									5	
FC	1992	280	438	49	16669	295*	42.85	46	74	1417	775	6	129.16	3-25	0	0	3.28	276	1
Int	1996	16	16	0	354	118	22.12	1	1	6	5	0					5.00	6	
Lim	1990	399	381	19	11168	268	30.85	19	50	520	561	14	40.07	3-39	0	0	6.47	130	
20T	2003	79	79	2	1758	83	22.83	0	12	2	2	0					6.00	41	
BROWN, Ben Christopher (Sussex) b Crawley, Sussex 23.11.1988 RHB WK																			
FC		9	14	2	515	112	42.91	2	2									9	2
Lim		2	2	1	81	58	81.00	0	1									3	
FC	2007	10	15	2	561	112	43.15	2	2									9	2
Lim	2007	11	7	3	112	58	28.00	0	1									8	1
20T	2008	9	5	1	19	7	4.75	0	0									3	
BROWN, Christopher (Unicorns) b Oldham, Lancashire 16.8.1974 RHB OB																			
Lim		3	2	1	20	19	20.00	0	0	136	103	2	51.50	2-50	0	0	4.54	1	
FC	2005/06	4	6	1	45	21	9.00	0	0	366	163	6	27.16	2-10	0	0	2.67	2	
Lim	2001	9	7	2	88	33	17.60	0	0	412	302	7	43.14	2-39	0	0	4.39	3	
BROWN, David Owen (Glamorgan) b Burnley, Lancashire 8.12.1982 RHB RM																			
FC		1	2	0	114	99	57.00	0	1									1	
Lim		10	9	1	139	31*	17.37	0	0	228	283	2	141.50	1-31	0	0	7.44	3	
20T		12	7	1	66	21	11.00	0	0	78	143	2	71.50	2-30	0	0	11.00	4	
FC	2003	24	41	4	1089	99	29.43	0	8	1755	1251	28	44.67	5-38	1	0	4.27	13	
Lim	2006	38	31	7	500	63*	20.83	0	1	732	804	14	57.42	3-29	0	0	6.59	13	
20T	2006	30	22	2	329	56	16.45	0	1	138	214	6	35.66	2-30	0	0	9.30	10	
BROWN, Francis Andrew (Cambridge MCCU) b Nottingham 21.3.1990 RHB SLA																			
FC		2	2	0	30	30	15.00	0	0	270	194	4	48.50	2-70	0	0	4.31	0	
FC	2009	4	4	0	61	30	15.25	0	0	540	330	8	41.25	3-26	0	0	3.66	1	
BROWN, Karl Robert (Lancashire) b Bolton, Lancashire 17.5.1988 RHB RM																			
FC		2	3	0	25	21	8.33	0	0									0	
Lim		7	7	1	286	65*	47.66	0	3									2	
FC	2006	9	15	1	181	40	12.92	0	0	66	44	2	22.00	2-30	0	0	4.00	7	
Lim	2007	12	12	1	358	65*	32.54	0	3									3	
BROWN, Michael James (Surrey) b Burnley, Lancashire 9.2.1980 RHB OB																			
FC		1	2	0	64	47	32.00	0	0									0	
FC	1999	93	166	16	5195	133	34.63	9	28	18	20	0					6.66	71	
Lim	2002	30	29	2	922	96*	34.14	0	7									9	
20T	2004	12	12	1	284	77	25.81	0	1									4	
BRYAN, Thomas Edward (Oxford University) b Colchester, Essex 31.10.1988 RHB RMF																			
FC		1								30	11	0					2.20	1	
FC	2009	2	2	0	17	16	8.50	0	0	36	17	0					2.83	1	
BUCK, Nathan Liam (Leicestershire) b Leicester 26.4.1991 RHB RMF																			
FC		15	20	5	93	26	6.20	0	0	2291	1340	49	27.34	4-44	0	0	3.50	4	
Lim		5	1	1	5	5*		0	0	220	204	7	29.14	2-16	0	0	5.56	0	
20T		9	1	1	3	3*		0	0	180	251	10	25.10	3-20	0	0	8.36	2	
FC	2009	19	25	7	122	26	6.77	0	0	2819	1616	52	31.07	4-44	0	0	3.44	5	
Lim	2009	9	2	1	26	21	26.00	0	0	370	355	11	32.27	2-16	0	0	5.75	1	
BURTON, David Alexander (Northamptonshire) b Dulwich, Surrey 23.8.1985 RHB RMF																			
FC		1	2	1	2	2*	2.00	0	0	120	75	5	15.00	5-75	1	0	3.75	1	
FC	2006	5	8	4	58	52*	14.50	0	1	698	550	14	39.28	5-68	2	0	4.72	1	
Lim	2009	3	1	0	2	2	2.00	0	0	90	94	2	47.00	1-26	0	0	6.26	1	
20T	2008	3								54	51	4	12.75	2-13	0	0	5.66	1	
BUTLER, Ian Gareth (New Zealand, Otago, Gloucestershire, New Zealand to South Africa, New Zealand to United Arab Emirates, New Zealand to West Indies, Otago to India) b Middlemore, Auckland, New Zealand 24.11.1981 RHB RFM																			
20T		4	3	0	47	28	15.66	0	0	83	122	5	24.40	3-8	0	0	8.81	0	
Test	2001/02	8	10	2	76	26	9.50	0	0	1368	884	24	36.83	6-46	1	0	3.87	4	
FC	2001/02	43	56	18	648	68	17.05	0	2	6871	3989	126	31.65	6-46	2	0	3.48	11	
Int	2001/02	26	13	5	84	25	10.50	0	0	1109	1038	28	37.07	4-44	1	0	5.61	8	
Lim	2001/02	87	56	15	642	53*	15.65	0	1	3764	3403	100	34.03	5-55	2	1	5.42	16	
I20T	2008/09	14	5	4	4	2*	4.00	0	0	270	361	19	19.00	3-19	0	0	8.02	2	
20T	2004	42	29	12	252	36*	14.82	0	0	805	1074	54	19.88	6-28	0	1	8.00	10	

Cmp	Debut	M	I	NO	Runs	HS	Avge	100	50	Balls	Runs	Wkts	Avge	BB	5i	10m	RpO	ct	st
BUTTLER, Joseph Charles (Somerset, Somerset to India) b Taunton, Somerset 8.9.1990 RHB WK																			
FC		13	20	3	569	144	33.47	1	2									23	
Lim		15	14	5	443	90*	49.22	0	4									10	1
20T		19	14	6	240	55*	30.00	0	1									19	2
FC	2009	14	21	3	599	144	33.27	1	2									23	
Lim	2009	16	14	5	443	90*	49.22	0	4									11	1
20T	2009/10	20	15	7	246	55*	30.75	0	1									20	2
CAMERON, James Gair (Worcestershire) b Harare, Zimbabwe 31.1.1986 LHB RM																			
FC		10	17	1	576	105	36.00	1	3	563	332	8	41.50	2-18	0	0	3.53	7	
Lim		12	11	3	236	58	29.50	0	1	265	292	7	41.71	4-44	1	0	6.61	1	
20T		15	11	1	158	51*	15.80	0	1	179	239	8	29.87	3-22	0	0	8.01	2	
CARBERRY, Michael Alexander (Hampshire, England to Bangladesh, England Lions to United Arab Emirates, Hampshire to Scotland) b Croydon, Surrey 29.9.1980 LHB OB																			
FC		16	28	1	1385	164	51.29	6	4	252	110	4	27.50	1-0	0	0	2.61	9	
Lim		11	11	1	346	103	34.60	1	1	48	69	1	69.00	1-24	0	0	8.62	3	
20T		12	11	1	205	41	20.50	0	0	6	3	0					3.00	6	
Test	2009/10	1	2	0	64	34	32.00	0	0									1	
FC	2001	112	198	18	7832	204	43.51	23	36	1201	873	13	67.15	2-85	0	0	4.36	50	
Lim	1999	118	111	11	2901	121*	29.01	2	21	174	170	4	42.50	2-11	0	0	5.86	45	
20T	2003	66	61	9	1441	90	27.71	0	10	18	19	1	19.00	1-16	0	0	6.33	30	
CARTER, Andrew (Essex, Nottinghamshire, Nottinghamshire to Scotland) b Lincoln 27.8.1988 RHB RM																			
FC		3	5	1	45	16*	11.25	0	0	605	311	13	23.92	5-40	1	0	3.08	2	
Lim		3	1	1	5	5*		0	0	84	82	4	20.50	2-31	0	0	5.85	1	
20T		2								42	69	0					9.85	0	
FC	2009	5	6	1	49	16*	9.80	0	0	923	475	16	29.68	5-40	1	0	3.08	2	
Lim	2009	10	6	1	25	12	5.00	0	0	294	279	12	23.25	3-32	0	0	5.69	3	
CARTER, Neil Miller (Cape Cobras, Warwickshire, Warwickshire to Scotland) b Cape Town, Cape Province, South Africa 29.1.1975 LHB LMF																			
FC		11	20	3	617	99*	36.29	0	4	2138	1129	51	22.13	5-60	4	0	3.16	0	
Lim		12	12	0	418	101	34.83	1	2	542	539	12	44.91	2-28	0	0	5.96	0	
20T		17	17	0	231	39	13.58	0	0	360	383	16	23.93	3-28	0	0	6.38	2	
FC	1999/00	107	148	24	2872	103	23.16	1	13	17725	10258	297	34.53	6-63	13	0	3.47	24	
Lim	1999/00	167	142	15	2853	135	22.46	3	12	7187	5804	220	26.38	5-31	6	2	4.84	14	
20T	2003	79	76	2	1217	58	16.44	0	2	1606	1869	77	24.27	5-19	0	1	6.98	11	
CHADWICK, Michael Steven (Sussex) b Leeds, Yorkshire 24.5.1989 RHB RMF																			
FC		1								114	74	1	74.00	1-41	0	0	3.89	0	
CHAMBERS, Maurice Anthony (Essex) b Port Antonio, Portland, Jamaica 14.9.1987 RHB RF																			
FC		11	16	5	53	14	4.81	0	0	1617	909	38	23.92	6-68	2	1	3.37	5	
20T		6	1	1	9	9*		0	0	126	208	6	34.66	2-29	0	0	9.90	1	
FC	2005	22	30	16	83	14	5.92	0	0	2959	1770	62	28.54	6-68	2	1	3.58	7	
Lim	2008	3	1	1	1	1*		0	0	90	93	3	31.00	1-26	0	0	6.20	1	
20T	2008	18	8	5	28	10*	9.33	0	0	312	461	17	27.11	3-31	0	0	8.86	6	
CHANDERPAUL, Shivnarine (Guyana, West Indies, West Indies XI, Lancashire, West Indies to Australia) b Unity Village, East Coast, Demerara, Guyana 16.8.1974 LHB LB																			
FC		8	14	1	698	120	53.69	2	5									2	
Test	1993/94	126	215	33	8969	203*	49.28	22	54	1680	845	8	105.62	1-2	0	0	3.01	52	
FC	1991/92	261	424	75	19007	303*	54.46	55	97	4634	2453	56	43.80	4-48	0	0	3.17	146	
Int	1994/95	261	245	38	8648	150	41.77	11	59	740	636	14	45.42	3-18	0	0	5.15	73	
Lim	1991/92	374	348	60	12110	150	42.04	12	88	1681	1388	56	24.78	4-22	2	0	4.95	109	
I20T	2005/06	22	22	5	343	41	20.17	0	0									7	
20T	2005/06	35	34	5	534	64	18.41	0	1									13	
CHAPPLE, Glen (Lancashire) b Skipton, Yorkshire 23.1.1974 RHB RMF																			
FC		14	22	6	403	54*	25.18	0	2	2236	1027	52	19.75	5-27	2	0	2.75	4	
Lim		3	1	0	13	13	13.00	0	0	132	136	0					6.18	0	
20T		14	7	2	77	28*	15.40	0	0	275	397	13	30.53	3-36	0	0	8.66	2	
FC	1992	252	346	65	7104	155	25.28	6	33	42769	21124	780	27.08	7-53	31	2	2.96	83	
Int	2006	1	1	0	14	14	14.00	0	0	24	14	0					3.50	0	
Lim	1993	270	154	41	2000	81*	17.69	0	9	11583	8716	299	29.15	6-18	4	4	4.51	60	
20T	2003	50	28	9	280	55*	14.73	0	1	935	1197	50	23.94	3-36	0	0	7.68	14	
CHAWLA, Piyush Pramod (Central Zone to India, Kings XI Punjab, Sussex to India, Uttar Pradesh, India to West Indies, India to Zimbabwe) b Aligarh, Uttar Pradesh, India 24.12.1988 LHB LBG																			
Test	2005/06	2	2	0	5	4	2.50	0	0	205	137	3	45.66	2-66	0	0	4.01	0	
FC	2005/06	61	89	9	2257	102*	28.21	1	17	13495	6742	247	27.29	6-46	15	2	2.99	29	
Int	2007	21	10	5	28	13*	5.60	0	0	1102	911	28	32.53	4-23	2	0	4.96	9	
Lim	2005/06	73	47	13	702	93	20.64	0	4	3547	2938	108	27.20	6-46	5	1	4.97	24	
I20T	2010	3								66	69	2	34.50	1-14	0	0	6.27	2	
20T	2006/07	56	31	10	291	33	13.85	0	0	1131	1378	57	24.17	3-22	0	0	7.31	18	
CHEETHAM, Steven Philip (Lancashire, Surrey) b Oldham, Lancashire 5.9.1987 RHB RFM																			
FC		1	1	1	0	0*		0	0	96	71	2	35.50	2-71	0	0	4.43	0	
Lim		6	3	1	17	13*	8.50	0	0	210	273	7	39.00	4-32	1	0	7.80	1	

Cmp	Debut	M	I	NO	Runs	HS	Avge	100	50	Balls	Runs	Wkts	Avge	BB	5i	10m	RpO	ct	st
FC	2007	2	1	1	0	0*		0	0	240	198	3	66.00	2-71	0	0	4.95	1	
Lim	2008	10	5	3	20	13*	10.00	0	0	378	399	14	28.50	4-32	1	0	6.33	1	
CHIGUMBURA, Elton (Mashonaland Eagles, Zimbabwe, Northamptonshire, Northamptonshire to Netherlands, Zimbabwe to Bangladesh, Zimbabwe to South Africa, Zimbabwe to West Indies, Zimbabweans to Bangladesh) b Kwekwe, Midlands, Zimbabwe 14.3.1986 RHB RM																			
FC		6	10	1	189	44	21.00	0	0	684	482	20	24.10	5-92	1	0	4.22	0	
Lim		1	1	0	24	24	24.00	0	0	44	44	1	44.00	1-44	0	0	6.00	0	
20T		13	13	6	218	58*	31.14	0	1	198	244	10	24.40	4-14	1	0	7.39	8	
Test	2004	6	12	0	187	71	15.58	0	1	829	498	9	55.33	5-54	1	0	3.60	2	
FC	2001/02	70	122	7	4014	186	34.90	3	28	8580	4709	167	28.19	5-33	4	0	3.29	29	
Int	2004	113	105	11	2292	79	24.38	0	13	2971	2953	79	37.37	4-28	1	0	5.96	36	
Lim	2002/03	166	152	21	3447	97*	26.31	0	20	4413	4283	119	35.99	4-23	2	0	5.82	50	
I20T	2006/07	12	11	1	138	34	13.80	0	0	156	212	12	17.66	4-31	1	0	8.15	5	
20T	2006/07	46	45	11	834	103*	24.52	1	3	698	864	42	20.57	5-13	4	1	7.42	17	
CHILTON, Mark James (Lancashire) b Sheffield, Yorkshire 2.10.1976 RHB RM																			
FC		16	29	4	750	69	30.00	0	4									6	
Lim		8	6	0	124	68	20.66	0	1	24	19	1	19.00	1-19	0	0	4.75	4	
20T		11	10	5	82	34	16.40	0	0									4	
FC	1997	182	297	27	8909	131	32.99	20	36	1343	667	12	55.58	2-3	0	0	2.98	132	
Lim	1997	184	171	24	4480	115	30.47	5	21	1106	1011	42	24.07	5-26	1	1	5.48	57	
20T	2003	52	38	15	376	38	16.34	0	0									20	
CHOPRA, Varun (Warwickshire) b Barking, Essex 21.6.1987 RHB LB																			
FC		9	18	1	409	54	24.05	0	1									9	
Lim		4	4	0	156	76	39.00	0	2									0	
20T		4	3	1	13	10*	6.50	0	0									0	
FC	2006	57	99	6	2661	155	28.61	2	17	131	78	0					3.57	49	
Lim	2006	38	36	1	1335	102	38.14	2	12	18	18	0					6.00	10	
20T	2006	16	15	4	149	51	13.54	0	1									2	
CHOUDHRY, Shaaiq Hussain (Worcestershire) b Rotherham, Yorkshire 3.11.1985 RHB SLA																			
FC		1	1	0	63	63	63.00	0	1	60	32	1	32.00	1-32	0	0	3.20	1	
Lim		7	6	4	115	39	57.50	0	0	198	213	6	35.50	4-54	1	0	6.45	3	
20T		3	3	3	15	8*		0	0	42	51	2	25.50	1-24	0	0	7.28	0	
FC	2007	3	4	2	199	75	99.50	0	3	138	86	1	86.00	1-32	0	0	3.73	1	
CHRISTIAN, Daniel Trevor (Australia, South Australia, Australia to New Zealand, Hampshire) b Camperdown, New South Wales, Australia 4.5.1983 RHB RFM																			
FC		1	2	0	64	36	32.00	0	0	133	115	2	57.50	2-115	0	0	5.18	0	
Lim		1	1	1	4	4*		0	0	48	46	1	46.00	1-46	0	0	5.75	1	
20T		12	8	4	33	10*	8.25	0	0	218	284	9	31.55	2-37	0	0	7.81	7	
FC	2007/08	19	30	3	664	72	24.59	0	4	3020	1786	56	31.89	5-24	2	0	3.54	18	
Lim	2006/07	33	31	9	833	94*	37.86	0	3	850	839	21	39.95	4-32	1	0	5.92	8	
I20T	2009/10	3	1	1	4	4*		0	0	42	69	2	34.50	2-29	0	0	9.85	0	
20T	2005/06	38	31	9	335	54	15.22	0	1	530	717	30	23.90	4-23	1	0	8.11	15	
CLARE, Jonathan Luke (Derbyshire) b Burnley, Lancashire 14.6.1986 RHB RM																			
FC		4	6	0	45	24	7.50	0	0	417	324	11	29.45	4-42	0	0	4.66	4	
Lim		5	5	1	50	21*	12.50	0	0	72	72	0					6.00	2	
20T		6	5	1	53	18	13.25	0	0									5	
FC	2007	24	32	5	655	129*	24.25	1	5	2973	1805	62	29.11	7-74	2	0	3.64	10	
Lim	2007	24	19	2	193	34	11.35	0	0	787	736	15	49.06	3-39	0	0	5.61	7	
20T	2008	12	8	2	63	18	10.50	0	0	53	72	2	36.00	2-20	0	0	8.15	6	
CLARK, Jordan (Lancashire) b Whitehaven, Cumberland 14.10.1990 RHB RM WK																			
Lim		1	1	0	32	32	32.00	0	0									0	
CLARKE, Rikki (Warwickshire, Warwickshire to Scotland) b Orsett, Essex 29.9.1981 RHB RFM																			
FC		15	28	5	673	127*	29.26	1	3	1277	743	32	23.21	6-63	1	0	3.49	23	
Lim		11	8	1	169	49*	24.14	0	0	138	192	0					8.34	7	
20T		17	14	6	200	39	25.00	0	0	114	177	1	177.00	1-48	0	0	9.31	9	
Test	2003/04	2	3	0	96	55	32.00	0	1	174	60	4	15.00	2-7	0	0	2.06	1	
FC	2002	118	188	19	6023	214	35.63	12	28	9852	6598	168	39.27	6-63	1	0	4.01	161	
Int	2003	20	13	0	144	39	11.07	0	0	469	415	11	37.72	2-28	0	0	5.30	11	
Lim	2001	150	124	18	2694	98*	25.41	0	12	3461	3297	80	41.21	4-49	2	0	5.71	70	
20T	2003	64	59	19	926	79*	23.15	0	3	780	1047	42	24.92	3-11	0	0	8.05	30	
CLAYDON, Mitchell Eric (Durham, Durham to United Arab Emirates) b Fairfield, New South Wales, Australia 25.11.1982 LHB RMF																			
FC		12	15	4	185	38*	16.81	0	0	1723	1087	35	31.05	3-17	0	0	3.78	2	
Lim		6	5	3	20	9*	10.00	0	0	221	189	6	31.50	3-51	0	0	5.13	0	
20T		8	1	1	0	0*		0	0	138	209	4	52.25	1-17	0	0	9.08	1	
FC	2005	31	33	6	391	40	14.48	0	0	4111	2493	70	35.61	4-90	0	0	3.63	5	
Lim	2006	28	15	3	86	19	7.16	0	0	1207	973	28	34.75	3-31	0	0	4.83	0	
20T	2006	27	9	6	40	12*	13.33	0	0	541	711	26	27.34	5-26	0	1	7.88	7	
CLIFF, Samuel James (Leicestershire) b Nottingham 3.10.1987 RHB RMF																			
FC		1								126	54	1	54.00	1-29	0	0	2.57	0	
Lim		3	1	1	0	0*		0	0	114	71	4	17.75	3-27	0	0	3.73	0	

Cmp	Debut	M	I	NO	Runs	HS	Avge	100	50	Balls	Runs	Wkts	Avge	BB	5i	10m	RpO	ct	st
20T		1	1	1	1	1*		0	0	18	28	1	28.00	1-28	0	0	9.33	0	
FC	2007	7	7	2	71	26	14.20	0	0	878	513	14	36.64	4-42	0	0	3.50	1	
Lim	2008	10	4	2	10	9	5.00	0	0	432	379	10	37.90	4-26	1	0	5.26	1	
20T	2008	6	2	1	5	4	5.00	0	0	108	139	2	69.50	1-24	0	0	7.72	2	

COBB, Joshua James (Leicestershire) b Leicester 17.8.1990 RHB LB

Cmp	Debut	M	I	NO	Runs	HS	Avge	100	50	Balls	Runs	Wkts	Avge	BB	5i	10m	RpO	ct	st
FC		5	10	2	153	55*	19.12	0	1	48	38	0					4.75	3	
Lim		7	7	1	105	43*	17.50	0	0	126	107	2	53.50	1-25	0	0	5.09	3	
20T		8	5	1	31	15	7.75	0	0	54	101	2	50.50	2-16	0	0	11.22	3	
FC	2007	28	48	5	1105	148*	25.69	1	7	336	243	5	48.60	2-11	0	0	4.33	12	
Lim	2008	17	15	2	222	43*	17.07	0	0	132	119	3	39.66	1-12	0	0	5.40	5	
20T	2008	9	6	2	33	15	8.25	0	0	54	101	2	50.50	2-16	0	0	11.22	3	

COETZER, Kyle James (Scotland, Durham, Durham to United Arab Emirates, Scotland to Kenya, Scotland to United Arab Emirates) b Aberdeen, Scotland 14.4.1984 RHB RMF

Cmp	Debut	M	I	NO	Runs	HS	Avge	100	50	Balls	Runs	Wkts	Avge	BB	5i	10m	RpO	ct	st
FC		7	13	1	302	72	25.16	0	2	42	33	0					4.71	2	
Lim		2	2	1	43	35	43.00	0	0									1	
FC	2004	42	74	9	2248	172	34.58	5	7	150	71	2	35.50	2-16	0	0	2.84	26	
Int	2008	5	5	0	132	51	26.40	0	1	12	23	0					11.50	3	
Lim	2003	58	56	7	1479	127	30.18	1	9	96	96	0					6.00	22	
I20T	2008	9	9	1	234	48*	29.25	0	0	48	47	5	9.40	3-25	0	0	5.87	2	
20T	2007	23	22	2	469	64	23.45	0	1	78	85	6	14.16	3-25	0	0	6.53	5	

COLES, Matthew Thomas (Kent) b Maidstone, Kent 26.5.1990 LHB RM

Cmp	Debut	M	I	NO	Runs	HS	Avge	100	50	Balls	Runs	Wkts	Avge	BB	5i	10m	RpO	ct	st
FC		14	23	6	378	51	22.23	0	1	1680	1040	27	38.51	4-55	0	0	3.71	4	
Lim		6	1	0	1	1	1.00	0	0	144	148	14	10.57	4-45	1	0	6.16	1	
20T		14	9	1	60	16*	7.50	0	0	224	324	15	21.60	3-30	0	0	8.67	5	
FC	2009	16	25	6	408	51	21.47	0	1	1786	1170	29	40.34	4-55	0	0	3.93	4	
Lim	2009	10	3	0	11	5	3.66	0	0	246	275	18	15.27	4-45	1	0	6.70	1	

COLLINGWOOD, Paul David (Durham, England, Delhi Daredevils, England to Bangladesh, England to South Africa, England to Scotland, England to United Arab Emirates, England to West Indies) b Shotley Bridge, Co Durham 26.5.1976 RHB RM

Cmp	Debut	M	I	NO	Runs	HS	Avge	100	50	Balls	Runs	Wkts	Avge	BB	5i	10m	RpO	ct	st
Test		4	6	0	119	82	19.83	0	1	66	25	0					2.27	8	
FC		5	7	0	131	82	18.71	0	1	108	36	1	36.00	1-11	0	0	2.00	8	
Int		12	12	0	344	95	28.66	0	1	192	144	4	36.00	1-8	0	0	4.50	4	
Lim		12	12	0	344	95	28.66	0	1	192	144	4	36.00	1-8	0	0	4.50	4	
I20T		2	2	0	25	21	12.50	0	0	6	8	0					8.00	0	
20T		4	2	0	25	21	12.50	0	0	44	42	4	10.50	4-13	1	0	5.72	0	
Test	2003/04	63	109	10	4176	206	42.18	10	20	1719	945	15	63.00	3-23	0	0	3.29	87	
FC	1996	188	325	26	10977	206	36.71	24	56	9665	4928	121	40.72	5-52	1	0	3.05	214	
Int	2001	189	173	35	4978	120*	36.07	5	26	4898	4095	106	38.63	6-31	3	1	5.01	105	
Lim	1995	359	337	59	9469	120*	34.06	8	54	9444	7651	221	34.61	6-31	4	1	4.86	182	
I20T	2005	33	31	2	561	79	19.34	0	3	222	329	16	20.56	4-22	1	0	8.89	12	
20T	2005	52	47	5	855	79	20.35	0	6	463	579	36	16.08	5-14	2	1	7.50	16	

COLLINS, Pedro Tyrone (Barbados, Middlesex, Middlesex to Netherlands) b Boscobelle, St Peter, Barbados 12.8.1976 RHB LFM

Cmp	Debut	M	I	NO	Runs	HS	Avge	100	50	Balls	Runs	Wkts	Avge	BB	5i	10m	RpO	ct	st
FC		10	13	4	36	13	4.00	0	0	1708	999	36	27.75	4-46	0	0	3.50	0	
Lim		6	3	2	13	6*	13.00	0	0	234	219	9	24.33	3-42	0	0	5.61	2	
20T		16	2	1	1	1*	1.00	0	0	324	422	16	26.37	3-27	0	0	7.81	2	
Test	1998/99	32	47	7	235	24	5.87	0	0	6964	3671	106	34.63	6-53	3	0	3.16	7	
FC	1996/97	141	178	51	837	25	6.59	0	0	24193	12523	478	26.19	6-24	13	0	3.10	30	
Int	1999/00	30	12	5	30	10*	4.28	0	0	1577	1212	39	31.07	5-43	0	1	4.61	8	
Lim	1997/98	98	39	12	166	55*	6.14	0	1	4717	3444	149	23.11	7-11	3	2	4.38	17	
20T	2006	29	5	3	3	1*	1.50	0	0	598	777	26	29.88	3-13	0	0	7.79	3	

COLLYMORE, Corey Dalanelo (Sussex) b Boscobelle, St Peter, Barbados 21.12.1977 RHB RFM

Cmp	Debut	M	I	NO	Runs	HS	Avge	100	50	Balls	Runs	Wkts	Avge	BB	5i	10m	RpO	ct	st
FC		14	17	8	78	19*	8.66	0	0	2484	1133	57	19.87	6-48	2	0	2.73	3	
Test	1998/99	30	52	27	197	16*	7.88	0	0	6337	3004	93	32.30	7-57	4	1	2.84	6	
FC	1998/99	134	187	85	819	23	8.02	0	0	22970	10717	406	26.39	7-57	12	2	2.79	45	
Int	1999	84	35	17	104	13*	5.77	0	0	4074	2924	83	35.22	5-51	1	1	4.30	12	
Lim	1999	131	50	25	151	13*	6.04	0	0	6139	4374	139	31.46	5-27	1	2	4.27	20	
20T	2006	6	2	1	5	4	5.00	0	0	95	133	3	44.33	1-21	0	0	8.40	4	

COMBER, Michael Andrew (Essex) b Colchester, Essex 26.10.1989 RHB RMF

Cmp	Debut	M	I	NO	Runs	HS	Avge	100	50	Balls	Runs	Wkts	Avge	BB	5i	10m	RpO	ct	st
FC		2	3	0	19	19	6.33	0	0	134	94	4	23.50	2-34	0	0	4.20	1	
Lim		1	1	1	52	52*		0	1									0	
20T		1	1	0	5	5	5.00	0	0									0	

COMPTON, Nicholas Richard Denis (Somerset) b Durban, Natal, South Africa 26.6.1983 RHB OB

Cmp	Debut	M	I	NO	Runs	HS	Avge	100	50	Balls	Runs	Wkts	Avge	BB	5i	10m	RpO	ct	st
FC		11	17	3	465	72	33.21	0	2	86	87	2	43.50	1-1	0	0	6.07	5	
Lim		15	15	0	432	73	28.80	0	6									7	
20T		8	8	0	165	74	20.62	0	1									2	
FC	2004	65	114	12	3453	190	33.85	8	14	164	215	3	71.66	1-1	0	0	7.86	33	
Lim	2001	71	65	12	1957	131	36.92	4	12	61	53	1	53.00	1-0	0	0	5.21	36	
20T	2004	37	31	1	417	74	13.90	0	2									15	

CONWAY, Danny Oliver (Oxford MCCU) b Stockton-on-Tees, Co Durham 1.5.1985 RHB RM

Cmp	Debut	M	I	NO	Runs	HS	Avge	100	50	Balls	Runs	Wkts	Avge	BB	5i	10m	RpO	ct	st
FC		3	2	1	6	6	6.00	0	0	456	249	6	41.50	2-36	0	0	3.27	0	

Cmp	Debut	M	I	NO	Runs	HS	Avge	100	50	Balls	Runs	Wkts	Avge	BB	5i	10m	RpO	ct	st
COOK, Alastair Nathan (England, England Lions, Essex, England to Bangladesh, England to South Africa) b Gloucester 25.12.1984 LHB OB																			
Test		6	10	0	226	110	22.60	1	0									4	
FC		14	24	1	773	110	33.60	2	3	48	36	1	36.00	1-33	0	0	4.50	12	
Lim		8	8	1	242	101*	34.57	1	1									3	
20T		11	11	1	388	73	38.80	0	3									5	
Test	2005/06	60	108	6	4364	173	42.78	13	22	6	1	0					1.00	52	
FC	2003	133	237	18	9700	195	44.29	26	52	270	205	6	34.16	3-13	0	0	4.55	127	
Int	2006	26	26	0	858	102	33.00	1	5									10	
Lim	2003	75	74	6	2486	125	36.55	5	14	18	10	0					3.33	33	
I20T	2007	4	4	0	61	26	15.25	0	0									1	
20T	2005	28	27	2	834	100*	33.36	1	5									9	
COOK, Simon James (Kent, Kent to Scotland) b Oxford 15.1.1977 RHB RFM																			
FC		15	24	7	205	26*	12.05	0	0	1989	1132	37	30.59	4-62	0	0	3.41	2	
Lim		8	2	1	10	9	10.00	0	0	258	212	7	30.28	2-13	0	0	4.93	0	
20T		16	6	5	19	8*	19.00	0	0	342	413	21	19.66	3-13	0	0	7.24	5	
FC	1999	132	170	29	2312	93*	16.39	0	6	20094	10526	330	31.89	8-63	12	0	3.14	33	
Lim	1997	179	107	33	1244	67*	16.81	0	2	7873	6195	224	27.65	6-37	5	2	4.72	28	
20T	2003	67	21	13	134	25*	16.75	0	0	1429	1761	81	21.74	3-13	0	0	7.39	14	
COPE, Alan Charles (Loughborough MCCU) b Guildford, Surrey 17.7.1988 RHB RM																			
FC		2	3	0	33	18	11.00	0	0	24	24	0					6.00	0	
FC	2008	3	5	0	84	51	16.80	0	1	24	24	0					6.00	0	
CORK, Dominic Gerald (Hampshire, Hampshire to Scotland) b Newcastle-under-Lyme, Staffordshire 7.8.1971 RHB RFM																			
FC		13	17	3	380	55	27.14	0	2	2444	1042	45	23.15	5-50	2	0	2.55	8	
Lim		10	9	4	101	28	20.20	0	0	378	429	12	35.75	3-30	0	0	6.81	2	
20T		19	9	2	56	15	8.00	0	0	413	455	15	30.33	2-9	0	0	6.61	4	
Test	1995	37	56	8	864	59	18.00	0	3	7678	3906	131	29.81	7-43	5	0	3.05	18	
FC	1990	312	450	60	9797	200*	25.12	8	53	52643	25637	967	26.51	9-43	35	5	2.92	231	
Int	1992	32	21	3	180	31*	10.00	0	0	1772	1368	41	33.36	3-27	0	0	4.63	6	
Lim	1991	308	234	39	4157	93	21.31	0	19	14465	10406	380	27.38	6-21	13	4	4.31	112	
20T	2003	65	44	12	401	28	12.53	0	0	1187	1390	56	24.82	4-16	1	0	7.02	12	
COSGROVE, Mark James (South Australia, Glamorgan) b Elizabeth, Adelaide, South Australia, Australia 14.6.1984 LHB RM																			
FC		15	26	2	1187	142	49.45	5	4	210	140	3	46.66	1-12	0	0	4.00	10	
Lim		10	8	0	397	88	49.62	0	5	96	120	3	40.00	2-21	0	0	7.50	4	
20T		16	16	0	562	89	35.12	0	4	42	71	2	35.50	1-6	0	0	10.14	2	
FC	2002/03	90	160	11	6449	233	43.28	19	37	2520	1437	35	41.05	3-3	0	0	3.42	61	
Int	2005/06	3	3	0	112	74	37.33	0	1	30	13	1	13.00	1-1	0	0	2.60	0	
Lim	2002/03	96	93	4	3178	121	35.70	3	25	905	964	17	56.70	2-21	0	0	6.39	28	
20T	2005/06	41	40	2	1020	89	26.84	0	6	153	260	6	43.33	2-11	0	0	10.19	8	
COSKER, Dean Andrew (Glamorgan, MCC to United Arab Emirates) b Weymouth, Dorset 7.1.1978 RHB SLA																			
FC		16	24	10	268	49*	19.14	0	0	2592	1128	51	22.11	5-93	1	0	2.61	7	
Lim		11	7	5	51	22*	25.50	0	0	438	415	11	37.72	4-33	1	0	5.68	2	
20T		12	4	2	8	6	4.00	0	0	222	278	9	30.88	2-23	0	0	7.51	3	
FC	1996	178	232	71	2174	52	13.50	0	1	33117	15890	445	35.70	6-91	7	1	2.87	110	
Lim	1996	201	106	47	646	50*	10.94	0	1	8539	6822	205	33.27	5-54	3	1	4.79	78	
20T	2003	63	21	16	67	16*	13.40	0	0	1086	1459	49	29.77	3-18	0	0	8.06	19	
COUGHTRIE, Richard George (Oxford MCCU) b North Shields, Co Durham 1.9.1988 RHB WK																			
FC		3	5	1	84	43	21.00	0	0									4	
FC	2009	5	7	1	115	43	19.16	0	0									6	
COX, Oliver Benjamin (Worcestershire) b Wordsley, Stourbridge, Worcestershire 2.2.1992 RHB WK																			
FC		9	16	4	218	59	18.16	0	1									18	1
Lim		7	3	2	9	9*	9.00	0	0									7	2
20T		8	5	3	13	6*	6.50	0	0									2	2
FC	2009	10	17	4	279	61	21.46	0	2									22	2
CROFT, Robert Damien Bale (Glamorgan) b Morriston, Swansea, Glamorgan, Wales 25.5.1970 RHB OB																			
FC		9	14	3	244	63	22.18	0	2	1942	805	26	30.96	4-20	0	0	2.48	0	
Lim		3	3	1	74	53*	37.00	0	1	144	132	1	132.00	1-31	0	0	5.50	0	
20T		16	6	3	37	22*	12.33	0	0	347	343	22	15.59	3-19	0	0	5.93	3	
Test	1996	21	34	8	421	37*	16.19	0	0	4619	1825	49	37.24	5-95	1	0	2.37	10	
FC	1989	391	576	103	12609	143	26.65	8	54	86538	39995	1133	35.30	8-66	49	9	2.77	175	
Int	1996	50	36	12	345	32	14.37	0	0	2466	1743	45	38.73	3-51	0	0	4.24	11	
Lim	1989	402	337	61	6474	143	23.45	4	32	18349	13270	409	32.44	6-20	6	1	4.33	94	
20T	2003	68	44	11	670	62*	20.30	0	4	1371	1647	68	24.22	3-12	0	0	7.20	21	
CROFT, Steven John (Lancashire) b Blackpool, Lancashire 11.10.1984 RHB RMF																			
FC		16	26	3	883	93	38.39	0	8	84	51	1	51.00	1-17	0	0	3.64	13	
Lim		13	12	3	436	93*	48.44	0	4	150	176	3	58.66	1-17	0	0	7.04	5	
20T		17	16	1	394	88	26.26	0	2	53	70	5	14.00	3-18	0	0	7.92	13	
FC	2005	59	90	9	2509	122	30.97	1	17	2149	1375	31	44.35	4-51	0	0	3.83	48	
Lim	2002	76	67	15	1663	93*	31.98	0	11	1392	1241	39	31.82	4-24	2	0	5.34	27	
20T	2006	58	53	8	1174	88	26.08	0	5	423	580	22	26.36	3-6	0	0	8.22	31	

Cmp	Debut	M	I	NO	Runs	HS	Avge	100	50	Balls	Runs	Wkts	Avge	BB	5i	10m	RpO	ct	st
CROSS, Gareth David (Lancashire) b Bury, Lancashire 20.6.1984 RHB RMF WK																			
FC		7	11	1	290	100*	29.00	1	1									12	
Lim		7	5	0	108	30	21.60	0	0									3	2
20T		17	12	3	184	65*	20.44	0	1									7	2
FC	2005	15	24	2	599	100*	27.22	1	4									39	8
Lim	2002	42	34	3	599	76	19.32	0	1	36	26	2	13.00	2-26	0	0	4.33	24	11
20T	2006	51	37	9	497	65*	17.75	0	2									32	12
DAGGETT, Lee Martin (Northamptonshire, Northamptonshire to Netherlands) b Bury, Lancashire 1.10.1982 RHB RM																			
FC		12	17	8	167	48	18.55	0	0	1930	1058	30	35.26	4-25	0	0	3.28	3	
Lim		9	3	2	9	5	9.00	0	0	402	319	18	17.72	4-17	1	0	4.76	2	
20T		14	2	1	3	2*	3.00	0	0	120	190	5	38.00	1-14	0	0	9.50	1	
FC	2003	39	50	21	302	48	10.41	0	0	5673	3328	91	36.57	8-94	2	0	3.52	5	
Lim	2006	41	14	11	78	14*	26.00	0	0	1724	1419	54	26.27	4-17	2	0	4.93	6	
20T	2007	28	5	2	7	3*	2.33	0	0	288	420	11	38.18	2-19	0	0	8.75	6	
DALRYMPLE, James William Murray (Glamorgan) b Nairobi, Kenya 21.1.1981 RHB OB																			
FC		15	22	0	554	105	25.18	1	2	762	391	11	35.54	4-71	0	0	3.07	19	
Lim		7	7	1	142	54*	23.66	0	1	162	163	3	54.33	2-55	0	0	6.03	5	
20T		16	15	3	281	46*	23.41	0	0	192	246	8	30.75	3-25	0	0	7.68	4	
FC	2001	123	192	16	6013	244	34.16	10	32	12485	6893	160	43.08	5-49	1	0	3.31	82	
Int	2006	27	26	1	487	67	19.48	0	2	840	666	14	47.57	2-5	0	0	4.75	12	
Lim	2000	161	149	29	3252	107	27.10	2	19	4877	4136	113	36.60	4-14	2	0	5.08	65	
I20T	2006	3	3	0	60	32	20.00	0	0	30	39	2	19.50	1-10	0	0	7.80	1	
20T	2004	60	55	9	1171	63	25.45	0	4	685	929	39	23.82	3-25	0	0	8.13	16	
DANISH Parabha Shanker KANERIA (Habib Bank, Karachi Zebras, Sind Dolphins, Essex, Pakistan to Australia, Pakistan to England, Pakistan, Pakistan to New Zealand) b Karachi, Sind, Pakistan 16.12.1980 RHB LB																			
Test		3	5	1	54	16*	13.50	0	0	540	377	7	53.85	2-49	0	0	4.18	0	
FC		9	14	2	82	16*	6.83	0	0	1900	1130	30	37.66	4-51	0	0	3.56	1	
Lim		6	2	1	1	1*	1.00	0	0	246	213	5	42.60	2-41	0	0	5.19	1	
20T		12	4	1	24	9*	8.00	0	0	273	337	18	18.72	3-32	0	0	7.40	0	
Test	2000/01	61	84	33	360	29	7.05	0	0	17697	9082	261	34.79	7-77	15	2	3.07	18	
FC	1998/99	180	229	81	1508	65	10.18	0	1	47813	23489	884	26.57	8-59	61	10	2.94	61	
Int	2001/02	18	10	8	12	6*	6.00	0	0	854	682	15	45.46	3-31	0	0	4.79	2	
Lim	1998/99	153	69	33	348	64	9.66	0	1	7576	5401	232	23.28	6-33	7	7	4.27	29	
20T	2004/05	57	23	8	97	12	6.46	0	0	1183	1431	75	19.08	4-22	2	0	7.25	10	
DAVEY, Joshua Henry (Scotland, Middlesex, Middlesex to Netherlands, Scotland to Netherlands) b Aberdeen, Scotland 3.8.1990 RHB RM																			
FC		4	7	0	220	72	31.42	0	3	162	107	2	53.50	2-41	0	0	3.96	3	
Lim		2	2	0	26	15	13.00	0	0	18	24	0					8.00	1	
20T		2	2	1	7	7*	7.00	0	0	30	48	0					9.60	2	
Int	2010	4	4	0	46	24	11.50	0	0	122	94	6	15.66	5-9	0	1	4.62	2	
Lim	2010	7	7	1	74	24	12.33	0	0	140	118	6	19.66	5-9	0	1	5.05	3	
DAVIES, Anthony Mark (Durham) b Stockton-on-Tees, Co Durham 4.10.1980 RHB RM																			
FC		6	5	2	32	27	10.66	0	0	786	282	2	141.00	2-10	0	0	2.15	0	
Lim		1								48	51	0					6.37	0	
FC	2002	83	107	41	733	62	11.10	0	1	12540	5726	253	22.63	8-24	12	2	2.74	17	
Lim	1998	73	36	14	166	31*	7.54	0	0	2982	2087	68	30.69	4-13	1	0	4.19	10	
20T	2003	9	4	3	11	6	11.00	0	0	204	241	8	30.12	2-14	0	0	7.08	2	
DAVIES, Steven Michael (England, England Lions, Surrey, England to South Africa, England Lions to United Arab Emirates) b Bromsgrove, Worcestershire 17.6.1986 LHB WK																			
FC		14	22	3	1090	137	57.36	2	9									38	
Int		5	5	0	197	87	39.40	0	1									7	
Lim		19	19	1	854	101	47.44	1	7									21	2
I20T		2	2	0	42	33	21.00	0	0									2	1
20T		15	15	0	431	89	28.73	0	3									16	3
FC	2005	91	152	18	5371	192	40.08	8	28									275	14
Int	2009/10	6	6	0	202	87	33.66	0	1									8	
Lim	2002	107	97	12	3183	119	37.44	5	19									96	27
I20T	2008/09	3	3	0	69	33	23.00	0	0									2	1
20T	2006	53	48	5	989	89	23.00	0	5									30	7
DAVIS, Christian Arthur Linghorne (Northamptonshire) b Milton Keynes, Buckinghamshire 11.10.1992 RHB LFM																			
Lim		1								45	44	0					5.86	0	
DAWSON, Liam Andrew (Hampshire, Hampshire to Scotland) b Swindon, Wiltshire 1.3.1990 RHB SLA																			
FC		8	13	1	348	86	29.00	0	3	198	107	1	107.00	1-61	0	0	3.24	4	
Lim		9	9	2	162	47*	23.14	0	0	180	169	2	84.50	1-36	0	0	5.63	4	
20T		9	5	0	29	19	5.80	0	0	82	106	0					7.75	3	
FC	2007	29	44	6	1112	100*	29.26	1	7	1123	741	17	43.58	2-3	0	0	3.95	17	
Lim	2007	38	32	7	632	69*	25.28	0	2	1041	928	27	34.37	4-45	2	0	5.34	21	
20T	2008	25	17	4	105	23	8.07	0	0	232	305	8	38.12	3-25	0	0	7.88	12	
DAWSON, Richard Kevin James (Gloucestershire) b Doncaster, Yorkshire 4.8.1980 RHB OB																			
Lim		8	4	3	32	17*	32.00	0	0	291	271	10	27.10	3-41	0	0	5.58	6	
20T		8	5	1	38	24*	9.50	0	0	156	217	10	21.70	2-20	0	0	8.34	2	

Cmp	Debut	M	I	NO	Runs	HS	Avge	100	50	Balls	Runs	Wkts	Avge	BB	5i	10m	RpO	ct	st
Test	2001/02	7	13	3	114	19*	11.40	0	0	1116	677	11	61.54	4-134	0	0	3.64	3	
FC	2000	103	153	17	2927	87	21.52	0	12	15467	8770	199	44.07	6-82	5	0	3.40	63	
Lim	1999	127	78	18	626	41	10.43	0	0	4766	3918	128	30.60	4-13	5	0	4.93	45	
20T	2004	42	22	5	178	27*	10.47	0	0	809	1045	39	26.79	3-24	0	0	7.75	13	
DE BRUYN, Zander (Lions, Somerset, Somerset to India) b Johannesburg, Transvaal, South Africa 5.7.1975 RHB RFM																			
FC		14	21	0	814	95	38.76	0	5	566	386	12	32.16	4-23	0	0	4.09	10	
Lim		13	13	2	555	122*	50.45	2	3	320	329	16	20.56	3-27	0	0	6.16	4	
20T		19	18	8	303	95*	30.30	0	1	168	248	7	35.42	2-21	0	0	8.85	8	
Test	2004/05	3	5	1	155	83	38.75	0	1	216	92	3	30.66	2-32	0	0	2.55	0	
FC	1995/96	167	279	27	10008	266*	39.71	21	54	13123	7573	191	39.64	7-67	3	0	3.46	103	
Lim	1995/96	181	165	33	4829	122*	36.58	5	30	4471	4045	128	31.60	5-44	2	1	5.42	43	
20T	2004/05	79	72	21	1544	95*	30.27	0	6	678	995	34	29.26	4-18	1	0	8.80	17	
DENLY, Joseph Liam (Kent, England to South Africa, England to United Arab Emirates, Kent to Scotland) b Canterbury, Kent 16.3.1986 RHB LB																			
FC		18	33	0	848	106	25.69	1	5	318	215	3	71.66	2-100	0	0	4.05	10	
Lim		10	10	1	429	102*	47.66	1	2									3	
20T		12	12	0	382	65	31.83	0	1									6	
FC	2004	70	121	5	3906	149	33.67	10	19	1195	662	13	50.92	2-13	0	0	3.32	33	
Int	2009	9	9	0	268	67	29.77	0	2									5	
Lim	2004	77	75	7	2296	115	33.76	4	11	30	35	1	35.00	1-20	0	0	7.00	24	
I20T	2009	5	5	0	20	14	4.00	0	0	6	9	1	9.00	1-9	0	0	9.00	1	
20T	2004	60	57	3	1341	91	24.83	0	7	18	32	1	32.00	1-9	0	0	10.66	23	
DENT, Christopher David James (Gloucestershire, Gloucestershire to Netherlands) b Bristol 20.1.1991 LHB SLA																			
FC		16	31	3	725	98	25.89	0	4	66	43	0					3.90	24	
Lim		4	3	0	13	8	4.33	0	0									0	
20T		7	6	0	162	63	27.00	0	1									0	
Lim	2009	6	3	0	13	8	4.33	0	0	12	17	1	17.00	1-17	0	0	8.50	2	
DERNBACH, Jade Winston (Surrey) b Johannesburg, Transvaal, South Africa 3.3.1986 RHB RMF																			
FC		15	20	9	154	56*	14.00	0	1	2682	1390	51	27.25	5-68	2	0	3.11	1	
Lim		11	5	1	36	31	9.00	0	0	456	551	12	45.91	3-29	0	0	7.25	3	
20T		5	2	1	22	12	22.00	0	0	90	98	3	32.66	2-22	0	0	6.53	1	
FC	2003	49	62	23	404	56*	10.35	0	1	7453	4505	129	34.92	6-47	5	0	3.62	4	
Lim	2005	60	27	10	147	31	8.64	0	0	2456	2592	95	27.28	5-31	3	2	6.33	15	
20T	2005	34	8	2	36	12	6.00	0	0	589	894	21	42.57	3-32	0	0	9.10	7	
DEXTER, Neil John (Middlesex, Middlesex to Netherlands) b Johannesburg, Transvaal, South Africa 21.8.1984 RHB RM																			
FC		12	21	2	907	118	47.73	2	5	720	378	13	29.07	3-50	0	0	3.15	10	
Lim		11	9	2	255	56*	36.42	0	1	384	324	2	162.00	1-31	0	0	5.06	2	
20T		16	16	3	349	62*	26.84	0	1	275	317	14	22.64	2-8	0	0	6.91	6	
FC	2005	51	81	12	2955	146	42.82	7	15	2064	1167	28	41.67	3-50	0	0	3.39	44	
Lim	2005	52	45	8	1250	135*	33.78	2	5	1120	968	19	50.94	3-17	0	0	5.18	12	
20T	2006	53	47	6	870	73	21.21	0	2	419	555	19	29.21	3-27	0	0	7.94	22	
DINGLE, Lewis Allen (Oxford University) b Blackpool, Lancashire 16.9.1988 RHB RMF																			
FC		1								114	73	1	73.00	1-36	0	0	3.84	0	
FC	2007	3	3	1	7	6*	3.50	0	0	252	171	1	171.00	1-36	0	0	4.07	0	
DI VENUTO, Michael James (Durham, Durham to Scotland, Durham to United Arab Emirates) b Hobart, Tasmania, Australia 12.12.1973 LHB RM,LBG																			
FC		16	27	3	1092	129	45.50	3	7									29	
Lim		3	3	0	71	37	23.66	0	0									0	
FC	1991/92	315	556	41	23974	254*	46.55	57	141	807	484	5	96.80	1-0	0	0	3.59	379	
Int	1996/97	9	9	0	241	89	26.77	0	2									1	
Lim	1992/93	299	293	18	9082	173*	33.02	15	46	200	181	5	36.20	1-10	0	0	5.43	123	
20T	2003	46	44	4	951	95*	23.77	0	7	78	88	5	17.60	3-19	0	0	6.76	10	
DIXEY, Paul Garrod (Kent) b Canterbury, Kent 2.11.1987 RHB WK																			
FC		1	1	0	22	22	22.00	0	0									0	3
FC	2005	13	22	1	334	103	15.90	1	0									27	6
Lim	2007	4	3	2	32	16	32.00	0	0									4	
DUNN, Matthew Peter (Surrey) b Egham, Surrey 5.5.1992 LHB RFM																			
FC		1								89	48	3	16.00	3-48	0	0	3.23	0	
DURANDT, Luc Etienne (Durham MCCU) b Johannesburg, Transvaal, South Africa 1.9.1989 LHB RM																			
FC		2	3	2	53	20*	53.00	0	0									1	
DURSTON, Wesley John (Derbyshire, Unicorns, Derbyshire to Netherlands, Somerset to India) b Taunton, Somerset 6.10.1980 RHB OB																			
FC		6	11	0	240	69	21.81	0	1	96	76	1	76.00	1-9	0	0	4.75	9	
Lim		11	11	1	378	117	37.80	1	2	213	189	5	37.80	2-28	0	0	5.32	4	
20T		16	15	3	445	111	37.08	1	2	108	139	6	23.16	2-18	0	0	7.72	6	
FC	2002	40	68	12	1966	146*	35.10	1	14	2253	1496	25	59.84	3-23	0	0	3.98	43	
Lim	2000	68	58	17	1342	117	32.73	1	8	1023	1027	24	42.79	3-44	0	0	6.02	19	
20T	2003	54	45	10	831	111	23.74	1	3	322	477	23	20.73	3-25	0	0	8.88	20	

Cmp	Debut	M	I	NO	Runs	HS	Avge	100	50	Balls	Runs	Wkts	Avge	BB	5i	10m	RpO	ct	st
DU TOIT, Jacques (Leicestershire, Leicestershire to Scotland) b Port Elizabeth, Cape Province, South Africa 2.1.1980 RHB RMF																			
FC		13	20	1	899	154	47.31	2	6	12	20	0					10.00	16	
Lim		11	11	0	485	141	44.09	1	3									6	
20T		14	14	0	273	69	19.50	0	1									12	
FC	1998/99	28	43	3	1599	154	39.97	4	9	474	355	5	71.00	3-31	0	0	4.49	24	
Lim	2004/05	36	34	2	888	144	27.75	2	3	66	66	2	33.00	2-30	0	0	6.00	15	
20T	2008	31	30	3	480	69	17.77	0	1	32	41	2	20.50	2-15	0	0	7.68	22	
EDWARDS, Neil James (Nottinghamshire, Nottinghamshire to Scotland) b Treliske, Truro, Cornwall 14.10.1983 LHB RM																			
FC		7	11	0	255	85	23.18	0	1									17	
Lim		2	1	0	17	17	17.00	0	0									1	
FC	2002	56	93	0	3153	212	33.90	3	16	287	194	2	97.00	1-16	0	0	4.05	52	
Lim	2006	8	7	0	141	65	20.14	0	1									2	
20T	2003	1	1	0	1	1	1.00	0	0									0	
EDWARDS, Philip Duncan (Kent) b Minster, Isle of Sheppey, Kent 16.4.1984 RHB RFM																			
FC		2	3	1	20	13	10.00	0	0	204	145	3	48.33	2-60	0	0	4.26	0	
FC	2004	12	15	8	121	43	17.28	0	0	1482	965	15	64.33	3-72	0	0	3.90	2	
Lim	2009	7	3	2	3	2*	3.00	0	0	204	241	7	34.42	3-57	0	0	7.08	0	
ELSTONE, Scott Liam (Nottinghamshire) b Burton-on-Trent, Staffordshire 10.6.1990 RHB OB																			
Lim		4	4	1	66	30	22.00	0	0	22	22	1	22.00	1-22	0	0	6.00	1	
20T		1																0	
ERVINE, Sean Michael (Southern Rocks, Hampshire, Hampshire to Scotland) b Harare, Zimbabwe 6.12.1982 LHB RM																			
FC		17	27	4	976	237*	42.43	1	5	2177	1073	20	53.65	4-31	0	0	2.95	7	
Lim		9	9	0	296	96	32.88	0	1	372	380	12	31.66	4-39	1	0	6.12	1	
20T		19	19	6	470	74*	36.15	0	3	264	386	16	24.12	4-12	1	0	8.77	4	
Test	2003	5	8	0	261	86	32.62	0	3	570	388	9	43.11	4-146	0	0	4.08	7	
FC	2000/01	117	185	19	5863	237*	35.31	11	30	13145	7838	181	43.30	6-82	5	0	3.57	96	
Int	2001/02	42	34	7	698	100	25.85	1	2	1649	1561	41	38.07	3-29	0	0	5.68	5	
Lim	2000/01	169	151	24	4035	167*	31.77	6	17	5994	5578	166	33.60	5-50	5	2	5.58	46	
20T	2005	66	63	14	1229	74*	25.08	0	6	770	1103	47	23.46	4-12	2	0	8.59	24	
EVANS, Daniel (Middlesex) b Hartlepool, Co Durham 24.7.1987 RHB RMF																			
FC		4	5	2	23	19*	7.66	0	0	615	397	11	36.09	5-87	1	0	3.87	1	
Lim		1	1	0	0	0	0.00	0	0	60	51	3	17.00	3-51	0	0	5.10	0	
FC	2007	19	23	6	75	19*	4.41	0	0	2637	1710	49	34.89	6-35	3	0	3.89	4	
Lim	2008	7	2	1	1	1*	1.00	0	0	388	342	12	28.50	3-36	0	0	5.28	0	
20T	2009	4	3	2	6	5*	6.00	0	0	60	102	0					10.20	1	
EVANS, Luke (Durham, Northamptonshire) b Sunderland, Co Durham 26.4.1987 RHB RMF																			
FC		3	4	3	20	8*	20.00	0	0	354	212	5	42.40	3-53	0	0	3.59	1	
Lim		2	1	1	1	1*		0	0	60	61	1	61.00	1-28	0	0	6.10	1	
FC	2007	4	6	4	21	8*	10.50	0	0	475	327	9	36.33	3-53	0	0	4.13	1	
Lim	2009	5	2	1	1	1*	1.00	0	0	144	156	5	31.20	2-53	0	0	6.50	1	
EVANS, Laurie John (Surrey, Warwickshire) b Lambeth, Surrey 12.10.1987 RHB RFM																			
FC		3	6	0	155	98	25.83	0	1	36	30	1	30.00	1-30	0	0	5.00	2	
Lim		1	1	0	3	3	3.00	0	0									1	
FC	2007	9	18	1	543	133*	31.94	1	3	36	30	1	30.00	1-30	0	0	5.00	6	
Lim	2009	2	2	1	39	36*	39.00	0	0									2	
20T	2009	1	1	0	7	7	7.00	0	0									0	
EVANS, Rhodri Francis (Loughborough MCCU) b Swansea, Glamorgan, Wales 6.12.1989 LHB RM																			
FC		2	2	0	55	44	27.50	0	0	144	100	1	100.00	1-57	0	0	4.16	1	
FC	2009	4	4	0	67	44	16.75	0	0	264	217	2	108.50	1-57	0	0	4.93	2	
FERLEY, Robert Steven (Kent) b Norwich, Norfolk 4.2.1982 RHB SLA																			
FC		1	2	0	20	19	10.00	0	0	156	142	2	71.00	1-54	0	0	5.46	0	
Lim		2	1	0	52	52	52.00	0	1	54	47	0					5.22	0	
FC	2001	34	41	10	650	78*	20.96	0	2	5083	3018	66	45.72	6-136	1	0	3.56	10	
Lim	2001	56	28	7	337	52	16.04	0	1	2471	2030	66	30.75	4-33	1	0	4.92	21	
20T	2004	18	7	4	23	16*	7.66	0	0	339	415	14	29.64	3-17	0	0	7.34	4	
FINN, Steven Thomas (England, Middlesex, England to Bangladesh, England Lions to United Arab Emirates) b Watford, Hertfordshire 4.4.1989 RHB RMF																			
Test		6	8	6	13	9*	6.50	0	0	876	566	28	20.21	5-42	2	0	3.87	0	
FC		13	19	9	47	18	4.70	0	0	2443	1410	64	22.03	9-37	4	1	3.46	1	
Lim		2								96	71	4	17.75	2-31	0	0	4.43	1	
20T		1								12	30	0					15.00	0	
Test	2009/10	8	9	7	13	9*	6.50	0	0	1182	743	32	23.21	5-42	2	0	3.77	1	
FC	2005	46	62	21	245	26*	5.97	0	0	7607	4589	162	28.32	9-37	5	1	3.62	11	
Lim	2007	32	9	2	35	13	5.00	0	0	1290	1112	37	30.05	3-23	0	0	5.17	4	
20T	2008	16	3	2	14	8	14.00	0	0	308	431	15	28.73	3-22	0	0	8.39	4	
FLETCHER, Luke Jack (Nottinghamshire) b Nottingham 18.9.1988 RHB RMF																			
FC		6	9	3	96	23*	16.00	0	0	1016	563	12	46.91	3-39	0	0	3.32	2	
Lim		6	3	1	16	14*	8.00	0	0	207	236	6	39.33	2-41	0	0	6.84	1	
20T		1								18	13	1	13.00	1-13	0	0	4.33	0	
FC	2008	15	17	6	217	92	19.72	0	1	2609	1433	42	34.11	4-38	0	0	3.29	2	

Cmp	Debut	M	I	NO	Runs	HS	Avge	100	50	Balls	Runs	Wkts	Avge	BB	5i	10m	RpO	ct	st
Lim	2008	21	12	5	79	40*	11.28	0	0	858	743	20	37.15	2-35	0	0	5.19	2	
20T	2009	11	2	1	2	1*	2.00	0	0	240	311	9	34.55	2-23	0	0	7.77	2	
FLOWER, Grant William (Essex, Essex to Netherlands) b Salisbury (now Harare), Zimbabwe 20.12.1970 RHB SLA																			
FC		3	5	2	123	46	41.00	0	0	54	32	1	32.00	1-19	0	0	3.55	3	
Lim		11	10	3	511	116	73.00	2	2	228	228	5	45.60	2-31	0	0	6.00	6	
20T		19	15	5	185	54	18.50	0	1	78	106	2	53.00	1-16	0	0	8.15	5	
Test	1992/93	67	123	6	3457	201*	29.54	6	15	3378	1537	25	61.48	4-41	0	0	2.73	43	
FC	1989/90	188	318	25	10898	243*	37.19	23	58	12511	5605	166	33.76	7-31	3	0	2.68	174	
Int	1992/93	219	212	18	6536	142*	33.69	6	40	5420	4187	104	40.25	4-32	2	0	4.63	86	
Lim	1990/91	363	342	37	10713	148*	35.12	13	70	8914	6682	188	35.54	4-32	3	0	4.49	140	
20T	2005	57	43	10	692	61	20.96	0	2	352	460	24	19.16	3-20	0	0	7.84	17	
FOOTITT, Mark Harold Alan (Derbyshire, Derbyshire to Netherlands) b Nottingham 25.11.1985 RHB LFM																			
FC		9	12	3	69	30	7.66	0	0	1436	786	23	34.17	4-78	0	0	3.28	3	
Lim		7	2	1	1	1	1.00	0	0	246	246	7	35.14	3-20	0	0	6.00	0	
FC	2005	18	19	8	118	30	10.72	0	0	2367	1515	46	32.93	5-45	2	0	3.84	4	
Lim	2001	9	2	1	1	1	1.00	0	0	312	291	10	29.10	3-20	0	0	5.59	0	
20T	2005	1								12	34	0					17.00	0	
FOSTER, James Savin (Essex, Essex to Netherlands, MCC to United Arab Emirates) b Whipps Cross, Leytonstone, Essex 15.4.1980 RHB WK																			
FC		16	27	1	839	169	32.26	1	4									48	5
Lim		11	7	2	130	58	26.00	0	1									9	3
20T		19	16	6	194	54*	19.40	0	1									5	9
Test	2001/02	7	12	3	226	48	25.11	0	0									17	1
FC	2000	174	263	30	8213	212	35.24	14	41	84	128	1	128.00	1-122	0	0	9.14	484	44
Int	2001/02	11	6	3	41	13	13.66	0	0									13	7
Lim	2000	163	123	34	2411	83*	27.08	0	11									193	53
I20T	2009	5	5	2	37	14*	12.33	0	0									3	3
20T	2003	77	64	17	969	62*	20.61	0	4									30	30
FRANKLIN, James Edward Charles (New Zealand, Wellington to New Zealand, Gloucestershire, Gloucestershire to Netherlands, New Zealand to South Africa, New Zealand to United Arab Emirates) b Wellington, New Zealand 7.11.1980 LHB LFM																			
FC		16	29	3	862	108	33.15	1	4	2006	1083	46	23.54	7-14	1	0	3.23	7	
Lim		11	11	4	466	133*	66.57	2	2	306	251	3	83.66	1-9	0	0	4.92	2	
20T		15	15	3	470	90	39.16	0	2	216	318	8	39.75	2-33	0	0	8.83	3	
Test	2000/01	26	36	6	644	122*	21.46	1	2	4399	2612	80	32.65	6-119	3	0	3.56	11	
FC	1998/99	132	201	28	5949	219	34.38	11	26	20726	10871	411	26.45	7-14	13	1	3.14	50	
Int	2000/01	75	53	19	636	45*	18.70	0	0	3149	2677	69	38.79	5-42	0	1	5.10	20	
Lim	1999/00	180	147	48	3065	133*	30.95	2	14	7250	5819	169	34.43	5-42	3	1	4.81	57	
I20T	2005/06	13	11	4	128	43	18.28	0	0	144	183	7	26.14	3-23	0	0	7.62	5	
20T	2004	58	53	14	1309	90	33.56	0	6	941	1281	35	36.60	3-23	0	0	8.16	16	
FRANKS, Paul John (Nottinghamshire, Nottinghamshire to Scotland) b Mansfield, Nottinghamshire 3.2.1979 LHB RFM																			
FC		16	22	1	765	114	36.42	1	6	2462	1129	42	26.88	3-15	0	0	2.75	1	
Lim		10	6	0	44	22	7.33	0	0	288	304	10	30.40	3-22	0	0	6.33	2	
20T		9	4	2	34	23*	17.00	0	0	144	231	5	46.20	2-45	0	0	9.62	1	
FC	1996	175	249	44	5643	123*	27.52	4	30	26597	14685	460	31.92	7-56	11	0	3.31	56	
Int	2000	1	1	0	4	4	4.00	0	0	54	48	0					5.33	1	
Lim	1997	167	122	36	1802	84*	20.95	0	5	6176	5151	176	29.26	6-27	3	2	5.00	26	
20T	2003	44	25	10	235	29*	15.66	0	0	381	564	17	33.17	2-12	0	0	8.88	5	
GALE, Andrew William (England Lions, Yorkshire, England Lions to United Arab Emirates, Yorkshire to Netherlands) b Dewsbury, Yorkshire 28.11.1983 LHB LB																			
FC		14	24	4	950	151*	47.50	3	4									2	
Lim		16	16	2	548	125*	39.14	1	2									6	
20T		14	14	2	382	65*	31.83	0	4									7	
FC	2004	61	97	5	3290	151*	35.76	9	14	24	47	1	47.00	1-33	0	0	11.75	26	
Lim	2001	92	84	10	2285	125*	30.87	1	12									16	
20T	2004	56	51	9	1172	91	27.90	0	9									26	
GALE, Daniel James (Durham MCCU) b Tadworth, Surrey 15.6.1989 RHB SLA																			
FC		2	1	0	37	37	37.00	0	0	468	287	8	35.87	4-94	0	0	3.67	1	
FC	2008	7	9	7	59	37	29.50	0	0	725	435	9	48.33	4-94	0	0	3.60	4	
Lim	2008	1	1	1	1	1*		0	0	54	58	0					6.44	0	
GANDAM, Harveer Singh (Loughborough MCCU) b Slough, Buckinghamshire 21.1.1990 RHB RFM																			
FC		2	2	0	44	33	22.00	0	0									1	
GATTING, Joe Stephen (Sussex, Sussex to India) b Brighton, Sussex 25.11.1987 RHB OB																			
FC		8	11	0	155	31	14.09	0	0	30	19	1	19.00	1-19	0	0	3.80	4	
Lim		10	10	2	230	71	28.75	0	2									4	
20T		17	14	4	157	30*	15.70	0	0									6	
FC	2009	12	17	0	465	152	27.35	1	1	30	19	1	19.00	1-19	0	0	3.80	6	
Lim	2009	23	22	3	555	99*	29.21	0	4	8	5	0					3.75	7	
20T	2009	24	18	4	213	30*	15.21	0	0									6	
GELDART, Callum John (Yorkshire) b Huddersfield, Yorkshire 17.12.1991 LHB RM																			
FC		1	1	0	17	17	17.00	0	0									0	

Cmp	Debut	M	I	NO	Runs	HS	Avge	100	50	Balls	Runs	Wkts	Avge	BB	5i	10m	RpO	ct	st
GIBBS, Herschelle Herman (Cape Cobras, South Africa, South Africa A, Cape Cobras to India, Deccan Chargers, South Africa to India, South Africa to West Indies, Yorkshire) b Green Point, Cape Town, Cape Province, South Africa 23.2.1974 RHB LB																			
20T		15	15	3	443	101*	36.91	1	2									8	
Test	1996/97	90	154	7	6167	228	41.95	14	26	6	4	0					4.00	94	
FC	1990/91	193	331	13	13425	228	42.21	31	60	138	78	3	26.00	2-14	0	0	3.39	176	
Int	1996/97	248	240	16	8094	175	36.13	21	37									108	
Lim	1990/91	383	366	32	11860	175	35.50	27	62	66	57	2	28.50	1-16	0	0	5.18	169	
I20T	2005/06	23	23	1	400	90*	18.18	0	3									8	
20T	2003/04	100	98	9	2380	101*	26.74	1	16									54	
GIDMAN, Alexander Peter Richard (Gloucestershire, Gloucestershire to Netherlands, MCC to United Arab Emirates) b High Wycombe, Buckinghamshire 22.6.1981 RHB RM																			
FC		16	29	0	679	99	23.41	0	3	318	203	9	22.55	2-10	0	0	3.83	16	
Lim		11	11	1	438	104*	43.80	1	2	234	223	4	55.75	2-23	0	0	5.71	7	
20T		12	11	2	204	42	22.66	0	0	52	76	1	76.00	1-17	0	0	8.76	1	
FC	2002	130	227	20	7348	176	35.49	15	40	6857	4251	97	43.82	4-47	0	0	3.72	80	
Lim	2001	154	145	15	3420	116	26.30	4	17	2992	2593	61	42.50	5-42	0	1	5.20	50	
20T	2003	58	51	9	884	64	21.04	0	3	256	347	8	43.37	2-24	0	0	8.13	12	
GIDMAN, William Robert Simon (Durham) b High Wycombe, Buckinghamshire 14.2.1985 LHB RM																			
Lim		2								64	54	6	9.00	4-36	1	0	5.06	0	
FC	2007	1	2	0	8	8	4.00	0	0	138	86	4	21.50	3-37	0	0	3.73	0	
Lim	2002	18	10	2	105	21	13.12	0	0	562	423	19	22.26	4-36	1	0	4.51	6	
GILCHRIST, Adam Craig (Deccan Chargers, Middlesex) b Bellingen, New South Wales, Australia 14.11.1971 LHB OB WK																			
Lim		1	1	0	38	38	38.00	0	0									0	
20T		7	7	0	212	106	30.28	1	1									4	5
Test	1999/00	96	137	20	5570	204*	47.60	17	26									379	37
FC	1992/93	190	280	46	10334	204*	44.16	30	43									756	55
Int	1996/97	287	279	11	9619	172	35.89	16	55									417	55
Lim	1992/93	356	343	19	11326	172	34.95	18	63	12	10	0					5.00	526	65
I20T	2004/05	13	13	1	272	48	22.66	0	0									17	
20T	2004/05	68	68	2	1773	109*	26.86	2	9									48	19
GLOVER, John Charles (Durham MCCU) b Cardiff, Glamorgan, Wales 29.8.1989 RHB RMF																			
FC		2	1	1	4	4*		0	0	270	180	2	90.00	2-82	0	0	4.00	1	
FC	2008	8	10	2	41	14	5.12	0	0	1024	601	15	40.06	5-38	1	0	3.52	1	
GODDARD, Lee James (Derbyshire, Derbyshire to Netherlands) b Dewsbury, Yorkshire 22.10.1982 RHB WK																			
FC		8	11	1	165	67	16.50	0	1									24	
Lim		6	5	1	36	24*	9.00	0	0									1	
20T		16	9	7	63	22*	31.50	0	0									5	1
FC	2003	18	25	5	489	91	24.45	0	3									46	
Lim	2002	16	12	4	136	36	17.00	0	0									17	
20T	2007	17	9	7	63	22*	31.50	0	0									5	1
GODLEMAN, Billy Ashley (Essex, Essex to Netherlands) b Camden, Middlesex 11.2.1989 LHB LB																			
FC		12	22	0	569	106	25.86	1	2									12	
Lim		2	2	0	5	4	2.50	0	0									0	
FC	2005	48	81	3	2376	113*	30.46	3	12	30	35	0					7.00	42	
Lim	2007	17	17	1	342	82	21.37	0	1									4	
20T	2006	24	23	0	419	69	18.21	0	3									11	
GOODMAN, James Elliott (Kent) b Farnborough, Kent 19.11.1990 RHB RM																			
FC		1	2	1	59	59	59.00	0	1	36	16	1	16.00	1-16	0	0	2.66	0	
Lim	2007	3	2	1	38	26*	38.00	0	0									2	
GOODWIN, Daniel Michael (Cambridge University) b Lambeth, Surrey 26.10.1989 RHB RMF																			
FC		1	2	0	26	18	13.00	0	0	210	142	1	142.00	1-142	0	0	4.05	0	
GOODWIN, Murray William (Sussex) b Salisbury (now Harare), Zimbabwe 11.12.1972 RHB LB																			
FC		16	26	3	1201	142	52.21	4	5									5	
Lim		11	11	1	402	92*	40.20	0	4									1	
20T		17	17	1	405	76*	25.31	0	2									5	
Test	1997/98	19	37	4	1414	166*	42.84	3	8	119	69	0					3.47	10	
FC	1994/95	266	461	38	20381	344*	48.18	63	84	713	376	7	53.71	2-23	0	0	3.16	144	
Int	1997/98	71	70	3	1818	112*	27.13	2	8	248	210	4	52.50	1-12	0	0	5.08	20	
Lim	1994/95	340	326	38	10384	167	36.05	13	66	351	306	7	43.71	1-9	0	0	5.23	103	
20T	2003	73	68	8	1671	102*	27.85	1	9									16	
GRAY, Stephen Kevin (Cambridge MCCU) b Barking, Essex 6.7.1988 RHB																			
FC		3	6	2	131	35*	32.75	0	0									3	
FC	2008	8	13	4	190	35*	21.11	0	0									12	1
GREENWOOD, James Murray (Cambridge University) b Hammersmith, Middlesex 20.3.1985 RHB RMF																			
FC		1	2	1	24	23*	24.00	0	0	114	97	0					5.10	1	
GREGORY, Lewis (Somerset) b Plymouth, Devon 24.5.1992 RHB RM																			
Lim		1	1	0	0	0	0.00	0	0	60	49	4	12.25	4-49	1	0	4.90	1	
GRIFFITHS, David Andrew (Hampshire) b Newport, Isle of Wight 10.9.1985 LHB RFM																			
FC		5	9	6	34	9*	11.33	0	0	912	646	19	34.00	5-85	1	0	4.25	1	
Lim		1								48	56	1	56.00	1-56	0	0	7.00	1	

Cmp	Debut	M	I	NO	Runs	HS	Avge	100	50	Balls	Runs	Wkts	Avge	BB	5i	10m	RpO	ct	st
FC	2006	22	32	14	141	31*	7.83	0	0	3503	2303	65	35.43	5-85	1	0	3.94	2	
Lim	2008	5	1	1	3	3*		0	0	222	227	6	37.83	4-29	1	0	6.13	2	
20T	2007	3	1	1	4	4*		0	0	42	55	3	18.33	3-13	0	0	7.85	0	
GROENEWALD, Timothy Duncan (Derbyshire, Derbyshire to Netherlands) b Pietermaritzburg, Natal, South Africa 10.1.1984 RHB RFM																			
FC		13	19	9	216	35*	21.60	0	0	2483	1295	38	34.07	5-86	1	0	3.12	3	
Lim		8	6	3	45	13*	15.00	0	0	342	303	8	37.87	2-42	0	0	5.31	4	
20T		16	3	1	12	8	6.00	0	0	302	375	16	23.43	3-18	0	0	7.45	2	
FC	2006	39	51	14	778	78	21.02	0	3	6172	3345	98	34.13	6-50	4	0	3.25	16	
Lim	2006	46	33	8	330	36	13.20	0	0	1591	1483	41	36.17	3-25	0	0	5.59	10	
20T	2006	46	19	9	247	41	24.70	0	0	759	1020	39	26.15	3-18	0	0	8.06	12	
GROVES, Peter Richard (Loughborough MCCU) b Bromley, Kent 30.6.1988 RHB RMF																			
FC		2	2	1	80	43	80.00	0	0	174	142	3	47.33	2-55	0	0	4.89	0	
FC	2009	5	4	2	139	52	69.50	0	1	474	349	11	31.72	5-72	1	0	4.41	0	
GURNEY, Harry Frederick (Leicestershire, Leicestershire to Scotland) b Nottingham 25.10.1986 RHB LMF																			
FC		5	4	1	6	4	2.00	0	0	576	332	10	33.20	3-82	0	0	3.45	0	
Lim		5	2	0	7	7	3.50	0	0	198	154	7	22.00	5-24	0	1	4.66	0	
20T		5	1	1	5	5*		0	0	84	137	2	68.50	1-15	0	0	9.78	0	
FC	2007	16	17	8	61	24*	6.77	0	0	2165	1334	28	47.64	5-82	1	0	3.69	2	
Lim	2009	16	3	0	7	7	2.33	0	0	591	510	12	42.50	5-24	0	1	5.17	0	
20T	2009	14	1	1	5	5*		0	0	246	321	10	32.10	3-21	0	0	7.82	2	
HALES, Alexander Daniel (Nottinghamshire, Nottinghamshire to Scotland) b Hillingdon, Middlesex 3.1.1989 RHB RM																			
FC		12	20	1	677	136	35.63	1	4	35	26	0					4.45	12	
Lim		11	10	1	301	96*	33.44	0	1									5	
20T		18	18	2	466	83	29.12	0	4	2	5	0					15.00	8	
FC	2008	20	32	2	1124	136	37.46	1	8	275	166	3	55.33	2-63	0	0	3.62	15	
Lim	2008	26	24	2	797	150*	36.22	2	3									9	
20T	2009	24	24	2	515	83	23.40	0	4	2	5	0					15.00	10	
HALL, Andrew James (Dolphins, North West to South Africa, Northamptonshire, Northamptonshire to Netherlands) b Johannesburg, Transvaal, South Africa 31.7.1975 RHB RFM																			
FC		15	27	3	696	133	29.00	1	3	1908	1047	33	31.72	4-44	0	0	3.29	21	
Lim		10	10	2	152	37	19.00	0	0	373	396	13	30.46	4-39	1	0	6.37	6	
20T		17	16	10	252	40*	42.00	0	0	293	423	16	26.43	2-8	0	0	8.66	3	
Test	2001/02	21	33	4	760	163	26.20	1	3	3001	1617	45	35.93	3-1	0	0	3.23	16	
FC	1995/96	173	254	32	7606	163	34.26	8	47	26818	12863	490	26.25	6-77	15	1	2.87	156	
Int	1998/99	88	56	13	905	81	21.04	0	3	3341	2515	95	26.47	5-18	3	1	4.51	29	
Lim	1994/95	286	227	40	5451	129*	29.14	6	29	11547	9048	329	27.50	5-18	10	1	4.70	85	1
I20T	2005/06	2	1	0	11	11	11.00	0	0	48	60	3	20.00	3-22	0	0	7.50	0	
20T	2003	73	64	15	1204	66*	24.57	0	4	1435	1869	91	20.53	6-21	1	2	7.81	21	
HAMILTON-BROWN, Rory James (Surrey, Sussex to India) b St John's Wood, Middlesex 3.9.1987 RHB OB																			
FC		17	29	1	844	125	30.14	2	3	285	184	1	184.00	1-17	0	0	3.87	11	
Lim		11	11	0	478	115	43.45	1	4	126	134	4	33.50	2-50	0	0	6.38	2	
20T		16	16	2	397	87*	28.35	0	2	108	165	7	23.57	2-23	0	0	9.16	5	
FC	2005	25	42	3	1277	171*	32.74	4	4	644	378	7	54.00	2-49	0	0	3.52	17	
Lim	2005	48	41	2	1020	115	26.15	1	4	996	951	28	33.96	3-28	0	0	5.72	14	
20T	2008	41	38	3	711	87*	20.31	0	3	312	415	22	18.86	4-15	1	0	7.98	15	
HAMPTON, Thomas Robert Garth (Middlesex) b Kingston-upon-Thames, Surrey 5.10.1990 RHB RMF																			
FC		1	1	1	1	1*		0	0	84	42	1	42.00	1-15	0	0	3.00	0	
HANCOCK, Neil David (Unicorns) b Casino, New South Wales, Australia 13.4.1976 RHB RFM																			
Lim		10	8	1	113	29	16.14	0	0	277	241	10	24.10	5-64	0	1	5.22	3	
Lim	1999	21	19	4	449	113*	29.93	1	1	856	696	26	26.76	5-64	0	1	4.87	8	
20T	2004	2	2	0	9	7	4.50	0	0	12	25	1	25.00	1-9	0	0	12.50	0	
HANNON-DALBY, Oliver James (Yorkshire) b Halifax, Yorkshire 20.6.1989 LHB RMF																			
FC		17	15	7	29	11*	3.62	0	0	2296	1372	34	40.35	5-68	2	0	3.58	1	
FC	2008	18	16	7	30	11*	3.33	0	0	2470	1486	35	42.45	5-68	2	0	3.61	1	
HARINATH, Arun (Surrey) b Sutton, Surrey 26.3.1987 LHB OB																			
FC		14	25	1	621	63	25.87	0	4	12	12	0					6.00	3	
FC	2007	24	40	1	1001	69	25.66	0	7	36	30	0					5.00	7	
Lim	2009	1	1	1	21	21*		0	0									0	
HARMISON, Ben William (Durham, Durham to Scotland) b Ashington, Northumberland 9.1.1986 LHB RMF																			
FC		6	10	0	286	96	28.60	0	2	520	402	14	28.71	4-70	0	0	4.63	0	
Lim		10	10	0	311	52	31.10	0	1	246	240	6	40.00	2-13	0	0	5.85	3	
20T		11	6	3	51	24	17.00	0	0	162	228	8	28.50	2-22	0	0	8.44	2	
FC	2006	37	62	5	1488	110	26.10	3	7	1557	1144	33	34.66	4-27	0	0	4.40	23	
Lim	2005	47	43	4	950	67	24.35	0	3	859	840	24	35.00	3-43	0	0	5.86	17	
20T	2006	30	17	7	117	24	11.70	0	0	348	471	23	20.47	3-20	0	0	8.12	9	
HARMISON, Stephen James (Durham, Durham to Scotland, Durham to United Arab Emirates) b Ashington, Northumberland 23.10.1978 RHB RF																			
FC		9	12	6	36	11*	6.00	0	0	1474	819	30	27.30	7-29	1	0	3.33	2	
Lim		2	1	0	8	8	8.00	0	0	54	46	0					5.11	0	
20T		12	2	1	0	0*	0.00	0	0	198	283	14	20.21	5-41	1	1	8.57	0	

Cmp	*Debut*	*M*	*I*	*NO*	*Runs*	*HS*	*Avge*	*100*	*50*	*Balls*	*Runs*	*Wkts*	*Avge*	*BB*	*5i*	*10m*	*RpO*	*ct*	*st*
Test	2002	63	86	23	743	49*	11.79	0	0	13375	7192	226	31.82	7-12	8	1	3.22	7	
FC	1996	199	258	74	1812	49*	9.84	0	0	38079	19927	713	27.94	7-12	27	1	3.14	29	
Int	2002/03	58	25	14	91	18*	8.27	0	0	2899	2481	76	32.64	5-33	2	1	5.13	10	
Lim	1998	143	67	34	267	25*	8.09	0	0	6838	5658	184	30.75	5-33	6	1	4.96	23	
I20T	2005	2								39	42	1	42.00	1-13	0	0	6.46	1	
20T	2004	28	6	1	11	6	2.20	0	0	505	668	29	23.03	5-41	2	1	7.93	3	
HARPER, George Michael (Durham MCCU) b Minnesota, United States of America 5.12.1988 RHB LMF																			
FC		2	1	0	3	3	3.00	0	0	294	248	2	124.00	2-89	0	0	5.06	1	
FC	2009	3	3	0	3	3	1.00	0	0	383	297	6	49.50	4-49	0	0	4.65	1	
HARRIS, Andrew James (Leicestershire) b Ashton-under-Lyne, Lancashire 26.6.1973 RHB RM																			
FC		4	7	4	27	20*	9.00	0	0	580	385	9	42.77	3-43	0	0	3.98	2	
Lim		1								48	53	1	53.00	1-53	0	0	6.62	3	
FC	1994	147	197	50	1253	41*	8.52	0	0	24454	14733	451	32.66	7-54	17	3	3.61	38	
Lim	1994	150	57	25	224	34	7.00	0	0	6658	5635	195	28.89	5-35	8	1	5.07	31	
20T	2003	29	7	4	12	6*	4.00	0	0	524	737	28	26.32	2-13	0	0	8.43	4	
HARRIS, James Alexander Russell (England Lions, Glamorgan) b Morriston, Swansea, Glamorgan, Wales 16.5.1990 RHB RFM																			
FC		14	20	2	267	49	14.83	0	0	2782	1356	63	21.52	5-56	2	0	2.92	3	
Lim		3	1	0	1	1	1.00	0	0	126	141	4	35.25	2-41	0	0	6.71	1	
20T		10	5	2	37	18	12.33	0	0	180	285	7	40.71	2-23	0	0	9.50	0	
FC	2007	42	59	9	886	87*	17.72	0	2	7561	4027	150	26.84	7-66	4	1	3.19	8	
Lim	2007	21	14	1	98	21	7.53	0	0	887	770	27	28.51	4-48	1	0	5.20	5	
20T	2008	19	10	4	66	18	11.00	0	0	336	479	17	28.17	4-23	1	0	8.55	2	
HARRISON, David Stuart (Glamorgan) b Newport, Monmouthshire, Wales 30.7.1981 RHB RMF																			
FC		12	18	0	253	35	14.05	0	0	1941	1156	37	31.24	7-45	2	0	3.57	2	
Lim		4	3	0	31	12	10.33	0	0	178	265	3	88.33	3-54	0	0	8.93	0	
20T		2	1	0	8	8	8.00	0	0	30	61	2	30.50	2-45	0	0	12.20	0	
FC	1999	102	141	18	2017	88	16.39	0	7	16005	9276	257	36.09	7-45	8	0	3.47	30	
Lim	2000	85	55	19	454	37*	12.61	0	0	3583	3015	98	30.76	5-26	4	2	5.04	9	
20T	2003	27	8	2	20	8	3.33	0	0	477	714	23	31.04	2-17	0	0	8.98	4	
HARRISON, Paul William (Northamptonshire) b Cuckfield, Sussex 22.5.1984 RHB RM WK																			
FC		5	8	1	137	44	19.57	0	0									7	2
Lim		2	2	0	13	13	6.50	0	0									2	
20T		2	2	0	13	10	6.50	0	0									0	
FC	2004	18	28	5	488	54	21.21	0	1									23	2
Lim	2006	11	10	0	178	61	17.80	0	1									7	
20T	2005	14	13	1	132	26	11.00	0	0									2	
HATCHETT, Lewis James (Sussex) b Shoreham-by-Sea, Sussex 21.1.1990 LHB LMF																			
FC		4	4	0	30	20	7.50	0	0	400	256	12	21.33	5-47	1	0	3.84	1	
HENDERSON, Claude William (Cape Cobras to India, Leicestershire, Leicestershire to Scotland) b Worcester, Cape Province, South Africa 14.6.1972 RHB SLA																			
FC		16	21	1	265	33	13.25	0	0	2937	1179	56	21.05	6-21	3	0	2.40	6	
Lim		5	4	3	16	12*	16.00	0	0	204	194	8	24.25	2-28	0	0	5.70	1	
20T		15	9	5	77	32	19.25	0	0	342	396	14	28.28	3-33	0	0	6.94	3	
Test	2001/02	7	7	0	65	30	9.28	0	0	1962	928	22	42.18	4-116	0	0	2.83	2	
FC	1990/91	239	326	70	4775	81	18.65	0	15	57233	24413	791	30.86	7-57	30	1	2.55	82	
Int	2001/02	4								217	132	7	18.85	4-17	1	0	3.65	0	
Lim	1990/91	241	138	66	1110	45	15.41	0	0	10699	7674	304	25.24	6-29	13	2	4.30	52	
20T	2004	70	31	11	161	32	8.05	0	0	1354	1540	64	24.06	3-23	0	0	6.82	17	
HENDERSON, Tyron (Middlesex) b Durban, Natal, South Africa 1.8.1974 RHB RFM																			
20T		9	6	0	44	17	7.33	0	0	210	258	9	28.66	3-25	0	0	7.37	0	
FC	1998/99	86	137	17	1897	81	15.80	0	6	15744	7024	262	26.80	7-67	10	1	2.67	31	
Lim	1998/99	114	92	18	1608	126*	21.72	1	9	4915	3567	130	27.43	5-5	0	3	4.35	27	
I20T	2006/07	1	1	0	0	0	0.00	0	0	24	31	0					7.75	0	
20T	2003/04	84	74	10	1289	85	20.14	0	7	1824	2195	93	23.60	4-29	1	0	7.22	10	
HERATH, Herath Mudiyanselage Rangana Keerthi Bandara (Moors, Sri Lanka, Wayamba, Hampshire, Sri Lanka to India, Wayamba to India) b Kurunegala, Sri Lanka 19.3.1978 LHB SLA																			
FC		4	6	3	59	17*	19.66	0	0	1053	463	10	46.30	4-98	0	0	2.63	1	
Lim		5	2	1	6	6*	6.00	0	0	186	170	5	34.00	2-28	0	0	5.48	3	
Test	1999	22	28	5	287	80*	12.47	0	1	5383	2690	71	37.88	5-99	4	0	2.99	4	
FC	1996/97	184	262	60	3304	80*	16.35	0	12	36475	16602	668	24.85	8-43	38	5	2.73	84	
Int	2004	9	2	1	2	2	2.00	0	0	336	215	9	23.88	3-28	0	0	3.83	4	
Lim	1998/99	112	72	32	802	88*	20.05	0	1	4566	3051	141	21.63	4-19	3	0	4.00	28	
20T	2004/05	20	12	4	44	9	5.50	0	0	397	375	27	13.88	3-14	0	0	5.66	4	
HESKETH, Richard Lindsay (Cambridge MCCU, Cambridge University) b Cambridge 30.3.1988 RHB SLA																			
FC		2	3	0	38	20	12.66	0	0	18	21	0					7.00	1	
HILDRETH, James Charles (Somerset, Somerset to India) b Milton Keynes, Buckinghamshire 9.9.1984 RHB RFM																			
FC		16	23	1	1440	151	65.45	7	5	78	95	1	95.00	1-95	0	0	7.30	7	
Lim		15	15	5	658	100*	65.80	1	5									9	
20T		19	19	5	459	77*	32.78	0	2									8	
FC	2003	110	179	14	7110	303*	43.09	19	35	474	411	5	82.20	2-39	0	0	5.20	78	

Cmp	Debut	M	I	NO	Runs	HS	Avge	100	50	Balls	Runs	Wkts	Avge	BB	5i	10m	RpO	ct	st
Lim	2002	124	120	19	3332	151	32.99	4	14	150	185	6	30.83	2-26	0	0	7.40	39	
20T	2004	73	70	10	1272	77*	21.20	0	5	169	247	10	24.70	3-24	0	0	8.76	29	
HOCKLEY, James Bernard (Kent) b Beckenham, Kent 16.4.1979 RHB OB																			
FC		6	11	1	141	82	14.10	0	1	258	175	2	87.50	1-8	0	0	4.07	7	
Lim		2	1	1	9	9*		0	0	18	29	0					9.66	0	
20T		6	6	0	39	18	6.50	0	0	29	32	1	32.00	1-9	0	0	6.62	3	
FC	1998	30	49	5	804	82	18.27	0	4	624	408	5	81.60	1-8	0	0	3.92	21	
Lim	1999	71	68	7	1595	121	26.14	1	8	90	96	3	32.00	2-32	0	0	6.40	24	
20T	2009	10	8	0	53	18	6.62	0	0	29	32	1	32.00	1-9	0	0	6.62	4	
HODD, Andrew John (Sussex, Sussex to India) b Chichester, Sussex 12.1.1984 RHB WK																			
FC		10	14	1	319	109	24.53	1	1									29	1
Lim		10	8	2	225	91	37.50	0	1									7	6
20T		13	9	2	131	26	18.71	0	0									1	3
FC	2003	48	68	11	1686	123	29.57	4	8	10	7	0					4.20	93	11
Lim	2002	37	30	8	552	91	25.09	0	1									29	8
20T	2005	34	17	2	199	26	13.26	0	0									11	9
HODGE, Bradley John (Victoria to Australia, Kolkata Knight Riders, Leicestershire, Victoria to India) b Sandringham, Victoria, Australia 29.12.1974 RHB OB																			
20T		15	15	0	431	103	28.73	1	2	150	187	10	18.70	3-26	0	0	7.48	5	
Test	2005/06	6	11	2	503	203*	55.88	1	2	12	8	0					4.00	9	
FC	1993/94	223	388	38	17084	302*	48.81	51	64	5583	3086	74	41.70	4-17	0	0	3.31	127	
Int	2005/06	25	21	2	575	123	30.26	1	3	66	51	1	51.00	1-17	0	0	4.63	16	
Lim	1993/94	234	224	28	8255	164	42.11	25	35	1698	1508	40	37.70	5-28	0	1	5.32	90	
I20T	2007/08	8	5	2	94	36	31.33	0	0	12	20	0					10.00	3	
20T	2003	99	96	11	3077	106	36.20	2	21	720	917	43	21.32	4-17	2	0	7.64	38	
HODGSON, Lee John (Yorkshire) b Middlesborugh, Yorkshire 29.6.1986 RHB RMF																			
FC		2	2	0	67	34	33.50	0	0	185	128	2	64.00	1-42	0	0	4.15	1	
20T		2	1	1	39	39*		0	0	36	59	2	29.50	2-29	0	0	9.83	1	
FC	2008	4	5	0	165	63	33.00	0	1	299	216	2	108.00	1-42	0	0	4.33	3	
Lim	2008	6	1	0	9	9	9.00	0	0	156	160	2	80.00	2-44	0	0	6.15	4	
HOGG, Kyle William (Lancashire) b Birmingham, Warwickshire 2.7.1983 LHB RFM																			
FC		9	13	4	301	88	33.44	0	2	1214	650	20	32.50	4-53	0	0	3.21	3	
Lim		11	7	3	100	36*	25.00	0	0	428	423	14	30.21	2-27	0	0	5.93	2	
20T		1	1	1	2	2*		0	0	12	17	0					8.50	0	
FC	2001	64	78	11	1649	88	24.61	0	11	8466	4406	124	35.53	5-48	1	0	3.12	16	
Lim	2001	126	78	21	935	66*	16.40	0	1	4788	3785	127	29.80	4-20	2	0	4.74	22	
20T	2003	22	16	3	211	44	16.23	0	0	283	405	12	33.75	2-10	0	0	8.58	3	
HOGGARD, Matthew James (Leicestershire) b Leeds, Yorkshire 31.12.1976 RHB RFM																			
FC		15	17	6	31	6	2.81	0	0	2500	1222	50	24.44	6-63	3	0	2.93	5	
Lim		10	3	2	21	17*	21.00	0	0	402	364	11	33.09	3-43	0	0	5.43	2	
20T		15	3	2	27	12*	27.00	0	0	329	465	18	25.83	3-19	0	0	8.48	1	
Test	2000	67	92	27	473	38	7.27	0	0	13909	7564	248	30.50	7-61	7	1	3.26	24	
FC	1996	210	263	77	1684	89*	9.05	0	4	38061	19510	718	27.17	7-49	25	1	3.07	60	
Int	2001/02	26	6	2	17	7	4.25	0	0	1306	1152	32	36.00	5-49	0	1	5.29	5	
Lim	1998	140	43	24	88	17*	4.63	0	0	6529	4899	190	25.78	5-28	2	4	4.50	16	
20T	2004	30	5	3	46	18	23.00	0	0	653	937	31	30.22	3-19	0	0	8.60	5	
HOPKINS, Charles Edward Heughan (Cambridge MCCU, Cambridge University) b Peterborough 12.6.1987 RHB RM																			
FC		3	4	0	34	14	8.50	0	0	366	305	2	152.50	1-66	0	0	5.00	0	
HORTON, Paul James (Lancashire) b Sydney, New South Wales, Australia 20.9.1982 RHB RM																			
FC		16	30	2	634	123	22.64	1	3									19	
Lim		13	12	2	383	78*	38.30	0	4									5	
20T		17	16	3	270	44	20.76	0	0									5	
FC	2003	75	129	12	4319	173	36.91	9	23	12	10	0					5.00	68	1
Lim	2002	55	50	3	1376	111*	29.27	2	7									19	
20T	2005	31	29	4	464	44	18.56	0	0									12	
HOUSEGO, Daniel Mark (Middlesex) b Windsor, Berkshire 12.10.1988 RHB LB																			
FC		2	4	1	144	102*	48.00	1	0									1	
FC	2008	7	14	1	296	102*	22.76	1	0	7	17	0					14.57	3	
20T	2008	5	4	0	37	18	9.25	0	0									0	
HOWELL, Benny Alexander Cameron (Hampshire) b Bordeaux, France 5.10.1988 RHB RM																			
Lim		2	2	0	17	12	8.50	0	0	66	55	2	27.50	1-23	0	0	5.00	0	
HOWGEGO, Benjamin Harry Nicholas (Northamptonshire) b Kings Lynn, Norfolk 3.3.1988 LHB RM																			
FC		7	13	2	292	80	26.54	0	1	12	16	0					8.00	3	
20T		1	1	0	1	1	1.00	0	0									0	
FC	2008	14	26	4	527	80	23.95	0	1	12	16	0					8.00	6	
Lim	2009	1	1	0	7	7	7.00	0	0									0	
HUGHES, Chesney Francis (Leeward Islands, Derbyshire, Derbyshire to Netherlands) b Anguilla 20.1.1991 LHB SLA																			
FC		12	21	2	784	156	41.26	2	4	66	81	1	81.00	1-9	0	0	7.36	12	
Lim		11	11	0	350	64	31.81	0	4	30	26	0					5.20	4	
20T		12	10	0	164	65	16.40	0	1									3	

Cmp	Debut	M	I	NO	Runs	HS	Avge	100	50	Balls	Runs	Wkts	Avge	BB	5i	10m	RpO	ct	st
Lim	2007/08	20	19	1	492	72	27.33	0	5	186	162	2	81.00	1-17	0	0	5.22	6	
20T	2006	14	12	0	192	65	16.00	0	1	12	19	0					9.50	3	
HUGHES, Philip Heywood (Cambridge MCCU, Cambridge University) b Southampton, Hampshire 17.6.1991 RHB RM																			
FC		2	4	0	198	87	49.50	0	2									0	
HUGHES, Phillip Joel (Australia, New South Wales, Australia to New Zealand, Hampshire, New South Wales to India) b Macksville, New South Wales, Australia 30.11.1988 LHB OB																			
FC		3	6	0	85	38	14.16	0	0									0	
Lim		2	2	0	33	32	16.50	0	0									1	
Test	2008/09	7	13	1	615	160	51.25	2	2									3	
FC	2007/08	43	77	6	3967	198	55.87	13	21	18	9	0					3.00	30	
Lim	2007/08	37	37	4	1117	119	33.84	1	7									12	
20T	2008/09	13	13	3	486	83	48.60	0	4									8	
HUNTER, Ian David (Derbyshire) b Durham 11.9.1979 RHB RMF																			
Lim		1	1	0	14	14	14.00	0	0	30	25	0					5.00	0	
FC	2000	63	81	21	1064	65	17.73	0	2	9805	5835	150	38.90	5-46	3	0	3.57	18	
Lim	1999	88	53	13	339	39	8.47	0	0	3799	3138	96	32.68	4-29	2	0	4.95	17	
20T	2003	18	6	2	41	25*	10.25	0	0	378	542	19	28.52	3-26	0	0	8.60	3	
HUSSAIN, Gemaal Maqsood (Gloucestershire) b Waltham Forest, Essex 10.10.1983 RHB RM																			
FC		15	26	10	153	28*	9.56	0	0	2506	1497	67	22.34	5-36	2	0	3.58	1	
20T		4	2	0	5	3	2.50	0	0	78	147	2	73.50	1-41	0	0	11.30	1	
FC	2009	16	28	10	169	28*	9.38	0	0	2638	1604	69	23.24	5-36	2	0	3.64	2	
Lim	2009	1								30	17	2	8.50	2-17	0	0	3.40	0	
20T	2009	11	9	4	28	8	5.60	0	0	228	340	12	28.33	3-22	0	0	8.94	3	
HUSSEY, David John (Australia, Victoria, Australia to England, Australia to New Zealand, Australia to West Indies, Kolkata Knight Riders, Nottinghamshire, Victoria to India) b Morley, Western Australia, Australia 15.7.1977 RHB OB																			
FC		5	7	1	399	251*	66.50	1	1	108	82	0					4.55	7	
Lim		3	3	1	114	80	57.00	0	1	6	6	0					6.00	3	
I20T		2	2	0	67	34	33.50	0	0	42	49	2	24.50	1-16	0	0	7.00	1	
20T		19	19	5	591	81*	42.21	0	3	60	72	3	24.00	1-0	0	0	7.20	10	
FC	2002/03	147	227	22	11417	275	55.69	39	50	2348	1486	21	70.76	4-105	0	0	3.79	180	
Int	2008	23	21	0	598	111	28.47	1	4	257	230	3	76.66	1-6	0	0	5.37	12	
Lim	2001	174	163	23	5636	130	40.25	8	37	1480	1302	30	43.40	3-26	0	0	5.27	86	
I20T	2007/08	25	23	3	579	88*	28.95	0	3	252	267	15	17.80	3-25	0	0	6.35	14	
20T	2004	127	122	23	3219	100*	32.51	1	17	814	990	38	26.05	3-25	0	0	7.29	67	
IFTIKHAR ANJUM, Rao (Islamabad Leopards, ZTBL, Pakistan to Australia, Surrey) b Khanewal, Punjab, Pakistan 1.12.1980 RHB RM																			
FC		3	5	1	61	29	15.25	0	0	390	240	6	40.00	2-53	0	0	3.69	0	
Lim		2	1	1	4	4*		0	0	90	88	4	22.00	3-39	0	0	5.86	0	
Test	2005/06	1	1	1	9	9*		0	0	84	62	0					4.42	0	
FC	1999/00	99	149	33	1963	78	16.92	0	5	17795	9504	394	24.12	7-59	22	3	3.20	56	
Int	2004/05	62	34	19	234	32	15.60	0	0	2960	2430	77	31.55	5-30	2	1	4.92	10	
Lim	1998/99	111	63	29	472	39	13.88	0	0	5436	4306	140	30.75	5-30	3	1	4.75	27	
I20T	2007/08	2								48	67	1	67.00	1-34	0	0	8.37	0	
20T	2004/05	16	10	3	90	24	12.85	0	0	348	418	16	26.12	2-18	0	0	7.20	1	
IMRAN ARIF (Worcestershire) b Kotli, Azad Kashmir, Pakistan 15.1.1984 RHB RFM																			
FC		2	3	1	8	4*	4.00	0	0	198	141	4	35.25	2-63	0	0	4.27	1	
Lim		3	2	2	6	5*		0	0	108	141	3	47.00	2-43	0	0	7.83	4	
20T		9	3	2	11	6*	11.00	0	0	132	198	2	99.00	1-30	0	0	9.00	0	
FC	2008	17	19	9	102	35	10.20	0	0	2260	1615	43	37.55	5-50	2	0	4.28	6	
Lim	2008	13	4	4	23	16*		0	0	464	516	11	46.90	2-43	0	0	6.67	6	
IMRAN TAHIR, Mohammad (Easterns, Titans to South Africa, Warwickshire, Warwickshire to Scotland) b Lahore, Punjab, Pakistan 27.3.1979 RHB LBG																			
FC		16	27	4	384	69*	16.69	0	1	2584	1376	56	24.57	8-114	3	0	3.19	4	
Lim		12	2	1	8	8*	8.00	0	0	456	418	20	20.90	5-41	1	1	5.50	4	
20T		17	3	1	19	11	9.50	0	0	366	401	20	20.05	3-14	0	0	6.57	2	
FC	1996/97	123	155	32	1794	77*	14.58	0	3	23851	12765	505	25.27	8-76	35	7	3.21	56	
Lim	1997/98	87	30	9	304	41*	14.47	0	0	3840	2920	125	23.36	5-27	4	3	4.56	19	
20T	2005/06	37	11	4	47	13	6.71	0	0	822	868	40	21.70	3-13	0	0	6.33	9	
IRELAND, Anthony John (Southern Rocks, Gloucestershire) b Masvingo, Zimbabwe 30.8.1984 RHB RM																			
FC		8	12	2	21	11	2.10	0	0	1337	784	36	21.77	5-25	2	0	3.51	0	
Lim		8	4	1	8	3	2.66	0	0	282	357	12	29.75	3-36	0	0	7.59	0	
20T		13	4	1	5	2	1.66	0	0	237	389	12	32.41	3-35	0	0	9.84	4	
FC	2002/03	36	53	16	135	16*	3.64	0	0	5313	3271	113	28.94	7-36	4	1	3.69	9	
Int	2005/06	26	13	5	30	8*	3.75	0	0	1326	1115	38	29.34	3-41	0	0	5.04	2	
Lim	2004/05	65	31	15	90	17	5.62	0	0	2805	2520	88	28.63	4-16	2	0	5.39	9	
I20T	2006/07	1	1	1	2	2*		0	0	18	33	1	33.00	1-33	0	0	11.00	0	
20T	2006/07	31	10	4	32	8*	5.33	0	0	569	845	35	24.14	3-10	0	0	8.91	9	
JAMES, Nicholas Alexander (Glamorgan) b Sandwell, Warwickshire 17.9.1986 LHB SLA																			
FC		1	2	1	75	60*	75.00	0	1	6	1	0					1.00	0	
Lim		2	1	0	15	15	15.00	0	0	18	19	2	9.50	2-19	0	0	6.33	1	
FC	2008	2	3	1	109	60*	54.50	0	1	24	7	1	7.00	1-6	0	0	1.75	1	

Cmp	Debut	M	I	NO	Runs	HS	Avge	100	50	Balls	Runs	Wkts	Avge	BB	5i	10m	RpO	ct	st
Lim	2006	13	9	2	127	30	18.14	0	0	264	195	9	21.66	2-19	0	0	4.43	3	
20T	2007	2	2	1	13	12*	13.00	0	0									2	
JAQUES, Philip Anthony (New South Wales, Worcestershire) b Wollongong, New South Wales, Australia 3.5.1979 LHB SLC																			
FC		8	15	0	465	94	31.00	0	3									9	
Lim		5	5	0	249	110	49.80	1	1									3	
20T		14	13	3	330	78*	33.00	0	2									6	
Test	2005/06	11	19	0	902	150	47.47	3	6									7	
FC	2000/01	147	261	10	12808	244	51.02	36	61	68	87	0					7.67	109	
Int	2005/06	6	6	0	125	94	20.83	0	1									3	
Lim	2000/01	137	134	9	5366	171*	42.92	14	29	18	19	0					6.33	35	
20T	2003	49	48	5	1297	92	30.16	0	8	6	15	0					15.00	14	
JAVID, Ateeq (Warwickshire) b Birmingham, Warwickshire 15.10.1991 RHB OB																			
FC		4	7	0	91	48	13.00	0	0									3	
FC	2009	7	13	0	146	48	11.23	0	0	78	78	0					6.00	6	
JAYASURIYA, Sanath Teran (Bloomfield, Ruhuna, Mumbai Indians, Sri Lanka to India, Sri Lanka to South Africa, Sri Lanka to United States of America, Sri Lanka to West Indies, Worcestershire) b Matara, Sri Lanka 30.6.1969 LHB SLA																			
20T		10	10	0	267	87	26.70	0	2	234	278	5	55.60	1-20	0	0	7.12	2	
Test	1990/91	110	188	14	6973	340	40.07	14	31	8188	3366	98	34.34	5-34	2	0	2.46	78	
FC	1988/89	263	417	33	14782	340	38.49	29	70	15113	6719	205	32.77	5-34	2	0	2.66	162	
Int	1989/90	444	432	18	13428	189	32.43	28	68	14838	11825	322	36.72	6-29	8	4	4.78	123	
Lim	1989/90	545	530	25	15734	189	31.15	31	78	17730	14069	399	35.26	6-29	12	5	4.76	149	
I20T	2006	30	29	3	621	88	23.88	0	4	353	438	17	25.76	3-21	0	0	7.44	4	
20T	2004/05	92	91	6	2052	114*	24.14	1	11	1263	1634	62	26.35	4-24	1	0	7.76	16	
JEAVONS, Aaron Francis (Oxford MCCU) b Stafford 23.4.1989 LHB OB																			
FC		1	2	0	66	62	33.00	0	1									1	
JEFFERSON, William Ingleby (Leicestershire) b Derby 25.10.1979 RHB RMF																			
FC		11	20	1	722	135	38.00	2	4									14	
Lim		3	3	0	123	55	41.00	0	1									2	
20T		13	13	0	289	83	22.23	0	3									4	
FC	2000	102	179	13	6014	222	36.22	14	24	120	60	1	60.00	1-16	0	0	3.00	102	
Lim	2000	96	94	6	3092	132	35.13	4	18	24	9	2	4.50	2-9	0	0	2.25	43	
20T	2003	48	47	4	922	83	21.44	0	5									16	
JEWELL, Thomas Melvin (Surrey) b Reading, Berkshire 13.1.1991 RHB RFM																			
FC		3	2	1	5	4*	5.00	0	0	240	127	3	42.33	1-22	0	0	3.17	0	
FC	2008	4	2	1	5	4*	5.00	0	0	282	143	4	35.75	1-16	0	0	3.04	0	
Lim	2009	2	2	1	1	1	1.00	0	0	36	56	0					9.33	0	
JOHNSON, Richard Matthew (Warwickshire, Warwickshire to Scotland) b Solihull, Warwickshire 1.9.1988 RHB WK																			
FC		5	8	1	118	39	16.85	0	0									12	2
Lim		5	1	1	4	4*		0	0									3	2
20T		6	2	2	7	6*		0	0									1	2
FC	2008	7	11	1	223	72	22.30	0	1									20	2
Lim	2008	8	3	1	30	20	15.00	0	0									7	2
20T	2009	8	3	2	7	6*	7.00	0	0									1	2
JONES, Alexander John (Glamorgan) b Bridgend, Glamorgan, Wales 10.11.1988 RHB LM																			
Lim		1	1	0	5	5	5.00	0	0	48	74	0					9.25	0	
JONES, Christopher Robert (Somerset) b Harold Wood, Essex 5.11.1990 RHB																			
FC		1																0	
JONES, Geraint Owen (Kent, Kent to Scotland) b Kundiawa, Papua New Guinea 14.7.1976 RHB RM WK																			
FC		17	31	0	1003	178	32.35	3	2	6	8	0					8.00	49	6
Lim		10	8	1	133	40	19.00	0	0									2	7
20T		16	15	1	240	54	17.14	0	1									8	2
Test	2003/04	34	53	4	1172	100	23.91	1	6									128	5
FC	2001	143	218	20	6699	178	33.83	15	32	24	26	0					6.50	431	31
Int	2004	49	41	8	815	80	24.69	0	4									68	4
Lim	2001	160	135	23	2702	86	24.12	0	11									174	35
I20T	2005	2	2	1	33	19	33.00	0	0									2	
20T	2003	61	51	10	681	56	16.60	0	2									33	15
JONES, Philip Steffan (Derbyshire, Derbyshire to Netherlands) b Llanelli, Carmarthenshire, Wales 9.2.1974 RHB RFM																			
FC		12	18	4	427	86	30.50	0	1	1883	959	31	30.93	4-26	0	0	3.05	4	
Lim		3	2	0	37	22	18.50	0	0	114	115	1	115.00	1-22	0	0	6.05	0	
20T		16	7	4	103	40	34.33	0	0	288	393	11	35.72	3-20	0	0	8.18	1	
FC	1997	146	175	43	2655	114	20.11	2	8	24164	14122	384	36.77	6-25	10	1	3.50	33	
Lim	1994	184	98	45	676	42	12.75	0	0	8271	7256	245	29.61	6-56	7	3	5.26	31	
20T	2003	42	19	10	165	40	18.33	0	0	820	1169	38	30.76	3-20	0	0	8.55	6	
JONES, Richard Alan (Worcestershire) b Stourbridge, Worcestershire 6.11.1986 RHB RMF																			
FC		11	19	2	100	21*	5.88	0	0	1790	1281	38	33.71	7-115	2	0	4.29	7	
Lim		3	2	2	11	11*		0	0	126	129	1	129.00	1-47	0	0	6.14	0	
20T		6	2	1	14	9	14.00	0	0	66	119	2	59.50	1-17	0	0	10.81	7	
FC	2007	23	36	5	349	53*	11.25	0	1	3430	2461	68	36.19	7-115	3	0	4.30	11	
Lim	2008	7	4	2	19	11*	9.50	0	0	228	269	1	269.00	1-47	0	0	7.07	1	

Cmp	Debut	M	I	NO	Runs	HS	Avge	100	50	Balls	Runs	Wkts	Avge	BB	5i	10m	RpO	ct	st
JONES, Simon Philip (Hampshire) b Morriston, Swansea, Glamorgan, Wales 25.12.1978 LHB RF																			
FC		1	2	2	0	0*		0	0	132	60	4	15.00	4-60	0	0	2.72	0	
Lim		1								48	41	1	41.00	1-41	0	0	5.12	0	
20T		6	1	1	1	1*		0	0	138	195	8	24.37	3-20	0	0	8.47	0	
Test	2002	18	18	5	205	44	15.76	0	0	2821	1666	59	28.23	6-53	3	0	3.54	4	
FC	1998	89	110	37	899	46	12.31	0	0	13131	8007	264	30.32	6-45	15	1	3.65	17	
Int	2004/05	8	1	0	1	1	1.00	0	0	348	275	7	39.28	2-43	0	0	4.74	0	
Lim	1999	35	13	8	76	26	15.20	0	0	1502	1280	32	40.00	5-32	0	1	5.11	2	
20T	2008	10	3	2	23	11*	23.00	0	0	230	345	10	34.50	3-20	0	0	9.00	0	
JOSEPH, Robert Hartman (Kent) b St John's, Antigua 20.1.1982 RHB RFM																			
FC		2	3	2	30	18*	30.00	0	0	312	185	2	92.50	2-112	0	0	3.55	0	
20T		1								12	25	0					12.50	0	
FC	2000	46	59	22	414	36*	11.18	0	0	6982	4258	130	32.75	6-32	5	0	3.65	9	
Lim	2004	33	14	12	43	15	21.50	0	0	1307	1114	39	28.56	5-13	0	1	5.11	4	
20T	2008	9	1	1	1	1*		0	0	168	213	10	21.30	2-14	0	0	7.60	3	
JOSLIN, Andrew James Philip (Cambridge MCCU) b Leytonstone, Essex 18.12.1989 RHB RM																			
FC		1	2	0	12	11	6.00	0	0									0	
FC	2009	2	4	0	74	33	18.50	0	0									1	
JOYCE, Edmund Christopher (Sussex, Sussex to India) b Dublin, Ireland 22.9.1978 LHB RM																			
FC		10	17	3	738	164	52.71	2	3									17	
Lim		7	7	0	299	117	42.71	1	0									1	
20T		8	8	0	74	22	9.25	0	0									1	
FC	1997	152	251	21	10344	211	44.97	24	56	1287	1025	11	93.18	2-34	0	0	4.77	126	
Int	2006	17	17	0	471	107	27.70	1	3									6	
Lim	1998	191	181	19	5997	146	37.01	8	37	264	309	6	51.50	2-10	0	0	7.02	65	
I20T	2006	2	1	0	1	1	1.00	0	0									0	
20T	2003	57	53	9	709	47	16.11	0	0	6	12	0					12.00	15	
KARTIK, Murali (Kolkata Knight Riders, Railways, Somerset) b Madras (now Chennai), Tamil Nadu, India 11.9.1976 LHB SLA																			
FC		11	12	5	199	52*	28.42	0	2	2300	882	45	19.60	6-42	5	2	2.30	9	
Lim		10	3	1	34	26*	17.00	0	0	417	321	20	16.05	4-30	1	0	4.61	6	
20T		17	3	2	18	16*	18.00	0	0	366	402	13	30.92	3-18	0	0	6.59	4	
Test	1999/00	8	10	1	88	43	9.77	0	0	1932	820	24	34.16	4-44	0	0	2.54	2	
FC	1996/97	160	199	33	3249	96	19.57	0	16	34546	13738	537	25.58	9-70	31	5	2.38	117	
Int	2001/02	37	14	5	126	32*	14.00	0	0	1907	1612	37	43.56	6-27	0	1	5.07	10	
Lim	1996/97	180	86	28	669	44	11.53	0	0	9148	6652	233	28.54	6-27	4	2	4.36	60	
I20T	2007/08	1								24	27	0					6.75	0	
20T	2007	74	16	6	102	21	10.20	0	0	1558	1713	59	29.03	5-13	0	1	6.59	22	
KATICH, Simon Mathew (Australia, New South Wales, Australia to England, Australia to New Zealand, Lancashire, New South Wales to India) b Middle Swan, Western Australia, Australia 21.8.1975 LHB SLC																			
Test		2	4	0	187	83	46.75	0	2									1	
FC		3	6	0	227	83	37.83	0	2									2	
20T		9	8	1	185	41*	26.42	0	0	12	14	0					7.00	5	
Test	2001	52	91	6	3981	157	46.83	10	24	1009	617	21	29.38	6-65	1	0	3.66	38	
FC	1996/97	223	382	47	18134	306	54.13	50	97	5769	3462	95	36.44	7-130	3	0	3.60	204	
Int	2000/01	45	42	5	1324	107*	35.78	1	9									13	
Lim	1995/96	218	208	22	6900	136*	37.09	7	54	877	818	24	34.08	3-21	0	0	5.59	99	
I20T	2004/05	3	2	0	69	39	34.50	0	0									2	
20T	2003	52	48	9	1239	75	31.76	0	5	12	14	0					7.00	27	
KEEDY, Gary (Lancashire) b Sandal, Wakefield, Yorkshire 27.11.1974 LHB SLA																			
FC		7	9	2	89	34	12.71	0	0	1481	688	31	22.19	7-68	2	1	2.78	0	
Lim		7	3	1	12	11	6.00	0	0	318	257	12	21.41	4-41	1	0	4.84	2	
20T		4								73	105	4	26.25	2-27	0	0	8.63	0	
FC	1994	194	219	106	1290	64	11.41	0	2	39418	18498	585	31.62	7-68	29	6	2.81	46	
Lim	1995	75	26	11	141	33	9.40	0	0	3088	2383	90	26.47	5-30	3	1	4.63	11	
20T	2004	47	7	4	19	9*	6.33	0	0	910	995	43	23.13	4-15	1	0	6.56	4	
KEEGAN, Chad Blake (Sussex, Sussex to India) b Sandton, Johannesburg, Transvaal, South Africa 30.7.1979 RHB RFM																			
Lim		6	4	2	24	12	12.00	0	0	227	246	9	27.33	2-23	0	0	6.50	1	
20T		12	8	1	75	26	10.71	0	0	243	319	12	26.58	3-11	0	0	7.87	3	
FC	2001	47	57	6	607	44	11.90	0	0	8395	4887	140	34.90	6-114	6	0	3.49	14	
Lim	2001	95	62	21	673	50	16.41	0	1	4300	3499	145	24.13	6-33	3	3	4.88	22	
20T	2003	33	25	6	313	42	16.47	0	0	639	840	25	33.60	3-11	0	0	7.88	8	
KENNEDY, Augustus Damian John (Cambridge University) b London 10.8.1990 RHB WK																			
FC		1	2	1	62	48*	62.00	0	0									2	
KEOGH, Robert Ian (Northamptonshire) b Dunstable, Bedfordshire 21.10.1991 RHB OB																			
Lim		1	1	0	11	11	11.00	0	0									1	
KERRIGAN, Simon Christopher (Lancashire) b Preston, Lancashire 10.5.1989 RHB SLA																			
FC		13	15	5	45	16*	4.50	0	0	1914	967	30	32.23	6-74	3	0	3.03	3	
20T		12	1	1	4	4*		0	0	240	264	11	24.00	3-17	0	0	6.60	6	

Cmp	Debut	M	I	NO	Runs	HS	Avge	100	50	Balls	Runs	Wkts	Avge	BB	5i	10m	RpO	ct	st
KERVEZEE, Alexei Nicolaas (Netherlands, Netherlands to Kenya, Netherlands to Scotland, Netherlands to United Arab Emirates, Worcestershire) b Walvis Bay, Namibia 11.9.1989 RHB OB																			
FC		16	30	3	1190	155	44.07	3	6	27	63	0					14.00	14	
Lim		12	12	0	331	111	27.58	1	0									4	
20T		16	14	2	179	35	14.91	0	0									6	
FC	2005	36	62	5	2126	155	37.29	3	11	183	145	2	72.50	1-14	0	0	4.75	21	
Int	2006	30	27	2	664	92	26.56	0	3	24	34	0					8.50	12	
Lim	2006	52	49	3	1436	121*	31.21	2	6	48	73	0					9.12	21	
I20T	2009	6	6	0	135	39	22.50	0	0									4	
20T	2009	23	21	2	323	39	17.00	0	0									10	
KEY, Robert William Trevor (Kent, Kent to Scotland) b East Dulwich, Surrey 12.5.1979 RHB RM																			
FC		16	28	2	814	261	31.30	2	1	92	45	2	22.50	2-31	0	0	2.93	1	
Lim		9	9	0	285	87	31.66	0	1									0	
20T		12	12	1	277	98*	25.18	0	1									4	
Test	2002	15	26	1	775	221	31.00	1	3									11	
FC	1998	226	390	28	15039	270*	41.54	43	56	388	198	3	66.00	2-31	0	0	3.06	127	
Int	2003	5	5	0	54	19	10.80	0	0									0	
Lim	1998	194	187	13	5467	120*	31.41	5	34									38	
I20T	2009	1	1	1	10	10*		0	0									1	
20T	2004	58	58	9	1390	98*	28.36	0	8									15	
KHAN, Amjad (Kent, Kent to Scotland) b Copenhagen, Denmark 14.10.1980 RHB RFM																			
FC		12	18	5	115	24	8.84	0	0	2234	1258	38	33.10	5-43	1	0	3.37	4	
Lim		5	1	1	5	5*		0	0	127	119	3	39.66	3-32	0	0	5.62	2	
20T		4	3	2	6	2*	6.00	0	0	62	104	4	26.00	2-27	0	0	10.06	3	
Test	2008/09	1								174	122	1	122.00	1-111	0	0	4.20	0	
FC	2001	87	102	32	1138	78	16.25	0	4	14652	9151	286	31.99	6-52	8	0	3.74	16	
Lim	1999	62	31	8	281	65*	12.21	0	1	2448	2125	65	32.69	4-26	1	0	5.20	16	
I20T	2008/09	1	1	0	2	2	2.00	0	0	24	34	2	17.00	2-34	0	0	8.50	0	
20T	2004	26	11	4	38	15	5.42	0	0	453	684	30	22.80	3-11	0	0	9.06	6	
KIESWETTER, Craig (England, Somerset, England to Bangladesh, England to Scotland, England to West Indies, England Lions to United Arab Emirates, Somerset to India) b Johannesburg, Transvaal, South Africa 28.11.1987 RHB WK																			
FC		12	18	1	467	84	27.47	0	4									29	
Int		8	8	0	121	38	15.12	0	0									10	1
Lim		18	18	0	517	107	28.72	1	2									19	3
I20T		2	2	0	22	16	11.00	0	0									0	
20T		12	12	0	242	71	20.16	0	1									9	1
FC	2007	59	84	11	2721	153	37.27	4	16									171	2
Int	2009/10	12	12	0	320	107	26.66	1	1									11	2
Lim	2007	69	67	6	2359	143	38.67	6	9									67	15
I20T	2010	9	9	0	244	63	27.11	0	1									4	1
20T	2007	53	52	8	1236	84	28.09	0	7									30	10
KILLEEN, Neil (Durham) b Shotley Bridge, Co Durham 17.10.1975 RHB RMF																			
Lim		2	1	0	6	6	6.00	0	0	72	67	3	22.33	3-24	0	0	5.58	0	
20T		2								36	54	1	54.00	1-35	0	0	9.00	0	
FC	1995	102	145	31	1302	48	11.42	0	0	16499	8215	262	31.35	7-70	9	0	2.98	26	
Lim	1995	226	120	46	700	32	9.45	0	0	10631	7376	304	24.26	6-31	7	5	4.16	39	
20T	2003	45	17	12	88	17*	17.60	0	0	933	1141	47	24.27	4-7	2	0	7.33	9	
KING, Daniel Alexander (Oxford University) b Canberra, Australian Capital Territory, Australia 26.2.1983 LHB WK																			
FC		1	1	0	189	189	189.00	1	0									2	
FC	2009	2	3	0	191	189	63.66	1	0									4	
KING, Simon James (Surrey) b Warlingham, Surrey 4.9.1987 RHB OB																			
FC		1								168	134	1	134.00	1-134	0	0	4.78	0	
FC	2009	3	2	0	8	8	4.00	0	0	405	290	5	58.00	3-61	0	0	4.29	0	
20T	2009	1	1	1	5	5*		0	0	18	28	0					9.33	0	
KIRBY, Steven Paul (England Lions, Gloucestershire, England Lions to United Arab Emirates, Gloucestershire to Netherlands, MCC to United Arab Emirates) b Ainsworth, Bolton, Lancashire 4.10.1977 RHB RFM																			
FC		11	18	6	106	22*	8.83	0	0	1684	912	33	27.63	4-50	0	0	3.24	2	
Lim		10	3	0	12	9	4.00	0	0	432	388	17	22.82	3-41	0	0	5.38	2	
20T		10	6	2	10	3*	2.50	0	0	209	269	13	20.69	3-17	0	0	7.72	3	
FC	2001	130	181	58	1067	57	8.67	0	1	22995	13008	464	28.03	8-80	15	4	3.39	24	
Lim	2001	77	33	12	88	15	4.19	0	0	3201	2971	97	30.62	5-36	3	1	5.56	14	
20T	2004	38	17	4	55	25	4.23	0	0	786	1016	49	20.73	3-17	0	0	7.75	8	
KIRTLEY, Robert James (Sussex, Sussex to India) b Eastbourne, Sussex 10.1.1975 RHB RFM																			
Lim		11	2	2	7	5*		0	0	436	476	24	19.83	4-30	3	0	6.55	2	
20T		16	5	5	21	11*		0	0	313	423	13	32.53	3-3	0	0	8.10	2	
Test	2003	4	7	1	32	12	5.33	0	0	1079	561	19	29.52	6-34	1	0	3.12	3	
FC	1995	170	231	76	2040	59	13.16	0	4	31916	16607	614	27.04	7-21	29	4	3.12	60	
Int	2001/02	11	2	0	2	1	1.00	0	0	549	481	9	53.44	2-33	0	0	5.25	5	
Lim	1995	260	94	50	447	30*	10.15	0	0	11367	9135	395	23.12	6-50	14	9	4.82	71	
I20T	2007/08	1	1	1	2	2*		0	0	6	17	0					17.00	0	
20T	2003	70	21	13	33	11*	4.12	0	0	1252	1674	64	26.15	4-22	1	0	8.02	18	

Cmp	Debut	M	I	NO	Runs	HS	Avge	100	50	Balls	Runs	Wkts	Avge	BB	5i	10m	RpO	ct	st
KNAPPETT, Joshua Philip Thomas (Unicorns) b Westminster, Middlesex 15.4.1985 RHB WK																			
Lim		11	10	0	364	91	36.40	0	4									6	2
FC	2004	13	20	3	523	100*	30.76	1	3									26	3
KRUGER, Neil (Oxford University) b Cape Town, Cape Province, South Africa 15.8.1981 RHB RM																			
FC		1	1	0	48	48	48.00	0	0									2	
FC	2008	3	5	0	381	172	76.20	1	1									4	
LANCEFIELD, Thomas John (Surrey) b Epsom, Surrey 8.10.1990 LHB LM																			
FC		8	13	1	381	74	31.75	0	2	6	9	0					9.00	3	
20T		5	3	0	65	27	21.66	0	0									1	
Lim	2009	1	1	0	20	20	20.00	0	0									1	
LANGER, Justin Lee (Somerset to India) b Perth, Western Australia, Australia 21.11.1970 LHB RM																			
Test	1992/93	105	182	12	7696	250	45.27	23	30	6	3	0					3.00	73	
FC	1991/92	360	622	57	28382	342	50.23	86	110	386	210	5	42.00	2-17	0	0	3.26	324	
Int	1993/94	8	7	2	160	36	32.00	0	0									2	1
Lim	1992/93	239	226	22	7875	146	38.60	14	53	193	215	7	30.71	3-51	0	0	6.68	113	2
20T	2006	41	38	2	1015	97	28.19	0	5									8	
LANGEVELDT, Charl Kenneth (Cape Cobras, South Africa, Cape Cobras to India, Derbyshire, Kolkata Knight Riders, South Africa to India, South Africa to West Indies) b Stellenbosch, Cape Province, South Africa 17.12.1974 RHB RFM																			
20T		12	2	1	9	5*	9.00	0	0	252	309	13	23.76	3-36	0	0	7.35	1	
Test	2004/05	6	4	2	16	10	8.00	0	0	999	593	16	37.06	5-46	1	0	3.56	2	
FC	1997/98	93	116	39	1106	56	14.36	0	1	17559	8670	310	27.96	6-48	9	1	2.96	25	
Int	2001/02	68	20	9	69	12	6.27	0	0	3255	2728	93	29.33	5-39	1	2	5.02	10	
Lim	1997/98	195	77	31	359	33*	7.80	0	0	9121	7033	293	24.00	5-7	7	7	4.62	36	
I20T	2005/06	9	3	2	4	2*	4.00	0	0	198	241	17	14.17	4-19	1	0	7.30	1	
20T	2003/04	58	15	10	36	9*	7.20	0	0	1242	1408	86	16.37	5-16	4	1	6.80	17	
LAWSON, Mark Anthony Kenneth (Kent) b Leeds, Yorkshire 24.10.1985 RHB LB																			
FC		1	1	0	31	31	31.00	0	0	204	164	6	27.33	4-93	0	0	4.82	0	
FC	2004	24	29	8	311	44	14.80	0	0	3261	2279	52	43.82	6-88	4	0	4.19	10	
Lim	2005	12	6	2	37	20	9.25	0	0	469	452	9	50.22	2-36	0	0	5.78	4	
20T	2005	10	2	2	5	4*		0	0	174	252	9	28.00	2-20	0	0	8.69	2	
LEE, Nicholas Trevor (Cambridge MCCU) b Dartford, Kent 16.10.1983 RHB LB																			
FC		3	4	0	111	63	27.75	0	1									0	
FC	2004	13	20	4	490	79*	30.62	0	3	28	24	1	24.00	1-24	0	0	5.14	2	
LEES, Alexander Zak (Yorkshire) b Halifax, Yorkshire 14.4.1993 LHB LB																			
FC		1	1	0	38	38	38.00	0	0									0	
LEWIS, Jonathan (Gloucestershire, Gloucestershire to Netherlands, MCC to United Arab Emirates) b Aylesbury, Buckinghamshire 26.8.1975 RHB RMF																			
FC		16	28	2	419	50	16.11	0	1	2517	1222	54	22.62	4-25	0	0	2.91	7	
Lim		9	6	2	51	22*	12.75	0	0	390	347	13	26.69	3-45	0	0	5.33	2	
20T		13	10	0	78	26	7.80	0	0	270	372	8	46.50	2-26	0	0	8.26	1	
Test	2006	1	2	0	27	20	13.50	0	0	246	122	3	40.66	3-68	0	0	2.97	0	
FC	1995	212	302	61	3666	62	15.21	0	9	38197	19102	733	26.06	8-95	33	5	3.00	53	
Int	2005	13	8	2	50	17	8.33	0	0	716	500	18	27.77	4-36	1	0	4.19	0	
Lim	1995	209	122	44	873	54	11.19	0	1	9628	7287	277	26.30	5-19	10	2	4.54	39	
I20T	2005	2	2	1	1	1	1.00	0	0	42	55	4	13.75	4-24	1	0	7.85	1	
20T	2003	48	31	7	325	43	13.54	0	0	1014	1401	49	28.59	4-24	2	0	8.29	8	
LIDDLE, Christopher John (Sussex) b Middlesbrough, Yorkshire 1.2.1984 RHB LMF																			
Lim		3	1	0	3	3	3.00	0	0	108	126	5	25.20	4-49	1	0	7.00	2	
FC	2005	14	14	5	113	53	12.55	0	1	1706	962	17	56.58	3-42	0	0	3.38	5	
Lim	2006	17	4	0	16	11	4.00	0	0	612	658	15	43.86	4-49	1	0	6.45	8	
20T	2008	5	2	1	10	10*	10.00	0	0	116	165	10	16.50	4-15	2	0	8.53	2	
LINLEY, Timothy Edward (Surrey) b Leeds, Yorkshire 23.3.1982 RHB RFM																			
FC		7	10	4	55	16	9.16	0	0	1020	483	16	30.18	5-105	1	0	2.84	4	
Lim		4	3	2	0	0*	0.00	0	0	132	151	1	151.00	1-51	0	0	6.86	1	
20T		3	1	0	1	1	1.00	0	0	54	62	3	20.66	1-17	0	0	6.88	0	
FC	2003	20	24	5	228	42	12.00	0	0	2676	1461	38	38.44	5-105	1	0	3.27	6	
Lim	2009	12	5	4	37	20*	37.00	0	0	420	404	5	80.80	2-38	0	0	5.77	1	
20T	2009	5	2	0	9	8	4.50	0	0	86	104	3	34.66	1-17	0	0	7.25	1	
LODWICK, Jonathon Andrew (Oxford University) b Reading, Berkshire 14.10.1989 RHB RM																			
FC		1								108	60	0					3.33	1	
LONDON, Adam Brian (Middlesex) b Ashford, Middlesex 12.10.1988 LHB OB																			
FC		4	7	1	137	77	22.83	0	1	48	15	1	15.00	1-15	0	0	1.87	3	
FC	2009	8	15	2	327	77	25.15	0	3	96	54	1	54.00	1-15	0	0	3.37	4	
Lim	2009	2								6	5	0					5.00	0	
LOTAY, Jivan Daulat Singh (Cambridge MCCU) b High Wycombe, Buckinghamshire 25.7.1990 LHB OB																			
FC		2	3	1	43	34*	21.50	0	0	222	146	2	73.00	1-43	0	0	3.94	1	
FC	2009	5	6	1	87	34*	17.40	0	0	493	333	7	47.57	3-147	0	0	4.05	2	
LOWE, Jordan Richard (Yorkshire) b Rotherham, Yorkshire 19.10.1991 RHB WK																			
FC		1	1	0	5	5	5.00	0	0									0	

Cmp	Debut	M	I	NO	Runs	HS	Avge	100	50	Balls	Runs	Wkts	Avge	BB	5i	10m	RpO	ct	st
LOYE, Malachy Bernard (Northamptonshire, Northamptonshire to Netherlands) b Northampton 27.9.1972 RHB OB																			
FC		10	18	1	420	164	24.70	1	1									0	
Lim		7	7	0	208	66	29.71	0	2									0	
20T		3	3	0	115	54	38.33	0	1									1	
FC	1991	256	410	38	14936	322*	40.15	42	61	55	61	1	61.00	1-8	0	0	6.65	119	
Int	2006/07	7	7	0	142	45	20.28	0	0									0	
Lim	1992	299	292	32	8884	127	34.16	10	58									65	
20T	2003	42	41	4	1246	100	33.67	1	8									15	
LUCAS, David Scott (Northamptonshire) b Nottingham 19.8.1978 RHB LMF																			
FC		11	17	2	316	40*	21.06	0	0	1804	1038	32	32.43	5-64	1	0	3.45	1	
Lim		5	3	2	20	11*	20.00	0	0	198	201	5	40.20	1-23	0	0	6.09	4	
20T		2								27	33	0					7.33	1	
FC	1999	75	98	25	1391	55*	19.05	0	1	11359	6614	207	31.95	7-24	8	1	3.49	14	
Lim	1999	65	29	10	205	32*	10.78	0	0	2493	2342	77	30.41	4-27	3	0	5.63	15	
20T	2007	17	5	4	15	5*	15.00	0	0	219	338	8	42.25	2-37	0	0	9.26	2	
LUMB, Michael John (Hampshire, England to West Indies, England Lions to United Arab Emirates, Rajasthan Royals) b Johannesburg, Transvaal, South Africa 12.2.1980 LHB RM																			
FC		5	7	0	381	158	54.42	1	1									4	
Lim		4	4	0	130	75	32.50	0	2									3	
20T		10	10	0	76	21	7.60	0	0									3	
FC	2000	134	224	15	7266	219	34.76	12	45	318	242	6	40.33	2-10	0	0	4.56	92	
Lim	2001	164	158	11	4752	110	32.32	3	37	12	28	0					14.00	56	
I20T	2010	7	7	0	137	33	19.57	0	0									3	
20T	2003	86	86	5	1838	124*	22.69	1	11	36	65	3	21.66	3-32	0	0	10.83	29	
LUNGLEY, Tom (Derbyshire) b Derby 25.7.1979 LHB RM																			
FC		7	10	1	85	21	9.44	0	0	990	630	19	33.15	3-39	0	0	3.81	6	
Lim		5	3	2	12	6*	12.00	0	0	222	214	7	30.57	3-41	0	0	5.78	2	
20T		1								18	34	1	34.00	1-34	0	0	11.33	0	
FC	2000	55	77	16	885	50	14.50	0	1	7421	4784	149	32.10	5-20	3	0	3.86	25	
Lim	2000	81	48	13	396	45	11.31	0	0	3124	2736	89	30.74	4-28	1	0	5.25	21	
20T	2003	30	13	5	107	25	13.37	0	0	475	644	30	21.46	5-27	2	1	8.13	8	
LYTH, Adam (Yorkshire, Yorkshire to Netherlands) b Whitby, Yorkshire 25.9.1987 LHB RM																			
FC		16	29	0	1509	142	52.03	3	9	12	16	0					8.00	9	
Lim		12	11	0	325	91	29.54	0	2									5	
20T		10	10	0	227	59	22.70	0	1									4	
FC	2007	36	59	0	2425	142	41.10	4	16	313	171	3	57.00	1-12	0	0	3.27	21	
Lim	2006	42	36	3	883	109*	26.75	1	3	18	14	0					4.66	14	
20T	2008	19	17	0	244	59	14.35	0	1									6	
McCULLUM, Brendon Barrie (New Zealand, Otago, Kolkata Knight Riders, New Zealand to South Africa, New Zealand to United Arab Emirates, New Zealand to United States of America, New Zealand to West Indies, Otago to India, Sussex) b Dunedin, Otago, New Zealand 27.9.1981 RHB WK																			
20T		7	7	1	200	59*	33.33	0	1									4	
Test	2003/04	52	87	5	2862	185	34.90	5	16									162	11
FC	1999/00	95	163	9	5339	185	34.66	9	30	36	18	0					3.00	267	19
Int	2001/02	171	145	22	3569	166	29.01	2	17									189	13
Lim	2000/01	215	183	26	4617	170	29.40	5	21									232	15
I20T	2004/05	40	40	7	1100	116*	33.33	1	6									25	4
20T	2004/05	98	97	13	2695	158*	32.08	3	14									48	4
McCULLUM, Nathan Leslie (New Zealand, Otago, Lancashire, New Zealand to Sri Lanka, New Zealand to United Arab Emirates, New Zealand to United States of America, New Zealand to West Indies, Otago to India) b Dunedin, Otago, New Zealand 1.9.1980 RHB OB																			
20T		13	11	2	155	32*	17.22	0	0	300	325	11	29.54	3-31	0	0	6.50	5	
FC	1999/00	48	73	6	1804	106*	26.92	1	11	8850	4176	100	41.76	6-90	2	0	2.83	51	
Int	2009	6	5	0	58	36	11.60	0	0	244	185	5	37.00	3-35	0	0	4.54	2	
Lim	2000/01	95	76	13	1204	71	19.11	0	6	4347	3106	79	39.31	3-21	0	0	4.28	40	
I20T	2007/08	22	14	8	160	36*	26.66	0	0	344	370	21	17.61	3-15	0	0	6.45	9	
20T	2005/06	66	54	17	940	76*	25.40	0	3	1218	1426	66	21.60	4-16	1	0	7.02	27	
McDONALD, Andrew Barry (Australia A, Victoria to Australia, Delhi Daredevils, Leicestershire, Victoria to India) b Wodonga, Victoria, Australia 15.6.1981 RHB RFM																			
FC		6	11	1	442	176*	44.20	2	1	618	320	12	26.66	5-40	1	0	3.10	2	
Lim		5	5	0	90	46	18.00	0	0	168	192	3	64.00	1-40	0	0	6.85	4	
20T		3	3	1	174	67	87.00	0	2	60	80	7	11.42	5-13	0	1	8.00	1	
Test	2008/09	4	6	1	107	68	21.40	0	1	732	300	9	33.33	3-25	0	0	2.45	2	
FC	2001/02	69	112	25	3230	176*	37.12	6	18	9785	4602	159	28.94	6-34	4	0	2.82	51	
Lim	2001/02	77	67	21	1475	67	32.06	0	8	3116	2640	68	38.82	4-50	1	0	5.08	31	
20T	2005/06	39	34	14	678	67	33.90	0	2	678	872	45	19.37	5-13	1	1	7.71	12	
McGAIN, Bryce Edward (Victoria to Australia, Essex) b Mornington, Victoria, Australia 25.3.1972 RHB LBG																			
FC		2	4	2	46	24	23.00	0	0	387	260	10	26.00	5-151	1	0	4.03	0	
Lim		1								42	46	0					6.57	1	
Test	2008/09	1	2	0	2	2	1.00	0	0	108	149	0					8.27	0	
FC	2001/02	32	35	13	242	25	11.00	0	0	6129	3467	100	34.67	6-112	5	0	3.39	11	

Cmp	Debut	M	I	NO	Runs	HS	Avge	100	50	Balls	Runs	Wkts	Avge	BB	5i	10m	RpO	ct	st
Lim	2002	23	11	6	97	51	19.40	0	1	1218	964	34	28.35	3-11	0	0	4.74	7	
20T	2007/08	7	2	2	7	6*		0	0	156	168	9	18.66	2-10	0	0	6.46	4	
McGRATH, Anthony (Yorkshire, Yorkshire to Netherlands) b Bradford, Yorkshire 6.10.1975 RHB RM																			
FC		16	29	1	1219	124*	43.53	3	9	444	226	0					3.05	9	
Lim		11	10	3	405	77*	57.85	0	4	131	130	5	26.00	2-24	0	0	5.95	7	
20T		12	10	4	251	73*	41.83	0	1	60	92	3	30.66	2-19	0	0	9.20	7	
Test	2003	4	5	0	201	81	40.20	0	2	102	56	4	14.00	3-16	0	0	3.29	3	
FC	1995	231	389	27	13565	211	37.47	32	66	8436	4234	114	37.14	5-39	1	0	3.01	164	
Int	2003	14	12	2	166	52	16.60	0	1	228	175	4	43.75	1-13	0	0	4.60	4	
Lim	1995	288	266	40	7472	148	33.06	7	44	3095	2610	80	32.62	4-41	2	0	5.06	97	
20T	2004	57	54	12	1311	73*	31.21	0	8	451	656	20	32.80	3-27	0	0	8.72	24	
MACHAN, Matthew William (Sussex) b Brighton, Sussex 15.2.1991 LHB																			
FC		1	2	0	11	6	5.50	0	0									0	
Lim		1	1	0	10	10	10.00	0	0									0	
McKAY, Clinton James (Australia, Victoria, Australia to England, Australia to India, Australia to Ireland, Australia to New Zealand, Victoria to India, Yorkshire) b Melbourne, Victoria, Australia 22.2.1983 RHB RFM																			
Int		1								56	60	0					6.42	0	
Lim		2								116	120	1	120.00	1-60	0	0	6.20	0	
20T		8	6	3	54	21*	18.00	0	0	186	258	10	25.80	4-33	1	0	8.32	1	
Test	2009/10	1	1	0	10	10	10.00	0	0	168	101	1	101.00	1-56	0	0	3.60	1	
FC	2006/07	22	28	2	489	55	18.80	0	2	4508	2015	81	24.87	6-75	2	0	2.68	5	
Int	2009/10	12	3	2	6	4*	6.00	0	0	618	502	22	22.81	4-35	1	0	4.87	0	
Lim	2006/07	36	14	3	143	27	13.00	0	0	1987	1532	59	25.96	4-35	1	0	4.62	5	
20T	2007/08	25	13	6	105	21*	15.00	0	0	561	811	36	22.52	4-33	1	0	8.67	4	
McKENZIE, Neil Douglas (Lions, Hampshire, Hampshire to Scotland) b Johannesburg, Transvaal, South Africa 24.11.1975 RHB RM																			
FC		15	25	5	942	141*	47.10	3	4	192	95	2	47.50	2-30	0	0	2.96	20	
Lim		10	10	2	305	62*	38.12	0	2									3	
20T		17	17	6	440	73	40.00	0	5									7	
Test	2000	58	94	7	3253	226	37.39	5	16	90	68	0					4.53	54	
FC	1994/95	209	353	42	13563	226	43.61	35	66	864	464	9	51.55	2-13	0	0	3.22	184	
Int	1999/00	64	55	10	1688	131*	37.51	2	10	46	27	0					3.52	21	
Lim	1995/96	228	206	31	6365	131*	36.37	8	43	255	248	4	62.00	2-19	0	0	5.83	68	
I20T	2005/06	2	1	1	7	7*		0	0									0	
20T	2003/04	53	52	14	1290	85*	33.94	0	9	12	19	0					9.50	20	
MADDY, Darren Lee (Warwickshire, Warwickshire to Scotland) b Leicester 23.5.1974 RHB RM																			
FC		14	27	1	499	61	19.19	0	2	1241	523	21	24.90	4-37	0	0	2.52	16	
Lim		13	12	4	240	74	30.00	0	1	354	361	10	36.10	3-25	0	0	6.11	5	
20T		17	17	3	456	88	32.57	0	1	108	164	6	27.33	1-5	0	0	9.11	8	
Test	1999	3	4	0	46	24	11.50	0	0	84	40	0					2.85	4	
FC	1994	258	422	28	12807	229*	32.50	26	60	13800	7208	227	31.75	5-37	5	0	3.13	269	
Int	1998	8	6	0	113	53	18.83	0	1									1	
Lim	1993	337	311	34	8546	167*	30.85	11	51	6848	5852	198	29.55	4-16	3	0	5.12	131	
I20T	2007/08	4	4	0	113	50	28.25	0	1	18	26	3	8.66	2-6	0	0	8.66	1	
20T	2003	65	65	8	1874	111	32.87	1	12	671	899	32	28.09	2-6	0	0	8.03	36	
MADSEN, Wayne Lee (Derbyshire, Derbyshire to Netherlands) b Durban, Natal, South Africa 2.1.1984 RHB OB																			
FC		16	29	1	940	179	33.57	4	2	50	68	1	68.00	1-68	0	0	8.16	11	
Lim		9	9	1	402	71*	50.25	0	4									7	
20T		5	4	1	59	29	19.66	0	0									0	
FC	2003/04	49	86	7	3057	179	38.69	8	14	686	372	7	53.14	3-45	0	0	3.25	51	
Lim	2004/05	24	23	5	627	71*	34.83	0	5	102	74	5	14.80	2-18	0	0	4.35	22	
MAHMOOD, Sajid Iqbal (England Lions, Lancashire, England to South Africa, England Lions to United Arab Emirates) b Bolton, Lancashire 21.12.1981 RHB RFM																			
FC		15	20	2	564	72	31.33	0	5	2088	1263	33	38.27	5-55	1	0	3.62	2	
Lim		10	3	1	26	16	13.00	0	0	465	469	14	33.50	4-40	1	0	6.05	2	
20T		15	6	1	84	34	16.80	0	0	318	430	23	18.69	4-21	1	0	8.11	9	
Test	2006	8	11	1	81	34	8.10	0	0	1130	762	20	38.10	4-22	0	0	4.04	0	
FC	2002	96	122	18	1698	94	16.32	0	8	14230	8754	264	33.15	6-30	7	1	3.69	22	
Int	2004	26	15	4	85	22*	7.72	0	0	1197	1169	30	38.96	4-50	1	0	5.86	1	
Lim	2001	137	72	21	435	29	8.52	0	0	6017	5192	192	27.04	5-16	6	1	5.17	18	
I20T	2006	4	2	2	1	1*		0	0	84	155	3	51.66	1-31	0	0	11.07	1	
20T	2003	52	19	6	136	34	10.46	0	0	1103	1428	59	24.20	4-21	2	0	7.76	15	
MALAN, Charl Christiaan (Loughborough MCCU) b Wandsworth, Surrey 23.2.1989 RHB OB																			
FC		1	1	0	11	11	11.00	0	0	60	28	1	28.00	1-28	0	0	2.80	0	
FC	2009	4	4	0	43	24	10.75	0	0	402	178	4	44.50	1-28	0	0	2.65	0	
MALAN, Dawid Johannes (Middlesex, MCC to United Arab Emirates, Middlesex to Netherlands) b Roehampton, Surrey 3.9.1987 LHB LB																			
FC		16	29	3	1001	115	38.50	3	5	445	339	6	56.50	2-51	0	0	4.57	19	
Lim		12	12	1	242	42	22.00	0	0	42	46	0					6.57	5	
20T		16	16	5	364	86	33.09	0	1	36	63	0					10.50	2	
FC	2005/06	46	82	8	2699	132*	36.47	4	18	1642	1141	24	47.54	4-20	0	0	4.16	45	

Cmp	Debut	M	I	NO	Runs	HS	Avge	100	50	Balls	Runs	Wkts	Avge	BB	5i	10m	RpO	ct	st
Lim	2005/06	42	42	4	742	60	19.52	0	2	413	405	10	40.50	2-4	0	0	5.88	13	
20T	2006	43	41	13	916	103	32.71	1	2	240	276	12	23.00	2-10	0	0	6.90	8	
MALIK, Muhammad Nadeem (Leicestershire, Leicestershire to Scotland) b Nottingham 6.10.1982 RHB RMF																			
FC		8	9	3	88	35*	14.66	0	0	1160	599	21	28.52	4-32	0	0	3.09	0	
Lim		3	1	1	8	8*		0	0	113	115	6	19.16	4-40	1	0	6.10	0	
20T		14	3	1	6	3	3.00	0	0	277	371	13	28.53	4-25	1	0	8.03	1	
FC	2001	74	96	33	646	41	10.25	0	0	11730	7066	200	35.33	6-46	7	0	3.61	10	
Lim	2000	73	29	19	105	11	10.50	0	0	2872	2525	73	34.58	4-40	3	0	5.27	10	
20T	2004	38	9	4	12	3*	2.40	0	0	751	1021	41	24.90	4-16	2	0	8.15	3	
MANUEL, Jack Kenneth (Worcestershire) b Sutton Coldfield, Warwickshire 13.2.1991 LHB OB																			
Lim		2	2	0	26	22	13.00	0	0									2	
20T		11	9	1	86	31	10.75	0	0									3	
MARSHALL, Hamish John Hamilton (Northern Districts, Gloucestershire, Gloucestershire to Netherlands) b Warkworth, Auckland, New Zealand 15.2.1979 RHB RM																			
FC		15	27	2	884	89*	35.36	0	7	366	153	0					2.50	15	
Lim		11	10	0	333	85	33.30	0	2	12	15	0					7.50	5	
20T		13	12	2	283	52*	28.30	0	1	6	14	0					14.00	7	
Test	2000/01	13	19	2	652	160	38.35	2	2	6	4	0					4.00	1	
FC	1998/99	153	260	17	8709	170	35.83	18	43	2874	1483	30	49.43	4-24	0	0	3.09	88	
Int	2003/04	66	62	9	1454	101*	27.43	1	12									18	
Lim	1998/99	239	227	24	5770	122	28.42	6	38	248	258	4	64.50	2-21	0	0	6.24	90	
I20T	2004/05	3	3	0	12	8	4.00	0	0									1	
20T	2004/05	49	48	3	1080	100	24.00	1	3	6	14	0					14.00	26	
MARTIN, Christopher Stewart (Canterbury, New Zealand, Essex) b Christchurch, Canterbury, New Zealand 10.12.1974 RHB RFM																			
FC		1	2	1	11	11	11.00	0	0	150	84	1	84.00	1-84	0	0	3.36	0	
Lim		2	1	0	0	0	0.00	0	0	78	82	1	82.00	1-24	0	0	6.30	1	
Test	2000/01	56	81	42	89	12*	2.28	0	0	11069	6341	181	35.03	6-54	8	1	3.43	12	
FC	1997/98	155	192	95	389	25	4.01	0	0	29770	15434	477	32.35	6-54	18	1	3.11	30	
Int	2000/01	20	7	2	8	3	1.60	0	0	948	804	18	44.66	3-62	0	0	5.08	7	
Lim	1998/99	126	51	24	79	13	2.92	0	0	6183	4980	169	29.46	6-24	6	2	4.83	25	
I20T	2007/08	6	1	1	5	5*		0	0	138	193	7	27.57	2-14	0	0	8.39	1	
20T	2005/06	49	5	5	16	5*		0	0	1084	1352	43	31.44	3-33	0	0	7.48	10	
MARTIN, Jak (Oxford MCCU) b Kingston-upon-Thames, Surrey 7.9.1988 LHB RM																			
FC		3	5	0	195	81	39.00	0	2									2	
FC	2009	6	9	0	290	81	32.22	0	2									3	
MARTIN-JENKINS, Robin Simon Christopher (Sussex, Sussex to India) b Guildford, Surrey 28.10.1975 RHB RFM																			
FC		9	13	3	629	130	62.90	2	5	1207	593	30	19.76	5-45	1	0	2.94	4	
Lim		6	5	3	92	35*	46.00	0	0	216	196	3	65.33	1-17	0	0	5.44	2	
20T		7	2	1	12	11	12.00	0	0	144	200	4	50.00	1-16	0	0	8.33	4	
FC	1995	184	276	41	7448	205*	31.69	5	41	24758	12253	384	31.90	7-51	8	0	2.96	55	
Lim	1995	229	169	38	2014	68*	15.37	0	3	9902	7115	234	30.40	4-22	6	0	4.31	49	
20T	2003	47	26	8	237	56*	13.16	0	1	919	1153	34	33.91	4-20	1	0	7.52	15	
MASCARENHAS, Adrian Dimitri (Hampshire, Otago to India, Rajasthan Royals) b Chiswick, Middlesex 30.10.1977 RHB RMF																			
20T		1								18	21	1	21.00	1-21	0	0	7.00	0	
FC	1996	181	271	30	6185	131	25.66	8	22	26181	11818	418	28.27	6-25	16	0	2.70	72	
Int	2007	20	13	2	245	52	22.27	0	1	822	634	13	48.76	3-23	0	0	4.62	4	
Lim	1996	244	205	43	4107	79	25.35	0	27	10389	7376	281	26.24	5-27	9	1	4.26	62	
I20T	2007	14	13	5	123	31	15.37	0	0	252	309	12	25.75	3-18	0	0	7.35	7	
20T	2003	66	63	19	960	57*	21.81	0	3	1327	1587	81	19.59	5-14	1	1	7.17	20	
MASON, Matthew Sean (Worcestershire) b Claremont, Western Australia, Australia 20.3.1974 RHB RFM																			
FC		8	12	2	137	51*	13.70	0	1	1668	849	31	27.38	4-87	0	0	3.05	6	
Lim		1								48	38	3	12.66	3-38	0	0	4.75	0	
20T		1	1	0	0	0	0.00	0	0	7	1	0					0.85	1	
FC	1996/97	98	127	31	1320	63	13.75	0	4	18045	8410	311	27.04	8-45	10	1	2.79	27	
Lim	1996/97	81	38	15	171	25	7.43	0	0	3684	2646	94	28.14	4-34	2	0	4.30	16	
20T	2003	11	5	2	18	8*	6.00	0	0	227	291	9	32.33	3-42	0	0	7.69	3	
MASTERS, Daniel (Leicestershire) b Chatham, Kent 7.12.1986 RHB RFM																			
Lim		2	1	0	2	2	2.00	0	0	54	73	1	73.00	1-46	0	0	8.11	0	
Lim	2009	3	1	0	2	2	2.00	0	0	100	122	2	61.00	1-46	0	0	7.32	0	
MASTERS, David Daniel (Essex, Essex to Netherlands) b Chatham, Kent 22.4.1978 RHB RMF																			
FC		14	22	1	356	50	16.95	0	1	2922	1223	53	23.07	5-43	1	0	2.51	8	
Lim		10	3	0	18	16	6.00	0	0	468	361	15	24.06	4-41	1	0	4.62	1	
20T		16	6	4	11	10*	5.50	0	0	319	418	12	34.83	2-18	0	0	7.86	2	
FC	2000	132	165	27	2039	119	14.77	1	5	23560	10892	376	28.96	6-24	12	0	2.77	45	
Lim	2000	131	65	27	467	39	12.28	0	0	5463	4062	126	32.23	5-17	2	2	4.46	14	
20T	2003	70	24	10	77	14	5.50	0	0	1326	1663	57	29.17	3-7	0	0	7.52	16	
MAUNDERS, John Kenneth (Essex) b Ashford, Middlesex 4.4.1981 LHB RM																			
FC		7	12	0	307	126	25.58	1	1									6	
20T		5	4	1	49	25*	16.33	0	0									3	

Cmp	Debut	M	I	NO	Runs	HS	Avge	100	50	Balls	Runs	Wkts	Avge	BB	5i	10m	RpO	ct	st
FC	1999	90	159	3	4689	180	30.05	8	23	1525	928	24	38.66	4-15	0	0	3.65	56	
Lim	2001	36	33	3	748	109*	24.93	1	2	139	103	4	25.75	2-16	0	0	4.44	9	
20T	2005	19	11	4	73	25*	10.42	0	0	12	14	2	7.00	2-14	0	0	7.00	5	
MAYNARD, Thomas Lloyd (Glamorgan) b Cardiff, Glamorgan, Wales 25.3.1989 RHB OB																			
FC		11	18	0	495	98	27.50	0	4	18	20	0					6.66	11	
Lim		11	10	1	285	103*	31.66	1	1	12	32	0					16.00	5	
20T		16	16	3	380	78*	29.23	0	3									5	
FC	2007	24	35	1	727	98	21.38	0	5	30	38	0					7.60	22	
Lim	2007	41	39	3	1109	108	30.80	2	7	12	32	0					16.00	14	
20T	2007	29	28	4	517	78*	21.54	0	3									13	
MEADOWS, Nicholas Axel (Oxford University) b Brisbane, Queensland, Australia 26.9.1980 RHB OB																			
FC		1	1	0	38	38	38.00	0	0									4	
MEAKER, Stuart Christopher (Surrey) b Durban, Natal, South Africa 21.1.1989 RHB RMF																			
FC		11	14	1	175	94	13.46	0	1	1618	998	29	34.41	5-48	2	0	3.70	3	
Lim		4	2	0	2	2	1.00	0	0	144	152	2	76.00	1-34	0	0	6.33	0	
20T		3	1	1	10	10*		0	0	60	88	3	29.33	2-36	0	0	8.80	1	
FC	2008	18	25	2	411	94	17.86	0	3	2493	1635	43	38.02	5-48	2	0	3.93	3	
Lim	2008	15	4	2	16	10*	8.00	0	0	492	524	11	47.63	2-21	0	0	6.39	3	
MEES, Thomas (Unicorns) b Wolverhampton, Staffordshire 8.6.1981 RHB RMF																			
Lim		4	2	1	2	2*	2.00	0	0	143	167	2	83.50	2-47	0	0	7.00	2	
FC	2001	9	12	2	110	36*	11.00	0	0	1491	966	20	48.30	6-64	1	0	3.88	1	
Lim	1999	8	4	2	6	4*	3.00	0	0	341	311	5	62.20	3-19	0	0	5.47	2	
MICKLEBURGH, Jaik Charles (Essex, Essex to Netherlands) b Norwich, Norfolk 30.3.1990 RHB RM																			
FC		16	30	0	852	174	28.40	1	3	7	11	0					9.42	11	
Lim		3	3	0	38	34	12.66	0	0									2	
20T		10	5	2	76	32	25.33	0	0									7	
FC	2008	25	46	0	1287	174	27.97	1	7	78	50	0					3.84	17	
Lim	2010	4	4	0	84	46	21.00	0	0									2	
MIDDLEBROOK, James Daniel (Northamptonshire, MCC to United Arab Emirates) b Leeds, Yorkshire 13.5.1977 RHB OB																			
FC		12	21	3	459	84	25.50	0	3	1508	863	18	47.94	3-23	0	0	3.43	6	
Lim		11	10	5	150	57*	30.00	0	1	444	366	10	36.60	3-34	0	0	4.94	4	
20T		18	7	4	34	14*	11.33	0	0	330	356	13	27.38	2-12	0	0	6.47	6	
FC	1998	156	225	32	4884	127	25.30	4	19	25318	13313	341	39.04	6-82	8	1	3.15	78	
Lim	1998	157	105	33	1406	57*	19.52	0	1	5497	4264	122	34.95	4-27	2	0	4.65	46	
20T	2004	65	43	13	387	43	12.90	0	0	834	1062	28	37.92	3-13	0	0	7.64	16	
MILES, Jonathan Samuel (Unicorns) b Sutton Coldfield, Warwickshire 21.2.1986 RHB LM																			
Lim		11	3	3	9	5*		0	0	396	444	10	44.40	3-49	0	0	6.72	2	
Lim	2008	12	4	3	15	6	15.00	0	0	450	488	12	40.66	3-49	0	0	6.50	2	
MILLER, Andrew Stephen (Warwickshire) b Preston, Lancashire 27.9.1987 RHB RFM																			
FC		7	12	5	65	35	9.28	0	0	928	488	16	30.50	5-58	2	0	3.15	4	
FC	2008	11	16	7	70	35	7.77	0	0	1546	782	27	28.96	5-58	2	0	3.03	4	
MILLIGAN, Marc John (Oxford MCCU) b Pretoria, Transvaal, South Africa 1.8.1987 RHB RFM																			
FC		3	2	0	7	4	3.50	0	0	312	205	1	205.00	1-49	0	0	3.94	2	
FC	2009	5	3	0	9	4	3.00	0	0	450	280	2	140.00	1-17	0	0	3.73	2	
MITCHELL, Daryl Keith Henry (Worcestershire) b Badsey, Worcestershire 25.11.1983 RHB RM																			
FC		16	31	3	1180	165*	42.14	4	4	90	64	0					4.26	32	
Lim		12	12	3	283	70	31.44	0	1	216	187	4	46.75	2-30	0	0	5.19	6	
20T		16	12	1	215	39	19.54	0	0	152	210	5	42.00	1-15	0	0	8.28	6	
FC	2005	64	117	16	4002	298	39.62	9	18	1155	596	16	37.25	4-49	0	0	3.09	75	
Lim	2005	54	43	10	1030	92	31.21	0	7	1127	1102	28	39.35	4-42	1	0	5.86	18	
20T	2005	52	32	9	408	39	17.73	0	0	791	1056	36	29.33	4-11	1	0	8.01	17	
MONTGOMERY, Gary Stephen (Lancashire) b Leamington Spa, Warwickshire 8.10.1982																			
Lim		3	1	1	0	0*		0	0	102	127	1	127.00	1-61	0	0	7.47	1	
MOORE, Stephen Colin (Lancashire) b Johannesburg, Transvaal, South Africa 4.11.1980 RHB RM																			
FC		9	17	0	426	61	25.05	0	2									6	
Lim		8	8	1	337	118	48.14	2	1									2	
20T		17	16	3	331	83*	25.46	0	3									9	
FC	2003	112	204	16	7288	246	38.76	15	35	342	321	5	64.20	1-13	0	0	5.63	55	
Lim	2003	103	99	10	2536	118	28.49	4	13	41	53	1	53.00	1-1	0	0	7.75	28	
20T	2003	63	57	8	1231	83*	25.12	0	6									21	
MORGAN, Charlie Felix Derrington (Durham MCCU) b Leicester 9.7.1989 RHB WK																			
FC		2	1	0	16	16	16.00	0	0									4	1
FC	2008	5	6	0	61	38	10.16	0	0									5	1
MORGAN, Eoin Joseph Gerard (England, Middlesex, England to Bangladesh, England to South Africa, England to Scotland, England to United Arab Emirates, England to West Indies, Royal Challengers Bangalore) b Dublin, Ireland 10.9.1986 LHB RM																			
Test		6	8	0	256	130	32.00	1	0									4	
FC		7	10	1	372	130	41.33	1	2									4	
Int		13	13	2	488	107*	44.36	2	2									7	
Lim		13	13	2	488	107*	44.36	2	2									7	
I20T		2	2	2	56	38*		0	0									2	
20T		6	6	4	204	79*	102.00	0	1									3	

Cmp	Debut	M	I	NO	Runs	HS	Avge	100	50	Balls	Runs	Wkts	Avge	BB	5i	10m	RpO	ct	st
FC	2004	55	91	12	2930	209*	37.08	7	13	79	46	2	23.00	2-24	0	0	3.49	47	1
Int	2006	55	55	11	1798	115	40.86	4	10									24	
Lim	2003	135	128	21	4049	161	37.84	7	23	42	49	0					7.00	45	
I20T	2009	14	14	6	416	85*	52.00	0	3									8	
20T	2006	64	60	11	1343	85*	27.40	0	6									29	
MORKEL, Johannes Albertus (South Africa, Titans, Chennai Super Kings, Durham, South Africa to India, South Africa to West Indies) b Vereeniging, Transvaal, South Africa 10.6.1981 LHB RMF																			
20T		15	11	3	272	48	34.00	0	0	200	297	7	42.42	2-25	0	0	8.91	1	
Test	2008/09	1	1	0	58	58	58.00	0	1	192	132	1	132.00	1-44	0	0	4.12	0	
FC	1999/00	65	93	15	3296	204*	42.25	5	20	9779	5049	169	29.87	6-36	4	0	3.09	27	
Int	2003/04	47	34	8	621	97	23.88	0	2	1816	1629	48	33.93	4-29	2	0	5.38	12	
Lim	1999/00	158	121	32	2434	97	27.34	0	11	6174	5081	170	29.88	4-23	4	0	4.93	35	
I20T	2005/06	29	25	6	443	43	23.31	0	0	406	549	16	34.31	2-12	0	0	8.11	12	
20T	2003/04	127	104	31	1867	71	25.57	0	4	2137	2888	100	28.88	4-30	2	0	8.10	24	
MUCHALL, Gordon James (Durham, Durham to Scotland) b Newcastle upon Tyne, Northumberland 2.11.1982 RHB RM																			
FC		10	15	1	520	140*	37.14	2	1	6	2	0					2.00	3	
Lim		10	10	2	310	77	38.75	0	1									9	
20T		4	3	0	30	16	10.00	0	0									1	
FC	2002	115	200	10	5576	219	29.34	10	26	896	617	15	41.13	3-26	0	0	4.13	77	
Lim	2001	97	88	14	2153	101*	29.09	1	10	168	144	1	144.00	1-15	0	0	5.14	37	
20T	2003	40	34	8	706	64*	27.15	0	2	12	8	1	8.00	1-8	0	0	4.00	16	
MUCHALL, Paul Bernard (Kent) b Newcastle upon Tyne, Northumberland 17.3.1987 RHB RM																			
Lim		1	1	0	22	22	22.00	0	0	24	34	1	34.00	1-34	0	0	8.50	0	
MULLANEY, Steven John (Nottinghamshire, Nottinghamshire to Scotland) b Warrington, Cheshire 19.11.1986 RHB RM																			
FC		11	17	4	512	100*	39.38	1	3	562	321	9	35.66	4-31	0	0	3.42	6	
Lim		10	9	1	147	41	18.37	0	0	288	259	11	23.54	3-24	0	0	5.39	7	
20T		18	13	5	145	53	18.12	0	1	324	393	14	28.07	3-12	0	0	7.27	7	
FC	2006	15	22	5	769	165*	45.23	2	3	723	405	10	40.50	4-31	0	0	3.36	9	
Lim	2006	19	14	2	206	41	17.16	0	0	500	438	23	19.04	3-13	0	0	5.25	11	
20T	2006	21	14	5	150	53	16.66	0	1	342	414	15	27.60	3-12	0	0	7.26	8	
MUNDAY, Michael Kenneth (Somerset) b Nottingham 22.10.1984 RHB LB																			
FC		3	3	1	0	0*	0.00	0	0	313	238	6	39.66	4-105	0	0	4.56	1	
FC	2003	31	28	11	107	21	6.29	0	0	3795	2534	86	29.46	8-55	4	2	4.00	12	
Lim	2001	1								30	39	1	39.00	1-39	0	0	7.80	0	
MURPHY, David (Loughborough MCCU, Northamptonshire, Northamptonshire to Netherlands) b Welwyn Garden City, Hertfordshire 24.6.1989 RHB WK																			
FC		11	18	7	421	76	38.27	0	4									30	
Lim		7	5	4	69	31*	69.00	0	0									6	2
20T		7	1	0	0	0	0.00	0	0									4	
FC	2009	16	24	8	522	76	32.62	0	5									41	1
Lim	2010	8	5	4	69	31*	69.00	0	0									7	3
MURTAGH, Christopher Paul (Unicorns) b Lambeth, Surrey 14.10.1984 RHB OB																			
Lim		10	9	0	121	31	13.44	0	0									2	
FC	2005	14	20	3	316	107	18.58	1	0	6	8	0					8.00	9	
Lim	2005	17	15	2	243	74	18.69	0	1									6	
20T	2008	4	4	1	33	28	11.00	0	0									4	
MURTAGH, Timothy James (Middlesex, MCC to United Arab Emirates, Middlesex to Netherlands) b Lambeth, Surrey 2.8.1981 LHB RFM																			
FC		15	23	10	241	50*	18.53	0	1	2756	1405	38	36.97	5-52	2	0	3.05	4	
Lim		10	7	3	41	20	10.25	0	0	470	435	14	31.07	3-35	0	0	5.55	1	
20T		15	2	0	6	6	3.00	0	0	290	393	16	24.56	3-24	0	0	8.13	5	
FC	2000	98	139	43	2168	74*	22.58	0	9	15061	8641	280	30.86	7-82	12	1	3.44	29	
Lim	2000	115	76	27	595	35*	12.14	0	0	5112	4418	165	26.77	4-14	4	0	5.18	31	
20T	2003	66	28	10	182	40*	10.11	0	0	1329	1857	78	23.80	6-24	0	1	8.38	14	
MUSTARD, Philip (Durham, Durham to Scotland, Durham to United Arab Emirates) b Sunderland, Co Durham 8.10.1982 LHB WK																			
FC		16	24	5	742	120	39.05	2	4									40	2
Lim		10	10	0	292	90	29.20	0	3									8	6
20T		15	13	1	284	70*	23.66	0	2									11	3
FC	2002	118	182	20	4771	130	29.45	4	27									389	15
Int	2007/08	10	10	0	233	83	23.30	0	1									9	2
Lim	2000	128	114	6	3135	108	29.02	2	22									129	31
I20T	2007/08	2	2	0	60	40	30.00	0	0									0	
20T	2003	67	65	3	1431	70*	23.08	0	8									30	17
NAIK, Jigar Kumar Hakumatrai (Leicestershire, Leicestershire to Scotland) b Leicester 10.8.1984 RHB OB																			
FC		8	12	3	301	72	33.44	0	1	1230	619	35	17.68	7-96	1	0	3.02	5	
Lim		7	6	2	21	8*	5.25	0	0	259	245	5	49.00	1-35	0	0	5.67	2	
20T		1	1	0	1	1	1.00	0	0	18	27	0					9.00	0	
FC	2006	21	29	9	561	109*	28.05	1	1	2687	1500	51	29.41	7-96	1	0	3.34	11	
Lim	2002	21	15	6	85	18	9.44	0	0	809	694	19	36.52	3-21	0	0	5.14	3	
20T	2008	12	5	3	14	7*	7.00	0	0	180	230	4	57.50	2-22	0	0	7.66	2	

Cmp	Debut	M	I	NO	Runs	HS	Avge	100	50	Balls	Runs	Wkts	Avge	BB	5i	10m	RpO	ct	st
NANNES, Dirk Peter (Australia, Victoria, Australia to England, Australia to New Zealand, Australia to West Indies, Delhi Daredevils, Nottinghamshire) b Mount Waverly, Melbourne, Victoria, Australia 16.5.1976 RHB LFM																			
I20T		2	2	2	12	12*		0	0	48	71	5	14.20	3-30	0	0	8.87	1	
20T		18	4	4	13	12*		0	0	401	537	22	24.40	3-30	0	0	8.03	2	
FC	2005/06	23	24	8	108	31*	6.75	0	0	4139	2327	93	25.02	7-50	2	1	3.37	7	
Int	2009	1	1	0	1	1	1.00	0	0	42	20	1	20.00	1-20	0	0	2.85	0	
Lim	2005/06	23	10	5	18	5*	3.60	0	0	1224	965	31	31.12	4-38	1	0	4.73	0	
I20T	2009	16	5	3	22	12*	11.00	0	0	348	431	27	15.96	4-18	1	0	7.43	1	
20T	2007/08	87	12	9	33	12*	11.00	0	0	1947	2307	120	19.22	4-11	5	0	7.10	13	
NAPIER, Graham Richard (Essex, Central Districts, Essex to Netherlands) b Colchester, Essex 6.1.1980 RHB RM																			
FC		4	6	1	67	35	13.40	0	0	570	280	3	93.33	1-47	0	0	2.94	1	
Lim		2	1	0	6	6	6.00	0	0	96	103	5	20.60	3-54	0	0	6.43	1	
20T		1	1	0	12	12	12.00	0	0	22	40	2	20.00	2-40	0	0	10.90	0	
FC	1997	103	142	30	3350	125	29.91	3	20	13257	8134	210	38.73	6-103	3	0	3.68	39	
Lim	1997	196	151	19	2370	79	17.95	0	12	6600	5593	225	24.85	6-29	8	1	5.08	41	
20T	2003	67	49	7	697	152*	16.59	1	0	1419	1720	90	19.11	4-10	1	0	7.27	20	
NASH, Christopher David (Sussex, Sussex to India) b Cuckfield, Sussex 19.5.1983 RHB OB																			
FC		17	29	2	1051	184	38.92	3	1	336	126	8	15.75	4-12	0	0	2.25	12	
Lim		11	11	0	457	85	41.54	0	5	66	79	3	26.33	1-8	0	0	7.18	3	
20T		17	15	3	299	60*	24.91	0	1	198	226	13	17.38	2-17	0	0	6.84	3	
FC	2002	79	134	11	4734	184	38.48	9	24	1938	1167	27	43.22	4-12	0	0	3.61	32	
Lim	2006	50	47	0	1292	85	27.48	0	8	446	419	16	26.18	4-40	1	0	5.63	11	
20T	2006	49	45	8	834	60*	22.54	0	3	216	248	13	19.07	2-17	0	0	6.88	13	
NAVED-UL-HASAN, Rana (Sialkot Stallions, WAPDA, Pakistan to Australia, Pakistan to South Africa, Sussex, Tasmania) b Sheikhupura, Punjab, Pakistan 28.2.1978 RHB RFM																			
FC		5	8	2	208	101	34.66	1	1	976	532	20	26.60	4-28	0	0	3.27	0	
Lim		4	3	0	50	26	16.66	0	0	174	152	7	21.71	3-37	0	0	5.24	0	
Test	2004/05	9	15	3	239	42*	19.91	0	0	1565	1044	18	58.00	3-30	0	0	4.00	3	
FC	1995/96	122	174	20	3560	139	23.11	5	10	22636	12761	523	24.39	7-49	27	4	3.38	56	
Int	2002/03	74	51	18	524	33	15.87	0	0	3466	3221	110	29.28	6-27	6	1	5.57	16	
Lim	1999/00	170	130	34	2094	74	21.81	0	10	8032	7024	261	26.91	6-27	10	3	5.24	46	
I20T	2006	4	2	1	18	17*	18.00	0	0	85	101	5	20.20	3-19	0	0	7.12	2	
20T	2004/05	47	36	12	545	95	22.70	0	1	978	1122	52	21.57	4-23	1	0	6.88	21	
NEEDHAM, Jake (Derbyshire) b Portsmouth, Hampshire 30.9.1986 RHB OB																			
Lim		7	4	0	10	5	2.50	0	0	294	225	9	25.00	3-36	0	0	4.59	0	
FC	2005	19	31	12	384	48	20.21	0	0	2263	1268	35	36.22	6-49	1	0	3.36	10	
Lim	2005	41	28	11	223	42	13.11	0	0	1365	1176	26	45.23	3-36	0	0	5.16	13	
20T	2007	14	5	3	16	7*	8.00	0	0	159	212	8	26.50	4-21	1	0	8.00	4	
NEL, Andre (Lions, Surrey) b Germiston, Transvaal, South Africa 15.7.1977 RHB RFM																			
FC		7	10	0	219	96	21.90	0	1	1362	671	21	31.95	4-68	0	0	2.95	4	
Lim		3	2	1	4	3	4.00	0	0	144	140	7	20.00	3-29	0	0	5.83	1	
20T		14	8	4	30	9	7.50	0	0	312	381	7	54.42	2-30	0	0	7.32	1	
Test	2001/02	36	42	8	337	34	9.91	0	0	7630	3919	123	31.86	6-32	3	1	3.08	16	
FC	1996/97	132	153	43	1692	96	15.38	0	4	25915	12212	446	27.38	6-25	14	1	2.82	53	
Int	2000/01	79	22	12	127	30*	12.70	0	0	3801	2935	106	27.68	5-45	3	1	4.63	21	
Lim	1997/98	214	85	44	482	58	11.75	0	1	10454	7627	295	25.85	6-27	7	4	4.37	49	
I20T	2005/06	2	1	1	0	0*		0	0	48	42	2	21.00	2-19	0	0	5.25	1	
20T	2003	46	26	11	140	19	9.33	0	0	1038	1139	31	36.74	2-13	0	0	6.58	10	
NEL, Johann Dewald (Scotland, Kent, Scotland to Kenya, Scotland to United Arab Emirates) b Klerksdorp, Transvaal, South Africa 6.6.1980 RHB RMF																			
FC		3	2	0	6	4	3.00	0	0	324	190	10	19.00	6-62	1	0	3.51	2	
Lim		4	1	1	2	2*		0	0	113	137	3	45.66	1-20	0	0	7.27	1	
FC	2004	18	23	10	154	36	11.84	0	0	2424	1374	51	26.94	6-62	2	0	3.40	6	
Int	2006	19	10	8	31	11*	15.50	0	0	730	649	14	46.35	4-25	1	0	5.33	3	
Lim	2004	84	49	28	202	36*	9.61	0	0	3398	2969	83	35.77	4-25	1	0	5.24	15	
I20T	2007/08	10	5	2	34	13*	11.33	0	0	186	169	12	14.08	3-10	0	0	5.45	1	
20T	2007	15	5	2	34	13*	11.33	0	0	289	278	17	16.35	3-10	0	0	5.77	1	
NEW, Thomas James (Leicestershire, Leicestershire to Scotland) b Sutton-in-Ashfield, Nottinghamshire 18.1.1985 LHB WK																			
FC		17	27	4	746	91	32.43	0	6									46	1
Lim		9	7	2	166	47*	33.20	0	0									11	3
FC	2004	85	141	18	3926	125	31.91	2	29	229	211	5	42.20	2-18	0	0	5.52	141	7
Lim	2001	54	48	6	1114	68	26.52	0	4									26	7
20T	2008	1	1	0	18	18	18.00	0	0									1	1
NEWBY, Oliver James (Lancashire) b Blackburn, Lancashire 26.8.1984 RHB RFM																			
Lim		1	1	0	0	0	0.00	0	0	48	45	1	45.00	1-45	0	0	5.62	0	
FC	2003	43	37	8	238	38*	8.20	0	0	5509	3505	105	33.38	5-69	1	0	3.81	8	
Lim	2002	18	13	7	36	12*	6.00	0	0	692	677	16	42.31	4-41	1	0	5.87	3	
20T	2003	10	4	2	14	6*	7.00	0	0	162	216	6	36.00	2-34	0	0	8.00	3	

Cmp	Debut	M	I	NO	Runs	HS	Avge	100	50	Balls	Runs	Wkts	Avge	BB	5i	10m	RpO	ct	st
NEWMAN, Scott Alexander (Middlesex, MCC to United Arab Emirates, Middlesex to Netherlands) b Epsom, Surrey 3.11.1979 LHB RM																			
FC		15	27	0	945	126	35.00	2	6									8	
Lim		11	11	1	290	90	29.00	0	3									3	
20T		10	9	0	183	48	20.33	0	0									4	
FC	2002	116	199	3	7721	219	39.39	16	46	78	57	0					4.38	85	
Lim	2001	94	92	4	2692	177	30.59	4	16									22	
20T	2003	49	46	4	923	81*	21.97	0	4									18	
NEWTON, Daniel Charles Alexander (Durham MCCU) b Westminster, Middlesex 14.12.1990 RHB RM																			
FC		1	1	0	0	0	0.00	0	0									0	
NEWTON, Robert Irving (Northamptonshire, Northamptonshire to Netherlands) b Taunton, Somerset 18.1.1990 RHB LB																			
FC		6	11	0	357	102	32.45	1	2	13	19	0					8.76	1	
Lim		6	6	0	175	66	29.16	0	1									1	
20T		1	1	0	7	7	7.00	0	0									0	
Lim	2009	8	8	0	203	66	25.37	0	1									1	
NIXON, Paul Andrew (Leicestershire) b Carlisle, Cumberland 21.10.1970 LHB WK																			
FC		16	27	1	915	106	35.19	1	7	13	7	1	7.00	1-7	0	0	3.23	4	
Lim		5	5	1	166	40	41.50	0	0									2	
20T		15	14	3	214	44*	19.45	0	0									7	6
FC	1989	351	526	111	14401	173*	34.70	21	72	125	157	1	157.00	1-7	0	0	7.53	889	67
Int	2006/07	19	18	4	297	49	21.21	0	0									20	3
Lim	1989	406	349	72	7300	101	26.35	1	33	3	1	0					2.00	419	99
I20T	2006/07	1	1	1	31	31*		0	0									0	1
20T	2003	75	70	14	1309	65	23.37	0	4									40	19
NORTHEAST, Sam Alexander (Kent) b Ashford, Kent 16.10.1989 RHB OB																			
FC		17	30	0	719	71	23.96	0	4	36	8	0					1.33	6	
Lim		4	2	0	15	9	7.50	0	0									3	
20T		4	4	2	48	21	24.00	0	0									1	
FC	2007	29	51	2	1391	128*	28.38	1	7	42	10	0					1.42	16	
Lim	2007	11	8	0	159	69	19.87	0	1									4	
NTINI, Makhaya (South Africa, Warriors to South Africa, Kent, Kent to Scotland) b Mdingi, nr King William's Town, Cape Province, South Africa 6.7.1977 RHB RF																			
FC		5	8	3	25	13	5.00	0	0	984	474	24	19.75	6-51	2	1	2.89	0	
Lim		3	1	1	3	3*		0	0	90	61	2	30.50	1-28	0	0	4.06	0	
Test	1997/98	101	116	45	699	32*	9.84	0	0	20834	11242	390	28.82	7-37	18	4	3.23	25	
FC	1995/96	186	217	82	1274	34*	9.43	0	0	34468	18586	648	28.68	7-37	27	5	3.23	40	
Int	1997/98	173	47	24	199	42*	8.65	0	0	8687	6559	266	24.65	6-22	8	4	4.53	30	
Lim	1995/96	246	73	33	284	42*	7.10	0	0	11848	8878	357	24.86	6-22	9	6	4.49	45	
I20T	2005/06	9	3	1	9	5	4.50	0	0	168	252	6	42.00	2-22	0	0	9.00	1	
20T	2003/04	34	9	4	27	11	5.40	0	0	750	910	32	28.43	4-21	1	0	7.28	2	
O'BRIEN, Iain Edward (New Zealand, Wellington to New Zealand, Middlesex) b Lower Hutt, Wellington, New Zealand 10.7.1976 RHB RM																			
FC		7	9	1	39	14*	4.87	0	0	1231	628	23	27.30	7-48	1	0	3.06	1	
Lim		1								40	41	4	10.25	4-41	1	0	6.15	0	
20T		1	1	1	1	1*		0	0	14	27	0					11.57	0	
Test	2004/05	22	34	5	219	31	7.55	0	0	4394	2429	73	33.27	6-75	1	0	3.31	7	
FC	2000/01	91	113	26	756	44	8.68	0	0	16845	8392	322	26.06	8-55	14	1	2.98	17	
Int	2007/08	10	2	2	3	3*		0	0	453	488	14	34.85	3-68	0	0	6.46	1	
Lim	2003/04	58	21	17	99	19*	24.75	0	0	2818	2332	75	31.09	5-35	2	2	4.96	9	
I20T	2008/09	4								78	116	6	19.33	2-30	0	0	8.92	0	
20T	2006/07	18	5	4	6	3*	6.00	0	0	332	438	21	20.85	5-23	0	1	7.91	3	
O'BRIEN, Niall John (Ireland, Ireland to Sri Lanka, Ireland to United Arab Emirates, Ireland to West Indies, Northamptonshire) b Dublin, Ireland 8.11.1981 LHB WK																			
FC		3	6	0	216	49	36.00	0	0									7	1
Lim		2	2	0	55	52	27.50	0	1									3	
20T		11	10	0	215	37	21.50	0	0									9	4
FC	2004	83	126	14	3971	176	35.45	9	16	12	16	2	8.00	1-4	0	0	8.00	240	26
Int	2006	37	37	3	911	72	26.79	0	7									28	6
Lim	2002	112	91	11	2174	95	27.17	0	15									93	30
I20T	2008	16	15	1	260	50	18.57	0	1									10	8
20T	2004	70	59	9	1172	84	23.44	0	5									34	25
ONIONS, Graham (England to South Africa) b Gateshead, Co Durham 9.9.1982 RHB RMF																			
Test	2009	8	10	7	30	17*	10.00	0	0	1429	869	28	31.03	5-38	1	0	3.64	0	
FC	2004	72	93	32	758	41	12.42	0	0	11558	6923	230	30.10	8-101	9	0	3.59	17	
Int	2009	4	1	0	1	1	1.00	0	0	204	185	4	46.25	2-58	0	0	5.44	1	
Lim	2003	53	21	5	107	19	6.68	0	0	2203	1918	60	31.96	3-39	0	0	5.22	8	
20T	2004	19	8	3	54	31	10.80	0	0	408	437	15	29.13	3-25	0	0	6.42	4	
ORD, James Edward (Warwickshire) b Birmingham, Warwickshire 9.11.1987 RHB OB																			
FC		1	2	0	7	6	3.50	0	0									1	
FC	2009	2	4	0	17	9	4.25	0	0									1	
Lim	2009	2	1	0	27	27	27.00	0	0									0	

Cmp	Debut	M	I	NO	Runs	HS	Avge	100	50	Balls	Runs	Wkts	Avge	BB	5i	10m	RpO	ct	st
OSBORNE, Max (Essex) b Orsett, Essex 21.11.1990 RHB RMF																			
FC		2	3	2	5	5	5.00	0	0	216	151	6	25.16	3-35	0	0	4.19	0	
O'SHEA, Michael Peter (Unicorns) b Cardiff, Glamorgan, Wales 4.9.1987 RHB OB																			
Lim		8	7	0	355	90	50.71	0	3	116	121	1	121.00	1-38	0	0	6.25	2	
FC	2005	6	9	0	137	50	15.22	0	1									1	
Lim	2005	17	16	1	504	90	33.60	0	3	314	334	5	66.80	2-37	0	0	6.38	5	
20T	2009	2	1	0	5	5	5.00	0	0									1	
OWEN, Frederick Gerard (Cambridge University) b Chester, Cheshire 25.9.1985 RHB																			
FC		1	2	0	33	24	16.50	0	0									0	
FC	2006	5	9	0	174	50	19.33	0	1									0	
OWEN, William Thomas (Glamorgan) b St Asaph, Flintshire, Wales 2.9.1988 RHB RM																			
FC		3	4	1	38	38	12.66	0	0	324	232	3	77.33	3-65	0	0	4.29	0	
Lim		8	6	1	35	12	7.00	0	0	294	320	13	24.61	5-49	0	1	6.53	1	
20T		4	1	0	8	8	8.00	0	0	54	104	0					11.55	0	
FC	2007	4	4	1	38	38	12.66	0	0	372	269	3	89.66	3-65	0	0	4.33	0	
PALLADINO, Antonio Paul (Essex, Namibia, Namibia to South Africa, Namibia to Zimbabwe) b Tower Hamlets, Essex 29.6.1983 RHB RMF																			
FC		5	9	1	130	66	16.25	0	1	852	499	18	27.72	4-57	0	0	3.51	1	
Lim		7	3	1	4	2	2.00	0	0	246	255	2	127.50	1-21	0	0	6.22	2	
20T		1	1	0	1	1	1.00	0	0	18	29	0					9.66	1	
FC	2003	52	66	18	620	66	12.91	0	2	7225	3994	117	34.13	6-41	2	0	3.31	24	
Lim	2002	35	19	3	125	31	7.81	0	0	1308	1193	33	36.15	3-32	0	0	5.47	4	
20T	2005	16	5	3	21	8*	10.50	0	0	287	347	22	15.77	4-21	1	0	7.25	2	
PANESAR, Mudhsuden Singh (England Lions, Sussex, Lions) b Luton, Bedfordshire 25.4.1982 LHB SLA																			
FC		16	20	5	163	46*	10.86	0	0	3110	1336	52	25.69	5-44	2	0	2.57	2	
Lim		12	1	0	9	9	9.00	0	0	514	406	14	29.00	3-21	0	0	4.73	0	
Test	2005/06	39	51	17	187	26	5.50	0	0	9042	4331	126	34.37	6-37	8	1	2.87	9	
FC	2001	131	168	53	1021	46*	8.87	0	0	28767	13562	419	32.36	7-181	21	3	2.82	29	
Int	2006/07	26	8	3	26	13	5.20	0	0	1308	980	24	40.83	3-25	0	0	4.49	3	
Lim	2002	66	23	10	135	17*	10.38	0	0	2951	2226	65	34.24	5-20	0	1	4.52	10	
I20T	2006/07	1	1	0	1	1	1.00	0	0	24	40	2	20.00	2-40	0	0	10.00	0	
20T	2006	19	6	2	7	3*	1.75	0	0	366	461	12	38.41	2-22	0	0	7.55	2	
PARK, Craig Mitchell (Cambridge MCCU) b Empangeni, Natal, South Africa 1.3.1986 RHB RFM WK																			
FC		3	4	0	91	72	22.75	0	1	294	219	2	109.50	1-34	0	0	4.46	2	
PARK, Garry Terence (Derbyshire, Derbyshire to Netherlands) b Empangeni, Natal (Zululand), South Africa 19.4.1983 RHB RMF WK																			
FC		11	19	2	431	124*	25.35	1	2	501	327	9	36.33	2-20	0	0	3.91	6	
Lim		8	8	2	153	43	25.50	0	0	131	171	1	171.00	1-17	0	0	7.83	3	
20T		15	9	1	241	66	30.12	0	2	168	226	8	28.25	3-11	0	0	8.07	4	
FC	2003	45	76	10	2335	178*	35.37	4	14	1434	958	18	53.22	3-25	0	0	4.00	41	
Lim	2005	38	33	7	648	64	24.92	0	1	556	542	7	77.42	2-40	0	0	5.84	12	
20T	2007	34	23	3	485	66	24.25	0	3	336	428	19	22.52	3-11	0	0	7.64	7	
PARK, Sean Michael (Unicorns) b Umtata, Transkei, South Africa 24.4.1980 RHB RFM WK																			
Lim		8	7	1	62	21	10.33	0	0									2	
PARRY, Stephen David (England Lions, Lancashire) b Manchester, Lancashire 12.1.1986 RHB SLA																			
Lim		13	7	2	58	26	11.60	0	0	587	519	14	37.07	3-48	0	0	5.30	2	
20T		17	5	4	13	7	13.00	0	0	360	427	26	16.42	4-28	1	0	7.11	1	
FC	2007	3	2	0	3	2	1.50	0	0	523	256	9	28.44	5-23	1	0	2.93	1	
Lim	2009	22	11	2	102	31	11.33	0	0	983	771	27	28.55	3-48	0	0	4.70	2	
20T	2009	26	6	4	17	7	8.50	0	0	558	650	36	18.05	4-28	1	0	6.98	3	
PARSONS, Keith Alan (Unicorns) b Taunton, Somerset 2.5.1973 RHB RM																			
Lim		11	10	2	388	89	48.50	0	3	12	29	0					14.50	2	
FC	1992	130	209	23	5324	193*	28.62	6	28	8005	4646	106	43.83	5-13	2	0	3.48	115	
Lim	1993	258	226	42	5613	121	30.50	2	31	6345	5319	146	36.43	5-39	3	1	5.03	100	
20T	2003	31	30	7	464	57*	20.17	0	1	338	467	18	25.94	3-12	0	0	8.29	9	
PASCOE, Daniel Charles (Oxford MCCU, Oxford University) b Canberra, Australian Capital Territory, Australia 14.5.1983 RHB SLA																			
FC		2	2	2	64	33*		0	0	642	245	12	20.41	6-68	2	0	2.29	3	
FC	2009	3	4	2	131	37	65.50	0	0	809	324	14	23.14	6-68	2	0	2.40	3	
PATEL, Akhil (Nottinghamshire) b Nottingham 18.6.1990 LHB SLC																			
Lim		3	3	0	81	38	27.00	0	0									0	
FC	2007	3	6	2	153	69*	38.25	0	1	143	76	1	76.00	1-34	0	0	3.18	2	
Lim	2009	7	7	0	173	41	24.71	0	0	30	34	2	17.00	2-34	0	0	6.80	1	
PATEL, Luke Adam (Durham MCCU) b Wakefield, Yorkshire 6.10.1990 LHB OB																			
FC		1	1	0	26	26	26.00	0	0									0	
PATEL, Ravi Hasmukh (Middlesex) b Harrow, Middlesex 4.8.1991 RHB SLA																			
FC		1	1	1	19	19*		0	0	282	134	5	26.80	3-52	0	0	2.85	0	
Lim		1								30	38	0					7.60	0	

Cmp	Debut	M	I	NO	Runs	HS	Avge	100	50	Balls	Runs	Wkts	Avge	BB	5i	10m	RpO	ct	st
PATEL, Samit Rohit (Nottinghamshire, Nottinghamshire to Scotland) b Leicester 30.11.1984 RHB SLA																			
FC		17	28	2	750	104	28.84	1	4	2073	1044	26	40.15	4-55	0	0	3.02	9	
Lim		11	10	1	406	108*	45.11	1	2	386	329	11	29.90	2-19	0	0	5.11	2	
20T		18	18	2	459	63	28.68	0	3	348	377	17	22.17	3-26	0	0	6.50	3	
FC	2002	77	118	8	4430	176	40.27	10	24	7498	3805	93	40.91	6-84	2	0	3.04	41	
Int	2008	11	5	0	116	31	23.20	0	0	340	319	11	29.00	5-41	0	1	5.62	4	
Lim	2002	114	96	15	2559	114	31.59	2	13	3086	2647	97	27.28	6-13	0	2	5.14	29	
20T	2003	72	67	11	1462	84*	26.10	0	9	1135	1358	54	25.14	3-11	0	0	7.17	22	
PATTERSON, Steven Andrew (Yorkshire, Yorkshire to Netherlands) b Beverley, Yorkshire 3.10.1983 RHB RMF																			
FC		14	17	4	184	39*	14.15	0	0	2357	1201	45	26.68	5-50	1	0	3.05	3	
Lim		12	1	0	0	0	0.00	0	0	504	461	21	21.95	6-32	0	1	5.48	2	
20T		14	3	3	3	3*		0	0	304	450	15	30.00	4-30	1	0	8.88	1	
FC	2005	29	33	9	350	46	14.58	0	0	4163	2184	67	32.59	5-50	1	0	3.14	6	
Lim	2002	39	14	12	83	25*	41.50	0	0	1677	1413	44	32.11	6-32	0	1	5.05	5	
20T	2009	16	4	3	3	3*	3.00	0	0	340	507	16	31.68	4-30	1	0	8.94	1	
PATTINSON, Darren John (Nottinghamshire, Victoria to Australia) b Grimsby, Lincolnshire 2.8.1979 RHB RFM																			
FC		13	14	4	101	27	10.10	0	0	1862	1180	33	35.75	5-95	1	0	3.80	0	
Lim		5	1	0	8	8	8.00	0	0	186	200	6	33.33	3-70	0	0	6.45	3	
20T		15	3	1	5	4*	2.50	0	0	300	353	20	17.65	4-19	1	0	7.06	6	
Test	2008	1	2	0	21	13	10.50	0	0	181	96	2	48.00	2-95	0	0	3.18	0	
FC	2006/07	51	58	10	561	59	11.68	0	1	8130	4709	133	35.40	6-30	6	0	3.47	5	
Lim	2006/07	43	16	6	69	13*	6.90	0	0	1725	1515	56	27.05	4-29	2	0	5.27	13	
20T	2006/07	32	7	3	19	5	4.75	0	0	609	772	35	22.05	4-19	1	0	7.60	10	
PAYNE, David Alan (Gloucestershire, Gloucestershire to Netherlands) b Poole, Dorset 15.2.1991 LHB LFM																			
Lim		5	3	2	21	13	21.00	0	0	215	174	15	11.60	7-29	1	1	4.85	0	
20T		3	1	1	1	1*		0	0	66	81	6	13.50	3-25	0	0	7.36	0	
Lim	2009	9	5	4	25	13	25.00	0	0	299	253	22	11.50	7-29	1	1	5.07	2	
PEPLOE, Christopher Thomas (Unicorns) b Hammersmith, Middlesex 26.4.1981 LHB SLA																			
Lim		4	2	1	2	2	2.00	0	0	144	105	4	26.25	2-23	0	0	4.37	2	
FC	2003	30	41	7	530	46	15.58	0	0	5283	2839	56	50.69	4-31	0	0	3.22	11	
Lim	2001	22	12	4	38	14*	4.75	0	0	960	701	30	23.36	4-38	2	0	4.38	9	
20T	2005	15	6	4	12	7	6.00	0	0	221	378	10	37.80	3-35	0	0	10.26	4	
PETERS, Stephen David (Northamptonshire, Northamptonshire to Netherlands) b Harold Wood, Essex 10.12.1978 RHB LB																			
FC		16	30	2	1320	199	47.14	3	7									16	
Lim		9	9	1	231	56	28.87	0	2									2	
20T		2	2	1	79	40*	79.00	0	0									2	
FC	1996	194	334	27	10685	199	34.80	24	53	35	31	1	31.00	1-19	0	0	5.31	153	
Lim	1996	161	148	10	3063	107	22.19	2	18									45	
20T	2003	17	14	3	222	61*	20.18	0	1									6	
PETERSON, Robin John (Cape Cobras, Derbyshire, Derbyshire to Netherlands) b Port Elizabeth, Cape Province, South Africa 4.8.1979 LHB SLA																			
FC		15	24	3	484	58	23.04	0	2	3321	1566	51	30.70	4-10	0	0	2.82	9	
Lim		7	6	0	124	51	20.66	0	1	269	229	7	32.71	3-38	0	0	5.10	2	
20T		16	15	2	252	35*	19.38	0	0	307	380	8	47.50	2-38	0	0	7.42	2	
Test	2003	6	7	1	163	61	27.16	0	1	959	497	14	35.50	5-33	1	0	3.10	5	
FC	1998/99	114	177	22	3964	130	25.57	6	14	21038	10547	321	32.85	6-67	14	1	3.00	49	
Int	2002/03	35	15	4	147	36	13.36	0	0	1252	992	17	58.35	2-26	0	0	4.75	7	
Lim	1999/00	145	101	11	2294	101	25.48	1	14	5836	4427	152	29.12	7-24	1	4	4.55	49	
I20T	2005/06	5	2	0	42	34	21.00	0	0	65	86	6	14.33	3-30	0	0	7.93	2	
20T	2003/04	56	50	6	830	72*	18.86	0	3	1048	1202	47	25.57	3-24	0	0	6.88	10	
PETTINI, Mark Lewis (Essex, Essex to Netherlands) b Brighton, Sussex 7.8.1983 RHB RM																			
FC		15	27	3	599	96	24.95	0	2									7	
Lim		11	11	0	314	82	28.54	0	3									8	
20T		13	13	1	333	81	27.75	0	4									5	
FC	2001	93	158	20	4663	208*	33.78	5	26	113	191	0					10.14	67	
Lim	2001	112	103	6	2529	144	26.07	4	17									42	
20T	2003	62	59	5	1444	87	26.74	0	10									22	
PHILLIPS, Ben James (Somerset, Somerset to India) b Lewisham, Kent 30.9.1974 RHB RFM																			
FC		11	15	3	179	55	14.91	0	1	1665	661	29	22.79	5-72	1	0	2.38	5	
Lim		13	7	4	75	51*	25.00	0	1	503	466	19	24.52	4-31	1	0	5.55	4	
20T		18	6	1	16	5	3.20	0	0	360	466	19	24.52	3-33	0	0	7.76	6	
FC	1996	108	150	26	2581	100*	20.81	1	14	14825	7121	238	29.92	6-29	5	0	2.88	31	
Lim	1996	125	76	25	946	51*	18.54	0	1	5142	4166	147	28.34	4-25	3	0	4.86	34	
20T	2003	59	38	10	436	41*	15.57	0	0	1218	1645	59	27.88	4-18	2	0	8.10	19	
PHILLIPS, Timothy James (Essex, Essex to Netherlands) b Cambridge 13.3.1981 LHB SLA																			
FC		10	16	3	240	46*	18.46	0	0	1478	752	20	37.60	4-94	0	0	3.05	8	
Lim		5	2	0	0	0	0.00	0	0	177	177	6	29.50	4-37	1	0	6.00	1	
20T		16	9	4	98	57*	19.60	0	1	228	321	9	35.66	1-7	0	0	8.44	8	
FC	1999	61	85	11	1436	89	19.40	0	4	8393	5046	110	45.87	5-41	1	0	3.60	40	
Lim	1999	48	28	11	263	41	15.47	0	0	1439	1215	52	23.36	5-34	2	2	5.06	15	
20T	2006	33	17	6	163	57*	14.81	0	1	423	557	16	34.81	2-11	0	0	7.90	15	

Cmp	Debut	M	I	NO	Runs	HS	Avge	100	50	Balls	Runs	Wkts	Avge	BB	5i	10m	RpO	ct	st
PIESLEY, Christopher Damien (Kent) b Chatham, Kent 12.3.1992 LHB OB																			
FC		1	2	0	43	43	21.50	0	0									0	
PIETERSEN, Kevin Peter (England, Hampshire, Surrey, England to Bangladesh, England to South Africa, England to Scotland, England to United Arab Emirates, England to West Indies, Royal Challengers Bangalore) b Pietermaritzburg, Natal, South Africa 27.6.1980 RHB OB																			
Test		6	9	1	232	80	29.00	0	2	6	2	0					2.00	6	
FC		8	12	1	273	80	24.81	0	2	6	2	0					2.00	6	
Int		5	5	0	95	33	19.00	0	0									0	
Lim		7	7	0	249	116	35.57	1	0	6	17	0					17.00	0	
20T		1	1	0	15	15	15.00	0	0	6	14	0					14.00	1	
Test	2005	66	117	6	5306	226	47.80	16	20	843	568	4	142.00	1-0	0	0	4.04	39	
FC	1997/98	154	256	18	11726	254*	49.26	38	49	5647	3279	61	53.75	4-31	0	0	3.48	119	
Int	2004/05	104	94	15	3332	116	42.17	7	20	274	246	6	41.00	2-22	0	0	5.38	32	
Lim	1998/99	217	198	32	6931	147	41.75	13	41	2264	1998	40	49.95	3-14	0	0	5.29	76	
I20T	2005	28	28	4	911	79	37.95	0	5	18	36	1	36.00	1-27	0	0	12.00	10	
20T	2003	57	57	7	1636	79	32.72	0	9	312	408	17	24.00	3-33	0	0	7.84	19	
PIOLET, Steffan Andreas (Warwickshire) b Redhill, Surrey 8.8.1988 RHB RM																			
FC		1	2	0	10	6	5.00	0	0	102	80	1	80.00	1-67	0	0	4.70	2	
Lim		1								12	19	0					9.50	0	
20T		7	2	1	11	7	11.00	0	0	144	152	7	21.71	2-9	0	0	6.33	3	
FC	2009	2	4	1	41	26*	13.66	0	0	264	123	11	11.18	6-17	1	1	2.79	2	
Lim	2009	12	2	0	6	4	3.00	0	0	353	317	13	24.38	3-34	0	0	5.38	3	
20T	2009	18	4	1	14	7	4.66	0	0	354	389	17	22.88	2-9	0	0	6.59	8	
PLUNKETT, Liam Edward (Durham, England Lions, Durham to Scotland, England to Bangladesh) b Middlesbrough, Yorkshire 6.4.1985 RHB RFM																			
FC		15	18	0	238	51	13.22	0	1	2494	1499	40	37.47	4-107	0	0	3.60	10	
Lim		11	7	2	32	12*	6.40	0	0	353	355	11	32.27	4-58	1	0	6.03	2	
20T		13	7	3	102	31	25.50	0	0	192	291	7	41.57	2-18	0	0	9.09	2	
Test	2005/06	9	13	2	126	44*	11.45	0	0	1538	916	23	39.82	3-17	0	0	3.57	3	
FC	2003	100	136	24	2305	94*	20.58	0	10	15713	9520	306	31.11	6-63	8	1	3.63	60	
Int	2005/06	28	24	10	295	56	21.07	0	1	1303	1272	37	34.37	3-24	0	0	5.85	7	
Lim	2002	110	75	27	907	72	18.89	0	2	4632	4159	130	31.99	4-15	3	0	5.38	24	
I20T	2006	1								24	37	1	37.00	1-37	0	0	9.25	0	
20T	2003	38	21	11	175	31	17.50	0	0	680	880	29	30.34	3-16	0	0	7.76	10	
POLLARD, Kieron Adrian (Trinidad and Tobago, West Indies, Mumbai Indians, Somerset, South Australia, Trinidad and Tobago to India, West Indies to Australia) b Cacariqua, Trinidad 12.5.1987 RHB RM																			
20T		17	16	5	354	89*	32.18	0	2	350	438	29	15.10	4-15	1	0	7.50	8	
FC	2006/07	20	33	1	1199	174	37.46	3	5	571	313	6	52.16	2-29	0	0	3.28	32	
Int	2006/07	30	27	0	538	62	19.92	0	1	936	833	30	27.76	3-27	0	0	5.34	10	
Lim	2006/07	48	43	3	1109	87	27.72	0	7	1410	1214	57	21.29	4-32	1	0	5.16	22	
I20T	2008	20	17	2	190	38	12.66	0	0	258	360	11	32.72	2-22	0	0	8.37	11	
20T	2006	80	69	13	1391	89*	24.83	0	6	1178	1514	81	18.69	4-15	2	0	7.71	35	
POPE, Joel Ian (Leicestershire) b Ashford, Middlesex 23.10.1988 RHB WK																			
Lim		2	2	0	13	9	6.50	0	0									1	
Lim	2008	3	3	0	22	9	7.33	0	0									3	1
PORTERFIELD, William Thomas Stuart (Ireland, Gloucestershire, Gloucestershire to Netherlands, Ireland to Sri Lanka, Ireland to United Arab Emirates, Ireland to West Indies) b Londonderry, Ireland 6.9.1984 LHB OB																			
FC		7	14	0	531	175	37.92	2	1	30	49	0					9.80	6	
Lim		10	10	0	257	65	25.70	0	2									4	
20T		13	13	1	331	65	27.58	0	2									7	
FC	2006	43	75	2	2431	175	33.30	4	13	102	135	2	67.50	1-29	0	0	7.94	45	
Int	2006	41	41	3	1313	112*	34.55	5	4									21	
Lim	2006	96	95	4	3135	112*	34.45	5	17									41	
I20T	2008	17	16	1	263	46	17.53	0	0									4	
20T	2008	45	44	2	897	65	21.35	0	3									18	
POTHAS, Nic (Hampshire) b Johannesburg, Transvaal, South Africa 18.11.1973 RHB RM WK																			
FC		9	15	0	531	87	35.40	0	4									33	
Lim		6	6	0	96	40	16.00	0	0									7	1
20T		15	11	4	165	59	23.57	0	1									8	1
FC	1993/94	210	325	59	11135	165	41.86	24	58	120	63	1	63.00	1-16	0	0	3.15	592	45
Int	2000	3	1	0	24	24	24.00	0	0									4	1
Lim	1993/94	235	198	70	4552	114*	35.56	3	24									211	53
20T	2003	68	50	20	653	59	21.76	0	3									26	11
POWELL, Daren Brent Lyle (Jamaica, Lancashire) b Malvenn, St Elizabeth, Jamaica 15.4.1978 RHB RFM																			
FC		4	4	1	29	16*	9.66	0	0	594	343	7	49.00	2-45	0	0	3.46	0	
Lim		10	5	2	32	11*	10.66	0	0	358	333	9	37.00	4-49	1	0	5.58	5	
20T		4								54	87	0					9.66	0	
Test	2002	37	57	5	407	36*	7.82	0	0	7077	4068	85	47.85	5-25	1	0	3.44	8	
FC	2000/01	102	144	23	1525	69	12.60	0	4	16806	9318	276	33.76	6-49	6	0	3.32	31	
Int	2002/03	55	25	3	118	48*	5.36	0	0	2850	2239	71	31.53	4-27	2	0	4.71	13	
Lim	2002	108	48	11	274	48*	7.40	0	0	5212	4179	148	28.23	5-23	6	1	4.81	29	

Cmp	Debut	M	I	NO	Runs	HS	Avge	100	50	Balls	Runs	Wkts	Avge	BB	5i	10m	RpO	ct	st
I20T	2007	5	1	1	1	1*		0	0	102	131	2	65.50	1-6	0	0	7.70	2	
20T	2007	16	3	3	2	1*		0	0	307	373	7	53.28	2-15	0	0	7.29	3	
POWELL, Michael John (Glamorgan) b Abergavenny, Monmouthshire, Wales 3.2.1977 RHB OB																			
FC		7	12	1	275	55	25.00	0	1									1	
FC	1997	200	335	31	11786	299	38.76	25	59	164	132	2	66.00	2-39	0	0	4.82	122	
Lim	1997	204	193	20	4665	114*	26.96	1	25	24	26	1	26.00	1-26	0	0	6.50	79	
20T	2003	44	41	4	844	68*	22.81	0	5									16	
POYNTER, Stuart William (Middlesex) b Hammersmith, Middlesex 18.10.1990 RHB WK																			
FC		1	1	0	42	42	42.00	0	0									3	
POYNTON, Thomas (Derbyshire) b Burton-on-Trent, Staffordshire 25.11.1989 RHB WK																			
FC		4	6	0	88	25	14.66	0	0	48	96	2	48.00	2-96	0	0	12.00	5	
FC	2007	7	11	0	105	25	9.54	0	0	48	96	2	48.00	2-96	0	0	12.00	12	2
Lim	2007	6	3	1	52	24	26.00	0	0									5	1
20T	2007	2	1	0	3	3	3.00	0	0									0	2
PRINCE, Ashwell Gavin (South Africa, Warriors, Lancashire, South Africa to India, South Africa to West Indies) b Port Elizabeth, Cape Province, South Africa 28.5.1977 LHB OB																			
FC		7	13	2	450	115	40.90	1	4									7	
Lim		6	5	1	207	102*	51.75	1	0									1	
Test	2001/02	57	91	14	3355	162*	43.57	11	10	96	47	1	47.00	1-2	0	0	2.93	36	
FC	1995/96	189	304	41	11418	254	43.41	28	55	276	166	4	41.50	2-11	0	0	3.60	127	
Int	2002/03	52	41	12	1018	89*	35.10	0	3	12	3	0					1.50	26	
Lim	1996/97	206	180	35	4539	128	31.30	2	22	91	86	0					5.67	93	
I20T	2005/06	1	1	0	5	5	5.00	0	0									0	
20T	2003/04	22	20	3	476	69	28.00	0	1	4	5	0					7.50	7	
PRIOR, Matthew James (England, Sussex, England to Bangladesh, England to South Africa, England to United Arab Emirates) b Johannesburg, Transvaal, South Africa 26.2.1982 RHB WK																			
Test		6	8	2	343	102*	57.16	1	2									22	1
FC		13	19	3	639	123*	39.93	2	2									41	1
Lim		5	5	0	183	64	36.60	0	1									1	
20T		14	14	1	443	117	34.07	1	2									6	
Test	2007	35	55	10	1896	131*	42.13	3	15									94	4
FC	2001	173	272	29	9651	201*	39.71	22	55									416	26
Int	2004/05	55	50	8	1066	87	25.38	0	2									60	4
Lim	2000	203	186	16	4719	144	27.75	4	26									174	27
I20T	2007	10	8	2	127	32	21.16	0	0									6	3
20T	2003	64	59	5	1362	117	25.22	1	7									40	5
PROCTER, Luke Anthony (Lancashire) b Oldham, Lancashire 24.6.1988 LHB RM																			
FC		2	3	0	64	32	21.33	0	0	45	47	1	47.00	1-26	0	0	6.26	0	
Lim		6	4	1	165	97	55.00	0	2	228	203	9	22.55	3-29	0	0	5.34	2	
Lim	2009	7	5	1	167	97	41.75	0	2	228	203	9	22.55	3-29	0	0	5.34	2	
PYRAH, Richard Michael (Yorkshire, Yorkshire to Netherlands) b Dewsbury, Yorkshire 1.11.1982 RHB RM																			
FC		7	7	2	304	134*	60.80	1	1	508	326	7	46.57	2-8	0	0	3.85	4	
Lim		12	3	0	33	29	11.00	0	0	444	460	16	28.75	4-43	1	0	6.21	3	
20T		16	10	3	89	22*	12.71	0	0	348	408	21	19.42	3-12	0	0	7.03	8	
FC	2004	22	28	4	801	134*	33.37	2	4	1372	817	16	51.06	2-8	0	0	3.57	13	
Lim	2001	82	53	13	775	67	19.37	0	1	2590	2459	100	24.59	5-50	4	1	5.69	28	
20T	2005	47	31	9	250	33*	11.36	0	0	696	844	43	19.62	4-20	1	0	7.27	19	
QUERL, Reginald Glenn (Unicorns) b Harare, Zimbabwe 4.4.1988 RHB RM																			
Lim		11	8	3	64	28*	12.80	0	0	427	411	14	29.35	4-41	1	0	5.77	2	
RAMPRAKASH, Mark Ravin (Surrey) b Bushey, Hertfordshire 5.9.1969 RHB OB																			
FC		16	28	2	1595	248	61.34	5	5	6	6	0					6.00	5	
Lim		9	9	2	326	85*	46.57	0	2									5	
20T		11	11	2	331	63*	36.77	0	3									3	
Test	1991	52	92	6	2350	154	27.32	2	12	895	477	4	119.25	1-2	0	0	3.19	39	
FC	1987	442	729	91	34839	301*	54.60	113	144	4177	2202	34	64.76	3-32	0	0	3.16	249	
Int	1991	18	18	4	376	51	26.85	0	1	132	108	4	27.00	3-28	0	0	4.90	8	
Lim	1987	407	394	64	13273	147*	40.22	17	85	1734	1354	46	29.43	5-38	0	1	4.68	137	
20T	2003	63	63	10	1719	85*	32.43	0	13									21	
RANKIN, William Boyd (Ireland, Ireland to West Indies, Warwickshire, Warwickshire to Scotland) b Londonderry, Ireland 5.7.1984 LHB RMF																			
FC		9	16	7	63	13	7.00	0	0	873	594	22	27.00	5-16	1	0	4.08	3	
Lim		7	1	0	7	7	7.00	0	0	222	230	13	17.69	4-34	1	0	6.21	1	
20T		2								36	39	1	39.00	1-17	0	0	6.50	0	
FC	2006/07	34	42	17	128	13	5.12	0	0	4531	2867	101	28.38	5-16	3	0	3.79	12	
Int	2006/07	23	8	6	25	7*	12.50	0	0	1010	815	33	24.69	3-32	0	0	4.84	4	
Lim	2006	52	15	9	50	9	8.33	0	0	2051	1718	70	24.54	4-34	1	0	5.02	6	
I20T	2009	6	2	1	6	5*	6.00	0	0	144	162	7	23.14	2-25	0	0	6.75	3	
20T	2009	9	3	2	9	5*	9.00	0	0	204	223	9	24.77	2-25	0	0	6.55	3	

Cmp	Debut	M	I	NO	Runs	HS	Avge	100	50	Balls	Runs	Wkts	Avge	BB	5i	10m	RpO	ct	st
RASHID, Adil Usman (Yorkshire, England to South Africa, England Lions to United Arab Emirates, Yorkshire to Netherlands) b Bradford, Yorkshire 17.2.1988 RHB LB																			
FC		16	24	8	732	76	45.75	0	6	3028	1784	57	31.29	5-87	3	0	3.53	14	
Lim		12	5	2	44	22*	14.66	0	0	444	368	10	36.80	3-28	0	0	4.97	3	
20T		16	10	1	128	34	14.22	0	0	366	428	26	16.46	4-20	1	0	7.01	4	
FC	2006	69	97	21	2937	157*	38.64	4	19	12856	7593	228	33.30	7-107	13	0	3.54	37	
Int	2009	5	4	1	60	31*	20.00	0	0	204	191	3	63.66	1-16	0	0	5.61	2	
Lim	2006	55	34	10	343	41*	14.29	0	0	2001	1684	43	39.16	3-28	0	0	5.04	20	
I20T	2009	5	2	1	10	9*	10.00	0	0	84	120	3	40.00	1-11	0	0	8.57	0	
20T	2008	37	22	7	204	34	13.60	0	0	756	904	49	18.44	4-20	2	0	7.17	11	
RAYNER, Oliver Philip (Sussex, Mid West Rhinos) b Fallingbostel, Germany 1.11.1985 RHB OB																			
FC		7	10	2	256	67*	32.00	0	2	890	412	18	22.88	4-62	0	0	2.77	10	
Lim		5	4	3	62	35*	62.00	0	0	186	164	4	41.00	2-33	0	0	5.29	3	
20T		5	3	2	69	41*	69.00	0	0	96	105	5	21.00	1-16	0	0	6.56	0	
FC	2006	38	45	9	782	101	21.72	1	3	6034	3086	89	34.67	5-49	3	0	3.06	42	
Lim	2006	20	17	9	213	61	26.62	0	1	672	670	14	47.85	2-31	0	0	5.98	7	
20T	2006	17	9	2	115	41*	16.42	0	0	235	307	9	34.11	1-16	0	0	7.83	1	
READ, Christopher Mark Wells (Nottinghamshire, Nottinghamshire to Scotland) b Paignton, Devon 10.8.1978 RHB WK																			
FC		17	26	5	945	124*	45.00	2	5									60	4
Lim		11	9	3	241	69*	40.16	0	2									7	2
20T		14	12	5	145	28*	20.71	0	0									3	4
Test	1999	15	23	4	360	55	18.94	0	1									48	6
FC	1997/98	239	354	61	10700	240	36.51	18	57	96	90	0					5.62	707	40
Int	1999/00	36	24	7	300	30*	17.64	0	0									41	2
Lim	1995	262	209	52	4334	135	27.60	2	15									256	60
I20T	2006	1	1	0	13	13	13.00	0	0									1	
20T	2004	60	53	16	944	58*	25.51	0	1									34	11
REDFERN, Daniel James (Derbyshire) b Shrewsbury, Shropshire 18.4.1990 LHB OB																			
FC		9	15	1	331	85	23.64	0	1	18	14	0					4.66	3	
Lim		4	4	0	86	37	21.50	0	0									0	
FC	2007	32	51	4	1338	95	28.46	0	8	432	255	5	51.00	1-7	0	0	3.54	17	
Lim	2006	27	24	1	496	57*	21.56	0	2	226	188	5	37.60	2-10	0	0	4.99	5	
20T	2008	1	1	0	9	9	9.00	0	0									0	
REDMOND, Aaron James (Otago, Gloucestershire, New Zealand to South Africa, New Zealand to United Arab Emirates, New Zealand to United States of America, New Zealand to West Indies, Otago to India) b Auckland, New Zealand 23.9.1979 RHB LB																			
20T		8	8	0	132	33	16.50	0	0	107	184	4	46.00	2-38	0	0	10.31	4	
Test	2008	7	14	1	299	83	23.00	0	2	75	62	3	20.66	2-47	0	0	4.96	5	
FC	1999/00	86	147	10	4529	146	33.05	8	27	7898	4314	100	43.14	4-30	0	0	3.27	66	
Int	2009/10	5	5	0	136	52	27.20	0	1									2	
Lim	1999/00	86	83	7	1820	134*	23.94	2	8	998	839	20	41.95	3-40	0	0	5.04	23	
I20T	2009	7	6	0	126	63	21.00	0	1	17	24	2	12.00	2-24	0	0	8.47	3	
20T	2005/06	37	32	1	755	100*	24.35	1	4	251	380	14	27.14	4-24	1	0	9.08	15	
REES, Gareth Peter (Glamorgan) b Swansea, Glamorgan, Wales 8.4.1985 LHB LM																			
FC		17	30	4	918	106*	35.30	2	5	6	3	0					3.00	6	
Lim		5	4	1	66	51*	22.00	0	1									1	
20T		15	15	5	183	35	18.30	0	0									5	
FC	2006	63	106	8	3580	154	36.53	10	18	6	3	0					3.00	50	
Lim	2003	21	20	2	556	123*	30.88	1	4									4	
20T	2009	18	18	5	198	35	15.23	0	0									7	
RIAZUDDIN, Hamza (Hampshire, Hampshire to Scotland) b Hendon, Middlesex 19.12.1989 RHB RFM																			
FC		1								78	29	2	14.50	1-0	0	0	2.23	0	
Lim		4	4	1	40	23*	13.33	0	0	174	170	2	85.00	1-38	0	0	5.86	1	
FC	2008	3	2	0	7	4	3.50	0	0	384	200	5	40.00	1-0	0	0	3.12	0	
Lim	2008	17	6	3	42	23*	14.00	0	0	738	592	11	53.81	2-47	0	0	4.81	5	
20T	2008	11	4	3	16	13*	16.00	0	0	210	296	9	32.88	3-15	0	0	8.45	2	
RICHARDSON, Alan (Worcestershire) b Newcastle-under-Lyme, Staffordshire 6.5.1975 RHB RMF																			
FC		14	18	11	71	11	10.14	0	0	3144	1342	55	24.40	5-44	2	0	2.56	5	
Lim		2	1	1	1	1*		0	0	90	78	4	19.50	2-22	0	0	5.20	1	
20T		2								42	45	1	45.00	1-21	0	0	6.42	0	
FC	1995	122	127	53	832	91	11.24	0	1	22756	10699	369	28.99	8-46	11	1	2.82	38	
Lim	1995	64	28	18	105	21*	10.50	0	0	2806	2199	62	35.46	5-35	1	1	4.70	14	
20T	2004	11	2	1	6	6*	6.00	0	0	228	268	10	26.80	3-13	0	0	7.05	2	
RICHARDSON, Michael John (Durham) b Port Elizabeth, Eastern Province, South Africa 4.10.1986 RHB WK																			
FC		1	1	0	2	2	2.00	0	0									0	
ROBSON, Samuel David (Middlesex) b Paddington, New South Wales, Australia 1.7.1989 RHB LB																			
FC		8	15	0	513	204	34.20	1	2	12	17	0					8.50	8	
FC	2009	15	28	0	954	204	34.07	2	4	24	22	0					5.50	20	
Lim	2008	4	2	0	69	48	34.50	0	0									0	
ROEBUCK, Charles George (Yorkshire) b Huddersfield, Yorkshire 14.8.1991 RHB RM																			
FC		1	1	0	23	23	23.00	0	0									0	

Cmp	Debut	M	I	NO	Runs	HS	Avge	100	50	Balls	Runs	Wkts	Avge	BB	5i	10m	RpO	ct	st
ROGERS, Christopher John Llewellyn (Victoria to Australia, Derbyshire, Derbyshire to Netherlands) b St George, Sydney, New South Wales, Australia 31.8.1977 LHB LBG																			
FC		15	27	3	1285	200	53.54	4	5	6	5	0					5.00	19	
Lim		8	8	0	280	73	35.00	0	1									2	
20T		3	3	1	18	13*	9.00	0	0									1	
Test	2007/08	1	2	0	19	15	9.50	0	0									1	
FC	1998/99	173	305	22	14791	319	52.26	45	68	230	131	1	131.00	1-16	0	0	3.41	173	
Lim	1998/99	128	124	7	4173	140	35.66	4	28	24	26	2	13.00	2-22	0	0	6.50	63	
20T	2005	24	20	1	368	58	19.36	0	3									16	
ROLAND-JONES, Tobias Skelton (Middlesex) b Ashford, Middlesex 29.1.1988 RHB RMF																			
FC		8	12	1	124	26	11.27	0	0	1382	745	38	19.60	5-41	2	0	3.23	3	
Lim		8	6	2	56	23*	14.00	0	0	366	362	11	32.90	3-55	0	0	5.93	3	
ROOT, Joseph Edward (Yorkshire) b Sheffield, Yorkshire 30.12.1990 RHB RM																			
FC		2	3	1	38	20*	19.00	0	0	42	27	0					3.85	1	
Lim	2009	1	1	0	63	63	63.00	0	1									1	
ROPER, Christopher George William (Durham MCCU) b Bristol 20.5.1991 RHB RM																			
FC		2	1	0	0	0	0.00	0	0	252	249	2	124.50	1-61	0	0	5.92	1	
ROSE, Simon Alexander Leslie (Loughborough MCCU) b Huntingdon, Cambridgeshire 6.1.1989 RHB RMF																			
FC		2	2	1	14	14	14.00	0	0	318	216	1	216.00	1-72	0	0	4.07	0	
ROSSINGTON, Adam Matthew (Middlesex) b Edgware, Middlesex 5.5.1993 RHB WK																			
FC		1	1	0	1	1	1.00	0	0									1	
ROY, Jason Jonathan (Surrey) b Durban, Natal, South Africa 21.7.1990 RHB																			
FC		3	5	0	170	76	34.00	0	2	18	18	0					6.00	0	
Lim		6	5	0	92	60	18.40	0	1									2	
20T		9	9	1	242	101*	30.25	1	1									2	
Lim	2008	9	8	0	104	60	13.00	0	1	6	12	0					12.00	3	
20T	2008	10	10	1	246	101*	27.33	1	1									2	
RUDOLPH, Jacobus Andries (Titans, Yorkshire, Yorkshire to Netherlands) b Springs, Transvaal, South Africa 4.5.1981 LHB LBG																			
FC		16	29	2	1375	228*	50.92	4	6	66	43	0					3.90	20	
Lim		12	12	4	855	124*	106.87	4	5									4	
20T		12	12	0	227	53	18.91	0	1	6	13	0					13.00	5	
Test	2003	35	63	7	2028	222*	36.21	5	8	664	432	4	108.00	1-1	0	0	3.90	22	
FC	1997/98	186	317	21	13337	228*	45.05	38	61	4451	2521	58	43.46	5-80	3	0	3.39	174	
Int	2003	45	39	6	1174	81	35.57	0	7	24	26	0					6.50	11	
Lim	2000/01	192	180	28	7280	134*	47.89	12	49	388	351	12	29.25	4-40	1	0	5.42	75	
I20T	2005/06	1	1	1	6	6*		0	0									0	
20T	2003/04	64	58	9	1384	71	28.24	0	9	163	221	10	22.10	3-16	0	0	8.13	19	
RUSHWORTH, Christopher (Durham, Durham to Scotland) b Sunderland, Co Durham 11.7.1986 RHB RFM																			
FC		9	14	2	127	28	10.58	0	0	1288	821	21	39.09	4-90	0	0	3.82	1	
Lim		8	4	2	15	7*	7.50	0	0	288	212	14	15.14	3-6	0	0	4.41	0	
Lim	2004	10	5	3	16	7*	8.00	0	0	354	262	15	17.46	3-6	0	0	4.44	2	
RUSSELL, Christopher James (Worcestershire) b Newport, Isle of Wight 16.2.1989 RHB RMF																			
Lim		2								54	68	1	68.00	1-23	0	0	7.55	0	
SADLER, John Leonard (Derbyshire) b Dewsbury, Yorkshire 19.11.1981 LHB LBG																			
FC		3	4	0	45	16	11.25	0	0									3	
Lim		5	5	1	135	41	33.75	0	0	6	11	0					11.00	0	
20T		12	11	6	157	39	31.40	0	0									4	
FC	2003	66	111	15	3047	145	31.73	3	16	231	250	3	83.33	1-5	0	0	6.49	46	
Lim	1999	93	86	14	1956	113*	27.16	1	6	54	44	1	44.00	1-33	0	0	4.88	14	
20T	2003	64	56	19	785	73	21.21	0	1	30	49	0					9.80	20	
SAKER, Neil Clifford (Unicorns) b Tooting, Surrey 20.9.1984 RHB RM																			
Lim		7	6	2	87	40*	21.75	0	0	228	250	4	62.50	2-54	0	0	6.57	2	
FC	2003	18	23	4	272	58*	14.31	0	1	2159	1578	31	50.90	5-76	1	0	4.38	5	
Lim	2005	30	17	6	161	40*	14.63	0	0	1161	1192	22	54.18	4-43	1	0	6.16	4	
20T	2007	2	1	0	0	0	0.00	0	0	30	44	1	44.00	1-28	0	0	8.80	0	
SALES, David John Grimwood (Northamptonshire, MCC to United Arab Emirates, Northamptonshire to Netherlands) b Carshalton, Surrey 3.12.1977 RHB RM																			
FC		15	28	0	680	127	24.28	1	2	6	10	0					10.00	20	
Lim		11	11	1	380	84	38.00	0	4									5	
20T		10	10	1	128	49	14.22	0	0									3	
FC	1996	204	329	28	12145	303*	40.34	24	59	345	184	9	20.44	4-25	0	0	3.20	189	
Lim	1994	241	229	31	6761	161	34.14	4	48	84	67	0					4.78	108	
20T	2003	54	51	11	1202	78*	30.05	0	10	12	23	1	23.00	1-10	0	0	11.50	28	
SANDERSON, Ben William (Yorkshire) b Sheffield, Yorkshire 3.1.1989 RHB RMF																			
FC		1								108	50	5	10.00	5-50	1	0	2.77	0	
Lim		7	1	1	12	12*		0	0	174	167	7	23.85	2-17	0	0	5.75	4	
20T		2								28	26	1	26.00	1-13	0	0	5.57	0	
FC	2008	3	2	1	6	6	6.00	0	0	330	190	6	31.66	5-50	1	0	3.45	0	

Cmp	Debut	M	I	NO	Runs	HS	Avge	100	50	Balls	Runs	Wkts	Avge	BB	5i	10m	RpO	ct	st
SAYERS, Joseph John (Yorkshire) b Leeds, Yorkshire 5.11.1983 LHB OB																			
FC		9	14	0	395	63	28.21	0	5	144	61	0					2.54	3	
Lim		1	1	0	29	29	29.00	0	0									1	
FC	2002	85	139	10	4360	187	33.79	10	22	281	147	3	49.00	3-20	0	0	3.13	51	
Lim	2003	21	21	2	444	62	23.36	0	4	54	71	1	71.00	1-31	0	0	7.88	2	
20T	2005	5	3	0	18	12	6.00	0	0									2	
SCHOFIELD, Christopher Paul (Surrey) b Wardle, Rochdale, Lancashire 6.10.1978 LHB LBG																			
FC		8	13	0	341	90	26.23	0	2	1104	606	14	43.28	4-63	0	0	3.29	5	
Lim		8	5	1	127	64*	31.75	0	1	336	331	8	41.37	2-40	0	0	5.91	0	
20T		16	10	1	54	15	6.00	0	0	329	401	14	28.64	2-15	0	0	7.31	7	
Test	2000	2	3	0	67	57	22.33	0	1	108	73	0					4.05	0	
FC	1998	100	143	18	3644	144	29.15	1	26	15702	8399	232	36.20	6-120	6	0	3.20	57	
Lim	1999	137	102	27	1794	75*	23.92	0	8	4430	3857	141	27.35	5-31	6	2	5.22	35	
I20T	2007/08	4	4	3	24	9*	24.00	0	0	77	92	4	23.00	2-15	0	0	7.16	1	
20T	2003	54	37	9	274	27	9.78	0	0	939	1157	58	19.94	4-12	1	0	7.39	15	
SCOLLAY, Thomas Edward (Middlesex) b Alice Springs, Northern Territory, Australia 28.11.1987 RHB OB																			
Lim		6	6	0	78	32	13.00	0	0	24	21	1	21.00	1-21	0	0	5.25	2	
SCOTT, Alex James Denis (Oxford University) b Hong Kong 4.5.1990 RHB OB																			
FC		1								287	147	8	18.37	4-52	0	0	3.07	0	
SCOTT, Ben James Matthew (Middlesex, Worcestershire) b Isleworth, Middlesex 4.8.1981 RHB WK																			
FC		7	12	2	313	98	31.30	0	3									30	1
Lim		5	4	1	62	22	20.66	0	0									3	
20T		17	12	6	149	43*	24.83	0	0									6	3
FC	2003	77	119	22	2710	164*	27.93	3	16	3	1	0					2.00	211	22
Lim	1999	100	62	21	821	73*	20.02	0	4									81	30
20T	2004	72	51	24	443	43*	16.40	0	0									23	27
SHAFAYAT, Bilal Mustapha (Nottinghamshire) b Nottingham 10.7.1984 RHB RMF																			
FC		7	11	0	277	159	25.18	1	0									7	
Lim		1																0	
20T		4	2	0	10	8	5.00	0	0									2	
FC	2001	119	201	7	5828	161	30.04	9	31	926	642	8	80.25	2-25	0	0	4.16	107	9
Lim	2000	106	98	8	2016	104	22.40	1	7	790	730	24	30.41	4-33	2	0	5.54	40	5
20T	2003	44	33	5	455	40	16.25	0	0	120	191	4	47.75	2-13	0	0	9.55	13	1
SHAH, Owais Alam (Middlesex, Delhi Daredevils, England to South Africa, Kolkata Knight Riders, Middlesex to Netherlands, Wellington) b Karachi, Sind, Pakistan 22.10.1978 RHB OB																			
FC		13	23	1	804	156	36.54	2	3	263	133	4	33.25	1-16	0	0	3.03	10	
Lim		11	11	2	482	111	53.55	1	4	54	63	1	63.00	1-28	0	0	7.00	6	
20T		16	15	3	421	80	35.08	0	1	30	43	3	14.33	2-26	0	0	8.60	8	
Test	2005/06	6	10	0	269	88	26.90	0	2	30	31	0					6.20	2	
FC	1996	222	379	34	14521	203	42.08	39	72	2237	1489	26	57.26	3-33	0	0	3.99	170	
Int	2001	71	66	6	1834	107*	30.56	1	12	193	184	7	26.28	3-15	0	0	5.72	21	
Lim	1995	325	307	37	9406	134	34.83	13	60	912	896	27	33.18	4-11	1	0	5.89	112	
I20T	2007	17	15	1	347	55*	24.78	0	1									5	
20T	2003	89	85	17	2160	80	31.76	0	11	45	64	4	16.00	2-26	0	0	8.53	33	
SHAHZAD, Ajmal (England, England Lions, Yorkshire, England to Bangladesh, England to Scotland, England to United Arab Emirates, Yorkshire to Netherlands) b Huddersfield, Yorkshire 27.7.1985 RHB RMF																			
Test		1	1	0	5	5	5.00	0	0	102	63	4	15.75	3-45	0	0	3.70	2	
FC		10	13	3	243	45	24.30	0	0	1856	1076	38	28.31	5-51	1	0	3.47	3	
Int		2	1	0	5	5	5.00	0	0	84	65	5	13.00	3-41	0	0	4.64	0	
Lim		10	4	3	23	9*	23.00	0	0	486	435	15	29.00	4-34	1	0	5.37	1	
20T		3	1	0	12	12	12.00	0	0	72	93	2	46.50	1-21	0	0	7.75	2	
FC	2006	32	40	12	796	88	28.42	0	2	5165	2933	91	32.23	5-51	1	0	3.40	7	
Int	2009/10	4	1	0	5	5	5.00	0	0	197	151	8	18.87	3-41	0	0	4.59	1	
Lim	2004	30	16	6	149	43*	14.90	0	0	1415	1139	39	29.20	5-51	1	1	4.83	5	
I20T	2009/10	1								24	38	2	19.00	2-38	0	0	9.50	0	
20T	2006	14	9	2	47	17*	6.71	0	0	294	372	10	37.20	2-22	0	0	7.59	5	
SHAKIB AL HASAN (Bangladesh, Khulna to Bangladesh, Bangladesh to England, Bangladesh to Ireland, Bangladesh to New Zealand, Bangladesh to Scotland, Bangladesh to Sri Lanka, Bangladesh to West Indies, Worcestershire) b Magura, Khulna, Bangladesh 24.3.1987 LHB SLA																			
Test		2	4	0	52	25	13.00	0	0	483	278	8	34.75	5-121	1	0	3.45	0	
FC		11	20	2	415	90	23.05	0	1	2073	1088	43	25.30	7-32	4	0	3.14	4	
Int		3	3	0	27	20	9.00	0	0	180	150	4	37.50	2-35	0	0	5.00	3	
Lim		9	9	0	252	91	28.00	0	2	403	338	14	24.14	4-32	1	0	5.03	4	
Test	2007	21	40	2	1179	100	31.02	1	5	5083	2410	75	32.13	7-36	7	0	2.84	8	
FC	2004/05	54	100	9	2991	129	32.86	4	14	10706	4898	164	29.86	7-32	12	0	2.74	28	
Int	2006	94	90	15	2465	134*	32.86	4	14	4790	3350	109	30.73	4-33	1	0	4.19	24	
Lim	2005/06	117	113	16	3057	134*	31.51	4	19	5725	4010	132	30.37	4-30	4	0	4.20	34	
I20T	2006/07	14	14	0	207	47	14.78	0	0	294	328	17	19.29	4-34	1	0	6.69	4	
20T	2006/07	21	21	0	293	47	13.95	0	0	456	488	25	19.52	4-34	1	0	6.42	8	

Cmp	Debut	M	I	NO	Runs	HS	Avge	100	50	Balls	Runs	Wkts	Avge	BB	5i	10m	RpO	ct	st
SHANTRY, Adam John (Glamorgan) b Bristol 13.11.1982 LHB LFM																			
FC		1	1	0	22	22	22.00	0	0	84	41	1	41.00	1-21	0	0	2.92	0	
FC	2003	29	37	12	444	100	17.76	1	0	3684	1923	81	23.74	5-49	4	1	3.13	6	
Lim	2002	12	6	3	48	19*	16.00	0	0	408	325	13	25.00	5-37	0	1	4.77	6	
20T	2004	1								12	31	0					15.50	0	
SHANTRY, Jack David (Worcestershire) b Shrewsbury, Shropshire 29.1.1988 LHB LM																			
FC		11	15	5	55	13*	5.50	0	0	1848	945	27	35.00	5-49	1	0	3.06	3	
Lim		12	4	1	35	18	11.66	0	0	490	487	18	27.05	3-33	0	0	5.96	2	
20T		15	4	2	8	6*	4.00	0	0	294	345	18	19.16	3-23	0	0	7.04	4	
FC	2009	15	20	6	67	13*	4.78	0	0	2611	1327	35	37.91	5-49	1	0	3.04	5	
Lim	2009	17	5	2	42	18	14.00	0	0	694	699	23	30.39	3-33	0	0	6.04	2	
SHARMA, Avinash Sumil (Oxford University) b Whangarei, Northland, New Zealand 15.9.1981 RHB RM																			
FC		1	1	1	185	185*		1	0									2	
SHARMA, Rajiv (Oxford MCCU, Oxford University) b Auckland, New Zealand 10.6.1984 RHB RMF																			
FC		4	6	0	108	44	18.00	0	0	407	188	2	94.00	1-14	0	0	2.77	1	
FC	2009	8	12	2	287	58*	28.70	0	1	836	398	9	44.22	5-81	1	0	2.85	2	
SHARP, Thomas Granville (Unicorns) b Truro, Cornwall 7.11.1977 RHB OB																			
Lim		1	1	0	0	0	0.00	0	0	30	20	1	20.00	1-20	0	0	4.00	0	
Lim	1999	10	10	0	263	61	26.30	0	2	114	91	3	30.33	2-33	0	0	4.78	2	
SHAW, Stuart Ashley (Kent) b Crewe, Cheshire 15.4.1991 RHB LFM																			
20T		4	2	2	4	3*		0	0	60	84	2	42.00	1-10	0	0	8.40	2	
SHEIKH, Atif (Derbyshire) b Nottingham 18.2.1991 RHB LMF																			
FC		1	2	0	6	6	3.00	0	0	150	152	5	30.40	3-78	0	0	6.08	1	
SHRECK, Charles Edward (Nottinghamshire) b Truro, Cornwall 6.1.1978 RHB RFM																			
FC		5	7	1	10	7*	1.66	0	0	1194	577	18	32.05	4-81	0	0	2.89	4	
Lim		2								31	37	0					7.16	1	
FC	2003	85	97	54	154	19	3.58	0	0	17365	9390	307	30.58	8-31	18	2	3.24	31	
Lim	1999	52	19	12	45	9*	6.42	0	0	2309	2010	63	31.90	5-19	0	2	5.22	13	
20T	2003	22	6	5	10	6*	10.00	0	0	457	597	23	25.95	4-22	1	0	7.83	4	
SIDEBOTTOM, Ryan Jay (England, Nottinghamshire, England to Bangladesh, England to South Africa, England to United Arab Emirates, England to West Indies, Nottinghamshire to Scotland) b Huddersfield, Yorkshire 15.1.1978 LHB LFM																			
FC		9	7	7	66	22*		0	0	1416	630	30	21.00	5-35	1	0	2.66	3	
Lim		4	2	2	2	1*		0	0	144	124	5	24.80	3-45	0	0	5.16	0	
I20T		2								42	54	2	27.00	2-22	0	0	7.71	0	
20T		13	4	2	18	11	9.00	0	0	288	369	9	41.00	2-19	0	0	7.68	7	
Test	2001	22	31	11	313	31	15.65	0	0	4812	2231	79	28.24	7-47	5	1	2.78	5	
FC	1997	147	184	59	1592	54	12.73	0	1	25904	12106	475	25.48	7-47	20	2	2.80	49	
Int	2001/02	25	18	8	133	24	13.30	0	0	1277	1039	29	35.82	3-19	0	0	4.88	6	
Lim	1997	173	82	38	500	32	11.36	0	0	7662	5573	178	31.30	6-40	1	2	4.36	36	
I20T	2007	18	1	1	5	5*		0	0	367	437	23	19.00	3-16	0	0	7.14	5	
20T	2003	50	11	8	63	17*	21.00	0	0	1058	1216	58	20.96	3-16	0	0	6.89	17	
SIMPSON, John Andrew (Middlesex, Middlesex to Netherlands) b Bury, Lancashire 13.7.1988 LHB WK																			
FC		16	27	2	657	101*	26.28	1	2									42	2
Lim		11	8	0	207	82	25.87	0	1									8	3
FC	2009	19	33	2	827	101*	26.67	1	3									47	2
Lim	2009	18	14	1	327	82	25.15	0	1									11	4
20T	2009	1	1	0	13	13	13.00	0	0									0	
SMITH, Benjamin Francis (Worcestershire) b Corby, Northamptonshire 3.4.1972 RHB RM																			
FC		8	14	2	282	80	23.50	0	2									9	
Lim		5	5	0	30	19	6.00	0	0									2	
FC	1990	334	529	58	18777	204	39.86	40	100	653	488	4	122.00	1-5	0	0	4.48	214	
Lim	1990	399	382	54	9899	115	30.17	3	61	127	121	2	60.50	1-2	0	0	5.71	142	
20T	2003	51	49	6	866	105	20.13	1	1									23	
SMITH, Dwayne Romel (Barbados, West Indies, Deccan Chargers, New South Wales, Sussex, Sussex to India, West Indies to Australia) b Storey Gap, Codrington Hill, St Michael, Barbados 12.4.1983 RHB RM																			
20T		13	12	1	215	49	19.54	0	0	202	276	8	34.50	2-19	0	0	8.19	4	
Test	2003/04	10	14	1	320	105*	24.61	1	0	651	344	7	49.14	3-71	0	0	3.17	9	
FC	2001/02	81	134	9	3679	155	29.43	7	14	8096	4054	124	32.69	4-22	0	0	3.00	78	
Int	2003/04	77	61	4	925	68	16.22	0	3	2510	2060	56	36.78	5-45	3	1	4.92	26	
Lim	2003/04	133	113	9	2274	96	21.86	0	14	3871	3123	94	33.22	6-29	3	2	4.84	44	
I20T	2005/06	8	8	0	73	29	9.12	0	0	104	155	7	22.14	3-24	0	0	8.94	1	
20T	2005/06	74	70	7	1220	72*	19.36	0	4	1084	1411	55	25.65	4-9	1	0	7.81	28	
SMITH, David Thomas (Oxford MCCU) b Canterbury, Kent 13.9.1989 RHB RM																			
FC		1	2	1	16	12*	16.00	0	0	3	5	0					10.00	1	
FC	2009	2	3	1	22	12*	11.00	0	0	3	5	0					10.00	2	
SMITH, Gregory Marc (Derbyshire, Derbyshire to Netherlands, Mountaineers) b Johannesburg, Transvaal, South Africa 20.4.1983 RHB RM,OB																			
FC		16	27	1	721	165*	27.73	1	4	2487	1368	42	32.57	5-54	1	0	3.30	4	
Lim		10	10	0	179	46	17.90	0	0	342	328	7	46.85	2-34	0	0	5.75	1	
20T		15	14	0	225	38	16.07	0	0	235	307	13	23.61	3-19	0	0	7.83	11	
FC	2003/04	71	122	10	3308	165*	29.53	3	22	7334	4090	113	36.19	5-54	2	0	3.34	19	

Cmp	Debut	M	I	NO	Runs	HS	Avge	100	50	Balls	Runs	Wkts	Avge	BB	5i	10m	RpO	ct	st
Lim	2003/04	62	62	5	1346	88	23.61	0	5	1723	1653	49	33.73	4-53	1	0	5.75	24	
20T	2007	44	42	2	900	100*	22.50	1	4	454	594	25	23.76	5-27	0	1	7.85	18	
SMITH, Greg Phillip (Durham MCCU, Leicestershire, Leicestershire to Scotland) b Leicester 16.11.1988 RHB SLA																			
FC		7	12	5	652	158*	93.14	3	3									6	
Lim		6	6	1	63	26	12.60	0	0									3	
FC	2008	20	36	6	1098	158*	36.60	3	5	30	64	1	64.00	1-64	0	0	12.80	11	
Lim	2008	10	10	1	139	58	15.44	0	1									3	
SMITH, Steven Peter Devereux (Australia, New South Wales, Australia to England, Australia to New Zealand, Australia to West Indies, New South Wales to India, Worcestershire) b Sydney, New South Wales, Australia 2.6.1989 RHB LB																			
Test		2	4	0	100	77	25.00	0	1	186	82	3	27.33	3-51	0	0	2.64	1	
FC		2	4	0	100	77	25.00	0	1	186	82	3	27.33	3-51	0	0	2.64	1	
Int		4	4	1	94	41	31.33	0	0	216	182	7	26.00	2-34	0	0	5.05	0	
Lim		5	5	2	122	41	40.66	0	0	258	225	7	32.14	2-34	0	0	5.23	0	
I20T		1	1	0	12	12	12.00	0	0	24	34	1	34.00	1-34	0	0	8.50	0	
20T		6	5	0	79	34	15.80	0	0	120	150	7	21.42	2-20	0	0	7.50	3	
FC	2007/08	15	26	4	1112	177	50.54	4	3	2085	1352	29	46.62	7-64	1	0	3.89	22	
Int	2009/10	5	4	1	94	41	31.33	0	0	275	260	9	28.88	2-34	0	0	5.67	2	
Lim	2007/08	23	20	5	594	92	39.60	0	3	1031	923	24	38.45	3-43	0	0	5.37	11	
I20T	2009/10	13	8	2	62	27	10.33	0	0	240	300	15	20.00	3-20	0	0	7.50	12	
20T	2007/08	38	29	7	355	35*	16.13	0	0	567	686	41	16.73	4-13	2	0	7.25	21	
SMITH, Thomas Christopher (Lancashire) b Liverpool, Lancashire 26.12.1985 LHB RM																			
FC		14	25	3	576	128	26.18	2	2	1679	913	32	28.53	6-94	1	0	3.26	14	
Lim		8	8	0	175	61	21.87	0	1	330	339	13	26.07	3-49	0	0	6.16	2	
20T		17	17	2	543	92*	36.20	0	3	250	306	13	23.53	3-12	0	0	7.34	9	
FC	2005	56	78	16	1626	128	26.22	3	5	7588	3792	116	32.68	6-46	2	0	2.99	50	
Lim	2005	45	35	7	742	87*	26.50	0	6	1772	1467	57	25.73	3-8	0	0	4.96	12	
20T	2006	38	32	8	765	92*	31.87	0	4	578	690	28	24.64	3-12	0	0	7.16	18	
SMITH, Thomas Michael John (Middlesex, Middlesex to Netherlands) b Eastbourne, Sussex 22.8.1987 RHB SLA																			
FC		4	7	1	110	33	18.33	0	0	432	262	2	131.00	1-30	0	0	3.63	3	
Lim		7	3	0	31	18	10.33	0	0	246	217	6	36.16	3-26	0	0	5.29	1	
20T		14	6	4	22	9*	11.00	0	0	239	311	18	17.27	5-24	1	1	7.80	4	
FC	2007	6	10	1	123	33	13.66	0	0	586	411	3	137.00	1-30	0	0	4.20	3	
Lim	2006	18	6	0	118	65	19.66	0	1	654	617	15	41.13	3-26	0	0	5.66	9	
20T	2007	16	7	5	25	9*	12.50	0	0	251	325	18	18.05	5-24	1	1	7.76	4	
SMITH, William Rew (Durham, Durham to United Arab Emirates) b Luton, Bedfordshire 28.9.1982 RHB OB																			
FC		5	8	0	171	57	21.37	0	1	24	27	0					6.75	2	
Lim		5	5	2	88	50*	29.33	0	1									0	
20T		10	5	1	41	19	10.25	0	0	71	93	0					7.85	2	
FC	2002	76	122	8	3628	201*	31.82	8	12	729	552	8	69.00	3-34	0	0	4.54	36	
Lim	2002	70	65	5	1527	103	25.45	1	11	53	51	2	25.50	1-6	0	0	5.77	24	
20T	2003	55	44	9	624	55	17.82	0	3	95	132	1	132.00	1-31	0	0	8.33	32	
SNELL, Stephen David (Gloucestershire, Gloucestershire to Netherlands) b Winchester, Hampshire 27.2.1983 RHB WK																			
FC		10	19	1	322	71	17.88	0	2									18	
Lim		11	8	1	262	95	37.42	0	2									13	1
20T		15	12	3	166	50	18.44	0	1									8	3
FC	2005	41	69	7	1679	127	27.08	1	13	18	15	0					5.00	96	3
Lim	2001	25	19	2	328	95	19.29	0	2									32	1
20T	2009	17	14	4	179	50	17.90	0	1									9	3
SOLANKI, Vikram Singh (Worcestershire) b Udaipur, Rajasthan, India 1.4.1976 RHB OB																			
FC		15	28	1	717	114	26.55	1	4	174	96	1	96.00	1-22	0	0	3.31	18	
Lim		12	12	0	436	129	36.33	1	2	66	39	1	39.00	1-14	0	0	3.54	8	
20T		7	6	0	121	51	20.16	0	1	18	31	1	31.00	1-6	0	0	10.33	2	
FC	1995	267	446	26	15039	270	35.80	27	79	7105	4120	86	47.90	5-40	4	1	3.47	276	
Int	1999/00	51	46	5	1097	106	26.75	2	5	111	105	1	105.00	1-17	0	0	5.67	16	
Lim	1993	362	334	28	9775	164*	31.94	14	55	1115	973	28	34.75	4-14	1	0	5.23	139	
I20T	2005	3	3	0	76	43	25.33	0	0									3	
20T	2004	48	46	0	1231	100	26.76	1	8	84	131	4	32.75	1-6	0	0	9.35	25	
SPRIEGEL, Matthew Neil William (Surrey) b Epsom, Surrey 4.3.1987 LHB OB																			
FC		10	14	1	391	108*	30.07	2	0	393	207	5	41.40	1-5	0	0	3.16	10	
Lim		11	10	3	268	56*	38.28	0	2	234	266	5	53.20	1-20	0	0	6.82	6	
20T		12	7	4	67	25*	22.33	0	0	174	208	7	29.71	2-23	0	0	7.17	7	
FC	2007	31	50	3	1203	108*	25.59	3	3	1255	767	17	45.11	2-28	0	0	3.66	23	
Lim	2008	36	33	12	794	81*	37.80	0	6	1050	942	20	47.10	2-23	0	0	5.38	19	
20T	2008	31	23	11	219	25*	18.25	0	0	528	657	24	27.37	4-33	1	0	7.46	11	
STEBBINGS, Benjamin Robert William (Oxford MCCU) b Oxford 4.10.1989 RHB RM																			
FC		3	3	0	44	25	14.66	0	0									0	
STEVENS, Darren Ian (England Lions, Kent, Kent to Scotland, Mid West Rhinos) b Leicester 30.4.1976 RHB RM																			
FC		15	26	3	979	197	42.56	4	2	1681	768	28	27.42	4-38	0	0	2.74	6	
Lim		15	14	5	451	68	50.11	0	4	258	226	3	75.33	1-15	0	0	5.25	6	
20T		14	13	4	369	52*	41.00	0	2	234	287	12	23.91	3-17	0	0	7.35	5	
FC	1997	170	276	20	8836	208	34.51	21	42	6786	3407	94	36.24	4-36	0	0	3.01	128	

Cmp	Debut	M	I	NO	Runs	HS	Avge	100	50	Balls	Runs	Wkts	Avge	BB	5i	10m	RpO	ct	st
Lim	1997	218	204	24	5454	133	30.30	4	36	2183	1806	51	35.41	5-32	0	1	4.96	84	
20T	2003	84	78	19	1746	77	29.59	0	8	690	839	39	21.51	4-14	2	0	7.29	27	
STIFF, David Alexander (Somerset) b Dewsbury, Yorkshire 20.10.1984 RHB RF																			
FC		2	4	2	71	40	35.50	0	0	245	207	2	103.50	1-42	0	0	5.06	0	
FC	2004	20	24	10	321	49	22.92	0	0	2578	1906	43	44.32	5-91	1	0	4.43	1	
Lim	2001	1								30	27	1	27.00	1-27	0	0	5.40	0	
STIRLING, Paul Robert (Ireland, Ireland to Canada, Ireland to Netherlands, Ireland to Sri Lanka, Ireland to United Arab Emirates, Ireland to West Indies, Middlesex) b Belfast, Ireland 3.9.1990 RHB OB																			
20T		1	1	0	2	2	2.00	0	0									0	
FC	2008	8	12	0	338	100	28.16	1	1	195	113	3	37.66	2-45	0	0	3.47	6	
Int	2008	20	20	1	817	177	43.00	1	5	353	260	10	26.00	4-11	1	0	4.41	10	
Lim	2008	37	37	1	1130	177	31.38	1	8	395	299	10	29.90	4-11	1	0	4.54	16	
I20T	2009	6	6	0	77	22	12.83	0	0	18	25	0					8.33	1	
20T	2008	13	13	0	222	43	17.07	0	0	84	94	1	94.00	1-13	0	0	6.71	5	
STOKES, Benjamin Andrew (Durham, Durham to Scotland, Durham to United Arab Emirates) b Christchurch, Canterbury, New Zealand 4.6.1991 LHB RM																			
FC		13	19	3	740	161*	46.25	2	2	399	328	5	65.60	2-32	0	0	4.93	8	
Lim		9	9	1	143	39	17.87	0	0	24	22	2	11.00	2-22	0	0	5.50	3	
20T		15	12	1	180	44	16.36	0	0	30	37	1	37.00	1-23	0	0	7.40	4	
FC	2010	14	21	3	798	161*	44.33	2	3	453	365	6	60.83	2-32	0	0	4.83	8	
Lim	2009	13	13	2	204	39	18.54	0	0	84	79	5	15.80	2-22	0	0	5.64	4	
STONEMAN, Mark Daniel (Durham) b Newcastle upon Tyne, Northumberland 26.6.1987 LHB RM																			
FC		11	17	1	525	118	32.81	1	4									5	
Lim		4	4	0	73	25	18.25	0	0									2	
20T		3	3	0	85	46	28.33	0	0									1	
FC	2007	45	75	3	1789	118	24.84	2	9									28	
Lim	2008	5	5	0	94	25	18.80	0	0									2	
STRAUSS, Andrew John (England, Middlesex, England to South Africa, England to Scotland) b Johannesburg, Transvaal, South Africa 2.3.1977 LHB LM																			
Test		6	10	1	341	83	37.88	0	3									9	
FC		14	25	1	801	92	33.37	0	6									25	
Int		13	13	0	745	154	57.30	2	5									11	
Lim		17	17	0	812	154	47.76	2	5									11	
Test	2004	77	140	6	5777	177	43.11	18	21									86	
FC	1998	199	353	17	14061	177	41.84	35	63	102	89	2	44.50	1-16	0	0	5.23	175	
Int	2003/04	113	112	8	3692	154	35.50	5	24	6	3	0					3.00	49	
Lim	1997	240	233	14	7118	163	32.50	9	46	6	3	0					3.00	82	
I20T	2005	4	4	0	73	33	18.25	0	0									1	
20T	2003	28	28	0	519	60	18.53	0	2									12	
STYRIS, Scott Bernard (Auckland, New Zealand, Deccan Chargers, Essex, New Zealand to Sri Lanka, New Zealand to United Arab Emirates, New Zealand to United States of America, New Zealand to West Indies) b Brisbane, Queensland, Australia 10.7.1975 RHB RFM																			
20T		15	13	2	392	106*	35.63	1	1	294	408	13	31.38	2-28	0	0	8.32	2	
Test	2002	29	48	4	1586	170	36.04	5	6	1960	1015	20	50.75	3-28	0	0	3.10	23	
FC	1994/95	126	210	19	5964	212*	31.22	10	29	12657	6353	203	31.29	6-32	9	1	3.01	100	
Int	1999/00	169	146	22	4056	141	32.70	4	25	5642	4464	128	34.87	6-25	4	1	4.74	67	
Lim	1994/95	312	276	46	7667	141	33.33	5	52	11361	8714	287	30.36	6-25	8	1	4.60	121	
I20T	2004/05	28	26	2	492	66	20.50	0	1	279	327	17	19.23	3-5	0	0	7.03	7	
20T	2004/05	103	97	9	2135	106*	24.26	1	9	1639	2093	79	26.49	3-5	0	0	7.66	26	
SUPPIAH, Arul Vivasvan (Somerset, Somerset to India) b Kuala Lumpur, Malaysia 30.8.1983 RHB SLA																			
FC		16	26	3	771	125	33.52	1	4	594	300	3	100.00	1-21	0	0	3.03	5	
Lim		9	7	1	173	80	28.83	0	1	90	97	1	97.00	1-24	0	0	6.46	4	
20T		10	5	2	61	26*	20.33	0	0	48	50	2	25.00	1-6	0	0	6.25	6	
FC	2002	60	99	5	3296	151	35.06	5	18	3278	1932	32	60.37	3-46	0	0	3.53	34	
Lim	2002	68	59	11	1347	80	28.06	0	7	1235	1190	35	34.00	4-39	1	0	5.78	26	
20T	2005	48	30	9	273	32*	13.00	0	0	391	485	22	22.04	3-25	0	0	7.44	22	
SUTTON, Luke David (Lancashire) b Keynsham, Somerset 4.10.1976 RHB WK																			
FC		13	21	2	530	118	27.89	2	0									37	5
Lim		10	7	2	144	47	28.80	0	0									8	3
FC	1997	160	254	39	6780	151*	31.53	11	19									408	22
Lim	1998	159	132	28	2055	83	19.75	0	6									176	24
20T	2003	16	14	4	306	61*	30.60	0	1									9	7
SWANN, Graeme Peter (England, Nottinghamshire, England to Bangladesh, England to South Africa, England to Scotland, England to United Arab Emirates, England to West Indies) b Northampton 24.3.1979 RHB OB																			
Test		6	8	0	90	28	11.25	0	0	1045	479	28	17.10	6-65	3	0	2.75	9	
FC		7	9	0	91	28	10.11	0	0	1201	567	30	18.90	6-65	3	0	2.83	9	
Int		10	6	1	66	33	13.20	0	0	498	372	19	19.57	4-37	2	0	4.48	3	
Lim		10	6	1	66	33	13.20	0	0	498	372	19	19.57	4-37	2	0	4.48	3	
I20T		2								48	41	4	10.25	2-14	0	0	5.12	1	
20T		3	1	0	11	11	11.00	0	0	72	65	6	10.83	2-14	0	0	5.41	2	
Test	2008/09	24	31	5	653	85	25.11	0	4	6116	3001	113	26.55	6-65	9	1	2.94	19	

Cmp	Debut	M	I	NO	Runs	HS	Avge	100	50	Balls	Runs	Wkts	Avge	BB	5i	10m	RpO	ct	st
FC	1998	200	276	22	6740	183	26.53	4	35	35333	17608	553	31.84	7-33	24	4	2.99	146	
Int	1999/00	43	27	4	295	34	12.82	0	0	1902	1436	59	24.33	5-28	3	1	4.53	19	
Lim	1997	230	175	20	2945	83	19.00	0	14	9132	6720	259	25.94	5-17	11	3	4.41	78	
I20T	2007/08	20	8	6	42	15*	21.00	0	0	402	435	30	14.50	3-14	0	0	6.49	2	
20T	2003	61	46	10	729	90*	20.25	0	3	1284	1427	77	18.53	3-14	0	0	6.66	17	
SYMONDS, Andrew (Queensland, Deccan Chargers, Surrey) b Birmingham, Warwickshire 9.6.1975 RHB OB																			
20T		15	13	0	263	63	20.23	0	2	193	298	12	24.83	5-18	0	1	9.26	5	
Test	2003/04	26	41	5	1462	162*	40.61	2	10	2094	896	24	37.33	3-50	0	0	2.56	22	
FC	1994/95	227	376	33	14477	254*	42.20	40	65	17633	8714	242	36.00	6-105	2	0	2.96	159	
Int	1998/99	198	161	33	5088	156	39.75	6	30	5935	4955	133	37.25	5-18	2	1	5.00	82	
Lim	1993/94	424	377	51	11099	156	34.04	9	64	11713	9379	282	33.25	6-14	2	4	4.80	187	
I20T	2004/05	14	11	4	337	85*	48.14	0	2	185	277	8	34.62	2-14	0	0	8.98	3	
20T	2003	78	72	13	1980	117*	33.55	2	12	1201	1600	51	31.37	5-18	0	1	7.99	37	
TAHIR, Naqaash Sarosh (Warwickshire) b Birmingham, Warwickshire 14.11.1983 RHB RFM																			
FC		3	6	0	69	34	11.50	0	0	498	238	5	47.60	2-49	0	0	2.86	2	
Lim		1								37	49	0					7.94	0	
FC	2004	52	59	16	658	49	15.30	0	0	6963	3815	128	29.80	7-107	2	0	3.28	7	
Lim	2005	15	5	3	19	13*	9.50	0	0	523	439	5	87.80	2-47	0	0	5.03	1	
TAIT, Shaun William (Australia, South Australia, Australia to England, Australia to New Zealand, Australia to West Indies, Glamorgan, Rajasthan Royals) b Bedford Park, Adelaide, South Australia, Australia 22.2.1983 RHB RF																			
Int		3	1	1	1	1*		0	0	153	99	8	12.37	4-48	1	0	3.88	1	
Lim		3	1	1	1	1*		0	0	153	99	8	12.37	4-48	1	0	3.88	1	
I20T		2	2	0	8	6	4.00	0	0	48	62	2	31.00	2-25	0	0	7.75	0	
20T		12	4	1	14	6	4.66	0	0	264	347	9	38.55	2-25	0	0	7.88	1	
Test	2005	3	5	2	20	8	6.66	0	0	414	302	5	60.40	3-97	0	0	4.37	1	
FC	2002/03	50	70	29	509	68	12.41	0	2	9263	5661	198	28.59	7-29	7	1	3.66	15	
Int	2006/07	25	5	3	25	11	12.50	0	0	1233	1060	46	23.04	4-39	2	0	5.15	3	
Lim	2002/03	88	33	17	108	22*	6.75	0	0	4445	3770	162	23.27	8-43	6	3	5.08	18	
I20T	2007/08	17	5	1	10	6	2.50	0	0	382	419	26	16.11	3-13	0	0	6.58	3	
20T	2004/05	50	17	5	77	14*	6.41	0	0	1099	1363	70	19.47	4-14	1	0	7.44	10	
TAVARÉ, William Andrew (Loughborough MCCU) b Bristol 1.1.1990 RHB RM																			
FC		2	3	0	60	49	20.00	0	0									0	
TAYLOR, Christopher Glyn (Gloucestershire, Gloucestershire to Netherlands) b Bristol 27.9.1976 RHB OB																			
FC		15	27	2	803	89	32.12	0	6	314	172	3	57.33	1-19	0	0	3.28	11	
Lim		11	10	2	379	105	47.37	1	2	120	113	3	37.66	2-15	0	0	5.65	4	
20T		15	13	0	257	67	19.76	0	1	12	15	0					7.50	1	
FC	2000	144	250	18	7944	196	34.24	17	37	2497	1452	27	53.77	4-52	0	0	3.48	96	
Lim	1999	169	152	22	3383	105	26.02	1	20	700	613	16	38.31	2-5	0	0	5.25	70	1
20T	2003	65	59	10	1180	83	24.08	0	5	36	60	1	60.00	1-22	0	0	10.00	21	
TAYLOR, Jack Martin Robert (Gloucestershire) b Banbury, Oxfordshire 12.11.1991 RHB OB																			
FC		2	4	0	11	6	2.75	0	0	30	13	1	13.00	1-8	0	0	2.60	2	
TAYLOR, James William Arthur (England Lions, Leicestershire, England Lions to United Arab Emirates, Leicestershire to Scotland, MCC to United Arab Emirates) b Nottingham 6.1.1990 RHB LB																			
FC		18	29	4	1095	206*	43.80	3	4	24	15	0					3.75	15	
Lim		13	13	5	439	103*	54.87	1	3	66	98	5	19.60	4-61	1	0	8.90	3	
20T		14	14	3	407	62*	37.00	0	4	12	16	0					8.00	5	
FC	2008	40	64	11	2405	207*	45.37	6	11	216	160	0					4.44	29	
Lim	2008	36	33	8	1150	103*	46.00	2	7	138	170	5	34.00	4-61	1	0	7.39	5	
20T	2008	27	26	6	644	62*	32.20	0	4	74	100	2	50.00	1-10	0	0	8.10	7	
TAYLOR, Luteru Ross Poutoa Lote (Central Districts, New Zealand, Durham, New Zealand to South Africa, New Zealand to Sri Lanka, New Zealand to United Arab Emirates, New Zealand to United States of America, New Zealand to West Indies, Royal Challengers Bangalore, Victoria to Australia) b Lower Hutt, Wellington, New Zealand 8.3.1984 RHB OB																			
20T		11	9	1	315	80*	39.37	0	2									4	
Test	2007/08	25	46	1	1941	154*	43.13	5	9	32	14	0					2.62	45	
FC	2002/03	71	120	3	4774	217	40.80	10	26	602	330	4	82.50	2-34	0	0	3.28	89	
Int	2005/06	84	77	11	2376	128*	36.00	3	16	30	32	0					6.40	62	
Lim	2002/03	129	122	15	4028	132*	37.64	7	27	306	240	3	80.00	1-13	0	0	4.70	87	
I20T	2006/07	34	31	2	590	63	20.34	0	3									22	
20T	2005/06	92	87	14	2395	111*	32.80	1	14	180	269	8	33.62	3-28	0	0	8.96	47	
TAYLOR, Michael Hugh (Cambridge MCCU, Cambridge University) b Ballymena, Co Antrim, Ireland 6.12.1988 RHB LB																			
FC		2	4	2	42	16*	21.00	0	0	305	235	4	58.75	4-161	0	0	4.62	0	
TAYLOR, Robert Meadows L (Loughborough MCCU) b Northampton 21.12.1989 LHB LM																			
FC		2	2	0	39	22	19.50	0	0	276	202	5	40.40	2-60	0	0	4.39	2	
TEN DOESCHATE, Ryan Neil (Essex to Netherlands, Netherlands, Essex, Netherlands to Kenya, Netherlands to United Arab Emirates) b Port Elizabeth, Cape Province, South Africa 30.6.1980 RHB RMF																			
FC		11	19	2	577	85	33.94	0	5	1149	716	27	26.51	5-13	1	0	3.73	9	
Lim		9	9	4	270	109*	54.00	1	1	318	349	9	38.77	2-30	0	0	6.58	1	
20T		6	6	1	296	102	59.20	1	1	66	75	3	25.00	1-16	0	0	6.81	2	
FC	2003	81	118	15	4950	259*	48.05	16	17	7916	5258	158	33.27	6-20	7	0	3.98	44	
Int	2006	27	26	8	1234	109*	68.55	3	8	1268	1005	48	20.93	4-31	3	0	4.75	11	
Lim	2003	126	102	31	3328	134*	46.87	5	19	3632	3319	125	26.55	5-50	6	1	5.48	39	

Cmp	Debut	M	I	NO	Runs	HS	Avge	100	50	Balls	Runs	Wkts	Avge	BB	5i	10m	RpO	ct	st
I20T	2008	9	9	4	214	56	42.80	0	1	204	241	12	20.08	3-23	0	0	7.08	3	
20T	2003	64	55	16	1130	102	28.97	1	2	654	796	36	22.11	4-24	1	0	7.30	20	
THOMAS, Alfonso Clive (Dolphins, Somerset, Somerset to India) b Cape Town, Cape Province, South Africa 9.2.1977 RHB RFM																			
FC		15	20	4	328	44	20.50	0	0	2267	1202	49	24.53	5-40	2	0	3.18	1	
Lim		14	6	3	43	19	14.33	0	0	487	430	27	15.92	4-34	2	0	5.29	6	
20T		19	6	3	29	14*	9.66	0	0	437	460	33	13.93	3-11	0	0	6.31	5	
FC	1998/99	112	158	33	3158	119*	25.26	2	11	20188	9655	353	27.35	7-54	16	1	2.87	31	
Lim	2000/01	134	67	33	504	28*	14.82	0	0	5798	4917	178	27.62	4-18	6	0	5.08	30	
I20T	2006/07	1								24	25	3	8.33	3-25	0	0	6.25	0	
20T	2003/04	82	27	14	153	30*	11.76	0	0	1578	1892	99	19.11	4-27	1	0	7.19	25	
THOMPSON, Jackson Gladwin (Middlesex, Unicorns) b Nasik, Maharashtra, India 7.2.1986 LHB OB																			
Lim		12	11	0	249	54	22.63	0	1	60	65	0					6.50	2	
20T		2	2	0	46	32	23.00	0	0	6	8	1	8.00	1-8	0	0	8.00	0	
FC	2007	1	2	0	32	21	16.00	0	0									0	
Lim	2002	14	13	0	257	54	19.76	0	1	60	65	0					6.50	2	
20T	2008	6	6	0	68	32	11.33	0	0	6	8	1	8.00	1-8	0	0	8.00	3	
THORNELY, Michael Alistair (Sussex) b Camden, Middlesex 19.10.1987 RHB RM																			
FC		12	21	1	467	89	23.35	0	4	126	75	4	18.75	2-14	0	0	3.57	8	
Lim		6	6	0	186	67	31.00	0	2									2	
FC	2007	17	30	2	522	89	18.64	0	4	150	100	4	25.00	2-14	0	0	4.00	15	
Lim	2007	7	6	0	186	67	31.00	0	2									2	
THORP, Callum David (Durham, Durham to United Arab Emirates) b Mount Lawley, Perth, Western Australia, Australia 11.2.1975 RHB RM																			
FC		5	6	1	64	29	12.80	0	0	891	427	13	32.84	4-54	0	0	2.87	2	
FC	2002/03	56	74	9	976	79*	15.01	0	3	8417	4168	159	26.21	7-88	7	1	2.97	33	
Lim	2002/03	38	25	8	286	52	16.82	0	1	1765	1286	47	27.36	6-17	2	1	4.37	7	
20T	2005	9	6	0	63	13	10.50	0	0	162	266	3	88.66	2-32	0	0	9.85	1	
THORPE, James Ashley (Sussex) b Geneva, Switzerland 20.1.1991 RHB RMF																			
Lim		1	1	1	3	3*		0	0	18	26	1	26.00	1-26	0	0	8.66	0	
TIMMS, Richard Thomas (Cambridge University) b Bristol 9.9.1984 RHB RFM																			
FC		1	2	0	66	36	33.00	0	0	66	51	0					4.63	1	
FC	2005	8	15	0	308	57	20.53	0	2	162	126	0					4.66	6	
Lim	2002	1	1	1	38	38*		0	0									0	
TOMLINSON, James Andrew (Hampshire) b Winchester, Hampshire 12.6.1982 LHB LM																			
FC		15	21	5	198	42	12.37	0	0	3355	1624	46	35.30	7-85	2	0	2.90	3	
Lim		5	2	1	16	14	16.00	0	0	202	195	9	21.66	3-33	0	0	5.79	0	
FC	2002	65	85	35	530	42	10.60	0	0	11374	6735	190	35.44	8-46	8	1	3.55	16	
Lim	2000	27	14	5	34	14	3.77	0	0	1089	910	29	31.37	4-47	1	0	5.01	3	
20T	2006	2	1	0	5	5	5.00	0	0	42	48	1	48.00	1-20	0	0	6.85	0	
TOOR, Kabir Singh (Middlesex) b Watford, Hertfordshire 30.4.1990 RHB LB																			
FC		1	1	0	15	15	15.00	0	0	150	84	1	84.00	1-36	0	0	3.36	0	
Lim	2009	2	2	1	8	5	8.00	0	0	24	32	1	32.00	1-25	0	0	8.00	0	
TREDWELL, James Cullum (England, England Lions, Kent, England to Bangladesh, England Lions to United Arab Emirates, Kent to Scotland) b Ashford, Kent 27.2.1982 LHB OB																			
FC		12	20	2	489	115	27.16	1	1	2262	1151	38	30.28	7-22	2	0	3.05	21	
Int		1								18	18	0					6.00	0	
Lim		12	3	0	22	11	7.33	0	0	486	376	11	34.18	4-20	1	0	4.64	5	
20T		10	7	1	47	25	7.83	0	0	186	268	11	24.36	3-13	0	0	8.64	5	
Test	2009/10	1	1	0	37	37	37.00	0	0	390	181	6	30.16	4-82	0	0	2.78	1	
FC	2001	101	145	19	3004	123*	23.84	3	13	18033	9534	267	35.70	8-66	9	3	3.17	106	
Int	2009/10	2	1	1	2	2*		0	0	78	70	0					5.38	0	
Lim	2000	152	105	36	1253	88	18.15	0	4	6114	4809	144	33.39	6-27	3	1	4.71	63	
20T	2003	76	35	8	299	34	11.07	0	0	1380	1660	69	24.05	4-21	1	0	7.21	27	
TREGO, Peter David (England Lions, Somerset, England Lions to United Arab Emirates, Somerset to India) b Weston-super-Mare, Somerset 12.6.1981 RHB RM																			
FC		16	23	2	693	108	33.00	1	5	1363	729	22	33.13	4-26	0	0	3.20	12	
Lim		19	17	4	540	147	41.53	1	2	696	630	19	33.15	5-40	0	1	5.43	7	
20T		16	15	2	294	72*	22.61	0	1	186	277	11	25.18	2-19	0	0	8.93	6	
FC	2000	99	143	20	4352	140	35.38	8	27	9821	6256	166	37.68	6-59	1	0	3.82	37	
Lim	1999	108	89	18	1581	147	22.26	1	6	3800	3531	111	31.81	5-40	7	2	5.57	31	
20T	2003	59	51	9	999	79	23.78	0	3	698	1000	34	29.41	2-17	0	0	8.59	15	
TREMLETT, Christopher Timothy (Surrey) b Southampton, Hampshire 2.9.1981 RHB RFM																			
FC		12	17	6	230	53*	20.90	0	1	2171	969	48	20.18	4-29	0	0	2.67	1	
Lim		7	5	0	94	38	18.80	0	0	287	351	8	43.87	2-31	0	0	7.33	1	
20T		16	3	2	14	6*	14.00	0	0	360	411	24	17.12	3-17	0	0	6.85	0	
Test	2007	3	5	1	50	25*	12.50	0	0	859	386	13	29.69	3-12	0	0	2.69	1	
FC	2000	104	139	37	1868	64	18.31	0	7	17552	9252	337	27.45	6-44	7	0	3.16	28	
Int	2005	9	6	2	38	19*	9.50	0	0	479	419	9	46.55	4-32	1	0	5.24	2	
Lim	2000	119	71	22	509	38*	10.38	0	0	5482	4432	164	27.02	4-25	5	0	4.85	24	

Cmp	Debut	M	I	NO	Runs	HS	Avge	100	50	Balls	Runs	Wkts	Avge	BB	5i	10m	RpO	ct	st
I20T	2007/08	1								24	45	2	22.50	2-45	0	0	11.25	0	
20T	2004	41	15	6	72	13	8.00	0	0	891	1065	56	19.01	4-25	1	0	7.17	5	
TRESCOTHICK, Marcus Edward (Somerset, Somerset to India) b Keynsham, Somerset 25.12.1975 LHB RM																			
FC		16	28	4	1397	228*	58.20	4	6									26	
Lim		14	14	0	366	79	26.14	0	4									8	
20T		19	19	1	572	83	31.77	0	6									4	
Test	2000	76	143	10	5825	219	43.79	14	29	300	155	1	155.00	1-34	0	0	3.10	95	
FC	1993	271	466	27	18042	284	41.09	43	91	2704	1551	36	43.08	4-36	0	0	3.44	340	
Int	2000	123	122	6	4335	137	37.37	12	21	232	219	4	54.75	2-7	0	0	5.66	49	
Lim	1993	334	321	25	11136	184	37.62	27	55	2010	1644	57	28.84	4-50	1	0	4.90	131	
I20T	2005	3	3	0	166	72	55.33	0	2									2	
20T	2004	51	50	2	1613	107	33.60	1	14									18	
TRIPATHI, Vishal (Northamptonshire) b Burnley, Lancashire 3.3.1988 RHB LB																			
FC		4	7	1	196	71	32.66	0	2	36	28	0					4.66	3	
Lim		1	1	0	0	0	0.00	0	0									1	
20T		3	1	0	6	6	6.00	0	0									2	
TROTT, Ian Jonathan Leonard (England, England Lions, Warwickshire, England to Bangladesh, England to South Africa, England to United Arab Emirates) b Cape Town, Cape Province, South Africa 22.4.1981 RHB RM																			
Test		6	10	2	669	226	83.62	2	2	36	23	1	23.00	1-16	0	0	3.83	4	
FC		12	21	2	1084	226	57.05	3	5	150	94	5	18.80	2-20	0	0	3.76	14	
Int		7	7	0	335	110	47.85	1	3	18	18	0					6.00	1	
Lim		19	19	2	940	118	55.29	3	7	18	18	0					6.00	7	
20T		12	12	2	306	72*	30.60	0	2									2	
Test	2009	13	23	2	1155	226	55.00	3	4	114	86	1	86.00	1-16	0	0	4.52	8	
FC	2000/01	153	257	31	10183	226	45.05	23	51	4358	2471	56	44.12	7-39	1	0	3.40	148	
Int	2009	11	11	1	483	110	48.30	1	5	66	47	0					4.27	3	
Lim	1999/00	173	161	31	5952	125*	45.78	12	40	1423	1331	52	25.59	4-55	1	0	5.61	57	
I20T	2007	7	7	1	138	51	23.00	0	1									0	
20T	2003	76	71	16	2081	86*	37.83	0	13	144	234	8	29.25	2-19	0	0	9.75	18	
TROUGHTON, Jamie Oliver (Warwickshire, Warwickshire to Scotland) b Camden, Middlesex 2.3.1979 LHB SLA																			
FC		16	30	1	585	78	20.17	0	1									5	
Lim		13	13	4	297	66*	33.00	0	2									5	
20T		17	16	2	365	66	26.07	0	2									7	
FC	2001	126	196	15	6498	223	35.90	16	31	2357	1416	22	64.36	3-1	0	0	3.60	58	
Int	2003	6	5	1	36	20	9.00	0	0									1	
Lim	1999	137	121	14	3130	115*	29.25	2	18	736	644	25	25.76	4-23	2	0	5.25	48	
20T	2003	68	62	4	1291	66	22.25	0	8	96	127	6	21.16	2-10	0	0	7.93	31	
TURNBULL, Peter Thomas (Cambridge MCCU) b Pontypridd, Glamorgan, Wales 20.5.1989 RHB RMF																			
FC		3	4	0	25	13	6.25	0	0	650	366	10	36.60	5-92	1	0	3.37	0	
FC	2009	4	5	1	25	13	6.25	0	0	836	469	11	42.63	5-92	1	0	3.36	1	
TURNER, Mark Leif (Somerset) b Sunderland, Co Durham 23.10.1984 RHB RMF																			
Lim		7	3	1	11	8	5.50	0	0	245	286	12	23.83	4-36	1	0	7.00	3	
20T		15	3	1	12	11*	6.00	0	0	252	372	14	26.57	3-25	0	0	8.85	3	
FC	2005	9	8	2	89	57	14.83	0	1	1323	853	17	50.17	4-30	0	0	3.86	3	
Lim	2007	22	9	5	49	15*	12.25	0	0	802	820	31	26.45	4-36	1	0	6.13	5	
20T	2005	33	10	4	25	11*	4.16	0	0	564	837	30	27.90	3-25	0	0	8.90	6	
UDAL, Shaun David (Middlesex, Middlesex to Netherlands) b Cove, Farnborough, Hampshire 18.3.1969 RHB OB																			
FC		13	19	1	216	55	12.00	0	1	1707	917	27	33.96	5-128	1	0	3.22	6	
Lim		9	7	1	82	33*	13.66	0	0	300	279	5	55.80	2-18	0	0	5.58	2	
20T		8	4	2	3	3	1.50	0	0	126	146	5	29.20	3-24	0	0	6.95	2	
Test	2005/06	4	7	1	109	33*	18.16	0	0	596	344	8	43.00	4-14	0	0	3.46	1	
FC	1989	301	430	79	7931	117*	22.59	1	34	53921	26695	822	32.47	8-50	37	5	2.97	127	
Int	1994	11	7	4	35	11*	11.66	0	0	612	400	9	44.44	2-37	0	0	3.92	1	
Lim	1989	410	264	82	2966	79*	16.29	0	9	18667	13830	458	30.19	5-43	9	1	4.44	136	
20T	2003	60	39	15	382	40*	15.91	0	0	1155	1357	50	27.14	3-19	0	0	7.04	16	
VAAS, Warnakulasuriya Patabendige Ushantha Joseph Chaminda (Basnahira North, Colts, Deccan Chargers, Northamptonshire) b Mattumagala, Sri Lanka 27.1.1974 LHB LFM																			
FC		2	2	0	17	17	8.50	0	0	440	161	6	26.83	4-49	0	0	2.19	1	
20T		17	17	1	412	73	25.75	0	4	345	364	23	15.82	3-16	0	0	6.33	3	
Test	1994	111	162	35	3089	100*	24.32	1	13	23438	10501	355	29.58	7-71	12	2	2.68	31	
FC	1990/91	202	272	57	5525	134	25.69	4	24	37222	17068	683	24.98	7-54	27	3	2.75	57	
Int	1993/94	322	220	72	2025	50*	13.68	0	1	15775	11014	400	27.53	8-19	9	4	4.18	60	
Lim	1992/93	392	268	88	2903	76*	16.12	0	6	18664	12947	480	26.97	8-19	11	4	4.16	79	
I20T	2006/07	6	2	1	33	21	33.00	0	0	132	128	6	21.33	2-14	0	0	5.81	0	
20T	2005/06	45	39	8	622	73	20.06	0	4	927	1059	55	19.25	3-16	0	0	6.85	7	
VAN JAARSVELD, Martin (Kent, Kent to Scotland) b Klerksdorp, Transvaal, South Africa 18.6.1974 RHB OB																			
FC		17	29	2	1188	110*	44.00	3	6	738	332	5	66.40	2-50	0	0	2.69	36	
Lim		10	10	3	316	104*	45.14	1	3	82	65	5	13.00	3-23	0	0	4.75	5	
20T		16	16	1	421	82	28.06	0	4	72	75	3	25.00	3-25	0	0	6.25	5	
Test	2002/03	9	15	2	397	73	30.53	0	3	42	28	0					4.00	11	
FC	1994/95	239	402	36	16775	262*	45.83	51	81	3678	1848	47	39.31	5-33	1	0	3.01	364	

Cmp	Debut	M	I	NO	Runs	HS	Avge	100	50	Balls	Runs	Wkts	Avge	BB	5i	10m	RpO	ct	st
Int	2002/03	11	7	1	124	45	20.66	0	0	31	18	2	9.00	1-0	0	0	3.48	4	
Lim	1995/96	261	243	41	8361	132*	41.39	15	52	1471	1293	35	36.94	3-13	0	0	5.27	149	
20T	2003/04	96	87	11	1994	82	26.23	0	15	150	191	7	27.28	3-25	0	0	7.64	56	
VINCE, James Michael (Hampshire, Hampshire to Scotland) b Cuckfield, Sussex 14.3.1991 RHB RM																			
FC		16	27	4	891	180	38.73	1	4	32	24	0					4.50	11	
Lim		10	10	0	254	62	25.40	0	1									5	
20T		14	14	1	353	77	27.15	0	2									10	
FC	2009	25	40	5	1192	180	34.05	1	5	92	61	0					3.97	14	
Lim	2009	17	17	1	520	93	32.50	0	3									6	
VINCENT, Lou (Auckland, Northamptonshire) b Warkworth, Auckland, New Zealand 11.11.1978 RHB RM																			
20T		3	3	0	67	38	22.33	0	0									1	
Test	2001/02	23	40	1	1332	224	34.15	3	9	6	2	0					2.00	19	
FC	1997/98	92	151	11	4922	224	35.15	10	29	1003	527	10	52.70	2-37	0	0	3.15	109	
Int	2000/01	102	99	10	2413	172	27.11	3	11	20	25	1	25.00	1-0	0	0	7.50	41	
Lim	1998/99	199	193	13	5119	172	28.43	7	27	243	245	4	61.25	2-25	0	0	6.04	113	3
I20T	2005/06	9	9	0	174	42	19.33	0	0									1	
20T	2005/06	49	49	3	1222	105*	26.56	2	6	50	73	4	18.25	3-28	0	0	8.76	19	
VOGES, Adam Charles (Australia, Australia A, Western Australia, Australia to India, Australia to New Zealand, Nottinghamshire, Rajasthan Royals) b Perth, Western Australia, Australia 4.10.1979 RHB SLC																			
FC		3	5	0	254	126	50.80	1	1	6	2	0					2.00	1	
Lim		3	3	1	127	71*	63.50	0	2									1	
FC	2002/03	82	138	18	4867	180	40.55	10	27	2518	1370	40	34.25	4-92	0	0	3.26	100	
Int	2006/07	14	13	4	312	72	34.66	0	1	150	159	1	159.00	1-22	0	0	6.36	2	
Lim	2004/05	103	98	20	3219	104*	41.26	2	25	1244	1092	22	49.63	3-25	0	0	5.26	35	
I20T	2007/08	4	3	1	63	26	31.50	0	0	12	5	2	2.50	2-5	0	0	2.50	2	
20T	2005/06	59	55	11	1489	82*	33.84	0	7	281	405	12	33.75	2-4	0	0	8.64	22	
WAGG, Graham Grant (Derbyshire) b Rugby, Warwickshire 28.4.1983 RHB SLA,LM																			
FC		4	7	0	82	37	11.71	0	0	462	246	10	24.60	3-31	0	0	3.19	1	
Lim		5	5	3	137	48*	68.50	0	0	187	160	9	17.77	3-22	0	0	5.13	2	
FC	2002	68	94	11	2024	108	24.38	1	10	11603	7024	216	32.51	6-35	8	1	3.63	23	
Lim	2000	76	61	9	901	48*	17.32	0	0	2886	2632	86	30.60	4-35	5	0	5.47	21	
20T	2003	45	38	8	455	62	15.16	0	1	724	989	34	29.08	3-23	0	0	8.19	13	
WAGH, Mark Anant (Nottinghamshire) b Birmingham, Warwickshire 20.10.1976 RHB OB																			
FC		16	24	1	953	139	41.43	3	3									8	
Lim		2	2	0	5	3	2.50	0	0									0	
FC	1996	203	332	27	12187	315	39.95	31	58	8697	4611	100	46.11	7-222	2	0	3.18	88	
Lim	1996	113	109	9	2720	102*	27.20	1	21	1096	862	25	34.48	4-35	1	0	4.71	21	
20T	2003	18	15	0	288	56	19.20	0	1	75	106	5	21.20	2-16	0	0	8.48	5	
WAINWRIGHT, David John (Yorkshire, England Lions to United Arab Emirates) b Pontefract, Yorkshire 21.3.1985 LHB SLA																			
FC		7	6	3	108	39	36.00	0	0	1106	716	14	51.14	3-48	0	0	3.88	1	
Lim		7	3	2	16	9*	16.00	0	0	252	260	6	43.33	2-31	0	0	6.19	2	
20T		3	1	0	0	0	0.00	0	0	60	78	5	15.60	3-32	0	0	7.80	1	
FC	2004	31	37	11	925	104*	35.57	2	2	4498	2552	70	36.45	5-134	1	0	3.40	10	
Lim	2005	41	19	11	136	26	17.00	0	0	1494	1184	33	35.87	3-26	0	0	4.75	9	
20T	2007	18	6	3	9	3*	3.00	0	0	311	366	18	20.33	3-6	0	0	7.06	6	
WAKELY, Alexander George (Northamptonshire, Northamptonshire to Netherlands) b Hammersmith, Middlesex 3.11.1988 RHB OB																			
FC		13	22	0	627	108	28.50	1	4	55	57	1	57.00	1-4	0	0	6.21	6	
Lim		8	8	0	118	29	14.75	0	0	6	6	0					6.00	2	
20T		18	18	2	387	55	24.18	0	1	6	11	0					11.00	8	
FC	2007	34	58	2	1371	113*	24.48	2	9	301	252	4	63.00	2-62	0	0	5.02	21	
Lim	2005	21	20	2	256	35	14.22	0	0	24	20	2	10.00	2-14	0	0	5.00	4	
20T	2009	24	23	3	473	55	23.65	0	1	6	11	0					11.00	9	
WALKER, Matthew Jonathan (Essex, Essex to Netherlands) b Gravesend, Kent 2.1.1974 LHB RM																			
FC		12	24	2	838	105	38.09	1	4	108	71	3	23.66	3-35	0	0	3.94	8	
Lim		8	6	1	161	39	32.20	0	0									2	
20T		19	18	3	380	74*	25.33	0	2									2	
FC	1992/93	212	356	37	11610	275*	36.39	28	47	2004	1214	25	48.56	3-35	0	0	3.63	142	
Lim	1994	280	253	38	6153	117	28.61	3	36	904	759	30	25.30	4-24	1	0	5.03	74	
20T	2003	69	65	10	1302	74*	23.67	0	4									6	
WALLACE, Mark Alexander (Glamorgan) b Abergavenny, Monmouthshire, Wales 19.11.1981 LHB WK																			
FC		16	24	1	626	113	27.21	1	4	6	3	0					3.00	43	4
Lim		11	7	0	140	38	20.00	0	0									4	2
20T		16	13	5	130	42*	16.25	0	0									8	6
FC	1999	167	265	17	6848	139	27.61	9	32	6	3	0					3.00	418	37
Lim	1999	153	120	26	1829	85	19.45	0	3									142	38
20T	2003	68	55	17	717	42*	18.86	0	0									26	18
WALLER, Max Thomas Charles (Somerset, Somerset to India) b Salisbury, Wiltshire 3.3.1988 RHB LB																			
Lim		9	3	2	9	5	9.00	0	0	264	246	4	61.50	2-24	0	0	5.59	2	
20T		2								18	26	0					8.66	0	

Cmp	Debut	M	I	NO	Runs	HS	Avge	100	50	Balls	Runs	Wkts	Avge	BB	5i	10m	RpO	ct	st
FC	2009	4	6	1	67	28	13.40	0	0	496	320	5	64.00	2-27	0	0	3.87	1	
Lim	2009	16	5	4	12	5	12.00	0	0	504	465	11	42.27	2-24	0	0	5.53	3	
20T	2009	15	5	1	1	1	0.25	0	0	228	289	13	22.23	3-17	0	0	7.60	4	
WALTERS, Stewart Jonathan (Surrey) b Mornington, Victoria, Australia 25.6.1983 RHB RM																			
FC		6	10	0	242	53	24.20	0	1	18	15	0					5.00	8	
Lim		10	9	2	271	88	38.71	0	2									0	
20T		12	11	7	184	53*	46.00	0	1									9	
FC	2006	34	54	1	1336	188	25.20	2	4	426	239	3	79.66	1-4	0	0	3.36	38	
Lim	2005	45	42	7	1000	91	28.57	0	6	165	179	3	59.66	1-12	0	0	6.50	16	
20T	2006	33	26	9	376	53*	22.11	0	1	18	26	1	26.00	1-9	0	0	8.66	21	
WARNER, David Andrew (Australia, New South Wales, Australia to England, Australia to New Zealand, Australia to West Indies, Delhi Daredevils, Middlesex, New South Wales to India) b Paddington, Sydney, New South Wales, Australia 27.10.1986 LHB LB																			
Lim		1	1	0	5	5	5.00	0	0									0	
I20T		2	2	0	42	41	21.00	0	0									1	
20T		15	15	0	310	43	20.66	0	0									5	
FC	2008/09	4	6	1	131	48*	26.20	0	0	25	19	1	19.00	1-0	0	0	4.56	3	
Int	2008/09	7	7	0	106	69	15.14	0	1									1	
Lim	2006/07	29	29	2	827	165*	30.62	1	4	90	81	2	40.50	1-11	0	0	5.40	6	
I20T	2008/09	22	22	0	644	89	29.27	0	4									13	
20T	2006/07	79	79	2	2096	107*	27.22	1	11									32	
WATERS, Huw Thomas (Glamorgan) b Cardiff, Glamorgan, Wales 26.9.1986 RHB RM																			
FC		11	13	4	67	16	7.44	0	0	1786	898	26	34.53	4-39	0	0	3.01	1	
Lim		5								156	187	3	62.33	1-30	0	0	7.19	3	
20T		4	2	2	11	11*		0	0	85	118	3	39.33	3-30	0	0	8.32	0	
FC	2005	34	50	22	212	34	7.57	0	0	4318	2377	65	36.56	5-86	1	0	3.30	7	
Lim	2005	20	8	3	24	8	4.80	0	0	780	809	14	57.78	3-47	0	0	6.22	3	
WATERS, Seren Robert (Kenya, Durham MCCU) b Nairobi, Kenya 11.4.1990 RHB LB																			
FC		2	3	1	47	25*	23.50	0	0	96	65	2	32.50	1-18	0	0	4.06	2	
FC	2008	6	11	2	354	157*	39.33	1	1	102	68	2	34.00	1-18	0	0	4.00	5	
Int	2008/09	12	12	0	261	74	21.75	0	1									3	
Lim	2008/09	14	14	1	326	74	25.07	0	2									4	
WATKINS, Simon Joseph Vernon (Oxford MCCU) b Wandsworth, Surrey 20.1.1989 LHB OB																			
FC		1	2	1	54	46*	54.00	0	0	102	73	0					4.29	0	
WATSON, Matthew John Corbett (Oxford MCCU) b Barnet, Hertfordshire 4.4.1987 RHB LB																			
FC		3	4	0	26	22	6.50	0	0	186	128	0					4.12	1	
FC	2009	6	6	1	69	22	13.80	0	0	390	271	4	67.75	4-78	0	0	4.16	1	
WELLS, Luke William Peter (Sussex) b Eastbourne, Sussex 29.12.1990 LHB OB																			
FC		1	2	0	70	62	35.00	0	1	12	16	0					8.00	0	
Lim		1	1	0	9	9	9.00	0	0									1	
WELSH, Alex Stephen (Loughborough MCCU) b Sheffield, Yorkshire 1.9.1988 RHB SLA																			
FC		2	3	1	30	21	15.00	0	0	256	152	4	38.00	3-32	0	0	3.56	1	
WESTLEY, Thomas (Durham MCCU, Essex) b Cambridge 13.3.1989 RHB OB																			
FC		10	18	1	440	132	25.88	1	2	531	229	10	22.90	4-55	0	0	2.58	1	
Lim		2	1	0	4	4	4.00	0	0	66	59	1	59.00	1-34	0	0	5.36	0	
20T		1																0	
FC	2007	35	61	9	1517	132	29.17	2	7	825	415	14	29.64	4-55	0	0	3.01	15	
Lim	2006	6	4	0	41	36	10.25	0	0	66	59	1	59.00	1-34	0	0	5.36	0	
WESTWOOD, Ian James (Warwickshire, Warwickshire to Scotland) b Birmingham, Warwickshire 13.7.1982 LHB OB																			
FC		16	32	4	726	86*	25.92	0	5									6	
Lim		10	8	3	160	47	32.00	0	0	42	48	1	48.00	1-48	0	0	6.85	2	
20T		10	9	1	103	24*	12.87	0	0									0	
FC	2003	82	144	16	4149	178	32.41	7	23	371	222	6	37.00	2-39	0	0	3.59	40	
Lim	2001	59	49	9	929	65	23.22	0	3	252	215	3	71.66	1-28	0	0	5.11	6	
20T	2005	38	27	12	342	49*	22.80	0	0	54	91	5	18.20	3-29	0	0	10.11	5	
WHEATER, Adam Jack (Cambridge MCCU, Essex) b Whipps Cross, Essex 13.2.1990 RHB WK																			
FC		3	5	1	167	55	41.75	0	2									8	
Lim		7	3	1	96	55*	48.00	0	1									1	
FC	2008	7	8	1	225	55	32.14	0	2									17	
20T	2009	3	2	1	7	4	7.00	0	0									1	
WHEELDON, David Antony (Worcestershire) b Stoke-on-Trent, Staffordshire 12.4.1989 LHB LB																			
FC		7	14	1	269	65	20.69	0	2									2	
FC	2009	12	20	1	429	87	22.57	0	3									5	
WHELAN, Christopher David (Worcestershire) b Liverpool, Lancashire 8.5.1986 RHB RM																			
FC		1	2	0	5	5	2.50	0	0	54	34	1	34.00	1-21	0	0	3.77	1	
Lim		2	1	0	1	1	1.00	0	0	66	84	4	21.00	3-34	0	0	7.63	0	
FC	2005	22	27	6	302	58	14.38	0	1	2236	1715	44	38.97	5-95	1	0	4.60	4	
Lim	2004	24	12	2	41	11	4.10	0	0	750	758	27	28.07	4-27	2	0	6.06	4	
20T	2008	16	3	2	4	2*	4.00	0	0	302	407	16	25.43	2-24	0	0	8.08	2	

Cmp	Debut	M	I	NO	Runs	HS	Avge	100	50	Balls	Runs	Wkts	Avge	BB	5i	10m	RpO	ct	st
WHITE, Graeme Geoffrey (Nottinghamshire, Nottinghamshire to Scotland) b Milton Keynes, Buckinghamshire 18.4.1987 RHB SLA																			
FC		1	1	0	29	29	29.00	0	0	138	104	1	104.00	1-104	0	0	4.52	1	
Lim		11	6	3	29	14	9.66	0	0	288	271	6	45.16	1-6	0	0	5.64	2	
20T		16	7	3	56	26*	14.00	0	0	217	270	12	22.50	3-22	0	0	7.46	9	
FC	2006	9	11	2	169	65	18.77	0	1	948	498	6	83.00	2-35	0	0	3.15	2	
Lim	2007	20	11	4	52	14	7.42	0	0	632	552	21	26.28	5-35	0	1	5.24	9	
20T	2007	22	8	3	64	26*	12.80	0	0	265	361	13	27.76	3-22	0	0	8.17	10	
WHITE, Robert Allan (Northamptonshire) b Chelmsford, Essex 15.10.1979 RHB OB																			
FC		10	19	1	363	95	20.16	0	2	6	7	0					7.00	3	
Lim		7	7	0	248	69	35.42	0	3									0	
20T		13	13	1	277	80	23.08	0	2									3	
FC	2000	97	169	16	5045	277	32.97	7	26	1126	807	14	57.64	2-30	0	0	4.30	58	
Lim	2002	83	79	3	1782	111	23.44	2	10	54	55	2	27.50	2-18	0	0	6.11	16	
20T	2003	56	53	5	1122	94*	23.37	0	6									11	
WHITE, Wayne Andrew (Leicestershire, Leicestershire to Scotland) b Derby 22.4.1985 RHB RM																			
FC		9	13	2	394	101*	35.81	1	1	806	531	8	66.37	4-58	0	0	3.95	4	
Lim		6	6	1	99	36	19.80	0	0	150	189	8	23.62	6-29	0	1	7.56	0	
20T		8	8	2	84	26	14.00	0	0	61	124	1	124.00	1-42	0	0	12.19	4	
FC	2005	32	48	7	880	101*	21.46	1	2	3736	2583	58	44.53	5-87	1	0	4.14	14	
Lim	2006	36	28	11	345	46*	20.29	0	0	1144	1193	31	38.48	6-29	1	1	6.25	8	
20T	2009	18	14	3	117	26	10.63	0	0	249	367	11	33.36	3-27	0	0	8.84	12	
WIGLEY, David Harry (Northamptonshire) b Bradford, Yorkshire 26.10.1981 RHB RFM																			
Lim		1								24	29	1	29.00	1-29	0	0	7.25	0	
FC	2002	50	62	22	532	70	13.30	0	2	7249	4932	136	36.26	6-72	4	0	4.08	22	
Lim	2002	25	12	0	34	10	2.83	0	0	846	899	17	52.88	4-37	1	0	6.37	7	
20T	2004	2	1	0	1	1	1.00	0	0	30	33	1	33.00	1-8	0	0	6.60	0	
WILLEY, David Jonathan (Northamptonshire) b Northampton 28.2.1990 LHB SLA																			
FC		3	4	2	41	18*	20.50	0	0	341	218	6	36.33	2-47	0	0	3.83	1	
Lim		6	6	1	74	25	14.80	0	0	239	212	3	70.66	2-40	0	0	5.32	2	
20T		17	8	3	63	19	12.60	0	0	138	199	8	24.87	3-33	0	0	8.65	7	
FC	2009	13	21	3	372	60	20.66	0	1	753	513	12	42.75	2-21	0	0	4.08	4	
Lim	2009	18	15	3	149	25	12.41	0	0	347	338	6	56.33	2-40	0	0	5.84	5	
20T	2009	29	14	5	120	19	13.33	0	0	270	312	18	17.33	3-9	0	0	6.93	10	
WILLIAMS, Robert Edward Morgan (Middlesex) b Pembury, Kent 19.1.1987 RHB RMF																			
Lim		5	1	1	2	2*		0	0	149	199	2	99.50	2-60	0	0	8.01	0	
20T		2								24	55	0					13.75	0	
FC	2007	9	15	5	119	31	11.90	0	0	1241	755	23	32.82	5-70	2	0	3.65	4	
Lim	2007	6	1	1	2	2*		0	0	185	248	2	124.00	2-60	0	0	8.04	0	
WILLOUGHBY, Charl Myles (Somerset, Somerset to India) b Cape Town, Cape Province, South Africa 3.12.1974 LHB LFM																			
FC		16	18	6	85	16	7.08	0	0	3073	1582	58	27.27	6-101	1	0	3.08	1	
Lim		3	2	0	0	0	0.00	0	0	138	137	1	137.00	1-52	0	0	5.95	0	
20T		1	1	0	2	2	2.00	0	0	18	21	1	21.00	1-21	0	0	7.00	0	
Test	2003	2								300	125	1	125.00	1-47	0	0	2.50	0	
FC	1994/95	209	233	102	801	47	6.11	0	0	41933	19646	774	25.38	7-44	31	3	2.81	42	
Int	1999/00	3	2	0	0	0	0.00	0	0	168	148	2	74.00	2-39	0	0	5.28	0	
Lim	1994/95	209	61	32	147	15	5.06	0	0	10164	7094	255	27.81	6-16	3	5	4.18	26	
20T	2003/04	66	16	11	28	11	5.60	0	0	1457	1712	71	24.11	4-9	3	0	7.05	11	
WILSON, Gary Craig (Ireland, Ireland to Sri Lanka, Ireland to United Arab Emirates, Ireland to West Indies, Surrey) b Dundonald, Co Roscommon, Ireland 5.2.1986 RHB WK																			
FC		6	9	1	349	125	43.62	1	1	54	44	0					4.88	14	
Lim		5	3	0	15	9	5.00	0	0									3	2
20T		5	3	2	51	36*	51.00	0	0									5	1
FC	2005	16	23	2	583	125	27.76	1	2	66	46	0					4.18	31	1
Int	2007	22	21	2	519	113	27.31	1	3									16	6
Lim	2006	70	62	5	1287	113	22.57	1	9									51	15
I20T	2008	15	13	1	193	29	16.08	0	0									8	
20T	2008	38	31	7	372	36*	15.50	0	0									24	4
WINSLADE, Thomas Simon (Loughborough MCCU) b Epsom, Surrey 28.5.1990 RHB OB																			
FC		1	2	0	18	17	9.00	0	0									0	
WOAKES, Christopher Roger (England Lions, Warwickshire, England Lions to United Arab Emirates, Warwickshire to Scotland) b Birmingham, Warwickshire 2.3.1989 RHB RM																			
FC		14	22	3	457	136*	24.05	1	1	2546	1246	58	21.48	6-52	3	1	2.93	7	
Lim		16	7	2	82	49*	16.40	0	0	702	679	16	42.43	2-20	0	0	5.80	3	
20T		15	7	3	95	27*	23.75	0	0	252	310	15	20.66	3-21	0	0	7.38	7	
FC	2006	46	60	15	1226	136*	27.24	2	3	7589	3936	154	25.55	6-43	8	2	3.11	23	
Lim	2007	40	19	5	191	49*	13.64	0	0	1531	1334	37	36.05	4-38	1	0	5.22	8	
20T	2008	33	13	8	114	27*	22.80	0	0	557	767	26	29.50	4-21	1	0	8.26	14	
WOOD, Christopher Philip (Hampshire, Hampshire to Scotland) b Basingstoke, Hampshire 27.6.1990 RHB LM																			
FC		3	4	0	68	35	17.00	0	0	427	240	13	18.46	5-54	1	0	3.37	0	
Lim		9	6	2	5	3	1.25	0	0	379	335	14	23.92	3-32	0	0	5.30	1	

Cmp	Debut	M	I	NO	Runs	HS	Avge	100	50	Balls	Runs	Wkts	Avge	BB	5i	10m	RpO	ct	st
20T		19	6	2	41	18	10.25	0	0	391	551	20	27.55	3-27	0	0	8.45	7	
Lim	2010	10	6	2	5	3	1.25	0	0	427	368	18	20.44	4-33	1	0	5.17	3	
WOOD, Matthew James (Nottinghamshire, Nottinghamshire to Scotland) b Exeter, Devon 30.9.1980 RHB OB																			
FC		4	6	0	148	72	24.66	0	2	6	11	0					11.00	1	
Lim		5	4	0	50	20	12.50	0	0									0	
20T		18	17	2	328	61	21.86	0	2									1	
FC	2001	101	170	8	5332	297	32.91	9	34	91	79	0					5.20	31	
Lim	2000	97	91	4	2339	129	26.88	2	16									14	
20T	2004	52	51	3	1334	94	27.79	0	7									6	
WOOLLEY, Robert James Joseph (Cambridge MCCU) b Tameside, Manchester, Lancashire 6.8.1990 RHB RM																			
FC		3	4	1	117	55*	39.00	0	1	534	394	6	65.66	3-73	0	0	4.42	0	
FC	2009	6	6	1	135	55*	27.00	0	1	989	689	11	62.63	3-71	0	0	4.18	4	
WRIGHT, Ben James (Glamorgan) b Preston, Lancashire 5.12.1987 RHB RM																			
FC		17	27	1	847	172	32.57	2	4	12	7	0					3.50	7	
Lim		11	10	2	217	79	27.12	0	1									2	
20T		7	6	1	83	27	16.60	0	0									1	
FC	2006	38	60	3	1527	172	26.78	3	7	192	137	2	68.50	1-14	0	0	4.28	25	
Lim	2006	49	46	6	966	79	24.15	0	5	132	126	1	126.00	1-19	0	0	5.72	11	
20T	2007	27	24	9	394	55*	26.26	0	1	24	22	1	22.00	1-16	0	0	5.50	8	
WRIGHT, Christopher Julian Clement (Essex, Essex to Netherlands) b Chipping Norton, Oxfordshire 14.7.1985 RHB RFM																			
FC		11	17	5	161	28*	13.41	0	0	1811	1156	31	37.29	5-70	1	0	3.83	2	
Lim		10	4	2	3	3*	1.50	0	0	395	403	12	33.58	3-43	0	0	6.12	0	
20T		19	3	2	2	1*	2.00	0	0	420	641	21	30.52	4-25	1	0	9.15	2	
FC	2004	54	70	18	916	76	17.61	0	3	8097	5110	123	41.54	6-22	2	0	3.78	13	
Lim	2004	59	25	10	121	23	8.06	0	0	2273	2118	51	41.52	3-3	0	0	5.59	10	
20T	2004	31	7	6	15	6*	15.00	0	0	650	947	31	30.54	4-24	2	0	8.74	4	
WRIGHT, Damien Geoffrey (Victoria to Australia, Somerset) b Casino, New South Wales, Australia 25.7.1975 RHB RFM																			
FC		5	7	0	236	78	33.71	0	2	925	377	14	26.92	5-41	1	0	2.44	4	
Lim		2	1	1	4	4*		0	0	90	109	6	18.16	3-43	0	0	7.26	0	
FC	1997/98	108	163	22	3500	111	24.82	1	19	22029	9999	349	28.65	8-60	12	0	2.72	53	
Lim	1997/98	104	79	24	929	55	16.89	0	4	5311	3710	128	28.98	5-37	3	1	4.19	23	
20T	2004/05	22	16	3	174	38*	13.38	0	0	412	513	17	30.17	3-17	0	0	7.47	4	
WRIGHT, Luke James (England, Sussex, England to Bangladesh, England to South Africa, England to Scotland, England to United Arab Emirates, England to West Indies, Sussex to India) b Grantham, Lincolnshire 7.3.1985 RHB RM																			
FC		9	12	1	465	134	42.27	1	3	929	573	23	24.91	5-65	1	0	3.70	3	
Int		10	9	1	133	48*	16.62	0	0	300	243	4	60.75	2-34	0	0	4.86	3	
Lim		13	12	1	282	95	25.63	0	1	363	340	8	42.50	3-41	0	0	5.62	5	
I20T		2	1	0	0	0	0.00	0	0									0	
20T		10	9	0	155	39	17.22	0	0	120	169	2	84.50	2-33	0	0	8.45	1	
FC	2003	66	93	15	2867	155*	36.75	8	15	6672	3924	101	38.85	5-65	3	0	3.52	29	
Int	2007	42	31	3	600	52	21.42	0	2	906	769	15	51.26	2-34	0	0	5.09	16	
Lim	2001	140	107	17	2069	125	22.98	1	5	4341	3826	100	38.26	4-12	3	0	5.28	43	
I20T	2007/08	27	22	2	328	71	16.40	0	1	156	219	6	36.50	1-5	0	0	8.42	10	
20T	2004	79	64	6	1180	103	20.34	1	3	918	1230	43	28.60	3-17	0	0	8.03	27	
WYATT, Alexander Charles Frederick (Leicestershire) b Roehampton, Surrey 23.7.1990 RHB RMF																			
Lim		2	1	0	1	1	1.00	0	0	50	61	1	61.00	1-24	0	0	7.32	0	
FC	2009	3	3	1	4	3	2.00	0	0	366	159	7	22.71	3-42	0	0	2.60	1	
Lim	2009	4	1	0	1	1	1.00	0	0	116	123	3	41.00	1-24	0	0	6.36	1	
20T	2009	2								42	36	3	12.00	3-14	0	0	5.14	1	
YARDY, Michael Howard (England, Sussex, England to Scotland, England to West Indies, Sussex to India) b Pembury, Kent 27.11.1980 LHB SLA,LM																			
FC		9	13	2	345	100*	31.36	1	1									12	
Int		12	11	5	121	57	20.16	0	1	540	439	7	62.71	2-49	0	0	4.87	1	
Lim		18	17	8	337	66*	37.44	0	3	768	638	12	53.16	2-49	0	0	4.98	4	
I20T		2	2	2	41	35*		0	0	48	31	1	31.00	1-21	0	0	3.87	3	
20T		10	10	6	228	76*	57.00	0	1	222	190	9	21.11	2-14	0	0	5.13	6	
FC	2000	129	217	21	7606	257	38.80	15	38	3441	2003	26	77.03	5-83	1	0	3.49	99	
Int	2006	19	16	6	170	57	17.00	0	1	852	615	14	43.92	3-24	0	0	4.33	3	
Lim	1999	165	146	25	2893	98*	23.90	0	19	4787	3931	102	38.53	6-27	2	1	4.92	66	
I20T	2006	12	7	5	96	35*	48.00	0	0	228	252	7	36.00	2-19	0	0	6.63	8	
20T	2004	64	49	22	804	76*	29.77	0	2	1147	1194	45	26.53	3-21	0	0	6.24	26	
YASIR ARAFAT Satti (KRL, Otago, Pakistan to United Arab Emirates, Sussex, Sussex to India) b Rawalpindi, Punjab, Pakistan 12.3.1982 RHB RFM																			
FC		9	9	2	255	58	36.42	0	2	1536	896	36	24.88	5-74	2	0	3.50	1	
Lim		5	2	0	19	14	9.50	0	0	201	238	5	47.60	2-37	0	0	7.10	1	
20T		13	10	4	104	25*	17.33	0	0	284	391	13	30.07	4-34	1	0	8.26	4	
Test	2007/08	3	3	1	94	50*	47.00	0	1	627	438	9	48.66	5-161	1	0	4.19	0	
FC	1997/98	168	250	37	5788	122	27.17	4	31	28055	16236	674	24.08	9-35	39	5	3.47	45	
Int	1999/00	11	8	3	74	27	14.80	0	0	414	373	4	93.25	1-28	0	0	5.40	2	
Lim	1997/98	207	149	39	2333	110*	21.20	1	7	9990	8212	330	24.88	6-24	14	5	4.93	48	

Cmp	Debut	M	I	NO	Runs	HS	Avge	100	50	Balls	Runs	Wkts	Avge	BB	5i	10m	RpO	ct	st
I20T	2007/08	7	7	4	64	17	21.33	0	0	150	195	6	32.50	3-32	0	0	7.80	1	
20T	2005/06	82	57	17	667	49	16.67	0	0	1689	2168	103	21.04	4-17	5	0	7.70	12	
YOUNG, Edward George Christopher (Gloucestershire, Oxford MCCU, Unicorns, Gloucestershire to Netherlands) b Chertsey, Surrey 21.5.1989 RHB SLA																			
FC		4	6	0	225	79	37.50	0	2	324	228	1	228.00	1-75	0	0	4.22	5	
Lim		7	5	0	47	25	9.40	0	0	208	200	3	66.66	2-42	0	0	5.76	2	
FC	2009	7	9	1	265	79	33.12	0	2	588	379	3	126.33	2-74	0	0	3.86	6	
Lim	2010	8	5	0	47	25	9.40	0	0	220	206	3	68.66	2-42	0	0	5.61	2	
YOUNIS KHAN, Mohammad (Habib Bank, Pakistan to Australia, Pakistan to South Africa, Pakistan to United Arab Emirates, Surrey) b Mardan, North-West Frontier Province, Pakistan 29.11.1977 RHB RM,LB																			
FC		3	5	1	155	77*	38.75	0	1	108	64	0					3.55	2	
20T		11	10	0	154	59	15.40	0	1									2	
Test	1999/00	63	112	7	5260	313	50.09	16	21	540	341	7	48.71	2-23	0	0	3.78	67	
FC	1998/99	150	244	28	10873	313	50.33	34	44	2677	1560	35	44.57	4-52	0	0	3.49	158	
Int	1999/00	202	196	19	5765	144	32.57	6	37	224	224	2	112.00	1-3	0	0	6.00	107	
Lim	1998/99	264	252	29	7684	144	34.45	10	48	1085	1035	27	38.33	3-5	0	0	5.72	147	
I20T	2006	22	20	3	432	51	25.41	0	2	22	18	3	6.00	3-18	0	0	4.90	11	
20T	2004/05	47	44	8	962	70	26.72	0	4	82	105	6	17.50	3-18	0	0	7.68	19	

AUSTRALIA TO ENGLAND 2010

Cmp	Debut	M	I	NO	Runs	HS	Avge	100	50	Balls	Runs	Wkts	Avge	BB	5i	10m	RpO	ct	st
BOLLINGER, D.E.																			
Test		2	4	2	27	21	13.50	0	0	318	182	5	36.40	3-51	0	0	3.43	0	
FC		2	4	2	27	21	13.50	0	0	318	182	5	36.40	3-51	0	0	3.43	0	
Int		5	1	0	3	3	3.00	0	0	270	178	9	19.77	3-20	0	0	3.95	1	
Lim		6	1	0	3	3	3.00	0	0	318	202	12	16.83	3-20	0	0	3.81	2	
CLARKE, M.J.																			
Test		2	4	0	139	77	34.75	0	1									2	
FC		2	4	0	139	77	34.75	0	1									2	
Int		4	4	2	220	99*	110.00	0	2	24	25	0					6.25	0	
Lim		5	5	2	220	99*	73.33	0	2	24	25	0					6.25	0	
I20T		2	2	0	35	30	17.50	0	0									1	
20T		2	2	0	35	30	17.50	0	0									1	
HARRIS, R.J.																			
Int		4	3	2	1	1	1.00	0	0	214	171	10	17.10	5-32	0	1	4.79	1	
Lim		5	3	2	1	1	1.00	0	0	268	218	10	21.80	5-32	0	1	4.88	1	
HAURITZ, N.M.																			
Int		2	2	1	22	22	22.00	0	0	108	100	1	100.00	1-56	0	0	5.55	1	
Lim		3	2	1	22	22	22.00	0	0	162	141	1	141.00	1-56	0	0	5.22	1	
HAZLEWOOD, J.R.																			
Int		1								42	41	1	41.00	1-41	0	0	5.85	0	
Lim		1								42	41	1	41.00	1-41	0	0	5.85	0	
HILFENHAUS, B.W.																			
Test		2	4	1	77	56*	25.66	0	1	371	190	8	23.75	3-39	0	0	3.07	0	
FC		2	4	1	77	56*	25.66	0	1	371	190	8	23.75	3-39	0	0	3.07	0	
HOPES, J.R.																			
Int		5	4	1	61	34	20.33	0	0	217	202	2	101.00	1-30	0	0	5.58	2	
Lim		5	4	1	61	34	20.33	0	0	217	202	2	101.00	1-30	0	0	5.58	2	
I20T		1	1	0	30	30	30.00	0	0	6	8	0					8.00	0	
20T		1	1	0	30	30	30.00	0	0	6	8	0					8.00	0	
HUSSEY, D.J.																			
FC		5	7	1	399	251*	66.50	1	1	108	82	0					4.55	7	
Lim		3	3	1	114	80	57.00	0	1	6	6	0					6.00	3	
I20T		2	2	0	67	34	33.50	0	0	42	49	2	24.50	1-16	0	0	7.00	1	
20T		2	2	0	67	34	33.50	0	0	42	49	2	24.50	1-16	0	0	7.00	1	
HUSSEY, M.E.K.																			
Test		2	4	1	69	56*	23.00	0	1									3	
FC		2	4	1	69	56*	23.00	0	1									3	
Int		5	5	0	143	79	28.60	0	1	12	22	0					11.00	2	
Lim		6	6	1	215	79	43.00	0	2	12	22	0					11.00	3	
I20T		2	2	0	43	25	21.50	0	0									0	
20T		2	2	0	43	25	21.50	0	0									0	
JOHNSON, M.G.																			
Test		2	4	0	45	30	11.25	0	0	322	217	3	72.33	1-31	0	0	4.04	1	
FC		2	4	0	45	30	11.25	0	0	322	217	3	72.33	1-31	0	0	4.04	1	
I20T		2	2	0	3	3	1.50	0	0	48	72	1	72.00	1-39	0	0	9.00	0	
20T		2	2	0	3	3	1.50	0	0	48	72	1	72.00	1-39	0	0	9.00	0	

Cmp Debut	M	I	NO	Runs	HS	Avge	100	50	Balls	Runs	Wkts	Avge	BB	5i	10m	RpO	ct	st
KATICH, S.M.																		
Test	2	4	0	187	83	46.75	0	2									1	
FC	3	6	0	227	83	37.83	0	2									2	
McKAY, C.J.																		
Int	1								56	60	0					6.42	0	
Lim	2								116	120	1	120.00	1-60	0	0	6.20	0	
MARSH, S.E.																		
Int	1	1	0	59	59	59.00	0	1									2	
Lim	1	1	0	59	59	59.00	0	1									2	
NANNES, D.P.																		
I20T	2	2	2	12	12*		0	0	48	71	5	14.20	3-30	0	0	8.87	1	
20T	2	2	2	12	12*		0	0	48	71	5	14.20	3-30	0	0	8.87	1	
NORTH, M.J.																		
Test	2	4	0	36	20	9.00	0	0	109	55	6	9.16	6-55	1	0	3.02	3	
FC	2	4	0	36	20	9.00	0	0	109	55	6	9.16	6-55	1	0	3.02	3	
O'KEEFE, S.N.J.																		
I20T	1	1	0	5	5	5.00	0	0	24	29	3	9.66	3-29	0	0	7.25	1	
20T	1	1	0	5	5	5.00	0	0	24	29	3	9.66	3-29	0	0	7.25	1	
PAINE, T.D.																		
Test	2	4	0	104	47	26.00	0	0									11	1
FC	2	4	0	104	47	26.00	0	0									11	1
Int	5	5	0	148	54	29.60	0	1									8	
Lim	6	6	0	158	54	26.33	0	1									11	
I20T	2	2	0	1	1	0.50	0	0									2	
20T	2	2	0	1	1	0.50	0	0									2	
PONTING, R.T.																		
Test	2	4	0	98	66	24.50	0	1									2	
FC	2	4	0	98	66	24.50	0	1									2	
Int	5	5	0	144	92	28.80	0	1									3	
Lim	6	6	0	161	92	26.83	0	1									3	
SMITH, S.P.D.																		
Test	2	4	0	100	77	25.00	0	1	186	82	3	27.33	3-51	0	0	2.64	1	
FC	2	4	0	100	77	25.00	0	1	186	82	3	27.33	3-51	0	0	2.64	1	
Int	4	4	1	94	41	31.33	0	0	216	182	7	26.00	2-34	0	0	5.05	0	
Lim	5	5	2	122	41	40.66	0	0	258	225	7	32.14	2-34	0	0	5.23	0	
I20T	1	1	0	12	12	12.00	0	0	24	34	1	34.00	1-34	0	0	8.50	0	
20T	1	1	0	12	12	12.00	0	0	24	34	1	34.00	1-34	0	0	8.50	0	
TAIT, S.W.																		
Int	3	1	1	1	1*		0	0	153	99	8	12.37	4-48	1	0	3.88	1	
Lim	3	1	1	1	1*		0	0	153	99	8	12.37	4-48	1	0	3.88	1	
I20T	2	2	0	8	6	4.00	0	0	48	62	2	31.00	2-25	0	0	7.75	0	
20T	2	2	0	8	6	4.00	0	0	48	62	2	31.00	2-25	0	0	7.75	0	
WARNER, D.A.																		
Lim	1	1	0	5	5	5.00	0	0									0	
I20T	2	2	0	42	41	21.00	0	0									1	
20T	2	2	0	42	41	21.00	0	0									1	
WATSON, S.R.																		
Test	2	4	0	64	31	16.00	0	0	179	117	11	10.63	6-33	2	0	3.92	2	
FC	2	4	0	64	31	16.00	0	0	179	117	11	10.63	6-33	2	0	3.92	2	
Int	5	5	0	205	61	41.00	0	2	66	64	2	32.00	2-55	0	0	5.81	1	
Lim	6	6	0	229	61	38.16	0	2	108	108	3	36.00	2-55	0	0	6.00	1	
I20T	1	1	0	0	0	0.00	0	0									0	
20T	1	1	0	0	0	0.00	0	0									0	
WHITE, C.L.																		
Int	5	5	1	145	86*	36.25	0	1									1	
Lim	6	6	1	251	106	50.20	1	1									1	
I20T	2	2	0	24	17	12.00	0	0									1	
20T	2	2	0	24	17	12.00	0	0									1	

BANGLADESH TO ENGLAND 2010

Cmp Debut	M	I	NO	Runs	HS	Avge	100	50	Balls	Runs	Wkts	Avge	BB	5i	10m	RpO	ct	st
ABDUR RAZZAK																		
Test	1	2	1	19	19	19.00	0	0	180	109	2	54.50	2-109	0	0	3.63	1	
FC	3	6	1	99	30	19.80	0	0	438	241	6	40.16	2-67	0	0	3.30	1	
Int	3	3	1	31	27	15.50	0	0	174	170	3	56.66	2-43	0	0	5.86	0	
Lim	5	4	1	45	27	15.00	0	0	276	260	6	43.33	2-43	0	0	5.65	0	
FAISAL HOSSAIN																		
Int	1	1	1	8	8*		0	0	37	26	0					4.21	1	
Lim	3	3	1	14	8*	7.00	0	0	85	59	2	29.50	1-13	0	0	4.16	1	

Cmp Debut	M	I	NO	Runs	HS	Avge	100	50	Balls	Runs	Wkts	Avge	BB	5i	10m	RpO	ct	st
IMRUL KAYES																		
Test	2	4	0	163	75	40.75	0	1									2	
FC	5	9	0	242	75	26.88	0	1									5	
Int	3	3	0	94	76	31.33	0	1									0	
Lim	4	4	0	171	77	42.75	0	2									0	
JAHURUL ISLAM																		
Test	2	4	0	71	46	17.75	0	0									2	
FC	5	9	1	312	158	39.00	1	1									6	
Int	2	2	0	67	40	33.50	0	0									4	
Lim	4	4	0	174	88	43.50	0	1									4	
JUNAID SIDDIQUE																		
Test	2	4	0	139	74	34.75	0	2									2	
FC	4	8	0	223	74	27.87	0	2									3	
Int	3	3	0	97	51	32.33	0	1									2	
Lim	5	5	0	111	51	22.20	0	1									4	
MAHBUBUL ALAM																		
FC	1								144	88	2	44.00	1-38	0	0	3.66	0	
MAHMUDULLAH																		
Test	2	4	0	82	38	20.50	0	0	301	161	2	80.50	1-59	0	0	3.20	0	
FC	5	9	0	200	40	22.22	0	0	562	329	5	65.80	2-70	0	0	3.51	3	
Int	3	3	1	70	42	35.00	0	0	66	56	0					5.09	0	
Lim	5	5	2	92	42	30.66	0	0	144	117	1	117.00	1-39	0	0	4.87	0	
MASHRAFE MORTAZA																		
Int	3	3	0	41	22	13.66	0	0	156	103	5	20.60	3-31	0	0	3.96	1	
Lim	5	5	1	57	22	14.25	0	0	249	155	9	17.22	3-31	0	0	3.73	2	
MOHAMMAD ASHRAFUL																		
Test	2	4	0	50	21	12.50	0	0	12	13	0					6.50	0	
FC	5	9	0	260	89	28.88	0	3	96	81	0					5.06	0	
Int	2	2	0	27	14	13.50	0	0	6	9	0					9.00	1	
Lim	2	2	0	27	14	13.50	0	0	6	9	0					9.00	1	
MUSHFIQUR RAHIM																		
Test	2	4	0	40	16	10.00	0	0									2	1
FC	5	9	0	117	52	13.00	0	1									6	1
Int	1	1	0	22	22	22.00	0	0									0	
Lim	3	3	0	53	25	17.66	0	0									2	
NAEEM ISLAM																		
FC	2	3	0	13	8	4.33	0	0	186	133	0					4.29	0	
RAQIBUL HASAN																		
Int	1	1	0	76	76	76.00	0	1									0	
Lim	2	2	0	99	76	49.50	0	1									1	
ROBIUL ISLAM																		
Test	1	2	2	9	9*		0	0	138	119	0					5.17	0	
FC	4	6	4	29	17*	14.50	0	0	624	432	12	36.00	4-77	0	0	4.15	1	
RUBEL HOSSAIN																		
Test	1	2	0	13	9	6.50	0	0	144	117	1	117.00	1-109	0	0	4.87	1	
FC	3	4	0	23	9	5.75	0	0	349	250	5	50.00	2-30	0	0	4.29	2	
Int	2	1	1	1	1*		0	0	108	113	4	28.25	2-52	0	0	6.27	0	
Lim	3	2	1	1	1*	1.00	0	0	156	159	6	26.50	2-46	0	0	6.11	0	
SHAFIUL ISLAM																		
Test	1	2	0	8	4	4.00	0	0	126	63	2	31.50	2-63	0	0	3.00	0	
FC	3	6	1	56	24	11.20	0	0	398	187	5	37.40	2-44	0	0	2.81	1	
Int	3	1	0	16	16	16.00	0	0	141	181	4	45.25	2-38	0	0	7.70	1	
Lim	5	2	1	16	16	16.00	0	0	248	272	9	30.22	3-31	0	0	6.58	1	
SHAHADAT HOSSAIN																		
Test	2	4	1	24	20	8.00	0	0	306	201	6	33.50	5-98	1	0	3.94	0	
FC	4	6	1	80	33	16.00	0	0	651	416	13	32.00	5-98	1	0	3.83	0	
SHAKIB AL HASAN																		
Test	2	4	0	52	25	13.00	0	0	483	278	8	34.75	5-121	1	0	3.45	0	
FC	3	5	1	57	25	14.25	0	0	519	305	8	38.12	5-121	1	0	3.52	1	
Int	3	3	0	27	20	9.00	0	0	180	150	4	37.50	2-35	0	0	5.00	3	
Lim	4	4	0	65	38	16.25	0	0	228	178	5	35.36	2-35	0	0	4.68	3	
TAMIM IQBAL																		
Test	2	4	0	268	108	67.00	2	1									0	
FC	3	6	0	323	108	53.83	2	1									4	
Int	3	3	0	62	28	20.66	0	0									2	
Lim	5	5	0	107	28	21.40	0	0									3	

INDIA A TO ENGLAND 2010

Cmp	Debut	M	I	NO	Runs	HS	Avge	100	50	Balls	Runs	Wkts	Avge	BB	5i	10m	RpO	ct	st
DHAWAN, S.																			
FC		3	4	0	260	179	65.00	1	0	54	33	1	33.00	1-18	0	0	3.66	1	
Lim		4	4	0	166	59	41.50	0	1	102	95	2	47.50	1-22	0	0	5.58	3	
GANAPATHY, C.																			
FC		1	1	0	1	1	1.00	0	0	114	77	1	77.00	1-53	0	0	4.05	0	
IQBAL ABDULLA																			
FC		3	2	0	12	12	6.00	0	0	584	232	10	23.20	4-42	0	0	2.38	2	
Lim		5	4	1	31	13	10.33	0	0	294	275	3	91.66	2-56	0	0	5.61	0	
JASKARAN SINGH																			
FC		2	1	0	58	58	58.00	0	1	270	174	1	174.00	1-97	0	0	3.86	0	
Lim		5	5	1	99	51	24.75	0	1	276	289	6	48.16	2-73	0	0	6.28	0	
KULKARNI, D.S.																			
FC		3	2	1	15	13	15.00	0	0	525	253	7	36.14	5-31	1	0	2.89	0	
Lim		3	1	0	6	6	6.00	0	0	153	166	5	33.20	2-61	0	0	6.51	0	
MITHUN, A.																			
Lim		5	3	2	4	3	4.00	0	0	292	274	5	54.80	3-49	0	0	5.63	0	
MUKUND, A.																			
FC		3	4	0	201	91	50.25	0	2	18	3	0					1.00	2	
Lim		5	5	0	263	114	52.60	1	1									0	
PANDEY, M.K.																			
FC		3	4	2	54	36	27.00	0	0	12	12	0					6.00	2	
Lim		5	5	0	55	17	11.00	0	0	30	27	0					5.40	1	
PUJARA, C.A.																			
FC		3	4	2	322	208*	161.00	1	1									4	
Lim		5	5	1	332	114	83.00	1	2									2	
RAHANE, A.M.																			
FC		3	4	1	233	118	77.66	1	1	18	5	0					1.66	0	
Lim		5	5	0	165	90	33.00	0	1									0	
SAHA, W.P.																			
FC		3	2	0	112	62	56.00	0	2									2	1
Lim		5	5	2	89	36*	29.66	0	0									7	
TIWARY, M.K.																			
FC		3	3	0	57	36	19.00	0	0	192	93	2	46.50	2-72	0	0	2.90	3	
Lim		5	5	0	95	46	19.00	0	0	144	142	2	71.00	2-34	0	0	5.91	2	
TYAGI, S.																			
FC		1								30	4	0					0.80	0	
Lim		1	1	1	2	2*		0	0	60	81	0					8.10	0	
UNADKAT, J.D.																			
FC		2	1	1	12	12*		0	0	501	203	16	12.68	7-41	2	1	2.43	0	
Lim		2	1	0	2	2	2.00	0	0	114	119	3	39.66	2-46	0	0	6.26	0	

NETHERLANDS TO ENGLAND 2010

Cmp	Debut	M	I	NO	Runs	HS	Avge	100	50	Balls	Runs	Wkts	Avge	BB	5i	10m	RpO	ct	st
BARRESI, W.																			
Lim		2	2	0	42	39	21.00	0	0									1	
BORREN, P.W.																			
Lim		6	3	0	44	21	14.66	0	0	174	167	1	167.00	1-34	0	0	5.75	2	
BUURMAN, A.F.																			
Lim		4	2	0	17	17	8.50	0	0									3	1
COOPER, T.L.W.																			
Lim		4	3	0	23	15	7.66	0	0									2	
DE GROOTH, T.N.																			
Lim		5	3	0	34	17	11.33	0	0									0	
DIEPEVEEN, W.P.																			
Lim		2	2	1	37	23	37.00	0	0									0	
DIGHTON, M.G.																			
Lim		5	5	1	229	110*	57.25	1	2	156	124	5	24.80	2-27	0	0	4.76	3	
JONKMAN, M.B.S.																			
Lim		4	2	0	16	14	8.00	0	0	180	140	8	17.50	3-34	0	0	4.66	1	
KRUGER, B.P.																			
Lim		4	2	0	5	5	2.50	0	0	105	116	3	38.66	2-14	0	0	6.62	0	
LOOTS, B.P.																			
Lim		1	1	0	6	6	6.00	0	0	48	30	0					3.75	0	
MOHAMMAD KASHIF																			
Lim		3								90	102	3	34.00	2-41	0	0	6.80	0	
MUDASSAR BUKHARI																			
Lim		5	2	1	63	49*	63.00	0	0	171	165	2	82.50	2-45	0	0	5.78	2	

Cmp	Debut	M	I	NO	Runs	HS	Avge	100	50	Balls	Runs	Wkts	Avge	BB	5i	10m	RpO	ct	st
SEELAAR, P.M.																			
Lim		5	3	2	12	7*	12.00	0	0	219	194	6	32.33	3-39	0	0	5.31	1	
STATHAM, N.A.																			
Lim		2	1	0	4	4	4.00	0	0									0	
SZWARCZYNSKI, E.S.																			
Lim		6	5	0	56	18	11.20	0	0									0	
WESTDIJK, B.A.																			
Lim		2	1	1	3	3*		0	0	36	47	1	47.00	1-31	0	0	7.83	0	
ZUIDERENT, B.																			
Lim		6	5	2	122	42*	40.66	0	0									2	

PAKISTAN TO ENGLAND 2010

Cmp	Debut	M	I	NO	Runs	HS	Avge	100	50	Balls	Runs	Wkts	Avge	BB	5i	10m	RpO	ct	st
ABDUL RAZZAQ																			
Int		3	3	2	86	44*	86.00	0	0	106	106	2	53.00	2-38	0	0	6.00	0	
Lim		4	4	2	88	44*	44.00	0	0	106	106	2	53.00	2-38	0	0	6.00	0	
I20T		4	3	0	21	11	7.00	0	0	24	35	1	35.00	1-15	0	0	8.75	0	
20T		6	5	2	31	11	10.33	0	0	54	68	5	13.60	3-19	0	0	7.55	0	
ABDUR REHMAN																			
FC		1	1	0	30	30	30.00	0	0	150	99	1	99.00	1-54	0	0	3.96	0	
ASAD SHAFIQ																			
Int		5	5	0	120	50	24.00	0	1									0	
Lim		5	5	0	120	50	24.00	0	1									0	
AZHAR ALI																			
Test		6	12	1	291	92*	26.45	0	2	6	9	0					9.00	3	
FC		6	12	1	291	92*	26.45	0	2	6	9	0					9.00	3	
Lim		1	1	0	0	0	0.00	0	0									0	
DANISH KANERIA																			
Test		3	5	1	54	16*	13.50	0	0	540	377	7	53.85	2-49	0	0	4.18	0	
FC		9	14	2	82	16*	6.83	0	0	1900	1130	30	37.66	4-51	0	0	3.56	1	
Lim		6	2	1	1	1*	1.00	0	0	246	213	5	42.60	2-41	0	0	5.19	1	
FAWAD ALAM																			
FC		1	2	0	88	68	44.00	0	1	24	8	0					2.00	0	
Int		5	5	1	153	64	38.25	0	1									2	
Lim		6	6	1	250	97	50.00	0	2	18	13	0					4.33	2	
I20T		2	2	0	20	20	10.00	0	0									0	
20T		4	3	0	31	20	10.33	0	0	12	18	0					9.00	1	
IMRAN FARHAT																			
Test		6	12	0	256	67	21.33	0	1	84	40	0					2.85	5	
FC		6	12	0	256	67	21.33	0	1	84	40	0					2.85	5	
KAMRAN AKMAL																			
Test		5	10	0	98	46	9.80	0	0									25	
FC		6	12	0	128	46	10.66	0	0									27	1
Int		5	5	0	201	74	40.20	0	2									5	1
Lim		6	6	1	213	74	42.60	0	2									6	3
I20T		4	4	0	73	33	18.25	0	0									1	3
20T		6	6	0	110	33	18.33	0	0									2	5
MOHAMMAD AAMER																			
Test		6	12	2	91	25	9.10	0	0	1253	594	30	19.80	6-84	2	0	2.84	0	
FC		7	14	3	151	44*	13.72	0	0	1349	656	35	18.74	6-84	3	0	2.91	0	
I20T		2	2	2	32	21*		0	0	48	54	6	9.00	3-27	0	0	6.75	0	
20T		3	2	2	32	21*		0	0	66	64	6	10.66	3-27	0	0	5.81	0	
MOHAMMAD ASIF																			
Test		6	10	3	37	14	5.28	0	0	1267	657	23	28.56	5-77	1	0	3.11	1	
FC		6	10	3	37	14	5.28	0	0	1267	657	23	28.56	5-77	1	0	3.11	1	
MOHAMMAD HAFEEZ																			
Int		5	5	0	167	64	33.40	0	1	162	128	1	128.00	1-40	0	0	4.74	2	
Lim		6	6	0	167	64	27.83	0	1	216	156	1	156.00	1-40	0	0	4.33	2	
I20T		1	1	0	14	14	14.00	0	0	12	15	0					7.50	1	
20T		1	1	0	14	14	14.00	0	0	12	15	0					7.50	1	
MOHAMMAD IRFAN																			
Int		2	1	1	3	3*		0	0	75	77	0					6.16	0	
Lim		2	1	1	3	3*		0	0	75	77	0					6.16	0	
MOHAMMAD YOUSUF																			
Test		2	4	0	99	56	24.75	0	1									0	
FC		2	4	0	99	56	24.75	0	1									0	
Int		5	5	0	93	46	18.60	0	0									1	
Lim		6	6	0	119	46	19.83	0	0									2	
I20T		2	2	0	30	26	15.00	0	0									1	
20T		2	2	0	30	26	15.00	0	0									1	

Cmp Debut	M	I	NO	Runs	HS	Avge	100	50	Balls	Runs	Wkts	Avge	BB	5i	10m	RpO	ct	st
SAEED AJMAL																		
Test	3	5	2	67	50	22.33	0	1	751	353	12	29.41	5-82	1	0	2.82	2	
FC	3	5	2	67	50	22.33	0	1	751	353	12	29.41	5-82	1	0	2.82	2	
Int	5	4	1	17	9*	5.66	0	0	258	233	9	25.88	4-58	1	0	5.41	0	
Lim	6	5	1	17	9*	4.25	0	0	318	273	12	22.75	4-58	1	0	5.15	0	
I20T	4	2	2	6	6*		0	0	82	95	5	19.00	3-26	0	0	6.95	1	
20T	6	2	2	6	6*		0	0	124	128	8	16.00	3-26	0	0	6.19	2	
SALMAN BUTT																		
Test	6	12	0	341	92	28.41	0	2									0	
FC	7	14	0	376	92	26.85	0	2									1	
I20T	2	2	0	44	31	22.00	0	0									0	
20T	3	3	0	85	41	28.33	0	0									0	
SHAHID AFRIDI																		
Test	1	2	0	33	31	16.50	0	0	102	69	1	69.00	1-44	0	0	4.05	0	
FC	2	3	0	33	31	11.00	0	0	102	69	1	69.00	1-44	0	0	4.05	0	
Int	5	5	0	99	37	19.80	0	0	255	229	4	57.25	1-31	0	0	5.38	1	
Lim	6	6	0	101	37	16.83	0	0	315	276	6	46.00	2-47	0	0	5.25	3	
I20T	4	4	1	36	18	12.00	0	0	90	98	6	16.33	2-27	0	0	6.53	2	
20T	5	5	1	78	42	19.50	0	0	114	125	6	20.83	2-27	0	0	6.57	2	
SHAHZAIB HASAN																		
Lim	1	1	0	105	105	105.00	1	0									0	
I20T	4	4	0	24	21	6.00	0	0									0	
20T	6	6	0	137	64	22.83	0	1									0	
SHOAIB AKHTAR																		
Int	5	4	2	6	6*	3.00	0	0	276	219	8	27.37	3-40	0	0	4.76	0	
Lim	6	5	2	10	6*	3.33	0	0	324	274	8	34.25	3-40	0	0	5.07	0	
I20T	4	2	0	4	4	2.00	0	0	84	104	4	26.00	2-23	0	0	7.42	0	
20T	5	2	0	4	4	2.00	0	0	102	112	4	28.00	2-23	0	0	6.58	0	
SHOAIB MALIK																		
Test	3	6	0	89	38	14.83	0	0	159	90	2	45.00	2-31	0	0	3.39	0	
FC	4	8	1	164	48*	23.42	0	0	267	134	6	22.33	2-17	0	0	3.01	0	
I20T	2	2	0	33	21	16.50	0	0									2	
20T	4	4	2	71	38*	35.50	0	0	24	38	1	38.00	1-31	0	0	9.50	2	
UMAR AKMAL																		
Test	6	12	2	240	79*	24.00	0	1									4	
FC	7	13	2	393	153	35.72	1	1	6	10	0					10.00	5	
Int	5	5	0	125	43	25.00	0	0									0	
Lim	5	5	0	125	43	25.00	0	0									0	
I20T	4	4	1	141	64	47.00	0	1									1	
20T	6	5	1	179	64	44.75	0	1									2	
UMAR AMIN																		
Test	4	8	0	99	33	12.37	0	0	132	63	3	21.00	1-7	0	0	2.86	1	
FC	5	10	0	174	73	17.40	0	1	132	63	3	21.00	1-7	0	0	2.86	1	
UMAR GUL																		
Test	4	8	3	96	65*	19.20	0	1	628	315	12	26.25	4-61	0	0	3.01	0	
FC	5	9	4	126	65*	25.20	0	1	718	391	14	27.92	4-61	0	0	3.26	0	
Int	5	5	1	46	18	11.50	0	0	262	255	12	21.25	6-42	1	1	5.84	0	
Lim	6	6	1	46	18	9.20	0	0	322	321	15	21.40	6-42	1	1	5.98	0	
I20T	4	3	0	26	16	8.66	0	0	65	89	4	22.25	2-13	0	0	8.21	1	
20T	6	3	0	26	16	8.66	0	0	113	159	6	26.50	2-13	0	0	8.44	1	
WAHAB RIAZ																		
Test	2	3	0	29	27	9.66	0	0	320	195	7	27.85	5-63	1	0	3.65	0	
FC	3	4	0	35	27	8.75	0	0	428	283	8	35.37	5-63	1	0	3.96	2	
I20T	1								12	11	0					5.50	1	
20T	3								36	37	1	37.00	1-26	0	0	6.16	1	
YASIR HAMEED																		
Test	2	4	0	41	36	10.25	0	0	6	0	0					0.00	4	
FC	2	4	0	41	36	10.25	0	0	6	0	0					0.00	4	
ZULQARNAIN HAIDER																		
Test	1	2	0	88	88	44.00	0	1									2	
FC	1	2	0	88	88	44.00	0	1									2	

SCOTLAND TO ENGLAND 2010

Cmp Debut	M	I	NO	Runs	HS	Avge	100	50	Balls	Runs	Wkts	Avge	BB	5i	10m	RpO	ct	st
BAILEY, G.J.																		
Lim	6	6	1	340	123*	68.00	1	3									5	
BERRINGTON, R.D.																		
Lim	6	6	0	155	82	25.83	0	2	150	176	7	25.14	4-47	1	0	7.04	2	
DRUMMOND, G.D.																		
Lim	6	4	1	32	12	10.66	0	0	264	219	7	31.28	2-42	0	0	4.97	2	

Cmp	Debut	M	I	NO	Runs	HS	Avge	100	50	Balls	Runs	Wkts	Avge	BB	5i	10m	RpO	ct	st
FLANNIGAN, R.																			
Lim		1	1	0	1	1	1.00	0	0									0	
GOUDIE, G.																			
Lim		6	3	0	13	10	4.33	0	0	264	330	8	41.25	3-45	0	0	7.50	1	
HAIRS, O.J.																			
Lim		1	1	0	24	24	24.00	0	0									0	
HAMILTON, G.M.																			
Lim		4	4	0	45	16	11.25	0	0									1	
HAQ, R.M.																			
Lim		6	5	4	89	28	89.00	0	0	252	229	4	57.25	2-35	0	0	5.45	0	
HUSSAIN, R.O.																			
Lim		3	3	0	62	42	20.66	0	0									0	
IQBAL, M.M.																			
Lim		1	1	0	31	31	31.00	0	0	24	22	0					5.50	0	
LAIDLAW, N.J.W.																			
Lim		1								36	29	0					4.83	0	
LOCKHART, D.R.																			
Lim		4	4	1	64	37	21.33	0	0									4	1
LYONS, R.T.																			
Lim		4	2	1	1	1*	1.00	0	0	186	145	5	29.00	3-39	0	0	4.67	3	
McCALLUM, N.F.I.																			
Lim		5	4	1	83	45	27.66	0	0									4	
MAIDEN, G.I.																			
Lim		2	2	0	9	9	4.50	0	0	54	53	0					5.88	1	
MOMMSEN, P.L.																			
Lim		1	1	0	28	28	28.00	0	0									0	
PARKER, M.A.																			
Lim		3	3	0	10	7	3.33	0	0	126	127	7	18.14	3-27	0	0	6.04	0	
PETRIE, M.J.																			
Lim		1	1	0	0	0	0.00	0	0									0	
SMITH, S.J.S.																			
Lim		1																2	
WATSON, R.R.																			
Lim		1	1	0	24	24	24.00	0	0	36	34	2	17.00	2-34	0	0	5.66	1	
WATTS, D.F.																			
Lim		3	3	0	54	28	18.00	0	0									1	

WEST INDIES A TO ENGLAND 2010

Cmp	Debut	M	I	NO	Runs	HS	Avge	100	50	Balls	Runs	Wkts	Avge	BB	5i	10m	RpO	ct	st
BAKER, L.S.																			
FC		3	4	2	12	6	6.00	0	0	483	245	8	30.62	2-31	0	0	3.04	1	
Lim		5	2	1	26	18	26.00	0	0	254	256	6	42.66	2-32	0	0	6.04	4	
BERNARD, D.E.																			
FC		2	3	0	92	70	30.66	0	1	324	160	1	160.00	1-102	0	0	2.96	0	
Lim		1	1	0	33	33	33.00	0	0	30	22	0					4.40	0	
BRATHWAITE, K.C.																			
FC		2	3	0	17	13	5.66	0	0									1	
BRAVO, D.M.																			
Lim		3	3	0	172	83	57.33	0	2									1	
BROWN, O.V.																			
FC		1	1	1	0	0*		0	0	194	123	5	24.60	5-92	1	0	3.80	0	
EDWARDS, K.A.																			
FC		3	4	0	67	40	16.75	0	0									0	
Lim		5	5	0	165	147	33.00	1	0									2	
FLETCHER, A.D.S.																			
FC		3	4	0	183	123	45.75	1	0	30	19	0					3.80	1	
Lim		5	5	0	188	88	37.60	0	1									7	1
FUDADIN, A.B.																			
FC		1	1	0	3	3	3.00	0	0	84	42	0					3.00	0	
Lim		3	3	0	87	51	29.00	0	1									3	
GUILLEN, J.C.																			
FC		1	2	0	3	3	1.50	0	0									0	
KHAN, I.																			
FC		3	4	0	123	62	30.75	0	1	312	217	2	108.50	1-18	0	0	4.17	3	
Lim		5	5	2	89	74	29.66	0	1	210	206	4	51.50	1-16	0	0	5.88	1	
MARTIN, A.																			
Lim		5	2	1	2	2*	2.00	0	0	288	250	5	50.00	3-47	0	0	5.20	2	
PHILLIPS, O.J.																			
FC		3	5	1	91	35	22.75	0	0									1	
Lim		2	2	0	32	17	16.00	0	0									0	

Cmp Debut	M	I	NO	Runs	HS	Avge	100	50	Balls	Runs	Wkts	Avge	BB	5i	10m	RpO	ct	st
RUSSELL, A.D.																		
FC	2	3	0	37	19	12.33	0	0	408	207	11	18.81	5-68	2	0	3.04	0	
Lim	5	5	1	123	49	30.75	0	0	238	263	7	37.57	3-75	0	0	6.63	1	
SMITH, D.S.																		
FC	3	5	1	246	170	61.50	1	0	6	5	0					5.00	6	
Lim	3	3	0	106	104	35.33	1	0	24	26	0					6.50	2	
STOUTE, K.A.																		
Lim	5	5	2	177	64	59.00	0	2	104	107	9	11.88	8-52	0	1	6.17	3	
TONGE, G.C.																		
FC	3	4	1	128	54	42.66	0	1	570	321	9	35.66	3-53	0	0	3.37	0	
Lim	5	3	1	24	19	12.00	0	0	239	246	9	27.33	4-69	1	0	6.17	0	
WALTON, C.A.K.																		
FC	3	4	0	51	34	12.75	0	0									7	
Lim	3	3	0	30	25	10.00	0	0									4	

INDIA

Ranji Trophy winners 2009/10 (first-class): Mumbai
Duleep Trophy winners 2009/10 (first-class): West Zone
Irani Cup winners 2009/10 (first-class): Rest of India
Vijay Hazare Trophy winners 2009/10 (limited overs): Tamil Nadu
Deodhar Trophy winners 2009/10 (limited overs): West Zone
Indian Premier League winners 2010 (twenty20): Chennai Super Kings

2009/10 and 2010 AND CAREER RECORDS FOR INDIAN PLAYERS

Cmp	*Debut*	*M*	*I*	*NO*	*Runs*	*HS*	*Avge*	*100*	*50*	*Balls*	*Runs*	*Wkts*	*Avge*	*BB*	*5i*	*10m*	*RpO*	*ct*	*st*
AARON, Varun Raymond (Jharkhand) b Jamshedpur, Bihar 29.10.1989 RHB RM																			
FC		4	6	2	78	29	19.50	0	0	582	305	8	38.12	3-36	0	0	3.14	1	
Lim		3	2	1	17	17*	17.00	0	0	150	135	9	15.00	5-54	0	1	5.40	0	
20T		4	1	0	6	6	6.00	0	0	84	87	5	17.40	2-6	0	0	6.21	0	
FC	2008/09	6	9	3	115	29	19.16	0	0	971	539	12	44.91	3-36	0	0	3.33	2	
ABBAS ALI, Syed (Madhya Pradesh) b Indore, Madhya Pradesh 20.2.1976 LHB OB																			
FC		4	3	1	59	57*	29.50	0	1	104	73	3	24.33	2-31	0	0	4.21	7	
Lim		6	6	1	89	35	17.80	0	0	147	190	3	63.33	2-40	0	0	7.75	3	
20T		4	4	0	101	33	25.25	0	0	54	65	4	16.25	2-21	0	0	7.22	1	
FC	1996/97	86	132	23	5328	251	48.88	13	30	3371	1463	47	31.12	3-17	0	0	2.60	98	
Lim	1996/97	75	73	8	1996	125*	30.70	3	12	2266	1817	53	34.28	6-25	0	1	4.81	36	
20T	2006/07	11	10	1	204	55	22.66	0	1	175	199	13	15.30	2-5	0	0	6.82	4	
ABDUL BASEER, Mohammad (Hyderabad) b 9.2.1989 RHB RM																			
20T		3	1	0	8	8	8.00	0	0	42	76	1	76.00	1-30	0	0	10.85	1	
MOHAMMAD ABDUL KHADER (Hyderabad) b Hyderabad, Andhra Pradesh 6.11.1987 LHB RM																			
FC		5	6	1	74	34	14.80	0	0	1215	600	18	33.33	5-101	1	0	2.96	2	
FC	2007/08	6	8	2	113	34	18.83	0	0	1323	659	19	34.68	5-101	1	0	2.98	2	
ABDULLA, Yusuf Adam (Dolphins, South Africa, Kings XI Punjab) b Johannesburg, South Africa, South Africa 17.1.1983 LHB LFM																			
20T		2	1	1	0	0*		0	0	41	66	1	66.00	1-30	0	0	9.65	0	
FC	2005/06	23	28	8	182	54	9.10	0	1	3263	1902	54	35.22	5-62	2	0	3.49	4	
Lim	2005/06	51	15	11	88	31*	22.00	0	0	2146	1729	57	30.33	4-41	2	0	4.83	9	
I20T	2008/09	2								42	44	2	22.00	1-16	0	0	6.28	0	
20T	2005/06	38	3	2	4	3	4.00	0	0	809	895	50	17.90	4-31	2	0	6.63	3	
ABHINAV KUMAR (Deccan Chargers, Hyderabad) b Hyderabad, Andhra Pradesh 7.11.1984 RHB WK																			
FC		7	12	1	355	103*	32.27	1	1									11	
Lim		5	5	0	12	7	2.40	0	0									1	
20T		2	2	1	56	55*	56.00	0	1									0	
FC	2005/06	18	32	3	731	103*	25.20	1	4									30	3
Lim	2004/05	20	19	1	681	110	37.83	2	4									15	5
ABID KHAN, Mohammad (Uttar Pradesh) b Allahabad, Uttar Pradesh 1.12.1985 RHB RM																			
Lim		1	1	1	4	4*		0	0	27	25	0					5.55	0	
FC	2007/08	3	3	0	17	10	5.66	0	0	696	331	6	55.16	1-29	0	0	2.85	1	
ABID NABI (Jammu and Kashmir) b Srinagar, Jammu and Kashmir 26.12.1985 RHB RFM																			
FC		4	7	1	133	54	22.16	0	1	650	404	22	18.36	5-27	2	0	3.72	1	
Lim		5	5	0	23	12	4.60	0	0	253	292	2	146.00	2-75	0	0	6.92	3	
20T		5	4	0	57	26	14.25	0	0	103	133	3	44.33	1-22	0	0	7.74	0	
FC	2004/05	19	31	4	295	54	10.92	0	1	3662	2042	81	25.20	6-91	5	0	3.34	6	
Lim	2004/05	20	16	1	119	44	7.93	0	0	918	894	23	38.86	5-50	1	1	5.84	3	
20T	2006/07	10	9	0	115	26	12.77	0	0	211	245	5	49.00	2-24	0	0	6.96	2	
ABLASH, Lovesh (Kings XI Punjab, Punjab) b Ludhiana, Punjab 3.12.1982 RHB RM																			
FC		8	11	4	163	32	23.28	0	0	1559	860	36	23.88	6-79	3	1	3.31	2	
Lim		3	2	2	0	0*		0	0	150	103	5	20.60	3-28	0	0	4.12	0	
20T		7	1	1	1	1*		0	0	132	156	13	12.00	5-20	0	1	7.09	1	
FC	2004/05	16	20	6	279	76	19.92	0	1	2800	1414	57	24.80	6-79	4	1	3.03	2	
Lim	2006/07	4	2	2	0	0*		0	0	186	126	6	21.00	3-28	0	0	4.06	0	
20T	2006/07	14	1	1	1	1*		0	0	282	317	23	13.78	5-20	0	1	6.74	1	
ABSOLEM, Alfred (Hyderabad, South Zone) b Hyderabad, Andhra Pradesh 23.1.1986 RHB RM																			
FC		7	11	3	122	29	15.25	0	0	1673	865	29	29.82	5-89	2	0	3.10	2	
Lim		4	3	1	13	11*	6.50	0	0	204	225	4	56.25	3-53	0	0	6.61	1	
20T		1								24	20	1	20.00	1-20	0	0	5.00	2	
FC	2005/06	13	21	3	213	29	11.83	0	0	2833	1453	59	24.62	7-35	4	1	3.07	6	
Lim	2005/06	14	12	4	126	27*	15.75	0	0	736	632	21	30.09	3-30	0	0	5.15	4	
20T	2006/07	6	3	1	12	6	6.00	0	0	118	134	4	33.50	1-16	0	0	6.81	4	

Cmp	Debut	M	I	NO	Runs	HS	Avge	100	50	Balls	Runs	Wkts	Avge	BB	5i	10m	RpO	ct	st
ADHAV, Kiran Ramling (Maharashtra) b Kolhapur, Maharashtra 5.9.1983 RHB SLA																			
FC		6	11	2	105	28	11.66	0	0	1455	809	13	62.23	5-24	1	0	3.33	0	
Lim		4	3	1	62	37*	31.00	0	0	234	225	4	56.25	2-45	0	0	5.76	1	
20T		7	4	3	43	23*	43.00	0	0	156	177	7	25.28	3-29	0	0	6.80	3	
FC	2001/02	18	27	7	211	28	10.55	0	0	4094	2049	51	40.17	5-24	2	0	3.00	7	
ADITYA PRATAP SINGH Jamwal (Jammu and Kashmir) b Jammu 21.12.1989 RHB OB																			
FC		1	2	0	0	0	0.00	0	0									0	
FC	2008/09	4	8	1	84	56	12.00	0	1									0	
Lim	2008/09	1	1	1	32	32*		0	0									0	
AGARKAR, Ajit Bhalchandra (Kolkata Knight Riders, Mumbai) b Bombay (now Mumbai), Maharashtra 4.12.1977 RHB RFM																			
FC		10	13	3	406	102*	40.60	1	2	1669	781	22	35.50	5-81	1	0	2.80	6	
Lim		4	4	0	42	26	10.50	0	0	233	150	8	18.75	3-30	0	0	3.86	0	
20T		11	7	3	81	25	20.25	0	0	222	326	8	40.75	3-38	0	0	8.81	3	
Test	1998/99	26	39	5	571	109*	16.79	1	0	4857	2745	58	47.32	6-41	1	0	3.39	6	
FC	1996/97	95	124	22	2872	109*	28.15	3	14	16074	8158	271	30.10	6-41	12	0	3.04	35	
Int	1997/98	191	113	26	1269	95	14.58	0	3	9484	8021	288	27.85	6-42	10	2	5.07	53	
Lim	1996/97	258	163	40	2141	95	17.40	0	8	12695	10543	399	26.42	6-18	10	3	4.98	68	
I20T	2006/07	4	2	0	15	14	7.50	0	0	63	85	3	28.33	2-10	0	0	8.09	0	
20T	2006/07	39	25	11	222	39	15.85	0	0	705	988	30	32.93	3-25	0	0	8.40	4	
AHMED, Abu Nachim (Assam, East Zone, Mumbai Indians) b Guwahati, Assam 5.11.1988 RHB RFM																			
FC		8	10	3	88	24*	12.57	0	0	1468	615	28	21.96	5-40	3	1	2.51	3	
Lim		3	2	0	37	32	18.50	0	0	150	132	2	66.00	1-37	0	0	5.28	0	
20T		5	2	1	15	11	15.00	0	0	90	102	3	34.00	1-11	0	0	6.80	0	
FC	2005/06	16	21	5	230	24*	14.37	0	0	2774	1243	50	24.86	5-40	4	1	2.68	5	
Lim	2006/07	6	4	0	63	32	15.75	0	0	311	224	6	37.33	2-27	0	0	4.32	0	
20T	2006/07	9	6	1	33	11	6.60	0	0	174	213	5	42.60	1-11	0	0	7.34	0	
AJIT SINGH (Haryana) b Hansawas Khurd, Haryana 15.10.1985 RHB RM																			
Lim		1	1	0	0	0	0.00	0	0	24	34	0					8.50	0	
AKHIL, Balachandra (Karnataka, Royal Challengers Bangalore) b Bangalore, Karnataka 7.10.1977 RHB RMF																			
FC		4	6	2	178	52*	44.50	0	1	306	100	2	50.00	1-1	0	0	1.96	8	
20T		5	3	1	41	19	20.50	0	0	66	76	4	19.00	1-10	0	0	6.90	0	
FC	1998/99	51	72	9	1810	135	28.73	1	14	4283	1837	49	37.48	5-58	1	0	2.57	79	
Lim	1998/99	69	56	6	1382	91	27.64	0	8	2653	1960	57	34.38	4-31	1	0	4.43	33	
20T	2006/07	27	22	8	271	35	19.35	0	0	433	487	20	24.35	3-16	0	0	6.74	6	
AKSHATH REDDY, Produturi (Hyderabad) b Hyderabad, Andhra Pradesh 11.2.1991 RHB LBG																			
Lim		3	3	0	200	121	66.66	1	1									2	
20T		3	3	1	139	105*	69.50	1	0									1	
AKSHAY, Santhebennur Lokesh (Karnataka) b Shimoga, Karnataka 30.4.1987 RHB RFM																			
Lim		2								102	83	2	41.50	1-39	0	0	4.88	1	
AMARJEET SINGH (Madhya Pradesh) b Bhopal, Madhya Pradesh 22.5.1990 RHB RFM																			
Lim		6	4	2	51	19	25.50	0	0	292	292	14	20.85	4-46	1	0	6.00	1	
20T		3	2	1	1	1	1.00	0	0	66	67	2	33.50	1-25	0	0	6.09	0	
Lim	2008/09	8	5	3	62	19	31.00	0	0	364	350	15	23.33	4-46	1	0	5.76	2	
AMARNATH, Palani (Tamil Nadu) b Vellore, Tamil Nadu 1.6.1982 LHB RM																			
20T		2								48	71	3	23.66	2-36	0	0	8.87	1	
FC	2007/08	15	13	8	21	8	4.20	0	0	2261	1113	29	38.37	5-60	2	0	2.95	6	
Lim	2007/08	6	1	1	1	1*		0	0	314	234	9	26.00	4-16	1	0	4.47	1	
20T	2006/07	13	3	2	1	1	1.00	0	0	294	455	17	26.76	2-25	0	0	9.28	4	
AMIR KHAN, Mohammad (Uttar Pradesh) b Kanpur, Uttar Pradesh 27.1.1986 RHB RAB WK																			
FC		8	12	3	211	61	23.44	0	1									19	7
20T		3	2	1	4	4	4.00	0	0									2	
FC	2004/05	48	71	11	1294	70	21.56	0	5									151	15
Lim	2004/05	22	16	3	186	40	14.30	0	0									33	10
AMIT SINGH (Gujarat) b Bidar, Karnataka 21.6.1981 RHB RM																			
Lim		1								48	45	0					5.62	0	
20T		2	1	0	5	5	5.00	0	0	48	56	3	18.66	3-22	0	0	7.00	0	
FC	2005/06	5	8	2	107	37*	17.83	0	0	630	280	6	46.66	2-82	0	0	2.66	1	
Lim	2005/06	10	8	1	88	32	12.57	0	0	516	454	15	30.26	5-50	0	1	5.27	1	
20T	2009	8	3	1	6	5	3.00	0	0	165	156	12	13.00	4-19	1	0	5.67	0	
AMRINDER SINGH (Services) b Bokaro, Bihar 20.9.1983 LHB SLA																			
Lim		5	3	1	26	24	13.00	0	0	288	236	8	29.50	2-33	0	0	4.91	1	
FC	2005/06	5	8	2	107	37*	17.83	0	0	630	280	6	46.66	2-82	0	0	2.66	1	
Lim	2005/06	10	8	1	88	32	12.57	0	0	516	454	15	30.26	5-50	0	1	5.27	1	
ANAND SINGH (Madhya Pradesh) b Rewa, Madhya Pradesh 17.11.1986 RHB RFM																			
FC		2	2	1	36	30	36.00	0	0	36	3	2	1.50	2-1	0	0	0.50	1	
Lim		6	4	0	123	57	30.75	0	1	12	18	0					9.00	1	
20T		1	1	0	21	21	21.00	0	0	18	19	1	19.00	1-19	0	0	6.33	2	
ANIRUDH SINGH (Deccan Chargers, Hyderabad) b Hyderabad, Andhra Pradesh 2.8.1980 LHB RM																			
FC		5	7	1	317	75	52.83	0	3									7	
Lim		3	3	0	109	58	36.33	0	1									2	

Cmp	Debut	M	I	NO	Runs	HS	Avge	100	50	Balls	Runs	Wkts	Avge	BB	5i	10m	RpO	ct	st
20T		5	4	0	63	40	15.75	0	0									3	
FC	2000/01	46	76	2	2472	124	33.40	3	13	72	37	0					3.08	34	1
Lim	2001/02	33	33	5	769	86*	27.46	0	6	12	6	0					3.00	11	
20T	2006/07	8	7	0	67	40	9.57	0	0									4	
ANSARI, Azhar Ahmed (Maharashtra) b Malegaon, Maharashtra 18.1.1990 LHB RM																			
FC		3	5	0	93	52	18.60	0	1	331	176	2	88.00	2-33	0	0	3.19	2	
Lim		2	2	0	46	46	23.00	0	0	78	96	1	96.00	1-61	0	0	7.38	1	
20T		7	5	1	84	34	21.00	0	0	158	214	6	35.66	2-19	0	0	8.12	3	
Lim	2008/09	6	6	2	147	50*	36.75	0	1	222	225	5	45.00	2-22	0	0	6.08	2	
ANUREET SINGH, Kathuria (Railways) b Delhi 2.3.1988 RHB RFM																			
Lim		4	2	1	15	14*	15.00	0	0	213	227	6	37.83	2-43	0	0	6.39	1	
20T		1								7	9	0					7.71	0	
FC	2008/09	5	6	3	33	16*	11.00	0	0	1064	563	20	28.15	6-49	1	0	3.17	3	
Lim	2008/09	9	5	2	29	14*	9.66	0	0	423	420	14	30.00	3-45	0	0	5.95	2	
20T	2009	4								37	56	2	28.00	2-35	0	0	9.08	0	
APHALE, Kaushik Dattatray (Tripura) b Pune, Maharashtra 18.11.1978 RHB OB																			
FC		5	8	1	142	47	20.28	0	0	150	79	1	79.00	1-27	0	0	3.16	5	
Lim		4	4	0	92	33	23.00	0	0	60	39	4	9.75	2-22	0	0	3.90	1	
20T		4	4	0	77	51	19.25	0	1	24	37	1	37.00	1-13	0	0	9.25	3	
FC	1999/00	37	57	4	1753	215*	33.07	4	8	360	208	1	208.00	1-27	0	0	3.46	32	
Lim	1999/00	23	22	1	547	90	26.04	0	3	60	39	4	9.75	2-22	0	0	3.90	5	
APPANNA, Kotragada Prabhu (Karnataka, Royal Challengers Bangalore) b Virajpet, Karnataka 20.12.1988 RHB SLA																			
FC		1	1	1	0	0*		0	0	213	111	3	37.00	2-83	0	0	3.12	0	
Lim		7	2	2	3	3*		0	0	378	297	10	29.70	5-56	0	1	4.71	4	
20T		2	2	1	2	1*	2.00	0	0	42	51	1	51.00	1-24	0	0	7.28	0	
FC	2006/07	13	17	13	25	5*	6.25	0	0	2386	1204	39	30.87	5-79	1	0	3.02	4	
Lim	2007/08	18	8	6	16	8*	8.00	0	0	960	728	31	23.48	5-56	1	1	4.55	9	
20T	2006/07	10	4	3	11	9*	11.00	0	0	162	203	5	40.60	1-9	0	0	7.51	0	
ARAVIND, Sreesanth (Karnataka, South Zone) b Bangalore, Karnataka 8.4.1984 LHB LM																			
FC		9	8	1	58	15	8.28	0	0	1805	973	30	32.43	5-49	1	0	3.23	1	
Lim		3	1	1	38	38*		0	0	171	136	3	45.33	2-45	0	0	4.77	1	
20T		1								6	5	0					5.00	1	
FC	2008/09	10	10	1	68	15	7.55	0	0	1991	1038	32	32.43	5-49	1	0	3.12	1	
Lim	2008/09	10	6	2	53	38*	13.25	0	0	526	397	19	20.89	4-41	1	0	4.52	4	
20T	2006/07	10	1	1	4	4*		0	0	197	201	13	15.46	4-24	1	0	6.12	6	
ARGAL, Ajitesh Kamlesh (Baroda) b Bhopal, Madhya Pradesh 21.9.1988 RHB RM																			
FC		1	1	0	8	8	8.00	0	0	168	105	1	105.00	1-105	0	0	3.75	1	
Lim		3	2	0	2	1	1.00	0	0	107	113	1	113.00	1-50	0	0	6.33	0	
FC	2008/09	5	7	2	20	8	4.00	0	0	670	422	15	28.13	4-59	0	0	3.77	2	
ARJUN, Munagala Praneet (Hyderabad) b Hyderabad, Andhra Pradesh 11.1.1986 RHB RM																			
FC		7	10	0	205	71	20.50	0	1	1319	642	21	30.57	6-47	1	0	2.92	2	
20T		1								24	25	2	12.50	2-25	0	0	6.25	0	
FC	2006/07	21	34	3	436	71	14.06	0	1	3518	1652	55	30.03	7-56	2	0	2.81	4	
Lim	2005/06	16	13	5	113	23*	14.12	0	0	672	506	10	50.60	3-19	0	0	4.51	3	
20T	2006/07	6	4	2	16	7	8.00	0	0	102	117	2	58.50	2-25	0	0	6.88	1	
ARSHAD AHMED Seikh (Jammu and Kashmir) b Bhaderwah 12.4.1986 RHB RM																			
FC		2	4	3	10	10	10.00	0	0	234	136	1	136.00	1-87	0	0	3.48	0	
FC	2008/09	3	6	3	15	10	5.00	0	0	417	210	5	42.00	3-33	0	0	3.02	0	
Lim	2008/09	5	4	1	1	1	0.33	0	0	273	244	6	40.66	3-72	0	0	5.36	2	
ARUN KARTHIK, Konda Bhaskar (Chennai Super Kings, South Zone, Tamil Nadu) b Walajapet, Tamil Nadu 15.2.1986 RHB LBG																			
FC		10	15	0	637	118	42.46	1	5	48	27	0					3.37	11	
Lim		4	3	2	168	106*	168.00	1	0									1	
20T		3	3	1	105	58	52.50	0	1	12	13	1	13.00	1-13	0	0	6.50	1	
FC	2008/09	14	21	0	981	149	46.71	3	5	48	27	0					3.37	16	
Lim	2007/08	24	23	3	654	106*	32.70	1	1	114	74	3	24.66	2-19	0	0	3.89	8	
ASHISH REDDY, Ammana (Hyderabad) b Secunderabad, Andhra Pradesh 24.2.1991 RHB RM																			
Lim		5	5	0	36	17	7.20	0	0	222	219	3	73.00	2-36	0	0	5.91	0	
20T		1	1	1	19	19*		0	0	18	33	1	33.00	1-33	0	0	11.00	0	
Lim	2008/09	8	8	1	81	29*	11.57	0	0	294	273	4	68.25	2-36	0	0	5.57	1	
ASHWIN, Ravichandran (Chennai Super Kings, India Red, South Zone, Tamil Nadu, India to Zimbabwe) b Madras (now Chennai), Tamil Nadu 17.9.1986 RHB OB																			
FC		8	12	4	388	107*	48.50	1	3	2028	835	23	36.30	6-67	2	0	2.47	7	
Lim		10	5	1	149	79	37.25	0	1	564	428	14	30.57	2-31	0	0	4.55	1	
20T		14	6	2	30	11*	7.50	0	0	336	333	18	18.50	3-16	0	0	5.94	2	
FC	2006/07	28	41	11	1085	107*	36.16	2	6	6837	3032	103	29.43	6-64	7	2	2.66	13	
Int	2010	1	1	0	38	38	38.00	0	0	60	50	2	25.00	2-50	0	0	5.00	0	
Lim	2006/07	37	23	5	412	79	22.88	0	2	2018	1387	48	28.89	3-25	0	0	4.12	12	
I20T	2010	2								48	70	2	35.00	1-22	0	0	8.75	0	
20T	2006/07	28	11	3	45	11*	5.62	0	0	610	631	32	19.71	3-15	0	0	6.20	8	

Cmp	Debut	M	I	NO	Runs	HS	Avge	100	50	Balls	Runs	Wkts	Avge	BB	5i	10m	RpO	ct	st
ASIF RASOOL Zargav (Jammu and Kashmir) b Anantnag, Jammu 1.1.1987 RHB RFM																			
20T		2	1	0	0	0	0.00	0	0	18	19	0					6.33	0	
ASNODKAR, Swapnil Ashok (Goa, Rajasthan Royals) b Porvorim, Goa 29.3.1984 RHB OB																			
FC		3	4	0	250	136	62.50	1	1									0	
Lim		5	5	0	188	77	37.60	0	2									0	
20T		5	5	1	105	71*	26.25	0	1									3	
FC	2001/02	42	76	3	3232	254*	44.27	8	14	138	85	1	85.00	1-21	0	0	3.69	14	
Lim	2001/02	47	47	4	1656	120*	38.51	3	13	37	28	0					4.54	13	
20T	2006/07	28	28	1	624	71*	23.11	0	3									10	
ATCHUTI RAO, Tekkami (Andhra) b Visakhapatnam, Andhra Pradesh 21.8.1986 LHB LFM																			
FC		5	6	1	79	33*	15.80	0	0	816	332	12	27.66	5-43	1	0	2.44	4	
Lim		2	2	1	11	7	11.00	0	0	88	79	2	39.50	2-31	0	0	5.38	1	
FC	2008/09	6	8	1	115	33*	16.42	0	0	999	398	17	23.41	5-43	2	0	2.39	4	
Lim	2007/08	9	7	1	45	17	7.50	0	0	340	323	5	64.60	2-31	0	0	5.70	4	
ATITKAR, Sangram Diliprao (Maharashtra) b Ambedwadi, Maharashtra 23.1.1988 RHB RFM																			
FC		5	10	0	293	95	29.30	0	3	24	12	0					3.00	2	
Lim		4	4	1	134	55	44.66	0	1	4	12	0					18.00	1	
20T		3	3	0	38	33	12.66	0	0	24	31	2	15.50	1-8	0	0	7.75	2	
Lim	2008/09	7	7	1	242	89	40.33	0	2	4	12	0					18.00	1	
ATTRI, Digamber Singh (Services) b Faridabad, Haryana 18.4.1985 RHB RFM																			
20T		2	2	0	11	7	5.50	0	0	48	60	2	30.00	1-26	0	0	7.50	0	
Lim	2008/09	5	4	2	36	24	18.00	0	0	240	190	6	31.66	3-44	0	0	4.75	3	
AUSHIK SRINIVAS, Raju (South Zone, Tamil Nadu) b Coimbatore, Tamil Nadu 16.3.1993 RHB SLA																			
FC		9	10	6	37	21*	9.25	0	0	1735	839	25	33.56	7-107	1	0	2.90	3	
AWANA, Parvinder (Delhi, North Zone) b Noida, Delhi 19.7.1986 RHB RM																			
FC		9	11	2	105	28	11.66	0	0	1585	950	29	32.75	5-40	1	0	3.59	2	
Lim		2								102	99	2	49.50	1-43	0	0	5.82	0	
20T		2	1	1	7	7*		0	0	42	49	3	16.33	3-20	0	0	7.00	0	
FC	2007/08	21	25	7	173	28	9.61	0	0	3517	1995	69	28.91	5-40	3	1	3.40	5	
Lim	2007/08	11	2	1	8	7	8.00	0	0	545	505	11	45.90	4-30	1	0	5.56	1	
AZIZ, Parvez (Assam) b Guwahati, Assam 8.12.1987 LHB SLA																			
FC		7	11	0	309	85	28.09	0	2	18	18	0					6.00	8	
Lim		4	4	0	153	83	38.25	0	2	21	22	0					6.28	0	
20T		6	6	0	287	75	47.83	0	3	30	40	2	20.00	1-9	0	0	8.00	0	
FC	2004/05	21	34	1	828	85	25.09	0	7	264	112	0					2.54	11	
Lim	2004/05	20	20	1	567	108*	29.84	1	4	177	160	3	53.33	1-26	0	0	5.42	0	
20T	2006/07	10	10	1	373	75	41.44	0	4	54	71	4	17.75	2-25	0	0	7.88	2	
BADANI, Hemang Kamal (Rajasthan) b Madras (now Chennai), Tamil Nadu 14.11.1976 LHB SLA																			
Lim		4	4	1	144	73*	48.00	0	1	180	140	4	35.00	2-38	0	0	4.66	5	
Test	2001	4	7	1	94	38	15.66	0	0	48	17	0					2.12	6	
FC	1996/97	96	135	19	5558	164	47.91	13	36	762	431	6	71.83	1-6	0	0	3.39	72	
Int	2000	40	36	10	867	100	33.34	1	4	183	149	3	49.66	1-7	0	0	4.88	13	
Lim	1996/97	135	124	32	3944	111*	42.86	5	24	1171	1021	29	35.20	2-8	0	0	5.23	54	
20T	2006/07	6	5	3	87	26*	43.50	0	0	36	46	2	23.00	2-23	0	0	7.66	1	
BADDHAN, Harmeet Singh (Mumbai) b Bombay (now Mumbai), Maharashtra 7.9.1992 LHB SLA																			
FC		2	3	0	10	6	3.33	0	0	558	219	12	18.25	4-89	0	0	2.35	0	
BADHWAR, Sanjay (Haryana, North Zone) b Sunarian Khurd 2.10.1987 RHB LFM																			
FC		6	7	4	58	22	19.33	0	0	1231	629	23	27.34	5-69	1	0	3.06	2	
Lim		7	4	2	7	3*	3.50	0	0	369	263	11	23.90	4-27	1	0	4.27	1	
20T		3	1	0	0	0	0.00	0	0	60	90	1	90.00	1-21	0	0	9.00	2	
FC	2006/07	21	29	19	134	24*	13.40	0	0	3353	1680	63	26.66	5-30	3	0	3.00	5	
Lim	2006/07	16	9	7	40	17*	20.00	0	0	657	530	15	35.33	4-27	1	0	4.84	2	
20T	2006/07	12	5	1	22	9	5.50	0	0	270	330	14	23.57	3-26	0	0	7.33	8	
BADRINATH, Subramaniam (Chennai Super Kings, India, India Red, Rest of India, South Zone, Tamil Nadu) b Madras (now Chennai), Tamil Nadu 30.8.1980 RHB OB																			
Test		2	3	0	63	56	21.00	0	1									2	
FC		10	14	0	800	250	57.14	3	4	54	43	0					4.77	7	
Lim		7	7	2	226	105	45.20	1	1	60	46	1	46.00	1-12	0	0	4.60	3	
20T		18	17	4	372	55*	28.61	0	2									2	
FC	2000/01	85	123	14	6252	250	57.35	22	27	1095	601	13	46.23	2-19	0	0	3.29	57	
Int	2008	3	3	1	39	27*	19.50	0	0									2	
Lim	2000/01	96	88	15	3002	134	41.12	4	22	830	732	18	40.66	4-43	1	0	5.29	41	
20T	2006/07	53	44	13	872	64	28.12	0	5	12	6	0					3.00	15	
BAHUTULE, Sairaj Vasant (Assam) b Bombay (now Mumbai), Maharashtra 6.1.1973 LHB LB																			
FC		7	10	2	151	34	18.87	0	0	1436	536	28	19.14	6-61	2	0	2.24	1	
Lim		4	3	0	53	42	17.66	0	0	197	166	3	55.33	3-52	0	0	5.05	1	
20T		6	3	2	18	9	18.00	0	0	138	148	8	18.50	4-19	1	0	6.43	2	
Test	2000/01	2	4	1	39	21*	13.00	0	0	366	203	3	67.66	1-32	0	0	3.32	1	
FC	1991/92	172	223	42	5661	134*	31.27	8	23	36322	15439	604	25.56	8-71	27	4	2.55	76	
Int	1997/98	8	4	1	23	11	7.66	0	0	294	283	2	141.50	1-31	0	0	5.77	3	

Cmp	Debut	M	I	NO	Runs	HS	Avge	100	50	Balls	Runs	Wkts	Avge	BB	5i	10m	RpO	ct	st
Lim	1992/93	143	87	28	1366	105	23.15	1	2	7436	5156	197	26.17	5-24	9	1	4.16	47	
20T	2006/07	8	5	2	101	64	33.66	0	1	174	200	9	22.22	4-19	1	0	6.89	2	
BAIG, Salman Saeed (Madhya Pradesh) b Bhopal, Madhya Pradesh 7.5.1989 RHB RM																			
20T		1	1	0	2	2	2.00	0	0	6	13	0					13.00	0	
BAILEY, George John (Australia A, Tasmania, Chennai Super Kings, Scotland to England, Scotland) b Launceston, Tasmania, Australia 7.9.1982 RHB RM																			
20T		1	1	0	18	18	18.00	0	0									0	
FC	2004/05	61	112	11	4081	155	40.40	10	22	84	46	0					3.28	47	
Lim	2001/02	105	97	12	2739	123*	32.22	2	17	53	40	1	40.00	1-19	0	0	4.52	50	
20T	2005/06	25	21	3	529	60	29.38	0	4	12	24	0					12.00	8	
BAKSHI, Rahul Naresh (Madhya Pradesh) b Indore, Madhya Pradesh 10.12.1985 RHB RM																			
20T		2	2	1	33	19*	33.00	0	0									1	1
FC	2003/04	12	23	4	448	66*	23.57	0	3									11	1
Lim	2003/04	13	10	0	115	34	11.50	0	0									4	
20T	2006/07	10	10	3	156	40	22.28	0	0									3	1
BALAJI, Lakshmipathy (Chennai Super Kings, India Green, Tamil Nadu) b Madras (now Chennai), Tamil Nadu 27.9.1981 RHB RFM																			
FC		7	8	0	115	42	14.37	0	0	1242	532	16	33.25	4-29	0	0	2.57	3	
Lim		8	3	1	19	12	9.50	0	0	416	312	6	52.00	3-27	0	0	4.50	4	
20T		9	3	1	18	15	9.00	0	0	188	260	11	23.63	3-31	0	0	8.29	1	
Test	2003/04	8	9	0	51	31	5.66	0	0	1756	1004	27	37.18	5-76	1	0	3.43	1	
FC	2001/02	69	75	13	807	47	13.01	0	0	13457	6495	259	25.07	7-42	16	4	2.89	23	
Int	2002/03	30	16	6	120	21*	12.00	0	0	1447	1344	34	39.52	4-48	1	0	5.57	11	
Lim	2001/02	83	44	16	251	21*	8.96	0	0	4296	3659	115	31.81	5-36	2	2	5.11	22	
20T	2007/08	31	8	2	22	15	3.66	0	0	610	862	35	24.62	5-24	1	1	8.47	5	
BALI, Abhinav (Himachal Pradesh) b Delhi 2.6.1985 LHB SLA																			
FC		2	4	0	41	34	10.25	0	0	240	110	2	55.00	1-44	0	0	2.75	0	
Lim		3	3	0	50	21	16.66	0	0	54	41	1	41.00	1-30	0	0	4.55	1	
20T		6	5	0	85	54	17.00	0	1	30	34	3	11.33	2-19	0	0	6.80	2	
FC	2004/05	7	11	0	179	43	16.27	0	0	426	208	5	41.60	1-4	0	0	2.93	1	
Lim	2003/04	11	9	2	92	21	13.14	0	0	182	137	6	22.83	2-28	0	0	4.51	7	
BALORIA, Amit (Jammu and Kashmir) b Jammu 24.10.1984 RHB RFM																			
Lim		2	2	0	18	16	9.00	0	0									0	
20T		5	4	1	52	31*	17.33	0	0	54	66	2	33.00	1-18	0	0	7.33	0	
FC	2008/09	1	2	1	22	22*	22.00	0	0	84	28	1	28.00	1-28	0	0	2.00	0	
Lim	2008/09	3	3	0	20	16	6.66	0	0	12	19	0					9.50	0	
BAMEL, Sanjay (Haryana) b Karnal, Haryana 8.10.1984 RHB RAB																			
Lim		2	2	0	15	8	7.50	0	0									0	
FC	2006/07	1	2	0	1	1	0.50	0	0									1	
Lim	2003/04	6	6	1	76	41	15.20	0	0									3	
BANDEKAR, Saurabh Sushant (Goa) b Bombay (now Mumbai), Maharashtra 16.10.1987 RHB RFM																			
FC		5	6	0	222	100	37.00	1	0	612	394	10	39.40	3-72	0	0	3.86	1	
Lim		5	5	0	148	60	29.60	0	1	209	193	10	19.30	4-47	1	0	5.54	0	
20T		3	3	0	41	17	13.66	0	0	48	83	3	27.66	2-26	0	0	10.37	0	
FC	2005/06	20	28	0	661	100	23.60	1	1	3586	2073	69	30.04	6-75	5	0	3.46	7	
Lim	2003/04	21	19	4	362	101*	24.13	1	1	957	892	27	33.03	4-47	2	0	5.59	3	
20T	2006/07	8	8	1	97	26*	13.85	0	0	168	216	8	27.00	2-8	0	0	7.71	0	
BANERJEE, Rohan Bijesh (Bengal) b Bijpur, Bengal 10.12.1988 LHB RM																			
FC		3	6	0	205	107	34.16	1	1									1	
FC	2008/09	8	13	2	445	176	40.45	2	1									6	
BANGAR, Sanjay Bapusaheb (Central Zone, Railways) b Bid, Maharashtra 11.10.1972 RHB RM																			
FC		9	14	2	548	163*	45.66	3	0	1327	411	14	29.35	4-91	0	0	1.85	4	
Lim		4	4	0	153	115	38.25	1	0	224	205	7	29.28	3-25	0	0	5.49	0	
20T		4	4	0	83	57	20.75	0	1	76	97	4	24.25	2-23	0	0	7.65	0	
Test	2001/02	12	18	2	470	100*	29.37	1	3	762	343	7	49.00	2-23	0	0	2.70	4	
FC	1993/94	142	235	17	7234	212	33.18	12	39	18091	8054	249	32.34	6-41	7	1	2.67	123	
Int	2001/02	15	15	2	180	57*	13.84	0	1	442	384	7	54.85	2-39	0	0	5.21	4	
Lim	1993/94	104	97	8	2382	115	26.76	2	15	3906	3276	80	40.95	4-35	2	0	5.03	30	
20T	2006/07	24	20	1	261	67	13.73	0	2	404	488	21	23.23	5-16	0	1	7.24	5	
BANIK, Rajesh Dhrubalal (Tripura) b Agartala, Tripura 12.12.1984 RHB LB																			
FC		4	7	0	106	36	15.14	0	0	9	10	1	10.00	1-5	0	0	6.66	5	
FC	2000/01	24	45	2	907	76	21.09	0	4	153	114	2	57.00	1-5	0	0	4.47	27	
Lim	2001/02	16	15	2	318	101*	24.46	1	0	18	32	1	32.00	1-32	0	0	10.66	5	
20T	2006/07	4	4	0	37	18	9.25	0	0									1	
BANIK, Soumya Sukamal (Tripura) b Agartala, Tripura 14.12.1987 LHB OB																			
FC		1	2	0	1	1	0.50	0	0									0	
Lim	2006/07	4	4	0	36	24	9.00	0	0									0	
BANSAL, Harmeet Singh (Deccan Chargers, Punjab) b Jodhpur, Rajasthan 9.10.1987 RHB RM																			
FC		5	6	2	28	11	7.00	0	0	893	423	13	32.53	3-28	0	0	2.84	0	
20T		9	4	2	0	0*	0.00	0	0	150	187	8	23.37	2-24	0	0	7.48	1	

Cmp	Debut	M	I	NO	Runs	HS	Avge	100	50	Balls	Runs	Wkts	Avge	BB	5i	10m	RpO	ct	st
Lim	2008/09	2	1	0	4	4	4.00	0	0	90	70	2	35.00	2-33	0	0	4.66	0	
20T	2009	16	4	2	0	0*	0.00	0	0	287	379	11	34.45	2-23	0	0	7.92	4	
BANSAL, Neeraj (Haryana) b Devsar, Jammu and Kashmir 27.12.1988 RHB OB																			
Lim		1	1	1	6	6*		0	0									0	
BARATH, Adrian Boris (Trinidad and Tobago, West Indies, Kings XI Punjab, Trinidad and Tobago to India, West Indies to Australia) b Chaguanas, Trinidad 14.4.1990 RHB OB																			
20T		6	6	1	148	63	29.60	0	1									1	
Test	2009/10	2	4	0	139	104	34.75	1	0	6	3	0					3.00	2	
FC	2006/07	26	46	3	1963	192	45.65	6	10	12	3	0					1.50	17	
Int	2009/10	5	5	0	131	50	26.20	0	1									1	
Lim	2006/07	17	17	0	463	72	27.23	0	3	6	0	0					0.00	5	
I20T	2009/10	1	1	0	8	8	8.00	0	0									1	
20T	2009/10	12	12	3	329	66*	36.55	0	3									2	
BAWNE, Ankit Ramdas (Maharashtra) b Paitha, Aurangabad, Maharashtra 17.12.1992 RHB OB																			
FC		5	10	0	369	136	36.90	2	0									1	
Lim		3	3	0	45	31	15.00	0	0									0	
FC	2007/08	9	17	0	529	136	31.11	2	1	54	43	0					4.77	2	
Lim	2008/09	7	7	1	132	41*	22.00	0	0									1	
BEHERA, Deepak Rasananda (Orissa) b Cuttack, Orissa 15.1.1985 RHB RM																			
20T		4	1	1	2	2*		0	0	60	62	2	31.00	1-6	0	0	6.20	2	
BEHERA, Natraj Bhuban (Orissa) b Rourkela, Orissa 28.5.1988 RHB OB																			
Lim		4	4	0	152	61	38.00	0	2	6	14	0					14.00	0	
20T		4	4	0	34	27	8.50	0	0									2	
FC	2008/09	1	2	0	36	22	18.00	0	0	120	29	0					1.45	1	
Lim	2008/09	11	11	0	339	61	30.81	0	2	125	103	3	34.33	2-12	0	0	4.94	4	
20T	2006/07	5	5	1	41	27	10.25	0	0									3	
BEHERA, Niranjan Jayaram (Orissa) b Cuttack, Orissa 2.5.1984 RHB OB																			
FC		7	11	1	407	95	40.70	0	5	330	151	0					2.74	3	
Lim		2	2	0	82	44	41.00	0	0									0	
20T		4	4	1	121	57	40.33	0	1	66	75	2	37.50	1-18	0	0	6.81	1	
FC	2002/03	46	71	7	2053	103	32.07	1	19	3454	1077	29	37.13	4-16	0	0	1.87	27	
Lim	1999/00	30	25	2	649	90	28.21	0	4	1231	890	28	31.78	4-13	3	0	4.33	7	
20T	2006/07	12	12	1	346	57	31.45	0	3	240	259	14	18.50	3-11	0	0	6.47	3	
BEIGH, Samiullah (Jammu and Kashmir) b Srinigar, Jammu and Kashmir 15.4.1981 RHB RFM																			
FC		4	7	1	105	51*	17.50	0	1	565	336	9	37.33	2-51	0	0	3.56	0	
Lim		5	5	1	41	15	10.25	0	0	253	251	6	41.83	2-56	0	0	5.95	0	
20T		5	4	2	22	11*	11.00	0	0	114	138	7	19.71	3-15	0	0	7.26	2	
FC	2003/04	24	39	6	584	61	17.69	0	3	4305	2387	67	35.62	6-50	4	0	3.32	10	
Lim	2002/03	23	22	2	212	61	10.60	0	1	1141	1120	25	44.80	4-57	1	0	5.89	2	
20T	2006/07	9	7	5	29	11*	14.50	0	0	193	242	12	20.16	3-15	0	0	7.52	2	
BHAJA, Firdaush Daud (Baroda) b Valan, Gujarat 8.10.1988 RHB RM																			
FC		2	2	0	14	10	7.00	0	0	252	148	6	24.66	4-42	0	0	3.52	1	
20T		4	1	1	17	17*		0	0	66	107	5	21.40	3-43	0	0	9.72	1	
BHALLA, Vishwas (Punjab) b Chandigarh 15.12.1984 RHB RM																			
FC		7	12	4	383	116*	47.87	1	1	186	102	1	102.00	1-34	0	0	3.29	7	
Lim		1	1	0	20	20	20.00	0	0	6	8	0					8.00	0	
Lim	2008/09	2	2	1	128	108*	128.00	1	0	36	25	0					4.16	0	
BHANDARI, Akash Ashok (Hyderabad) b Secunderabad, Andhra Pradesh 10.6.1993 RHB LB																			
Lim		3	3	2	4	3*	4.00	0	0	155	162	2	81.00	1-45	0	0	6.27	0	
20T		3	1	0	20	20	20.00	0	0	70	61	5	12.20	3-25	0	0	5.22	2	
BHARADWAJ, Pawan (Haryana) b Mundhal, Haryana 13.1.1989 RHB SLA																			
Lim		1								18	21	0					7.00	0	
BHATI, Abhishek Rajendersingh (Haryana) b Gautam Budhnagar, Uttar Pradesh 8.9.1989 RHB RM																			
FC		1	1	1	0	0*		0	0	30	9	1	9.00	1-9	0	0	1.80	0	
20T		3	1	1	0	0*		0	0	42	44	1	44.00	1-26	0	0	6.28	0	
BHATI, Lalit Devendermukhiya (Haryana) b Ghaziabad, Uttar Pradesh 23.4.1990 RHB OB																			
20T		1								12	11	0					5.50	0	
BHATI, Naresh Shrinandkishor (Rajasthan) b Jodhpur, Rajasthan 23.11.1984 RHB LB																			
FC		1	2	1	0	0*	0.00	0	0	192	96	0					3.00	0	
BHATIA, Harpreet Singh (Central Zone, Kolkata Knight Riders, Madhya Pradesh) b Durg, Madhya Pradesh 11.8.1991 LHB RM																			
FC		2	1	0	1	1	1.00	0	0	6	5	0					5.00	0	
Lim		8	7	2	306	111*	61.20	1	1	6	9	0					9.00	3	
20T		1																0	
Lim	2007/08	13	12	3	405	111*	45.00	1	1	6	9	0					9.00	4	
BHATIA, Rajat (Delhi, Delhi Daredevils, North Zone) b Delhi 22.10.1979 RHB RMF																			
FC		9	11	1	582	99	58.20	0	7	1014	498	9	55.33	2-51	0	0	2.94	4	
Lim		7	6	2	226	59*	56.50	0	2	270	208	6	34.66	3-35	0	0	4.62	3	
20T		14	12	5	203	44	29.00	0	0	232	297	9	33.00	3-33	0	0	7.68	5	
FC	1999/00	64	89	12	3665	185	47.59	9	18	5463	2099	73	28.75	5-29	1	0	2.30	19	

Cmp	Debut	M	I	NO	Runs	HS	Avge	100	50	Balls	Runs	Wkts	Avge	BB	5i	10m	RpO	ct	st
Lim	2000/01	60	53	14	1449	106*	37.15	2	8	1563	1251	31	40.35	3-35	0	0	4.80	21	
20T	2006/07	34	22	6	260	44	16.25	0	0	518	661	26	25.42	4-15	1	0	7.65	10	
BHATIA, Vishal (Himachal Pradesh) b Hamirpur, Himachal Pradesh 6.12.1981 RHB SLA																			
FC		1								114	65	0					3.42	0	
Lim		2								120	70	2	35.00	2-39	0	0	3.50	0	
FC	2001/02	45	61	17	455	44*	10.34	0	0	8280	3764	143	26.32	6-57	8	0	2.72	11	
Lim	2001/02	41	25	11	91	10*	6.50	0	0	1912	1271	55	23.10	6-15	4	1	3.98	13	
20T	2006/07	2								12	22	0					11.00	0	
BHATKAL, Raju Ravi (Karnataka) b Belgaum, Karnataka 1.9.1985 RHB RM																			
Lim		4	3	1	77	38	38.50	0	0	121	99	6	16.50	3-21	0	0	4.90	1	
FC	2006/07	2	3	1	74	42	37.00	0	0	210	85	3	28.33	3-53	0	0	2.42	1	
Lim	2005/06	15	12	2	207	46	20.70	0	0	355	256	10	25.60	3-21	0	0	4.32	2	
20T	2006/07	9	5	3	22	8	11.00	0	0	111	117	8	14.62	3-8	0	0	6.32	7	
BHATT, Bhargav Ashokbhai (Baroda) b Baroda (now Vadodara), Gujarat 13.5.1990 RHB OB																			
FC		1	1	0	9	9	9.00	0	0	222	112	3	37.33	2-75	0	0	3.02	1	
BHATT, Rujul Haren (Gujarat) b Ahmedabad, Gujarat 24.4.1986 LHB OB																			
FC		7	12	1	410	186	37.27	1	1	270	128	3	42.66	2-44	0	0	2.84	3	
Lim		1	1	0	4	4	4.00	0	0	30	15	0					3.00	0	
20T		3	3	1	32	18*	16.00	0	0	42	71	2	35.50	2-27	0	0	10.14	2	
Lim	2008/09	5	5	0	125	58	25.00	0	2	258	202	5	40.40	2-49	0	0	4.69	1	
20T	2006/07	6	5	2	40	18*	13.33	0	0	84	141	2	70.50	2-27	0	0	10.07	2	
BHIKANE, Kishor Prakash (Maharashtra) b Latur, Maharashtra 18.12.1987 RHB RFM																			
FC		1	2	0	62	47	31.00	0	0	162	106	2	53.00	2-89	0	0	3.92	0	
Lim		3	3	1	23	16*	11.50	0	0	162	156	5	31.20	3-76	0	0	5.77	2	
20T		3	1	0	1	1	1.00	0	0	66	67	3	22.33	3-19	0	0	6.09	1	
BHONDEKAR, Shailesh Namdeo (Vidarbha) b Ramtek, Maharashtra 9.12.1991 RHB RFM																			
Lim		1	1	0	5	5	5.00	0	0	30	24	0					4.80	0	
BHOSALE, Rohan Udaysingh (Maharashtra) b Bombay (now Mumbai), Maharashtra 30.9.1988 RHB RM																			
FC		6	12	0	217	82	18.08	0	1									2	
20T		4	4	1	121	54*	40.33	0	1									0	
FC	2008/09	12	24	1	526	82	22.86	0	3									3	
Lim	2008/09	1	1	0	140	140	140.00	1	0									0	
BHOWMIK, Gopesh Barun (Tripura) b Chandrapur, Tripura 2.4.1987 RHB RFM																			
Lim		3	1	0	23	23	23.00	0	0	160	106	4	26.50	2-37	0	0	3.97	0	
20T		1								24	42	0					10.50	0	
FC	2008/09	2	4	1	9	5	3.00	0	0	198	81	2	40.50	2-43	0	0	2.45	1	
Lim	2007/08	8	5	1	30	23	7.50	0	0	304	223	7	31.85	2-37	0	0	4.40	1	
BHUVNESHWAR Kumar SINGH (Royal Challengers Bangalore, Uttar Pradesh) b Meerut, Uttar Pradesh 5.2.1990 RHB RM																			
FC		8	13	0	295	75	22.69	0	2	1332	678	19	35.68	5-27	1	0	3.05	1	
Lim		4	4	0	44	35	11.00	0	0	78	65	1	65.00	1-21	0	0	5.00	0	
20T		4	2	0	24	17	12.00	0	0	84	106	1	106.00	1-16	0	0	7.57	1	
FC	2007/08	22	36	4	827	80	25.84	0	4	3793	1760	60	29.33	5-27	4	0	2.78	4	
Lim	2007/08	16	15	5	270	72	27.00	0	1	647	477	17	28.05	3-31	0	0	4.42	2	
BILAKHIA, Azharuddin Arjun (Baroda, Deccan Chargers) b Mohwa, Bhavnagar, Gujarat 31.5.1986 RHB RM																			
FC		5	10	0	199	91	19.90	0	1									2	
20T		5	5	1	131	80*	32.75	0	1									2	
FC	2005/06	25	44	0	1433	157	32.56	2	5	111	64	0					3.45	15	
Lim	2005/06	16	16	0	495	96	30.93	0	5									4	
20T	2006/07	19	19	3	377	80*	23.56	0	3									4	
BILLA, Jitender (Haryana) b Raisinghnagar, Haryana 14.12.1986 RHB RM																			
20T		4	2	2	6	6*		0	0	74	72	7	10.28	3-10	0	0	5.83	0	
FC	2007/08	8	11	5	73	20	12.16	0	0	1665	772	37	20.86	6-58	2	0	2.78	1	
Lim	2006/07	11	7	3	20	12*	5.00	0	0	412	410	9	45.55	3-35	0	0	5.97	4	
20T	2006/07	13	5	3	24	11	12.00	0	0	286	317	25	12.68	4-26	1	0	6.65	9	
BINNY, Stuart Terence Roger (Karnataka, Mumbai Indians) b Bangalore, Karnataka 3.6.1984 RHB RM																			
FC		3	5	1	116	66	29.00	0	1	198	86	2	43.00	2-20	0	0	2.60	3	
Lim		5	4	1	99	41	33.00	0	0	204	181	3	60.33	2-34	0	0	5.32	4	
20T		3	3	1	13	8	6.50	0	0	36	45	3	15.00	2-26	0	0	7.50	0	
FC	2003/04	21	34	2	629	66	19.65	0	2	1158	586	12	48.83	2-20	0	0	3.03	13	
Lim	2003/04	23	19	5	307	74	21.92	0	1	678	585	13	45.00	4-29	1	0	5.17	11	
BIRLA, Udit Alok (Madhya Pradesh) b Calcutta (now Kolkata), Bengal 17.11.1989 RHB RM																			
20T		3	3	1	13	10*	6.50	0	0									2	
BISATI, Rauf Ahmed (Jammu and Kashmir) b Srinigar, Kashmir 12.9.1979 RHB																			
Lim		2	2	0	37	31	18.50	0	0									0	
Lim	2004/05	7	7	1	119	31	19.83	0	0									0	
BISHNOI, Rajesh Kinyaram (Rajasthan) b Bikaner, Rajasthan 10.8.1987 RHB RM																			
FC		2	3	0	2	2	0.66	0	0	18	14	0					4.66	2	
Lim		4	4	1	51	27	17.00	0	0	54	46	0					5.11	1	
FC	2006/07	17	29	3	619	97	23.80	0	4	180	111	1	111.00	1-27	0	0	3.70	5	
Lim	2005/06	16	16	2	427	94	30.50	0	2	208	183	1	183.00	1-47	0	0	5.27	3	
20T	2006/07	4	4	0	32	18	8.00	0	0									1	

Cmp	Debut	M	I	NO	Runs	HS	Avge	100	50	Balls	Runs	Wkts	Avge	BB	5i	10m	RpO	ct	st
BISHT, Punit (Delhi) b Delhi 15.6.1986 RHB OB																			
FC		8	11	3	543	128*	67.87	2	2									30	2
Lim		5	3	1	75	51	37.50	0	1									4	3
20T		7	5	1	68	27	17.00	0	0									6	
FC	2006/07	31	39	4	1150	156	32.85	3	4									97	3
Lim	2005/06	23	12	3	273	118	30.33	1	1									28	5
20T	2006/07	12	9	2	122	27	17.42	0	0									9	3
BISLA, Manvinder Sultansingh (Jammu and Kashmir, Kings XI Punjab) b Hisar, Haryana 27.12.1984 RHB WK																			
FC		4	7	0	103	46	14.71	0	0									23	1
20T		15	15	1	352	75*	25.14	0	2									7	1
FC	2002/03	35	60	5	1640	168	29.81	4	6	120	63	0					3.15	104	13
Lim	2003/04	29	28	3	531	81	21.24	0	3	36	15	0					2.50	21	11
20T	2006/07	20	20	2	430	75*	23.88	0	2									15	1
BIST, Neeraj Ramprasad (Hyderabad) b Hyderabad, Andhra Pradesh 3.4.1990 RHB RFM																			
Lim		2	2	1	133	70*	133.00	0	2	30	21	0					4.20	0	
20T		3	3	0	41	29	13.66	0	0	30	37	1	37.00	1-25	0	0	7.40	1	
BIST, Robin Dinesh (Rajasthan) b Delhi 2.11.1987 RHB OB																			
FC		3	5	1	64	47*	16.00	0	0	12	8	0					4.00	0	
Lim		4	4	1	143	57	47.66	0	2	36	46	1	46.00	1-46	0	0	7.66	1	
FC	2007/08	16	28	4	901	136	37.54	1	5	42	30	1	30.00	1-13	0	0	4.28	4	
Lim	2006/07	12	12	3	239	57	26.55	0	2	36	46	1	46.00	1-46	0	0	7.66	2	
20T	2006/07	4	4	1	42	25*	14.00	0	0	60	74	5	14.80	2-19	0	0	7.40	1	
BISWAL, Subit Subodha (Orissa) b Cuttack, Orissa 8.10.1984 RHB OB																			
FC		1	2	0	8	6	4.00	0	0									1	
Lim		3	3	0	52	28	17.33	0	0									2	
FC	2002/03	23	37	2	872	122	24.91	1	7	18	10	0					3.33	2	
Lim	2003/04	19	18	1	484	105	28.47	1	2									8	
20T	2006/07	6	6	2	65	20*	16.25	0	0									3	
BOLLINGER, Douglas Erwin (Australia, New South Wales, Australia to England, Australia to India, Australia to Ireland, Australia to New Zealand, Chennai Super Kings, New South Wales to India) b Baulkham Hills, Sydney, New South Wales, Australia 24.7.1981 LHB LFM																			
Int		4	1	0	0	0	0.00	0	0	234	174	9	19.33	5-35	0	1	4.46	2	
Lim		4	1	0	0	0	0.00	0	0	234	174	9	19.33	5-35	0	1	4.46	2	
20T		14	2	2	18	16*		0	0	330	337	16	21.06	4-13	1	0	6.12	4	
Test	2008/09	10	10	4	42	21	7.00	0	0	2083	1085	44	24.65	5-28	2	0	3.12	2	
FC	2002/03	64	69	30	301	31*	7.71	0	0	11574	6324	222	28.48	6-47	12	2	3.27	23	
Int	2008/09	26	4	2	4	3	2.00	0	0	1288	930	42	22.14	5-35	1	2	4.33	5	
Lim	2002/03	80	22	11	51	7*	4.63	0	0	3932	3023	113	26.75	5-35	3	2	4.61	15	
20T	2005/06	27	3	2	23	16*	23.00	0	0	571	701	27	25.96	4-13	1	0	7.36	6	
BOND, Shane Edward (Canterbury, New Zealand, Kolkata Knight Riders, New Zealand to South Africa, New Zealand to United Arab Emirates, New Zealand to West Indies) b Christchurch, Canterbury, New Zealand 7.6.1975 RHB RF																			
20T		8	1	0	1	1	1.00	0	0	186	224	9	24.88	2-24	0	0	7.22	1	
Test	2001/02	18	20	7	168	41*	12.92	0	0	3372	1922	87	22.09	6-51	5	1	3.42	8	
FC	1996/97	60	70	20	830	100	16.60	1	2	10263	5478	225	24.34	7-66	12	1	3.20	24	
Int	2001/02	82	40	22	292	31*	16.22	0	0	4295	3070	147	20.88	6-19	7	4	4.28	15	
Lim	1997/98	135	70	33	498	40	13.45	0	0	6903	5083	214	23.75	6-19	9	5	4.41	18	
I20T	2005/06	20	8	3	21	8*	4.20	0	0	465	543	25	21.72	3-18	0	0	7.00	4	
20T	2005/06	40	14	6	32	8*	4.00	0	0	939	1109	51	21.74	4-19	1	0	7.08	9	
BOPARA, Ravinder Singh (England, England Lions, Essex, Auckland, England to South Africa, England to West Indies, Kings XI Punjab) b Forest Gate, Essex, England 4.5.1985 RHB RM																			
20T		10	9	1	248	77	31.00	0	2	78	127	5	25.40	3-31	0	0	9.76	4	
Test	2007/08	10	15	0	502	143	33.46	3	0	296	199	1	199.00	1-39	0	0	4.03	5	
FC	2002	103	172	22	6332	229	42.21	17	25	6946	4585	107	42.85	5-75	1	0	3.96	67	
Int	2006/07	54	50	10	1140	60	28.50	0	4	391	331	10	33.10	4-38	1	0	5.07	18	
Lim	2001	164	155	32	4607	201*	37.45	6	24	3303	2943	109	27.00	4-38	3	0	5.34	49	
I20T	2008	11	10	0	191	55	19.10	0	1									4	
20T	2003	91	81	9	1807	105*	25.09	1	10	1108	1431	60	23.85	3-13	0	0	7.74	29	
BOSE, Ranadeb Ranjit (Bengal, East Zone) b Calcutta (now Kolkata), Bengal 27.2.1979 RHB RMF																			
FC		7	8	2	21	6*	3.50	0	0	1403	748	30	24.93	5-18	3	1	3.19	4	
Lim		8	2	2	1	1*		0	0	402	367	8	45.87	4-39	1	0	5.47	0	
20T		2	1	0	7	7	7.00	0	0	30	44	2	22.00	1-19	0	0	8.80	0	
FC	1998/99	80	93	19	338	21	4.56	0	0	15719	7195	300	23.98	7-24	24	6	2.74	17	
Lim	1998/99	82	35	11	121	17	5.04	0	0	4052	3144	126	24.95	6-35	6	3	4.65	13	
20T	2006/07	11	3	1	7	7	3.50	0	0	234	334	11	30.36	4-40	1	0	8.56	0	
BOUCHER, Mark Verdon (South Africa, Warriors, Royal Challengers Bangalore, South Africa, South Africa to India, South Africa to West Indies) b East London, Cape Province, South Africa 3.12.1976 RHB RM WK																			
Test		1	1	0	39	39	39.00	0	0									3	
FC		1	1	0	39	39	39.00	0	0									3	
Int		3	2	0	19	14	9.50	0	0									6	1
Lim		3	2	0	19	14	9.50	0	0									6	1
20T		9	3	1	18	11*	9.00	0	0									5	3

Cmp	Debut	M	I	NO	Runs	HS	Avge	100	50	Balls	Runs	Wkts	Avge	BB	5i	10m	RpO	ct	st
Test	1997/98	134	189	22	5171	125	30.96	5	33	8	6	1	6.00	1-6	0	0	4.50	482	22
FC	1995/96	196	285	40	8279	134	33.79	9	51	26	26	1	26.00	1-6	0	0	6.00	660	36
Int	1997/98	292	218	56	4664	147*	28.79	1	26									400	22
Lim	1995/96	357	281	67	6137	147*	28.67	2	35									473	30
I20T	2005/06	25	21	6	268	36*	17.86	0	0									18	1
20T	2003/04	64	51	18	871	57*	26.39	0	2									38	9
BRAHMBHATT, Tatsat Mayankbhai (Gujarat) b Ahmedabad, Gujarat 27.12.1986 RHB RFM																			
FC		2	3	0	14	12	4.66	0	0	342	196	5	39.20	3-39	0	0	3.43	1	
BRAVO, Dwayne John (Trinidad and Tobago, West Indies, Essex, Mumbai Indians, Trinidad and Tobago to India, Victoria, West Indies to Australia) b Santa Cruz, Trinidad 7.10.1983 RHB RFM																			
20T		16	14	3	157	58*	14.27	0	1	289	418	16	26.12	4-23	1	0	8.67	6	
Test	2004	37	68	1	2175	113	32.46	3	13	6164	3270	83	39.39	6-55	2	0	3.18	39	
FC	2001/02	94	173	7	5193	197	31.28	8	29	10461	5621	168	33.45	6-11	7	0	3.22	81	
Int	2003/04	107	87	16	1715	112*	24.15	1	5	4260	3721	129	28.84	4-19	4	0	5.24	44	
Lim	2002	144	121	20	2312	112*	22.89	1	7	5489	4677	172	27.19	6-46	6	1	5.11	60	
I20T	2005/06	22	20	5	344	66*	22.93	0	2	338	491	19	25.84	4-38	1	0	8.71	5	
20T	2005/06	74	64	15	1208	70*	24.65	0	8	1315	1811	70	25.87	4-23	2	0	8.26	32	
BUNDELA, Devendrasingh (Madhya Pradesh) b Indore, Madhya Pradesh 22.2.1977 RHB RM																			
FC		4	3	0	281	153	93.66	1	1	42	31	0					4.42	1	
FC	1995/96	99	161	24	6039	167*	44.08	15	30	4819	2287	50	45.74	6-37	2	1	2.84	55	
Lim	1995/96	79	75	21	2283	125*	42.27	1	13	1419	1144	27	42.37	4-32	2	0	4.83	29	
20T	2006/07	8	8	0	110	32	13.75	0	0	24	24	0					6.00	4	
CHAHAL, Yuzvendra Singh (Haryana) b Jind, Haryana 23.7.1990 RHB LBG																			
FC		3	4	0	19	17	4.75	0	0	181	81	5	16.20	4-22	0	0	2.68	0	
Lim		5	4	2	8	5	4.00	0	0	150	109	1	109.00	1-13	0	0	4.36	0	
20T		5	2	1	3	3*	3.00	0	0	105	76	5	15.20	2-6	0	0	4.34	1	
CHAHAR, Deepak Lokandersingh (Rajasthan) b Agra, Uttar Pradesh 17.8.1992 RHB RM																			
Lim		1	1	0	5	5	5.00	0	0	60	61	2	30.50	2-61	0	0	6.10	0	
CHAKRABARTY, Dibyendu Pratul (Bengal) b Howrah (now Haora), Bengal 15.11.1982 RHB RM																			
FC		2	3	1	48	19	24.00	0	0	18	8	0					2.66	1	
20T		2	1	0	37	37	37.00	0	0									1	
FC	2008/09	6	10	1	332	82	36.88	0	3	18	8	0					2.66	2	
Lim	2003/04	8	6	1	106	28	21.20	0	0	24	27	0					6.75	1	
20T	2006/07	9	5	0	84	37	16.80	0	0									3	
CHAND, Unmukt (Delhi) b Delhi 25.3.1993 RHB RAB																			
Lim		3	3	0	116	74	38.66	0	1									0	
20T		2	2	0	5	5	2.50	0	0									0	
CHANDA, Timir Kajal (Tripura) b Agartala, Tripura 25.6.1978 RHB RM																			
FC		3	4	2	60	26*	30.00	0	0	564	211	14	15.07	5-56	2	0	2.24	2	
Lim		4	3	0	32	21	10.66	0	0	210	133	4	33.25	2-42	0	0	3.80	0	
FC	1995/96	49	89	5	1871	134	22.27	1	10	4662	2439	84	29.03	5-56	2	0	3.13	25	
Lim	1995/96	43	42	5	540	58*	14.59	0	1	1492	1290	38	33.94	4-28	1	0	5.18	6	
20T	2006/07	4	3	0	16	13	5.33	0	0	83	118	4	29.50	3-37	0	0	8.53	0	
CHANDILA, Ajit (Haryana) b Faridabad, Punjab 5.12.1983 RHB OB																			
Lim		4	4	1	20	9	6.66	0	0	181	131	4	32.75	3-25	0	0	4.34	2	
Lim	2003/04	5	5	1	26	9	6.50	0	0	205	159	5	31.80	3-25	0	0	4.65	2	
CHANWARIA, Vinod Seetaram (Rajasthan) b Bikaner, Rajasthan 25.11.1985 RHB RM																			
FC		2	3	0	5	4	1.66	0	0	288	118	6	19.66	2-33	0	0	2.45	4	
FC	2008/09	4	7	0	112	88	16.00	0	1	480	242	8	30.25	2-33	0	0	3.02	4	
Lim	2004/05	6	6	1	156	59	31.20	0	1	93	71	2	35.50	1-10	0	0	4.58	2	
CHATARJEE, Soomik (Services) b Howrah, Bengal 27.9.1988 LHB LB																			
Lim		4	4	1	60	33	20.00	0	0	56	56	1	56.00	1-27	0	0	6.00	1	
FC	2006/07	12	24	2	606	118	27.54	2	2	78	48	0					3.69	6	
Lim	2007/08	13	13	2	344	71*	31.27	0	2	68	69	1	69.00	1-27	0	0	6.08	4	
CHATTERJEE, Sudip Dipen (Bengal) b Barasat, Bengal 11.11.1991 LHB LB																			
Lim		2	2	0	60	53	30.00	0	1									0	
CHAUHAN, Abhimanyu Ravindrapalsingh (Baroda) b Bhilai, Madhya Pradesh 29.9.1986 RHB RFM																			
FC		1	1	0	37	37	37.00	0	0	78	36	2	18.00	1-6	0	0	2.76	1	
Lim		4	4	2	95	53*	47.50	0	1	144	134	5	26.80	3-28	0	0	5.58	0	
FC	2005/06	7	7	1	139	37	23.16	0	0	438	192	3	64.00	1-6	0	0	2.63	3	
CHAUHAN, Bhushan Maheshbhai (Saurashtra) b Rajkot, Saurashtra 29.10.1984 RHB RAB																			
FC		1	2	0	37	33	18.50	0	0									1	
FC	2004/05	12	17	0	472	114	27.76	2	1	6	2	0					2.00	9	
Lim	2008/09	3	3	0	22	22	7.33	0	0									2	
CHAUHAN, Neeraj (Himachal Pradesh) b Tropher, Himachal Pradesh 21.10.1987 RHB OB																			
Lim		2	2	0	42	31	21.00	0	0	48	53	1	53.00	1-34	0	0	6.62	1	
20T		2	2	1	10	6*	10.00	0	0	12	17	0					8.50	1	
CHAUHAN, Nileshkumar Babulal (Gujarat) b Rajkot, Saurashtra 30.9.1983 RHB LBG WK																			
Lim		4	3	2	37	21*	37.00	0	0	228	193	6	32.16	3-50	0	0	5.07	1	
CHAUHAN, Rikin Pareshbhai (Gujarat) b Mansa, Gujarat 18.6.1986 LHB SLA																			
FC		3	4	0	87	53	21.75	0	1	66	48	1	48.00	1-19	0	0	4.36	2	

Cmp	Debut	M	I	NO	Runs	HS	Avge	100	50	Balls	Runs	Wkts	Avge	BB	5i	10m	RpO	ct	st
CHAVAN, Ankeet Anil (Mumbai) b Bombay (now Mumbai), Maharashtra 28.10.1985 LHB SLA																			
20T		1	1	1	23	23*		0	0	6	17	0					17.00	1	
FC	2008/09	2	2	0	21	20	10.50	0	0	289	142	3	47.33	2-19	0	0	2.94	1	
Lim	2007/08	8	6	2	83	24*	20.75	0	0	270	262	2	131.00	1-39	0	0	5.82	3	
CHAWDA, Krushnasinh Gajendrasinh (Services) b Varsoda, Gandhinagar, Gujarat 2.10.1981 RHB WK																			
20T		3	3	2	41	24	41.00	0	0									0	1
FC	2001/02	20	30	1	555	56	19.13	0	3									25	4
Lim	2002/03	9	8	0	73	27	9.12	0	0									8	2
CHAWLA, Himanshu (Punjab) b Delhi 31.5.1991 RHB LBG																			
Lim		4	1	0	6	6	6.00	0	0	78	86	2	43.00	2-43	0	0	6.61	1	
CHAWLA, Piyush Pramod (Central Zone, Kings XI Punjab, Sussex to India, Uttar Pradesh, India to West Indies, India to Zimbabwe) b Aligarh, Uttar Pradesh 24.12.1988 LHB LBG																			
FC		9	14	2	493	90*	41.08	0	5	1928	1059	36	29.41	5-73	1	0	3.29	7	
Lim		7	5	0	65	48	13.00	0	0	354	281	10	28.10	6-46	0	1	4.76	3	
20T		19	11	2	120	25	13.33	0	0	401	498	19	26.21	3-24	0	0	7.45	4	
Test	2005/06	2	2	0	5	4	2.50	0	0	205	137	3	45.66	2-66	0	0	4.01	0	
FC	2005/06	61	89	9	2257	102*	28.21	1	17	13495	6742	247	27.29	6-46	15	2	2.99	29	
Int	2007	21	10	5	28	13*	5.60	0	0	1102	911	28	32.53	4-23	2	0	4.96	9	
Lim	2005/06	73	47	13	702	93	20.64	0	4	3547	2938	108	27.20	6-46	5	1	4.97	24	
I20T	2010	3								66	69	2	34.50	1-14	0	0	6.27	2	
20T	2006/07	56	31	10	291	33	13.85	0	0	1131	1378	57	24.17	3-22	0	0	7.31	18	
CHELUVARAJ, Vairamudi Gowda (Railways) b Bangalore, Karnataka 5.9.1986 RHB WK																			
FC		7	11	1	372	93	37.20	0	3									7	
Lim		4	3	0	59	38	19.66	0	0									3	2
FC	2008/09	9	14	1	466	93	35.84	0	4									8	1
Lim	2008/09	9	8	0	245	76	30.62	0	1									5	2
CHERUVATHUR, Sony Kuriakose (Kerala) b Chengannur, Kerala 26.8.1978 RHB RM																			
FC		4	5	1	60	28	15.00	0	0	602	276	12	23.00	6-31	1	1	2.75	0	
FC	2003/04	23	34	7	436	49	16.14	0	0	3920	1871	72	25.98	7-30	5	2	2.86	9	
Lim	2001/02	15	13	1	197	80	16.41	0	1	638	574	16	35.87	4-38	1	0	5.39	2	
20T	2006/07	5	4	0	25	20	6.25	0	0	96	114	3	38.00	2-21	0	0	7.12	0	
CHHABRA, Gaurav (Delhi) b Delhi 19.11.1987 RHB RM																			
FC		6	9	0	292	100	32.44	1	1									2	
FC	2008/09	7	10	0	355	100	35.50	1	2									2	
Lim	2005/06	4	3	0	25	23	8.33	0	0									1	
20T	2006/07	1	1	0	10	10	10.00	0	0									1	
CHIMKARA, Pravesh (Delhi) b Delhi 11.11.1985 RHB RM																			
Lim		2								84	43	5	8.60	4-19	1	0	3.07	0	
20T		1								18	28	1	28.00	1-28	0	0	9.33	0	
CHITNIS, Siddharth Dilip (Mumbai) b Bombay (now Mumbai), Maharashtra 6.5.1987 RHB OB																			
20T		4	3	2	96	89*	96.00	0	1	18	30	1	30.00	1-24	0	0	10.00	0	
20T	2007/08	8	6	2	120	89*	30.00	0	1	54	90	3	30.00	2-40	0	0	10.00	1	
CHOPRA, Aakash Shyamlal (Delhi) b Agra, Uttar Pradesh 19.9.1977 RHB RM																			
FC		4	6	0	65	22	10.83	0	0									6	
20T		5	5	0	98	31	19.60	0	0									0	
Test	2003/04	10	19	0	437	60	23.00	0	2									15	
FC	1997/98	133	220	22	9073	239*	45.82	24	44	534	297	6	49.50	2-5	0	0	3.33	164	
Lim	1996/97	58	55	7	2293	130*	47.77	7	16	84	58	1	58.00	1-17	0	0	4.14	28	
20T	2007/08	12	11	0	151	31	13.72	0	0									2	
CHOUDHARY, Kishan Jogindersingh (Rajasthan) b Udaipur, Rajasthan 22.12.1981 RHB RM																			
Lim		2	2	0	11	10	5.50	0	0	120	107	3	35.66	3-47	0	0	5.35	2	
FC	2002/03	8	12	4	70	19	8.75	0	0	1164	559	17	32.88	4-28	0	0	2.88	1	
Lim	2000/01	11	8	3	23	10	4.60	0	0	570	473	15	31.53	4-61	1	0	4.97	6	
CHOUDHARY, Rohit (Uttar Pradesh) b Chhilora, Uttar Pradesh 14.12.1987 RHB RFM																			
Lim		3	3	2	10	5*	10.00	0	0	156	131	5	26.20	2-47	0	0	5.03	2	
CHOWDHARY, Ishwar Haribhai (Gujarat) b Sagthala, Gujarat 10.7.1988 RHB RFM																			
FC		1	1	0	4	4	4.00	0	0	222	173	2	86.50	2-118	0	0	4.67	0	
Lim		3	2	0	2	2	1.00	0	0	180	162	3	54.00	2-64	0	0	5.40	1	
FC	2008/09	4	5	2	21	15	7.00	0	0	594	368	8	46.00	3-55	0	0	3.71	1	
20T	2006/07	2								22	53	1	53.00	1-16	0	0	14.45	0	
CHOWDHURY, Debabrata Dilip (Tripura) b Udaipur, Tripura 27.3.1987 LHB RFM																			
FC		6	9	1	166	78	20.75	0	1	180	93	1	93.00	1-4	0	0	3.10	2	
FC	2005/06	8	13	1	173	78	14.41	0	1	180	93	1	93.00	1-4	0	0	3.10	2	
CHOWDHURY, Subal Dwijendrakishore (Tripura) b Agartala, Tripura 6.12.1979 RHB LB																			
FC		6	8	0	68	22	8.50	0	0	486	259	13	19.92	5-35	1	0	3.19	5	
20T		2	2	0	11	8	5.50	0	0									0	
FC	1995/96	44	82	2	1420	118	17.75	1	5	2311	1474	41	35.95	5-35	2	0	3.82	42	
Lim	1995/96	38	38	4	564	64	16.58	0	1	342	318	4	79.50	2-37	0	0	5.57	14	
20T	2006/07	6	6	0	97	43	16.16	0	0	49	53	2	26.50	2-21	0	0	6.49	0	

Cmp	Debut	M	I	NO	Runs	HS	Avge	100	50	Balls	Runs	Wkts	Avge	BB	5i	10m	RpO	ct	st
CHOWHAN, Dinesh Surbir (Services) b Dehra Dun, Uttar Pradesh 3.3.1975 RHB RM																			
20T		1	1	1	4	4*		0	0	24	32	0					8.00	0	
Lim	1998/99	1	1	0	11	11	11.00	0	0									0	
20T	2006/07	4	4	2	21	14*	10.50	0	0	54	63	2	31.50	2-20	0	0	7.00	1	
COLLINGWOOD, Paul David (Durham, England, Delhi Daredevils, England to Bangladesh, England to South Africa, England to Scotland, England to United Arab Emirates, England to West Indies) b Shotley Bridge, Co Durham, England 26.5.1976 RHB RM																			
20T		8	7	2	203	75*	40.60	0	3	89	101	5	20.20	2-19	0	0	6.80	4	
Test	2003/04	63	109	10	4176	206	42.18	10	20	1719	945	15	63.00	3-23	0	0	3.29	87	
FC	1996	188	325	26	10977	206	36.71	24	56	9665	4928	121	40.72	5-52	1	0	3.05	214	
Int	2001	189	173	35	4978	120*	36.07	5	26	4898	4095	106	38.63	6-31	3	1	5.01	105	
Lim	1995	359	337	59	9469	120*	34.06	8	54	9444	7651	221	34.61	6-31	4	1	4.86	182	
I20T	2005	33	31	2	561	79	19.34	0	3	222	329	16	20.56	4-22	1	0	8.89	12	
20T	2005	52	47	5	855	79	20.35	0	6	463	579	36	16.08	5-14	2	1	7.50	16	
DAGAR, Mukul (Haryana) b Delhi 17.12.1990 LHB RAB																			
Lim		1	1	0	0	0	0.00	0	0									0	
DAHIYA, Rohit Pradeepbhai (Gujarat) b Khanda, Gujarat 31.3.1988 RHB RFM																			
Lim		2	2	0	46	36	23.00	0	0	102	98	1	98.00	1-39	0	0	5.76	0	
20T		3	3	0	7	4	2.33	0	0	66	86	6	14.33	3-27	0	0	7.81	0	
Lim	2008/09	6	5	2	126	36	42.00	0	0	314	289	8	36.12	3-46	0	0	5.52	3	
DARBAR, Rajdeep Dilipbhai (Gujarat) b Gadhda, Gujarat 14.9.1987 RHB WK																			
Lim		4	4	0	105	46	26.25	0	0									4	1
DAS, Anup Kamalkantaa (Assam) b Barpeta, Assam 27.7.1991 RHB RM																			
Lim		1	1	0	1	1	1.00	0	0	48	43	1	43.00	1-43	0	0	5.37	0	
20T		2	1	0	0	0	0.00	0	0	48	67	2	33.50	1-33	0	0	8.37	0	
Lim	2008/09	3	3	0	8	6	2.66	0	0	150	134	3	44.66	1-39	0	0	5.36	2	
DAS, Arindam Shibendranarayan (Bengal, East Zone) b Calcutta (now Kolkata), Bengal 16.10.1981 RHB RM																			
FC		7	12	2	571	144	57.10	2	3	6	2	0					2.00	6	
Lim		3	3	0	88	59	29.33	0	1									1	
FC	2001/02	57	98	8	3096	215*	34.40	6	17	12	7	0					3.50	63	
Lim	2001/02	24	24	1	935	78	40.65	0	8									8	
DAS, Bappa Santiranjan (Tripura) b Udaipur, Tripura 15.10.1985 RHB RFM																			
Lim		2	2	1	108	61*	108.00	0	1	24	19	0					4.75	0	
20T		4	4	0	37	18	9.25	0	0									2	
FC	2005/06	4	6	1	55	18*	11.00	0	0	60	19	0					1.90	1	
Lim	2005/06	10	10	1	257	61*	28.55	0	2	126	72	0					3.42	1	
20T	2006/07	7	6	1	41	18	8.20	0	0	12	24	0					12.00	2	
DAS, Halhadar Michu (East Zone, Orissa) b Dhenkamal, Orissa 10.12.1986 RHB WK																			
FC		6	9	2	380	144	54.28	1	1									24	
Lim		6	6	0	192	88	32.00	0	1									7	1
FC	2006/07	29	46	8	1407	144	37.02	2	9									89	5
Lim	2005/06	23	20	3	582	88*	34.23	0	4									28	6
20T	2006/07	9	8	5	36	13*	12.00	0	0									7	6
DAS, Pritamjeet (Orissa) b Rourkela, Orissa 15.11.1986 RHB LFM																			
FC		2	2	0	9	9	4.50	0	0	321	212	3	70.66	1-55	0	0	3.96	0	
20T		3								66	43	2	21.50	1-10	0	0	3.90	0	
FC	2006/07	11	17	7	101	27	10.10	0	0	1652	865	25	34.60	5-63	1	0	3.14	1	
Lim	2005/06	13	6	4	24	20*	12.00	0	0	670	517	20	25.85	4-27	2	0	4.63	2	
20T	2006/07	11	2	0	3	2	1.50	0	0	221	208	9	23.11	2-13	0	0	5.64	2	
DAS, Pritamkumar Laru (Assam) b Tarapur, Assam 16.10.1988 RHB RM																			
FC		1	2	0	0	0	0.00	0	0	126	67	0					3.19	0	
Lim		2	1	1	3	3*		0	0	108	146	1	146.00	1-77	0	0	8.11	0	
20T		3								55	48	4	12.00	2-15	0	0	5.23	2	
FC	2006/07	2	4	0	4	4	1.00	0	0	363	172	5	34.40	5-65	1	0	2.84	1	
Lim	2006/07	5	3	1	14	10	7.00	0	0	204	241	4	60.25	2-40	0	0	7.08	0	
20T	2006/07	7	4	0	10	7	2.50	0	0	140	164	8	20.50	3-27	0	0	7.02	6	
DAS, Rajdeep Nabendu (Assam) b Bhagabhazar, Assam 11.3.1990 RHB WK																			
FC		1	1	0	0	0	0.00	0	0									0	
20T		2	1	0	4	4	4.00	0	0									2	
FC	2007/08	5	8	2	159	49	26.50	0	0									12	1
Lim	2007/08	3	3	0	19	17	6.33	0	0									3	
DAS, Rashmi Ranjan (Orissa) b Cuttack, Orissa 7.10.1981 RHB RM																			
FC		4	3	0	37	18	12.33	0	0									2	
Lim		4	4	0	135	104	33.75	1	0									3	
20T		4	4	0	94	45	23.50	0	0									2	
FC	1999/00	20	27	3	576	101	24.00	1	3									10	
Lim	1999/00	22	18	3	444	104	29.60	1	1									13	
20T	2006/07	12	12	1	248	56	22.54	0	1									7	
DAS, Swapan Chintaharan (Tripura) b Sonamura, South Tripura 12.10.1990 RHB RM																			
FC		1	1	0	8	8	8.00	0	0									1	
Lim		4	3	0	49	35	16.33	0	0	36	19	0					3.16	4	

Cmp	Debut	M	I	NO	Runs	HS	Avge	100	50	Balls	Runs	Wkts	Avge	BB	5i	10m	RpO	ct	st
20T		4	4	1	31	15*	10.33	0	0	30	44	2	22.00	2-25	0	0	8.80	1	
Lim	2008/09	6	5	1	113	41*	28.25	0	0	60	46	1	46.00	1-8	0	0	4.60	4	
DAS, Subhomoy Gopinath (Bengal) b Calcutta (now Kolkata), Bengal 26.12.1981 RHB OB																			
Lim		3	3	0	18	12	6.00	0	0									2	
FC	2001/02	36	59	4	1911	129	34.74	3	11	12	1	0					0.50	31	
Lim	2001/02	39	37	5	941	126*	29.40	1	4									8	
20T	2006/07	5	5	1	107	79*	26.75	0	1									1	
DAS, Shiv Sunder (Orissa) b Bhubaneswar, Orissa 5.11.1977 RHB RM																			
FC		7	11	0	294	119	26.72	1	0									5	
Test	2000/01	23	40	2	1326	110	34.89	2	9	66	35	0					3.18	34	
FC	1993/94	163	272	14	10364	300*	40.17	24	48	382	194	4	48.50	1-0	0	0	3.04	154	
Int	2001/02	4	4	1	39	30	13.00	0	0									0	
Lim	1994/95	81	80	6	2421	133*	32.71	4	13	190	136	0					4.29	21	
DASGUPTA, Deep Biplab (Bengal) b Calcutta (now Kolkata), Bengal 7.6.1977 RHB WK																			
FC		5	9	1	230	61	28.75	0	4									5	
20T		3	3	0	69	42	23.00	0	0									0	
Test	2001/02	8	13	1	344	100	28.66	1	2									13	
FC	1998/99	83	136	9	3801	171	29.92	6	21									191	22
Int	2001/02	5	4	1	51	24*	17.00	0	0									2	1
Lim	1999/00	53	42	8	776	65	22.82	0	3									45	11
20T	2006/07	9	8	1	97	42	13.85	0	0									1	6
DATTA, Rana Kajal (Tripura) b Udaipur, Tripura 15.5.1989 RHB RFM																			
FC		6	7	1	43	15	7.16	0	0	762	406	13	31.23	3-54	0	0	3.19	1	
Lim		4	2	2	3	2*		0	0	204	148	5	29.60	2-22	0	0	4.35	0	
20T		3	3	3	17	12*		0	0	60	76	2	38.00	2-22	0	0	7.60	1	
FC	2008/09	7	9	2	87	43	12.42	0	0	990	500	13	38.46	3-54	0	0	3.03	1	
Lim	2008/09	8	6	3	99	51	33.00	0	1	404	311	11	28.27	4-43	1	0	4.61	1	
DEB, Rahul Ratan (Railways) b Calcutta (now Kolkata), Bengal 31.8.1978 RHB RAB WK																			
FC		1	1	0	13	13	13.00	0	0									3	1
Lim	2005/06	12	8	3	111	32*	22.20	0	0									10	5
20T	2006/07	8	4	2	38	17*	19.00	0	0									6	7
DEBNATH, Jayanta Shantibhushan (Tripura) b Agartala, Tripura 29.7.1983 RHB OB																			
FC		4	6	4	34	10*	17.00	0	0	609	291	6	48.50	2-32	0	0	2.86	1	
FC	2000/01	29	47	25	175	36	7.95	0	0	5378	2224	76	29.26	6-101	3	0	2.48	11	
Lim	2001/02	19	9	2	41	13	5.85	0	0	883	643	15	42.86	3-39	0	0	4.36	6	
DEBNATH, Pritam Khokhan (Assam) b Guwahati, Assam 25.7.1987 RHB OB																			
FC		1	1	1	11	11*		0	0									0	
Lim		1	1	0	20	20	20.00	0	0									1	
20T		2	2	0	56	55	28.00	0	1									0	
FC	2008/09	2	3	1	18	11*	9.00	0	0									0	
DEEPAK KUMAR, Mukkerila (Andhra) b Srikakulam, Andhra Pradesh 5.8.1988 RHB RM																			
20T		3	3	0	13	9	4.33	0	0									0	
DESAI, Aniket Kamlakar (Goa) b Mapusa, Goa 29.8.1988 LHB RFM																			
FC		2	1	0	9	9	9.00	0	0	30	6	0					1.20	0	
FC	2007/08	6	8	0	60	37	7.50	0	0	30	6	0					1.20	3	
Lim	2007/08	2	1	0	0	0	0.00	0	0									1	
20T	2006/07	4	4	0	35	19	8.75	0	0									0	
DESAI, Jaykumar Dineshchandra (Gujarat) b Kathodia, Gujarat 30.1.1987 RHB OB																			
FC		7	12	0	295	108	24.58	1	1	24	22	0					5.50	5	
Lim		3	3	0	55	35	18.33	0	0									1	
20T		4	4	1	108	41	36.00	0	0	2	4	0					12.00	1	
FC	2007/08	10	18	1	349	108	20.52	1	1	36	31	0					5.16	6	
Lim	2006/07	4	4	0	75	35	18.75	0	0	30	28	0					5.60	1	
20T	2006/07	12	11	2	212	51*	23.55	0	1	30	66	0					13.20	4	
DEVDHAR, Kedar Hemant (Baroda) b Baroda (now Vadodara), Gujarat 14.12.1989 RHB WK																			
FC		1	2	1	55	53*	55.00	0	1									0	
Lim		4	4	0	110	62	27.50	0	1									3	
Lim	2007/08	14	14	0	266	69	19.00	0	2									5	
DE VILLIERS, Abraham Benjamin (South Africa, Titans to South Africa, Delhi Daredevils, South Africa to India, South Africa to West Indies) b Pretoria, Transvaal, South Africa 17.2.1984 RHB RM																			
Test		2	3	0	68	53	22.66	0	1									2	
FC		2	3	0	68	53	22.66	0	1									2	
Int		3	3	2	241	114*	241.00	2	0									1	
Lim		3	3	2	241	114*	241.00	2	0									1	
20T		7	7	0	111	45	15.85	0	0									6	
Test	2004/05	61	105	12	4232	217*	45.50	10	23	198	99	2	49.50	2-49	0	0	3.00	86	1
FC	2003/04	85	148	17	6081	217*	46.41	13	37	228	133	2	66.50	2-49	0	0	3.50	132	2
Int	2004/05	101	97	14	3616	146	43.56	7	22	12	22	0					11.00	63	
Lim	2003/04	126	121	17	4642	146	44.63	9	30	12	22	0					11.00	84	
I20T	2005/06	30	29	6	579	79*	25.17	0	4									32	4
20T	2003/04	69	65	12	1574	105*	29.69	1	9									62	6

Cmp	Debut	M	I	NO	Runs	HS	Avge	100	50	Balls	Runs	Wkts	Avge	BB	5i	10m	RpO	ct	st
DEV SINGH, Ian Chauhan (Jammu and Kashmir) b Gandhinagar, Gujarat 1.3.1989 RHB OB																			
FC		3	5	0	106	64	21.20	0	1									0	
Lim		5	5	0	156	112	31.20	1	0									1	
FC	2007/08	11	21	0	606	104	28.85	1	5	24	24	0					6.00	6	
Lim	2006/07	17	16	1	565	112	37.66	1	3	36	41	0					6.83	2	
20T	2006/07	4	4	0	87	48	21.75	0	0	1	4	0					24.00	3	
DEWAN, Rahul (Haryana, North Zone) b Delhi 15.7.1986 RHB OB																			
FC		7	11	1	489	133*	48.90	1	4	240	172	0					4.30	6	
Lim		8	8	1	368	131*	52.57	1	2	125	90	4	22.50	4-18	1	0	4.32	4	
20T		5	5	0	152	47	30.40	0	0	6	3	1	3.00	1-3	0	0	3.00	2	
FC	2008/09	13	21	2	1003	254*	52.78	2	7	294	210	0					4.28	11	
Lim	2008/09	15	15	1	547	131*	39.07	1	3	125	90	4	22.50	4-18	1	0	4.32	5	
DEY, Abhijit Apanchandra (Tripura) b Belnia 30.12.1987 RHB OB																			
FC		2	2	0	39	35	19.50	0	0	174	120	1	120.00	1-100	0	0	4.13	0	
Lim		2	2	0	13	13	6.50	0	0									0	
FC	2005/06	10	17	1	300	37	18.75	0	0	846	418	11	38.00	3-16	0	0	2.96	8	
Lim	2005/06	10	9	0	60	20	6.66	0	0	147	113	5	22.60	2-34	0	0	4.61	2	
DHARMANI, Pankaj (Punjab) b Delhi 27.9.1974 RHB WK																			
FC		8	12	0	385	83	32.08	0	3									4	
FC	1992/93	141	204	25	8989	305*	50.21	24	41	26	11	0					2.53	261	20
Int	1996/97	1	1	0	8	8	8.00	0	0									0	
Lim	1994/95	121	106	25	3211	95	39.64	0	23	3	9	0					18.00	113	27
20T	2006/07	11	7	2	47	16*	9.40	0	0									9	9
DHAWAN, Rishi (Himachal Pradesh) b Mandi, Himachal Pradesh 19.2.1990 RHB RM																			
FC		2	4	0	24	13	6.00	0	0	102	63	1	63.00	1-17	0	0	3.70	1	
Lim		5	3	1	37	31	18.50	0	0	246	191	6	31.83	2-41	0	0	4.65	0	
20T		7	6	3	92	49	30.66	0	0	72	106	3	35.33	1-14	0	0	8.83	0	
Lim	2007/08	11	6	2	62	31	15.50	0	0	401	300	9	33.33	2-41	0	0	4.48	1	
20T	2006/07	8	6	3	92	49	30.66	0	0	72	106	3	35.33	1-14	0	0	8.83	1	
DHAWAN, Shikhar (Delhi, India Red, Mumbai Indians, North Zone, India A to England, India A to Scotland) b Delhi 5.12.1985 LHB																			
FC		6	7	0	453	224	64.71	2	0	24	20	0					5.00	4	
Lim		10	10	2	605	155*	75.62	1	4									8	
20T		15	15	1	380	75*	27.14	0	4									7	
FC	2004/05	50	79	5	3408	224	46.05	9	15	126	62	1	62.00	1-18	0	0	2.95	45	
Lim	2004/05	69	69	10	2704	155*	45.83	7	13	104	96	3	32.00	1-1	0	0	5.53	32	
20T	2006/07	39	38	6	856	75*	26.75	0	8									20	
DHIRAJ KUMAR Singh (Orissa) b Cuttack, Orissa 21.11.1987 RHB SLA																			
FC		6	6	4	4	4	2.00	0	0	1299	751	25	30.04	4-29	0	0	3.46	2	
Lim		5	2	2	2	1*		0	0	180	157	1	157.00	1-37	0	0	5.23	2	
FC	2008/09	11	15	5	9	4	0.90	0	0	2409	1221	38	32.13	7-83	1	0	3.04	5	
Lim	2008/09	9	2	2	2	1*		0	0	366	314	5	62.80	2-25	0	0	5.14	2	
DHONI, Mahendra Singh (Chennai Super Kings, India, India Blue, India to Bangladesh, India to South Africa, India to Sri Lanka, India to West Indies) b Ranchi, Bihar (now Jharkhand) 7.7.1981 RHB WK																			
Test		5	6	2	377	132*	94.25	3	0									15	
FC		5	6	2	377	132*	94.25	3	0									15	
Int		12	11	2	567	124	63.00	2	3									7	5
Lim		15	14	3	661	124	60.09	2	3	27	22	1	22.00	1-14	0	0	4.88	8	5
I20T		2	2	0	55	46	27.50	0	0									0	
20T		15	13	2	342	66*	31.09	0	2									5	6
Test	2005/06	46	70	9	2556	148	41.90	4	18	12	14	0					7.00	119	20
FC	1999/00	87	136	12	4734	148	38.17	7	32	42	34	0					4.85	226	41
Int	2004/05	171	153	40	5733	183*	50.73	7	37	12	14	1	14.00	1-14	0	0	7.00	170	55
Lim	1999/00	227	205	50	7735	183*	49.90	13	48	39	36	2	18.00	1-14	0	0	5.53	237	70
I20T	2006/07	25	24	7	441	46	25.94	0	0									11	3
20T	2006/07	72	66	20	1597	73*	34.71	0	7									29	13
DHRUVE, Rakesh Vinubhai (Saurashtra) b Jamnagar, Gujarat 12.5.1981 LHB SLA																			
FC		5	7	1	108	42	18.00	0	0	1047	531	16	33.18	5-107	1	0	3.04	1	
Lim		2	1	1	2	2*		0	0	84	85	1	85.00	1-50	0	0	6.07	0	
20T		4	4	2	69	27*	34.50	0	0	66	98	5	19.60	4-20	1	0	8.90	0	
FC	1999/00	63	93	12	2125	117	26.23	1	9	10275	4641	154	30.13	5-20	5	0	2.71	28	
Lim	1999/00	41	34	9	621	70*	24.84	0	3	2096	1782	41	43.46	3-23	0	0	5.10	14	
20T	2006/07	8	7	3	94	27*	23.50	0	0	156	192	8	24.00	4-20	1	0	7.38	3	
DHRUV SINGH (Haryana) b Gurgaon, Haryana 2.5.1986 RHB RMF																			
FC		5	6	0	85	33	14.16	0	0	414	196	3	65.33	2-11	0	0	2.84	3	
Lim		2	1	0	33	33	33.00	0	0	66	47	5	9.40	5-32	0	1	4.27	0	
FC	2008/09	10	13	1	279	74*	23.25	0	1	967	403	15	26.86	5-56	1	0	2.50	5	
Lim	2006/07	13	11	2	368	68*	40.88	0	3	144	133	6	22.16	5-32	0	1	5.54	3	
20T	2006/07	9	6	2	51	18*	12.75	0	0	18	27	0					9.00	4	

Cmp	Debut	M	I	NO	Runs	HS	Avge	100	50	Balls	Runs	Wkts	Avge	BB	5i	10m	RpO	ct	st
DHURI, Saheel Suhas (Goa) b Panjim, Goa 25.6.1983 RHB RFM																			
Lim		1	1	1	27	27*		0	0	32	18	1	18.00	1-18	0	0	3.37	1	
FC	2004/05	11	19	1	363	107*	20.16	1	0	557	223	8	27.87	3-21	0	0	2.40	3	
Lim	2005/06	17	16	2	207	46	14.78	0	0	650	537	9	59.66	2-34	0	0	4.95	6	
20T	2006/07	5	5	1	133	65*	33.25	0	1	114	140	5	28.00	2-24	0	0	7.36	1	
DILSHAN, Tillakaratne Mudiyanselage (Basnahira South, Bloomfield, Sri Lanka, Delhi Daredevils, Northern Districts, Sri Lanka to Bangladesh, Sri Lanka to India, Sri Lanka to South Africa, Sri Lanka to United States of America, Sri Lanka to West Indies, Sri Lanka to Zimbabwe) b Kalutara, Sri Lanka 14.10.1976 RHB OB																			
Test		3	5	0	248	112	49.60	2	0	48	38	0					4.75	4	
FC		3	5	0	248	112	49.60	2	0	48	38	0					4.75	4	
Int		5	5	0	353	160	70.60	2	0	48	59	0					7.37	4	
Lim		5	5	0	353	160	70.60	2	0	48	59	0					7.37	4	
I20T		2	2	0	35	34	17.50	0	0	12	24	1	24.00	1-14	0	0	12.00	1	
20T		12	12	0	128	34	10.66	0	0	121	143	7	20.42	2-16	0	0	7.09	9	
Test	1999/00	63	101	11	3906	168	43.40	11	15	1184	590	16	36.87	4-10	0	0	2.99	73	
FC	1993/94	198	320	22	11572	200*	38.83	30	48	3796	1844	59	31.25	5-49	1	0	2.91	334	27
Int	1999/00	188	165	29	4860	160	35.73	8	20	2881	2281	54	42.24	4-29	2	0	4.75	80	1
Lim	1996/97	272	243	41	7654	188	37.89	13	36	3972	3084	83	37.15	4-17	3	0	4.65	154	8
I20T	2006	31	30	5	717	96*	28.68	0	5	120	151	4	37.75	2-4	0	0	7.55	13	2
20T	2004/05	77	74	9	1606	96*	24.70	0	11	433	491	17	28.88	3-23	0	0	6.80	37	3
DINDA, Ashok Bhimchandra (Bengal, East Zone, India, India Blue, Kolkata Knight Riders, India to Sri Lanka, India to Zimbabwe) b Medinipur, Calcutta (now Kolkata), Bengal 25.3.1984 RHB RMF																			
FC		5	5	2	57	41	19.00	0	0	1047	630	11	57.27	3-65	0	0	3.61	3	
Lim		11	6	3	55	28*	18.33	0	0	594	571	18	31.72	3-52	0	0	5.76	3	
I20T		1	1	0	19	19	19.00	0	0	18	34	1	34.00	1-34	0	0	11.33	0	
20T		12	4	1	21	19	7.00	0	0	241	279	14	19.92	2-15	0	0	6.94	0	
FC	2005/06	31	39	17	246	41	11.18	0	0	6189	3307	99	33.40	6-52	7	0	3.20	13	
Int	2010	5	3	0	18	16	6.00	0	0	227	228	3	76.00	2-44	0	0	6.02	0	
Lim	2008/09	28	16	4	107	28*	8.91	0	0	1421	1317	39	33.76	3-52	0	0	5.56	4	
I20T	2009/10	3	1	0	19	19	19.00	0	0	60	76	5	15.20	2-15	0	0	7.60	0	
20T	2007/08	36	9	3	25	19	4.16	0	0	661	774	31	24.96	3-33	0	0	7.02	1	
DIWAKAR, Mihir Singh (Jharkhand) b Siwan, Bihar 10.12.1982 RHB RFM																			
FC		1	1	0	7	7	7.00	0	0	174	65	1	65.00	1-65	0	0	2.24	0	
20T		3	1	0	1	1	1.00	0	0	61	58	6	9.66	5-6	0	1	5.70	2	
FC	1999/00	39	61	6	926	86	16.83	0	5	7578	4142	129	32.10	7-47	7	1	3.27	14	
Lim	2000/01	36	29	6	280	31	12.17	0	0	1870	1372	59	23.25	4-33	3	0	4.40	8	
20T	2006/07	7	4	0	9	7	2.25	0	0	148	185	11	16.81	5-6	0	1	7.50	3	
DIWAN, Kuldeep (Himachal Pradesh) b Gurgaon, Haryana 21.12.1984 LHB SLA																			
FC		5	7	1	195	83	32.50	0	2	658	333	8	41.62	2-16	0	0	3.03	1	
Lim		5	2	0	9	9	4.50	0	0	299	250	11	22.72	5-39	0	1	5.01	2	
20T		7	2	1	8	8	8.00	0	0	168	190	5	38.00	1-21	0	0	6.78	0	
FC	2004/05	11	15	3	284	83	23.66	0	2	1132	518	20	25.90	3-2	0	0	2.74	1	
Lim	2004/05	15	11	2	149	34*	16.55	0	0	794	579	23	25.17	5-39	0	1	4.37	5	
20T	2006/07	9	3	1	9	8	4.50	0	0	198	229	5	45.80	1-21	0	0	6.93	1	
DOGRA, Hemant (Himachal Pradesh) b Palampur, Himachal Pradesh 6.3.1982 RHB RM																			
FC		2	4	0	74	42	18.50	0	0									1	
Lim		5	5	0	172	64	34.40	0	3									0	
20T		2	2	0	77	41	38.50	0	0									0	
FC	2007/08	4	8	0	235	71	29.37	0	1	6	9	0					9.00	1	
Lim	2007/08	11	11	0	283	74	25.72	0	4									0	
DOGRA, Manish Kumar (Jammu and Kashmir) b Jammu 18.2.1987 LHB RAB WK																			
20T		1	1	0	15	15	15.00	0	0									0	
DOGRA, Paras (Himachal Pradesh, North Zone, Rajasthan Royals) b Palampur, Himachal Pradesh 19.11.1984 RHB LB																			
FC		7	13	1	381	123	31.75	1	1	18	9	0					3.00	10	
Lim		7	6	2	319	109	79.75	1	2									3	
20T		14	13	3	264	58*	26.40	0	2									7	
FC	2001/02	38	63	3	2049	123	34.15	4	9	264	145	1	145.00	1-25	0	0	3.29	44	
Lim	2002/03	39	36	9	1247	109	46.18	1	10									26	
20T	2006/07	19	17	5	408	58*	34.00	0	2									8	
DOLE, Aditya Pradeep (Rajasthan Royals) b Pimpri, Maharashtra 9.10.1987 RHB RM																			
20T		3	2	0	34	30	17.00	0	0	66	112	5	22.40	2-36	0	0	10.18	2	
FC	2006/07	6	6	1	58	31*	11.60	0	0	1031	509	6	84.83	2-15	0	0	2.96	3	
Lim	2005/06	3								48	21	2	10.50	2-11	0	0	2.62	0	
DONGAONKAR, Jayesh Satish (Vidarbha) b Nagpur, Maharashtra 17.2.1987 RHB RFM																			
FC		2	3	1	65	37*	32.50	0	0									3	
DORU, Nikhil Sanat (Rajasthan) b Udaipur, Rajasthan 23.1.1979 RHB RAB WK																			
FC		3	6	0	213	104	35.50	1	0									6	1
FC	1999/00	65	112	11	3137	128*	31.05	7	13	3	4	0					8.00	64	2
Lim	1999/00	36	35	0	772	72	22.05	0	4									4	
20T	2006/07	3	3	0	29	27	9.66	0	0									0	

Cmp	Debut	M	I	NO	Runs	HS	Avge	100	50	Balls	Runs	Wkts	Avge	BB	5i	10m	RpO	ct	st
DOSHI, Nayan Dilip (Royal Challengers Bangalore) b Nottingham, England 6.10.1978 RHB SLA																			
20T		1								24	17	1	17.00	1-17	0	0	4.25	0	
FC	2001/02	62	77	20	530	37	9.29	0	0	10872	5851	149	39.26	7-110	6	3	3.22	11	
Lim	2001	69	31	8	200	38*	8.69	0	0	2887	2619	59	44.38	5-30	1	1	5.44	18	
20T	2004	45	9	5	10	5	2.50	0	0	892	992	62	16.00	4-22	4	0	6.67	12	
DRAVID, Rahul Sharad (India, Karnataka, Royal Challengers Bangalore, India to Bangladesh, India to South Africa, India to Sri Lanka) b Indore, Madhya Pradesh 11.1.1973 RHB OB																			
Test		3	4	0	433	177	108.25	2	1									4	
FC		7	11	3	909	209*	113.62	3	4									12	
Lim		2	2	0	106	77	53.00	0	1									3	
20T		20	14	3	349	52	31.72	0	1									5	
Test	1996	142	245	28	11490	270	52.94	29	58	120	39	1	39.00	1-18	0	0	1.95	196	
FC	1990/91	274	453	63	21873	270	56.08	60	112	617	273	5	54.60	2-16	0	0	2.65	337	1
Int	1995/96	339	313	40	10765	153	39.43	12	82	186	170	4	42.50	2-43	0	0	5.48	196	14
Lim	1992/93	444	411	55	15147	153	42.54	21	111	477	421	4	105.25	2-43	0	0	5.29	233	17
20T	2006/07	49	42	4	1046	75*	27.52	0	5									9	
D'SOUZA, Robin Rone (Goa) b Dubai, United Arab Emirates 2.10.1982 RHB RM																			
FC		4	6	2	113	40*	28.25	0	0	402	219	5	43.80	2-65	0	0	3.26	2	
Lim		4	3	1	45	16	22.50	0	0	108	96	2	48.00	1-22	0	0	5.33	1	
20T		3	3	1	11	9*	5.50	0	0	42	57	1	57.00	1-10	0	0	8.14	4	
FC	2002/03	29	49	8	947	79	23.09	0	4	4065	1933	66	29.28	4-40	0	0	2.85	17	
Lim	2002/03	30	28	4	504	70	21.00	0	2	1088	933	26	35.88	5-38	0	1	5.14	5	
D'SOUZA, Ryan Sunil (Goa) b Panaji, Goa 16.12.1987 RHB RM																			
20T		3	2	1	8	7	8.00	0	0	24	27	1	27.00	1-16	0	0	6.75	0	
FC	2007/08	3	6	0	59	27	9.83	0	0	366	182	4	45.50	2-25	0	0	2.98	1	
Lim	2006/07	13	11	7	65	32*	16.25	0	0	576	457	10	45.70	2-23	0	0	4.76	1	
20T	2006/07	8	5	2	31	13	10.33	0	0	128	186	5	37.20	2-27	0	0	8.71	1	
DUMINY, Jean-Paul (Cape Cobras, Cape Cobras to India, South Africa, Mumbai Indians, South Africa to India, South Africa to West Indies) b Strandfontein, Cape Town, Cape Province, South Africa 14.4.1984 LHB OB																			
Test		2	3	0	15	9	5.00	0	0	138	114	1	114.00	1-73	0	0	4.95	1	
FC		2	3	0	15	9	5.00	0	0	138	114	1	114.00	1-73	0	0	4.95	1	
Int		1	1	0	0	0	0.00	0	0	30	38	0					7.60	0	
Lim		1	1	0	0	0	0.00	0	0	30	38	0					7.60	0	
20T		12	12	5	381	99*	54.42	0	2	88	120	5	24.00	2-10	0	0	8.18	3	
Test	2008/09	12	20	2	518	166	28.77	1	3	671	408	11	37.09	3-89	0	0	3.64	12	
FC	2001/02	61	102	17	4085	169	48.05	12	21	2324	1384	35	39.54	5-108	1	0	3.57	47	
Int	2004	58	51	12	1391	111*	35.66	1	7	697	581	16	36.31	3-31	0	0	5.00	23	
Lim	2002/03	107	92	15	2709	111*	35.18	2	18	1055	880	23	38.26	3-31	0	0	5.00	33	
I20T	2007/08	25	24	5	456	78	24.00	0	2	42	52	4	13.00	1-3	0	0	7.42	12	
20T	2003/04	81	77	18	1961	99*	33.23	0	14	373	444	22	20.18	4-24	1	0	7.14	26	
DUTTA, Raman (Jammu and Kashmir) b Jammu 23.6.1982 RHB RM																			
FC		3	5	0	70	22	14.00	0	0	325	158	9	17.55	3-5	0	0	2.91	1	
20T		5	3	1	5	4	2.50	0	0	120	130	3	43.33	1-20	0	0	6.50	2	
FC	2005/06	9	14	0	139	31	9.92	0	0	1297	577	22	26.22	3-5	0	0	2.66	3	
Lim	2005/06	6	5	1	47	28*	11.75	0	0	251	230	1	230.00	1-46	0	0	5.49	1	
DUTTA, Rajib Kajalkumar (Tripura) b Agartala, Tripura 17.11.1980 RHB OB WK																			
FC		6	8	1	180	60	25.71	0	1									13	1
Lim		4	3	0	64	26	21.33	0	0									9	2
20T		4	4	0	30	13	7.50	0	0									1	
FC	1999/00	43	77	11	1145	81	17.34	0	5									70	14
Lim	1999/00	34	32	6	490	54	18.84	0	1									41	8
20T	2006/07	8	7	0	44	13	6.28	0	0									6	1
DWIVEDI, Eklavya Rakesh (Uttar Pradesh) b Allahabad, Uttar Pradesh 22.7.1988 RHB WK																			
Lim		5	5	1	175	86	43.75	0	2									3	1
Lim	2007/08	9	9	1	290	86	36.25	0	2									10	1
20T	2006/07	2																1	
EDWARDS, Fidel Henderson (Deccan Chargers) b Gays, St Peter, Barbados 6.2.1982 RHB RF																			
20T		2	2	1	8	8*	8.00	0	0	36	55	3	18.33	3-32	0	0	9.16	0	
Test	2003	43	69	21	248	21	5.16	0	0	7259	4811	122	39.43	7-87	8	0	3.97	7	
FC	2001/02	63	97	34	394	40	6.25	0	0	9992	6634	187	35.47	7-87	10	1	3.98	11	
Int	2003/04	50	22	14	73	13	9.12	0	0	2138	1812	60	30.20	6-22	0	2	5.08	4	
Lim	2003/04	65	27	18	105	21*	11.66	0	0	2835	2368	78	30.35	6-22	0	3	5.01	7	
I20T	2007/08	12	2	1	3	2*	3.00	0	0	219	308	10	30.80	3-24	0	0	8.43	2	
20T	2006	24	8	3	20	8*	4.00	0	0	454	579	20	28.95	3-24	0	0	7.65	2	
FALLAH, Samad Mohammed (Maharashtra) b Hyderabad, Andhra Pradesh 2.5.1985 LHB LM																			
FC		6	11	5	63	28	10.50	0	0	1359	807	26	31.03	8-98	2	0	3.56	1	
Lim		3	2	1	1	1	1.00	0	0	173	194	1	194.00	1-56	0	0	6.72	0	
20T		7	1	1	0	0*		0	0	168	196	11	17.81	4-12	1	0	7.00	1	
FC	2007/08	18	29	13	141	28	8.81	0	0	3966	2138	81	26.39	8-98	7	0	3.23	5	
Lim	2007/08	11	6	4	33	32	16.50	0	0	631	600	11	54.54	3-29	0	0	5.70	0	

Cmp	Debut	M	I	NO	Runs	HS	Avge	100	50	Balls	Runs	Wkts	Avge	BB	5i	10m	RpO	ct	st
FARMAN AHMED (Delhi) b Delhi 8.10.1983 RHB RM																			
20T		7	7	0	184	54	26.28	0	1	114	142	6	23.66	4-25	1	0	7.47	2	
FAZAL, Faiz Yakub (Railways, Rajasthan Royals) b Nagpur, Maharashtra 7.9.1985 LHB RMF																			
FC		7	11	0	434	87	39.45	0	3	25	10	0					2.40	0	
Lim		4	4	0	90	40	22.50	0	0	108	94	1	94.00	1-28	0	0	5.22	4	
20T		13	12	1	233	55	21.18	0	1	12	20	0					10.00	8	
FC	2003/04	35	64	5	2339	200*	39.64	3	12	151	83	2	41.50	2-14	0	0	3.29	28	
Lim	2004/05	33	33	1	942	129*	29.43	2	6	264	214	3	71.33	1-12	0	0	4.86	14	
20T	2006/07	18	17	1	285	55	17.81	0	1	12	20	0					10.00	9	
FAZIL MOHAMMAD (Services) b Kurukone, Kollam, Kerala 28.12.1979 RHB RFM																			
Lim		4	3	1	7	4	3.50	0	0	206	161	4	40.25	2-33	0	0	4.68	1	
FC	2003/04	24	31	7	316	51	13.16	0	1	4420	2052	69	29.73	5-58	3	0	2.78	2	
Lim	2000/01	26	17	5	78	24	6.50	0	0	1112	851	29	29.34	6-38	0	1	4.59	4	
20T	2006/07	4	3	0	43	30	14.33	0	0	96	143	3	47.66	3-30	0	0	8.93	0	
FERNANDEZ, Robert Martin (Kerala) b Ernakulam, Kerala 29.9.1986 RHB RM																			
FC		1	2	0	4	2	2.00	0	0									2	
Lim		5	4	0	135	62	33.75	0	1									1	
FC	2005/06	12	21	2	547	124	28.78	1	4	84	63	0					4.50	6	
Lim	2005/06	18	15	1	393	83	28.07	0	3	144	106	1	106.00	1-31	0	0	4.41	1	
FERNANDO, Congenige Randhi Dilhara (Kandurata, Sinhalese, Sri Lanka, Sri Lanka Board President's XI, Mumbai Indians, Sri Lanka to India, Sri Lanka to Zimbabwe) b Colombo, Sri Lanka 19.7.1979 RHB RFM																			
Int		1								54	66	2	33.00	2-66	0	0	7.33	0	
Lim		1								54	66	2	33.00	2-66	0	0	7.33	0	
I20T		2								42	55	1	55.00	1-29	0	0	7.85	0	
20T		7	1	1	2	2*		0	0	156	193	8	24.12	2-23	0	0	7.42	1	
Test	2000	34	40	13	198	36*	7.33	0	0	5314	3188	89	35.82	5-42	3	0	3.60	10	
FC	1997	100	98	28	505	42	7.21	0	0	13440	7979	269	29.66	6-29	6	0	3.56	38	
Int	2000/01	139	56	32	237	20	9.87	0	0	6080	5270	176	29.94	6-27	3	1	5.20	26	
Lim	1998/99	197	82	43	320	21*	8.20	0	0	8764	7287	272	26.79	6-27	5	2	4.98	41	
I20T	2006	15	5	2	24	21	8.00	0	0	318	392	16	24.50	3-19	0	0	7.39	2	
20T	2004/05	38	13	7	36	21	6.00	0	0	834	1024	49	20.89	4-14	2	0	7.36	9	
FINCH, Aaron James (Australia A, Victoria, Rajasthan Royals) b Colac, Victoria, Australia 17.11.1986 RHB LM																			
20T		1	1	0	21	21	21.00	0	0	7	5	0					4.28	0	
FC	2007/08	7	11	0	416	102	37.81	1	3	42	21	0					3.00	4	
Lim	2007/08	19	19	2	489	87*	28.76	0	2									6	
20T	2008/09	13	10	1	291	58*	32.33	0	1	7	5	0					4.28	5	
GADEKAR, Harshad Hanumant (Goa) b Povorim, Goa 5.12.1986 RHB RM																			
Lim		4	1	0	0	0	0.00	0	0	144	134	2	67.00	1-24	0	0	5.58	1	
FC	2007/08	6	6	3	34	11*	11.33	0	0	1086	527	20	26.35	3-27	0	0	2.91	4	
Lim	2007/08	7	3	0	24	15	8.00	0	0	312	278	9	30.88	3-38	0	0	5.34	2	
GAEKWAD, Shatrunjay Anshuman (Baroda) b Baroda, Gujarat 3.9.1983 LHB OB																			
FC		2	4	0	141	118	35.25	1	0									1	
Lim		4	4	0	53	19	13.25	0	0									1	
20T		2	2	2	77	45*		0	0									0	
FC	2003/04	20	34	3	904	118	29.16	1	5									16	
Lim	2007/08	8	8	1	161	39*	23.00	0	0									1	
20T	2006/07	6	6	3	99	45*	33.00	0	0									1	
GAGANDEEP SINGH Toor (Punjab) b Ludhiana, Punjab 3.10.1981 RHB RMF																			
FC		1	1	0	3	3	3.00	0	0	240	101	2	50.50	1-39	0	0	2.52	0	
FC	1999/00	67	85	22	965	50	15.31	0	1	13446	5648	267	21.15	6-14	16	3	2.52	12	
Lim	2000/01	45	16	6	102	12*	10.20	0	0	2285	1462	52	28.11	4-15	2	0	3.83	9	
20T	2006/07	14	2	0	24	15	12.00	0	0	306	370	12	30.83	2-21	0	0	7.25	0	
GAIKWAD, Ganesh Babanrao (Maharashtra) b Pune, Maharashtra 4.12.1987 RHB OB																			
FC		6	12	1	318	63	28.90	0	1	474	309	0					3.91	2	
Lim		4	4	0	68	33	17.00	0	0	174	141	6	23.50	2-35	0	0	4.86	1	
20T		6	5	1	99	34	24.75	0	0	144	127	11	11.54	3-27	0	0	5.29	2	
FC	2008/09	7	14	1	323	63	24.84	0	1	612	406	3	135.33	3-65	0	0	3.98	3	
Lim	2008/09	8	6	1	127	58*	25.40	0	1	396	312	10	31.20	3-40	0	0	4.72	2	
GAJENDRA SINGH Parihar (Rajasthan) b Bikaner, Rajasthan 10.9.1988 RHB SLA																			
FC		2	3	1	18	11	9.00	0	0	355	143	7	20.42	4-46	0	0	2.41	1	
FC	2007/08	9	12	2	68	25*	6.80	0	0	1863	909	22	41.31	4-46	0	0	2.92	7	
Lim	2007/08	2	2	1	20	12	20.00	0	0	82	71	4	17.75	4-22	1	0	5.19	0	
GAMBHIR, Gaurav (Punjab) b Chandigarh, Punjab 26.11.1987 RHB OB																			
FC		2	4	1	118	50*	39.33	0	1	126	81	0					3.85	0	
Lim	2008/09	2	1	1	1	1*		0	0	101	67	2	33.50	2-35	0	0	3.98	1	
GAMBHIR, Gautam (Delhi Daredevils, India, India to Bangladesh, India to South Africa, India to Sri Lanka, India to West Indies) b Delhi 14.10.1981 LHB LB																			
Test		4	6	0	320	167	53.33	2	0									1	
FC		4	6	0	320	167	53.33	2	0									1	
Int		10	9	1	353	150*	44.12	1	2									2	
Lim		10	9	1	353	150*	44.12	1	2									2	

Cmp	Debut	M	I	NO	Runs	HS	Avge	100	50	Balls	Runs	Wkts	Avge	BB	5i	10m	RpO	ct	st
I20T		2	2	0	76	55	38.00	0	1									0	
20T		17	16	1	371	72	24.73	0	3									3	
Test	2004/05	32	57	4	2800	206	52.83	9	11									25	
FC	1999/00	115	195	19	9797	233*	55.66	32	40	385	277	7	39.57	3-12	0	0	4.31	74	
Int	2003	100	96	8	3351	150*	38.07	7	21	6	13	0					13.00	30	
Lim	2000/01	202	196	14	6690	150*	36.75	15	39	37	36	1	36.00	1-7	0	0	5.83	60	
I20T	2007/08	23	22	0	621	75	28.22	0	6									5	
20T	2006/07	72	70	5	1844	86	28.36	0	15									12	
GANAPATHY, Chandrasekharan (Chennai Super Kings, South Zone, Tamil Nadu, India A to England, India A to Scotland) b Madras (now Chennai), Tamil Nadu 10.6.1981 RHB RM																			
FC		10	13	3	594	126	59.40	2	1	1518	682	25	27.28	5-61	2	0	2.69	6	
Lim		7	2	0	13	12	6.50	0	0	342	309	10	30.90	3-41	0	0	5.42	2	
20T		3	2	1	0	0*	0.00	0	0	42	61	2	30.50	1-19	0	0	8.71	0	
FC	2003/04	31	43	17	1101	126	42.34	2	3	4548	2118	72	29.41	5-59	3	0	2.79	13	
Lim	2003/04	33	16	5	120	27*	10.90	0	0	1499	1233	42	29.35	3-34	0	0	4.93	10	
20T	2006/07	12	6	1	4	4	0.80	0	0	214	240	17	14.11	4-12	1	0	6.72	6	
GANESH KUMAR, Timmeri Kuppu (Andhra) b Vijayawada, Andhra Pradesh 22.10.1992 LHB SLA																			
Lim		1	1	0	5	5	5.00	0	0	60	55	0					5.50	1	
GANGULY, Sourav Chandidas (Bengal, Kolkata Knight Riders) b Calcutta (now Kolkata), Bengal 8.7.1972 LHB RM																			
FC		4	5	0	310	152	62.00	1	2	66	36	0					3.27	2	
Lim		5	5	1	253	87*	63.25	0	3	78	73	0					5.61	0	
20T		14	14	1	493	88	37.92	0	4	24	43	0					10.75	7	
Test	1996	113	188	17	7212	239	42.17	16	35	3117	1681	32	52.53	3-28	0	0	3.23	71	
FC	1989/90	246	388	43	15243	239	44.18	32	87	11034	6076	164	37.04	6-46	4	0	3.30	168	
Int	1991/92	311	300	23	11363	183	41.02	22	72	4561	3849	100	38.49	5-16	1	2	5.06	100	
Lim	1989/90	431	415	43	15531	183	41.75	31	97	8027	6527	168	38.85	5-16	4	2	4.87	129	
20T	2005	58	55	3	1408	91	27.07	0	8	513	661	27	24.48	3-27	0	0	7.73	21	
GAUTAM, Chidambaram Muralidharan (Karnataka, South Zone) b Bangalore, Karnataka 8.3.1986 RHB WK																			
FC		10	15	3	533	108*	44.41	2	2									29	1
Lim		8	5	2	174	72	58.00	0	2									7	3
FC	2008/09	13	20	3	731	108*	43.00	3	2									32	1
Lim	2007/08	17	13	3	428	76	42.80	0	4									12	4
GAUTAM, Shiv Prakash (Jharkhand) b Ranchi, Bihar 29.10.1988 RHB WK																			
FC		5	8	2	250	95*	41.66	0	1									11	
Lim		4	3	0	77	40	25.66	0	0									4	1
20T		5	4	3	43	18*	43.00	0	0									3	
Lim	2005/06	8	7	1	198	62	33.00	0	1									6	2
GAVASKAR, Rohan Sunil (Bengal, Kolkata Knight Riders) b Kanpur, Uttar Pradesh 20.2.1976 LHB SLA																			
FC		3	5	2	109	46*	36.33	0	0	144	66	1	66.00	1-56	0	0	2.75	1	
20T		5	4	1	26	19	8.66	0	0	9	12	0					8.00	1	
FC	1996/97	117	181	24	6938	212*	44.19	18	34	3890	1913	38	50.34	5-3	1	0	2.95	63	
Int	2003/04	11	10	2	151	54	18.87	0	1	72	74	1	74.00	1-56	0	0	6.16	5	
Lim	1996/97	126	116	14	3156	101*	30.94	1	18	2492	2062	58	35.55	5-35	0	1	4.96	43	
20T	2005	10	8	1	113	47	16.14	0	0	87	112	3	37.33	1-16	0	0	7.72	1	
GAYLE, Christopher Henry (Jamaica, West Indies, Kolkata Knight Riders, West Indies to Australia, Western Australia) b Kingston, Jamaica 21.9.1979 LHB OB																			
20T		9	9	0	292	88	32.44	0	2	96	152	4	38.00	1-9	0	0	9.50	2	
Test	1999/00	88	155	6	6007	317	40.31	12	33	6851	2992	72	41.55	5-34	2	0	2.62	84	
FC	1998/99	162	288	21	11761	317	44.04	28	59	12127	5012	129	38.85	5-34	2	0	2.48	142	
Int	1999	220	215	15	7885	153*	39.42	19	42	6816	5395	156	34.58	5-46	3	1	4.74	95	
Lim	1998/99	278	272	22	9957	153*	39.82	21	56	8810	6667	209	31.89	5-46	4	1	4.54	115	
I20T	2005/06	20	20	1	617	117	32.47	1	5	209	254	12	21.16	2-15	0	0	7.29	5	
20T	2005	51	50	5	1357	117	30.15	1	8	634	775	30	25.83	3-13	0	0	7.33	17	
GEHLOT, Naresh Gokul (Rajasthan) b Bikaner, Rajasthan 24.12.1982 LHB SLA																			
FC		1	2	0	30	23	15.00	0	0	60	31	2	15.50	2-31	0	0	3.10	0	
FC	2004/05	11	19	2	316	47	18.58	0	0	138	81	2	40.50	2-31	0	0	3.52	5	
Lim	2003/04	11	11	1	230	69	23.00	0	3	99	83	1	83.00	1-39	0	0	5.03	3	
GEHLOT, Shailender Gopalsingh (Railways) b Bhilwara, Rajasthan 23.11.1980 RHB RMF																			
FC		5	5	1	1	1*	0.25	0	0	608	238	10	23.80	3-70	0	0	2.34	1	
Lim		2	1	0	9	9	9.00	0	0	114	114	0					6.00	1	
20T		3								66	72	5	14.40	3-30	0	0	6.54	0	
FC	2004/05	14	19	4	104	47	6.93	0	0	2158	1029	28	36.75	4-97	0	0	2.86	2	
Lim	2002/03	18	10	4	42	15*	7.00	0	0	1002	838	27	31.03	4-25	3	0	5.01	3	
20T	2006/07	7	2	2	1	1*		0	0	150	166	8	20.75	3-30	0	0	6.64	3	
GHOSH, Arindam Nanigopal (Bengal) b Barasat, Bengal 19.10.1986 RHB RM																			
FC		1	1	0	10	10	10.00	0	0									3	
20T		1	1	1	2	2*		0	0									0	
FC	2008/09	4	6	1	91	50	18.20	0	1									4	
Lim	2007/08	2																2	
20T	2006/07	4	3	1	9	7	4.50	0	0									2	

Cmp	Debut	M	I	NO	Runs	HS	Avge	100	50	Balls	Runs	Wkts	Avge	BB	5i	10m	RpO	ct	st
GIBBS, Herschelle Herman (Cape Cobras, Cape Cobras to India, South Africa, South Africa A, Deccan Chargers, South Africa to India, South Africa to West Indies, Yorkshire) b Green Point, Cape Town, Cape Province, South Africa 23.2.1974 RHB LB																			
Int		3	2	0	34	27	17.00	0	0									2	
Lim		3	2	0	34	27	17.00	0	0									2	
20T		14	14	0	310	50	22.14	0	1									9	
Test	1996/97	90	154	7	6167	228	41.95	14	26	6	4	0					4.00	94	
FC	1990/91	193	331	13	13425	228	42.21	31	60	138	78	3	26.00	2-14	0	0	3.39	176	
Int	1996/97	248	240	16	8094	175	36.13	21	37									108	
Lim	1990/91	383	366	32	11860	175	35.50	27	62	66	57	2	28.50	1-16	0	0	5.18	169	
I20T	2005/06	23	23	1	400	90*	18.18	0	3									8	
20T	2003/04	100	98	9	2380	101*	26.74	1	16									54	
GILCHRIST, Adam Craig (Deccan Chargers, Middlesex) b Bellingen, New South Wales, Australia 14.11.1971 LHB OB WK																			
20T		18	18	0	358	54	19.88	0	2									11	5
Test	1999/00	96	137	20	5570	204*	47.60	17	26									379	37
FC	1992/93	190	280	46	10334	204*	44.16	30	43									756	55
Int	1996/97	287	279	11	9619	172	35.89	16	55									417	55
Lim	1992/93	356	343	19	11326	172	34.95	18	63	12	10	0					5.00	526	65
I20T	2004/05	13	13	1	272	48	22.66	0	0									17	
20T	2004/05	68	68	2	1773	109*	26.86	2	9									48	19
GIRAP, Akshay Abhay (Railways) b Bombay (now Mumbai), Maharashtra 5.3.1985 RHB OB																			
FC		1	1	0	23	23	23.00	0	0	48	31	0					3.87	0	
GNANESWARA RAO, Yalaka (Andhra) b Visakhapatnam, Andhra Pradesh 25.8.1984 RHB OB																			
Lim		5	5	0	169	71	33.80	0	2	84	82	1	82.00	1-16	0	0	5.85	2	
20T		3	3	1	93	71*	46.50	0	1									2	
FC	2000/01	40	68	6	1548	111	24.96	1	12	946	433	18	24.05	5-16	1	0	2.74	24	
Lim	2003/04	35	35	3	933	159*	29.15	1	7	462	385	15	25.66	3-42	0	0	5.00	24	
20T	2006/07	8	8	1	235	71*	33.57	0	2	30	42	1	42.00	1-18	0	0	8.40	4	
GODARA, Sandeep (Haryana) b Bhiwani, Haryana 8.12.1987 RHB RFM																			
Lim		2	2	0	7	4	3.50	0	0									0	
Lim	2008/09	3	3	0	27	20	9.00	0	0									0	
GOEL, Karan (Kings XI Punjab, Punjab) b Ludhiana, Punjab 24.12.1986 LHB OB																			
Lim		6	6	1	265	100*	53.00	1	2	126	122	3	40.66	1-17	0	0	5.81	1	
20T		6	2	1	18	17*	18.00	0	0	6	7	0					7.00	2	
FC	2005/06	22	39	2	972	127	26.27	1	5	370	273	5	54.60	2-34	0	0	4.42	10	
Lim	2006/07	26	25	3	989	122	44.95	3	6	318	255	4	63.75	1-17	0	0	4.81	8	
20T	2006/07	32	27	4	531	82	23.08	0	3	97	116	6	19.33	4-13	1	0	7.17	10	
GOMEZ, Raiphi Vincent (Kerala) b Trivandrum (now Thiruvananthapuram), Kerala 16.10.1985 RHB RM																			
FC		4	5	0	120	39	24.00	0	0	438	203	5	40.60	3-33	0	0	2.78	1	
Lim		5	5	1	208	88*	52.00	0	2	117	119	2	59.50	2-43	0	0	6.10	2	
20T		1	1	0	20	20	20.00	0	0	6	14	0					14.00	0	
FC	2006/07	17	28	1	590	108	21.85	2	0	798	392	9	43.55	3-33	0	0	2.94	10	
Lim	2004/05	26	24	2	766	105	34.81	1	5	310	329	3	109.66	2-43	0	0	6.36	5	
20T	2006/07	6	6	0	102	29	17.00	0	0	66	97	1	97.00	1-33	0	0	8.81	2	
GONY, Manpreet Singh (Chennai Super Kings, North Zone, Punjab) b Roopnagar, Punjab 4.1.1984 RHB RM																			
FC		7	9	1	148	41	18.50	0	0	1374	702	33	21.27	5-21	2	1	3.06	2	
Lim		5	2	0	55	42	27.50	0	0	266	225	4	56.25	3-36	0	0	5.07	2	
20T		8	5	1	69	34*	17.25	0	0	163	194	9	21.55	4-16	1	0	7.14	1	
FC	2007/08	20	27	3	406	69	16.91	0	1	3918	2120	65	32.61	5-21	2	1	3.24	4	
Int	2008	2								78	76	2	38.00	2-65	0	0	5.84	0	
Lim	2007/08	17	10	3	75	42	10.71	0	0	859	695	25	27.80	4-35	2	0	4.85	4	
20T	2007/08	31	13	6	117	34*	16.71	0	0	625	809	31	26.09	4-16	1	0	7.76	5	
GOPINATH, Harikrishnan (Tamil Nadu) b Madras (now Chennai), Tamil Nadu 16.6.1988 RHB WK																			
Lim		5	3	3	51	28*		0	0									4	3
20T		4	3	2	33	25*	33.00	0	0									2	1
FC	2007/08	6	8	0	103	37	12.87	0	0									10	1
Lim	2006/07	15	7	4	71	28*	23.66	0	0									20	7
GOSWAMI, Dhiraj Satyen (Assam, East Zone, India Blue) b Nagaon, Assam 1.5.1985 RHB RM																			
FC		7	9	0	102	29	11.33	0	0	794	416	18	23.11	5-57	1	0	3.14	5	
Lim		6	4	1	27	22*	9.00	0	0	244	210	6	35.00	2-23	0	0	5.16	0	
20T		6	4	1	43	26*	14.33	0	0	130	147	10	14.70	3-19	0	0	6.78	2	
FC	2002/03	22	31	2	435	79	15.00	0	1	2993	1549	49	31.61	5-57	1	0	3.10	10	
Lim	2002/03	27	21	6	326	61	21.73	0	1	1212	1010	38	26.57	4-35	2	0	5.00	1	
20T	2006/07	8	6	1	56	26*	11.20	0	0	172	197	12	16.41	3-19	0	0	6.87	3	
GOSWAMI, Shreevats Pratyush (Bengal, East Zone, Royal Challengers Bangalore) b Calcutta (now Kolkata), Bengal 18.5.1989 LHB WK																			
Lim		8	8	2	568	149*	94.66	3	1									4	
20T		4	4	0	59	19	14.75	0	0									0	
FC	2008/09	2	3	0	38	22	12.66	0	0									1	
Lim	2007/08	16	16	2	844	149*	60.28	3	3									4	
20T	2007/08	10	9	0	194	52	21.55	0	1									3	2

Cmp	Debut	M	I	NO	Runs	HS	Avge	100	50	Balls	Runs	Wkts	Avge	BB	5i	10m	RpO	ct	st
GOUD, Yere Karekal Thippana (Railways) b Raichur, Karnataka 27.11.1971 RHB LBG																			
FC		7	9	1	341	79	42.62	0	4									1	
Lim		4	4	0	159	77	39.75	0	1									2	
FC	1994/95	125	199	42	7351	221*	46.82	16	37	961	562	9	62.44	2-29	0	0	3.50	60	
Lim	1995/96	49	39	11	1051	85*	37.53	0	5	66	56	0					5.09	16	
20T	2006/07	7	2	0	17	15	8.50	0	0									2	
GUPTA, Anupan Mithlesh (Baroda) b Bhopal, Madhya Pradesh 26.1.1989 LHB SLA WK																			
Lim		1	1	0	18	18	18.00	0	0									0	
GUPTA, Arjit Ramesh (Rajasthan) b Suratgarh, Rajasthan 12.9.1989 RHB RM																			
FC		2	4	0	165	77	41.25	0	2	28	11	0					2.35	1	
GUPTA, Manik (Jammu and Kashmir) b Dar Khem Chand, Jammu 16.12.1990 LHB LBG																			
Lim		5	5	3	24	10	12.00	0	0	234	224	5	44.80	2-51	0	0	5.74	0	
GUPTA, Praveen Pawan (Uttar Pradesh) b Meerut, Uttar Pradesh 8.12.1986 LHB SLA																			
FC		7	10	5	176	55*	35.20	0	1	966	484	12	40.33	4-83	0	0	3.00	2	
20T		1	1	0	7	7	7.00	0	0	12	17	0					8.50	0	
FC	2002/03	39	59	16	688	74	16.00	0	3	7001	2994	100	29.94	5-11	3	0	2.56	14	
Lim	2002/03	31	20	7	121	21	9.30	0	0	1506	1021	42	24.30	4-18	2	0	4.06	5	
GUPTA, Sunny (Jharkhand) b Jamshedpur, Bihar 27.9.1988 RHB OB																			
FC		3	4	0	23	15	5.75	0	0	847	400	7	57.14	3-40	0	0	2.83	1	
Lim		3	2	1	9	8*	9.00	0	0	112	109	2	54.50	1-7	0	0	5.83	2	
20T		4								72	65	4	16.25	2-15	0	0	5.41	1	
FC	2003/04	19	29	6	318	51	13.82	0	1	3094	1632	40	40.80	4-128	0	0	3.16	9	
Lim	2005/06	13	11	5	86	19*	14.33	0	0	586	429	13	33.00	3-28	0	0	4.39	6	
20T	2006/07	6	2	0	24	22	12.00	0	0	78	85	4	21.25	2-15	0	0	6.53	1	
GURAV, Omkar Dattaram (Mumbai) b Bombay (now Mumbai), Maharashtra 29.6.1988 RHB WK																			
20T		1	1	0	5	5	5.00	0	0									0	1
FC	2007/08	2	3	1	10	10*	5.00	0	0									4	1
HADIYAL, Dilipsinh Madarsinh (Gujarat) b Palanpur, Gujarat 7.9.1982 RHB RMF																			
Lim		1	1	0	21	21	21.00	0	0									0	
20T		3	3	0	27	18	9.00	0	0									0	
Lim	2002/03	11	10	0	149	31	14.90	0	0									2	
HARBHAJAN SINGH (India, India Blue, Mumbai Indians, India to Bangladesh, India to South Africa, India to Sri Lanka, India to West Indies) b Jullundur (now Jalandhar), Punjab 3.7.1980 RHB OB																			
Test		5	5	0	75	39	15.00	0	0	1661	822	23	35.73	5-59	1	0	2.96	2	
FC		5	5	0	75	39	15.00	0	0	1661	822	23	35.73	5-59	1	0	2.96	2	
Int		11	7	1	92	49	15.33	0	0	618	481	14	34.35	2-23	0	0	4.67	0	
Lim		14	9	1	136	49	17.00	0	0	772	584	22	26.54	3-23	0	0	4.53	0	
20T		15	7	3	105	49*	26.25	0	0	321	377	17	22.17	3-31	0	0	7.04	6	
Test	1997/98	85	117	20	1594	66	16.43	0	7	23928	11289	357	31.62	8-84	24	5	2.83	41	
FC	1997/98	149	198	37	3002	84	18.64	0	11	37867	17810	634	28.09	8-84	38	7	2.82	74	
Int	1997/98	212	112	30	1083	49	13.20	0	0	11075	7949	242	32.84	5-31	2	3	4.30	60	
Lim	1997/98	262	143	38	1425	49	13.57	0	0	13567	9661	310	31.16	5-31	4	3	4.27	79	
I20T	2006/07	22	9	2	84	21	12.00	0	0	480	516	16	32.25	3-30	0	0	6.45	6	
20T	2005	66	36	10	386	49*	14.84	0	0	1359	1474	58	25.41	4-17	1	0	6.50	20	
HARDEEP SINGH (Jammu and Kashmir) b Jammu and Kashmir 13.12.1981 RHB RM WK																			
FC		4	7	1	165	41	27.50	0	0	114	56	0					2.94	2	
Lim		3	3	0	39	23	13.00	0	0	24	15	0					3.75	1	
20T		1	1	0	6	6	6.00	0	0									1	
FC	2004/05	13	22	1	532	78	25.33	0	3	444	209	1	209.00	1-11	0	0	2.82	10	
Lim	2001/02	13	12	2	172	35	17.20	0	0	159	128	3	42.66	3-33	0	0	4.83	4	
20T	2006/07	6	6	1	111	51	22.20	0	1	6	12	0					12.00	3	
HARRIS, Ryan James (Australia, Queensland, Australia to England, Australia to Ireland, Australia to New Zealand, Australia to West Indies, Deccan Chargers) b Nowra, New South Wales, Australia 11.10.1979 RHB RFM																			
20T		8	5	1	45	15	11.25	0	0	184	233	14	16.64	3-18	0	0	7.59	5	
Test	2009/10	2	2	1	28	18*	28.00	0	0	423	207	9	23.00	4-77	0	0	2.93	1	
FC	2001/02	40	66	8	1175	94	20.25	0	6	7373	3860	118	32.71	7-108	2	0	3.14	19	
Int	2008/09	17	11	6	43	21	8.60	0	0	845	661	41	16.12	5-19	0	3	4.69	4	
Lim	2000/01	72	45	17	379	39	13.53	0	0	3440	2795	100	27.95	5-19	1	4	4.87	27	
I20T	2009/10	3	1	1	2	2*		0	0	70	95	4	23.75	2-27	0	0	8.14	0	
20T	2006/07	38	22	9	148	31	11.38	0	0	841	1015	50	20.30	3-18	0	0	7.24	12	
HAYDEN, Matthew Lawrence (Chennai Super Kings) b Kingaroy, Queensland, Australia 29.10.1971 LHB RM																			
20T		16	16	0	346	93	21.62	0	1									6	
Test	1993/94	103	184	14	8625	380	50.73	30	29	54	40	0					4.44	128	
FC	1991/92	295	515	47	24603	380	52.57	79	100	1097	671	17	39.47	3-10	0	0	3.67	296	
Int	1993	161	155	15	6133	181*	43.80	10	36	6	18	0					18.00	68	
Lim	1991/92	308	299	29	12051	181*	44.63	27	67	339	358	10	35.80	2-16	0	0	6.33	129	
I20T	2005	9	9	3	308	73*	51.33	0	4									1	
20T	2005	41	41	5	1415	93	39.30	0	12									12	

Cmp	Debut	M	I	NO	Runs	HS	Avge	100	50	Balls	Runs	Wkts	Avge	BB	5i	10m	RpO	ct	st
HEGDE, Abhishek Manjunath (Kerala) b Hyderabad, Andhra Pradesh 1.7.1987 RHB LB																			
Lim		5	5	0	219	121	43.80	1	0									0	
FC	2004/05	2	4	0	49	22	12.25	0	0	18	11	0					3.66	0	
Lim	2004/05	12	12	0	347	121	28.91	1	0									2	
HENRIQUES, Moises Constantino (Australia A, New South Wales, Australia, Australia to India, Delhi Daredevils, New South Wales to India) b Funchal, Portugal 1.2.1987 RHB RFM																			
Int		2	2	0	18	12	9.00	0	0	90	84	1	84.00	1-51	0	0	5.60	0	
Lim		2	2	0	18	12	9.00	0	0	90	84	1	84.00	1-51	0	0	5.60	0	
20T		7	7	1	130	51*	21.66	0	1	123	151	11	13.72	3-11	0	0	7.36	3	
FC	2006/07	16	28	2	799	82	30.73	0	5	1931	1011	28	36.10	5-17	2	0	3.14	7	
Lim	2005/06	36	31	5	538	59	20.69	0	1	1391	1278	29	44.06	3-29	0	0	5.51	15	
I20T	2008/09	1	1	0	1	1	1.00	0	0									0	
20T	2005/06	32	28	4	398	51*	16.58	0	1	502	689	25	27.56	3-11	0	0	8.23	17	
HODGE, Bradley John (Victoria, Kolkata Knight Riders, Leicestershire, Victoria to India) b Sandringham, Victoria, Australia 29.12.1974 RHB OB																			
20T		9	9	1	177	50	22.12	0	1	48	66	2	33.00	1-4	0	0	8.25	3	
Test	2005/06	6	11	2	503	203*	55.88	1	2	12	8	0					4.00	9	
FC	1993/94	223	388	38	17084	302*	48.81	51	64	5583	3086	74	41.70	4-17	0	0	3.31	127	
Int	2005/06	25	21	2	575	123	30.26	1	3	66	51	1	51.00	1-17	0	0	4.63	16	
Lim	1993/94	234	224	28	8255	164	42.11	25	35	1698	1508	40	37.70	5-28	0	1	5.32	90	
I20T	2007/08	8	5	2	94	36	31.33	0	0	12	20	0					10.00	3	
20T	2003	99	96	11	3077	106	36.20	2	21	720	917	43	21.32	4-17	2	0	7.64	38	
HUSSEY, David John (Australia, Victoria, Victoria to India, Australia to England, Australia to New Zealand, Australia to West Indies, Kolkata Knight Riders, Nottinghamshire) b Morley, Western Australia, Australia 15.7.1977 RHB OB																			
20T		11	11	3	174	31*	21.75	0	0	72	97	0					8.08	4	
FC	2002/03	147	227	22	11417	275	55.69	39	50	2348	1486	21	70.76	4-105	0	0	3.79	180	
Int	2008	23	21	0	598	111	28.47	1	4	257	230	3	76.66	1-6	0	0	5.37	12	
Lim	2001	174	163	23	5636	130	40.25	8	37	1480	1302	30	43.40	3-26	0	0	5.27	86	
I20T	2007/08	25	23	3	579	88*	28.95	0	3	252	267	15	17.80	3-25	0	0	6.35	14	
20T	2004	127	122	23	3219	100*	32.51	1	17	814	990	38	26.05	3-25	0	0	7.29	67	
HUSSEY, Michael Edward Killeen (Australia, Australia to England, Australia to India, Australia to Ireland, Australia to New Zealand, Australia to South Africa, Australia to West Indies, Chennai Super Kings) b Morley, Western Australia, Australia 27.5.1975 LHB RM																			
Int		6	6	3	313	81*	104.33	0	3	18	26	0					8.66	1	
Lim		6	6	3	313	81*	104.33	0	3	18	26	0					8.66	1	
20T		3	3	1	37	15	18.50	0	0									0	
Test	2005/06	52	90	12	3981	182	51.03	11	21	180	103	2	51.50	1-3	0	0	3.43	50	
FC	1994/95	235	419	43	19906	331*	52.94	52	92	1620	875	22	39.77	3-34	0	0	3.24	255	
Int	2003/04	146	121	38	4287	109*	51.65	2	31	234	227	2	113.50	1-22	0	0	5.82	82	
Lim	1996/97	339	307	65	10933	123	45.17	11	82	780	821	20	41.05	3-52	0	0	6.31	176	
I20T	2004/05	27	20	7	457	60*	35.15	0	2	6	5	0					5.00	18	
20T	2003	42	34	10	1009	116*	42.04	1	5	6	5	0					5.00	26	
HUWAID Ahmed RONGA (Jammu and Kashmir) b Srinagar, Jammu and Kashmir 4.10.1979 RHB LBG																			
Lim		2	2	0	4	2	2.00	0	0									0	
FC	2004/05	7	13	0	208	41	16.00	0	0									1	
Lim	2003/04	8	8	1	69	21	9.85	0	0									1	
IMRAN KHAN (Services) b Kanpur, Uttar Pradesh 15.5.1973 RHB RM																			
20T		3	3	0	45	31	15.00	0	0									1	
Lim	2006/07	4	4	0	40	31	10.00	0	0									0	
20T	2006/07	8	8	0	125	40	15.62	0	0									1	
IMTIYAZ AHMED (Uttar Pradesh) b Bhadohi, Uttar Pradesh 10.11.1985 RHB RFM																			
Lim		1	1	1	14	14*		0	0	30	32	0					6.40	0	
20T		1	1	0	0	0	0.00	0	0	18	39	0					13.00	0	
FC	2008/09	4	5	2	49	17	16.33	0	0	558	288	9	32.00	3-32	0	0	3.09	2	
Lim	2007/08	7	4	2	22	14*	11.00	0	0	318	214	3	71.33	2-37	0	0	4.03	0	
INDER SINGH, Ravi Mehra (India Green, North Zone, Punjab) b Patiala, Punjab 4.11.1987 LHB OB																			
FC		9	15	0	476	104	31.73	1	2	349	166	3	55.33	1-0	0	0	2.85	5	
Lim		7	7	0	311	98	44.42	0	3	6	8	0					8.00	5	
20T		5	5	1	167	69*	41.75	0	2									0	
FC	2007/08	22	38	2	1289	142	35.80	4	4	511	237	3	79.00	1-0	0	0	2.78	19	
Lim	2007/08	18	18	1	744	126	43.76	2	4	42	36	0					5.14	8	
INDULKAR, Vinit Ajit (Himachal Pradesh) b Sholapur, Maharashtra 26.8.1984 RHB RM																			
FC		7	13	1	466	165	38.83	1	2									3	
Lim		5	4	2	104	40*	52.00	0	0									2	
20T		7	7	1	165	47	27.50	0	0									4	
FC	2004/05	33	54	7	1843	165	39.21	4	8	42	27	0					3.85	30	
Lim	2003/04	23	21	5	628	103	39.25	1	4									7	
20T	2006/07	13	12	1	305	69	27.72	0	1	6	14	1	14.00	1-14	0	0	14.00	7	

Cmp	Debut	M	I	NO	Runs	HS	Avge	100	50	Balls	Runs	Wkts	Avge	BB	5i	10m	RpO	ct	st
IQBAL ABDULLA, Sayed (Kolkata Knight Riders, Mumbai, West Zone, India A to England, India A to Scotland) b Bombay (now Mumbai), Maharashtra 2.12.1989 LHB SLA																			
FC		10	11	3	300	69	37.50	0	3	2155	978	35	27.94	4-48	0	0	2.72	4	
Lim		8	7	3	136	29*	34.00	0	0	390	260	11	23.63	2-24	0	0	4.00	4	
20T		7	2	1	1	1	1.00	0	0	135	148	3	49.33	1-19	0	0	6.57	3	
FC	2007/08	19	20	5	437	69	29.13	0	4	4198	1806	61	29.60	4-42	0	0	2.58	10	
Lim	2006/07	29	23	9	273	29*	19.50	0	0	1444	1052	47	22.38	4-35	1	0	4.37	10	
20T	2006/07	15	6	5	19	10*	19.00	0	0	298	323	14	23.07	5-10	0	1	6.50	4	
IRFAN KHAN (Services) b Secunderabad, Andhra Pradesh 2.7.1988 RHB RM																			
Lim		2	2	0	17	9	8.50	0	0	60	51	0					5.10	1	
20T		2	2	1	4	2*	4.00	0	0	48	57	0					7.12	0	
ISRANI, Devendra Sohanlal (Services) b Varanasi, Uttar Pradesh 1.12.1987 LHB WK																			
20T		1	1	0	0	0	0.00	0	0									0	
FC	2007/08	10	20	1	506	115	26.63	1	1									10	2
Lim	2007/08	5	5	1	64	33	16.00	0	0									3	1
IYER, Shridhar Ramesh (Madhya Pradesh) b 1.1.1988 RHB LB																			
FC		1	1	0	22	22	22.00	0	0	206	158	1	158.00	1-90	0	0	4.60	1	
JACKSON, Sheldon Philip (Saurashtra) b Bhavnagar, Saurashtra 27.9.1986 RHB RAB WK																			
Lim		2	1	0	4	4	4.00	0	0									1	
20T		3	3	0	25	21	8.33	0	0									3	
Lim	2005/06	7	5	0	51	30	10.20	0	0									4	
JADEJA, Balkrishna Nirubha (Saurashtra) b Khambbalia, Gujarat 25.10.1987 RHB LM																			
FC		3	3	0	11	5	3.66	0	0	480	237	1	237.00	1-73	0	0	2.96	1	
20T		4	2	1	4	4	4.00	0	0	95	102	3	34.00	2-17	0	0	6.44	0	
FC	2008/09	9	10	4	40	13*	6.66	0	0	1512	747	19	39.31	6-29	1	0	2.96	2	
Lim	2007/08	8	3	3	19	16*		0	0	423	356	10	35.60	3-68	0	0	5.05	3	
JADEJA, Ravindrasinh Anirudhsinh (India, India Red, Rest of India, Saurashtra, West Zone, India to Bangladesh, India to Sri Lanka, India to West Indies, India to Zimbabwe) b Navagam-Khed, Saurashtra 6.12.1988 LHB SLA																			
FC		7	12	1	417	122*	37.90	1	3	1032	393	16	24.56	4-71	0	0	2.28	7	
Int		14	8	2	192	57	32.00	0	1	669	543	15	36.20	4-32	1	0	4.87	5	
Lim		23	16	5	311	57	28.27	0	1	1099	856	31	27.61	4-8	3	0	4.67	9	
I20T		1								24	30	0					7.50	1	
20T		1								24	30	0					7.50	1	
FC	2006/07	29	44	3	1547	232*	37.73	3	8	5854	2313	81	28.55	7-31	5	1	2.37	22	
Int	2008/09	34	22	5	535	61*	31.47	0	4	1492	1205	29	41.55	4-32	1	0	4.84	11	
Lim	2005/06	62	43	15	959	70	34.25	0	6	2683	2025	69	29.34	4-8	4	0	4.52	22	
I20T	2008/09	9	6	2	65	25	16.25	0	0	186	232	5	46.40	2-26	0	0	7.48	5	
20T	2006/07	40	31	6	549	42	21.96	0	0	393	485	13	37.30	3-15	0	0	7.40	17	
JADHAV, Ashutosh Chandrasekhar (Madhya Pradesh) b Gwalior, Madhya Pradesh 27.1.1987 LHB SLA																			
20T		1																2	
FC	2006/07	5	8	3	196	93*	39.20	0	1	758	313	9	34.77	3-30	0	0	2.47	3	
Lim	2006/07	7	5	0	23	12	4.60	0	0	330	255	7	36.42	3-43	0	0	4.63	1	
20T	2006/07	9	1	1	5	5*		0	0	132	138	5	27.60	2-13	0	0	6.27	2	
JADHAV, Dheeraj Subash (Assam, East Zone) b Malegaon, Maharashtra 16.9.1979 LHB OB																			
FC		8	10	2	631	165*	78.87	3	2	6	2	0					2.00	4	
Lim		4	4	1	222	148*	74.00	1	0									2	
20T		6	5	2	124	69*	41.33	0	1	12	23	0					11.50	0	
FC	1999/00	61	97	12	4576	260*	53.83	14	14	60	28	0					2.80	51	
Lim	2004	31	31	3	1259	148*	44.96	2	9									16	
JADHAV, Kedar Mahadeo (Delhi Daredevils, India Blue, Maharashtra) b Pune, Maharashtra 26.3.1985 RHB OB																			
FC		5	10	1	267	111*	29.66	1	0	12	18	0					9.00	0	
Lim		5	5	0	268	141	53.60	1	1									2	
20T		9	9	3	159	60*	26.50	0	2									4	
FC	2007/08	19	34	6	1282	114*	45.78	2	7	24	35	0					8.75	10	
Lim	2007/08	13	13	1	567	141	47.25	2	2	18	34	0					11.33	8	
20T	2006/07	13	13	4	191	60*	21.22	0	2	54	78	4	19.50	2-23	0	0	8.66	6	
JAFFER, Wasim (India Blue, Mumbai, West Zone) b Bombay (now Mumbai), Maharashtra 16.2.1978 RHB OB																			
FC		13	19	2	801	165*	47.11	3	4									17	
Lim		9	9	0	434	143	48.22	2	1									7	
20T		4	4	0	177	95	44.25	0	1									3	
Test	1999/00	31	58	1	1944	212	34.10	5	11	66	18	2	9.00	2-18	0	0	1.63	27	
FC	1996/97	184	308	28	13868	314*	49.52	39	67	138	74	2	37.00	2-18	0	0	3.21	214	
Int	2006/07	2	2	0	10	10	5.00	0	0									0	
Lim	1996/97	80	80	5	3360	178*	44.80	8	22									39	
20T	2006/07	13	13	0	311	95	23.92	0	2									7	
JAGADEESH, Vasudevanpillai Arundhathiamma (Kerala) b Kottarakara, Kerala 25.5.1983 RHB RM																			
FC		3	3	0	58	50	19.33	0	1	144	42	1	42.00	1-35	0	0	1.75	2	
Lim		5	5	1	288	113	72.00	2	0	198	178	2	89.00	1-26	0	0	5.39	2	
20T		1	1	0	12	12	12.00	0	0	18	28	0					9.33	1	
FC	2004/05	21	35	2	650	109	19.69	1	3	348	128	3	42.66	1-0	0	0	2.20	10	

Cmp	Debut	M	I	NO	Runs	HS	Avge	100	50	Balls	Runs	Wkts	Avge	BB	5i	10m	RpO	ct	st
Lim	2004/05	25	25	6	996	113	52.42	3	4	810	686	14	49.00	2-9	0	0	5.08	5	
20T	2006/07	6	6	2	107	33*	26.75	0	0	102	121	5	24.20	3-23	0	0	7.11	3	
JAGGI, Ishank Rajiv (East Zone, India Red, Jharkhand) b Bacheli, Bihar 27.1.1989 RHB LBG																			
FC		4	7	0	103	31	14.71	0	0									1	
Lim		6	5	1	247	109	61.75	1	2									3	
20T		5	4	0	45	24	11.25	0	0									3	
FC	2008/09	9	16	1	402	101	26.80	1	2									2	
Lim	2006/07	20	19	4	938	159*	62.53	3	5									7	
JAIN, Aditya (Delhi) b Agra, Uttar Pradesh 11.6.1986 RHB SLA																			
FC		5	7	0	232	76	33.14	0	2	374	226	4	56.50	4-43	0	0	3.62	4	
Lim		1	1	0	11	11	11.00	0	0	36	27	0					4.50	0	
FC	2005/06	12	16	1	428	76	28.53	0	3	824	504	6	84.00	4-43	0	0	3.67	9	
Lim	2007/08	3	2	0	12	11	6.00	0	0	42	39	0					5.57	1	
20T	2006/07	1	1	0	4	4	4.00	0	0									0	
JAKATI, Shadab Bashir (Chennai Super Kings, Goa, India Green, South Zone) b Vasco da Gama, Goa 27.11.1980 LHB SLA																			
FC		6	7	1	218	63	36.33	0	1	786	293	12	24.41	4-41	0	0	2.23	3	
Lim		7	7	3	81	29	20.25	0	0	312	289	2	144.50	1-28	0	0	5.55	3	
20T		11	2	2	0	0*		0	0	228	291	13	22.38	2-17	0	0	7.65	1	
FC	1998/99	47	75	5	1508	100*	21.54	1	7	8929	4041	115	35.13	6-42	6	1	2.71	30	
Lim	1998/99	48	45	8	781	77	21.10	0	4	2157	1763	50	35.26	5-61	1	1	4.90	16	
20T	2006/07	25	9	2	107	43	15.28	0	0	522	624	32	19.50	4-22	2	0	7.17	6	
JAMATIA, Debabhakta Shibabhakta (Tripura) b Udaipur, Tripura 12.12.1985 LHB LM																			
20T		1	1	1	4	4*		0	0	12	22	0					11.00	0	
JANGID, Ravi Lakshmichand (Vidarbha) b Ratannagar, Maharashtra 13.6.1987 LHB SLA																			
FC		5	8	0	188	63	23.50	0	1	702	264	9	29.33	3-59	0	0	2.25	3	
Lim		4	4	0	163	58	40.75	0	2	126	113	0					5.38	1	
20T		3	3	0	42	19	14.00	0	0	64	50	5	10.00	5-11	0	1	4.68	0	
FC	2007/08	10	18	0	343	63	19.05	0	2	816	314	10	31.40	3-59	0	0	2.30	6	
Lim	2007/08	14	14	2	467	87*	38.91	0	4	622	446	10	44.60	3-27	0	0	4.30	5	
JASKARAN SINGH Butta (Deccan Chargers, North Zone, Punjab, India A to England, India A to Scotland) b Mohali, Punjab 4.9.1989 RHB RM																			
Lim		8	4	2	45	25*	22.50	0	0	417	377	17	22.17	4-72	1	0	5.42	1	
20T		6	4	3	8	4*	8.00	0	0	84	139	6	23.16	2-18	0	0	9.92	0	
FC	2010	2	1	0	58	58	58.00	0	1	270	174	1	174.00	1-97	0	0	3.86	0	
Lim	2008/09	16	12	4	181	51	22.62	0	1	840	790	27	29.25	4-72	1	0	5.64	1	
20T	2009	8	5	4	8	4*	8.00	0	0	102	171	6	28.50	2-18	0	0	10.05	0	
JASVIR SINGH (Services) b Bhiwani, Haryana 29.9.1978 RHB OB																			
Lim		5	5	1	204	112*	51.00	1	1									0	
FC	1998/99	57	96	7	3347	120	37.60	7	22	186	132	1	132.00	1-14	0	0	4.25	38	1
Lim	1998/99	53	52	6	1246	112*	27.08	1	7	14	16	0					6.85	17	1
20T	2006/07	2	2	0	9	9	4.50	0	0									0	
JATHAR, Gaurav Ashok (Mumbai) b Bombay (now Mumbai), Maharashtra 30.1.1991 RHB SLA																			
20T		1	1	0	16	16	16.00	0	0	24	31	0					7.75	0	
JAVED AHMED Ali Mir (Jammu and Kashmir) b Srinagar, Kashmir 26.5.1984 RHB LB																			
FC		3	6	0	94	38	15.66	0	0									1	
20T		4	4	0	44	22	11.00	0	0									2	
FC	2008/09	5	10	0	202	55	20.20	0	1	6	7	0					7.00	1	
Lim	2008/09	3	3	0	37	23	12.33	0	0									2	
JAYASURIYA, Sanath Teran (Bloomfield, Ruhuna, Mumbai Indians, Sri Lanka, Sri Lanka to India, Sri Lanka to South Africa, Sri Lanka to United States of America, Sri Lanka to West Indies, Worcestershire) b Matara, Sri Lanka 30.6.1969 LHB SLA																			
Int		3	3	0	51	31	17.00	0	0	84	118	0					8.42	1	
Lim		3	3	0	51	31	17.00	0	0	84	118	0					8.42	1	
I20T		2	2	0	57	31	28.50	0	0	24	19	2	9.50	2-19	0	0	4.75	0	
20T		6	6	0	90	31	15.00	0	0	78	87	4	21.75	2-17	0	0	6.69	0	
Test	1990/91	110	188	14	6973	340	40.07	14	31	8188	3366	98	34.34	5-34	2	0	2.46	78	
FC	1988/89	263	417	33	14782	340	38.49	29	70	15113	6719	205	32.77	5-34	2	0	2.66	162	
Int	1989/90	444	432	18	13428	189	32.43	28	68	14838	11825	322	36.72	6-29	8	4	4.78	123	
Lim	1989/90	545	530	25	15734	189	31.15	31	78	17730	14069	399	35.26	6-29	12	5	4.76	149	
I20T	2006	30	29	3	621	88	23.88	0	4	353	438	17	25.76	3-21	0	0	7.44	4	
20T	2004/05	92	91	6	2052	114*	24.14	1	11	1263	1634	62	26.35	4-24	1	0	7.76	16	
JAYAWARDENE, Denagamage Proboth Mahela de Silva (Sinhalese, Sri Lanka, Wayamba, Wayamba to India, Kings XI Punjab, Sri Lanka to Bangladesh, Sri Lanka to India, Sri Lanka to South Africa, Sri Lanka to United States of America, Sri Lanka to West Indies) b Colombo, Sri Lanka 27.5.1977 RHB RM																			
Test		3	5	0	373	275	74.60	1	0									1	
FC		3	5	0	373	275	74.60	1	0									1	
Int		4	4	0	77	39	19.25	0	0									0	
Lim		4	4	0	77	39	19.25	0	0									0	
I20T		2	2	0	21	12	10.50	0	0									0	
20T		17	17	3	516	110*	36.85	1	2									5	
Test	1997	113	187	13	9408	374	54.06	28	36	547	292	6	48.66	2-32	0	0	3.20	161	

Cmp	Debut	M	I	NO	Runs	HS	Avge	100	50	Balls	Runs	Wkts	Avge	BB	5i	10m	RpO	ct	st
FC	1995	195	310	22	15177	374	52.69	45	64	2959	1611	52	30.98	5-72	1	0	3.26	256	
Int	1997/98	326	307	32	9003	128	32.73	12	55	582	558	7	79.71	2-56	0	0	5.75	168	
Lim	1995	401	375	41	10787	128	32.29	12	67	1239	1094	23	47.56	3-25	0	0	5.29	202	
I20T	2006	31	31	4	760	100	28.14	1	4	6	8	0					8.00	9	
20T	2004/05	84	81	16	2049	110*	31.52	2	11	69	82	3	27.33	2-22	0	0	7.13	38	
JESURAJ, Rajamani (Tamil Nadu) b Madras (now Chennai), Tamil Nadu 24.5.1983 RHB RM																			
FC		3	2	0	47	39	23.50	0	0	408	171	0					2.51	1	
FC	2003/04	18	17	7	76	39	7.60	0	0	3097	1290	51	25.29	7-76	4	1	2.49	2	
Lim	2004/05	11	5	5	21	16*		0	0	570	434	19	22.84	4-24	1	0	4.56	3	
JHALANI, Rohit Banwarilal (Rajasthan) b Jaipur, Rajasthan 1.9.1978 RHB OB WK																			
FC		3	5	0	34	15	6.80	0	0									10	1
FC	1997/98	55	94	8	1575	85	18.31	0	8									170	20
Lim	1998/99	46	38	4	497	50	14.61	0	1									56	16
20T	2006/07	4	4	2	85	28	42.50	0	0									1	3
JHUNJHUNWALA, Abhishek Arunkumar (Bengal, Rajasthan Royals) b Calcutta (now Kolkata), Bengal 1.12.1982 RHB OB																			
FC		3	4	0	138	95	34.50	0	1	168	133	2	66.50	2-80	0	0	4.75	3	
Lim		6	5	1	116	83*	29.00	0	1	102	83	0					4.88	0	
20T		17	15	3	226	53*	18.83	0	1	61	98	1	98.00	1-9	0	0	9.63	4	
FC	2005/06	18	27	0	1010	139	37.40	3	4	246	184	3	61.33	2-80	0	0	4.48	12	
Lim	2005/06	24	22	4	529	84	29.38	0	4	300	269	3	89.66	2-58	0	0	5.38	2	
20T	2006/07	23	21	4	332	53*	19.52	0	1	67	107	1	107.00	1-9	0	0	9.58	10	
JOBANPUTRA, Sandeep Pravinkumar (Saurashtra) b Rajkot, Saurashtra 13.3.1981 RHB LM																			
FC		6	8	2	137	53*	22.83	0	1	1103	601	20	30.05	4-55	0	0	3.26	4	
Lim		5	1	0	3	3	3.00	0	0	252	180	4	45.00	2-25	0	0	4.28	2	
FC	2000/01	64	89	18	1293	82	18.21	0	5	11424	6101	189	32.28	7-83	8	0	3.20	27	
Lim	2001/02	29	19	4	197	31	13.13	0	0	1337	1154	25	46.16	3-33	0	0	5.17	6	
20T	2006/07	4	3	0	10	5	3.33	0	0	90	113	8	14.12	4-27	1	0	7.53	2	
JOGINDER SINGH (Delhi) b Delhi 11.7.1980 RHB RM																			
Lim		4	3	2	72	52*	72.00	0	1	126	91	1	91.00	1-26	0	0	4.33	0	
20T		5	3	2	31	24*	31.00	0	0	48	60	1	60.00	1-3	0	0	7.50	0	
JOGIYANI, Sagar Dipakbhai (Saurashtra) b Gondal, Gujarat 20.6.1984 RHB RAB WK																			
FC		6	10	0	243	103	24.30	1	0	6	8	0					8.00	16	3
Lim		6	4	1	245	102*	81.66	1	2									7	1
20T		2	2	0	79	55	39.50	0	1									2	
FC	2004/05	41	66	3	1729	103	27.44	1	8	18	16	0					5.33	135	16
Lim	2003/04	30	28	1	750	102*	27.77	1	6									32	13
20T	2006/07	6	6	0	149	55	24.83	0	1									5	2
JONATHAN, Rongsen (Karnataka) b Umaga, Karnataka 4.10.1986 RHB																			
Lim		4	4	0	120	64	30.00	0	2									2	
20T		2	1	0	19	19	19.00	0	0									1	
JOSHI, Himanshu Sanjay (Vidarbha) b Nagpur, Maharashtra 21.2.1987 LHB OB																			
FC		1	2	0	38	38	19.00	0	0									0	
Lim		4	4	0	77	37	19.25	0	0									1	
20T		3	3	1	47	28	23.50	0	0									3	
FC	2007/08	4	6	0	63	38	10.50	0	0	60	33	0					3.30	0	
20T	2006/07	6	6	2	82	33	20.50	0	0	29	37	0					7.65	3	
JOSHI, Sunil Bandacharya (Karnataka) b Gadag, Karnataka 6.6.1969 LHB SLA																			
FC		8	10	2	172	42	21.50	0	0	1325	529	16	33.06	4-62	0	0	2.39	2	
Test	1996	15	19	2	352	92	20.70	0	1	3451	1470	41	35.85	5-142	1	0	2.55	7	
FC	1992/93	152	210	29	4947	118	27.33	4	25	36754	14845	583	25.46	7-29	29	5	2.42	86	
Int	1996	69	45	11	584	61*	17.17	0	1	3386	2509	69	36.36	5-6	1	1	4.44	19	
Lim	1993/94	163	117	29	1729	64	19.64	0	5	8164	5593	192	29.13	5-6	3	2	4.11	47	
20T	2006/07	10	6	2	31	10*	7.75	0	0	175	223	7	31.85	2-11	0	0	7.64	2	
JOSHI, Vishal Harishbhai (Saurashtra) b Jamnagar, Saurashtra 1.5.1989 RHB OB																			
FC		2	3	1	71	45	35.50	0	0	331	182	6	30.33	4-77	0	0	3.29	1	
20T		4	3	0	18	9	6.00	0	0	84	109	4	27.25	2-29	0	0	7.78	1	
JOSHIPURA, Hem Ravindra (Gujarat) b Ahmedabad, Gujarat 14.7.1980 RHB OB																			
FC		2	4	0	86	39	21.50	0	0									1	
FC	2001/02	17	29	1	568	113	20.28	1	2	12	3	0					1.50	11	
JULKA, Ankur (Delhi) b Delhi 30.3.1987 RHB RM																			
FC		3	4	0	103	36	25.75	0	0									4	
20T		2	2	1	84	79*	84.00	0	1									0	
JUND, Ankur (Punjab) b Patiala, Punjab 26.10.1986 RHB OB																			
20T		1	1	1	4	4*		0	0	6	10	0					10.00	0	
Lim	2007/08	1								60	42	2	21.00	2-42	0	0	4.20	0	
JUNGADE, Amol Ganesh (Vidarbha) b Nandura, Maharashtra 6.2.1989 RHB RM																			
Lim		3	2	2	3	2*		0	0	78	76	1	76.00	1-39	0	0	5.84	1	
KAIF, Mohammad (Central Zone, Kings XI Punjab, Uttar Pradesh) b Allahabad, Uttar Pradesh 1.12.1980 RHB OB																			
FC		10	17	2	684	202*	45.60	2	3	30	29	0					5.80	10	
Lim		7	6	1	156	72*	31.20	0	1									3	
20T		7	6	0	102	57	17.00	0	1									4	

Cmp	Debut	M	I	NO	Runs	HS	Avge	100	50	Balls	Runs	Wkts	Avge	BB	5i	10m	RpO	ct	st
Test	1999/00	13	22	3	624	148*	32.84	1	3	18	4	0					1.33	14	
FC	1997/98	121	192	21	7253	202*	42.41	14	43	1466	702	20	35.10	3-4	0	0	2.87	105	
Int	2001/02	125	110	24	2753	111*	32.01	2	17									55	
Lim	1998/99	245	225	38	6742	151*	36.05	6	49	1154	1002	33	30.36	4-23	2	0	5.21	112	
20T	2003	33	30	5	493	59*	19.72	0	3									15	
KAKKAR, Ankur (Punjab) b Chandigarh 28.7.1979 LHB SLA																			
FC		3	6	0	87	33	14.50	0	0	54	17	1	17.00	1-10	0	0	1.88	2	
FC	2000/01	41	61	7	1916	124*	35.48	3	13	1945	986	26	37.92	4-55	0	0	3.04	11	
Lim	1999/00	26	21	5	394	74	24.62	0	2	354	243	7	34.71	2-18	0	0	4.11	15	
KALLIS, Jacques Henry (South Africa, Warriors, Royal Challengers Bangalore, South Africa to India, South Africa to West Indies) b Pinelands, Cape Town, Cape Province, South Africa 16.10.1975 RHB RFM																			
Test		2	3	0	203	173	67.66	1	0	180	73	1	73.00	1-19	0	0	2.43	3	
FC		2	3	0	203	173	67.66	1	0	180	73	1	73.00	1-19	0	0	2.43	3	
Int		3	3	1	204	104*	102.00	1	1	72	73	3	24.33	3-29	0	0	6.08	1	
Lim		3	3	1	204	104*	102.00	1	1	72	73	3	24.33	3-29	0	0	6.08	1	
20T		18	18	5	653	89*	50.23	0	7	378	512	16	32.00	3-18	0	0	8.12	8	
Test	1995/96	140	237	35	11126	189*	55.07	35	53	17887	8403	266	31.59	6-54	5	0	2.81	159	
FC	1993/94	230	377	52	17478	200	53.77	52	91	26622	12367	401	30.84	6-54	8	0	2.78	222	
Int	1995/96	303	289	52	10838	139	45.72	17	78	10108	8142	254	32.05	5-30	2	2	4.83	115	
Lim	1994/95	397	379	63	14019	155*	44.36	23	100	12917	10148	330	30.75	5-30	3	3	4.71	144	
I20T	2005/06	16	16	1	512	73	34.13	0	4	186	229	5	45.80	2-20	0	0	7.38	6	
20T	2003/04	65	65	9	1920	89*	34.28	0	17	1064	1427	32	44.59	3-18	0	0	8.04	24	
KALYANKRISHNA, Doddapaneni (Andhra) b Vijayawada, Andhra Pradesh 16.12.1983 RHB RFM																			
FC		2	1	0	3	3	3.00	0	0	192	87	1	87.00	1-29	0	0	2.71	0	
Lim		4	1	0	2	2	2.00	0	0	186	157	5	31.40	2-27	0	0	5.06	1	
20T		3	2	2	0	0*		0	0	54	71	3	23.66	3-23	0	0	7.88	0	
FC	2002/03	47	65	15	382	40*	7.64	0	0	7909	3636	139	26.15	6-43	5	0	2.75	10	
Lim	2003/04	39	31	6	286	53	11.44	0	1	1735	1521	49	31.04	4-29	2	0	5.26	6	
20T	2006/07	11	7	3	9	5	2.25	0	0	216	313	11	28.45	4-16	1	0	8.69	3	
KAMAT, Madhu Yeshwant (Goa) b Santa Cruz, Goa 22.3.1990 RHB RM																			
FC		1																0	
Lim	2008/09	3	3	0	72	47	24.00	0	0									1	
KAMAT, Sagun Krishna (Goa) b Ribandar, Goa 11.5.1983 LHB LBG																			
FC		4	6	0	90	26	15.00	0	0	24	19	1	19.00	1-13	0	0	4.75	3	
20T		3	3	0	96	41	32.00	0	0									2	
FC	1999/00	34	63	1	1522	130	24.54	1	7	234	139	2	69.50	1-11	0	0	3.56	27	
Lim	1999/00	25	25	1	643	92*	26.79	0	4	42	71	0					10.14	9	
20T	2006/07	8	8	0	260	78	32.50	0	1	5	10	0					12.00	3	
KAMATH, Vidhyadhar Surendra (Goa) b Thane, Maharashtra 15.6.1989 RHB OB																			
Lim		3	1	1	4	4*		0	0	54	55	2	27.50	1-19	0	0	6.11	1	
KAMRAN KHAN (Rajasthan Royals) b Azamgarh, Uttar Pradesh 10.3.1991 RHB LFM																			
20T		3	1	1	0	0*		0	0	36	53	3	17.66	2-13	0	0	8.83	0	
20T	2009	8	2	1	3	3	3.00	0	0	142	177	9	19.66	3-18	0	0	7.47	4	
KANITKAR, Hrishikesh Hemant (Madhya Pradesh) b Pune, Maharashtra 14.11.1974 LHB OB																			
FC		4	4	1	203	72	67.66	0	3									0	
Test	1999/00	2	4	0	74	45	18.50	0	0	6	2	0					2.00	0	
FC	1994/95	115	176	18	8421	290	53.29	26	37	7645	3462	73	47.42	3-21	0	0	2.71	71	
Int	1997/98	34	27	8	339	57	17.84	0	1	1006	803	17	47.23	2-22	0	0	4.78	14	
Lim	1994/95	125	113	16	3443	133	35.49	6	20	3476	2775	70	39.64	4-35	1	0	4.79	48	
KANJANIA, Dharshan (Delhi) b Delhi 15.10.1989 LHB SLA																			
FC		1	1	1	1	1*		0	0	222	157	1	157.00	1-85	0	0	4.24	0	
Lim	2008/09	6								313	255	6	42.50	3-46	0	0	4.88	2	
KANWAT, Rahul Jagdishprasad (Rajasthan) b Jaipur, Rajasthan 21.10.1974 RHB OB																			
FC		3	5	1	141	60*	35.25	0	1	246	97	1	97.00	1-7	0	0	2.36	1	
FC	1992/93	89	145	9	3527	143	25.93	2	23	13329	6007	162	37.08	5-37	5	0	2.70	43	
Lim	1994/95	50	48	5	777	73	18.06	0	3	2353	1609	67	24.01	4-48	2	0	4.10	21	
KARAMBELKAR, Abhijit Sanjay (Baroda) b Baroda (now Vadodara), Gujarat 4.6.1991 RHB RM																			
Lim		4	3	1	31	24	15.50	0	0	84	69	1	69.00	1-23	0	0	4.92	2	
Lim	2008/09	7	5	2	34	24	11.33	0	0	222	153	4	38.25	2-38	0	0	4.13	3	
KARTHIK, Krishankumar Dinesh (Delhi Daredevils, India, South Zone, Tamil Nadu, India to Bangladesh, India to South Africa, India to Sri Lanka, India to West Indies, India to Zimbabwe) b Madras (now Chennai), Tamil Nadu 1.6.1985 RHB RAB WK																			
FC		7	10	0	776	183	77.60	4	2	84	97	0					6.92	15	2
Int		6	5	2	185	79	61.66	0	1									2	2
Lim		9	6	2	273	88	68.25	0	2									3	2
I20T		1	1	1	4	4*		0	0									1	
20T		19	19	2	374	69	22.00	0	2									7	6
Test	2004/05	23	37	1	1000	129	27.77	1	7									51	5
FC	2002/03	79	125	6	4660	213	39.15	13	23	114	125	0					6.57	215	19
Int	2004	52	44	7	1008	79	27.24	0	5									31	5
Lim	2002/03	114	96	10	2509	117*	29.17	2	13									96	21

Cmp	Debut	M	I	NO	Runs	HS	Avge	100	50	Balls	Runs	Wkts	Avge	BB	5i	10m	RpO	ct	st
I20T	2006/07	9	8	2	100	31*	16.66	0	0									5	2
20T	2006/07	65	56	12	1056	69	24.00	0	4	12	10	1	10.00	1-10	0	0	5.00	40	20
KARTIK, Murali (Kolkata Knight Riders, Railways, Somerset) b Madras (now Chennai), Tamil Nadu 11.9.1976 LHB SLA																			
FC		7	8	0	97	44	12.12	0	0	1504	426	17	25.05	5-81	1	0	1.69	6	
Lim		4	2	1	23	12*	23.00	0	0	210	168	5	33.60	4-31	1	0	4.80	4	
20T		13	3	1	26	21	13.00	0	0	294	320	10	32.00	2-20	0	0	6.53	6	
Test	1999/00	8	10	1	88	43	9.77	0	0	1932	820	24	34.16	4-44	0	0	2.54	2	
FC	1996/97	160	199	33	3249	96	19.57	0	16	34546	13738	537	25.58	9-70	31	5	2.38	117	
Int	2001/02	37	14	5	126	32*	14.00	0	0	1907	1612	37	43.56	6-27	0	1	5.07	10	
Lim	1996/97	180	86	28	669	44	11.53	0	0	9148	6652	233	28.54	6-27	4	2	4.36	60	
I20T	2007/08	1								24	27	0					6.75	0	
20T	2007	74	16	6	102	21	10.20	0	0	1558	1713	59	29.03	5-13	0	1	6.59	22	
KATKAR, Advait Navinchandra (Goa) b Zambia 12.1.1981 RHB LFM																			
Lim		5	5	0	86	22	17.20	0	0									2	
FC	2003/04	9	16	0	257	76	16.06	0	1	168	73	1	73.00	1-42	0	0	2.60	2	
Lim	2003/04	10	10	0	174	30	17.40	0	0									3	
20T	2006/07	3	3	0	30	28	10.00	0	0									2	
KAUL, Uday (India Green, North Zone, Punjab) b Kangra, Himachal Pradesh 2.12.1987 LHB OB WK																			
FC		9	15	2	625	123	48.07	1	5	6	4	0					4.00	24	
Lim		9	7	1	251	101*	41.83	1	2									9	4
20T		4	2	1	13	9	13.00	0	0									1	
FC	2005/06	35	53	8	2210	162	49.11	6	9	12	8	0					4.00	65	2
Lim	2005/06	33	26	5	1064	107	50.66	3	8									30	7
20T	2007/08	9	3	2	13	9	13.00	0	0									3	
KAW, Vimarash (Jammu and Kashmir) b Nadigam, Jammu 1.1.1985 RHB OB																			
Lim		2	2	0	24	19	12.00	0	0									0	
FC	2005/06	2	3	0	28	20	9.33	0	0									0	
Lim	2003/04	5	5	0	89	33	17.80	0	0									0	
20T	2006/07	2	2	0	5	4	2.50	0	0									0	
KEMP, Justin Miles (Cape Cobras, Chennai Super Kings) b Queenstown, Cape Province, South Africa 2.10.1977 RHB RFM																			
20T		5	2	0	26	22	13.00	0	0	44	54	3	18.00	3-12	0	0	7.36	1	
Test	2000/01	4	6	0	80	55	13.33	0	1	479	222	9	24.66	3-33	0	0	2.78	3	
FC	1996/97	128	205	24	6422	188	35.48	14	30	12149	5771	203	28.42	6-56	5	0	2.85	181	
Int	2000/01	85	66	18	1512	100*	31.50	1	10	1303	1015	32	31.71	3-20	0	0	4.67	33	
Lim	1997/98	266	225	60	5934	107*	35.96	3	42	6704	5405	182	29.69	6-20	6	3	4.83	114	
I20T	2005/06	8	7	3	203	89*	50.75	0	1	6	5	0					5.00	3	
20T	2003/04	64	53	13	1079	89*	26.97	0	3	494	620	32	19.37	3-12	0	0	7.53	25	
KENI, Rahul Viraj (Goa) b Mapusa, Goa 24.4.1988 LHB WK																			
FC		5	6	0	199	69	33.16	0	2									3	1
Lim		4	3	0	53	23	17.66	0	0									2	
Lim	2004/05	12	11	3	106	23	13.25	0	0									10	
KESHAV KUMAR (Jharkhand) b Nalanda, Bihar 13.12.1988 RHB OB																			
FC		1	1	0	16	16	16.00	0	0	48	18	1	18.00	1-18	0	0	2.25	0	
20T		1								12	14	0					7.00	1	
FC	2008/09	3	4	0	65	34	16.25	0	0	150	101	1	101.00	1-18	0	0	4.04	2	
Lim	2003/04	13	11	2	147	56	16.33	0	1	534	404	9	44.88	2-26	0	0	4.53	6	
20T	2006/07	5	3	1	42	15	21.00	0	0	66	87	2	43.50	2-16	0	0	7.90	3	
KHADIWALE, Harshad Hemantkumar (India Red, Maharashtra, West Zone) b Pune, Maharashtra 21.10.1988 RHB RM																			
FC		7	14	0	483	114	34.50	2	1	210	75	0					2.14	1	
Lim		6	6	1	206	66	41.20	0	2	2	4	0					12.00	1	
20T		4	4	0	104	75	26.00	0	1	6	13	0					13.00	1	
FC	2006/07	25	45	1	1515	126	34.43	4	7	1247	536	9	59.55	3-46	0	0	2.57	16	
Lim	2007/08	14	14	1	485	66	37.30	0	6	314	324	11	29.45	3-55	0	0	6.19	6	
KHALEEL, Mohammad Ibrahim (Hyderabad) b Hyderabad, Andhra Pradesh 9.10.1982 RHB WK																			
FC		2	4	1	73	35	24.33	0	0									5	
20T		3	3	1	44	28	22.00	0	0									3	2
FC	2002/03	36	60	7	1466	128*	27.66	2	7									121	15
Lim	2002/03	27	25	5	474	78	23.70	0	3									37	9
20T	2006/07	8	8	2	185	68*	30.83	0	1									5	7
KHAN, Zaheer (India, Mumbai, Mumbai Indians, India to Bangladesh, India to Sri Lanka, India to West Indies) b Shrirampur, Maharashtra 7.10.1978 RHB LFM																			
Test		5	5	0	55	33	11.00	0	0	978	583	17	34.29	5-72	1	0	3.57	0	
FC		7	6	0	72	33	12.00	0	0	1376	835	27	30.92	5-72	1	0	3.64	0	
Int		5								270	280	7	40.00	3-63	0	0	6.22	0	
Lim		5								270	280	7	40.00	3-63	0	0	6.22	0	
20T		18	6	4	25	23*	12.50	0	0	386	486	19	25.57	3-21	0	0	7.55	5	
Test	2000/01	72	94	22	970	75	13.47	0	3	14417	7983	242	32.98	7-87	9	1	3.32	18	
FC	1999/00	136	176	37	2004	75	14.41	0	4	27899	15505	561	27.63	9-138	31	8	3.33	42	
Int	2000/01	175	91	35	719	34*	12.83	0	0	8754	7183	241	29.80	5-42	7	1	4.92	37	
Lim	1999/00	228	119	43	974	42	12.81	0	0	11402	9285	316	29.38	5-42	10	1	4.88	51	

Cmp	Debut	M	I	NO	Runs	HS	Avge	100	50	Balls	Runs	Wkts	Avge	BB	5i	10m	RpO	ct	st
I20T	2006/07	12	4	2	13	9	6.50	0	0	250	327	13	25.15	4-19	1	0	7.84	2	
20T	2006	56	29	16	136	26	10.46	0	0	1218	1562	58	26.93	4-19	1	0	7.69	13	
KHANAPURKAR, Parag Prakash (Mumbai) b Dhanbad, Karnataka 31.3.1986 LHB LB																			
Lim		2	2	0	125	123	62.50	1	0	54	56	1	56.00	1-34	0	0	6.22	0	
KHANNA, Varun (Punjab) b Chandigarh, Punjab 12.10.1984 RHB SLA																			
FC		1	2	2	30	30*		0	0	162	122	2	61.00	2-122	0	0	4.51	0	
FC	2008/09	5	8	5	49	30*	16.33	0	0	1047	621	9	69.00	3-38	0	0	3.55	0	
KHANOLKAR, Shreyas Narasimha (Railways) b Vengurla, Maharashtra 15.10.1977 RHB OB																			
20T		4	4	0	73	47	18.25	0	0	42	39	2	19.50	1-4	0	0	5.57	1	
FC	2000/01	42	70	9	1890	120	30.98	2	11	2069	1003	30	33.43	5-21	1	0	2.90	39	
Lim	1999/00	36	30	5	805	76*	32.20	0	6	837	660	17	38.82	3-35	0	0	4.73	14	
20T	2006/07	12	12	2	284	66*	28.40	0	1	150	143	7	20.42	2-18	0	0	5.72	4	
KHANWILKAR, Onkar Jagannath (Mumbai) b Bombay (now Mumbai), Maharashtra 8.9.1982 LHB OB																			
FC		6	8	0	252	87	31.50	0	2	36	20	1	20.00	1-11	0	0	3.33	12	
FC	2003/04	12	16	1	430	87	28.66	0	3	309	128	5	25.60	2-14	0	0	2.48	14	
Lim	2003/04	2	2	1	11	6	11.00	0	0	48	40	1	40.00	1-27	0	0	5.00	0	
KHATRI, Madhur Surendra (Rajasthan) b Bikaner, Rajasthan 25.6.1987 RHB OB																			
FC		5	9	1	135	35	16.87	0	0	1122	461	16	28.81	6-49	1	1	2.46	3	
KHODA, Gagan Kishanlal (Rajasthan) b Barmer, Rajasthan 24.10.1974 RHB OB																			
FC		4	7	0	305	106	43.57	1	2	6	8	0					8.00	2	
FC	1991/92	132	225	7	8521	300*	39.08	20	42	1154	685	14	48.92	3-24	0	0	3.56	91	
Int	1997/98	2	2	0	115	89	57.50	0	1									0	
Lim	1993/94	119	119	7	4487	166*	40.06	10	27	363	357	9	39.66	3-30	0	0	5.90	39	
KIRAN KUMAR Chinta (Services) b West Godavari, Andhra Pradesh 29.7.1984 RHB OB																			
Lim		1								42	36	0					5.14	1	
KODOTH, Akshay Gopalkrishna (Kerala) b Kollam, Kerala 20.3.1992 RHB WK																			
Lim		5	3	1	44	30*	22.00	0	0									5	1
KOHLI, Taruwar (Punjab) b Jalanhar, Punjab 17.12.1988 RHB RM																			
FC		7	12	1	272	118	24.72	1	0	180	98	2	49.00	2-37	0	0	3.26	0	
Lim		5	3	1	58	24*	29.00	0	0	186	138	5	27.60	5-38	0	1	4.45	0	
20T		3	3	1	20	14*	10.00	0	0									3	
FC	2008/09	9	15	1	352	118	25.14	1	1	249	159	2	79.50	2-37	0	0	3.83	3	
Lim	2008/09	10	8	3	152	58	30.40	0	1	384	300	12	25.00	5-38	0	1	4.68	1	
20T	2007/08	7	7	2	31	14*	6.20	0	0									4	
KOHLI, Virat (Delhi, India, North Zone, Royal Challengers Bangalore, India to Bangladesh, India to South Africa, India to Sri Lanka, India to Zimbabwe) b Delhi 5.11.1988 RHB OB																			
FC		4	7	2	430	145	86.00	1	3	114	91	0					4.78	7	
Int		9	7	0	316	107	45.14	1	2	12	11	0					5.50	4	
Lim		16	14	0	640	107	45.71	1	5	37	45	0					7.29	9	
20T		20	17	3	386	58	27.57	0	1	44	73	0					9.95	5	
FC	2006/07	25	36	6	1673	197	55.76	5	7	180	157	1	157.00	1-23	0	0	5.23	21	
Int	2008	34	31	4	1127	107	41.74	2	8	58	60	0					6.20	15	
Lim	2005/06	62	58	7	2382	124	46.70	6	14	83	94	0					6.79	29	
I20T	2010	2	1	1	26	26*		0	0									0	
20T	2006/07	56	48	7	1002	76	24.43	0	3	126	180	2	90.00	2-25	0	0	8.57	19	
KOLAMBKAR, Anup Shashikant (Goa) b Karwar, Karnataka 27.9.1984 LHB LB																			
FC		2	2	0	53	38	26.50	0	0									0	
FC	2006/07	5	8	0	112	38	14.00	0	0	204	114	5	22.80	2-9	0	0	3.35	0	
KOLHAR, Akshay Venkatesh (Vidarbha) b Dharwad, Maharashtra 5.5.1988 RHB OB																			
FC		3	6	0	157	84	26.16	0	1	24	16	0					4.00	4	
Lim		4	4	0	55	27	13.75	0	0	6	11	0					11.00	1	
KONWAR, Arlan (Assam) b Sibsagar, Assam 1.1.1981 RHB OB																			
FC		7	9	5	54	22	13.50	0	0	1509	542	31	17.48	6-72	2	0	2.15	3	
Lim		1	1	0	0	0	0.00	0	0									0	
20T		4								36	50	2	25.00	1-6	0	0	8.33	2	
FC	2001/02	47	63	21	450	34	10.71	0	0	9537	4031	145	27.80	6-46	8	0	2.53	12	
Lim	2001/02	28	17	5	71	12*	5.91	0	0	1309	905	28	32.32	4-37	2	0	4.14	7	
KOTAK, Shitanshu Hargovindbhai (Saurashtra) b Rajkot, Saurashtra 19.10.1972 LHB SLA																			
FC		6	10	0	305	103	30.50	1	1	128	73	0					3.42	3	
Lim		6	5	2	193	82*	64.33	0	2									3	
20T		3	3	0	66	27	22.00	0	0									3	
FC	1992/93	104	174	15	6814	168*	42.85	14	46	4014	2286	61	37.47	6-81	1	0	3.41	81	
Lim	1993/94	82	79	13	2964	122*	44.90	3	26	1467	1205	51	23.62	7-43	1	1	4.92	38	
20T	2006/07	6	6	1	88	27	17.60	0	0	12	10	0					5.00	4	
KRISHANATRY, Yajuvendra (Jharkhand) b Meerut, Uttar Pradesh 14.12.1983 RHB RM																			
Lim		4	1	0	7	7	7.00	0	0	180	133	3	44.33	2-26	0	0	4.43	2	
20T		1								24	31	4	7.75	4-31	1	0	7.75	0	
FC	2008/09	1	1	1	0	0*		0	0	150	92	1	92.00	1-92	0	0	3.68	0	

Cmp	Debut	M	I	NO	Runs	HS	Avge	100	50	Balls	Runs	Wkts	Avge	BB	5i	10m	RpO	ct	st
KUKREJA, Sahil Omprakash (Mumbai) b Bombay (now Mumbài), Maharashtra 9.7.1985 RHB OB																			
FC		11	17	1	617	122	38.56	1	4	6	7	0					7.00	4	
FC	2005/06	45	73	6	2543	229*	37.95	6	12	32	14	1	14.00	1-0	0	0	2.62	41	
Lim	2007/08	2	2	0	94	69	47.00	0	1									0	
KULDEEP SINGH (Rajasthan) b Jaipur, Rajasthan 26.10.1978 LHB SLA																			
FC		2	4	0	56	26	14.00	0	0	65	17	2	8.50	2-16	0	0	1.56	2	
FC	1997/98	12	23	2	553	92	26.33	0	3	95	52	2	26.00	2-16	0	0	3.28	8	
Lim	1997/98	16	16	1	209	33	13.93	0	0	395	305	7	43.57	2-36	0	0	4.63	2	
20T	2006/07	4	4	1	43	15	14.33	0	0	84	84	2	42.00	1-23	0	0	6.00	3	
KULKARNI, Dhawal Sunil (India Green, Mumbai, Mumbai Indians, West Zone, India A to England, India A to Scotland) b Bombay (now Mumbai), Maharashtra 10.12.1988 RHB RM																			
FC		12	12	5	279	87	39.85	0	2	2202	983	33	29.78	5-58	1	0	2.67	7	
Lim		7	4	3	24	9	24.00	0	0	276	253	9	28.11	3-23	0	0	5.50	1	
20T		5	2	2	5	5*		0	0	90	142	5	28.40	2-14	0	0	9.46	0	
FC	2008/09	29	27	14	411	87	31.61	0	2	5082	2396	92	26.04	7-50	6	0	2.82	10	
Lim	2007/08	24	11	8	54	15*	18.00	0	0	1097	956	36	26.55	5-29	0	1	5.22	8	
20T	2006/07	24	7	5	16	7*	8.00	0	0	435	597	22	27.13	3-33	0	0	8.23	4	
KUMAR, Praveenkumar Sakat Singh (Central Zone, India, Royal Challengers Bangalore, Uttar Pradesh, India to South Africa, India to Sri Lanka, India to West Indies) b Meerut, Uttar Pradesh 2.10.1986 RHB RFM																			
FC		5	8	2	237	58*	39.50	0	1	1014	468	22	21.27	6-68	2	0	2.76	0	
Int		10	7	3	138	54*	34.50	0	1	440	441	8	55.12	2-37	0	0	6.01	1	
Lim		14	10	3	201	54*	28.71	0	1	656	579	15	38.60	3-52	0	0	5.29	2	
20T		16	4	2	4	3*	2.00	0	0	342	470	14	33.57	3-18	0	0	8.24	1	
FC	2005/06	37	59	4	1387	98	25.21	0	8	8254	3845	166	23.16	8-68	12	1	2.79	5	
Int	2007/08	45	24	7	225	54*	13.23	0	1	2132	1801	56	32.16	4-31	3	0	5.06	11	
Lim	2004/05	96	67	9	1225	64	21.12	0	5	4712	3652	142	25.71	5-32	4	2	4.65	19	
I20T	2007/08	3	1	0	6	6	6.00	0	0	36	32	3	10.66	2-14	0	0	5.33	0	
20T	2006/07	49	29	8	294	76*	14.00	0	1	1036	1331	46	28.93	3-18	0	0	7.70	6	
KUMARAN, Dakshinamoorthy <u>Tamil</u> (Tamil Nadu) b Thanjavur, Tamil Nadu 24.11.1983 RHB RM																			
Lim		1	1	1	0	0*		0	0	48	43	1	43.00	1-43	0	0	5.37	0	
FC	2003/04	7	10	3	60	14	8.57	0	0	1325	729	20	36.45	5-57	1	0	3.30	0	
Lim	2003/04	15	6	4	28	12	14.00	0	0	789	620	28	22.14	5-37	0	1	4.71	1	
20T	2006/07	4	1	1	9	9*		0	0	84	124	7	17.71	3-39	0	0	8.85	2	
KUMBLE, Anil (Karnataka, Royal Challengers Bangalore) b Bangalore, Karnataka 17.10.1970 RHB LBG																			
20T		21	6	6	7	2*		0	0	493	561	22	25.50	4-16	1	0	6.82	7	
Test	1990	132	173	32	2506	110*	17.77	1	5	40850	18355	619	29.65	10-74	35	8	2.69	60	
FC	1989/90	244	318	61	5572	154*	21.68	7	17	66931	29347	1136	25.83	10-74	72	19	2.63	120	
Int	1989/90	271	136	47	938	26	10.53	0	0	14496	10412	337	30.89	6-12	8	2	4.31	85	
Lim	1989/90	380	203	73	1456	30*	11.20	0	0	20247	14178	514	27.58	6-12	14	3	4.20	122	
20T	2006	49	19	15	44	8	11.00	0	0	1125	1258	54	23.29	5-5	2	1	6.70	14	
KUSH, Arnav (Services) b Karnal, Haryana 15.10.1988 RHB OB																			
20T		1	1	1	7	7*		0	0	6	9	0					9.00	0	
Lim	2007/08	5	2	1	5	4	5.00	0	0	248	197	5	39.40	3-37	0	0	4.76	0	
LAHIRI, Saurasish Sukanta (Bengal, East Zone) b Howrah (now Haora), Bengal 9.9.1981 RHB OB																			
FC		7	9	2	92	37	13.14	0	0	1371	754	19	39.68	5-157	1	0	3.30	0	
Lim		3	2	1	27	20	27.00	0	0	144	124	2	62.00	1-23	0	0	5.16	1	
20T		4	2	1	11	7*	11.00	0	0	84	103	4	25.75	3-20	0	0	7.35	0	
FC	1999/00	76	107	17	1496	62	16.62	0	3	15849	7912	216	36.62	7-93	9	1	2.99	27	
Lim	1999/00	54	31	9	251	40	11.40	0	0	2850	2023	54	37.46	5-43	0	1	4.25	12	
20T	2006/07	12	10	2	94	44	11.75	0	0	240	269	13	20.69	3-20	0	0	6.72	2	
LALITH MOHAN, Akkaraju (Hyderabad) b Hyderabad, Andhra Pradesh 19.3.1990 RHB SLA																			
FC		1	2	2	6	4*		0	0	36	13	0					2.16	0	
FC	2007/08	8	10	5	28	9	5.60	0	0	1447	771	10	77.10	4-132	0	0	3.19	1	
LAMBA, Ankit Satyaveer (Rajasthan) b Khetri, Rajasthan 3.12.1991 RHB LBG																			
FC		2	4	0	68	41	17.00	0	0									2	
LANGEVELDT, Charl Kenneth (Cape Cobras, South Africa, Derbyshire, Kolkata Knight Riders, South Africa to India, South Africa to West Indies) b Stellenbosch, Cape Province, South Africa 17.12.1974 RHB RFM																			
Int		2	2	1	16	12	16.00	0	0	120	118	1	118.00	1-48	0	0	5.90	0	
Lim		2	2	1	16	12	16.00	0	0	120	118	1	118.00	1-48	0	0	5.90	0	
20T		5	1	0	0	0	0.00	0	0	108	127	6	21.16	2-26	0	0	7.05	0	
Test	2004/05	6	4	2	16	10	8.00	0	0	999	593	16	37.06	5-46	1	0	3.56	2	
FC	1997/98	93	116	39	1106	56	14.36	0	1	17559	8670	310	27.96	6-48	9	1	2.96	25	
Int	2001/02	68	20	9	69	12	6.27	0	0	3255	2728	93	29.33	5-39	1	2	5.02	10	
Lim	1997/98	195	77	31	359	33*	7.80	0	0	9121	7033	293	24.00	5-7	7	7	4.62	36	
I20T	2005/06	9	3	2	4	2*	4.00	0	0	198	241	17	14.17	4-19	1	0	7.30	1	
20T	2003/04	58	15	10	36	9*	7.20	0	0	1242	1408	86	16.37	5-16	4	1	6.80	17	
LAXMAN, Vangipurappu Venkata Sai (Deccan Chargers, Hyderabad, India, India to Bangladesh, India to Sri Lanka) b Hyderabad, Andhra Pradesh 1.11.1974 RHB OB																			
Test		4	5	2	319	143*	106.33	1	3									3	
FC		6	8	2	409	143*	68.16	1	4									5	
20T		8	8	1	114	46	16.28	0	0									2	

Cmp	Debut	M	I	NO	Runs	HS	Avge	100	50	Balls	Runs	Wkts	Avge	BB	5i	10m	RpO	ct	st
Test	1996/97	113	186	29	7415	281	47.22	16	45	324	126	2	63.00	1-2	0	0	2.33	118	
FC	1992/93	244	394	49	18154	353	52.62	53	86	1835	754	22	34.27	3-11	0	0	2.46	260	1
Int	1997/98	86	83	7	2338	131	30.76	6	10	42	40	0					5.71	39	
Lim	1994/95	173	166	19	5078	131	34.54	9	28	698	548	8	68.50	2-42	0	0	4.71	74	
20T	2007/08	22	22	3	447	78*	23.52	0	3									4	

LEE, Brett (New South Wales, New South Wales to India, Australia, Australia to India, Australia to South Africa, Kings XI Punjab) b Wollongong, New South Wales, Australia 8.11.1976 RHB RF

Cmp	Debut	M	I	NO	Runs	HS	Avge	100	50	Balls	Runs	Wkts	Avge	BB	5i	10m	RpO	ct	st
Int		1	1	0	0	0	0.00	0	0	36	28	1	28.00	1-28	0	0	4.66	1	
Lim		1	1	0	0	0	0.00	0	0	36	28	1	28.00	1-28	0	0	4.66	1	
20T		10	6	3	59	48	19.66	0	0	213	228	8	28.50	2-10	0	0	6.42	4	
Test	1999/00	76	90	18	1451	64	20.15	0	5	16531	9554	310	30.81	5-30	10	0	3.46	23	
FC	1994/95	116	139	25	2120	97	18.59	0	8	24193	13747	487	28.22	7-114	20	2	3.40	35	
Int	1999/00	186	92	37	897	57	16.30	0	2	9478	7456	324	23.01	5-22	11	9	4.72	44	
Lim	1997/98	219	112	46	1071	57	16.22	0	2	11274	8721	366	23.82	5-22	12	9	4.64	49	
I20T	2004/05	17	9	4	91	43*	18.20	0	0	355	454	17	26.70	3-27	0	0	7.67	5	
20T	2004/05	36	22	11	195	48	17.72	0	0	784	905	34	26.61	3-15	0	0	6.92	13	

LENIN, Vemu (Andhra) b Vijayawada, Andhra Pradesh 14.1.1983 RHB OB

Cmp	Debut	M	I	NO	Runs	HS	Avge	100	50	Balls	Runs	Wkts	Avge	BB	5i	10m	RpO	ct	st
Lim		5	4	1	161	78*	53.66	0	1									1	

LINGWAL, Bhupinder (Haryana) b Delhi 4.3.1987 RHB RM

Cmp	Debut	M	I	NO	Runs	HS	Avge	100	50	Balls	Runs	Wkts	Avge	BB	5i	10m	RpO	ct	st
FC		2	2	0	33	24	16.50	0	0	36	16	1	16.00	1-16	0	0	2.66	0	
20T		1								12	21	0					10.50	1	

LUMB, Michael John (Hampshire, England to West Indies, England Lions to United Arab Emirates, Rajasthan Royals) b Johannesburg, Transvaal, South Africa 12.2.1980 LHB RM

Cmp	Debut	M	I	NO	Runs	HS	Avge	100	50	Balls	Runs	Wkts	Avge	BB	5i	10m	RpO	ct	st
20T		11	11	0	278	83	25.27	0	1									4	
FC	2000	134	224	15	7266	219	34.76	12	45	318	242	6	40.33	2-10	0	0	4.56	92	
Lim	2001	164	158	11	4752	110	32.32	3	37	12	28	0					14.00	56	
I20T	2010	7	7	0	137	33	19.57	0	0									3	
20T	2003	86	86	5	1838	124*	22.69	1	11	36	65	3	21.66	3-32	0	0	10.83	29	

LUMBA, Bharat (Punjab) b Ludhiana, Punjab 10.10.1987 RHB RM

Cmp	Debut	M	I	NO	Runs	HS	Avge	100	50	Balls	Runs	Wkts	Avge	BB	5i	10m	RpO	ct	st
FC		1	2	0	4	3	2.00	0	0	144	90	0					3.75	1	
20T		4	2	0	17	17	8.50	0	0	66	82	3	27.33	2-16	0	0	7.45	3	
Lim	2007/08	1								54	50	0					5.55	0	

McCULLUM, Brendon Barrie (New Zealand, Otago, Otago to India, Kolkata Knight Riders, New Zealand to South Africa, New Zealand to United Arab Emirates, New Zealand to United States of America, New Zealand to West Indies, Sussex) b Dunedin, Otago, New Zealand 27.9.1981 RHB WK

Cmp	Debut	M	I	NO	Runs	HS	Avge	100	50	Balls	Runs	Wkts	Avge	BB	5i	10m	RpO	ct	st
20T		7	7	1	140	57*	23.33	0	1									2	
Test	2003/04	52	87	5	2862	185	34.90	5	16									162	11
FC	1999/00	95	163	9	5339	185	34.66	9	30	36	18	0					3.00	267	19
Int	2001/02	171	145	22	3569	166	29.01	2	17									189	13
Lim	2000/01	215	183	26	4617	170	29.40	5	21									232	15
I20T	2004/05	40	40	7	1100	116*	33.33	1	6									25	4
20T	2004/05	98	97	13	2695	158*	32.08	3	14									48	4

McDONALD, Andrew Barry (Australia A, Victoria, Delhi Daredevils, Leicestershire) b Wodonga, Victoria, Australia 15.6.1981 RHB RFM

Cmp	Debut	M	I	NO	Runs	HS	Avge	100	50	Balls	Runs	Wkts	Avge	BB	5i	10m	RpO	ct	st
20T		9	6	5	130	33*	130.00	0	0	198	252	14	18.00	4-21	1	0	7.63	3	
Test	2008/09	4	6	1	107	68	21.40	0	1	732	300	9	33.33	3-25	0	0	2.45	2	
FC	2001/02	69	112	25	3230	176*	37.12	6	18	9785	4602	159	28.94	6-34	4	0	2.82	51	
Lim	2001/02	77	67	21	1475	67	32.06	0	8	3116	2640	68	38.82	4-50	1	0	5.08	31	
20T	2005/06	39	34	14	678	67	33.90	0	2	678	872	45	19.37	5-13	1	1	7.71	12	

McGRATH, Glenn Donald (Delhi Daredevils) b Dubbo, New South Wales, Australia 9.2.1970 RHB RFM

Cmp	Debut	M	I	NO	Runs	HS	Avge	100	50	Balls	Runs	Wkts	Avge	BB	5i	10m	RpO	ct	st
20T		2								36	45	2	22.50	2-20	0	0	7.50	0	
Test	1993/94	124	138	51	641	61	7.36	0	1	29248	12186	563	21.64	8-24	29	3	2.50	38	
FC	1992/93	189	193	67	977	61	7.75	0	2	41759	17414	835	20.85	8-24	42	7	2.50	54	
Int	1993/94	250	68	38	115	11	3.83	0	0	12970	8391	381	22.02	7-15	9	7	3.88	37	
Lim	1992/93	305	80	43	124	11	3.35	0	0	15808	10004	463	21.60	7-15	15	7	3.79	48	
I20T	2004/05	2	1	0	5	5	5.00	0	0	48	79	5	15.80	3-31	0	0	9.87	1	
20T	2004/05	19	5	2	9	5	3.00	0	0	432	492	20	24.60	4-29	1	0	6.83	5	

McLAREN, Ryan (Eagles, Eagles to India, South Africa, Mumbai Indians, South Africa to West Indies) b Kimberley, Cape Province, South Africa 9.2.1983 LHB RMF

Cmp	Debut	M	I	NO	Runs	HS	Avge	100	50	Balls	Runs	Wkts	Avge	BB	5i	10m	RpO	ct	st
20T		14	11	7	136	40	34.00	0	0	294	386	5	77.20	2-28	0	0	7.87	5	
Test	2009/10	1	1	1	33	33*		0	0	78	43	1	43.00	1-30	0	0	3.30	0	
FC	2003/04	80	115	19	2711	140	28.23	2	14	12627	6361	255	24.94	8-38	10	1	3.02	40	
Int	2009/10	10	8	2	37	12	6.16	0	0	432	366	8	45.75	3-51	0	0	5.08	5	
Lim	2003/04	105	78	30	1561	82*	32.52	0	8	3919	3322	105	31.63	5-46	4	1	5.08	35	
I20T	2009/10	4	3	3	8	6*		0	0	95	107	9	11.88	5-19	0	1	6.75	1	
20T	2004/05	81	55	27	583	46*	20.82	0	0	1554	1944	68	28.58	5-19	1	1	7.50	33	

MADAN, Chandan (Mumbai Indians, Punjab) b Amritsar, Punjab 15.10.1982 RHB OB WK

Cmp	Debut	M	I	NO	Runs	HS	Avge	100	50	Balls	Runs	Wkts	Avge	BB	5i	10m	RpO	ct	st
FC		3	4	0	51	36	12.75	0	0									8	
20T		6	5	2	152	69*	50.66	0	1									6	1
FC	2003/04	16	20	1	379	67	19.94	0	1									37	1
Lim	2002/03	4	3	1	22	11	11.00	0	0									5	

Cmp	Debut	M	I	NO	Runs	HS	Avge	100	50	Balls	Runs	Wkts	Avge	BB	5i	10m	RpO	ct	st
MAHAJAN, Dhruv (Jammu and Kashmir) b Jammu 9.9.1976 RHB RM																			
FC		3	5	0	53	24	10.60	0	0	66	29	1	29.00	1-16	0	0	2.63	3	
Lim		5	5	0	192	127	38.40	1	0	108	81	0					4.50	2	
20T		5	4	0	44	27	11.00	0	0	60	70	5	14.00	2-23	0	0	7.00	2	
FC	1998/99	43	75	5	1891	123	27.01	2	11	1578	752	9	83.55	3-16	0	0	2.85	29	
Lim	1998/99	37	35	2	894	127	27.09	1	3	497	369	9	41.00	3-34	0	0	4.45	9	
20T	2006/07	10	9	0	110	27	12.22	0	0	126	157	7	22.42	2-23	0	0	7.47	3	
MAHAROOF, Mohamed Farveez (Nondescripts, Sri Lanka, Sri Lanka A, Wayamba, Wayamba to India, Delhi Daredevils) b Colombo, Sri Lanka 7.9.1984 RHB RFM																			
20T		9	6	1	35	28	7.00	0	0	192	259	9	28.77	2-13	0	0	8.09	1	
Test	2004	20	31	4	538	72	19.92	0	3	2628	1458	24	60.75	4-52	0	0	3.32	6	
FC	2001/02	49	72	7	1442	115*	22.18	2	4	5958	3234	99	32.66	7-73	1	0	3.25	25	
Int	2004	94	64	15	984	69*	20.08	0	2	3932	3133	121	25.89	6-14	4	2	4.78	20	
Lim	2002/03	149	110	23	1866	70*	21.44	0	6	6072	4875	173	28.17	6-14	6	2	4.81	34	
I20T	2006	7	4	1	23	13*	7.66	0	0	144	173	7	24.71	2-18	0	0	7.20	2	
20T	2004/05	44	29	11	288	39	16.00	0	0	900	1101	45	24.46	3-21	0	0	7.34	13	
MAHESH, Vijaykumar Yo (Delhi Daredevils, Tamil Nadu) b Madras (now Chennai), Tamil Nadu 21.12.1987 RHB RMF																			
FC		4	7	3	91	23*	22.75	0	0	513	281	9	31.22	3-58	0	0	3.28	3	
Lim		8	2	1	21	19*	21.00	0	0	385	367	20	18.35	5-55	0	1	5.71	5	
20T		1								18	23	1	23.00	1-23	0	0	7.66	0	
FC	2005/06	27	31	8	330	47	14.34	0	0	3879	2260	60	37.66	6-71	1	0	3.49	13	
Lim	2004/05	32	15	6	109	30*	12.11	0	0	1434	1211	54	22.42	5-55	1	1	5.06	13	
20T	2006/07	23	10	5	45	13	9.00	0	0	505	696	27	25.77	4-36	1	0	8.26	8	
MAJMUDAR, Hitesh Akash (Gujarat) b Ahmedabad, Gujarat 21.7.1974 RHB RFM																			
FC		1	2	1	5	5*	5.00	0	0	133	50	0					2.25	0	
FC	1999/00	38	52	7	357	35	7.93	0	0	6393	3156	95	33.22	6-74	3	0	2.96	12	
Lim	1999/00	20	11	5	107	29*	17.83	0	0	864	725	11	65.90	2-22	0	0	5.03	2	
20T	2006/07	4	3	2	27	17*	27.00	0	0	84	79	6	13.16	2-19	0	0	5.64	1	
MAJUMDAR, Anustup Prabir (Bengal) b Chandannagore, Hooghly, Bengal 30.4.1984 RHB LBG																			
Lim		1	1	0	66	66	66.00	0	1									0	
FC	2004/05	15	26	1	691	103	27.64	1	4	186	131	0					4.22	10	
Lim	2007/08	10	10	0	465	109	46.50	2	2	6	10	0					10.00	5	
20T	2006/07	1	1	0	6	6	6.00	0	0									0	
MAKDA, Ashraf Mohammad (Gujarat) b Valsad, Gujarat 28.8.1978 LHB LMF																			
FC		4	5	1	125	53	31.25	0	1	564	254	5	50.80	2-39	0	0	2.70	2	
20T		4	4	2	19	8*	9.50	0	0	90	110	3	36.66	1-20	0	0	7.33	0	
FC	2004/05	34	45	5	522	73	13.05	0	4	6515	2890	109	26.51	7-90	5	0	2.66	6	
Lim	2004/05	13	8	4	68	19	17.00	0	0	576	411	15	27.40	3-33	0	0	4.28	6	
20T	2006/07	12	11	5	41	8*	6.83	0	0	271	292	11	26.54	3-15	0	0	6.46	3	
MAKLA, Jayeshkumar Tulsidas (Gujarat) b Bulsar (now Valsad), Gujarat 27.5.1981 RHB OB																			
Lim		4	3	0	27	21	9.00	0	0	174	167	3	55.66	2-57	0	0	5.75	0	
20T		1	1	0	2	2	2.00	0	0	24	33	1	33.00	1-33	0	0	8.25	0	
FC	2004/05	6	9	4	79	19	15.80	0	0	780	397	11	36.09	4-25	0	0	3.05	1	
Lim	2003/04	8	6	1	28	21	5.60	0	0	312	278	3	92.66	2-57	0	0	5.34	1	
MAKWANA, Kamlesh Rasikbhai (Saurashtra) b Rajkot, Saurashtra 31.8.1983 RHB OB																			
FC		2	2	0	30	20	15.00	0	0	350	182	3	60.66	3-82	0	0	3.12	1	
Lim		6	3	1	12	11*	6.00	0	0	347	263	4	65.75	1-30	0	0	4.54	0	
FC	2004/05	34	46	10	518	56*	14.38	0	2	5176	2563	71	36.09	6-41	3	0	2.97	15	
Lim	2003/04	25	16	3	180	64	13.84	0	1	1329	981	27	36.33	3-32	0	0	4.42	4	
20T	2006/07	4	3	1	21	10	10.50	0	0	78	95	6	15.83	2-12	0	0	7.30	2	
MAKWANA, Rakesh Prabhudas (Gujarat) b Bombay (now Mumbai), Maharashtra 10.1.1981 RHB RM																			
20T		3	3	0	34	20	11.33	0	0									1	
MALI, Ranjit Laxman (Assam) b Sonitpur, Assam 5.11.1988 RHB RFM																			
FC		1	1	0	4	4	4.00	0	0	234	123	5	24.60	4-89	0	0	3.15	2	
20T		1								12	31	0					15.50	1	
FC	2008/09	5	7	2	16	5	3.20	0	0	1128	579	19	30.47	4-89	0	0	3.08	2	
Lim	2008/09	2	1	1	1	1*		0	0	114	106	0					5.57	0	
MALIK, Abdulahad (Gujarat) b Hansot, Gujarat 9.8.1986 LHB OB WK																			
20T		1	1	0	1	1	1.00	0	0									2	
Lim	2007/08	1	1	0	35	35	35.00	0	0									0	
20T	2006/07	9	9	0	116	51	12.88	0	1									5	
MALIK, Vikramjeet (Himachal Pradesh, India Green, Kings XI Punjab, North Zone) b Solan, Himachal Pradesh 9.5.1983 RHB RM																			
FC		8	12	0	246	72	20.50	0	1	1652	726	33	22.00	6-33	2	0	2.63	0	
Lim		1	1	1	11	11*		0	0	42	81	0					11.57	0	
20T		8	5	0	82	48	16.40	0	0	161	219	10	21.90	3-21	0	0	8.16	1	
FC	2002/03	47	63	8	677	72	12.30	0	1	9094	4333	189	22.92	7-29	10	2	2.85	6	
Lim	2004/05	32	24	5	180	31	9.47	0	0	1631	1265	40	31.62	4-35	1	0	4.65	11	
20T	2006/07	17	6	0	89	48	14.83	0	0	322	445	14	31.78	3-21	0	0	8.29	4	

Cmp	Debut	M	I	NO	Runs	HS	Avge	100	50	Balls	Runs	Wkts	Avge	BB	5i	10m	RpO	ct	st
MALINGA, Separamadu Lasith Swarnajith (Nondescripts, Ruhuna, Sri Lanka, Mumbai Indians, Sri Lanka to India, Sri Lanka to South Africa, Sri Lanka to United States of America, Sri Lanka to West Indies) b Galle, Sri Lanka 4.9.1983 RHB RF																			
Int		2	1	0	13	13	13.00	0	0	112	131	0					7.01	0	
Lim		2	1	0	13	13	13.00	0	0	112	131	0					7.01	0	
I20T		2								36	57	1	57.00	1-28	0	0	9.50	1	
20T		15	2	2	1	1*		0	0	330	401	16	25.06	4-22	1	0	7.29	3	
Test	2004	30	37	13	275	64	11.45	0	1	5209	3349	101	33.15	5-50	3	0	3.85	7	
FC	2001/02	83	100	41	584	64	9.89	0	1	11885	7755	255	30.41	6-17	7	0	3.91	23	
Int	2004	72	34	12	152	16	6.90	0	0	3494	2896	106	27.32	5-34	5	1	4.97	12	
Lim	2001/02	115	61	20	276	23*	6.73	0	0	5519	4600	182	25.27	5-34	8	2	5.00	20	
I20T	2006	28	12	7	63	27	12.60	0	0	564	702	34	20.64	3-12	0	0	7.46	12	
20T	2004/05	66	20	11	68	27	7.55	0	0	1363	1577	77	20.48	4-22	1	0	6.94	19	
MALVI, Usman Rizwan (Mumbai) b Thana, Maharashtra 22.11.1981 RHB RFM																			
FC		3	5	1	45	20	11.25	0	0	384	215	7	30.71	3-108	0	0	3.35	3	
Lim		6	3	1	24	17	12.00	0	0	313	270	4	67.50	2-51	0	0	5.17	2	
20T		1								24	45	1	45.00	1-45	0	0	11.25	0	
FC	2002/03	21	25	8	287	56	16.88	0	1	3092	1456	53	27.47	4-55	0	0	2.82	4	
Lim	2003/04	22	9	3	50	17	8.33	0	0	1142	923	26	35.50	3-25	0	0	4.84	11	
MANDEEP SINGH (Kolkata Knight Riders, North Zone, Punjab) b Jalandhar, Punjab 18.12.1991 RHB RFM																			
Lim		8	7	1	277	73	46.16	0	3									4	
20T		3	2	0	4	4	2.00	0	0									0	
MANDHANI, Ashwani Raju Das (Railways) b Kanpur, Uttar Pradesh 20.12.1987 RHB RFM																			
Lim		1	1	0	8	8	8.00	0	0	60	64	3	21.33	3-64	0	0	6.40	0	
20T		1	1	0	5	5	5.00	0	0	6	15	0					15.00	0	
Lim	2005/06	2	2	0	10	8	5.00	0	0	60	64	3	21.33	3-64	0	0	6.40	0	
MANE, Vinayak Ramesh (Jammu and Kashmir) b Bombay (now Mumbai), Maharashtra 10.6.1982 RHB OB																			
FC		3	5	0	104	59	20.80	0	1									2	
20T		5	4	0	38	17	9.50	0	0									2	
FC	2000/01	57	93	7	2971	154	34.54	4	20	186	86	1	86.00	1-4	0	0	2.77	78	
Lim	2000/01	33	33	3	1436	114*	47.86	4	9	31	16	0					3.09	20	
20T	2006/07	7	5	1	60	22*	15.00	0	0									4	
MANHAS, Mithun (Delhi, Delhi Daredevils, North Zone) b Jammu 12.9.1977 RHB OB																			
FC		6	8	2	464	170	77.33	1	2	414	217	3	72.33	1-2	0	0	3.14	1	
Lim		5	5	0	251	148	50.20	1	1	71	84	2	42.00	2-52	0	0	7.09	1	
20T		10	9	4	182	32*	36.40	0	0									5	
FC	1997/98	110	169	23	6424	205*	44.00	17	31	2840	1427	33	43.24	3-15	0	0	3.01	87	1
Lim	1997/98	104	97	27	3513	148	50.18	5	23	922	763	21	36.33	3-36	0	0	4.96	41	
20T	2006/07	26	19	7	356	32*	29.66	0	0	30	47	3	15.66	3-33	0	0	9.40	8	
MANIAR, Sandeep Manubhai (Saurashtra) b Sihor, Gujarat 28.12.1976 RHB RFM																			
FC		6	8	1	88	37	12.57	0	0	1098	606	15	40.40	3-28	0	0	3.31	2	
Lim		1								60	73	1	73.00	1-73	0	0	7.30	0	
20T		4	3	0	12	8	4.00	0	0	90	109	6	18.16	3-32	0	0	7.26	0	
FC	2002/03	38	53	19	463	57	13.61	0	1	6785	3535	123	28.73	7-81	6	2	3.12	8	
Lim	2002/03	29	18	8	97	22	9.70	0	0	1376	1147	28	40.96	4-37	1	0	5.00	5	
20T	2006/07	8	5	2	13	8	4.33	0	0	174	218	10	21.80	3-32	0	0	7.51	2	
MANIKANTAN, Padmaja Vasudevan (Kerala) b Trivandrum (now Thiruvananthapuram), Kerala 19.11.1975 RHB RM																			
Lim		2	2	0	21	15	10.50	0	0									0	
Lim	2005/06	16	15	0	445	84	29.66	0	2									3	
20T	2006/07	5	5	0	125	42	25.00	0	0									2	
MANNU, Ajaymannu Bhardwaj (Himachal Pradesh) b Chamba, Himachal Pradesh 15.5.1977 RHB RM																			
FC		7	12	1	205	68	18.63	0	1									31	1
Lim		5	3	1	48	22*	24.00	0	0									3	9
20T		7	6	2	70	41	17.50	0	0									3	2
FC	1996/97	51	85	9	2117	103	27.85	1	15	30	15	0					3.00	63	3
Lim	1996/97	50	42	5	672	72	18.16	0	2	88	85	2	42.50	2-48	0	0	5.79	18	14
20T	2006/07	12	10	4	97	41	16.16	0	0	24	17	1	17.00	1-11	0	0	4.25	6	2
MANTRI, Dinesh Laxman (Services) b Jodhpur, Rajasthan 10.1.1984 RHB																			
20T		1	1	0	4	4	4.00	0	0									1	
FC	2008/09	1	2	0	23	20	11.50	0	0									0	
MANZOOR ILAHI Gudoo (Jammu and Kashmir) b Srinagar, Kashmir 5.6.1987 RHB RFM																			
20T		2	2	1	32	23*	32.00	0	0	12	11	1	11.00	1-11	0	0	5.50	1	
MARATHE, Sushant Hemant (Mumbai) b Bombay (now Mumbai), Maharashtra 16.10.1985 RHB LBG WK																			
FC		3	5	0	237	144	47.40	1	1									1	
Lim		6	6	0	270	108	45.00	1	2									9	1
20T		1	1	0	8	8	8.00	0	0									0	
FC	2005/06	7	13	0	374	144	28.76	1	2									5	
Lim	2006/07	10	10	0	332	108	33.20	1	2									16	3
MARSH, Mitchell Ross (Western Australia, Deccan Chargers) b Armadale, Perth, Western Australia, Australia 20.10.1991 RHB RM																			
20T		3	2	0	28	15	14.00	0	0	60	88	2	44.00	1-19	0	0	8.80	0	
FC	2009/10	6	11	1	219	59*	21.90	0	2	306	204	2	102.00	1-13	0	0	4.00	3	

Cmp	Debut	M	I	NO	Runs	HS	Avge	100	50	Balls	Runs	Wkts	Avge	BB	5i	10m	RpO	ct	st
Lim	2008/09	8	8	1	309	92	44.14	0	3	186	176	5	35.20	3-37	0	0	5.67	5	
20T	2009/10	6	4	0	52	21	13.00	0	0	74	94	6	15.66	4-6	1	0	7.62	5	
MARSH, Shaun Edward (Australia, Western Australia, Australia to England, Australia to India, Kings XI Punjab) b Narrogin, Western Australia, Australia 9.7.1983 LHB SLA																			
Int		4	4	0	144	112	36.00	1	0									0	
Lim		4	4	0	144	112	36.00	1	0									0	
20T		4	4	1	147	88*	49.00	0	2									1	
FC	2000/01	56	104	15	3232	166*	36.31	5	17	174	131	2	65.50	2-20	0	0	4.51	46	
Int	2008	27	27	1	1008	112	38.76	1	7									6	
Lim	2002/03	74	72	3	2487	116	36.04	3	16	36	31	1	31.00	1-14	0	0	5.16	18	
I20T	2008	3	3	0	53	29	17.66	0	0									0	
20T	2005/06	38	38	5	1429	115	43.30	2	10	12	13	0					6.50	12	
MARTIN, Jacob Joseph (Baroda) b Baroda, Gujarat 11.5.1972 RHB LBG																			
FC		6	11	1	293	52	29.30	0	1	24	23	1	23.00	1-23	0	0	5.75	1	
20T		2	2	0	14	10	7.00	0	0									1	
FC	1991/92	138	227	30	9192	271	46.65	23	47	618	459	10	45.90	5-51	1	0	4.45	120	4
Int	1999	10	8	1	158	39	22.57	0	0									6	
Lim	1993/94	101	96	21	2968	133	39.57	3	20	373	283	9	31.44	2-15	0	0	4.55	37	2
MARTYN, Damien Richard (Rajasthan Royals) b Darwin, Northern Territory, Australia 21.10.1971 RHB RM																			
20T		1	1	0	19	19	19.00	0	0									0	
Test	1992/93	67	109	14	4406	165	46.37	13	23	348	168	2	84.00	1-0	0	0	2.89	36	
FC	1990/91	204	343	46	14630	238	49.25	44	73	3365	1563	37	42.24	4-30	0	0	2.78	158	2
Int	1992/93	208	182	51	5346	144*	40.80	5	37	794	704	12	58.66	2-21	0	0	5.32	69	
Lim	1991/92	299	266	64	8644	144*	42.79	10	61	1549	1300	41	31.70	3-3	0	0	5.03	104	
I20T	2004/05	4	4	0	120	96	30.00	0	1									1	
20T	2004/05	6	6	0	175	96	29.16	0	1									3	
MASCARENHAS, Adrian Dimitri (Hampshire, Otago, Otago to India, Rajasthan Royals) b Chiswick, Middlesex, England 30.10.1977 RHB RMF																			
20T		4	4	1	25	10	8.33	0	0	96	122	6	20.33	2-20	0	0	7.62	0	
FC	1996	181	271	30	6185	131	25.66	8	22	26181	11818	418	28.27	6-25	16	0	2.70	72	
Int	2007	20	13	2	245	52	22.27	0	1	822	634	13	48.76	3-23	0	0	4.62	4	
Lim	1996	244	205	43	4107	79	25.35	0	27	10389	7376	281	26.24	5-27	9	1	4.26	62	
I20T	2007	14	13	5	123	31	15.37	0	0	252	309	12	25.75	3-18	0	0	7.35	7	
20T	2003	66	63	19	960	57*	21.81	0	3	1327	1587	81	19.59	5-14	1	1	7.17	20	
MATHEWS, Angelo Davis (Basnahira North, Colts, Sri Lanka, Kolkata Knight Riders, Sri Lanka to India, Sri Lanka to South Africa, Sri Lanka to United States of America, Sri Lanka to West Indies, Sri Lanka to Zimbabwe) b Colombo, Sri Lanka 2.6.1987 RHB RFM																			
Test		3	5	0	149	99	29.80	0	1	300	164	1	164.00	1-29	0	0	3.28	2	
FC		3	5	0	149	99	29.80	0	1	300	164	1	164.00	1-29	0	0	3.28	2	
Int		2	2	1	75	38	75.00	0	0	102	120	2	60.00	1-60	0	0	7.05	1	
Lim		2	2	1	75	38	75.00	0	0	102	120	2	60.00	1-60	0	0	7.05	1	
I20T		2	2	2	41	26*		0	0	43	79	2	39.50	2-30	0	0	11.02	1	
20T		16	13	6	274	65*	39.14	0	1	268	393	10	39.30	4-19	1	0	8.79	4	
Test	2009	10	14	1	470	99	36.15	0	2	696	376	6	62.66	1-13	0	0	3.24	2	
FC	2006/07	40	60	6	2770	270	51.29	8	11	3159	1503	36	41.75	5-47	1	0	2.85	24	
Int	2008/09	29	23	4	563	75	29.63	0	5	1002	765	27	28.33	6-20	0	1	4.58	9	
Lim	2005/06	55	45	10	1065	75	30.42	0	10	1533	1149	44	26.11	6-20	1	1	4.49	19	
I20T	2009	20	18	8	293	58	29.30	0	1	283	346	15	23.06	3-16	0	0	7.33	7	
20T	2006/07	52	46	13	857	65*	25.96	0	3	673	894	32	27.93	4-19	1	0	7.97	19	
MATHUR, Sumit Omprakash (Rajasthan) b Kota, Rajasthan 26.11.1980 RHB RFM																			
FC		4	8	2	31	10	5.16	0	0	870	349	11	31.72	3-49	0	0	2.40	0	
Lim		4	2	2	10	5*		0	0	216	194	1	194.00	1-58	0	0	5.38	1	
FC	2002/03	39	62	21	248	31	6.04	0	0	6808	3300	125	26.40	7-49	7	1	2.90	9	
Lim	2003/04	29	17	9	60	19*	7.50	0	0	1423	1210	38	31.84	4-62	1	0	5.10	7	
MEHRA, Puneet (Delhi) b Delhi 6.10.1988 RHB SLA																			
Lim		3	2	0	37	29	18.50	0	0	114	119	2	59.50	2-30	0	0	6.26	0	
20T		2	2	0	45	35	22.50	0	0	24	30	1	30.00	1-12	0	0	7.50	2	
MEHTA, Jitender (Himachal Pradesh) b Shimla, Himachal Pradesh 11.3.1982 RHB RM																			
FC		3	6	3	14	4*	4.66	0	0	486	247	4	61.75	2-22	0	0	3.04	0	
Lim		5	2	1	4	4*	4.00	0	0	266	265	7	37.85	3-42	0	0	5.97	2	
20T		5								120	128	8	16.00	2-14	0	0	6.40	0	
FC	2005/06	10	18	5	60	19	4.61	0	0	1364	738	18	41.00	3-87	0	0	3.24	1	
Lim	2005/06	18	8	3	34	13*	6.80	0	0	824	738	22	33.54	3-42	0	0	5.37	2	
20T	2006/07	10	1	0	0	0	0.00	0	0	231	232	18	12.88	4-31	1	0	6.02	2	
MEHTA, Pratik Satishbhai (Saurashtra) b Rajkot, Saurashtra 2.1.1978 LHB SLA																			
FC		6	9	3	335	77*	55.83	0	3	6	7	0					7.00	3	
Lim		4	2	1	153	134*	153.00	1	0									1	
20T		2	2	1	31	19*	31.00	0	0									0	
FC	1998/99	22	36	4	656	77*	20.50	0	4	146	95	1	95.00	1-6	0	0	3.90	9	
Lim	1998/99	28	24	6	650	134*	36.11	1	2	198	154	5	30.80	1-9	0	0	4.66	9	
20T	2006/07	5	4	1	43	19*	14.33	0	0	24	12	1	12.00	1-8	0	0	3.00	1	

Cmp	Debut	M	I	NO	Runs	HS	Avge	100	50	Balls	Runs	Wkts	Avge	BB	5i	10m	RpO	ct	st
MENARIA, Ashok Lakshminarayan (Rajasthan) b Udaipur, Rajasthan 29.10.1990 LHB LBG																			
Lim		4	4	0	115	72	28.75	0	1	12	22	0					11.00	2	
FC	2008/09	3	6	0	32	11	5.33	0	0	78	39	3	13.00	3-7	0	0	3.00	1	
Lim	2008/09	8	8	0	176	72	22.00	0	2	60	76	1	76.00	1-27	0	0	7.60	3	
MENDIS, Balapuwaduge Ajantha Winslo (Sri Lanka, Sri Lanka Army, Sri Lanka Board President's XI, Wayamba, Wayamba to India, Kolkata Knight Riders, Sri Lanka to India, Sri Lanka to South Africa, Sri Lanka to United States of America, Sri Lanka to West Indies, Sri Lanka to Zimbabwe) b Moratuwa, Sri Lanka 11.3.1985 RHB RS																			
Test		1	2	1	33	27	33.00	0	0	228	162	2	81.00	2-162	0	0	4.26	0	
FC		1	2	1	33	27	33.00	0	0	228	162	2	81.00	2-162	0	0	4.26	0	
Int		2	2	1	8	6	8.00	0	0	114	124	1	124.00	1-57	0	0	6.52	0	
Lim		2	2	1	8	6	8.00	0	0	114	124	1	124.00	1-57	0	0	6.52	0	
20T		4	2	2	2	1*		0	0	96	122	5	24.40	2-22	0	0	7.62	1	
Test	2008	12	13	4	145	78	16.11	0	1	3228	1644	50	32.88	6-117	2	1	3.05	2	
FC	2006/07	35	47	4	572	78	13.30	0	1	7545	3597	185	19.44	7-37	11	2	2.86	11	
Int	2007/08	44	21	9	91	15*	7.58	0	0	2073	1511	78	19.37	6-13	3	3	4.37	5	
Lim	2006/07	69	39	12	450	71*	16.66	0	2	3150	2144	123	17.43	6-13	5	3	4.08	10	
I20T	2008/09	19	4	2	7	4*	3.50	0	0	432	409	33	12.39	4-15	2	0	5.68	2	
20T	2006/07	46	15	8	25	9	3.57	0	0	1020	1043	64	16.29	4-9	3	0	6.13	12	
MERAI, Bhargav Hemantkumar (Gujarat) b Anand, Gujarat 17.9.1990 RHB RM																			
Lim		1	1	0	16	16	16.00	0	0									0	
MILIND KUMAR (Delhi) b Delhi 15.2.1991 RHB OB																			
20T		2	1	0	19	19	19.00	0	0									1	
MIRANDO, Magina Thilan Thushara (Kandurata, Sinhalese, Sri Lanka A, Chennai Super Kings, Sri Lanka to Bangladesh, Sri Lanka to South Africa, Sri Lanka to West Indies, Sri Lanka to Zimbabwe) b Balapitiya, Sri Lanka 1.3.1981 LHB LFM																			
20T		4	2	1	10	8	10.00	0	0	87	101	5	20.20	2-16	0	0	6.96	2	
Test	2003	9	13	2	90	15*	8.18	0	0	1542	961	28	34.32	5-83	1	0	3.73	3	
FC	1998/99	99	146	15	2032	103*	15.51	1	6	12698	7536	256	29.43	6-50	8	1	3.56	38	
Int	2007/08	38	27	6	392	54*	18.66	0	1	1676	1393	50	27.86	5-47	0	1	4.98	4	
Lim	1999/00	124	84	20	1139	75*	17.79	0	3	4841	3916	147	26.63	6-28	1	4	4.85	18	
I20T	2008/09	6	2	0	4	3	2.00	0	0	132	179	7	25.57	2-37	0	0	8.13	2	
20T	2004/05	33	21	7	134	33*	9.57	0	0	687	824	38	21.68	3-23	0	0	7.19	12	
MISHRA, Amit (Delhi Daredevils, Haryana, India, India to Bangladesh, India to South Africa, India to Sri Lanka, India to Zimbabwe) b Delhi 24.11.1982 RHB LB																			
Test		3	5	1	59	28	14.75	0	0	1032	491	5	98.20	3-78	0	0	2.85	2	
FC		6	9	3	96	28	16.00	0	0	1728	751	20	37.55	5-41	1	0	2.60	2	
20T		18	9	5	54	12	13.50	0	0	414	489	21	23.28	3-25	0	0	7.08	5	
Test	2008/09	10	13	2	205	50	18.63	0	1	2850	1429	36	39.69	5-71	1	0	3.00	6	
FC	2000/01	95	127	18	2132	84	19.55	0	10	21021	10019	371	27.00	6-66	19	1	2.86	55	
Int	2003	10	1	0	0	0	0.00	0	0	463	376	8	47.00	3-40	0	0	4.87	1	
Lim	2001/02	76	52	18	438	45	12.88	0	0	3960	2946	109	27.02	6-25	3	3	4.46	22	
I20T	2010	1								24	21	1	21.00	1-21	0	0	5.25	0	
20T	2006/07	45	26	7	274	49	14.42	0	0	995	1141	62	18.40	5-17	0	1	6.88	11	
MISHRA, Durgesh Kripashankar (Vidarbha) b Nagpur, Maharashtra 4.11.1991 RHB OB																			
Lim		1	1	0	2	2	2.00	0	0									0	
MISHRA, Mohnish Dinesh (Central Zone, Deccan Chargers, Madhya Pradesh) b Bhopal, Madhya Pradesh 9.2.1984 RHB OB																			
FC		4	3	0	158	131	52.66	1	0									0	
Lim		8	8	0	442	117	55.25	1	2									6	
20T		14	14	0	262	84	18.71	0	1									1	
FC	2000/01	13	19	2	625	131	36.76	1	4	78	40	0					3.07	3	
Lim	2005/06	16	15	1	735	117	52.50	2	4									8	
20T	2006/07	17	17	1	375	84	23.43	0	2									4	
MISHRA, Vikas (Delhi, North Zone) b Delhi 27.12.1992 RHB LAB																			
FC		4	3	1	2	2	1.00	0	0	1208	645	24	26.87	6-49	2	1	3.20	0	
Lim		4								198	143	6	23.83	4-50	1	0	4.33	1	
MITHUN, Abhimanyu (India, Karnataka, Royal Challengers Bangalore, South Zone, India to Sri Lanka, India A to England) b Dasarahalli, Karnataka 25.10.1989 RHB RM																			
FC		10	10	3	95	39*	13.57	0	0	2017	1210	52	23.26	6-71	3	1	3.59	1	
Int		1	1	0	24	24	24.00	0	0	48	63	0					7.87	0	
Lim		5	3	0	32	24	10.66	0	0	240	237	4	59.25	2-50	0	0	5.92	0	
20T		3	2	0	5	5	2.50	0	0	36	64	1	64.00	1-39	0	0	10.66	0	
Test	2010	3	4	0	120	46	30.00	0	0	552	372	6	62.00	4-105	0	0	4.04	0	
FC	2009/10	14	15	4	224	46	20.36	0	0	2755	1723	59	29.20	6-71	3	1	3.75	1	
Int	2009/10	2	2	0	28	24	14.00	0	0	72	87	0					7.25	0	
Lim	2007/08	16	9	2	46	24	6.57	0	0	790	707	13	54.38	3-49	0	0	5.37	0	
20T	2009	4	2	0	5	5	2.50	0	0	60	106	1	106.00	1-39	0	0	10.60	0	
MOHAMMAD HASHIM Rizvi (Vidarbha) b Nagpur, Maharashtra 13.9.1984 RHB RM																			
20T		1								24	28	2	14.00	2-28	0	0	7.00	0	
FC	2007/08	8	12	3	43	23	4.77	0	0	1398	660	36	18.33	7-26	1	1	2.83	1	
Lim	2005/06	13	7	3	21	14*	5.25	0	0	583	441	18	24.50	4-58	1	0	4.53	3	
20T	2006/07	3	2	2	8	7*		0	0	66	74	3	24.66	2-28	0	0	6.72	0	

Cmp	Debut	M	I	NO	Runs	HS	Avge	100	50	Balls	Runs	Wkts	Avge	BB	5i	10m	RpO	ct	st
MOHANTY, Basantkumar Chintamani (Orissa) b Bhubaneswar, Orissa 24.11.1986 RHB RFM																			
FC		6	7	2	75	27*	15.00	0	0	1277	594	20	29.70	6-65	1	0	2.79	1	
FC	2007/08	17	25	8	210	27*	12.35	0	0	3412	1510	69	21.88	7-27	5	0	2.65	4	
MOHANTY, Debasis Sarbeswar (East Zone, Orissa) b Bhubaneswar, Orissa 20.7.1976 RHB RM																			
FC		7	9	3	101	26	16.83	0	0	1373	525	22	23.86	4-48	0	0	2.29	1	
Lim		6	5	2	40	16	13.33	0	0	288	189	10	18.90	4-14	2	0	3.93	2	
Test	1997	2	1	1	0	0*		0	0	430	239	4	59.75	4-78	0	0	3.33	0	
FC	1996/97	111	148	42	1490	97	14.05	0	5	21070	8388	405	20.71	10-46	19	3	2.38	45	
Int	1997	45	11	6	28	18*	5.60	0	0	1996	1662	57	29.15	4-56	1	0	4.99	10	
Lim	1996/97	129	56	26	218	22	7.26	0	0	6024	4295	160	26.84	5-22	6	1	4.27	26	
20T	2006/07	8	3	0	12	12	4.00	0	0	163	183	9	20.33	2-24	0	0	6.73	1	
MOHANTY, Rakesh Kishorechandra (East Zone, Orissa) b Cuttack, Orissa 19.9.1985 RHB OB																			
FC		7	11	3	331	71*	41.37	0	2	300	222	2	111.00	2-79	0	0	4.44	6	
Lim		6	6	2	150	73	37.50	0	1	182	150	6	25.00	3-38	0	0	4.94	1	
20T		4	3	0	15	9	5.00	0	0	66	71	6	11.83	3-28	0	0	6.45	3	
FC	2004/05	14	20	3	465	71*	27.35	0	2	780	494	6	82.33	2-61	0	0	3.80	10	
Lim	2002/03	15	13	4	295	73	32.77	0	2	602	486	15	32.40	3-31	0	0	4.84	3	
MONDAL, Sayan Shekhar (Bengal) b Burdwan, Bengal 10.11.1989 RHB RM																			
FC		2	3	0	21	11	7.00	0	0	220	167	2	83.50	2-97	0	0	4.55	1	
Lim		3	1	0	31	31	31.00	0	0	145	102	7	14.57	3-25	0	0	4.22	0	
MORGAN, Eoin Joseph Gerard (England, Middlesex, England to Bangladesh, England to South Africa, England to Scotland, England to United Arab Emirates, England to West Indies, Royal Challengers Bangalore) b Dublin, Ireland 10.9.1986 LHB RM																			
20T		6	4	1	35	17	11.66	0	0									4	
Test	2010	6	8	0	256	130	32.00	1	0									4	
FC	2004	55	91	12	2930	209*	37.08	7	13	79	46	2	23.00	2-24	0	0	3.49	47	1
Int	2006	55	55	11	1798	115	40.86	4	10									24	
Lim	2003	135	128	21	4049	161	37.84	7	23	42	49	0					7.00	45	
I20T	2009	14	14	6	416	85*	52.00	0	3									8	
20T	2006	64	60	11	1343	85*	27.40	0	6									29	
MORKEL, Johannes Albertus (South Africa, Titans to South Africa, Chennai Super Kings, Durham, South Africa to India, South Africa to West Indies) b Vereeniging, Transvaal, South Africa 10.6.1981 LHB RMF																			
Int		1	1	0	2	2	2.00	0	0	48	59	1	59.00	1-59	0	0	7.37	1	
Lim		1	1	0	2	2	2.00	0	0	48	59	1	59.00	1-59	0	0	7.37	1	
20T		14	11	3	198	62	24.75	0	1	286	405	11	36.81	2-23	0	0	8.49	3	
Test	2008/09	1	1	0	58	58	58.00	0	1	192	132	1	132.00	1-44	0	0	4.12	0	
FC	1999/00	65	93	15	3296	204*	42.25	5	20	9779	5049	169	29.87	6-36	4	0	3.09	27	
Int	2003/04	47	34	8	621	97	23.88	0	2	1816	1629	48	33.93	4-29	2	0	5.38	12	
Lim	1999/00	158	121	32	2434	97	27.34	0	11	6174	5081	170	29.88	4-23	4	0	4.93	35	
I20T	2005/06	29	25	6	443	43	23.31	0	0	406	549	16	34.31	2-12	0	0	8.11	12	
20T	2003/04	127	104	31	1867	71	25.57	0	4	2137	2888	100	28.88	4-30	2	0	8.10	24	
MORKEL, Morné (South Africa, South Africa A, Titans, Rajasthan Royals, South Africa to India, South Africa to West Indies) b Vereeniging, Transvaal, South Africa 6.10.1984 LHB RFM																			
Test		2	2	1	23	12	23.00	0	0	372	238	4	59.50	2-115	0	0	3.83	1	
FC		2	2	1	23	12	23.00	0	0	372	238	4	59.50	2-115	0	0	3.83	1	
Int		1								42	48	0					6.85	0	
Lim		1								42	48	0					6.85	0	
20T		2	2	1	9	7*	9.00	0	0	42	66	0					9.42	1	
Test	2006/07	26	31	3	370	40	13.21	0	0	4855	2831	92	30.77	5-50	2	0	3.49	7	
FC	2003/04	58	72	9	1027	82*	16.30	0	4	10134	5778	212	27.25	6-43	9	2	3.42	24	
Int	2007	28	10	3	102	25	14.57	0	0	1439	1216	45	27.02	4-21	2	0	5.07	6	
Lim	2005/06	49	20	6	207	35	14.78	0	0	2336	1922	72	26.69	5-34	3	1	4.93	10	
I20T	2007/08	14	2	1	2	1*	2.00	0	0	317	346	23	15.04	4-17	2	0	6.54	1	
20T	2005	42	12	7	36	8	7.20	0	0	874	1027	44	23.34	4-17	2	0	7.05	7	
MOTA, Wilkin Arvind (Tripura) b Bombay (now Mumbai), Maharashtra 20.9.1981 RHB RM																			
FC		6	9	0	195	43	21.66	0	0	1105	491	23	21.34	6-26	1	0	2.66	3	
Lim		4	4	0	77	34	19.25	0	0	210	166	8	20.75	4-52	1	0	4.74	1	
20T		4	4	0	65	50	16.25	0	1	74	93	3	31.00	2-20	0	0	7.54	0	
FC	2004/05	15	24	4	471	74	23.55	0	2	2275	1008	41	24.58	6-26	1	0	2.65	6	
Lim	2003/04	16	13	3	175	34	17.50	0	0	612	532	18	29.55	4-52	1	0	5.21	2	
20T	2006/07	17	13	2	135	50	12.27	0	1	170	224	7	32.00	2-20	0	0	7.90	5	
MOTWANI, Rohit Heero (Maharashtra) b Pune, Maharashtra 13.12.1990 LHB WK																			
FC		6	12	0	430	78	35.83	0	5									18	1
Lim		4	4	0	93	48	23.25	0	0									3	2
20T		7	7	0	147	36	21.00	0	0									5	1
FC	2008/09	12	24	5	592	78	31.15	0	5									33	2
Lim	2006/07	12	10	0	180	48	18.00	0	0									11	2
20T	2006/07	11	11	0	198	36	18.00	0	0									6	1
MUHURI, Kishore Sankar (Tripura) b Agartala, Tripura 5.1.1986 RHB OB																			
20T		2	2	0	0	0	0.00	0	0									0	
FC	2007/08	2	4	0	26	10	6.50	0	0									1	

Cmp	Debut	M	I	NO	Runs	HS	Avge	100	50	Balls	Runs	Wkts	Avge	BB	5i	10m	RpO	ct	st

MUKUND, Abhinav (India Blue, Rest of India, South Zone, Tamil Nadu, India A to England, India A to Scotland) b Madras (now Chennai), Tamil Nadu 6.1.1990 LHB LBG

Cmp	Debut	M	I	NO	Runs	HS	Avge	100	50	Balls	Runs	Wkts	Avge	BB	5i	10m	RpO	ct	st
FC		9	14	0	689	257	49.21	2	2	303	169	7	24.14	3-5	0	0	3.34	6	
Lim		10	10	0	739	130	73.90	2	6	61	55	2	27.50	1-4	0	0	5.41	5	
20T		2	2	0	41	32	20.50	0	0									1	
FC	2007/08	28	43	1	2235	300*	53.21	8	6	333	183	7	26.14	3-5	0	0	3.29	19	
Lim	2008/09	22	22	0	1280	130	58.18	4	9	73	62	3	20.66	1-4	0	0	5.09	11	
20T	2007/08	4	3	0	41	32	13.66	0	0	33	39	5	7.80	2-4	0	0	7.09	4	

MULLICK, Pravanjan Madhabnanda (Orissa) b Bhubaneswar, Orissa 12.9.1976 RHB RM

Cmp	Debut	M	I	NO	Runs	HS	Avge	100	50	Balls	Runs	Wkts	Avge	BB	5i	10m	RpO	ct	st
FC		7	11	0	282	77	25.63	0	2	165	91	1	91.00	1-22	0	0	3.30	4	
20T		2	2	1	79	45	79.00	0	0									4	
FC	1996/97	88	141	18	5818	207*	47.30	18	27	2975	1302	31	42.00	3-45	0	0	2.62	62	
Lim	1996/97	56	49	8	1159	99	28.26	0	7	840	634	16	39.62	2-24	0	0	4.52	22	
20T	2006/07	9	7	2	164	45	32.80	0	0	6	6	0					6.00	6	

MUMTAZ QADIR (Services) b Allahabad, Uttar Pradesh 17.11.1986 RHB OB

Cmp	Debut	M	I	NO	Runs	HS	Avge	100	50	Balls	Runs	Wkts	Avge	BB	5i	10m	RpO	ct	st
Lim		5	4	0	54	50	13.50	0	1									2	
20T		5	5	0	88	51	17.60	0	1									1	
FC	2007/08	3	5	1	50	37	12.50	0	0									2	

MURALITHARAN, Muttiah (Kandurata, Sri Lanka, Tamil Union, Chennai Super Kings, Sri Lanka to India, Sri Lanka to South Africa, Sri Lanka to West Indies) b Kandy, Sri Lanka 17.4.1972 RHB OB

Cmp	Debut	M	I	NO	Runs	HS	Avge	100	50	Balls	Runs	Wkts	Avge	BB	5i	10m	RpO	ct	st
Test		3	4	1	53	29	17.66	0	0	911	591	9	65.66	4-195	0	0	3.89	2	
FC		3	4	1	53	29	17.66	0	0	911	591	9	65.66	4-195	0	0	3.89	2	
20T		12	1	0	1	1	1.00	0	0	288	329	15	21.93	3-16	0	0	6.85	3	
Test	1992	133	164	56	1261	67	11.67	0	1	44039	18180	800	22.72	9-51	67	22	2.47	72	
FC	1990	232	276	83	2192	67	11.35	0	1	66933	26997	1374	19.64	9-51	119	34	2.42	123	
Int	1993	337	159	61	663	33*	6.76	0	0	18169	11885	515	23.07	7-30	14	10	3.92	128	
Lim	1991/92	434	200	73	924	33*	7.27	0	0	22802	14637	654	22.38	7-30	16	12	3.85	155	
I20T	2006/07	11	2	0	1	1	0.50	0	0	258	266	13	20.46	3-29	0	0	6.18	0	
20T	2005	66	15	3	38	11	3.16	0	0	1523	1569	83	18.90	4-16	3	0	6.18	16	

MURASINGH, Manisankar Bhagyamani (Tripura) b Abhoynagar, Tripura 1.1.1993 LHB RM

Cmp	Debut	M	I	NO	Runs	HS	Avge	100	50	Balls	Runs	Wkts	Avge	BB	5i	10m	RpO	ct	st
FC		2	2	0	36	18	18.00	0	0	288	137	3	45.66	2-58	0	0	2.85	1	
Lim		1	1	1	24	24*		0	0	18	2	1	2.00	1-2	0	0	0.66	0	
20T		4	3	0	3	2	1.00	0	0	72	119	3	39.66	2-44	0	0	9.91	0	
Lim	2008/09	3	3	2	74	46*	74.00	0	0	78	56	2	28.00	1-2	0	0	4.30	0	

MURTAZA, Ali Ghulam (Mumbai Indians, Uttar Pradesh) b Allahabad, Uttar Pradesh 1.1.1990 LHB LM

Cmp	Debut	M	I	NO	Runs	HS	Avge	100	50	Balls	Runs	Wkts	Avge	BB	5i	10m	RpO	ct	st
FC		1	2	0	16	11	8.00	0	0	78	23	1	23.00	1-13	0	0	1.76	0	
Lim		5	4	2	148	67	74.00	0	2	76	62	0					4.89	1	
20T		5	2	0	33	21	16.50	0	0	114	125	7	17.85	3-9	0	0	6.57	3	
FC	2006/07	4	7	0	171	68	24.42	0	1	318	121	4	30.25	2-9	0	0	2.28	2	
Lim	2005/06	16	13	5	268	67	33.50	0	2	457	287	13	22.07	3-20	0	0	3.76	2	
20T	2006/07	9	5	2	92	39*	30.66	0	0	150	175	9	19.44	3-9	0	0	7.00	3	

MURTUZA ALI (Madhya Pradesh) b Bhopal, Madhya Pradesh 14.10.1986 RHB RMF

Cmp	Debut	M	I	NO	Runs	HS	Avge	100	50	Balls	Runs	Wkts	Avge	BB	5i	10m	RpO	ct	st
20T		3	1	1	20	20*		0	0									1	
FC	2006/07	7	12	1	299	88	27.18	0	1	162	100	2	50.00	2-38	0	0	3.70	5	
Lim	2007/08	9	8	1	266	86	38.00	0	2	204	170	6	28.33	3-31	0	0	5.00	2	
20T	2006/07	11	8	2	127	29*	21.16	0	0	12	16	0					8.00	5	

MURTUZA Rehman HUSSAIN (Mumbai) b Motihari, Bihar 1.10.1986 RHB RFM

Cmp	Debut	M	I	NO	Runs	HS	Avge	100	50	Balls	Runs	Wkts	Avge	BB	5i	10m	RpO	ct	st
Lim		1	1	0	1	1	1.00	0	0	48	50	0					6.25	0	
FC	2007/08	5	5	1	41	16	10.25	0	0	1155	566	17	33.29	6-58	1	0	2.94	0	
Lim	2007/08	3	2	1	4	3*	4.00	0	0	162	174	1	174.00	1-65	0	0	6.44	1	

MUZUMDAR, Amol Anil (Assam) b Bombay (now Mumbai), Maharashtra 11.11.1974 RHB LBG

Cmp	Debut	M	I	NO	Runs	HS	Avge	100	50	Balls	Runs	Wkts	Avge	BB	5i	10m	RpO	ct	st
FC		7	11	1	336	119*	33.60	1	1									3	
Lim		4	4	0	65	28	16.25	0	0									0	
20T		4	4	1	35	16	11.66	0	0									2	
FC	1993/94	151	230	27	9894	260	48.73	25	56	348	179	5	35.80	1-1	0	0	3.08	152	
Lim	1994/95	108	101	19	3168	109	38.63	3	25	96	91	2	45.50	1-11	0	0	5.68	37	
20T	2006/07	10	9	2	137	57	19.57	0	1									2	

NADEEM, Shahbaz (Jharkhand) b Patna, Bihar 12.8.1989 RHB SLA

Cmp	Debut	M	I	NO	Runs	HS	Avge	100	50	Balls	Runs	Wkts	Avge	BB	5i	10m	RpO	ct	st
FC		5	7	0	126	33	18.00	0	0	1362	526	21	25.04	6-74	1	0	2.31	5	
Lim		4	3	0	32	22	10.66	0	0	204	152	2	76.00	1-35	0	0	4.47	1	
20T		5	1	1	30	30*		0	0	96	71	4	17.75	1-4	0	0	4.43	1	
FC	2004/05	23	35	1	528	59	15.52	0	2	5131	2069	65	31.83	6-74	2	0	2.41	16	
Lim	2004/05	19	14	6	124	22	15.50	0	0	1015	675	25	27.00	5-30	0	1	3.99	4	
20T	2006/07	9	3	1	43	30*	21.50	0	0	192	172	11	15.63	3-20	0	0	5.37	3	

NADKARNI, Sachin Damodar (Services) b Mandsaur, Madhya Pradesh 24.8.1976 RHB OB

Cmp	Debut	M	I	NO	Runs	HS	Avge	100	50	Balls	Runs	Wkts	Avge	BB	5i	10m	RpO	ct	st
20T		5	5	0	42	21	8.40	0	0	102	105	7	15.00	3-23	0	0	6.17	0	
FC	2000/01	6	12	2	221	38	22.10	0	0	650	347	9	38.55	3-30	0	0	3.20	0	
Lim	1999/00	12	12	2	157	51	15.70	0	1	510	414	12	34.50	3-26	0	0	4.87	1	

NAGAR, Yogesh (Delhi, Delhi Daredevils) b Wazirabad, Delhi 6.1.1990 RHB OB

Cmp	Debut	M	I	NO	Runs	HS	Avge	100	50	Balls	Runs	Wkts	Avge	BB	5i	10m	RpO	ct	st
FC		3	4	0	86	55	21.50	0	1	78	35	2	17.50	1-0	0	0	2.69	1	
Lim		1	1	0	15	15	15.00	0	0									1	

Cmp	Debut	M	I	NO	Runs	HS	Avge	100	50	Balls	Runs	Wkts	Avge	BB	5i	10m	RpO	ct	st
20T		7	3	0	13	10	4.33	0	0	111	109	10	10.90	3-15	0	0	5.89	2	
FC	2008/09	6	7	0	182	79	26.00	0	2	372	162	5	32.40	1-0	0	0	2.61	1	
Lim	2008/09	8	6	3	43	15	14.33	0	0	367	297	15	19.80	5-48	0	1	4.85	6	
20T	2009	8	4	0	33	20	8.25	0	0	123	129	12	10.75	3-15	0	0	6.29	3	
NAIDU, Alind Shriniwas (Vidarbha) b Yavatmal, Maharashtra 11.10.1983 RHB OB																			
FC		5	9	1	170	76	21.25	0	1	312	179	6	29.83	3-23	0	0	3.44	2	
20T		3	3	0	82	55	27.33	0	1	18	30	0					10.00	1	
FC	1999/00	45	80	7	2437	118*	33.38	3	14	2634	1264	45	28.08	4-18	0	0	2.87	41	
Lim	1999/00	37	37	2	912	114	26.05	1	4	630	507	12	42.25	2-28	0	0	4.82	13	
20T	2006/07	7	7	0	161	55	23.00	0	1	36	56	0					9.33	3	
NAIDU, Pagadala Kaneshuk Kaushik K (Hyderabad) b Secunderabad, Andhra Pradesh 7.10.1990 RHB RM																			
Lim		2	2	1	3	3	3.00	0	0	95	82	3	27.33	2-26	0	0	5.17	0	
20T		1								24	67	1	67.00	1-67	0	0	16.75	0	
NAIDU, Venkatswamy Suryaprakash Thilak (Karnataka) b Bangalore, Karnataka 27.1.1978 RHB WK																			
FC		2	3	0	40	22	13.33	0	0									4	
FC	1998/99	93	140	14	4386	167*	34.80	8	24									220	17
Lim	1999/00	53	44	9	1108	77	31.65	0	7	1	4	0					24.00	56	14
20T	2006/07	1	1	0	44	44	44.00	0	0									0	
NAIK, Prashant Tukuram (Mumbai) b Pune, Maharashtra 2.9.1986 RHB LBG																			
FC		2	2	0	68	67	34.00	0	1									2	
20T		1	1	0	4	4	4.00	0	0									0	
FC	2007/08	8	11	1	417	118	41.70	1	3	66	56	0					5.09	3	
Lim	2006/07	7	5	1	141	58	35.25	0	1									0	
20T	2006/07	3	3	0	24	13	8.00	0	0									0	
NAIR, Sreekumar Rajagopalan (Kerala) b Trichur (now Thrissur), Kerala 2.11.1978 LHB SLA																			
FC		4	5	0	48	24	9.60	0	0	372	111	4	27.75	3-52	0	0	1.79	1	
FC	1997/98	67	102	8	3648	306*	38.80	5	23	10688	4077	122	33.41	5-66	3	0	2.28	36	
Lim	1997/98	67	60	8	1122	68	21.57	0	7	2946	2247	76	29.56	5-8	1	2	4.57	26	
NAIR, Vinan Gopinathan (Kerala) b Trivandrum (now Thiruvananthapuram), Kerala 18.11.1976 RHB WK																			
FC		4	5	1	67	44	16.75	0	0	6	1	0					1.00	5	
20T		1	1	0	9	9	9.00	0	0									2	
FC	2005/06	17	22	4	461	70	25.61	0	4	6	1	0					1.00	36	2
Lim	2005/06	17	14	3	235	44*	21.36	0	0									16	2
NANDA, Chetanya (Delhi, India Green) b Delhi 29.3.1979 RHB LBG																			
Lim		5	2	1	6	4*	6.00	0	0	208	187	2	93.50	1-43	0	0	5.39	0	
20T		7	1	1	13	13*		0	0	120	148	6	24.66	2-17	0	0	7.40	6	
FC	2004/05	30	35	7	436	58	15.57	0	2	6290	2825	103	27.42	6-67	4	0	2.69	11	
Lim	2004/05	31	15	4	141	52*	12.81	0	1	1488	1062	21	50.57	3-44	0	0	4.28	10	
20T	2006/07	15	4	1	20	13*	6.66	0	0	282	338	14	24.14	2-17	0	0	7.19	6	
NANDY, Arnab Arun (Bengal) b Babugang, Bengal 11.9.1987 RHB OB																			
Lim		5	2	0	27	20	13.50	0	0	112	91	1	91.00	1-39	0	0	4.87	4	
NANNES, Dirk Peter (Australia, Victoria, Australia to England, Australia to New Zealand, Australia to West Indies, Delhi Daredevils, Nottinghamshire) b Mount Waverly, Melbourne, Victoria, Australia 16.5.1976 RHB LFM																			
20T		13	2	1	4	3	4.00	0	0	295	303	16	18.93	4-24	1	0	6.16	0	
FC	2005/06	23	24	8	108	31*	6.75	0	0	4139	2327	93	25.02	7-50	2	1	3.37	7	
Int	2009	1	1	0	1	1	1.00	0	0	42	20	1	20.00	1-20	0	0	2.85	0	
Lim	2005/06	23	10	5	18	5*	3.60	0	0	1224	965	31	31.12	4-38	1	0	4.73	0	
I20T	2009	16	5	3	22	12*	11.00	0	0	348	431	27	15.96	4-18	1	0	7.43	1	
20T	2007/08	87	12	9	33	12*	11.00	0	0	1947	2307	120	19.22	4-11	5	0	7.10	13	
NARAYANAN KUTTY, Vilas (Kerala) b Northampton, England 19.4.1984 RHB RM																			
20T		1	1	0	2	2	2.00	0	0									0	
Lim	2007/08	2	2	0	38	38	19.00	0	0	18	28	0					9.33	0	
NARENDER KUMAR (Services) b Bhiwani, Haryana 4.10.1984 RHB RM																			
20T		3	3	0	12	7	4.00	0	0	54	73	1	73.00	1-37	0	0	8.11	0	
FC	2007/08	1	2	0	13	11	6.50	0	0	203	117	3	39.00	2-48	0	0	3.45	0	
Lim	2005/06	15	12	2	56	15*	5.60	0	0	543	445	18	24.72	5-29	1	1	4.91	5	
20T	2006/07	8	7	0	44	18	6.28	0	0	168	226	5	45.20	2-38	0	0	8.07	3	
NARENDER SINGH (Services) b Kanpur, Uttar Pradesh 16.8.1975 RHB																			
Lim		1	1	0	8	8	8.00	0	0									0	
FC	1996/97	32	59	3	1322	229*	23.60	1	3	12	1	0					0.50	16	
Lim	1996/97	31	31	1	654	86	21.80	0	3									6	
NARWAL, Sumit (Delhi, Rajasthan Royals) b Chirao, Karnal, Haryana 16.4.1982 LHB RM																			
FC		6	8	1	77	34*	11.00	0	0	981	485	17	28.52	5-71	1	0	2.96	2	
Lim		1								36	33	1	33.00	1-33	0	0	5.50	0	
20T		10	6	2	50	16	12.50	0	0	201	292	11	26.54	3-23	0	0	8.71	3	
FC	2001/02	22	29	2	591	137	21.88	1	1	3848	1755	66	26.59	5-71	2	0	2.73	6	
Lim	2001/02	17	12	2	140	29*	14.00	0	0	769	622	18	34.55	2-12	0	0	4.85	2	
NASEER WANT (Jammu and Kashmir) b Anantnag, Jammu 1.7.1982 RHB OB																			
FC		1	1	0	7	7	7.00	0	0									1	
Lim	2004/05	4	4	0	36	17	9.00	0	0									2	

Cmp	Debut	M	I	NO	Runs	HS	Avge	100	50	Balls	Runs	Wkts	Avge	BB	5i	10m	RpO	ct	st
NAYAR, Abhishek Mohan (India Blue, Mumbai, Mumbai Indians, West Zone, India to South Africa) b Secunderabad, Andhra Pradesh 26.10.1983 LHB RM																			
FC		8	11	1	610	259	61.00	2	2	756	344	6	57.33	2-63	0	0	2.73	3	
Lim		6	5	1	142	49*	35.50	0	0	114	98	3	32.66	2-23	0	0	5.15	2	
20T		3	3	1	58	27	29.00	0	0									1	
FC	2005/06	31	44	4	1917	259	47.92	5	8	4108	1819	60	30.31	6-45	2	0	2.65	11	
Int	2009	3	1	1	0	0*		0	0	18	17	0					5.66	0	
Lim	2003/04	54	46	7	1062	102	27.23	1	3	1541	1325	41	32.31	6-28	1	1	5.15	10	
20T	2006/07	31	24	5	457	45*	24.05	0	0	126	170	6	28.33	3-13	0	0	8.09	10	
NAZAR, Shadab (Services) b Bijnor, Uttar Pradesh 14.6.1987 RHB RM																			
Lim		2	2	1	1	1*	1.00	0	0	120	138	5	27.60	5-71	0	1	6.90	0	
NEGI, Ritesh (Services) b Delhi 29.12.1987 RHB RM																			
20T		1	1	0	0	0	0.00	0	0	24	35	0					8.75	1	
NEHRA, Ashish (Delhi, Delhi Daredevils, India, India to Bangladesh, India to South Africa, India to Sri Lanka, India to West Indies) b Delhi 29.4.1979 RHB LMF																			
Int		13	5	2	30	16*	10.00	0	0	632	692	16	43.25	3-37	0	0	6.57	2	
Lim		15	7	3	55	20	13.75	0	0	752	803	19	42.26	3-37	0	0	6.40	3	
I20T		2	1	0	22	22	22.00	0	0	42	96	1	96.00	1-52	0	0	13.71	1	
20T		9	3	1	45	22*	22.50	0	0	187	258	7	36.85	3-26	0	0	8.27	3	
Test	1998/99	17	25	11	77	19	5.50	0	0	3447	1866	44	42.40	4-72	0	0	3.24	5	
FC	1997/98	78	92	30	515	43	8.30	0	0	14829	7677	257	29.87	7-14	12	4	3.10	24	
Int	2001	107	40	20	132	24	6.60	0	0	5153	4399	144	30.54	6-23	5	2	5.12	16	
Lim	1997/98	164	69	31	333	24	8.76	0	0	7950	6511	207	31.45	6-23	7	2	4.91	24	
I20T	2009/10	7	3	0	22	22	7.33	0	0	162	252	11	22.90	3-19	0	0	9.33	2	
20T	2007/08	41	11	6	49	22*	9.80	0	0	882	1108	48	23.08	3-13	0	0	7.53	14	
NEMAT, Rameez Khan (Jharkhand) b Sitamarhi, Bihar 14.11.1986 RHB RM																			
FC		2	4	0	89	44	22.25	0	0									0	
Lim		2	2	0	34	34	17.00	0	0	6	6	0					6.00	1	
20T		4	4	2	96	62*	48.00	0	1									1	
Lim	2008/09	6	6	0	181	80	30.16	0	1	6	6	0					6.00	3	
NINAN, Ryan (Karnataka) b Thinuvanathapuram, Karnataka 19.11.1985 RHB OB																			
Lim		1	1	1	15	15*		0	0	60	51	2	25.50	2-51	0	0	5.10	0	
FC	2008/09	4	6	2	205	88*	51.25	0	2	910	349	10	34.90	3-46	0	0	2.30	0	
NIRANJAN, Pagadala Saikumar (Hyderabad) b Hyderabad, Andhra Pradesh 16.12.1984 LHB LB																			
20T		3	1	0	11	11	11.00	0	0	18	21	2	10.50	1-10	0	0	7.00	0	
FC	2004/05	3	6	0	79	41	13.16	0	0	107	71	4	17.75	2-4	0	0	3.98	0	
Lim	2004/05	7	6	0	68	31	11.33	0	0	147	133	4	33.25	2-8	0	0	5.42	2	
NIYAS, Nizar (Kerala) b Balaramapuram, Thiruvananthapuram, Kerala 19.9.1989 RHB RFM																			
FC		1	2	0	6	5	3.00	0	0	204	109	2	54.50	2-60	0	0	3.20	0	
Lim		4	2	1	8	7*	8.00	0	0	168	230	7	32.85	4-80	1	0	8.21	0	
20T		1	1	0	7	7	7.00	0	0	24	26	3	8.66	3-26	0	0	6.50	0	
Lim	2008/09	7	4	3	8	7*	8.00	0	0	304	360	12	30.00	4-80	1	0	7.10	0	
OBAID AHMED Haroon (Jammu and Kashmir) b Srinagar, Kashmir 2.12.1986 RHB RAB WK																			
Lim		5	5	1	73	26	18.25	0	0									4	
20T		4	3	0	13	12	4.33	0	0									3	
Lim	2007/08	11	11	1	166	26	16.60	0	0									14	
ODEDRA, Jayesh Arashibhai (Saurashtra, West Zone) b Bagvadar, Saurashtra 20.10.1987 RHB RFM																			
FC		2	4	2	16	16*	8.00	0	0	330	173	11	15.72	6-92	2	0	3.14	0	
Lim		8	2	1	10	5*	10.00	0	0	420	323	16	20.18	3-18	0	0	4.61	1	
20T		4	3	2	11	9	11.00	0	0	83	113	2	56.50	1-27	0	0	8.16	2	
FC	2008/09	5	7	3	32	16*	8.00	0	0	1008	485	17	28.52	6-92	2	0	2.88	0	
Lim	2006/07	20	6	5	25	13*	25.00	0	0	1044	806	37	21.78	4-16	2	0	4.63	4	
OJHA, Naman Vijaykumar (Central Zone, India Blue, Madhya Pradesh, Rajasthan Royals, India to Zimbabwe) b Ujjain, Madhya Pradesh 20.7.1983 RHB RAB WK																			
FC		6	7	1	216	87*	36.00	0	1									11	3
Lim		10	10	1	432	167	48.00	3	0									17	1
20T		17	17	3	480	94*	34.28	0	3									8	2
FC	2000/01	63	109	7	3380	214*	33.13	2	27									172	25
Int	2010	1	1	0	1	1	1.00	0	0									0	1
Lim	2001/02	66	64	2	2181	167	35.17	6	10									79	22
I20T	2010	2	2	0	12	10	6.00	0	0									0	
20T	2006/07	32	32	4	718	94*	25.64	0	5									13	7
OJHA, Pragyan Prayish (Deccan Chargers, Hyderabad, India, Rest of India, South Zone, India to Bangladesh, India to Sri Lanka, India to Zimbabwe) b Khurda, Orissa 5.9.1986 LHB SLA																			
Test		2	2	2	6	5*		0	0	511	258	9	28.66	3-101	0	0	3.02	3	
FC		5	6	3	37	15	12.33	0	0	1241	557	19	29.31	5-52	1	0	2.69	4	
Lim		2	2	1	16	15	16.00	0	0	114	112	1	112.00	1-56	0	0	5.89	0	
I20T		1	1	1	10	10*		0	0	12	27	0					13.50	0	
20T		20	9	5	14	10*	3.50	0	0	437	528	25	21.12	3-26	0	0	7.24	4	
Test	2009/10	6	7	5	42	18*	21.00	0	0	1723	899	21	42.80	4-115	0	0	3.13	3	
FC	2004/05	42	56	20	376	35	10.44	0	0	9756	4823	165	29.23	7-114	10	0	2.96	17	

Cmp	Debut	M	I	NO	Runs	HS	Avge	100	50	Balls	Runs	Wkts	Avge	BB	5i	10m	RpO	ct	st
Int	2008	16	9	8	41	16*	41.00	0	0	835	601	20	30.05	4-38	1	0	4.31	7	
Lim	2005/06	53	32	19	146	20	11.23	0	0	2740	2036	65	31.32	5-21	1	1	4.45	19	
I20T	2009	6	1	1	10	10*		0	0	126	132	10	13.20	4-21	1	0	6.28	1	
20T	2006/07	57	19	10	32	11*	3.55	0	0	1190	1371	73	18.78	4-21	1	0	6.91	11	
PAI, Srinivas Anoop (Hyderabad) b Addis Ababa, Ethiopia 20.12.1984 LHB LBG																			
FC		4	7	0	79	51	11.28	0	1	12	9	0					4.50	4	
20T		4	4	0	92	31	23.00	0	0									0	
FC	2005/06	19	36	1	1047	130	29.91	2	8	36	30	0					5.00	15	
Lim	2005/06	12	12	0	356	102	29.66	1	2	66	59	2	29.50	1-14	0	0	5.36	4	
PAKRAY, Saumya Lakshminarayan (Bengal) b Tribeny, Bengal 18.3.1989 LHB OB																			
Lim		2	1	1	2	2*		0	0	108	109	4	27.25	2-34	0	0	6.05	0	
PANCHAL, Ketan Narottam (Baroda) b Bombay (now Mumbai), Maharashtra 4.10.1986 LHB RFM																			
FC		1	2	0	28	25	14.00	0	0	150	78	2	39.00	2-78	0	0	3.12	0	
20T		4	2	1	53	33	53.00	0	0	54	75	2	37.50	1-16	0	0	8.33	3	
FC	2006/07	13	20	1	267	72	14.05	0	1	864	338	4	84.50	2-78	0	0	2.34	5	
Lim	2005/06	17	15	1	298	102	21.28	1	0	579	497	15	33.13	5-20	0	1	5.15	8	
20T	2006/07	8	5	1	82	33	20.50	0	0	83	107	3	35.66	1-14	0	0	7.73	5	
PANCHAL, Priyank Kiritbhai (Gujarat) b Ahmedabad, Gujarat 9.4.1990 RHB RM																			
Lim		4	4	0	99	35	24.75	0	0	12	7	0					3.50	1	
FC	2008/09	8	12	0	241	59	20.08	0	1	126	67	2	33.50	2-27	0	0	3.19	7	
Lim	2007/08	10	10	0	436	123	43.60	1	2	12	7	0					3.50	6	
PANDA, Bibhudutta Lingaraj (Orissa) b Cuttack, Orissa 14.3.1989 RHB RM																			
Lim		5	4	0	54	37	13.50	0	0	225	191	6	31.83	2-28	0	0	5.09	5	
FC	2008/09	1	2	0	23	14	11.50	0	0	222	109	2	54.50	2-109	0	0	2.94	0	
Lim	2008/09	8	5	0	66	37	13.20	0	0	387	344	9	38.22	2-28	0	0	5.33	6	
PANDEY, Abhishek Ramanath (Railways) b Darekhu, Uttar Pradesh 7.8.1988 RHB RFM																			
20T		1								6	9	0					9.00	0	
PANDEY, Ishwar Chand (Madhya Pradesh) b Rewa, Madhya Pradesh 15.8.1989 RHB RFM																			
Lim		6	3	0	0	0	0.00	0	0	300	256	3	85.33	1-33	0	0	5.12	1	
PANDEY, Manish Krishnanand (Karnataka, Royal Challengers Bangalore, South Zone, India A to England, India A to Scotland) b Nainital, Uttaranchal 10.9.1989 RHB OB																			
FC		10	16	0	956	194	59.75	4	5	6	1	0					1.00	14	
Lim		8	8	0	285	95	35.62	0	2									5	
20T		18	18	3	356	44	23.73	0	0									9	
FC	2008/09	18	28	3	1203	194	48.12	4	7	36	21	0					3.50	22	
Lim	2007/08	20	20	1	544	95	28.63	0	3	30	27	0					5.40	11	
20T	2006/07	33	31	5	656	114*	25.23	1	1									14	
PANDEY, Sanjay Panchanand (Madhya Pradesh) b Bhopal, Madhya Pradesh 14.12.1976 RHB RM																			
FC		4	2	0	64	46	32.00	0	0	449	269	5	53.80	3-53	0	0	3.59	0	
FC	1996/97	72	86	16	843	52*	12.04	0	1	14437	6830	240	28.45	8-132	10	1	2.83	24	
Lim	1996/97	52	28	16	172	28*	14.33	0	0	2636	2088	65	32.12	4-38	2	0	4.75	13	
PANKAJ SINGH (Central Zone, India Green, Rajasthan, Royal Challengers Bangalore, India to Zimbabwe) b Sultanpur, Uttar Pradesh 6.5.1985 RHB RM																			
FC		6	10	2	21	6	2.62	0	0	1342	638	32	19.93	7-56	2	1	2.85	0	
Lim		7	3	0	2	2	0.66	0	0	383	270	16	16.87	4-38	2	0	4.23	1	
20T		2	1	0	1	1	1.00	0	0	48	81	2	40.50	2-27	0	0	10.12	0	
FC	2004/05	39	57	10	543	74	11.55	0	1	7224	3608	138	26.14	7-56	8	3	2.99	9	
Int	2010	1	1	1	3	3*		0	0	42	45	0					6.42	1	
Lim	2005/06	38	28	8	327	66	16.35	0	1	1996	1621	57	28.43	4-29	3	0	4.87	6	
20T	2006/07	11	5	3	7	4*	3.50	0	0	180	292	5	58.40	2-27	0	0	9.73	4	
PARAB, Satyajit Sudhir (Baroda) b Baroda, Gujarat 1.9.1975 RHB OB																			
FC		5	9	0	234	154	26.00	1	0									2	
FC	1997/98	84	143	6	4782	154	34.90	16	16	281	188	2	94.00	1-6	0	0	4.01	62	
Lim	1997/98	35	33	0	1114	142	33.75	1	7	76	86	0					6.78	9	
PARADKAR, Nikhil Sandesh (Maharashtra) b Daund, Maharashtra 24.9.1987 LHB OB																			
Lim		3	3	0	53	39	17.66	0	0	126	106	1	106.00	1-36	0	0	5.04	2	
FC	2006/07	8	12	0	150	92	12.50	0	1	460	240	6	40.00	2-63	0	0	3.13	7	
Lim	2006/07	11	10	1	262	71	29.11	0	1	356	312	3	104.00	1-23	0	0	5.25	4	
20T	2006/07	4	4	0	16	10	4.00	0	0	72	86	2	43.00	1-17	0	0	7.16	0	
PARADKAR, Ranjit Satish (Vidarbha) b Nagpur, Maharashtra 7.7.1982 RHB OB																			
FC		5	8	0	260	72	32.50	0	2	24	20	0					5.00	2	
Lim		4	4	0	135	67	33.75	0	1	4	10	0					15.00	1	
FC	1999/00	32	55	4	1458	75	28.58	0	9	84	56	0					4.00	19	1
Lim	2002/03	29	29	8	801	103*	38.14	1	4	10	11	0					6.60	5	
PARAMESWARAN, Prasanth (Kerala) b Thanner Mukham, Allepey, Kerala 30.5.1985 RHB RM																			
FC		1	2	0	0	0	0.00	0	0	164	80	2	40.00	2-80	0	0	2.92	0	
Lim		5	2	2	0	0*		0	0	246	238	5	47.60	3-46	0	0	5.80	0	
Lim	2006/07	13	8	4	20	11*	5.00	0	0	684	556	21	26.47	6-35	0	1	4.87	1	
20T	2006/07	5	2	2	1	1*		0	0	102	119	7	17.00	3-34	0	0	7.00	1	

Cmp	Debut	M	I	NO	Runs	HS	Avge	100	50	Balls	Runs	Wkts	Avge	BB	5i	10m	RpO	ct	st
PARIDA, Kulamani Shankar (Railways) b Cuttack, Orissa 9.3.1977 RHB OB																			
FC		1	1	0	8	8	8.00	0	0	36	10	0					1.66	0	
FC	1996/97	107	129	34	1025	84	10.78	0	1	21723	9115	319	28.57	8-65	13	4	2.51	39	
Lim	1997/98	39	21	10	84	20	7.63	0	0	1875	1288	38	33.89	5-23	0	1	4.12	19	
20T	2006/07	5	1	1	0	0*		0	0	90	97	5	19.40	2-12	0	0	6.46	0	
PARIDA, Rashmi Ranjan (Rajasthan) b Bhubaneswar, Orissa 7.9.1974 RHB LB																			
Lim		4	4	0	273	122	68.25	1	2									2	
FC	1994/95	94	155	16	6273	220	45.12	14	36	24	15	0					3.75	94	
Lim	1994/95	58	53	6	1826	122	38.85	2	13	18	13	0					4.33	24	
PARMAR, Hardikkumar Shankarbhai (Baroda) b Borsad, Gujarat 22.9.1982 RHB RM																			
Lim		2	1	0	3	3	3.00	0	0	72	83	1	83.00	1-64	0	0	6.91	0	
FC	2001/02	1	1	1	0	0*		0	0	180	140	3	46.66	3-71	0	0	4.66	0	
Lim	2005/06	6	2	0	3	3	1.50	0	0	274	237	10	23.70	5-47	0	1	5.19	1	
PARMAR, Mohnish Bipinbhai (Gujarat, Kolkata Knight Riders) b Gandhinagar, Gujarat 12.4.1988 RHB OB																			
FC		1	1	0	7	7	7.00	0	0	108	87	0					4.83	0	
20T		1								18	33	0					11.00	0	
FC	2007/08	19	24	3	289	41	13.76	0	0	4217	1644	89	18.47	6-44	8	2	2.33	7	
Lim	2005/06	9	8	1	53	16	7.57	0	0	400	341	10	34.10	4-41	1	0	5.11	4	
20T	2006/07	5	3	1	12	7	6.00	0	0	102	148	2	74.00	1-25	0	0	8.70	1	
PARMAR, Vishwanath Mohanbhai (Baroda) b Baroda (now Vadodara), Gujarat 20.10.1983 RHB SLA																			
Lim		4	2	0	13	11	6.50	0	0	132	110	4	27.50	2-18	0	0	5.00	1	
FC	2007/08	1	1	0	9	9	9.00	0	0	96	40	0					2.50	0	
Lim	2005/06	10	6	2	63	23*	15.75	0	0	410	295	9	32.77	4-32	1	0	4.31	3	
PARVEZ RASOOL Zarghav (Jammu and Kashmir) b Bijbehara, Jammu and Kashmir 13.2.1989 RHB OB																			
FC		2	4	0	56	28	14.00	0	0	30	24	0					4.80	1	
Lim		5	5	1	225	81*	56.25	0	2	132	101	0					4.59	0	
FC	2008/09	3	6	0	115	40	19.16	0	0	192	167	0					5.21	1	
Lim	2008/09	9	9	1	306	81*	38.25	0	3	264	232	2	116.00	1-48	0	0	5.27	1	
PARVINDER SINGH (Central Zone, Uttar Pradesh) b Meerut, Uttar Pradesh 8.12.1981 RHB RM																			
FC		10	16	0	682	122	42.62	4	1	72	44	0					3.66	2	
Lim		5	4	0	74	36	18.50	0	0									2	
20T		3	3	1	93	51*	46.50	0	1	24	22	1	22.00	1-17	0	0	5.50	0	
FC	1999/00	26	44	0	1360	138	30.90	5	5	354	189	4	47.25	3-46	0	0	3.20	19	
Lim	2001/02	28	25	7	628	75	34.88	0	3	216	182	6	30.33	2-14	0	0	5.05	3	
20T	2006/07	4	4	1	108	51*	36.00	0	1	42	48	1	48.00	1-17	0	0	6.85	0	
PATEL, Anupam Sukhabhai (Gujarat) b Jamshedpur, Bihar 1.5.1985 RHB RM																			
20T		2	1	1	0	0*		0	0	42	67	0					9.57	0	
PATEL, Harshal Vikram (Gujarat) b Sanand, Gujarat 23.11.1990 RHB RFM																			
Lim		2	2	0	52	37	26.00	0	0	108	117	1	117.00	1-60	0	0	6.50	0	
Lim	2008/09	6	3	1	53	37	26.50	0	0	312	321	5	64.20	2-41	0	0	6.17	1	
PATEL, Munaf Musa (Baroda, India, India Red, Rajasthan Royals, Rest of India, West Zone, India to Sri Lanka) b Ikhar, Gujarat 12.7.1983 RHB RMF																			
FC		6	8	3	60	36*	12.00	0	0	911	489	23	21.26	5-48	2	0	3.22	1	
Int		2	2	1	2	2*	2.00	0	0	78	86	1	86.00	1-13	0	0	6.61	0	
Lim		10	6	2	13	7	3.25	0	0	441	371	12	30.91	4-21	1	0	5.04	4	
20T		4	2	1	4	4*	4.00	0	0	78	118	3	39.33	1-20	0	0	9.07	1	
Test	2005/06	12	13	5	56	15*	7.00	0	0	2394	1230	34	36.17	4-25	0	0	3.08	6	
FC	2003/04	48	55	17	545	78	14.34	0	1	8556	4124	171	24.11	6-50	7	1	2.89	13	
Int	2005/06	45	19	10	61	15	6.77	0	0	1999	1614	52	31.03	4-49	1	0	4.84	6	
Lim	2003/04	91	36	16	153	28	7.65	0	0	4182	3196	110	29.05	4-21	2	0	4.58	22	
20T	2007/08	31	9	5	37	23*	9.25	0	0	635	800	33	24.24	3-17	0	0	7.55	7	
PATEL, Mehul Suryakantbhai (Gujarat) b Surat, Gujarat 17.11.1984 RHB RM																			
FC		7	10	5	47	14	9.40	0	0	1255	620	15	41.33	3-21	0	0	2.96	2	
Lim		2	2	0	35	21	17.50	0	0	80	84	1	84.00	1-57	0	0	6.30	0	
PATEL, Niraj Kanubhai (Gujarat) b Ahmedabad, Gujarat 26.3.1981 LHB SLA																			
FC		7	12	0	477	107	39.75	2	2	208	143	5	28.60	3-35	0	0	4.12	2	
Lim		4	4	0	258	92	64.50	0	2	96	83	2	41.50	1-22	0	0	5.18	2	
20T		4	4	1	167	96*	55.66	0	2	60	84	2	42.00	1-9	0	0	8.40	1	
FC	1997/98	77	130	7	4788	173	38.92	12	24	781	412	10	41.20	3-35	0	0	3.16	50	
Lim	1998/99	57	52	7	1876	111	41.68	1	13	606	599	8	74.87	2-28	0	0	5.93	23	
20T	2006/07	21	18	5	588	96*	45.23	0	5	150	223	9	24.77	4-29	1	0	8.92	9	
PATEL, Parthiv Ajay (Chennai Super Kings, Gujarat, India Green, West Zone) b Ahmedabad, Gujarat 9.3.1985 LHB OB WK																			
FC		8	13	0	813	166	62.53	3	5	6	0	0					0.00	24	1
Lim		6	6	1	58	20	11.60	0	0									3	2
20T		8	8	0	159	57	19.87	0	1									2	4
Test	2002	20	30	7	683	69	29.69	0	4									41	8
FC	2001/02	110	161	19	5806	206	40.88	13	33	24	9	0					2.25	273	43
Int	2002/03	14	10	1	132	28	14.66	0	0									12	3
Lim	2001/02	93	83	6	1906	71	24.75	0	12									97	39
20T	2005	39	38	2	762	57	21.16	0	4									15	7

Cmp	Debut	M	I	NO	Runs	HS	Avge	100	50	Balls	Runs	Wkts	Avge	BB	5i	10m	RpO	ct	st
PATEL, Paresh Chunilal (East Zone, Orissa) b Bhubaneswar, Orissa 18.9.1985 LHB SLA																			
FC		1	2	0	13	9	6.50	0	0	144	108	2	54.00	2-64	0	0	4.50	1	
Lim		4	4	1	307	123*	102.33	1	2	154	140	2	70.00	1-29	0	0	5.45	0	
20T		4	4	0	71	41	17.75	0	0	84	91	10	9.10	3-16	0	0	6.50	1	
FC	2005/06	9	14	0	326	88	23.28	0	1	772	273	6	45.50	2-42	0	0	2.12	5	
Lim	2004/05	11	11	1	378	123*	37.80	1	2	496	401	9	44.55	5-41	0	1	4.85	0	
20T	2006/07	12	12	1	201	51	18.27	0	1	255	272	27	10.07	4-11	1	0	6.40	5	
PATEL, Sunny Jayantibhai (Gujarat) b Surat, Gujarat 10.4.1987 RHB LBG																			
FC		2	3	0	67	37	22.33	0	0	24	16	0					4.00	1	
20T		2	2	1	40	29*	40.00	0	0									0	
FC	2008/09	8	12	1	256	90	23.27	0	1	84	52	0					3.71	14	
Lim	2007/08	7	7	3	179	53*	44.75	0	2									3	
20T	2006/07	5	5	1	77	29*	19.25	0	0									0	
PATEL, Timil Kaushik (Gujarat) b Ahmedabad, Gujarat 1.12.1983 RHB LBG																			
FC		4	8	1	119	31	17.00	0	0	278	192	5	38.40	2-47	0	0	4.14	3	
FC	2002/03	38	60	11	1169	104*	23.85	1	4	4551	2800	72	38.88	5-15	2	0	3.69	24	
PATEL, Udit Brijesh (Karnataka) b Baroda, Gujarat 31.8.1984 RHB OB																			
FC		2	2	0	15	10	7.50	0	0	372	202	5	40.40	3-96	0	0	3.25	0	
Lim		6	4	1	31	16*	10.33	0	0	306	211	7	30.14	2-33	0	0	4.13	3	
20T		2	1	0	21	21	21.00	0	0	12	15	0					7.50	0	
FC	2002/03	17	20	8	136	35	11.33	0	0	2944	1613	40	40.32	4-38	0	0	3.28	2	
Lim	2002/03	16	7	3	45	16*	11.25	0	0	638	505	13	38.84	2-33	0	0	4.74	3	
PATHAK, Chirag Rajeshbhai (Saurashtra, West Zone) b Keshod, Saurashtra 2.2.1987 LHB RAB																			
FC		7	12	0	735	138	61.25	3	3	12	13	0					6.50	9	
Lim		8	8	0	223	101	27.87	1	0									1	
20T		3	3	0	37	26	12.33	0	0									0	
FC	2008/09	13	21	0	1102	170	52.47	4	4	18	14	0					4.66	9	
Lim	2006/07	23	23	0	645	101	28.04	1	4									7	
20T	2006/07	7	7	0	147	55	21.00	0	1									0	
PATHAN, Asadullah Khan (Railways) b Ankleshwar, Gujarat 17.6.1984 RHB RM																			
20T		4	4	1	46	35	15.33	0	0									0	
PATHAN, Irfan Khan (Baroda, Kings XI Punjab, West Zone) b Baroda, Gujarat 27.10.1984 LHB LMF																			
FC		7	13	1	465	81	38.75	0	4	1020	647	31	20.87	5-100	1	0	3.80	1	
20T		14	13	5	276	60	34.50	0	1	278	426	15	28.40	3-24	0	0	9.19	4	
Test	2003/04	29	40	5	1105	102	31.57	1	6	5884	3226	100	32.26	7-59	7	2	3.29	8	
FC	2000/01	87	119	24	2946	111*	31.01	2	18	16348	8726	301	28.99	7-35	14	3	3.20	25	
Int	2003/04	107	78	18	1368	83	22.80	0	5	5194	4546	152	29.90	5-27	4	1	5.25	18	
Lim	2001/02	152	109	26	1870	83	22.53	0	7	7471	6309	220	28.67	5-27	6	1	5.06	27	
I20T	2006/07	16	12	7	133	33*	26.60	0	0	306	395	16	24.68	3-16	0	0	7.74	2	
20T	2005	69	55	19	818	60	22.72	0	1	1420	1818	78	23.30	4-27	1	0	7.68	16	
PATHAN, Yusuf Khan (Baroda, India, India Blue, Rajasthan Royals, West Zone, India to South Africa, India to West Indies, India to Zimbabwe) b Baroda, Gujarat 27.11.1984 RHB OB																			
FC		6	12	2	541	210*	54.10	2	2	730	447	7	63.85	3-148	0	0	3.67	7	
Int		3	3	0	59	36	19.66	0	0	174	154	4	38.50	2-37	0	0	5.31	0	
Lim		12	12	2	443	108*	44.30	1	2	557	440	12	36.66	3-7	0	0	4.74	1	
I20T		2	1	0	0	0	0.00	0	0	42	83	2	41.50	1-29	0	0	11.85	0	
20T		20	19	2	447	100	26.29	1	2	330	459	15	30.60	3-30	0	0	8.34	9	
FC	2001/02	42	67	8	2323	210*	39.37	6	10	7293	3348	96	34.87	6-47	7	1	2.75	44	
Int	2008	37	26	9	376	59*	22.11	0	2	890	854	21	40.66	3-56	0	0	5.75	9	
Lim	2004/05	102	86	17	2256	148	32.69	4	11	3546	2984	74	40.32	5-52	1	2	5.04	38	
I20T	2007/08	18	15	4	205	37*	18.63	0	0	239	351	10	35.10	2-23	0	0	8.81	8	
20T	2006/07	69	65	8	1410	100	24.73	1	8	972	1285	47	27.34	4-10	2	0	7.93	26	
PATI, Bikas Swarup (Orissa) b Jeybone, Orissa 17.5.1985 RHB RAB																			
FC		7	11	0	202	55	18.36	0	2									4	
Lim		3	3	0	11	6	3.66	0	0									0	
FC	2006/07	25	41	0	841	72	20.51	0	5	40	37	0					5.55	17	
Lim	2006/07	11	10	0	265	80	26.50	0	3									5	
20T	2006/07	5	5	0	59	30	11.80	0	0									2	
PATIL, Devraj Thyagaraj (Karnataka) b Shimoga, Karnataka 6.12.1984 RHB WK																			
20T		2	1	0	2	2	2.00	0	0									0	
FC	2007/08	2	1	0	7	7	7.00	0	0									0	
Lim	2005/06	14	11	4	286	106*	40.85	1	1									17	1
20T	2006/07	13	12	0	231	44	19.25	0	0									6	3
PATIL, Jitendra Arun (Maharashtra) b Pachora, Maharashtra 9.9.1989 RHB LM																			
FC		2	4	0	39	39	9.75	0	0	342	254	7	36.28	4-113	0	0	4.45	0	
Lim	2006/07	12	7	3	33	16*	8.25	0	0	480	458	11	41.63	3-49	0	0	5.72	4	
20T	2006/07	3	2	1	4	4*	4.00	0	0	60	67	4	16.75	2-18	0	0	6.70	0	
PAUNIKAR, Amit Gajanan (Rajasthan Royals, Vidarbha) b Nagpur, Maharashtra 18.4.1988 RHB WK																			
FC		5	9	0	211	98	23.44	0	1									3	
Lim		4	4	0	86	40	21.50	0	0									4	
20T		4	4	0	18	18	4.50	0	0									0	

Cmp	Debut	M	I	NO	Runs	HS	Avge	100	50	Balls	Runs	Wkts	Avge	BB	5i	10m	RpO	ct	st
FC	2007/08	7	13	1	349	102	29.08	1	1									4	
Lim	2007/08	14	14	0	362	63	25.85	0	3									7	6
PAWAN, Kolar Balasubramanya (Karnataka, South Zone) b Bangalore, Karnataka 19.12.1987 RHB WK																			
FC		10	17	1	651	152	40.68	2	2									7	
FC	2006/07	24	42	3	1417	152	36.33	4	6									19	
Lim	2006/07	3	3	0	25	16	8.33	0	0									1	
PAWAR, Prateek (Haryana) b Delhi 28.1.1989 RHB RAB																			
Lim		5	4	0	63	35	15.75	0	0									2	
PAWAR, Rajesh Vithal (Baroda) b Bombay (now Mumbai), Maharashtra 6.9.1979 LHB SLA																			
FC		1	1	0	45	45	45.00	0	0	132	80	0					3.63	0	
20T		4	2	1	5	3	5.00	0	0	72	109	3	36.33	2-21	0	0	9.08	1	
FC	1996/97	76	101	14	1484	95*	17.05	0	4	17158	7715	272	28.36	7-87	11	2	2.69	35	
Lim	1996/97	36	19	3	432	89	27.00	0	3	1719	1355	39	34.74	3-38	0	0	4.72	13	
20T	2006/07	8	4	1	7	3	2.33	0	0	132	179	6	29.83	2-21	0	0	8.13	1	
PAWASKAR, Ninad Shamsundar (Goa) b Duler, Goa 15.12.1988 LHB SLA																			
Lim		1	1	0	6	6	6.00	0	0									0	
PERERA, Narangoda Liyanaarachchilage Tissara Chirantha (Colts, Sri Lanka, Wayamba, Wayamba to India, Chennai Super Kings, Sri Lanka to Bangladesh, Sri Lanka to India, Sri Lanka to United States of America, Sri Lanka to West Indies, Sri Lanka to Zimbabwe, Sri Lanka A to Australia) b Colombo, Sri Lanka 3.4.1989 LHB RMF																			
Int		2	1	0	31	31	31.00	0	0	54	66	0					7.33	0	
Lim		2	1	0	31	31	31.00	0	0	54	66	0					7.33	0	
20T		2	1	0	6	6	6.00	0	0	24	29	0					7.25	1	
FC	2008/09	14	24	6	745	113*	41.38	1	5	1373	818	24	34.08	5-69	1	0	3.57	10	
Int	2009/10	12	7	2	130	36*	26.00	0	0	414	378	15	25.20	5-28	0	1	5.47	5	
Lim	2008/09	38	26	7	449	50	23.63	0	1	1356	1264	49	25.79	5-28	1	2	5.59	15	
I20T	2010	6	5	2	57	24	19.00	0	0	78	80	3	26.66	2-19	0	0	6.15	0	
20T	2007/08	30	23	8	142	24	9.46	0	0	512	592	32	18.50	3-17	0	0	6.93	11	
PIETERSEN, Kevin Peter (England, Hampshire, Surrey, England to Bangladesh, England to South Africa, England to Scotland, England to United Arab Emirates, England to West Indies, Royal Challengers Bangalore) b Pietermaritzburg, Natal, South Africa 27.6.1980 RHB OB																			
20T		7	7	3	236	66*	59.00	0	2	60	77	3	25.66	1-10	0	0	7.70	3	
Test	2005	66	117	6	5306	226	47.80	16	20	843	568	4	142.00	1-0	0	0	4.04	39	
FC	1997/98	154	256	18	11726	254*	49.26	38	49	5647	3279	61	53.75	4-31	0	0	3.48	119	
Int	2004/05	104	94	15	3332	116	42.17	7	20	274	246	6	41.00	2-22	0	0	5.38	32	
Lim	1998/99	217	198	32	6931	147	41.75	13	41	2264	1998	40	49.95	3-14	0	0	5.29	76	
I20T	2005	28	28	4	911	79	37.95	0	5	18	36	1	36.00	1-27	0	0	12.00	10	
20T	2003	57	57	7	1636	79	32.72	0	9	312	408	17	24.00	3-33	0	0	7.84	19	
PINTO, Reagan John (Goa) b Bombay (now Mumbai), Maharashtra 21.9.1991 RHB LBG																			
FC		4	5	0	125	46	25.00	0	0	128	76	3	25.33	2-15	0	0	3.56	0	
20T		3	2	0	18	12	9.00	0	0	4	1	2	0.50	2-1	0	0	1.50	1	
Lim	2008/09	5	5	0	54	24	10.80	0	0	198	180	2	90.00	1-32	0	0	5.45	4	
POLLARD, Kieron Adrian (Trinidad and Tobago, Trinidad and Tobago to India, West Indies, Mumbai Indians, Somerset, South Australia, West Indies to Australia) b Cacariqua, Trinidad 12.5.1987 RHB RM																			
20T		20	19	3	419	54*	26.18	0	1	294	371	19	19.52	3-17	0	0	7.57	11	
FC	2006/07	20	33	1	1199	174	37.46	3	5	571	313	6	52.16	2-29	0	0	3.28	32	
Int	2006/07	30	27	0	538	62	19.92	0	1	936	833	30	27.76	3-27	0	0	5.34	10	
Lim	2006/07	48	43	3	1109	87	27.72	0	7	1410	1214	57	21.29	4-32	1	0	5.16	22	
I20T	2008	20	17	2	190	38	12.66	0	0	258	360	11	32.72	2-22	0	0	8.37	11	
20T	2006	80	69	13	1391	89*	24.83	0	6	1178	1514	81	18.69	4-15	2	0	7.71	35	
POPAT, Digant Manoj (Gujarat) b Ahmedabad, Gujarat 27.11.1982 LHB LM																			
FC		2	3	0	47	24	15.66	0	0									2	
FC	2007/08	11	17	2	326	63	21.73	0	2	6	3	0					3.00	9	
POULOSE, Arun Manavalan (Kerala) b Aluva, Ernakulam, Kerala 22.7.1986 RHB RMF																			
Lim		1	1	0	3	3	3.00	0	0									0	
20T		1	1	0	9	9	9.00	0	0									0	
20T	2006/07	4	4	0	84	42	21.00	0	0									0	
POWAR, Ramesh Rajaram (Kings XI Punjab, Mumbai, West Zone) b Bombay (now Mumbai), Maharashtra 20.5.1978 RHB OB																			
FC		10	12	3	432	125*	48.00	2	1	1797	1010	22	45.90	5-47	1	0	3.37	2	
Lim		4	3	1	19	15	9.50	0	0	208	145	9	16.11	4-44	1	0	4.18	2	
20T		7	2	1	5	3	5.00	0	0	138	160	3	53.33	2-28	0	0	6.95	0	
Test	2007	2	2	0	13	7	6.50	0	0	252	118	6	19.66	3-33	0	0	2.81	0	
FC	1999/00	111	141	20	3679	131	30.40	7	17	22576	11023	378	29.16	7-44	21	3	2.93	45	
Int	2003/04	31	19	5	163	54	11.64	0	1	1536	1191	34	35.02	3-24	0	0	4.65	3	
Lim	2000/01	113	80	17	1081	80*	17.15	0	4	5557	4392	142	30.92	5-53	4	1	4.74	25	
20T	2006/07	22	8	5	61	28*	20.33	0	0	360	418	12	34.83	2-11	0	0	6.96	5	
PRABHU, Murthy (Tamil Nadu) b Madras (now Chennai), Tamil Nadu 14.12.1987 RHB OB																			
Lim		2								108	58	4	14.50	4-34	1	0	3.22	3	
20T		2								42	34	3	11.33	3-17	0	0	4.85	0	

Cmp	Debut	M	I	NO	Runs	HS	Avge	100	50	Balls	Runs	Wkts	Avge	BB	5i	10m	RpO	ct	st
PRASAD, Garikina Venkata Satya (Andhra) b Visakhapatnam, Andhra Pradesh 2.12.1989 RHB OB																			
FC		3	3	3	15	8*		0	0	650	282	9	31.33	5-100	1	0	2.60	1	
Lim		1								24	32	2	16.00	2-32	0	0	8.00	1	
20T		1																0	
FC	2008/09	4	4	4	16	8*		0	0	722	340	9	37.77	5-100	1	0	2.82	1	
Lim	2008/09	4	2	2	42	41*		0	0	121	125	4	31.25	2-10	0	0	6.19	2	
PRASAD, Sachin Chandra (Jharkhand) b Ranchi, Bihar 18.11.1987 RHB																			
FC		2	4	1	141	106	47.00	1	0									1	
Lim		2	2	0	21	12	10.50	0	0									0	
PRASANNA, Ramaswamy (Tamil Nadu) b Madras (now Chennai), Tamil Nadu 7.4.1982 LHB RMF																			
FC		1	2	0	60	32	30.00	0	0									1	
Lim		1	1	0	30	30	30.00	0	0	12	13	0					6.50	0	
20T		2	1	0	4	4	4.00	0	0	30	48	1	48.00	1-13	0	0	9.60	0	
FC	2004/05	16	27	2	957	134	38.28	2	5	90	25	0					1.66	26	
Lim	2004/05	15	13	2	350	72	31.81	0	1	192	152	5	30.40	2-33	0	0	4.75	8	
20T	2006/07	7	6	1	58	34	11.60	0	0	72	83	4	20.75	2-12	0	0	6.91	0	
PRASANTH, Padmanabhan (Kerala) b Trivandrum (now Thiruvananthapuram), Kerala 22.5.1985 LHB SLA																			
FC		3	3	1	40	35	20.00	0	0	277	114	5	22.80	2-20	0	0	2.46	0	
Lim		5	4	1	103	41*	34.33	0	0	258	243	6	40.50	3-56	0	0	5.65	2	
20T		1	1	1	9	9*		0	0	24	27	1	27.00	1-27	0	0	6.75	0	
FC	2006/07	13	18	4	346	83	24.71	0	2	1176	477	13	36.69	2-20	0	0	2.43	5	
Lim	2005/06	15	11	4	247	73	35.28	0	1	664	581	15	38.73	3-34	0	0	5.25	5	
20T	2006/07	3	3	1	17	9*	8.50	0	0	72	85	6	14.16	3-20	0	0	7.08	1	
PRATAP SINGH, Prabal (Madhya Pradesh) b Morena, Madhya Pradesh 9.12.1986 RHB RM																			
20T		3	1	0	8	8	8.00	0	0	42	55	2	27.50	1-23	0	0	7.85	1	
PRINCE, Dany Derek Rudrapathi (Hyderabad) b Nizamabad, Andhra Pradesh 14.3.1986 LHB OB																			
20T		3	3	0	48	28	16.00	0	0									0	
FC	2007/08	1	2	0	8	8	4.00	0	0									1	
PUJARA, Cheteshwar Arvind (Kolkata Knight Riders, Saurashtra, West Zone, India A to England, India A to Scotland) b Rajkot, Saurashtra 25.1.1988 RHB LB																			
FC		6	10	1	741	204*	82.33	2	5									1	
Lim		8	8	2	424	110	70.66	2	2									2	
20T		10	6	2	122	45*	30.50	0	0									2	
FC	2005/06	49	78	13	3925	302*	60.38	14	13	153	83	5	16.60	2-4	0	0	3.25	24	1
Lim	2005/06	44	44	10	1941	122*	57.08	6	12									13	
20T	2006/07	14	10	3	232	45*	33.14	0	0									4	
PUJARI, Hanumant Ningappa (Maharashtra) b Solapur, Maharashtra 1.1.1989 RHB RM																			
20T		1	1	0	2	2	2.00	0	0									1	
PURKAYASTHA, Sarupam Phanindra (Assam) b Guwahati, Assam 15.9.1989 RHB OB																			
FC		2	3	1	53	21	26.50	0	0	54	24	0					2.66	1	
Lim		2	2	1	7	6	7.00	0	0	48	51	0					6.37	0	
20T		4								64	82	4	20.50	2-25	0	0	7.68	2	
FC	2008/09	6	11	2	281	77	31.22	0	2	242	124	5	24.80	2-1	0	0	3.07	4	
Lim	2007/08	8	8	1	132	60	18.85	0	1	273	244	0					5.36	1	
QUADRI, Syed Ahmed (Hyderabad) b Hyderabad, Andhra Pradesh 2.12.1981 LHB RM																			
FC		7	11	3	376	76*	47.00	0	3	749	417	4	104.25	1-51	0	0	3.34	4	
Lim		4	4	0	108	76	27.00	0	1	90	108	2	54.00	2-55	0	0	7.20	0	
FC	2008/09	13	21	5	764	100*	47.75	1	6	1289	734	9	81.55	2-120	0	0	3.41	5	
Lim	2002/03	15	14	2	316	76	26.33	0	2	386	409	8	51.12	4-40	1	0	6.35	1	
QUADRI, Samar Safdar (Jharkhand) b Patna, Bihar 27.7.1989 LBG																			
FC		2	3	1	23	12*	11.50	0	0	372	180	6	30.00	3-6	0	0	2.90	0	
QURESHI, Sameer Parvesh (Saurashtra) b Dholpur, Rajasthan 29.11.1986 RHB RAB																			
20T		4	4	0	122	80	30.50	0	1									1	
RAHANE, Ajinkya Madhukar (India Green, Mumbai, West Zone, India A to England, India A to Scotland) b Ashwi Khurd, Maharashtra 6.6.1988 RHB RM																			
FC		11	17	3	887	265*	63.35	3	3	60	43	0					4.30	1	
Lim		8	8	0	233	76	29.12	0	2	11	8	1	8.00	1-8	0	0	4.36	2	
20T		5	5	0	54	24	10.80	0	0									1	
FC	2007/08	39	64	7	3670	265*	64.38	12	16	102	63	0					3.70	27	
Lim	2006/07	40	40	0	1552	187	38.80	3	9	53	51	4	12.75	2-36	0	0	5.77	12	
20T	2006/07	22	21	2	322	62*	16.94	0	3	6	5	1	5.00	1-5	0	0	5.00	5	
RAHUL, Kannur Lokesh (Karnataka) b Bangalore, Karnataka 18.4.1992 RHB OB WK																			
Lim		1	1	0	36	36	36.00	0	0									0	
RAINA, Suresh Kumar (Central Zone, Chennai Super Kings, India, India Green, Uttar Pradesh, India to Bangladesh, India to South Africa, India to Sri Lanka, India to West Indies, India to Zimbabwe) b Ghaziabad, Uttar Pradesh 27.11.1986 LHB OB																			
FC		5	7	0	292	98	41.71	0	3	174	81	3	27.00	3-31	0	0	2.79	5	
Int		14	10	1	347	68	38.55	0	4	114	130	3	43.33	1-13	0	0	6.84	6	
Lim		18	14	2	412	68	34.33	0	4	240	276	3	92.00	1-13	0	0	6.90	8	
I20T		2	2	0	30	21	15.00	0	0	6	10	0					10.00	0	
20T		18	18	5	550	83*	42.30	0	4	149	188	6	31.33	1-0	0	0	7.57	10	
Test	2010	2	3	1	223	120	111.50	1	1	30	21	0					4.20	4	

Cmp	Debut	M	I	NO	Runs	HS	Avge	100	50	Balls	Runs	Wkts	Avge	BB	5i	10m	RpO	ct	st
FC	2002/03	53	89	4	3907	203	45.96	7	26	966	425	12	35.41	3-31	0	0	2.64	57	
Int	2005	103	86	17	2444	116*	35.42	3	15	344	309	6	51.50	1-13	0	0	5.39	45	
Lim	2004/05	146	128	21	3959	129	37.00	4	27	1044	873	24	36.37	4-23	2	0	5.01	60	
I20T	2006/07	18	17	3	468	101	33.42	1	3	24	39	1	39.00	1-6	0	0	9.75	5	
20T	2006/07	64	61	11	1843	101	36.86	1	12	353	411	15	27.40	2-17	0	0	6.98	32	
RAJAN, Anand (Madhya Pradesh) b Nagpur, Maharashtra 17.4.1987 RHB RMF																			
FC		4	2	2	27	17*		0	0	420	271	5	54.20	3-85	0	0	3.87	1	
20T		3								72	89	8	11.12	4-26	1	0	7.41	4	
FC	2005/06	18	19	9	82	17*	8.20	0	0	3432	1856	60	30.93	6-45	3	1	3.24	6	
Lim	2005/06	4								102	100	1	100.00	1-27	0	0	5.88	0	
20T	2006/07	7								168	194	14	13.85	4-26	1	0	6.92	6	
RAJE, Rohan Ravindra (Mumbai) b Neral, Maharashtra 3.9.1986 RHB RFM																			
20T		1								18	17	0					5.66	0	
Lim	2007/08	1	1	0	11	11	11.00	0	0	48	55	0					6.87	0	
20T	2006/07	13	7	5	22	11*	11.00	0	0	187	273	7	39.00	2-16	0	0	8.75	6	
RAJIV KUMAR (Jharkhand) b Patna, Bihar 2.12.1976 RHB RM																			
FC		5	8	2	304	87*	50.66	0	2	12	12	1	12.00	1-12	0	0	6.00	5	
Lim		4	3	1	121	61*	60.50	0	2	12	23	0					11.50	1	
20T		5	3	2	87	45*	87.00	0	0									4	
FC	1994/95	79	133	14	4940	164	41.51	10	27	114	65	1	65.00	1-12	0	0	3.42	66	
Lim	1995/96	63	60	12	1956	106*	40.75	1	15	108	124	2	62.00	2-35	0	0	6.88	30	
RAJWINDER SINGH Golu (Punjab) b Patiala, Punjab 7.5.1989 LHB SLA																			
FC		1	1	0	7	7	7.00	0	0	402	133	3	44.33	2-76	0	0	1.98	2	
Lim	2008/09	1	1	1	2	2*		0	0	42	48	1	48.00	1-48	0	0	6.85	0	
RAKESH, Avadhanam (Andhra) b Chittoor, Andhra Pradesh 19.6.1986 RHB WK																			
FC		3	5	0	127	66	25.40	0	1									0	
Lim		2	2	0	23	20	11.50	0	0									1	
20T		3	2	0	5	4	2.50	0	0									0	
Lim	2008/09	7	7	0	107	64	15.28	0	1									4	
RAKESH, Karimuttath Jagadeesapanicker (Kerala) b Thiruvalla, Kerala 12.5.1983 LHB OB																			
FC		1	2	0	38	38	19.00	0	0									1	
Lim		3	3	0	74	41	24.66	0	0	12	12	0					6.00	0	
20T		1	1	0	21	21	21.00	0	0									0	
FC	2008/09	5	7	0	147	44	21.00	0	0	381	228	4	57.00	2-26	0	0	3.59	4	
Lim	2007/08	10	10	1	290	75	32.22	0	1	274	210	8	26.25	3-32	0	0	4.59	4	
20T	2006/07	5	4	1	40	21	13.33	0	0	79	116	5	23.20	2-19	0	0	8.81	3	
RAKESH KUMAR (Services) b Sikar 20.6.1983 LHB LM																			
20T		3	2	0	3	3	1.50	0	0	67	69	3	23.00	3-23	0	0	6.17	0	
FC	2007/08	7	13	8	72	27*	14.40	0	0	1643	848	35	24.22	6-36	5	0	3.09	0	
Lim	2007/08	9	4	2	14	9	7.00	0	0	438	332	12	27.66	3-36	0	0	4.54	3	
RANA, Abhimanyu (Himachal Pradesh) b Delhi 21.9.1991 LHB SLA																			
20T		1	1	0	0	0	0.00	0	0									0	
RANA, Sachin (Haryana) b Gurgaon, Haryana 18.9.1984 RHB RFM																			
FC		6	9	2	315	163*	45.00	1	1	888	333	19	17.52	4-27	0	0	2.25	6	
Lim		6	6	1	158	81	31.60	0	1	264	160	3	53.33	2-23	0	0	3.63	3	
20T		4	4	1	74	33	24.66	0	0	12	15	0					7.50	0	
FC	2004/05	35	59	4	1847	163*	33.58	4	8	4968	2062	93	22.17	5-32	4	0	2.49	36	
Lim	2003/04	34	31	3	717	81	25.60	0	3	1336	1021	25	40.84	3-33	0	0	4.58	13	
20T	2006/07	13	12	1	249	62	22.63	0	1	198	234	11	21.27	3-22	0	0	7.09	3	
RAO, Shiv Shankar (Jharkhand) b Dhanbad, Bihar 6.12.1982 RHB RM																			
FC		1	1	1	2	2*		0	0	126	66	1	66.00	1-22	0	0	3.14	0	
FC	2000/01	33	46	12	234	31	6.88	0	0	6701	3295	132	24.96	6-28	4	2	2.95	11	
Lim	2000/01	18	12	4	29	13	3.62	0	0	912	696	16	43.50	4-53	1	0	4.57	4	
RATAN KUMAR Singh (Jharkhand) b Muzaffarpur, Bihar 3.12.1983 RHB RM																			
20T		1	1	0	9	9	9.00	0	0	6	16	0					16.00	0	
FC	1999/00	21	41	3	796	107	20.94	1	5	264	121	5	24.20	1-7	0	0	2.75	14	
Lim	2005/06	5	5	0	111	36	22.20	0	0	6	7	0					7.00	0	
RATHEE, Vineet (Haryana) b Banla, Haryana 19.11.1988 RHB OB																			
Lim		1	1	0	4	4	4.00	0	0	1	5	0					30.00	0	
RATHOD, Nikhil Rajendrakumar (Saurashtra) b Rajkot, Saurashtra 3.9.1984 RHB LB																			
20T		1	1	0	17	17	17.00	0	0									0	
FC	2004/05	10	15	0	294	43	19.60	0	0	18	11	0					3.66	7	
Lim	2003/04	8	8	2	229	74*	38.16	0	2									3	
RATRA, Ajay (Goa) b Faridabad, Haryana 13.12.1981 RHB RAB WK																			
FC		5	6	1	343	170*	68.60	2	0									4	
Lim		5	5	0	96	45	19.20	0	0									1	
20T		3	3	0	18	10	6.00	0	0									2	
Test	2001/02	6	10	1	163	115*	18.11	1	0	6	1	0					1.00	11	2
FC	1998/99	80	129	21	3053	170*	28.26	5	13	6	1	0					1.00	188	24
Int	2001/02	12	8	1	90	30	12.85	0	0									11	5
Lim	1999/00	76	61	12	1209	103	24.67	1	6									63	28

Cmp	Debut	M	I	NO	Runs	HS	Avge	100	50	Balls	Runs	Wkts	Avge	BB	5i	10m	RpO	ct	st
RAUT, Abhishek Santosh (Mumbai, Rajasthan Royals) b Jaipur Road, Maharashtra 3.3.1987 RHB LBG																			
Lim		6	6	1	40	12*	8.00	0	0	101	80	3	26.66	2-30	0	0	4.75	2	
20T		10	7	3	99	43	24.75	0	0	12	18	1	18.00	1-18	0	0	9.00	2	
FC	2005/06	2	3	0	28	17	9.33	0	0									0	
Lim	2005/06	15	14	3	197	35	17.90	0	0	131	107	4	26.75	2-30	0	0	4.90	6	
20T	2009	20	14	6	177	43	22.12	0	0	54	76	2	38.00	1-18	0	0	8.44	5	
RAVI TEJA, Dharaka Bhanidipati (Hyderabad) b Kakinada, Andhra Pradesh 5.9.1987 RHB LBG																			
FC		2	4	1	15	14	5.00	0	0	42	16	1	16.00	1-16	0	0	2.28	2	
Lim		5	5	0	288	131	57.60	1	1	114	151	1	151.00	1-40	0	0	7.94	5	
20T		1	1	0	6	6	6.00	0	0	12	21	1	21.00	1-21	0	0	10.50	0	
FC	2006/07	22	43	4	1640	133*	42.05	4	10	432	207	5	41.40	3-33	0	0	2.87	15	
Lim	2005/06	23	23	1	800	131	36.36	1	5	445	386	9	42.88	3-16	0	0	5.20	13	
20T	2006/07	20	16	3	242	40	18.61	0	0	36	54	2	27.00	1-19	0	0	9.00	7	
RAWAT, Ankit (Haryana) b Krishnanagar, Haryana 8.9.1986 RHB OB																			
FC		5	9	2	256	114*	36.57	2	0	207	111	4	27.75	2-12	0	0	3.21	4	
Lim		3	3	0	55	33	18.33	0	0	28	13	2	6.50	2-13	0	0	2.78	2	
20T		5	5	0	173	56	34.60	0	2	24	20	0					5.00	2	
FC	2006/07	10	18	2	449	114*	28.06	2	1	231	123	4	30.75	2-12	0	0	3.19	10	
RAWAT, Kuldeep Balbirsingh (Delhi) b Uttaranchal, Uttar Pradesh 16.10.1984 RHB RM																			
20T		2	2	1	6	6	6.00	0	0	36	40	1	40.00	1-19	0	0	6.66	1	
FC	2002/03	4	5	2	22	15*	7.33	0	0	424	229	5	45.80	1-18	0	0	3.24	0	
Lim	2003/04	3	1	0	1	1	1.00	0	0	136	94	9	10.44	5-39	0	1	4.14	0	
20T	2006/07	5	5	2	12	6	4.00	0	0	96	117	2	58.50	1-19	0	0	7.31	2	
RAWAT, Mahesh (Railways) b Faridabad, Haryana 25.10.1985 RHB WK																			
FC		3	3	1	40	39*	20.00	0	0									5	2
FC	2003/04	41	60	10	1895	115	37.90	3	13	210	89	5	17.80	2-5	0	0	2.54	94	16
Lim	2003/04	25	23	5	481	83*	26.72	0	2	126	90	5	18.00	2-9	0	0	4.28	15	9
20T	2006/07	25	18	8	160	39*	16.00	0	0									24	5
RAWLE, Harshad Dinkar (Railways) b Bombay (now Mumbai), Maharashtra 27.7.1984 RHB OB																			
FC		2	4	0	92	40	23.00	0	0	78	21	1	21.00	1-14	0	0	1.61	2	
FC	2007/08	16	25	3	804	110	36.54	2	3	186	77	2	38.50	1-8	0	0	2.48	12	
Lim	2007/08	3	3	0	10	10	3.33	0	0									0	
RAYUDU, Ambati Thirupathi (Hyderabad, Mumbai Indians) b Guntur, Andhra Pradesh 23.9.1985 RHB OB																			
FC		7	11	0	473	106	43.00	1	3	27	16	0					3.55	6	
Lim		5	4	0	174	68	43.50	0	2									3	
20T		15	15	1	409	55*	29.21	0	3									8	1
FC	2001/02	54	87	8	3188	210	40.35	8	16	594	391	8	48.87	4-43	0	0	3.94	38	1
Lim	2001/02	45	41	1	1256	117	31.40	1	10	216	202	8	25.25	4-45	1	0	5.61	19	
20T	2006/07	20	20	2	523	75*	29.05	0	4									10	1
REANG, Sukanta Khanaram (Tripura) b West Manu, Tripura 7.2.1986 RHB RFM																			
Lim		4	4	1	78	45	26.00	0	0									0	
20T		2	2	0	68	53	34.00	0	1									1	
REDDY, Lindala Narasimha Prasad (Andhra) b Anantapur, Andhra Pradesh 29.12.1977 RHB RAB WK																			
FC		5	9	2	177	53	25.28	0	1									0	
FC	1998/99	49	92	8	2895	148	34.46	6	14	30	9	0					1.80	42	4
Lim	1997/98	29	28	0	772	93	27.57	0	6									15	4
ROACH, Kemar Andre Jamal (Barbados, West Indies, Deccan Chargers, West Indies to Australia, West Indies to South Africa) b Checker Hall, St Lucy, Barbados 30.6.1988 RHB RF																			
20T		2	1	0	10	10	10.00	0	0	48	80	0					10.00	1	
Test	2009	7	13	4	57	17	6.33	0	0	1472	772	26	29.69	6-48	1	0	3.14	4	
FC	2007/08	26	35	8	266	52*	9.85	0	1	4007	2365	73	32.39	7-23	3	0	3.54	14	
Int	2008	13	8	4	20	10	5.00	0	0	677	554	26	21.30	5-44	1	1	4.91	1	
Lim	2006/07	18	10	6	40	13*	10.00	0	0	843	706	29	24.34	5-44	1	1	5.02	1	
I20T	2008	10	1	1	3	3*		0	0	210	248	9	27.55	2-25	0	0	7.08	1	
20T	2008	14	2	1	13	10	13.00	0	0	288	375	9	41.66	2-25	0	0	7.81	2	
ROHAN PREM, Preambhasan (Kerala, South Zone) b Trivandrum (now Thiruvananthapuram), Kerala 13.9.1986 LHB OB																			
FC		5	7	0	228	91	32.57	0	1	200	140	3	46.66	1-18	0	0	4.20	3	
Lim		5	4	1	102	54	34.00	0	1	84	85	0					6.07	2	
20T		1	1	0	30	30	30.00	0	0	6	11	0					11.00	0	
FC	2005/06	22	32	1	1264	138	40.77	4	4	452	290	6	48.33	2-52	0	0	3.85	17	
Lim	2004/05	20	18	2	396	76	24.75	0	5	252	237	3	79.00	1-14	0	0	5.64	6	
20T	2006/07	3	3	0	46	30	15.33	0	0	18	30	1	30.00	1-19	0	0	10.00	0	
ROY, Avijit Singha (Assam) b Kamrup, Assam 20.2.1987 LHB RAB																			
FC		1	1	0	12	12	12.00	0	0									0	
20T		4	4	0	59	32	14.75	0	0									5	1
ROY, Sibsankar Arabinda (Assam) b Kamrup, Assam 10.10.1990 RHB OB																			
FC		1	2	0	15	15	7.50	0	0									2	
Lim		3	3	0	41	30	13.66	0	0	96	75	1	75.00	1-37	0	0	4.68	2	
FC	2008/09	3	6	0	75	29	12.50	0	0									4	
Lim	2007/08	9	9	0	225	111	25.00	1	0	120	97	2	48.50	1-14	0	0	4.85	4	

Cmp	Debut	M	I	NO	Runs	HS	Avge	100	50	Balls	Runs	Wkts	Avge	BB	5i	10m	RpO	ct	st
ROY, Sujitkumar Ramkumar (Jharkhand) b Jamshedpur, Bihar 10.11.1984 RHB LBG																			
FC		1	1	0	5	5	5.00	0	0	136	80	1	80.00	1-80	0	0	3.52	0	
FC	2001/02	10	17	8	80	22	8.88	0	0	1466	943	26	36.26	5-77	2	0	3.85	4	
Lim	2008/09	2								120	67	5	13.40	4-28	1	0	3.35	0	
RUSHI RAJ, Doddapaneni (Hyderabad) b Nacharam, Andhra Pradesh 3.4.1986 LHB LBG																			
FC		1	2	0	44	29	22.00	0	0									0	
FC	2008/09	5	10	0	200	56	20.00	0	1									0	
Lim	2007/08	4	4	0	29	16	7.25	0	0									1	
20T	2006/07	4	4	0	111	46	27.75	0	0									1	
SACHIN BABY (Kerala) b Thodupuzha, Kerala 18.12.1988 LHB OB																			
FC		4	5	0	87	32	17.40	0	0	96	57	1	57.00	1-17	0	0	3.56	3	
SAHA, Rajib Haradhan (Tripura) b Agartala, Tripura 23.7.1984 RHB RM																			
FC		4	5	0	92	51	18.40	0	1	174	108	0					3.72	0	
20T		2	2	0	14	14	7.00	0	0									0	
FC	2002/03	20	35	2	715	66	21.66	0	7	324	198	2	99.00	2-13	0	0	3.66	24	
Lim	2002/03	9	9	2	130	35	18.57	0	0	66	55	1	55.00	1-26	0	0	5.00	2	
20T	2006/07	5	4	1	18	14	6.00	0	0	30	41	2	20.50	2-3	0	0	8.20	1	
SAHA, Tushar Swapan (Tripura) b Agartala, Tripura 20.9.1985 LHB LM																			
FC		4	5	1	137	53*	34.25	0	1	636	292	7	41.71	2-22	0	0	2.75	4	
Lim		4	3	1	35	19*	17.50	0	0	181	133	7	19.00	2-21	0	0	4.40	2	
20T		3	3	1	13	6	6.50	0	0	48	65	1	65.00	1-35	0	0	8.12	0	
FC	2000/01	36	59	5	924	73*	17.11	0	2	7872	3508	105	33.40	6-51	4	1	2.67	19	
Lim	2001/02	31	24	3	256	29	12.19	0	0	1288	1007	25	40.28	3-13	0	0	4.69	8	
20T	2006/07	7	5	1	24	6	6.00	0	0	136	168	7	24.00	2-19	0	0	7.41	1	
SAHA, Wriddhaman Prasanta (Bengal, East Zone, India, India Red, Kolkata Knight Riders, Rest of India, India A to England, India A to Scotland) b Siliguri, Bengal 24.10.1984 RHB WK																			
Test		1	2	0	36	36	18.00	0	0									0	
FC		8	14	2	363	120	30.25	1	1									20	1
Lim		10	7	3	230	58	57.50	0	2									6	
20T		17	11	4	199	71	28.42	0	1									5	3
FC	2007/08	28	44	5	1404	159	36.00	3	7									67	4
Lim	2006/07	47	42	14	1208	102*	43.14	1	6									49	7
20T	2006/07	41	32	13	486	71	25.57	0	2									17	6
SAHABUDDIN, Khatib Syeb (Andhra) b Kadiri, Andhra Pradesh 1.1.1979 RHB RMF																			
FC		5	7	0	211	120	30.14	1	1	966	341	13	26.23	4-55	0	0	2.11	3	
Lim		5	5	1	135	40	33.75	0	0	240	201	5	40.20	2-37	0	0	5.02	1	
20T		3	3	1	60	31	30.00	0	0	48	59	4	14.75	2-20	0	0	7.37	0	
FC	1998/99	59	86	7	1915	120	24.24	2	9	12464	5266	191	27.57	7-35	13	2	2.53	15	
Lim	1998/99	50	45	6	692	77	17.74	0	1	2454	1861	59	31.54	4-29	2	0	4.55	10	
20T	2006/07	8	8	1	131	31	18.71	0	0	149	187	6	31.16	2-20	0	0	7.53	1	
SAHNI, Vishal (Haryana) b Panchkula, Haryana 3.12.1983 RHB RAB																			
FC		1	1	1	41	41*		0	0									1	
FC	2007/08	5	8	1	236	58	33.71	0	2									1	
Lim	2006/07	3	3	0	101	53	33.66	0	1									1	
20T	2006/07	9	9	2	199	41	28.42	0	0									2	
SAHOO, Alok Chandra (Orissa) b Cuttack, Orissa 5.11.1989 RHB RM																			
FC		5	6	0	141	58	23.50	0	1	1008	537	17	31.58	3-100	0	0	3.19	2	
Lim		5	4	1	68	22	22.66	0	0	246	213	3	71.00	2-56	0	0	5.19	0	
20T		4	4	2	69	32*	34.50	0	0	60	74	1	74.00	1-7	0	0	7.40	1	
Lim	2006/07	7	5	1	73	22	18.25	0	0	348	296	5	59.20	2-37	0	0	5.10	0	
20T	2006/07	7	5	3	73	32*	36.50	0	0	132	158	3	52.66	1-7	0	0	7.18	3	
SAHOO, Prasanta Brundaban (Orissa) b Cuttack, Orissa 5.12.1984 RHB RM																			
20T		1	1	0	0	0	0.00	0	0	1	4	0					24.00	0	
SAHOO, Subhrajit Dayanidhi (Orissa) b Paradeep, Orissa 12.11.1988 RHB RAB WK																			
FC		4	7	0	181	62	25.85	0	1									4	
20T		4	2	0	6	6	3.00	0	0									0	2
SAHU, Pardeep (Haryana) b Rohtak, Haryana 21.8.1985 RHB LB																			
Lim		5	5	0	148	47	29.60	0	0	52	40	2	20.00	1-2	0	0	4.61	1	
20T		4	4	1	52	27	17.33	0	0	24	19	1	19.00	1-15	0	0	4.75	2	
FC	2002/03	12	19	3	430	72	26.87	0	1	1012	475	13	36.53	6-96	1	0	2.81	4	
Lim	2004/05	12	12	0	190	47	15.83	0	0	146	116	7	16.57	3-24	0	0	4.76	1	
SAI, Vemula Manoj (Andhra) b Guntur, Andhra Pradesh 10.10.1982 RHB RAB WK																			
FC		5	7	0	113	34	16.14	0	0									16	
Lim		5	5	0	109	47	21.80	0	0	30	23	0					4.60	4	
20T		3	3	0	7	7	2.33	0	0									2	
FC	2004/05	15	24	0	362	70	15.08	0	1									32	6
Lim	2004/05	24	23	1	600	104	27.27	1	3	30	23	0					4.60	12	3
20T	2006/07	8	8	0	102	40	12.75	0	0									5	2
SAIKIA, Kunal Naren (Assam) b North Lakhimpur, Assam 19.6.1988 RHB WK																			
FC		6	10	0	232	58	23.20	0	1									21	2
Lim		4	4	0	22	11	5.50	0	0									4	1

Cmp	Debut	M	I	NO	Runs	HS	Avge	100	50	Balls	Runs	Wkts	Avge	BB	5i	10m	RpO	ct	st
20T		2	2	1	8	8	8.00	0	0									1	
FC	2006/07	17	29	0	462	58	15.93	0	1									47	4
Lim	2005/06	8	8	0	52	13	6.50	0	0									7	1
SAINI, Nitin (Haryana) b Rohtak, Haryana 28.10.1988 RHB WK																			
FC		6	9	0	188	61	20.88	0	2									18	2
Lim		6	6	0	168	105	28.00	1	0									3	3
20T		5	5	0	95	31	19.00	0	0									4	3
FC	2006/07	13	21	0	510	125	24.28	1	2	91	51	3	17.00	2-28	0	0	3.36	34	2
Lim	2007/08	12	12	0	280	105	23.33	1	0									15	5
SALVI, Aavishkar Madhav (Delhi Daredevils, Mumbai, West Zone) b Bombay (now Mumbai), Maharashtra 20.10.1981 RHB RM																			
FC		6	6	3	23	16	7.66	0	0	852	408	13	31.38	5-31	1	0	2.87	2	
Lim		3	1	1	2	2*		0	0	108	75	4	18.75	3-21	0	0	4.16	1	
20T		1																0	
FC	2001/02	50	59	34	277	25	11.08	0	0	8616	3698	149	24.81	5-31	7	1	2.57	19	
Int	2003	4	3	1	4	4*	2.00	0	0	172	120	4	30.00	2-15	0	0	4.18	2	
Lim	2001/02	43	15	10	45	20*	9.00	0	0	2072	1588	63	25.20	5-45	1	1	4.59	15	
20T	2006/07	10								180	226	8	28.25	3-28	0	0	7.53	2	
SALVI, Dhiran Pradip (Railways) b Baroda (now Vadodara), Gujarat 10.10.1979 RHB WK																			
Lim		4	4	1	61	21	20.33	0	0									1	
20T		4	4	3	107	60*	107.00	0	1									1	
FC	2002/03	1	2	0	0	0	0.00	0	0									0	
Lim	2005/06	16	15	4	306	48*	27.81	0	0									16	1
SAMAL, Lagnajit Lalatendu (Orissa) b Cuttack, Orissa 29.9.1989 RHB RM																			
Lim		1	1	0	0	0	0.00	0	0	18	17	0					5.66	0	
20T		4	2	1	1	1*	1.00	0	0	46	33	1	33.00	1-13	0	0	4.30	1	
SAMANT, Vinayak Radhakrishna (Mumbai) b Bombay (now Mumbai), Maharashtra 25.10.1972 RHB WK																			
FC		11	15	3	257	67	21.41	0	2									26	7
FC	1995/96	96	139	24	2953	113	25.67	1	18	2	4	0					12.00	296	37
Lim	1995/96	41	31	7	643	81	26.79	0	3									44	15
20T	2006/07	8	3	1	12	9*	6.00	0	0									4	3
SAMANTRAY, Biplab Bipin (Orissa) b Cuttack, Orissa 14.9.1988 RHB RM																			
Lim		5	4	0	64	27	16.00	0	0	246	207	7	29.57	3-24	0	0	5.04	4	
20T		2	1	0	14	14	14.00	0	0									0	
SAMEER ALI, Mohammad (Jammu and Kashmir) b Srinagar, Jammu and Kashmir 9.1.1986 RHB RFM																			
FC		3	5	1	42	23	10.50	0	0	294	169	8	21.12	4-74	0	0	3.44	1	
Lim		5	4	1	13	11	4.33	0	0	221	207	2	103.50	2-53	0	0	5.62	0	
FC	2005/06	10	17	3	129	32	9.21	0	0	1252	723	24	30.12	4-74	0	0	3.46	4	
Lim	2006/07	13	9	4	54	12*	10.80	0	0	556	464	9	51.55	2-32	0	0	5.00	1	
20T	2006/07	3	1	0	0	0	0.00	0	0	65	83	4	20.75	2-15	0	0	7.66	0	
SANDEEP SINGH Dhull (Services) b Mundhal, Haryana 10.10.1988 RHB WK																			
20T		4	4	2	34	15	17.00	0	0									1	1
FC	2005/06	11	19	2	210	58	12.35	0	1									10	3
Lim	2006/07	8	6	0	57	34	9.50	0	0									6	2
20T	2006/07	13	9	4	83	25*	16.60	0	0									3	2
SANGAKKARA, Kumar Chokshanada (Kandurata, Nondescripts, Sri Lanka, Kings XI Punjab, Sri Lanka to Bangladesh, Sri Lanka to India, Sri Lanka to South Africa, Sri Lanka to United States of America, Sri Lanka to West Indies) b Matale, Sri Lanka 27.10.1977 LHB OB WK																			
Test		3	5	0	241	137	48.20	1	0									1	
FC		3	5	0	241	137	48.20	1	0									1	
Int		5	5	0	218	90	43.60	0	2									3	2
Lim		5	5	0	218	90	43.60	0	2									3	2
I20T		2	2	0	137	78	68.50	0	2									0	
20T		15	14	0	494	78	35.28	0	4									6	5
Test	2000	91	152	11	8016	287	56.85	23	33	66	38	0					3.45	163	20
FC	1997/98	176	281	21	12400	287	47.69	31	57	192	108	1	108.00	1-13	0	0	3.37	324	33
Int	2000	276	259	28	8510	138*	36.83	10	58									272	68
Lim	1997/98	359	338	37	11672	156*	38.77	16	76									355	91
I20T	2006	28	27	2	733	78	29.32	0	6									12	8
20T	2004/05	79	75	5	2138	94	30.54	0	16									40	21
SANGRAM SINGH (Himachal Pradesh) b Nahan, Himachal Pradesh 30.1.1978 RHB RM																			
FC		6	11	0	185	50	16.81	0	1	18	7	0					2.33	3	
Lim		5	5	0	172	110	34.40	1	0									0	
20T		7	7	1	171	65*	28.50	0	1									2	
FC	1995/96	73	125	7	3743	215*	31.72	10	13	2449	1260	23	54.78	4-28	0	0	3.08	64	1
Lim	1995/96	65	63	2	1748	110	28.65	1	10	750	544	14	38.85	3-16	0	0	4.35	21	
20T	2006/07	12	12	3	254	65*	28.22	0	1									2	
SANGWAN, Pradeep (Delhi, Delhi Daredevils) b Najafgarh, Delhi 5.11.1990 RHB LM																			
FC		7	9	2	154	57	22.00	0	1	1345	820	20	41.00	5-107	1	0	3.65	4	
Lim		2	1	1	18	18*		0	0	115	121	2	60.50	2-57	0	0	6.31	0	
20T		15	4	1	11	6*	3.66	0	0	318	404	18	22.44	3-22	0	0	7.62	4	

Cmp	Debut	M	I	NO	Runs	HS	Avge	100	50	Balls	Runs	Wkts	Avge	BB	5i	10m	RpO	ct	st
FC	2007/08	24	30	5	462	57	18.48	0	2	4333	2401	77	31.18	5-46	3	0	3.32	8	
Lim	2006/07	19	13	5	179	69*	22.37	0	1	978	857	30	28.56	4-43	1	0	5.25	4	
20T	2006/07	40	15	8	28	6*	4.00	0	0	847	1106	40	27.65	3-18	0	0	7.83	10	
SANKLECHA, Anupam Amrutlal (Maharashtra) b Ahmednagar, Maharashtra 17.7.1982 LHB RMF																			
Lim		1	1	1	0	0*		0	0	60	74	2	37.00	2-74	0	0	7.40	0	
FC	2004/05	16	24	8	255	54	15.93	0	1	2746	1451	47	30.87	6-60	4	0	3.17	2	
Lim	2004/05	13	8	5	79	34*	26.33	0	0	530	429	12	35.75	3-34	0	0	4.85	4	
20T	2006/07	1	1	1	3	3*		0	0	12	19	0					9.50	0	
SANTOSH LAL (Jharkhand) b Ranchi, Bihar 4.12.1983 RHB RM																			
20T		2	2	0	27	14	13.50	0	0	24	40	1	40.00	1-28	0	0	10.00	1	
FC	2004/05	8	13	0	280	63	21.53	0	2	525	324	9	36.00	4-48	0	0	3.70	3	
Lim	2003/04	16	15	1	225	54	16.07	0	1	318	301	6	50.16	2-37	0	0	5.67	1	
20T	2006/07	6	5	0	44	14	8.80	0	0	90	125	8	15.62	3-23	0	0	8.33	2	
SANYAL, Sanjib Chandrasekhar (Railways) b Howrah (now Haora), Bengal 25.7.1977 RHB RM																			
FC		6	8	0	221	92	27.62	0	1	390	131	3	43.66	1-14	0	0	2.01	0	
FC	2001/02	50	74	12	2328	123	37.54	3	16	3765	1868	53	35.24	4-26	0	0	2.97	19	
Lim	2000/01	44	34	9	550	66	22.00	0	4	1568	1267	54	23.46	4-21	6	0	4.84	13	
20T	2006/07	8	8	4	139	48*	34.75	0	0	168	188	14	13.42	3-15	0	0	6.71	2	
SARABJIT SINGH (Services) b Palampur, Himachal Pradesh 25.10.1974 RHB WK																			
Lim		4	3	1	16	16*	8.00	0	0									4	1
FC	1993/94	69	119	5	2389	89	20.95	0	15	18	12	0					4.00	130	28
Lim	1993/94	67	63	6	1610	88	28.24	0	13									45	16
20T	2006/07	5	5	1	43	11	10.75	0	0									1	5
SARABJIT SINGH Ladda (Delhi Daredevils, Punjab) b Patiala, Punjab 10.7.1986 RHB LBG																			
FC		2	3	1	15	15	7.50	0	0	366	218	7	31.14	4-144	0	0	3.57	3	
20T		5	2	1	0	0*	0.00	0	0	90	143	4	35.75	2-44	0	0	9.53	0	
FC	2007/08	9	12	3	31	15	3.44	0	0	1808	904	29	31.17	5-39	1	0	3.00	4	
Lim	2007/08	10	3	1	0	0*	0.00	0	0	482	322	11	29.27	2-24	0	0	4.00	3	
SARANDEEP SINGH (Himachal Pradesh) b Amritsar, Punjab 21.10.1979 RHB OB																			
FC		4	6	1	100	39	20.00	0	0	779	360	12	30.00	7-120	1	0	2.77	1	
Lim		3	2	0	7	4	3.50	0	0	150	127	2	63.50	2-32	0	0	5.08	1	
20T		5								108	102	8	12.75	3-20	0	0	5.66	4	
Test	2000/01	3	2	1	43	39*	43.00	0	0	678	340	10	34.00	4-136	0	0	3.00	1	
FC	1998/99	92	118	22	2216	94	23.08	0	7	19898	9100	314	28.98	8-180	18	2	2.74	28	
Int	2001/02	5	4	1	47	19	15.66	0	0	258	180	3	60.00	2-34	0	0	4.18	2	
Lim	1999/00	77	46	13	474	50*	14.36	0	1	3754	2700	97	27.83	5-11	1	2	4.31	31	
20T	2006/07	10	2	1	53	30	53.00	0	0	204	213	11	19.36	3-20	0	0	6.26	6	
SARKAR, Sourav Subrata (Bengal) b Calcutta (now Kolkata), Bengal 15.12.1984 RHB RM																			
FC		3	4	0	28	27	7.00	0	0	593	344	10	34.40	3-20	0	0	3.48	0	
Lim		1	1	0	7	7	7.00	0	0	30	31	0					6.20	0	
20T		2								42	70	1	70.00	1-44	0	0	10.00	0	
FC	2006/07	16	18	1	201	60	11.82	0	1	3061	1566	63	24.85	5-21	2	0	3.07	1	
Lim	2008/09	2	2	0	11	7	5.50	0	0	60	56	0					5.60	0	
20T	2006/07	5								79	127	2	63.50	1-15	0	0	9.64	0	
SARMA, Sambasiva Krishna (Kerala) b Madras (now Chennai), Tamil Nadu 13.10.1984 LHB LM																			
FC		4	5	0	33	16	6.60	0	0	12	13	0					6.50	0	
FC	2007/08	10	16	1	437	111*	29.13	2	1	48	38	0					4.75	6	
Lim	2006/07	4	4	0	79	32	19.75	0	0									1	
SARVESH KUMAR, Patangay Manikrao (Hyderabad) b Hyderabad, Andhra Pradesh 26.4.1989 RHB RM																			
FC		2	3	2	19	14*	19.00	0	0	433	265	2	132.50	1-62	0	0	3.67	2	
Lim	2007/08	7	2	2	9	7*		0	0	287	253	10	25.30	5-47	0	1	5.28	1	
20T	2007/08	2	1	1	1	1*		0	0	30	42	1	42.00	1-18	0	0	8.40	0	
SATHISH, Rajagopal (Mumbai Indians, Tamil Nadu) b Trichy (now Tiruchchirappali), Tamil Nadu 14.1.1981 RHB RM																			
FC		3	4	0	113	50	28.25	0	1	174	57	1	57.00	1-31	0	0	1.96	1	
Lim		7	6	1	157	48	31.40	0	0	147	113	6	18.83	4-16	1	0	4.61	7	
20T		14	13	4	152	24	16.88	0	0	72	109	2	54.50	1-11	0	0	9.08	6	
FC	2000/01	25	41	4	1335	204*	36.08	4	4	1210	468	13	36.00	3-18	0	0	2.32	25	
Lim	2000/01	35	29	7	699	91*	31.77	0	1	765	599	20	29.95	4-16	1	0	4.69	20	
SATISH, Ganesh (Karnataka, South Zone) b Davanagere, Karnataka 15.3.1988 RHB																			
FC		8	13	2	698	141	63.45	2	4	48	32	0					4.00	5	
Lim		8	8	1	438	121*	62.57	2	2	24	26	0					6.50	1	
FC	2008/09	11	19	2	824	141	48.47	2	4	48	32	0					4.00	5	
Lim	2007/08	12	11	1	458	121*	45.80	2	2	24	26	0					6.50	3	
SAXENA, Iresh (Bengal) b Faridabad, Haryana 14.3.1981 RHB SLA																			
FC		2	3	1	9	4*	4.50	0	0	235	77	5	15.40	5-72	1	0	1.96	0	
Lim		4	1	0	2	2	2.00	0	0	156	110	1	110.00	1-49	0	0	4.23	1	
20T		2	1	1	0	0*		0	0	24	29	0					7.25	1	
FC	2008/09	4	6	3	13	4*	4.33	0	0	469	117	8	14.62	5-72	1	0	1.49	0	
Lim	2007/08	20	7	4	12	6*	4.00	0	0	879	530	23	23.04	4-50	1	0	3.61	6	

Cmp	Debut	M	I	NO	Runs	HS	Avge	100	50	Balls	Runs	Wkts	Avge	BB	5i	10m	RpO	ct	st
SAXENA, Jalaj Sahai (Central Zone, India Blue, Madhya Pradesh) b Indore, Madhya Pradesh 15.12.1986 RHB OB																			
FC		6	7	0	259	142	37.00	1	1	462	246	4	61.50	2-56	0	0	3.19	0	
Lim		9	8	1	146	69	20.85	0	1	348	286	4	71.50	1-19	0	0	4.93	0	
20T		4	4	0	73	35	18.25	0	0	72	88	2	44.00	1-17	0	0	7.33	0	
FC	2005/06	23	38	4	1072	142	31.52	4	5	2748	1148	31	37.03	4-54	0	0	2.50	6	
Lim	2005/06	22	19	3	371	114*	23.18	1	1	847	618	19	32.52	3-50	0	0	4.37	2	
SAXENA, Jatin Sahay (Madhya Pradesh) b Indore, Madhya Pradesh 4.8.1982 RHB LB																			
20T		1								6	13	0					13.00	0	
FC	2001/02	14	25	2	649	125*	28.21	2	2	338	227	3	75.66	1-7	0	0	4.03	7	
Lim	2007/08	6	6	1	111	29	22.20	0	0	72	51	3	17.00	3-32	0	0	4.25	5	
SAXENA, Santosh Ramesh (Railways) b Bombay (now Mumbai), Maharashtra 20.4.1976 RHB RMF																			
FC		2	2	2	1	1*		0	0	336	128	7	18.28	3-19	0	0	2.28	0	
FC	1997/98	40	41	17	196	30	8.16	0	0	6045	2879	94	30.62	6-65	2	0	2.85	8	
Lim	1999/00	21	10	5	54	27	10.80	0	0	1017	770	30	25.66	3-37	0	0	4.54	3	
SAXENA, Vineet Ashokkumar (Rajasthan) b Margao, Goa 3.12.1980 RHB OB																			
FC		5	9	1	318	115	39.75	2	1	24	28	0					7.00	5	
Lim		2	2	0	100	66	50.00	0	1									0	
FC	1998/99	58	104	5	3279	122	33.12	6	17	246	156	2	78.00	1-3	0	0	3.80	47	
Lim	2000/01	11	11	2	303	66	33.66	0	2	6	11	0					11.00	2	
SEHWAG, Virender (Delhi Daredevils, India, Rest of India, India to Bangladesh, India to Sri Lanka) b Delhi 20.10.1978 RHB OB																			
Test		5	7	0	781	293	111.57	4	1	264	122	2	61.00	1-4	0	0	2.77	1	
FC		6	8	0	791	293	98.87	4	1	264	122	2	61.00	1-4	0	0	2.77	1	
Int		13	12	0	397	146	33.08	1	0	84	74	1	74.00	1-26	0	0	5.28	2	
Lim		13	12	0	397	146	33.08	1	0	84	74	1	74.00	1-26	0	0	5.28	2	
I20T		2	2	0	90	64	45.00	0	1									0	
20T		19	19	0	580	75	30.52	0	5	34	23	3	7.66	2-18	0	0	4.05	2	
Test	2001/02	79	135	5	7039	319	54.14	21	22	3139	1598	39	40.97	5-104	1	0	3.05	61	
FC	1997/98	143	236	9	11544	319	50.85	35	40	7878	4098	104	39.40	5-104	1	0	3.12	119	
Int	1998/99	228	222	9	7380	146	34.64	13	36	4230	3716	92	40.39	4-6	1	0	5.27	84	
Lim	1997/98	298	287	14	9333	146	34.18	14	53	5835	5009	138	36.29	4-6	3	0	5.15	108	
I20T	2006/07	14	13	0	313	68	24.07	0	2	6	20	0					20.00	1	
20T	2003	66	65	4	1609	94*	26.37	0	11	292	393	19	20.68	3-14	0	0	8.07	10	
SHADAB Maqsood KHAN (Madhya Pradesh) b Indore, Madhya Pradesh 14.4.1985 RHB RM																			
Lim		6	5	2	133	40*	44.33	0	0									2	
20T		3	3	1	31	22	15.50	0	0									0	
Lim	2006/07	17	15	4	475	58	43.18	0	2	30	32	0					6.40	4	
SHAFQAT Mahmood MALIK (Jammu and Kashmir) b Doda, Jammu and Kashmir 5.5.1980 LHB LFM																			
Lim		1	1	0	3	3	3.00	0	0	60	44	0					4.40	0	
20T		1	1	0	1	1	1.00	0	0	24	39	1	39.00	1-39	0	0	9.75	0	
FC	2007/08	1	2	0	15	9	7.50	0	0	90	59	1	59.00	1-59	0	0	3.93	1	
Lim	2004/05	11	9	2	56	30	8.00	0	0	482	412	5	82.40	3-30	0	0	5.12	2	
20T	2006/07	4	3	0	5	4	1.66	0	0	84	97	1	97.00	1-39	0	0	6.92	0	
SHAH, Hiken Naresh (Jammu and Kashmir) b Bombay (now Mumbai), Maharashtra 15.11.1984 LHB LM																			
FC		4	7	0	242	80	34.57	0	2	6	6	0					6.00	2	
20T		5	5	1	109	33	27.25	0	0	84	102	2	51.00	1-23	0	0	7.28	1	
FC	2006/07	12	19	1	607	112	33.72	1	2	12	13	0					6.50	8	
Lim	2005/06	6	6	1	75	35	15.00	0	0									1	
20T	2006/07	6	6	1	162	53	32.40	0	1	84	102	2	51.00	1-23	0	0	7.28	1	
SHAH, Jaydev Niranjan (Saurashtra) b Rajkot, Saurashtra 4.5.1983 RHB OB																			
FC		6	9	0	187	59	20.77	0	1	114	96	0					5.05	5	
Lim		6	6	0	72	46	12.00	0	0	18	26	0					8.66	2	
20T		4	4	0	22	21	5.50	0	0	12	25	1	25.00	1-25	0	0	12.50	4	
FC	2002/03	53	86	6	2205	178	27.56	3	9	1057	663	10	66.30	2-21	0	0	3.76	25	
Lim	2002/03	34	34	0	778	101	22.88	2	1	317	315	2	157.50	1-34	0	0	5.96	8	
20T	2006/07	8	8	0	108	49	13.50	0	0	75	106	7	15.14	2-11	0	0	8.48	10	
SHAH, Owais Alam (Middlesex, Delhi Daredevils, England to South Africa, Kolkata Knight Riders, Middlesex to Netherlands, Wellington) b Karachi, Sind, Pakistan 22.10.1978 RHB OB																			
20T		9	9	4	189	58*	37.80	0	1									2	
Test	2005/06	6	10	0	269	88	26.90	0	2	30	31	0					6.20	2	
FC	1996	222	379	34	14521	203	42.08	39	72	2237	1489	26	57.26	3-33	0	0	3.99	170	
Int	2001	71	66	6	1834	107*	30.56	1	12	193	184	7	26.28	3-15	0	0	5.72	21	
Lim	1995	325	307	37	9406	134	34.83	13	60	912	896	27	33.18	4-11	1	0	5.89	112	
I20T	2007	17	15	1	347	55*	24.78	0	1									5	
20T	2003	89	85	17	2160	80	31.76	0	11	45	64	4	16.00	2-26	0	0	8.53	33	
SHAH, Pinal Rohitbhai (Baroda, West Zone) b Baroda, Gujarat 3.11.1987 RHB WK																			
FC		7	12	3	311	63	34.55	0	3									22	
Lim		4	3	0	108	77	36.00	0	1									0	
20T		4	3	1	25	11	12.50	0	0									3	
FC	2005/06	34	54	8	1578	217*	34.30	2	7									97	8

Cmp	Debut	M	I	NO	Runs	HS	Avge	100	50	Balls	Runs	Wkts	Avge	BB	5i	10m	RpO	ct	st
Lim	2004/05	25	22	3	755	157*	39.73	1	5									19	8
20T	2006/07	22	16	4	218	71	18.16	0	1									16	3
SHAHID, Agha Hussain (Railways) b Lucknow, Uttar Pradesh 13.1.1984 LHB SLA																			
20T		3	1	1	0	0*		0	0	42	49	1	49.00	1-17	0	0	7.00	1	
Lim	2008/09	4	3	0	50	29	16.66	0	0	204	140	6	23.33	3-34	0	0	4.11	2	
SHAIKH, Rahil Akhilahmed (Mumbai) b Bombay (now Mumbai), Maharashtra 12.6.1985 LHB LM																			
FC		1	1	1	0	0*		0	0	186	104	1	104.00	1-57	0	0	3.35	0	
FC	2008/09	4	4	3	26	20*	26.00	0	0	511	340	10	34.00	4-50	0	0	3.99	0	
20T	2009	1								6	11	0					11.00	0	
SHAIKH, Shoaib Shabbir (Mumbai) b Bombay (now Mumbai), Maharashtra 18.1.1987 RHB RM																			
20T		1	1	1	2	2*		0	0	12	19	0					9.50	0	
20T	2009	3	2	1	8	6	8.00	0	0	12	19	0					9.50	2	
SHAMSHER SINGH Rathore (Rajasthan) b Udaipur, Rajasthan 28.12.1983 RHB OB																			
Lim		1	1	0	5	5	5.00	0	0	48	53	0					6.62	0	
FC	2003/04	14	22	5	120	18*	7.05	0	0	2427	1170	35	33.42	4-52	0	0	2.89	7	
Lim	2002/03	12	8	5	22	8*	7.33	0	0	471	422	7	60.28	2-29	0	0	5.37	3	
SHANKAR RAO, Gorrela (Andhra) b Visakhapatnam, Andhra Pradesh 10.4.1984 LHB LFM																			
FC		5	7	1	188	66	31.33	0	1	852	403	7	57.57	3-44	0	0	2.83	3	
Lim		5	5	1	46	19	11.50	0	0	270	171	4	42.75	3-28	0	0	3.80	1	
20T		3	2	0	25	24	12.50	0	0	48	70	5	14.00	2-13	0	0	8.75	2	
FC	2002/03	27	38	3	798	91	22.80	0	5	4604	1771	54	32.79	5-36	2	0	2.30	11	
Lim	2003/04	31	30	4	557	50	21.42	0	1	1164	895	16	55.93	3-28	0	0	4.61	6	
20T	2006/07	11	8	2	66	24	11.00	0	0	198	216	13	16.61	3-20	0	0	6.54	5	
SHARMA, Abhishek (Delhi) b Delhi 10.8.1985 RHB LB																			
FC		2	4	0	49	34	12.25	0	0	210	167	2	83.50	1-22	0	0	4.77	0	
FC	2001/02	16	19	3	280	73	17.50	0	1	2203	1116	30	37.20	5-37	2	0	3.03	5	
Lim	2002/03	5	2	1	40	34*	40.00	0	0	146	126	4	31.50	3-40	0	0	5.17	0	
SHARMA, Ankit Nagendra (Madhya Pradesh) b Gwalior, Madhya Pradesh 20.4.1991 LHB SLA																			
FC		3	1	0	7	7	7.00	0	0	272	108	5	21.60	2-40	0	0	2.38	1	
Lim		6	4	2	32	21*	16.00	0	0	306	244	10	24.40	3-22	0	0	4.78	5	
20T		1	1	0	14	14	14.00	0	0	18	30	1	30.00	1-30	0	0	10.00	0	
SHARMA, Bipul (Kings XI Punjab, North Zone, Punjab, India A to Scotland) b Chandigarh, Punjab 28.9.1983 LHB SLA																			
Lim		8	6	3	166	61*	55.33	0	1	402	318	12	26.50	5-36	0	1	4.74	5	
20T		10	5	2	39	23	13.00	0	0	168	193	5	38.60	1-10	0	0	6.89	3	
FC	2005/06	4	6	1	197	93	39.40	0	2	528	188	5	37.60	3-24	0	0	2.13	2	
Lim	2003/04	36	20	6	426	61*	30.42	0	3	1536	1059	42	25.21	5-36	0	1	4.13	15	
20T	2006/07	18	13	6	141	26*	20.14	0	0	210	243	5	48.60	1-10	0	0	6.94	5	
SHARMA, Deepak (Assam) b Delhi 1.5.1984 RHB WK																			
FC		3	5	0	54	23	10.80	0	0									3	
Lim		4	4	1	127	50	42.33	0	1									0	
20T		6	6	2	102	33	25.50	0	0	18	34	0					11.33	1	
FC	2008/09	7	13	1	255	46	21.25	0	0									6	
Lim	2008/09	11	11	1	429	88	42.90	0	5	30	37	1	37.00	1-37	0	0	7.40	4	
SHARMA, Ishant (Delhi, India, India Red, Kolkata Knight Riders, India to Bangladesh, India to South Africa, India to Sri Lanka) b Delhi 2.9.1988 RHB RFM																			
Test		3	3	2	0	0*	0.00	0	0	624	371	5	74.20	2-84	0	0	3.56	1	
FC		5	5	2	17	16	5.66	0	0	978	529	9	58.77	3-77	0	0	3.24	2	
Int		6	1	1	3	3*		0	0	252	280	7	40.00	3-50	0	0	6.66	1	
Lim		9	2	1	4	3*	4.00	0	0	391	403	13	31.00	4-56	1	0	6.18	2	
I20T		2	1	1	5	5*		0	0	48	64	2	32.00	2-42	0	0	8.00	1	
20T		9	3	2	11	6*	11.00	0	0	198	300	9	33.33	2-33	0	0	9.09	2	
Test	2007	26	35	17	238	31*	13.22	0	0	4818	2738	73	37.50	5-118	1	0	3.41	8	
FC	2006/07	47	54	27	293	31*	10.85	0	0	8755	4634	155	29.89	7-24	3	1	3.17	13	
Int	2007	45	14	6	47	13	5.87	0	0	2035	1948	63	30.92	4-38	3	0	5.74	11	
Lim	2005/06	59	18	9	52	13	5.77	0	0	2751	2513	88	28.55	4-34	5	0	5.48	13	
I20T	2007/08	11	2	2	8	5*		0	0	206	291	6	48.50	2-34	0	0	8.47	2	
20T	2006/07	45	14	10	41	9	10.25	0	0	939	1204	32	37.62	2-15	0	0	7.69	6	
SHARMA, Joginder (Chennai Super Kings, Haryana, North Zone) b Rohtak, Haryana 23.10.1983 RHB RFM																			
FC		6	8	0	205	110	25.62	1	0	996	422	14	30.14	3-15	0	0	2.54	2	
Lim		8	7	0	215	87	30.71	0	1	350	222	9	24.66	2-16	0	0	3.80	2	
20T		8	4	1	50	24	16.66	0	0	144	175	9	19.44	3-17	0	0	7.29	3	
FC	2002/03	50	82	7	2248	139	29.97	5	9	9968	4433	214	20.71	8-24	14	5	2.66	6	
Int	2004/05	4	3	2	35	29*	35.00	0	0	150	115	1	115.00	1-28	0	0	4.60	3	
Lim	2001/02	56	46	8	785	87	20.65	0	1	2494	1925	77	25.00	4-13	3	0	4.63	11	
I20T	2007/08	4								87	138	4	34.50	2-20	0	0	9.51	2	
20T	2006/07	32	16	5	159	35	14.45	0	0	565	778	29	26.82	3-17	0	0	8.26	10	
SHARMA, Kuldeep Sharwan (Jharkhand) b Sundargarh, Orissa 1.10.1985 RHB RM																			
FC		2	4	0	10	5	2.50	0	0	159	69	4	17.25	3-44	0	0	2.60	0	
Lim		2	2	2	48	33*		0	0	120	99	2	49.50	2-48	0	0	4.95	2	
20T		5	1	0	12	12	12.00	0	0	108	108	5	21.60	3-30	0	0	6.00	0	

Cmp	Debut	M	I	NO	Runs	HS	Avge	100	50	Balls	Runs	Wkts	Avge	BB	5i	10m	RpO	ct	st
FC	2006/07	14	24	2	174	35*	7.90	0	0	2455	1188	31	38.32	4-38	0	0	2.90	3	
Lim	2005/06	11	9	3	91	33*	15.16	0	0	522	430	13	33.07	4-33	2	0	4.94	3	
SHARMA, Karan Vinod (Railways) b Meerut, Uttar Pradesh 23.10.1987 LHB LBG																			
FC		6	8	2	174	59*	29.00	0	1	654	261	7	37.28	4-93	0	0	2.39	3	
Lim		4	3	1	34	21*	17.00	0	0	132	119	5	23.80	2-32	0	0	5.40	0	
20T		4	4	0	60	29	15.00	0	0	42	58	2	29.00	1-11	0	0	8.28	1	
FC	2007/08	18	22	3	578	120	30.42	1	4	1704	719	25	28.76	4-37	0	0	2.53	7	
Lim	2006/07	16	13	2	220	65*	20.00	0	1	420	344	15	22.93	3-24	0	0	4.91	3	
20T	2006/07	10	8	0	92	29	11.50	0	0	42	58	2	29.00	1-11	0	0	8.28	2	
SHARMA, Manav (Haryana) b Delhi 13.8.1986 RHB RM																			
FC		4	6	0	147	42	24.50	0	0	6	6	0					6.00	0	
FC	2008/09	5	8	0	259	98	32.37	0	1	6	6	0					6.00	1	
SHARMA, Mohinderraj (Himachal Pradesh) b Kulu, Himachal Pradesh 17.2.1985 LHB LM																			
FC		4	6	3	9	8	3.00	0	0	927	442	17	26.00	5-31	2	0	2.86	1	
FC	2003/04	8	11	4	31	16	4.42	0	0	1458	726	27	26.88	5-31	3	0	2.98	2	
SHARMA, Mohit (Delhi) b Bahadurgarh, Haryana 19.12.1991 LHB OB																			
20T		2	2	0	19	11	9.50	0	0									0	
SHARMA, Mukesh (Himachal Pradesh, North Zone) b Khiah, Himachal Pradesh 5.8.1983 LHB SLA																			
FC		7	13	2	267	78	24.27	0	2	455	205	13	15.76	4-95	0	0	2.70	8	
Lim		4	3	0	139	96	46.33	0	1	234	196	10	19.60	5-59	0	1	5.02	3	
20T		5	5	1	83	41	20.75	0	0	76	101	2	50.50	1-19	0	0	7.97	3	
FC	2006/07	24	37	5	1090	161	34.06	2	8	539	272	14	19.42	4-95	0	0	3.02	13	
Lim	2006/07	18	16	2	401	96	28.64	0	3	503	465	19	24.47	5-59	1	1	5.54	4	
SHARMA, Naman (Uttar Pradesh) b Ghaziabad, Uttar Pradesh 11.12.1986 RHB LB																			
20T		2	2	1	7	7*	7.00	0	0									1	
SHARMA, Pranay Inder (Rajasthan) b Jaipur, Rajasthan 16.3.1988 LHB RFM																			
FC		3	5	0	175	64	35.00	0	1	6	9	0					9.00	1	
Lim		1	1	0	1	1	1.00	0	0									1	
Lim	2008/09	5	5	0	191	92	38.20	0	2									2	
SHARMA, Rahul (Deccan Chargers, Punjab) b Jullundur (now Jalandhar), Punjab 30.11.1986 RHB LBG																			
FC		7	10	1	271	95	30.11	0	2	1077	535	13	41.15	6-92	1	0	2.98	10	
Lim		6	2	0	8	7	4.00	0	0	310	213	13	16.38	3-37	0	0	4.12	5	
20T		11	7	2	40	14*	8.00	0	0	226	262	12	21.83	3-14	0	0	6.95	2	
FC	2006/07	8	11	1	303	95	30.30	0	2	1197	588	14	42.00	6-92	1	0	2.94	10	
SHARMA, Rohit Gangasahai (Rajasthan) b Jaipur, Rajasthan 7.11.1983 RHB LB																			
FC		1	2	0	20	10	10.00	0	0	12	12	0					6.00	1	
FC	2004/05	7	13	0	166	36	12.76	0	0	156	105	0					4.03	2	
Lim	2003/04	29	28	3	872	147*	34.88	2	3	76	74	1	74.00	1-14	0	0	5.84	15	
20T	2006/07	4	4	0	131	81	32.75	0	1	36	47	6	7.83	3-7	0	0	7.83	2	
SHARMA, Rohit Gurunath (Deccan Chargers, India, Mumbai, West Zone, India to Sri Lanka, India to West Indies, India to Zimbabwe) b Bansod, Nagpur, Maharashtra 30.4.1987 RHB OB																			
FC		8	10	1	718	309*	79.77	3	2	270	122	3	40.66	1-7	0	0	2.71	2	
Int		1	1	0	48	48	48.00	0	0	18	28	0					9.33	0	
Lim		6	6	0	161	96	26.83	0	1	102	98	3	32.66	2-27	0	0	5.76	2	
I20T		1	1	0	3	3	3.00	0	0	18	22	1	22.00	1-22	0	0	7.33	0	
20T		23	23	3	592	73	29.60	0	3	204	260	6	43.33	1-15	0	0	7.64	9	
FC	2006	36	52	4	2641	309*	55.02	8	11	648	328	5	65.60	1-1	0	0	3.03	25	
Int	2007	54	51	11	1155	114	28.87	2	5	221	179	3	59.66	2-27	0	0	4.86	21	
Lim	2005/06	102	96	16	2685	142*	33.56	5	13	702	601	13	46.23	2-27	0	0	5.13	37	
I20T	2007/08	19	16	6	335	79*	33.50	0	3	30	37	1	37.00	1-22	0	0	7.40	6	
20T	2006/07	78	74	15	1942	101*	32.91	1	11	492	584	26	22.46	4-6	1	0	7.12	31	
SHARMA, Sumeet (Haryana) b Bhiwani, Haryana 26.1.1982 RHB OB																			
FC		6	8	0	201	45	25.12	0	0	36	13	0					2.16	1	
FC	2002/03	29	48	1	1341	126	28.53	2	5	144	39	0					1.62	14	
Lim	2001/02	27	27	4	1048	142	45.56	2	7	108	75	3	25.00	2-20	0	0	4.16	7	
20T	2006/07	9	6	1	53	26*	10.60	0	0	10	17	0					10.20	1	
SHARMA, Vishal Gopal (Hyderabad) b Hyderabad, Andhra Pradesh 14.11.1987 RHB OB																			
FC		1	2	1	36	32	36.00	0	0	324	215	0					3.98	1	
FC	2007/08	2	4	1	52	32	17.33	0	0	531	350	4	87.50	4-73	0	0	3.95	1	
Lim	2007/08	1	1	1	1	1*		0	0	18	15	0					5.00	1	
SHASHANK NAG, Padala (Hyderabad) b Gollapudi, Andhra Pradesh 20.8.1982 LHB																			
FC		3	5	0	122	57	24.40	0	2									1	
FC	2004/05	13	24	1	407	60	17.69	0	3									10	
Lim	2003/04	6	6	0	184	66	30.66	0	2									3	
20T	2006/07	2	2	0	55	32	27.50	0	0									1	
SHEIKH, Azhar Mohammad Ishaq (Vidarbha) b Chandrapur, Maharashtra 11.3.1985 RHB LB																			
FC		3	5	0	61	23	12.20	0	0	429	182	9	20.22	4-27	0	0	2.54	1	
20T		2	2	1	29	27*	29.00	0	0	12	15	0					7.50	0	
FC	2002/03	5	8	1	102	25	14.57	0	0	795	415	12	34.58	4-27	0	0	3.13	2	
Lim	2002/03	3	2	1	15	9*	15.00	0	0	123	106	2	53.00	2-35	0	0	5.17	1	

Cmp	Debut	M	I	NO	Runs	HS	Avge	100	50	Balls	Runs	Wkts	Avge	BB	5i	10m	RpO	ct	st
SHETTY, Nishit Sudhakar (Tripura) b Bombay (now Mumbai), Maharashtra 28.5.1972 LHB SLA																			
FC		6	9	1	257	104	32.12	1	0	54	38	0					4.22	5	
Lim		4	4	1	119	81*	39.66	0	1									1	
20T		4	4	0	67	40	16.75	0	0	36	59	2	29.50	1-29	0	0	9.83	1	
FC	2000/01	41	65	2	2422	165	38.44	7	12	724	274	6	45.66	3-31	0	0	2.27	17	
Lim	2002/03	33	32	6	1124	128	43.23	2	6	595	458	8	57.25	2-43	0	0	4.61	6	
SHIBSAGAR SINGH (Bengal) b Burdwan (now Bardhhaman), Orissa 15.9.1979 RHB SLA																			
FC		2	2	0	5	4	2.50	0	0	282	137	2	68.50	2-12	0	0	2.91	0	
20T		2	1	1	5	5*		0	0	48	42	4	10.50	2-18	0	0	5.25	1	
FC	1996/97	26	24	5	247	46	13.00	0	0	5206	2112	43	49.11	4-47	0	0	2.43	13	
Lim	1996/97	27	13	2	158	32*	14.36	0	0	1269	743	27	27.51	3-29	0	0	3.51	11	
SHILAMKAR, Deepak Vijay (Maharashtra) b Pune, Maharashtra 29.10.1987 LHB LBG																			
20T		3	3	1	24	14*	12.00	0	0									0	
FC	2008/09	4	8	1	139	56	19.85	0	1	108	109	1	109.00	1-19	0	0	6.05	4	
Lim	2006/07	6	6	1	115	29	23.00	0	0	12	16	0					8.00	3	
20T	2006/07	7	7	2	73	27	14.60	0	0									4	
SHINDE, Amol Jayawant (Hyderabad) b Hyderabad, Andhra Pradesh 6.11.1985 RHB OB																			
FC		2	3	0	43	23	14.33	0	0	486	284	0					3.50	0	
Lim		5	5	2	100	35*	33.33	0	0	276	209	8	26.12	3-55	0	0	4.54	2	
20T		4	2	1	18	13	18.00	0	0	84	106	4	26.50	2-12	0	0	7.57	5	
FC	2005/06	13	25	1	580	90	24.16	0	3	1500	769	14	54.92	4-13	0	0	3.07	7	
Lim	2005/06	23	23	7	590	61	36.87	0	1	1056	876	22	39.81	3-55	0	0	4.97	9	
20T	2006/07	9	7	2	56	23	11.20	0	0	174	192	9	21.33	3-17	0	0	6.62	7	
SHITOOT, Harshal Vinod (Vidarbha) b Nagpur, Maharashtra 23.1.1982 RHB OB																			
FC		2	4	1	110	86	36.66	0	1									1	
Lim		3	3	0	21	13	7.00	0	0									1	
20T		3	3	0	24	12	8.00	0	0	42	49	2	24.50	1-16	0	0	7.00	1	
FC	2000/01	26	46	3	907	114	21.09	1	6	957	451	16	28.18	4-38	0	0	2.82	18	
Lim	2001/02	15	14	1	336	62	25.84	0	2	296	280	3	93.33	1-14	0	0	5.67	2	
20T	2006/07	7	7	0	103	28	14.71	0	0	66	84	3	28.00	1-16	0	0	7.63	2	
SHOAIB AHMED, Syed Mohammad (Hyderabad) b Hyderabad, Andhra Pradesh 19.11.1987 RHB RFM																			
FC		1	1	0	0	0	0.00	0	0	144	102	0					4.25	0	
FC	2007/08	13	19	3	151	32	9.43	0	0	1820	769	18	42.72	3-50	0	0	2.53	2	
Lim	2008/09	8	3	1	11	8	5.50	0	0	371	288	24	12.00	7-15	0	3	4.65	0	
20T	2009	8	3	1	1	1*	0.50	0	0	102	152	5	30.40	2-20	0	0	8.94	4	
SHRIKHANDE, Ameya Jayprakash (Maharashtra) b Pune, Maharashtra 25.7.1986 RHB RFM																			
FC		2	4	0	20	9	5.00	0	0									1	
20T		3	3	0	46	35	15.33	0	0									1	
FC	2007/08	9	17	0	607	195	35.70	3	1									8	
Lim	2007/08	8	8	0	258	124	32.25	1	1									1	
SHRIVASTAVA, Rohan Pradeep (Madhya Pradesh) b Mhow, Madhya Pradesh 9.3.1989 RHB LM																			
20T		1	1	0	2	2	2.00	0	0	6	8	0					8.00	0	
SHRIVASTAVA, Shalabh Umeshchandra (Vidarbha) b Nagpur, Maharashtra 2.2.1986 RHB RFM																			
FC		4	6	1	211	78	42.20	0	1									4	
20T		3	3	0	82	44	27.33	0	0									0	
FC	2005/06	20	35	7	954	78	34.07	0	5									17	
Lim	2005/06	8	7	1	241	83*	40.16	0	3									2	
SHUKLA, Laxmi Ratan (Bengal, Kolkata Knight Riders) b Howrah (now Haora), Bengal 6.5.1981 RHB RM																			
FC		4	5	0	296	132	59.20	1	1	350	154	7	22.00	3-47	0	0	2.64	0	
Lim		6	3	0	29	18	9.66	0	0	342	273	9	30.33	3-35	0	0	4.78	3	
20T		8	6	0	104	35	17.33	0	0	156	203	6	33.83	2-35	0	0	7.80	3	
FC	1997/98	97	134	12	3967	141	32.51	4	25	8350	4038	113	35.73	6-86	2	0	2.90	48	
Int	1998/99	3	2	0	18	13	9.00	0	0	114	94	1	94.00	1-25	0	0	4.94	1	
Lim	1998/99	104	85	14	2240	136	31.54	2	12	3677	2719	100	27.19	4-13	4	0	4.43	40	
20T	2006/07	37	31	8	523	76	22.73	0	1	426	568	23	24.69	3-6	0	0	8.00	9	
SHUKLA, Rahul (Jharkhand) b Padia, Bihar 28.8.1990 RHB RFM																			
FC		4	5	2	26	19	8.66	0	0	707	375	11	34.09	5-90	1	0	3.18	1	
Lim		2	1	0	28	28	28.00	0	0	89	53	5	10.60	5-29	0	1	3.57	0	
20T		1	1	0	0	0	0.00	0	0	24	27	4	6.75	4-27	1	0	6.75	1	
Lim	2008/09	4	2	0	28	28	14.00	0	0	161	139	6	23.16	5-29	0	1	5.18	0	
SHUKLA, Ravikant Udaybhan (Uttar Pradesh) b Rae Bareli, Uttar Pradesh 7.7.1987 LHB OB																			
FC		2	4	0	77	27	19.25	0	0									0	
20T		3	3	0	25	24	8.33	0	0									1	
FC	2005/06	25	40	3	1169	135	31.59	1	7	174	82	1	82.00	1-31	0	0	2.82	13	
Lim	2004/05	29	27	6	748	94*	35.61	0	6	6	4	0					4.00	16	
20T	2006/07	5	5	0	37	24	7.40	0	0	6	9	0					9.00	4	
SHUKLA, Shivakant (Uttar Pradesh) b Allahabad, Uttar Pradesh 26.1.1986 LHB OB																			
FC		8	15	2	335	119	25.76	1	0	264	126	4	31.50	3-28	0	0	2.86	8	
20T		1	1	0	8	8	8.00	0	0									0	
FC	2003/04	42	77	6	1970	178*	27.74	4	5	972	479	15	31.93	3-12	0	0	2.95	33	
Lim	2003/04	18	18	0	403	66	22.38	0	2	113	87	5	17.40	2-20	0	0	4.61	6	

Cmp	Debut	M	I	NO	Runs	HS	Avge	100	50	Balls	Runs	Wkts	Avge	BB	5i	10m	RpO	ct	st
SIDANA, Mayank (Punjab) b Delhi 4.12.1986 RHB OB																			
FC		3	4	1	194	54	64.66	0	3	24	11	0					2.75	0	
Lim		5	5	1	81	30	20.25	0	0									1	
20T		3	3	0	56	35	18.66	0	0									2	
FC	2008/09	4	5	1	235	54	58.75	0	3	24	11	0					2.75	1	
Lim	2007/08	13	10	2	217	62	27.12	0	1									4	
SINDHI, Irshad Akbarkan (Baroda) b Baroda, Gujarat 28.12.1985 RHB WK																			
20T		4	4	0	141	88	35.25	0	1									0	
FC	2005/06	3	5	1	21	9	5.25	0	0									4	
Lim	2006/07	3	3	0	57	44	19.00	0	0									0	
SINGH, Rudra Pratap (Central Zone, Deccan Chargers, Uttar Pradesh, India to South Africa) b Rae Bareli, Uttar Pradesh 6.12.1985 RHB LMF																			
FC		10	13	3	101	24	10.10	0	0	2207	1113	35	31.80	4-47	0	0	3.02	5	
Lim		3	2	0	9	5	4.50	0	0	168	197	6	32.83	3-60	0	0	7.03	1	
20T		17	10	4	28	8	4.66	0	0	372	502	20	25.10	3-17	0	0	8.09	6	
Test	2005/06	13	17	3	91	30	6.50	0	0	2330	1564	40	39.10	5-59	1	0	4.02	6	
FC	2003/04	55	73	15	545	41*	9.39	0	0	10256	5669	191	29.68	5-33	7	1	3.31	26	
Int	2005/06	55	20	10	104	23	10.40	0	0	2433	2201	65	33.86	4-35	2	0	5.42	12	
Lim	2004/05	109	52	17	377	35	10.77	0	0	5039	4319	147	29.38	5-30	3	3	5.14	33	
I20T	2007/08	10	2	2	3	2*		0	0	198	225	15	15.00	4-13	1	0	6.81	2	
20T	2006/07	60	30	15	73	10	4.86	0	0	1308	1685	74	22.77	4-13	2	0	7.72	21	
SINGH, Sandeep Rampyare (Vidarbha) b Nagpur, Maharashtra 18.2.1981 RHB RM																			
FC		2	2	0	31	16	15.50	0	0	300	157	3	52.33	2-70	0	0	3.14	1	
20T		3	1	1	0	0*		0	0	69	77	3	25.66	2-27	0	0	6.69	0	
FC	2001/02	37	54	24	221	29	7.36	0	0	7142	3095	132	23.44	8-82	5	1	2.60	11	
Lim	2001/02	36	20	9	80	13*	7.27	0	0	1745	1218	44	27.68	4-20	2	0	4.18	12	
20T	2006/07	7	4	3	12	6*	12.00	0	0	145	168	7	24.00	3-34	0	0	6.95	0	
SINGH, Tejinder Pal (Central Zone, Railways) b Amritsar, Punjab 16.1.1978 LHB SLA																			
FC		7	11	2	369	102	41.00	2	1	54	37	1	37.00	1-28	0	0	4.11	2	
Lim		6	5	0	193	81	38.60	0	2	54	40	0					4.44	2	
20T		4	4	0	74	34	18.50	0	0	6	13	0					13.00	4	
FC	1999/00	62	109	7	3810	186	37.35	7	18	3133	1615	44	36.70	6-95	2	1	3.09	26	
Lim	1998/99	63	56	5	1611	156*	31.58	3	8	1046	773	27	28.62	4-21	1	0	4.43	30	
20T	2006/07	12	12	0	203	40	16.91	0	0	60	82	6	13.66	3-12	0	0	8.20	13	
SINGH, Vikram Rajvir (Kings XI Punjab) b Chandigarh, Punjab 17.9.1984 RHB RMF																			
20T		1								18	40	0					13.33	0	
Test	2006	5	6	2	47	29	11.75	0	0	669	427	8	53.37	3-48	0	0	3.83	1	
FC	2004/05	25	30	6	360	47	15.00	0	0	4055	2621	101	25.95	7-75	8	2	3.87	6	
Int	2005/06	2	1	0	8	8	8.00	0	0	72	105	0					8.75	3	
Lim	2003/04	37	15	8	126	30*	18.00	0	0	1757	1533	55	27.87	5-38	3	1	5.23	8	
20T	2006/07	29	6	3	39	22*	13.00	0	0	571	784	23	34.08	3-16	0	0	8.23	6	
SINHA, Avishek (Services) b Siwan, Bihar 18.10.1985 RHB SLA																			
Lim		3	3	0	65	37	21.66	0	0	138	99	0					4.30	1	
20T		3	3	0	19	9	6.33	0	0	54	79	2	39.50	1-21	0	0	8.77	0	
FC	2008/09	2	4	0	57	26	14.25	0	0	216	107	2	53.50	1-16	0	0	2.97	0	
Lim	2007/08	8	7	1	114	37	19.00	0	0	336	249	6	41.50	2-33	0	0	4.44	2	
SINHA, Amit Sumanta (Assam) b Khutikatia, Assam 26.11.1988 RHB LBG																			
FC		4	6	0	170	51	28.33	0	1	24	15	0					3.75	4	
20T		2	2	0	33	28	16.50	0	0									0	
Lim	2006/07	3	2	0	46	33	23.00	0	0	72	56	0					4.66	0	
SINHA, Siddhartha Raj (Jharkhand) b Patna, Bihar 30.12.1986 RHB LBG																			
FC		5	10	1	347	89	38.55	0	3									1	
Lim		4	4	0	97	39	24.25	0	0									0	
20T		1	1	0	31	31	31.00	0	0									0	
Lim	2008/09	5	5	0	159	62	31.80	0	1									2	
SIVAKUMAR, Duwarapu (Andhra) b Sidhanthah, Andhra Pradesh 11.2.1990 RHB RFM																			
FC		3	5	2	92	38	30.66	0	0	484	156	10	15.60	3-33	0	0	1.93	0	
Lim		5	5	2	106	67*	35.33	0	1	198	208	3	69.33	3-53	0	0	6.30	0	
20T		3	2	1	26	22	26.00	0	0	42	50	1	50.00	1-32	0	0	7.14	2	
Lim	2008/09	10	10	3	196	67*	28.00	0	2	396	348	10	34.80	5-20	0	1	5.27	0	
SIVAKUMAR, Mooverjanthali Kasipandian (Tamil Nadu) b Madras (now Chennai), Tamil Nadu 5.9.1981 RHB RM																			
20T		2	2	1	27	21	27.00	0	0	24	41	1	41.00	1-30	0	0	10.25	2	
Lim	2004/05	12	5	4	102	56*	102.00	0	1	345	297	9	33.00	2-23	0	0	5.16	4	
20T	2006/07	4	4	3	54	24*	54.00	0	0	54	83	3	27.66	1-15	0	0	9.22	2	
SIVARAMAKRISHNAN, Vidyut (Tamil Nadu) b Madras (now Chennai), Tamil Nadu 3.12.1981 LHB SLA																			
20T		2	2	0	44	37	22.00	0	0	30	31	2	15.50	1-11	0	0	6.20	0	
FC	1999/00	50	74	6	2254	193	33.14	4	10	5079	2586	86	30.06	6-24	3	0	3.05	27	
Lim	2003/04	53	52	4	1950	158	40.62	6	7	1251	975	32	30.46	3-16	0	0	4.67	15	
20T	2006/07	20	16	1	345	54	23.00	0	1	192	226	14	16.14	4-24	1	0	7.06	5	

Cmp	Debut	M	I	NO	Runs	HS	Avge	100	50	Balls	Runs	Wkts	Avge	BB	5i	10m	RpO	ct	st
SMITH, Dwayne Romel (Barbados, West Indies, Deccan Chargers, New South Wales, Sussex, Sussex to India, West Indies to Australia) b Storey Gap, Codrington Hill, St Michael, Barbados 12.4.1983 RHB RM																			
20T		5	5	1	44	13*	11.00	0	0	65	75	1	75.00	1-22	0	0	6.92	0	
Test	2003/04	10	14	1	320	105*	24.61	1	0	651	344	7	49.14	3-71	0	0	3.17	9	
FC	2001/02	81	134	9	3679	155	29.43	7	14	8096	4054	124	32.69	4-22	0	0	3.00	78	
Int	2003/04	77	61	4	925	68	16.22	0	3	2510	2060	56	36.78	5-45	3	1	4.92	26	
Lim	2003/04	133	113	9	2274	96	21.86	0	14	3871	3123	94	33.22	6-29	3	2	4.84	44	
I20T	2005/06	8	8	0	73	29	9.12	0	0	104	155	7	22.14	3-24	0	0	8.94	1	
20T	2005/06	74	70	7	1220	72*	19.36	0	4	1084	1411	55	25.65	4-9	1	0	7.81	28	
SMITH, Graeme Craig (Cape Cobras, South Africa, Rajasthan Royals, South Africa to India, South Africa to West Indies) b Johannesburg, Transvaal, South Africa 1.2.1981 LHB OB																			
Test		2	3	0	30	20	10.00	0	0									1	
FC		2	3	0	30	20	10.00	0	0									1	
20T		2	2	0	44	26	22.00	0	0									2	
Test	2001/02	86	151	9	7170	277	50.49	21	28	1322	805	8	100.62	2-145	0	0	3.65	114	
FC	1999/00	123	213	14	10121	311	50.85	29	38	1690	1052	11	95.63	2-145	0	0	3.73	169	
Int	2001/02	154	152	9	5732	141	40.08	8	41	1026	951	18	52.83	3-30	0	0	5.56	81	
Lim	1999/00	211	207	14	7958	141	41.23	12	60	1968	1796	47	38.21	3-30	0	0	5.47	110	
I20T	2005/06	27	27	2	803	89*	32.12	0	4	24	57	0					14.25	15	
20T	2003/04	71	71	6	2061	105	31.70	1	10	96	148	4	37.00	3-23	0	0	9.25	31	
SODHI, Reetinder Singh (Kings XI Punjab, Punjab) b Patiala, Punjab 18.10.1980 RHB RM																			
20T		8	5	1	25	8	6.25	0	0	84	104	4	26.00	3-23	0	0	7.42	3	
FC	1996/97	70	105	9	3699	251*	38.53	6	19	6838	3039	104	29.22	5-30	3	0	2.66	23	
Int	2000/01	18	14	3	280	67	25.45	0	2	462	365	5	73.00	2-31	0	0	4.74	9	
Lim	1996/97	109	89	25	2922	125	45.65	4	23	3259	2568	61	42.09	5-22	1	1	4.72	39	
20T	2006/07	12	8	1	37	12	5.28	0	0	96	126	5	25.20	3-23	0	0	7.87	4	
SOHAL, Sunny (India Red, Kings XI Punjab, Punjab) b Mohali, Punjab 10.11.1987 RHB LBG																			
FC		7	11	0	271	89	24.63	0	2	24	4	0					1.00	4	
Lim		3	2	0	6	6	3.00	0	0									0	
20T		6	5	0	120	42	24.00	0	0									2	
FC	2005/06	21	35	2	1202	110	36.42	3	7	60	13	1	13.00	1-8	0	0	1.30	7	
Lim	2005/06	15	13	0	215	56	16.53	0	1									3	
20T	2006/07	21	17	0	262	43	15.41	0	0									6	
SOLANKI, Rakesh Kantilai (Baroda) b Baroda, Gujarat 1.6.1985 LHB OB																			
FC		4	7	2	264	69*	52.80	0	3	144	73	3	24.33	3-73	0	0	3.04	3	
Lim		3	3	1	135	94	67.50	0	1									1	
FC	2002/03	45	74	5	2640	186	38.26	4	19	349	174	6	29.00	3-73	0	0	2.99	21	
Lim	2005/06	21	20	2	627	94	34.83	0	6	18	20	0					6.66	5	
20T	2006/07	4	4	0	81	39	20.25	0	0									0	
SOLANKI, Shailesh Ratilal (Baroda) b Baroda (now Vadodara), Gujarat 25.11.1989 RHB LBG																			
20T		4	3	1	56	30	28.00	0	0	12	19	0					9.50	0	
Lim	2008/09	3	3	0	101	59	33.66	0	1									3	
SONKAR, Amaradeep Bankelal (Haryana) b Kanpur, Uttar Pradesh 6.3.1984 LHB SLA																			
Lim		2	1	0	14	14	14.00	0	0	77	54	4	13.50	3-9	0	0	4.20	1	
20T		5	4	2	2	1*	1.00	0	0	104	93	5	18.60	2-7	0	0	5.36	2	
FC	2008/09	1	2	0	8	7	4.00	0	0	24	7	0					1.75	1	
Lim	2007/08	11	10	0	334	73	33.40	0	3	550	419	17	24.64	4-31	1	0	4.57	2	
SREEJITH, Kanakkatharaparambu Ramachandran (Kerala) b Cochin (now Kochi), Kerala 27.10.1986 RHB SLA																			
FC		1	2	1	0	0*	0.00	0	0	135	65	4	16.25	4-65	0	0	2.88	0	
Lim		4	1	0	0	0	0.00	0	0	205	191	3	63.66	1-38	0	0	5.59	2	
SREESANTH, Shanthakumaran (India, India Blue, Kerala, Kings XI Punjab, Rest of India, South Zone, India to Bangladesh) b Kothamangalam, Kerala 6.2.1983 RHB RFM																			
Test		2	2	0	8	8	4.00	0	0	372	240	8	30.00	5-75	1	0	3.87	0	
FC		5	4	1	46	22*	15.33	0	0	708	432	12	36.00	5-75	1	0	3.66	1	
Int		3	2	1	1	1	1.00	0	0	150	206	5	41.20	3-49	0	0	8.24	0	
Lim		7	6	1	17	14	3.40	0	0	330	352	6	58.66	3-49	0	0	6.40	0	
20T		7	3	3	27	15*		0	0	132	228	3	76.00	2-24	0	0	10.36	0	
Test	2005/06	17	24	7	226	35	13.29	0	0	3385	1921	60	32.01	5-40	2	0	3.40	2	
FC	2002/03	56	74	22	524	35	10.07	0	0	9840	5565	170	32.73	5-40	5	0	3.39	12	
Int	2005/06	49	20	10	40	10*	4.00	0	0	2312	2326	68	34.20	6-55	1	1	6.03	7	
Lim	2002/03	78	35	15	123	33	6.15	0	0	3710	3508	97	36.16	6-55	2	1	5.67	8	
I20T	2006/07	10	3	2	20	19*	20.00	0	0	204	288	7	41.14	2-12	0	0	8.47	2	
20T	2006/07	42	14	9	71	19*	14.20	0	0	841	1234	38	32.47	3-29	0	0	8.80	5	
SRIKKANTH, Anirudh (Chennai Super Kings, India Green, South Zone, Tamil Nadu) b Madras (now Chennai), Tamil Nadu 14.4.1987 RHB OB																			
FC		7	10	0	462	113	46.20	1	4	78	60	3	20.00	1-6	0	0	4.61	5	
Lim		11	11	0	522	134	47.45	1	4	19	17	0					5.36	5	
20T		8	7	2	121	42	24.20	0	0									4	
FC	2003/04	17	27	0	780	113	28.88	1	6	78	60	3	20.00	1-6	0	0	4.61	16	
Lim	2003/04	36	36	1	1128	134	32.22	1	7	19	17	0					5.36	14	
20T	2006/07	18	17	2	407	50	27.13	0	1									8	

Cmp	Debut	M	I	NO	Runs	HS	Avge	100	50	Balls	Runs	Wkts	Avge	BB	5i	10m	RpO	ct	st
SRIRAM, Sridharan (Goa, Royal Challengers Bangalore) b Madras (now Chennai), Tamil Nadu 21.2.1976 LHB SLA																			
FC		5	6	0	182	69	30.33	0	2	72	26	1	26.00	1-15	0	0	2.16	0	
Lim		5	5	2	343	148*	114.33	1	2	168	135	4	33.75	2-12	0	0	4.82	3	
20T		4	4	0	75	27	18.75	0	0	66	88	3	29.33	1-19	0	0	8.00	3	
FC	1993/94	120	175	13	8885	288	54.84	30	33	7909	3700	83	44.57	4-26	0	0	2.80	63	
Int	1999/00	8	7	1	81	57	13.50	0	1	324	274	9	30.44	3-43	0	0	5.07	1	
Lim	1993/94	143	134	14	4070	148*	33.91	4	26	4637	3509	115	30.51	5-43	2	1	4.54	43	
20T	2006/07	5	5	0	75	27	15.00	0	0	78	110	3	36.66	1-19	0	0	8.46	3	
SRIVASTAVA, Rohit Prakash (Uttar Pradesh) b Allahabad, Uttar Pradesh 8.5.1980 RHB OB																			
FC		3	6	2	120	55	30.00	0	1	42	19	0					2.71	0	
FC	2000/01	38	69	6	1879	186	29.82	2	8	348	147	4	36.75	2-16	0	0	2.53	18	
Lim	2002/03	19	19	0	490	67	25.78	0	5	36	22	0					3.66	10	
20T	2006/07	2	1	0	3	3	3.00	0	0	42	51	2	25.50	1-21	0	0	7.28	0	
SRIVASTAVA, Shalabh Jagdishprasad (Kings XI Punjab, Uttar Pradesh) b Allahabad, Uttar Pradesh 22.9.1981 RHB LFM																			
FC		3	5	1	43	14	10.75	0	0	597	318	14	22.71	4-75	0	0	3.19	1	
Lim		3	1	0	1	1	1.00	0	0	135	110	3	36.66	1-29	0	0	4.88	1	
20T		10	4	2	2	1*	1.00	0	0	210	305	8	38.12	2-23	0	0	8.71	1	
FC	1999/00	39	54	19	189	24*	5.40	0	0	7520	3901	129	30.24	6-82	4	0	3.11	17	
Lim	1999/00	33	14	5	46	14*	5.11	0	0	1549	1145	44	26.02	4-18	2	0	4.43	6	
20T	2006/07	14	5	2	2	1*	0.66	0	0	290	395	11	35.90	3-29	0	0	8.17	3	
SRIVASTAVA, Tanmay Manoj (Central Zone, India Green, Uttar Pradesh) b Lucknow, Uttar Pradesh 7.11.1989 LHB RM																			
FC		10	18	0	438	109	24.33	1	0	72	40	1	40.00	1-40	0	0	3.33	6	
Lim		9	9	0	464	118	51.55	3	1	42	45	0					6.42	3	
20T		3	3	0	51	34	17.00	0	0									2	
FC	2006/07	32	55	1	1828	159	33.85	4	10	72	40	1	40.00	1-40	0	0	3.33	22	
Lim	2006/07	20	20	2	905	124*	50.27	5	3	48	52	0					6.50	7	
20T	2006/07	12	8	2	66	34	11.00	0	0									4	
STEYN, Dale Willem (South Africa, Titans to South Africa, Royal Challengers Bangalore, South Africa to India, South Africa to West Indies) b Phalaborwa, Northern Province, South Africa 27.6.1983 RHB RF																			
Test		2	3	1	6	5	3.00	0	0	389	223	11	20.27	7-51	1	1	3.44	0	
FC		2	3	1	6	5	3.00	0	0	389	223	11	20.27	7-51	1	1	3.44	0	
Int		3	2	0	35	35	17.50	0	0	168	172	3	57.33	3-37	0	0	6.14	2	
Lim		3	2	0	35	35	17.50	0	0	168	172	3	57.33	3-37	0	0	6.14	2	
20T		17	4	0	13	8	3.25	0	0	402	463	17	27.23	3-18	0	0	6.91	1	
Test	2004/05	41	52	12	540	76	13.50	0	1	8273	4881	211	23.13	7-51	14	4	3.54	11	
FC	2003/04	82	98	24	1044	82	14.10	0	3	15723	8875	365	24.31	8-41	22	6	3.38	17	
Int	2005/06	41	14	5	86	35	9.55	0	0	2012	1778	58	30.65	4-16	3	0	5.30	7	
Lim	2004/05	85	29	12	131	35	7.70	0	0	4072	3246	127	25.55	5-20	4	2	4.78	13	
I20T	2007/08	21	4	2	8	5	4.00	0	0	468	531	29	18.31	4-9	1	0	6.80	8	
20T	2004/05	66	16	5	51	22	4.63	0	0	1476	1670	70	23.85	4-9	1	0	6.78	17	
STYRIS, Scott Bernard (Auckland, New Zealand, Deccan Chargers, Essex, New Zealand to Sri Lanka, New Zealand to United Arab Emirates, New Zealand to United States of America, New Zealand to West Indies) b Brisbane, Queensland, Australia 10.7.1975 RHB RFM																			
20T		2	2	0	27	14	13.50	0	0	24	34	2	17.00	2-24	0	0	8.50	2	
Test	2002	29	48	4	1586	170	36.04	5	6	1960	1015	20	50.75	3-28	0	0	3.10	23	
FC	1994/95	126	210	19	5964	212*	31.22	10	29	12657	6353	203	31.29	6-32	9	1	3.01	100	
Int	1999/00	169	146	22	4056	141	32.70	4	25	5642	4464	128	34.87	6-25	4	1	4.74	67	
Lim	1994/95	312	276	46	7667	141	33.33	5	52	11361	8714	287	30.36	6-25	8	1	4.60	121	
I20T	2004/05	28	26	2	492	66	20.50	0	1	279	327	17	19.23	3-5	0	0	7.03	7	
20T	2004/05	103	97	9	2135	106*	24.26	1	9	1639	2093	79	26.49	3-5	0	0	7.66	26	
SUBRAMANIA SIVA, V (Tamil Nadu, Badureliya) b Surandai, Tamil Nadu 3.3.1984 RHB RM																			
20T		1	1	0	12	12	12.00	0	0									0	
FC	2009/10	8	12	0	328	64	27.33	0	2	54	36	0					4.00	5	
Lim	2009/10	4	4	0	152	57	38.00	0	1									2	
SUDHINDRA, Taduri Prakashchandra (Madhya Pradesh) b Hindupur, Andhra Pradesh 24.8.1984 LHB RM																			
FC		4	2	0	44	26	22.00	0	0	630	283	12	23.58	5-39	1	0	2.69	0	
Lim		6	1	1	2	2*		0	0	328	301	10	30.10	4-58	1	0	5.50	3	
20T		4	2	1	14	11*	14.00	0	0	96	96	2	48.00	1-20	0	0	6.00	0	
FC	2005/06	11	11	2	115	26	12.77	0	0	2484	946	39	24.25	5-39	1	0	2.28	3	
Lim	2006/07	9	3	1	35	20	17.50	0	0	454	403	12	33.58	4-58	1	0	5.32	3	
20T	2006/07	12	9	4	56	11*	11.20	0	0	279	301	11	27.36	2-16	0	0	6.47	4	
SUMAN, Tirumalasetti Laxminarayana (Deccan Chargers, Hyderabad) b Hyderabad, Andhra Pradesh 15.12.1983 RHB																			
FC		3	6	1	147	46	29.40	0	0	138	77	3	25.66	2-26	0	0	3.34	2	
20T		17	17	6	341	78*	31.00	0	2	48	75	3	25.00	2-15	0	0	9.37	5	
FC	2003/04	23	42	3	958	131	24.56	1	4	433	264	6	44.00	3-63	0	0	3.65	12	
Lim	2002/03	24	24	0	582	104	24.25	1	3	270	223	8	27.87	3-31	0	0	4.95	5	
20T	2006/07	32	32	8	623	78*	25.95	0	2	192	252	11	22.90	2-14	0	0	7.87	7	
SUMANTH, Bodapati Apparao (Andhra, Deccan Chargers) b Visakhapatnam, Andhra Pradesh 10.5.1988 RHB RMF																			
FC		5	7	1	230	117	38.33	1	1	24	4	1	4.00	1-3	0	0	1.00	4	
Lim		5	5	0	24	11	4.80	0	0	18	18	0					6.00	2	
20T		8	6	4	103	46*	51.50	0	0	6	5	0					5.00	4	

Cmp	Debut	M	I	NO	Runs	HS	Avge	100	50	Balls	Runs	Wkts	Avge	BB	5i	10m	RpO	ct	st
FC	2006/07	18	30	4	840	117	32.30	1	4	42	18	1	18.00	1-3	0	0	2.57	11	
Lim	2007/08	15	14	1	125	51	9.61	0	1	18	18	0					6.00	3	
20T	2006/07	13	11	7	121	46*	30.25	0	0	6	5	0					5.00	6	
SUMIT SINGH (Services) b Delhi 10.9.1987 RHB RM																			
Lim		5	5	0	169	77	33.80	0	1	174	136	4	34.00	2-37	0	0	4.69	1	
20T		3	3	0	15	7	5.00	0	0	60	65	2	32.50	1-15	0	0	6.50	1	
SUNIL SINGH (Services) b Fatehpur, Uttar Pradesh 31.7.1984 RHB LM																			
20T		2								42	63	2	31.50	2-34	0	0	9.00	0	
SUNNY SINGH (Haryana) b Mirch, Bhiwani, Haryana 18.12.1986 RHB RMF																			
FC		6	9	1	617	312	77.12	3	0									4	
Lim		1	1	0	2	2	2.00	0	0									0	
20T		5	5	1	69	33*	17.25	0	0									2	
FC	2003/04	34	58	4	2287	312	42.35	9	8	1216	583	14	41.64	3-34	0	0	2.87	26	
Lim	2001/02	28	27	0	826	103	30.59	1	5	480	323	7	46.14	2-19	0	0	4.03	7	
20T	2006/07	14	14	2	329	65*	27.41	0	3									3	
SURESH, Maripuri (Railways) b Cuddapah, Andhra Pradesh 21.12.1983 LHB SLA																			
FC		5	7	2	312	89*	62.40	0	3	318	153	1	153.00	1-60	0	0	2.88	1	
Lim		4	4	2	67	33*	33.50	0	0	54	60	1	60.00	1-12	0	0	6.66	0	
FC	2002/03	31	51	12	1182	89*	30.30	0	8	3063	1567	47	33.34	6-84	2	0	3.07	11	
Lim	2008/09	9	9	3	138	35	23.00	0	0	242	210	1	210.00	1-12	0	0	5.20	2	
SURESH KUMAR, Selvam (India Blue, Tamil Nadu) b Madras (now Chennai), Tamil Nadu 20.3.1985 RHB OB																			
FC		5	7	1	85	23*	14.16	0	0	270	168	4	42.00	2-12	0	0	3.73	1	
Lim		11	9	5	122	87	30.50	0	1	270	229	10	22.90	7-46	0	1	5.08	9	
20T		4	4	1	107	82*	35.66	0	1	48	64	3	21.33	3-20	0	0	8.00	5	
FC	2007/08	18	23	4	588	90	30.94	0	4	989	518	18	28.77	4-31	0	0	3.14	5	
Lim	2007/08	21	17	9	328	94	41.00	0	3	479	387	14	27.64	7-46	0	1	4.84	12	
SURESHNATH, Sajin (Maharashtra) b Nasik, Maharashtra 6.9.1987 RHB RM																			
FC		4	7	4	38	12*	12.66	0	0	774	378	4	94.50	2-38	0	0	2.93	2	
Lim		1	1	0	3	3	3.00	0	0	57	56	1	56.00	1-56	0	0	5.89	0	
20T		4	1	1	5	5*		0	0	91	113	8	14.12	3-31	0	0	7.45	1	
SUSHIL, Umashankar (Tamil Nadu) b Madras (now Chennai), Tamil Nadu 31.7.1989 RHB RAB WK																			
FC		2	3	1	47	30	23.50	0	0									2	2
Lim	2008/09	3	2	0	34	20	17.00	0	0									4	
SUTHESH, Rangaraj (Tamil Nadu) b Palani, Tamil Nadu 8.4.1987 LHB LM																			
FC		2	2	1	1	1*	1.00	0	0	222	143	3	47.66	2-78	0	0	3.86	0	
Lim		2								120	102	3	34.00	3-51	0	0	5.10	0	
20T		2	1	1	17	17*		0	0	46	47	3	15.66	2-22	0	0	6.13	1	
Lim	2008/09	10	3	1	11	10*	5.50	0	0	510	448	21	21.33	3-25	0	0	5.27	0	
SUYAL, Pawan (Delhi) b Delhi 15.10.1989 RHB LMF																			
FC		3	4	2	13	8*	6.50	0	0	465	315	13	24.23	4-41	0	0	4.06	0	
Lim		1								42	48	2	24.00	2-48	0	0	6.85	1	
SWAPNIL Kamlesh SINGH (Baroda) b Lalupur, Punjab 22.1.1991 RHB LBG																			
FC		3	5	1	135	43*	33.75	0	0	144	62	2	31.00	2-37	0	0	2.58	0	
Lim		4	3	0	43	36	14.33	0	0	193	155	5	31.00	2-44	0	0	4.81	2	
FC	2005/06	5	9	1	159	43*	19.87	0	0	324	161	4	40.25	2-37	0	0	2.98	2	
Lim	2007/08	9	7	1	106	36	17.66	0	0	425	335	11	30.45	3-25	0	0	4.72	3	
20T	2006/07	3	1	1	5	5*		0	0	36	48	1	48.00	1-31	0	0	8.00	1	
SYED MOHAMMAD, Jamaluddin (Tamil Nadu) b Madras (now Chennai), Tamil Nadu 3.8.1983 LHB LM																			
20T		2	2	2	11	11*		0	0	24	39	1	39.00	1-15	0	0	9.75	0	
Lim	2005/06	1	1	0	10	10	10.00	0	0	39	21	3	7.00	3-21	0	0	3.23	0	
SYMONDS, Andrew (Queensland, Deccan Chargers, Surrey) b Birmingham, Warwickshire, England 9.6.1975 RHB OB																			
20T		18	18	2	439	54	27.43	0	4	348	406	13	31.23	3-21	0	0	7.00	13	
Test	2003/04	26	41	5	1462	162*	40.61	2	10	2094	896	24	37.33	3-50	0	0	2.56	22	
FC	1994/95	227	376	33	14477	254*	42.20	40	65	17633	8714	242	36.00	6-105	2	0	2.96	159	
Int	1998/99	198	161	33	5088	156	39.75	6	30	5935	4955	133	37.25	5-18	2	1	5.00	82	
Lim	1993/94	424	377	51	11099	156	34.04	9	64	11713	9379	282	33.25	6-14	2	4	4.80	187	
I20T	2004/05	14	11	4	337	85*	48.14	0	2	185	277	8	34.62	2-14	0	0	8.98	3	
20T	2003	78	72	13	1980	117*	33.55	2	12	1201	1600	51	31.37	5-18	0	1	7.99	37	
TAHIR KHAN (Services) b Udaipur, Rajasthan 28.7.1983 RHB WK																			
Lim		5	5	0	154	67	30.80	0	1									2	
20T		3	3	0	45	33	15.00	0	0									1	
FC	2007/08	9	18	0	550	142	30.55	2	3									7	
Lim	2006/07	17	17	1	436	75	27.25	0	3									6	
20T	2006/07	8	8	0	183	70	22.87	0	1									2	
TAIT, Shaun William (Australia, South Australia, Australia to England, Australia to New Zealand, Australia to West Indies, Glamorgan, Rajasthan Royals) b Bedford Park, Adelaide, South Australia, Australia 22.2.1983 RHB RF																			
20T		8	2	1	12	11	12.00	0	0	187	264	10	26.40	3-22	0	0	8.47	2	
Test	2005	3	5	2	20	8	6.66	0	0	414	302	5	60.40	3-97	0	0	4.37	1	
FC	2002/03	50	70	29	509	68	12.41	0	2	9263	5661	198	28.59	7-29	7	1	3.66	15	
Int	2006/07	25	5	3	25	11	12.50	0	0	1233	1060	46	23.04	4-39	2	0	5.15	3	
Lim	2002/03	88	33	17	108	22*	6.75	0	0	4445	3770	162	23.27	8-43	6	3	5.08	18	

Cmp	Debut	M	I	NO	Runs	HS	Avge	100	50	Balls	Runs	Wkts	Avge	BB	5i	10m	RpO	ct	st
I20T	2007/08	17	5	1	10	6	2.50	0	0	382	419	26	16.11	3-13	0	0	6.58	3	
20T	2004/05	50	17	5	77	14*	6.41	0	0	1099	1363	70	19.47	4-14	1	0	7.44	10	
TANDEL, Vimalkumar Jagdish (Gujarat) b Umbargaon, Gujarat 13.5.1980 RHB WK																			
FC		1	2	0	26	19	13.00	0	0									1	
Lim	2003/04	3	3	1	42	33	21.00	0	0									4	
TARAFDAR, Sujay Subhash (Assam) b Chhattamguri, Bongaigon, Assam 6.12.1989 RHB RM																			
FC		4	4	0	17	10	4.25	0	0	498	203	7	29.00	2-22	0	0	2.44	2	
Lim		2	2	0	9	5	4.50	0	0	66	79	1	79.00	1-57	0	0	7.18	0	
20T		2	1	1	8	8*		0	0	48	61	2	30.50	1-29	0	0	7.62	1	
FC	2006/07	8	9	1	64	27	8.00	0	0	1020	452	20	22.60	3-30	0	0	2.65	4	
Lim	2005/06	11	6	1	29	11	5.80	0	0	515	384	15	25.60	4-41	1	0	4.47	2	
20T	2006/07	3	2	2	22	14*		0	0	60	83	2	41.50	1-29	0	0	8.30	2	
TARANJEET SINGH Matharu (Maharashtra) b Malkapo, Hyderabad, Andhra Pradesh 28.3.1987 LHB LM																			
20T		7	5	0	30	21	6.00	0	0	10	16	0					9.60	2	
TARE, Aditya Prakash (Mumbai, Mumbai Indians) b Bombay (now Mumbai), Maharashtra 7.11.1987 LHB RAB WK																			
FC		1																0	
Lim		3	3	0	26	12	8.66	0	0									1	1
20T		11	8	1	124	49*	17.71	0	0									3	4
Lim	2007/08	14	13	3	265	65	26.50	0	1									20	2
TARJINDER SINGH (Assam) b Kamrup, Assam 22.12.1987 RHB OB																			
FC		4	6	0	164	117	27.33	1	0									7	
Lim		1	1	0	15	15	15.00	0	0	6	5	0					5.00	0	
FC	2005/06	12	20	0	418	117	20.90	1	1	156	80	0					3.07	17	
Lim	2006/07	8	8	0	85	27	10.62	0	0	144	98	2	49.00	1-14	0	0	4.08	2	
TAYLOR, Luteru Ross Poutoa Lote (Central Districts, New Zealand, Durham, New Zealand to South Africa, New Zealand to Sri Lanka, New Zealand to United Arab Emirates, New Zealand to United States of America, New Zealand to West Indies, Royal Challengers Bangalore, Victoria) b Lower Hutt, Wellington, New Zealand 8.3.1984 RHB OB																			
20T		11	11	5	240	65	40.00	0	2									4	
Test	2007/08	25	46	1	1941	154*	43.13	5	9	32	14	0					2.62	45	
FC	2002/03	71	120	3	4774	217	40.80	10	26	602	330	4	82.50	2-34	0	0	3.28	89	
Int	2005/06	84	77	11	2376	128*	36.00	3	16	30	32	0					6.40	62	
Lim	2002/03	129	122	15	4028	132*	37.64	7	27	306	240	3	80.00	1-13	0	0	4.70	87	
I20T	2006/07	34	31	2	590	63	20.34	0	3									22	
20T	2005/06	92	87	14	2395	111*	32.80	1	14	180	269	8	33.62	3-28	0	0	8.96	47	
TEHLAN, Mayank (Delhi) b Delhi 11.10.1986 RHB OB																			
FC		5	8	0	184	55	23.00	0	1	210	88	1	88.00	1-56	0	0	2.51	2	
20T		5	3	1	46	25*	23.00	0	0									0	
FC	2005/06	24	37	3	1051	200	30.91	3	2	216	93	1	93.00	1-56	0	0	2.58	12	
Lim	2003/04	10	8	1	114	45	16.28	0	0									1	
20T	2006/07	6	4	1	53	25*	17.66	0	0									0	
TENDULKAR, Sachin Ramesh (India, Mumbai Indians, India to Bangladesh, India to South Africa, India to Sri Lanka) b Bombay (now Mumbai), Maharashtra 24.4.1973 RHB RM,OB,LB																			
Test		5	7	1	410	106	68.33	3	1	60	27	0					2.70	2	
FC		5	7	1	410	106	68.33	3	1	60	27	0					2.70	2	
Int		12	12	2	695	200*	69.50	2	2	5	11	0					13.20	4	
Lim		12	12	2	695	200*	69.50	2	2	5	11	0					13.20	4	
20T		15	15	2	618	89*	47.53	0	5									3	
Test	1989/90	169	276	29	13837	248*	56.02	48	56	3994	2299	44	52.25	3-10	0	0	3.45	106	
FC	1988/89	272	428	45	22730	248*	59.34	75	102	7359	4191	69	60.73	3-10	0	0	3.41	174	
Int	1989/90	442	431	41	17598	200*	45.12	46	93	8020	6817	154	44.26	5-32	4	2	5.10	134	
Lim	1989/90	529	516	55	21150	200*	45.87	57	111	10196	8445	201	42.01	5-32	4	2	4.97	169	
I20T	2006/07	1	1	0	10	10	10.00	0	0	15	12	1	12.00	1-12	0	0	4.80	1	
20T	2006/07	40	40	5	1368	89*	39.08	0	10	93	123	2	61.50	1-12	0	0	7.93	17	
THAKER, Bhavik Dinbandhubhai (Gujarat, West Zone) b Bhavnagar, Gujarat 23.10.1982 RHB OB																			
FC		8	14	1	402	122	30.92	1	3	6	0	0					0.00	8	
Lim		3	2	0	95	56	47.50	0	1									0	
20T		4	4	0	90	34	22.50	0	0									0	
FC	2003/04	44	71	13	2573	192	44.36	6	16	6	0	0					0.00	38	
Lim	2003/04	32	29	3	853	87*	32.80	0	7									11	
20T	2006/07	10	9	1	184	34	23.00	0	0									3	
THAKKAR, Bhavin Jitendra (Himachal Pradesh) b Bombay (now Mumbai), Maharashtra 22.1.1982 RHB RM																			
FC		7	13	0	307	88	23.61	0	3	54	25	0					2.77	4	
20T		2	1	0	0	0	0.00	0	0	42	51	0					7.28	0	
FC	2001/02	32	48	2	1761	166	38.28	5	9	372	167	1	167.00	1-18	0	0	2.69	18	
Lim	2001/02	11	8	1	164	60	23.42	0	1	73	65	2	32.50	1-8	0	0	5.34	4	
THAKUR, Ashok Kumar (Himachal Pradesh) b Una, Himachal Pradesh 10.4.1977 RHB LM																			
FC		6	9	3	77	26	12.83	0	0	1180	521	22	23.68	6-38	2	0	2.64	3	
Lim		2	1	1	7	7*		0	0	114	74	3	24.66	2-59	0	0	3.89	0	
20T		4								90	117	5	23.40	2-29	0	0	7.80	0	
FC	2001/02	51	72	22	668	70	13.36	0	1	9638	4185	184	22.74	6-30	10	1	2.60	16	

Cmp	Debut	M	I	NO	Runs	HS	Avge	100	50	Balls	Runs	Wkts	Avge	BB	5i	10m	RpO	ct	st
Lim	2002/03	25	14	8	65	17*	10.83	0	0	1273	807	38	21.23	5-21	3	1	3.80	2	
20T	2006/07	7								156	200	6	33.33	2-29	0	0	7.69	0	
THAKUR, Imraj (Jammu and Kashmir) b Srinagar, Kashmir 10.2.1982 RHB WK																			
Lim		3	3	0	50	43	16.66	0	0									0	
Lim	2008/09	6	6	0	217	117	36.16	1	0									1	
THERON, Juan (South Africa A, Warriors to South Africa, Kings XI Punjab, South Africa A to Sri Lanka) b Potchefstroom, Transvaal, South Africa 24.7.1985 RHB RMF																			
20T		7	2	0	2	2	1.00	0	0	144	187	6	31.16	2-17	0	0	7.79	1	
FC	2005/06	40	51	10	570	66	13.90	0	2	6371	2994	131	22.85	7-46	7	0	2.82	12	
Lim	2005/06	59	33	13	371	41	18.55	0	0	2460	2052	102	20.11	4-33	7	0	5.00	17	
20T	2007/08	31	11	3	52	24*	6.50	0	0	650	746	32	23.31	3-16	0	0	6.88	13	
THOMAS, Benjamin Christopher (Hyderabad) b Hyderabad, Andhra Pradesh 20.6.1989 RHB OB																			
Lim		1	1	0	1	1	1.00	0	0									1	
TIWARI, Vishnu (Services) b Allahabad, Uttar Pradesh 11.11.1987 RHB																			
Lim		1	1	0	44	44	44.00	0	0									0	
20T		1	1	0	11	11	11.00	0	0									0	
TIWARY, Manoj Kumar (Bengal, Delhi Daredevils, East Zone, Kolkata Knight Riders, Rest of India, India A to England, India A to Scotland) b Howrah, Bengal 14.11.1985 RHB LBG																			
FC		7	12	4	590	107	73.75	2	4	114	84	0					4.42	6	
Lim		7	6	1	204	86	40.80	0	2	107	97	3	32.33	1-22	0	0	5.43	2	
20T		20	18	3	366	75*	24.40	0	3	54	73	1	73.00	1-11	0	0	8.11	6	
FC	2004/05	42	62	7	2903	210*	52.78	11	7	1472	760	14	54.28	2-42	0	0	3.09	46	
Int	2007/08	1	1	0	2	2	2.00	0	0									0	
Lim	2003/04	63	58	8	1760	96*	35.20	0	14	1055	1001	22	45.50	2-29	0	0	5.69	37	
20T	2006/07	37	32	6	740	75*	28.46	0	5	132	169	7	24.14	3-19	0	0	7.68	17	
TIWARY, Saurabh Sunil (East Zone, India Green, Jharkhand, Mumbai Indians) b Jamshedpur, Bihar 30.12.1989 LHB OB																			
FC		6	9	2	615	136	87.85	3	2	18	15	0					5.00	5	
Lim		7	7	1	176	66	29.33	0	1	94	84	3	28.00	2-40	0	0	5.36	3	
20T		20	19	2	573	61	33.70	0	3									5	
FC	2006/07	19	33	2	1579	169	50.93	6	5	48	49	0					6.12	9	
Lim	2005/06	19	19	1	759	76	42.16	0	8	118	109	4	27.25	2-40	0	0	5.54	6	
20T	2006/07	31	28	4	748	69	31.16	0	5									7	
TRIPATHI, Rahul Ajay (Maharashtra) b Ranchi, Maharastra 2.3.1991 RHB RM																			
Lim		1	1	0	0	0	0.00	0	0									0	
TRIVEDI, Siddharth Kishorkumar (Gujarat, India Blue, Rajasthan Royals) b Ahmedabad, Gujarat 4.9.1982 RHB RM																			
FC		6	10	2	76	22	9.50	0	0	1008	327	19	17.21	6-32	2	0	1.94	1	
Lim		5	4	3	19	13*	19.00	0	0	204	191	6	31.83	2-41	0	0	5.61	1	
20T		15	6	3	28	9	9.33	0	0	300	394	17	23.17	4-37	1	0	7.88	5	
FC	2002/03	60	82	30	678	51*	13.03	0	2	11703	5144	220	23.38	6-32	14	1	2.63	10	
Lim	2002/03	61	36	14	168	21*	7.63	0	0	2868	2283	81	28.18	4-40	1	0	4.77	17	
20T	2006/07	44	15	8	59	12	8.42	0	0	864	1147	42	27.30	4-37	1	0	7.96	10	
TYAGI, Sudeep (Central Zone, Chennai Super Kings, India, India Red, Rest of India, Uttar Pradesh, India to Bangladesh, India A to England, India A to Scotland) b Ghaziabad, Uttar Pradesh 19.9.1987 RHB RM																			
FC		3	3	0	7	6	2.33	0	0	402	275	5	55.00	2-56	0	0	4.10	0	
Int		2	1	1	1	1*		0	0	87	74	1	74.00	1-15	0	0	5.10	0	
Lim		10	4	3	1	1*	1.00	0	0	477	413	17	24.29	5-44	0	1	5.19	3	
I20T		1								12	21	0					10.50	1	
20T		7	1	1	3	3*		0	0	107	180	1	180.00	1-20	0	0	10.09	3	
FC	2007/08	19	22	7	32	12	2.13	0	0	3044	1690	60	28.16	6-46	2	1	3.33	1	
Int	2009/10	4	1	1	1	1*		0	0	165	144	3	48.00	1-15	0	0	5.23	1	
Lim	2007/08	18	5	4	3	2*	3.00	0	0	834	732	24	30.50	5-44	0	1	5.26	5	
20T	2009	15	3	3	3	3*		0	0	221	316	6	52.66	2-18	0	0	8.57	4	
UBARHANDE, Amol Vishwasrao (Vidarbha) b Buldhana, Maharashtra 28.9.1988 RHB WK																			
FC		3	4	0	40	16	10.00	0	0									10	
20T		3	3	0	46	25	15.33	0	0									4	1
UNADKAT, Jaydev Dipakbhai (Kolkata Knight Riders, Saurashtra, West Zone, India A to England, India A to Scotland) b Porbandar, Saurashtra 18.10.1991 RHB LFM																			
Lim		7	2	1	4	4*	4.00	0	0	354	251	9	27.88	3-36	0	0	4.25	2	
20T		3								62	85	4	21.25	3-26	0	0	8.22	1	
FC	2010	2	1	1	12	12*		0	0	501	203	16	12.68	7-41	2	1	2.43	0	
Lim	2009/10	10	3	1	6	4*	3.00	0	0	509	398	13	30.61	3-36	0	0	4.69	2	
UNIYAL, Amit (Rajasthan Royals) b Chandigarh 21.11.1981 LHB LFM																			
20T		2	2	1	4	4*	4.00	0	0	36	66	2	33.00	2-41	0	0	11.00	0	
FC	2001/02	29	40	6	808	68	23.76	0	3	5159	2725	91	29.94	6-92	3	0	3.16	10	
Lim	2001/02	40	21	6	301	49*	20.06	0	0	1566	1141	40	28.52	3-16	0	0	4.37	11	
20T	2006/07	4	3	2	18	14*	18.00	0	0	60	88	5	17.60	3-22	0	0	8.80	0	
UPADHYAY, Krishnakant (Railways) b Agra, Uttar Pradesh 18.6.1986 RHB RM																			
FC		3	3	1	53	49*	26.50	0	0	402	187	5	37.40	4-93	0	0	2.79	0	
20T		1								24	19	1	19.00	1-19	0	0	4.75	0	

Cmp	Debut	M	I	NO	Runs	HS	Avge	100	50	Balls	Runs	Wkts	Avge	BB	5i	10m	RpO	ct	st
UPADHYAY, Satish (Services) b Vijayawada, Andhra Pradesh 27.8.1977 RHB OB																			
20T		1	1	0	7	7	7.00	0	0	6	11	0					11.00	1	
FC	2004/05	9	14	3	347	92	31.54	0	2	54	41	0					4.55	2	
Lim	2005/06	7	7	1	85	33*	14.16	0	0	12	13	0					6.50	2	
20T	2006/07	6	6	1	55	29	11.00	0	0	66	56	3	18.66	3-15	0	0	5.09	3	
UPADHYAYA, Gaurav (Vidarbha) b Jamnagar, Punjab 26.3.1988 LHB OB																			
Lim		4	4	0	81	37	20.25	0	0	108	93	4	23.25	3-45	0	0	5.16	0	
FC	2008/09	2	4	0	34	16	8.50	0	0	24	18	1	18.00	1-6	0	0	4.50	2	
Lim	2007/08	12	12	2	188	40	18.80	0	0	318	249	10	24.90	4-20	1	0	4.69	5	
20T	2006/07	3	3	0	17	10	5.66	0	0	30	41	0					8.20	0	
UTHAPPA, Robin Venu (Karnataka, Royal Challengers Bangalore, South Zone) b Coorg, Karnataka 11.11.1985 RHB RM																			
FC		9	14	0	414	91	29.57	0	4	114	74	2	37.00	2-22	0	0	3.89	9	
Lim		7	7	0	262	117	37.42	1	2									6	
20T		22	20	3	528	68*	31.05	0	4									10	3
FC	2002/03	61	102	4	3958	162	40.38	10	22	490	292	10	29.20	3-26	0	0	3.57	60	
Int	2005/06	38	34	5	786	86	27.10	0	5									15	
Lim	2002/03	99	94	7	2877	160	33.06	4	21	150	152	2	76.00	1-23	0	0	6.08	42	
I20T	2007/08	9	8	0	149	50	18.62	0	1									1	
20T	2006/07	69	64	10	1363	68*	25.24	0	6									29	4
VAAS, Warnakulasuriya Patabendige Ushantha Joseph Chaminda (Basnahira North, Colts, Deccan Chargers, Northamptonshire) b Mattumagala, Sri Lanka 27.1.1974 LHB LFM																			
20T		6	5	1	30	16	7.50	0	0	132	139	9	15.44	3-21	0	0	6.31	0	
Test	1994	111	162	35	3089	100*	24.32	1	13	23438	10501	355	29.58	7-71	12	2	2.68	31	
FC	1990/91	202	272	57	5525	134	25.69	4	24	37222	17068	683	24.98	7-54	27	3	2.75	57	
Int	1993/94	322	220	72	2025	50*	13.68	0	1	15775	11014	400	27.53	8-19	9	4	4.18	60	
Lim	1992/93	392	268	88	2903	76*	16.12	0	6	18664	12947	480	26.97	8-19	11	4	4.16	79	
I20T	2006/07	6	2	1	33	21	33.00	0	0	132	128	6	21.33	2-14	0	0	5.81	0	
20T	2005/06	45	39	8	622	73	20.06	0	4	927	1059	55	19.25	3-16	0	0	6.85	7	
VAHORA, Murtuja Yakubbhai (Baroda) b Navapur, Maharashtra 1.12.1985 RHB RM																			
FC		6	8	2	70	14	11.66	0	0	814	362	13	27.84	4-35	0	0	2.66	3	
20T		4	2	0	1	1	0.50	0	0	90	112	2	56.00	2-27	0	0	7.46	6	
FC	2005/06	9	11	2	82	14	9.11	0	0	1301	553	18	30.72	4-35	0	0	2.55	6	
Lim	2008/09	6	3	0	98	50	32.66	0	1	335	286	7	40.85	2-44	0	0	5.12	3	
20T	2006/07	6	3	0	8	7	2.66	0	0	127	168	2	84.00	2-27	0	0	7.93	7	
VALTHATY, Paul Chandrasekhar (Mumbai) b Bombay (now Mumbai), Maharashtra 7.12.1983 RHB RM																			
20T		5	5	0	166	70	33.20	0	1	84	115	4	28.75	2-23	0	0	8.21	2	
Lim	2005/06	1	1	0	16	16	16.00	0	0	18	11	0					3.66	1	
20T	2009	7	7	0	172	70	24.57	0	1	84	115	4	28.75	2-23	0	0	8.21	2	
VAN DER MERWE, Roelof Erasmus (Northerns, South Africa, Titans, Royal Challengers Bangalore, South Africa to India, South Africa to West Indies) b Johannesburg, Transvaal, South Africa 31.12.1984 RHB SLA																			
Int		2	1	0	12	12	12.00	0	0	120	109	3	36.33	2-47	0	0	5.45	0	
Lim		2	1	0	12	12	12.00	0	0	120	109	3	36.33	2-47	0	0	5.45	0	
20T		5	2	1	4	3*	4.00	0	0	114	120	6	20.00	2-27	0	0	6.31	1	
FC	2006/07	16	23	5	568	81	31.55	0	3	2273	1168	30	38.93	4-59	0	0	3.08	9	
Int	2008/09	13	7	3	39	12	9.75	0	0	705	561	17	33.00	3-27	0	0	4.77	3	
Lim	2006/07	64	53	16	905	72	24.45	0	4	2908	2278	98	23.24	5-31	6	1	4.70	24	
I20T	2008/09	13	6	3	57	48	19.00	0	0	264	305	14	21.78	2-14	0	0	6.93	6	
20T	2007/08	43	27	6	397	70*	18.90	0	2	865	1025	47	21.80	3-18	0	0	7.11	17	
VARDHAN, Manish Singh (Jharkhand) b Purnea, Bihar 6.10.1983 RHB OB																			
FC		3	6	1	203	108	40.60	1	1	60	19	1	19.00	1-11	0	0	1.90	3	
FC	2004/05	30	55	3	1747	179	33.59	4	9	433	239	2	119.50	1-11	0	0	3.31	20	
Lim	2004/05	14	14	0	343	84	24.50	0	4	120	84	2	42.00	1-15	0	0	4.20	6	
20T	2006/07	4	4	1	88	64*	29.33	0	1	6	11	0					11.00	1	
VASUDEVADAS, Kuthethurshri (Tamil Nadu) b Madras (now Chennai), Tamil Nadu 26.1.1985 LHB LB																			
Lim		7	5	1	224	94	56.00	0	2									4	
20T		1	1	0	11	11	11.00	0	0									2	
FC	2003/04	19	34	4	968	103*	32.26	1	5	330	213	4	53.25	2-40	0	0	3.87	20	1
Lim	2003/04	27	19	3	642	94	40.12	0	5	54	57	1	57.00	1-12	0	0	6.33	15	
20T	2006/07	8	6	0	65	25	10.83	0	0	24	20	2	10.00	2-20	0	0	5.00	5	
VEER, Bharat (Delhi) b Saharanpur, Delhi 2.2.1988 RHB RM																			
20T		1								22	34	1	34.00	1-34	0	0	9.27	0	
VENUGOPAL RAO, Yalaka (Andhra, Deccan Chargers) b Visakhapatnam, Andhra Pradesh 26.2.1982 RHB OB																			
FC		5	7	0	201	69	28.71	0	1									5	
Lim		5	5	0	185	113	37.00	1	0									1	
20T		11	10	1	98	30	10.88	0	0	12	19	0					9.50	1	
FC	1998/99	90	148	17	5527	228*	42.19	13	24	4685	2147	57	37.66	4-34	0	0	2.75	76	
Int	2005	16	11	2	218	61*	24.22	0	1									5	
Lim	1998/99	119	104	13	3421	113	37.59	10	20	2935	2383	51	46.72	5-20	0	1	4.87	38	
20T	2006/07	43	37	6	587	71*	18.93	0	3	270	380	8	47.50	2-23	0	0	8.44	9	

Cmp	*Debut*	*M*	*I*	*NO*	*Runs*	*HS*	*Avge*	*100*	*50*	*Balls*	*Runs*	*Wkts*	*Avge*	*BB*	*5i*	*10m*	*RpO*	*ct*	*st*
VERAGI, Salim Yusuf (Baroda) b Tankariya, Bharuch, Gujarat 28.7.1986 RHB RM																			
FC		1	1	1	0	0*		0	0	60	34	1	34.00	1-34	0	0	3.40	0	
20T		4								84	105	2	52.50	1-23	0	0	7.50	0	
FC	2007/08	8	11	6	35	10*	7.00	0	0	1161	632	22	28.72	5-24	1	0	3.26	0	
VERMA, Amit Anil (Karnataka) b Bangalore, Karnataka 30.6.1987 LHB LBG																			
FC		9	14	1	560	157	43.07	2	1	392	185	5	37.00	1-11	0	0	2.83	7	
Lim		5	5	4	51	38*	51.00	0	0	216	171	2	85.50	2-45	0	0	4.75	1	
20T		2	1	0	29	29	29.00	0	0									0	
FC	2007/08	11	15	1	561	157	40.07	2	1	488	227	5	45.40	1-11	0	0	2.79	9	
Lim	2007/08	12	10	4	150	45	25.00	0	0	312	260	2	130.00	2-45	0	0	5.00	4	
20T	2006/07	5	2	0	32	29	16.00	0	0	18	26	0					8.66	2	
VERMA, Alliuri Satyakumar (Andhra) b Appanapalli, Andhra Pradesh 1.4.1984 RHB RM																			
FC		2	2	0	12	8	6.00	0	0									0	
FC	2002/03	34	57	3	1324	105*	24.51	2	9	504	251	6	41.83	2-21	0	0	2.98	16	
Lim	2003/04	14	14	2	324	75	27.00	0	2	170	189	3	63.00	1-19	0	0	6.67	3	
20T	2006/07	5	5	1	54	26	13.50	0	0	84	101	3	33.66	1-22	0	0	7.21	1	
VETTORI, Daniel Luca (New Zealand, Northern Districts, Delhi Daredevils, New Zealand to South Africa, New Zealand to United Arab Emirates, New Zealand to United States of America, New Zealand to West Indies, Queensland) b Auckland, New Zealand 27.1.1979 LHB SLA																			
20T		3	3	2	33	19*	33.00	0	0	70	97	2	48.50	1-30	0	0	8.31	0	
Test	1996/97	100	152	23	3962	140	30.71	5	22	24997	11007	325	33.86	7-87	18	3	2.64	55	
FC	1996/97	152	220	31	5809	140	30.73	8	32	35722	15920	499	31.90	7-87	28	3	2.67	79	
Int	1996/97	255	160	49	1895	83	17.07	0	4	12111	8367	268	31.22	5-7	7	2	4.14	71	
Lim	1996/97	322	211	57	3149	138	20.44	2	10	15529	10550	347	30.40	5-7	7	2	4.07	102	
I20T	2007/08	28	20	6	187	38	13.35	0	0	649	580	35	16.57	4-20	1	0	5.36	8	
20T	2005/06	57	43	11	669	57	20.90	0	1	1282	1321	67	19.71	4-20	1	0	6.18	22	
VIHARI, Gade Hanuma (Hyderabad) b Kakinada, Andhra Pradesh 13.10.1993 RHB OB																			
20T		2	2	1	8	4*	8.00	0	0	48	50	5	10.00	3-28	0	0	6.25	1	
VIJAY, Murali (Chennai Super Kings, India, India Red, Rest of India, Tamil Nadu, India to Bangladesh, India to Sri Lanka, India to West Indies, India to Zimbabwe) b Madras (now Chennai), Tamil Nadu 1.4.1984 RHB OB																			
Test		3	4	0	130	87	32.50	0	1									3	
FC		9	12	0	770	154	64.16	2	5	78	47	0					3.61	7	
Int		1	1	0	25	25	25.00	0	0									1	
Lim		6	6	0	311	104	51.83	2	0	12	7	1	7.00	1-7	0	0	3.50	3	
20T		17	17	2	519	127	34.60	1	3									12	
Test	2008/09	7	10	0	333	87	33.30	0	2									6	
FC	2006/07	38	61	2	3033	243	51.40	7	14	186	118	1	118.00	1-16	0	0	3.80	39	
Int	2009/10	4	4	0	71	25	17.75	0	0									3	
Lim	2005/06	34	34	1	1417	112	42.93	5	5	87	61	5	12.20	3-13	0	0	4.20	19	
I20T	2010	6	6	0	108	48	18.00	0	0									3	
20T	2006/07	36	34	2	815	127	25.46	1	3	6	2	0					2.00	18	
VIJAYKUMAR, Paidikalva David (Andhra) b Paidikalva, Andhra Pradesh 20.10.1986 RHB RM																			
FC		2	3	0	9	4	3.00	0	0	579	238	10	23.80	3-56	0	0	2.46	0	
Lim		2	1	1	7	7*		0	0	112	114	3	38.00	2-55	0	0	6.10	0	
20T		2								42	72	1	72.00	1-27	0	0	10.28	0	
FC	2006/07	19	28	15	47	16*	3.61	0	0	3838	1600	61	26.22	6-51	3	1	2.50	4	
Lim	2007/08	7	5	4	8	7*	8.00	0	0	316	313	6	52.16	2-42	0	0	5.94	0	
20T	2006/07	15	4	3	7	6	7.00	0	0	284	383	10	38.30	2-16	0	0	8.09	0	
VINAY KUMAR, Ranganath (Karnataka, Royal Challengers Bangalore, South Zone, India to West Indies, India to Zimbabwe) b Davanagere, Karnataka 12.2.1984 RHB RM																			
FC		9	11	3	217	51*	27.12	0	1	2044	1058	53	19.96	8-32	3	1	3.10	4	
Lim		7	4	0	107	43	26.75	0	0	363	355	12	29.58	4-45	1	0	5.86	1	
20T		18	6	1	27	10*	5.40	0	0	346	493	19	25.94	4-40	1	0	8.54	3	
FC	2004/05	54	71	15	805	51*	14.37	0	1	10172	4888	202	24.19	8-32	10	2	2.88	18	
Int	2010	1								48	51	2	25.50	2-51	0	0	6.37	0	
Lim	2004/05	43	27	8	454	82	23.89	0	2	2176	1699	72	23.59	4-24	4	0	4.68	12	
I20T	2010	3								66	82	5	16.40	3-24	0	0	7.45	0	
20T	2006/07	47	24	8	170	25*	10.62	0	0	899	1214	47	25.82	4-40	1	0	8.10	8	
VIVEK KRISHNA, Kattar (Hyderabad) b Hannam Konda, Andhra Pradesh 12.9.1990 RHB RFM																			
20T		3	1	1	9	9*		0	0	48	51	5	10.20	4-25	1	0	6.37	1	
VOGES, Adam Charles (Australia, Australia A, Western Australia, Australia to India, Australia to New Zealand, Nottinghamshire, Rajasthan Royals) b Perth, Western Australia, Australia 4.10.1979 RHB SLC																			
Int		5	4	1	79	36	26.33	0	0	90	91	1	91.00	1-22	0	0	6.06	1	
Lim		5	4	1	79	36	26.33	0	0	90	91	1	91.00	1-22	0	0	6.06	1	
20T		9	7	3	181	45*	45.25	0	0	54	76	0					8.44	1	
FC	2002/03	82	138	18	4867	180	40.55	10	27	2518	1370	40	34.25	4-92	0	0	3.26	100	
Int	2006/07	14	13	4	312	72	34.66	0	1	150	159	1	159.00	1-22	0	0	6.36	2	
Lim	2004/05	103	98	20	3219	104*	41.26	2	25	1244	1092	22	49.63	3-25	0	0	5.26	35	
I20T	2007/08	4	3	1	63	26	31.50	0	0	12	5	2	2.50	2-5	0	0	2.50	2	
20T	2005/06	59	55	11	1489	82*	33.84	0	7	281	405	12	33.75	2-4	0	0	8.64	22	

Cmp	Debut	M	I	NO	Runs	HS	Avge	100	50	Balls	Runs	Wkts	Avge	BB	5i	10m	RpO	ct	st
WAGH, Shrikant Bhaskar (Rajasthan Royals, Vidarbha) b Chikhli, Maharashtra 9.10.1988 LHB LM																			
FC		5	8	3	111	37*	22.20	0	0	756	306	10	30.60	2-29	0	0	2.42	0	
Lim		4	4	1	90	44	30.00	0	0	206	161	6	26.83	2-38	0	0	4.68	2	
20T		4	3	2	27	17*	27.00	0	0	60	93	3	31.00	1-16	0	0	9.30	1	
FC	2007/08	8	14	5	304	110*	33.77	1	0	1284	591	13	45.46	2-29	0	0	2.76	1	
Lim	2006/07	9	7	1	95	44	15.83	0	0	422	362	9	40.22	2-38	0	0	5.14	2	
20T	2006/07	7	4	3	50	23*	50.00	0	0	120	179	6	29.83	2-37	0	0	8.95	1	
WAGHELA, Praful Giju (Mumbai) b Bombay (now Mumbai), Maharashtra 19.11.1984 LHB LBG																			
FC		1	1	0	24	24	24.00	0	0	48	42	0					5.25	0	
Lim		2	2	0	92	92	46.00	0	1									0	
Lim	2004/05	6	6	0	177	92	29.50	0	1									0	
20T	2006/07	1	1	0	5	5	5.00	0	0									0	
WAGHMARE, Atul Bholanath (Vidarbha) b Nagpur, Maharashtra 7.3.1980 RHB SLA																			
20T		1								6	13	0					13.00	0	
FC	2001/02	2	4	0	4	4	1.00	0	0	294	100	4	25.00	3-58	0	0	2.04	2	
WAGHMARE, Digambar Kisanrao (Maharashtra) b Manjaram, Maharashtra 5.1.1984 RHB LBG																			
FC		3	6	1	107	46	21.40	0	0	235	177	3	59.00	2-24	0	0	4.51	0	
Lim		3	3	1	40	29	20.00	0	0	48	53	0					6.62	0	
20T		7	5	3	91	31*	45.50	0	0	12	16	0					8.00	5	
FC	2008/09	7	12	1	196	46	17.81	0	0	613	445	8	55.62	2-24	0	0	4.35	4	
Lim	2007/08	5	5	1	50	29	12.50	0	0	72	120	1	120.00	1-53	0	0	10.00	2	
20T	2006/07	11	8	3	114	31*	22.80	0	0	39	53	2	26.50	1-12	0	0	8.15	6	
WAINGANKAR, Kshemal Makarand (Goa) b Andheri, Maharashtra 5.4.1985 RHB RMF																			
FC		5	4	3	31	12	31.00	0	0	595	316	8	39.50	3-72	0	0	3.18	0	
Lim		1	1	1	6	6*		0	0	36	48	2	24.00	2-48	0	0	8.00	0	
20T		3	2	2	2	1*		0	0	42	57	3	19.00	2-21	0	0	8.14	1	
FC	2006/07	7	7	4	57	19*	19.00	0	0	836	428	13	32.92	3-72	0	0	3.07	0	
WAKHARE, Akshay Anilrao (Vidarbha) b Nagpur, Maharashtra 3.10.1985 RHB OB																			
FC		5	5	1	93	56	23.25	0	1	1187	439	23	19.08	6-56	3	1	2.21	2	
Lim		4	3	0	18	10	6.00	0	0	166	118	3	39.33	1-26	0	0	4.26	1	
FC	2006/07	8	8	1	110	56	15.71	0	1	1709	656	29	22.62	6-56	3	1	2.30	4	
WARNE, Shane Keith (Rajasthan Royals) b Ferntree Gully, Victoria, Australia 13.9.1969 RHB LBG																			
20T		14	7	2	10	4	2.00	0	0	300	381	11	34.63	4-21	1	0	7.62	2	
Test	1991/92	145	199	17	3154	99	17.32	0	12	40704	17995	708	25.41	8-71	37	10	2.65	125	
FC	1990/91	301	404	48	6919	107*	19.43	2	26	74829	34449	1319	26.11	8-71	69	12	2.76	264	
Int	1992/93	194	107	29	1018	55	13.05	0	1	10642	7541	293	25.73	5-33	12	1	4.25	80	
Lim	1991/92	311	200	41	1879	55	11.81	0	1	16419	11642	473	24.61	6-42	20	3	4.25	126	
20T	2004	45	27	7	200	34*	10.00	0	0	984	1225	46	26.63	4-21	1	0	7.47	14	
WARNER, David Andrew (Australia, New South Wales, Australia to England, Australia to New Zealand, Australia to West Indies, Delhi Daredevils, Middlesex, New South Wales to India) b Paddington, Sydney, New South Wales, Australia 27.10.1986 LHB LB																			
20T		17	17	1	489	107*	30.56	1	2									9	
FC	2008/09	4	6	1	131	48*	26.20	0	0	25	19	1	19.00	1-0	0	0	4.56	3	
Int	2008/09	7	7	0	106	69	15.14	0	1									1	
Lim	2006/07	29	29	2	827	165*	30.62	1	4	90	81	2	40.50	1-11	0	0	5.40	6	
I20T	2008/09	22	22	0	644	89	29.27	0	4									13	
20T	2006/07	79	79	2	2096	107*	27.22	1	11									32	
WATEKAR, Hemal Haribhai (Andhra) b Gandhinagar, Gujarat 1.12.1977 RHB OB																			
FC		5	9	2	179	59	25.57	0	1									8	
Lim		3	3	0	98	53	32.66	0	1									0	
FC	1999/00	56	91	16	1965	142	26.20	3	7	6877	3021	94	32.13	5-32	2	0	2.63	47	
Lim	1999/00	46	38	9	739	71	25.48	0	4	1777	1377	52	26.48	4-21	2	0	4.64	12	
WATSON, Shane Robert (Australia, Australia to England, Australia to India, Australia to Ireland, Australia to New Zealand, Australia to South Africa, Australia to West Indies, Rajasthan Royals) b Ipswich, Queensland, Australia 17.6.1981 RHB RMF																			
Int		6	6	0	256	93	42.66	0	1	236	220	10	22.00	3-29	0	0	5.59	4	
Lim		6	6	0	256	93	42.66	0	1	236	220	10	22.00	3-29	0	0	5.59	4	
20T		6	5	0	185	60	37.00	0	2	132	184	6	30.66	3-37	0	0	8.36	3	
Test	2004/05	20	35	1	1247	120*	36.67	1	9	1995	1048	38	27.57	6-33	2	0	3.15	15	
FC	2000/01	84	146	16	5940	203*	45.69	14	32	7872	4478	159	28.16	7-69	5	1	3.41	69	
Int	2001/02	114	96	22	2982	136*	40.29	4	17	4051	3296	118	27.93	4-36	3	0	4.88	33	
Lim	2000/01	179	158	30	4851	136*	37.89	6	28	5937	4976	160	31.10	4-36	3	0	5.02	52	
I20T	2005/06	19	18	2	375	81	23.43	0	3	249	347	10	34.70	2-23	0	0	8.36	7	
20T	2004	52	49	9	1306	97*	32.65	0	12	850	1071	43	24.90	3-10	0	0	7.56	18	
WHITE, Cameron Leon (Australia, Victoria, Victoria to India, Australia to England, Australia to India, Australia to Ireland, Australia to New Zealand, Australia to South Africa, Australia to West Indies, Royal Challengers Bangalore) b Bairnsdale, Victoria, Australia 18.8.1983 RHB LBG																			
Int		6	6	0	218	62	36.33	0	3									2	
Lim		6	6	0	218	62	36.33	0	3									2	
20T		12	10	5	122	24	24.40	0	0	6	19	0					19.00	5	
Test	2008/09	4	7	2	146	46	29.20	0	0	558	342	5	68.40	2-71	0	0	3.67	1	
FC	2000/01	108	181	23	6680	260*	42.27	15	31	11730	6901	172	40.12	6-66	2	1	3.53	101	

Cmp	Debut	M	I	NO	Runs	HS	Avge	100	50	Balls	Runs	Wkts	Avge	BB	5i	10m	RpO	ct	st
Int	2005/06	68	56	11	1642	105	36.48	2	10	325	345	12	28.75	3-5	0	0	6.36	32	
Lim	2001/02	177	152	22	4586	126*	35.27	6	29	3712	3292	92	35.78	4-15	4	0	5.32	77	
I20T	2006/07	22	21	8	505	85*	38.84	0	3	24	25	1	25.00	1-11	0	0	6.25	11	
20T	2004/05	78	74	20	1816	141*	33.62	2	10	322	477	22	21.68	4-10	1	0	8.88	32	
WILLIAMS, Connor Cecil (Baroda) b Baroda, Gujarat 7.8.1973 LHB SLA																			
FC		6	12	0	375	129	31.25	1	1									5	
FC	1995/96	115	194	8	7504	237*	40.34	18	39									89	
Lim	1995/96	57	57	4	2075	114*	39.15	3	14	30	6	1	6.00	1-4	0	0	1.20	25	
YADAV, Ashwin Dhannulal (Hyderabad) b Hyderabad, Andhra Pradesh 10.9.1987 RHB RMF																			
FC		3	4	1	21	11	7.00	0	0	432	281	2	140.50	1-59	0	0	3.90	0	
Lim		4	2	0	8	7	4.00	0	0	174	180	2	90.00	2-50	0	0	6.20	2	
FC	2007/08	14	19	6	120	28*	9.23	0	0	2013	1112	34	32.70	6-52	1	0	3.31	2	
Lim	2007/08	10	4	2	17	7*	8.50	0	0	360	366	4	91.50	2-50	0	0	6.10	3	
YADAV, Ashish Kumara (Uttar Pradesh) b Varanasi, Uttar Pradesh 1.9.1985 LHB SLA																			
Lim		5	4	1	83	46	27.66	0	0	108	90	2	45.00	1-17	0	0	5.00	1	
Lim	2007/08	6	5	1	94	46	23.50	0	0	126	102	2	51.00	1-17	0	0	4.85	1	
YADAV, Amit Ramkumar (Goa) b Khar Khari, Goa 10.10.1989 RHB OB																			
FC		5	5	2	62	39*	20.66	0	0	571	241	7	34.42	4-60	0	0	2.53	5	
Lim		5	4	1	142	119	47.33	1	0	242	204	6	34.00	3-40	0	0	5.05	2	
20T		3	3	1	21	16	10.50	0	0	72	63	6	10.50	3-20	0	0	5.25	1	
Lim	2008/09	10	9	3	209	119	34.83	1	0	512	403	12	33.58	3-40	0	0	4.72	4	
20T	2006/07	8	8	2	48	21	8.00	0	0	174	197	10	19.70	3-20	0	0	6.79	4	
YADAV, Arjun Shivlal (Hyderabad) b Palghat (now Palakkad), Kerala 23.12.1981 RHB OB																			
FC		4	7	1	113	57*	18.83	0	1	18	13	0					4.33	5	
Lim		3	3	0	42	28	14.00	0	0									0	
20T		1	1	0	5	5	5.00	0	0									0	
FC	1999/00	72	126	9	3350	155	28.63	4	18	591	309	12	25.75	3-25	0	0	3.13	22	
Lim	1999/00	68	66	3	1393	96*	22.11	0	9	318	331	8	41.37	2-5	0	0	6.24	22	
20T	2006/07	12	10	1	71	16	7.88	0	0									2	
YADAV, Deepak Kishanlal (Railways) b Lucknow, Uttar Pradesh 3.9.1984 RHB OB																			
Lim		1								42	41	1	41.00	1-41	0	0	5.85	0	
FC	2008/09	2	3	1	53	24*	26.50	0	0	72	54	1	54.00	1-24	0	0	4.50	0	
Lim	2007/08	6	4	1	201	69	67.00	0	3	54	49	2	24.50	1-8	0	0	5.44	0	
YADAV, Jai Prakash (Railways) b Bhopal, Madhya Pradesh 7.8.1974 RHB RM																			
20T		4	4	2	48	33*	24.00	0	0	96	111	2	55.50	1-20	0	0	6.93	2	
FC	1994/95	117	193	12	7027	265	38.82	13	36	16166	5866	258	22.73	8-80	16	2	2.17	79	
Int	2002/03	12	7	3	81	69	20.25	0	1	396	326	6	54.33	2-32	0	0	4.93	3	
Lim	1994/95	126	119	11	3546	128	32.83	4	23	5236	3728	131	28.45	5-49	4	1	4.27	45	
YADAV, Rahul Mahesh (Delhi) b Ghaziabad, Uttar Pradesh 15.1.1989 RHB WK																			
FC		1	1	0	7	7	7.00	0	0									0	
Lim	2008/09	5																8	3
YADAV, Suraj (Services) b New Delhi 26.10.1987 RHB RM																			
Lim		3	2	1	2	1*	2.00	0	0	150	134	3	44.66	2-44	0	0	5.36	2	
20T		2	2	0	4	2	2.00	0	0	48	50	0					6.25	0	
YADAV, Suryakumar Ashok (Mumbai) b Bombay (now Mumbai), Maharashtra 14.9.1990 RHB RM																			
Lim		2	2	0	50	41	25.00	0	0									0	
20T		1	1	0	5	5	5.00	0	0									0	
YADAV, Salil Girishchandra (Gujarat) b Gandhinagar, Gujarat 3.4.1982 RHB LBG																			
FC		6	9	2	15	5	2.14	0	0	1309	743	17	43.70	6-123	1	0	3.40	2	
FC	2001/02	14	20	9	136	33*	12.36	0	0	2803	1422	30	47.40	6-123	1	0	3.04	3	
Lim	2003/04	8	5	1	2	2	0.50	0	0	455	355	11	32.27	3-37	0	0	4.68	3	
YADAV, Sherbahadur Shyamlal (Goa) b Vasco da Gama, Goa 4.12.1984 LHB SLA																			
Lim		2	2	0	17	15	8.50	0	0	37	50	0					8.10	0	
20T		3	2	1	4	2*	4.00	0	0	36	54	3	18.00	2-18	0	0	9.00	0	
FC	2004/05	10	19	6	138	33*	10.61	0	0	1836	823	21	39.19	4-57	0	0	2.69	4	
Lim	2003/04	15	13	2	105	19	9.54	0	0	649	499	12	41.58	3-13	0	0	4.61	6	
YADAV, Tejashwi Prasad (Jharkhand) b Patna, Bihar 9.11.1989 RHB OB																			
FC		1	2	0	20	19	10.00	0	0	30	17	0					3.40	0	
Lim		2	2	0	14	9	7.00	0	0	24	23	1	23.00	1-10	0	0	5.75	1	
20T		4	1	0	3	3	3.00	0	0	36	50	0					8.33	1	
YADAV, Umeshkumar Tilak (Central Zone, Delhi Daredevils, Vidarbha, India to Zimbabwe) b Nagpur, Maharashtra 25.10.1987 RHB RFM																			
FC		6	6	4	50	24*	25.00	0	0	866	466	16	29.12	6-40	1	0	3.22	4	
Lim		4	4	2	32	13*	16.00	0	0	198	150	6	25.00	3-40	0	0	4.54	0	
20T		9	1	1	3	3*		0	0	187	257	7	36.71	2-24	0	0	8.24	1	
FC	2008/09	11	14	9	82	24*	16.40	0	0	1879	922	42	21.95	6-40	3	0	2.94	5	
Int	2010	3	1	1	3	3*		0	0	132	129	1	129.00	1-61	0	0	5.86	1	
Lim	2008/09	11	8	5	55	13*	18.33	0	0	523	446	10	44.60	3-40	0	0	5.11	2	
YADAV, Vivek (Rajasthan) b Rohtak, Haryana 9.12.1984 RHB LBG																			
FC		2	4	0	53	27	13.25	0	0	327	135	7	19.28	4-28	0	0	2.47	1	
Lim		2	2	0	10	10	5.00	0	0	66	78	2	39.00	2-29	0	0	7.09	0	

Cmp	Debut	M	I	NO	Runs	HS	Avge	100	50	Balls	Runs	Wkts	Avge	BB	5i	10m	RpO	ct	st
FC	2008/09	5	9	2	107	41*	15.28	0	0	727	308	17	18.11	4-28	0	0	2.54	1	
Lim	2004/05	5	5	2	38	15*	12.66	0	0	198	185	5	37.00	2-29	0	0	5.60	0	
YADAV, Vikrant Sajjan (Rajasthan) b Udaipur, Rajasthan 14.12.1982 RHB RM																			
FC		1	2	1	6	5*	6.00	0	0	120	26	1	26.00	1-11	0	0	1.30	0	
Lim		3	2	1	13	8*	13.00	0	0	152	172	2	86.00	2-66	0	0	6.78	2	
FC	2006/07	4	7	3	38	15	9.50	0	0	648	370	6	61.66	2-81	0	0	3.42	1	
Lim	2002/03	7	5	2	27	14*	9.00	0	0	332	337	7	48.14	3-55	0	0	6.09	2	
YAGNIK, Dishant Harendra (Rajasthan) b Banswara, Rajasthan 22.6.1983 LHB WK																			
Lim		4	4	0	97	40	24.25	0	0									3	
FC	2004/05	14	23	0	476	79	20.69	0	3									36	2
Lim	2002/03	14	13	1	290	50	24.16	0	1									14	2
20T	2006/07	2	2	0	42	29	21.00	0	0									1	
YASHPAL SINGH (Services) b Delhi 27.11.1981 RHB RM																			
Lim		5	5	0	182	63	36.40	0	2	150	129	3	43.00	2-39	0	0	5.16	1	
20T		5	5	0	157	58	31.40	0	2	12	21	0					10.50	1	
FC	2001/02	57	97	11	4409	240	51.26	10	23	2213	1207	31	38.93	4-31	0	0	3.27	38	
Lim	2001/02	49	46	4	1942	126*	46.23	4	16	990	877	18	48.72	3-28	0	0	5.31	24	
20T	2006/07	17	13	0	286	58	22.00	0	2	68	96	4	24.00	3-26	0	0	8.47	6	
YOHANNAN, Tinu (Kerala) b Quilon (now Kollam), Kerala 18.2.1979 RHB RMF																			
FC		3	3	0	42	28	14.00	0	0	240	148	0					3.70	1	
20T		1	1	0	6	6	6.00	0	0	24	33	2	16.50	2-33	0	0	8.25	1	
Test	2001/02	3	4	4	13	8*		0	0	486	256	5	51.20	2-56	0	0	3.16	1	
FC	1999/00	59	71	26	524	43	11.64	0	0	9404	4868	145	33.57	6-61	6	0	3.10	28	
Int	2001/02	3	2	2	7	5*		0	0	120	122	5	24.40	3-33	0	0	6.10	0	
Lim	1999/00	45	28	16	93	13*	7.75	0	0	2302	1810	63	28.73	3-22	0	0	4.71	10	
YUVRAJ SINGH (India, Kings XI Punjab, India to Bangladesh, India to Sri Lanka, India to West Indies) b Chandigarh 12.12.1981 LHB SLA,LM																			
Test		3	3	0	158	68	52.66	0	2	138	90	1	90.00	1-7	0	0	3.91	1	
FC		3	3	0	158	68	52.66	0	2	138	90	1	90.00	1-7	0	0	3.91	1	
Int		6	6	0	151	78	25.16	0	1	246	193	2	96.50	1-30	0	0	4.70	0	
Lim		6	6	0	151	78	25.16	0	1	246	193	2	96.50	1-30	0	0	4.70	0	
I20T		2	2	1	66	60*	66.00	0	1	18	23	3	7.66	3-23	0	0	7.66	0	
20T		16	16	3	321	60*	24.69	0	1	156	175	8	21.87	3-23	0	0	6.73	2	
Test	2003/04	34	52	6	1639	169	35.63	3	9	751	431	8	53.87	2-9	0	0	3.44	30	
FC	1996/97	91	144	17	5523	209	43.48	17	26	1813	987	19	51.94	3-25	0	0	3.26	89	
Int	2000/01	254	234	32	7420	139	36.73	12	43	4004	3374	84	40.16	4-6	2	0	5.05	72	
Lim	1999/00	321	296	42	9566	172	37.66	16	56	5001	4195	116	36.16	4-6	2	0	5.03	93	
I20T	2007/08	22	21	4	555	70	32.64	0	5	120	174	7	24.85	3-23	0	0	8.70	6	
20T	2003	78	76	9	1775	71	26.49	0	10	540	680	30	22.66	3-13	0	0	7.55	21	
ZALA, Abhiraj Balbhadrasinh (Saurashtra) b Khambalia, Saurashtra 6.12.1986 RHB RFM																			
20T		2	2	0	0	0	0.00	0	0	36	41	1	41.00	1-25	0	0	6.83	0	

AUSTRALIA TO INDIA 2009/10

Cmp	Debut	M	I	NO	Runs	HS	Avge	100	50	Balls	Runs	Wkts	Avge	BB	5i	10m	RpO	ct	st
BOLLINGER, D.E.																			
Int		4	1	0	0	0	0.00	0	0	234	174	9	19.33	5-35	0	1	4.46	2	
Lim		4	1	0	0	0	0.00	0	0	234	174	9	19.33	5-35	0	1	4.46	2	
HAURITZ, N.M.																			
Int		6	2	2	39	30*		0	0	312	229	4	57.25	2-31	0	0	4.40	3	
Lim		6	2	2	39	30*		0	0	312	229	4	57.25	2-31	0	0	4.40	3	
HENRIQUES, M.C.																			
Int		2	2	0	18	12	9.00	0	0	90	84	1	84.00	1-51	0	0	5.60	0	
Lim		2	2	0	18	12	9.00	0	0	90	84	1	84.00	1-51	0	0	5.60	0	
HILFENHAUS, B.W.																			
Int		2	1	0	16	16	16.00	0	0	120	155	2	77.50	1-72	0	0	7.75	3	
Lim		2	1	0	16	16	16.00	0	0	120	155	2	77.50	1-72	0	0	7.75	3	
HOPES, J.R.																			
Int		1	1	0	14	14	14.00	0	0	12	10	0					5.00	0	
Lim		1	1	0	14	14	14.00	0	0	12	10	0					5.00	0	
HUSSEY, M.E.K.																			
Int		6	6	3	313	81*	104.33	0	3	18	26	0					8.66	1	
Lim		6	6	3	313	81*	104.33	0	3	18	26	0					8.66	1	
JOHNSON, M.G.																			
Int		5	4	2	52	21	26.00	0	0	284	290	9	32.22	3-39	0	0	6.12	1	
Lim		5	4	2	52	21	26.00	0	0	284	290	9	32.22	3-39	0	0	6.12	1	
LEE, B.																			
Int		1	1	0	0	0	0.00	0	0	36	28	1	28.00	1-28	0	0	4.66	1	
Lim		1	1	0	0	0	0.00	0	0	36	28	1	28.00	1-28	0	0	4.66	1	

Cmp Debut	M	I	NO	Runs	HS	Avge	100	50	Balls	Runs	Wkts	Avge	BB	5i	10m	RpO	ct	st
McKAY, C.J.																		
Int	2								120	103	3	34.33	3-59	0	0	5.15	0	
Lim	2								120	103	3	34.33	3-59	0	0	5.15	0	
MANOU, G.A.																		
Int	4	1	0	7	7	7.00	0	0									5	
Lim	4	1	0	7	7	7.00	0	0									5	
MARSH, S.E.																		
Int	4	4	0	144	112	36.00	1	0									0	
Lim	4	4	0	144	112	36.00	1	0									0	
PAINE, T.D.																		
Int	2	2	0	58	50	29.00	0	1									3	
Lim	2	2	0	58	50	29.00	0	1									3	
PONTING, R.T.																		
Int	6	6	0	267	74	44.50	0	3									1	
Lim	6	6	0	267	74	44.50	0	3									1	
SIDDLE, P.M.																		
Int	4	2	0	4	3	2.00	0	0	204	166	2	83.00	1-55	0	0	4.88	0	
Lim	4	2	0	4	3	2.00	0	0	204	166	2	83.00	1-55	0	0	4.88	0	
VOGES, A.C.																		
Int	5	4	1	79	36	26.33	0	0	90	91	1	91.00	1-22	0	0	6.06	1	
Lim	5	4	1	79	36	26.33	0	0	90	91	1	91.00	1-22	0	0	6.06	1	
WATSON, S.R.																		
Int	6	6	0	256	93	42.66	0	1	236	220	10	22.00	3-29	0	0	5.59	4	
Lim	6	6	0	256	93	42.66	0	1	236	220	10	22.00	3-29	0	0	5.59	4	
WHITE, C.L.																		
Int	6	6	0	218	62	36.33	0	3									2	
Lim	6	6	0	218	62	36.33	0	3									2	

CAPE COBRAS TO INDIA 2009/10

Cmp Debut	M	I	NO	Runs	HS	Avge	100	50	Balls	Runs	Wkts	Avge	BB	5i	10m	RpO	ct	st
BRAND, D.																		
20T	1	1	0	29	29	29.00	0	0									0	
CANNING, R.C.C.																		
20T	4	2	0	23	20	11.50	0	0									2	1
DAVIDS, H.																		
20T	5	5	1	137	69*	34.25	0	1									2	
DUMINY, J.P.																		
20T	5	5	3	224	99*	112.00	0	2	55	83	4	20.75	2-10	0	0	9.05	0	
ENGELBRECHT, S.A.																		
20T	1								6	9	0					9.00	0	
GIBBS, H.H.																		
20T	4	4	0	43	42	10.75	0	0									3	
HENDERSON, C.W.																		
20T	5	1	0	0	0	0.00	0	0	120	129	2	64.50	1-19	0	0	6.45	1	
KLEINVELDT, R.K.																		
20T	5	4	1	35	21	11.66	0	0	98	158	6	26.33	3-24	0	0	9.67	3	
LANGEVELDT, C.K.																		
20T	2								42	39	1	39.00	1-12	0	0	5.57	0	
ONTONG, J.L.																		
20T	5	4	1	74	39*	24.66	0	0	48	74	3	24.66	2-8	0	0	9.25	1	
PHILANDER, V.D.																		
20T	5	2	1	25	13*	25.00	0	0	60	91	2	45.50	1-12	0	0	9.10	1	
PLAATJIES, F.C.																		
20T	1	1	1	0	0*		0	0	24	13	0					3.25	0	
PUTTICK, A.G.																		
20T	5	5	1	135	104*	33.75	1	0									0	
VAN ZYL, S.																		
20T	2																0	
ZONDEKI, M.																		
20T	5	1	0	0	0	0.00	0	0	108	129	4	32.25	2-21	0	0	7.16	1	

EAGLES TO INDIA 2009/10

Cmp Debut	M	I	NO	Runs	HS	Avge	100	50	Balls	Runs	Wkts	Avge	BB	5i	10m	RpO	ct	st
BAILEY, R.T.																		
20T	4	3	1	58	29	29.00	0	0	54	54	3	18.00	1-10	0	0	6.00	0	
COETZEE, J.																		
20T	1								24	24	2	12.00	2-24	0	0	6.00	0	
DE VILLIERS, C.J.D.																		
20T	3								66	73	6	12.16	4-17	1	0	6.63	1	

Cmp Debut	M	I	NO	Runs	HS	Avge	100	50	Balls	Runs	Wkts	Avge	BB	5i	10m	RpO	ct	st
DIPPENAAR, H.H.																		
20T	4	4	0	65	33	16.25	0	0									0	
DU PREEZ, D.																		
20T	3	3	1	45	35	22.50	0	0	72	109	4	27.25	2-23	0	0	9.08	0	
ELGAR, D.																		
20T	1	1	0	2	2	2.00	0	0									0	
KRUGER, A.K.																		
20T	3	1	1	0	0*		0	0	30	29	1	29.00	1-14	0	0	5.80	2	
McLAREN, A.P.																		
20T	4	4	0	49	16	12.25	0	0									2	
McLAREN, R.																		
20T	4	4	3	70	40	70.00	0	0	90	116	1	116.00	1-29	0	0	7.73	3	
MPITSANG, P.V.																		
20T	3	1	1	0	0*		0	0	54	59	2	29.50	1-11	0	0	6.55	1	
ROSSOUW, R.R.																		
20T	4	4	0	123	65	30.75	0	1									2	
TSHABALALA, M.S.																		
20T	4	1	1	8	8*		0	0	66	84	2	42.00	1-18	0	0	7.63	0	
VAN SCHALKWYK, S.C.																		
20T	2	1	0	3	3	3.00	0	0	24	31	2	15.50	2-22	0	0	7.75	0	
VAN WYK, M.N.																		
20T	4	4	0	74	47	18.50	0	0									0	

NEW SOUTH WALES TO INDIA 2009/10

Cmp Debut	M	I	NO	Runs	HS	Avge	100	50	Balls	Runs	Wkts	Avge	BB	5i	10m	RpO	ct	st
BOLLINGER, D.E.																		
20T	6								144	130	4	32.50	1-13	0	0	5.41	2	
CLARK, S.R.																		
20T	6	1	1	0	0*		0	0	137	112	9	12.44	3-12	0	0	4.90	1	
HAURITZ, N.M.																		
20T	6	2	1	11	10	11.00	0	0	96	100	7	14.28	2-23	0	0	6.25	3	
HENRIQUES, M.C.																		
20T	6	6	1	119	51*	23.80	0	1	99	116	10	11.60	3-11	0	0	9.90	2	
HUGHES, P.J.																		
20T	6	6	1	202	83	40.40	0	2									4	
KATICH, S.M.																		
20T	6	4	1	113	53	37.66	0	1									5	
LEE, B.																		
20T	6	3	1	48	48	24.00	0	0	126	79	8	9.87	2-10	0	0	3.76	2	
ROHRER, B.J.																		
20T	6	4	1	59	22*	19.66	0	0									0	
SMITH, D.L.R.																		
20T	6	5	1	45	20	11.25	0	0									1	3
SMITH, S.P.D.																		
20T	6	5	2	53	33	17.66	0	0	84	106	4	26.50	2-32	0	0	7.57	3	
WARNER, D.A.																		
20T	6	6	0	207	63	34.50	0	1									1	

OTAGO TO INDIA 2009/10

Cmp Debut	M	I	NO	Runs	HS	Avge	100	50	Balls	Runs	Wkts	Avge	BB	5i	10m	RpO	ct	st
BROOM, N.T.																		
20T	2	2	0	12	7	6.00	0	0									0	
BUTLER, I.G.																		
20T	2	2	0	2	1	1.00	0	0	45	90	1	90.00	1-48	0	0	12.00	0	
CUMMING, C.D.																		
20T	2	2	0	38	20	19.00	0	0	6	14	0					14.00	1	
DE BOORDER, D.C.																		
20T	2	2	0	28	16	14.00	0	0									1	
McCULLUM, B.B.																		
20T	2	2	0	26	21	13.00	0	0									0	
McCULLUM, N.L.																		
20T	2	2	0	46	38	23.00	0	0	36	59	0					9.83	1	
McSKIMMING, W.C.																		
20T	2	2	2	14	12*		0	0	39	68	0					10.46	1	
MASCARENHAS, A.D.																		
20T	2	2	0	13	10	6.50	0	0	48	57	2	28.50	2-20	0	0	7.12	0	
REDMOND, A.J.																		
20T	2	2	0	25	14	12.50	0	0	18	23	1	23.00	1-23	0	0	7.66	1	

Cmp Debut	M	I	NO	Runs	HS	Avge	100	50	Balls	Runs	Wkts	Avge	BB	5i	10m	RpO	ct	st
RUTHERFORD, H.D.																		
20T	2	2	0	28	14	14.00	0	0									1	
WAGNER, N.																		
20T	2	2	0	2	1	1.00	0	0	48	69	2	34.50	1-27	0	0	8.62	0	

SOMERSET TO INDIA 2009/10

Cmp Debut	M	I	NO	Runs	HS	Avge	100	50	Balls	Runs	Wkts	Avge	BB	5i	10m	RpO	ct	st
BANKS, O.A.C.																		
20T	1	1	0	15	15	15.00	0	0	12	28	1	28.00	1-28	0	0	14.00	0	
BUTTLER, J.C.																		
20T	1	1	1	6	6*		0	0									1	
DE BRUYN, Z.																		
20T	4	4	1	87	43*	29.00	0	0	36	53	3	17.66	2-19	0	0	8.83	0	
DURSTON, W.J.																		
20T	2	2	1	77	57	77.00	0	1									3	
HILDRETH, J.C.																		
20T	4	4	0	62	31	15.50	0	0									2	
KIESWETTER, C.																		
20T	4	4	0	30	13	7.50	0	0									2	
LANGER, J.L.																		
20T	4	4	0	47	15	11.75	0	0									0	
PHILLIPS, B.J.																		
20T	3	3	0	10	5	3.33	0	0	72	96	4	24.00	3-31	0	0	8.00	0	
SUPPIAH, A.V.																		
20T	4	4	0	33	19	8.25	0	0	24	19	0					4.75	3	
THOMAS, A.C.																		
20T	4	3	2	40	30*	40.00	0	0	93	90	6	15.00	2-20	0	0	5.80	3	
TREGO, P.D.																		
20T	4	4	0	27	12	6.75	0	0	48	60	2	30.00	2-19	0	0	7.50	0	
TRESCOTHICK, M.E.																		
20T	2	2	0	17	14	8.50	0	0									2	
WALLER, M.T.C.																		
20T	3	3	1	1	1	0.50	0	0	48	55	3	18.33	2-27	0	0	6.87	1	
WILLOUGHBY, C.M.																		
20T	4	2	1	0	0*	0.00	0	0	90	138	6	23.00	3-35	0	0	9.20	1	

SOUTH AFRICA TO INDIA 2009/10

Cmp Debut	M	I	NO	Runs	HS	Avge	100	50	Balls	Runs	Wkts	Avge	BB	5i	10m	RpO	ct	st
AMLA, H.M.																		
Test	2	3	2	490	253*	490.00	3	0									0	
FC	2	3	2	490	253*	490.00	3	0									0	
Int	2	2	0	121	87	60.50	0	1									1	
Lim	2	2	0	121	87	60.50	0	1									1	
BOSMAN, L.E.																		
Int	2	2	0	97	68	48.50	0	1									0	
Lim	2	2	0	97	68	48.50	0	1									0	
BOTHA, J.																		
Int	2	1	0	10	10	10.00	0	0	96	120	2	60.00	2-80	0	0	7.50	0	
Lim	2	1	0	10	10	10.00	0	0	96	120	2	60.00	2-80	0	0	7.50	0	
BOUCHER, M.V.																		
Test	1	1	0	39	39	39.00	0	0									3	
FC	1	1	0	39	39	39.00	0	0									3	
Int	3	2	0	19	14	9.50	0	0									6	1
Lim	3	2	0	19	14	9.50	0	0									6	1
DE VILLIERS, A.B.																		
Test	2	3	0	68	53	22.66	0	1									2	
FC	2	3	0	68	53	22.66	0	1									2	
Int	3	3	2	241	114*	241.00	2	0									1	
Lim	3	3	2	241	114*	241.00	2	0									1	
DUMINY, J.P.																		
Test	2	3	0	15	9	5.00	0	0	138	114	1	114.00	1-73	0	0	4.95	1	
FC	2	3	0	15	9	5.00	0	0	138	114	1	114.00	1-73	0	0	4.95	1	
Int	1	1	0	0	0	0.00	0	0	30	38	0					7.60	0	
Lim	1	1	0	0	0	0.00	0	0	30	38	0					7.60	0	
GIBBS, H.H.																		
Int	3	2	0	34	27	17.00	0	0									2	
Lim	3	2	0	34	27	17.00	0	0									2	
HARRIS, P.L.																		
Test	2	2	0	5	4	2.50	0	0	630	297	5	59.40	3-76	0	0	2.82	1	
FC	2	2	0	5	4	2.50	0	0	630	297	5	59.40	3-76	0	0	2.82	1	

Cmp Debut	M	I	NO	Runs	HS	Avge	100	50	Balls	Runs	Wkts	Avge	BB	5i	10m	RpO	ct	st
KALLIS, J.H.																		
Test	2	3	0	203	173	67.66	1	0	180	73	1	73.00	1-19	0	0	2.43	3	
FC	2	3	0	203	173	67.66	1	0	180	73	1	73.00	1-19	0	0	2.43	3	
Int	3	3	1	204	104*	102.00	1	1	72	73	3	24.33	3-29	0	0	6.08	1	
Lim	3	3	1	204	104*	102.00	1	1	72	73	3	24.33	3-29	0	0	6.08	1	
LANGEVELDT, C.K.																		
Int	2	2	1	16	12	16.00	0	0	120	118	1	118.00	1-48	0	0	5.90	0	
Lim	2	2	1	16	12	16.00	0	0	120	118	1	118.00	1-48	0	0	5.90	0	
MORKEL, J.A.																		
Int	1	1	0	2	2	2.00	0	0	48	59	1	59.00	1-59	0	0	7.37	1	
Lim	1	1	0	2	2	2.00	0	0	48	59	1	59.00	1-59	0	0	7.37	1	
MORKEL, M.																		
Test	2	2	1	23	12	23.00	0	0	372	238	4	59.50	2-115	0	0	3.83	1	
FC	2	2	1	23	12	23.00	0	0	372	238	4	59.50	2-115	0	0	3.83	1	
Int	1								42	48	0					6.85	0	
Lim	1								42	48	0					6.85	0	
PARNELL, W.D.																		
Test	2	2	0	34	22	17.00	0	0	240	192	3	64.00	2-58	0	0	4.80	0	
FC	2	2	0	34	22	17.00	0	0	240	192	3	64.00	2-58	0	0	4.80	0	
Int	2	2	0	67	49	33.50	0	0	114	164	3	54.66	2-95	0	0	8.63	0	
Lim	2	2	0	67	49	33.50	0	0	114	164	3	54.66	2-95	0	0	8.63	0	
PETERSEN, A.N.																		
Test	1	2	0	121	100	60.50	1	0									0	
FC	1	2	0	121	100	60.50	1	0									0	
Int	2	2	0	18	9	9.00	0	0									1	
Lim	2	2	0	18	9	9.00	0	0									1	
PRINCE, A.G.																		
Test	2	3	0	24	23	8.00	0	0									2	
FC	2	3	0	24	23	8.00	0	0									2	
SMITH, G.C.																		
Test	2	3	0	30	20	10.00	0	0									1	
FC	2	3	0	30	20	10.00	0	0									1	
STEYN, D.W.																		
Test	2	3	1	6	5	3.00	0	0	389	223	11	20.27	7-51	1	1	3.44	0	
FC	2	3	1	6	5	3.00	0	0	389	223	11	20.27	7-51	1	1	3.44	0	
Int	3	2	0	35	35	17.50	0	0	168	172	3	57.33	3-37	0	0	6.14	2	
Lim	3	2	0	35	35	17.50	0	0	168	172	3	57.33	3-37	0	0	6.14	2	
TSOTSOBE, L.L.																		
Int	1								57	58	3	19.33	3-58	0	0	6.10	1	
Lim	1								57	58	3	19.33	3-58	0	0	6.10	1	
VAN DER MERWE, R.E.																		
Int	2	1	0	12	12	12.00	0	0	120	109	3	36.33	2-47	0	0	5.45	0	
Lim	2	1	0	12	12	12.00	0	0	120	109	3	36.33	2-47	0	0	5.45	0	

SRI LANKA TO INDIA 2009/10

Cmp Debut	M	I	NO	Runs	HS	Avge	100	50	Balls	Runs	Wkts	Avge	BB	5i	10m	RpO	ct	st
DILSHAN, T.M.																		
Test	3	5	0	248	112	49.60	2	0	48	38	0					4.75	4	
FC	3	5	0	248	112	49.60	2	0	48	38	0					4.75	4	
Int	5	5	0	353	160	70.60	2	0	48	59	0					7.37	4	
Lim	5	5	0	353	160	70.60	2	0	48	59	0					7.37	4	
I20T	2	2	0	35	34	17.50	0	0	12	24	1	24.00	1-14	0	0	12.00	1	
20T	2	2	0	35	34	17.50	0	0	12	24	1	24.00	1-14	0	0	12.00	1	
FERNANDO, C.R.D.																		
Int	1								54	66	2	33.00	2-66	0	0	7.33	0	
Lim	1								54	66	2	33.00	2-66	0	0	7.33	0	
I20T	2								42	55	1	55.00	1-29	0	0	7.85	0	
20T	2								42	55	1	55.00	1-29	0	0	7.85	0	
HERATH, H.M.R.K.B.																		
Test	3	4	0	28	13	7.00	0	0	891	537	11	48.81	5-121	1	0	3.61	0	
FC	3	4	0	28	13	7.00	0	0	891	537	11	48.81	5-121	1	0	3.61	0	
JAYASINGHE, C.U.																		
I20T	2	1	0	38	38	38.00	0	0									0	
20T	2	1	0	38	38	38.00	0	0									0	
JAYASURIYA, S.T.																		
Int	3	3	0	51	31	17.00	0	0	84	118	0					8.42	1	
Lim	3	3	0	51	31	17.00	0	0	84	118	0					8.42	1	
I20T	2	2	0	57	31	28.50	0	0	24	19	2	9.50	2-19	0	0	4.75	0	
20T	2	2	0	57	31	28.50	0	0	24	19	2	9.50	2-19	0	0	4.75	0	

Cmp	Debut	M	I	NO	Runs	HS	Avge	100	50	Balls	Runs	Wkts	Avge	BB	5i	10m	RpO	ct	st
JAYAWARDENE, D.P.M.D.																			
Test		3	5	0	373	275	74.60	1	0									1	
FC		3	5	0	373	275	74.60	1	0									1	
Int		4	4	0	77	39	19.25	0	0									0	
Lim		4	4	0	77	39	19.25	0	0									0	
I20T		2	2	0	21	12	10.50	0	0									0	
20T		2	2	0	21	12	10.50	0	0									0	
JAYAWARDENE, H.A.P.W.																			
Test		3	5	1	297	154*	74.25	1	0									2	1
FC		3	5	1	297	154*	74.25	1	0									2	1
KALUHALAMULLA, H.K.S.R.																			
Int		4	2	0	5	5	2.50	0	0	168	141	5	28.20	3-51	0	0	5.03	3	
Lim		4	2	0	5	5	2.50	0	0	168	141	5	28.20	3-51	0	0	5.03	3	
KANDAMBY, S.H.T.																			
Int		5	5	2	108	27	36.00	0	0	30	49	0					9.80	0	
Lim		5	5	2	108	27	36.00	0	0	30	49	0					9.80	0	
KAPUGEDERA, C.K.																			
Int		2	2	0	17	15	8.50	0	0									0	
Lim		2	2	0	17	15	8.50	0	0									0	
I20T		2	2	0	49	47	24.50	0	0									0	
20T		2	2	0	49	47	24.50	0	0									0	
KULASEKARA, K.M.D.N.																			
Test		1	2	0	31	19	15.50	0	0	120	105	1	105.00	1-105	0	0	5.25	2	
FC		1	2	0	31	19	15.50	0	0	120	105	1	105.00	1-105	0	0	5.25	2	
Int		2	2	1	12	10	12.00	0	0	108	112	2	56.00	2-65	0	0	6.22	1	
Lim		2	2	1	12	10	12.00	0	0	108	112	2	56.00	2-65	0	0	6.22	1	
I20T		2	1	1	10	10*		0	0	42	86	1	86.00	1-36	0	0	12.28	1	
20T		2	1	1	10	10*		0	0	42	86	1	86.00	1-36	0	0	12.28	1	
LAKMAL, R.A.S.																			
Int		3								108	112	2	56.00	2-55	0	0	6.22	0	
Lim		3								108	112	2	56.00	2-55	0	0	6.22	0	
MALINGA, S.L.																			
Int		2	1	0	13	13	13.00	0	0	112	131	0					7.01	0	
Lim		2	1	0	13	13	13.00	0	0	112	131	0					7.01	0	
I20T		2								36	57	1	57.00	1-28	0	0	9.50	1	
20T		2								36	57	1	57.00	1-28	0	0	9.50	1	
MATHEWS, A.D.																			
Test		3	5	0	149	99	29.80	0	1	300	164	1	164.00	1-29	0	0	3.28	2	
FC		3	5	0	149	99	29.80	0	1	300	164	1	164.00	1-29	0	0	3.28	2	
Int		2	2	1	75	38	75.00	0	0	102	120	2	60.00	1-60	0	0	7.05	1	
Lim		2	2	1	75	38	75.00	0	0	102	120	2	60.00	1-60	0	0	7.05	1	
I20T		2	2	2	41	26*		0	0	43	79	2	39.50	2-30	0	0	11.02	1	
20T		2	2	2	41	26*		0	0	43	79	2	39.50	2-30	0	0	11.02	1	
MENDIS, B.A.W.																			
Test		1	2	1	33	27	33.00	0	0	228	162	2	81.00	2-162	0	0	4.26	0	
FC		1	2	1	33	27	33.00	0	0	228	162	2	81.00	2-162	0	0	4.26	0	
Int		2	2	1	8	6	8.00	0	0	114	124	1	124.00	1-57	0	0	6.52	0	
Lim		2	2	1	8	6	8.00	0	0	114	124	1	124.00	1-57	0	0	6.52	0	
MURALITHARAN, M.																			
Test		3	4	1	53	29	17.66	0	0	911	591	9	65.66	4-195	0	0	3.89	2	
FC		3	4	1	53	29	17.66	0	0	911	591	9	65.66	4-195	0	0	3.89	2	
PARANAVITANA, N.T.																			
Test		3	5	0	200	54	40.00	0	2	6	7	0					7.00	0	
FC		3	5	0	200	54	40.00	0	2	6	7	0					7.00	0	
PERERA, N.L.T.C.																			
Int		2	1	0	31	31	31.00	0	0	54	66	0					7.33	0	
Lim		2	1	0	31	31	31.00	0	0	54	66	0					7.33	0	
PRASAD, K.T.G.D.																			
Test		1	1	0	21	21	21.00	0	0	210	162	2	81.00	2-106	0	0	4.62	1	
FC		1	1	0	21	21	21.00	0	0	210	162	2	81.00	2-106	0	0	4.62	1	
PUSHPAKUMARA, M.																			
Int		1	1	1	7	7*		0	0									0	
Lim		1	1	1	7	7*		0	0									0	
I20T		1								18	27	1	27.00	1-27	0	0	9.00	1	
20T		1								18	27	1	27.00	1-27	0	0	9.00	1	
SAMARAWEERA, T.T.																			
Test		3	5	1	151	78*	37.75	0	2									1	
FC		3	5	1	151	78*	37.75	0	2									1	
Int		3	3	1	15	13*	7.50	0	0									0	
Lim		3	3	1	15	13*	7.50	0	0									0	

Cmp Debut	M	I	NO	Runs	HS	Avge	100	50	Balls	Runs	Wkts	Avge	BB	5i	10m	RpO	ct	st
SANGAKKARA, K.C.																		
Test	3	5	0	241	137	48.20	1	0									1	
FC	3	5	0	241	137	48.20	1	0									1	
Int	5	5	0	218	90	43.60	0	2									3	2
Lim	5	5	0	218	90	43.60	0	2									3	2
I20T	2	2	0	137	78	68.50	0	2									0	
20T	2	2	0	137	78	68.50	0	2									0	
THARANGA, W.U.																		
Int	5	5	0	295	118	59.00	1	2									0	
Lim	5	5	0	295	118	59.00	1	2									0	
WEERARATNE, K.																		
I20T	1	1	0	3	3	3.00	0	0	18	43	0					14.33	1	
20T	1	1	0	3	3	3.00	0	0	18	43	0					14.33	1	
WELAGEDARA, U.W.M.B.C.A.																		
Test	3	4	1	19	8	6.33	0	0	594	397	6	66.16	4-87	0	0	4.01	0	
FC	3	4	1	19	8	6.33	0	0	594	397	6	66.16	4-87	0	0	4.01	0	
Int	4	2	2	3	2*		0	0	162	151	5	30.20	2-35	0	0	5.59	0	
Lim	4	2	2	3	2*		0	0	162	151	5	30.20	2-35	0	0	5.59	0	

SUSSEX TO INDIA 2009/10

Cmp Debut	M	I	NO	Runs	HS	Avge	100	50	Balls	Runs	Wkts	Avge	BB	5i	10m	RpO	ct	st
CHAWLA, P.P.																		
20T	2	2	1	9	9*	9.00	0	0	36	38	3	12.66	2-17	0	0	6.33	0	
GATTING, J.S.																		
20T	2	2	0	34	25	17.00	0	0									0	
HAMILTON-BROWN, R.J.																		
20T	2	2	0	19	13	9.50	0	0	24	23	2	11.50	2-15	0	0	5.75	0	
HODD, A.J.																		
20T	2	1	0	12	12	12.00	0	0									1	
JOYCE, E.C.																		
20T	2	2	0	21	21	10.50	0	0									1	
KEEGAN, C.B.																		
20T	1	1	1	10	10*		0	0	24	25	0					6.25	0	
KIRTLEY, R.J.																		
20T	2								30	28	0					5.60	0	
MARTIN-JENKINS, R.S.C.																		
20T	1	1	1	2	2*		0	0	12	14	0					7.00	1	
NASH, C.D.																		
20T	2	2	0	31	24	15.50	0	0									0	
SMITH, D.R.																		
20T	2	2	0	22	13	11.00	0	0	42	39	0					5.57	0	
WRIGHT, L.J.																		
20T	1	1	0	19	19	19.00	0	0	6	8	0					8.00	0	
YARDY, M.H.																		
20T	1	1	0	12	12	12.00	0	0	24	13	0					3.25	0	
YASIR ARAFAT																		
20T	2	2	1	2	1*	2.00	0	0	42	51	0					7.28	0	

TRINIDAD AND TOBAGO TO INDIA 2009/10

Cmp Debut	M	I	NO	Runs	HS	Avge	100	50	Balls	Runs	Wkts	Avge	BB	5i	10m	RpO	ct	st
BADREE, S.																		
20T	3	1	1	1	1*		0	0	48	69	1	69.00	1-25	0	0	8.62	0	
BARATH, A.B.																		
20T	3	3	0	106	63	35.33	0	1									1	
BRAVO, D.J.																		
20T	6	6	2	96	58*	24.00	0	1	132	190	12	15.83	4-23	1	0	8.63	2	
BRAVO, D.M.																		
20T	3	3	0	50	27	16.66	0	0									2	
GANGA, D.																		
20T	6	5	1	118	44*	29.50	0	0									0	
GANGA, S.																		
20T	6	4	3	40	18*	40.00	0	0	120	132	6	22.00	2-16	0	0	6.60	2	
MOHAMMED, D.																		
20T	6	3	1	3	2*	1.50	0	0	114	125	5	25.00	2-18	0	0	6.57	2	
PERKINS, W.K.D.																		
20T	6	6	0	129	38	21.50	0	0									2	
POLLARD, K.A.																		
20T	6	5	1	146	54*	36.50	0	1	72	97	4	24.25	2-25	0	0	8.08	5	

Cmp Debut	M	I	NO	Runs	HS	Avge	100	50	Balls	Runs	Wkts	Avge	BB	5i	10m	RpO	ct	st
RAMDIN, D.																		
20T	6	4	0	93	39	23.25	0	0									4	
RAMPAUL, R.																		
20T	6	2	1	2	2	2.00	0	0	120	150	4	37.50	3-20	0	0	7.50	0	
SIMMONS, L.M.P.																		
20T	6	6	0	96	40	16.00	0	0	84	112	4	28.00	2-17	0	0	8.00	4	
STEWART, N.D.																		
20T	3	2	1	37	33*	37.00	0	0	30	46	0					9.20	1	

VICTORIA TO INDIA 2009/10

Cmp Debut	M	I	NO	Runs	HS	Avge	100	50	Balls	Runs	Wkts	Avge	BB	5i	10m	RpO	ct	st
BLIZZARD, A.C.																		
20T	5	5	1	69	22	17.25	0	0									3	
HARWOOD, S.M.																		
20T	5	1	0	10	10	10.00	0	0	114	123	6	20.50	3-14	0	0	6.47	0	
HODGE, B.J.																		
20T	5	5	1	78	44*	19.50	0	0	18	25	0					8.33	0	
HOLLAND, J.M.																		
20T	5	1	0	0	0	0.00	0	0	78	97	0					7.46	0	
HUSSEY, D.J.																		
20T	5	5	1	80	31*	20.00	0	0	12	17	0					8.50	0	
McDONALD, A.B.																		
20T	5	3	2	65	29*	65.00	0	0	114	114	9	12.66	3-17	0	0	6.00	3	
McKAY, C.J.																		
20T	5	1	0	8	8	8.00	0	0	120	120	10	12.00	3-17	0	0	6.00	1	
QUINEY, R.J.																		
20T	5	5	0	69	40	13.80	0	0									2	
SIDDLE, P.M.																		
20T	5	1	1	1	1*		0	0	120	121	2	60.50	1-12	0	0	6.05	0	
WADE, M.S.																		
20T	5	2	2	41	23*		0	0									1	
WHITE, C.L.																		
20T	5	5	2	74	24	24.66	0	0									1	

WAYAMBA TO INDIA 2009/10

Cmp Debut	M	I	NO	Runs	HS	Avge	100	50	Balls	Runs	Wkts	Avge	BB	5i	10m	RpO	ct	st
DE ZOYSA, R.S.S.S.																		
20T	1	1	1	21	21*		0	0									0	1
HERATH, H.M.R.K.B.																		
20T	1	1	0	3	3	3.00	0	0	24	10	0					2.50	0	
JAYAWARDENE, D.P.M.D.																		
20T	2	2	0	56	53	28.00	0	1									0	
KULATUNGA, H.G.J.M.																		
20T	2	2	0	51	41	25.50	0	0									0	
LOKUARACHCHI, K.S.																		
20T	2	2	0	4	4	2.00	0	0	24	49	0					12.25	0	
MAHAROOF, M.F.																		
20T	2	2	0	4	3	2.00	0	0	48	53	1	53.00	1-19	0	0	6.62	0	
MENDIS, B.A.W.																		
20T	2	1	1	1	1*		0	0	48	56	3	18.66	2-35	0	0	7.00	1	
MUBARAK, J.																		
20T	2	2	0	10	10	5.00	0	0	6	7	0					7.00	1	
PERERA, N.L.T.C.																		
20T	1	1	0	6	6	6.00	0	0	18	10	0					3.33	1	
UDANA, I.																		
20T	1	1	1	11	11*		0	0	24	38	0					9.50	0	
UDAWATTE, M.L.																		
20T	2	2	0	3	2	1.50	0	0									0	
VANDORT, M.G.																		
20T	2	2	0	51	42	25.50	0	0									0	
WELAGEDARA, U.W.M.B.C.A.																		
20T	2	1	1	7	7*		0	0	48	42	4	10.50	2-18	0	0	5.25	1	

IRELAND

2010 AND CAREER RECORDS FOR IRELAND PLAYERS

Cmp	*Debut*	*M*	*I*	*NO*	*Runs*	*HS*	*Avge*	*100*	*50*	*Balls*	*Runs*	*Wkts*	*Avge*	*BB*	*5i*	*10m*	*RpO*	*ct*	*st*
BALBIRNIE, Andrew (Ireland to Netherlands) b Dublin 28.12.1990 RHB OB WK																			
Int	2010	4	4	0	29	17	7.25	0	0									1	
Lim	2010	4	4	0	29	17	7.25	0	0									1	
BOTHA, Andre Cornelius (Ireland to Canada, Ireland to Sri Lanka, Ireland to United Arab Emirates, Ireland to West Indies) b Johannesburg, Transvaal, South Africa 12.9.1975 LHB RM																			
FC	1998/99	29	46	3	1755	186	40.81	5	7	2649	1148	45	25.51	4-52	0	0	2.60	13	
Int	2006	38	34	4	624	56	20.80	0	2	1380	997	37	26.94	4-19	2	0	4.33	9	
Lim	1996/97	87	71	8	1258	139	19.96	1	4	3050	2368	82	28.87	4-19	4	0	4.65	19	
I20T	2008	14	11	1	130	38	13.00	0	0	204	184	21	8.76	3-14	0	0	5.41	8	
20T	2008	19	15	3	209	62*	17.41	0	1	307	294	26	11.30	3-14	0	0	5.74	11	
CONNELL, Peter (Ireland, Ireland to Sri Lanka, Ireland to United Arab Emirates, Ireland to West Indies) b Dannevirke, Manawatu, New Zealand 13.8.1981 RHB RMF																			
Int		1	1	0	0	0	0.00	0	0	30	37	0					7.40	0	
Lim		1	1	0	0	0	0.00	0	0	30	37	0					7.40	0	
FC	2008	8	7	0	37	18	5.28	0	0	1169	602	35	17.20	6-28	2	1	3.09	4	
Int	2008	13	5	3	40	22*	20.00	0	0	564	518	13	39.84	3-68	0	0	5.51	1	
Lim	2008	26	12	8	71	22*	17.75	0	0	1169	1026	37	27.72	5-19	1	1	5.26	1	
I20T	2008	9	3	2	4	3*	4.00	0	0	153	156	10	15.60	3-8	0	0	6.11	3	
20T	2008	16	4	3	10	6*	10.00	0	0	291	330	20	16.50	4-14	1	0	6.80	3	
CUSACK, Alex Richard (Ireland, Ireland to Netherlands, Ireland to Sri Lanka, Ireland to United Arab Emirates, Ireland to West Indies) b Brisbane, Queensland, Australia 29.10.1980 RHB RM																			
FC		1	1	0	43	43	43.00	0	0									0	
Int		5	5	2	135	45*	45.00	0	0	120	95	3	31.66	2-38	0	0	4.75	2	
Lim		7	7	2	153	45*	30.60	0	0	198	155	5	31.00	2-38	0	0	4.69	2	
FC	2007	12	17	3	630	130	45.00	1	4	605	241	8	30.12	3-19	0	0	2.39	9	
Int	2007	31	25	8	441	59*	25.94	0	1	964	691	34	20.32	5-20	0	1	4.30	13	
Lim	2007	52	40	9	683	59*	22.03	0	1	1676	1207	50	24.14	5-20	0	1	4.32	19	
I20T	2008	16	11	1	155	65	15.50	0	1	270	321	17	18.88	4-18	2	0	7.13	4	
20T	2008	24	19	2	258	65	15.17	0	1	387	485	28	17.32	4-18	2	0	7.51	9	
DOCKRELL, George Henry (Ireland, Ireland to Canada, Ireland to Netherlands, Ireland to Sri Lanka, Ireland to United Arab Emirates, Ireland to West Indies) b Dublin 22.7.1992 RHB SLA																			
FC		1	1	0	2	2	2.00	0	0	108	43	4	10.75	4-36	0	0	2.38	0	
Int		4	1	1	5	5*		0	0	149	108	2	54.00	1-21	0	0	4.34	1	
Lim		5	2	2	15	10*		0	0	209	155	2	77.50	1-21	0	0	4.45	2	
FC	2010	2	2	0	4	2	2.00	0	0	180	93	4	23.25	4-36	0	0	3.10	1	
Int	2009/10	13	4	2	7	5*	3.50	0	0	593	417	13	32.07	4-35	1	0	4.21	6	
Lim	2009/10	15	6	3	18	10*	6.00	0	0	713	503	13	38.69	4-35	1	0	4.23	7	
I20T	2009/10	7	2	1	0	0*	0.00	0	0	147	132	12	11.00	4-20	1	0	5.38	0	
20T	2009/10	11	2	1	0	0*	0.00	0	0	219	232	15	15.46	4-20	1	0	6.35	0	
EAGLESTONE, Philip Steven (Ireland, Ireland to Canada, Ireland to Sri Lanka) b Beckenham, Kent, England 17.6.1982 LHB LFM																			
Lim		2	2	1	7	4	7.00	0	0	110	121	4	30.25	3-48	0	0	6.60	0	
FC	2010	1	1	1	0	0*		0	0	102	66	1	66.00	1-44	0	0	3.88	0	
Int	2008	1	1	0	4	4	4.00	0	0	42	60	1	60.00	1-60	0	0	8.57	0	
Lim	2008	11	8	4	15	4	3.75	0	0	392	379	12	31.58	3-48	0	0	5.80	0	
I20T	2009/10	1								12	16	0					8.00	0	
20T	2009/10	1								12	16	0					8.00	0	
EASTWOOD, Allan William (Ireland, Ireland to Canada) b Port Laoise, Co Laoise 22.10.1979 RHB RF																			
FC		1	1	1	8	8*		0	0	192	108	5	21.60	4-62	0	0	3.37	0	
FC	2010	2	2	1	8	8*	8.00	0	0	366	200	9	22.22	4-62	0	0	3.27	0	
HALL, James Douglas (Ireland, Ireland to Netherlands) b Preston, Lancashire, England 19.10.1988 RHB OB																			
FC		1	1	0	7	7	7.00	0	0									1	
Int	2010	3	3	0	28	15	9.33	0	0									0	
Lim	2008	7	7	0	91	27	13.00	0	0	32	22	1	22.00	1-22	0	0	4.12	0	
JOHNSTON, David Trent (Ireland, Ireland to Canada, Ireland to Netherlands, Ireland to Sri Lanka, Ireland to United Arab Emirates, Ireland to West Indies) b Wollongong, New South Wales, Australia 29.4.1974 RHB RFM																			
FC		1	1	0	4	4	4.00	0	0	174	89	5	17.80	3-41	0	0	3.06	3	
Int		5	3	0	11	10	3.66	0	0	180	118	5	23.60	2-19	0	0	3.93	3	
Lim		5	3	0	11	10	3.66	0	0	180	118	5	23.60	2-19	0	0	3.93	3	
FC	1998/99	26	33	7	638	71	24.53	0	6	3472	1650	84	19.64	6-23	3	0	2.85	17	
Int	2006	44	32	8	483	45*	20.12	0	0	1875	1292	43	30.04	5-14	1	1	4.13	17	
Lim	1999/00	75	56	11	878	67	19.51	0	2	3269	2348	78	30.10	5-14	2	1	4.31	29	
I20T	2008	16	12	3	89	18	9.88	0	0	318	335	20	16.75	4-22	1	0	6.32	1	
20T	2008	22	18	5	220	39	16.92	0	0	456	459	27	17.00	4-22	1	0	6.03	3	

Cmp	Debut	M	I	NO	Runs	HS	Avge	100	50	Balls	Runs	Wkts	Avge	BB	5i	10m	RpO	ct	st
JONES, Nigel Geoffrey (Ireland, Ireland to Canada, Ireland to Netherlands, Ireland to Sri Lanka, Ireland to United Arab Emirates, Ireland to West Indies) b Timaru, Canterbury, New Zealand 22.4.1982 RHB RM																			
Int		2	1	1	5	5*		0	0	72	41	2	20.50	2-20	0	0	3.41	1	
Lim		3	2	1	16	11	16.00	0	0	114	80	2	40.00	2-20	0	0	4.21	1	
Int	2010	10	5	2	62	25*	20.66	0	0	266	148	8	18.50	2-19	0	0	3.33	5	
Lim	2009/10	12	7	2	103	30	20.60	0	0	368	236	9	26.22	2-19	0	0	3.84	7	
I20T	2009/10	1	1	0	14	14	14.00	0	0	6	8	0					8.00	0	
20T	2009/10	4	4	0	37	21	9.25	0	0	42	56	1	56.00	1-22	0	0	8.00	0	
KIDD, Gary Edward (Ireland to Sri Lanka, Ireland to West Indies) b Craigavon, Co Armagh 18.9.1985 LHB SLA																			
FC	2008	3	3	0	5	4	1.66	0	0	444	313	7	44.71	3-102	0	0	4.23	5	
Int	2007	6	1	0	15	15	15.00	0	0	216	172	1	172.00	1-27	0	0	4.77	1	
Lim	2006	14	7	0	37	15	5.28	0	0	606	433	10	43.30	3-32	0	0	4.28	4	
I20T	2009/10	1	1	1	1	1*		0	0	18	32	0					10.66	0	
20T	2009/10	5	2	1	2	1*	2.00	0	0	78	115	3	38.33	2-13	0	0	8.84	1	
McCANN, Rory Desmond (Ireland, Ireland to Canada, Ireland to Netherlands) b Belfast, Co Antrim 11.1.1985 RHB WK																			
Lim		2	2	0	7	6	3.50	0	0									2	
FC	2010	1	2	0	4	4	2.00	0	0									9	
Int	2010	8	5	1	44	18	11.00	0	0									9	
Lim	2010	10	7	1	51	18	8.50	0	0									11	
MOONEY, John Francis (Ireland, Ireland to Canada, Ireland to Netherlands, Ireland to Sri Lanka, Ireland to United Arab Emirates, Ireland to West Indies) b Dublin 10.2.1982 LHB RM																			
FC		1	1	0	107	107	107.00	1	0									1	
Int		5	3	0	77	38	25.66	0	0	48	16	2	8.00	2-16	0	0	2.00	2	
Lim		7	5	0	93	38	18.60	0	0	84	39	2	19.50	2-16	0	0	2.78	5	
FC	2004	5	7	2	202	107	40.40	1	1	110	69	1	69.00	1-37	0	0	3.76	2	
Int	2006	26	22	8	457	54	32.64	0	1	468	433	11	39.36	3-79	0	0	5.55	10	
Lim	2006	48	41	9	719	54	22.46	0	1	1117	992	26	38.15	4-43	1	0	5.32	20	
I20T	2009	13	12	4	140	31*	17.50	0	0	12	16	0					8.00	7	
20T	2009	20	18	7	202	31*	18.36	0	0	24	35	1	35.00	1-19	0	0	8.75	11	
O'BRIEN, Kevin Joseph (Ireland, Ireland to Canada, Ireland to Netherlands, Ireland to Sri Lanka, Ireland to United Arab Emirates, Ireland to West Indies) b Dublin 4.3.1984 RHB RMF																			
FC		1	1	0	41	41	41.00	0	0	36	25	0					4.16	2	
Int		5	4	1	53	26	17.66	0	0	234	158	8	19.75	3-18	0	0	4.05	0	
Lim		7	6	1	97	37	19.40	0	0	329	234	11	21.27	3-18	0	0	4.26	2	
FC	2006/07	17	23	1	670	171*	30.45	1	4	939	424	18	23.55	5-39	1	0	2.70	13	
Int	2006	49	44	7	1227	142	33.16	1	6	1476	1178	37	31.83	3-18	0	0	4.78	22	
Lim	2006	91	84	15	2141	142	31.02	2	10	2626	2221	61	36.40	4-31	1	0	5.07	38	
I20T	2008	17	15	3	129	39*	10.75	0	0	213	264	8	33.00	2-15	0	0	7.43	7	
20T	2008	28	24	5	211	39*	11.10	0	0	321	414	14	29.57	2-14	0	0	7.73	8	
O'BRIEN, Niall John (Ireland, Ireland to Sri Lanka, Ireland to United Arab Emirates, Ireland to West Indies, Northamptonshire) b Dublin 8.11.1981 LHB WK																			
Int		3	3	0	47	27	15.66	0	0									4	
Lim		3	3	0	47	27	15.66	0	0									4	
FC	2004	83	126	14	3971	176	35.45	9	16	12	16	2	8.00	1-4	0	0	8.00	240	26
Int	2006	37	37	3	911	72	26.79	0	7									28	6
Lim	2002	112	91	11	2174	95	27.17	0	15									93	30
I20T	2008	16	15	1	260	50	18.57	0	1									10	8
20T	2004	70	59	9	1172	84	23.44	0	5									34	25
PORTERFIELD, William Thomas Stuart (Ireland, Gloucestershire, Gloucestershire to Netherlands, Ireland to Sri Lanka, Ireland to United Arab Emirates, Ireland to West Indies) b Londonderry 6.9.1984 LHB OB																			
Int		3	3	0	153	108	51.00	1	0									1	
Lim		3	3	0	153	108	51.00	1	0									1	
FC	2006	43	75	2	2431	175	33.30	4	13	102	135	2	67.50	1-29	0	0	7.94	45	
Int	2006	41	41	3	1313	112*	34.55	5	4									21	
Lim	2006	96	95	4	3135	112*	34.45	5	17									41	
I20T	2008	17	16	1	263	46	17.53	0	0									4	
20T	2008	45	44	2	897	65	21.35	0	3									18	
POYNTER, Andrew David (Ireland, Ireland to Canada, Ireland to Netherlands) b Hammersmith, Middlesex, England 25.4.1987 RHB OB																			
Int		2	1	1	0	0*		0	0									2	
Lim		4	3	1	77	64	38.50	0	1									3	
FC	2005	3	3	1	100	76*	50.00	0	1	6	2	0					2.00	4	
Int	2008	14	11	3	149	78	18.62	0	1									8	
Lim	2008	23	20	3	301	78	17.70	0	2									12	
20T	2008	1	1	1	0	0*		0	0									0	
RANKIN, William Boyd (Ireland, Ireland to West Indies, Warwickshire, Warwickshire to Scotland) b Londonderry 5.7.1984 LHB RMF																			
Int		3	2	2	9	6*		0	0	174	122	5	24.40	3-43	0	0	4.20	0	
Lim		3	2	2	9	6*		0	0	174	122	5	24.40	3-43	0	0	4.20	0	
FC	2006/07	34	42	17	128	13	5.12	0	0	4531	2867	101	28.38	5-16	3	0	3.79	12	
Int	2006/07	23	8	6	25	7*	12.50	0	0	1010	815	33	24.69	3-32	0	0	4.84	4	

Cmp	Debut	M	I	NO	Runs	HS	Avge	100	50	Balls	Runs	Wkts	Avge	BB	5i	10m	RpO	ct	st
Lim	2006	52	15	9	50	9	8.33	0	0	2051	1718	70	24.54	4-34	1	0	5.02	6	
I20T	2009	6	2	1	6	5*	6.00	0	0	144	162	7	23.14	2-25	0	0	6.75	3	
20T	2009	9	3	2	9	5*	9.00	0	0	204	223	9	24.77	2-25	0	0	6.55	3	
STIRLING, Paul Robert (Ireland, Ireland to Canada, Ireland to Netherlands, Ireland to Sri Lanka, Ireland to United Arab Emirates, Ireland to West Indies, Middlesex) b Belfast 3.9.1990 RHB OB																			
FC		1	1	0	5	5	5.00	0	0									2	
Int		5	5	0	196	62	39.20	0	2	192	142	4	35.50	2-34	0	0	4.43	2	
Lim		7	7	0	211	62	30.14	0	2	222	165	4	41.25	2-34	0	0	4.45	2	
FC	2008	8	12	0	338	100	28.16	1	1	195	113	3	37.66	2-45	0	0	3.47	6	
Int	2008	20	20	1	817	177	43.00	1	5	353	260	10	26.00	4-11	1	0	4.41	10	
Lim	2008	37	37	1	1130	177	31.38	1	8	395	299	10	29.90	4-11	1	0	4.54	16	
I20T	2009	6	6	0	77	22	12.83	0	0	18	25	0					8.33	1	
20T	2008	13	13	0	222	43	17.07	0	0	84	94	1	94.00	1-13	0	0	6.71	5	
VAN DER MERWE, Albert (Ireland, Ireland to Canada, Ireland to Netherlands) b Bellville, Cape Town, Cape Province, South Africa 1.6.1979 RHB OB																			
FC		1	1	0	7	7	7.00	0	0	114	40	6	6.66	3-15	0	0	2.10	1	
Int		2								84	54	3	18.00	2-31	0	0	3.85	0	
Lim		4	2	0	16	8	8.00	0	0	162	124	4	31.00	2-31	0	0	4.59	1	
FC	2010	2	2	0	11	7	5.50	0	0	288	120	7	17.14	3-15	0	0	2.50	2	
Int	2010	5	3	2	5	4*	5.00	0	0	204	142	8	17.75	5-49	0	1	4.17	1	
Lim	2010	7	5	2	21	8	7.00	0	0	282	212	9	23.55	5-49	0	1	4.51	2	
WHITE, Andrew Roland (Ireland, Ireland to Canada, Ireland to Netherlands, Ireland to Sri Lanka, Ireland to United Arab Emirates, Ireland to West Indies) b Newtownards, Co Down 3.7.1980 RHB OB																			
FC		1	1	0	144	144	144.00	1	0									0	
Int		5	2	0	28	24	14.00	0	0	98	61	6	10.16	4-44	1	0	3.73	4	
Lim		7	4	0	160	75	40.00	0	2	98	61	6	10.16	4-44	1	0	3.73	4	
FC	2004	22	28	7	1061	152*	50.52	3	6	1230	662	21	31.52	4-99	0	0	3.22	15	
Int	2006	46	34	1	620	79	18.78	0	1	745	573	25	22.92	4-44	1	0	4.61	15	
Lim	2002	92	75	9	1460	79	22.12	0	7	1608	1234	43	28.69	4-22	2	0	4.60	30	
I20T	2008	12	10	5	131	29	26.20	0	0									2	
20T	2006	22	16	8	198	29	24.75	0	0	60	98	1	98.00	1-17	0	0	9.80	4	
WILSON, Gary Craig (Ireland, Ireland to Sri Lanka, Ireland to United Arab Emirates, Ireland to West Indies, Surrey) b Dundonald, Co Roscommon 5.2.1986 RHB WK																			
FC		1	1	0	21	21	21.00	0	0									3	1
Int		5	4	1	225	113	75.00	1	1									6	2
Lim		7	6	1	239	113	47.80	1	1									6	2
FC	2005	16	23	2	583	125	27.76	1	2	66	46	0					4.18	31	1
Int	2007	22	21	2	519	113	27.31	1	3									16	6
Lim	2006	70	62	5	1287	113	22.57	1	9									51	15
I20T	2008	15	13	1	193	29	16.08	0	0									8	
20T	2008	38	31	7	372	36*	15.50	0	0									24	4

AUSTRALIA TO IRELAND 2010

Cmp	Debut	M	I	NO	Runs	HS	Avge	100	50	Balls	Runs	Wkts	Avge	BB	5i	10m	RpO	ct	st
BOLLINGER, D.E.																			
Int		1								36	30	0					5.00	0	
Lim		1								36	30	0					5.00	0	
CLARKE, M.J.																			
Int		1	1	0	0	0	0.00	0	0									0	
Lim		1	1	0	0	0	0.00	0	0									0	
HARRIS, R.J.																			
Int		1	1	0	6	6	6.00	0	0	42	40	2	20.00	2-40	0	0	5.71	0	
Lim		1	1	0	6	6	6.00	0	0	42	40	2	20.00	2-40	0	0	5.71	0	
HAURITZ, N.M.																			
Int		1	1	0	19	19	19.00	0	0	60	40	2	20.00	2-40	0	0	4.00	0	
Lim		1	1	0	19	19	19.00	0	0	60	40	2	20.00	2-40	0	0	4.00	0	
HOPES, J.R.																			
Int		1	1	0	12	12	12.00	0	0	54	14	5	2.80	5-14	0	1	1.55	0	
Lim		1	1	0	12	12	12.00	0	0	54	14	5	2.80	5-14	0	1	1.55	0	
HUSSEY, M.E.K.																			
Int		1	1	0	8	8	8.00	0	0									0	
Lim		1	1	0	8	8	8.00	0	0									0	
McKAY, C.J.																			
Int		1	1	1	4	4*		0	0	36	39	0					6.50	0	
Lim		1	1	1	4	4*		0	0	36	39	0					6.50	0	
PAINE, T.D.																			
Int		1	1	0	81	81	81.00	0	1									3	
Lim		1	1	0	81	81	81.00	0	1									3	

Cmp Debut	M	I	NO	Runs	HS	Avge	100	50	Balls	Runs	Wkts	Avge	BB	5i	10m	RpO	ct	st
PONTING, R.T.																		
Int	1	1	0	33	33	33.00	0	0									1	
Lim	1	1	0	33	33	33.00	0	0									1	
WATSON, S.R.																		
Int	1	1	0	13	13	13.00	0	0	24	26	1	26.00	1-26	0	0	6.50	0	
Lim	1	1	0	13	13	13.00	0	0	24	26	1	26.00	1-26	0	0	6.50	0	
WHITE, C.L.																		
Int	1	1	0	42	42	42.00	0	0									0	
Lim	1	1	0	42	42	42.00	0	0									0	

BANGLADESH TO IRELAND 2010

Cmp Debut	M	I	NO	Runs	HS	Avge	100	50	Balls	Runs	Wkts	Avge	BB	5i	10m	RpO	ct	st
ABDUR RAZZAK																		
Int	2	1	1	9	9*		0	0	114	77	2	38.50	1-30	0	0	4.05	0	
Lim	2	1	1	9	9*		0	0	114	77	2	38.50	1-30	0	0	4.05	0	
FAISAL HOSSAIN																		
Int	1								36	27	1	27.00	1-27	0	0	4.50	0	
Lim	1								36	27	1	27.00	1-27	0	0	4.50	0	
IMRUL KAYES																		
Int	2	2	0	10	5	5.00	0	0									0	
Lim	2	2	0	10	5	5.00	0	0									0	
JAHURUL ISLAM																		
Int	2	2	0	37	34	18.50	0	0									2	
Lim	2	2	0	37	34	18.50	0	0									2	
JUNAID SIDDIQUE																		
Int	2	2	0	113	100	56.50	1	0									0	
Lim	2	2	0	113	100	56.50	1	0									0	
MAHMUDULLAH																		
Int	2	1	0	14	14	14.00	0	0	36	33	0					5.50	0	
Lim	2	1	0	14	14	14.00	0	0	36	33	0					5.50	0	
MASHRAFE MORTAZA																		
Int	2	1	0	15	15	15.00	0	0	90	48	1	48.00	1-28	0	0	3.20	1	
Lim	2	1	0	15	15	15.00	0	0	90	48	1	48.00	1-28	0	0	3.20	1	
MUSHFIQUR RAHIM																		
Int	2	2	1	22	13*	22.00	0	0									3	1
Lim	2	2	1	22	13*	22.00	0	0									3	1
RUBEL HOSSAIN																		
Int	1	1	0	4	4	4.00	0	0	42	42	0					6.00	0	
Lim	1	1	0	4	4	4.00	0	0	42	42	0					6.00	0	
SHAFIUL ISLAM																		
Int	1								60	59	4	14.75	4-59	1	0	5.90	1	
Lim	1								60	59	4	14.75	4-59	1	0	5.90	1	
SHAKIB AL HASAN																		
Int	2	2	1	83	50	83.00	0	1	114	73	3	24.33	2-21	0	0	3.84	0	
Lim	2	2	1	83	50	83.00	0	1	114	73	3	24.33	2-21	0	0	3.84	0	
SYED RASEL																		
Int	1	1	1	2	2*		0	0	54	53	1	53.00	1-53	0	0	5.88	0	
Lim	1	1	1	2	2*		0	0	54	53	1	53.00	1-53	0	0	5.88	0	
TAMIM IQBAL																		
Int	2	2	0	79	74	39.50	0	1									0	
Lim	2	2	0	79	74	39.50	0	1									0	

NETHERLANDS TO IRELAND 2010

Cmp Debut	M	I	NO	Runs	HS	Avge	100	50	Balls	Runs	Wkts	Avge	BB	5i	10m	RpO	ct	st
ADEEL RAJA																		
Int	2	2	0	9	6	4.50	0	0	66	77	0					7.00	0	
Lim	2	2	0	9	6	4.50	0	0	66	77	0					7.00	0	
BARRESI, W.																		
FC	1	2	0	23	13	11.50	0	0									0	
Int	2	2	0	15	9	7.50	0	0									0	
Lim	2	2	0	15	9	7.50	0	0									0	
BORREN, P.W.																		
FC	1	2	0	76	39	38.00	0	0	54	38	0					4.22	0	
Int	2	2	0	17	10	8.50	0	0	54	47	0					5.22	0	
Lim	2	2	0	17	10	8.50	0	0	54	47	0					5.22	0	
COOPER, T.L.W.																		
Int	2	2	0	93	68	46.50	0	1	9	6	0					4.00	2	
Lim	2	2	0	93	68	46.50	0	1	9	6	0					4.00	2	
DE GROOTH, T.N.																		
FC	1	2	0	37	29	18.50	0	0									0	

Cmp Debut	M	I	NO	Runs	HS	Avge	100	50	Balls	Runs	Wkts	Avge	BB	5i	10m	RpO	ct	st
DIEPEVEEN, W.P.																		
FC	1	2	0	53	41	26.50	0	0									2	
HEGGELMAN, T.J.																		
FC	1	2	0	46	30	23.00	0	0	72	54	0					4.50	0	
Int	2	2	0	3	2	1.50	0	0									0	
Lim	2	2	0	3	2	1.50	0	0									0	
JONKMAN, M.M.A.																		
FC	1	2	0	1	1	0.50	0	0	126	90	2	45.00	2-90	0	0	4.28	0	
Int	2	2	0	20	13	10.00	0	0	60	56	3	18.66	2-35	0	0	5.60	0	
Lim	2	2	0	20	13	10.00	0	0	60	56	3	18.66	2-35	0	0	5.60	0	
KRUGER, B.P.																		
Int	1	1	0	9	9	9.00	0	0	42	43	0					6.14	1	
Lim	1	1	0	9	9	9.00	0	0	42	43	0					6.14	1	
LOOTS, B.P.																		
FC	1	2	1	3	3	3.00	0	0	132	86	2	43.00	2-86	0	0	3.90	0	
Int	1	1	1	9	9*		0	0	18	19	0					6.33	0	
Lim	1	1	1	9	9*		0	0	18	19	0					6.33	0	
MOHAMMAD KASHIF																		
FC	1	2	1	2	2	2.00	0	0	121	53	5	10.60	5-53	1	0	2.62	1	
MUDASSAR BUKHARI																		
Int	2	2	0	36	29	18.00	0	0	84	68	1	68.00	1-50	0	0	4.85	0	
Lim	2	2	0	36	29	18.00	0	0	84	68	1	68.00	1-50	0	0	4.85	0	
SEELAAR, P.M.																		
FC	1	2	0	24	20	12.00	0	0	96	49	1	49.00	1-49	0	0	3.06	0	
Int	2	2	1	68	34*	68.00	0	0	90	76	2	38.00	2-53	0	0	5.06	1	
Lim	2	2	1	68	34*	68.00	0	0	90	76	2	38.00	2-53	0	0	5.06	1	
STATHAM, N.A.																		
FC	1	2	0	26	26	13.00	0	0									0	
SZWARCZYNSKI, E.S.																		
FC	1	2	0	9	8	4.50	0	0	30	22	0					4.40	1	
Int	2	2	0	12	10	6.00	0	0									0	
Lim	2	2	0	12	10	6.00	0	0									0	
ZUIDERENT, B.																		
Int	2	2	0	16	16	8.00	0	0									0	
Lim	2	2	0	16	16	8.00	0	0									0	

WEST INDIES A TO IRELAND 2010

Cmp Debut	M	I	NO	Runs	HS	Avge	100	50	Balls	Runs	Wkts	Avge	BB	5i	10m	RpO	ct	st
BERNARD, D.E.																		
Lim	2	1	0	7	7	7.00	0	0	96	41	4	10.25	3-24	0	0	2.56	1	
BRATHWAITE, K.C.																		
Lim	1	1	0	15	15	15.00	0	0									0	
EDWARDS, K.A.																		
Lim	2	2	1	0	0*	0.00	0	0									1	
FLETCHER, A.D.S.																		
Lim	2	2	1	89	81*	89.00	0	1									0	
FUDADIN, A.B.																		
Lim	2	1	0	50	50	50.00	0	1	42	36	2	18.00	2-28	0	0	5.14	2	
KHAN, I.																		
Lim	1								60	44	3	14.66	3-44	0	0	4.40	0	
MARTIN, A.																		
Lim	2	1	1	1	1*		0	0	120	84	1	84.00	1-47	0	0	4.20	0	
PHILLIPS, O.J.																		
Lim	1	1	0	9	9	9.00	0	0									0	
RUSSELL, A.D.																		
Lim	2	1	0	64	64	64.00	0	1	102	85	7	12.14	6-42	0	1	5.00	1	
SMITH, D.S.																		
Lim	2	2	0	117	114	58.50	1	0									4	
STOUTE, K.A.																		
Lim	2	1	0	61	61	61.00	0	1	96	79	2	39.50	1-36	0	0	4.93	1	
TONGE, G.C.																		
Lim	1	1	0	28	28	28.00	0	0	49	25	1	25.00	1-25	0	0	3.06	0	
WALTON, C.A.K.																		
Lim	2	1	0	10	10	10.00	0	0									1	1

KENYA

2009/10 AND CAREER RECORDS FOR KENYA PLAYERS

Cmp	Debut	M	I	NO	Runs	HS	Avge	100	50	Balls	Runs	Wkts	Avge	BB	5i	10m	RpO	ct	st
AGA, Ragheb Gul (Kenya to Zimbabwe, Sussex) b Nairobi 10.7.1984 RHB RMF																			
FC	2003/04	19	29	5	340	66*	14.16	0	1	1782	1024	29	35.31	4-63	0	0	3.44	7	
Int	2004	2	2	0	1	1	0.50	0	0	78	87	2	43.50	2-17	0	0	6.69	0	
Lim	2004	16	13	2	118	23*	10.72	0	0	482	495	15	33.00	4-14	2	0	6.16	3	
I20T	2008	4	4	1	51	28	17.00	0	0	83	83	3	27.66	2-12	0	0	6.00	1	
20T	2008	4	4	1	51	28	17.00	0	0	83	83	3	27.66	2-12	0	0	6.00	1	
KAMANDE, James Kabatha (Kenya, Kenya to Netherlands, Kenya to United Arab Emirates, Kenya to Zimbabwe) b Muranga 12.12.1978 RHB RM,OB																			
FC		2	4	1	97	75	32.33	0	1	204	99	2	49.50	2-31	0	0	2.91	2	
Int		2	2	1	48	42	48.00	0	0	48	36	0					4.50	0	
Lim		2	2	1	48	42	48.00	0	0	48	36	0					4.50	0	
I20T		2								44	43	3	14.33	3-28	0	0	5.86	0	
20T		4								92	93	5	18.60	3-28	0	0	6.06	0	
FC	2000/01	21	37	3	630	75	18.52	0	3	2394	1173	24	48.87	4-56	0	0	2.94	16	
Int	1999	78	65	10	997	74	18.12	0	3	2385	1950	44	44.31	4-36	1	0	4.90	17	
Lim	1999	101	82	10	1215	74	16.87	0	5	2789	2260	50	45.20	4-36	1	0	4.86	27	
I20T	2007/08	12	9	0	83	42	9.22	0	0	206	212	13	16.30	3-28	0	0	6.17	1	
20T	2007/08	15	10	1	105	42	11.66	0	0	278	296	15	19.73	3-28	0	0	6.38	1	
LUSENO, Alfred Sorongo (Kenya to Netherlands, Kenya to Zimbabwe) b Kakemaga 20.12.1981 RHB RM																			
FC	2000/01	12	16	9	43	11	6.14	0	0	1260	747	17	43.94	3-40	0	0	3.55	2	
Int	2002/03	10	9	7	34	16*	17.00	0	0	330	316	9	35.11	4-32	1	0	5.74	1	
Lim	2001/02	11	10	8	41	16*	20.50	0	0	378	353	9	39.22	4-32	1	0	5.60	1	
NGOCHE, James Otieno (Kenya, Kenya to Netherlands) b 29.1.1988 RHB OB																			
FC		2	3	0	3	3	1.00	0	0	294	135	1	135.00	1-17	0	0	2.75	0	
Int	2010	6	5	1	22	21*	5.50	0	0	330	167	8	20.87	3-18	0	0	3.03	1	
Lim	2010	6	5	1	22	21*	5.50	0	0	330	167	8	20.87	3-18	0	0	3.03	1	
NGOCHE, Shem Obado (Kenya, Kenya to Netherlands, Kenya to United Arab Emirates) b 6.6.1989 RHB SLA																			
Int		2	1	0	0	0	0.00	0	0	114	65	2	32.50	1-32	0	0	3.42	0	
Lim		2	1	0	0	0	0.00	0	0	114	65	2	32.50	1-32	0	0	3.42	0	
I20T		2								36	27	2	13.50	2-10	0	0	4.50	0	
20T		4								72	86	4	21.50	2-10	0	0	7.16	0	
Int	2009/10	5	4	1	15	7*	5.00	0	0	252	143	4	35.75	2-28	0	0	3.40	0	
Lim	2009/10	5	4	1	15	7*	5.00	0	0	252	143	4	35.75	2-28	0	0	3.40	0	
I20T	2009/10	4	1	0	0	0	0.00	0	0	60	59	3	19.66	2-10	0	0	5.90	0	
20T	2009/10	6	1	0	0	0	0.00	0	0	96	118	5	23.60	2-10	0	0	7.37	0	
OBANDA, Alex Auma (Kenya, Kenya to Netherlands, Kenya to United Arab Emirates, Kenya to Zimbabwe) b Nairobi 25.12.1987 RHB RMF																			
FC		1	2	0	43	40	21.50	0	0									0	
Int		2	2	0	76	61	38.00	0	1									2	
Lim		2	2	0	76	61	38.00	0	1									2	
I20T		2																1	
20T		4	2	1	74	43	74.00	0	0									1	
FC	2006/07	15	29	1	753	114	26.89	1	4									6	
Int	2007	36	33	2	1017	96*	32.80	0	7									13	
Lim	2007	46	41	3	1140	96*	30.00	0	8									17	
I20T	2007/08	10	8	1	126	79	18.00	0	1									2	
20T	2007/08	13	11	2	213	79	23.66	0	1									3	
OBUYA, Collins Omondi (Kenya, Kenya to Netherlands, Kenya to United Arab Emirates, Kenya to Zimbabwe) b Nairobi 27.7.1981 RHB LB																			
FC		2	4	0	246	89	61.50	0	2									2	
Int		2	2	0	28	21	14.00	0	0									1	
Lim		2	2	0	28	21	14.00	0	0									1	
I20T		2																0	
20T		4	1	1	79	79*		0	1									0	
FC	2000	45	73	8	1954	103	30.06	2	10	3872	2416	64	37.75	5-97	1	0	3.74	29	
Int	2001	83	68	7	1354	78*	22.19	0	6	1640	1472	29	50.75	5-24	0	1	5.38	34	
Lim	2000	121	96	12	1765	78*	21.01	0	7	2571	2292	50	45.84	5-24	0	1	5.34	45	
I20T	2007/08	9	7	2	106	33	21.20	0	0									3	
20T	2003	19	14	5	311	79*	34.55	0	1	120	177	10	17.70	5-24	0	1	8.85	9	
OBUYA, David Oluoch (Kenya, Kenya to United Arab Emirates, Kenya to Zimbabwe) b Nairobi 14.8.1979 RHB WK																			
FC		1	2	0	173	115	86.50	1	1									0	
Int		2	2	0	32	32	16.00	0	0									0	
Lim		2	2	0	32	32	16.00	0	0									0	
I20T		2	2	2	125	65*		0	2									0	
20T		4	4	2	167	65*	83.50	0	2									0	1
FC	2001	22	41	2	1117	115	28.64	2	5									31	3

Cmp	Debut	M	I	NO	Runs	HS	Avge	100	50	Balls	Runs	Wkts	Avge	BB	5i	10m	RpO	ct	st
Int	2001	64	63	3	1211	93	20.18	0	5									32	5
Lim	2001	81	79	6	1472	93	20.16	0	6									44	12
I20T	2007/08	6	6	2	170	65*	42.50	0	2									2	
20T	2007/08	9	9	2	214	65*	30.57	0	2									2	1
ODHIAMBO, Nelson Mandela (Kenya, Kenya to Netherlands, Kenya to United Arab Emirates) b 21.3.1989 RHB RM																			
FC		2	3	1	10	7	5.00	0	0	278	171	4	42.75	2-53	0	0	3.69	1	
Int		2	1	0	1	1	1.00	0	0	90	92	1	92.00	1-63	0	0	6.13	0	
Lim		2	1	0	1	1	1.00	0	0	90	92	1	92.00	1-63	0	0	6.13	0	
I20T		1								24	33	2	16.50	2-33	0	0	8.25	0	
20T		2								48	58	6	9.66	4-25	1	0	7.25	0	
Int	2009/10	5	3	0	34	29	11.33	0	0	216	189	4	47.25	1-22	0	0	5.25	1	
Lim	2009/10	5	3	0	34	29	11.33	0	0	216	189	4	47.25	1-22	0	0	5.25	1	
20T	2009/10	3								72	91	8	11.37	4-25	1	0	7.58	0	
ODHIAMBO, Nehemiah Ngoche (Kenya, Kenya to Netherlands, Kenya to United Arab Emirates, Kenya to Zimbabwe) b Nairobi 7.8.1983 RHB RMF																			
FC		2	4	2	52	50*	26.00	0	1	420	258	7	36.85	3-60	0	0	3.68	0	
Int		2	1	0	19	19	19.00	0	0	114	81	4	20.25	3-35	0	0	4.26	0	
Lim		2	1	0	19	19	19.00	0	0	114	81	4	20.25	3-35	0	0	4.26	0	
I20T		2								36	33	5	6.60	5-20	0	1	5.50	0	
20T		3								54	61	7	8.71	5-20	0	1	6.77	0	
FC	2006	16	28	4	324	50*	13.50	0	1	2409	1446	48	30.12	5-54	1	0	3.60	7	
Int	2005/06	50	40	8	424	66	13.25	0	1	1992	1870	51	36.66	4-61	1	0	5.63	7	
Lim	2005/06	59	45	9	501	66	13.91	0	1	2308	2119	61	34.73	4-61	1	0	5.50	7	
I20T	2007/08	9	6	0	47	18	7.83	0	0	97	139	9	15.44	5-20	0	1	8.59	2	
20T	2007/08	11	6	0	47	18	7.83	0	0	139	201	12	16.75	5-20	0	1	8.67	2	
ODOYO, Thomas Migai (Kenya to Netherlands, Kenya to Zimbabwe, Southern Rocks) b Nairobi 12.5.1978 RHB RMF																			
FC	1997	40	63	7	1476	137	26.35	2	8	4367	2138	86	24.86	5-21	3	0	2.93	13	
Int	1995/96	126	110	16	2307	111*	24.54	1	7	5262	4016	133	30.19	4-25	5	0	4.57	25	
Lim	1995/96	186	165	27	3574	111*	25.89	1	16	7478	5603	200	28.01	5-27	6	1	4.49	41	
I20T	2007/08	8	7	0	85	22	12.14	0	0	150	122	6	20.33	2-13	0	0	4.88	4	
20T	2007/08	8	7	0	85	22	12.14	0	0	150	122	6	20.33	2-13	0	0	4.88	4	
ONGONDO, Peter Jimmy (Kenya to Zimbabwe) b Nairobi 10.2.1977 RHB RFM																			
FC	2000	36	52	16	273	37	7.58	0	0	4806	2474	79	31.31	5-13	4	0	3.08	16	
Int	1999/00	77	60	18	385	36	9.16	0	0	3024	2269	77	29.46	5-51	1	1	4.50	17	
Lim	1999/00	115	85	29	533	36	9.51	0	0	4411	3399	114	29.81	5-30	2	2	4.62	25	
I20T	2007/08	8	6	0	28	16	4.66	0	0	156	177	5	35.40	2-18	0	0	6.80	0	
20T	2007/08	8	6	0	28	16	4.66	0	0	156	177	5	35.40	2-18	0	0	6.80	0	
ONYANGO, Lameck Ngoche (Kenya, Kenya to United Arab Emirates, Kenya to Zimbabwe) b Nairobi 22.9.1973 RHB RM																			
20T		2								36	55	0					9.16	0	
FC	1997/98	23	33	8	339	67	13.56	0	1	2489	1484	35	42.40	6-21	2	0	3.57	8	
Int	1995/96	27	18	7	144	34*	13.09	0	0	887	901	21	42.90	3-29	0	0	6.09	3	
Lim	1995/96	56	40	15	286	34*	11.44	0	0	1725	1630	42	38.80	6-14	1	1	5.67	8	
I20T	2007/08	5	4	2	17	5	8.50	0	0	78	128	4	32.00	2-17	0	0	9.84	0	
20T	2007/08	8	4	2	17	5	8.50	0	0	138	215	6	35.83	2-17	0	0	9.34	0	
OTIENO, Elijah Asoyo (Kenya, Kenya to Netherlands, Kenya to Zimbabwe) b Nairobi 3.1.1988 RHB RM																			
FC		2	3	1	15	13	7.50	0	0	416	191	9	21.22	4-57	0	0	2.75	0	
Int		2	1	1	0	0*		0	0	114	71	4	17.75	3-39	0	0	3.73	0	
Lim		2	1	1	0	0*		0	0	114	71	4	17.75	3-39	0	0	3.73	0	
20T		1								12	15	1	15.00	1-15	0	0	7.50	0	
FC	2006/07	9	14	5	31	13	3.44	0	0	1060	492	14	35.14	4-57	0	0	2.78	6	
Int	2007	13	8	4	23	11	5.75	0	0	429	420	10	42.00	3-39	0	0	5.87	2	
Lim	2007	17	11	6	32	11	6.40	0	0	614	601	15	40.06	3-39	0	0	5.87	4	
OTIENO, Francis Ndege (Kenya to Netherlands) b Nairobi 25.8.1979 RHB RM																			
FC	2000/01	5	9	2	29	8*	4.14	0	0	288	150	3	50.00	3-78	0	0	3.12	6	
Int	2010	4	4	0	16	8	4.00	0	0	6	2	0					2.00	2	
Lim	1999/00	13	13	0	118	35	9.07	0	0	223	183	4	45.75	1-0	0	0	4.92	2	
OUMA, Morris Amollo (Kenya, Kenya to Netherlands, Kenya to United Arab Emirates, Kenya to Zimbabwe) b Kiambli 8.11.1982 RHB OB WK																			
FC		2	4	0	216	130	54.00	1	1									7	
Int		2	2	1	15	12*	15.00	0	0									4	2
Lim		2	2	1	15	12*	15.00	0	0									4	2
I20T		2																2	
20T		4	2	1	41	39	41.00	0	0									4	
FC	2003/04	33	59	1	1657	130	28.56	3	9									51	4
Int	2004	64	62	3	1237	61	20.96	0	6									41	8
Lim	1999/00	82	78	4	1555	62	21.01	0	8									56	10
I20T	2007/08	10	7	0	34	13	4.85	0	0									4	2
20T	2007/08	13	10	1	114	39	12.66	0	0									6	2

Cmp	Debut	M	I	NO	Runs	HS	Avge	100	50	Balls	Runs	Wkts	Avge	BB	5i	10m	RpO	ct	st
PATEL, Rakep Rajendrabhai (Kenya, Kenya to Netherlands, Kenya to United Arab Emirates, Kenya to Zimbabwe) b Nairobi 12.7.1989 RHB OB																			
FC		2	4	0	130	87	32.50	0	1									0	
Int		2	2	0	98	92	49.00	0	1									0	
Lim		2	2	0	98	92	49.00	0	1									0	
I20T		2																1	
20T		4	1	1	1	1*		0	0									4	
FC	2006/07	5	10	0	208	87	20.80	0	1	24	13	0					3.25	1	
Int	2008	21	18	0	320	92	17.77	0	1	78	61	0					4.69	8	
Lim	2008	22	18	0	320	92	17.77	0	1	90	65	0					4.33	8	
I20T	2008	5	2	0	13	7	6.50	0	0									3	
20T	2008	8	4	1	14	7	4.66	0	0									6	
SUJI, Otieno Ondik (Kenya, Kenya to United Arab Emirates) b Nairobi 5.2.1976 RHB RM																			
I20T		1								12	9	1	9.00	1-9	0	0	4.50	1	
20T		2								36	34	3	11.33	2-25	0	0	5.66	2	
FC	1997/98	26	44	6	574	103*	15.10	1	1	1340	800	17	47.05	4-62	0	0	3.58	12	
Int	1996/97	60	46	7	506	67	12.97	0	1	1295	1175	21	55.95	2-14	0	0	5.44	19	
Lim	1996/97	92	70	13	699	67	12.26	0	1	2241	1880	39	48.20	4-36	1	0	5.03	25	
I20T	2007/08	8	5	2	15	7	5.00	0	0	97	116	4	29.00	2-23	0	0	7.17	3	
20T	2007/08	9	5	2	15	7	5.00	0	0	121	141	6	23.50	2-23	0	0	6.99	4	
TIKOLO, Stephen Ogonji (Kenya, Kenya to United Arab Emirates, Kenya to Zimbabwe, Southern Rocks) b Nairobi 25.6.1971 RHB RM																			
FC		1	2	0	41	34	20.50	0	0	120	45	1	45.00	1-45	0	0	2.25	0	
I20T		2	2	2	102	56*		0	1	36	25	1	25.00	1-10	0	0	4.16	1	
20T		3	3	2	165	63	165.00	0	2	54	42	1	42.00	1-10	0	0	4.66	2	
FC	1995/96	56	92	5	4276	220	49.14	11	21	5464	2879	78	36.91	6-80	1	0	3.16	57	
Int	1995/96	126	121	10	3304	111	29.76	3	23	3794	3010	90	33.44	4-41	2	0	4.76	64	
Lim	1995/96	192	184	13	5541	133	32.40	9	34	5903	4560	143	31.88	4-41	4	0	4.63	92	
I20T	2007/08	11	11	3	260	56*	32.50	0	2	102	121	3	40.33	1-10	0	0	7.11	5	
20T	2007/08	17	17	3	471	65	33.64	0	4	204	252	4	63.00	1-10	0	0	7.41	8	
VARAIYA, Hiren Ashok (Kenya, Kenya to Netherlands, Kenya to United Arab Emirates, Kenya to Zimbabwe) b 9.4.1984 RHB SLA																			
FC		2	3	0	53	44	17.66	0	0	336	223	2	111.50	1-38	0	0	3.98	3	
Int		2	1	0	3	3	3.00	0	0	112	62	5	12.40	4-33	1	0	3.32	2	
Lim		2	1	0	3	3	3.00	0	0	112	62	5	12.40	4-33	1	0	3.32	2	
I20T		2								48	46	0					5.75	0	
20T		3								72	55	2	27.50	2-9	0	0	4.58	0	
FC	2006	19	31	6	318	44	12.72	0	0	3392	1746	79	22.10	6-45	5	1	3.08	10	
Int	2006	51	30	15	219	34	14.60	0	0	2334	1591	57	27.91	4-25	2	0	4.09	14	
Lim	2006	60	34	16	256	34	14.22	0	0	2664	1818	63	28.85	4-25	2	0	4.09	15	
I20T	2007/08	10	4	4	14	6*		0	0	192	178	5	35.60	2-24	0	0	5.56	5	
20T	2007/08	12	4	4	14	6*		0	0	228	204	7	29.14	2-9	0	0	5.36	8	
WATERS, Seren Robert (Kenya, Durham MCCU) b Nairobi 11.4.1990 RHB LB																			
FC		1	2	0	13	12	6.50	0	0									1	
FC	2008	6	11	2	354	157*	39.33	1	1	102	68	2	34.00	1-18	0	0	4.00	5	
Int	2008/09	12	12	0	261	74	21.75	0	1									3	
Lim	2008/09	14	14	1	326	74	25.07	0	2									4	
WESONGA, Dominic Saleti (Kenya to Netherlands) b Nairobi 16.7.1988 RHB RFM																			
Int	2010	3	3	0	59	33	19.66	0	0									1	
Lim	2010	3	3	0	59	33	19.66	0	0									1	

NETHERLANDS TO KENYA 2009/10

Cmp	Debut	M	I	NO	Runs	HS	Avge	100	50	Balls	Runs	Wkts	Avge	BB	5i	10m	RpO	ct	st
BORREN, P.W.																			
FC		1	2	0	65	44	32.50	0	0	126	91	0					4.33	1	
Int		2	2	0	18	17	9.00	0	0	42	30	3	10.00	2-10	0	0	4.28	0	
Lim		2	2	0	18	17	9.00	0	0	42	30	3	10.00	2-10	0	0	4.28	0	
BUURMAN, A.F.																			
FC		1	2	1	55	29*	55.00	0	0									4	1
Int		2	2	1	39	30*	39.00	0	0									3	1
Lim		2	2	1	39	30*	39.00	0	0									3	1
DE GROOTH, T.N.																			
Int		2	2	0	17	9	8.50	0	0									1	
Lim		2	2	0	17	9	8.50	0	0									1	
GRUIJTERS, T.G.J.																			
Int		2	2	0	35	29	17.50	0	0	42	34	0					4.85	1	
Lim		2	2	0	35	29	17.50	0	0	42	34	0					4.85	1	

Cmp	Debut	M	I	NO	Runs	HS	Avge	100	50	Balls	Runs	Wkts	Avge	BB	5i	10m	RpO	ct	st
JONKMAN, M.B.S.																			
FC		1	1	0	7	7	7.00	0	0	144	94	3	31.33	3-54	0	0	3.91	1	
Int		2	2	0	10	8	5.00	0	0	89	81	4	20.25	3-24	0	0	5.46	0	
Lim		2	2	0	10	8	5.00	0	0	89	81	4	20.25	3-24	0	0	5.46	0	
KERVEZEE, A.N.																			
FC		1	2	0	131	89	65.50	0	1	36	23	0					3.83	1	
Int		2	2	0	17	11	8.50	0	0									2	
Lim		2	2	0	17	11	8.50	0	0									2	
MUDASSAR BUKHARI																			
FC		1	2	0	6	5	3.00	0	0	114	98	0					5.15	0	
Int		2	2	0	6	6	3.00	0	0	78	54	3	18.00	3-17	0	0	4.15	1	
Lim		2	2	0	6	6	3.00	0	0	78	54	3	18.00	3-17	0	0	4.15	1	
NIJMAN, R.G.																			
FC		1	1	0	5	5	5.00	0	0	78	58	0					4.46	0	
SEELAAR, P.M.																			
FC		1	1	0	0	0	0.00	0	0	306	186	4	46.50	2-87	0	0	3.64	0	
Int		2	2	1	6	6*	6.00	0	0	78	85	2	42.50	1-37	0	0	6.53	0	
Lim		2	2	1	6	6*	6.00	0	0	78	85	2	42.50	1-37	0	0	6.53	0	
STATHAM, N.A.																			
FC		1	2	1	76	62*	76.00	0	1									0	
SZWARCZYNSKI, E.S.																			
FC		1	2	0	93	93	46.50	0	1									0	
Int		2	2	0	41	23	20.50	0	0									0	
Lim		2	2	0	41	23	20.50	0	0									0	
TEN DOESCHATE, R.N.																			
FC		1	2	1	241	212*	241.00	1	0	228	174	7	24.85	5-104	1	0	4.57	0	
Int		2	2	1	118	109*	118.00	1	0	72	49	2	24.50	1-13	0	0	4.08	0	
Lim		2	2	1	118	109*	118.00	1	0	72	49	2	24.50	1-13	0	0	4.08	0	
ZUIDERENT, B.																			
FC		1	2	0	27	24	13.50	0	0									1	
Int		2	2	0	77	56	38.50	0	1									0	
Lim		2	2	0	77	56	38.50	0	1									0	

SCOTLAND TO KENYA 2009/10

Cmp	Debut	M	I	NO	Runs	HS	Avge	100	50	Balls	Runs	Wkts	Avge	BB	5i	10m	RpO	ct	st
BERRINGTON, R.D.																			
FC		1	1	0	80	80	80.00	0	1	138	39	3	13.00	3-13	0	0	1.69	1	
I20T		2	2	0	6	6	3.00	0	0	15	16	0					6.40	0	
20T		4	4	1	9	6	3.00	0	0	45	51	2	25.50	2-12	0	0	6.80	1	
CHALMERS, E.F.																			
FC		1	2	1	32	18*	32.00	0	0									2	
COETZER, K.J.																			
FC		1	2	0	46	34	23.00	0	0	54	16	2	8.00	2-16	0	0	1.77	0	
I20T		2	2	0	15	9	7.50	0	0	6	8	0					8.00	0	
20T		4	4	0	91	64	22.75	0	1	24	32	1	32.00	1-12	0	0	8.00	0	
DRUMMOND, G.D.																			
FC		1	1	0	5	5	5.00	0	0	144	44	3	14.66	3-18	0	0	1.83	0	
I20T		1	1	0	0	0	0.00	0	0	12	22	0					11.00	0	
20T		3	2	1	6	6*	6.00	0	0	48	54	3	18.00	2-14	0	0	6.75	0	
GOUDIE, G.																			
FC		1	1	1	5	5*		0	0	217	84	2	42.00	2-30	0	0	2.32	0	
I20T		1	1	0	4	4	4.00	0	0	6	20	0					20.00	0	
20T		1	1	0	4	4	4.00	0	0	6	20	0					20.00	0	
HAMILTON, G.M.																			
I20T		2	2	0	36	28	18.00	0	0									0	
20T		4	4	1	58	28	19.33	0	0									2	
HAQ, R.M.																			
FC		1	1	0	8	8	8.00	0	0	178	46	3	15.33	3-46	0	0	1.55	0	
I20T		2	2	1	23	21*	23.00	0	0	36	37	0					6.16	0	
20T		4	3	2	24	21*	24.00	0	0	84	73	4	18.25	2-15	0	0	5.21	1	
LOCKHART, D.R.																			
FC		1	2	1	73	51*	73.00	0	1									0	
LYONS, R.T.																			
FC		1	1	0	23	23	23.00	0	0	84	34	0					2.42	1	
I20T		1	1	0	4	4	4.00	0	0	12	14	0					7.00	0	
20T		3	1	0	4	4	4.00	0	0	54	64	4	16.00	3-28	0	0	7.11	1	
McCALLUM, N.F.I.																			
I20T		1	1	0	3	3	3.00	0	0									0	
20T		3	3	0	7	3	2.33	0	0									1	

Cmp Debut	M	I	NO	Runs	HS	Avge	100	50	Balls	Runs	Wkts	Avge	BB	5i	10m	RpO	ct	st
NEL, J.D.																		
FC	1	1	0	5	5	5.00	0	0	276	135	7	19.28	5-107	1	0	2.93	0	
I20T	2	2	1	16	9	16.00	0	0	30	37	0					7.40	0	
20T	3	2	1	16	9	16.00	0	0	54	49	2	24.50	2-12	0	0	5.44	0	
POONIA, N.S.																		
20T	1	1	0	20	20	20.00	0	0									0	
SHEIKH, M.Q.																		
FC	1	2	0	108	108	54.00	1	0									0	
SMITH, S.J.S.																		
FC	1	1	0	0	0	0.00	0	0									6	
I20T	2	2	1	13	9	13.00	0	0									0	
20T	3	2	1	13	9	13.00	0	0									2	1
STANDER, J.H.																		
I20T	2	2	0	45	45	22.50	0	0	27	43	0					9.55	0	
20T	3	3	0	70	45	23.33	0	0	45	55	0					7.33	0	
WATSON, R.R.																		
I20T	2	2	0	26	13	13.00	0	0	18	34	0					11.33	0	
20T	4	4	0	50	17	12.50	0	0	42	44	2	22.00	1-1	0	0	6.28	1	
WATTS, D.F.																		
I20T	2	2	0	16	16	8.00	0	0									0	
20T	4	4	0	99	73	24.75	0	1									1	

UGANDA TO KENYA 2009/10

Cmp Debut	M	I	NO	Runs	HS	Avge	100	50	Balls	Runs	Wkts	Avge	BB	5i	10m	RpO	ct	st
ARINAITWE, D.K.																		
20T	4	4	2	27	16*	13.50	0	0	84	72	4	18.00	2-18	0	0	5.14	1	
BAIG, A.M.																		
20T	3	3	0	75	38	25.00	0	0	18	21	0					7.00	1	
ISABIRYE, F.																		
20T	1	1	0	2	2	2.00	0	0									0	
KYOBE, A.S.																		
20T	4	4	1	71	51*	23.66	0	1									0	
MUHUMZA, D.																		
20T	3	3	1	39	17	19.50	0	0	68	71	2	35.50	1-14	0	0	6.26	1	
MUKASA, R.G.																		
20T	4	4	0	96	66	24.00	0	1	12	24	0					12.00	2	2
MUSOKE, B.																		
20T	2	2	0	1	1	0.50	0	0									0	
NSUBUGA, F.																		
20T	4	4	0	56	22	14.00	0	0	72	92	3	30.66	2-9	0	0	7.66	0	
OTIM, R.																		
20T	2	2	0	34	25	17.00	0	0									1	
SEBANJA, J.																		
20T	2	2	0	1	1	0.50	0	0	42	67	0					9.57	0	
SEIGA, A.																		
20T	2	2	1	1	1*	1.00	0	0	36	50	1	50.00	1-34	0	0	8.33	1	
SEMATIMBA, L.																		
20T	2	2	0	14	12	7.00	0	0									0	1
SENYONDO, H.																		
20T	2	2	1	4	2*	4.00	0	0	48	57	3	19.00	3-20	0	0	7.12	0	
SSEMANDA, R.																		
20T	1	1	0	14	14	14.00	0	0	24	40	1	40.00	1-40	0	0	10.00	0	
TABBY, D.																		
20T	2	1	0	0	0	0.00	0	0	30	42	2	21.00	2-21	0	0	8.40	1	
THAWITHEMWIRA, I.																		
20T	3	3	0	18	17	6.00	0	0									2	
WAISWA, C.																		
20T	2	2	0	9	9	4.50	0	0	30	37	1	37.00	1-25	0	0	7.40	1	
ZIRABA, A.																		
20T	1	1	0	7	7	7.00	0	0									0	

NAMIBIA

2009/10 AND CAREER RECORDS FOR NAMIBIA PLAYERS

Cmp	*Debut*	*M*	*I*	*NO*	*Runs*	*HS*	*Avge*	*100*	*50*	*Balls*	*Runs*	*Wkts*	*Avge*	*BB*	*5i*	*10m*	*RpO*	*ct*	*st*
AMBAMBI, Nasimabe Elton (Namibia, Namibia to South Africa) b Okakundu 15.9.1990 RHB RFM																			
FC		2	3	2	5	4	5.00	0	0	132	82	0					3.72	0	
Lim		1	1	0	0	0	0.00	0	0	36	26	0					4.33	0	
FC	2009/10	4	6	4	18	8	9.00	0	0	342	213	2	106.50	1-44	0	0	3.73	0	
Lim	2009/10	5	1	0	0	0	0.00	0	0	102	104	2	52.00	2-23	0	0	6.11	0	
BAARD, Stephen Julian (Namibia to South Africa) b South Africa 20.4.1992 RHB RMF																			
FC	2009/10	1	2	0	65	45	32.50	0	0	6	5	0					5.00	1	
Lim	2009/10	1	1	0	18	18	18.00	0	0									0	
BARNARD, Pieter Jacobus (Namibia to South Africa) b Windhoek 28.3.1988 RHB RM																			
Lim	2009/10	1								36	49	1	49.00	1-49	0	0	8.16	0	
BURGER, Louis Jacobus (Namibia, Namibia to South Africa) b Windhoek 12.3.1978 RHB RM																			
FC		3	5	0	41	34	8.20	0	0	30	15	0					3.00	3	
Lim		4	3	0	52	29	17.33	0	0	78	73	1	73.00	1-30	0	0	5.61	3	
FC	2003/04	28	50	6	1266	125	28.77	3	6	1081	598	16	37.37	3-15	0	0	3.31	18	
Int	2002/03	6	6	1	11	5	2.20	0	0	330	297	6	49.50	3-39	0	0	5.40	6	
Lim	2001/02	50	48	3	809	69	17.97	0	4	1226	1020	28	36.42	3-39	0	0	4.99	23	
BURGER, Sarel Francois (Namibia, Namibia to South Africa) b Windhoek 13.2.1983 RHB RMF																			
FC		5	9	1	223	90*	27.87	0	2	809	361	13	27.76	4-49	0	0	2.67	6	
Lim		9	8	1	302	91	43.14	0	2	348	282	9	31.33	3-40	0	0	4.86	2	
FC	2003/04	28	50	4	1305	123*	28.36	1	9	3462	1483	59	25.13	4-22	0	0	2.57	26	
Int	2002/03	2	2	0	11	6	5.50	0	0	66	67	0					6.09	1	
Lim	2001/02	47	44	2	993	91	23.64	0	6	1764	1256	52	24.15	5-23	1	2	4.27	17	
GELDENHUYS, Hendrik W (Namibia) b Windhoek LHB LFM																			
FC		1	1	0	9	9	9.00	0	0	72	50	0					4.16	0	
FC	2007/08	2	1	0	9	9	9.00	0	0	126	81	1	81.00	1-31	0	0	3.85	0	
GROENEWALD, Pieter Coetzee (Namibia) b Outjo 1.7.1992 RHB OB																			
Lim		1								24	38	1	38.00	1-38	0	0	9.50	0	
GROENEWALD, Willem Johannes (Namibia, Namibia to South Africa, Namibia to Zimbabwe) b 27.6.1990 RHB OB																			
FC		4	8	1	104	31	14.85	0	0	114	107	0					5.63	1	
Lim		5	3	1	33	18	16.50	0	0	96	75	1	75.00	1-18	0	0	4.68	2	
FC	2009/10	9	17	1	172	33	10.75	0	0	276	222	4	55.50	1-14	0	0	4.82	4	
Lim	2009/10	10	7	1	101	44	16.83	0	0	226	177	2	88.50	1-18	0	0	4.69	4	
20T	2009/10	5	1	1	2	2*		0	0	36	50	0					8.33	1	
KLAZINGA, Louis (Namibia, Namibia to South Africa, Namibia to Zimbabwe) b Pretoria, Gauteng, South Africa 4.12.1985 RHB RFM																			
FC		8	13	4	154	30	17.11	0	0	1403	802	35	22.91	6-70	3	0	3.43	3	
Lim		8	6	3	25	11	8.33	0	0	330	299	16	18.68	4-62	1	0	5.43	4	
FC	2006/07	44	63	24	541	32	13.87	0	0	5503	3170	138	22.97	6-70	6	0	3.45	19	
Lim	2006/07	46	32	17	118	18	7.86	0	0	1930	1748	68	25.70	4-41	2	0	5.43	12	
20T	2009/10	6	3	2	25	22*	25.00	0	0	121	116	7	16.57	3-41	0	0	5.75	3	
LOTTER, Gerhard Petrus (Namibia) b Windhoek 3.1.1993 RHB WK																			
Lim		1																0	
LOUW, Tiaan (Namibia, Namibia to South Africa, Namibia to Zimbabwe) b 10.6.1988 RHB RM																			
Lim		1	1	0	12	12	12.00	0	0									0	
Lim	2009/10	2	2	0	12	12	6.00	0	0									0	
20T	2009/10	1	1	0	19	19	19.00	0	0									2	
MANYANDE, Rangarirai Norbert (Namibia to Zimbabwe, Namibia, Namibia to South Africa) b Bikita, Masvingo, Zimbabwe 29.8.1982 RHB RM																			
FC		5	10	0	286	91	28.60	0	2	12	13	0					6.50	1	
Lim		5	5	0	63	26	12.60	0	0									2	
FC	2000/01	21	38	1	809	148	21.86	1	2	1137	559	13	43.00	5-29	1	0	2.95	12	
Lim	2003/04	17	14	1	144	31	11.07	0	0	164	136	7	19.42	3-34	0	0	4.97	6	
20T	2009/10	6	5	0	79	51	15.80	0	1									2	
MYBURGH, Wessel (Namibia, Namibia to South Africa) b Windhoek 31.5.1990 RHB WK																			
FC		1	2	0	2	2	1.00	0	0									0	
Lim		1	1	0	33	33	33.00	0	0									1	
Lim	2009/10	2	2	0	38	33	19.00	0	0									1	
OLLEWAGEN, Andre (Namibia) b Windhoek 25.3.1985 RHB RM																			
Lim		1								55	32	1	32.00	1-32	0	0	3.49	0	
PALLADINO, Antonio Paul (Essex, Namibia, Namibia to South Africa, Namibia to Zimbabwe) b Tower Hamlets, Essex, England 29.6.1983 RHB RMF																			
FC		4	6	1	108	53*	21.60	0	1	581	289	11	26.27	4-33	0	0	2.98	2	
Lim		4	3	1	44	31	22.00	0	0	180	171	5	34.20	2-33	0	0	5.70	0	
FC	2003	52	66	18	620	66	12.91	0	2	7225	3994	117	34.13	6-41	2	0	3.31	24	
Lim	2002	35	19	3	125	31	7.81	0	0	1308	1193	33	36.15	3-32	0	0	5.47	4	
20T	2005	16	5	3	21	8*	10.50	0	0	287	347	22	15.77	4-21	1	0	7.25	2	

Cmp	Debut	M	I	NO	Runs	HS	Avge	100	50	Balls	Runs	Wkts	Avge	BB	5i	10m	RpO	ct	st
PRETORIUS, Dwaine (Namibia to Zimbabwe) b Randfontein, Transvaal, South Africa 29.3.1989 RHB RMF																			
20T	2009/10	6	6	1	193	48*	38.60	0	0	54	67	3	22.33	1-13	0	0	7.44	4	
ROSSOUW, Pieter (Namibia, Namibia to South Africa) b Keetmanshoop 19.6.1980 RHB RMF																			
FC		2	4	0	17	11	4.25	0	0	171	69	4	17.25	3-35	0	0	2.42	0	
Lim		5	2	2	16	11*		0	0	120	121	3	40.33	1-17	0	0	6.05	1	
FC	2009/10	3	6	0	19	11	3.16	0	0	309	137	5	27.40	3-35	0	0	2.66	1	
Lim	2009/10	6	3	3	27	11*		0	0	138	141	3	47.00	1-17	0	0	6.13	2	
RUDOLPH, Gerhardus Johannes (Namibia to South Africa, Namibia, Namibia to Zimbabwe) b Pretoria, Transvaal, South Africa 2.3.1988 RHB LB																			
FC		6	12	1	423	118	38.45	1	2									2	
Lim		8	7	0	134	73	19.14	0	1									5	
FC	2006/07	29	56	2	1319	118	24.42	1	7	54	59	1	59.00	1-33	0	0	6.55	31	
Lim	2006/07	27	26	1	577	87	23.08	0	4									10	
20T	2009/10	6	6	0	45	19	7.50	0	0									1	
SCHOLTZ, Bernard Martinus (Namibia, Namibia to South Africa, Namibia to Zimbabwe) b Keetmanshoop 10.3.1990 RHB SLA																			
FC		4	5	4	23	17*	23.00	0	0	401	201	8	25.12	2-15	0	0	3.00	2	
Lim		4	1	1	6	6*		0	0	114	81	4	20.25	2-43	0	0	4.26	0	
FC	2008/09	13	20	12	119	23	14.87	0	0	1230	689	25	27.56	5-65	1	0	3.36	4	
Lim	2008/09	10	5	2	37	24	12.33	0	0	286	232	6	38.66	2-43	0	0	4.86	2	
20T	2009/10	6	1	0	7	7	7.00	0	0	30	47	2	23.50	2-15	0	0	9.40	0	
SCHOLTZ, Nicolaas Reimert Petrus (Namibia, Namibia to South Africa) b Keemanshoop 5.11.1986 LHB LB																			
FC		4	7	0	145	56	20.71	0	1	97	65	2	32.50	2-8	0	0	4.02	1	
Lim		6	5	2	138	58	46.00	0	1	138	119	3	39.66	3-56	0	0	5.17	0	
FC	2003/04	31	52	10	852	64	20.28	0	4	2058	1288	28	46.00	4-62	0	0	3.75	12	
Lim	2006/07	38	31	9	641	64	29.13	0	5	921	796	19	41.89	3-28	0	0	5.18	13	
SLABBER, Wilbur (Namibia, Namibia to South Africa) b Windhoek 2.12.1980 RHB OB																			
Lim		2	1	0	4	4	4.00	0	0	84	71	0					5.07	1	
FC	2007/08	7	12	2	39	20*	3.90	0	0	348	214	1	214.00	1-57	0	0	3.69	3	
Lim	2007/08	4	3	0	8	4	2.66	0	0	96	86	0					5.37	1	
SNYMAN, Gerrie (Namibia, Namibia to South Africa) b Windhoek 30.4.1981 RHB RFM																			
FC		2	3	0	108	55	36.00	0	1	142	72	1	72.00	1-49	0	0	3.04	2	
Lim		3	2	0	82	56	41.00	0	1	17	11	1	11.00	1-11	0	0	3.88	0	
FC	2003/04	37	66	5	2278	230	37.34	2	14	3634	1954	62	31.51	5-53	1	0	3.22	25	
Int	2002/03	5	4	0	5	5	1.25	0	0	288	281	6	46.83	3-69	0	0	5.85	0	
Lim	2001/02	65	63	9	2188	196	40.51	4	14	2430	2010	65	30.92	5-36	2	1	4.96	17	
STEENKAMP, Ewald (Namibia, Namibia to South Africa) b Windhoek 18.4.1988 RHB WK																			
FC		2	3	0	248	206	82.66	1	0									2	
Lim		3	3	0	48	26	16.00	0	0									3	
FC	2007/08	6	10	1	377	206	41.88	1	1									7	
Lim	2009/10	5	5	0	108	43	21.60	0	0									5	
VANDER MERWE, Lowaldo van der Merwe (Namibia) b Paarl, Cape Province, South Africa 24.12.1986 RHB RM																			
FC		2	3	0	27	20	9.00	0	0									0	
Lim		2																0	
VAN DER WESTHUIZEN, Louis Petrus (Namibia, Namibia to South Africa) b Windhoek 31.3.1988 LHB SLA																			
FC		5	9	2	303	70*	43.28	0	3	528	310	10	31.00	5-90	1	0	3.52	4	
Lim		6	5	0	67	29	13.40	0	0	189	161	10	16.10	4-63	1	0	5.11	5	
FC	2006	19	34	4	643	85*	21.43	0	4	990	548	14	39.14	5-90	1	0	3.32	7	
Lim	2006/07	29	26	5	392	68	18.66	0	2	859	740	27	27.40	4-48	2	0	5.16	15	
VAN ROOI, Ashley (Namibia to South Africa) b 6.4.1988 RHB RM																			
FC	2009/10	2	1	1	1	1*		0	0	96	45	0					2.81	0	
VAN SCHOOR, Raymond (Namibia, Namibia to South Africa, Namibia to Zimbabwe) b 23.5.1990 RHB OB WK																			
FC		8	15	1	623	157	44.50	2	3									19	1
Lim		10	10	0	379	90	37.90	0	3	20	23	1	23.00	1-9	0	0	6.90	4	2
FC	2007	25	48	1	1329	157	28.27	2	6	70	59	2	29.50	2-22	0	0	5.05	58	2
Lim	2007/08	37	37	2	1029	90	29.40	0	8	50	56	2	28.00	1-9	0	0	6.72	22	5
20T	2009/10	6	6	0	139	46	23.16	0	0	24	24	2	12.00	2-24	0	0	6.00	4	
VAN VUUREN, Wian (Namibia, Namibia to South Africa) b Windhoek 15.4.1993 RHB																			
FC		4	8	0	173	55	21.62	0	1									4	
Lim		5	3	0	26	13	8.66	0	0									3	
FC	2009/10	6	12	0	238	55	19.83	0	1	12	22	0					11.00	5	
Lim	2009/10	9	7	0	94	26	13.42	0	0									3	
VERWEY, Tobias (Namibia, Namibia to South Africa, Namibia to Zimbabwe) b Emelo, South Africa 2.11.1981 RHB LB																			
FC		5	9	1	130	35	16.25	0	0	457	293	10	29.30	5-46	1	0	3.84	9	
Lim		5	5	1	84	42	21.00	0	0	120	102	5	20.40	3-49	0	0	5.10	2	
FC	2005	25	40	8	784	114	24.50	1	2	667	433	10	43.30	5-46	1	0	3.89	46	3
Lim	2006/07	18	14	3	196	42	17.81	0	0	126	106	5	21.20	3-49	0	0	5.04	14	
20T	2009/10	6	6	2	91	22*	22.75	0	0	18	28	0					9.33	3	

Cmp	Debut	M	I	NO	Runs	HS	Avge	100	50	Balls	Runs	Wkts	Avge	BB	5i	10m	RpO	ct	st
VILJOEN, Christoffel (Namibia to South Africa, Namibia, Namibia to Zimbabwe) b Pretoria, Transvaal, South Africa 28.9.1987 RHB RM																			
FC		2	4	0	62	47	15.50	0	0	324	138	5	27.60	2-9	0	0	2.55	1	
Lim		4	2	1	12	11	12.00	0	0	198	155	6	25.83	4-45	1	0	4.69	3	
FC	2009/10	7	13	0	148	47	11.38	0	0	1165	570	20	28.50	4-36	0	0	2.93	4	
Lim	2009/10	9	6	1	17	11	3.40	0	0	396	340	14	24.28	4-45	1	0	5.15	4	
20T	2009/10	6	3	1	61	41	30.50	0	0	120	101	6	16.83	2-14	0	0	5.05	0	
VORSTER, Louis Phillippus (Namibia to South Africa, Namibia) b Potchefstroom, Transvaal, South Africa 2.11.1966 LHB OB																			
FC		1	2	0	29	17	14.50	0	0									0	
Lim		2	2	0	27	17	13.50	0	0									0	
FC	1985/86	95	165	21	4786	188	33.23	7	26	69	41	1	41.00	1-10	0	0	3.56	59	
Lim	1986/87	96	88	16	2186	93*	30.36	0	15									25	
WILLIAMS, Craig George (Namibia, Namibia to South Africa, Namibia to Zimbabwe) b Oshakati 25.2.1984 RHB RM																			
FC		8	15	1	567	110*	40.50	1	3	792	451	9	50.11	5-41	1	0	3.41	8	
Lim		10	10	3	362	114*	51.71	1	1	342	304	9	33.77	4-24	1	0	5.33	8	
FC	2007/08	32	59	4	2135	134	38.81	4	12	2566	1588	42	37.80	5-41	1	0	3.71	30	
Lim	2007/08	37	36	4	861	114*	26.90	1	3	672	616	17	36.23	4-24	1	0	5.50	19	
20T	2009/10	6	6	0	132	50	22.00	0	1	93	96	6	16.00	3-28	0	0	6.19	2	

BERMUDA TO NAMIBIA 2010

Cmp	Debut	M	I	NO	Runs	HS	Avge	100	50	Balls	Runs	Wkts	Avge	BB	5i	10m	RpO	ct	st
CROCKWELL, F.S.																			
FC		1	2	0	23	17	11.50	0	0	42	27	0					3.85	1	
Lim		2	2	0	25	20	12.50	0	0									0	
DESILVA, J.A.																			
Lim		1	1	0	20	20	20.00	0	0	48	32	0					4.00	0	
EDNESS, J.																			
FC		1	2	0	14	14	7.00	0	0									2	
Lim		2	2	0	17	9	8.50	0	0									1	
FOGGO, C.R.																			
FC		1	2	0	49	34	24.50	0	0	55	38	1	38.00	1-38	0	0	4.14	0	
Lim		2	2	0	13	13	6.50	0	0	30	28	1	28.00	1-28	0	0	5.60	0	
HEMP, D.L.																			
FC		1	2	0	117	65	58.50	0	2									1	
Lim		2	2	0	19	13	9.50	0	0									0	
JONES, M.O.																			
FC		1	2	0	0	0	0.00	0	0	126	141	3	47.00	3-141	0	0	6.71	0	
Lim		2	2	0	47	25	23.50	0	0	78	80	0					6.15	1	
KELLY, S.K.W.																			
FC		1	2	1	0	0*	0.00	0	0	131	107	1	107.00	1-107	0	0	4.90	2	
Lim		1	1	1	8	8*		0	0	60	51	0					5.10	1	
OUTERBRIDGE, S.D.																			
FC		1	2	0	67	46	33.50	0	0									0	
Lim		2	2	0	22	22	11.00	0	0	30	30	1	30.00	1-30	0	0	6.00	0	
PITCHER, J.E.																			
FC		1	2	0	18	9	9.00	0	0	83	57	0					4.12	0	
Lim		2	2	0	15	13	7.50	0	0	99	82	4	20.50	3-45	0	0	4.97	2	
RAYNER, S.																			
Lim		1	1	0	4	4	4.00	0	0									0	
ROMAINE, I.H.																			
FC		1	2	0	35	34	17.50	0	0									0	
Lim		2	2	0	104	100	52.00	1	0									0	
STEEDE, R.D.																			
FC		1	2	0	2	2	1.00	0	0	54	46	1	46.00	1-46	0	0	5.11	0	
TROTT, R.J.																			
FC		1	2	1	30	24*	30.00	0	0	198	148	2	74.00	2-148	0	0	4.48	0	
Lim		2	2	0	11	9	5.50	0	0	96	90	1	90.00	1-33	0	0	5.62	0	
WEST, J.																			
Lim		1	1	1	0	0*		0	0	25	24	0					5.76	0	

BOLAND TO NAMIBIA 2009/10

Cmp	Debut	M	I	NO	Runs	HS	Avge	100	50	Balls	Runs	Wkts	Avge	BB	5i	10m	RpO	ct	st
AUGUST, C.J.																			
Lim		1	1	1	5	5*		0	0	48	34	3	11.33	3-34	0	0	4.25	0	
CHILDS, D.B.																			
FC		1	1	0	0	0	0.00	0	0	103	49	4	12.25	4-15	0	0	2.85	0	
Lim		1								24	6	0					1.50	0	

Cmp Debut	M	I	NO	Runs	HS	Avge	100	50	Balls	Runs	Wkts	Avge	BB	5i	10m	RpO	ct	st
CLOETE, T.W.R.																		
FC	1	1	0	36	36	36.00	0	0	18	7	0					2.33	1	
Lim	1	1	1	39	39*		0	0									0	
DAVIDS, H.																		
FC	1	2	1	69	48	69.00	0	0	102	64	2	32.00	2-26	0	0	3.76	1	
Lim	1	1	0	8	8	8.00	0	0	48	57	0					7.12	0	
ERASMUS, O.J.																		
Lim	1	1	0	0	0	0.00	0	0	48	27	2	13.50	2-27	0	0	3.37	1	
JEFTHA, P.J.N.																		
FC	1	1	0	51	51	51.00	0	1	54	23	0					2.55	2	
JORDAAN, H.																		
FC	1	1	0	10	10	10.00	0	0									0	
Lim	1	1	0	18	18	18.00	0	0									1	
KRIEK, E.C.																		
FC	1	1	0	26	26	26.00	0	0									0	
Lim	1	1	0	12	12	12.00	0	0									1	
PAULSE, H.H.																		
FC	1	1	0	0	0	0.00	0	0	120	69	5	13.80	3-34	0	0	3.45	0	
Lim	1								42	32	3	10.66	3-32	0	0	4.57	1	
RAMELA, O.A.																		
FC	1	2	1	42	37	42.00	0	0									1	
Lim	1	1	0	79	79	79.00	0	1									0	
RAUBENHEIMER, C.H.																		
FC	1	1	1	9	9*		0	0	174	86	7	12.28	6-65	1	0	2.96	0	
Lim	1																0	
STEVENS, G.C.																		
FC	1	1	0	10	10	10.00	0	0	90	41	2	20.50	2-16	0	0	2.73	0	
Lim	1	1	0	2	2	2.00	0	0	30	23	0					4.60	1	
WALTERS, L.R.																		
FC	1	1	0	82	82	82.00	0	1									4	1
Lim	1	1	0	4	4	4.00	0	0									1	

BORDER TO NAMIBIA 2009/10

Cmp Debut	M	I	NO	Runs	HS	Avge	100	50	Balls	Runs	Wkts	Avge	BB	5i	10m	RpO	ct	st
BENNETT, B.L.																		
FC	1	2	0	48	40	24.00	0	0	72	39	0					3.25	0	
Lim	1	1	0	44	44	44.00	0	0									0	
BENNETT, K.D.																		
FC	1	2	1	75	71	75.00	0	1									0	
Lim	1	1	1	3	3*		0	0									0	
BROWN, D.L.																		
FC	1	2	0	96	56	48.00	0	1	72	28	0					2.33	2	
Lim	1	1	0	2	2	2.00	0	0	48	60	0					7.50	0	
DE KOCK, S.																		
FC	1	2	0	53	33	26.50	0	0	192	72	3	24.00	3-51	0	0	2.25	2	
Lim	1	1	0	4	4	4.00	0	0	18	9	0					3.00	2	
FOJELA, P.																		
FC	1								90	34	2	17.00	2-24	0	0	2.26	0	
Lim	1	1	0	2	2	2.00	0	0	48	35	1	35.00	1-35	0	0	4.37	0	
LWANA, L.L.																		
Lim	1								12	15	0					7.50	0	
MBANE, L.																		
FC	1	2	1	51	26	51.00	0	0	120	50	2	25.00	1-21	0	0	2.50	0	
Lim	1	1	0	2	2	2.00	0	0	48	25	0					3.12	0	
MNYANDA, L.L.																		
FC	1	1	0	21	21	21.00	0	0	210	107	5	21.40	3-52	0	0	3.05	2	
Lim	1	1	0	7	7	7.00	0	0	24	27	1	27.00	1-27	0	0	6.75	0	
PANGABANTU, Y.																		
FC	1	1	1	0	0*		0	0	192	63	6	10.50	3-30	0	0	1.96	0	
Lim	1								42	29	2	14.50	2-29	0	0	4.14	0	
SEYIBOKWE, S.																		
FC	1	2	0	0	0	0.00	0	0									0	
Lim	1	1	1	6	6*		0	0									0	
SODUMO, A.M.																		
FC	1	2	1	101	65*	101.00	0	1									2	2
Lim	1	1	0	34	34	34.00	0	0									0	
THOMAS, B.J.																		
FC	1	2	0	19	18	9.50	0	0									0	
Lim	1	1	0	84	84	84.00	0	1									0	

EASTERNS TO NAMIBIA 2009/10

Cmp Debut	M	I	NO	Runs	HS	Avge	100	50	Balls	Runs	Wkts	Avge	BB	5i	10m	RpO	ct	st
BODIBE, T.M.																		
FC	1	1	0	18	18	18.00	0	0									3	
Lim	1	1	0	10	10	10.00	0	0									1	
BOOYSEN, J.																		
FC	1	1	0	61	61	61.00	0	1	42	22	1	22.00	1-22	0	0	3.14	3	
Lim	1	1	0	33	33	33.00	0	0									0	
DU PLESSIS, R.A.																		
FC	1	1	0	40	40	40.00	0	0									0	
Lim	1	1	0	34	34	34.00	0	0									0	
HLENGANI, I.C.																		
FC	1	1	1	1	1*		0	0	216	105	1	105.00	1-83	0	0	2.91	2	
Lim	1	1	0	4	4	4.00	0	0	30	31	2	15.50	2-31	0	0	6.20	1	
JAPPIE, R.																		
FC	1	1	1	62	62*		0	1									0	
Lim	1	1	0	22	22	22.00	0	0									0	
MATHEBULA, B.M.																		
FC	1								138	117	3	39.00	2-39	0	0	5.08	0	
Lim	1								48	30	0					3.75	1	
O'CONNOR, S.P.																		
FC	1	1	0	11	11	11.00	0	0	54	25	0					2.77	0	
Lim	1	1	1	16	16*		0	0	24	16	1	16.00	1-16	0	0	4.00	0	
PIENAAR, J.J.																		
FC	1	1	0	154	154	154.00	1	0	6	3	0					3.00	0	
Lim	1	1	0	20	20	20.00	0	0									0	
SEKHOTO, M.R.																		
Lim	1	1	0	6	6	6.00	0	0									0	
VILJOEN, G.C.																		
FC	1	1	0	5	5	5.00	0	0	186	114	5	22.80	5-54	1	0	3.67	0	
Lim	1	1	0	2	2	2.00	0	0	48	67	2	33.50	2-67	0	0	8.37	0	
WALTERS, B.D.																		
FC	1	1	0	39	39	39.00	0	0	228	116	2	58.00	2-57	0	0	3.05	0	
Lim	1	1	0	4	4	4.00	0	0	42	60	0					8.57	1	
WIESE, D.																		
FC	1	1	0	20	20	20.00	0	0	212	115	2	57.50	1-41	0	0	3.25	3	
Lim	1	1	0	9	9	9.00	0	0	48	37	1	37.00	1-37	0	0	4.62	0	

GAUTENG TO NAMIBIA 2009/10

Cmp Debut	M	I	NO	Runs	HS	Avge	100	50	Balls	Runs	Wkts	Avge	BB	5i	10m	RpO	ct	st
BAVUMA, T.																		
FC	1	1	0	42	42	42.00	0	0	36	41	1	41.00	1-41	0	0	6.83	1	
Lim	1	1	0	79	79	79.00	0	1									0	
BURGER, S.																		
FC	1	1	1	94	94*		0	1	84	41	1	41.00	1-21	0	0	2.92	5	
Lim	1	1	0	10	10	10.00	0	0	18	10	1	10.00	1-10	0	0	3.33	1	
CAMERON, R.																		
FC	1	1	0	13	13	13.00	0	0	66	36	0					3.27	2	
Lim	1	1	0	18	18	18.00	0	0									1	
DAS NEVES, R.																		
Lim	1	1	1	7	7*		0	0	30	28	4	7.00	4-28	1	0	5.60	0	
FRYLINCK, R.																		
FC	1	1	0	74	74	74.00	0	1	78	45	0					3.46	2	
Lim	1	1	0	2	2	2.00	0	0	12	7	0					3.50	0	
HENDRICKS, D.A.																		
Lim	1	1	1	8	8*		0	0									1	
MAFA, J.T.																		
FC	1								120	51	2	25.50	1-21	0	0	2.55	0	
Lim	1								36	29	2	14.50	2-29	0	0	4.83	0	
MATSHIKWE, P.																		
FC	1	1	0	0	0	0.00	0	0	150	85	1	85.00	1-45	0	0	3.40	1	
Lim	1								30	16	1	16.00	1-16	0	0	3.20	0	
MOKOENA, T.G.																		
FC	1	1	0	22	22	22.00	0	0	6	4	0					4.00	1	
Lim	1	1	0	6	6	6.00	0	0									0	
PHANGISO, A.M.																		
FC	1	1	0	9	9	9.00	0	0	336	146	6	24.33	4-59	0	0	2.60	1	
Lim	1	1	0	18	18	18.00	0	0	24	12	0					3.00	0	
SHAMSI, T.																		
FC	1	1	0	0	0	0.00	0	0	309	146	6	24.33	4-60	0	0	2.83	0	

Cmp	Debut	M	I	NO	Runs	HS	Avge	100	50	Balls	Runs	Wkts	Avge	BB	5i	10m	RpO	ct	st
SYMES, J.																			
FC		1	1	0	4	4	4.00	0	0	54	28	0					3.11	0	
Lim		1	1	0	0	0	0.00	0	0	30	15	1	15.00	1-15	0	0	3.00	1	
VILAS, D.J.																			
FC		1	1	0	69	69	69.00	0	1									1	
Lim		1	1	0	120	120	120.00	1	0									1	1

KWAZULU-NATAL INLAND TO NAMIBIA 2009/10

Cmp	Debut	M	I	NO	Runs	HS	Avge	100	50	Balls	Runs	Wkts	Avge	BB	5i	10m	RpO	ct	st
ADDICOTT, G.N.																			
FC		1	2	0	28	22	14.00	0	0									1	
Lim		1	1	0	28	28	28.00	0	0									0	
BARENDS, B.L.																			
FC		1	1	1	9	9*		0	0	144	69	4	17.25	2-23	0	0	2.87	1	
Lim		1								18	21	1	21.00	1-21	0	0	7.00	0	
BARRON, C.A.H.																			
FC		1	2	0	34	21	17.00	0	0									0	
Lim		1	1	1	34	34*		0	0									0	
CHETTY, K.																			
FC		1	2	0	20	19	10.00	0	0	210	102	4	25.50	3-73	0	0	2.91	0	
Lim		1								12	12	0					6.00	0	
DRUMMOND, T.J.																			
FC		1	2	0	4	3	2.00	0	0									7	
Lim		1	1	0	35	35	35.00	0	0									2	
GQADUSHE, M.																			
Lim		1	1	1	5	5*		0	0									0	
HARRIDAVE, N.																			
FC		1	2	1	48	47	48.00	0	0	48	27	1	27.00	1-1	0	0	3.37	1	
Lim		1								48	24	1	24.00	1-24	0	0	3.00	1	
HLELA, R.T.																			
FC		1	2	1	9	9	9.00	0	0	60	43	0					4.30	0	
MOSES, B.																			
FC		1	2	0	102	93	51.00	0	1	36	11	0					1.83	2	
Lim		1	1	0	18	18	18.00	0	0	30	19	1	19.00	1-19	0	0	3.80	0	
NHLAPO, C.E.M.																			
Lim		1																0	
NIPPER, K.																			
FC		1	2	0	49	38	24.50	0	0	170	47	6	7.83	4-7	0	0	1.65	3	
Lim		1	1	0	54	54	54.00	0	1	33	23	1	23.00	1-23	0	0	4.18	1	
OLIVIER, M.																			
FC		1	2	0	37	22	18.50	0	0	3	0	1	0.00	1-0	0	0	0.00	0	
Lim		1	1	0	23	23	23.00	0	0									0	
SAVAGE, C.P.																			
FC		1	2	0	11	7	5.50	0	0	204	97	4	24.25	2-36	0	0	2.85	0	
Lim		1								48	24	2	12.00	2-24	0	0	3.00	0	

SOUTH WESTERN DISTRICTS TO NAMIBIA 2009/10

Cmp	Debut	M	I	NO	Runs	HS	Avge	100	50	Balls	Runs	Wkts	Avge	BB	5i	10m	RpO	ct	st
BAARTMAN, D.D.G.																			
FC		1	2	1	10	6	10.00	0	0	126	70	3	23.33	2-42	0	0	3.33	1	
Lim		1								12	20	0					10.00	1	
BREDENKAMP, N.																			
FC		1	2	0	24	15	12.00	0	0	18	21	2	10.50	2-21	0	0	7.00	0	
Lim		1	1	0	1	1	1.00	0	0	24	33	2	16.50	2-33	0	0	8.25	0	
DEWETT, B.C.																			
FC		1	2	0	88	63	44.00	0	1	56	33	3	11.00	2-33	0	0	3.53	2	
Lim		1	1	0	6	6	6.00	0	0									0	
GROBLER, S.F.																			
FC		1	2	0	46	44	23.00	0	0	174	49	3	16.33	2-4	0	0	1.69	0	
Lim		1	1	0	27	27	27.00	0	0	48	55	0					6.87	1	
HANTAM, W.C.																			
FC		1	2	0	45	45	22.50	0	0	96	62	1	62.00	1-39	0	0	3.87	1	
Lim		1	1	0	29	29	29.00	0	0	36	40	1	40.00	1-40	0	0	6.66	0	
HARTSLIEF, W.																			
FC		1	2	1	17	13*	17.00	0	0	171	87	2	43.50	2-29	0	0	3.05	0	
Lim		1	1	1	1	1*		0	0	24	14	0					3.50	0	
HILLERMANN, R.E.																			
FC		1	2	0	52	45	26.00	0	0	60	43	2	21.50	2-34	0	0	4.30	1	
Lim		1	1	0	4	4	4.00	0	0									0	

Cmp Debut	M	I	NO	Runs	HS	Avge	100	50	Balls	Runs	Wkts	Avge	BB	5i	10m	RpO	ct	st
HUGO, R.P.																		
FC	1	2	0	33	24	16.50	0	0									7	
Lim	1	1	0	11	11	11.00	0	0									0	1
JORDAAN, J.J.																		
Lim	1								48	32	1	32.00	1-32	0	0	4.00	0	
MURRAY, N.M.																		
FC	1	2	0	38	31	19.00	0	0	24	30	1	30.00	1-30	0	0	7.50	0	
Lim	1								48	43	0					5.37	0	
STRYDOM, J.G.																		
FC	1	2	0	18	9	9.00	0	0									0	
Lim	1	1	0	104	104	104.00	1	0									0	
STUURMAN, P.A.																		
FC	1	2	0	47	35	23.50	0	0									2	
Lim	1	1	1	45	45*		0	0									0	

UNITED ARAB EMIRATES TO NAMIBIA 2009/10

Cmp Debut	M	I	NO	Runs	HS	Avge	100	50	Balls	Runs	Wkts	Avge	BB	5i	10m	RpO	ct	st
ABDUL REHMAN																		
FC	1	2	1	76	46	76.00	0	0									3	
Lim	2	2	0	83	71	41.50	0	1									1	1
AHMED RAZA																		
Lim	1	1	0	7	7	7.00	0	0	51	62	3	20.66	3-62	0	0	7.29	0	
AMJAD ALI																		
Lim	2	2	0	51	35	25.50	0	0									2	
AMJAD JAVED																		
FC	1	2	0	45	35	22.50	0	0	132	50	0					2.27	0	
Lim	2	2	0	39	31	19.50	0	0	66	41	1	41.00	1-23	0	0	3.72	0	
ARFAN HAIDER																		
FC	1	2	0	91	84	45.50	0	1	18	5	1	5.00	1-5	0	0	1.66	0	
ARSHAD ALI																		
FC	1	2	0	90	47	45.00	0	0	48	17	0					2.12	0	
Lim	1	1	0	75	75	75.00	0	1	54	47	2	23.50	2-47	0	0	5.22	0	
FAHAD ALHASHMI																		
Lim	2	1	0	4	4	4.00	0	0	42	43	0					6.14	2	
FAYYAZ AHMED																		
FC	1	2	0	58	52	29.00	0	1	367	152	7	21.71	4-75	0	0	2.48	1	
Lim	2	2	1	58	58*	58.00	0	1	120	84	4	21.00	3-42	0	0	4.20	1	
KHURRAM KHAN																		
FC	1	2	0	153	109	76.50	1	0	210	86	0					2.45	2	
Lim	2	2	0	66	48	33.00	0	0	57	67	1	67.00	1-35	0	0	7.05	1	
MOHAMMAD IQBAL																		
Lim	2	2	0	51	33	25.50	0	0									0	
MOHAMMAD TAUQIR																		
FC	1	2	1	26	25	26.00	0	0	228	117	6	19.50	5-40	1	0	3.07	1	
Lim	2	2	0	1	1	0.50	0	0	102	82	2	41.00	2-47	0	0	4.82	1	
MOIZ SHAHID																		
FC	1	1	1	8	8*		0	0	36	25	0					4.16	1	
Lim	1	1	1	17	17*		0	0	36	21	0					3.50	0	
QASIM ZUBAIR																		
FC	1	1	0	1	1	1.00	0	0	132	50	2	25.00	2-44	0	0	2.27	0	
SAQIB ALI																		
FC	1	2	0	22	13	11.00	0	0	12	7	0					3.50	2	
Lim	2	2	0	31	30	15.50	0	0	44	34	3	11.33	2-19	0	0	4.63	0	
SHOAIB SARWAR																		
FC	1	1	0	0	0	0.00	0	0	126	74	2	37.00	2-68	0	0	3.52	1	
Lim	1	1	1	13	13*		0	0	24	30	1	30.00	1-30	0	0	7.50	0	

NETHERLANDS

2010 AND CAREER RECORDS FOR NETHERLANDS PLAYERS

Cmp	*Debut*	*M*	*I*	*NO*	*Runs*	*HS*	*Avge*	*100*	*50*	*Balls*	*Runs*	*Wkts*	*Avge*	*BB*	*5i*	*10m*	*RpO*	*ct*	*st*
ADEEL Khalid RAJA, Mohammad (Netherlands, Netherlands to Ireland, Netherlands to Scotland) b Lahore, Punjab, Pakistan 15.8.1980 RHB OB																			
FC		1	2	0	0	0	0.00	0	0	198	82	2	41.00	2-82	0	0	2.48	0	
Int		6	2	0	0	0	0.00	0	0	246	126	7	18.00	2-3	0	0	3.07	1	
Lim		9	4	1	24	19	8.00	0	0	342	188	8	23.50	2-3	0	0	3.29	1	
FC	2004	7	9	0	62	28	6.88	0	0	752	419	7	59.85	2-82	0	0	3.34	0	
Int	2002/03	19	10	2	28	8*	3.50	0	0	756	615	17	36.17	4-42	1	0	4.88	3	
Lim	2001	31	17	6	90	19	8.18	0	0	1254	995	24	41.45	4-42	1	0	4.76	5	
BARRESI, Wesley (Netherlands to England, Netherlands to Ireland, Netherlands, Netherlands to Scotland) b Johannesburg, Transvaal, South Africa 3.5.1984 RHB																			
FC		2	4	0	146	81	36.50	0	1									5	1
Int		6	6	1	129	51*	25.80	0	1	18	20	0					6.66	0	
Lim		11	11	2	238	51*	26.44	0	1	18	20	0					6.66	5	
FC	2004/05	9	18	0	317	81	17.61	0	2	12	3	0					1.50	13	1
Int	2010	9	9	2	208	64*	29.71	0	2	18	20	0					6.66	0	
Lim	2004/05	19	19	3	379	64*	23.68	0	2	18	20	0					6.66	8	
BORREN, Peter William (Netherlands, Netherlands to England, Netherlands to Ireland, Netherlands to Kenya, Netherlands to Scotland, Netherlands to United Arab Emirates) b Christchurch, Canterbury, New Zealand 21.8.1983 RHB RM																			
FC		2	4	0	171	109	42.75	1	0	306	165	5	33.00	3-61	0	0	3.23	3	
Int		7	6	1	81	47	16.20	0	0	281	200	6	33.33	2-26	0	0	4.27	6	
Lim		13	12	2	145	47	14.50	0	0	503	353	10	35.30	2-18	0	0	4.21	8	
FC	2006/07	15	27	0	856	109	31.70	2	3	2085	1095	27	40.55	3-21	0	0	3.15	18	
Int	2006	39	33	1	477	96	14.90	0	2	1337	1164	35	33.25	3-30	0	0	5.22	17	
Lim	2006	60	50	3	759	96	16.14	0	2	2194	1869	50	37.38	3-30	0	0	5.11	24	
I20T	2008	10	8	2	107	37*	17.83	0	0	210	237	7	33.85	2-19	0	0	6.77	5	
20T	2008	11	9	3	139	37*	23.16	0	0	228	267	7	38.14	2-19	0	0	7.02	5	
BUURMAN, Atse F (Netherlands, Netherlands to England, Netherlands to Kenya, Netherlands to Scotland, Netherlands to United Arab Emirates) b 21.3.1982 RHB WK																			
Int		7	4	1	31	23	10.33	0	0									7	2
Lim		10	6	1	40	23	8.00	0	0									10	3
FC	2007	5	10	1	176	41	19.55	0	0									16	1
Int	2007	15	9	2	114	34	16.28	0	0									14	3
Lim	2002	27	18	2	236	53	14.75	0	1									22	5
I20T	2009/10	4	2	0	0	0	0.00	0	0									1	1
20T	2009/10	5	3	0	3	3	1.00	0	0									3	1
COOPER, Tom Lexley William (Netherlands, Netherlands to England, Netherlands to Ireland, Netherlands to Scotland, South Australia) b Wollongong, New South Wales, Australia 26.11.1986 RHB OB																			
Int		7	7	1	488	101	81.33	1	4	150	103	5	20.60	2-19	0	0	4.12	4	
Lim		12	12	1	605	101	55.00	1	4	156	105	5	21.00	2-19	0	0	4.03	8	
FC	2008/09	6	8	0	160	49	20.00	0	0	31	23	0					4.45	4	
Int	2010	10	10	1	589	101	65.44	1	5	171	119	5	23.80	2-19	0	0	4.17	6	
Lim	2008/09	34	33	3	1235	101	41.16	2	10	177	121	5	24.20	2-19	0	0	4.10	15	
20T	2008/09	11	11	0	185	50	16.81	0	1									4	
DE BRUIN, Steven Thijs (Netherlands) b Amstelveen 5.9.1988 LHB WK																			
FC		1	2	0	40	32	20.00	0	0									5	
DE GROOTH, Tom Nico (Netherlands, Netherlands to England, Netherlands to Ireland, Netherlands to Kenya, Netherlands to United Arab Emirates) b The Hague 15.5.1979 RHB OB																			
FC		2	4	0	34	20	8.50	0	0	3	9	0					18.00	1	
Int		3	3	0	44	22	14.66	0	0									0	
Lim		4	4	0	54	22	13.50	0	0									0	
FC	2004	18	33	1	844	196	26.37	1	5	45	36	1	36.00	1-2	0	0	4.80	6	
Int	2006	22	21	3	387	97	21.50	0	1	6	2	1	2.00	1-2	0	0	2.00	6	
Lim	2005	42	38	4	601	97	17.67	0	2	42	34	3	11.33	2-32	0	0	4.85	8	
I20T	2008	7	5	1	96	49	24.00	0	0									3	
20T	2008	8	6	1	96	49	19.20	0	0									3	
DIEPEVEEN, Wilfred Patrick (Netherlands, Netherlands to England, Netherlands to Ireland) b Utrecht 18.6.1985 RHB LB																			
FC		2	4	1	118	72*	39.33	0	1									0	
FC	2010	3	6	1	171	72*	34.20	0	1									2	
Lim	2010	2	2	1	37	23	37.00	0	0									0	
DIGHTON, Michael Gray (Tasmania, Netherlands to England, Netherlands) b Toowoomba, Queensland, Australia 24.4.1976 RHB RM																			
Lim		6	6	0	140	85	23.33	0	1	162	168	5	33.60	2-23	0	0	6.22	0	
FC	1997/98	71	130	6	4208	182*	33.93	8	21	570	322	6	53.66	2-47	0	0	3.38	50	
Lim	1997/98	99	98	3	3190	146*	33.57	4	23	522	462	15	30.80	2-23	0	0	5.31	34	1
20T	2006/07	22	22	3	455	111	23.94	1	0	96	121	9	13.44	6-25	0	1	7.56	6	

Cmp	Debut	M	I	NO	Runs	HS	Avge	100	50	Balls	Runs	Wkts	Avge	BB	5i	10m	RpO	ct	st
GRUIJTERS, Timothy George Johannus (Netherlands to Kenya) b The Hague 28.8.1991 RHB RM																			
Int	2009/10	2	2	0	35	29	17.50	0	0	42	34	0					4.85	1	
Lim	2009/10	2	2	0	35	29	17.50	0	0	42	34	0					4.85	1	
HEGGELMAN, Thomas Josephus (Netherlands, Netherlands to Ireland) b Schiedam 16.1.1987 RHB RM																			
Lim		2	1	0	3	3	3.00	0	0									0	
FC	2010	1	2	0	46	30	23.00	0	0	72	54	0					4.50	0	
Int	2010	2	2	0	3	2	1.50	0	0									0	
Lim	2010	4	3	0	6	3	2.00	0	0									0	
JONKMAN, Mark Benjamin Sebastiaan (Netherlands, Netherlands to England, Netherlands to Kenya, Netherlands to Scotland, Netherlands to United Arab Emirates) b The Hague 20.3.1986 RHB RMF																			
FC		1	2	0	13	9	6.50	0	0	228	83	7	11.85	5-21	1	0	2.18	0	
Int		6	3	2	18	16	18.00	0	0	323	234	10	23.40	3-28	0	0	4.34	1	
Lim		8	4	3	26	16	26.00	0	0	407	320	13	24.61	3-28	0	0	4.71	1	
FC	2006/07	6	10	3	144	43*	20.57	0	0	858	419	15	27.93	5-21	1	0	2.93	3	
Int	2006/07	16	9	4	59	16	11.80	0	0	719	565	24	23.54	3-24	0	0	4.71	1	
Lim	2006	24	14	6	95	16	11.87	0	0	1091	898	37	24.27	3-24	0	0	4.93	3	
I20T	2009/10	3	1	0	1	1	1.00	0	0	48	47	4	11.75	2-21	0	0	5.87	2	
20T	2009/10	3	1	0	1	1	1.00	0	0	48	47	4	11.75	2-21	0	0	5.87	2	
JONKMAN, Maurits Maarten Alexander (Netherlands, Netherlands to Ireland) b The Hague 20.3.1986 RHB RM																			
FC		1	2	0	13	9	6.50	0	0	150	101	3	33.66	2-63	0	0	4.04	0	
Lim		4	4	1	35	25*	11.66	0	0	124	85	4	21.25	3-18	0	0	4.11	1	
FC	2007	4	7	1	62	18*	10.33	0	0	420	297	8	37.12	2-63	0	0	4.24	1	
Int	2007	4	2	0	20	13	10.00	0	0	136	114	6	19.00	3-23	0	0	5.02	1	
Lim	2007	8	6	1	55	25*	11.00	0	0	260	199	10	19.90	3-18	0	0	4.59	2	
KERVEZEE, Alexei Nicolaas (Netherlands, Netherlands to Kenya, Netherlands to Scotland, Netherlands to United Arab Emirates, Worcestershire) b Walvis Bay, Namibia 11.9.1989 RHB OB																			
Int		3	3	0	127	92	42.33	0	1	18	26	0					8.66	1	
Lim		3	3	0	127	92	42.33	0	1	18	26	0					8.66	1	
FC	2005	36	62	5	2126	155	37.29	3	11	183	145	2	72.50	1-14	0	0	4.75	21	
Int	2006	30	27	2	664	92	26.56	0	3	24	34	0					8.50	12	
Lim	2006	52	49	3	1436	121*	31.21	2	6	48	73	0					9.12	21	
I20T	2009	6	6	0	135	39	22.50	0	0									4	
20T	2009	23	21	2	323	39	17.00	0	0									10	
KRUGER, Bradley Peter (Netherlands, Netherlands to England, Netherlands to Ireland, Netherlands to Scotland) b Pretoria, Transvaal, South Africa 17.9.1988 RHB RFM																			
Int		2	1	0	15	15	15.00	0	0	97	39	3	13.00	3-21	0	0	2.41	0	
Lim		2	1	0	15	15	15.00	0	0	97	39	3	13.00	3-21	0	0	2.41	0	
Int	2010	4	2	0	24	15	12.00	0	0	163	108	3	36.00	3-21	0	0	3.97	4	
Lim	2010	8	4	0	29	15	7.25	0	0	268	224	6	37.33	3-21	0	0	5.01	4	
LOOTS, Bernardus Pieters (Netherlands, Netherlands to England, Netherlands to Ireland) b Prieska, South Africa 19.4.1979 RHB RM																			
FC		1	2	0	8	5	4.00	0	0	168	83	3	27.66	2-48	0	0	2.96	0	
Int		2	1	0	1	1	1.00	0	0	96	61	4	15.25	3-16	0	0	3.81	3	
Lim		5	3	2	15	13*	15.00	0	0	186	132	8	16.50	3-16	0	0	4.25	4	
FC	2010	2	4	1	11	5	3.66	0	0	300	169	5	33.80	2-48	0	0	3.38	0	
Int	2010	3	2	1	10	9*	10.00	0	0	114	80	4	20.00	3-16	0	0	4.21	3	
Lim	2010	7	5	3	30	13*	15.00	0	0	252	181	8	22.62	3-16	0	0	4.31	4	
MOHAMMAD KASHIF Hussain (Netherlands, Netherlands to England, Netherlands to Ireland, Netherlands to United Arab Emirates) b Khanewal, Punjab, Pakistan 3.12.1984 RHB SLA																			
Int		3	1	0	0	0	0.00	0	0	144	127	1	127.00	1-52	0	0	5.29	1	
Lim		5	2	0	1	1	0.50	0	0	222	202	3	67.33	1-35	0	0	5.45	3	
FC	2005/06	6	9	4	59	24*	11.80	0	0	919	502	16	31.37	5-53	1	0	3.27	3	
Int	2006	11	3	0	1	1	0.33	0	0	450	410	9	45.55	3-42	0	0	5.46	2	
Lim	2006	19	7	0	16	9	2.28	0	0	774	747	16	46.68	3-42	0	0	5.79	5	
I20T	2009/10	3	1	1	0	0*		0	0	42	55	4	13.75	2-28	0	0	7.85	1	
20T	2009/10	4	1	1	0	0*		0	0	66	81	4	20.25	2-28	0	0	7.36	1	
MUDASSAR BUKHARI (Netherlands, Netherlands to England, Netherlands to Ireland, Netherlands to Kenya, Netherlands to Scotland, Netherlands to United Arab Emirates) b Gujrat, Punjab, Pakistan 26.12.1983 RHB RFM																			
Int		6	4	1	34	12	11.33	0	0	306	199	8	24.87	3-31	0	0	3.90	1	
Lim		13	11	2	141	69*	15.66	0	1	516	390	13	30.00	3-31	0	0	4.53	3	
FC	2007	8	15	2	309	66*	23.76	0	2	1216	595	18	33.05	4-85	0	0	2.93	1	
Int	2007	27	19	2	283	71	16.64	0	2	1158	818	33	24.78	3-17	0	0	4.23	5	
Lim	2006	50	37	4	610	84	18.48	0	4	2071	1627	53	30.69	3-17	0	0	4.71	10	
I20T	2008	8	5	2	14	9	4.66	0	0	154	180	6	30.00	4-33	1	0	7.01	1	
20T	2008	9	6	2	14	9	3.50	0	0	177	218	7	31.14	4-33	1	0	7.39	1	
NIJMAN, Ruud Gerard (Netherlands, Netherlands to Kenya) b 15.6.1982 RHB RMF																			
FC		2	3	0	25	23	8.33	0	0	210	98	1	98.00	1-43	0	0	2.80	0	
Lim		1	1	0	23	23	23.00	0	0	36	33	1	33.00	1-33	0	0	5.50	0	
FC	2009/10	3	4	0	30	23	7.50	0	0	288	156	1	156.00	1-43	0	0	3.25	0	
Int	2008/09	1								49	31	3	10.33	3-31	0	0	3.79	0	
Lim	2008/09	3	2	0	25	23	12.50	0	0	133	113	4	28.25	3-31	0	0	5.09	1	

Cmp	Debut	M	I	NO	Runs	HS	Avge	100	50	Balls	Runs	Wkts	Avge	BB	5i	10m	RpO	ct	st
SCHIFERLI, Edgar (Netherlands to United Arab Emirates) b The Hague 17.5.1976 RHB RMF																			
FC	2004	12	17	4	257	69	19.76	0	1	2142	1121	41	27.34	5-48	2	0	3.14	6	
Int	2002/03	27	19	6	153	41	11.76	0	0	1210	934	31	30.12	4-23	3	0	4.63	3	
Lim	2001	54	38	9	472	89*	16.27	0	1	2670	1995	82	24.32	5-20	6	2	4.48	11	
I20T	2008	7	3	1	7	5*	3.50	0	0	138	146	6	24.33	3-23	0	0	6.34	5	
20T	2008	7	3	1	7	5*	3.50	0	0	138	146	6	24.33	3-23	0	0	6.34	5	
SEELAAR, Pieter Marinus (Netherlands, Netherlands to England, Netherlands to Ireland, Netherlands to Kenya, Netherlands to United Arab Emirates) b Schiedam 2.7.1987 RHB SLA																			
FC		2	4	3	156	81*	156.00	0	1	292	190	3	63.33	3-67	0	0	3.90	0	
Int		4	1	1	2	2*		0	0	156	119	2	59.50	1-1	0	0	4.57	2	
Lim		11	6	3	24	12	8.00	0	0	402	319	10	31.90	3-31	0	0	4.76	6	
FC	2006/07	12	21	5	264	81*	16.50	0	1	1791	1053	26	40.50	5-57	1	0	3.52	3	
Int	2006	21	11	7	85	34*	21.25	0	0	866	689	21	32.80	3-22	0	0	4.77	6	
Lim	2005	45	25	12	155	34*	11.92	0	0	1979	1566	43	36.41	3-22	0	0	4.74	12	
I20T	2008	9	3	0	2	1	0.66	0	0	210	215	13	16.53	4-19	1	0	6.14	5	
20T	2008	10	4	1	2	1	0.66	0	0	234	251	13	19.30	4-19	1	0	6.43	5	
STATHAM, Nickholas Alexander (Netherlands, Netherlands to England, Netherlands to Ireland, Netherlands to Kenya) b Dahek 15.3.1975 RHB OB																			
FC		1	2	0	3	3	1.50	0	0									1	
Lim		5	5	0	30	11	6.00	0	0									2	
FC	2007	8	16	1	258	62*	17.20	0	2	6	1	0					1.00	4	
Int	2002/03	3	3	0	7	7	2.33	0	0									0	
Lim	1999	21	17	0	117	37	6.88	0	0	60	72	1	72.00	1-60	0	0	7.20	5	
SZWARCZYNSKI, Eric Stefan (Netherlands, Netherlands to England, Netherlands to Ireland, Netherlands to Kenya, Netherlands to Scotland, Netherlands to United Arab Emirates) b Vanderbijlpark, Transvaal, South Africa 13.2.1983 RHB RM																			
FC		2	4	0	144	72	36.00	0	2	54	46	1	46.00	1-37	0	0	5.11	1	
Int		7	7	1	135	84*	22.50	0	1									0	
Lim		14	14	1	250	84*	19.23	0	2	12	10	0					5.00	1	
FC	2005	13	22	0	450	93	20.45	0	3	136	98	3	32.66	2-24	0	0	4.32	5	
Int	2006	30	29	2	748	84*	27.70	0	7									5	
Lim	2006	52	50	2	1097	84*	22.85	0	10	36	32	0					5.33	15	
I20T	2008	8	7	0	185	45	26.42	0	0									2	
20T	2008	9	8	0	191	45	23.87	0	0									2	
TEN DOESCHATE, Ryan Neil (Essex, Netherlands, Netherlands to Kenya, Netherlands to United Arab Emirates) b Port Elizabeth, Cape Province, South Africa 30.6.1980 RHB RMF																			
Int		1	1	0	90	90	90.00	0	1	60	38	2	19.00	2-38	0	0	3.80	0	
Lim		2	2	0	92	90	46.00	0	1	96	80	3	26.66	2-38	0	0	5.00	0	
FC	2003	81	118	15	4950	259*	48.05	16	17	7916	5258	158	33.27	6-20	7	0	3.98	44	
Int	2006	27	26	8	1234	109*	68.55	3	8	1268	1005	48	20.93	4-31	3	0	4.75	11	
Lim	2003	126	102	31	3328	134*	46.87	5	19	3632	3319	125	26.55	5-50	6	1	5.48	39	
I20T	2008	9	9	4	214	56	42.80	0	1	204	241	12	20.08	3-23	0	0	7.08	3	
20T	2003	64	55	16	1130	102	28.97	1	2	654	796	36	22.11	4-24	1	0	7.30	20	
VAN BUNGE, Daan Lodewijk Samuel (Netherlands to United Arab Emirates) b Voorburg 19.10.1982 RHB LB																			
FC	2004	10	17	2	351	98*	23.40	0	2	891	563	20	28.15	4-163	0	0	3.79	13	
Int	2002/03	32	27	1	564	80	21.69	0	3	319	321	11	29.18	3-16	0	0	6.03	11	
Lim	2002/03	60	53	5	1341	137	27.93	1	7	540	541	17	31.82	3-16	0	0	6.01	24	
I20T	2008	10	9	2	60	24	8.57	0	0	12	14	1	14.00	1-14	0	0	7.00	4	
20T	2004	14	12	2	144	76	14.40	0	1	18	21	1	21.00	1-14	0	0	7.00	4	
WESTDIJK, Berend Arnold (Netherlands, Netherlands to England) b The Hague 5.3.1985 RHB RMF																			
FC		2	4	0	22	17	5.50	0	0	294	164	6	27.33	4-46	0	0	3.34	1	
Lim		1								12	27	0					13.50	0	
FC	2009	3	5	0	22	17	4.40	0	0	456	291	10	29.10	4-46	0	0	3.82	3	
Lim	2010	3	1	1	3	3*		0	0	48	74	1	74.00	1-31	0	0	9.25	0	
ZUIDERENT, Bastiaan (Netherlands, Netherlands to England, Netherlands to Ireland, Netherlands to Kenya, Netherlands to Scotland, Netherlands to United Arab Emirates) b Utrecht 3.3.1977 RHB RM																			
Int		7	7	2	160	55*	32.00	0	1									2	
Lim		14	14	2	349	56	29.08	0	2									2	
FC	2001	31	50	4	1328	149*	28.86	2	9									23	
Int	1995/96	53	52	10	1080	77*	25.71	0	8									26	
Lim	1995/96	134	129	19	3255	119	29.59	4	19	12	15	0					7.50	51	
I20T	2009	6	6	1	108	43*	21.60	0	0									2	
20T	2003	12	12	1	242	43*	22.00	0	0									4	

AFGHANISTAN TO NETHERLANDS 2010

Cmp	Debut	M	I	NO	Runs	HS	Avge	100	50	Balls	Runs	Wkts	Avge	BB	5i	10m	RpO	ct	st
AFTAB ALAM																			
Int		1								54	52	1	52.00	1-52	0	0	5.77	0	
Lim		1								54	52	1	52.00	1-52	0	0	5.77	0	

Cmp	Debut	M	I	NO	Runs	HS	Avge	100	50	Balls	Runs	Wkts	Avge	BB	5i	10m	RpO	ct	st
ASGHAR STANIKZAI																			
Int		6	6	1	188	64	37.60	0	1	60	22	1	22.00	1-22	0	0	2.20	2	
Lim		6	6	1	188	64	37.60	0	1	60	22	1	22.00	1-22	0	0	2.20	2	
DAWLAT AHMADZAI																			
Int		1								60	53	0					5.30	0	
Lim		1								60	53	0					5.30	0	
HAMID HASSAN																			
Int		6	3	0	32	17	10.66	0	0	318	230	10	23.00	3-32	0	0	4.34	1	
Lim		6	3	0	32	17	10.66	0	0	318	230	10	23.00	3-32	0	0	4.34	1	
JAVED AHMADI																			
Int		2	2	0	6	3	3.00	0	0									1	
Lim		2	2	0	6	3	3.00	0	0									1	
KARIM SADIQ																			
Int		6	5	1	74	26	18.50	0	0	30	19	0					3.80	3	
Lim		6	5	1	74	26	18.50	0	0	30	19	0					3.80	3	
KHALIQ DAD																			
Int		5	3	1	40	20	20.00	0	0	216	125	7	17.85	3-30	0	0	3.47	0	
Lim		5	3	1	40	20	20.00	0	0	216	125	7	17.85	3-30	0	0	3.47	0	
MIRWAIS ASHRAF																			
Int		1								36	20	2	10.00	2-20	0	0	3.33	0	
Lim		1								36	20	2	10.00	2-20	0	0	3.33	0	
MOHAMMAD NABI																			
Int		6	5	2	95	47	31.66	0	0	312	237	4	59.25	2-31	0	0	4.55	4	
Lim		6	5	2	95	47	31.66	0	0	312	237	4	59.25	2-31	0	0	4.55	4	
MOHAMMAD SHAHZAD																			
Int		6	6	0	250	82	41.66	0	3									6	2
Lim		6	6	0	250	82	41.66	0	3									6	2
NAWROZ MANGAL																			
Int		6	6	3	205	70*	68.33	0	2	156	92	2	46.00	2-22	0	0	3.53	3	
Lim		6	6	3	205	70*	68.33	0	2	156	92	2	46.00	2-22	0	0	3.53	3	
NOOR ALI ZADRAN																			
Int		5	5	0	101	50	20.20	0	1									3	
Lim		5	5	0	101	50	20.20	0	1									3	
SAMIULLAH SHENWARI																			
Int		6	3	0	97	82	32.33	0	1	330	234	8	29.25	3-43	0	0	4.25	0	
Lim		6	3	0	97	82	32.33	0	1	330	234	8	29.25	3-43	0	0	4.25	0	
SHABIR NOORI																			
Int		5	5	0	65	38	13.00	0	0									3	
Lim		5	5	0	65	38	13.00	0	0									3	
SHAPOOR ZADRAN																			
Int		4	3	2	0	0*	0.00	0	0	191	158	7	22.57	2-19	0	0	4.96	0	
Lim		4	3	2	0	0*	0.00	0	0	191	158	7	22.57	2-19	0	0	4.96	0	

CANADA TO NETHERLANDS 2010

Cmp	Debut	M	I	NO	Runs	HS	Avge	100	50	Balls	Runs	Wkts	Avge	BB	5i	10m	RpO	ct	st
BAGAI, A.																			
Int		6	6	1	284	82	56.80	0	3									1	3
Lim		6	6	1	284	82	56.80	0	3									1	3
BAIDWAN, H.S.																			
Int		4	2	1	15	11*	15.00	0	0	228	108	8	13.50	3-24	0	0	2.84	0	
Lim		4	2	1	15	11*	15.00	0	0	228	108	8	13.50	3-24	0	0	2.84	0	
BARNETT, G.E.F.																			
Int		6	6	0	123	34	20.50	0	0									2	
Lim		6	6	0	123	34	20.50	0	0									2	
BASTIAMPILLAI, T.C.																			
Int		3	3	0	26	16	8.66	0	0									0	
Lim		3	3	0	26	16	8.66	0	0									0	
DESAI, P.A.																			
Int		6	3	3	3	2*		0	0	306	202	6	33.66	3-35	0	0	3.96	1	
Lim		6	3	3	3	2*		0	0	306	202	6	33.66	3-35	0	0	3.96	1	
DHANIRAM, S.																			
Int		3	3	0	30	16	10.00	0	0	108	80	0					4.44	0	
Lim		3	3	0	30	16	10.00	0	0	108	80	0					4.44	0	
HANSRA, A.S.																			
Int		5	4	2	52	30*	26.00	0	0	96	50	1	50.00	1-23	0	0	3.12	1	
Lim		5	4	2	52	30*	26.00	0	0	96	50	1	50.00	1-23	0	0	3.12	1	
HOOPER, C.K.																			
Int		4	4	2	45	27	22.50	0	0	120	115	2	57.50	1-17	0	0	5.75	1	
Lim		4	4	2	45	27	22.50	0	0	120	115	2	57.50	1-17	0	0	5.75	1	

Cmp Debut	M	I	NO	Runs	HS	Avge	100	50	Balls	Runs	Wkts	Avge	BB	5i	10m	RpO	ct	st
KHURRAM CHAUHAN																		
Int	2	1	0	2	2	2.00	0	0	118	109	1	109.00	1-57	0	0	5.54	0	
Lim	2	1	0	2	2	2.00	0	0	118	109	1	109.00	1-57	0	0	5.54	0	
KUMAR, N.R.																		
Int	3	3	0	57	38	19.00	0	0									2	
Lim	3	3	0	57	38	19.00	0	0									2	
PATEL, H.																		
Int	6	6	0	120	43	20.00	0	0	198	130	3	43.33	1-18	0	0	3.93	3	
Lim	6	6	0	120	43	20.00	0	0	198	130	3	43.33	1-18	0	0	3.93	3	
RIZWAN CHEEMA																		
Int	6	5	0	18	6	3.60	0	0	246	169	6	28.16	3-39	0	0	4.12	0	
Lim	6	5	0	18	6	3.60	0	0	246	169	6	28.16	3-39	0	0	4.12	0	
SURKARI, Z.E.																		
Int	6	6	1	100	49	20.00	0	0									0	
Lim	6	6	1	100	49	20.00	0	0									0	
UMAR BHATTI																		
Int	6	5	1	85	32	21.25	0	0	235	167	4	41.75	2-29	0	0	4.26	0	
Lim	6	5	1	85	32	21.25	0	0	235	167	4	41.75	2-29	0	0	4.26	0	

DERBYSHIRE TO NETHERLANDS 2010

Cmp Debut	M	I	NO	Runs	HS	Avge	100	50	Balls	Runs	Wkts	Avge	BB	5i	10m	RpO	ct	st
DURSTON, W.J.																		
Lim	1	1	1	12	12*		0	0									0	
FOOTITT, M.H.A.																		
Lim	1								48	27	3	9.00	3-27	0	0	3.37	0	
GODDARD, L.J.																		
Lim	1																0	
GROENEWALD, T.D.																		
Lim	1								36	42	2	21.00	2-42	0	0	7.00	0	
HUGHES, C.F.																		
Lim	1	1	0	72	72	72.00	0	1									1	
JONES, P.S.																		
Lim	1								42	27	3	9.00	3-27	0	0	3.85	0	
MADSEN, W.L.																		
Lim	1	1	1	2	2*		0	0									1	
PARK, G.T.																		
Lim	1								48	28	0					3.50	0	
PETERSON, R.J.																		
Lim	1								48	31	0					3.87	1	
ROGERS, C.J.L.																		
Lim	1	1	0	56	56	56.00	0	1									1	
SMITH, G.M.																		
Lim	1	1	0	12	12	12.00	0	0	18	16	0					5.33	1	

ESSEX TO NETHERLANDS 2010

Cmp Debut	M	I	NO	Runs	HS	Avge	100	50	Balls	Runs	Wkts	Avge	BB	5i	10m	RpO	ct	st
FLOWER, G.W.																		
Lim	1	1	0	16	16	16.00	0	0	36	27	0					4.50	0	
FOSTER, J.S.																		
Lim	1	1	0	24	24	24.00	0	0									1	1
GODLEMAN, B.A.																		
Lim	1	1	0	16	16	16.00	0	0									0	
MASTERS, D.D.																		
Lim	1	1	1	0	0*		0	0	42	31	0					4.42	0	
MICKLEBURGH, J.C.																		
Lim	1	1	0	46	46	46.00	0	0									0	
NAPIER, G.R.																		
Lim	1	1	0	2	2	2.00	0	0	48	40	2	20.00	2-40	0	0	5.00	0	
PETTINI, M.L.																		
Lim	1	1	0	28	28	28.00	0	0									0	
PHILLIPS, T.J.																		
Lim	1	1	1	3	3*		0	0	36	32	0					5.33	1	
TEN DOESCHATE, R.N.																		
Lim	1	1	0	2	2	2.00	0	0	36	42	1	42.00	1-42	0	0	7.00	0	
WALKER, M.J.																		
Lim	1	1	0	71	71	71.00	0	1									0	
WRIGHT, C.J.C.																		
Lim	1								42	39	1	39.00	1-39	0	0	5.57	0	

GLOUCESTERSHIRE TO NETHERLANDS 2010

Cmp	Debut	M	I	NO	Runs	HS	Avge	100	50	Balls	Runs	Wkts	Avge	BB	5i	10m	RpO	ct	st
DENT, C.D.J.																			
Lim		1								12	17	1	17.00	1-17	0	0	8.50	0	
FRANKLIN, J.E.C.																			
Lim		1	1	1	45	45*		0	0	6	12	0					12.00	1	
GIDMAN, A.P.R.																			
Lim		1	1	0	14	14	14.00	0	0									0	
KIRBY, S.P.																			
Lim		1								6	12	0					12.00	0	
LEWIS, J.																			
Lim		1								12	3	3	1.00	3-3	0	0	1.50	0	
MARSHALL, H.J.H.																			
Lim		1																0	
PAYNE, D.A.																			
Lim		1								6	5	1	5.00	1-5	0	0	5.00	1	
PORTERFIELD, W.T.S.																			
Lim		1	1	0	46	46	46.00	0	0									3	
SNELL, S.D.																			
Lim		1	1	1	5	5*		0	0									0	
TAYLOR, C.G.																			
Lim		1	1	0	6	6	6.00	0	0	6	10	1	10.00	1-10	0	0	10.00	1	
YOUNG, E.G.C.																			
Lim		1								12	6	0					3.00	0	

IRELAND TO NETHERLANDS 2010

Cmp	Debut	M	I	NO	Runs	HS	Avge	100	50	Balls	Runs	Wkts	Avge	BB	5i	10m	RpO	ct	st
BALBIRNIE, A.																			
Int		4	4	0	29	17	7.25	0	0									1	
Lim		4	4	0	29	17	7.25	0	0									1	
CUSACK, A.R.																			
Int		5	4	1	61	59*	20.33	0	1	222	127	10	12.70	5-20	0	1	3.43	3	
Lim		5	4	1	61	59*	20.33	0	1	222	127	10	12.70	5-20	0	1	3.43	3	
DOCKRELL, G.H.																			
Int		6	1	0	0	0	0.00	0	0	312	186	10	18.60	4-35	1	0	3.57	4	
Lim		6	1	0	0	0	0.00	0	0	312	186	10	18.60	4-35	1	0	3.57	4	
HALL, J.D.																			
Int		3	3	0	28	15	9.33	0	0									0	
Lim		3	3	0	28	15	9.33	0	0									0	
JOHNSTON, D.T.																			
Int		5	1	1	42	42*		0	0	276	126	8	15.75	2-18	0	0	2.73	0	
Lim		5	1	1	42	42*		0	0	276	126	8	15.75	2-18	0	0	2.73	0	
JONES, N.G.																			
Int		6	2	1	27	25*	27.00	0	0	161	83	5	16.60	2-19	0	0	3.09	2	
Lim		6	2	1	27	25*	27.00	0	0	161	83	5	16.60	2-19	0	0	3.09	2	
McCANN, R.D.																			
Int		6	3	0	24	18	8.00	0	0									7	
Lim		6	3	0	24	18	8.00	0	0									7	
MOONEY, J.F.																			
Int		6	5	3	132	54	66.00	0	1	126	88	4	22.00	2-26	0	0	4.19	2	
Lim		6	5	3	132	54	66.00	0	1	126	88	4	22.00	2-26	0	0	4.19	2	
O'BRIEN, K.J.																			
Int		6	6	3	226	98*	75.33	0	1	276	182	8	22.75	2-21	0	0	3.95	4	
Lim		6	6	3	226	98*	75.33	0	1	276	182	8	22.75	2-21	0	0	3.95	4	
POYNTER, A.D.																			
Int		6	5	1	79	78	19.75	0	1									4	
Lim		6	5	1	79	78	19.75	0	1									4	
STIRLING, P.R.																			
Int		6	6	0	230	87	38.33	0	1	131	88	5	17.60	4-11	1	0	4.03	5	
Lim		6	6	0	230	87	38.33	0	1	131	88	5	17.60	4-11	1	0	4.03	5	
VAN DER MERWE, A.																			
Int		1	1	0	0	0	0.00	0	0	36	20	0					3.33	1	
Lim		1	1	0	0	0	0.00	0	0	36	20	0					3.33	1	
WHITE, A.R.																			
Int		6	5	0	135	79	27.00	0	1	126	78	4	19.50	2-28	0	0	3.71	2	
Lim		6	5	0	135	79	27.00	0	1	126	78	4	19.50	2-28	0	0	3.71	2	

KENYA TO NETHERLANDS 2010

Cmp Debut	M	I	NO	Runs	HS	Avge	100	50	Balls	Runs	Wkts	Avge	BB	5i	10m	RpO	ct	st
KAMANDE, J.K.																		
Int	6	6	1	87	34	17.40	0	0	230	151	6	25.16	4-36	1	0	3.93	2	
Lim	6	6	1	87	34	17.40	0	0	230	151	6	25.16	4-36	1	0	3.93	2	
LUSENO, A.S.																		
Int	2	2	2	16	16*		0	0	66	53	3	17.66	2-23	0	0	4.81	0	
Lim	2	2	2	16	16*		0	0	66	53	3	17.66	2-23	0	0	4.81	0	
NGOCHE, J.O.																		
Int	6	5	1	22	21*	5.50	0	0	330	167	8	20.87	3-18	0	0	3.03	1	
Lim	6	5	1	22	21*	5.50	0	0	330	167	8	20.87	3-18	0	0	3.03	1	
NGOCHE, S.O.																		
Int	3	3	1	15	7*	7.50	0	0	138	78	2	39.00	2-28	0	0	3.39	0	
Lim	3	3	1	15	7*	7.50	0	0	138	78	2	39.00	2-28	0	0	3.39	0	
OBANDA, A.A.																		
Int	6	6	0	127	40	21.16	0	0									2	
Lim	6	6	0	127	40	21.16	0	0									2	
OBUYA, C.O.																		
Int	6	6	0	177	60	29.50	0	1									4	
Lim	6	6	0	177	60	29.50	0	1									4	
ODHIAMBO, N.M.																		
Int	3	2	0	33	29	16.50	0	0	126	97	3	32.33	1-22	0	0	4.61	1	
Lim	3	2	0	33	29	16.50	0	0	126	97	3	32.33	1-22	0	0	4.61	1	
ODHIAMBO, N.N.																		
Int	5	5	0	23	8	4.60	0	0	244	216	5	43.20	3-53	0	0	5.31	2	
Lim	5	5	0	23	8	4.60	0	0	244	216	5	43.20	3-53	0	0	5.31	2	
ODOYO, T.M.																		
Int	6	6	1	140	52*	28.00	0	1	284	172	9	19.11	3-43	0	0	3.63	1	
Lim	6	6	1	140	52*	28.00	0	1	284	172	9	19.11	3-43	0	0	3.63	1	
OTIENO, E.																		
Int	2	2	0	11	11	5.50	0	0	66	51	0					4.63	0	
Lim	2	2	0	11	11	5.50	0	0	66	51	0					4.63	0	
OTIENO, F.N.																		
Int	4	4	0	16	8	4.00	0	0	6	2	0					2.00	2	
Lim	4	4	0	16	8	4.00	0	0	6	2	0					2.00	2	
OUMA, M.A.																		
Int	5	5	0	109	40	21.80	0	0									6	
Lim	5	5	0	109	40	21.80	0	0									6	
PATEL, R.R.																		
Int	6	6	0	81	34	13.50	0	0									2	
Lim	6	6	0	81	34	13.50	0	0									2	
VARAIYA, H.A.																		
Int	3	3	1	33	23	16.50	0	0	156	117	1	117.00	1-20	0	0	4.50	0	
Lim	3	3	1	33	23	16.50	0	0	156	117	1	117.00	1-20	0	0	4.50	0	
WESONGA, D.S.																		
Int	3	3	0	59	33	19.66	0	0									1	
Lim	3	3	0	59	33	19.66	0	0									1	

MIDDLESEX TO NETHERLANDS 2010

Cmp Debut	M	I	NO	Runs	HS	Avge	100	50	Balls	Runs	Wkts	Avge	BB	5i	10m	RpO	ct	st
BERG, G.K.																		
Lim	1	1	0	21	21	21.00	0	0	30	29	0					5.80	1	
COLLINS, P.T.																		
Lim	1								40	25	4	6.25	4-25	1	0	3.75	1	
DAVEY, J.H.																		
Lim	1	1	1	2	2*		0	0									0	
DEXTER, N.J.																		
Lim	1	1	0	40	40	40.00	0	0	6	12	0					12.00	1	
MALAN, D.J.																		
Lim	1	1	0	23	23	23.00	0	0	18	15	0					5.00	0	
MURTAGH, T.J.																		
Lim	1								42	39	3	13.00	3-39	0	0	5.57	0	
NEWMAN, S.A.																		
Lim	1	1	0	122	122	122.00	1	0									1	
SHAH, O.A.																		
Lim	1	1	0	8	8	8.00	0	0									0	
SIMPSON, J.A.																		
Lim	1	1	1	12	12*		0	0									0	

Cmp	Debut	M	I	NO	Runs	HS	Avge	100	50	Balls	Runs	Wkts	Avge	BB	5i	10m	RpO	ct	st
SMITH, T.M.J.																			
Lim		1								42	36	2	18.00	2-36	0	0	5.14	1	
UDAL, S.D.																			
Lim		1								42	36	1	36.00	1-36	0	0	5.14	1	

NORTHAMPTONSHIRE TO NETHERLANDS 2010

Cmp	Debut	M	I	NO	Runs	HS	Avge	100	50	Balls	Runs	Wkts	Avge	BB	5i	10m	RpO	ct	st
BOJE, N.																			
Lim		1	1	1	24	24*		0	0	30	25	1	25.00	1-25	0	0	5.00	0	
BRETT, T.																			
Lim		1								24	24	1	24.00	1-24	0	0	6.00	1	
CHIGUMBURA, E.																			
Lim		1	1	0	5	5	5.00	0	0	24	22	2	11.00	2-22	0	0	5.50	0	
DAGGETT, L.M.																			
Lim		1								24	11	2	5.50	2-11	0	0	2.75	0	
HALL, A.J.																			
Lim		1	1	1	15	15*		0	0	30	22	2	11.00	2-22	0	0	4.40	0	
LOYE, M.B.																			
Lim		1	1	0	15	15	15.00	0	0									0	
MURPHY, D.																			
Lim		1																1	1
NEWTON, R.I.																			
Lim		1	1	0	19	19	19.00	0	0									0	
PETERS, S.D.																			
Lim		1																0	
SALES, D.J.G.																			
Lim		1	1	0	28	28	28.00	0	0									0	
WAKELY, A.G.																			
Lim		1	1	0	35	35	35.00	0	0									0	

SCOTLAND TO NETHERLANDS 2010

Cmp	Debut	M	I	NO	Runs	HS	Avge	100	50	Balls	Runs	Wkts	Avge	BB	5i	10m	RpO	ct	st
BERRINGTON, R.D.																			
FC		1	2	0	83	82	41.50	0	1	156	91	3	30.33	3-48	0	0	3.50	1	
Int		7	7	0	201	84	28.71	0	2	286	177	8	22.12	2-14	0	0	3.71	4	
Lim		7	7	0	201	84	28.71	0	2	286	177	8	22.12	2-14	0	0	3.71	4	
DAVEY, J.H.																			
Int		1	1	0	24	24	24.00	0	0	42	27	1	27.00	1-27	0	0	3.85	0	
Lim		1	1	0	24	24	24.00	0	0	42	27	1	27.00	1-27	0	0	3.85	0	
DRUMMOND, G.D.																			
FC		1	1	0	4	4	4.00	0	0	204	63	3	21.00	2-20	0	0	1.85	0	
Int		7	5	1	72	33*	18.00	0	0	360	192	9	21.33	2-23	0	0	3.20	1	
Lim		7	5	1	72	33*	18.00	0	0	360	192	9	21.33	2-23	0	0	3.20	1	
GOUDIE, G.																			
FC		1	1	1	44	44*		0	0	126	46	0					2.19	0	
Int		6	5	2	8	4	2.66	0	0	269	205	9	22.77	3-18	0	0	4.57	1	
Lim		6	5	2	8	4	2.66	0	0	269	205	9	22.77	3-18	0	0	4.57	1	
HAIRS, O.J.																			
Int		5	5	0	68	27	13.60	0	0									0	
Lim		5	5	0	68	27	13.60	0	0									0	
HAQ, R.M.																			
FC		1	2	1	64	34*	64.00	0	0	348	100	3	33.33	3-45	0	0	1.72	1	
Int		1								60	28	0					2.80	0	
Lim		1								60	28	0					2.80	0	
HUSSAIN, R.O.																			
Int		2	2	0	19	17	9.50	0	0									0	
Lim		2	2	0	19	17	9.50	0	0									0	
IQBAL, M.M.																			
Int		6	6	2	121	63	30.25	0	1	132	109	2	54.50	2-35	0	0	4.95	1	
Lim		6	6	2	121	63	30.25	0	1	132	109	2	54.50	2-35	0	0	4.95	1	
LOCKHART, D.R.																			
FC		1	2	0	5	5	2.50	0	0									1	
Int		7	6	1	82	31*	16.40	0	0									3	
Lim		7	6	1	82	31*	16.40	0	0									3	
LYONS, R.T.																			
Int		7	3	3	3	2*		0	0	264	177	7	25.28	3-21	0	0	4.02	1	
Lim		7	3	3	3	2*		0	0	264	177	7	25.28	3-21	0	0	4.02	1	

Cmp Debut	M	I	NO	Runs	HS	Avge	100	50	Balls	Runs	Wkts	Avge	BB	5i	10m	RpO	ct	st
McCALLUM, N.F.I.																		
FC	1	2	1	85	51	85.00	0	1									1	
Int	7	7	1	191	89*	31.83	0	1									4	
Lim	7	7	1	191	89*	31.83	0	1									4	
MAIDEN, G.I.																		
FC	1	2	0	40	40	20.00	0	0	24	36	0					9.00	3	
Int	3	3	0	66	31	22.00	0	0	48	38	0					4.75	0	
Lim	3	3	0	66	31	22.00	0	0	48	38	0					4.75	0	
MOMMSEN, P.L.																		
FC	1	2	0	20	18	10.00	0	0									1	
Int	6	6	0	137	80	22.83	0	1	12	19	1	19.00	1-19	0	0	9.50	2	
Lim	6	6	0	137	80	22.83	0	1	12	19	1	19.00	1-19	0	0	9.50	2	
PARKER, M.A.																		
FC	1	2	0	70	65	35.00	0	1	260	119	7	17.00	4-63	0	0	2.74	0	
Int	7	6	2	40	22	10.00	0	0	330	256	9	28.44	4-33	1	0	4.65	2	
Lim	7	6	2	40	22	10.00	0	0	330	256	9	28.44	4-33	1	0	4.65	2	
SHEIKH, M.Q.																		
FC	1	2	0	16	15	8.00	0	0									1	
Int	1	1	0	14	14	14.00	0	0									1	
Lim	1	1	0	14	14	14.00	0	0									1	
SMITH, S.J.S.																		
FC	1	1	0	7	7	7.00	0	0									0	
WATTS, D.F.																		
Int	4	4	0	202	98	50.50	0	2									1	
Lim	4	4	0	202	98	50.50	0	2									1	

YORKSHIRE TO NETHERLANDS 2010

Cmp Debut	M	I	NO	Runs	HS	Avge	100	50	Balls	Runs	Wkts	Avge	BB	5i	10m	RpO	ct	st
BAIRSTOW, J.M.																		
Lim	1	1	1	46	46*		0	0									1	
BRESNAN, T.T.																		
Lim	1	1	1	5	5*		0	0	48	45	2	22.50	2-45	0	0	5.62	1	
BROPHY, G.L.																		
Lim	1	1	0	25	25	25.00	0	0									2	
GALE, A.W.																		
Lim	1	1	0	32	32	32.00	0	0									0	
LYTH, A.																		
Lim	1	1	0	23	23	23.00	0	0									0	
McGRATH, A.																		
Lim	1	1	0	9	9	9.00	0	0	6	7	0					7.00	0	
PATTERSON, S.A.																		
Lim	1								48	9	0					1.12	0	
PYRAH, R.M.																		
Lim	1								42	24	4	6.00	4-24	1	0	3.42	0	
RASHID, A.U.																		
Lim	1								48	28	2	14.00	2-28	0	0	3.50	0	
RUDOLPH, J.A.																		
Lim	1	1	0	6	6	6.00	0	0									0	
SHAHZAD, A.																		
Lim	1								48	32	1	32.00	1-32	0	0	4.00	0	

ZIMBABWE XI TO NETHERLANDS 2010

Cmp Debut	M	I	NO	Runs	HS	Avge	100	50	Balls	Runs	Wkts	Avge	BB	5i	10m	RpO	ct	st
CHAKABVA, R.W.																		
FC	1	2	2	88	54*		0	1									1	1
Lim	1	1	0	10	10	10.00	0	0									2	1
CHIBHABHA, C.J.																		
FC	1	2	0	16	15	8.00	0	0									1	
COVENTRY, C.K.																		
FC	1	2	0	26	17	13.00	0	0									1	
Lim	1	1	0	31	31	31.00	0	0									0	
ERVINE, C.R.																		
FC	1	2	1	204	145	204.00	1	1									1	
Lim	1	1	0	10	10	10.00	0	0	6	7	0					7.00	1	
MARUMA, T.																		
FC	1	2	0	6	4	3.00	0	0	138	73	5	14.60	3-44	0	0	3.17	0	
MASAKADZA, S.W.																		
FC	1	1	0	0	0	0.00	0	0	216	81	1	81.00	1-52	0	0	2.25	0	
Lim	1	1	0	14	14	14.00	0	0	60	41	2	20.50	2-41	0	0	4.10	0	

Cmp Debut	*M*	*I*	*NO*	*Runs*	*HS*	*Avge*	*100*	*50*	*Balls*	*Runs*	*Wkts*	*Avge*	*BB*	*5i*	*10m*	*RpO*	*ct*	*st*
MATSIKENYERI, S.																		
FC	1	2	0	112	68	56.00	0	1	30	24	0					4.80	0	
Lim	1	1	0	22	22	22.00	0	0	30	14	0					2.80	1	
MUSHANGWE, N.																		
FC	1	1	0	11	11	11.00	0	0	257	145	4	36.25	3-47	0	0	3.38	0	
Lim	1	1	0	7	7	7.00	0	0	60	38	0					3.80	0	
MUTIZWA, F.																		
Lim	1	1	0	8	8	8.00	0	0	6	5	0					5.00	0	
RAINSFORD, E.C.																		
FC	1	1	0	20	20	20.00	0	0	246	83	4	20.75	2-37	0	0	2.02	0	
Lim	1	1	1	2	2*		0	0	60	39	3	13.00	3-39	0	0	3.90	0	
SIBANDA, V.																		
FC	1	2	0	88	88	44.00	0	1	6	2	0					2.00	2	
Lim	1	1	0	14	14	14.00	0	0									0	
WALLER, N.																		
FC	1	1	0	0	0	0.00	0	0	126	45	2	22.50	2-16	0	0	2.14	0	
Lim	1	1	0	3	3	3.00	0	0	60	24	2	12.00	2-24	0	0	2.40	0	
WILLIAMS, S.C.																		
Lim	1								18	14	1	14.00	1-14	0	0	4.66	0	

NEW ZEALAND

Plunket Shield winners 2009/10 (first-class): Northern Districts
New Zealand Cricket One-Day Competition winners 2009/10 (limited overs): Northern Districts
HRV Cup 2009/10 (twenty20): Central Districts

2009/10 AND CAREER RECORDS FOR NEW ZEALAND PLAYERS

Cmp	*Debut*	*M*	*I*	*NO*	*Runs*	*HS*	*Avge*	*100*	*50*	*Balls*	*Runs*	*Wkts*	*Avge*	*BB*	*5i*	*10m*	*RpO*	*ct*	*st*
ALDRIDGE, Graeme William (Northern Districts) b Christchurch, Canterbury 15.11.1977 RHB RFM																			
FC		9	10	3	183	52	26.14	0	1	1749	968	42	23.04	6-49	3	1	3.32	4	
Lim		10	6	3	68	27*	22.66	0	0	486	405	11	36.81	3-40	0	0	5.00	0	
20T		1	1	0	2	2	2.00	0	0	12	31	0					15.50	0	
FC	1998/99	79	103	33	1542	75	22.02	0	4	12922	6416	218	29.43	6-49	8	1	2.97	35	
Lim	1998/99	96	50	25	396	36	15.84	0	0	4411	3505	135	25.96	5-34	4	2	4.76	19	
20T	2005/06	17	11	4	68	22	9.71	0	0	332	464	18	25.77	4-19	1	0	8.38	6	
ANDERSON, Corey James (Canterbury) b Christchurch, Canterbury 13.12.1990 LHB LMF																			
FC		4	6	1	135	42*	27.00	0	0	342	167	10	16.70	5-22	1	0	2.93	6	
Lim		2	2	1	73	52*	73.00	0	1	90	61	6	10.16	5-26	0	1	4.06	0	
FC	2006/07	15	26	5	590	88*	28.09	0	2	936	508	13	39.07	5-22	1	0	3.25	10	
Lim	2007/08	12	12	2	191	71	19.10	0	2	90	61	6	10.16	5-26	0	1	4.06	3	
20T	2008/09	7	7	0	76	23	10.85	0	0									2	
ARNEL, Brent John (New Zealand, Northern Districts) b Te Awamutu, Waikato 3.1.1979 RHB RMF																			
Test		2	4	0	10	7	2.50	0	0	444	250	5	50.00	3-77	0	0	3.37	1	
FC		9	12	4	62	32	7.75	0	0	1855	818	34	24.05	6-18	2	0	2.64	2	
Lim		9	3	2	7	6*	7.00	0	0	444	345	8	43.12	2-23	0	0	4.66	0	
20T		10	3	3	5	3*		0	0	215	230	8	28.75	2-23	0	0	6.41	1	
FC	2005/06	34	42	13	164	32	5.65	0	0	6271	2800	111	25.22	6-18	4	1	2.67	8	
Lim	2005/06	37	14	10	54	11*	13.50	0	0	1814	1486	46	32.30	4-26	1	0	4.91	4	
20T	2005/06	27	7	4	7	3*	2.33	0	0	558	672	17	39.52	2-18	0	0	7.22	3	
ASTLE, Todd Duncan (Canterbury) b Palmerston North, Manawatu 24.9.1986 RHB LB																			
FC		5	9	2	169	55*	24.14	0	1	798	458	18	25.44	6-103	3	0	3.44	7	
FC	2005/06	36	65	4	1407	101	23.06	1	7	3731	2154	59	36.50	6-103	3	0	3.46	28	
Lim	2006/07	1	1	0	9	9	9.00	0	0	36	43	0					7.16	0	
20T	2008/09	4	3	3	7	6*		0	0	48	66	2	33.00	2-12	0	0	8.25	3	
AUSTIN-SMELLIE, Joseph (Wellington) b Dunedin, Otago 17.10.1989 RHB WK																			
FC		3	5	1	162	97	40.50	0	1									5	
Lim		1	1	0	10	10	10.00	0	0									2	
BARTLETT, Dean Joseph (Auckland) b Auckland 10.10.1987 RHB RMF																			
FC		2	2	1	12	10*	12.00	0	0	354	207	6	34.50	3-70	0	0	3.50	1	
BASSETT-GRAHAM, Jonathan Rhys McGowan (Auckland) b Auckland 28.11.1989 RHB WK																			
FC		1	2	0	22	15	11.00	0	0									5	
BATES, Michael David (Auckland) b Auckland 11.10.1983 RHB LM																			
FC		10	12	7	119	57	23.80	0	1	2141	1016	37	27.45	6-55	3	0	2.84	2	
Lim		9	6	4	27	14*	13.50	0	0	417	340	14	24.28	4-27	1	0	4.89	3	
20T		11	3	1	1	1	0.50	0	0	240	367	15	24.46	3-24	0	0	9.17	2	
FC	2003/04	17	19	9	191	57	19.10	0	1	2963	1495	52	28.75	6-55	3	0	3.02	3	
Lim	2007/08	13	8	6	52	15*	26.00	0	0	585	503	14	35.92	4-27	1	0	5.15	3	
BEARD, Nicholas Brendan (Otago) b Dunedin, Otago 16.9.1989 LHB SLA																			
FC		10	13	7	143	42	23.83	0	0	2187	1033	27	38.25	6-107	1	0	2.83	2	
Lim		4	2	1	2	2*	2.00	0	0	234	206	3	68.66	1-31	0	0	5.28	0	
20T		5	2	2	11	9*		0	0	105	113	7	16.14	2-16	0	0	6.45	2	
FC	2008/09	12	16	9	180	42	25.71	0	0	2529	1222	28	43.64	6-107	1	0	2.89	3	
BELL, Matthew David (Wellington) b Dunedin, Otago 25.2.1977 RHB OB																			
FC		7	14	0	265	94	18.92	0	1									10	
Lim		5	5	1	111	40*	27.75	0	0									3	
20T		6	4	1	33	25	11.00	0	0									2	
Test	1998/99	18	32	2	729	107	24.30	2	3									19	
FC	1993/94	168	287	18	9811	265	36.47	24	53	31	23	0					4.45	137	
Int	1998/99	7	7	0	133	66	19.00	0	1									1	
Lim	1995/96	161	155	15	3831	124	27.36	4	22	2	4	0					12.00	74	
20T	2005/06	18	12	3	195	46	21.66	0	0									10	
BENNETT, Hamish Kyle (Canterbury) b Timaru, Canterbury 22.2.1987 LHB RMF																			
FC		5	4	1	1	1	0.33	0	0	898	486	18	27.00	4-39	0	0	3.24	1	
Lim		2	1	1	7	7*		0	0	96	119	1	119.00	1-57	0	0	7.43	0	
20T		1								24	36	0					9.00	0	
FC	2005/06	33	33	14	108	27	5.68	0	0	5579	3395	91	37.30	7-50	1	0	3.65	8	

Cmp	Debut	M	I	NO	Runs	HS	Avge	100	50	Balls	Runs	Wkts	Avge	BB	5i	10m	RpO	ct	st
Lim	2005/06	21	5	3	13	7*	6.50	0	0	899	895	24	37.29	6-45	0	1	5.97	0	
20T	2006	5	1	0	0	0	0.00	0	0	84	131	0					9.35	1	
BHUPINDER SINGH (Auckland) b Kurputala, Punjab, India 31.10.1986 RHB OB																			
FC		4	3	1	27	14*	13.50	0	0	1215	571	17	33.58	4-93	0	0	2.82	2	
Lim		7	3	2	1	1	1.00	0	0	361	279	7	39.85	2-36	0	0	4.63	2	
20T		2								24	42	0					10.50	1	
BOAM, Harry Kenneth Perrott (Wellington) b Birmingham, Warwickshire, England 15.10.1990 RHB RM																			
FC		2	4	0	26	13	6.50	0	0	108	60	1	60.00	1-36	0	0	3.33	1	
Lim		2	2	0	60	37	30.00	0	0	42	47	1	47.00	1-26	0	0	6.71	0	
FC	2008/09	6	10	3	142	49*	20.28	0	0	357	175	5	35.00	3-56	0	0	2.94	4	
Lim	2008/09	7	5	1	114	37	28.50	0	0	156	164	2	82.00	1-26	0	0	6.30	3	
20T	2008/09	6	2	1	4	2*	4.00	0	0	36	50	1	50.00	1-32	0	0	8.33	0	
BOND, Shane Edward (Canterbury, New Zealand, Kolkata Knight Riders, New Zealand to South Africa, New Zealand to United Arab Emirates, New Zealand to West Indies) b Christchurch, Canterbury 7.6.1975 RHB RF																			
Test		1	2	0	29	22	14.50	0	0	293	153	8	19.12	5-107	1	0	3.13	2	
FC		2	3	0	56	27	18.66	0	0	533	301	14	21.50	5-107	1	0	3.38	2	
Int		5	5	2	53	19	17.66	0	0	259	189	9	21.00	4-26	1	0	4.37	0	
Lim		9	6	2	55	19	13.75	0	0	463	372	14	26.57	4-26	1	0	4.82	0	
I20T		2	1	1	1	1*		0	0	48	59	3	19.66	2-32	0	0	7.37	0	
20T		2	1	1	1	1*		0	0	48	59	3	19.66	2-32	0	0	7.37	0	
Test	2001/02	18	20	7	168	41*	12.92	0	0	3372	1922	87	22.09	6-51	5	1	3.42	8	
FC	1996/97	60	70	20	830	100	16.60	1	2	10263	5478	225	24.34	7-66	12	1	3.20	24	
Int	2001/02	82	40	22	292	31*	16.22	0	0	4295	3070	147	20.88	6-19	7	4	4.28	15	
Lim	1997/98	135	70	33	498	40	13.45	0	0	6903	5083	214	23.75	6-19	9	5	4.41	18	
I20T	2005/06	20	8	3	21	8*	4.20	0	0	465	543	25	21.72	3-18	0	0	7.00	4	
20T	2005/06	40	14	6	32	8*	4.00	0	0	939	1109	51	21.74	4-19	1	0	7.08	9	
BOPARA, Ravinder Singh (England, England Lions, Essex, Auckland, England to South Africa, England to West Indies, Kings XI Punjab) b Forest Gate, Essex, England 4.5.1985 RHB RM																			
FC		5	9	0	294	90	32.66	0	2	546	369	6	61.50	3-109	0	0	4.05	3	
Lim		9	9	0	496	102	55.11	1	4	417	349	11	31.72	3-34	0	0	5.02	1	
20T		11	10	2	137	55*	17.12	0	1	192	251	12	20.91	3-21	0	0	7.84	5	
Test	2007/08	10	15	0	502	143	33.46	3	0	296	199	1	199.00	1-39	0	0	4.03	5	
FC	2002	103	172	22	6332	229	42.21	17	25	6946	4585	107	42.85	5-75	1	0	3.96	67	
Int	2006/07	54	50	10	1140	60	28.50	0	4	391	331	10	33.10	4-38	1	0	5.07	18	
Lim	2001	164	155	32	4607	201*	37.45	6	24	3303	2943	109	27.00	4-38	3	0	5.34	49	
I20T	2008	11	10	0	191	55	19.10	0	1									4	
20T	2003	91	81	9	1807	105*	25.09	1	10	1108	1431	60	23.85	3-13	0	0	7.74	29	
BOULT, Jonathan James (Northern Districts) b Rotorua, Bay of Plenty 29.11.1985 LHB OB																			
FC		2	2	0	121	76	60.50	0	1	246	182	5	36.40	3-47	0	0	4.43	0	
FC	2008/09	3	4	0	157	76	39.25	0	1	414	260	9	28.88	4-78	0	0	3.76	1	
BOULT, Trent Alexander (Northern Districts) b Rotorua, Bay of Plenty 22.7.1989 RHB LMF																			
FC		3	2	1	5	5	5.00	0	0	486	238	9	26.44	4-15	0	0	2.93	3	
Lim		3	1	0	4	4	4.00	0	0	144	164	4	41.00	3-42	0	0	6.83	1	
FC	2008/09	9	11	4	64	35	9.14	0	0	1284	639	22	29.04	5-58	1	0	2.98	8	
Lim	2008/09	12	3	0	14	10	4.66	0	0	629	562	20	28.10	4-50	1	0	5.36	7	
20T	2008/09	2	1	1	3	3*		0	0	36	52	0					8.66	1	
BOWDEN, DeWayne Jamie (Wellington) b Wellington 27.2.1982 LHB LFM																			
FC		5	9	1	81	32*	10.12	0	0	835	536	17	31.52	4-48	0	0	3.85	2	
Lim		8	6	1	45	20	9.00	0	0	324	282	8	35.25	2-41	0	0	5.22	0	
20T		8	4	1	57	34	19.00	0	0	96	178	4	44.50	2-23	0	0	11.12	3	
FC	2005/06	31	45	9	1071	106*	29.75	1	4	4024	2305	68	33.89	4-48	0	0	3.43	9	
Lim	2006/07	29	23	10	260	32*	20.00	0	0	1236	920	25	36.80	2-37	0	0	4.46	5	
20T	2005/06	25	14	3	141	34	12.81	0	0	378	522	11	47.45	2-13	0	0	8.28	10	
BRACEWELL, Douglas Andrew John (Central Districts) b Tauranga, Bay of Plenty 28.9.1990 RHB RM																			
FC		7	11	1	204	60*	20.40	0	1	1157	725	16	45.31	5-47	1	0	3.76	3	
FC	2008/09	12	17	1	274	60*	17.12	0	1	1923	1235	26	47.50	5-47	1	0	3.85	4	
Lim	2008/09	8	6	0	87	55	14.50	0	1	208	203	4	50.75	2-24	0	0	5.85	3	
BRODIE, Joshua Michael (Wellington) b Wellington 8.6.1987 LHB																			
FC		5	9	0	402	103	44.66	1	4									3	
FC	2007/08	14	22	0	770	110	35.00	2	5									16	
BROOM, Darren John (Otago) b Christchurch, Canterbury 16.9.1985 RHB RM																			
FC		2	3	0	119	119	39.66	1	0	30	29	0					5.80	0	
Lim		8	7	1	149	73	24.83	0	1	12	10	0					5.00	5	
20T		7	3	2	2	1*	2.00	0	0									1	
Lim	2007/08	11	9	1	150	73	18.75	0	1	12	10	0					5.00	6	
20T	2008/09	8	4	2	22	20	11.00	0	0									1	
BROOM, Neil Trevor (New Zealand, Otago, New Zealand to South Africa, New Zealand to United Arab Emirates, Otago to India) b Christchurch, Canterbury 20.11.1983 RHB RM																			
FC		7	10	1	608	196	67.55	3	0	66	36	0					3.27	11	
Int		6	6	0	132	71	22.00	0	1									0	
Lim		11	11	1	452	164	45.20	1	3	60	62	1	62.00	1-27	0	0	6.20	1	

Cmp	Debut	M	I	NO	Runs	HS	Avge	100	50	Balls	Runs	Wkts	Avge	BB	5i	10m	RpO	ct	st
20T		9	8	0	201	58	25.12	0	1	18	19	2	9.50	2-19	0	0	6.33	4	
FC	2002/03	55	87	8	3301	196	41.78	8	15	570	371	5	74.20	1-8	0	0	3.90	43	
Int	2008/09	22	22	3	333	71	17.52	0	1									2	
Lim	2003/04	77	72	11	1959	164	32.11	1	12	290	302	5	60.40	2-59	0	0	6.24	22	
I20T	2008/09	9	5	1	61	36	15.25	0	0									4	
20T	2005/06	35	29	2	451	58	16.70	0	1	138	214	7	30.57	2-19	0	0	9.30	11	
BROWNLIE, Dean Graham (Canterbury) b Perth, Western Australia, Australia 30.7.1984 RHB RM																			
FC		5	9	2	364	112*	52.00	1	2	102	82	0					4.82	9	
Lim		3	3	1	112	86*	56.00	0	1									0	
20T		7	6	2	118	45*	29.50	0	0									6	
BULLICK, Anthony David (Otago) b Hamilton, Waikato 30.7.1985 RHB RMF																			
FC		4	6	1	119	42	23.80	0	0	753	402	11	36.54	3-51	0	0	3.20	2	
Lim		5	3	1	46	33*	23.00	0	0	202	206	14	14.71	4-60	1	0	6.11	1	
FC	2007/08	6	9	2	130	42	18.57	0	0	963	538	12	44.83	3-51	0	0	3.35	2	
BURNS, Michael (Wellington) b Balclutha, Otago 6.7.1979 RHB RFM																			
FC		3	5	2	6	4	2.00	0	0	277	201	5	40.20	2-40	0	0	4.35	0	
FC	2006/07	13	16	5	48	8	4.36	0	0	1517	894	32	27.93	4-41	0	0	3.53	4	
Lim	2006/07	9	1	0	6	6	6.00	0	0	325	246	7	35.14	2-15	0	0	4.54	0	
20T	2006/07	4								30	67	0					13.40	1	
BURSON, Ryan David (Canterbury) b Christchurch, Canterbury 27.8.1978 RHB RFM																			
Lim		6	2	0	2	2	1.00	0	0	289	293	7	41.85	2-23	0	0	6.08	0	
20T		6	4	2	16	7*	8.00	0	0	120	163	6	27.16	4-16	1	0	8.15	3	
FC	1997/98	18	29	11	292	41*	16.22	0	0	3317	1670	47	35.53	6-35	1	0	3.02	7	
Lim	1997/98	45	17	10	94	15*	13.42	0	0	2085	1578	57	27.68	4-45	1	0	4.54	6	
20T	2007/08	11	6	3	23	7*	7.66	0	0	222	273	13	21.00	4-16	1	0	7.37	4	
BURTT, Leighton McGregor (Canterbury) b Christchurch, Canterbury 17.4.1984 RHB RM																			
FC		5	6	3	53	27	17.66	0	0	819	492	17	28.94	5-57	2	0	3.60	0	
Lim		2	1	1	0	0*		0	0	72	106	1	106.00	1-45	0	0	8.83	1	
FC	2006/07	24	28	9	212	29*	11.15	0	0	4171	2509	76	33.01	6-108	5	1	3.60	6	
Lim	2005/06	22	7	5	25	8*	12.50	0	0	998	948	35	27.08	5-26	0	2	5.69	1	
20T	2005/06	12	1	0	1	1	1.00	0	0	252	354	12	29.50	2-16	0	0	8.42	5	
BUTLER, Ian Gareth (New Zealand, Otago, Gloucestershire, New Zealand to South Africa, New Zealand to United Arab Emirates, New Zealand to West Indies, Otago to India) b Middlemore, Auckland 24.11.1981 RHB RFM																			
FC		2	3	0	58	45	19.33	0	0	365	180	6	30.00	2-18	0	0	2.95	0	
Int		2	1	1	13	13*		0	0	108	101	3	33.66	3-43	0	0	5.61	0	
Lim		6	5	2	154	53*	51.33	0	1	267	289	7	41.28	4-45	1	0	6.49	1	
20T		9	7	3	96	36*	24.00	0	0	156	179	14	12.78	6-28	0	1	6.88	1	
Test	2001/02	8	10	2	76	26	9.50	0	0	1368	884	24	36.83	6-46	1	0	3.87	4	
FC	2001/02	43	56	18	648	68	17.05	0	2	6871	3989	126	31.65	6-46	2	0	3.48	11	
Int	2001/02	26	13	5	84	25	10.50	0	0	1109	1038	28	37.07	4-44	1	0	5.61	8	
Lim	2001/02	87	56	15	642	53*	15.65	0	1	3764	3403	100	34.03	5-55	2	1	5.42	16	
I20T	2008/09	14	5	4	4	2*	4.00	0	0	270	361	19	19.00	3-19	0	0	8.02	2	
20T	2004	42	29	12	252	36*	14.82	0	0	805	1074	54	19.88	6-28	0	1	8.00	10	
CHAN, Sunnie Percival (Wellington) b Wellington 4.2.1982 RHB RMF																			
FC		1	2	0	17	11	8.50	0	0	96	74	0					4.62	1	
Lim		2	2	1	7	7*	7.00	0	0	78	96	0					7.38	1	
FC	2006/07	3	4	0	52	35	13.00	0	0	447	289	6	48.16	3-58	0	0	3.87	1	
Lim	2005/06	8	5	2	18	7*	6.00	0	0	270	309	3	103.00	1-21	0	0	6.86	2	
20T	2005/06	3	1	1	0	0*		0	0	42	66	1	66.00	1-30	0	0	9.42	1	
CROOK, Brendon-John (Wellington) b Lower Hutt, Wellington 29.6.1984 LHB RM																			
Lim		3	3	0	49	27	16.33	0	0	24	17	1	17.00	1-17	0	0	4.25	0	
FC	2007/08	9	13	1	333	101*	27.75	1	1	12	2	1	2.00	1-2	0	0	1.00	5	
Lim	2008/09	12	12	0	299	75	24.91	0	3	24	17	1	17.00	1-17	0	0	4.25	2	
20T	2008/09	6	6	1	81	21	16.20	0	0									2	
CUMMING, Craig Derek (Otago, Otago to India) b Timaru, Canterbury 31.8.1975 RHB RSM																			
FC		9	16	1	924	160	61.60	4	4	214	112	2	56.00	1-6	0	0	3.14	10	
Lim		8	8	1	251	52*	35.85	0	1	198	202	2	101.00	1-17	0	0	6.12	6	
20T		9	8	1	196	56*	28.00	0	2	6	4	0					4.00	5	
Test	2004/05	11	19	2	441	74	25.94	0	1									3	
FC	1995/96	127	226	18	7790	187	37.45	19	36	3699	1704	32	53.25	3-31	0	0	2.76	62	
Int	2003/04	13	13	1	161	45*	13.41	0	0	18	17	0					5.66	6	
Lim	1993/94	130	123	7	3061	112	26.38	3	16	2687	2116	42	50.38	2-18	0	0	4.72	59	
20T	2005/06	28	26	1	596	76	23.84	0	3	131	168	13	12.92	4-24	1	0	7.69	15	
DE BOORDER, Andrew Philip (Auckland) b Hastings, Hawke's Bay 6.7.1988 RHB RM																			
FC		10	14	2	508	125*	42.33	1	2	306	248	5	49.60	2-56	0	0	4.86	8	
Lim		6	5	1	172	57	43.00	0	2									2	
FC	2007/08	15	22	2	689	125*	34.45	1	3	318	263	5	52.60	2-56	0	0	4.96	8	
DE BOORDER, Derek Charles (Otago, Otago to India) b Hastings, Hawke's Bay 25.10.1985 RHB WK																			
FC		10	16	2	345	70*	24.64	0	2									31	4
Lim		8	6	0	69	26	11.50	0	0									7	
20T		9	4	2	23	9	11.50	0	0									9	1

Cmp	Debut	M	I	NO	Runs	HS	Avge	100	50	Balls	Runs	Wkts	Avge	BB	5i	10m	RpO	ct	st
FC	2007/08	22	32	6	843	74	32.42	0	6									64	10
Lim	2005/06	30	20	3	350	52*	20.58	0	1									33	2
20T	2007/08	23	12	5	59	16	8.42	0	0									15	5
DE GRANDHOMME, Colin (Auckland) b Harare, Zimbabwe 22.7.1986 RHB RFM																			
FC		4	5	2	203	106*	67.66	1	0	453	204	5	40.80	2-34	0	0	2.70	0	
Lim		5	4	0	85	36	21.25	0	0	192	206	2	103.00	2-58	0	0	6.43	2	
20T		11	10	3	145	40	20.71	0	0	168	271	10	27.10	3-22	0	0	9.67	4	
FC	2005/06	32	49	7	1418	109	33.76	4	5	2698	1283	42	30.54	4-65	0	0	2.85	24	
Lim	2004/05	31	29	3	468	96*	18.00	0	1	606	518	7	74.00	3-38	0	0	5.12	9	
20T	2006/07	19	17	3	266	40	19.00	0	0	257	422	15	28.13	3-22	0	0	9.85	8	
DE TERTE, James William (Central Districts) b Sydney, New South Wales, Australia 16.1.1983 RHB RM																			
FC		2	4	1	135	77*	45.00	0	1									0	
FC	2007/08	3	6	1	153	77*	30.60	0	1									0	
DEVCICH, Anton Paul (Northern Districts) b Hamilton, Waikato 28.9.1985 LHB SLA																			
FC		4	7	1	73	39*	12.16	0	0	114	72	2	36.00	2-30	0	0	3.78	0	
Lim		9	8	0	218	54	27.25	0	2	161	111	4	27.75	3-25	0	0	4.13	1	
20T		10	10	2	138	37*	17.25	0	0									6	
FC	2004/05	10	17	2	282	94*	18.80	0	1	344	214	5	42.80	2-20	0	0	3.73	9	
Lim	2005/06	12	11	0	275	54	25.00	0	2	281	226	5	45.20	3-25	0	0	4.82	3	
20T	2005/06	16	16	2	223	37*	15.92	0	0	30	43	0					8.60	6	
DIAMANTI, Brendon John (Central Districts) b Blenheim, Marlborough 30.4.1981 RHB RM																			
FC		4	7	0	261	94	37.28	0	2									2	
Lim		6	5	1	224	68	56.00	0	3	138	139	3	46.33	3-55	0	0	6.04	2	
FC	2003/04	27	42	5	952	136	25.72	2	3	4317	1982	57	34.77	6-73	3	1	2.75	7	
Int	2008/09	1	1	1	26	26*		0	0	12	25	0					12.50	1	
Lim	2004/05	59	42	13	815	68	28.10	0	5	2656	2101	73	28.78	5-58	3	1	4.74	21	
I20T	2009	1								12	19	0					9.50	0	
20T	2005/06	17	10	4	125	36*	20.83	0	0	354	461	25	18.44	3-14	0	0	7.81	3	
DILSHAN, Tillakaratne Mudiyanselage (Basnahira South, Bloomfield, Sri Lanka, Delhi Daredevils, Northern Districts, Sri Lanka to Bangladesh, Sri Lanka to India, Sri Lanka to South Africa, Sri Lanka to United States of America, Sri Lanka to West Indies, Sri Lanka to Zimbabwe) b Kalutara, Sri Lanka 14.10.1976 RHB OB																			
20T		5	5	0	125	59	25.00	0	1	30	32	1	32.00	1-12	0	0	6.40	1	
Test	1999/00	63	101	11	3906	168	43.40	11	15	1184	590	16	36.87	4-10	0	0	2.99	73	
FC	1993/94	198	320	22	11572	200*	38.83	30	48	3796	1844	59	31.25	5-49	1	0	2.91	334	27
Int	1999/00	188	165	29	4860	160	35.73	8	20	2881	2281	54	42.24	4-29	2	0	4.75	80	1
Lim	1996/97	272	243	41	7654	188	37.89	13	36	3972	3084	83	37.15	4-17	3	0	4.65	154	8
I20T	2006	31	30	5	717	96*	28.68	0	5	120	151	4	37.75	2-4	0	0	7.55	13	2
20T	2004/05	77	74	9	1606	96*	24.70	0	11	433	491	17	28.88	3-23	0	0	6.80	37	3
DONNELLY, Jason Patrick Thomas (Canterbury) b Auckland 24.4.1987 RHB SLA																			
FC		5	5	1	20	13	5.00	0	0	1372	704	14	50.28	4-150	0	0	3.07	1	
EATHORNE, Sean William (Otago) b Dunedin, Otago 5.5.1986 RHB OB																			
Lim		1	1	0	9	9	9.00	0	0									0	
FC	2004/05	5	10	0	72	28	7.20	0	0									4	
Lim	2004/05	6	5	2	103	37*	34.33	0	0	24	28	2	14.00	2-28	0	0	7.00	0	
20T	2008/09	5	1	0	4	4	4.00	0	0									3	
EDWARDS, Lee Jonathan (Wellington) b Wellington 21.4.1979 RHB RFM																			
FC		1	1	0	0	0	0.00	0	0	254	104	5	20.80	3-71	0	0	2.45	0	
FC	1998/99	4	4	0	34	27	8.50	0	0	722	355	8	44.37	3-71	0	0	2.95	3	
ELLIOTT, Grant David (New Zealand, Wellington, New Zealand to South Africa, New Zealand to Sri Lanka) b Johannesburg, Transvaal, South Africa 21.3.1979 RHB RFM																			
Test		2	4	0	59	25	14.75	0	0	42	11	2	5.50	2-8	0	0	1.57	0	
FC		3	6	0	95	33	15.83	0	0	78	31	2	15.50	2-8	0	0	2.38	0	
Test	2007/08	5	9	1	86	25	10.75	0	0	282	140	4	35.00	2-8	0	0	2.97	2	
FC	1996/97	52	82	4	2288	196*	29.33	5	12	5343	2424	65	37.29	4-56	0	0	2.72	31	
Int	2008	31	22	6	628	115	39.25	1	3	458	376	17	22.11	4-31	1	0	4.92	5	
Lim	1998/99	108	87	19	2121	115	31.19	2	11	2760	2374	79	30.05	5-34	3	1	5.16	32	
I20T	2008/09	1	1	1	23	23*		0	0	6	11	1	11.00	1-11	0	0	11.00	0	
20T	2005/06	22	20	6	339	57	24.21	0	2	309	430	16	26.87	2-13	0	0	8.35	10	
ELLIS, Andrew Malcolm (Canterbury) b Christchurch, Canterbury 24.3.1982 RHB RFM																			
FC		4	6	1	122	58	24.40	0	1	738	277	11	25.18	3-37	0	0	2.25	2	
Lim		1	1	1	5	5*		0	0	60	66	2	33.00	2-66	0	0	6.60	0	
20T		7	5	2	20	12	6.66	0	0	150	233	7	33.28	3-32	0	0	9.32	1	
FC	2002/03	42	66	9	1545	78	27.10	0	10	5442	2437	73	33.38	5-63	1	0	2.68	22	
Lim	2003/04	27	20	2	358	52	19.88	0	1	902	807	23	35.08	3-50	0	0	5.36	4	
20T	2006/07	24	18	6	124	20	10.33	0	0	412	553	23	24.04	3-32	0	0	8.05	9	
ERASMUS, Pieter Bernardus (Auckland) b Ceres, Cape Province, South Africa 19.3.1983 RHB LFM																			
FC		3	3	0	74	60	24.66	0	1	282	105	2	52.50	1-7	0	0	2.23	0	
Lim		1	1	1	1	1*		0	0	48	45	3	15.00	3-45	0	0	5.62	0	
FC	2006/07	4	4	0	89	60	22.25	0	1	336	120	4	30.00	2-15	0	0	2.14	0	

Cmp	Debut	M	I	NO	Runs	HS	Avge	100	50	Balls	Runs	Wkts	Avge	BB	5i	10m	RpO	ct	st
FLYNN, Daniel Raymond (New Zealand, Northern Districts) b Rotorua, Bay of Plenty 16.4.1985 LHB SLC																			
Test		3	5	0	62	29	12.40	0	0									1	
FC		9	13	0	266	65	20.46	0	2	43	56	1	56.00	1-37	0	0	7.81	2	
Lim		10	10	1	233	81	25.88	0	2	24	19	0					4.75	3	
20T		8	7	0	89	22	12.71	0	0									4	
Test	2008	16	29	5	689	95	28.70	0	4									7	
FC	2004/05	54	91	10	2528	110	31.20	5	12	241	143	1	143.00	1-37	0	0	3.56	20	
Int	2007/08	16	13	2	167	35	15.18	0	0	6	6	0					6.00	4	
Lim	2004/05	60	57	6	1280	149	25.09	2	6	378	369	6	61.50	2-45	0	0	5.85	16	
I20T	2007/08	4	4	0	37	23	9.25	0	0	6	7	0					7.00	2	
20T	2005/06	31	30	2	432	47	15.42	0	0	90	106	0					7.06	8	
FRANKLIN, James Edward Charles (New Zealand, Wellington, Gloucestershire, Gloucestershire to Netherlands, New Zealand to South Africa, New Zealand to United Arab Emirates) b Wellington 7.11.1980 LHB LFM																			
FC		2	3	0	212	162	70.66	1	0	484	215	6	35.83	3-27	0	0	2.66	2	
Int		6	6	2	65	20*	16.25	0	0	153	139	3	46.33	1-26	0	0	5.45	1	
Lim		10	10	3	208	84*	29.71	0	1	183	155	4	38.75	1-16	0	0	5.08	5	
I20T		3	2	0	50	43	25.00	0	0	24	40	3	13.33	2-32	0	0	10.00	1	
20T		12	10	2	264	72	33.00	0	1	186	255	9	28.33	2-20	0	0	8.22	3	
Test	2000/01	26	36	6	644	122*	21.46	1	2	4399	2612	80	32.65	6-119	3	0	3.56	11	
FC	1998/99	132	201	28	5949	219	34.38	11	26	20726	10871	411	26.45	7-14	13	1	3.14	50	
Int	2000/01	75	53	19	636	45*	18.70	0	0	3149	2677	69	38.79	5-42	0	1	5.10	20	
Lim	1999/00	180	147	48	3065	133*	30.95	2	14	7250	5819	169	34.43	5-42	3	1	4.81	57	
I20T	2005/06	13	11	4	128	43	18.28	0	0	144	183	7	26.14	3-23	0	0	7.62	5	
20T	2004	58	53	14	1309	90	33.56	0	6	941	1281	35	36.60	3-23	0	0	8.16	16	
FRAUENSTEIN, Carl (Canterbury) b Stutterheim, Cape Province, South Africa 23.10.1985 RHB RMF																			
Lim		7	5	1	40	16	10.00	0	0	284	304	11	27.63	4-48	1	0	6.42	3	
20T		10	7	1	62	23	10.33	0	0	192	259	10	25.90	2-19	0	0	8.09	6	
Lim	2006/07	15	12	2	131	48	13.10	0	0	525	527	21	25.09	4-48	1	0	6.02	5	
20T	2006/07	27	20	2	187	27	10.38	0	0	356	505	18	28.05	3-20	0	0	8.51	13	
FULLER, James Kerr (Otago) b Cape Town, Cape Province, South Africa 24.1.1990 RHB RFM																			
FC		2	3	0	31	24	10.33	0	0	342	231	2	115.50	1-33	0	0	4.05	1	
FULTON, Peter Gordon (Canterbury, New Zealand) b Christchurch, Canterbury 1.2.1979 RHB RM																			
Test		2	4	0	42	29	10.50	0	0									4	
FC		10	19	1	691	172	38.38	1	3	6	3	0					3.00	9	
Lim		9	9	0	279	88	31.00	0	2									8	
20T		10	10	1	193	43	21.44	0	0									2	
Test	2005/06	10	16	1	314	75	20.93	0	1									12	
FC	2000/01	84	143	12	5652	301*	43.14	9	31	679	402	11	36.54	4-49	0	0	3.55	66	
Int	2004/05	49	46	5	1334	112	32.53	1	8									18	
Lim	2001/02	124	117	12	3631	115*	34.58	2	26	18	25	0					8.33	47	
I20T	2005/06	11	11	1	118	25	11.80	0	0									3	
20T	2005/06	31	31	3	464	43	16.57	0	0									8	
GILLESPIE, Mark Raymond (Wellington) b Wanganui 17.10.1979 RHB RFM																			
FC		1								36	30	1	30.00	1-30	0	0	5.00	0	
Lim		3	2	2	2	2*		0	0	118	128	6	21.33	2-30	0	0	6.50	0	
Test	2007/08	3	5	1	25	16*	6.25	0	0	516	380	11	34.54	5-136	1	0	4.41	0	
FC	1999/00	53	66	11	915	81*	16.63	0	3	9795	5200	213	24.41	6-42	10	0	3.18	8	
Int	2006/07	32	14	8	93	28	15.50	0	0	1521	1369	37	37.00	4-58	1	0	5.40	6	
Lim	2001/02	92	53	19	375	28	11.02	0	0	4440	3826	131	29.20	5-35	4	1	5.17	16	
I20T	2006/07	11	6	4	21	7	10.50	0	0	210	255	10	25.50	4-7	1	0	7.28	1	
20T	2005/06	13	8	4	27	7	6.75	0	0	256	323	13	24.84	4-7	1	0	7.57	1	
GRIGGS, Bevan Barry John (Central Districts) b Palmerston North, Manawatu 29.3.1978 RHB WK																			
FC		10	16	5	394	85	35.81	0	4									30	
Lim		10	9	0	182	51	20.22	0	1									11	
20T		11	3	2	10	5*	10.00	0	0									11	
FC	2000/01	83	130	16	3155	143	27.67	2	19									236	7
Lim	2000/01	90	73	10	1222	74	19.39	0	4									109	7
20T	2005/06	27	12	3	129	34	14.33	0	0									17	4
GUPTILL, Martin James (Auckland, New Zealand, New Zealand to South Africa, New Zealand to Sri Lanka, New Zealand to United Arab Emirates, New Zealand to United States of America, New Zealand to West Indies) b Auckland 30.9.1986 RHB OB																			
Test		6	11	1	431	189	43.10	1	3	86	47	3	15.66	3-37	0	0	3.27	7	
FC		7	13	1	484	189	40.33	1	3	104	64	3	21.33	3-37	0	0	3.69	8	
Int		8	8	0	210	91	26.25	0	1	47	28	2	14.00	2-7	0	0	3.57	4	
Lim		9	9	0	366	156	40.66	1	1	47	28	2	14.00	2-7	0	0	3.57	4	
I20T		3	2	0	47	30	23.50	0	0	6	11	0					11.00	1	
20T		11	10	1	300	97*	33.33	0	2	6	11	0					11.00	8	
Test	2008/09	11	20	1	672	189	35.36	1	3	86	47	3	15.66	3-37	0	0	3.27	8	
FC	2005/06	33	57	2	1694	189	30.80	2	9	206	127	4	31.75	3-37	0	0	3.69	20	
Int	2008/09	33	32	3	959	122*	33.06	1	7	65	53	2	26.50	2-7	0	0	4.89	16	
Lim	2005/06	67	64	5	2115	156	35.84	5	11	65	53	2	26.50	2-7	0	0	4.89	35	

Cmp	Debut	M	I	NO	Runs	HS	Avge	100	50	Balls	Runs	Wkts	Avge	BB	5i	10m	RpO	ct	st
I20T	2008/09	20	18	2	341	45*	21.31	0	0	6	11	0					11.00	8	
20T	2005/06	40	37	4	906	97*	27.45	0	3	6	11	0					11.00	24	
HAIG, Shaun Barry (Otago) b Auckland 19.3.1982 RHB RM																			
FC		10	18	1	507	153	29.82	1	2									8	
Lim		8	8	1	292	93*	41.71	0	2									5	
FC	2005/06	25	41	2	1229	153	31.51	3	5									22	
Lim	2005/06	24	23	1	558	93*	25.36	0	4									10	1
20T	2006/07	1	1	0	0	0	0.00	0	0									0	
HARRIS, Chris Zinzan (Canterbury) b Christchurch, Canterbury 20.11.1969 LHB RM,OB																			
FC		3	4	0	149	105	37.25	1	0	219	64	3	21.33	2-23	0	0	1.75	5	
Lim		8	7	3	97	32	24.25	0	0	373	322	4	80.50	2-25	0	0	5.18	2	
Test	1992/93	23	42	4	777	71	20.44	0	5	2560	1170	16	73.12	2-16	0	0	2.74	14	
FC	1989/90	131	204	42	7377	251*	45.53	15	41	14887	5720	160	35.75	4-22	0	0	2.30	120	
Int	1990/91	250	213	62	4379	130	29.00	1	16	10667	7613	203	37.50	5-42	2	1	4.28	96	
Lim	1989/90	449	395	116	9584	130	34.35	3	47	20244	13502	396	34.09	5-42	5	1	4.00	197	
20T	2005/06	13	13	8	449	100	89.80	1	1	293	322	11	29.27	3-14	0	0	6.59	6	
HARVIE, Mathew James (Otago) b Dunedin, Otago 6.12.1984 RHB RFM																			
FC		7	8	3	34	16*	6.80	0	0	1224	724	19	38.10	3-45	0	0	3.54	5	
Lim		1								18	16	1	16.00	1-16	0	0	5.33	0	
FC	2003/04	26	29	9	233	37*	11.65	0	0	4078	2441	60	40.68	4-73	0	0	3.59	8	
Lim	2003/04	14	9	5	60	19*	15.00	0	0	599	516	21	24.57	5-40	0	1	5.16	0	
20T	2006/07	5	3	1	26	14*	13.00	0	0	84	123	5	24.60	2-15	0	0	8.78	1	
HIINI, Brandon Christopher (Canterbury) b Invercargill, Southland 11.12.1981 RHB RMF																			
FC		9	10	1	191	64*	21.22	0	1	1389	674	22	30.63	4-34	0	0	2.91	5	
20T		2	1	0	1	1	1.00	0	0	40	65	1	65.00	1-35	0	0	9.75	0	
FC	2005/06	32	43	10	910	103*	27.57	2	2	5779	2683	92	29.16	5-32	2	0	2.78	15	
Lim	2006/07	23	17	8	190	33	21.11	0	0	1074	955	21	45.47	3-38	0	0	5.33	5	
20T	2006/07	7	3	1	2	1*	1.00	0	0	148	210	9	23.33	3-17	0	0	8.51	2	
HIRA, Roneel Magan (Auckland) b Auckland 23.1.1987 LHB SLA																			
Lim		9	6	3	63	28*	21.00	0	0	432	377	10	37.70	3-54	0	0	5.23	6	
20T		11	4	2	28	14*	14.00	0	0	174	213	11	19.36	4-13	1	0	7.34	5	
FC	2006/07	4	5	1	106	45*	26.50	0	0	420	205	1	205.00	1-27	0	0	2.92	1	
Lim	2006/07	39	24	12	212	44*	17.66	0	0	1884	1490	39	38.20	4-31	3	0	4.74	13	
20T	2006/07	22	10	5	79	28	15.80	0	0	384	470	21	22.38	4-13	1	0	7.34	11	
HITCHCOCK, Paul Anthony (Wellington) b Whangarei, Northland 23.1.1975 RHB RM																			
Lim		1								48	50	2	25.00	2-50	0	0	6.25	0	
20T		7	6	0	50	23	8.33	0	0	135	199	8	24.87	3-17	0	0	8.84	5	
FC	1999/00	11	16	3	298	51	22.92	0	1	1389	747	14	53.35	3-27	0	0	3.22	1	
Int	2002	14	7	3	41	11*	10.25	0	0	558	468	12	39.00	3-30	0	0	5.03	4	
Lim	1997/98	105	88	21	1424	108	21.25	2	2	4829	3930	139	28.27	5-10	5	1	4.88	22	
I20T	2007/08	1	1	0	13	13	13.00	0	0	18	43	2	21.50	2-43	0	0	14.33	0	
20T	2005/06	22	21	0	442	77	21.04	0	2	453	641	22	29.13	3-17	0	0	8.49	8	
HOPKINS, Gareth James (Auckland, New Zealand, New Zealand to South Africa, New Zealand to Sri Lanka, New Zealand to United States of America, New Zealand to West Indies) b Lower Hutt, Wellington 24.11.1976 RHB WK																			
FC		7	8	0	463	201	57.87	1	3	11	36	0					19.63	14	
Int		4	4	0	126	45	31.50	0	0									2	1
Lim		13	13	2	372	70	33.81	0	2									9	1
I20T		3	2	0	57	36	28.50	0	0									2	
20T		14	13	2	277	71*	25.18	0	2									4	1
Test	2008	1	2	0	27	15	13.50	0	0									3	
FC	1997/98	117	181	28	5336	201	34.87	11	23	17	49	0					17.29	304	20
Int	2004	22	14	0	203	45	14.50	0	0									24	1
Lim	1995/96	163	137	22	2867	130*	24.93	1	11									164	23
I20T	2007/08	10	8	0	86	36	10.75	0	0									4	2
20T	2005/06	41	37	8	650	71*	22.41	0	2									16	6
HOUGHTON, Mark Vincent (Wellington) b Upper Hutt, Wellington 3.11.1984 RHB SLA																			
20T		7	4	1	41	32	13.66	0	0	114	146	4	36.50	1-19	0	0	7.68	2	
FC	2007/08	9	9	1	192	81	24.00	0	1	1520	612	14	43.71	3-20	0	0	2.41	2	
Lim	2007/08	9	5	2	44	23*	14.66	0	0	325	310	2	155.00	2-50	0	0	5.72	0	
20T	2006/07	18	7	3	65	32	16.25	0	0	333	407	14	29.07	3-24	0	0	7.33	5	
HOW, Jamie Michael (Central Districts) b New Plymouth, Taranaki 19.5.1981 RHB OB																			
FC		9	17	1	695	176	43.43	1	4	240	123	0					3.07	12	
Lim		10	10	1	306	94	34.00	0	2	12	12	0					6.00	12	
20T		11	11	0	171	50	15.54	0	1									4	
Test	2005/06	19	35	1	772	92	22.70	0	4	12	4	0					2.00	18	
FC	2000/01	92	161	12	5281	190*	35.44	12	28	2142	1202	20	60.10	3-57	0	0	3.36	96	
Int	2005/06	31	28	1	930	139	34.44	1	7									13	
Lim	2000/01	118	114	6	3497	139	32.37	2	26	428	388	8	48.50	2-15	0	0	5.43	65	
I20T	2007/08	5	5	0	56	31	11.20	0	0									1	
20T	2005/06	36	36	2	869	78*	25.55	0	6	84	135	5	27.00	1-12	0	0	9.64	14	

Cmp	Debut	M	I	NO	Runs	HS	Avge	100	50	Balls	Runs	Wkts	Avge	BB	5i	10m	RpO	ct	st
INGRAM, Peter John (Central Districts, New Zealand, New Zealand to Sri Lanka) b Hawera, Taranaki 25.10.1978 RHB OB																			
Test		2	4	0	61	42	15.25	0	0									0	
FC		9	17	2	916	245*	61.06	3	3									5	
Int		6	6	0	181	69	30.16	0	1									3	
Lim		11	11	0	335	69	30.45	0	3									5	
I20T		3	3	1	22	20*	11.00	0	0									1	
20T		12	12	2	338	77*	33.80	0	4									2	
FC	2001/02	67	122	8	4290	247	37.63	12	15	96	47	0					2.93	39	
Int	2009/10	8	7	0	193	69	27.57	0	1									3	
Lim	2001/02	50	49	1	1625	135	33.85	3	9									11	
20T	2006/07	26	25	3	518	77*	23.54	0	4									4	
JONES, Richard Andrew (Auckland) b Auckland 22.10.1973 RHB																			
FC		10	17	1	953	170*	59.56	4	2									7	
Lim		5	5	0	103	36	20.60	0	0									3	
20T		2	2	1	22	14	22.00	0	0									1	
Test	2003/04	1	2	0	23	16	11.50	0	0									0	
FC	1993/94	124	215	12	7254	201	35.73	19	33	1	0	1	0.00	1-0	0	0	0.00	105	
Int	2003/04	5	5	0	168	63	33.60	0	1									0	
Lim	1992/93	133	132	7	3218	108	25.74	1	16	3	5	0					10.00	37	
20T	2005/06	23	22	5	399	75	23.47	0	2									6	
KITCHEN, Anaru Kyle (Auckland) b Auckland 21.2.1984 RHB SLA																			
FC		10	16	2	436	116	31.14	1	1	90	88	2	44.00	2-31	0	0	5.86	5	
Lim		8	7	1	86	37	14.33	0	0									3	
20T		10	7	1	188	61*	31.33	0	2									8	
FC	2008/09	15	24	2	878	132	39.90	4	1	90	88	2	44.00	2-31	0	0	5.86	14	
Lim	2008/09	14	12	1	248	69	22.54	0	2									4	
20T	2008/09	13	10	2	252	61*	31.50	0	2									10	
KURU, Jeremy Newton (Central Districts) b Napier, Hawke's Bay 17.2.1985 RHB RMF																			
FC		4	5	2	18	15*	6.00	0	0	438	316	6	52.66	2-48	0	0	4.32	0	
LAMB, Andrew Robert (Wellington) b Bathurst, New South Wales, Australia 1.1.1978 RHB RFM																			
FC		4	7	0	114	28	16.28	0	0	660	469	10	46.90	3-48	0	0	4.26	1	
FC	2008/09	7	7	0	114	28	16.28	0	0	966	632	14	45.14	3-48	0	0	3.92	1	
Lim	2008/09	2	1	1	7	7*		0	0	78	99	1	99.00	1-47	0	0	7.61	1	
McCONE, Ryan James (Canterbury) b Christchurch, Canterbury 5.9.1987 LHB LM																			
FC		3	5	0	60	24	12.00	0	0	546	336	5	67.20	2-39	0	0	3.69	0	
FC	2008/09	4	6	0	162	102	27.00	1	0	606	369	5	73.80	2-39	0	0	3.65	1	
McCULLUM, Brendon Barrie (New Zealand, Otago, Kolkata Knight Riders, New Zealand to South Africa, New Zealand to United Arab Emirates, New Zealand to United States of America, New Zealand to West Indies, Otago to India, Sussex) b Dunedin, Otago 27.9.1981 RHB WK																			
Test		6	11	1	579	185	57.90	2	3									23	2
FC		7	13	1	607	185	50.58	2	3									23	2
Int		8	8	0	182	61	22.75	0	1									11	
Lim		8	8	0	182	61	22.75	0	1									11	
I20T		3	3	2	174	116*	174.00	1	1									1	1
20T		12	11	3	481	116*	60.12	2	2									3	1
Test	2003/04	52	87	5	2862	185	34.90	5	16									162	11
FC	1999/00	95	163	9	5339	185	34.66	9	30	36	18	0					3.00	267	19
Int	2001/02	171	145	22	3569	166	29.01	2	17									189	13
Lim	2000/01	215	183	26	4617	170	29.40	5	21									232	15
I20T	2004/05	40	40	7	1100	116*	33.33	1	6									25	4
20T	2004/05	98	97	13	2695	158*	32.08	3	14									48	4
McCULLUM, Nathan Leslie (New Zealand, Otago, Lancashire, New Zealand to Sri Lanka, New Zealand to United Arab Emirates, New Zealand to United States of America, New Zealand to West Indies, Otago to India) b Dunedin, Otago 1.9.1980 RHB OB																			
FC		2	3	0	142	88	47.33	0	2	615	356	4	89.00	3-139	0	0	3.47	1	
Int		1	1	0	17	17	17.00	0	0	48	31	1	31.00	1-31	0	0	3.87	0	
Lim		5	4	0	81	26	20.25	0	0	288	207	6	34.50	2-32	0	0	4.31	8	
I20T		3	2	1	15	14*	15.00	0	0	48	53	3	17.66	2-15	0	0	6.62	0	
20T		12	10	4	145	61	24.16	0	1	228	279	12	23.25	2-15	0	0	7.34	3	
FC	1999/00	48	73	6	1804	106*	26.92	1	11	8850	4176	100	41.76	6-90	2	0	2.83	51	
Int	2009	6	5	0	58	36	11.60	0	0	244	185	5	37.00	3-35	0	0	4.54	2	
Lim	2000/01	95	76	13	1204	71	19.11	0	6	4347	3106	79	39.31	3-21	0	0	4.28	40	
I20T	2007/08	22	14	8	160	36*	26.66	0	0	344	370	21	17.61	3-15	0	0	6.45	9	
20T	2005/06	66	54	17	940	76*	25.40	0	3	1218	1426	66	21.60	4-16	1	0	7.02	27	
McGLASHAN, Peter Donald (Northern Districts) b Napier, Hawke's Bay 22.6.1979 RHB WK																			
FC		10	12	0	493	115	41.08	1	2									37	4
Lim		10	9	1	184	53	23.00	0	2									11	4
20T		10	10	0	160	43	16.00	0	0									7	3
FC	2000/01	56	82	7	2198	115	29.30	2	11									141	12
Int	2008/09	4	2	1	63	56*	63.00	0	1									7	
Lim	1999/00	83	73	18	1834	112	33.34	1	11									82	14

Cmp	Debut	M	I	NO	Runs	HS	Avge	100	50	Balls	Runs	Wkts	Avge	BB	5i	10m	RpO	ct	st
I20T	2006/07	8	6	0	23	8	3.83	0	0									4	
20T	2005/06	37	35	2	679	94	20.57	0	2									20	9
McINTOSH, Timothy Gavin (Auckland, New Zealand) b Auckland 4.12.1979 LHB																			
Test		6	12	1	345	89	31.36	0	3									6	
FC		10	20	2	889	171	49.38	1	7	66	17	0					1.54	11	
Lim		5	5	0	227	138	45.40	1	1									4	
Test	2008/09	13	25	2	683	136	29.69	1	4									9	
FC	1998/99	98	167	12	5459	268	35.21	15	23	190	97	0					3.06	82	
Lim	1999/00	30	29	0	751	138	25.89	1	4									16	
McKAY, Andrew John (New Zealand, Wellington, New Zealand to Sri Lanka, New Zealand to United States of America) b Auckland 17.4.1980 RHB LFM																			
FC		5	6	4	27	11*	13.50	0	0	1067	600	15	40.00	4-60	0	0	3.37	0	
Int		3	1	1	3	3*		0	0	156	105	5	21.00	2-17	0	0	4.03	1	
Lim		8	3	2	15	12	15.00	0	0	391	332	16	20.75	4-47	1	0	5.09	1	
20T		9	3	3	8	6*		0	0	160	249	11	22.63	4-38	1	0	9.33	0	
FC	2002/03	24	27	12	175	36*	11.66	0	0	4278	2248	69	32.57	4-37	0	0	3.15	2	
Int	2009/10	6	4	4	10	4*		0	0	264	173	7	24.71	2-17	0	0	3.93	2	
Lim	2004/05	20	8	5	30	12	10.00	0	0	913	750	27	27.77	4-41	2	0	4.92	6	
I20T	2010	2	1	0	0	0	0.00	0	0	34	31	2	15.50	2-20	0	0	5.47	0	
20T	2007/08	12	5	4	8	6*	8.00	0	0	218	308	13	23.69	4-38	1	0	8.47	0	
McMILLAN, Craig Douglas (Canterbury) b Christchurch, Canterbury 13.9.1976 RHB RM																			
Lim		3	3	0	66	57	22.00	0	1	54	58	3	19.33	3-47	0	0	6.44	1	
20T		7	7	1	104	38	17.33	0	0	84	110	3	36.66	2-27	0	0	7.85	0	
Test	1997/98	55	91	10	3116	142	38.46	6	19	2502	1257	28	44.89	3-48	0	0	3.01	22	
FC	1994/95	138	226	27	7817	168*	39.28	16	42	6572	3167	88	35.98	6-71	1	0	2.89	58	
Int	1996/97	197	183	16	4707	117	28.18	3	28	1879	1717	49	35.04	3-20	0	0	5.48	44	
Lim	1994/95	326	307	33	8457	125	30.86	12	43	3651	3158	106	29.79	5-38	1	1	5.19	89	
I20T	2004/05	8	7	1	187	57	31.16	0	1									3	
20T	2004/05	27	25	3	605	65*	27.50	0	2	144	212	9	23.55	2-21	0	0	8.83	6	
McMILLAN, James Michael (Otago) b Christchurch, Canterbury 14.6.1978 RHB RFM																			
FC		3	3	0	34	20	11.33	0	0	474	302	5	60.40	2-84	0	0	3.82	2	
FC	2000/01	40	49	23	232	21*	8.92	0	0	6031	3352	95	35.28	7-105	1	0	3.33	7	
Lim	2001/02	37	20	13	52	9*	7.42	0	0	1658	1345	49	27.44	3-30	0	0	4.86	8	
20T	2006/07	8	1	1	0	0*		0	0	145	170	7	24.28	3-15	0	0	7.03	1	
McSKIMMING, Warren Charles (Otago, Otago to India) b Ranfurly, Otago 21.6.1979 RHB RM																			
FC		6	11	0	134	70	12.18	0	1	1247	653	23	28.39	5-17	1	0	3.14	2	
Lim		6	4	1	30	16	10.00	0	0	246	265	5	53.00	2-29	0	0	6.46	2	
20T		8	3	2	42	23	42.00	0	0	138	200	4	50.00	1-17	0	0	8.69	3	
FC	1999/00	60	90	13	1548	111	20.10	1	7	11964	5248	210	24.99	6-39	9	1	2.63	25	
Lim	1999/00	92	67	19	669	59*	13.93	0	2	4494	3527	115	30.66	5-9	0	1	4.70	25	
20T	2005/06	24	11	9	106	23	53.00	0	0	463	645	19	33.94	3-28	0	0	8.35	11	
MARSHALL, Hamish John Hamilton (Northern Districts, Gloucestershire, Gloucestershire to Netherlands) b Warkworth, Auckland 15.2.1979 RHB RM																			
FC		5	7	0	434	170	62.00	2	1	468	247	3	82.33	2-12	0	0	3.16	4	
Lim		4	3	0	87	66	29.00	0	1									0	
Test	2000/01	13	19	2	652	160	38.35	2	2	6	4	0					4.00	1	
FC	1998/99	153	260	17	8709	170	35.83	18	43	2874	1483	30	49.43	4-24	0	0	3.09	88	
Int	2003/04	66	62	9	1454	101*	27.43	1	12									18	
Lim	1998/99	239	227	24	5770	122	28.42	6	38	248	258	4	64.50	2-21	0	0	6.24	90	
I20T	2004/05	3	3	0	12	8	4.00	0	0									1	
20T	2004/05	49	48	3	1080	100	24.00	1	3	6	14	0					14.00	26	
MARSHALL, James Andrew Hamilton (Northern Districts) b Warkworth, Auckland 15.2.1979 RHB RM																			
FC		10	14	4	531	178*	53.10	1	2	12	9	1	9.00	1-9	0	0	4.50	1	
Lim		8	6	1	128	37*	25.60	0	0									5	
20T		10	10	2	166	59*	20.75	0	2									8	
Test	2004/05	7	11	0	218	52	19.81	0	1									5	
FC	1997/98	121	207	14	5992	235	31.04	11	29	561	333	5	66.60	1-5	0	0	3.56	110	
Int	2004/05	10	10	0	250	161	25.00	1	1									0	
Lim	1999/00	138	132	12	4317	161	35.97	6	28	289	269	4	67.25	1-20	0	0	5.58	51	
I20T	2005/06	3	2	0	14	13	7.00	0	0									0	
20T	2005/06	30	29	5	586	59*	24.41	0	5	24	31	0					7.75	12	
MARTIN, Bruce Philip (Northern Districts) b Whangarei, Northland 25.4.1980 RHB SLA																			
FC		4	5	2	78	25*	26.00	0	0	962	454	5	90.80	2-45	0	0	2.83	2	
Lim		7	3	1	41	37	20.50	0	0	336	282	7	40.28	2-45	0	0	5.03	1	
20T		3	2	1	16	9	16.00	0	0	54	71	4	17.75	2-18	0	0	7.88	0	
FC	1999/00	89	118	32	1547	113*	17.98	1	4	17384	7964	220	36.20	7-33	13	2	2.74	37	
Lim	1999/00	73	46	10	456	37	12.66	0	0	3508	2431	77	31.57	4-28	1	0	4.15	24	
20T	2005/06	21	15	6	98	19	10.88	0	0	474	591	27	21.88	3-16	0	0	7.48	3	
MARTIN, Christopher Stewart (Canterbury, New Zealand, Essex) b Christchurch, Canterbury 10.12.1974 RHB RFM																			
Test		6	9	5	7	5*	1.75	0	0	1296	767	16	47.93	4-52	0	0	3.55	1	
FC		11	13	7	25	10*	4.16	0	0	2352	1355	32	42.34	4-35	0	0	3.45	2	

Cmp	Debut	M	I	NO	Runs	HS	Avge	100	50	Balls	Runs	Wkts	Avge	BB	5i	10m	RpO	ct	st
Lim		6	2	0	1	1	0.50	0	0	316	306	10	30.60	4-25	1	0	5.81	0	
20T		10	2	2	6	4*		0	0	220	269	8	33.62	2-22	0	0	7.33	2	
Test	2000/01	56	81	42	89	12*	2.28	0	0	11069	6341	181	35.03	6-54	8	1	3.43	12	
FC	1997/98	155	192	95	389	25	4.01	0	0	29770	15434	477	32.35	6-54	18	1	3.11	30	
Int	2000/01	20	7	2	8	3	1.60	0	0	948	804	18	44.66	3-62	0	0	5.08	7	
Lim	1998/99	126	51	24	79	13	2.92	0	0	6183	4980	169	29.46	6-24	6	2	4.83	25	
I20T	2007/08	6	1	1	5	5*		0	0	138	193	7	27.57	2-14	0	0	8.39	1	
20T	2005/06	49	5	5	16	5*		0	0	1084	1352	43	31.44	3-33	0	0	7.48	10	
MASCARENHAS, Adrian Dimitri (Hampshire, Otago to India, Rajasthan Royals) b Chiswick, Middlesex, England 30.10.1977 RHB RMF																			
FC	1996	181	271	30	6185	131	25.66	8	22	26181	11818	418	28.27	6-25	16	0	2.70	72	
Int	2007	20	13	2	245	52	22.27	0	1	822	634	13	48.76	3-23	0	0	4.62	4	
Lim	1996	244	205	43	4107	79	25.35	0	27	10389	7376	281	26.24	5-27	9	1	4.26	62	
I20T	2007	14	13	5	123	31	15.37	0	0	252	309	12	25.75	3-18	0	0	7.35	7	
20T	2003	66	63	19	960	57*	21.81	0	3	1327	1587	81	19.59	5-14	1	1	7.17	20	
MASON, Michael James (Central Districts, New Zealand) b Carterton, Wairarapa 27.8.1974 RHB RFM																			
FC		9	11	3	63	19	7.87	0	0	1585	758	30	25.26	5-42	2	0	2.86	0	
Int		1	1	1	2	2*		0	0	60	68	1	68.00	1-68	0	0	6.80	0	
Lim		11	7	5	11	4*	5.50	0	0	590	488	15	32.53	3-48	0	0	4.96	2	
20T		11	3	1	4	2*	2.00	0	0	258	322	13	24.76	3-34	0	0	7.48	4	
Test	2003/04	1	2	0	3	3	1.50	0	0	132	105	0					4.77	0	
FC	1997/98	81	109	33	1194	64*	15.71	0	1	15186	6474	260	24.90	6-56	11	1	2.55	18	
Int	2003/04	26	7	4	24	13*	8.00	0	0	1179	1024	31	33.03	4-24	1	0	5.21	4	
Lim	1997/98	121	60	29	287	20	9.25	0	0	5686	4295	161	26.67	6-25	5	1	4.53	27	
I20T	2006/07	3	1	0	2	2	2.00	0	0	54	65	2	32.50	1-18	0	0	7.22	0	
20T	2005/06	29	7	2	8	2*	1.60	0	0	657	819	33	24.81	4-23	1	0	7.47	9	
MERCHANT, Cameron James (Wellington) b Darlinghurst, Sydney, New South Wales, Australia 4.1.1984 LHB OB																			
FC		10	20	1	764	108	40.21	2	4									6	
Lim		8	8	0	129	43	16.12	0	0									3	
20T		8	7	0	144	57	20.57	0	1									2	
FC	2007/08	18	34	1	1158	108	35.09	2	7	12	6	0					3.00	11	
Lim	2007/08	9	9	0	129	43	14.33	0	0									3	
MILLS, Kyle David (New Zealand to South Africa, New Zealand to Sri Lanka, New Zealand to United Arab Emirates, New Zealand to United States of America, New Zealand to West Indies) b Auckland 15.3.1979 RHB RM																			
Test	2004	19	30	5	289	57	11.56	0	1	2902	1453	44	33.02	4-16	0	0	3.00	4	
FC	1998/99	66	94	23	1840	117*	25.91	1	12	10456	5059	176	28.74	5-33	3	1	2.90	22	
Int	2000/01	114	65	24	661	54	16.12	0	2	5663	4425	170	26.02	5-25	7	1	4.68	32	
Lim	1998/99	177	116	39	1553	57*	20.16	0	5	8736	6573	255	25.77	5-25	9	1	4.51	47	
I20T	2004/05	19	13	4	119	33*	13.22	0	0	424	594	21	28.28	3-44	0	0	8.40	4	
20T	2004/05	26	17	4	159	33*	12.23	0	0	580	809	32	25.28	3-32	0	0	8.36	4	
MILNE, Adam Fraser (Central Districts) b Palmerston North, Manawatu 13.4.1992 RHB RMF																			
FC		3	5	4	55	36	55.00	0	0	458	303	11	27.54	4-49	0	0	3.96	0	
MORGAN, Greg Jan (Auckland) b East London, Border, South Africa 6.2.1989 RHB RM																			
FC		1	1	0	11	11	11.00	0	0	78	34	0					2.61	0	
Lim		1	1	0	1	1	1.00	0	0	36	38	0					6.33	0	
FC	2007/08	4	4	1	102	83*	34.00	0	1	430	197	5	39.40	2-46	0	0	2.74	3	
Lim	2007/08	4	3	1	34	22	17.00	0	0	108	114	0					6.33	1	
20T	2008/09	7	3	3	9	6*		0	0	150	163	8	20.37	3-16	0	0	6.52	1	
MORGAN, Leighton James (Otago) b Wellington 16.2.1981 RHB SLA																			
FC		7	14	1	382	71*	29.38	0	4									5	
Lim		2	2	0	6	4	3.00	0	0									0	
FC	2001/02	18	31	1	844	81	28.13	0	7									10	
Lim	2007/08	5	5	0	55	38	11.00	0	0									2	
MURDOCH, Stephen Joseph (Wellington) b Wellington 6.8.1983 RHB RM																			
FC		4	8	0	280	88	35.00	0	3	6	5	0					5.00	4	
Lim		1	1	0	7	7	7.00	0	0									0	
Lim	2008/09	6	6	0	49	19	8.16	0	0									1	
MYBURGH, Johannes Gerhardus (Canterbury) b Pretoria, Transvaal, South Africa 22.10.1980 RHB OB																			
FC		9	15	0	758	120	50.53	2	3	308	155	3	51.66	2-60	0	0	3.01	6	
Lim		9	9	0	281	112	31.22	1	0	198	143	5	28.60	2-22	0	0	4.33	3	
20T		10	10	3	186	40	26.57	0	0	97	136	3	45.33	1-19	0	0	8.41	4	
FC	1997/98	73	132	18	5180	203	45.43	13	30	2610	1326	30	44.20	4-56	0	0	3.04	50	
Lim	1999/00	90	85	9	2239	112	29.46	1	13	1648	1381	23	60.04	2-22	0	0	5.02	19	
20T	2005	30	28	6	575	73*	26.13	0	2	235	316	8	39.50	3-16	0	0	8.06	8	
NAPIER, Graham Richard (Essex, Central Districts, Essex to Netherlands) b Colchester, Essex, England 6.1.1980 RHB RM																			
Lim		8	6	1	111	73*	22.20	0	1	454	368	13	28.30	3-40	0	0	4.86	0	
20T		11	8	3	44	17*	8.80	0	0	254	294	18	16.33	3-22	0	0	6.94	6	
FC	1997	103	142	30	3350	125	29.91	3	20	13257	8134	210	38.73	6-103	3	0	3.68	39	
Lim	1997	196	151	19	2370	79	17.95	0	12	6600	5593	225	24.85	6-29	8	1	5.08	41	
20T	2003	67	49	7	697	152*	16.59	1	0	1419	1720	90	19.11	4-10	1	0	7.27	20	

Cmp	Debut	M	I	NO	Runs	HS	Avge	100	50	Balls	Runs	Wkts	Avge	BB	5i	10m	RpO	ct	st
NEESHAM, James Douglas Sheehan (Auckland) b Auckland 17.9.1990 LHB RFM																			
FC		1	1	0	0	0	0.00	0	0	66	73	0					6.63	2	
Lim		1	1	1	11	11*		0	0	48	44	2	22.00	2-44	0	0	5.50	0	
20T		1	1	0	39	39	39.00	0	0	6	20	0					20.00	0	
NETHULA, Tarun Sai (Auckland) b Kurnool, Andhra Pradesh, India 8.5.1983 RHB LBG																			
FC		7	8	1	64	28	9.14	0	0	956	655	12	54.58	4-17	0	0	4.11	3	
FC	2008/09	16	20	5	170	33	11.33	0	0	2752	1782	41	43.46	4-17	0	0	3.88	10	
NEVIN, Christopher John (Wellington) b Dunedin, Otago 3.8.1975 RHB WK																			
FC		7	13	3	303	53	30.30	0	1									29	
Lim		7	7	1	215	63	35.83	0	1									6	1
20T		9	7	2	97	41	19.40	0	0									2	1
FC	1995/96	112	172	26	5058	143*	34.64	4	28	6	0	0					0.00	304	9
Int	1999/00	37	36	0	732	74	20.33	0	4									16	3
Lim	1995/96	188	177	10	4481	149	26.83	5	24	18	26	0					8.66	191	18
20T	2005/06	28	23	3	386	87*	19.30	0	1									11	5
NICOL, Robert James (Canterbury, New Zealand to United States of America) b Auckland 28.5.1983 RHB OB,RM																			
FC		10	20	3	545	134	32.05	1	2	1182	598	9	66.44	3-65	0	0	3.03	8	
Lim		9	9	0	327	132	36.33	1	2	306	258	3	86.00	1-24	0	0	5.05	7	
20T		10	10	0	237	58	23.70	0	2	240	294	8	36.75	5-22	0	1	7.35	1	
FC	2001/02	76	122	14	3823	160	35.39	8	19	2991	1668	24	69.50	3-65	0	0	3.34	54	
Lim	2002/03	69	68	6	1915	135	30.88	2	11	1751	1340	39	34.35	5-54	0	1	4.59	29	
I20T	2010	2	2	0	10	10	5.00	0	0	9	9	0					6.00	1	
20T	2005/06	30	24	5	609	78*	32.05	0	3	447	589	20	29.45	5-22	1	1	7.90	10	
NOEMA-BARNETT, Kieran (Central Districts) b Dunedin, Otago 4.6.1987 LHB RM																			
FC		3	4	1	43	32*	14.33	0	0	492	231	1	231.00	1-29	0	0	2.81	0	
Lim		10	8	1	199	45	28.42	0	0	207	170	4	42.50	2-43	0	0	4.92	6	
20T		11	10	0	126	49	12.60	0	0	180	273	11	24.81	2-13	0	0	9.10	1	
FC	2008/09	4	5	1	54	32*	13.50	0	0	666	328	1	328.00	1-29	0	0	2.95	0	
Lim	2008/09	16	13	1	299	63	24.91	0	1	333	294	9	32.66	2-30	0	0	5.29	7	
20T	2006/07	24	22	1	247	49	11.76	0	0	294	459	15	30.60	2-13	0	0	9.36	4	
O'BRIEN, Iain Edward (New Zealand, Wellington, Middlesex to England) b Lower Hutt, Wellington 10.7.1976 RHB RM																			
Test		3	5	1	67	31	16.75	0	0	861	448	15	29.86	4-35	0	0	3.12	1	
FC		4	7	1	68	31	11.33	0	0	1131	560	21	26.66	5-75	1	0	2.97	1	
Lim		1	1	1	10	10*		0	0	60	45	2	22.50	2-45	0	0	4.50	0	
Test	2004/05	22	34	5	219	31	7.55	0	0	4394	2429	73	33.27	6-75	1	0	3.31	7	
FC	2000/01	91	113	26	756	44	8.68	0	0	16845	8392	322	26.06	8-55	14	1	2.98	17	
Int	2007/08	10	2	2	3	3*		0	0	453	488	14	34.85	3-68	0	0	6.46	1	
Lim	2003/04	58	21	17	99	19*	24.75	0	0	2818	2332	75	31.09	5-35	2	2	4.96	9	
I20T	2008/09	4								78	116	6	19.33	2-30	0	0	8.92	0	
20T	2006/07	18	5	4	6	3*	6.00	0	0	332	438	21	20.85	5-23	0	1	7.91	3	
ORAM, Jacob David Philip (Central Districts, New Zealand, New Zealand to Sri Lanka, New Zealand to United Arab Emirates, New Zealand to United States of America, New Zealand to West Indies) b Palmerston North, Manawatu 28.7.1978 LHB RM																			
Int		4	2	0	95	83	47.50	0	1	174	109	4	27.25	2-33	0	0	3.75	0	
Lim		9	7	0	258	83	36.85	0	2	420	332	11	30.18	3-48	0	0	4.74	3	
I20T		3	2	0	1	1	0.50	0	0	51	83	2	41.50	2-16	0	0	9.76	0	
20T		13	11	1	73	22	7.30	0	0	286	392	19	20.63	5-14	0	1	8.22	2	
Test	2002/03	33	59	10	1780	133	36.32	5	6	4964	1983	60	33.05	4-41	0	0	2.39	15	
FC	1997/98	85	136	18	3992	155	33.83	8	18	10682	4172	155	26.91	6-45	3	0	2.34	36	
Int	2000/01	141	102	13	2203	101*	24.75	1	12	5999	4334	142	30.52	5-26	2	2	4.33	42	
Lim	1997/98	219	171	18	4086	127	26.70	3	22	8161	5853	188	31.13	5-26	2	2	4.30	66	
I20T	2005/06	27	24	5	396	66*	20.84	0	2	387	564	12	47.00	3-33	0	0	8.74	10	
20T	2005/06	62	54	11	804	66*	18.69	0	4	964	1375	41	33.53	5-14	0	1	8.55	23	
PAPPS, Michael Hugh William (Canterbury) b Christchurch, Canterbury 2.7.1979 RHB WK																			
FC		10	20	1	927	180	48.78	4	4	14	11	0					4.71	14	
Lim		9	9	0	511	150	56.77	2	2									3	
20T		10	10	0	183	30	18.30	0	0									0	
Test	2003/04	8	16	1	246	86	16.40	0	2									11	
FC	1998/99	110	200	16	6996	192	38.02	20	29	26	17	0					3.92	128	4
Int	2003/04	6	6	2	207	92*	51.75	0	2									1	
Lim	1999/00	107	107	9	3896	150	39.75	9	21									53	3
20T	2005/06	30	28	0	577	66	20.60	0	2									3	
PARLANE, Michael Edward (Northern Districts) b Pukekohe, Auckland 22.7.1972 RHB																			
FC		9	16	3	551	68	42.38	0	7	6	4	0					4.00	11	
Lim		10	10	0	277	80	27.70	0	1									2	
20T		2	2	0	26	15	13.00	0	0									0	
FC	1992/93	135	231	15	7204	203	33.35	15	33	84	60	1	60.00	1-14	0	0	4.28	87	
Lim	1992/93	164	162	10	4415	132	29.04	5	25	3	5	0					10.00	41	
20T	2005/06	20	19	0	330	48	17.36	0	0									4	

Cmp	Debut	M	I	NO	Runs	HS	Avge	100	50	Balls	Runs	Wkts	Avge	BB	5i	10m	RpO	ct	st
PARLANE, Neal Ronald (Wellington) b Whangarei, Northland 9.8.1978 RHB																			
FC		10	20	1	763	193	40.15	2	2									11	
Lim		5	5	0	92	57	18.40	0	1									2	
20T		9	8	0	315	85	39.37	0	3									2	
FC	1996/97	85	138	11	4803	193	37.81	10	29	54	46	0					5.11	100	
Lim	1996/97	101	94	6	2264	105	25.72	1	14									48	
20T	2005/06	21	18	1	581	85	34.17	0	4									5	
PATEL, Jeetan Shashi (New Zealand, Wellington, New Zealand to South Africa) b Wellington 7.5.1980 RHB OB																			
Test		2	3	1	22	12*	11.00	0	0	468	298	4	74.50	2-75	0	0	3.82	1	
FC		9	14	2	214	71*	17.83	0	1	2379	1078	26	41.46	4-48	0	0	2.71	2	
Lim		7	5	1	9	5	2.25	0	0	372	257	7	36.71	3-38	0	0	4.14	1	
20T		9	5	2	13	6*	4.33	0	0	141	219	5	43.80	2-30	0	0	9.31	2	
Test	2005/06	11	15	3	153	27*	12.75	0	0	3024	1587	37	42.89	5-110	1	0	3.14	6	
FC	1999/00	90	109	35	1438	120	19.43	1	4	17035	8237	197	41.81	6-32	5	0	2.90	29	
Int	2005/06	39	13	7	88	34	14.66	0	0	1804	1513	42	36.02	3-11	0	0	5.03	12	
Lim	1999/00	104	53	19	304	34	8.94	0	0	5011	3942	107	36.84	4-16	2	0	4.72	30	
I20T	2005/06	11	4	1	9	5	3.00	0	0	199	269	16	16.81	3-20	0	0	8.11	4	
20T	2005/06	42	15	5	53	12	5.30	0	0	817	1009	47	21.46	3-15	0	0	7.41	14	
PATTON, Bradley Michael King (Central Districts) b Hastings, Hawke's Bay 9.11.1979 LHB RMF																			
FC		10	18	1	520	65	30.58	0	6	210	110	3	36.66	1-29	0	0	3.14	6	
Lim		3	3	0	44	20	14.66	0	0									1	
FC	2006/07	18	31	3	1041	142	37.17	2	7	360	238	6	39.66	2-19	0	0	3.96	12	
Lim	2008/09	4	4	0	47	20	11.75	0	0									1	
POLLARD, Michael Alan (Wellington) b Wellington 2.11.1989 RHB																			
FC		5	10	1	193	60	21.44	0	1									1	
Lim		4	4	0	126	53	31.50	0	1									0	
RANCE, Seth Hayden Arnold (Central Districts) b Wellington 23.8.1987 RHB RM																			
FC		6	8	0	180	71	22.50	0	2	894	499	8	62.37	2-24	0	0	3.34	2	
Lim		5	3	1	15	11	7.50	0	0	274	258	10	25.80	4-71	1	0	5.65	0	
20T		6	1	1	1	1*		0	0	144	153	11	13.90	4-13	1	0	6.37	6	
FC	2008/09	7	9	0	211	71	23.44	0	2	1074	624	9	69.33	2-24	0	0	3.48	3	
RAVAL, Jeet Ashokbhai (Auckland) b Ahmedabad, Gujarat, India 22.5.1988 LHB LB																			
FC		7	13	1	520	134	43.33	1	4	258	150	4	37.50	2-10	0	0	3.48	4	
FC	2008/09	11	17	1	821	256	51.31	2	4	258	150	4	37.50	2-10	0	0	3.48	6	
REDMOND, Aaron James (Otago, Gloucestershire, New Zealand to South Africa, New Zealand to United Arab Emirates, New Zealand to United States of America, New Zealand to West Indies, Otago to India) b Auckland 23.9.1979 RHB LB																			
FC		2	2	0	148	136	74.00	1	0									1	
Lim		2	2	0	31	18	15.50	0	0									0	
Test	2008	7	14	1	299	83	23.00	0	2	75	62	3	20.66	2-47	0	0	4.96	5	
FC	1999/00	86	147	10	4529	146	33.05	8	27	7898	4314	100	43.14	4-30	0	0	3.27	66	
Int	2009/10	5	5	0	136	52	27.20	0	1									2	
Lim	1999/00	86	83	7	1820	134*	23.94	2	8	998	839	20	41.95	3-40	0	0	5.04	23	
I20T	2009	7	6	0	126	63	21.00	0	1	17	24	2	12.00	2-24	0	0	8.47	3	
20T	2005/06	37	32	1	755	100*	24.35	1	4	251	380	14	27.14	4-24	1	0	9.08	15	
RHODES, Stewart John (Wellington) b Orange, New South Wales, Australia 1.12.1986 LHB RM																			
FC		5	10	1	391	142*	43.44	2	1	354	229	5	45.80	2-38	0	0	3.88	2	
Lim		6	6	2	186	50	46.50	0	1	184	167	4	41.75	2-31	0	0	5.44	4	
RUTHERFORD, Hamish Duncan (Otago, Otago to India) b Dunedin, Otago 27.4.1989 LHB																			
FC		1	2	0	14	12	7.00	0	0									0	
Lim		4	4	0	49	30	12.25	0	0									1	
20T		9	8	0	144	38	18.00	0	0									5	
FC	2008/09	6	11	0	131	41	11.90	0	0									3	
Lim	2008/09	7	6	0	76	30	12.66	0	0									2	
20T	2008/09	18	17	0	392	87	23.05	0	1									8	
RYDER, Jesse Daniel (Wellington, New Zealand to South Africa, New Zealand to West Indies) b Masterton, Wairarapa 6.8.1984 LHB RM																			
FC		1	1	0	103	103	103.00	1	0	46	11	0					1.43	1	
Test	2008/09	11	20	2	898	201	49.88	2	4	378	212	4	53.00	2-7	0	0	3.36	8	
FC	2002/03	53	85	6	3514	236	44.48	8	17	2789	1294	45	28.75	4-23	0	0	2.78	44	
Int	2007/08	21	19	1	637	105	35.38	1	3	256	282	8	35.25	3-29	0	0	6.60	5	
Lim	2002/03	78	75	3	1933	114	26.84	3	9	1180	1154	39	29.58	4-39	1	0	5.86	24	
I20T	2007/08	14	14	0	324	62	23.14	0	2	60	68	2	34.00	1-2	0	0	6.80	5	
20T	2005/06	32	31	2	628	66	21.65	0	4	362	492	9	54.66	2-14	0	0	8.15	10	
SCHAW, Robert James (Wellington) b Waipukurau, Hawke's Bay 12.5.1984 LHB LB																			
FC		4	6	1	38	16	7.60	0	0	464	361	7	51.57	2-44	0	0	4.66	2	
Lim		3	2	1	7	5*	7.00	0	0	78	78	1	78.00	1-26	0	0	6.00	1	
FC	2006/07	18	27	3	357	34	14.87	0	0	2657	1828	33	55.39	5-130	1	0	4.12	9	
Lim	2006/07	21	12	4	71	18*	8.87	0	0	1084	882	17	51.88	2-36	0	0	4.88	2	
20T	2006/07	17	7	4	71	19*	23.66	0	0	284	428	16	26.75	3-21	0	0	9.04	4	

Cmp	Debut	M	I	NO	Runs	HS	Avge	100	50	Balls	Runs	Wkts	Avge	BB	5i	10m	RpO	ct	st
SCOTT, Bradley Esmond (Northern Districts) b Ashburton, Canterbury 16.9.1979 LHB LFM																			
FC		6	8	0	158	65	19.75	0	1	930	459	8	57.37	2-51	0	0	2.96	1	
Lim		7	4	2	37	17*	18.50	0	0	318	252	12	21.00	3-40	0	0	4.75	1	
20T		8	5	3	69	20*	34.50	0	0	165	184	15	12.26	4-13	1	0	6.69	4	
FC	2000/01	56	72	17	1246	96	22.65	0	6	10443	4427	157	28.19	6-20	5	0	2.54	19	
Lim	2003/04	73	44	18	485	44	18.65	0	0	3672	2900	90	32.22	4-63	1	0	4.73	18	
20T	2005/06	26	18	11	177	22*	25.28	0	0	498	651	28	23.25	4-13	1	0	7.84	9	
SHAH, Owais Alam (Middlesex, Delhi Daredevils, England to South Africa, Kolkata Knight Riders, Middlesex to Netherlands, Wellington) b Karachi, Sind, Pakistan 22.10.1978 RHB OB																			
Lim		2	2	0	37	29	18.50	0	0	6	9	0					9.00	3	
20T		9	8	1	200	65*	28.57	0	1	2	10	0					30.00	5	
Test	2005/06	6	10	0	269	88	26.90	0	2	30	31	0					6.20	2	
FC	1996	222	379	34	14521	203	42.08	39	72	2237	1489	26	57.26	3-33	0	0	3.99	170	
Int	2001	71	66	6	1834	107*	30.56	1	12	193	184	7	26.28	3-15	0	0	5.72	21	
Lim	1995	325	307	37	9406	134	34.83	13	60	912	896	27	33.18	4-11	1	0	5.89	112	
I20T	2007	17	15	1	347	55*	24.78	0	1									5	
20T	2003	89	85	17	2160	80	31.76	0	11	45	64	4	16.00	2-26	0	0	8.53	33	
SHAW, Gareth Simon (Auckland) b Auckland 14.2.1982 RHB RMF																			
FC		5	6	1	79	28	15.80	0	0	1013	587	13	45.15	5-101	1	0	3.47	1	
FC	2001/02	19	24	9	158	28	10.53	0	0	2993	1823	62	29.40	5-49	3	0	3.65	4	
Lim	2001/02	8	5	5	26	14*		0	0	306	244	12	20.33	3-24	0	0	4.78	0	
20T	2005/06	2								40	93	4	23.25	2-34	0	0	13.95	2	
SHAW, Lance Joseph (Auckland) b Auckland 24.8.1983 RHB RMF																			
FC		4	5	1	42	18	10.50	0	0	758	484	9	53.77	2-69	0	0	3.83	2	
Lim		5	3	0	15	13	5.00	0	0	245	211	10	21.10	4-49	1	0	5.16	1	
FC	2005/06	27	33	8	254	52*	10.16	0	1	4176	2381	83	28.68	5-59	2	0	3.42	5	
Lim	2005/06	10	7	0	52	20	7.42	0	0	401	344	14	24.57	4-49	1	0	5.14	1	
20T	2005/06	1								18	20	1	20.00	1-20	0	0	6.66	0	
SHERLOCK, Richard Roland (Auckland) b Palmerston North, Manawatu 15.9.1983 RHB RF																			
FC		1	1	0	9	9	9.00	0	0	216	178	7	25.42	7-133	1	0	4.94	0	
Lim		2	1	0	12	12	12.00	0	0	90	99	3	33.00	2-57	0	0	6.60	0	
FC	2003/04	13	18	5	173	64	13.30	0	1	1780	1227	38	32.28	7-133	1	0	4.13	3	
Lim	2004/05	6	4	1	37	15	12.33	0	0	306	282	4	70.50	2-57	0	0	5.52	0	
20T	2006	1	1	0	2	2	2.00	0	0	24	47	2	23.50	2-47	0	0	11.75	0	
SINCLAIR, Mathew Stuart (Central Districts, New Zealand) b Katherine, Northern Territory, Australia 9.11.1975 RHB RM																			
Test		1	2	0	40	29	20.00	0	0	18	1	0					0.33	0	
FC		10	17	2	818	165	54.53	3	3	772	339	8	42.37	3-29	0	0	2.63	8	
Lim		10	10	2	396	105*	49.50	1	3	60	47	0					4.70	9	
20T		11	11	2	306	69	34.00	0	3									5	
Test	1999/00	33	56	5	1635	214	32.05	3	4	42	14	0					2.00	31	
FC	1995/96	158	268	28	11680	268	48.66	30	59	2197	955	22	43.40	3-29	0	0	2.60	157	1
Int	1999/00	54	50	4	1304	118*	28.34	2	8									17	
Lim	1995/96	209	199	25	5912	118*	33.97	6	43	172	183	3	61.00	1-15	0	0	6.38	98	2
I20T	2004/05	2	2	0	0	0	0.00	0	0									0	
20T	2004/05	34	34	4	821	85*	27.36	0	8	6	13	0					13.00	17	
SOUTHEE, Timothy Grant (New Zealand, Northern Districts, New Zealand to Sri Lanka, New Zealand to United Arab Emirates, New Zealand to United States of America, New Zealand to West Indies) b Whangarei, Northland 11.12.1988 RHB RFM																			
Test		4	5	1	72	45	18.00	0	0	816	447	13	34.38	4-61	0	0	3.28	2	
FC		6	7	1	116	45	19.33	0	0	1200	594	23	25.82	8-27	1	0	2.97	3	
Int		7	5	2	8	4*	2.66	0	0	355	328	9	36.44	4-36	1	0	5.54	4	
Lim		10	7	2	21	13	4.20	0	0	473	462	12	38.50	4-36	1	0	5.86	5	
I20T		2								36	59	0					9.83	1	
20T		12	7	3	98	35*	24.50	0	0	245	312	14	22.28	3-15	0	0	7.64	6	
Test	2007/08	9	14	3	199	77*	18.09	0	1	1743	1022	25	40.88	5-55	1	0	3.51	3	
FC	2006/07	31	39	6	476	77*	14.42	0	2	6199	3103	106	29.27	8-27	5	0	3.00	7	
Int	2008	33	19	5	132	32	9.42	0	0	1645	1469	44	33.38	4-36	3	0	5.35	6	
Lim	2007/08	44	28	5	197	32	8.56	0	0	2210	1985	57	34.82	4-36	3	0	5.38	9	
I20T	2007/08	16	6	2	25	12*	6.25	0	0	330	473	14	33.78	3-28	0	0	8.60	6	
20T	2006/07	33	17	5	139	35*	11.58	0	0	698	937	34	27.55	3-15	0	0	8.05	12	
STEWART, Shanan Luke (Canterbury, New Zealand) b Christchurch, Canterbury 21.6.1982 RHB RM																			
FC		8	14	3	812	227*	73.81	3	3									2	
Int		2	2	0	10	6	5.00	0	0									0	
Lim		11	11	0	411	101	37.36	1	2									1	
20T		10	10	0	199	57	19.90	0	2									1	
FC	2001/02	64	113	10	3870	227*	37.57	7	22	618	344	4	86.00	2-52	0	0	3.34	22	
Lim	2001/02	88	86	5	2676	120	33.03	4	12	36	51	2	25.50	2-51	0	0	8.50	14	
20T	2005/06	25	23	2	548	88*	26.09	0	5									3	

Cmp	Debut	M	I	NO	Runs	HS	Avge	100	50	Balls	Runs	Wkts	Avge	BB	5i	10m	RpO	ct	st
STYRIS, Scott Bernard (Auckland, New Zealand, Deccan Chargers, Essex, New Zealand to Sri Lanka, New Zealand to United Arab Emirates, New Zealand to United States of America, New Zealand to West Indies) b Brisbane, Queensland, Australia 10.7.1975 RHB RFM																			
FC		3	5	1	178	112	44.50	1	0									1	
Int		5	5	1	199	55	49.75	0	1	161	138	0					5.14	2	
Lim		13	12	1	419	71	38.09	0	3	472	345	6	57.50	3-24	0	0	4.38	6	
20T		11	11	1	274	59	27.40	0	2	252	301	12	25.08	3-15	0	0	7.16	2	
Test	2002	29	48	4	1586	170	36.04	5	6	1960	1015	20	50.75	3-28	0	0	3.10	23	
FC	1994/95	126	210	19	5964	212*	31.22	10	29	12657	6353	203	31.29	6-32	9	1	3.01	100	
Int	1999/00	169	146	22	4056	141	32.70	4	25	5642	4464	128	34.87	6-25	4	1	4.74	67	
Lim	1994/95	312	276	46	7667	141	33.33	5	52	11361	8714	287	30.36	6-25	8	1	4.60	121	
I20T	2004/05	28	26	2	492	66	20.50	0	1	279	327	17	19.23	3-5	0	0	7.03	7	
20T	2004/05	103	97	9	2135	106*	24.26	1	9	1639	2093	79	26.49	3-5	0	0	7.66	26	
TAYLOR, Luteru Ross Poutoa Lote (Central Districts, New Zealand, Durham, New Zealand to South Africa, New Zealand to Sri Lanka, New Zealand to United Arab Emirates, New Zealand to United States of America, New Zealand to West Indies, Royal Challengers Bangalore, Victoria) b Lower Hutt, Wellington 8.3.1984 RHB OB																			
Test		6	11	0	598	138	54.36	1	4									11	
FC		7	13	0	693	138	53.30	1	5									13	
Int		7	7	0	309	78	44.14	0	4									4	
Lim		7	7	0	309	78	44.14	0	4									4	
I20T		3	2	0	15	9	7.50	0	0									1	
20T		14	13	3	398	80	39.80	0	3	66	93	1	93.00	1-9	0	0	8.45	10	
Test	2007/08	25	46	1	1941	154*	43.13	5	9	32	14	0					2.62	45	
FC	2002/03	71	120	3	4774	217	40.80	10	26	602	330	4	82.50	2-34	0	0	3.28	89	
Int	2005/06	84	77	11	2376	128*	36.00	3	16	30	32	0					6.40	62	
Lim	2002/03	129	122	15	4028	132*	37.64	7	27	306	240	3	80.00	1-13	0	0	4.70	87	
I20T	2006/07	34	31	2	590	63	20.34	0	3									22	
20T	2005/06	92	87	14	2395	111*	32.80	1	14	180	269	8	33.62	3-28	0	0	8.96	47	
THOMPSON, Ewen Paul (Central Districts) b Warkworth, Auckland 17.12.1979 LHB LFM																			
FC		8	11	0	190	41	17.27	0	0	1669	819	34	24.08	5-64	3	0	2.94	3	
Lim		10	7	1	70	24	11.66	0	0	531	398	14	28.42	6-20	0	1	4.49	2	
20T		6	3	0	15	7	5.00	0	0	138	179	3	59.66	1-30	0	0	7.78	2	
FC	2000/01	52	75	9	1734	126	26.27	3	8	10156	5310	177	30.00	7-55	6	1	3.13	18	
Int	2008/09	1								24	42	0					10.50	0	
Lim	1999/00	69	48	15	599	62*	18.15	0	3	3385	2648	104	25.46	6-20	3	2	4.69	17	
I20T	2008/09	1	1	1	1	1*		0	0	18	18	1	18.00	1-18	0	0	6.00	0	
20T	2005/06	26	19	7	228	59	19.00	0	1	570	718	31	23.16	5-32	2	1	7.55	6	
TODD, Gregory Rex (Otago) b Masterton, Wairarapa 17.6.1982 LHB RM																			
FC		10	17	2	561	95	37.40	0	5	481	303	5	60.60	2-73	0	0	3.78	7	
Lim		3	2	1	108	69	108.00	0	1									0	
FC	2000/01	55	97	15	3063	165	37.35	4	18	2043	1212	19	63.78	2-26	0	0	3.55	22	
Lim	2000/01	58	53	6	1297	95	27.59	0	7	459	414	12	34.50	2-23	0	0	5.41	19	
20T	2005/06	17	16	4	341	39	28.41	0	0									5	
TODD, Keeley William Martin (Auckland) b Auckland 31.7.1982 LHB RM																			
Lim		2	2	0	30	19	15.00	0	0	60	64	2	32.00	1-20	0	0	6.40	0	
FC	2004/05	5	8	0	129	84	16.12	0	1									2	
Lim	2004/05	5	5	0	48	19	9.60	0	0	60	64	2	32.00	1-20	0	0	6.40	0	
20T	2006/07	4	3	1	30	29	15.00	0	0	12	17	0					8.50	0	
TUFFEY, Daryl Raymond (Auckland, New Zealand, New Zealand to South Africa, New Zealand to Sri Lanka) b Milton, Otago 11.6.1978 RHB RFM																			
Test		4	6	3	164	80*	54.66	0	1	767	388	11	35.27	4-52	0	0	3.03	3	
FC		5	7	3	220	80*	55.00	0	2	959	469	13	36.07	4-52	0	0	2.93	4	
Int		6	5	1	112	36	28.00	0	0	288	295	6	49.16	3-58	0	0	6.14	1	
Lim		8	7	2	150	36	30.00	0	0	396	343	10	34.30	3-12	0	0	5.19	3	
I20T		2	1	0	0	0	0.00	0	0	36	43	2	21.50	2-16	0	0	7.16	0	
20T		13	7	5	52	17*	26.00	0	0	296	317	16	19.81	3-19	0	0	6.42	1	
Test	1999/00	26	36	10	427	80*	16.42	0	1	4877	2445	77	31.75	6-54	2	0	3.00	15	
FC	1996/97	84	100	25	1232	89*	16.42	0	6	15661	7274	280	25.97	7-12	10	1	2.78	37	
Int	2000/01	92	50	21	291	36	10.03	0	0	4248	3447	106	32.51	4-24	2	0	4.86	20	
Lim	1997/98	208	114	52	806	38*	13.00	0	0	9885	7708	246	31.33	5-21	3	2	4.67	49	
I20T	2004/05	3	2	1	5	5*	5.00	0	0	60	93	3	31.00	2-16	0	0	9.30	0	
20T	2004/05	23	13	8	72	17*	14.40	0	0	524	621	24	25.87	3-19	0	0	7.11	3	
TUGAGA, Malaesaili Julian (Wellington) b Wellington 16.2.1990 LHB RFM																			
FC		8	13	2	156	103	14.18	1	0	1255	887	23	38.56	5-77	1	0	4.24	2	
Lim		2								66	97	2	48.50	1-23	0	0	8.81	1	
FC	2008/09	11	17	5	204	103	17.00	1	0	1549	1065	26	40.96	5-77	1	0	4.12	3	
TURNER, Nicholas Mirek (Auckland) b Invercargill, Southland 3.8.1983 LHB RFM																			
FC		1	1	0	0	0	0.00	0	0	210	97	2	48.50	2-66	0	0	2.77	0	
FC	2006/07	4	5	2	53	27*	17.66	0	0	762	338	9	37.55	3-57	0	0	2.66	1	
Lim	2006/07	10	3	2	3	2*	3.00	0	0	429	342	12	28.50	3-32	0	0	4.78	3	
20T	2006/07	6	2	1	4	3	4.00	0	0	72	97	3	32.33	2-39	0	0	8.08	1	

Cmp	Debut	M	I	NO	Runs	HS	Avge	100	50	Balls	Runs	Wkts	Avge	BB	5i	10m	RpO	ct	st
VAN BEEK, Logan Verjus (Canterbury) b Christchurch, Canterbury 7.9.1990 RHB RFM																			
FC		2	1	0	11	11	11.00	0	0	87	53	1	53.00	1-30	0	0	3.65	1	
Lim		1								12	25	0					12.50	0	
VAN WYK, Cornelius Francoius Kruger (Canterbury) b Wolmaransstad, North-West, South Africa 7.2.1980 RHB WK																			
FC		10	15	6	518	178*	57.55	1	2									30	2
Lim		9	9	4	172	46	34.40	0	0									9	2
20T		10	9	2	62	14	8.85	0	0									7	1
FC	2000/01	83	125	26	3466	178*	35.01	4	18	18	9	1	9.00	1-7	0	0	3.00	249	13
Lim	2000/01	102	82	43	1681	90*	43.10	0	8									111	14
20T	2004/05	34	24	6	347	40	19.27	0	0									22	5
VERMEULEN, Michael John (Canterbury) b Christchurch, Canterbury 30.12.1982 RHB RMF																			
FC		1	2	2	10	10*		0	0	194	132	4	33.00	2-65	0	0	4.08	0	
VETTORI, Daniel Luca (New Zealand, Northern Districts, Delhi Daredevils, New Zealand to South Africa, New Zealand to United Arab Emirates, New Zealand to United States of America, New Zealand to West Indies, Queensland) b Auckland 27.1.1979 LHB SLA																			
Test		6	11	0	470	134	42.72	1	2	1872	851	22	38.68	4-36	0	0	2.72	7	
FC		6	11	0	470	134	42.72	1	2	1872	851	22	38.68	4-36	0	0	2.72	7	
Int		7	7	1	180	70	30.00	0	1	402	247	12	20.58	3-33	0	0	3.68	3	
Lim		7	7	1	180	70	30.00	0	1	402	247	12	20.58	3-33	0	0	3.68	3	
I20T		3	1	0	3	3	3.00	0	0	72	60	4	15.00	3-6	0	0	5.00	0	
20T		13	11	0	249	57	22.63	0	1	298	333	18	18.50	3-6	0	0	6.70	5	
Test	1996/97	100	152	23	3962	140	30.71	5	22	24997	11007	325	33.86	7-87	18	3	2.64	55	
FC	1996/97	152	220	31	5809	140	30.73	8	32	35722	15920	499	31.90	7-87	28	3	2.67	79	
Int	1996/97	255	160	49	1895	83	17.07	0	4	12111	8367	268	31.22	5-7	7	2	4.14	71	
Lim	1996/97	322	211	57	3149	138	20.44	2	10	15529	10550	347	30.40	5-7	7	2	4.07	102	
I20T	2007/08	28	20	6	187	38	13.35	0	0	649	580	35	16.57	4-20	1	0	5.36	8	
20T	2005/06	57	43	11	669	57	20.90	0	1	1282	1321	67	19.71	4-20	1	0	6.18	22	
VINCENT, Lou (Auckland, Northamptonshire) b Warkworth, Auckland 11.11.1978 RHB RM																			
Lim		5	5	0	83	32	16.60	0	0	30	28	0					5.60	4	
20T		11	11	1	290	105*	29.00	1	2									3	
Test	2001/02	23	40	1	1332	224	34.15	3	9	6	2	0					2.00	19	
FC	1997/98	92	151	11	4922	224	35.15	10	29	1003	527	10	52.70	2-37	0	0	3.15	109	
Int	2000/01	102	99	10	2413	172	27.11	3	11	20	25	1	25.00	1-0	0	0	7.50	41	
Lim	1998/99	199	193	13	5119	172	28.43	7	27	243	245	4	61.25	2-25	0	0	6.04	113	3
I20T	2005/06	9	9	0	174	42	19.33	0	0									1	
20T	2005/06	49	49	3	1222	105*	26.56	2	6	50	73	4	18.25	3-28	0	0	8.76	19	
WAGNER, Neil (Otago to India, Otago) b Pretoria, Transvaal, South Africa 13.3.1986 LHB LMF																			
FC		8	11	1	284	70	28.40	0	1	1810	1047	28	37.39	4-62	0	0	3.47	3	
Lim		8	6	2	98	27	24.50	0	0	384	415	12	34.58	3-43	0	0	6.48	1	
20T		8	4	0	3	2	0.75	0	0	150	219	12	18.25	3-21	0	0	8.76	1	
FC	2005/06	35	42	9	556	70	16.84	0	1	6150	3376	138	24.46	5-28	4	0	3.29	8	
Lim	2005/06	38	20	5	154	27	10.26	0	0	1824	1555	61	25.49	5-34	3	1	5.11	7	
20T	2008/09	17	7	1	5	2	0.83	0	0	355	479	20	23.95	3-21	0	0	8.09	1	
WATLING, Bradley-John (New Zealand, Northern Districts, New Zealand to Sri Lanka, New Zealand to United Arab Emirates) b Durban, Natal, South Africa 9.7.1985 RHB WK																			
Test		4	8	1	195	60*	27.85	0	1									5	
FC		9	16	2	547	136	39.07	1	3	6	3	0					3.00	10	
Lim		8	8	1	384	145*	54.85	1	3									9	
20T		10	10	0	207	73	20.70	0	1									4	
FC	2004/05	47	86	4	2460	153	30.00	5	11	11	8	0					4.36	56	
Int	2010	3	2	0	57	55	28.50	0	1									2	
Lim	2004/05	50	49	5	1754	145*	39.86	5	12									24	
I20T	2009/10	2	2	0	29	22	14.50	0	0									2	
20T	2007/08	25	24	4	440	73	22.00	0	1									11	
WELLS, Samuel Raymond (Otago) b Dunedin, Otago 13.7.1984 LHB RM																			
FC		7	12	4	478	115*	59.75	2	3	891	513	21	24.42	5-26	2	0	3.45	2	
Lim		1	1	0	14	14	14.00	0	0	18	24	1	24.00	1-24	0	0	8.00	0	
FC	2007/08	13	21	5	598	115*	37.37	2	3	1351	758	27	28.07	5-26	2	0	3.36	5	
Lim	2008/09	2	2	0	27	14	13.50	0	0	42	42	1	42.00	1-24	0	0	6.00	0	
WESTON, Timothy Ian (Central Districts) b Stratford, Taranaki 6.6.1982 RHB WK																			
FC		8	14	1	456	82	35.07	0	2									2	
Lim		8	7	0	148	60	21.14	0	1									1	
20T		9	7	3	87	35	21.75	0	0									7	
FC	2005/06	36	61	9	2083	152	40.05	1	14									18	
Lim	2006/07	23	22	2	542	77*	27.10	0	3									6	
20T	2008/09	14	11	3	135	35	16.87	0	0									9	
WHEELER, Ben Matthew (Central Districts) b Blenheim, Marlborough 10.11.1991 RHB LM																			
FC		2	3	1	24	10*	12.00	0	0	294	167	3	55.66	2-67	0	0	3.40	2	
WILLIAMSON, Kane Stuart (Northern Districts, New Zealand to Sri Lanka) b Tauranga, Bay of Plenty 8.8.1990 RHB OB																			
FC		10	15	2	614	192	47.23	2	1	1016	592	13	45.53	3-48	0	0	3.49	12	
Lim		11	11	3	621	108*	77.62	2	5	403	325	13	25.00	5-51	0	1	4.83	5	

Cmp	Debut	M	I	NO	Runs	HS	Avge	100	50	Balls	Runs	Wkts	Avge	BB	5i	10m	RpO	ct	st
20T		3	3	1	13	13	6.50	0	0	36	41	0					6.83	1	
FC	2007/08	20	33	2	1428	192	46.06	4	6	2290	1282	30	42.73	5-75	1	0	3.35	24	
Int	2010	4	3	0	13	13	4.33	0	0	84	48	1	48.00	1-2	0	0	3.42	1	
Lim	2007/08	30	27	7	982	108*	49.10	3	6	913	674	18	37.44	5-51	0	1	4.42	13	
20T	2008/09	7	7	1	70	30	11.66	0	0	90	106	1	106.00	1-21	0	0	7.06	5	
WILSON, Bradley Svend (Northern Districts) b Auckland 10.4.1985 RHB OB																			
FC		8	15	3	435	107	36.25	2	0									11	
Lim		1	1	0	37	37	37.00	0	0									0	
FC	2004/05	32	58	3	1529	109	27.80	4	5	18	26	0					8.66	27	
Lim	2007/08	2	2	0	61	37	30.50	0	0									2	
20T	2008/09	2	2	0	103	91	51.50	0	1									2	
WOODCOCK, Luke James (Wellington) b Wellington 19.3.1982 LHB SLA																			
FC		10	20	5	988	220*	65.86	1	7	1277	560	8	70.00	2-21	0	0	2.63	4	
Lim		8	6	0	183	53	30.50	0	2	360	239	2	119.50	1-29	0	0	3.98	1	
20T		9	5	0	43	25	8.60	0	0	84	112	3	37.33	3-36	0	0	8.00	3	
FC	2001/02	71	118	15	3433	220*	33.33	4	20	7566	3259	78	41.78	4-3	0	0	2.58	34	
Lim	2003/04	63	49	8	902	71	22.00	0	5	2192	1685	40	42.12	4-36	2	0	4.61	15	
20T	2005/06	24	15	5	223	36*	22.30	0	0	324	444	19	23.36	3-27	0	0	8.22	4	
WORKER, George Herrick (Central Districts) b Palmerston North, Manawatu 23.8.1989 LHB SLA																			
FC		9	15	0	238	61	15.86	0	2	1803	1118	13	86.00	3-204	0	0	3.72	10	
Lim		10	10	2	235	84	29.37	0	1	366	311	4	77.75	2-49	0	0	5.09	1	
20T		4	3	1	22	12*	11.00	0	0	12	18	2	9.00	2-9	0	0	9.00	1	
FC	2007/08	22	38	1	840	71	22.70	0	6	3561	2016	28	72.00	3-54	0	0	3.39	21	
Lim	2007/08	20	20	2	533	86	29.61	0	3	671	559	10	55.90	2-30	0	0	4.99	3	
20T	2008/09	8	7	1	43	12*	7.16	0	0	84	139	4	34.75	2-9	0	0	9.92	4	
YASIR ARAFAT Satti (KRL, Otago, Pakistan to United Arab Emirates, Sussex, Sussex to India) b Rawalpindi, Punjab, Pakistan 12.3.1982 RHB RFM																			
Lim		6	5	1	156	110*	39.00	1	0	300	345	8	43.12	2-22	0	0	6.90	1	
20T		8	3	0	13	6	4.33	0	0	168	186	8	23.25	3-16	0	0	6.64	0	
Test	2007/08	3	3	1	94	50*	47.00	0	1	627	438	9	48.66	5-161	1	0	4.19	0	
FC	1997/98	168	250	37	5788	122	27.17	4	31	28055	16236	674	24.08	9-35	39	5	3.47	45	
Int	1999/00	11	8	3	74	27	14.80	0	0	414	373	4	93.25	1-28	0	0	5.40	2	
Lim	1997/98	207	149	39	2333	110*	21.20	1	7	9990	8212	330	24.88	6-24	14	5	4.93	48	
I20T	2007/08	7	7	4	64	17	21.33	0	0	150	195	6	32.50	3-32	0	0	7.80	1	
20T	2005/06	82	57	17	667	49	16.67	0	0	1689	2168	103	21.04	4-17	5	0	7.70	12	
YOUNG, Reece Alan (Auckland) b Auckland 15.9.1979 RHB WK																			
FC		9	15	4	574	126*	52.18	1	5	30	65	1	65.00	1-65	0	0	13.00	20	
Lim		10	10	1	393	94	43.66	0	3									4	1
20T		10	8	0	58	18	7.25	0	0									9	2
FC	1998/99	94	127	23	3031	126*	29.14	5	19	42	68	1	68.00	1-65	0	0	9.71	265	5
Lim	1999/00	75	63	14	1377	119	28.10	1	5									74	14
20T	2005/06	24	15	2	131	26	10.07	0	0									14	4
YOVICH, Joseph Adam Frank (Northern Districts) b Whangarei, Northland 15.12.1976 LHB RFM																			
FC		10	12	2	409	128*	40.90	1	3	1033	617	16	38.56	3-29	0	0	3.58	3	
Lim		11	9	4	153	39	30.60	0	0	420	426	12	35.50	3-50	0	0	6.08	7	
20T		10	8	2	88	22*	14.66	0	0	156	221	10	22.10	3-26	0	0	8.50	1	
FC	1996/97	99	151	29	3552	144	29.11	3	20	14652	8432	253	33.32	7-64	8	1	3.45	30	
Lim	1997/98	107	90	24	1469	78*	22.25	0	6	3543	3193	122	26.17	4-44	3	0	5.40	34	
20T	2005/06	26	23	6	225	33*	13.23	0	0	447	638	31	20.58	4-36	1	0	8.56	2	

AUSTRALIA TO NEW ZEALAND 2009/10

Cmp	Debut	M	I	NO	Runs	HS	Avge	100	50	Balls	Runs	Wkts	Avge	BB	5i	10m	RpO	ct	st
BIRT, T.R.																			
I20T		1																0	
20T		1																0	
BOLLINGER, D.E.																			
Test		2	1	0	4	4	4.00	0	0	420	252	12	21.00	5-28	1	0	3.60	0	
FC		2	1	0	4	4	4.00	0	0	420	252	12	21.00	5-28	1	0	3.60	0	
Int		5	1	1	1	1*		0	0	236	231	4	57.75	2-58	0	0	5.87	2	
Lim		5	1	1	1	1*		0	0	236	231	4	57.75	2-58	0	0	5.87	2	
CHRISTIAN, D.T.																			
I20T		2								18	40	0					13.33	0	
20T		2								18	40	0					13.33	0	
CLARKE, M.J.																			
Test		2	3	0	259	168	86.33	1	1	96	27	1	27.00	1-27	0	0	1.68	3	
FC		2	3	0	259	168	86.33	1	1	96	27	1	27.00	1-27	0	0	1.68	3	
Int		2	2	0	33	22	16.50	0	0	12	8	0					4.00	0	
Lim		2	2	0	33	22	16.50	0	0	12	8	0					4.00	0	
I20T		2	2	1	85	67	85.00	0	1									1	
20T		2	2	1	85	67	85.00	0	1									1	

Cmp Debut	M	I	NO	Runs	HS	Avge	100	50	Balls	Runs	Wkts	Avge	BB	5i	10m	RpO	ct	st
HADDIN, B.J.																		
Test	2	3	1	71	48	35.50	0	0									9	
FC	2	3	1	71	48	35.50	0	0									9	
Int	5	5	0	192	110	38.40	1	1									9	
Lim	5	5	0	192	110	38.40	1	1									9	
I20T	2	1	0	47	47	47.00	0	0									3	
20T	2	1	0	47	47	47.00	0	0									3	
HARRIS, R.J.																		
Test	2	2	1	28	18*	28.00	0	0	423	207	9	23.00	4-77	0	0	2.93	1	
FC	2	2	1	28	18*	28.00	0	0	423	207	9	23.00	4-77	0	0	2.93	1	
Int	4	1	1	0	0*		0	0	194	176	8	22.00	3-34	0	0	5.44	2	
Lim	4	1	1	0	0*		0	0	194	176	8	22.00	3-34	0	0	5.44	2	
I20T	1								24	40	1	40.00	1-40	0	0	10.00	0	
20T	1								24	40	1	40.00	1-40	0	0	10.00	0	
HAURITZ, N.M.																		
Test	2	2	2	53	41*		0	0	558	263	4	65.75	3-119	0	0	2.82	0	
FC	2	2	2	53	41*		0	0	558	263	4	65.75	3-119	0	0	2.82	0	
Int	5	2	0	13	9	6.50	0	0	198	185	6	30.83	3-46	0	0	5.60	1	
Lim	5	2	0	13	9	6.50	0	0	198	185	6	30.83	3-46	0	0	5.60	1	
HOPES, J.R.																		
Int	5	3	0	102	40	34.00	0	0	216	184	4	46.00	2-38	0	0	5.11	1	
Lim	5	3	0	102	40	34.00	0	0	216	184	4	46.00	2-38	0	0	5.11	1	
HUGHES, P.J.																		
Test	1	2	1	106	86*	106.00	0	1									0	
FC	1	2	1	106	86*	106.00	0	1									0	
HUSSEY, D.J.																		
I20T	2	2	0	56	46	28.00	0	0	24	27	0					6.75	1	
20T	2	2	0	56	46	28.00	0	0	24	27	0					6.75	1	
HUSSEY, M.E.K.																		
Test	2	3	0	93	67	31.00	0	1									2	
FC	2	3	0	93	67	31.00	0	1									2	
Int	5	5	1	198	59	49.50	0	2									4	
Lim	5	5	1	198	59	49.50	0	2									4	
JOHNSON, M.G.																		
Test	2	2	0	0	0	0.00	0	0	463	277	12	23.08	6-73	1	1	3.59	0	
FC	2	2	0	0	0	0.00	0	0	463	277	12	23.08	6-73	1	1	3.59	0	
Int	5	3	2	43	21*	43.00	0	0	279	220	12	18.33	4-51	1	0	4.73	1	
Lim	5	3	2	43	21*	43.00	0	0	279	220	12	18.33	4-51	1	0	4.73	1	
I20T	1	1	0	1	1	1.00	0	0	24	19	3	6.33	3-19	0	0	4.75	0	
20T	1	1	0	1	1	1.00	0	0	24	19	3	6.33	3-19	0	0	4.75	0	
KATICH, S.M.																		
Test	2	4	1	291	106	97.00	1	2									1	
FC	2	4	1	291	106	97.00	1	2									1	
McKAY, C.J.																		
Int	1	1	0	2	2	2.00	0	0	60	57	2	28.50	2-57	0	0	5.70	0	
Lim	1	1	0	2	2	2.00	0	0	60	57	2	28.50	2-57	0	0	5.70	0	
NANNES, D.P.																		
I20T	2								48	73	3	24.33	2-22	0	0	9.12	0	
20T	2								48	73	3	24.33	2-22	0	0	9.12	0	
NORTH, M.J.																		
Test	2	3	1	211	112*	105.50	1	1	66	15	0					1.36	3	
FC	2	3	1	211	112*	105.50	1	1	66	15	0					1.36	3	
PONTING, R.T.																		
Test	2	3	0	69	41	23.00	0	0									6	
FC	2	3	0	69	41	23.00	0	0									6	
Int	5	5	0	164	69	32.80	0	2									4	
Lim	5	5	0	164	69	32.80	0	2									4	
SMITH, S.P.D.																		
I20T	2								30	33	1	33.00	1-24	0	0	6.60	2	
20T	2								30	33	1	33.00	1-24	0	0	6.60	2	
TAIT, S.W.																		
I20T	2								48	61	4	15.25	2-21	0	0	7.62	0	
20T	2								48	61	4	15.25	2-21	0	0	7.62	0	
VOGES, A.C.																		
Int	3	3	1	52	34	26.00	0	0									0	
Lim	3	3	1	52	34	26.00	0	0									0	
WARNER, D.A.																		
I20T	2	2	0	39	20	19.50	0	0									0	
20T	2	2	0	39	20	19.50	0	0									0	

Cmp Debut	M	I	NO	Runs	HS	Avge	100	50	Balls	Runs	Wkts	Avge	BB	5i	10m	RpO	ct	st
WATSON, S.R.																		
Test	1	2	0	77	65	38.50	0	1	66	48	0					4.36	0	
FC	1	2	0	77	65	38.50	0	1	66	48	0					4.36	0	
Int	5	5	0	192	53	38.40	0	1	204	171	8	21.37	2-26	0	0	5.02	4	
Lim	5	5	0	192	53	38.40	0	1	204	171	8	21.37	2-26	0	0	5.02	4	
I20T	1	1	0	19	19	19.00	0	0	24	23	2	11.50	2-23	0	0	5.75	2	
20T	1	1	0	19	19	19.00	0	0	24	23	2	11.50	2-23	0	0	5.75	2	
WHITE, C.L.																		
Int	5	5	2	168	54	56.00	0	2									3	
Lim	5	5	2	168	54	56.00	0	2									3	
I20T	2	2	2	75	64*		0	1									0	
20T	2	2	2	75	64*		0	1									0	

BANGLADESH TO NEW ZEALAND 2009/10

Cmp Debut	M	I	NO	Runs	HS	Avge	100	50	Balls	Runs	Wkts	Avge	BB	5i	10m	RpO	ct	st
AFTAB AHMED																		
Test	1	2	0	41	33	20.50	0	0	24	10	0					2.50	0	
FC	1	2	0	41	33	20.50	0	0	24	10	0					2.50	0	
Int	2	2	0	28	18	14.00	0	0									1	
Lim	2	2	0	28	18	14.00	0	0									1	
I20T	1	1	0	12	12	12.00	0	0	2	8	0					24.00	0	
20T	1	1	0	12	12	12.00	0	0	2	8	0					24.00	0	
IMRUL KAYES																		
Test	1	2	0	57	29	28.50	0	0									2	
FC	1	2	0	57	29	28.50	0	0									2	
Int	3	3	0	143	101	47.66	1	0									0	
Lim	3	3	0	143	101	47.66	1	0									0	
JUNAID SIDDIQUE																		
Test	1	2	0	29	21	14.50	0	0									1	
FC	1	2	0	29	21	14.50	0	0									1	
MAHMUDULLAH																		
Test	1	2	0	157	115	78.50	1	0	156	105	2	52.50	2-84	0	0	4.03	0	
FC	1	2	0	157	115	78.50	1	0	156	105	2	52.50	2-84	0	0	4.03	0	
Int	3	3	0	37	23	12.33	0	0	36	51	1	51.00	1-33	0	0	8.50	2	
Lim	3	3	0	37	23	12.33	0	0	36	51	1	51.00	1-33	0	0	8.50	2	
I20T	1	1	0	11	11	11.00	0	0									0	
20T	1	1	0	11	11	11.00	0	0									0	
MOHAMMAD ASHRAFUL																		
Test	1	2	0	14	12	7.00	0	0	18	9	0					3.00	1	
FC	1	2	0	14	12	7.00	0	0	18	9	0					3.00	1	
Int	3	3	0	37	31	12.33	0	0									1	
Lim	3	3	0	37	31	12.33	0	0									1	
I20T	1	1	0	11	11	11.00	0	0									0	
20T	1	1	0	11	11	11.00	0	0									0	
MUSHFIQUR RAHIM																		
Test	1	2	0	29	22	14.50	0	0									2	
FC	1	2	0	29	22	14.50	0	0									2	
Int	3	3	0	98	86	32.66	0	1									2	2
Lim	3	3	0	98	86	32.66	0	1									2	2
I20T	1	1	0	0	0	0.00	0	0									0	
20T	1	1	0	0	0	0.00	0	0									0	
NAEEM ISLAM																		
Int	3	3	0	68	43	22.66	0	0	114	97	2	48.50	1-32	0	0	5.10	0	
Lim	3	3	0	68	43	22.66	0	0	114	97	2	48.50	1-32	0	0	5.10	0	
I20T	1	1	0	5	5	5.00	0	0									0	
20T	1	1	0	5	5	5.00	0	0									0	
NAZMUL HOSSAIN																		
Int	1	1	1	0	0*		0	0	54	78	0					8.66	0	
Lim	1	1	1	0	0*		0	0	54	78	0					8.66	0	
I20T	1	1	1	0	0*		0	0	12	18	0					9.00	0	
20T	1	1	1	0	0*		0	0	12	18	0					9.00	0	
RAQIBUL HASAN																		
Int	1	1	0	9	9	9.00	0	0									1	
Lim	1	1	0	9	9	9.00	0	0									1	
I20T	1	1	0	18	18	18.00	0	0									0	
20T	1	1	0	18	18	18.00	0	0									0	
RUBEL HOSSAIN																		
Test	1	2	0	0	0	0.00	0	0	246	210	5	42.00	5-166	1	0	5.12	0	
FC	1	2	0	0	0	0.00	0	0	246	210	5	42.00	5-166	1	0	5.12	0	

Cmp Debut	M	I	NO	Runs	HS	Avge	100	50	Balls	Runs	Wkts	Avge	BB	5i	10m	RpO	ct	st
Int	2								117	123	3	41.00	2-68	0	0	6.30	0	
Lim	2								117	123	3	41.00	2-68	0	0	6.30	0	
SHAFIUL ISLAM																		
Test	1	2	1	25	13	25.00	0	0	270	158	1	158.00	1-111	0	0	3.51	0	
FC	1	2	1	25	13	25.00	0	0	270	158	1	158.00	1-111	0	0	3.51	0	
Int	3	3	2	14	11	14.00	0	0	150	163	7	23.28	4-68	1	0	6.52	0	
Lim	3	3	2	14	11	14.00	0	0	150	163	7	23.28	4-68	1	0	6.52	0	
I20T	1	1	0	1	1	1.00	0	0	6	7	0					7.00	0	
20T	1	1	0	1	1	1.00	0	0	6	7	0					7.00	0	
SHAHADAT HOSSAIN																		
Test	1	2	1	30	17*	30.00	0	0	210	168	0					4.80	1	
FC	1	2	1	30	17*	30.00	0	0	210	168	0					4.80	1	
Int	3	3	1	21	16*	10.50	0	0	131	133	1	133.00	1-56	0	0	6.09	0	
Lim	3	3	1	21	16*	10.50	0	0	131	133	1	133.00	1-56	0	0	6.09	0	
I20T	1	1	0	1	1	1.00	0	0	18	28	0					9.33	0	
20T	1	1	0	1	1	1.00	0	0	18	28	0					9.33	0	
SHAKIB AL HASAN																		
Test	1	2	0	187	100	93.50	1	1	312	133	1	133.00	1-89	0	0	2.55	0	
FC	1	2	0	187	100	93.50	1	1	312	133	1	133.00	1-89	0	0	2.55	0	
Int	3	3	0	44	36	14.66	0	0	132	108	5	21.60	4-33	1	0	4.90	1	
Lim	3	3	0	44	36	14.66	0	0	132	108	5	21.60	4-33	1	0	4.90	1	
I20T	1	1	0	3	3	3.00	0	0	12	16	0					8.00	0	
20T	1	1	0	3	3	3.00	0	0	12	16	0					8.00	0	
TAMIM IQBAL																		
Test	1	2	0	98	68	49.00	0	1									0	
FC	1	2	0	98	68	49.00	0	1									0	
Int	3	3	0	71	62	23.66	0	1									1	
Lim	3	3	0	71	62	23.66	0	1									1	
I20T	1	1	0	14	14	14.00	0	0									0	
20T	1	1	0	14	14	14.00	0	0									0	

PAKISTAN TO NEW ZEALAND 2009/10

Cmp Debut	M	I	NO	Runs	HS	Avge	100	50	Balls	Runs	Wkts	Avge	BB	5i	10m	RpO	ct	st
DANISH KANERIA																		
Test	2	4	1	27	16	9.00	0	0	570	269	13	20.69	7-168	1	0	2.83	1	
FC	2	4	1	27	16	9.00	0	0	570	269	13	20.69	7-168	1	0	2.83	1	
FAISAL IQBAL																		
Test	1	2	0	73	67	36.50	0	1									1	
FC	1	2	0	73	67	36.50	0	1									1	
FAWAD ALAM																		
Test	1	2	0	34	29	17.00	0	0									2	
FC	1	2	0	34	29	17.00	0	0									2	
IMRAN FARHAT																		
Test	3	6	1	268	117*	53.60	1	1									2	
FC	3	6	1	268	117*	53.60	1	1									2	
KAMRAN AKMAL																		
Test	3	6	1	257	82	51.40	0	3									12	1
FC	3	6	1	257	82	51.40	0	3									12	1
KHURRAM MANZOOR																		
Test	1	2	0	10	6	5.00	0	0									0	
FC	1	2	0	10	6	5.00	0	0									0	
MISBAH-UL-HAQ																		
Test	2	4	0	61	33	15.25	0	0									2	
FC	2	4	0	61	33	15.25	0	0									2	
MOHAMMAD AAMER																		
Test	3	6	0	101	26	16.83	0	0	570	306	7	43.71	2-29	0	0	3.22	0	
FC	3	6	0	101	26	16.83	0	0	570	306	7	43.71	2-29	0	0	3.22	0	
MOHAMMAD ASIF																		
Test	3	6	1	14	10	2.80	0	0	760	376	19	19.78	5-67	1	0	2.96	0	
FC	3	6	1	14	10	2.80	0	0	760	376	19	19.78	5-67	1	0	2.96	0	
MOHAMMAD YOUSUF																		
Test	3	6	0	230	89	38.33	0	2									2	
FC	3	6	0	230	89	38.33	0	2									2	
SAEED AJMAL																		
Test	1	2	2	2	1*		0	0	329	117	2	58.50	2-91	0	0	2.13	0	
FC	1	2	2	2	1*		0	0	329	117	2	58.50	2-91	0	0	2.13	0	
SALMAN BUTT																		
Test	2	4	0	122	66	30.50	0	1									1	
FC	2	4	0	122	66	30.50	0	1									1	

Cmp Debut	M	I	NO	Runs	HS	Avge	100	50	Balls	Runs	Wkts	Avge	BB	5i	10m	RpO	ct	st
SHOAIB MALIK																		
Test	2	4	0	46	32	11.50	0	0	6	5	0					5.00	2	
FC	2	4	0	46	32	11.50	0	0	6	5	0					5.00	2	
UMAR AKMAL																		
Test	3	6	0	379	129	63.16	1	3									3	
FC	3	6	0	379	129	63.16	1	3									3	
UMAR GUL																		
Test	3	6	0	66	31	11.00	0	0	624	370	8	46.25	3-41	0	0	3.55	0	
FC	3	6	0	66	31	11.00	0	0	624	370	8	46.25	3-41	0	0	3.55	0	

PAKISTAN

Quaid-e-Azam Trophy winners 2009/10 (first-class): Karachi Blues
RBS Pentangular Cup winners 2009/10 (first-class): Sui Northern Gas Pipelines Limited
RBS Pentangular One Day Cup 2009/10 (limited overs): Sind Dolphins
Royal Bank of Scotland Cup winners 2009/10 (limited overs): Sui Northern Gas Pipelines Limited
Royal Bank of Scotland Twenty-20 Cup winners 2009/10 (twenty20): Sialkot Stallions

2009/10 AND CAREER RECORDS FOR PAKISTAN PLAYERS

Cmp	*Debut*	*M*	*I*	*NO*	*Runs*	*HS*	*Avge*	*100*	*50*	*Balls*	*Runs*	*Wkts*	*Avge*	*BB*	*5i*	*10m*	*RpO*	*ct*	*st*
AAMER GULZAR, Rana (Sialkot) b Gujranwala, Punjab 27.10.1985 RHB LB																			
FC		2	4	1	41	23	13.66	0	0	60	29	0					2.90	0	
FC	2002/03	3	4	1	41	23	13.66	0	0	60	29	0					2.90	0	
Lim	2002/03	3	3	0	71	41	23.66	0	0	42	38	2	19.00	1-9	0	0	5.42	0	
AAMER HAYAT, Mohammad (Lahore Ravi) b Lahore, Punjab 23.8.1982 RHB RMF																			
FC		6	8	4	58	15	14.50	0	0	843	421	23	18.30	6-29	3	1	2.99	1	
FC	2008/09	11	13	6	72	15	10.28	0	0	1557	756	29	26.06	6-29	3	1	2.91	4	
Lim	2008/09	5	2	2	6	4*		0	0	204	188	2	94.00	2-20	0	0	5.52	0	
AAMER IQBAL, Hafiz (Lahore Eagles) b Lahore, Punjab 21.12.1990 RHB LB																			
Lim		2	2	0	10	7	5.00	0	0									0	
AAMER SAJJAD (Lahore Eagles, Punjab Stallions, The Rest, WAPDA, Pakistan A to Sri Lanka, Pakistan A to United Arab Emirates) b Lahore, Punjab 5.2.1981 RHB OB																			
FC		14	25	4	1435	289	68.33	5	5	42	30	1	30.00	1-15	0	0	4.28	10	
Lim		4	4	0	88	64	22.00	0	1	24	13	1	13.00	1-7	0	0	3.25	2	
20T		2	2	0	33	32	16.50	0	0									0	
FC	2001/02	75	118	12	4549	289	42.91	10	23	450	272	1	272.00	1-15	0	0	3.62	54	
Lim	2000/01	65	65	11	2000	122*	37.03	3	10	310	230	9	25.55	2-23	0	0	4.45	31	
20T	2004/05	20	20	1	255	49	13.42	0	0	41	81	2	40.50	2-42	0	0	11.85	12	
AAMER YAMIN (Customs) b Multan, Punjab 26.6.1990 RHB OB																			
FC		2	3	1	63	36	31.50	0	0	83	52	2	26.00	2-33	0	0	3.75	1	
Lim		4	4	0	76	43	19.00	0	0	198	189	4	47.25	3-46	0	0	5.72	0	
AAMER YOUSUF (Customs) b Gujranwala, Punjab 1.1.1985 RHB RMF																			
FC		2	3	1	1	1*	0.50	0	0	222	145	3	48.33	2-37	0	0	3.91	0	
FC	2008/09	9	15	7	24	6	3.00	0	0	1382	755	19	39.73	5-68	1	0	3.27	2	
Lim	2008/09	1	1	1	12	12*		0	0	18	35	0					11.66	0	
ABDUL AMEER (Karachi Blues) b Karachi, Sind 20.3.1992 LHB LMF																			
FC		1	2	0	1	1	0.50	0	0	96	53	1	53.00	1-37	0	0	3.31	2	
FC	2007/08	12	16	9	31	13*	4.42	0	0	1783	915	32	28.59	5-55	2	0	3.07	4	
Lim	2007/08	3	2	1	4	2*	4.00	0	0	114	158	1	158.00	1-38	0	0	8.31	0	
20T	2008/09	1	1	1	1	1*		0	0	24	59	1	59.00	1-59	0	0	14.75	0	
ABDUL GHAFFAR (Lahore Ravi) b Lahore, Punjab 20.12.1990 LHB LMF																			
FC		2	2	0	13	10	6.50	0	0	360	181	7	25.85	4-69	0	0	3.01	1	
FC	2008/09	3	3	0	19	10	6.33	0	0	498	285	9	31.66	4-69	0	0	3.43	1	
ABDUL JABBAR (Quetta Bears) b Chaman, Baluchistan 24.4.1987 RHB OB																			
Lim		2	1	0	0	0	0.00	0	0	102	73	1	73.00	1-35	0	0	4.29	0	
20T		2	2	2	1	1*		0	0	48	58	0					7.25	1	
ABDUL MAJEED Khan (Quetta Bears) b Quetta, Baluchistan 1.2.1986 RHB RMF																			
Lim		2	2	0	1	1	0.50	0	0									0	
20T		2	2	0	32	32	16.00	0	0									0	
Lim	2004/05	5	5	0	29	26	5.80	0	0									0	
20T	2004/05	4	4	0	40	32	10.00	0	0									0	
ABDUL QADEER Khan (Quetta) b Loralai, Baluchistan 5.2.1980 RHB RMF																			
FC		1	2	0	20	13	10.00	0	0									0	
ABDUL RAUF (Faisalabad) b Faisalabad, Punjab 5.12.1988 RHB WK																			
FC		3	4	1	55	35	18.33	0	0									8	2
FC	2005/06	6	9	2	108	35	15.42	0	0									17	2
ABDUL RAZZAQ (Sialkot Stallions, ZTBL, Hampshire, Pakistan to England, Pakistan to Sri Lanka, Pakistan to United Arab Emirates, Pakistan to West Indies) b Lahore, Punjab 2.12.1979 RHB RFM																			
FC		3	5	0	36	20	7.20	0	0	486	285	12	23.75	4-60	0	0	3.51	0	
Lim		1	1	0	0	0	0.00	0	0	42	25	2	12.50	2-25	0	0	3.57	0	
20T		4	4	1	93	38	31.00	0	0	96	132	4	33.00	2-25	0	0	8.25	1	
Test	1999/00	46	77	9	1946	134	28.61	3	7	7008	3694	100	36.94	5-35	1	0	3.16	15	
FC	1996/97	116	182	27	5195	203*	33.51	8	27	18516	10778	340	31.70	7-51	11	2	3.49	32	
Int	1996/97	243	210	53	4726	112	30.10	2	22	10329	8103	258	31.40	6-35	8	3	4.70	33	
Lim	1996/97	303	261	63	6005	112	30.32	2	32	13245	10632	355	29.94	6-35	13	3	4.81	46	

Cmp	Debut	M	I	NO	Runs	HS	Avge	100	50	Balls	Runs	Wkts	Avge	BB	5i	10m	RpO	ct	st
I20T	2006	21	19	8	268	46*	24.36	0	0	261	300	14	21.42	3-20	0	0	6.89	2	
20T	2003	61	57	14	1160	109	26.97	1	3	1097	1331	67	19.86	4-13	2	0	7.28	9	
ABDUR RAUF Khan (Baluchistan Bears, Multan, Multan Tigers, Pakistan to Australia) b Renala Khurd, Punjab 9.12.1978 RHB RFM																			
FC		3	5	0	182	83	36.40	0	2	642	378	13	29.07	5-76	1	0	3.53	4	
Lim		10	8	1	166	65	23.71	0	2	390	355	7	50.71	2-34	0	0	5.46	2	
20T		3	2	1	7	7*	7.00	0	0	60	81	1	81.00	1-24	0	0	8.10	1	
Test	2009	3	6	0	52	31	8.66	0	0	450	278	6	46.33	2-59	0	0	3.70	0	
FC	1999/00	103	162	28	2148	98	16.02	0	10	20200	11838	468	25.29	8-40	38	5	3.51	44	
Int	2007/08	4								214	212	8	26.50	3-24	0	0	5.94	2	
Lim	1999/00	77	49	8	539	91	13.14	0	3	3551	3168	77	41.14	4-47	2	0	5.35	14	
I20T	2008/09	1								18	21	0					7.00	0	
20T	2004/05	16	10	1	20	7*	2.22	0	0	318	426	13	32.76	3-34	0	0	8.03	2	
ABDUR REHMAN (Habib Bank, Punjab Stallions, Sialkot Stallions, Pakistan to England, Pakistan to Sri Lanka, Pakistan to West Indies, Pakistan A to United Arab Emirates) b Sialkot, Punjab 1.3.1980 LHB SLA																			
FC		14	23	1	421	85	19.13	0	3	3431	1493	88	16.96	6-52	5	1	2.61	11	
Lim		1	1	0	13	13	13.00	0	0	60	46	2	23.00	2-46	0	0	4.60	0	
20T		4	1	0	6	6	6.00	0	0	84	105	4	26.25	2-17	0	0	7.50	3	
Test	2007/08	2	3	1	34	25*	17.00	0	0	750	352	11	32.00	4-105	0	0	2.81	1	
FC	1997/98	104	142	16	2288	96	18.15	0	11	21588	9529	363	26.25	8-53	18	4	2.64	47	
Int	2006/07	12	9	2	60	31	8.57	0	0	654	474	12	39.50	2-20	0	0	4.34	2	
Lim	1998/99	111	76	18	804	50	13.86	0	1	5905	4229	163	25.94	4-25	6	0	4.29	24	
I20T	2006/07	5	3	2	8	4*	8.00	0	0	102	130	8	16.25	2-7	0	0	7.64	5	
20T	2004/05	30	13	5	76	16*	9.50	0	0	657	732	35	20.91	2-7	0	0	6.68	17	
ABDUR REHMAN Muzammil (Multan) b Lahore, Punjab 31.7.1989 RHB OB																			
FC		2	3	0	41	27	13.66	0	0	120	70	0					3.50	3	
Lim	2007/08	1	1	0	32	32	32.00	0	0									0	
ABID ALI (Baluchistan Bears, Lahore Shalimar, The Rest, Pakistan A to Sri Lanka) b Lahore, Punjab 16.10.1987 RHB LB																			
FC		11	21	1	853	91	42.65	0	7	6	12	0					12.00	13	
Lim		5	5	0	167	94	33.40	0	2									1	
FC	2007/08	24	43	3	1651	141	41.27	3	9	24	17	1	17.00	1-2	0	0	4.25	28	
Lim	2004/05	25	25	1	599	96	24.95	0	6	8	3	1	3.00	1-3	0	0	2.25	15	
20T	2004/05	8	8	1	100	42	14.28	0	0									8	
ADEEL MALIK (Sialkot, Sialkot Stallions) b Sialkot, Punjab 17.10.1985 RHB LB																			
FC		5	8	0	234	79	29.25	0	2	228	170	4	42.50	2-24	0	0	4.47	4	
Lim		7	6	1	295	70	59.00	0	3	282	227	5	45.40	2-43	0	0	4.83	2	
20T		4	3	1	20	14*	10.00	0	0	24	26	0					6.50	0	
FC	2002/03	14	24	1	486	79	21.13	0	3	510	349	8	43.62	2-24	0	0	4.10	14	
Lim	2002/03	14	13	2	454	70	41.27	0	4	498	428	7	61.14	2-43	0	0	5.15	6	
20T	2004/05	11	7	2	79	23*	15.80	0	0	66	79	7	11.28	4-15	1	0	7.18	1	
ADIL AMIN (Peshawar, Peshawar Panthers) b Peshawar, North-West Frontier Province 13.12.1990 RHB OB																			
FC		4	8	0	161	60	20.12	0	1									6	
Lim		3	3	0	45	32	15.00	0	0	12	21	0					10.50	1	
20T		1	1	0	25	25	25.00	0	0									0	
FC	2008/09	9	15	0	396	93	26.40	0	2	12	16	0					8.00	9	
Lim	2008/09	5	5	0	62	32	12.40	0	0	24	37	0					9.25	3	
ADIL NISAR (WAPDA) b Lahore, Punjab 1.6.1978 LHB LB																			
FC		6	10	1	261	104	29.00	1	1	6	2	0					2.00	6	
Lim		4	4	0	59	20	14.75	0	0									2	
FC	1995/96	105	180	13	6232	232	37.31	10	31	2470	1244	27	46.07	4-27	0	0	3.02	91	
Lim	1997/98	88	88	9	2995	131	37.91	5	17	1525	1283	44	29.15	4-28	1	0	5.04	44	
20T	2005/06	5	5	0	57	26	11.40	0	0	48	67	5	13.40	4-21	1	0	8.37	1	
ADIL RAZA (Sui Northern Gas) b Gujranwala, Punjab 10.12.1991 RHB RFM																			
FC		3	3	2	29	17*	29.00	0	0	463	255	12	21.25	4-71	0	0	3.30	2	
FC	2007/08	13	12	4	58	17*	7.25	0	0	1744	1106	35	31.60	5-42	1	0	3.80	7	
Lim	2007/08	1	1	1	4	4*		0	0	36	53	0					8.83	1	
ADNAN AKMAL (Sui Northern Gas) b Lahore, Punjab 13.3.1985 RHB WK																			
FC		14	23	3	567	120	28.35	1	2									53	1
Lim		6	3	1	28	18	14.00	0	0									11	5
FC	2003/04	70	112	10	2134	120	20.92	1	7									256	8
Lim	2002/03	51	38	8	645	70	21.50	0	2									59	18
20T	2004/05	7	5	1	51	29	12.75	0	0									6	3
ADNAN ASHRAF (Faisalabad) b Kasur, Punjab 26.5.1981 RHB RAB																			
FC		1	1	0	0	0	0.00	0	0									0	
ADNAN BAIG, Mirza (Karachi Blues, Karachi Dolphins) b Karachi, Sind 19.5.1984 RHB RAB WK																			
FC		4	6	0	151	71	25.16	0	1									5	
Lim		4	4	0	198	71	49.50	0	2									1	
FC	2008/09	8	13	2	322	71	29.27	0	2									15	
Lim	2008/09	5	5	0	199	71	39.80	0	2									4	
ADNAN BUTT (Sialkot) b Gujranwala, Punjab 4.4.1979 RHB OB																			
FC		1	1	0	4	4	4.00	0	0									0	

Cmp	Debut	M	I	NO	Runs	HS	Avge	100	50	Balls	Runs	Wkts	Avge	BB	5i	10m	RpO	ct	st
ADNAN BUTT (Sialkot) b Lahore, Punjab 10.5.1985 RHB LB																			
FC		4	8	0	96	25	12.00	0	0									4	
FC	2000/01	6	12	0	133	25	11.08	0	0									6	
Lim	2000/01	3	3	0	54	26	18.00	0	0									2	
ADNAN BUTT (Sialkot) b Sialkot, Punjab 27.7.1986 RHB																			
FC		1	2	0	68	41	34.00	0	0									0	
ADNAN KALEEM, Mohammad (Karachi Whites) b Karachi, Sind 6.7.1978 RHB SLA																			
FC		1	2	1	2	2*	2.00	0	0	96	42	1	42.00	1-42	0	0	2.62	0	
FC	2001/02	9	14	4	110	38	11.00	0	0	2099	877	24	36.54	4-90	0	0	2.50	3	
Lim	2001/02	5	2	0	10	7	5.00	0	0	270	256	4	64.00	3-52	0	0	5.68	1	
ADNAN MALIK, Mohammad (Karachi Zebras, Sui Southern Gas) b Karachi, Sind 5.10.1976 LHB SLA																			
FC		2	4	1	61	25	20.33	0	0	368	174	7	24.85	3-30	0	0	2.83	1	
Lim		5	4	1	72	41*	24.00	0	0	258	233	4	58.25	2-22	0	0	5.41	0	
20T		1								24	39	2	19.50	2-39	0	0	9.75	0	
FC	1994/95	27	36	6	368	44	12.26	0	0	4235	2079	54	38.50	5-47	1	0	2.94	13	
Lim	1993/94	31	20	6	148	41*	10.57	0	0	1457	1161	39	29.76	5-42	0	1	4.78	4	
20T	2004/05	4	1	0	0	0	0.00	0	0	60	87	3	29.00	2-39	0	0	8.70	0	
ADNAN MUFTI (Rawalpindi, Rawalpindi Rams) b Kharian Cantt 30.12.1984 LHB RMF																			
FC		5	9	0	273	87	30.33	0	2									9	
Lim		4	4	0	114	47	28.50	0	0									4	
FC	2007/08	15	25	0	640	87	25.60	0	4	84	37	1	37.00	1-19	0	0	2.64	17	
Lim	2006/07	15	14	0	309	58	22.07	0	1									10	
ADNAN MUNIR (Faisalabad Wolves) b Faisalabad, Punjab 15.5.1988 LHB SLA																			
Lim		2	2	1	12	9*	12.00	0	0	120	88	4	22.00	2-42	0	0	4.40	0	
ADNAN RAEES (Abbottabad, Abbottabad Rhinos, Khyber Pakhtunkhwa Panthers) b Mardan, North-West Frontier Province 10.3.1981 LHB RMF																			
FC		9	17	1	704	200*	44.00	3	1	439	187	8	23.37	5-20	1	0	2.55	9	
Lim		9	9	0	218	52	24.22	0	1	94	82	2	41.00	2-24	0	0	5.23	6	
20T		1	1	0	1	1	1.00	0	0									0	
FC	2001/02	55	87	4	3137	205	37.79	8	10	1254	615	16	38.43	5-20	1	0	2.94	52	
Lim	2001/02	31	29	1	497	56	17.75	0	2	238	215	3	71.66	2-24	0	0	5.42	7	
20T	2005/06	10	10	0	187	42	18.70	0	0	34	42	0					7.41	2	
ADNAN RASOOL (Sui Northern Gas) b Faisalabad, Punjab 1.5.1981 RHB OB																			
FC		2	3	0	41	22	13.66	0	0	336	201	8	25.12	5-93	1	0	3.58	0	
FC	2002/03	11	10	2	71	22	8.87	0	0	1810	938	37	25.35	5-62	3	0	3.10	5	
Lim	2001/02	8	6	1	77	26	15.40	0	0	426	364	8	45.50	4-48	1	0	5.12	3	
ADNAN RAZA Ali (Lahore Lions, ZTBL) b Lahore, Punjab 5.12.1987 LHB OB																			
FC		4	7	2	103	61*	20.60	0	1	18	8	0					2.66	0	
Lim		1	1	0	6	6	6.00	0	0									1	
20T		1	1	0	5	5	5.00	0	0									0	
FC	2006/07	29	44	6	1694	137	44.57	4	11	228	144	2	72.00	1-5	0	0	3.78	10	
Lim	2002/03	26	24	6	821	91	45.61	0	8	216	180	7	25.71	2-45	0	0	5.00	11	
20T	2004/05	13	10	4	168	51*	28.00	0	1	6	15	1	15.00	1-15	0	0	15.00	7	
ADNAN ZAHEER (Sialkot Stallions) b Sialkot, Punjab 2.2.1987 RHB																			
Lim		2	2	0	14	10	7.00	0	0									0	
FC	2008/09	2	2	0	19	19	9.50	0	0									1	
Lim	2001/02	6	6	0	72	50	12.00	0	1									0	
AFAQ AHMED (Peshawar) b Malakand, North-West Frontier Province 7.1.1990 RHB RMF																			
FC		1	2	1	3	2*	3.00	0	0	126	86	1	86.00	1-86	0	0	4.09	1	
FC	2008/09	2	4	1	3	2*	1.00	0	0	240	178	4	44.50	3-92	0	0	4.45	1	
Lim	2007/08	2	1	0	1	1	1.00	0	0	96	87	2	43.50	1-31	0	0	5.43	0	
AFSAR NAWAZ Khan (Karachi Dolphins, Karachi Whites) b Karachi, Sind 7.10.1976 RHB RM WK																			
FC		10	17	2	826	121*	55.06	1	8	261	191	5	38.20	1-0	0	0	4.39	8	
Lim		4	3	0	72	38	24.00	0	0	141	103	3	34.33	1-4	0	0	4.38	2	
20T		3	2	0	20	20	10.00	0	0									4	
FC	1997/98	88	152	8	5432	178	37.72	10	30	987	664	19	34.94	3-19	0	0	4.03	119	6
Lim	1996/97	50	44	5	1252	119	32.10	2	4	873	705	24	29.37	3-27	0	0	4.84	15	1
20T	2004/05	14	13	1	354	71	29.50	0	3	80	118	5	23.60	2-6	0	0	8.85	13	6
AFTAB ALAM Khan (Habib Bank) b Peshawar, North-West Frontier Province 27.4.1984 RHB OB																			
FC		6	11	0	147	70	13.36	0	1	24	7	0					1.75	6	
FC	2000/01	95	147	9	3737	178*	27.07	4	21	606	293	4	73.25	1-2	0	0	2.90	84	2
Lim	2000/01	58	54	10	1694	122	38.50	1	10	770	595	19	31.31	3-20	0	0	4.63	21	
20T	2004/05	13	11	2	170	52	18.88	0	1	66	78	3	26.00	2-18	0	0	7.09	4	
AGHA SABIR Ali (PIA) b Karachi, Sind 8.4.1981 LHB SLA																			
FC		7	14	1	511	98	39.30	0	4	36	32	1	32.00	1-17	0	0	5.33	5	
Lim		3	2	0	27	23	13.50	0	0	96	86	2	43.00	2-37	0	0	5.37	2	
FC	2000/01	77	129	3	4001	196	31.75	9	19	360	212	3	70.66	1-17	0	0	3.53	52	
Lim	2000/01	30	29	1	634	103	22.64	1	3	174	162	4	40.50	2-37	0	0	5.58	11	
20T	2004/05	12	12	1	304	51*	27.63	0	1	6	4	0					4.00	7	
AHMED (Faisalabad Wolves) b Faisalabad, Punjab RHB SLA																			
Lim		1	1	0	2	2	2.00	0	0	48	40	1	40.00	1-40	0	0	5.00	0	

Cmp	Debut	M	I	NO	Runs	HS	Avge	100	50	Balls	Runs	Wkts	Avge	BB	5i	10m	RpO	ct	st
AHMED BUTT (Sialkot) b Gujranwala, Punjab 26.1.1981 RHB WK																			
FC		13	19	0	343	94	18.05	0	2	12	9	0					4.50	50	2
FC	2000/01	26	35	2	490	94	14.84	0	2	12	9	0					4.50	94	6
Lim	1999/00	5	4	2	117	65	58.50	0	1									6	2
AHMED DAR (Lahore Shalimar) b Lahore, Punjab 2.7.1982 LHB OB																			
FC		6	12	0	212	66	17.66	0	2	9	7	0					4.66	5	
FC	2002/03	13	24	0	522	73	21.75	0	4	9	7	0					4.66	11	
Lim	2008/09	5	5	0	183	61	36.60	0	2									0	
20T	2009	3	3	0	62	34	20.66	0	0									1	
AHMED HAYAT Gondal (Faisalabad, Faisalabad Wolves) b Sargodha, Punjab 1.10.1977 RHB RFM																			
FC		8	13	0	190	47	14.61	0	0	1396	752	26	28.92	5-47	2	0	3.23	3	
Lim		4	3	0	45	23	15.00	0	0	180	173	3	57.66	1-25	0	0	5.76	1	
FC	1993/94	105	145	14	2394	84	18.27	0	10	14666	8652	320	27.03	6-42	15	1	3.54	41	
Lim	1992/93	50	42	7	393	57	11.22	0	1	2150	1903	55	34.60	5-31	1	1	5.31	15	
20T	2004/05	16	9	2	40	11	5.71	0	0	257	387	15	25.80	3-29	0	0	9.03	1	
AHMED JAMAL (Abbottabad Rhinos, Customs) b Abbottabad, North-West Frontier Province 3.9.1988 RHB RFM																			
FC		4	8	3	52	31*	10.40	0	0	654	463	10	46.30	4-93	0	0	4.24	1	
Lim		1	1	1	1	1*		0	0	30	41	0					8.20	2	
20T		1	1	0	2	2	2.00	0	0	12	27	0					13.50	0	
AHMED RASHEED (Customs) b Mian Channu, Punjab 8.6.1991 RHB LB																			
Lim		1	1	0	5	5	5.00	0	0									0	
AHMED RAZA (Multan) b Rahimyar Khan, Punjab 18.3.1983 RHB SLA																			
FC		1	2	0	14	10	7.00	0	0	78	19	0					1.46	1	
FC	2004/05	8	13	4	95	23	10.55	0	0	1133	598	15	39.86	5-111	1	0	3.16	4	
Lim	2007/08	5	1	1	0	0*		0	0	234	227	5	45.40	2-53	0	0	5.82	5	
20T	2009	1	1	1	14	14*		0	0	18	25	1	25.00	1-25	0	0	8.33	0	
AHMED SAID (Khyber Pakhtunkhwa Panthers, WAPDA) b Mardan, North-West Frontier Province 15.4.1976 RHB WK																			
FC		10	16	2	466	101	33.28	1	2									47	
Lim		8	7	1	214	56*	35.66	0	2									10	
FC	1999/00	78	127	8	2849	106	23.94	4	12	12	13	0					6.50	241	16
Lim	1997/98	55	42	6	932	59	25.88	0	5									77	8
20T	2005/06	4	4	2	47	22*	23.50	0	0									3	2
AHMED SHEHZAD (Habib Bank) b Lahore, Punjab 23.11.1991 RHB LB																			
FC		5	8	0	106	39	13.25	0	0	120	75	2	37.50	1-1	0	0	3.75	8	
FC	2006/07	20	33	0	1114	175	33.75	2	6	306	198	2	99.00	1-1	0	0	3.88	20	
Int	2008/09	4	4	0	106	43	26.50	0	0									0	
Lim	2007/08	22	22	2	868	130*	43.40	1	6	318	291	4	72.75	1-11	0	0	5.49	10	
I20T	2008/09	2	2	0	8	4	4.00	0	0									0	
20T	2008/09	9	9	0	87	28	9.66	0	0	12	21	2	10.50	2-21	0	0	10.50	3	
AHMED ZEESHAN Malik (Sui Southern Gas) b Karachi, Sind 26.10.1979 RHB OB WK																			
FC		10	18	0	301	79	16.72	0	1									27	
Lim		5	5	1	27	21	6.75	0	0									5	3
FC	1997/98	87	134	15	2810	104*	23.61	2	9	18	21	0					7.00	241	19
Lim	1997/98	47	30	7	329	50	14.30	0	1									48	21
20T	2008/09	2	2	0	32	30	16.00	0	0									3	
AIZAZ Bin Ilyas CHEEMA (Lahore Lions, PIA) b Lahore, Punjab 5.9.1979 RHB RMF																			
FC		9	9	2	49	11	7.00	0	0	1709	845	40	21.12	6-75	2	0	2.96	3	
Lim		4	2	1	5	5*	5.00	0	0	182	161	3	53.66	2-58	0	0	5.30	1	
20T		4	1	1	6	6*		0	0	96	98	11	8.90	4-17	2	0	6.12	0	
FC	2001/02	53	51	17	268	33	7.88	0	0	7182	3866	163	23.71	7-24	9	1	3.23	11	
Lim	2001/02	25	9	7	46	13*	23.00	0	0	1111	967	40	24.17	5-37	2	1	5.22	4	
20T	2004/05	10	2	2	6	6*		0	0	180	229	15	15.26	4-17	2	0	7.63	2	
AKBAR-UR-REHMAN (Karachi Whites, Karachi Zebras) b Karachi, Sind 14.9.1983 RHB LB																			
FC		8	14	0	379	98	27.07	0	3	595	336	10	33.60	2-34	0	0	3.38	6	
Lim		5	5	1	274	126*	68.50	1	2	150	150	4	37.50	3-42	0	0	6.00	4	
20T		2	2	0	22	19	11.00	0	0	30	46	2	23.00	2-30	0	0	9.20	1	
FC	2006/07	18	31	2	820	98	28.27	0	6	997	579	13	44.53	2-34	0	0	3.48	21	
Lim	2007/08	15	15	2	685	126*	52.69	2	5	510	487	12	40.58	3-42	0	0	5.72	6	
20T	2009	4	4	0	33	19	8.25	0	0	71	105	3	35.00	2-30	0	0	8.87	1	
AKHTAR AYUB Awan (KRL) b Langer, Attock, Punjab 10.12.1987 RHB RMF																			
FC		6	6	1	21	8	4.20	0	0	902	604	19	31.78	3-30	0	0	4.01	1	
FC	2006/07	23	22	9	128	33	9.84	0	0	3084	1892	63	30.03	4-72	0	0	3.68	3	
Lim	2005/06	13	8	3	39	15	7.80	0	0	513	501	14	35.78	3-44	0	0	5.86	1	
20T	2006/07	2	1	1	7	7*		0	0	24	28	2	14.00	1-10	0	0	7.00	1	
ALI AKBAR Bhatti (Sialkot Stallions) b Hafizabad, Punjab 25.11.1984 RHB LB																			
Lim		1	1	0	0	0	0.00	0	0	18	28	0					9.33	0	
ALI ASAD (Karachi Blues, Karachi Dolphins, Khyber Pakhtunkhwa Panthers) b Karachi, Sind 25.12.1988 LHB LB WK																			
FC		11	22	1	741	113	35.28	2	4									15	
Lim		5	5	1	181	117*	45.25	1	0									3	
FC	2007/08	27	49	2	1851	172	39.38	6	9	6	2	0					2.00	27	
Lim	2005/06	17	17	1	561	117*	35.06	1	3									8	

Cmp	Debut	M	I	NO	Runs	HS	Avge	100	50	Balls	Runs	Wkts	Avge	BB	5i	10m	RpO	ct	st
ALI AZMAT (Lahore Eagles, WAPDA) b Lahore, Punjab 1.1.1979 LHB SLA																			
FC		8	12	3	522	128*	58.00	1	3	313	179	5	35.80	2-28	0	0	3.43	4	
Lim		4	4	1	72	33*	24.00	0	0	42	36	0					5.14	0	
20T		1	1	0	5	5	5.00	0	0	12	20	0					10.00	0	
FC	2004/05	32	45	7	1617	128*	42.55	3	9	1225	749	19	39.42	2-27	0	0	3.66	10	
Lim	2004/05	29	23	7	440	49	27.50	0	0	801	687	17	40.41	4-28	1	0	5.14	7	
20T	2004/05	12	9	2	105	21	15.00	0	0	246	299	13	23.00	3-15	0	0	7.29	2	
ALI IMRAN Pasha (PIA) b Gujranwala, Punjab 18.7.1985 RHB RFM																			
FC		7	9	2	27	10*	3.85	0	0	1285	741	25	29.64	4-53	0	0	3.46	4	
Lim		4	2	1	13	8	13.00	0	0	192	170	9	18.88	3-31	0	0	5.31	1	
FC	2002/03	25	30	13	197	69	11.58	0	1	3632	2245	72	31.18	5-84	1	0	3.70	6	
Lim	2002/03	26	13	8	84	17*	16.80	0	0	1217	1031	46	22.41	5-68	1	1	5.08	7	
20T	2004/05	7	4	2	7	3	3.50	0	0	136	198	5	39.60	2-11	0	0	8.73	2	
ALI Shamsher KHAN (KRL) b Sialkot, Punjab 1.8.1989 RHB RMF																			
FC		5	9	3	204	117*	34.00	1	1	102	67	2	33.50	1-10	0	0	3.94	5	
Lim		4	4	2	88	45	44.00	0	0	70	66	1	66.00	1-12	0	0	5.65	2	
FC	2007/08	13	20	5	404	117*	26.93	1	1	354	187	3	62.33	1-10	0	0	3.16	11	
Lim	2007/08	16	13	4	284	54	31.55	0	1	250	232	4	58.00	2-42	0	0	5.56	9	
20T	2008/09	1	1	0	6	6	6.00	0	0									0	
ALI MOAZZAM (Multan Tigers) b Okara, Punjab 15.6.1988 RHB SLA																			
20T		1								18	27	0					9.00	0	
20T	2009	2								30	44	1	44.00	1-17	0	0	8.80	0	
ALI MUDASSAR, Syed (Karachi Whites) b Karachi, Sind 2.4.1989 RHB RMF																			
FC		5	8	5	58	24*	19.33	0	0	616	386	19	20.31	6-61	1	0	3.76	3	
ALI Urooj NAQVI, Syed (KRL) b Lahore, Punjab 19.3.1977 RHB OB																			
FC		2	2	0	37	36	18.50	0	0	216	84	1	84.00	1-23	0	0	2.33	0	
Test	1997/98	5	9	1	242	115	30.25	1	0	12	11	0					5.50	1	
FC	1997	100	155	9	5086	137	34.83	12	20	5680	2557	88	29.05	5-65	1	0	2.70	42	
Lim	1996/97	52	52	7	2068	128*	45.95	7	11	1121	1005	19	52.89	3-17	0	0	5.37	14	
20T	2005/06	5	5	1	183	54	45.75	0	1	102	138	2	69.00	1-30	0	0	8.11	0	
ALI RAZA (Faisalabad) b Faisalabad, Punjab 28.5.1987 LHB RFM																			
FC		4	6	1	53	26*	10.60	0	0	582	364	11	33.09	3-60	0	0	3.75	1	
FC	2004/05	15	24	3	339	59	16.14	0	2	1722	1151	35	32.88	4-26	0	0	4.01	1	
Lim	2005/06	8	8	1	27	7	3.85	0	0	278	299	5	59.80	2-35	0	0	6.45	1	
20T	2009	1								24	28	3	9.33	3-28	0	0	7.00	0	
ALI RAZA, Syed (Lahore Lions, Lahore Shalimar) b Lahore, Punjab 4.2.1977 RHB OB WK																			
FC		8	15	1	479	98	34.21	0	3									15	
Lim		4	4	0	44	30	11.00	0	0									8	1
FC	1997/98	52	78	11	1644	126*	24.53	1	9									139	4
Lim	1998/99	27	22	4	321	41	17.83	0	0									38	7
20T	2008/09	6	4	1	74	29	24.66	0	0									6	3
ALI SARFRAZ (Islamabad, Islamabad Leopards) b Rawalpindi, Punjab 21.12.1987 LHB OB WK																			
FC		6	11	1	329	96	32.90	0	2									6	
Lim		4	4	0	95	45	23.75	0	0									2	
FC	2007/08	13	20	2	529	96	29.38	0	4									11	
Lim	2006/07	11	11	1	253	65*	25.30	0	1									7	
ALI TAHIR Zaidi (Lahore Shalimar) b Lahore, Punjab 29.6.1989 RHB																			
FC		2	4	0	40	22	10.00	0	0									1	
ALI WAQAS (Faisalabad Wolves, Sui Northern Gas) b Sargodha, Punjab 26.12.1989 LHB OB																			
FC		11	19	1	640	147	35.55	1	3									12	
Lim		6	6	0	190	60	31.66	0	2									3	
20T		4	4	0	86	32	21.50	0	0									1	
FC	2008/09	16	29	2	805	147	29.81	1	4									15	
Lim	2006/07	12	12	1	335	81*	30.45	0	3									4	
ALI ZAHID (Lahore Lions) b Lahore, Punjab 4.10.1989 RHB RMF																			
Lim		3	3	0	109	72	36.33	0	1									0	
AMEER KHAN (Islamabad) b Islamabad, Punjab 18.12.1982 RHB LB																			
FC		6	11	1	290	69	29.00	0	4	474	266	13	20.46	3-67	0	0	3.36	9	
FC	2000/01	28	47	4	901	92	20.95	0	6	777	455	22	20.68	3-14	0	0	3.51	16	
Lim	2000/01	20	17	4	600	111*	46.15	2	3	399	360	12	30.00	4-24	1	0	5.41	7	
20T	2004/05	2	2	0	43	42	21.50	0	0									2	
AMIN-UR-REHMAN (National Bank) b Karachi, Sind 22.9.1983 RHB WK																			
FC		7	9	0	195	49	21.66	0	0									26	1
FC	2001/02	43	59	3	1217	107	21.73	1	5									129	8
Lim	2000/01	49	38	7	599	72	19.32	0	4									62	23
20T	2004/05	13	13	4	96	21	10.66	0	0									7	12
AMJAD WAQAS (Abbottabad Rhinos) b Pharhari, Haripur, North-West Frontier Province 22.3.1983 LHB SLA																			
Lim		3	3	0	32	13	10.66	0	0	111	66	4	16.50	2-41	0	0	3.56	2	
FC	2005/06	8	11	3	115	23*	14.37	0	0	1201	600	20	30.00	6-92	1	0	2.99	3	
Lim	2005/06	11	8	2	66	25*	11.00	0	0	498	418	12	34.83	4-46	1	0	5.03	2	
20T	2005/06	7	3	1	13	9	6.50	0	0	132	153	8	19.12	3-22	0	0	6.95	1	

Cmp	Debut	M	I	NO	Runs	HS	Avge	100	50	Balls	Runs	Wkts	Avge	BB	5i	10m	RpO	ct	st
AMMAR MAHMOOD (Faisalabad) b Faisalabad, Punjab 4.4.1979 RHB OB																			
FC		7	11	2	386	78	42.88	0	4	354	190	2	95.00	1-13	0	0	3.22	6	
FC	2007/08	26	42	3	1369	106	35.10	1	10	438	237	2	118.50	1-13	0	0	3.24	16	
Lim	1998/99	10	9	0	106	32	11.77	0	0	40	46	1	46.00	1-11	0	0	6.90	2	
20T	2008/09	1	1	0	19	19	19.00	0	0									0	
ANOP Ravi SANTOSH Kumar (PIA) b Karachi, Sind 23.6.1991 RHB WK																			
FC		2	4	1	33	21*	11.00	0	0									9	
Lim		2	1	0	2	2	2.00	0	0									3	
FC	2007/08	7	10	1	60	21*	6.66	0	0									23	1
ANSAR JAVED (Multan, Multan Tigers) b Tibbi Lal Beg, Punjab 23.10.1980 RHB LFM																			
FC		7	9	0	144	42	16.00	0	0	1176	673	25	26.92	6-34	1	0	3.43	4	
Lim		4	2	1	0	0*	0.00	0	0	126	119	1	119.00	1-32	0	0	5.66	6	
FC	2007/08	23	30	5	406	43*	16.24	0	0	3233	1853	65	28.50	6-34	2	0	3.43	11	
Lim	2007/08	10	6	3	63	38*	21.00	0	0	318	316	5	63.20	2-61	0	0	5.96	7	
20T	2009	1	1	0	6	6	6.00	0	0									0	
ANWAAR HAFEEZ (National Bank) b Lahore, Punjab 17.12.1984 RHB OB																			
FC		3	4	0	80	43	20.00	0	0									0	
FC	2008/09	5	7	1	153	71	25.50	0	1									2	
Lim	2005/06	1	1	0	23	23	23.00	0	0	42	80	1	80.00	1-80	0	0	11.42	0	
ANWAR ALI (Karachi Zebras, PIA, Sind Dolphins) b Karachi, Sind 25.11.1987 RHB RMF																			
FC		7	9	2	171	68	24.42	0	1	1486	831	30	27.70	6-62	2	1	3.35	2	
Lim		9	7	5	140	79*	70.00	0	1	468	419	21	19.95	4-45	1	0	5.37	2	
20T		2	2	2	11	8*		0	0	48	55	5	11.00	3-24	0	0	6.87	3	
FC	2006/07	38	50	14	838	100*	23.27	1	3	6863	3797	137	27.71	6-54	9	3	3.32	9	
Lim	2005/06	32	21	9	255	79*	21.25	0	1	1531	1393	49	28.42	4-45	1	0	5.45	10	
I20T	2008/09	1								12	19	0					9.50	0	
20T	2005/06	16	9	5	46	11	11.50	0	0	318	364	17	21.41	3-8	0	0	6.86	9	
ANWARULLAH (Peshawar Panthers) b Swat, North-West Frontier Province 1.1.1983 RHB RAB																			
Lim		1	1	0	3	3	3.00	0	0									0	
AQEEL AHMED (Faisalabad Wolves) b Faisalabad, Punjab 1.10.1982 RHB OB																			
Lim		5	4	2	11	6	5.50	0	0	270	203	9	22.55	3-21	0	0	4.51	4	
FC	1999/00	49	65	21	430	61	9.77	0	1	8859	4860	182	26.70	7-98	13	4	3.29	31	
Lim	1999/00	45	23	12	59	9	5.36	0	0	2359	1649	70	23.55	4-12	3	0	4.19	13	
AQEEL Ahmed ANJUM (Hyderabad, Hyderabad Hawks, Sind Dolphins) b Mirpurkhas, Sind 7.3.1987 LHB RM																			
FC		9	17	0	542	92	31.88	0	3	120	74	3	24.66	3-25	0	0	3.70	2	
Lim		5	5	0	241	106	48.20	1	1	18	13	0					4.33	2	
20T		2	2	0	37	25	18.50	0	0									0	
FC	2005/06	30	51	1	1822	204	36.44	2	9	186	109	4	27.25	3-25	0	0	3.51	13	
Lim	2004/05	25	24	1	941	106	40.91	1	6	36	33	1	33.00	1-20	0	0	5.50	12	
20T	2004/05	11	11	1	217	39	21.70	0	0									6	
AQEEL ARSHAD, Mohammad (PIA) b Sheikhupura, Punjab 26.11.1985 RHB LB																			
FC		1	2	0	18	18	9.00	0	0	36	24	0					4.00	0	
FC	2003/04	11	15	1	241	105	17.21	1	0	720	438	13	33.69	3-59	0	0	3.65	2	
Lim	2003/04	2								114	74	4	18.50	2-33	0	0	3.89	1	
ARMAGHAN ELAHI Hashmi (Abbottabad, Abbottabad Rhinos, Khyber Pakhtunkhwa Panthers) b Abbottabad, North-West Frontier Province 1.1.1981 LHB LMF																			
FC		9	15	5	59	13	5.90	0	0	1843	950	30	31.66	5-64	1	0	3.09	4	
Lim		5	5	5	20	8*		0	0	246	156	4	39.00	2-32	0	0	3.80	1	
FC	2007/08	23	29	6	156	21*	6.78	0	0	4011	2047	85	24.08	9-38	5	2	3.06	7	
Lim	2007/08	11	11	8	37	13	12.33	0	0	498	375	7	53.57	2-32	0	0	4.51	3	
20T	2008/09	3	3	1	1	1	0.50	0	0	36	44	0					7.33	0	
ARSHAD KHAN (Quetta) b Peshawar, North-West Frontier Province 22.3.1971 RHB OB																			
FC		9	17	2	209	39	13.93	0	0	1759	731	25	29.24	5-85	1	0	2.49	3	
Test	1997/98	9	8	2	31	9*	5.16	0	0	2538	960	32	30.00	5-38	1	0	2.27	0	
FC	1988/89	187	250	37	2762	79*	12.96	0	6	34887	14470	601	24.07	8-80	30	6	2.48	85	
Int	1992/93	58	29	18	133	20	12.09	0	0	2823	1948	56	34.78	4-33	1	0	4.14	10	
Lim	1990/91	161	92	40	568	35*	10.92	0	0	8166	5194	187	27.77	5-21	5	1	3.81	43	
20T	2004/05	9	5	1	26	11	6.50	0	0	190	236	7	33.71	2-40	0	0	7.45	0	
ARUN LAL (Quetta, Quetta Bears, The Rest) b Quetta, Baluchistan 26.8.1985 RHB RMF																			
FC		11	22	3	376	98	19.78	0	1	2056	1145	46	24.89	7-87	3	0	3.34	5	
Lim		4	4	0	32	22	8.00	0	0	240	206	6	34.33	2-36	0	0	5.15	1	
20T		3	3	1	39	32	19.50	0	0	72	100	1	100.00	1-39	0	0	8.33	0	
FC	2001/02	45	85	9	1336	98	17.57	0	5	6499	3885	103	37.71	7-87	3	0	3.58	20	
Lim	2004/05	17	17	2	186	35*	12.40	0	0	620	630	14	45.00	3-59	0	0	6.09	1	
20T	2004/05	14	13	3	148	32	14.80	0	0	222	308	5	61.60	2-20	0	0	8.32	3	
ASAD ALI (Faisalabad Wolves, Punjab Stallions, Sui Northern Gas) b 14.10.1988 RHB RMF																			
FC		13	16	5	110	22	10.00	0	0	2702	1386	54	25.66	7-98	4	0	3.07	4	
Lim		10	4	0	11	7	2.75	0	0	480	353	14	25.21	4-39	1	0	4.41	4	
20T		4	1	1	1	1*		0	0	84	82	6	13.66	2-21	0	0	5.85	3	
FC	2005/06	44	57	17	335	53	8.37	0	1	8442	4399	190	23.15	7-98	12	2	3.12	12	

Cmp	Debut	M	I	NO	Runs	HS	Avge	100	50	Balls	Runs	Wkts	Avge	BB	5i	10m	RpO	ct	st
Lim	2005/06	32	13	3	53	22	5.30	0	0	1593	1180	61	19.34	4-20	6	0	4.44	12	
20T	2006/07	13	4	4	3	1*		0	0	276	294	14	21.00	2-12	0	0	6.39	3	
ASAD BAIG, Hafiz (Customs) b Karachi, Sind 26.11.1988 RHB OB																			
FC		10	20	1	497	96	26.15	0	4	42	34	0					4.85	3	
Lim		4	4	0	45	32	11.25	0	0	12	14	0					7.00	1	
ASAD IQBAL (Customs) b Karachi, Sind 14.8.1985 RHB RFM																			
FC		2	4	1	63	26	21.00	0	0	60	33	1	33.00	1-5	0	0	3.30	0	
Lim	2008/09	3	3	0	32	23	10.66	0	0	150	134	1	134.00	1-53	0	0	5.36	1	
ASAD SHAFIQ, Sheikh Mohammad (Karachi Blues, Karachi Zebras, Sind Dolphins, Pakistan to England, Pakistan to Sri Lanka, Pakistan A to Sri Lanka, Pakistan A to United Arab Emirates) b Karachi, Sind 28.1.1986 RHB LB WK																			
FC		15	28	3	1244	147*	49.76	4	4	14	10	0					4.28	13	
Lim		3	3	0	151	59	50.33	0	2	66	65	2	32.50	2-37	0	0	5.90	2	
20T		1	1	0	4	4	4.00	0	0									1	
FC	2007/08	35	63	5	2535	223	43.70	8	7	68	66	0					5.82	28	
Int	2010	6	6	0	137	50	22.83	0	1									0	
Lim	2007/08	27	27	1	1046	110	40.23	3	6	140	141	3	47.00	2-37	0	0	6.04	14	
20T	2008/09	7	7	0	64	31	9.14	0	0									4	
ASHAR Ahmed ZAIDI, Syed (Islamabad) b Karachi, Sind 13.7.1981 LHB LM																			
FC		8	13	3	656	202	65.60	3	1	469	250	9	27.77	4-50	0	0	3.19	5	
FC	1999/00	88	147	12	5180	202	38.37	11	26	3120	1490	49	30.40	4-50	0	0	2.86	75	
Lim	1999/00	54	53	4	1696	109	34.61	3	9	1446	1020	38	26.84	4-42	1	0	4.23	22	
20T	2005/06	9	9	1	166	42*	20.75	0	0	150	203	4	50.75	2-16	0	0	8.12	4	
ASHRAF ALI (Lahore Ravi) b Lahore, Punjab 4.4.1979 RHB RM																			
FC		2	4	0	105	47	26.25	0	0									3	
FC	2003/04	39	66	6	2256	141	37.60	8	10	12	3	0					1.50	22	
Lim	2000/01	29	25	5	892	156*	44.60	1	5	32	47	2	23.50	2-8	0	0	8.81	10	
20T	2005/06	5	5	2	62	33	20.66	0	0									2	
ASHRAF ALI Khan (Sui Southern Gas) b Karachi, Sind 4.5.1982 RHB LB																			
FC		1	2	0	16	9	8.00	0	0									1	
Lim		4	4	1	126	71	42.00	0	2									1	
FC	2001/02	16	25	1	470	49	19.58	0	0	6	5	0					5.00	14	
Lim	2002/03	19	19	2	453	81	26.64	0	5									7	
20T	2005/06	6	6	1	231	78	46.20	0	3									3	
ASHRAF KHAN (Quetta) b Killa Abdullah, Baluchistan 16.8.1986 LHB																			
FC		5	10	0	161	46	16.10	0	0									4	
ASIF Khan AFRIDI (Abbottabad Rhinos) b Peshawar, North-West Frontier Province 25.12.1986 LHB LMF																			
20T		2	2	1	4	4*	4.00	0	0	42	43	5	8.60	5-27	0	1	6.14	0	
FC	2008/09	3	3	0	17	8	5.66	0	0	240	156	6	26.00	3-69	0	0	3.90	2	
ASIF ALI (Abbottabad) b South Waziristan Agency 13.4.1989 LHB SLA																			
FC		2	4	0	2	1	0.50	0	0	91	41	1	41.00	1-0	0	0	2.70	0	
FC	2008/09	5	7	1	64	28	10.66	0	0	355	172	5	34.40	2-54	0	0	2.90	2	
ASIF ASHFAQ Ahmed Khan (Lahore Lions) b Lahore, Punjab 24.10.1990 RHB RMF																			
Lim		2	2	0	1	1	0.50	0	0	90	84	4	21.00	3-49	0	0	5.60	1	
Lim	2008/09	4	4	0	20	19	5.00	0	0	198	165	6	27.50	3-49	0	0	5.00	1	
ASIF HUSSAIN, Mohammad (Faisalabad Wolves, WAPDA) b Faisalabad, Punjab 20.11.1979 RHB OB																			
FC		5	9	1	253	100*	31.62	1	0									0	
Lim		1	1	0	11	11	11.00	0	0									0	
20T		4	4	0	123	54	30.75	0	1									1	
FC	1999/00	80	135	8	3523	198*	27.74	8	13	168	88	2	44.00	1-19	0	0	3.14	45	
Lim	1998/99	40	40	2	1087	139	28.60	2	5	766	603	10	60.30	2-31	0	0	4.72	9	
20T	2004/05	26	26	3	805	84	35.00	0	5	6	10	1	10.00	1-10	0	0	10.00	4	
ASIF KHAN, Mohammad (Lahore Ravi) b Lahore, Punjab 15.2.1990 RHB OB																			
FC		7	12	2	210	63	21.00	0	1	30	15	0					3.00	11	
FC	2007/08	12	21	2	389	63	20.47	0	1	30	15	0					3.00	13	
Lim	2007/08	5	5	0	203	100	40.60	1	0									1	
20T	2008/09	2	2	0	44	28	22.00	0	0									1	
ASIF MUMTAZ (Rawalpindi) b Sialkot, Punjab 3.10.1988 RHB OB																			
FC		1	2	0	31	31	15.50	0	0	78	77	1	77.00	1-45	0	0	5.92	0	
ASIF RAZA (Lahore Eagles) b Lahore, Punjab 11.1.1987 LHB RFM																			
20T		1	1	0	3	3	3.00	0	0									0	
FC	2006/07	16	27	1	354	55	13.61	0	1	2428	1346	31	43.41	5-82	2	0	3.32	5	
Lim	2005/06	10	9	2	86	28	12.28	0	0	498	497	8	62.12	2-53	0	0	5.98	1	
20T	2006/07	8	7	3	105	53*	26.25	0	1	132	188	4	47.00	2-15	0	0	8.54	3	
ASIF YOUSUF (Lahore Eagles) b Lahore, Punjab 1.9.1982 RHB OB																			
Lim		4	4	1	84	54*	28.00	0	1	222	168	1	168.00	1-47	0	0	4.54	0	
ASIF ZAKIR, Mohammad (Sui Southern Gas) b Karachi, Sind 1.9.1983 RHB RMF																			
FC		10	19	1	614	122*	34.11	2	2	222	146	3	48.66	1-7	0	0	3.94	5	
Lim		5	5	0	164	87	32.80	0	1	36	42	0					7.00	0	
FC	2002/03	65	113	5	3528	170	32.66	9	14	773	465	14	33.21	4-40	0	0	3.60	41	1
Lim	2003/04	36	36	2	1520	176*	44.70	3	10	138	132	0					5.73	9	2
20T	2006/07	4	4	2	80	58*	40.00	0	1	18	41	2	20.50	2-41	0	0	13.66	1	

Cmp	Debut	M	I	NO	Runs	HS	Avge	100	50	Balls	Runs	Wkts	Avge	BB	5i	10m	RpO	ct	st
ASIM KAMAL, Mohammad (Karachi Blues, Karachi Zebras) b Karachi, Sind 31.5.1976 LHB OB																			
FC		12	21	1	592	87	29.60	0	4									6	
Lim		1																1	
Test	2003/04	12	20	1	717	99	37.73	0	8									10	
FC	1997/98	114	183	16	5890	164	35.26	9	37	135	95	2	47.50	1-6	0	0	4.22	83	
Lim	1999/00	36	31	4	850	63	31.48	0	6	12	30	0					15.00	12	1
20T	2005/06	8	7	1	151	49	25.16	0	0									4	
ATA-UR-REHMAN (Quetta) b Lasbela, Hub Chowk, Baluchistan 29.10.1986 RHB OB WK																			
FC		9	18	0	363	74	20.16	0	3									10	2
FC	2008/09	16	32	0	645	74	20.15	0	4									12	2
Lim	2008/09	2	2	1	63	40*	63.00	0	0									1	
ATIF ALI Zaidi (Karachi Whites) b Karachi, Sind 26.6.1984 RHB OB																			
FC		8	12	0	373	70	31.08	0	3	6	14	0					14.00	4	
FC	2001/02	39	69	3	1784	98	27.03	0	13	20	31	0					9.30	21	
Lim	2000/01	27	25	3	732	81*	33.27	0	5									3	
ATIF ASHRAF Qureshi (ZTBL) b Islamabad, Punjab 26.5.1980 RHB OB																			
FC		2	4	0	44	15	11.00	0	0									4	
Lim		2	2	0	116	66	58.00	0	2									1	
FC	1999/00	56	86	8	2145	177	27.50	1	13	66	50	0					4.54	35	
Lim	1999/00	27	25	4	756	91	36.00	0	6									10	
20T	2005/06	3	3	0	39	29	13.00	0	0									2	
ATIF MANZOOR, Mohammad (Faisalabad) b Jhang, Punjab 26.1.1989 RHB LB																			
FC		2	3	0	46	24	15.33	0	0	30	33	2	16.50	2-16	0	0	6.60	1	
ATIF MAQBOOL (Karachi Blues) b Karachi, Sind 21.11.1981 RHB OB																			
FC		5	7	1	96	45	16.00	0	0	752	409	14	29.21	5-33	1	0	3.26	1	
FC	2001/02	24	38	4	393	45	11.55	0	0	4090	2331	66	35.31	5-33	2	0	3.42	12	
Lim	2001/02	21	12	4	58	15	7.25	0	0	1063	901	33	27.30	5-21	0	1	5.08	4	
20T	2004/05	3	1	0	4	4	4.00	0	0	60	63	7	9.00	3-20	0	0	6.30	0	
ATIQ-UR-REHMAN (WAPDA) b Gujranwala, Punjab 24.4.1984 RHB OB																			
Lim		2	2	0	30	25	15.00	0	0									1	
FC	2000/01	51	85	5	1996	157	24.95	2	10	100	46	1	46.00	1-8	0	0	2.76	46	
Lim	1999/00	43	42	0	1024	114	24.38	3	3	60	44	1	44.00	1-44	0	0	4.40	13	
ATTAULLAH (Quetta) b Anambar, Baluchistan 22.2.1989 RHB RMF																			
FC		1	2	0	0	0	0.00	0	0									1	
AWAIS KHAN (Abbottabad Rhinos) b Haripur, North-West Frontier Province 2.10.1991 RHB																			
20T		1	1	0	3	3	3.00	0	0									0	
AWAIS ZIA (KRL) b Bhown, Chakwal, Punjab 1.9.1986 LHB OB																			
FC		1	1	0	32	32	32.00	0	0									0	
Lim		1																0	
FC	2006/07	16	23	4	938	147*	49.36	2	4	42	33	0					4.71	13	
Lim	2006/07	15	11	0	115	37	10.45	0	0									9	
20T	2008/09	5	5	2	98	50*	32.66	0	1	18	19	0					6.33	2	
AYAZ Hussain JAMALI (Hyderabad Hawks) b Larkana, Sind 4.3.1987 RHB WK																			
20T		1	1	0	0	0	0.00	0	0									3	1
20T	2009	3	2	0	4	4	2.00	0	0									5	1
AYAZ TASAWWAR (Sialkot) b Sheikhupura, Punjab 10.12.1990 LHB LB																			
FC		7	10	0	231	83	23.10	0	2	102	51	1	51.00	1-36	0	0	3.00	4	
FC	2007/08	18	25	1	740	100*	30.83	1	5	228	126	1	126.00	1-36	0	0	3.31	15	
Lim	2007/08	7	5	1	80	27	20.00	0	0	169	154	4	38.50	3-39	0	0	5.46	2	
AZAM HUSSAIN, Syed Mohammad (Karachi Blues, Karachi Dolphins, Sind Dolphins) b Karachi, Sind 7.9.1985 LHB SLA																			
FC		9	14	6	233	48*	29.12	0	0	1151	592	21	28.19	4-50	0	0	3.08	3	
Lim		9	3	0	8	5	2.66	0	0	521	388	15	25.86	4-35	2	0	4.46	4	
20T		1	1	0	1	1	1.00	0	0	24	25	2	12.50	2-25	0	0	6.25	1	
FC	2001/02	46	66	15	814	49	15.96	0	0	8516	4232	148	28.59	8-113	5	3	2.98	12	
Lim	2000/01	44	27	4	236	30	10.26	0	0	2251	1792	56	32.00	4-35	5	0	4.77	11	
20T	2005/06	11	3	1	3	2	1.50	0	0	228	284	13	21.84	3-19	0	0	7.47	2	
AZAM JAN (Khyber Pakhtunkhwa Panthers, Peshawar, Peshawar Panthers) b Charsadda, North-West Frontier Province 5.7.1983 RHB RAB																			
FC		9	16	2	612	115	43.71	2	3									2	
Lim		5	5	0	183	57	36.60	0	3									2	
20T		3	3	0	5	4	1.66	0	0									0	
FC	2007/08	16	27	4	764	115	33.21	2	4									6	
Lim	2007/08	9	8	0	256	57	32.00	0	3									4	
AZAM KHAN, Mohammad (Peshawar, Peshawar Panthers) b Lower Dir, North-West Frontier Province 1.6.1987 RHB RFM																			
FC		5	8	3	41	14	8.20	0	0	698	537	14	38.35	5-45	1	0	4.61	1	
Lim		1	1	0	2	2	2.00	0	0	36	20	1	20.00	1-20	0	0	3.33	0	
Lim	2008/09	3	1	0	2	2	2.00	0	0	84	84	2	42.00	1-20	0	0	6.00	0	
AZEEM GHUMMAN, Mohammad (Hyderabad Hawks, Sui Southern Gas, Pakistan A to Sri Lanka) b Hyderabad, Sind 24.1.1991 RHB LB																			
FC		4	8	0	332	183	41.50	1	1	24	14	0					3.50	1	
Lim		5	5	0	302	133	60.40	1	2									3	

Cmp	Debut	M	I	NO	Runs	HS	Avge	100	50	Balls	Runs	Wkts	Avge	BB	5i	10m	RpO	ct	st
20T		2	2	0	10	10	5.00	0	0	24	22	2	11.00	2-22	0	0	5.50	0	
FC	2007/08	19	32	0	1469	199	45.90	5	4	108	78	0					4.33	13	
Lim	2007/08	15	15	0	420	133	28.00	1	2	24	30	0					7.50	4	
20T	2009	4	4	0	65	40	16.25	0	0	24	22	2	11.00	2-22	0	0	5.50	0	
AZHAR ALI (KRL, Punjab Stallions, Pakistan to England) b Lahore, Punjab 19.2.1985 RHB LB																			
FC		10	17	2	445	153*	29.66	2	0	24	15	0					3.75	13	
Lim		5	5	0	252	102	50.40	1	1	12	11	0					5.50	2	
Test	2010	6	12	1	291	92*	26.45	0	2	6	9	0					9.00	3	
FC	2001/02	56	92	12	3080	153*	38.50	11	11	996	639	17	37.58	4-34	0	0	3.84	52	
Lim	2000/01	61	48	11	1667	119	45.05	4	11	1318	1098	35	31.37	5-23	2	2	4.99	17	
20T	2005/06	11	11	1	188	40	18.80	0	0	78	74	6	12.33	2-13	0	0	5.69	7	
AZHAR ATTARI (ZTBL) b Lahore, Punjab 12.12.1990 RHB RMF																			
FC		5	6	2	3	2*	0.75	0	0	830	423	9	47.00	4-73	0	0	3.05	2	
Lim		1	1	0	0	0	0.00	0	0	60	55	1	55.00	1-55	0	0	5.50	0	
FC	2007/08	16	18	10	24	8*	3.00	0	0	2464	1295	45	28.77	4-47	0	0	3.15	4	
20T	2008/09	2								48	35	2	17.50	2-14	0	0	4.37	2	
AZHAR MAHMOOD Sagar (Islamabad Leopards, Kent, Kent to Scotland) b Rawalpindi, Punjab 28.2.1975 RHB RFM																			
Lim		3	3	0	48	24	16.00	0	0	117	99	0					5.07	2	
20T		2	1	0	2	2	2.00	0	0	36	37	3	12.33	3-17	0	0	6.16	0	
Test	1997/98	21	34	4	900	136	30.00	3	1	3015	1402	39	35.94	4-50	0	0	2.79	14	
FC	1993/94	163	254	29	6952	204*	30.89	9	35	27559	14277	566	25.22	8-61	24	3	3.10	127	
Int	1996	143	110	26	1521	67	18.10	0	3	6242	4813	123	39.13	6-18	2	3	4.62	37	
Lim	1993/94	291	233	47	3946	101*	21.21	2	15	12836	9919	310	31.99	6-18	11	5	4.63	87	
20T	2003	78	68	20	1219	65*	25.39	0	3	1586	1928	86	22.41	4-20	1	0	7.29	12	
AZHAR SHAFIQ, Mohammad (Sui Northern Gas) b Sadiqabad, Punjab 31.12.1978 LHB RM																			
FC		11	16	1	403	78*	26.86	0	3	48	24	0					3.00	6	
FC	1994/95	169	285	13	7464	128*	27.44	10	42	12148	6373	258	24.70	7-93	12	2	3.14	99	
Lim	1996/97	81	76	4	2030	103	28.19	1	14	1322	1106	20	55.30	2-40	0	0	5.02	18	
20T	2005/06	8	8	0	91	29	11.37	0	0	18	27	1	27.00	1-10	0	0	9.00	3	
AZHARULLAH, Mohammad (WAPDA) b Burewala, Punjab 25.12.1983 RHB RFM																			
FC		8	9	4	94	35*	18.80	0	0	1479	922	33	27.93	5-51	2	0	3.74	2	
FC	2004/05	49	63	35	432	41	15.42	0	0	7964	4714	182	25.90	7-74	11	1	3.55	12	
Lim	2004/05	23	11	7	39	9	9.75	0	0	1138	997	35	28.48	5-56	1	1	5.25	8	
20T	2004/05	8	5	4	6	5*	6.00	0	0	152	193	1	193.00	1-15	0	0	7.61	1	
BABAR ALI (Multan, Multan Tigers) b Multan, Punjab 8.11.1986 RHB OB																			
FC		5	8	0	142	42	17.75	0	0	24	16	0					4.00	4	
Lim		2	2	0	28	18	14.00	0	0									0	
20T		2	2	0	2	2	1.00	0	0									0	
Lim	2008/09	7	7	0	145	38	20.71	0	0									3	
20T	2009	4	4	0	60	58	15.00	0	1									1	
BABAR AZAM, Mohammad (ZTBL) b Lahore, Punjab 15.10.1994 RHB OB																			
Lim		4	4	0	122	68	30.50	0	1	48	45	2	22.50	1-11	0	0	5.62	2	
BABAR HUSSAIN Agha (Karachi Zebras) b Karachi, Sind 23.9.1984 RHB OB																			
Lim		2	2	0	17	17	8.50	0	0									0	
BABAR NAEEM (Rawalpindi, Rawalpindi Rams) b Rawalpindi, Punjab 1.1.1983 LHB SLA																			
FC		10	17	0	615	117	36.17	2	3	360	211	5	42.20	1-8	0	0	3.51	13	
Lim		5	5	0	240	82	48.00	0	3	216	184	5	36.80	2-49	0	0	5.11	3	
20T		2	2	0	20	20	10.00	0	0	6	15	0					15.00	0	
FC	1999/00	102	179	6	5287	227	30.56	10	25	4902	2444	67	36.47	4-64	0	0	2.99	78	
Lim	1998/99	84	83	2	2475	109	30.55	1	20	2757	2286	61	37.47	4-31	2	0	4.97	21	
20T	2005/06	12	12	0	175	48	14.58	0	0	120	190	4	47.50	1-15	0	0	9.50	2	
BABAR REHMAN (Karachi Whites, Karachi Zebras) b Karachi, Sind 14.8.1984 RHB RFM																			
FC		5	9	1	196	98	24.50	0	1	513	304	9	33.77	3-58	0	0	3.55	3	
Lim		5	5	1	105	52*	26.25	0	1	180	183	2	91.50	1-42	0	0	6.10	2	
20T		1	1	0	26	26	26.00	0	0	18	38	1	38.00	1-38	0	0	12.66	2	
FC	2007/08	11	17	1	373	98	23.31	0	2	1551	875	32	27.34	5-73	1	0	3.38	5	
Lim	2007/08	11	11	2	274	52*	30.44	0	1	438	458	8	57.25	3-34	0	0	6.27	7	
BASIT ALI (Multan Tigers) b Burewala, Punjab 10.6.1979 LHB OB																			
Lim		1								12	5	0					2.50	0	
BAZID KHAN (Federal Areas Leopards, KRL) b Lahore, Punjab 25.3.1981 RHB OB																			
FC		10	14	1	558	92	42.92	0	5	42	17	0					2.42	14	
Lim		8	8	0	249	94	31.12	0	2									2	
Test	2004/05	1	2	0	32	23	16.00	0	0									2	
FC	1997/98	124	184	10	6331	300*	36.38	12	29	606	313	5	62.60	2-23	0	0	3.09	118	1
Int	2004/05	5	5	0	131	66	26.20	0	2	12	11	0					5.50	1	
Lim	1997/98	104	98	15	3721	116	44.83	5	30	483	410	7	58.57	2-38	0	0	5.09	50	
20T	2005/06	12	12	0	272	90	22.66	0	2	36	42	2	21.00	1-6	0	0	7.00	3	
BEHRAM Hasan KHAN (Karachi Whites) b Karachi, Sind 31.12.1987 RHB RMF																			
FC		2	3	0	13	5	4.33	0	0									4	
FC	2008/09	4	7	0	57	21	8.14	0	0									5	
Lim	2007/08	4	4	0	52	47	13.00	0	0									1	

Cmp	Debut	M	I	NO	Runs	HS	Avge	100	50	Balls	Runs	Wkts	Avge	BB	5i	10m	RpO	ct	st
BILAL AHMED (Faisalabad Wolves) b Sargodha, Punjab 15.9.1989 RHB OB																			
Lim		1	1	0	0	0	0.00	0	0	48	45	2	22.50	2-45	0	0	5.62	0	
BILAL ASAD (Sui Southern Gas) b Jhang, Punjab 17.11.1978 RHB RM																			
FC		8	14	0	287	81	20.50	0	1	389	181	4	45.25	3-45	0	0	2.79	2	
Lim		2	2	0	49	26	24.50	0	0	24	22	0					5.50	0	
FC	1995/96	115	191	13	6072	151	34.11	11	34	6353	3253	122	26.66	5-37	2	0	3.07	85	
Lim	1993/94	73	67	6	1931	140*	31.65	1	11	1279	1132	27	41.92	4-40	1	0	5.31	26	1
20T	2004/05	9	9	0	259	51	28.77	0	1	78	92	5	18.40	3-19	0	0	7.07	3	
BILAL AZMAT (Sialkot) b Gujranwala, Punjab 10.10.1984 RHB OB																			
FC		3	4	0	56	26	14.00	0	0									3	
FC	2007/08	8	12	0	245	100	20.41	1	0									9	
Lim	2003/04	1	1	0	6	6	6.00	0	0									0	
BILAL BUTT (Sialkot, Sialkot Stallions) b Sialkot, Punjab 22.10.1988 RHB WK																			
FC		1	2	0	45	30	22.50	0	0									2	3
Lim		7	3	0	23	12	7.66	0	0									11	1
Lim	2001/02	9	5	1	34	12	8.50	0	0									11	2
BILAL HUSSAIN (WAPDA) b Gujranwala, Punjab 22.2.1984 RHB OB																			
FC		1	2	0	8	8	4.00	0	0									0	
FC	2000/01	27	44	4	830	117	20.75	1	3	485	247	7	35.28	2-23	0	0	3.05	13	
Lim	1998/99	37	35	2	912	119*	27.63	1	2	679	519	22	23.59	4-16	2	0	4.58	18	
20T	2004/05	3	3	0	62	34	20.66	0	0									1	
BILAL KHAN (Peshawar Panthers) b Peshawar, North-West Frontier Province 10.4.1987 LHB LMF																			
Lim		4	4	0	19	7	4.75	0	0	186	139	6	23.16	4-44	1	0	4.48	0	
FC	2007/08	6	10	3	85	20	12.14	0	0	642	352	11	32.00	4-63	0	0	3.29	3	
Lim	2007/08	5	5	0	45	26	9.00	0	0	216	174	7	24.85	4-44	1	0	4.83	0	
BILAL Moin-ul-Haq KHILJI (WAPDA) b Bahawalpur, Punjab 10.9.1975 LHB RM																			
FC		8	13	2	483	161	43.90	2	1	420	193	5	38.60	1-3	0	0	2.75	3	
Lim		2	2	0	93	62	46.50	0	1									0	
FC	1994/95	132	209	20	6433	161	34.03	12	38	3736	1703	53	32.13	5-9	1	0	2.73	90	
Lim	1997/98	66	61	7	1835	102*	33.98	1	12	771	572	16	35.75	3-35	0	0	4.45	28	
20T	2005/06	7	7	0	139	46	19.85	0	0									3	
BILAWAL BHATTI (Punjab Stallions, Sialkot, Sialkot Stallions) b Muridke, Punjab 17.9.1991 RHB RMF																			
FC		11	15	2	275	70	21.15	0	1	2281	1326	50	26.52	6-94	3	0	3.48	4	
Lim		9	6	5	52	23*	52.00	0	0	466	368	16	23.00	4-49	1	0	4.73	1	
FC	2008/09	17	23	3	393	70	19.65	0	1	3313	1932	73	26.46	6-94	3	0	3.49	7	
Lim	2007/08	16	10	5	105	34	21.00	0	0	778	658	23	28.60	4-49	1	0	5.07	3	
BISMILLAH KHAN (Quetta, Quetta Bears) b Quetta, Baluchistan 1.3.1990 RHB WK																			
FC		6	12	1	276	69	25.09	0	2									11	
Lim		4	4	0	67	27	16.75	0	0									7	3
20T		2	2	0	13	13	6.50	0	0									2	1
Lim	2008/09	9	8	0	177	72	22.12	0	1									8	5
20T	2009	5	5	0	50	26	10.00	0	0									3	1
DABEER ALI Khan (Faisalabad Wolves) b Bhakkar, Punjab 15.5.1988 RHB RFM																			
Lim		1	1	1	8	8*		0	0	48	43	0					5.37	0	
DANISH Parabha Shanker KANERIA (Habib Bank, Karachi Zebras, Sind Dolphins, Essex, Pakistan to Australia, Pakistan to England, Pakistan to New Zealand) b Karachi, Sind 16.12.1980 RHB LB																			
FC		4	5	1	89	36	22.25	0	0	1029	519	27	19.22	6-59	2	1	3.02	2	
Lim		9	3	1	73	64	36.50	0	1	540	357	16	22.31	6-33	0	1	3.96	1	
20T		2								48	60	2	30.00	2-21	0	0	7.50	1	
Test	2000/01	61	84	33	360	29	7.05	0	0	17697	9082	261	34.79	7-77	15	2	3.07	18	
FC	1998/99	180	229	81	1508	65	10.18	0	1	47813	23489	884	26.57	8-59	61	10	2.94	61	
Int	2001/02	18	10	8	12	6*	6.00	0	0	854	682	15	45.46	3-31	0	0	4.79	2	
Lim	1998/99	153	69	33	348	64	9.66	0	1	7576	5401	232	23.28	6-33	7	7	4.27	29	
20T	2004/05	57	23	8	97	12	6.46	0	0	1183	1431	75	19.08	4-22	2	0	7.25	10	
DANIYAL AHSAN (Karachi Blues, Karachi Dolphins) b Karachi, Sind 23.11.1985 RHB OB																			
FC		1	2	0	66	42	33.00	0	0									1	
Lim		2	2	0	39	33	19.50	0	0									1	
FC	2004/05	12	22	2	355	63	17.75	0	1	30	19	0					3.80	7	
Lim	2007/08	11	11	1	409	96	40.90	0	3									3	
DILAWAR KHAN Orakzai (Sui Southern Gas) b Peshawar, North-West Frontier Province 23.5.1984 RHB LB																			
FC		6	8	4	17	10	4.25	0	0	1072	586	20	29.30	4-13	0	0	3.28	2	
Lim		4	2	1	3	3*	3.00	0	0	141	130	1	130.00	1-40	0	0	5.53	0	
FC	2004/05	26	38	14	87	14*	3.62	0	0	4673	2854	87	32.80	7-33	4	1	3.66	9	
Lim	2001/02	10	5	3	10	7*	5.00	0	0	453	401	9	44.55	2-38	0	0	5.31	2	
20T	2005/06	6	2	1	7	6	7.00	0	0	102	141	9	15.66	3-30	0	0	8.29	2	
EHTESHAMUDDIN (Abbottabad) b Peshawar, North-West Frontier Province 3.5.1982 RHB OB																			
FC		4	8	0	185	58	23.12	0	1	6	3	0					3.00	0	
FC	2002/03	5	10	0	205	58	20.50	0	1	6	3	0					3.00	0	
EMMAD ALI (Lahore Eagles) b Lahore, Punjab 29.11.1991 LHB LMF																			
Lim		4	4	2	77	41	38.50	0	0	192	159	6	26.50	3-32	0	0	4.96	1	

Cmp	Debut	M	I	NO	Runs	HS	Avge	100	50	Balls	Runs	Wkts	Avge	BB	5i	10m	RpO	ct	st
FAHAD AKRAM (Islamabad) b Mirpur, Azad Kashmir 2.5.1979 RHB RAB WK																			
FC		2	4	0	108	59	27.00	0	1									0	
FAHAD IQBAL (PIA) b Karachi, Sind 25.2.1986 RHB RMF																			
FC		10	15	0	399	92	26.60	0	3	42	46	0					6.57	8	
Lim		4	3	1	46	36	23.00	0	0	10	8	0					4.80	1	
FC	2003/04	44	67	5	2195	200*	35.40	3	16	85	82	1	82.00	1-21	0	0	5.78	24	
Lim	2003/04	39	33	3	808	92*	26.93	0	4	142	155	4	38.75	2-75	0	0	6.54	11	
20T	2004/05	7	5	1	171	58*	42.75	0	1									1	
FAHAD KHAN, Mohammad (Karachi Blues) b Karachi, Sind 25.11.1983 RHB RMF																			
FC		2	3	1	10	8*	5.00	0	0	240	156	3	52.00	2-77	0	0	3.90	1	
FC	2003/04	33	44	21	71	8*	3.08	0	0	5027	3104	93	33.37	5-55	2	0	3.70	14	
Lim	2003/04	15	7	6	14	7*	14.00	0	0	636	716	16	44.75	3-57	0	0	6.75	1	
20T	2004/05	5	4	2	11	5*	5.50	0	0	102	147	7	21.00	4-21	1	0	8.64	3	
FAHAD MASOOD (Habib Bank, Lahore Eagles) b Gaggu Mandi, Punjab 14.8.1981 RHB RFM																			
FC		11	17	3	180	39*	12.85	0	0	1572	790	24	32.91	4-32	0	0	3.01	8	
20T		2	1	0	23	23	23.00	0	0	36	35	1	35.00	1-17	0	0	5.83	0	
FC	1999/00	97	138	26	1358	48	12.12	0	0	14689	7536	327	23.04	7-27	12	1	3.07	30	
Lim	1999/00	55	31	11	266	64	13.30	0	1	2367	2060	62	33.22	6-33	2	1	5.22	11	
20T	2004/05	10	7	1	70	39	11.66	0	0	185	256	10	25.60	3-28	0	0	8.30	3	
FAHADULLAH KHAN (Karachi Dolphins) b Karachi, Sind 18.8.1977 RHB OB																			
Lim		3	3	0	90	66	30.00	0	1									1	
20T		1	1	1	13	13*		0	0									0	
FC	1997/98	22	38	1	604	106	16.32	1	2	135	57	3	19.00	1-7	0	0	2.53	21	
Lim	1998/99	28	25	2	743	85	32.30	0	5	114	58	2	29.00	1-14	0	0	3.05	10	
20T	2004/05	8	8	1	158	61	22.57	0	1									1	
FAHEEM AKBAR Khan Niazi, Mohammad (Rawalpindi Rams) b Mianwali, Punjab 9.7.1983 RHB RMF																			
Lim		1								30	16	1	16.00	1-16	0	0	3.20	0	
FAISAL ATHAR (Hyderabad, Hyderabad Hawks) b Hyderabad, Sind 15.10.1975 RHB RM																			
FC		10	20	0	479	81	23.95	0	5	408	258	5	51.60	2-30	0	0	3.79	6	
Lim		2	2	0	46	35	23.00	0	0									0	
FC	1998/99	105	181	10	6300	171	36.84	14	30	1360	905	12	75.41	3-40	0	0	3.99	63	
Int	2003	1	1	0	9	9	9.00	0	0									0	
Lim	1998/99	46	46	3	1573	102*	36.58	1	10	112	116	2	58.00	2-59	0	0	6.21	16	1
20T	2005/06	11	11	2	253	66*	28.11	0	2	12	7	3	2.33	3-7	0	0	3.50	1	
FAISAL ELAHI (Multan Tigers) b Bahawalpur, Punjab 10.9.1976 LHB SLA																			
Lim		5	4	2	41	15	20.50	0	0	210	184	11	16.72	4-33	1	0	5.25	1	
FC	1994/95	27	46	6	645	96	16.12	0	2	2571	1292	31	41.67	5-46	1	0	3.01	8	
Lim	1996/97	22	19	2	193	40	11.35	0	0	1058	729	32	22.78	4-14	3	0	4.13	4	
FAISAL IQBAL (Karachi Zebras, PIA, Sind Dolphins, Pakistan to Australia, Pakistan to New Zealand, Sylhet) b Karachi, Sind 30.12.1981 RHB RM																			
FC		4	6	1	144	53	28.80	0	1									2	
Lim		9	9	0	237	58	26.33	0	1	12	10	0					5.00	3	
20T		2	2	0	80	58	40.00	0	1									1	
Test	2000/01	26	44	2	1124	139	26.76	1	8	6	7	0					7.00	22	
FC	1998/99	148	233	24	8247	200*	39.45	15	49	162	126	1	126.00	1-6	0	0	4.66	119	1
Int	1999/00	18	16	2	314	100*	22.42	1	0	18	33	0					11.00	3	
Lim	1997/98	130	118	21	3655	123	37.68	4	27	72	108	1	108.00	1-15	0	0	9.00	41	1
20T	2005/06	16	16	2	322	58	23.00	0	1									3	
FAISAL IQBAL (Rawalpindi Rams) b Rawalpindi, Punjab 23.7.1990 RHB SLA																			
Lim		3	1	1	29	29*		0	0	118	100	2	50.00	2-35	0	0	5.08	3	
Lim	2008/09	7	3	2	44	29*	44.00	0	0	301	238	5	47.60	2-15	0	0	4.74	4	
20T	2009	3	2	1	14	8*	14.00	0	0	60	77	1	77.00	1-22	0	0	7.70	2	
FAISAL IRFAN Butt (Quetta) b Quetta, Baluchistan 28.2.1979 RHB RFM																			
FC		7	14	4	276	77	27.60	0	1	574	363	6	60.50	2-32	0	0	3.79	2	
FC	2000/01	81	134	29	2335	102	22.23	1	6	11585	5615	204	27.52	6-19	5	1	2.90	23	
Lim	1998/99	34	26	9	351	78	20.64	0	1	1488	1196	32	37.37	5-35	1	1	4.82	5	
20T	2005/06	9	7	0	169	50	24.14	0	1	156	172	10	17.20	3-22	0	0	6.61	2	
FAISAL JAVED (Sialkot) b Sialkot, Punjab 23.12.1986 RHB OB																			
FC		2	4	0	15	15	3.75	0	0									0	
FAISAL KHAN (Sialkot, Sialkot Stallions) b Sialkot, Punjab 6.12.1983 RHB RM,OB																			
FC		9	16	1	713	202*	47.53	1	5									12	
Lim		5	5	0	74	34	14.80	0	0									2	
FC	2001/02	46	76	4	2255	202*	31.31	2	17	96	67	2	33.50	1-14	0	0	4.18	44	
Lim	2001/02	20	20	3	589	115*	34.64	1	2	231	224	5	44.80	2-41	0	0	5.81	8	
FAISAL NAVED (ZTBL) b Sialkot, Punjab 2.3.1980 RHB RM																			
FC		3	4	1	56	27	18.66	0	0	6	4	0					4.00	1	
FC	1997/98	87	150	8	3960	151*	27.88	8	16	1905	1079	18	59.94	3-17	0	0	3.39	49	
Lim	1999/00	56	54	5	1671	108	34.10	3	14	692	598	17	35.17	4-8	1	0	5.18	15	
20T	2005/06	5	5	0	92	37	18.40	0	0									0	

Cmp	Debut	M	I	NO	Runs	HS	Avge	100	50	Balls	Runs	Wkts	Avge	BB	5i	10m	RpO	ct	st
FAISAL RASHEED (Sialkot) b Sheikhupura, Punjab 29.11.1987 RHB RFM																			
FC		9	15	6	101	30	11.22	0	0	1412	924	38	24.31	5-45	3	0	3.92	2	
FC	2007/08	12	17	6	140	39	12.72	0	0	1712	1095	44	24.88	5-45	3	0	3.83	6	
Lim	2002/03	1								54	52	1	52.00	1-52	0	0	5.77	0	
FAISAL VIRK (Customs) b Sheikhupura, Punjab 30.10.1983 LHB SLA																			
Lim		2	2	0	20	14	10.00	0	0	78	62	0					4.76	0	
FC	2000/01	7	10	3	42	14	6.00	0	0	690	302	11	27.45	3-56	0	0	2.62	3	
Lim	2000/01	3	3	0	24	14	8.00	0	0	138	119	1	119.00	1-57	0	0	5.17	0	
FAIZAN RIAZ (Islamabad, Islamabad Leopards) b Islamabad, Punjab 2.7.1988 RHB LB																			
FC		2	3	0	64	39	21.33	0	0									2	
Lim		3	3	0	55	50	18.33	0	1									0	
20T		2	1	0	25	25	25.00	0	0									0	
20T	2009	5	4	1	47	25	15.66	0	0									2	
FAKHAR HUSSAIN (Islamabad, Islamabad Leopards) b Gujrat, Punjab 8.7.1978 RHB RMF																			
FC		5	7	0	226	74	32.28	0	2	411	221	4	55.25	2-30	0	0	3.22	2	
Lim		4	4	2	45	19*	22.50	0	0	78	80	1	80.00	1-26	0	0	6.15	2	
FC	2005/06	17	27	1	536	74	20.61	0	4	879	577	11	52.45	3-34	0	0	3.93	7	
Lim	2006/07	11	11	3	238	94	29.75	0	1	144	155	4	38.75	3-40	0	0	6.45	5	
20T	2006/07	4	3	0	14	9	4.66	0	0	48	57	0					7.12	2	
FARAZ AHMED Khan (Karachi Blues, Karachi Dolphins) b Karachi, Sind 16.10.1984 RHB SLA																			
FC		2	4	2	11	5*	5.50	0	0	142	99	2	49.50	1-22	0	0	4.18	0	
Lim		3	2	0	3	3	1.50	0	0	180	139	4	34.75	3-48	0	0	4.63	0	
FC	2007/08	5	8	2	78	44	13.00	0	0	622	393	5	78.60	3-110	0	0	3.79	2	
Lim	2007/08	10	6	0	73	31	12.16	0	0	582	498	12	41.50	3-48	0	0	5.13	3	
20T	2008/09	3	1	0	2	2	2.00	0	0	57	67	4	16.75	3-15	0	0	7.05	1	
FARAZ PATEL (Karachi Whites) b Karachi, Sind 2.12.1986 RHB OB																			
FC		2	4	0	35	32	8.75	0	0									0	
FC	2002/03	21	38	7	698	69*	22.51	0	4	282	206	5	41.20	3-96	0	0	4.38	8	
Lim	2007/08	5	5	0	215	80	43.00	0	1	108	81	0					4.50	0	
FARHAN ASGHAR (Lahore Ravi) b Lahore, Punjab 15.9.1980 RHB WK																			
FC		6	8	2	191	52*	31.83	0	1									23	
FC	2002/03	15	19	5	391	75*	27.92	0	2									38	
Lim	1998/99	6	5	0	81	59	16.20	0	1									6	5
FARHAN AYUB (Hyderabad) b Hyderabad, Sind 27.3.1985 LHB LMF																			
FC		4	7	4	19	14*	6.33	0	0	497	329	7	47.00	2-60	0	0	3.97	0	
FC	2003/04	27	48	14	226	22	6.64	0	0	4337	2702	78	34.64	7-71	5	1	3.73	6	
Lim	2003/04	13	9	3	19	10*	3.16	0	0	578	488	14	34.85	4-47	1	0	5.06	1	
20T	2005/06	8	3	2	1	1*	1.00	0	0	162	175	10	17.50	4-20	1	0	6.48	2	
FARHAN IQBAL (Habib Bank) b Karachi, Sind 3.12.1981 RHB WK																			
FC		8	14	4	332	70	33.20	0	3									26	6
Lim		1	1	0	20	20	20.00	0	0									1	
FC	2001/02	44	65	11	1169	70	21.64	0	6									105	14
Lim	2001/02	38	28	7	431	51	20.52	0	1									41	15
FARRUKH HAYAT (Islamabad Leopards) b Islamabad, Punjab 10.7.1983 RHB LB																			
Lim		1	1	0	0	0	0.00	0	0									0	
FC	2001/02	12	23	1	335	51*	15.22	0	1									4	
Lim	2000/01	3	3	0	31	26	10.33	0	0									0	
FARRUKH NAWAZ (Faisalabad Wolves) b Jhang, Punjab 20.1.1983 RHB RAB																			
Lim		1	1	0	1	1	1.00	0	0									0	
FARRUKH SHEHZAD (Faisalabad, Faisalabad Wolves) b Sargodha, Punjab 12.10.1984 RHB RMF																			
FC		3	5	0	121	81	24.20	0	1									1	
Lim		5	5	0	178	64	35.60	0	1									0	
Lim	2002/03	7	7	0	253	64	36.14	0	1	5	8	0					9.60	0	
FAWAD AHMED Khan (Abbottabad) b Merguz 10.3.1979 RHB LB																			
FC		3	5	1	17	7	4.25	0	0	177	113	4	28.25	3-24	0	0	3.83	1	
FC	2005/06	10	18	5	125	23	9.61	0	0	1196	802	23	34.86	6-109	1	0	4.02	3	
Lim	2008/09	1	1	0	35	35	35.00	0	0	14	16	0					6.85	1	
FAWAD ALAM (Karachi Dolphins, National Bank, Pakistan to Australia, Pakistan to England, Pakistan to New Zealand, Pakistan to United Arab Emirates, Pakistan to West Indies) b Karachi, Sind 8.10.1985 LHB SLA																			
FC		4	6	1	418	154*	83.60	2	1	66	18	0					1.63	1	
20T		3	2	0	42	41	21.00	0	0	24	20	2	10.00	2-20	0	0	5.00	2	
Test	2009	3	6	0	250	168	41.66	1	0									3	
FC	2003/04	57	98	19	4423	296*	55.98	8	28	1580	745	22	33.86	4-27	0	0	2.82	32	
Int	2007	22	20	8	480	64	40.00	0	3	362	332	4	83.00	1-8	0	0	5.50	7	
Lim	2003/04	72	65	15	2206	127	44.12	3	12	1941	1647	40	41.17	5-53	0	1	5.09	31	
I20T	2007/08	23	16	6	185	28	18.50	0	0	90	95	8	11.87	3-7	0	0	6.33	7	
20T	2004/05	48	36	12	721	70	30.04	0	4	400	470	31	15.16	5-27	0	1	7.05	14	
FAWAD ALI (Khyber Pakhtunkhwa Panthers, Peshawar, Peshawar Panthers) b Peshawar, North-West Frontier Province 12.11.1986 RHB RAB																			
FC		6	12	1	430	110	39.09	1	3									2	
Lim		1	1	0	21	21	21.00	0	0									0	

Cmp	Debut	M	I	NO	Runs	HS	Avge	100	50	Balls	Runs	Wkts	Avge	BB	5i	10m	RpO	ct	st
20T		2	2	0	9	9	4.50	0	0									1	
FC	2006/07	14	26	1	742	110	29.68	1	5									5	
Lim	2007/08	7	7	0	201	76	28.71	0	1									2	
20T	2009	3	3	0	21	12	7.00	0	0									1	
FAWAD HUSSAIN, Syed (Rawalpindi, Rawalpindi Rams) b Rawalpindi, Punjab 28.8.1989 RHB OB																			
FC		8	13	1	353	150	29.41	1	1									4	
Lim		1	1	0	19	19	19.00	0	0									0	
FC	2007/08	18	24	2	814	150	37.00	4	2									5	
Lim	2008/09	4	3	0	47	27	15.66	0	0									0	
20T	2009	1																0	
FAWAD Ahmed KHAN (Abbottabad, Abbottabad Rhinos) b Bannu, North-West Frontier Province 20.11.1986 RHB RM WK																			
FC		10	20	0	416	89	20.80	0	2	6	8	0					8.00	17	1
Lim		2	2	0	51	51	25.50	0	1									0	
FC	2007/08	30	47	1	1265	111	27.50	1	7	18	16	0					5.33	59	8
Lim	2004/05	10	10	0	220	69	22.00	0	3									5	4
20T	2004/05	6	6	1	113	40	22.60	0	0									3	1
FAYYAZ AHMED, Mohammad (Islamabad, Islamabad Leopards) b Islamabad, Punjab 28.12.1988 LHB SLA																			
FC		4	8	0	196	74	24.50	0	1	30	30	0					6.00	2	
Lim		2	2	0	50	35	25.00	0	0									1	
20T		2	1	0	20	20	20.00	0	0									0	
FC	2003/04	33	55	5	1248	118	24.96	1	5	411	318	11	28.90	4-63	0	0	4.64	25	
Lim	2001/02	18	15	3	275	65	22.91	0	1	230	208	10	20.80	3-47	0	0	5.42	8	
20T	2004/05	10	8	2	179	58*	29.83	0	1	12	14	2	7.00	2-14	0	0	7.00	2	
FAYYAZ-UL-HASAN (Multan) b Rahimyar Khan, Punjab 10.10.1988 LHB LB																			
FC		4	7	0	124	41	17.71	0	0	12	6	1	6.00	1-6	0	0	3.00	2	
FC	2008/09	6	11	1	200	41	20.00	0	0	12	6	1	6.00	1-6	0	0	3.00	3	
Lim	2008/09	4	4	0	70	52	17.50	0	1									1	
FAZAL SUBHAN (Karachi Whites, Karachi Zebras) b Karachi, Sind 1.1.1988 RHB RMF																			
FC		3	4	0	212	107	53.00	1	1	12	16	0					8.00	2	
Lim		2	2	0	26	26	13.00	0	0									0	
FC	2007/08	4	5	0	218	107	43.60	1	1	12	16	0					8.00	2	
Lim	2007/08	4	3	0	32	26	10.66	0	0									0	
FAZL-E-RABBI (Rawalpindi) b Swabi, North-West Frontier Province 10.1.1987 RHB RFM																			
FC		1	1	1	0	0*		0	0	48	48	0					6.00	0	
GAUHAR ALI Habib (Abbottabad Rhinos) b Mardan, North-West Frontier Province 13.12.1982 LHB SLA																			
20T		1	1	0	4	4	4.00	0	0									0	
Lim	2006/07	2	2	0	12	10	6.00	0	0									0	
GHULAM FAREED (Multan) b Sahiwal, Punjab 21.12.1988 RHB RMF																			
FC		5	9	0	266	88	29.55	0	2	318	154	6	25.66	2-39	0	0	2.90	2	
Lim	2008/09	1	1	0	8	8	8.00	0	0									1	
GHULAM MOHAMMAD (Abbottabad, Abbottabad Rhinos) b Dera Ismail Khan, North-West Frontier Province 6.9.1976 RHB RM WK																			
FC		10	20	0	437	85	21.85	0	2	78	42	3	14.00	3-38	0	0	3.23	6	
Lim		5	5	0	112	45	22.40	0	0	12	22	0					11.00	1	
FC	2007/08	25	39	3	1171	133	32.52	2	5	84	50	3	16.66	3-38	0	0	3.57	16	2
Lim	2007/08	15	15	0	355	65	23.66	0	1	26	41	1	41.00	1-1	0	0	9.46	5	
20T	2008/09	3	3	0	4	2	1.33	0	0									1	
GHULAM MUSTAFA (Lahore Ravi) b Sahiwal, Punjab 30.10.1988 LHB SLA																			
FC		6	9	7	44	27*	22.00	0	0	1178	558	8	69.75	1-0	0	0	2.84	2	
FC	2008/09	13	16	8	94	31	11.75	0	0	2606	1429	34	42.02	6-97	2	1	3.29	5	
Lim	2008/09	3	2	1	14	14*	14.00	0	0	102	78	1	78.00	1-38	0	0	4.58	0	
GHULAM SHABBIR (Faisalabad Wolves) b Jhang, Punjab 12.12.1985 LHB WK																			
Lim		1	1	0	19	19	19.00	0	0									0	
Lim	2008/09	2	1	0	19	19	19.00	0	0									1	
GHULAM SHABIR (Hyderabad Hawks) b 6.2.1991 RMF																			
20T		1	1	0	5	5	5.00	0	0	6	16	0					16.00	0	
GHULAM YASIN (Hyderabad Hawks) b Shikarpur, Sind 8.6.1986 RHB RFM																			
Lim		3	3	1	56	27	28.00	0	0	114	114	2	57.00	2-55	0	0	6.00	1	
20T	2009	1								24	30	1	30.00	1-30	0	0	7.50	0	
GOHAR FAIZ (Quetta) b Quetta, Baluchistan 27.9.1986 RHB RFM																			
FC		1	1	0	0	0	0.00	0	0	132	80	1	80.00	1-45	0	0	3.63	0	
FC	2006/07	13	23	11	132	35	11.00	0	0	1755	1189	20	59.45	4-86	0	0	4.06	2	
Lim	2006/07	3	2	0	9	7	4.50	0	0	78	104	1	104.00	1-66	0	0	8.00	0	
20T	2006/07	7	5	3	15	8*	7.50	0	0	144	232	4	58.00	3-19	0	0	9.66	2	
GULRAIZ SADAF (Baluchistan Bears, Multan, Multan Tigers) b Burewala, Punjab 27.12.1989 RHB WK																			
FC		10	17	1	516	118*	32.25	1	2									32	3
Lim		10	10	0	263	103	26.30	1	1									11	2
20T		3	3	0	43	20	14.33	0	0									5	1
FC	2006/07	39	66	4	1620	118*	26.12	1	10									107	6
Lim	2006/07	28	26	1	522	103	20.88	1	2									28	5
20T	2008/09	7	6	1	51	20	10.20	0	0									8	2

Cmp	Debut	M	I	NO	Runs	HS	Avge	100	50	Balls	Runs	Wkts	Avge	BB	5i	10m	RpO	ct	st
HAARIS AYAZ, Syed (Karachi Zebras, Sui Southern Gas) b Karachi, Sind 16.10.1975 RHB OB																			
FC		3	5	0	132	68	26.40	0	1	381	195	3	65.00	1-57	0	0	3.07	0	
Lim		5	5	1	25	9	6.25	0	0	250	239	6	39.83	3-47	0	0	5.73	1	
20T		1								24	20	3	6.66	3-20	0	0	5.00	0	
FC	1998/99	27	43	4	490	68	12.56	0	4	4222	2109	41	51.43	4-63	0	0	2.99	11	
Lim	1998/99	46	35	4	491	107	15.83	1	1	2096	1744	42	41.52	3-37	0	0	4.99	21	
20T	2004/05	7	5	1	29	13	7.25	0	0	151	200	15	13.33	3-20	0	0	7.94	1	
HAMAD-UL-HASAN (Peshawar, Peshawar Panthers) b Peshawar, North-West Frontier Province 2.4.1988 RHB OB																			
FC		10	16	2	106	19	7.57	0	0	1338	824	13	63.38	3-100	0	0	3.69	3	
Lim		4	4	3	67	28*	67.00	0	0	240	193	1	193.00	1-50	0	0	4.82	3	
20T		3	2	1	3	2	3.00	0	0	60	75	2	37.50	1-18	0	0	7.50	4	
Lim	2008/09	8	5	4	76	28*	76.00	0	0	372	365	6	60.83	3-72	0	0	5.88	3	
HAMMAD ALI Shah, Syed (Abbottabad) b Swabi, North-West Frontier Province 11.9.1990 RHB OB																			
FC		4	8	0	153	36	19.12	0	0									2	
FC	2006/07	12	21	3	581	100	32.27	1	1									10	
Lim	2008/09	4	4	0	158	81	39.50	0	1	5	10	0					12.00	2	
20T	2006/07	3	3	0	23	18	7.66	0	0									0	
HAMMAD AZAM (Rawalpindi, Rawalpindi Rams, Pakistan A to Sri Lanka, Pakistan A to United Arab Emirates) b Attock, Punjab 16.3.1991 RHB RM																			
FC		2	3	0	33	16	11.00	0	0	36	20	1	20.00	1-8	0	0	3.33	1	
Lim		4	4	1	90	60*	30.00	0	1	138	122	3	40.66	2-29	0	0	5.30	2	
20T		2	2	1	52	36*	52.00	0	0	30	57	2	28.50	2-23	0	0	11.40	2	
FC	2008/09	7	12	0	232	62	19.33	0	1	277	119	7	17.00	4-19	0	0	2.57	13	
Lim	2008/09	14	14	2	296	63*	24.66	0	2	420	352	8	44.00	2-29	0	0	5.02	7	
HAMMAD TARIQ Chaudhry (Multan) b Bahawalpur, Punjab 22.12.1980 LHB RM																			
FC		1	2	0	1	1	0.50	0	0									0	
FC	1999/00	44	71	2	1868	138	27.07	6	5	330	171	3	57.00	2-46	0	0	3.10	19	
Lim	1996/97	36	36	0	1007	77	27.97	0	8	68	86	0					7.58	7	
20T	2008/09	1	1	0	8	8	8.00	0	0									0	
HAMZA Haroon PARACHA (Lahore Shalimar) b Lahore, Punjab 21.9.1988 RHB RAB																			
FC		3	6	0	75	24	12.50	0	0									0	
HANIF MALIK (Customs) b Hyderabad, Sind 19.2.1981 RHB LB WK																			
FC		10	19	2	165	35	9.70	0	0	151	115	3	38.33	2-28	0	0	4.57	34	5
Lim		4	4	0	91	40	22.75	0	0									3	
FC	2001/02	74	131	11	2042	90	17.01	0	8	205	140	3	46.66	2-28	0	0	4.09	194	18
Lim	2001/02	40	32	6	389	40	14.96	0	0									28	16
20T	2004/05	11	8	1	80	22	11.42	0	0									7	3
HANIF-UR-REHMAN (Hyderabad, Hyderabad Hawks) b Moro, Sind 31.3.1976 RHB OB																			
FC		9	17	0	533	123	31.35	1	3	668	420	12	35.00	6-65	1	0	3.77	10	
Lim		2	2	0	40	39	20.00	0	0	18	20	0					6.66	1	
FC	1995/96	81	139	4	3708	123	27.46	4	23	3242	1721	48	35.85	6-65	2	0	3.18	39	
Lim	1996/97	52	51	1	1039	107	20.78	1	6	1293	1110	30	37.00	4-50	1	0	5.15	22	
20T	2004/05	9	9	0	160	43	17.77	0	0	52	72	2	36.00	2-29	0	0	8.30	4	
HARIS SOHAIL (ZTBL) b Sialkot, Punjab 9.1.1989 LHB LM																			
FC		6	8	0	242	81	30.25	0	2	48	31	0					3.87	2	
Lim		3	3	1	30	18*	15.00	0	0									2	
FC	2007/08	19	28	3	1165	155	46.60	1	10	54	33	1	33.00	1-2	0	0	3.66	12	
Lim	2007/08	9	9	3	183	75*	30.50	0	1									2	
HAROON AHMED (Peshawar, Peshawar Panthers) b Peshawar, North-West Frontier Province 15.11.1982 LHB RMF																			
FC		2	4	0	67	46	16.75	0	0	24	11	0					2.75	0	
Lim		4	4	0	180	67	45.00	0	2	42	36	0					5.14	1	
Lim	2008/09	5	5	0	194	67	38.80	0	2	42	36	0					5.14	1	
HASAN ADNAN Syed, Mohammad (Customs) b Lahore, Punjab 15.5.1975 RHB OB																			
FC		3	6	0	139	84	23.16	0	1	10	15	0					9.00	1	
FC	1994/95	130	219	24	7350	191	37.69	10	49	463	333	4	83.25	1-4	0	0	4.31	68	
Lim	1997/98	73	70	9	1875	113*	30.73	2	14	187	162	6	27.00	2-13	0	0	5.19	26	
20T	2004	11	9	2	167	54*	23.85	0	1	54	68	2	34.00	1-18	0	0	7.55	4	
HASAN Ahmed DAR (Lahore Eagles, Lahore Shalimar) b Lahore, Punjab 18.7.1989 RHB RMF																			
FC		5	9	3	23	6	3.83	0	0	787	591	16	36.93	7-53	1	0	4.50	0	
Lim		2	2	1	8	5*	8.00	0	0	36	45	0					7.50	0	
FC	2008/09	6	10	3	23	6	3.28	0	0	901	684	18	38.00	7-53	1	0	4.55	0	
HASAN JAVED Akhtar (Lahore Ravi) b Jeddah, Saudi Arabia 19.3.1990 RHB OB																			
FC		2	4	0	76	37	19.00	0	0									0	
HASAN MAHMOOD (Faisalabad) b Faisalabad, Punjab 11.5.1988 RHB OB																			
FC		4	6	0	161	56	26.83	0	1									5	
Lim	2008/09	2	1	0	67	67	67.00	0	1									0	
HASAN MAHMOOD (Faisalabad Wolves) b Sargodha, Punjab 1.1.1991 LHB SLA																			
Lim		5	4	1	41	16	13.66	0	0	279	212	12	17.66	4-62	1	0	4.55	2	
FC	2007/08	1	1	1	8	8*		0	0	42	10	0					1.42	0	
Lim	2007/08	6	5	1	42	16	10.50	0	0	327	257	12	21.41	4-62	1	0	4.71	2	

Cmp	Debut	M	I	NO	Runs	HS	Avge	100	50	Balls	Runs	Wkts	Avge	BB	5i	10m	RpO	ct	st
HASAN RAZA (Habib Bank, Karachi Zebras, Sind Dolphins) b Karachi, Sind 11.3.1982 RHB OB																			
FC		16	26	1	1087	124	43.48	2	8	90	70	1	70.00	1-42	0	0	4.66	22	
Lim		8	8	5	380	107	126.66	1	3									5	
20T		2	2	0	28	19	14.00	0	0									0	
Test	1996/97	7	10	1	235	68	26.11	0	2	6	1	0					1.00	5	
FC	1996/97	177	274	40	11564	256	49.41	34	51	1595	1020	17	60.00	2-11	0	0	3.83	148	
Int	1996/97	16	13	0	242	77	18.61	0	1									1	
Lim	1996/97	157	138	32	4182	115*	39.45	8	22	1000	921	26	35.42	3-17	0	0	5.52	65	2
20T	2005/06	14	14	1	261	49	20.07	0	0	108	157	9	17.44	3-13	0	0	8.72	7	
HASAN SAJJAD (Customs) b Karachi, Sind 11.10.1991 RHB LB																			
Lim		1	1	0	0	0	0.00	0	0									0	
Lim	2008/09	4	4	0	95	59	23.75	0	1									1	
HASEEB AZAM (Rawalpindi) b Fatehjang, Punjab 7.10.1986 LHB RMF																			
FC		2	3	0	44	32	14.66	0	0	203	154	6	25.66	3-20	0	0	4.55	3	
FC	2007/08	7	7	2	47	32	9.40	0	0	782	483	20	24.15	6-64	1	0	3.70	5	
HUMAYUN FARHAT (Habib Bank, Lahore Eagles) b Lahore, Punjab 24.1.1981 RHB RM WK																			
FC		11	18	0	498	156	27.66	1	2	144	95	0					3.95	30	1
Lim		3	2	0	13	13	6.50	0	0									4	
20T		2	2	0	20	20	10.00	0	0									3	1
Test	2000/01	1	2	0	54	28	27.00	0	0									0	
FC	1997/98	118	188	4	4905	188	26.65	4	33	449	256	4	64.00	2-52	0	0	3.42	342	36
Int	2000/01	5	3	0	60	39	20.00	0	0									4	3
Lim	1997/98	84	70	5	1787	150	27.49	3	9									95	43
20T	2005/06	11	10	1	127	24	14.11	0	0									10	6
IFTIKHAR ANJUM, Rao (Islamabad Leopards, ZTBL, Pakistan to Australia, Surrey) b Khanewal, Punjab 1.12.1980 RHB RM																			
FC		4	6	2	93	33	23.25	0	0	660	356	13	27.38	5-44	1	0	3.23	4	
Lim		1								48	36	2	18.00	2-36	0	0	4.50	0	
20T		2	1	0	7	7	7.00	0	0	36	34	2	17.00	2-18	0	0	5.66	0	
Test	2005/06	1	1	1	9	9*		0	0	84	62	0					4.42	0	
FC	1999/00	99	149	33	1963	78	16.92	0	5	17795	9504	394	24.12	7-59	22	3	3.20	56	
Int	2004/05	62	34	19	234	32	15.60	0	0	2960	2430	77	31.55	5-30	2	1	4.92	10	
Lim	1998/99	111	63	29	472	39	13.88	0	0	5436	4306	140	30.75	5-30	3	1	4.75	27	
I20T	2007/08	2								48	67	1	67.00	1-34	0	0	8.37	0	
20T	2004/05	16	10	3	90	24	12.85	0	0	348	418	16	26.12	2-18	0	0	7.20	1	
IJAZ AHMED (Faisalabad) b Lyallpur (now Faisalabad), Punjab 2.2.1969 RHB OB																			
FC		10	14	0	499	149	35.64	1	2	1177	544	24	22.66	5-59	1	0	2.77	11	
Test	1995/96	2	3	0	29	16	9.66	0	0	24	6	0					1.50	3	
FC	1989/90	220	340	30	12602	229*	40.65	33	57	9751	4112	164	25.07	6-62	6	1	2.53	229	
Int	1996/97	2	1	1	3	3*		0	0	30	25	1	25.00	1-9	0	0	5.00	1	
Lim	1989/90	149	139	17	4389	134	35.97	5	33	3223	2434	77	31.61	5-42	2	1	4.53	62	
20T	2004/05	11	8	1	125	44	17.85	0	0	12	15	0					7.50	6	
IKRAMULLAH KHAN, Mohammad (Abbottabad, Abbottabad Rhinos) b Mianwali, Punjab 12.7.1992 RHB LMF																			
FC		1	2	1	29	17*	29.00	0	0	144	72	3	24.00	2-41	0	0	3.00	1	
Lim		2								60	80	4	20.00	2-40	0	0	8.00	0	
FC	2008/09	2	2	1	29	17*	29.00	0	0	258	133	4	33.25	2-41	0	0	3.09	1	
IMAD WASIM, Syed (Federal Areas Leopards, Islamabad, Islamabad Leopards) b Swansea, Glamorgan, Wales 18.12.1988 LHB SLA																			
FC		5	9	2	190	44*	27.14	0	0	843	522	8	65.25	2-128	0	0	3.71	5	
Lim		8	7	1	145	41	24.16	0	0	403	307	12	25.58	4-24	1	0	4.57	3	
20T		2	1	0	2	2	2.00	0	0	48	47	1	47.00	1-22	0	0	5.87	0	
FC	2006/07	21	28	9	701	88	36.89	0	3	2433	1416	31	45.67	3-67	0	0	3.49	16	
Lim	2005/06	16	11	3	192	41	24.00	0	0	769	597	19	31.42	4-24	1	0	4.65	5	
20T	2005/06	12	7	3	57	24*	14.25	0	0	240	262	10	26.20	2-16	0	0	6.55	4	
IMRAN ABBAS (Sui Southern Gas) b Gujranwala, Punjab 25.3.1978 RHB OB																			
FC		4	7	0	141	66	20.14	0	1									2	
FC	1998/99	78	132	12	3883	204*	32.35	8	17	578	266	4	66.50	2-19	0	0	2.76	57	
Int	1999/00	2	2	0	29	28	14.50	0	0									1	
Lim	1997/98	20	20	4	452	90*	28.25	0	3	18	27	0					9.00	2	
IMRAN AHMED (Faisalabad) b Sargodha, Punjab 9.7.1979 RHB OB																			
FC		3	5	0	58	42	11.60	0	0									0	
FC	2007/08	8	14	2	313	84	26.08	0	2	6	7	0					7.00	1	
Lim	2007/08	1	1	0	18	18	18.00	0	0									0	
IMRAN ALI (Lahore Lions, Punjab Stallions, Sui Northern Gas) b Lahore, Punjab 21.10.1980 RHB RFM																			
FC		12	16	2	167	39	11.92	0	0	1811	865	40	21.62	6-87	2	0	2.86	2	
Lim		9	5	1	15	8	3.75	0	0	421	325	19	17.10	4-26	1	0	4.63	0	
20T		4	1	0	0	0	0.00	0	0	96	117	6	19.50	4-21	1	0	7.31	1	
FC	1999/00	61	79	27	572	39	11.00	0	0	10624	5128	219	23.41	6-41	9	0	2.89	22	
Lim	1999/00	48	29	18	143	18*	13.00	0	0	2350	1733	84	20.63	5-33	4	1	4.42	12	
20T	2006/07	11	3	2	2	2*	2.00	0	0	258	303	11	27.54	4-21	1	0	7.04	2	

Cmp	Debut	M	I	NO	Runs	HS	Avge	100	50	Balls	Runs	Wkts	Avge	BB	5i	10m	RpO	ct	st
IMRAN ALI (Faisalabad, Faisalabad Wolves) b Jaranwala, Punjab 15.4.1983 LHB SLA																			
FC		10	17	2	578	90*	38.53	0	5	12	14	0					7.00	4	
Lim		1	1	0	1	1	1.00	0	0									0	
FC	2003/04	56	98	8	3004	152*	33.37	5	16	108	64	2	32.00	2-6	0	0	3.55	43	
Lim	2003/04	20	19	1	572	83	31.77	0	3	84	80	1	80.00	1-59	0	0	5.71	8	
20T	2004/05	9	8	1	177	44	25.28	0	0									3	
IMRAN ALI Khan (PIA) b Sahiwal, Punjab 27.8.1987 RHB OB																			
FC		2	2	0	17	17	8.50	0	0	12	8	0					4.00	0	
FC	2006/07	5	6	1	36	17	7.20	0	0	12	8	0					4.00	1	
IMRAN FARHAT (Habib Bank, Lahore Eagles, Punjab Stallions, Pakistan to Australia, Pakistan to England, Pakistan to New Zealand, Pakistan to Sri Lanka, Pakistan to United Arab Emirates) b Lahore, Punjab 20.5.1982 LHB LB																			
FC		3	5	0	179	141	35.80	1	0	114	88	2	44.00	2-53	0	0	4.63	2	
Lim		4	4	1	138	105*	46.00	1	0	150	131	3	43.66	1-16	0	0	5.24	0	
20T		2	2	0	45	27	22.50	0	0	36	44	6	7.33	5-26	0	1	7.33	1	
Test	2000/01	39	75	2	2327	128	31.87	3	14	427	284	3	94.66	2-69	0	0	3.99	40	
FC	1998/99	135	234	13	9029	242	40.85	20	39	5158	2900	97	29.89	7-31	2	0	3.37	129	
Int	2000/01	35	35	1	1065	107	31.32	1	7	116	110	6	18.33	3-10	0	0	5.69	12	
Lim	1997/98	132	130	9	4145	138	34.25	9	20	2669	2310	80	28.87	4-13	3	0	5.19	59	
I20T	2009/10	3	3	0	22	14	7.33	0	0									1	
20T	2004/05	18	18	1	510	115	30.00	1	2	250	305	24	12.70	5-26	0	1	7.32	9	
IMRAN JAVED (National Bank) b Karachi, Sind 20.4.1975 RHB RFM																			
FC		5	6	0	211	167	35.16	1	0	144	116	3	38.66	1-9	0	0	4.83	3	
FC	2000/01	49	64	10	1768	167	32.74	4	8	4537	2264	71	31.88	5-49	1	0	2.99	35	
Lim	1998/99	52	37	9	979	104*	34.96	1	5	1704	1487	49	30.34	7-40	2	2	5.23	18	
IMRAN KHALID (Sui Northern Gas) b Kot Radha Kishan, Punjab 29.12.1982 LHB SLA																			
Lim		6	4	2	23	14*	11.50	0	0	315	172	10	17.20	4-29	1	0	3.27	2	
FC	2004/05	26	37	7	595	66	19.83	0	2	4113	1924	66	29.15	6-94	3	1	2.80	8	
Lim	2004/05	41	28	5	432	44*	18.78	0	0	2041	1492	56	26.64	4-22	2	0	4.38	10	
20T	2004/05	20	13	5	91	27*	11.37	0	0	420	447	29	15.41	4-21	1	0	6.38	8	
IMRAN KHAN (Quetta) b Sibi, Baluchistan 12.1.1990 LHB LM																			
FC		1	2	1	3	2*	3.00	0	0	24	13	2	6.50	2-13	0	0	3.25	0	
FC	2008/09	5	9	2	69	15	9.85	0	0	384	322	9	35.77	4-72	0	0	5.03	0	
Lim	2008/09	4	4	0	108	46	27.00	0	0	174	202	4	50.50	3-48	0	0	6.96	0	
IMRAN KHAN, Mohammad (Khyber Pakhtunkhwa Panthers, Peshawar, Peshawar Panthers) b Lower Dir, North-West Frontier Province 15.7.1987 RHB RMF																			
FC		8	13	4	74	27*	8.22	0	0	1237	704	34	20.70	6-29	3	0	3.41	1	
Lim		4	4	1	16	6	5.33	0	0	159	105	6	17.50	3-25	0	0	3.96	1	
FC	2007/08	22	32	10	117	27*	5.31	0	0	2950	1604	60	26.73	6-29	3	0	3.26	3	
Lim	2007/08	6	5	1	33	17	8.25	0	0	231	176	7	25.14	3-25	0	0	4.57	1	
20T	2009	1								6	9	0					9.00	0	
IMRAN NAZIR (Khyber Pakhtunkhwa Panthers, Sialkot Stallions, ZTBL, Dhaka, Pakistan to Australia, Pakistan to South Africa, Pakistan to United Arab Emirates) b Gujranwala, Punjab 16.12.1981 RHB LB																			
FC		8	13	0	441	73	33.92	0	5	113	70	2	35.00	2-36	0	0	3.71	3	
Lim		3	3	0	36	24	12.00	0	0									3	
20T		4	4	0	54	38	13.50	0	0									2	
Test	1998/99	8	13	0	427	131	32.84	2	1									4	
FC	1998/99	106	173	9	5338	164	32.54	7	30	424	339	7	48.42	3-61	0	0	4.79	75	
Int	1998/99	79	79	2	1895	160	24.61	2	9	49	48	1	48.00	1-3	0	0	5.87	26	
Lim	1998/99	148	148	3	3797	160	26.18	7	15	331	306	11	27.81	3-34	0	0	5.54	64	
I20T	2006/07	16	15	1	324	59	23.14	0	2									6	
20T	2004/05	41	39	5	1018	76*	29.94	0	7	8	3	3	1.00	1-0	0	0	2.25	15	
IMRAN NAZIR Malik (Habib Bank) b Lahore, Punjab 25.5.1983 RHB LB																			
FC		4	8	0	177	66	22.12	0	1	160	104	6	17.33	3-55	0	0	3.90	3	
FC	1999/00	17	28	0	530	66	18.92	0	2	232	163	6	27.16	3-55	0	0	4.21	14	
Lim	1998/99	10	10	1	274	74	30.44	0	3									6	
IMRANULLAH ASLAM (WAPDA) b Bahawalpur, Punjab 14.8.1980 RHB LB																			
FC		4	8	1	247	85	35.28	0	1	215	139	6	23.16	2-9	0	0	3.87	0	
Lim		4	4	0	81	76	20.25	0	1	203	204	7	29.14	3-42	0	0	6.03	0	
FC	2001/02	25	36	3	858	115	26.00	1	5	3118	1813	50	36.26	5-82	1	0	3.48	11	
Lim	2000/01	26	22	5	355	76	20.88	0	2	1219	931	35	26.60	4-12	1	0	4.58	5	
20T	2006/07	4	3	2	23	14*	23.00	0	0	78	93	7	13.28	5-17	0	1	7.15	3	
IMTIAZ HUSSAIN (Hyderabad) b Khairpur, Sind 20.4.1987 RHB WK																			
FC		1	2	1	34	27*	34.00	0	0									1	
INAM JAVED (Lahore Lions) b Lahore, Punjab 13.11.1991 RHB LMF																			
Lim		1	1	1	17	17*		0	0	48	45	2	22.50	2-45	0	0	5.62	1	
INAM KHAN (Abbottabad, Abbottabad Rhinos) b Mardan, North-West Frontier Province 6.9.1981 RHB OB																			
FC		3	5	1	42	18	10.50	0	0	264	140	0					3.18	1	
Lim		2	2	0	2	2	1.00	0	0	120	101	4	25.25	3-40	0	0	5.05	1	
FC	2008/09	5	8	1	74	30	10.57	0	0	594	313	5	62.60	4-99	0	0	3.16	2	
20T	2009	2	1	1	4	4*		0	0	48	69	1	69.00	1-41	0	0	8.62	0	

Cmp	Debut	M	I	NO	Runs	HS	Avge	100	50	Balls	Runs	Wkts	Avge	BB	5i	10m	RpO	ct	st
INAM-UL-HAQ (ZTBL) b Sialkot, Punjab 7.1.1979 RHB OB																			
FC		9	15	0	355	81	23.66	0	2	108	77	1	77.00	1-6	0	0	4.27	5	
FC	1997/98	74	130	5	3648	145	29.18	6	17	1846	1004	25	40.16	3-10	0	0	3.26	36	
Lim	1997/98	40	39	4	1258	104*	35.94	2	8	1352	1058	38	27.84	5-44	0	1	4.69	21	
IRAD ALI (Abbottabad) b Mardan, North-West Frontier Province 23.10.1990 LHB LMF																			
FC		1	2	0	0	0	0.00	0	0	108	81	0					4.50	0	
FC	2008/09	3	3	1	2	2*	1.00	0	0	282	196	1	196.00	1-39	0	0	4.17	0	
IRFAN FAZIL, Mohammad (Habib Bank) b Lahore, Punjab 2.11.1981 RHB RFM																			
FC		9	16	6	301	61*	30.10	0	2	862	593	28	21.17	5-56	1	0	4.12	2	
Test	1999/00	1	2	1	4	3	4.00	0	0	48	65	2	32.50	1-30	0	0	8.12	2	
FC	1997	81	123	32	1458	61*	16.02	0	5	9483	6430	212	30.33	6-38	9	0	4.06	33	
Int	1999/00	1	1	0	15	15	15.00	0	0	36	46	0					7.66	0	
Lim	1997	42	21	5	129	29	8.06	0	0	1808	1626	46	35.34	4-38	1	0	5.39	13	
20T	2004/05	4	2	1	9	8*	9.00	0	0	84	95	2	47.50	1-21	0	0	6.78	1	
IRFAN KHAN, Ali (Lahore Lions) b Lahore, Punjab 5.1.1984 RHB WK																			
Lim		2	2	0	29	29	14.50	0	0									6	
IRFAN TALIB (Islamabad Leopards) b Mirpur, Azad Kashmir 26.1.1986 LHB SLA																			
Lim		4	4	1	103	65*	34.33	0	1	141	87	6	14.50	4-37	1	0	3.70	0	
IRFANUDDIN (Karachi Dolphins, National Bank) b Karachi, Sind 21.9.1982 RHB OB																			
FC		1	1	0	0	0	0.00	0	0	91	49	2	24.50	2-39	0	0	3.23	1	
Lim		5	2	2	6	6*		0	0	240	215	7	30.71	3-48	0	0	5.37	0	
20T		1								20	24	1	24.00	1-24	0	0	7.20	1	
FC	2001/02	34	42	13	241	32*	8.31	0	0	5548	2950	97	30.41	6-76	4	0	3.19	12	
Lim	2000/01	45	24	12	85	17*	7.08	0	0	2347	1891	53	35.67	4-58	1	0	4.83	13	
20T	2005/06	9	1	1	5	5*		0	0	211	225	21	10.71	6-25	2	1	6.39	2	
IRFAN ZAMAN (Lahore Eagles) b Lahore, Punjab 11.11.1991 RHB OB																			
Lim		4	4	0	203	142	50.75	1	0	30	24	0					4.80	3	
FC	2008/09	1	2	0	36	29	18.00	0	0	6	12	0					12.00	0	
ISRARULLAH (Peshawar, Peshawar Panthers) b Manogai, North-West Frontier Province 15.1.1990 LHB SLA																			
FC		3	6	0	298	136	49.66	1	2	96	68	0					4.25	0	
Lim		2	2	0	76	41	38.00	0	0	56	47	0					5.03	1	
20T		3	3	0	78	48	26.00	0	0	12	31	0					15.50	0	
FC	2008/09	9	17	1	625	136	39.06	1	4	96	68	0					4.25	3	
Lim	2008/09	4	4	0	104	41	26.00	0	0	68	67	0					5.91	1	
JAFFAR NAZIR (KRL) b Muridke, Punjab 16.8.1977 RHB RFM																			
FC		8	12	3	176	49	19.55	0	0	1659	840	34	24.70	5-45	2	0	3.03	2	
FC	1997/98	127	168	31	2026	80	14.78	0	4	22062	10984	477	23.02	7-42	29	1	2.98	35	
Lim	1997/98	70	43	14	473	40	16.31	0	0	3286	2679	81	33.07	5-30	1	1	4.89	16	
JAHANDAD KHAN (Faisalabad Wolves) b Faisalabad, Punjab 4.4.1983 RHB RAB																			
Lim		3	3	0	59	24	19.66	0	0									0	
Lim	2008/09	4	4	1	71	24	23.66	0	0									0	
JAHANGIR MIRZA (Lahore Eagles, WAPDA) b Lahore, Punjab 28.2.1987 RHB OB																			
FC		8	15	0	431	52	28.73	0	1	96	73	1	73.00	1-15	0	0	4.56	4	
Lim		4	4	0	194	88	48.50	0	3	150	123	4	30.75	2-27	0	0	4.92	1	
20T		2	2	1	67	38*	67.00	0	0	12	7	1	7.00	1-7	0	0	3.50	0	
FC	2005/06	27	45	6	1255	135*	32.17	2	3	446	262	2	131.00	1-15	0	0	3.52	16	
Lim	2001/02	40	38	5	1262	96	38.24	0	12	873	764	22	34.72	3-15	0	0	5.25	10	
20T	2004/05	17	13	7	163	38*	27.16	0	0	178	214	13	16.46	4-28	1	0	7.21	2	
JAHANZEB ABDULLAH (Lahore Eagles) b Firozwala, Punjab 20.9.1989 RHB RAB																			
Lim		1	1	0	2	2	2.00	0	0									1	
JALAT KHAN (Baluchistan Bears, Quetta, Quetta Bears) b Sibi, Baluchistan 3.2.1986 LHB SLA																			
FC		10	19	0	399	78	21.00	0	1	1355	596	24	24.83	6-35	1	0	2.63	5	
Lim		9	9	0	125	43	13.88	0	0	441	315	9	35.00	3-43	0	0	4.28	4	
20T		2	2	0	13	13	6.50	0	0	48	46	2	23.00	1-16	0	0	5.75	0	
FC	2003/04	52	94	3	2071	170	22.75	2	6	6587	3474	95	36.56	6-35	3	0	3.16	24	
Lim	2002/03	37	35	2	425	43	12.87	0	0	1587	1387	28	49.53	4-44	1	0	5.24	12	
20T	2004/05	16	15	3	161	37	13.41	0	0	330	446	11	40.54	3-25	0	0	8.10	5	
JAMAL ANWAR (Rawalpindi, Rawalpindi Rams) b Rawalpindi, Punjab 31.12.1990 RHB WK																			
FC		9	14	1	221	35	17.00	0	0									30	1
Lim		4	2	0	31	22	15.50	0	0									3	2
20T		2	1	0	0	0	0.00	0	0									2	
FC	2008/09	21	31	5	473	52	18.19	0	1									78	2
Lim	2008/09	8	5	0	153	59	30.60	0	1									14	2
20T	2008/09	7	5	1	58	35*	14.50	0	0									6	1
JAMALUDDIN (Peshawar) b Swat, North-West Frontier Province 4.11.1985 RHB OB																			
FC		6	12	2	224	58*	22.40	0	2									2	
FC	2007/08	12	22	3	499	102*	26.26	1	3	84	20	1	20.00	1-20	0	0	1.42	3	
Lim	2007/08	5	5	1	138	81*	34.50	0	1	36	46	0					7.66	1	

Cmp	Debut	M	I	NO	Runs	HS	Avge	100	50	Balls	Runs	Wkts	Avge	BB	5i	10m	RpO	ct	st
JAMSHED AHMED, Mohammad (PIA) b Lahore, Punjab 10.12.1988 LHB LFM																			
FC		3	3	0	18	14	6.00	0	0	367	236	13	18.15	4-46	0	0	3.85	1	
FC	2005/06	15	20	4	70	14	4.37	0	0	2246	1188	47	25.27	5-47	1	0	3.17	3	
Lim	2005/06	7	3	0	9	6	3.00	0	0	378	247	9	27.44	3-39	0	0	3.92	0	
JANNISAR KHAN (Peshawar Panthers, PIA) b Peshawar, North-West Frontier Province 6.10.1981 RHB RM																			
FC		4	7	0	197	47	28.14	0	0	204	119	4	29.75	2-18	0	0	3.50	3	
Lim		1	1	0	13	13	13.00	0	0	44	36	5	7.20	5-36	0	1	4.90	0	
20T		3	3	1	65	55*	32.50	0	1	60	79	7	11.28	4-16	1	0	7.90	0	
FC	1996/97	58	88	11	1998	159	25.94	2	8	4384	2817	90	31.30	5-44	2	0	3.85	32	
Lim	1996/97	44	37	11	645	63	24.80	0	4	1579	1462	46	31.78	5-20	0	3	5.55	16	
20T	2004/05	11	10	1	156	55*	17.33	0	1	181	230	17	13.52	4-16	1	0	7.62	2	
JAVED HUSSAIN, Mohammad (Lahore Lions, Lahore Ravi) b Muridke, Punjab 3.6.1985 RHB OB																			
FC		6	9	0	100	49	11.11	0	0									4	
Lim		2	2	0	7	4	3.50	0	0									0	
FC	2000/01	8	12	0	131	49	10.91	0	0									5	
Lim	2000/01	16	16	2	196	54	14.00	0	1	36	43	0					7.16	6	
JAVED MANSOOR (Karachi Blues, Karachi Dolphins, Karachi Zebras) b Karachi, Sind 11.4.1982 RHB WK																			
FC		13	23	3	390	60*	19.50	0	3									48	1
Lim		4	3	1	56	40*	28.00	0	0									6	1
20T		2	1	1	6	6*		0	0									1	1
FC	2007/08	26	44	5	874	77*	22.41	0	6									91	4
Lim	2007/08	12	8	1	135	40*	19.28	0	0									20	2
20T	2009	4	3	1	35	29	17.50	0	0									1	2
JAVEDULLAH (Abbottabad Rhinos) b Upper Dir, North-West Frontier Province 24.10.1980 RHB OB																			
Lim		2	2	0	8	8	4.00	0	0	1	4	0					24.00	0	
FC	2008/09	1	2	1	38	34	38.00	0	0									0	
JIBRAN Hussain KHAN (Customs) b Crawley, Sussex, England 13.8.1984 RHB OB																			
FC		9	17	0	518	98	30.47	0	4	63	53	0					5.04	6	
Lim		4	4	0	108	53	27.00	0	1									0	
FC	2008/09	10	19	0	522	98	27.47	0	4	63	53	0					5.04	8	
Lim	2008/09	6	6	1	294	100*	58.80	1	2									0	
JIBRAN KHAN (Peshawar Panthers) b Peshawar, North-West Frontier Province 20.10.1990 RHB SLA																			
Lim		3	3	1	26	16*	13.00	0	0	168	134	5	26.80	3-35	0	0	4.78	0	
FC	2007/08	2	4	1	30	17	10.00	0	0	156	77	3	25.66	3-67	0	0	2.96	0	
Lim	2007/08	7	5	3	46	16*	23.00	0	0	360	319	10	31.90	3-35	0	0	5.31	3	
JIBRAN YOUSUF (Customs) b Karachi, Sind 25.4.1991 RHB LB																			
Lim		3	3	3	0	0*		0	0	93	100	3	33.33	2-36	0	0	6.45	0	
JUNAID ILYAS, Mohammad (Karachi Dolphins) b Karachi, Sind 4.11.1990 RHB OB																			
Lim		1	1	1	3	3*		0	0	60	47	2	23.50	2-47	0	0	4.70	0	
JUNAID IQBAL (Multan Tigers) b Multan, Punjab 25.12.1989 RHB																			
20T		1	1	0	9	9	9.00	0	0									0	
FC	2008/09	1	2	1	60	38	60.00	0	0									1	
JUNAID JAN (Lahore Eagles) b Lahore, Punjab 11.12.1989 LHB OB																			
Lim		4	4	0	106	56	26.50	0	1									1	
JUNAID KHAN, Mohammad (Abbottabad, Abbottabad Rhinos, Khyber Pakhtunkhwa Panthers, The Rest, Pakistan A to Sri Lanka) b Matra, North-West Frontier Province 24.12.1989 RHB LMF																			
FC		12	20	4	149	32*	9.31	0	0	3373	1795	75	23.93	7-94	7	2	3.19	2	
Lim		7	6	2	42	19	10.50	0	0	347	302	9	33.55	3-51	0	0	5.22	1	
20T		2	1	0	1	1	1.00	0	0	48	49	1	49.00	1-27	0	0	6.12	0	
FC	2006/07	32	45	16	340	71	11.72	0	1	6617	3355	159	21.10	7-46	12	3	3.04	5	
Lim	2006/07	21	15	4	94	32	8.54	0	0	1037	842	26	32.38	4-16	1	0	4.87	2	
20T	2006/07	7	5	2	15	7	5.00	0	0	144	175	5	35.00	2-23	0	0	7.29	1	
JUNAID NADIR Khan (Federal Areas Leopards, ZTBL) b Okara, Punjab 7.1.1989 RHB RMF																			
FC		5	8	2	80	22	13.33	0	0	675	370	14	26.42	6-60	1	0	3.28	2	
Lim		1	1	1	2	2*		0	0	27	23	0					5.11	0	
FC	2007/08	18	25	2	436	90	18.95	0	2	2663	1344	69	19.47	6-30	5	1	3.02	6	
Lim	2007/08	9	7	1	90	30	15.00	0	0	387	311	11	28.27	3-28	0	0	4.82	2	
JUNAID ZIA (Lahore Lions, Lahore Ravi) b Lahore, Punjab 11.12.1983 RHB RMF																			
FC		8	13	1	182	39	15.16	0	0	1595	860	39	22.05	6-48	2	1	3.23	3	
Lim		5	5	0	128	43	25.60	0	0	247	244	6	40.66	3-48	0	0	5.92	3	
FC	2002/03	73	110	14	1905	67	19.84	0	6	12714	7037	236	29.81	7-7	11	1	3.32	21	
Int	2003/04	4	2	1	2	2*	2.00	0	0	145	127	3	42.33	3-21	0	0	5.25	0	
Lim	2000/01	90	66	12	870	59*	16.11	0	4	3903	3423	117	29.25	5-53	5	1	5.26	29	
20T	2005/06	14	8	2	35	17	5.83	0	0	253	379	15	25.26	3-15	0	0	8.98	5	
KALEEM AHMED (Sui Northern Gas) b Muridke, Punjab 26.10.1991 RHB WK																			
FC		1	1	0	13	13	13.00	0	0									4	
FC	2008/09	2	2	1	54	41*	54.00	0	0									7	

Cmp	Debut	M	I	NO	Runs	HS	Avge	100	50	Balls	Runs	Wkts	Avge	BB	5i	10m	RpO	ct	st
KAMRAN AKMAL (Lahore Lions, National Bank, Pakistan to Australia, Pakistan to England, Pakistan to New Zealand, Pakistan to South Africa, Pakistan to Sri Lanka, Pakistan to United Arab Emirates, Pakistan to West Indies) b Lahore, Punjab 13.1.1982 RHB WK																			
FC		3	4	1	182	109	60.66	1	1									14	1
Lim		5	4	0	87	45	21.75	0	0									9	1
20T		4	3	1	118	68*	59.00	0	1									5	
Test	2002/03	53	92	6	2648	158*	30.79	6	12									184	22
FC	1997/98	152	240	27	6623	174	31.09	12	30									518	45
Int	2002/03	123	108	13	2577	124	27.12	5	7									124	21
Lim	1997/98	218	189	20	4748	133	28.09	9	16									243	59
I20T	2006	38	33	3	704	73	23.46	0	5									17	28
20T	2004/05	70	61	9	1353	73	26.01	0	8									40	45
KAMRAN HUSSAIN Shah (Islamabad, Islamabad Leopards) b Islamabad, Punjab 24.12.1990 RHB OB																			
FC		2	4	0	94	64	23.50	0	1	131	104	7	14.85	5-101	1	0	4.76	1	
Lim		2	2	0	6	6	3.00	0	0	108	71	5	14.20	4-24	1	0	3.94	1	
20T		2	1	1	0	0*		0	0	45	50	0					6.66	1	
FC	2007/08	6	10	1	185	64	20.55	0	2	457	289	16	18.06	5-41	2	0	3.79	5	
Lim	2007/08	9	8	2	101	30	16.83	0	0	415	277	15	18.46	4-18	2	0	4.00	4	
20T	2009	5	2	2	3	3*		0	0	102	123	2	61.50	1-19	0	0	7.23	3	
KAMRAN HUSSAIN, Mohammad (Habib Bank) b Bahawalpur, Punjab 9.5.1977 RHB LM																			
FC		12	22	2	437	63	21.85	0	3	1242	685	25	27.40	7-25	1	0	3.30	4	
Lim		4	3	0	33	28	11.00	0	0	189	166	7	23.71	3-54	0	0	5.27	2	
FC	1995/96	128	209	16	4524	156	23.44	2	26	17779	9250	368	25.13	7-25	17	2	3.12	56	
Int	2007/08	2	1	1	28	28*		0	0	102	67	3	22.33	2-32	0	0	3.94	0	
Lim	1996/97	91	80	12	1776	94*	26.11	0	9	3680	2880	91	31.64	5-51	2	1	4.69	21	
20T	2004/05	15	14	3	244	66	22.18	0	1	246	321	11	29.18	3-10	0	0	7.82	5	
KAMRAN SAJID (Lahore Eagles, PIA) b Lahore, Punjab 22.12.1983 LHB RM																			
FC		8	13	1	574	133	47.83	1	4	654	217	8	27.12	3-12	0	0	1.99	2	
Lim		3	1	0	14	14	14.00	0	0	84	63	2	31.50	1-19	0	0	4.50	1	
20T		1	1	0	11	11	11.00	0	0									2	
FC	2000/01	87	136	9	4227	147	33.28	7	29	4498	2012	66	30.48	6-70	1	0	2.68	29	
Lim	2000/01	72	65	10	1928	105	35.05	1	15	1231	1064	25	42.56	3-30	0	0	5.18	18	
20T	2005/06	6	6	0	118	44	19.66	0	0									4	
KAMRAN YOUNIS (Punjab Stallions, Sialkot, Sialkot Stallions) b Gujranwala, Punjab 20.1.1985 RHB SLA																			
FC		12	21	1	741	182	37.05	2	1	519	287	9	31.88	2-1	0	0	3.31	12	
Lim		8	8	0	202	127	25.25	1	0	258	176	2	88.00	1-33	0	0	4.09	3	
20T		2	2	0	10	10	5.00	0	0									0	
FC	1999/00	49	80	6	2347	182	31.71	2	12	2064	947	31	30.54	3-23	0	0	2.75	61	
Lim	2000/01	44	37	6	999	142*	32.22	3	3	1638	1252	29	43.17	3-8	0	0	4.58	11	
20T	2008/09	10	10	1	263	65*	29.22	0	2	150	177	5	35.40	2-16	0	0	7.08	5	
KASHIF BHATTI, Mohammad (Hyderabad, Hyderabad Hawks) b Nawabshah, Sind 25.7.1986 RHB SLA																			
FC		2	4	1	46	41	15.33	0	0	358	145	4	36.25	3-49	0	0	2.43	2	
Lim		4	3	1	31	24*	15.50	0	0	229	147	7	21.00	4-37	1	0	3.85	2	
20T		1	1	0	3	3	3.00	0	0	17	32	1	32.00	1-32	0	0	11.29	1	
FC	2007/08	9	16	4	284	41	23.66	0	0	1646	743	20	37.15	5-35	1	0	2.70	4	
Lim	2004/05	12	6	2	73	42	18.25	0	0	605	401	16	25.06	4-37	1	0	3.97	5	
20T	2009	2	2	1	6	3*	6.00	0	0	41	51	3	17.00	2-19	0	0	7.46	1	
KASHIF DAUD (ZTBL) b Sialkot, Punjab 10.2.1986 RHB RMF																			
FC		5	9	2	126	36*	18.00	0	0	1129	574	31	18.51	6-52	3	1	3.05	0	
Lim		4	3	1	24	17*	12.00	0	0	210	204	2	102.00	1-32	0	0	5.82	0	
FC	2005/06	25	35	8	379	36*	14.03	0	0	4302	2440	103	23.68	6-52	9	2	3.40	9	
Lim	2005/06	23	12	6	82	25	13.66	0	0	1165	1037	29	35.75	4-16	1	0	5.34	5	
20T	2009	4	2	1	5	5	5.00	0	0	76	105	7	15.00	3-16	0	0	8.28	4	
KASHIF HAYAT (Peshawar, Peshawar Panthers) b Peshawar, North-West Frontier Province 3.10.1985 RHB WK																			
FC		5	8	0	85	39	10.62	0	0									20	1
20T		3	2	1	8	8*	8.00	0	0									1	
FC	2002/03	8	13	0	125	39	9.61	0	0									26	2
Lim	2001/02	4	3	0	94	60	31.33	0	1									4	
KASHIF NAVED (Baluchistan Bears, Multan, Multan Tigers) b Chichawatni, Punjab 15.8.1983 RHB SLA																			
FC		8	13	0	254	61	19.53	0	1	54	31	0					3.44	12	
Lim		10	10	2	265	78*	33.12	0	2	294	196	3	65.33	2-22	0	0	4.00	5	
20T		3	3	0	90	58	30.00	0	1	26	19	1	19.00	1-9	0	0	4.38	1	
FC	1999/00	31	52	4	1599	199	33.31	2	9	356	245	5	49.00	2-36	0	0	4.12	31	
Lim	1998/99	33	29	3	887	134	34.11	1	5	612	498	11	45.27	4-30	1	0	4.88	12	
20T	2005/06	11	10	0	154	58	15.40	0	1	121	167	11	15.18	3-20	0	0	8.28	7	
KASHIF RAZA (WAPDA) b Sheikhupura, Punjab 29.12.1979 RHB RM																			
FC		5	6	4	92	32*	46.00	0	0	744	401	10	40.10	3-94	0	0	3.23	3	
Lim		3	2	1	4	2*	4.00	0	0	161	158	5	31.60	4-53	1	0	5.88	0	
FC	1999/00	97	131	34	1311	64*	13.51	0	2	15614	7634	329	23.20	8-84	15	1	2.93	30	
Int	2000/01	1	1	1	2	2*		0	0	30	36	1	36.00	1-36	0	0	7.20	0	

Cmp	Debut	M	I	NO	Runs	HS	Avge	100	50	Balls	Runs	Wkts	Avge	BB	5i	10m	RpO	ct	st
Lim	1999/00	70	38	17	204	24	9.71	0	0	3462	2624	100	26.24	4-27	7	0	4.54	7	
20T	2004/05	10	6	5	28	20*	28.00	0	0	215	224	8	28.00	3-25	0	0	6.25	1	
KASHIF SIDDIQ Khan (Lahore Lions, Lahore Ravi, The Rest, Pakistan A to United Arab Emirates) b Lahore, Punjab 31.12.1981 LHB LB																			
FC		12	22	2	925	178	46.25	3	3	820	369	17	21.70	3-24	0	0	2.70	11	
20T		4	3	0	42	23	14.00	0	0	36	41	1	41.00	1-16	0	0	6.83	0	
FC	1998/99	97	163	6	5489	178	34.96	13	28	3388	1609	54	29.79	4-33	0	0	2.84	70	
Lim	1997/98	59	57	5	1305	94*	25.09	0	9	1233	928	35	26.51	3-29	0	0	4.51	28	
20T	2006/07	10	9	1	92	26	11.50	0	0	126	111	4	27.75	2-17	0	0	5.28	2	
KHADIM HUSSAIN Shah (Hyderabad) b Shikarpur, Sind 1.2.1976 RHB OB																			
FC		1	2	1	35	31	35.00	0	0									1	
FC	2003/04	7	13	1	140	31	11.66	0	0	12	15	0					7.50	2	
Lim	2003/04	4	4	0	34	11	8.50	0	0	30	25	1	25.00	1-25	0	0	5.00	1	
20T	2005/06	4	3	2	33	21*	33.00	0	0									0	
KHALID LATIF (Karachi Blues, Karachi Dolphins, Pakistan to Australia, Pakistan to United Arab Emirates, Pakistan to West Indies) b Karachi, Sind 4.11.1985 RHB OB																			
FC		10	17	2	878	254*	58.53	3	2	30	24	0					4.80	2	
20T		3	3	1	108	75*	54.00	0	1									2	
FC	2000/01	70	130	11	4333	254*	36.41	12	17	468	358	9	39.77	3-22	0	0	4.59	45	
Int	2007/08	5	5	0	147	64	29.40	0	1									1	
Lim	2001/02	46	45	4	1905	204*	46.46	9	4	54	50	0					5.55	22	
I20T	2008/09	5	5	0	30	13	6.00	0	0									1	
20T	2004/05	30	29	2	628	81	23.25	0	3	18	21	2	10.50	2-11	0	0	7.00	12	
KHALID MAHMOOD (Karachi Blues, Karachi Zebras) b Karachi, Sind 13.12.1990 RHB RMF																			
FC		4	6	1	10	8*	2.00	0	0	537	415	9	46.11	3-33	0	0	4.63	0	
Lim		3	2	1	13	7*	13.00	0	0	128	131	2	65.50	1-37	0	0	6.14	1	
FC	2008/09	7	9	3	12	8*	2.00	0	0	999	686	22	31.18	6-65	1	0	4.12	0	
Lim	2008/09	6	3	2	18	7*	18.00	0	0	236	229	8	28.62	5-56	0	1	5.82	2	
KHALID USMAN (Abbottabad, Abbottabad Rhinos, Khyber Pakhtunkhwa Panthers) b Maneri, North-West Frontier Province 1.3.1986 RHB SLA																			
FC		9	16	4	409	68	34.08	0	3	1060	611	18	33.94	5-51	1	0	3.45	6	
Lim		8	7	1	162	47	27.00	0	0	407	267	12	22.25	3-32	0	0	3.93	5	
20T		2	1	1	23	23*		0	0	45	54	0					7.20	3	
FC	2007/08	18	26	6	574	68	28.70	0	5	1474	804	22	36.54	5-51	1	0	3.27	12	
Lim	2007/08	17	15	1	279	55	19.92	0	1	763	576	25	23.04	4-53	1	0	4.52	8	
20T	2008/09	7	6	1	72	23*	14.40	0	0	150	166	6	27.66	3-21	0	0	6.64	3	
KHALIL AHMED (Quetta Bears) b Chagi, Baluchistan 12.9.1983 RHB RMF																			
Lim		4	4	2	10	6*	5.00	0	0	192	162	7	23.14	4-34	1	0	5.06	0	
20T		3	3	1	2	2*	1.00	0	0	72	107	2	53.50	1-22	0	0	8.91	1	
FC	2004/05	1	2	0	0	0	0.00	0	0	96	52	3	17.33	3-52	0	0	3.25	0	
Lim	2003/04	7	5	3	11	6*	5.50	0	0	255	272	8	34.00	4-34	1	0	6.40	0	
20T	2009	6	4	2	3	2*	1.50	0	0	126	198	6	33.00	3-31	0	0	9.42	2	
KHAN, Rawait Mahmood (Customs) b Birmingham, Warwickshire, England 5.3.1982 RHB RM																			
FC		9	18	1	301	67	17.70	0	1	228	149	2	74.50	2-44	0	0	3.92	3	
FC	2001	36	65	2	1243	91	19.73	0	5	264	177	2	88.50	2-44	0	0	4.02	16	
Lim	2000	5	5	0	40	29	8.00	0	0	12	20	0					10.00	1	
KHAQAN ARSAL Raja (Habib Bank, Lahore Eagles) b Lahore, Punjab 10.12.1984 RHB RMF																			
FC		8	15	0	373	65	24.86	0	2	47	36	0					4.59	8	
20T		2	2	0	12	11	6.00	0	0									0	
FC	2002/03	66	101	6	2459	236	25.88	5	9	127	78	0					3.68	57	
Lim	2001/02	43	38	5	930	75	28.18	0	5									8	
20T	2004/05	10	10	4	156	56	26.00	0	1	18	20	1	20.00	1-20	0	0	6.66	3	
KHURRAM MANZOOR (Karachi Zebras, PIA, Sind Dolphins, Chittagong to Bangladesh, Pakistan to Australia, Pakistan to New Zealand, Pakistan A to Sri Lanka) b Karachi, Sind 10.6.1986 RHB OB																			
FC		6	11	2	620	241	68.88	3	1									4	
Lim		9	9	1	533	125*	66.62	1	3	15	8	2	4.00	2-8	0	0	3.20	4	
20T		2	2	0	127	74	63.50	0	2									0	
Test	2008/09	7	12	1	326	93	29.63	0	3									3	
FC	2002/03	64	110	8	4275	241	41.91	12	16	156	62	1	62.00	1-14	0	0	2.38	45	
Int	2007/08	7	7	0	236	83	33.71	0	3									3	
Lim	2002/03	60	60	6	2430	163*	45.00	4	17	27	28	2	14.00	2-8	0	0	6.22	35	
20T	2004/05	25	25	1	565	100	23.54	1	3	6	17	0					17.00	15	
KHURRAM SHEHZAD (Faisalabad Wolves, Sui Northern Gas) b Faisalabad, Punjab 19.1.1982 RHB OB																			
FC		1	2	0	7	6	3.50	0	0									0	
Lim		6	5	2	212	70	70.66	0	3	159	122	6	20.33	2-23	0	0	4.60	2	
20T		4	4	1	18	8*	6.00	0	0	30	26	2	13.00	2-10	0	0	5.20	2	
FC	2004/05	44	63	6	2030	166	35.61	3	13	354	198	2	99.00	1-16	0	0	3.35	28	
Lim	2000/01	38	34	5	1062	86	36.62	0	7	533	405	20	20.25	3-30	0	0	4.55	14	
20T	2004/05	18	16	2	227	65	16.21	0	1	61	65	4	16.25	2-10	0	0	6.39	9	

Cmp	Debut	M	I	NO	Runs	HS	Avge	100	50	Balls	Runs	Wkts	Avge	BB	5i	10m	RpO	ct	st
LAL KUMAR (Hyderabad, Hyderabad Hawks, Sind Dolphins) b Mithi, Sind 29.12.1989 LHB LFM																			
FC		8	16	0	472	97	29.50	0	2	1222	789	19	41.52	7-100	1	0	3.87	2	
Lim		8	7	2	117	38	23.40	0	0	372	333	14	23.78	3-22	0	0	5.37	2	
20T		2	2	1	48	38	48.00	0	0	36	67	1	67.00	1-25	0	0	11.16	0	
FC	2006/07	17	31	1	791	97	26.36	0	3	2576	1559	50	31.18	7-100	2	0	3.63	7	
Lim	2005/06	18	16	4	195	38	16.25	0	0	788	711	27	26.33	3-22	0	0	5.41	4	
20T	2006/07	6	3	1	49	38	24.50	0	0	108	177	2	88.50	1-25	0	0	9.83	2	
LIAQAT ALI Khan (Abbottabad Rhinos) b Tank, North-West Frontier Province 20.4.1987 RHB WK																			
Lim		2	2	0	1	1	0.50	0	0									0	
MAHFOOZ Ahmed SABRI (Peshawar, Peshawar Panthers) b Peshawar, North-West Frontier Province 20.5.1985 RHB LB																			
FC		4	7	0	20	15	2.85	0	0	48	35	1	35.00	1-20	0	0	4.37	6	
20T		1	1	1	17	17*		0	0	12	19	0					9.50	0	
FC	2007/08	20	31	5	905	95	34.80	0	8	365	257	8	32.12	4-56	0	0	4.22	17	
Lim	2005/06	7	7	0	183	66	26.14	0	1	88	110	2	55.00	1-37	0	0	7.50	4	
20T	2009	3	2	1	22	17*	22.00	0	0	60	76	2	38.00	2-32	0	0	7.60	0	
MAJID JAHANGIR, Haafiz (Sialkot, Sialkot Stallions) b Sialkot, Punjab 3.12.1980 RHB RM																			
FC		14	25	2	859	124	37.34	2	4	444	274	4	68.50	2-15	0	0	3.70	18	
Lim		7	7	1	214	58	35.66	0	1									4	
FC	1998/99	73	127	8	3493	156	29.35	4	15	1770	1057	27	39.14	3-64	0	0	3.58	60	
Lim	1997/98	36	35	4	1098	83*	35.41	0	9	60	56	1	56.00	1-12	0	0	5.60	10	
MALIK AFTAB Alam (Karachi Whites, Karachi Zebras) b Karachi, Sind 24.6.1982 LHB LMF																			
FC		3	5	3	9	9*	4.50	0	0	522	257	6	42.83	3-57	0	0	2.95	2	
Lim		3	1	1	16	16*		0	0	111	120	2	60.00	2-35	0	0	6.48	4	
FC	2003/04	31	45	17	167	21*	5.96	0	0	5406	2852	82	34.78	5-34	5	0	3.16	8	
Lim	2004/05	14	9	5	38	16*	9.50	0	0	638	541	8	67.62	2-35	0	0	5.08	5	
20T	2004/05	17	3	2	18	9*	18.00	0	0	360	385	19	20.26	4-17	1	0	6.41	4	
MANSOOR AHMED (Customs) b Karachi, Sind 10.9.1981 RHB LB																			
FC		2	4	0	8	4	2.00	0	0	264	168	5	33.60	3-72	0	0	3.81	2	
FC	1999/00	24	33	7	357	60	13.73	0	1	4642	2634	75	35.12	6-95	3	1	3.40	18	
Lim	2002/03	9	6	2	26	18*	6.50	0	0	409	384	11	34.90	5-40	0	2	5.63	1	
MANSOOR AMJAD (National Bank, Sialkot Stallions) b Sialkot, Punjab 25.12.1986 RHB LBG																			
FC		4	6	1	252	85	50.40	0	2	379	259	12	21.58	4-94	0	0	4.10	0	
Lim		5	4	2	65	46*	32.50	0	0	171	147	6	24.50	3-3	0	0	5.15	2	
20T		2	2	0	11	11	5.50	0	0									0	
FC	2003/04	66	100	14	2609	122*	30.33	4	10	9228	5406	168	32.17	6-19	6	0	3.51	31	
Int	2008	1	1	0	5	5	5.00	0	0	48	44	1	44.00	1-44	0	0	5.50	0	
Lim	2001/02	96	70	19	1277	56	25.03	0	3	4408	3672	121	30.34	5-37	3	2	4.99	32	
I20T	2007/08	1								6	3	3	1.00	3-3	0	0	3.00	2	
20T	2005/06	24	16	3	182	39*	14.00	0	0	150	188	13	14.46	3-3	0	0	7.52	14	
MANZOOR AHMED Badini (Quetta Bears) b Naushki, Baluchistan 5.4.1983 RHB OB																			
Lim		3	3	1	59	27	29.50	0	0									2	
20T		1	1	0	3	3	3.00	0	0									1	
FC	2001/02	6	12	0	138	33	11.50	0	0									4	
Lim	2001/02	7	7	1	126	45	21.00	0	0									2	
20T	2004/05	2	2	0	14	11	7.00	0	0									1	
MAQBOOL HUSSAIN (Abbottabad Rhinos) b Dera Ismail Khan, North-West Frontier Province 25.11.1989 RHB SLA																			
Lim		3	3	0	16	10	5.33	0	0	90	75	0					5.00	1	
MAQBOOL UMAID (Quetta) b Chahsar, Turbat, Baluchistan 1.6.1992 RHB LB																			
FC		1	2	0	5	5	2.50	0	0	60	50	0					5.00	1	
Lim	2008/09	2	2	1	0	0*	0.00	0	0	96	83	1	83.00	1-51	0	0	5.18	1	
20T	2009	1								17	26	0					9.17	0	
MAROOF AZIZ (Customs) b Karachi, Sind 22.11.1991 RHB RMF																			
FC		4	8	4	16	6	4.00	0	0	635	346	6	57.66	2-64	0	0	3.26	0	
Lim		1	1	0	0	0	0.00	0	0	60	59	0					5.90	0	
Lim	2008/09	3	3	1	2	2*	1.00	0	0	132	138	0					6.27	0	
MIR ALI Khan Talpur (Hyderabad, Hyderabad Hawks) b Hyderabad, Sind 9.10.1988 RHB RMF																			
FC		10	20	2	428	79	23.77	0	3	1439	995	25	39.80	5-80	1	0	4.14	1	
Lim		4	3	0	58	37	19.33	0	0	200	200	5	40.00	4-52	1	0	6.00	0	
20T		2	2	0	12	11	6.00	0	0	48	80	2	40.00	1-40	0	0	10.00	0	
FC	2007/08	12	22	2	475	79	23.75	0	3	1499	1058	25	42.32	5-80	1	0	4.23	1	
Lim	2007/08	7	5	0	62	37	12.40	0	0	305	326	6	54.33	4-52	1	0	6.41	1	
20T	2008/09	5	4	0	27	12	6.75	0	0	114	170	4	42.50	1-28	0	0	8.94	0	
MIR AZAM Khan (Abbottabad, Abbottabad Rhinos) b Parmoli, Swabi, North-West Frontier Province 15.1.1978 RHB WK																			
FC		6	12	1	223	37	20.27	0	0									25	3
Lim		4	4	0	114	61	28.50	0	1									2	3
20T		1	1	0	11	11	11.00	0	0									0	3
Lim	2008/09	8	8	0	240	61	30.00	0	1									3	3
20T	2008/09	4	4	0	64	28	16.00	0	0									0	6

Cmp	Debut	M	I	NO	Runs	HS	Avge	100	50	Balls	Runs	Wkts	Avge	BB	5i	10m	RpO	ct	st
MIR Mohammad USMAN Ali Khan (Islamabad) b Mirpur, Azad Kashmir 1.12.1983 RHB RMF																			
FC		1	2	1	33	21	33.00	0	0	96	57	0					3.56	0	
FC	2001/02	5	6	3	61	21*	20.33	0	0	333	175	8	21.87	3-41	0	0	3.15	1	
Lim	2001/02	1	1	1	0	0*		0	0	42	31	1	31.00	1-31	0	0	4.42	0	
MISBAH KHAN (Karachi Whites, Karachi Zebras) b Karachi, Sind 1.12.1986 RHB OB																			
FC		7	12	0	157	65	13.08	0	1	1120	598	19	31.47	5-101	1	0	3.20	2	
Lim		4	4	0	59	22	14.75	0	0	210	140	6	23.33	2-24	0	0	4.00	1	
FC	2007/08	17	27	3	355	65	14.79	0	1	2801	1520	43	35.34	5-49	2	0	3.25	4	
Lim	2008/09	8	6	1	63	22	12.60	0	0	438	342	7	48.85	2-24	0	0	4.68	2	
20T	2008/09	1								24	43	0					10.75	1	
MISBAH-UL-HAQ Khan Niazi (Faisalabad Wolves, Sui Northern Gas, Pakistan to Australia, Pakistan to New Zealand, Pakistan to South Africa, Pakistan to West Indies) b Mianwali, Punjab 28.5.1974 RHB LB																			
FC		6	10	3	521	284	74.42	1	2									11	
Lim		6	6	3	490	119*	163.33	2	3									5	
20T		4	3	0	78	40	26.00	0	0									3	
Test	2000/01	19	33	3	1008	161*	33.60	2	4									24	
FC	1998/99	155	250	27	11231	284	50.36	32	53	318	242	3	80.66	1-2	0	0	4.56	157	
Int	2002	56	50	11	1523	79*	39.05	0	9	24	30	0					7.50	32	
Lim	1998/99	164	149	32	5708	129*	48.78	10	34	144	179	1	179.00	1-10	0	0	7.45	86	
I20T	2007/08	29	25	9	577	87*	36.06	0	3									9	
20T	2005/06	57	49	15	1210	107*	35.58	1	5									22	
MOED AHMED Sheikh (Islamabad Leopards) b Islamabad, Punjab 11.7.1990 RHB SLA																			
Lim		2	2	0	57	32	28.50	0	0									2	
MOHAMMAD AAMER (National Bank, Rawalpindi Rams, Pakistan to Australia, Pakistan to England, Pakistan to New Zealand, Pakistan to South Africa, Pakistan to Sri Lanka, Pakistan to United Arab Emirates, Pakistan to West Indies) b Gujjar Khan, Punjab 13.4.1992 LHB LFM																			
FC		2	3	0	66	37	22.00	0	0	323	159	6	26.50	3-22	0	0	2.95	3	
20T		2	2	2	12	11*		0	0	48	66	1	66.00	1-37	0	0	8.25	0	
Test	2009	14	28	6	278	30*	12.63	0	0	2867	1484	51	29.09	6-84	3	0	3.10	0	
FC	2008/09	28	45	9	508	44*	14.11	0	0	4991	2578	120	21.48	7-61	7	1	3.09	5	
Int	2009	15	12	4	167	73*	20.87	0	1	789	600	25	24.00	4-28	1	0	4.56	6	
Lim	2007/08	30	17	8	204	73*	22.66	0	1	1633	1188	50	23.76	4-28	1	0	4.36	10	
I20T	2009	18	6	2	39	21*	9.75	0	0	390	457	23	19.86	3-23	0	0	7.03	3	
20T	2008/09	26	10	5	67	21*	13.40	0	0	575	662	32	20.68	3-13	0	0	6.90	3	
MOHAMMAD ALI Butta (Sialkot Stallions) b Sialkot, Punjab 12.8.1989 RHB RMF																			
Lim		6	1	0	0	0	0.00	0	0	348	233	15	15.53	4-32	2	0	4.01	1	
FC	2007/08	10	13	5	19	9	2.37	0	0	1779	1044	41	25.46	5-38	3	0	3.52	1	
Lim	2007/08	10	3	1	0	0*	0.00	0	0	548	386	21	18.38	4-32	2	0	4.22	2	
20T	2008/09	1								18	40	1	40.00	1-40	0	0	13.33	0	
MOHAMMAD ALI Niazi (Multan, Multan Tigers) b Multan, Punjab 22.12.1982 RHB SLA																			
FC		5	8	1	218	77	31.14	0	2	12	6	0					3.00	3	
Lim		3	3	0	42	21	14.00	0	0	30	22	0					4.40	1	
FC	2001/02	23	42	1	852	84	20.78	0	6	276	178	3	59.33	2-5	0	0	3.87	13	
Lim	2002/03	26	25	4	794	207	37.80	1	3	198	152	4	38.00	2-21	0	0	4.60	10	
20T	2004/05	5	5	0	20	13	4.00	0	0									1	
MOHAMMAD ASIF Khan (Peshawar Panthers) b Peshawar, North-West Frontier Province 10.11.1972 LHB SLA																			
20T		1								6	9	0					9.00	2	
MOHAMMAD ASIF (National Bank, Sialkot Stallions, Pakistan to Australia, Pakistan to England, Pakistan to New Zealand, Pakistan to South Africa, Pakistan to Sri Lanka, Pakistan to West Indies) b Sheikhupura, Punjab 20.12.1982 LHB RFM																			
FC		5	4	0	49	18	12.25	0	0	1048	538	23	23.39	5-35	2	0	3.08	3	
Lim		4	1	0	0	0	0.00	0	0	192	147	5	29.40	2-46	0	0	4.59	0	
20T		4								96	117	7	16.71	3-37	0	0	7.31	0	
Test	2004/05	23	38	13	141	29	5.64	0	0	5171	2583	106	24.36	6-41	7	1	2.99	3	
FC	2000/01	87	120	44	598	42	7.86	0	0	16480	8848	360	24.57	7-35	22	5	3.22	30	
Int	2005/06	38	16	7	34	6	3.77	0	0	1941	1524	46	33.13	3-28	0	0	4.71	5	
Lim	1999/00	70	30	17	109	13	8.38	0	0	3486	2754	84	32.78	4-30	1	0	4.74	17	
I20T	2006	11	3	3	9	5*		0	0	257	343	13	26.38	4-18	1	0	8.00	3	
20T	2005/06	35	7	4	13	5*	4.33	0	0	832	1058	50	21.16	5-11	3	1	7.63	8	
MOHAMMAD ASIM Nazir (Lahore Lions, Lahore Ravi) b Lahore, Punjab 10.3.1988 RHB RMF																			
FC		9	14	2	513	71	42.75	0	5	6	1	0					1.00	5	
Lim		4	4	0	44	41	11.00	0	0									1	
FC	2008/09	12	20	4	658	71	41.12	0	6	6	1	0					1.00	7	
MOHAMMAD ASLAM Khan (Quetta) b Kalat, Baluchistan 1.1.1987 RHB OB																			
FC		3	6	0	44	20	7.33	0	0	66	31	0					2.81	0	
FC	2008/09	11	21	0	300	60	14.28	0	2	420	171	5	34.20	4-82	0	0	2.44	3	
Lim	2004/05	12	12	0	231	51	19.25	0	1	102	107	1	107.00	1-36	0	0	6.29	2	
20T	2004/05	5	5	0	23	16	4.60	0	0									0	
MOHAMMAD ASLAM Qureshi (Habib Bank) b Peshawar, North-West Frontier Province 4.11.1979 RHB SLA																			
FC		9	14	4	271	74*	27.10	0	1	1445	613	30	20.43	7-37	1	0	2.54	4	
Lim		4	2	0	5	5	2.50	0	0	204	152	6	25.33	3-42	0	0	4.47	2	

Cmp	Debut	M	I	NO	Runs	HS	Avge	100	50	Balls	Runs	Wkts	Avge	BB	5i	10m	RpO	ct	st
FC	1998/99	49	66	17	687	74*	14.02	0	1	9155	3691	164	22.50	7-37	11	2	2.41	18	
Lim	1996/97	52	21	6	148	38	9.86	0	0	2424	1764	60	29.40	4-38	1	0	4.36	13	
20T	2004/05	15	5	2	11	4	3.66	0	0	325	361	20	18.05	4-13	1	0	6.66	4	
MOHAMMAD AWAIS (Hyderabad, Hyderabad Hawks) b Hyderabad, Sind 25.10.1992 RHB WK																			
FC		2	4	0	142	113	35.50	1	0									9	1
Lim		2	2	0	61	34	30.50	0	0									5	1
20T		1	1	0	0	0	0.00	0	0									0	
FC	2008/09	4	7	0	201	113	28.71	1	0									12	1
Lim	2008/09	3	3	0	84	34	28.00	0	0									5	1
MOHAMMAD AYAZ (Rawalpindi, Rawalpindi Rams) b Jhelum, Punjab 13.10.1987 LHB LMF																			
FC		3	5	4	0	0*	0.00	0	0	471	238	7	34.00	3-57	0	0	3.03	3	
Lim		1								42	25	0					3.57	1	
FC	2007/08	9	14	9	8	2*	1.60	0	0	1350	647	25	25.88	4-99	0	0	2.87	4	
Lim	2008/09	2	1	1	1	1*		0	0	102	59	4	14.75	4-34	1	0	3.47	1	
MOHAMMAD AYUB Dogar (Punjab Stallions, Sialkot, Sialkot Stallions) b Nankana Sahib, Punjab 13.9.1979 RHB OB																			
FC		14	23	3	1193	179*	59.65	4	5	364	244	5	48.80	2-2	0	0	4.02	6	
Lim		9	9	0	259	64	28.77	0	2	108	92	3	30.66	1-16	0	0	5.11	4	
FC	2001/02	61	99	11	3741	179*	42.51	9	20	753	487	11	44.27	2-2	0	0	3.88	44	
Lim	2000/01	43	37	5	715	64	22.34	0	3	423	415	10	41.50	3-33	0	0	5.88	23	
20T	2008/09	2	1	0	21	21	21.00	0	0									1	
MOHAMMAD FARHAN (Lahore Ravi) b Lahore, Punjab 30.12.1987 LHB LMF																			
FC		1	1	1	1	1*		0	0	30	25	0					5.00	0	
MOHAMMAD FAYYAZ Khan (Peshawar, Peshawar Panthers) b Peshawar, North-West Frontier Province 19.10.1984 RHB LB																			
FC		5	10	1	247	100	27.44	1	0	394	184	10	18.40	6-54	1	0	2.80	4	
Lim		2	2	0	20	19	10.00	0	0	36	33	0					5.50	1	
FC	2001/02	40	73	1	1434	100	19.91	1	6	1813	967	37	26.13	6-54	1	0	3.20	41	
Lim	2001/02	45	44	5	1412	117*	36.20	1	11	1090	966	20	48.30	3-52	0	0	5.31	18	
20T	2005/06	6	5	0	91	45	18.20	0	0	46	45	3	15.00	2-9	0	0	5.87	1	
MOHAMMAD GULFRAZ (Faisalabad) b Sargodha, Punjab 10.7.1991 RHB LMF																			
FC		3	4	1	31	19	10.33	0	0	454	226	6	37.66	3-49	0	0	2.98	0	
MOHAMMAD HAFEEZ (Multan, Multan Tigers) b Okara, Punjab 8.9.1974 LHB SLA																			
FC		5	8	0	199	105	24.87	1	0	78	40	1	40.00	1-23	0	0	3.07	4	
Lim		5	4	1	93	32*	31.00	0	0	266	194	9	21.55	3-45	0	0	4.37	5	
20T		3	2	1	46	32*	46.00	0	0	66	55	6	9.16	4-17	1	0	5.00	3	
FC	2007/08	10	14	0	350	105	25.00	1	1	192	85	3	28.33	1-3	0	0	2.65	9	
Lim	2007/08	14	13	5	356	66*	44.50	0	1	728	534	18	29.66	4-47	1	0	4.40	12	
20T	2008/09	4	2	1	46	32*	46.00	0	0	66	55	6	9.16	4-17	1	0	5.00	3	
MOHAMMAD HAFEEZ (Faisalabad Wolves, Sui Northern Gas, Pakistan to England, Pakistan to West Indies, Pakistan A to United Arab Emirates) b Sargodha, Punjab 17.10.1980 RHB OB																			
FC		15	27	0	1043	110	38.62	1	8	1535	665	26	25.57	5-63	1	0	2.59	17	
20T		4	4	0	187	100	46.75	1	1	84	68	2	34.00	1-13	0	0	4.85	2	
Test	2003/04	11	21	1	677	104	33.85	2	3	750	319	4	79.75	1-11	0	0	2.55	4	
FC	1998/99	135	226	7	7476	180	34.13	16	37	9657	4451	151	29.47	8-57	4	1	2.76	118	
Int	2002/03	53	53	1	1041	92	20.01	0	5	1883	1406	39	36.05	3-17	0	0	4.48	22	
Lim	1998/99	141	141	6	4443	137*	32.91	5	29	6193	4317	127	33.99	4-23	2	0	4.18	67	
I20T	2006	16	14	0	235	46	16.78	0	0	228	320	9	35.55	2-19	0	0	8.42	8	
20T	2004/05	60	58	5	1404	100	26.49	1	8	1014	1123	42	26.73	3-5	0	0	6.64	22	
MOHAMMAD HAMZA Mubeen (Sui Northern Gas) b Lahore, Punjab 18.12.1991 RHB RAB																			
FC		4	8	1	126	48	18.00	0	0									2	
MOHAMMAD HAROON Khan (Customs) b Multan, Punjab 12.8.1987 RHB RF																			
FC		2	4	0	31	16	7.75	0	0	198	131	5	26.20	2-46	0	0	3.97	0	
FC	2007/08	3	5	0	50	19	10.00	0	0	300	183	5	36.60	2-46	0	0	3.66	0	
Lim	2008/09	1	1	0	0	0	0.00	0	0	60	87	1	87.00	1-87	0	0	8.70	0	
MOHAMMAD HASAN (Karachi Whites, Karachi Zebras) b Karachi, Sind 4.10.1990 RHB WK																			
FC		8	14	1	316	88	24.30	0	1									22	3
Lim		3	3	1	58	38	29.00	0	0									3	1
FC	2007/08	19	30	1	705	88	24.31	0	3									47	4
Lim	2007/08	12	12	4	272	52	34.00	0	1									14	2
MOHAMMAD HUSSAIN (Customs) b Lahore, Punjab 8.10.1976 LHB SLA																			
FC		5	9	0	169	36	18.77	0	0	861	274	16	17.12	5-7	1	0	1.90	2	
Test	1996/97	2	3	0	18	17	6.00	0	0	180	87	3	29.00	2-66	0	0	2.90	1	
FC	1994/95	131	205	17	4996	132	26.57	2	29	26250	10504	454	23.13	7-53	29	7	2.40	64	
Int	1996/97	14	12	7	154	31*	30.80	0	0	672	547	13	42.07	4-33	1	0	4.88	5	
Lim	1994/95	92	80	18	1390	82	22.41	0	7	4692	3347	130	25.74	6-29	5	2	4.28	26	
MOHAMMAD IBRAHIM (Rawalpindi) b Rawalpindi, Punjab 26.12.1988 RHB RMF																			
FC		2	4	0	36	19	9.00	0	0									1	
FC	2006/07	14	24	2	453	51	20.59	0	1	54	24	1	24.00	1-7	0	0	2.66	15	
Lim	2005/06	9	9	0	187	53	20.77	0	1	13	12	0					5.53	6	

Cmp	Debut	M	I	NO	Runs	HS	Avge	100	50	Balls	Runs	Wkts	Avge	BB	5i	10m	RpO	ct	st
MOHAMMAD IDREES (KRL, Peshawar, Peshawar Panthers) b Charsadda, North-West Frontier Province 5.5.1983 RHB RMF																			
FC		8	15	0	390	102	26.00	1	2									8	
Lim		4	4	1	114	104	38.00	1	0									0	
20T		3	3	0	41	30	13.66	0	0	6	11	0					11.00	1	
FC	2008/09	13	23	0	627	102	27.26	1	4	2	0	0					0.00	11	
Lim	2001/02	7	7	2	142	104	28.40	1	0	18	18	0					6.00	1	
MOHAMMAD IFTIKHAR Ahmed (Customs) b Karachi, Sind 8.9.1985 RHB RMF																			
FC		5	9	1	135	41	16.87	0	0	735	353	11	32.09	5-68	1	0	2.88	0	
Lim		2	2	0	10	9	5.00	0	0	83	94	4	23.50	3-57	0	0	6.79	0	
Lim	2008/09	4	4	0	66	54	16.50	0	1	149	167	8	20.87	4-47	1	0	6.72	0	
20T	2009	1	1	0	0	0	0.00	0	0	12	12	0					6.00	0	
MOHAMMAD IRFAN (Baluchistan Bears, KRL, Multan Tigers, Pakistan to England, Pakistan A to Sri Lanka) b Gaggu Mandi, Punjab 6.6.1982 RHB LMF																			
FC		10	10	6	24	8*	6.00	0	0	2056	1237	43	28.76	7-113	4	1	3.61	3	
Lim		9	6	3	12	5	4.00	0	0	456	384	12	32.00	2-37	0	0	5.05	3	
20T		3								65	68	6	11.33	3-14	0	0	6.27	2	
Int	2010	2	1	1	3	3*		0	0	75	77	0					6.16	0	
Lim	2009/10	15	9	5	17	5	4.25	0	0	757	605	19	31.84	3-30	0	0	4.79	3	
MOHAMMAD IRFAN (ZTBL) b Rawalpindi, Punjab 25.10.1985 RHB LB																			
FC		1	1	0	23	23	23.00	0	0	132	99	3	33.00	3-71	0	0	4.50	0	
FC	2008/09	2	2	1	42	23	42.00	0	0	168	118	3	39.33	3-71	0	0	4.21	1	
MOHAMMAD IRSHAD (Lahore Eagles, Lahore Ravi) b Khanewal, Punjab 10.4.1983 RHB RMF																			
FC		10	14	1	216	65	16.61	0	1	1899	1134	43	26.37	6-42	3	1	3.58	7	
Lim		4	4	0	47	29	11.75	0	0	212	233	12	19.41	5-58	1	1	6.59	4	
20T		2	2	0	4	3	2.00	0	0	30	51	2	25.50	2-16	0	0	10.20	1	
FC	2002/03	73	101	24	871	65	11.31	0	2	10884	6692	213	31.41	6-42	7	1	3.68	19	
Lim	2002/03	49	36	12	261	32	10.87	0	0	2257	2217	61	36.34	5-58	3	1	5.89	20	
20T	2005/06	14	9	3	40	14*	6.66	0	0	222	349	14	24.92	3-33	0	0	9.43	5	
MOHAMMAD KASHIF Khan (Abbottabad, Abbottabad Rhinos) b Kohat, North-West Frontier Province 10.12.1975 RHB WK																			
FC		6	12	1	289	49	26.27	0	0									3	
Lim		2	2	1	112	78*	112.00	0	1									0	
20T		1	1	0	34	34	34.00	0	0									0	
FC	2007/08	16	23	2	549	72	26.14	0	2									6	
Lim	2007/08	5	4	1	135	78*	45.00	0	1									1	
20T	2008/09	3	3	0	38	34	12.66	0	0									0	
MOHAMMAD KASHIF Rana (Sui Southern Gas) b Bahawalpur, Punjab 1.1.1983 LHB LFM																			
FC		3	6	1	58	25	11.60	0	0	222	163	0					4.40	0	
Lim		4	3	2	19	18	19.00	0	0	186	217	2	108.50	1-64	0	0	7.00	0	
FC	2007/08	16	25	4	254	48	12.09	0	0	2390	1426	33	43.21	5-54	1	0	3.58	4	
Lim	2002/03	10	8	4	65	26	16.25	0	0	419	436	7	62.28	2-23	0	0	6.24	1	
MOHAMMAD KASHIF Khan, Raja (Islamabad Leopards) b Islamabad, Punjab 20.5.1983 RHB WK																			
Lim		4	2	1	39	29*	39.00	0	0									5	1
FC	2001/02	22	31	6	240	53	9.60	0	1									73	3
Lim	2001/02	9	2	1	39	29*	39.00	0	0									8	6
MOHAMMAD KHALIL (Lahore Eagles, ZTBL) b Lahore, Punjab 11.11.1982 LHB LM																			
FC		6	8	1	91	22	13.00	0	0	1155	598	13	46.00	3-69	0	0	3.10	3	
Lim		2	1	0	4	4	4.00	0	0	96	80	4	20.00	3-24	0	0	5.00	2	
20T		1	1	1	1	1*		0	0	12	12	0					6.00	0	
Test	2004/05	2	4	1	9	5	3.00	0	0	290	200	0					4.13	0	
FC	1999/00	74	103	38	798	55*	12.27	0	1	13008	6952	245	28.37	7-71	10	3	3.20	27	
Int	2004/05	3	1	1	0	0*		0	0	144	144	5	28.80	2-55	0	0	6.00	2	
Lim	2001/02	51	30	9	157	39	7.47	0	0	2564	2041	72	28.34	4-26	3	0	4.77	14	
20T	2004/05	13	6	1	34	21	6.80	0	0	234	357	11	32.45	3-40	0	0	9.15	4	
MOHAMMAD MASROOR (Sui Southern Gas) b Karachi, Sind 6.8.1975 RHB OB																			
FC		4	8	1	107	27	15.28	0	0	24	13	0					3.25	2	
FC	1995/96	55	95	8	2423	171*	27.85	3	14	360	178	5	35.60	3-14	0	0	2.96	54	
Lim	1994/95	20	15	1	460	101*	32.85	1	3	213	169	2	84.50	2-14	0	0	4.76	2	
MOHAMMAD NABI Eisakhil (Afghanistan to Netherlands, Afghanistan to Scotland, Afghanistan to Sri Lanka, Afghanistan to United Arab Emirates, Afghanistan to West Indies, Afghanistan to Zimbabwe, Customs) b Loger, Afghanistan 7.3.1985 RHB OB																			
FC		3	6	1	144	70*	28.80	0	1	330	168	10	16.80	4-25	0	0	3.05	1	
FC	2007	14	24	2	637	102	28.95	1	3	1691	818	31	26.38	4-25	0	0	2.90	6	
Int	2008/09	13	11	3	241	62	30.12	0	2	606	421	8	52.62	2-23	0	0	4.16	9	
Lim	2007/08	27	25	4	606	112*	28.85	1	3	1281	893	22	40.59	2-23	0	0	4.18	14	
I20T	2009/10	8	7	1	69	43*	11.50	0	0	168	208	11	18.90	3-23	0	0	7.42	3	
20T	2009/10	11	10	2	98	43*	12.25	0	0	234	274	17	16.11	3-17	0	0	7.02	5	
MOHAMMAD NAEEM (Lahore Eagles) LB																			
Lim		1	1	1	20	20*		0	0	18	16	0					5.33	0	

Cmp	Debut	M	I	NO	Runs	HS	Avge	100	50	Balls	Runs	Wkts	Avge	BB	5i	10m	RpO	ct	st
MOHAMMAD NAEEM (Abbottabad Rhinos) b Mardan, North-West Frontier Province 4.9.1990 RHB RMF																			
20T		1	1	0	0	0	0.00	0	0	12	26	0					13.00	0	
MOHAMMAD NAVED (Lahore Eagles, Lahore Lions, Lahore Shalimar, The Rest) b Lahore, Punjab 1.9.1988 RHB RFM																			
FC		10	17	6	152	75	13.81	0	1	2100	1118	42	26.61	6-114	3	0	3.19	3	
Lim		5	5	3	29	18	14.50	0	0	268	217	11	19.72	4-41	1	0	4.85	3	
20T		1	1	1	0	0*		0	0	6	26	0					26.00	0	
FC	2007/08	25	37	14	204	75	8.86	0	1	5867	3340	123	27.15	8-128	11	1	3.41	8	
Lim	2007/08	13	11	6	57	18	11.40	0	0	668	651	21	31.00	4-41	1	0	5.84	6	
20T	2008/09	9	3	2	7	7*	7.00	0	0	169	207	11	18.81	3-33	0	0	7.34	4	
MOHAMMAD RAMEEZ (Federal Areas Leopards, Rawalpindi, Rawalpindi Rams, The Rest, Pakistan A to Sri Lanka) b Rawalpindi, Punjab 19.2.1990 RHB RFM																			
FC		13	20	6	187	30*	13.35	0	0	3042	1602	79	20.27	8-27	9	3	3.16	14	
Lim		7	5	1	6	4	1.50	0	0	325	276	7	39.42	4-43	1	0	5.09	0	
20T		2	1	1	1	1*		0	0	42	54	1	54.00	1-24	0	0	7.71	1	
FC	2006/07	25	34	11	299	30*	13.00	0	0	5180	2569	126	20.38	8-27	11	3	2.97	20	
Lim	2007/08	19	13	6	134	31*	19.14	0	0	884	723	18	40.16	4-43	1	0	4.90	3	
20T	2009	4	3	1	5	2	2.50	0	0	78	111	1	111.00	1-24	0	0	8.53	2	
MOHAMMAD RIZWAN (Peshawar, Peshawar Panthers) b Peshawar, North-West Frontier Province 1.6.1992 RHB WK																			
FC		5	9	0	231	53	25.66	0	1									15	
Lim		4	4	0	74	37	18.50	0	0									5	
FC	2008/09	14	23	6	643	68*	37.82	0	6									41	1
Lim	2008/09	7	7	2	252	77*	50.40	0	2									5	
20T	2009	1	1	1	6	6*		0	0									1	1
MOHAMMAD SAAD (Lahore Shalimar) b Gujranwala, Punjab 24.3.1990 RHB LB																			
FC		4	8	0	172	43	21.50	0	0	6	5	0					5.00	1	
FC	2008/09	8	15	0	295	48	19.66	0	0	66	41	1	41.00	1-36	0	0	3.72	2	
MOHAMMAD SAEED (Lahore Eagles, Lahore Shalimar) b Lahore, Punjab 12.10.1983 RHB RFM																			
FC		5	10	1	228	96	25.33	0	1	723	481	13	37.00	6-82	1	0	3.99	0	
Lim		4	4	0	123	49	30.75	0	0	184	164	7	23.42	3-28	0	0	5.34	2	
FC	2004/05	20	36	3	858	96	26.00	0	4	2907	1940	51	38.03	6-82	1	0	4.00	4	
Lim	2002/03	12	11	0	276	67	25.09	0	1	544	523	16	32.68	3-28	0	0	5.76	6	
20T	2008/09	1	1	0	6	6	6.00	0	0	24	41	1	41.00	1-41	0	0	10.25	0	
MOHAMMAD SAEED (Sialkot, Sialkot Stallions) b 5.12.1990 RHB RMF																			
FC		5	9	0	159	44	17.66	0	0	6	6	0					6.00	2	
Lim		1	1	0	3	3	3.00	0	0									0	
MOHAMMAD SALMAN (Faisalabad, Faisalabad Wolves, Punjab Stallions) b Karachi, Sind 7.8.1981 RHB LB WK																			
FC		7	12	2	367	89	36.70	0	2	48	34	2	17.00	2-34	0	0	4.25	20	1
Lim		7	7	1	230	68	38.33	0	2	6	1	0					1.00	6	4
20T		4	3	2	10	5	10.00	0	0									3	2
FC	1999/00	92	138	22	2932	126*	25.27	1	19	102	54	3	18.00	2-34	0	0	3.17	256	17
Lim	1997/98	71	62	11	1496	113*	29.33	2	7	6	1	0					1.00	64	23
20T	2004/05	28	25	7	401	48	22.27	0	0									17	17
MOHAMMAD SAMI (Karachi Blues, Karachi Dolphins, Pakistan to Australia, Pakistan to West Indies) b Karachi, Sind 24.2.1981 RHB RF																			
FC		11	16	2	142	41*	10.14	0	0	1720	855	41	20.85	6-38	4	0	2.98	10	
Lim		3	2	0	19	10	9.50	0	0	162	104	6	17.33	3-26	0	0	3.85	2	
20T		3	1	0	21	21	21.00	0	0	60	74	3	24.66	3-27	0	0	7.40	3	
Test	2000/01	34	53	13	473	49	11.82	0	0	7175	4262	84	50.73	5-36	2	0	3.56	7	
FC	1999/00	108	148	39	1509	49	13.84	0	0	19634	11179	366	30.54	8-39	21	2	3.41	48	
Int	2000/01	83	46	19	314	46	11.62	0	0	4094	3357	118	28.44	5-10	3	1	4.92	18	
Lim	1999/00	125	71	27	541	46	12.29	0	0	6228	5129	186	27.57	6-20	5	2	4.94	27	
I20T	2010	3	1	1	5	5*		0	0	66	108	6	18.00	3-29	0	0	9.81	2	
20T	2003	18	8	3	57	21	11.40	0	0	401	524	20	26.20	3-27	0	0	7.84	10	
MOHAMMAD SAMI Afridi (Abbottabad Rhinos) b Khyber Agency 5.2.1992 RHB OB																			
20T		1	1	0	1	1	1.00	0	0	12	23	1	23.00	1-23	0	0	11.50	0	
MOHAMMAD SHAHID (Faisalabad Wolves) b Faisalabad, Punjab 1.5.1986 RHB OB																			
Lim		4	4	0	204	92	51.00	0	3	36	24	2	12.00	2-17	0	0	4.00	3	
FC	2008/09	1	2	0	47	47	23.50	0	0	6	4	0					4.00	0	
MOHAMMAD SHEHROZ (Hyderabad Hawks) b Hyderabad, Sind 16.10.1991 LHB OB																			
Lim		1	1	0	18	18	18.00	0	0	24	23	0					5.75	1	
MOHAMMAD TALHA (Faisalabad Wolves, National Bank, Punjab Stallions, The Rest, Pakistan A to Sri Lanka, Pakistan A to United Arab Emirates) b Faisalabad, Punjab 15.10.1988 RHB RFM																			
FC		11	10	1	43	17	4.77	0	0	1820	1175	45	26.11	5-37	2	0	3.87	2	
Lim		3	2	1	2	2	2.00	0	0	158	102	9	11.33	4-28	1	0	3.87	0	
20T		1	1	0	7	7	7.00	0	0	18	45	1	45.00	1-45	0	0	15.00	0	
Test	2008/09	1								102	88	1	88.00	1-88	0	0	5.17	0	
FC	2007/08	34	35	9	227	30	8.73	0	0	5942	3719	128	29.05	6-59	8	1	3.75	5	
Lim	2007/08	33	23	9	88	21	6.28	0	0	1634	1541	50	30.82	4-28	2	0	5.65	3	
20T	2008/09	8	2	0	7	7	3.50	0	0	167	232	9	25.77	3-26	0	0	8.33	3	

Cmp	Debut	M	I	NO	Runs	HS	Avge	100	50	Balls	Runs	Wkts	Avge	BB	5i	10m	RpO	ct	st
MOHAMMAD URS (Hyderabad Hawks) b Khairpur, Sind 4.6.1985 RHB SLA																			
Lim		2	2	0	26	15	13.00	0	0	66	55	1	55.00	1-36	0	0	5.00	0	
20T		1	1	0	4	4	4.00	0	0									0	
Lim	2008/09	6	6	2	169	58*	42.25	0	1	186	151	5	30.20	2-22	0	0	4.87	2	
20T	2009	3	2	0	15	11	7.50	0	0									1	
MOHAMMAD WAQAS (Karachi Zebras) b Karachi, Sind 14.12.1990 LHB LAB WK																			
Lim		4	4	0	58	34	14.50	0	0									3	2
MOHAMMAD WASIM (KRL) b Rawalpindi, Punjab 8.8.1977 RHB LBG																			
FC		9	12	1	586	123	53.27	3	1	132	96	1	96.00	1-9	0	0	4.36	6	
Test	1996/97	18	28	2	783	192	30.11	2	2									22	2
FC	1994/95	179	284	16	9322	192	34.78	24	43	1137	613	15	40.86	2-12	0	0	3.23	184	5
Int	1996/97	25	25	2	543	76	23.60	0	3									9	
Lim	1994/95	128	125	7	3269	129*	27.70	4	21	175	133	3	44.33	2-30	0	0	4.56	61	
20T	2005/06	8	8	1	297	86*	42.42	0	2									3	1
MOHAMMAD YASIN (Sialkot) b Sialkot, Punjab 2.12.1989 LHB																			
FC		2	3	0	37	21	12.33	0	0									0	
MOHAMMAD YOUSUF (Islamabad Leopards, WAPDA, Pakistan to Australia, Pakistan to England, Pakistan to New Zealand, Pakistan to South Africa, Pakistan to United Arab Emirates) b Lahore, Punjab 27.8.1974 RHB OB																			
FC		1	2	0	38	35	19.00	0	0									1	
20T		2	2	1	31	27*	31.00	0	0									0	
Test	1997/98	90	156	12	7530	223	52.29	24	33	6	3	0					3.00	65	
FC	1996/97	134	226	20	10152	223	49.28	29	49	18	24	0					8.00	84	
Int	1997/98	287	272	40	9717	141*	41.88	15	64	2	1	1	1.00	1-0	0	0	3.00	58	
Lim	1996/97	327	311	45	10584	141*	39.78	15	69	8	13	1	13.00	1-0	0	0	9.75	69	
I20T	2006	3	3	0	50	26	16.66	0	0									1	
20T	2004/05	15	14	1	228	30	17.53	0	0	1	1	0					6.00	3	
MOHAMMAD ZAHID (National Bank) b Multan, Punjab 20.11.1985 RHB RF																			
FC		1								84	68	4	17.00	2-32	0	0	4.85	1	
Lim		1								36	26	2	13.00	2-26	0	0	4.33	0	
FC	2005/06	6	8	3	30	8	6.00	0	0	642	408	18	22.66	5-49	1	0	3.81	4	
Lim	2004/05	4								180	187	5	37.40	2-26	0	0	6.23	1	
MOHAMMAD ZAMAN (Peshawar Panthers) b Mingora, Swat, North-West Frontier Province 9.4.1975 RHB																			
Lim		2	2	0	13	13	6.50	0	0									0	
MOHAMMAD ZOHAIB, Hafiz (Lahore Eagles, Lahore Shalimar) b Lahore, Punjab 1.1.1986 RHB WK																			
FC		3	6	2	39	23*	9.75	0	0									6	1
Lim		3	3	0	61	25	20.33	0	0									5	1
FC	2007/08	4	8	2	44	23*	7.33	0	0									9	1
MOHSIN SALEH (Lahore Eagles)																			
Lim		1	1	0	13	13	13.00	0	0									1	
MOHTASHIM ALI, Syed (Karachi Whites, Karachi Zebras) b Karachi, Sind 21.7.1981 LHB SLA																			
FC		9	16	0	577	95	36.06	0	5	357	167	3	55.66	2-61	0	0	2.80	11	
Lim		5	5	0	113	46	22.60	0	0	192	146	3	48.66	2-30	0	0	4.56	1	
FC	2001/02	61	108	4	3140	123*	30.19	3	20	759	440	6	73.33	3-4	0	0	3.47	42	
Lim	1998/99	28	28	3	735	90*	29.40	0	4	402	342	9	38.00	3-58	0	0	5.10	8	1
MURTAZA MAJEED (Karachi Whites, Karachi Zebras) b Karachi, Sind 30.3.1986 RHB LB																			
FC		3	5	1	84	60	21.00	0	1									2	
Lim		2	2	1	30	21*	30.00	0	0									1	
FC	2008/09	6	10	1	209	67	23.22	0	2									2	
MUSTAFA IQBAL (WAPDA) b Abu Dhabi, United Arab Emirates 30.8.1989 LHB SLA																			
FC		1	2	0	17	9	8.50	0	0	114	84	1	84.00	1-57	0	0	4.42	0	
FC	2008/09	4	7	1	48	10	8.00	0	0	586	232	10	23.20	4-39	0	0	2.37	1	
Lim	2008/09	2	2	1	28	26	28.00	0	0	102	119	2	59.50	1-56	0	0	7.00	0	
MUZAFFAR MAHBOOB (Lahore Shalimar) b Faisalabad, Punjab 1.1.1979 RHB RFM																			
FC		4	8	0	86	36	10.75	0	0	96	93	0					5.81	1	
FC	2008/09	10	16	0	278	54	17.37	0	1	216	199	0					5.52	1	
Lim	2001/02	1	1	0	0	0	0.00	0	0	12	14	0					7.00	0	
MUZAMMIL NIZAM (Rawalpindi Rams) b Rawalpindi, Punjab 29.10.1990 RHB RAB																			
Lim		3	2	0	9	8	4.50	0	0									1	
NABEEL MALIK (Sialkot) b Sialkot, Punjab 21.4.1988 LHB SLA																			
FC		2	4	0	35	18	8.75	0	0	165	160	4	40.00	2-71	0	0	5.81	0	
NAEEM ANJUM (Federal Areas Leopards, Islamabad, Islamabad Leopards, The Rest, Pakistan A to Sri Lanka, Pakistan A to United Arab Emirates) b Mandi Bahauddin, Punjab 15.9.1987 RHB WK																			
FC		14	23	4	522	88	27.47	0	2									55	
Lim		4	4	1	141	52*	47.00	0	1									10	
20T		2	1	0	16	16	16.00	0	0									3	
FC	2006/07	33	49	10	1197	88	30.69	0	7									124	3
Lim	2006/07	24	20	3	388	53*	22.82	0	2									24	6
20T	2006/07	13	10	2	181	38	22.62	0	0									6	1

Cmp	Debut	M	I	NO	Runs	HS	Avge	100	50	Balls	Runs	Wkts	Avge	BB	5i	10m	RpO	ct	st
NAEEM ARSHAD (Lahore Shalimar) b Lahore, Punjab 24.1.1986 RHB OB																			
FC		3	6	0	65	31	10.83	0	0									2	
Lim	2008/09	1	1	0	27	27	27.00	0	0									0	
NAEEMUDDIN (Punjab Stallions, Sui Northern Gas) b Gujranwala, Punjab 17.6.1981 LHB OB																			
FC		12	22	3	809	139	42.57	1	6									5	
Lim		8	8	1	467	103*	66.71	1	4									1	
FC	2007/08	31	52	5	2020	216*	42.97	5	9									16	
Lim	2007/08	15	15	2	778	103*	59.84	2	6									1	
20T	2008/09	2	2	0	1	1	0.50	0	0									1	
NAEEM-UR-REHMAN (Hyderabad) b Mardan, North-West Frontier Province 6.8.1982 RHB RMF																			
FC		5	9	3	89	33	14.83	0	0	591	424	18	23.55	5-56	1	0	4.30	2	
FC	2005/06	30	45	16	386	38	13.31	0	0	4142	2722	91	29.91	6-68	6	1	3.94	12	
Lim	2001/02	11	8	3	69	21	13.80	0	0	465	459	10	45.90	4-47	1	0	5.92	5	
20T	2005/06	6	1	1	4	4*		0	0	120	150	5	30.00	2-17	0	0	7.50	5	
NAJAF Hussain SHAH, Syed (PIA) b Gujarkhan, Punjab 17.12.1984 LHB LMF																			
FC		5	4	2	4	3	2.00	0	0	1004	467	19	24.57	6-39	1	0	2.79	3	
FC	2000/01	84	97	36	553	38*	9.06	0	0	16028	7608	315	24.15	7-57	16	1	2.84	22	
Int	2007	1	1	0	0	0	0.00	0	0	60	59	0					5.90	0	
Lim	2000/01	60	22	5	68	16*	4.00	0	0	3013	2193	67	32.73	4-35	1	0	4.36	10	
20T	2005/06	8	3	1	12	10	6.00	0	0	170	276	5	55.20	2-34	0	0	9.74	2	
NASIM KHAN, Mohammad (Quetta) b Quetta, Baluchistan 1.6.1976 LHB SLA																			
FC		2	4	0	55	31	13.75	0	0									0	
FC	1999/00	86	150	11	4354	151	31.32	9	24	288	160	2	80.00	2-17	0	0	3.33	32	
Lim	1998/99	55	54	2	2008	123	38.61	4	12	156	141	2	70.50	1-4	0	0	5.42	12	
20T	2004/05	11	11	0	154	32	14.00	0	0									0	
NASIR AHMED (Peshawar) b Peshawar, North-West Frontier Province 18.12.1989 LHB LMF																			
FC		5	9	4	69	14*	13.80	0	0	811	411	15	27.40	4-48	0	0	3.04	2	
Lim	2007/08	5	5	2	50	20	16.66	0	0	234	257	5	51.40	3-62	0	0	6.59	2	
NASIR IQBAL, Mohammad (Sialkot Stallions) b Sialkot, Punjab 4.1.1990 RHB																			
Lim		1	1	0	0	0	0.00	0	0									0	
NASIR JAMSHED (Lahore Lions, National Bank, Punjab Stallions) b Lahore, Punjab 6.12.1989 LHB OB																			
FC		7	12	0	340	108	28.33	1	2									4	
Lim		9	9	0	342	101	38.00	1	1									4	
20T		4	4	0	77	33	19.25	0	0									4	
FC	2004/05	42	71	5	2938	182	44.51	11	11	6	8	0					8.00	33	
Int	2007/08	12	12	2	353	74	35.30	0	4									4	
Lim	2004/05	59	58	4	1874	128	34.70	4	9									23	
20T	2004/05	17	16	0	329	58	20.56	0	1									8	
NASIR MALIK (Rawalpindi) b Rawalpindi, Punjab 22.11.1990 RHB LMF																			
FC		1	1	1	27	27*		0	0	66	70	0					6.36	0	
FC	2008/09	2	3	3	34	27*		0	0	288	191	5	38.20	4-80	0	0	3.97	1	
NASRULLAH KHAN (Quetta Bears) b Chaman, Baluchistan 14.9.1990 RHB RMF																			
Lim		4	4	1	119	104*	39.66	1	0	98	94	1	94.00	1-53	0	0	5.75	2	
20T		3	3	0	6	4	2.00	0	0	24	23	2	11.50	2-23	0	0	5.75	0	
NASRULLAH KHAN Farrukh (Islamabad, Islamabad Leopards) b Islamabad, Punjab 26.3.1984 LHB LFM																			
FC		9	15	7	47	14*	5.87	0	0	1723	1022	47	21.74	5-54	2	0	3.55	0	
Lim		2	2	1	19	17*	19.00	0	0	108	85	1	85.00	1-39	0	0	4.72	1	
NASRULLAH MEMON (Hyderabad, Hyderabad Hawks) b Shikarpur, Sind 2.3.1978 RHB OB WK																			
FC		9	18	0	560	144	31.11	1	1									21	
20T		1	1	0	10	10	10.00	0	0									0	
FC	2001/02	18	33	0	775	144	23.48	1	2									31	1
Lim	2008/09	2	2	0	33	23	16.50	0	0									0	
NAUMAN Ahmed ALAVI (PIA) b Karachi, Sind 23.8.1986 LHB SLA																			
FC		2	2	0	9	9	4.50	0	0	270	126	7	18.00	5-42	1	0	2.80	0	
FC	2006/07	9	10	2	64	23	8.00	0	0	1609	792	27	29.33	5-42	1	0	2.95	2	
Lim	2005/06	9	5	2	58	32	19.33	0	0	464	332	13	25.53	3-31	0	0	4.29	5	
20T	2005/06	5								120	155	4	38.75	1-15	0	0	7.75	3	
NAUMAN ALI (KRL) b Sanghar, Sind 7.10.1986 LHB SLA																			
FC		8	10	1	142	53	15.77	0	1	1404	576	26	22.15	5-26	2	0	2.46	1	
Lim		4	2	0	28	23	14.00	0	0	216	124	4	31.00	2-28	0	0	3.44	2	
FC	2006/07	13	17	3	296	67	21.14	0	2	1884	882	34	25.94	5-26	2	0	2.80	4	
Lim	2005/06	17	11	1	141	43	14.10	0	0	840	584	20	29.20	3-26	0	0	4.17	6	
20T	2005/06	11	8	3	103	26*	20.60	0	0	243	266	12	22.16	2-16	0	0	6.56	8	
NAUMAN HABIB (Peshawar) b Peshawar, North-West Frontier Province 13.9.1979 RHB RM																			
FC		7	11	1	217	61	21.70	0	1	1137	648	23	28.17	5-40	1	0	3.42	3	
FC	1999/00	54	76	6	868	61	12.40	0	2	8251	4859	190	25.57	7-57	9	3	3.53	11	
Lim	1997/98	30	18	2	147	33	9.18	0	0	1407	1235	40	30.87	4-43	1	0	5.26	4	
NAUMAN KHAN, Mohammad (Hyderabad) b Hyderabad, Sind 16.10.1985 RHB RMF																			
FC		3	5	1	26	14	6.50	0	0	340	347	6	57.83	4-122	0	0	6.12	2	
FC	2008/09	4	6	1	27	14	5.40	0	0	430	405	8	50.62	4-122	0	0	5.65	2	
Lim	2008/09	2	1	1	1	1*		0	0	84	70	2	35.00	2-27	0	0	5.00	0	

Cmp	Debut	M	I	NO	Runs	HS	Avge	100	50	Balls	Runs	Wkts	Avge	BB	5i	10m	RpO	ct	st
NAUMANULLAH (Karachi Zebras, National Bank) b Karachi, Sind 20.5.1975 RHB OB																			
FC		10	15	2	280	110	21.53	1	1	120	43	0					2.15	9	
Lim		5	3	0	91	48	30.33	0	0									1	
20T		2	1	0	5	5	5.00	0	0	12	25	0					12.50	1	
FC	1995/96	144	226	13	7579	176	35.58	14	47	1724	794	15	52.93	3-13	0	0	2.76	119	
Int	2007/08	1	1	0	5	5	5.00	0	0									0	
Lim	1996/97	115	108	12	3399	112	35.40	3	27	1066	969	20	48.45	3-28	0	0	5.45	47	
20T	2005/06	19	15	3	290	56*	24.16	0	1	108	174	2	87.00	1-27	0	0	9.66	4	
NAUSHAD IRSHAD (Quetta Bears) b Turbat, Baluchistan 15.12.1993 LHB WK																			
Lim		1	1	0	1	1	1.00	0	0									0	
20T		1	1	0	1	1	1.00	0	0									0	
NAVED ARIF Gondal (Sialkot, Sialkot Stallions) b Mandi Bahauddin, Punjab 2.11.1981 LHB LMF																			
FC		9	12	2	138	49	13.80	0	0	1888	993	41	24.21	7-66	2	1	3.15	3	
Lim		2								60	81	2	40.50	2-45	0	0	8.10	0	
FC	2001/02	30	38	12	410	49	15.76	0	0	6167	3375	145	23.27	7-66	10	1	3.28	11	
Lim	2002/03	10	4	0	77	49	19.25	0	0	330	361	9	40.11	3-19	0	0	6.56	3	
20T	2009	5	2	2	1	1*		0	0	108	103	6	17.16	2-13	0	0	5.72	1	
NAVED ASHRAF Qureshi, Mohammad (Rawalpindi, Rawalpindi Rams) b Rawalpindi, Punjab 4.9.1974 RHB OB																			
FC		9	15	1	714	230*	51.00	1	3	42	35	0					5.00	2	
Lim		5	4	0	59	30	14.75	0	0	60	47	2	23.50	2-28	0	0	4.70	2	
20T		2	2	0	21	14	10.50	0	0									0	
Test	1998/99	2	3	0	64	32	21.33	0	0									0	
FC	1992/93	162	263	11	7790	230*	30.91	10	42	1295	773	12	64.41	2-17	0	0	3.58	80	
Lim	1992/93	109	103	13	2946	122*	32.73	4	18	1450	1207	34	35.50	4-38	1	0	4.99	38	
20T	2004/05	17	16	0	315	57	19.68	0	2	42	64	3	21.33	2-20	0	0	9.14	1	
NAVED KHAN (Peshawar) b Nowshehra, North-West Frontier Province 17.7.1982 RHB LB																			
FC		1	2	0	18	18	9.00	0	0									2	
FC	1999/00	13	25	1	361	70	15.04	0	2	6	8	0					8.00	8	
Lim	2007/08	2	2	0	61	57	30.50	0	1									1	
NAVED KHAN (Karachi Whites, Karachi Zebras, The Rest) b Karachi, Sind 25.6.1985 RHB LB																			
FC		11	20	1	703	120	37.00	2	4	6	2	0					2.00	10	
Lim		4	4	0	60	24	15.00	0	0									1	
FC	2005/06	14	24	1	716	120	31.13	2	4	6	2	0					2.00	14	
Lim	2007/08	6	6	0	101	24	16.83	0	0									2	1
NAVED LATIF (Faisalabad, Faisalabad Wolves) b Sargodha, Punjab 21.2.1976 RHB RM																			
FC		7	10	1	344	105	38.22	1	3	78	48	0					3.69	6	
Lim		4	4	0	36	16	9.00	0	0	120	98	2	49.00	2-31	0	0	4.90	2	
Test	2001/02	1	2	0	20	20	10.00	0	0									0	
FC	1993/94	143	216	11	7322	394	35.71	15	38	2335	1243	34	36.55	3-41	0	0	3.19	107	
Int	2001/02	11	11	0	262	113	23.81	1	0	48	51	0					6.37	2	
Lim	1992/93	129	116	9	3993	128	37.31	8	21	1246	1087	21	51.76	3-37	0	0	5.23	45	1
20T	2004/05	21	17	5	287	45*	23.91	0	0									12	
NAVED MALIK Zamurad (Federal Areas Leopards, Rawalpindi, Rawalpindi Rams) b Rawalpindi, Punjab 28.1.1982 RHB RMF																			
FC		6	11	1	355	116*	35.50	1	2	30	25	0					5.00	3	
Lim		6	6	0	175	67	29.16	0	1	54	42	2	21.00	1-20	0	0	4.66	3	
20T		2	2	0	43	28	21.50	0	0									0	
Lim	2006/07	10	10	1	244	67	27.11	0	1	96	84	4	21.00	2-33	0	0	5.25	4	
20T	2006/07	7	7	1	202	73*	33.66	0	2									0	
NAVED SAFDAR (Lahore Lions) b Lahore, Punjab 24.10.1987 RHB SLA																			
Lim		1	1	0	13	13	13.00	0	0									0	
NAVED-UL-HASAN, Rana (Sialkot Stallions, WAPDA, Pakistan to Australia, Pakistan to South Africa, Sussex, Tasmania) b Sheikhupura, Punjab 28.2.1978 RHB RFM																			
FC		2	4	0	89	45	22.25	0	0	298	202	9	22.44	3-48	0	0	4.06	1	
20T		4	4	0	144	95	36.00	0	1	87	111	4	27.75	1-16	0	0	7.65	1	
Test	2004/05	9	15	3	239	42*	19.91	0	0	1565	1044	18	58.00	3-30	0	0	4.00	3	
FC	1995/96	122	174	20	3560	139	23.11	5	10	22636	12761	523	24.39	7-49	27	4	3.38	56	
Int	2002/03	74	51	18	524	33	15.87	0	0	3466	3221	110	29.28	6-27	6	1	5.57	16	
Lim	1999/00	170	130	34	2094	74	21.81	0	10	8032	7024	261	26.91	6-27	10	3	5.24	46	
I20T	2006	4	2	1	18	17*	18.00	0	0	85	101	5	20.20	3-19	0	0	7.12	2	
20T	2004/05	47	36	12	545	95	22.70	0	1	978	1122	52	21.57	4-23	1	0	6.88	21	
NAVED Ahmed YASIN (Multan, Multan Tigers, The Rest, Pakistan A to Sri Lanka, Pakistan A to United Arab Emirates) b Gaggu Mandi, Punjab 15.7.1987 LHB SLA																			
FC		12	20	1	1230	154	64.73	6	4									10	
20T		3	3	1	52	35	26.00	0	0									1	
FC	2006/07	30	46	4	2136	154	50.85	8	9	18	10	0					3.33	17	
Lim	2007/08	7	6	1	158	47	31.60	0	0									2	
20T	2004/05	4	4	1	60	35	20.00	0	0									2	

Cmp	Debut	M	I	NO	Runs	HS	Avge	100	50	Balls	Runs	Wkts	Avge	BB	5i	10m	RpO	ct	st
NAWAZ AHMED, Mohammad (Peshawar, Peshawar Panthers) b Peshawar, North-West Frontier Province 10.12.1986 RHB RMF																			
FC		2	4	0	30	21	7.50	0	0	78	35	2	17.50	2-35	0	0	2.69	1	
Lim		2	2	0	22	20	11.00	0	0	24	34	1	34.00	1-34	0	0	8.50	1	
FC	2005/06	16	28	1	450	109	16.66	1	3	428	280	4	70.00	2-35	0	0	3.92	10	
Lim	2007/08	9	9	1	282	67	35.25	0	3	96	97	4	24.25	3-44	0	0	6.06	3	
20T	2009	1	1	1	10	10*		0	0									0	
NAWAZ SARDAR (WAPDA) b Sheikhupura, Punjab 27.10.1987 RHB RMF																			
FC		2	4	0	83	28	20.75	0	0	140	75	0					3.21	0	
Lim		3	3	0	18	7	6.00	0	0	168	123	2	61.50	1-21	0	0	4.39	0	
FC	2003/04	17	27	1	822	147	31.61	1	5	1258	751	16	46.93	4-33	0	0	3.58	5	
Lim	2002/03	17	15	3	162	28	13.50	0	0	878	715	16	44.68	3-35	0	0	4.88	3	
20T	2004/05	2	1	0	10	10	10.00	0	0	24	38	0					9.50	2	
NAYYER ABBAS (Sialkot, Sialkot Stallions) b Abbas Nagar, Punjab 15.1.1990 LHB SLA																			
FC		13	20	1	515	66	27.10	0	5	2493	1126	41	27.46	5-37	1	0	2.71	9	
Lim		7	6	3	70	20*	23.33	0	0	357	287	9	31.88	4-30	1	0	4.82	2	
FC	2007/08	31	46	2	1093	93*	24.84	0	7	5415	2505	102	24.55	5-37	3	0	2.77	25	
Lim	2007/08	15	11	3	211	65	26.37	0	1	685	557	15	37.13	4-30	1	0	4.87	5	
NAZAR HUSSAIN (Quetta, Quetta Bears) b Pishin, Baluchistan 24.8.1988 LHB LFM																			
FC		10	18	9	123	38	13.66	0	0	2114	1132	37	30.59	5-93	1	0	3.21	5	
Lim		2	2	0	36	20	18.00	0	0	120	73	2	36.50	1-28	0	0	3.65	0	
20T		2	2	0	26	13	13.00	0	0	42	65	3	21.66	2-24	0	0	9.28	0	
FC	2007/08	31	53	23	398	38*	13.26	0	0	5544	2876	98	29.34	6-54	5	0	3.11	9	
Lim	2007/08	11	11	3	103	20	12.87	0	0	580	507	16	31.68	3-38	0	0	5.24	2	
20T	2008/09	6	5	1	45	13	11.25	0	0	126	193	5	38.60	2-24	0	0	9.19	1	
NOOR MOHAMMAD Khokhar (Hyderabad) b Dadu, Sind 2.6.1988 RHB OB																			
FC		1	2	0	22	22	11.00	0	0									0	
Lim	2008/09	3	3	1	108	68	54.00	0	1									0	
NOOR-UL-AMIN (WAPDA) b Mardan, North-West Frontier Province 4.2.1975 LHB SLA																			
Lim		2	2	1	1	1	1.00	0	0	120	106	1	106.00	1-50	0	0	5.30	0	
FC	2001/02	27	30	11	212	23*	11.15	0	0	5758	2745	93	29.51	6-49	6	1	2.86	6	
Lim	2001/02	20	17	6	78	23	7.09	0	0	1077	833	18	46.27	4-59	1	0	4.64	1	
20T	2008/09	2	2	1	2	1*	2.00	0	0	42	30	1	30.00	1-9	0	0	4.28	0	
PIR ZULFIQAR Ali (Hyderabad) b Dadu, Sind 3.1.1984 LHB SLA																			
FC		8	15	4	197	42	17.90	0	0	1267	737	16	46.06	4-85	0	0	3.49	4	
FC	2002/03	38	68	8	975	76	16.25	0	2	5560	3033	73	41.54	5-53	1	0	3.27	21	
Lim	2001/02	20	14	0	162	31	11.57	0	0	921	791	15	52.73	2-34	0	0	5.15	7	
20T	2005/06	3								64	86	5	17.20	4-29	1	0	8.06	1	
PRINCE ABBAS (Sialkot, Sialkot Stallions) b Hafizabad, Punjab 21.10.1989 RHB RMF																			
FC		9	13	10	36	11	12.00	0	0	1802	937	35	26.77	4-32	0	0	3.12	3	
Lim		5	2	1	4	4	4.00	0	0	240	174	7	24.85	3-26	0	0	4.35	1	
Lim	2007/08	7	3	2	8	4*	8.00	0	0	282	233	8	29.12	3-26	0	0	4.95	1	
QAISER ABBAS (National Bank, Sialkot Stallions, Rajshahi) b Muridke, Punjab 7.5.1982 LHB SLA																			
FC		10	14	2	583	136*	48.58	2	1	850	336	16	21.00	5-20	1	0	2.37	7	
Lim		5	5	2	108	64	36.00	0	1	201	157	4	39.25	2-34	0	0	4.68	0	
20T		1	1	1	2	2*		0	0									0	
Test	2000/01	1	1	0	2	2	2.00	0	0	96	35	0					2.18	0	
FC	1999/00	109	170	17	5055	168	33.03	5	31	6000	2320	75	30.93	5-20	2	0	2.32	60	
Lim	1999/00	118	107	27	2894	106*	36.17	2	21	4434	3380	105	32.19	4-33	4	0	4.57	48	
20T	2004/05	26	20	5	381	75*	25.40	0	2	222	287	13	22.07	3-17	0	0	7.75	6	
RAFATULLAH MOHMAND (Abbottabad Rhinos, Khyber Pakhtunkhwa Panthers, WAPDA) b Peshawar, North-West Frontier Province 6.11.1976 RHB SLA																			
FC		9	16	1	698	302*	46.53	2	1	64	55	4	13.75	2-23	0	0	5.15	5	
Lim		8	8	0	303	90	37.87	0	3									7	
20T		2	2	0	5	5	2.50	0	0									0	
FC	1996/97	126	204	14	5693	302*	29.96	10	24	566	328	9	36.44	2-23	0	0	3.47	83	
Lim	1996/97	104	103	7	3616	141*	37.66	2	29	470	378	14	27.00	3-34	0	0	4.82	51	
20T	2004/05	16	15	0	331	68	22.06	0	1	30	36	2	18.00	2-23	0	0	7.20	9	
RAHAT ALI (KRL) b Multan, Punjab 12.9.1988 RHB LFM																			
FC		1	1	1	1	1*		0	0	150	85	1	85.00	1-85	0	0	3.40	0	
Lim		4	2	2	0	0*		0	0	144	101	3	33.66	1-18	0	0	4.20	0	
FC	2007/08	6	6	4	9	6*	4.50	0	0	850	423	18	23.50	4-31	0	0	2.98	2	
Lim	2007/08	8	5	4	26	12*	26.00	0	0	300	269	8	33.62	3-58	0	0	5.38	1	
RAHEEL MAJEED (Federal Areas Leopards, Islamabad, Islamabad Leopards) b Islamabad, Punjab 9.9.1983 RHB LB																			
FC		10	19	0	532	75	28.00	0	1	336	276	5	55.20	2-44	0	0	4.92	11	
Lim		9	9	0	263	73	29.22	0	2	69	55	0					4.78	3	
20T		2	2	0	39	35	19.50	0	0									1	
FC	2001/02	52	96	3	2744	107	29.50	2	16	2581	1867	46	40.58	5-66	1	0	4.34	42	
Lim	2000/01	48	47	1	1405	129	30.54	1	10	1336	1286	35	36.74	4-47	2	0	5.77	18	
20T	2004/05	16	16	0	252	45	15.75	0	0	57	101	4	25.25	3-21	0	0	10.63	4	

Cmp	Debut	M	I	NO	Runs	HS	Avge	100	50	Balls	Runs	Wkts	Avge	BB	5i	10m	RpO	ct	st
RAJESH RAMESH (Sui Southern Gas) b Karachi, Sind 2.7.1982 RHB RFM																			
FC		4	4	1	16	9	5.33	0	0	600	292	8	36.50	2-37	0	0	2.92	0	
Lim		1								42	50	0					7.14	0	
FC	2001/02	56	76	14	886	100	14.29	1	2	9892	5761	204	28.24	6-48	9	1	3.49	18	
Lim	2000/01	29	20	4	130	29*	8.12	0	0	1239	1236	25	49.44	4-36	1	0	5.98	7	
20T	2005/06	3	2	2	11	8*		0	0	54	101	2	50.50	2-35	0	0	11.22	1	
RAMEEZ ALAM (Baluchistan Bears, Multan, Multan Tigers) b Sahiwal, Punjab 7.12.1988 RHB OB																			
FC		9	15	2	647	222*	49.76	2	2	6	4	0					4.00	6	
Lim		10	10	1	389	86	43.22	0	4									5	
20T		2	2	1	85	52*	85.00	0	1									1	
FC	2007/08	28	48	8	1639	222*	40.97	4	7	6	4	0					4.00	16	
Lim	2007/08	14	14	1	466	86	35.84	0	4									7	
20T	2009	4	3	1	102	52*	51.00	0	1									1	
RAMEEZ AZIZ Panjara (Customs) b Karachi, Sind 15.9.1990 LHB OB																			
FC		5	10	1	345	87	38.33	0	4	114	67	1	67.00	1-13	0	0	3.52	1	
Lim		4	4	0	146	58	36.50	0	2	12	16	0					8.00	1	
FC	2008/09	15	29	1	959	141	34.25	1	6	185	128	2	64.00	1-13	0	0	4.15	10	
Lim	2006/07	8	8	0	195	58	24.37	0	2	24	32	0					8.00	1	
RAMEEZ RAJA (Customs) b Karachi, Sind 31.7.1987 RHB OB																			
FC		8	15	0	215	84	14.33	0	1	12	9	0					4.50	4	
Lim		4	4	0	258	133	64.50	1	1	6	8	0					8.00	2	
FC	2005/06	19	36	1	741	117	21.17	1	2	18	14	0					4.66	15	
Lim	2007/08	9	9	1	388	133	48.50	1	2	6	8	0					8.00	2	
RANA ADNAN Shahbaz (Lahore Lions) b Lahore, Punjab 14.3.1990 RHB OB																			
Lim		5	5	0	186	65	37.20	0	3									0	
FC	2008/09	4	6	1	118	63	23.60	0	1									4	
Lim	2008/09	10	8	0	251	65	31.37	0	3									3	
RASHID ALI (Customs) b Karachi, Sind 20.12.1980 RHB OB																			
FC		4	7	0	77	42	11.00	0	0									5	
FC	1999/00	13	23	1	352	59	16.00	0	1									14	
Lim	2004/05	1	1	0	13	13	13.00	0	0									0	
RASHID LATIF (Rawalpindi, Rawalpindi Rams) b Wah Cantonment, Punjab 24.10.1974 RHB RMF																			
FC		10	15	1	216	50	15.42	0	1	1954	940	53	17.73	9-42	4	2	2.88	2	
Lim		4	2	2	17	13*		0	0	174	135	7	19.28	4-37	1	0	4.65	0	
FC	2008/09	15	20	1	330	82	17.36	0	2	2446	1096	64	17.12	9-42	4	2	2.68	2	
Lim	2008/09	6	3	2	23	13*	23.00	0	0	269	206	15	13.73	5-30	1	1	4.59	0	
RASHID MANSOOR (Abbottabad) b Kohat, North-West Frontier Province 6.4.1979 RHB RMF																			
FC		7	12	1	120	33	10.90	0	0	800	455	12	37.91	2-14	0	0	3.41	3	
FC	2007/08	21	26	4	312	68	14.18	0	1	2582	1420	54	26.29	6-76	3	1	3.30	9	
Lim	2007/08	8	7	1	90	27	15.00	0	0	330	274	4	68.50	2-55	0	0	4.98	2	
20T	2008/09	3	3	1	13	7	6.50	0	0	60	92	2	46.00	2-26	0	0	9.20	0	
RASHID RIAZ (National Bank) b Chiniot, Punjab 27.2.1976 RHB OB																			
FC		7	11	2	479	101	53.22	1	4									7	
Lim		1	1	0	10	10	10.00	0	0									0	
FC	2000/01	38	59	4	1896	128	34.47	3	14	15	16	0					6.40	34	
Lim	2001/02	25	21	2	576	108*	30.31	1	3	6	9	0					9.00	9	1
20T	2004/05	7	7	2	124	32	24.80	0	0									1	
RAUF AKBAR Khan (Islamabad) b Multan, Punjab 22.7.1977 RHB RFM																			
FC		10	17	1	258	70	16.12	0	1	1431	917	28	32.75	5-32	1	0	3.84	4	
FC	1997/98	56	86	15	1755	116	24.71	1	12	9008	4890	203	24.08	7-27	10	2	3.25	28	
Lim	1997/98	28	17	2	219	46	14.60	0	0	1199	1032	23	44.86	4-44	1	0	5.16	7	
20T	2005/06	7	7	4	45	19	15.00	0	0	156	206	11	18.72	4-28	1	0	7.92	2	
RAZA ALI DAR, Khwaja (Sui Northern Gas) b Lahore, Punjab 11.12.1987 LHB SLA																			
FC		5	10	1	287	85	31.88	0	2	45	33	2	16.50	2-16	0	0	4.40	5	
Lim		6	5	0	223	86	44.60	0	2	101	73	6	12.16	4-14	1	0	4.33	2	
FC	2003/04	16	28	1	815	183	30.18	1	3	325	188	5	37.60	2-16	0	0	3.47	10	
Lim	2002/03	12	11	1	289	86	28.90	0	2	293	245	8	30.62	4-14	1	0	5.01	2	
RAZA HASAN (Punjab Stallions, Rawalpindi Rams, ZTBL, Pakistan A to United Arab Emirates) b Sialkot, Punjab 8.7.1992 RHB SLA																			
Lim		5	4	2	15	6	7.50	0	0	280	190	7	27.14	2-32	0	0	4.07	2	
20T		2								48	64	4	16.00	2-27	0	0	8.00	1	
FC	2008/09	2	2	1	6	4*	6.00	0	0	283	129	8	16.12	3-24	0	0	2.73	1	
Lim	2007/08	9	5	3	18	6	9.00	0	0	481	324	17	19.05	3-13	0	0	4.04	2	
RAZA-UL-HASAN (Karachi Whites) b Karachi, Sind 26.11.1987 RHB OB																			
FC		1	1	0	3	3	3.00	0	0	183	71	3	23.66	2-32	0	0	2.32	0	
REHAN AFRIDI (Abbottabad Rhinos) b Khyber Agency 10.5.1992 RHB WK																			
Lim		1	1	0	4	4	4.00	0	0									0	
FC	2008/09	1	2	0	10	10	5.00	0	0									1	
REHAN NIZAMUDDIN (Hyderabad Hawks) b Mirpurkhas, Sind 2.1.1985 RHB LB																			
20T		1	1	1	1	1*		0	0	18	26	1	26.00	1-26	0	0	8.66	0	

Cmp	Debut	M	I	NO	Runs	HS	Avge	100	50	Balls	Runs	Wkts	Avge	BB	5i	10m	RpO	ct	st
REHAN RAFIQ (Habib Bank) b Bahawalpur, Punjab 15.10.1978 LHB SLA																			
FC		4	7	1	66	28	11.00	0	0									0	
FC	1994/95	99	163	24	3959	197*	28.48	6	20	2154	989	19	52.05	4-28	0	0	2.75	78	
Lim	1993/94	41	37	5	925	82	28.90	0	6	576	624	13	48.00	7-40	0	1	6.50	10	
REHAN RIAZ (ZTBL) b Hyderabad, Sind 14.1.1977 RHB RMF																			
FC		7	8	3	75	26	15.00	0	0	846	490	16	30.62	4-68	0	0	3.47	4	
Lim		3	3	0	12	6	4.00	0	0	132	151	6	25.16	3-39	0	0	6.86	1	
FC	2004/05	17	24	8	164	29*	10.25	0	0	1764	1029	22	46.77	4-68	0	0	3.50	9	
REHMAN QADIR (National Bank) b Lahore, Punjab 1.12.1978 RHB LB																			
FC		1	2	0	32	26	16.00	0	0									0	
Lim	2004/05	5	3	1	9	8*	4.50	0	0	182	185	3	61.66	1-30	0	0	6.09	2	
RIAZ AFRIDI, Mohammad (Peshawar, Peshawar Panthers) b Peshawar, North-West Frontier Province 21.1.1985 RHB RMF																			
FC		4	6	0	98	29	16.33	0	0	1052	698	27	25.85	6-31	3	1	3.98	2	
Lim		3	3	0	77	64	25.66	0	1	150	87	6	14.50	4-29	1	0	3.48	0	
20T		2	2	0	5	5	2.50	0	0	42	40	3	13.33	2-18	0	0	5.71	0	
Test	2004/05	1	1	0	9	9	9.00	0	0	186	87	2	43.50	2-42	0	0	2.80	0	
FC	2001/02	51	65	9	918	66	16.39	0	4	9802	5392	229	23.54	7-78	14	2	3.30	12	
Lim	2001/02	32	23	4	305	66	16.05	0	2	1409	1129	45	25.08	4-29	2	0	4.80	3	
20T	2005/06	9	7	2	59	23	11.80	0	0	168	232	7	33.14	2-16	0	0	8.28	2	
RIAZ KAIL (Abbottabad, Abbottabad Rhinos) b Peshawar, North-West Frontier Province 10.11.1988 RHB OB																			
FC		9	18	4	372	94	26.57	0	2	234	105	4	26.25	2-36	0	0	2.69	7	
Lim		2	2	0	17	17	8.50	0	0									0	
FC	2006/07	39	59	10	1679	153	34.26	2	11	1214	615	12	51.25	2-36	0	0	3.04	21	
Lim	2005/06	17	16	2	310	71	22.14	0	3	420	430	6	71.66	2-38	0	0	6.14	5	
20T	2005/06	10	8	0	55	25	6.87	0	0	96	114	5	22.80	3-17	0	0	7.12	2	
RIZWAN AHMED (Lahore Shalimar) b Lahore, Punjab 4.3.1983 LHB OB																			
FC		4	8	0	168	53	21.00	0	1									1	
RIZWAN AHMED Farid (Hyderabad Hawks, Sui Southern Gas) b Hyderabad, Sind 1.10.1978 RHB LBG																			
FC		9	16	2	548	117*	39.14	2	3	246	226	2	113.00	2-72	0	0	5.51	4	
Lim		5	5	0	91	53	18.20	0	1	42	51	1	51.00	1-23	0	0	7.28	1	
20T		1	1	0	16	16	16.00	0	0									0	
FC	1998/99	82	142	10	4622	149	35.01	9	24	7991	5172	125	41.37	6-88	4	0	3.88	44	
Int	2007/08	1								24	26	0					6.50	1	
Lim	1998/99	46	44	10	1236	158	36.35	1	5	1648	1395	46	30.32	4-29	3	0	5.07	17	
20T	2004/05	9	9	3	228	57*	38.00	0	2	90	99	2	49.50	2-24	0	0	6.60	0	
RIZWAN AKBAR (Sui Northern Gas) b Rawalpindi, Punjab 15.12.1986 RHB RMF																			
FC		5	6	2	49	30	12.25	0	0	660	474	12	39.50	3-35	0	0	4.30	3	
FC	2003/04	42	57	14	367	38	8.53	0	0	7425	3997	177	22.58	7-39	12	1	3.23	14	
Lim	2004/05	12	5	3	7	4	3.50	0	0	522	446	12	37.16	3-44	0	0	5.12	0	
20T	2005/06	2	1	1	1	1*		0	0	30	35	0					7.00	0	
RIZWAN HAIDER (Baluchistan Bears, Multan, Multan Tigers) b Renala Khurd, Punjab 16.6.1985 LHB LMF																			
FC		9	14	3	271	55	24.63	0	1	1395	777	33	23.54	5-60	2	0	3.34	8	
Lim		10	10	2	167	45*	20.87	0	0	372	281	14	20.07	5-31	0	1	4.53	4	
20T		3	2	0	34	21	17.00	0	0	48	59	2	29.50	1-11	0	0	7.37	0	
FC	2008/09	13	20	7	463	73	35.61	0	3	1749	999	35	28.54	5-60	2	0	3.42	13	
Lim	2008/09	16	15	4	319	51	29.00	0	1	546	383	17	22.52	5-31	0	1	4.20	5	
20T	2009	5	4	1	91	30*	30.33	0	0	78	117	2	58.50	1-11	0	0	9.00	2	
RIZWAN MALIK (Lahore Ravi) b Gujranwala, Punjab 2.8.1980 RHB OB																			
FC		4	8	0	87	38	10.87	0	0									1	
FC	1999/00	43	76	3	1938	169*	26.54	4	7	55	49	0					5.34	25	
Lim	1998/99	36	33	4	992	86	34.20	0	8	12	15	0					7.50	19	
RIZWAN SAEED (Karachi Whites) b Karachi, Sind 14.3.1978 RHB RM																			
FC		3	5	1	33	10*	8.25	0	0	173	104	0					3.60	5	
FC	1999/00	35	51	6	886	85	19.68	0	2	3871	2270	65	34.92	5-70	2	0	3.51	9	
Lim	1999/00	28	21	3	202	44	11.22	0	0	850	890	16	55.62	3-36	0	0	6.28	4	
20T	2005/06	5	2	1	35	32*	35.00	0	0	78	112	6	18.66	3-18	0	0	8.61	0	
RIZWAN SULTAN (Sialkot) b Hafizabad, Punjab 14.11.1989 RHB OB																			
FC		1	2	0	54	36	27.00	0	0									1	
Lim	2008/09	1	1	0	65	65	65.00	0	1	6	14	1	14.00	1-14	0	0	14.00	0	
RUMMAN RAEES Khan (Karachi Dolphins) b Karachi, Sind 18.10.1991 RHB LMF																			
Lim		4	3	1	35	28*	17.50	0	0	228	212	8	26.50	2-38	0	0	5.57	0	
SAAD ALI (Lahore Eagles) b Sheikhupura, Punjab 27.12.1990 RHB LB																			
Lim		1	1	0	6	6	6.00	0	0									0	
SAAD ALTAF (Sui Northern Gas) b Margala, Punjab 25.12.1983 RHB LMF																			
FC		5	7	3	31	15*	7.75	0	0	952	567	15	37.80	3-75	0	0	3.57	1	
FC	2001/02	35	42	19	191	24*	8.30	0	0	6575	3692	145	25.46	7-63	10	3	3.36	7	
Lim	2003/04	14	4	2	2	2*	1.00	0	0	678	608	27	22.51	4-40	2	0	5.38	1	
20T	2005/06	7	1	0	1	1	1.00	0	0	137	182	9	20.22	3-12	0	0	7.97	0	

Cmp	Debut	M	I	NO	Runs	HS	Avge	100	50	Balls	Runs	Wkts	Avge	BB	5i	10m	RpO	ct	st
SAADAT MUNIR Ahmed (Faisalabad) b Sialkot, Punjab 24.8.1982 LHB SLA																			
FC		6	7	1	94	42	15.66	0	0	1375	536	17	31.52	4-26	0	0	2.33	1	
FC	2007/08	20	21	4	239	42	14.05	0	0	3305	1422	68	20.91	6-39	3	0	2.58	5	
Lim	2007/08	7	5	1	20	11	5.00	0	0	366	317	12	26.41	3-41	0	0	5.19	0	
SAAD NASIM, Hafiz (Lahore Eagles, Lahore Lions, Lahore Shalimar) b Lahore, Punjab 29.4.1990 RHB LB																			
FC		9	18	0	400	86	22.22	0	2	891	715	12	59.58	3-53	0	0	4.81	12	
Lim		5	5	0	75	25	15.00	0	0	166	139	7	19.85	4-35	1	0	5.02	1	
20T		2	1	0	2	2	2.00	0	0	23	37	0					9.65	1	
FC	2007/08	19	36	1	808	95	23.08	0	4	1845	1249	25	49.96	3-53	0	0	4.06	18	
SAAD SUKHAIL Khilji (Karachi Whites) b Karachi, Sind 15.12.1987 LHB RMF																			
FC		1	2	0	44	30	22.00	0	0									2	
SAADULLAH GHAURI (Lahore Ravi) b Lahore, Punjab 17.9.1989 RHB OB																			
FC		2	3	0	56	41	18.66	0	0									0	
FC	2008/09	5	9	1	118	58*	14.75	0	1									0	
SAADULLAH KHAN (Lahore Shalimar) b Lahore, Punjab 26.11.1987 RHB RMF																			
FC		3	5	0	25	11	5.00	0	0	426	342	4	85.50	3-111	0	0	4.81	1	
SABIR HUSSAIN, Mohammad (WAPDA) b Lyallpur (now Faisalabad), Punjab 15.11.1979 LHB LM																			
Lim		1	1	0	22	22	22.00	0	0									0	
FC	2002/03	3	3	1	13	9*	6.50	0	0									0	
Lim	1995/96	21	20	3	247	68	14.52	0	1	84	111	1	111.00	1-28	0	0	7.92	3	
SABIR HUSSAIN Khosa (Quetta Bears) b Quetta, Baluchistan 15.3.1983 RHB LB																			
Lim		2	2	0	125	72	62.50	0	2									0	
20T		2	2	0	13	13	6.50	0	0									0	
FC	2001/02	23	43	0	833	92	19.37	0	3	12	19	0					9.50	5	
Lim	2001/02	12	12	0	238	72	19.83	0	2									2	
20T	2005/06	11	11	0	125	40	11.36	0	0									3	
SADAF HUSSAIN (Rawalpindi, Rawalpindi Rams) b Chakwal, Punjab 7.12.1989 LHB LMF																			
FC		3	4	0	6	6	1.50	0	0	555	249	18	13.83	5-51	1	0	2.69	1	
Lim		1								60	58	4	14.50	4-58	1	0	5.80	0	
FC	2008/09	4	5	0	6	6	1.20	0	0	603	264	21	12.57	5-51	1	0	2.62	1	
SAEED AJMAL (Faisalabad Wolves, ZTBL, Pakistan to Australia, Pakistan to England, Pakistan to New Zealand, Pakistan to South Africa, Pakistan to Sri Lanka, Pakistan to United Arab Emirates, Pakistan to West Indies) b Faisalabad, Punjab 14.10.1977 RHB OB																			
FC		2	3	1	33	33	16.50	0	0	472	198	10	19.80	4-53	0	0	2.51	1	
20T		4	1	0	5	5	5.00	0	0	82	58	9	6.44	4-20	1	0	4.24	1	
Test	2009	8	15	7	96	50	12.00	0	1	2375	1114	30	37.13	5-82	1	0	2.81	2	
FC	1996/97	91	122	42	963	53	12.03	0	3	18103	8354	299	27.93	7-63	18	1	2.76	30	
Int	2008	32	21	10	109	33	9.90	0	0	1692	1230	42	29.28	4-33	2	0	4.36	5	
Lim	1995/96	130	69	33	296	33	8.22	0	0	6765	5073	184	27.57	5-18	6	1	4.49	29	
I20T	2008/09	24	6	5	24	13*	24.00	0	0	539	571	36	15.86	4-19	2	0	6.35	4	
20T	2004/05	55	13	8	45	13*	9.00	0	0	1183	1312	81	16.19	4-19	3	0	6.65	8	
SAEED ANWAR, Mohammad (Baluchistan Bears, KRL, Multan Tigers, The Rest) b Burewala, Punjab 12.12.1978 LHB SLA																			
FC		13	24	3	919	126	43.76	2	5	748	300	11	27.27	4-18	0	0	2.40	8	
Lim		8	8	0	138	36	17.25	0	0	210	149	6	24.83	3-41	0	0	4.25	8	
20T		2	1	0	12	12	12.00	0	0									2	
FC	1997/98	138	234	16	7528	177	34.53	18	34	6726	2809	71	39.56	4-18	0	0	2.50	65	
Lim	1997/98	94	92	5	3350	166	38.50	5	27	3818	2961	82	36.10	4-45	2	0	4.65	36	
20T	2005/06	14	12	1	338	73	30.72	0	3	240	306	7	43.71	2-32	0	0	7.65	2	
SAEED BIN NASIR (Sind Dolphins, Sui Southern Gas, The Rest) b Karachi, Sind 19.12.1979 RHB OB																			
FC		14	24	0	986	129	41.08	3	5	324	230	1	230.00	1-6	0	0	4.25	14	
Lim		3	3	0	16	14	5.33	0	0									2	
FC	1997/98	118	199	21	7600	163	42.69	19	38	846	634	9	70.44	2-4	0	0	4.49	73	
Lim	1998/99	75	72	10	2844	186*	45.87	4	15	129	136	1	136.00	1-44	0	0	6.32	23	
20T	2008/09	2	2	0	12	12	6.00	0	0									0	
SAJID AFRIDI (Abbottabad Rhinos) b Kohat, North-West Frontier Province 1.8.1985 RHB																			
Lim		1	1	0	7	7	7.00	0	0									1	
20T		1	1	1	9	9*		0	0									0	
SAJID MAHMOOD (Rawalpindi) b Islamabad, Punjab 10.1.1981 RHB OB WK																			
FC		1	2	0	14	14	7.00	0	0									2	
FC	2001/02	28	44	5	510	44	13.07	0	0									97	2
Lim	2004/05	12	9	1	142	62	17.75	0	1									15	2
20T	2004/05	3	1	1	1	1*		0	0									1	
SAJJAD AHMED Jan (Khyber Pakhtunkhwa Panthers, Peshawar, Peshawar Panthers) b Peshawar, North-West Frontier Province 2.4.1978 RHB OB																			
FC		10	19	3	604	117*	37.75	2	3	108	86	0					4.77	8	
Lim		1	1	0	24	24	24.00	0	0									0	
20T		2	2	0	23	20	11.50	0	0									0	
FC	1997/98	48	81	8	2087	117*	28.58	4	11	288	200	1	200.00	1-27	0	0	4.16	42	
Lim	1997/98	38	37	5	837	92	26.15	0	4	24	24	0					6.00	17	
20T	2009	4	4	0	75	38	18.75	0	0									0	

Cmp	Debut	M	I	NO	Runs	HS	Avge	100	50	Balls	Runs	Wkts	Avge	BB	5i	10m	RpO	ct	st
SAJJAD ALI (Abbottabad Rhinos) b Mardan, North-West Frontier Province 1.8.1984 RHB RMF																			
Lim		1	1	0	12	12	12.00	0	0	18	14	0					4.66	0	
FC	2005/06	6	8	0	56	24	7.00	0	0	36	35	1	35.00	1-35	0	0	5.83	2	
Lim	2007/08	5	4	0	33	12	8.25	0	0	120	122	2	61.00	2-56	0	0	6.10	0	
20T	2005/06	4	4	0	99	36	24.75	0	0	6	9	0					9.00	2	
SAJJAD ALI Khan (Hyderabad) b Mirpurkhas, Sind 10.1.1987 RHB RMF																			
FC		3	5	1	34	28	8.50	0	0	438	324	8	40.50	6-104	1	0	4.43	0	
FC	2008/09	9	13	3	72	28	7.20	0	0	1086	779	21	37.09	6-104	1	0	4.30	0	
Lim	2008/09	2	1	0	0	0	0.00	0	0	102	107	2	53.50	2-55	0	0	6.29	0	
SAJJAD HUSSAIN (Multan) b Multan, Punjab 1.9.1986 RHB RFM																			
FC		3	4	2	11	10	5.50	0	0	438	296	5	59.20	2-56	0	0	4.05	4	
FC	2006/07	18	27	11	123	23	7.68	0	0	2739	1596	54	29.55	5-20	2	0	3.49	10	
Lim	2006/07	4	3	2	4	4*	4.00	0	0	198	152	3	50.66	2-46	0	0	4.60	0	
SAJJAD Hussain LAGHARI (Hyderabad Hawks) b Hyderabad, Sind 30.1.1988 RHB OB																			
Lim		1								60	65	0					6.50	0	
Lim	2008/09	5	3	1	2	1*	1.00	0	0	258	246	5	49.20	2-27	0	0	5.72	1	
SALEEM ELAHI (Habib Bank) b Sahiwal, Punjab 21.11.1976 RHB OB																			
FC		10	18	2	401	178*	25.06	1	0									4	
Lim		4	3	0	88	67	29.33	0	1									1	
Test	1995/96	13	24	1	436	72	18.95	0	1									10	1
FC	1995/96	101	170	11	5071	229	31.89	7	24	42	54	0					7.71	70	1
Int	1995/96	48	47	4	1579	135	36.72	4	9	6	10	0					10.00	10	
Lim	1994/95	134	132	16	5963	172	51.40	18	34	12	16	1	16.00	1-6	0	0	8.00	36	
SALEEM MUGHAL, Mohammad (Sui Northern Gas) b Sheikhupura, Punjab 4.3.1978 RHB OB																			
FC		6	9	1	303	102*	37.87	1	1									4	
Lim		3	1	0	19	19	19.00	0	0	60	53	3	17.66	2-31	0	0	5.30	0	
FC	1998/99	66	101	10	3028	193	33.27	6	18	1982	930	18	51.66	3-40	0	0	2.81	45	
Lim	1998/99	51	42	8	1408	133*	41.41	1	10	1534	1189	28	42.46	3-30	0	0	4.65	23	
SALMAN ALI (Sialkot) b Muridke, Punjab 1.4.1987 RHB OB																			
FC		5	8	1	140	46	20.00	0	0	654	302	13	23.23	3-58	0	0	2.77	8	
Lim	2008/09	4	3	0	12	11	4.00	0	0	132	97	5	19.40	3-26	0	0	4.40	2	
SALMAN BUTT (Lahore Lions, National Bank, Pakistan to Australia, Pakistan to England, Pakistan to New Zealand, Pakistan to Sri Lanka, Pakistan to United Arab Emirates, Pakistan to West Indies) b Lahore, Punjab 7.10.1984 LHB OB																			
FC		3	5	1	209	177	52.25	1	0	12	7	0					3.50	1	
Lim		4	3	1	220	113*	110.00	1	1									0	
20T		4	4	1	112	59	37.33	0	1									0	
Test	2003/04	33	62	0	1889	122	30.46	3	10	137	106	1	106.00	1-36	0	0	4.64	12	
FC	2000/01	90	159	7	6232	290	41.00	17	24	938	653	11	59.36	4-82	0	0	4.17	33	
Int	2004	78	78	4	2725	136	36.82	8	14	69	90	0					7.82	20	
Lim	2000/01	149	148	12	6049	150*	44.47	19	29	535	488	10	48.80	2-26	0	0	5.47	39	
I20T	2007/08	24	23	2	595	74	28.33	0	3									3	
20T	2004/05	52	51	5	1337	99*	29.06	0	7	108	141	5	28.20	2-25	0	0	7.83	8	
SALMAN HUSSAIN (Customs) b Karachi, Sind 20.11.1985 RHB																			
Lim		1	1	0	5	5	5.00	0	0									0	
SAMIULLAH AGHA, Syed (Quetta) b Pishin, Baluchistan 1.1.1981 RHB RMF																			
FC		3	6	0	87	20	14.50	0	0									1	
FC	2003/04	21	41	0	854	99	20.82	0	3	12	10	0					5.00	6	
Lim	2003/04	8	8	1	149	104*	21.28	1	0	20	38	0					11.40	0	
20T	2008/09	2	2	0	33	31	16.50	0	0									0	
SAMIULLAH KHAN Niazi, Mohammad (Faisalabad Wolves, Sui Northern Gas) b Mianwali, Punjab 4.8.1982 RHB LMF																			
FC		8	10	4	63	25	10.50	0	0	1494	715	45	15.88	7-55	5	0	2.87	2	
Lim		6	1	1	6	6*		0	0	323	196	11	17.81	3-25	0	0	3.64	0	
20T		3								60	87	4	21.75	3-33	0	0	8.70	2	
FC	2002/03	65	76	28	334	25	6.95	0	0	12029	5694	298	19.10	7-55	15	3	2.84	17	
Int	2007/08	2								120	115	0					5.75	0	
Lim	1999/00	46	19	8	83	10	7.54	0	0	2293	1588	55	28.87	4-23	2	0	4.15	6	
20T	2004/05	22	3	2	12	6*	12.00	0	0	468	591	32	18.46	4-27	1	0	7.57	12	
SANAULLAH KHAN (Quetta) b Quetta, Baluchistan 12.5.1978 RHB WK																			
FC		2	3	1	86	38	43.00	0	0									3	
FC	2001/02	27	47	7	547	50*	13.67	0	1									59	4
Lim	1998/99	14	12	2	140	37	14.00	0	0									9	4
20T	2004/05	5	3	1	13	6*	6.50	0	0									1	1
SARFRAZ AHMED (Sialkot Stallions, WAPDA) b Gujranwala, Punjab 11.12.1978 LHB LFM																			
FC		7	7	3	129	29	32.25	0	0	1436	488	30	16.26	5-40	1	0	2.03	2	
Lim		3	2	0	10	7	5.00	0	0	168	118	0					4.21	0	
20T		3								72	73	5	14.60	2-23	0	0	6.08	1	
FC	1998/99	113	140	27	1901	84	16.82	0	6	22582	9112	407	22.38	7-50	20	3	2.42	49	
Lim	1997/98	89	56	17	555	45	14.23	0	0	4680	2843	134	21.21	5-19	3	1	3.64	23	
20T	2005/06	15	4	2	6	5	3.00	0	0	342	412	23	17.91	3-16	0	0	7.22	6	

Cmp	Debut	M	I	NO	Runs	HS	Avge	100	50	Balls	Runs	Wkts	Avge	BB	5i	10m	RpO	ct	st
SARFRAZ AHMED (Karachi Dolphins, PIA, Sind Dolphins, The Rest, Pakistan to Australia, Pakistan to United Arab Emirates) b Karachi, Sind 22.5.1987 RHB WK																			
FC		7	10	3	238	73	34.00	0	2									32	1
Lim		6	6	2	167	79	41.75	0	1									15	2
20T		3	2	1	13	13*	13.00	0	0									2	2
Test	2009/10	1	2	0	6	5	3.00	0	0									4	
FC	2005/06	49	76	18	2514	117	43.34	2	22									162	17
Int	2007/08	9	3	0	32	19	10.66	0	0									7	3
Lim	2005/06	54	40	9	866	101	27.93	1	5									62	14
I20T	2009/10	2	1	0	5	5	5.00	0	0									0	
20T	2005/06	19	10	3	97	19*	13.85	0	0									9	6
SARMAD ANWAR (Habib Bank) b Sialkot, Punjab 19.8.1988 RHB RFM																			
FC		11	16	6	53	19	5.30	0	0	1781	990	40	24.75	7-33	2	0	3.33	2	
Lim		4	1	1	3	3*		0	0	194	192	6	32.00	3-30	0	0	5.93	0	
FC	2008/09	17	21	9	54	19	4.50	0	0	2855	1581	59	26.79	7-33	2	0	3.32	5	
SARMAD BHATTI (National Bank) b Khairpur, Sind 26.9.1991 LHB RM																			
Lim		5	3	1	105	45*	52.50	0	0	216	182	6	30.33	2-21	0	0	5.05	1	
SHABBIR AHMED Khan (WAPDA) b Khanewal, Punjab 21.4.1976 RHB RFM																			
FC		6	6	1	37	12	7.40	0	0	807	436	21	20.76	4-56	0	0	3.24	6	
Lim		1	1	0	4	4	4.00	0	0	60	77	0					7.70	0	
Test	2003/04	10	15	5	88	24*	8.80	0	0	2576	1175	51	23.03	5-48	2	0	2.73	3	
FC	1997/98	81	109	25	930	50	11.07	0	1	15435	7688	342	22.47	7-70	17	0	2.98	24	
Int	1999	32	11	5	10	2	1.66	0	0	1642	1192	33	36.12	3-32	0	0	4.35	10	
Lim	1997/98	115	62	22	421	42	10.52	0	0	5983	4467	149	29.97	5-24	3	2	4.48	25	
I20T	2006/07	1								12	19	0					9.50	0	
20T	2004/05	6	5	1	23	7*	5.75	0	0	115	134	5	26.80	3-15	0	0	6.99	2	
SHADAB KABIR Siddiqi, Mohammad (Karachi Whites) b Karachi, Sind 12.11.1977 LHB OB																			
FC		4	7	0	101	53	14.42	0	1	40	56	0					8.40	0	
Test	1996	5	7	0	148	55	21.14	0	1	6	9	0					9.00	11	
FC	1995/96	135	228	11	6947	176	32.01	11	42	747	519	10	51.90	2-9	0	0	4.16	100	
Int	1996	3	3	0	0	0	0.00	0	0									1	
Lim	1995/96	81	81	8	2813	152*	38.53	4	18	197	215	4	53.75	1-26	0	0	6.54	30	
20T	2004/05	10	10	1	257	45	28.55	0	0									4	
SHAHAB BASHARAT (Lahore Eagles) b Lahore, Punjab 5.11.1987 RHB RMF																			
Lim		2	2	0	30	27	15.00	0	0									0	
FC	2007/08	1								18	20	0					6.66	0	
Lim	2007/08	3	3	0	44	27	14.66	0	0	18	26	0					8.66	0	
20T	2008/09	1	1	0	22	22	22.00	0	0									1	
SHAHBAZ BUTT (Lahore Ravi) b Lahore, Punjab 14.4.1980 RHB WK																			
FC		5	8	1	127	67*	18.14	0	1									20	1
FC	2002/03	24	39	5	619	67*	18.20	0	1	138	86	2	43.00	2-58	0	0	3.73	76	4
Lim	2002/03	28	22	6	460	81*	28.75	0	2									27	9
20T	2009	1	1	0	0	0	0.00	0	0									0	1
SHAHBAZ HUSSAIN (Multan) b Khanewal, Punjab 15.1.1985 RHB LMF																			
FC		1	2	2	0	0*		0	0	48	38	0					4.75	0	
Lim	2008/09	1								18	10	1	10.00	1-10	0	0	3.33	0	
SHAHID Pervez ABBASI (Multan) b Bahawalpur, Punjab 4.2.1986 RHB LB																			
FC		3	6	0	174	56	29.00	0	1	24	29	0					7.25	0	
SHAHID Khan AFRIDI, Sahibzada Mohammad (Karachi Dolphins, Pakistan to Australia, Pakistan to England, Pakistan to South Africa, Pakistan to Sri Lanka, Pakistan to United Arab Emirates, Pakistan to West Indies, South Australia) b Khyber Agency 1.3.1980 RHB LBG																			
20T		3	2	1	33	29	33.00	0	0	72	68	6	11.33	3-21	0	0	5.66	0	
Test	1998/99	27	48	1	1716	156	36.51	5	8	3194	1709	48	35.60	5-52	1	0	3.21	10	
FC	1995/96	111	183	4	5631	164	31.45	12	30	13493	7023	258	27.22	6-101	8	0	3.12	75	
Int	1996/97	301	283	18	6321	124	23.85	6	30	12810	9888	282	35.06	6-38	2	3	4.63	100	
Lim	1995/96	392	371	21	8971	124	25.63	8	49	16905	13046	386	33.79	6-38	3	5	4.63	123	
I20T	2006	37	35	3	602	54*	18.81	0	3	858	884	47	18.80	4-11	2	0	6.18	11	
20T	2004	72	65	5	1049	54*	17.48	0	3	1575	1645	88	18.69	4-11	3	0	6.26	21	
SHAHID AKRAM (Multan Tigers) b Arifwala, Punjab 17.6.1978 RHB RFM																			
Lim		1	1	0	19	19	19.00	0	0									0	
20T		1	1	0	0	0	0.00	0	0									0	
SHAHID JALAL (Faisalabad) b Faisalabad, Punjab 4.3.1982 RHB LB																			
FC		2	4	1	51	25*	17.00	0	0									3	
FC	2002/03	4	7	1	64	25*	10.66	0	0	12	10	0					5.00	6	
Lim	2002/03	1	1	0	21	21	21.00	0	0									1	
SHAHID NAZIR Bajwa (Faisalabad Wolves, Habib Bank) b Faisalabad, Punjab 4.12.1977 RHB RFM																			
FC		5	6	2	76	33	19.00	0	0	546	255	9	28.33	2-23	0	0	2.80	6	
Lim		3	1	0	0	0	0.00	0	0	156	132	5	26.40	3-48	0	0	5.07	0	
20T		4	2	1	18	18*	18.00	0	0	69	70	6	11.66	2-6	0	0	6.08	1	
Test	1996/97	15	19	3	194	40	12.12	0	0	2234	1272	36	35.33	5-53	1	0	3.41	5	
FC	1995/96	124	155	31	1585	60*	12.78	0	2	18205	9353	443	21.11	7-39	18	1	3.08	40	

Cmp	Debut	M	I	NO	Runs	HS	Avge	100	50	Balls	Runs	Wkts	Avge	BB	5i	10m	RpO	ct	st
Int	1996	17	8	7	25	8	25.00	0	0	810	649	19	34.15	3-14	0	0	4.80	4	
Lim	1995/96	83	39	20	259	31	13.63	0	0	3797	2621	108	24.26	5-30	1	1	4.14	24	
20T	2004/05	9	3	1	18	18*	9.00	0	0	174	176	14	12.57	4-11	1	0	6.06	2	
SHAHID Ali QAMBRANI (Hyderabad, Hyderabad Hawks) b Kotri, Sind 2.2.1978 RHB RM																			
FC		9	18	1	464	150*	27.29	1	2	60	33	2	16.50	2-16	0	0	3.30	5	
Lim		2	2	1	65	55*	65.00	0	1									0	
20T		2	2	0	23	12	11.50	0	0									1	
FC	1998/99	85	153	12	4097	150*	29.05	8	23	1183	691	17	40.64	4-137	0	0	3.50	51	
Lim	1998/99	41	40	7	1394	112*	42.24	3	9	308	271	3	90.33	1-28	0	0	5.27	10	
20T	2004/05	13	13	2	249	48*	22.63	0	0									2	
SHAHID SIDDIQ (Faisalabad Wolves) b Kasur, Punjab 20.9.1987 LHB LB																			
Lim		1	1	0	79	79	79.00	0	1	6	10	0					10.00	1	
SHAHID YOUSUF (Sialkot Stallions, ZTBL) b Sialkot, Punjab 15.6.1986 RHB RM																			
FC		9	14	1	540	104	41.53	1	4	324	149	4	37.25	1-8	0	0	2.75	13	
Lim		4	4	0	80	46	20.00	0	0	6	7	0					7.00	2	
20T		4	4	1	84	31	28.00	0	0									5	
FC	2002/03	73	118	13	3488	125*	33.21	4	18	700	334	8	41.75	2-22	0	0	2.86	78	1
Lim	2001/02	81	80	6	2560	113	34.59	2	20	367	305	6	50.83	2-12	0	0	4.98	33	
20T	2004/05	24	23	3	404	68	20.20	0	1									11	
SHAHNAWAZ Atray MALIK (Lahore Ravi) b Lahore, Punjab 10.1.1984 RHB LB																			
FC		1	2	1	81	43*	81.00	0	0									1	
FC	2001/02	36	59	4	1160	104*	21.09	1	5	262	262	8	32.75	5-78	1	0	6.00	7	
Lim	2000/01	27	26	2	651	105	27.12	1	3	81	88	4	22.00	4-29	1	0	6.51	3	
20T	2004/05	9	9	1	210	61*	26.25	0	2									2	
SHAHZAD TAREEN, Mohammad (Quetta) b Quetta, Baluchistan 24.12.1988 RHB OB WK																			
FC		9	18	0	375	70	20.83	0	2	18	16	0					5.33	2	
FC	2006/07	19	37	1	545	70	15.13	0	2	150	103	0					4.12	16	1
Lim	2006/07	3	3	0	102	57	34.00	0	1	1	4	0					24.00	1	
SHAHZAIB AHMED Khan (Karachi Whites) b Karachi, Sind 8.9.1991 RHB LB																			
FC		2	1	0	8	8	8.00	0	0	305	208	4	52.00	2-38	0	0	4.09	1	
FC	2007/08	6	5	2	81	51*	27.00	0	1	791	467	10	46.70	3-94	0	0	3.54	2	
Lim	2007/08	2	1	0	7	7	7.00	0	0	96	67	4	16.75	3-38	0	0	4.18	2	
20T	2008/09	1	1	1	2	2*		0	0	24	26	0					6.50	0	
SHAHZAIB HASAN Khan, Mohammad (Karachi Blues, Karachi Dolphins, Sind Dolphins, Pakistan to England, Pakistan to Sri Lanka, Pakistan A to United Arab Emirates) b Karachi, Sind 25.12.1989 RHB OB																			
FC		14	26	0	880	127	33.84	2	3	186	127	4	31.75	2-13	0	0	4.09	10	
Lim		5	5	0	246	78	49.20	0	3	72	74	0					6.16	1	
20T		3	3	0	85	46	28.33	0	0									0	
FC	2008/09	24	44	1	1487	156	34.58	3	7	294	180	4	45.00	2-13	0	0	3.67	16	
Int	2010	2	2	0	61	50	30.50	0	1									0	
Lim	2007/08	16	16	0	670	111	41.87	2	5	152	143	2	71.50	1-1	0	0	5.64	7	
I20T	2009	8	8	0	101	35	12.62	0	0									3	
20T	2008/09	20	20	0	525	64	26.25	0	4	6	11	0					11.00	5	
SHAKEEL ANSAR (Sialkot Stallions, ZTBL) b Sialkot, Punjab 11.11.1978 RHB WK																			
FC		2	3	0	30	16	10.00	0	0									8	1
20T		4	2	2	11	11*		0	0									3	
FC	1997/98	42	61	6	651	54	11.83	0	1									123	7
Lim	1997/98	34	26	6	401	80*	20.05	0	2									47	9
20T	2008/09	12	4	2	18	11*	9.00	0	0									7	1
SHAKEEL SHAH, Syed (Abbottabad Rhinos) b Kohat, North-West Frontier Province 13.1.1988 LHB SLA																			
Lim		2	2	0	18	15	9.00	0	0	89	73	2	36.50	2-44	0	0	4.92	2	
SHAKEEL-UR-REHMAN (Sui Southern Gas) b Peshawar, North-West Frontier Province 1.6.1982 RHB RM																			
FC		10	15	6	73	15	8.11	0	0	1903	1042	28	37.21	6-105	1	0	3.28	2	
FC	1999/00	45	63	20	344	45	8.00	0	0	7288	4156	149	27.89	6-28	9	2	3.42	8	
Lim	1999/00	25	16	5	25	8	2.27	0	0	1025	809	16	50.56	3-23	0	0	4.73	3	
20T	2005/06	6	2	1	5	5	5.00	0	0	114	177	4	44.25	3-30	0	0	9.31	2	
SHAN MASOOD (Habib Bank) b Kuwait 14.10.1989 LHB RMF																			
FC		9	16	2	516	98*	36.85	0	4	12	27	0					13.50	7	
Lim		3	3	0	129	72	43.00	0	1									1	
FC	2007/08	13	22	2	639	98*	31.95	0	5	12	27	0					13.50	10	
Lim	2007/08	4	4	0	154	72	38.50	0	1									1	
SHARJEEL KHAN (Hyderabad, Hyderabad Hawks, The Rest) b Hyderabad, Sind 14.8.1989 LHB LB																			
FC		12	23	0	797	135	34.65	2	3	66	49	2	24.50	2-3	0	0	4.45	6	
Lim		4	4	0	139	109	34.75	1	0									1	
20T		2	2	0	43	39	21.50	0	0									1	
Lim	2008/09	5	5	0	151	109	30.20	1	0									1	
20T	2005/06	3	3	0	48	39	16.00	0	0									2	
SHEHARYAR GHANI (Karachi Blues, Karachi Dolphins, Sind Dolphins, Pakistan A to Sri Lanka) b Karachi, Sind 9.9.1985 LHB RMF																			
FC		9	15	1	463	159	33.07	1	1	102	46	1	46.00	1-32	0	0	2.70	4	
Lim		5	5	1	244	86	61.00	0	2									1	

Cmp	Debut	M	I	NO	Runs	HS	Avge	100	50	Balls	Runs	Wkts	Avge	BB	5i	10m	RpO	ct	st
20T		2	1	0	4	4	4.00	0	0									0	
FC	2007/08	22	35	2	1433	181*	43.42	4	5	114	59	1	59.00	1-32	0	0	3.10	10	
Lim	2007/08	22	22	1	622	93	29.61	0	5	31	29	1	29.00	1-25	0	0	5.61	8	
20T	2009	4	3	0	26	22	8.66	0	0									0	
SHEHZAD AZAM Rana (Federal Areas Leopards, Islamabad, Islamabad Leopards) b Sialkot, Punjab 1.11.1985 RHB RFM																			
FC		8	14	2	177	36*	14.75	0	0	1700	1170	49	23.87	7-36	3	1	4.12	8	
Lim		8	5	1	31	23	7.75	0	0	315	274	13	21.07	4-65	1	0	5.21	2	
20T		1								24	29	0					7.25	0	
FC	2007/08	28	40	11	403	36*	13.89	0	0	4111	3095	102	30.34	7-36	5	1	4.51	14	
Lim	2007/08	14	9	3	48	23	8.00	0	0	525	512	17	30.11	4-65	1	0	5.85	7	
20T	2009	3								66	85	3	28.33	2-35	0	0	7.72	1	
SHEHZAD BUTT, Mohammad (Sui Southern Gas) b Lahore, Punjab 4.2.1974 RHB RFM																			
FC		3	5	0	143	88	28.60	0	1	267	156	2	78.00	1-36	0	0	3.50	0	
FC	1994/95	58	89	21	1299	88	19.10	0	6	7929	4651	160	29.06	6-72	5	0	3.51	25	
Lim	1994/95	18	12	6	50	13*	8.33	0	0	772	656	32	20.50	6-36	0	1	5.09	3	
20T	2005/06	5	3	1	11	7*	5.50	0	0	107	163	5	32.60	2-28	0	0	9.14	2	
SHEHZAD MALIK (Sialkot Stallions) b Sialkot, Punjab 8.4.1977 RHB RM																			
Lim		7	6	2	217	80	54.25	0	3									7	
FC	1997/98	77	123	20	4226	131*	41.02	7	28	120	80	0					4.00	63	1
Lim	1997/98	71	65	11	2111	105	39.09	1	16	125	115	2	57.50	1-10	0	0	5.52	25	
20T	2005/06	12	8	2	101	30	16.83	0	0									5	
SHEHZAR MOHAMMAD (PIA) b Karachi, Sind 12.11.1991 RHB OB WK																			
FC		2	3	1	151	70	75.50	0	2	12	16	0					8.00	3	
Lim		1	1	0	14	14	14.00	0	0									1	
SHERAZ Riaz BUTT (Lahore Shalimar) b Lahore, Punjab 8.7.1978 RHB OB																			
FC		5	10	1	174	65	19.33	0	1	523	390	7	55.71	3-54	0	0	4.47	1	
FC	2001/02	14	23	5	420	96	23.33	0	2	755	476	12	39.66	5-65	1	0	3.78	7	
Lim	1999/00	11	10	1	152	30	16.88	0	0	126	131	1	131.00	1-32	0	0	6.23	5	
SHOAIB AKHTAR (Federal Areas Leopards, Islamabad Leopards, KRL, Chittagong, Pakistan to England, Pakistan to Sri Lanka) b Rawalpindi, Punjab 13.8.1975 RHB RF																			
Lim		6	4	0	41	24	10.25	0	0	307	253	13	19.46	6-52	0	1	4.94	2	
20T		1	1	0	0	0	0.00	0	0	24	21	1	21.00	1-21	0	0	5.25	0	
Test	1997/98	46	67	13	544	47	10.07	0	0	8143	4574	178	25.69	6-11	12	2	3.37	12	
FC	1994/95	133	186	50	1670	59*	12.27	0	1	20460	12265	467	26.26	6-11	28	2	3.59	41	
Int	1997/98	152	76	35	383	43	9.34	0	0	7242	5659	235	24.08	6-16	6	4	4.68	18	
Lim	1993/94	210	115	40	866	56	11.54	0	1	10105	8012	326	24.57	6-16	13	7	4.75	33	
I20T	2006	11	3	1	5	4	2.50	0	0	222	287	12	23.91	2-11	0	0	7.75	2	
20T	2003	31	16	3	59	14	4.53	0	0	636	763	31	24.61	5-23	1	1	7.19	7	
SHOAIB KHAN (PIA) b Peshawar, North-West Frontier Province 27.7.1978 RHB OB																			
FC		8	13	1	309	73	25.75	0	3									14	
FC	1999/00	96	156	17	4982	300*	35.84	9	26	231	74	4	18.50	2-11	0	0	1.92	114	1
Lim	1996/97	56	50	6	1012	82	23.00	0	5	60	78	0					7.80	22	
20T	2004/05	2	1	0	23	23	23.00	0	0									1	
SHOAIB KHAN (Quetta, Quetta Bears) b Bostan, Baluchistan 13.4.1985 LHB RMF																			
FC		10	20	2	647	111*	35.94	2	2	3	5	0					10.00	8	
Lim		4	4	0	80	43	20.00	0	0	105	93	5	18.60	3-28	0	0	5.31	0	
20T		3	3	0	48	21	16.00	0	0	33	49	3	16.33	3-36	0	0	8.90	2	
FC	2003/04	52	99	3	3184	185	33.16	7	11	238	190	2	95.00	1-11	0	0	4.79	44	
Lim	2003/04	30	30	0	734	75	24.46	0	5	218	209	6	34.83	3-28	0	0	5.75	6	
I20T	2008/09	4	4	0	65	50	16.25	0	1									1	
20T	2004/05	20	20	0	466	85	23.30	0	4	45	73	4	18.25	3-36	0	0	9.73	8	
SHOAIB LAGHARI (Hyderabad) b Hyderabad, Sind 21.3.1986 RHB OB																			
FC		1	2	0	78	47	39.00	0	0	150	110	2	55.00	2-92	0	0	4.40	0	
FC	2005/06	12	17	2	454	117	30.26	1	0	1760	957	29	33.00	5-46	1	0	3.26	3	
Lim	2004/05	9	5	1	17	12	4.25	0	0	390	305	10	30.50	6-46	0	1	4.69	3	
20T	2004/05	8	7	0	56	18	8.00	0	0	131	184	3	61.33	2-15	0	0	8.42	0	
SHOAIB MALIK (PIA, Sialkot Stallions, Pakistan to Australia, Pakistan to England, Pakistan to New Zealand, Pakistan to South Africa, Pakistan to Sri Lanka, Pakistan to United Arab Emirates) b Sialkot, Punjab 1.2.1982 RHB OB																			
FC		2	3	0	66	30	22.00	0	0	186	65	3	21.66	2-10	0	0	2.09	0	
Lim		1	1	0	102	102	102.00	1	0	54	41	2	20.50	2-41	0	0	4.55	3	
20T		4	4	2	141	67	70.50	0	1	12	18	0					9.00	2	
Test	2001/02	32	54	6	1606	148*	33.45	2	8	2245	1291	21	61.47	4-42	0	0	3.45	16	
FC	1997	95	147	17	3856	148*	29.66	8	17	11144	5559	179	31.05	7-81	5	1	2.99	44	
Int	1999/00	192	172	21	5188	143	34.35	7	31	6384	4863	134	36.29	4-19	1	0	4.57	68	
Lim	1997	270	231	37	7371	143	37.99	12	44	10388	7744	250	30.97	5-35	6	1	4.47	107	
I20T	2006	32	31	6	636	57	25.44	0	2	258	286	14	20.42	2-14	0	0	6.65	14	
20T	2004/05	67	63	20	1676	88*	38.97	0	10	692	803	39	20.58	5-13	0	1	6.96	33	
SOHAIB MAQSOOD (KRL) b Multan, Punjab 15.4.1987 RHB OB																			
FC		2	4	1	116	71	38.66	0	1	18	23	0					7.66	2	
FC	2003/04	14	25	4	766	123	36.47	1	5	492	367	3	122.33	2-52	0	0	4.47	9	

Cmp	Debut	M	I	NO	Runs	HS	Avge	100	50	Balls	Runs	Wkts	Avge	BB	5i	10m	RpO	ct	st
Lim	2003/04	13	10	1	247	53	27.44	0	1	426	370	14	26.42	4-49	1	0	5.21	7	
20T	2004/05	5	5	0	148	59	29.60	0	1	60	64	0					6.40	2	
SOHAIL AHMED (Lahore Lions, Lahore Ravi) b Lahore, Punjab 5.11.1985 LHB SLA																			
FC		10	16	0	395	111	24.68	2	1	456	298	4	74.50	2-36	0	0	3.92	2	
Lim		3	3	1	108	81	54.00	0	1	167	162	1	162.00	1-41	0	0	5.82	1	
20T		4	3	1	52	25	26.00	0	0	72	93	0					7.75	1	
FC	2003/04	45	76	3	1795	126	24.58	5	5	2479	1362	35	38.91	4-38	0	0	3.29	8	
Lim	2003/04	37	31	8	896	91	38.95	0	5	1802	1490	36	41.38	3-20	0	0	4.96	4	
20T	2004/05	26	18	5	216	31	16.61	0	0	556	581	37	15.70	4-13	4	0	6.27	6	
SOHAIL IDREES, Mohammad (Lahore Shalimar) b Lahore, Punjab 3.6.1972 RHB OB																			
FC		10	20	1	587	104*	30.89	1	4	28	21	0					4.50	5	
FC	1994/95	49	84	3	2111	154	26.06	2	13	94	47	1	47.00	1-7	0	0	3.00	28	
Lim	1995/96	34	33	2	1180	111	38.06	3	6	60	52	1	52.00	1-36	0	0	5.20	11	
SOHAIL KHAN (Islamabad Leopards) b Islamabad, Punjab 16.1.1982 LHB SLA																			
Lim		2	1	0	7	7	7.00	0	0	72	81	3	27.00	2-57	0	0	6.75	0	
SOHAIL KHAN (Karachi Dolphins, Khyber Pakhtunkhwa Panthers, Sui Southern Gas) b Malakand, North-West Frontier Province 6.3.1984 RHB RMF																			
FC		7	11	3	67	17*	8.37	0	0	1329	736	21	35.04	6-34	2	0	3.32	1	
Lim		7	4	0	37	14	9.25	0	0	354	333	12	27.75	4-35	1	0	5.64	1	
20T		2	1	1	0	0*		0	0	42	42	2	21.00	1-17	0	0	6.00	0	
Test	2008/09	1								162	164	0					6.07	0	
FC	2007/08	28	36	13	268	29	11.65	0	0	5888	3379	139	24.30	9-109	14	2	3.44	6	
Int	2007/08	4	1	0	4	4	4.00	0	0	199	163	5	32.60	3-30	0	0	4.91	0	
Lim	2007/08	22	13	2	83	14	7.54	0	0	1128	910	36	25.27	4-35	2	0	4.84	3	
I20T	2008/09	1								6	7	0					7.00	0	
20T	2008/09	9	3	2	8	7	8.00	0	0	172	160	10	16.00	2-5	0	0	5.58	3	
SOHAIL NASIR (WAPDA) b Rawalpindi, Punjab 13.1.1982 LHB OB																			
FC		1	2	0	22	22	11.00	0	0									2	
FC	2003/04	14	27	1	327	29	12.57	0	0									9	
Lim	2001/02	19	19	0	695	122	36.57	2	2	24	21	1	21.00	1-21	0	0	5.25	8	
SOHAIL TANVIR (ZTBL, Pakistan to United Arab Emirates) b Rawalpindi, Punjab 12.12.1984 LHB LMF																			
FC		2	4	0	116	116	29.00	1	0	321	167	5	33.40	2-32	0	0	3.12	1	
Test	2007/08	2	3	0	17	13	5.66	0	0	504	316	5	63.20	3-83	0	0	3.76	2	
FC	2004/05	35	58	9	1466	132	29.91	4	7	7525	4121	149	27.65	8-54	9	2	3.28	15	
Int	2007/08	31	18	5	182	59	14.00	0	1	1542	1272	44	28.90	5-48	2	1	4.94	8	
Lim	2005/06	56	36	6	495	93	16.50	0	2	2876	2482	88	28.20	7-34	4	2	5.17	12	
I20T	2007/08	15	5	1	29	12	7.25	0	0	306	365	11	33.18	3-31	0	0	7.15	3	
20T	2004/05	46	25	7	227	38	12.61	0	0	901	1074	47	22.85	6-14	1	1	7.15	15	
SULAMAN QADIR (Habib Bank, Lahore Lions) b Lahore, Punjab 28.12.1984 RHB OB																			
FC		2	4	1	77	34	25.66	0	0	114	97	1	97.00	1-66	0	0	5.10	2	
Lim		1	1	0	6	6	6.00	0	0	60	32	2	16.00	2-32	0	0	3.20	2	
20T		4	4	2	29	12*	14.50	0	0	48	52	2	26.00	1-17	0	0	6.50	1	
FC	2002/03	21	36	4	676	125	21.12	1	0	792	461	10	46.10	3-66	0	0	3.49	13	
Lim	2000/01	36	31	9	548	45*	24.90	0	0	1175	830	23	36.08	4-48	1	0	4.23	9	
20T	2004/05	9	8	3	55	23*	11.00	0	0	138	179	7	25.57	2-31	0	0	7.78	1	
SULEMAN KHAN (Lahore Shalimar) b Lahore, Punjab 4.6.1983 RHB SLA																			
FC		8	16	2	403	61*	28.78	0	4	509	274	4	68.50	1-13	0	0	3.23	5	
FC	2002/03	26	46	5	1268	129*	30.92	1	10	645	379	7	54.14	2-43	0	0	3.52	16	
Lim	2001/02	11	9	1	184	42*	23.00	0	0	426	353	10	35.30	3-39	0	0	4.97	7	
20T	2008/09	3	2	0	26	14	13.00	0	0	34	36	3	12.00	2-18	0	0	6.35	0	
TABISH KHAN (Karachi Whites, Karachi Zebras, Sind Dolphins, The Rest, Pakistan A to Sri Lanka, Pakistan A to United Arab Emirates) b Karachi, Sind 12.12.1984 RHB RFM																			
FC		14	22	4	187	37	10.38	0	0	3090	1819	77	23.62	7-72	7	1	3.53	1	
Lim		1								42	32	1	32.00	1-32	0	0	4.57	0	
20T		1								24	37	0					9.25	0	
FC	2002/03	40	57	12	484	57	10.75	0	2	8095	4443	160	27.76	7-72	8	1	3.29	6	
Lim	2002/03	15	10	4	38	19*	6.33	0	0	666	651	15	43.40	2-19	0	0	5.86	2	
20T	2005/06	7	3	1	13	10	6.50	0	0	132	174	4	43.50	2-26	0	0	7.90	0	
TABISH NAWAB (Karachi Blues) b Karachi, Sind 27.2.1981 RHB OB																			
FC		2	2	0	5	3	2.50	0	0	150	99	2	49.50	2-99	0	0	3.96	1	
FC	1999/00	39	43	14	184	24*	6.34	0	0	8705	4305	137	31.42	7-64	8	1	2.96	15	
Lim	1998/99	52	25	14	98	20	8.90	0	0	2585	2050	65	31.53	4-28	1	0	4.75	8	
TAHIR KHAN, Mohammad (Karachi Dolphins, PIA) b Karachi, Sind 9.1.1981 RHB OB																			
FC		7	8	5	222	50*	74.00	0	1	936	512	11	46.54	5-150	1	0	3.28	5	
Lim		4	2	0	29	21	14.50	0	0	240	164	3	54.66	2-35	0	0	4.10	6	
20T		1								18	22	1	22.00	1-22	0	0	7.33	0	
FC	1999/00	69	90	25	1797	85	27.64	0	7	12519	6149	218	28.20	8-48	9	0	2.94	63	
Lim	1999/00	66	32	8	403	65	16.79	0	1	3491	2500	73	34.24	5-17	3	1	4.29	31	
20T	2005/06	14	6	1	51	19	10.20	0	0	269	321	15	21.40	2-6	0	0	7.16	4	

Cmp	Debut	M	I	NO	Runs	HS	Avge	100	50	Balls	Runs	Wkts	Avge	BB	5i	10m	RpO	ct	st
TAHIR MAQSOOD (Multan, Multan Tigers) b Bahawalpur, Punjab 3.3.1981 RHB RMF																			
FC		6	8	4	22	11*	5.50	0	0	921	473	14	33.78	5-76	1	0	3.08	1	
Lim		1								30	32	0					6.40	0	
FC	2001/02	34	46	19	259	32	9.59	0	0	4883	2882	91	31.67	7-61	3	0	3.54	6	
Lim	2001/02	11	5	1	12	6	3.00	0	0	482	455	13	35.00	4-26	1	0	5.66	0	
20T	2004/05	2	1	0	1	1	1.00	0	0	48	69	2	34.50	1-25	0	0	8.62	0	
TAHIR Mahmood MUGHAL (Customs, Rawalpindi Rams) b Daska, Punjab 25.4.1977 RHB RFM																			
FC		6	11	2	213	41*	23.66	0	0	1031	439	23	19.08	5-101	1	0	2.55	3	
Lim		3	3	0	16	14	5.33	0	0	126	96	0					4.57	0	
20T		2	2	0	92	58	46.00	0	1	24	42	0					10.50	0	
FC	1997/98	102	157	20	2820	70	20.58	0	12	19252	10282	476	21.60	7-50	36	7	3.20	44	
Lim	1997/98	77	57	13	944	118*	21.45	1	3	3499	2845	83	34.27	3-26	0	0	4.87	25	
20T	2005/06	18	12	2	309	94	30.90	0	2	275	364	10	36.40	2-22	0	0	7.94	3	
TAIMUR AHMED Dogar (Multan Tigers) b Lahore, Punjab 24.7.1983 RHB OB																			
Lim		3	3	0	55	42	18.33	0	0									0	
FC	2008/09	5	9	0	142	38	15.77	0	0									3	
TAIMUR ALI (Quetta, Quetta Bears) b Usta Mohammad, Jacobabad, Sind 1.6.1991 RHB OB																			
FC		10	20	0	353	54	17.65	0	2	6	7	0					7.00	6	
Lim		4	4	0	112	81	28.00	0	1									3	
20T		3	3	0	9	4	3.00	0	0									1	
FC	2007/08	27	50	0	964	110	19.28	1	4	6	7	0					7.00	12	
Lim	2006/07	13	13	0	285	81	21.92	0	1									4	
20T	2009	6	6	0	89	42	14.83	0	0									1	
TAIMUR KHAN (Baluchistan Bears, Quetta Bears) b Quetta, Baluchistan 25.1.1991 RHB OB WK																			
Lim		3	3	2	113	55*	113.00	0	2									1	
20T		2	2	0	30	29	15.00	0	0									0	
Lim	2008/09	6	6	2	160	55*	40.00	0	2									2	
TAIMUR SIDDIQ (Quetta Bears) b Quetta, Baluchistan 12.8.1988 RHB WK																			
Lim		2	2	0	14	11	7.00	0	0									0	
20T		2	2	0	47	32	23.50	0	0									0	
TALIB ALI, Syed (Karachi Whites, Karachi Zebras) b Karachi, Sind 25.12.1986 LHB LAB																			
FC		2	4	0	63	24	15.75	0	0									2	
Lim		2	2	0	14	12	7.00	0	0									0	
FC	2008/09	3	6	0	73	24	12.16	0	0									3	
TANVIR AHMED (Karachi Blues, Karachi Dolphins, Sind Dolphins, Pakistan A to United Arab Emirates) b Kuwait City, Kuwait 20.12.1978 RHB RFM																			
FC		15	24	2	440	88	20.00	0	2	3055	1962	97	20.22	8-53	8	3	3.85	5	
Lim		4	2	1	53	47	53.00	0	0	216	231	4	57.75	2-62	0	0	6.41	0	
20T		3	1	0	15	15	15.00	0	0	66	87	3	29.00	1-11	0	0	7.90	2	
FC	1999/00	102	157	23	2801	90	20.90	0	13	19360	11253	400	28.13	8-53	24	7	3.48	33	
Lim	1998/99	64	37	5	347	47	10.84	0	0	2935	2736	81	33.77	5-33	0	1	5.59	15	
20T	2005/06	15	9	3	107	35	17.83	0	0	271	433	10	43.30	2-50	0	0	9.58	6	
TANZEEL ALTAF, Mohammad (Lahore Eagles) b Lahore, Punjab 16.6.1991 RHB LB																			
Lim		3	2	1	0	0*	0.00	0	0	72	69	2	34.50	2-28	0	0	5.75	1	
Lim	2008/09	5	4	1	3	2	1.00	0	0	120	127	3	42.33	2-28	0	0	6.35	2	
TARIQ HAROON, Mohammad (Karachi Blues, Karachi Dolphins) b Karachi, Sind 3.2.1977 RHB RM																			
FC		12	21	3	348	53	19.33	0	1	2009	1122	46	24.39	6-127	2	0	3.35	7	
Lim		2	1	0	6	6	6.00	0	0	66	42	1	42.00	1-29	0	0	3.81	1	
20T		1								24	21	1	21.00	1-21	0	0	5.25	0	
FC	2001/02	44	75	5	1720	142*	24.57	1	5	6186	3207	127	25.25	6-127	4	0	3.11	27	
Lim	2000/01	37	34	5	984	120	33.93	3	3	913	830	23	36.08	3-13	0	0	5.45	11	
20T	2004/05	7	5	2	45	18	15.00	0	0	78	93	1	93.00	1-21	0	0	7.15	0	
TARIQ MAHMOOD (KRL) b Gujranwala, Punjab 22.4.1985 RHB OB																			
FC		2	1	0	32	32	32.00	0	0	218	115	5	23.00	3-45	0	0	3.16	2	
FC	2003/04	17	20	5	300	46	20.00	0	0	2356	1257	33	38.09	4-26	0	0	3.20	9	
Lim	2001/02	11	6	0	20	9	3.33	0	0	528	449	12	37.41	3-50	0	0	5.10	2	
20T	2004/05	1								24	29	1	29.00	1-29	0	0	7.25	0	
TAUFEEQ UMAR (Baluchistan Bears, Habib Bank, Lahore Eagles) b Lahore, Punjab 20.6.1981 LHB OB																			
FC		11	20	2	756	154*	42.00	3	1	78	41	1	41.00	1-12	0	0	3.15	7	
Lim		9	9	1	345	100*	43.12	1	2	36	25	1	25.00	1-18	0	0	4.16	4	
20T		1	1	0	34	34	34.00	0	0									1	
Test	2001/02	25	46	2	1729	135	39.29	4	9	78	44	0					3.38	33	
FC	1998/99	110	190	9	6951	176	38.40	14	38	820	452	13	34.76	3-33	0	0	3.30	113	
Int	2001/02	19	19	1	447	81*	24.83	0	3	72	85	1	85.00	1-49	0	0	7.08	9	
Lim	1997/98	111	111	14	3913	151*	40.34	9	19	1223	1108	31	35.74	5-39	0	1	5.43	70	
20T	2004/05	8	8	1	285	100*	40.71	1	1	72	73	7	10.42	4-11	1	0	6.08	5	
TAUQEER HUSSAIN (Faisalabad) b Faisalabad, Punjab 6.10.1981 RHB RFM																			
FC		2	3	0	5	3	1.66	0	0	198	92	2	46.00	1-37	0	0	2.78	1	
FC	2002/03	26	38	3	687	100	19.62	1	3	1871	1058	47	22.51	6-65	2	0	3.39	12	
Lim	2000/01	40	33	4	478	51	16.48	0	1	1448	1260	35	36.00	5-35	1	1	5.22	12	
20T	2004/05	14	8	5	43	18*	14.33	0	0	168	239	8	29.87	2-27	0	0	8.53	5	

Cmp	Debut	M	I	NO	Runs	HS	Avge	100	50	Balls	Runs	Wkts	Avge	BB	5i	10m	RpO	ct	st
UMAID ASIF (WAPDA) b Gujranwala, Punjab 30.4.1984 RHB RMF																			
FC		8	10	2	181	67	22.62	0	1	976	629	19	33.10	4-60	0	0	3.86	6	
Lim		2	2	1	5	3	5.00	0	0	120	117	3	39.00	2-51	0	0	5.85	0	
UMAIR KHAN, Mohammad (Abbottabad) b Haripur, North-West Frontier Province 17.9.1982 RHB RMF																			
FC		1	2	0	0	0	0.00	0	0	96	79	0					4.93	0	
FC	2001/02	8	15	2	37	13	2.84	0	0	758	542	17	31.88	4-54	0	0	4.29	1	
Lim	2001/02	7	6	1	30	13*	6.00	0	0	294	253	10	25.30	3-29	0	0	5.16	0	
UMAIR KHAN (Federal Areas Leopards, Islamabad, Islamabad Leopards, The Rest, Pakistan A to United Arab Emirates) b Kohat, North-West Frontier Province 31.7.1985 LHB OB																			
FC		14	26	1	1175	194	47.00	3	6	126	69	1	69.00	1-9	0	0	3.28	8	
Lim		4	4	0	75	46	18.75	0	0									2	
20T		2	2	1	52	40*	52.00	0	0									1	
FC	2007/08	39	70	6	2346	194	36.65	4	13	132	70	2	35.00	1-1	0	0	3.18	18	
Lim	2006/07	18	17	1	522	109	32.62	2	2									6	
20T	2008/09	8	8	1	199	49	28.42	0	0									1	
UMAIR Sajid MIR (Islamabad Leopards) b Islamabad, Punjab 27.1.1990 LHB WK																			
Lim		1	1	0	17	17	17.00	0	0									0	1
FC	2007/08	1	2	0	22	13	11.00	0	0									2	1
UMAR AKMAL, Mohammad (Lahore Lions, Sui Northern Gas, Pakistan to Australia, Pakistan to England, Pakistan to New Zealand, Pakistan to South Africa, Pakistan to Sri Lanka, Pakistan to United Arab Emirates, Pakistan to West Indies) b Lahore, Punjab 26.5.1990 RHB OB																			
FC		2	3	0	98	52	32.66	0	1									1	
Lim		2	2	0	2	2	1.00	0	0									2	
20T		4	3	1	122	64*	61.00	0	1									5	
Test	2009/10	12	24	2	818	129	37.18	1	5									7	
FC	2007/08	42	72	7	3061	248	47.09	7	18	6	10	0					10.00	34	
Int	2009	23	23	3	724	102*	36.20	1	5									7	
Lim	2007/08	48	47	6	1487	104	36.26	3	9	24	13	0					3.25	21	
I20T	2009	16	15	3	455	64	37.91	0	4									11	
20T	2008/09	31	28	6	778	64*	35.36	0	5	24	36	1	36.00	1-36	0	0	9.00	23	
UMAR AMIN (Federal Areas Leopards, National Bank, Rawalpindi Rams, Pakistan to England, Pakistan to Sri Lanka) b Rawalpindi, Punjab 16.10.1989 LHB RM																			
FC		10	15	1	512	147	36.57	1	3	106	55	2	27.50	1-0	0	0	3.11	7	
Lim		9	9	1	274	85*	34.25	0	4	165	167	2	83.50	1-5	0	0	6.07	7	
20T		2	2	0	68	37	34.00	0	0									0	
Test	2010	4	8	0	99	33	12.37	0	0	132	63	3	21.00	1-7	0	0	2.86	1	
FC	2007/08	34	60	4	2113	153	37.73	4	13	500	261	9	29.00	1-0	0	0	3.13	17	
Int	2010	3	3	0	34	22	11.33	0	0									1	
Lim	2007/08	37	36	3	1171	125*	35.48	1	10	165	167	2	83.50	1-5	0	0	6.07	24	
20T	2008/09	7	7	0	161	50	23.00	0	1									0	
UMAR GUL (Habib Bank, Peshawar Panthers, Pakistan to Australia, Pakistan to England, Pakistan to New Zealand, Pakistan to South Africa, Pakistan to United Arab Emirates) b Peshawar, North-West Frontier Province 14.4.1984 RHB RFM																			
FC		2	3	0	63	47	21.00	0	0	324	173	6	28.83	3-35	0	0	3.20	0	
20T		3	3	0	34	17	11.33	0	0	66	73	4	18.25	2-15	0	0	6.63	2	
Test	2003/04	30	44	6	421	65*	11.07	0	1	6144	3639	108	33.69	6-135	4	0	3.55	7	
FC	2001/02	61	78	12	864	65*	13.09	0	1	11783	6844	249	27.48	8-78	14	1	3.48	15	
Int	2002/03	74	36	10	241	33	9.26	0	0	3578	3056	115	26.57	6-42	3	2	5.12	9	
Lim	2002/03	119	56	19	358	33	9.67	0	0	5796	4824	178	27.10	6-42	4	2	4.99	15	
I20T	2007/08	30	11	6	56	16	11.20	0	0	625	640	47	13.61	5-6	3	1	6.14	10	
20T	2004/05	58	31	11	213	24	10.65	0	0	1250	1409	92	15.31	5-6	6	1	6.76	21	
UMAR ISHAQ (Peshawar Panthers) b Peshawar, North-West Frontier Province 20.12.1988 RHB RMF																			
Lim		1	1	0	23	23	23.00	0	0									0	
UMAR WAHEED (Lahore Lions) b Lahore, Punjab 3.5.1990 RHB																			
Lim		1	1	0	31	31	31.00	0	0									0	
USAMA BASHARAT, Mohammad (Karachi Whites, Karachi Zebras) b Karachi, Sind 11.11.1989 LHB SLA																			
FC		1	2	1	32	19	32.00	0	0	216	142	1	142.00	1-142	0	0	3.94	2	
Lim		5	3	1	47	32	23.50	0	0	247	201	10	20.10	3-36	0	0	4.88	0	
USAMA SHAHROON Khan Niazi (Faisalabad) b Mianwali, Punjab 5.2.1991 RHB RMF																			
FC		2	3	0	63	54	21.00	0	1	12	7	0					3.50	3	
FC	2007/08	5	6	0	122	55	20.33	0	2	12	7	0					3.50	5	
20T	2009	1	1	0	0	0	0.00	0	0									0	
USMAN ARSHAD (Punjab Stallions, Sui Northern Gas) b Sargodha, Punjab 18.10.1983 RHB LBG																			
FC		14	22	3	857	183	45.10	2	2	24	19	0					4.75	19	
Lim		4	3	0	24	16	8.00	0	0	18	15	0					5.00	4	
FC	2000/01	51	82	10	2809	183	39.01	7	16	311	193	4	48.25	2-50	0	0	3.72	49	
Lim	2001/02	22	20	2	482	81	26.77	0	5	317	298	5	59.60	3-37	0	0	5.64	12	
20T	2008/09	1	1	0	13	13	13.00	0	0									0	
USMAN ASHRAF (ZTBL) b Rawalpindi, Punjab 29.1.1987 RHB OB																			
FC		3	4	0	70	37	17.50	0	0									1	
FC	2007/08	4	5	0	70	37	14.00	0	0									1	

Cmp	Debut	M	I	NO	Runs	HS	Avge	100	50	Balls	Runs	Wkts	Avge	BB	5i	10m	RpO	ct	st
USMAN MALIK, Mohammad (Lahore Lions, Lahore Shalimar) b Lahore, Punjab 20.7.1988 LHB OB																			
FC		6	12	3	124	74	13.77	0	1	648	392	6	65.33	2-50	0	0	3.63	3	
Lim		4	4	1	70	29*	23.33	0	0	192	135	3	45.00	2-22	0	0	4.21	1	
FC	2004/05	20	30	8	344	74	15.63	0	2	2525	1391	32	43.46	6-84	1	1	3.30	12	
Lim	2005/06	23	15	10	122	29*	24.40	0	0	1158	807	29	27.82	4-21	1	0	4.18	5	
20T	2004/05	7	4	3	18	16	18.00	0	0	160	183	8	22.87	3-22	0	0	6.86	3	
USMAN QADIR, Hafiz (ZTBL) b Lahore, Punjab 10.8.1993 LHB LB																			
Lim		3	3	2	71	42*	71.00	0	0	96	96	2	48.00	2-52	0	0	6.00	1	
USMAN SAEED, Mohammad (Federal Areas Leopards, Rawalpindi, Rawalpindi Rams) b Rawalpindi, Punjab 8.10.1986 RHB LB																			
FC		10	17	2	327	80*	21.80	0	3									4	
Lim		8	8	2	208	46*	34.66	0	0	24	25	0					6.25	1	
FC	2003/04	70	117	15	3527	243	34.57	7	20	156	94	1	94.00	1-19	0	0	3.61	27	
Lim	2003/04	44	39	10	1356	120*	46.75	2	6	102	81	0					4.76	9	
20T	2005/06	11	10	3	111	29*	15.85	0	0									3	
USMAN SALAHUDDIN (Sui Northern Gas) b Lahore, Punjab 2.12.1990 RHB LB																			
FC		4	7	0	147	116	21.00	1	0									3	
FC	2007/08	11	18	0	308	116	17.11	1	0									8	
Lim	2007/08	3	3	1	38	38*	19.00	0	0	30	32	0					6.40	0	
UZAIR-UL-HAQ (Karachi Zebras, National Bank, Pakistan A to United Arab Emirates) b Karachi, Sind 15.4.1986 RHB RMF																			
FC		8	8	5	14	4*	4.66	0	0	1348	771	34	22.67	6-65	3	1	3.43	2	
20T		1								12	23	0					11.50	0	
FC	2003/04	39	46	25	115	9	5.47	0	0	5819	3193	110	29.02	6-65	5	1	3.29	12	
Lim	2006/07	16	6	1	21	16	4.20	0	0	669	665	21	31.66	4-27	2	0	5.96	5	
20T	2009	4	1	0	0	0	0.00	0	0	48	88	0					11.00	0	
WAHAB RIAZ (Lahore Lions, National Bank, Pakistan to England, Pakistan A to United Arab Emirates) b Lahore, Punjab 28.6.1985 RHB LFM																			
FC		6	8	3	97	44	19.40	0	0	977	581	14	41.50	2-52	0	0	3.56	3	
20T		4	2	1	4	2*	4.00	0	0	84	106	4	26.50	3-32	0	0	7.57	1	
Test	2010	2	3	0	29	27	9.66	0	0	320	195	7	27.85	5-63	1	0	3.65	0	
FC	2001/02	67	92	15	1156	68	15.01	0	3	11663	6579	228	28.85	6-64	10	2	3.38	22	
Int	2007/08	5	4	1	4	3	1.33	0	0	241	202	10	20.20	3-22	0	0	5.02	1	
Lim	2001/02	57	35	16	286	42*	15.05	0	0	2576	2187	73	29.95	5-24	2	2	5.09	16	
I20T	2007/08	2								24	18	1	18.00	1-7	0	0	4.50	1	
20T	2004/05	26	14	5	95	28*	10.55	0	0	490	593	22	26.95	3-32	0	0	7.26	7	
WAHAJ ASLAM (Lahore Ravi) b Islamabad, Punjab 10.11.1988 RHB LB																			
FC		5	6	0	127	65	21.16	0	1									2	
WAJAHATULLAH WASTI, Syed (ZTBL) b Peshawar, North-West Frontier Province 11.11.1974 RHB OB																			
FC		8	12	2	274	57	27.40	0	1	144	61	4	15.25	3-13	0	0	2.54	17	
Lim		4	4	1	83	41	27.66	0	0	18	14	0					4.66	1	
Test	1998/99	6	10	1	329	133	36.55	2	0	18	8	0					2.66	7	
FC	1994/95	161	250	29	8214	196	37.16	15	46	1683	798	19	42.00	3-13	0	0	2.84	175	
Int	1998/99	15	15	0	349	84	23.26	0	1	55	69	3	23.00	3-36	0	0	7.52	5	
Lim	1994/95	106	98	6	3054	112	33.19	4	16	761	656	13	50.46	4-34	1	0	5.17	38	
20T	2005/06	11	10	1	152	48	16.88	0	0	54	59	0					6.55	2	
WAJID ALI (Abbottabad Rhinos, Khyber Pakhtunkhwa Panthers, Sui Southern Gas) b Lahore, Punjab 12.1.1981 RHB RMF																			
FC		9	17	3	477	143	34.07	1	1	48	43	0					5.37	4	
Lim		6	6	0	110	57	18.33	0	1									0	
20T		1	1	0	8	8	8.00	0	0									0	
FC	2001/02	43	72	8	2151	143	33.60	8	7	216	167	0					4.63	29	
Lim	2000/01	28	27	1	748	131	28.76	1	4	2	2	0					6.00	10	
20T	2006/07	7	7	0	81	27	11.57	0	0									1	
WAJIHUDDIN, Mohammad (Karachi Blues, Karachi Zebras) b Karachi, Sind 7.6.1980 RHB OB																			
FC		8	15	2	491	142	37.76	2	1	135	57	0					2.53	5	
Lim		5	5	0	119	50	23.80	0	1	60	64	2	32.00	2-41	0	0	6.40	1	
FC	2003/04	21	37	2	1025	142	29.28	3	4	225	128	0					3.41	14	
Lim	2006/07	16	16	0	399	80	24.93	0	3	82	96	2	48.00	2-41	0	0	7.02	6	
WAQAR AHMED (Peshawar Panthers, Sui Southern Gas) b Peshawar, North-West Frontier Province 1.4.1980 LHB LFM																			
FC		3	6	1	15	10	3.00	0	0	378	195	3	65.00	2-62	0	0	3.09	0	
Lim		1	1	0	8	8	8.00	0	0	36	63	1	63.00	1-63	0	0	10.50	0	
FC	1997/98	72	103	22	886	46	10.93	0	0	11916	6915	300	23.05	7-67	19	4	3.48	17	
Lim	1996/97	47	30	9	221	41	10.52	0	0	1873	1712	59	29.01	4-26	3	0	5.48	7	
20T	2005/06	3	1	1	1	1*		0	0	60	113	2	56.50	2-44	0	0	11.30	0	
WAQAR KHAN (Peshawar Panthers) b Mohalla Mera Khel, Charsadda, North-West Frontier Province 27.4.1987 LHB SLA																			
Lim		1	1	0	21	21	21.00	0	0	12	12	0					6.00	0	
FC	2008/09	1	2	0	15	15	7.50	0	0									0	
WAQAR KHAN (Islamabad, Islamabad Leopards) b Islamabad, Punjab 21.4.1993 RMF																			
FC		1	1	1	1	1*		0	0	90	105	1	105.00	1-33	0	0	7.00	0	
Lim		1	1	0	4	4	4.00	0	0	48	56	1	56.00	1-56	0	0	7.00	0	

Cmp	Debut	M	I	NO	Runs	HS	Avge	100	50	Balls	Runs	Wkts	Avge	BB	5i	10m	RpO	ct	st
WAQAR ORAKZAI (Abbottabad, Abbottabad Rhinos) b Abbottabad, North-West Frontier Province 25.10.1986 RHB WK																			
FC		4	8	0	242	86	30.25	0	2									4	
Lim		2	2	0	0	0	0.00	0	0									1	
Lim	2008/09	4	4	1	51	39*	17.00	0	0									2	1
WAQAS AHMED (Lahore Lions, Lahore Ravi) b Lahore, Punjab 24.1.1979 RHB RFM																			
FC		7	10	0	161	33	16.10	0	0	1189	660	26	25.38	4-117	0	0	3.33	5	
Lim		3	3	0	26	19	8.66	0	0	168	125	3	41.66	2-21	0	0	4.46	0	
20T		3	3	0	29	20	9.66	0	0	48	70	4	17.50	4-22	1	0	8.75	1	
FC	1996/97	83	126	10	1939	114	16.71	1	5	13213	7108	297	23.93	7-45	14	4	3.22	36	
Lim	1997/98	69	56	8	708	67*	14.75	0	3	2942	2536	82	30.92	5-54	1	2	5.17	17	
20T	2004/05	20	15	2	164	46	12.61	0	0	210	363	11	33.00	4-22	1	0	10.37	4	
WAQAS AUSAF, Mohammad (Karachi Blues, Karachi Dolphins) b Karachi, Sind 5.9.1984 RHB LMF																			
FC		3	6	1	55	23*	11.00	0	0	60	48	3	16.00	2-34	0	0	4.80	1	
Lim		1	1	0	5	5	5.00	0	0	18	17	0					5.66	0	
FC	2008/09	4	8	2	97	31	16.16	0	0	60	48	3	16.00	2-34	0	0	4.80	2	
Lim	2008/09	2	2	0	14	9	7.00	0	0	18	17	0					5.66	1	
WAQAS SATTI, Mohammad (Lahore Eagles) b Islamabad, Punjab 21.2.1987 LHB LB																			
Lim		1	1	0	15	15	15.00	0	0	30	37	0					7.40	0	
WASIM ABBAS Baig, Mirza (Islamabad) b Gujrat, Punjab 12.9.1986 RHB OB																			
FC		2	3	0	17	12	5.66	0	0									1	
FC	2008/09	4	7	0	73	20	10.42	0	0									3	
WASIM BUTT, Mohammad (Lahore Eagles) b Lahore, Punjab 24.4.1983 RHB OB																			
Lim		3	3	0	54	42	18.00	0	0									0	
WASIM ISHTIAQ (Lahore Ravi) b Lahore, Punjab 17.8.1989 RHB OB																			
FC		1	2	0	28	16	14.00	0	0									0	
WASIM KHAN (National Bank) b Lahore, Punjab 3.2.1978 RHB RFM																			
FC		3	3	0	28	27	9.33	0	0	512	254	13	19.53	5-71	1	0	2.97	1	
Lim		5	3	1	4	4	2.00	0	0	288	232	9	25.77	3-41	0	0	4.83	1	
FC	2001/02	71	96	12	1125	62	13.39	0	3	13237	7232	302	23.94	7-70	22	4	3.27	24	
Lim	2000/01	54	30	9	169	30	8.04	0	0	2625	2295	64	35.85	4-39	2	0	5.24	15	
20T	2004/05	12	5	2	19	16*	6.33	0	0	240	346	9	38.44	2-15	0	0	8.65	5	
WASIM MAJEED (Multan) b Vehari, Punjab 25.10.1980 RHB OB																			
FC		2	2	0	31	20	15.50	0	0	36	23	2	11.50	2-14	0	0	3.83	1	
FC	1997/98	9	15	0	241	81	16.06	0	1	174	99	6	16.50	2-7	0	0	3.41	6	
Lim	1998/99	10	9	0	210	56	23.33	0	1	306	301	7	43.00	5-35	0	1	5.90	4	
YASIM MURTAZA (Federal Areas Leopards, Rawalpindi, Rawalpindi Rams) b Sialkot, Punjab 4.12.1990 LHB SLA																			
FC		7	11	1	266	60*	26.60	0	1	575	292	6	48.66	3-37	0	0	3.04	7	
Lim		9	9	3	179	63	29.83	0	1	426	323	13	24.84	5-35	0	1	4.54	3	
20T		2	2	0	22	18	11.00	0	0	42	57	0					8.14	0	
FC	2006/07	24	35	2	775	75	23.48	0	4	2289	1034	33	31.33	5-52	1	0	2.71	23	
Lim	2005/06	29	25	5	460	63	23.00	0	3	1448	1094	30	36.46	5-13	0	2	4.53	10	
20T	2006/07	6	4	0	24	18	6.00	0	0	120	142	5	28.40	2-16	0	0	7.10	3	
YASIR AJMAL (Lahore Lions) b Lahore, Punjab 2.8.1990 RHB OB																			
Lim		5	5	0	155	46	31.00	0	0	48	30	2	15.00	2-21	0	0	3.75	2	
YASIR ALI (KRL) b Hazro, Attock, Punjab 15.10.1985 RHB RFM																			
FC		5	6	0	95	61	15.83	0	1	716	463	12	38.58	5-43	1	0	3.88	2	
Lim		2	1	0	26	26	26.00	0	0	96	83	6	13.83	3-41	0	0	5.18	1	
Test	2003/04	1	2	2	1	1*		0	0	120	55	2	27.50	1-12	0	0	2.75	0	
FC	2003/04	36	49	9	728	129	18.20	1	3	5729	3000	102	29.41	5-43	3	0	3.14	12	
Lim	2003/04	19	14	2	176	51	14.66	0	1	879	669	28	23.89	5-16	1	1	4.56	7	
20T	2008/09	2	1	0	3	3	3.00	0	0	30	39	0					7.80	0	
YASIR ARAFAT Satti (KRL, Otago, Pakistan to United Arab Emirates, Sussex, Sussex to India) b Rawalpindi, Punjab 12.3.1982 RHB RFM																			
FC		2	4	0	57	32	14.25	0	0	384	242	10	24.20	6-67	1	0	3.78	0	
Test	2007/08	3	3	1	94	50*	47.00	0	1	627	438	9	48.66	5-161	1	0	4.19	0	
FC	1997/98	168	250	37	5788	122	27.17	4	31	28055	16236	674	24.08	9-35	39	5	3.47	45	
Int	1999/00	11	8	3	74	27	14.80	0	0	414	373	4	93.25	1-28	0	0	5.40	2	
Lim	1997/98	207	149	39	2333	110*	21.20	1	7	9990	8212	330	24.88	6-24	14	5	4.93	48	
I20T	2007/08	7	7	4	64	17	21.33	0	0	150	195	6	32.50	3-32	0	0	7.80	1	
20T	2005/06	82	57	17	667	49	16.67	0	0	1689	2168	103	21.04	4-17	5	0	7.70	12	
YASIR HAMEED Qureshi (Abbottabad Rhinos, Khyber Pakhtunkhwa Panthers, PIA, Pakistan to England) b Peshawar, North-West Frontier Province 28.2.1978 RHB OB																			
FC		8	14	2	513	180	42.75	1	2	18	8	0					2.66	6	
Lim		8	8	0	162	45	20.25	0	0	66	60	0					5.45	3	
20T		2	2	0	73	54	36.50	0	1									0	
Test	2003/04	25	49	3	1491	170	32.41	2	8	78	72	0					5.53	20	
FC	1996/97	137	227	14	7733	300	36.30	16	35	921	735	7	105.00	2-46	0	0	4.78	108	
Int	2003	56	56	1	2028	127*	36.87	3	12	18	26	0					8.66	14	
Lim	1995/96	175	169	11	5884	128*	37.24	10	34	454	394	14	28.14	4-38	2	0	5.20	54	
20T	2004/05	18	18	1	404	69	23.76	0	3	1	4	0					24.00	1	

Cmp	Debut	M	I	NO	Runs	HS	Avge	100	50	Balls	Runs	Wkts	Avge	BB	5i	10m	RpO	ct	st
YASIR HUSSAIN (Customs) b Karachi, Sind 14.12.1988 RHB OB																			
FC		6	11	0	209	74	19.00	0	1	746	472	9	52.44	4-28	0	0	3.79	1	
Lim		4	4	0	19	14	4.75	0	0	186	179	4	44.75	3-28	0	0	5.77	3	
FC	2002/03	19	32	1	578	77	18.64	0	2	2126	1416	32	44.25	7-91	1	0	3.99	5	
Lim	2007/08	9	9	0	92	28	10.22	0	0	378	399	5	79.80	3-28	0	0	6.33	3	
YASIR SHAH (Abbottabad Rhinos, Khyber Pakhtunkhwa Panthers, Sui Northern Gas, Pakistan A to Sri Lanka, Pakistan A to United Arab Emirates) b Swabi, North-West Frontier Province 2.5.1986 RHB LB																			
FC		11	14	1	271	59*	20.84	0	1	2221	1081	41	26.36	6-40	1	0	2.92	9	
Lim		4	4	1	70	35*	23.33	0	0	240	194	6	32.33	2-39	0	0	4.85	0	
20T		2	1	0	0	0	0.00	0	0	48	59	1	59.00	1-31	0	0	7.37	0	
FC	2001/02	37	47	5	768	71	18.28	0	4	6548	3343	113	29.58	6-40	4	0	3.06	19	
Lim	2001/02	19	16	4	250	51	20.83	0	1	977	786	25	31.44	3-26	0	0	4.82	5	
20T	2008/09	8	7	1	59	22	9.83	0	0	179	224	4	56.00	2-16	0	0	7.50	4	
YAWAR ABBAS Khan (Lahore Shalimar) b Mianwali, Punjab 25.10.1988 RHB RMF																			
FC		3	5	3	16	12*	8.00	0	0	502	372	8	46.50	2-31	0	0	4.44	0	
YAWAR BASHIR (KRL)																			
Lim		1	1	0	2	2	2.00	0	0									2	
YOUNIS KHAN, Mohammad (Habib Bank, Pakistan to Australia, Pakistan to South Africa, Pakistan to United Arab Emirates, Surrey) b Mardan, North-West Frontier Province 29.11.1977 RHB RM,LB																			
FC		2	4	0	29	9	7.25	0	0	222	114	4	28.50	2-8	0	0	3.08	5	
Lim		4	3	1	161	81*	80.50	0	2	78	77	2	38.50	1-11	0	0	5.92	3	
Test	1999/00	63	112	7	5260	313	50.09	16	21	540	341	7	48.71	2-23	0	0	3.78	67	
FC	1998/99	150	244	28	10873	313	50.33	34	44	2677	1560	35	44.57	4-52	0	0	3.49	158	
Int	1999/00	202	196	19	5765	144	32.57	6	37	224	224	2	112.00	1-3	0	0	6.00	107	
Lim	1998/99	264	252	29	7684	144	34.45	10	48	1085	1035	27	38.33	3-5	0	0	5.72	147	
I20T	2006	22	20	3	432	51	25.41	0	2	22	18	3	6.00	3-18	0	0	4.90	11	
20T	2004/05	47	44	8	962	70	26.72	0	4	82	105	6	17.50	3-18	0	0	7.68	19	
YOUSUF KHAN (Abbottabad Rhinos) b Wah Cantonment, Punjab 11.7.1977 RHB RAB																			
Lim		2	2	0	40	36	20.00	0	0									0	
ZAFAR ALI Katper (Hyderabad Hawks) b Naudero, Sind 2.3.1986 RHB WK																			
Lim		3	3	0	46	23	15.33	0	0									3	1
FC	2004/05	5	10	0	140	41	14.00	0	0									16	3
Lim	2005/06	6	6	0	112	38	18.66	0	0									4	2
ZAFAR IQBAL (Multan)																			
FC		1	2	0	46	44	23.00	0	0									0	
ZAHID MAHMOOD (Hyderabad, Hyderabad Hawks) b Dadu, Sind 20.3.1988 RHB LB																			
FC		3	5	3	29	16*	14.50	0	0	378	230	4	57.50	2-105	0	0	3.65	2	
Lim		4	3	3	7	5*		0	0	228	155	6	25.83	2-31	0	0	4.07	4	
20T		2	2	1	9	7*	9.00	0	0	30	36	2	18.00	1-8	0	0	7.20	0	
ZAHID MANSOOR (Rawalpindi, Rawalpindi Rams) b Rawalpindi, Punjab 29.12.1989 RHB OB WK																			
FC		10	17	0	420	84	24.70	0	3	12	6	0					3.00	9	
Lim		1	1	0	87	87	87.00	0	1									1	2
FC	2007/08	20	33	1	811	146	25.34	1	3	24	14	0					3.50	23	
Lim	2007/08	10	8	2	304	87	50.66	0	2									8	2
ZAHOOR ELAHI (KRL) b Sahiwal, Punjab 1.3.1971 RHB RM																			
FC		10	15	1	569	105	40.64	1	3	6	7	0					7.00	5	
Lim		4	4	0	137	60	34.25	0	1									0	
Test	1996/97	2	3	0	30	22	10.00	0	0									1	
FC	1985/86	243	409	27	14176	203	37.10	31	78	3290	1689	40	42.22	5-55	1	0	3.08	148	
Int	1996/97	14	14	1	297	86	22.84	0	3									2	
Lim	1986/87	187	185	20	6301	133*	38.18	13	36	1455	1195	39	30.64	5-31	0	2	4.92	51	
ZAHOOR KHAN (Faisalabad, Faisalabad Wolves) b Faisalabad, Punjab 25.5.1989 RHB RMF																			
FC		10	13	6	22	10*	3.14	0	0	2693	1462	42	34.80	5-55	2	0	3.25	0	
Lim		4	3	1	2	1	1.00	0	0	192	182	3	60.66	1-29	0	0	5.68	0	
FC	2008/09	17	21	9	38	10*	3.16	0	0	3694	2016	68	29.64	7-86	5	1	3.27	0	
Lim	2008/09	8	4	1	2	1	0.66	0	0	360	345	10	34.50	3-41	0	0	5.75	1	
ZEESHAN ALI (Customs) b Lahore, Punjab 16.6.1989 RHB WK																			
FC		3	6	0	122	68	20.33	0	1									2	
Lim		1	1	0	14	14	14.00	0	0									1	
FC	2008/09	8	16	3	288	68	22.15	0	2									11	2
Lim	2008/09	4	4	0	45	30	11.25	0	0									2	
ZEESHAN Asif BUTT (Faisalabad, Faisalabad Wolves, Punjab Stallions) b Faisalabad, Punjab 20.2.1978 RHB RMF																			
FC		10	17	1	866	221	54.12	3	3	290	166	6	27.66	2-16	0	0	3.43	11	
Lim		7	7	1	215	80	35.83	0	3									1	
20T		4	4	2	3	2	1.50	0	0									1	
FC	1995/96	32	50	4	1791	221	38.93	5	7	536	308	11	28.00	3-38	0	0	3.44	23	
Lim	1997/98	17	17	2	710	170*	47.33	1	6	72	78	2	39.00	2-18	0	0	6.50	8	
20T	2009	7	6	2	31	20	7.75	0	0	12	21	0					10.50	3	

Cmp	Debut	M	I	NO	Runs	HS	Avge	100	50	Balls	Runs	Wkts	Avge	BB	5i	10m	RpO	ct	st
ZEESHAN GUL (Hyderabad, Hyderabad Hawks) b Tando Bago, Sind 12.3.1991 RHB RAB WK																			
FC		2	4	1	38	18	12.66	0	0									6	
Lim		1	1	0	1	1	1.00	0	0									2	
Lim	2008/09	4	4	0	41	18	10.25	0	0									3	
ZEESHAN MUSHTAQ, Mirza (Islamabad, Islamabad Leopards) b Gujrat, Punjab 1.10.1989 RHB RFM																			
FC		4	8	0	162	60	20.25	0	1									0	
Lim		3	3	0	54	47	18.00	0	0									1	
FC	2007/08	10	18	1	606	230	35.64	2	1	6	5	0					5.00	5	
Lim	2008/09	6	6	0	157	60	26.16	0	1									1	
ZEESHAN NADIR Masood (Customs) b Quetta, Baluchistan 1.1.1986 RHB RMF																			
FC		6	12	4	23	8*	2.87	0	0	845	558	23	24.26	6-63	3	1	3.96	2	
FC	2007/08	9	15	6	30	8*	3.33	0	0	1457	889	30	29.63	6-63	3	1	3.66	2	
ZIA-UL-HAQ (Abbottabad) b Battagaram, North West Frontier Province 5.12.1980 RHB LB																			
FC		2	4	1	15	7	5.00	0	0									1	
Lim	2008/09	2	2	0	51	29	25.50	0	0									0	
ZOHAIB AHMED (Islamabad, Islamabad Leopards) b Islamabad, Punjab 2.3.1986 RHB RMF																			
FC		5	10	0	123	63	12.30	0	1	24	16	0					4.00	1	
Lim		3	3	1	65	33*	32.50	0	0	24	33	0					8.25	0	
FC	2005/06	26	37	2	450	63	12.85	0	2	1665	1129	33	34.21	5-62	1	0	4.06	4	
Lim	2005/06	16	9	2	167	64	23.85	0	1	336	339	10	33.90	3-36	0	0	6.05	8	
20T	2005/06	10	7	3	29	17	7.25	0	0	78	132	0					10.15	7	
ZOHAIB KHAN (Khyber Pakhtunkhwa Panthers, Peshawar Panthers, ZTBL) b Peshawar, North-West Frontier Province 20.3.1984 RHB SLA																			
FC		8	12	1	567	143	51.54	2	2	1615	711	26	27.34	5-57	1	0	2.64	8	
Lim		8	7	1	179	47	29.83	0	0	438	326	6	54.33	3-46	0	0	4.46	1	
20T		3	3	0	38	28	12.66	0	0	42	47	3	15.66	3-21	0	0	6.71	2	
FC	2007/08	25	33	9	1008	143	42.00	2	4	4615	2081	69	30.15	5-49	3	0	2.70	24	
Lim	2004/05	25	16	3	366	59	28.15	0	1	1344	917	45	20.37	6-37	1	1	4.09	7	
20T	2008/09	5	5	0	60	28	12.00	0	0	90	109	6	18.16	3-21	0	0	7.26	3	
ZOHAIB SHERA (Karachi Blues, Karachi Dolphins, Karachi Whites) b Karachi, Sind 18.8.1990 RHB LMF																			
FC		4	6	3	4	2	1.33	0	0	688	455	13	35.00	4-49	0	0	3.96	0	
Lim		1	1	1	8	8*		0	0	60	55	0					5.50	1	
ZULFIQAR BABAR, Mohammad (Baluchistan Bears, Multan, Multan Tigers, The Rest, Pakistan A to Sri Lanka) b Okara, Punjab 10.12.1978 RHB SLA																			
FC		14	20	4	331	51	20.68	0	1	3757	1613	96	16.80	10-143	9	3	2.57	9	
Lim		10	7	3	66	39	16.50	0	0	553	343	20	17.15	6-10	0	1	3.72	2	
20T		3	2	2	9	6*		0	0	72	69	8	8.62	4-26	1	0	5.75	0	
FC	2001/02	31	44	7	634	51	17.13	0	2	6632	2892	145	19.94	10-143	11	3	2.61	18	
Lim	2005/06	21	16	8	142	39	17.75	0	0	1082	827	25	33.08	6-10	0	1	4.58	5	
ZULFIQAR GOPANG (Hyderabad Hawks) RHB																			
Lim		1	1	0	0	0	0.00	0	0									0	
ZULFIQAR JAN (KRL) b Charsadda, North-West Frontier Province 10.11.1979 RHB RM WK																			
FC		10	15	2	270	57	20.76	0	1									41	2
Lim		2	2	1	6	5	6.00	0	0									3	
FC	1999/00	113	161	24	3205	101*	23.39	3	13	12	13	0					6.50	400	23
Lim	1998/99	60	44	16	642	76	22.92	0	2									68	15
20T	2005/06	6	4	3	22	13*	22.00	0	0									3	2
ZULQARNAIN (Faisalabad, Faisalabad Wolves) b Faisalabad, Punjab 28.12.1990 RHB RMF																			
FC		6	7	3	159	77*	39.75	0	1	1202	707	18	39.27	5-91	1	0	3.52	3	
Lim		2	2	0	5	4	2.50	0	0	102	115	4	28.75	3-72	0	0	6.76	0	
FC	2007/08	14	16	7	263	77*	29.22	0	2	2140	1288	35	36.80	5-91	1	0	3.61	5	
Lim	2008/09	5	3	1	12	7*	6.00	0	0	228	254	10	25.40	6-57	0	1	6.68	1	
ZULQARNAIN HAIDER (Punjab Stallions, ZTBL, Pakistan to England) b Lahore, Punjab 23.4.1986 RHB RM WK																			
FC		8	12	3	495	161	55.00	1	2	24	26	0					6.50	25	2
Lim		6	5	0	63	36	12.60	0	0									8	
Test	2010	1	2	0	88	88	44.00	0	1									2	
FC	2003/04	71	109	18	3172	161	34.85	3	18	24	26	0					6.50	211	13
Lim	2001/02	62	45	5	629	90	15.72	0	2									72	18
I20T	2006/07	1	1	0	5	5	5.00	0	0									0	
20T	2005/06	5	4	0	58	35	14.50	0	0									3	2

SCOTLAND

2010 AND CAREER RECORDS FOR SCOTLAND PLAYERS

Cmp	Debut	M	I	NO	Runs	HS	Avge	100	50	Balls	Runs	Wkts	Avge	BB	5i	10m	RpO	ct	st
BAILEY, George John (Australia A, Tasmania, Chennai Super Kings, Scotland to England, Scotland) b Launceston, Tasmania, Australia 7.9.1982 RHB RM																			
Lim		6	6	0	82	43	13.66	0	0									4	
FC	2004/05	61	112	11	4081	155	40.40	10	22	84	46	0					3.28	47	
Lim	2001/02	105	97	12	2739	123*	32.22	2	17	53	40	1	40.00	1-19	0	0	4.52	50	
20T	2005/06	25	21	3	529	60	29.38	0	4	12	24	0					12.00	8	
BERRINGTON, Richard Douglas (Scotland, Scotland to England, Scotland to Kenya, Scotland to Netherlands, Scotland to United Arab Emirates) b Pretoria, Transvaal, South Africa 3.4.1987 RHB RMF																			
FC		1	2	0	29	22	14.50	0	0	120	110	2	55.00	1-43	0	0	5.50	1	
Int		3	3	0	40	33	13.33	0	0	34	38	0					6.70	0	
Lim		11	11	0	376	106	34.18	1	2	262	284	7	40.57	3-45	0	0	6.50	3	
FC	2007	8	13	1	278	82	23.16	0	2	682	367	13	28.23	3-13	0	0	3.22	11	
Int	2008	16	14	1	292	84	22.46	0	2	470	346	10	34.60	2-14	0	0	4.41	9	
Lim	2007	34	31	1	838	106	27.93	1	6	872	802	24	33.41	4-47	1	0	5.51	15	
I20T	2008	8	6	1	44	19*	8.80	0	0	112	103	5	20.60	2-21	0	0	5.51	0	
20T	2008	11	9	2	55	19*	7.85	0	0	154	149	7	21.28	2-12	0	0	5.80	2	
CHALMERS, Ewan Fraser (Scotland, Scotland to Kenya) b Edinburgh, Midlothian 19.10.1989 RHB RM																			
FC		1	2	0	77	67	38.50	0	1									1	
Lim		1	1	0	8	8	8.00	0	0									0	
FC	2009	4	8	1	155	67	22.14	0	1									4	
COETZER, Kyle James (Scotland, Durham, Durham to United Arab Emirates, Scotland to Kenya, Scotland to United Arab Emirates) b Aberdeen 14.4.1984 RHB RMF																			
Int		1	1	0	51	51	51.00	0	1	12	23	0					11.50	1	
Lim		1	1	0	51	51	51.00	0	1	12	23	0					11.50	1	
FC	2004	42	74	9	2248	172	34.58	5	7	150	71	2	35.50	2-16	0	0	2.84	26	
Int	2008	5	5	0	132	51	26.40	0	1	12	23	0					11.50	3	
Lim	2003	58	56	7	1479	127	30.18	1	9	96	96	0					6.00	22	
I20T	2008	9	9	1	234	48*	29.25	0	0	48	47	5	9.40	3-25	0	0	5.87	2	
20T	2007	23	22	2	469	64	23.45	0	1	78	85	6	14.16	3-25	0	0	6.53	5	
COLEMAN, Frederick Robert John (Scotland) b Edinburgh, Midlothian 15.12.1991 RHB WK																			
Lim		1	1	0	0	0	0.00	0	0									0	
DAVEY, Joshua Henry (Scotland, Middlesex, Middlesex to Netherlands, Scotland to Netherlands) b Aberdeen 3.8.1990 RHB RM																			
Int		3	3	0	22	11	7.33	0	0	80	67	5	13.40	5-9	0	1	5.02	2	
Lim		3	3	0	22	11	7.33	0	0	80	67	5	13.40	5-9	0	1	5.02	2	
FC	2010	4	7	0	220	72	31.42	0	3	162	107	2	53.50	2-41	0	0	3.96	3	
Int	2010	4	4	0	46	24	11.50	0	0	122	94	6	15.66	5-9	0	1	4.62	2	
Lim	2010	7	7	1	74	24	12.33	0	0	140	118	6	19.66	5-9	0	1	5.05	3	
20T	2010	2	2	1	7	7*	7.00	0	0	30	48	0					9.60	2	
DRUMMOND, Gordon David (Scotland, Scotland to England, Scotland to Kenya, Scotland to Netherlands, Scotland to United Arab Emirates) b Meigle, Perthshire 21.4.1980 RHB RM																			
FC		1	2	0	17	15	8.50	0	0	216	89	2	44.50	2-60	0	0	2.47	0	
Int		3	2	2	43	35*		0	0	108	87	1	87.00	1-31	0	0	4.83	1	
Lim		11	10	3	92	35*	13.14	0	0	360	295	5	59.00	1-23	0	0	4.91	2	
FC	2007	7	9	0	138	52	15.33	0	1	1062	401	13	30.84	3-18	0	0	2.26	3	
Int	2007	21	14	6	182	35*	22.75	0	0	903	621	20	31.05	4-41	1	0	4.12	3	
Lim	2007	42	33	10	289	35*	12.56	0	0	1719	1284	36	35.66	4-41	1	0	4.48	6	
I20T	2008	9	6	0	54	35	9.00	0	0	179	221	7	31.57	2-14	0	0	7.40	0	
20T	2008	12	8	1	66	35	9.42	0	0	233	264	10	26.40	2-14	0	0	6.79	0	
EVANS, Alasdair Campbell (Scotland) b Tunbridge Wells, Kent, England 12.1.1989 RHB RMF																			
Lim		1	1	1	1	1*		0	0	36	38	1	38.00	1-38	0	0	6.33	0	
FC	2009	3	1	0	2	2	2.00	0	0	252	210	4	52.50	2-41	0	0	5.00	0	
Int	2009	2								102	99	1	99.00	1-55	0	0	5.82	0	
Lim	2009	3	1	1	1	1*		0	0	138	137	2	68.50	1-38	0	0	5.95	0	
FLANNIGAN, Ryan (Scotland, Scotland to England) b Kelso, Roxburghshire 30.6.1988 RHB RM																			
FC		1	2	0	48	32	24.00	0	0									1	
Int		1	1	0	0	0	0.00	0	0									0	
Lim		4	4	0	41	22	10.25	0	0									3	
Lim	2010	5	5	0	42	22	8.40	0	0									3	
GOUDIE, Gordon (Scotland, Scotland to England, Scotland to Kenya, Scotland to Netherlands) b Aberdeen 12.8.1987 RHB RMF																			
Lim		7	6	2	57	26*	14.25	0	0	260	257	13	19.76	4-46	2	0	5.93	2	
FC	2005	7	8	2	87	44*	14.50	0	0	829	356	14	25.42	4-58	0	0	2.57	2	
Int	2008	10	8	3	40	17*	8.00	0	0	447	374	17	22.00	5-73	0	1	5.02	3	
Lim	2004	33	24	8	125	26*	7.81	0	0	1366	1304	46	28.34	5-73	2	1	5.72	7	

Cmp	Debut	M	I	NO	Runs	HS	Avge	100	50	Balls	Runs	Wkts	Avge	BB	5i	10m	RpO	ct	st
I20T	2009/10	1	1	0	4	4	4.00	0	0	6	20	0					20.00	0	
20T	2009/10	1	1	0	4	4	4.00	0	0	6	20	0					20.00	0	
HAIRS, Oliver James (Scotland, Scotland to England, Scotland to Netherlands) b Redhill, Surrey, England 14.4.1991 LHB OB																			
Lim		1	1	0	18	18	18.00	0	0									0	
Int	2010	5	5	0	68	27	13.60	0	0									0	
Lim	2010	7	7	0	110	27	15.71	0	0									0	
HAMILTON, Gavin Mark (Scotland to England, Scotland to Kenya, Scotland, Scotland to United Arab Emirates) b Broxburn, West Lothian 16.9.1974 LHB RMF																			
Int		3	3	0	81	48	27.00	0	0									0	
Lim		9	9	0	240	64	26.66	0	1									1	
Test	1999/00	1	2	0	0	0	0.00	0	0	90	63	0					4.20	0	
FC	1993	95	133	21	2939	125	26.24	2	18	12348	6415	249	25.76	7-50	9	2	3.11	34	
Int	1999	38	38	3	1231	119	35.17	2	7	220	160	3	53.33	2-36	0	0	4.36	6	1
Lim	1993	211	177	28	4209	131	28.24	4	22	4124	3227	128	25.21	5-16	4	2	4.69	43	1
I20T	2007/08	12	8	0	90	32	11.25	0	0									3	
20T	2003	18	14	2	194	41*	16.16	0	0									6	
HAQ, Rana Majid Khan (Scotland, Scotland to England, Scotland to Kenya, Scotland to Netherlands, Scotland to United Arab Emirates) b Paisley, Renfrewshire 11.2.1983 LHB OB																			
FC		1	2	0	25	25	12.50	0	0	318	148	4	37.00	2-66	0	0	2.79	0	
Int		3	2	0	23	12	11.50	0	0	144	105	3	35.00	2-35	0	0	4.37	0	
Lim		9	7	3	76	29*	19.00	0	0	378	301	6	50.16	2-35	0	0	4.77	0	
FC	2004	11	15	2	261	46	20.07	0	0	2053	768	29	26.48	5-30	1	0	2.24	4	
Int	2006/07	27	23	0	411	71	17.86	0	3	1301	1042	31	33.61	4-28	1	0	4.80	5	
Lim	2002	81	62	11	939	71	18.41	0	4	3385	2873	72	39.90	4-28	2	0	5.09	7	
I20T	2007/08	8	7	3	54	21*	13.50	0	0	150	180	6	30.00	2-16	0	0	7.20	2	
20T	2007/08	11	8	4	55	21*	13.75	0	0	222	245	10	24.50	2-15	0	0	6.62	3	
HUSSAIN, Rana Omer (Scotland, Scotland to England, Scotland to Netherlands) b Paisley, Renfrewshire 3.12.1984 LHB WK																			
Lim		1	1	0	7	7	7.00	0	0									0	
FC	2007	3	2	0	10	8	5.00	0	0									1	
Int	2006	8	8	1	63	17	9.00	0	0									1	
Lim	2005	17	16	2	193	52	13.78	0	1									3	
IQBAL, Moneeb Mohammed (Scotland, Scotland to England, Scotland to Netherlands) b Glasgow, Lanarkshire 28.2.1986 RHB LB																			
FC		1	2	0	42	42	21.00	0	0	107	82	2	41.00	1-37	0	0	4.59	0	
Int		2	2	1	14	9*	14.00	0	0	36	49	0					8.16	0	
Lim		4	4	1	114	67	38.00	0	1	102	122	0					7.17	0	
FC	2006	6	12	3	110	42	12.22	0	0	636	529	13	40.69	4-36	0	0	4.99	2	
Int	2008/09	10	10	3	156	63	22.28	0	1	258	249	4	62.25	2-35	0	0	5.79	1	
Lim	2002	19	18	4	316	67	22.57	0	2	516	450	5	90.00	2-35	0	0	5.23	3	
LAIDLAW, Neil John William (Scotland, Scotland to England) b Edinburgh, Midlothian 3.7.1987 LHB RFM																			
Lim		1								18	21	0					7.00	0	
Lim	2010	2								54	50	0					5.55	0	
LOCKHART, Douglas Ross (Scotland, Scotland to England, Scotland to Kenya, Scotland to Netherlands) b Glasgow, Lanarkshire 19.1.1976 RHB RM WK																			
Int		3	2	0	72	46	36.00	0	0									3	
Lim		9	8	0	87	46	10.87	0	0									5	
FC	1996	24	40	3	849	151	22.94	1	4									34	1
Int	2006	14	11	2	218	46	24.22	0	0									11	
Lim	1997	105	93	10	1484	88*	17.87	0	5									59	9
LYONS, Ross Thomas (Scotland, Scotland to England, Scotland to Kenya, Scotland to Netherlands, Scotland to United Arab Emirates) b Greenock, Renfrewshire 8.12.1984 LHB SLA																			
Int		2	1	0	1	1	1.00	0	0	114	80	2	40.00	1-16	0	0	4.21	0	
Lim		8	6	2	16	8	4.00	0	0	380	289	6	48.16	1-15	0	0	4.56	2	
FC	2006	7	7	6	66	23	66.00	0	0	884	424	21	20.19	4-10	0	0	2.87	6	
Int	2006	25	14	10	90	28	22.50	0	0	1093	901	20	45.05	3-21	0	0	4.94	4	
Lim	2005	51	31	18	152	28	11.69	0	0	2165	1813	38	47.71	3-21	0	0	5.02	13	
I20T	2009/10	2	2	0	4	4	2.00	0	0	36	40	1	40.00	1-26	0	0	6.66	0	
20T	2009/10	4	2	0	4	4	2.00	0	0	78	90	5	18.00	3-28	0	0	6.92	1	
MCCALLUM, Neil Francis Ian (Scotland, Scotland to England, Scotland to Kenya, Scotland to Netherlands, Scotland to United Arab Emirates) b Edinburgh, Midlothian 22.11.1977 RHB																			
Int		1	1	0	22	22	22.00	0	0									1	
Lim		6	6	0	113	41	18.83	0	0									4	
FC	2006	12	18	4	609	181	43.50	2	1									11	
Int	2006	41	40	6	977	121*	28.73	2	4									13	
Lim	2001	84	80	9	1807	121*	25.45	4	8									29	
I20T	2007/08	11	7	0	76	38	10.85	0	0									0	
20T	2007/08	13	9	0	80	38	8.88	0	0									1	
MAIDEN, Gregor Ian (Scotland to England, Scotland to Netherlands) b Glasgow, Lanarkshire 22.7.1979 RHB OB																			
FC	1999	7	9	1	111	40	13.87	0	0	445	239	11	21.72	3-24	0	0	3.22	5	
Int	2010	3	3	0	66	31	22.00	0	0	48	38	0					4.75	0	
Lim	1999	46	32	2	437	62	14.56	0	1	1338	1094	23	47.56	2-27	0	0	4.90	12	

Cmp	Debut	M	I	NO	Runs	HS	Avge	100	50	Balls	Runs	Wkts	Avge	BB	5i	10m	RpO	ct	st
I20T	2008	3	1	0	0	0	0.00	0	0	60	58	2	29.00	1-20	0	0	5.80	1	
20T	2003	4	2	1	2	2*	2.00	0	0	84	87	4	21.75	2-29	0	0	6.21	2	
MOMMSEN, Preston Luke (Scotland to England, Scotland to Netherlands, Scotland) b Durban, Natal, South Africa 14.10.1987 RHB OB																			
Int		1	1	0	5	5	5.00	0	0									0	
Lim		5	5	0	32	19	6.40	0	0	30	29	0					5.80	5	
FC	2010	1	2	0	20	18	10.00	0	0									1	
Int	2010	7	7	0	142	80	20.28	0	1	12	19	1	19.00	1-19	0	0	9.50	2	
Lim	2010	12	12	0	197	80	16.41	0	1	42	48	1	48.00	1-19	0	0	6.85	7	
NEL, Johann Dewald (Scotland, Kent, Scotland to Kenya, Scotland to United Arab Emirates) b Klerksdorp, Transvaal, South Africa 6.6.1980 RHB RMF																			
FC		1	2	1	36	36	36.00	0	0	179	118	2	59.00	1-30	0	0	3.95	1	
Int		1	1	1	11	11*		0	0	18	27	0					9.00	0	
Lim		1	1	1	11	11*		0	0	18	27	0					9.00	0	
FC	2004	18	23	10	154	36	11.84	0	0	2424	1374	51	26.94	6-62	2	0	3.40	6	
Int	2006	19	10	8	31	11*	15.50	0	0	730	649	14	46.35	4-25	1	0	5.33	3	
Lim	2004	84	49	28	202	36*	9.61	0	0	3398	2969	83	35.77	4-25	1	0	5.24	15	
I20T	2007/08	10	5	2	34	13*	11.33	0	0	186	169	12	14.08	3-10	0	0	5.45	1	
20T	2007	15	5	2	34	13*	11.33	0	0	289	278	17	16.35	3-10	0	0	5.77	1	
PARKER, Matthew Archibald (Scotland, Scotland to England, Scotland to Netherlands) b Dundee, Angus 2.3.1989 LHB RMF																			
FC		1	2	0	43	42	21.50	0	0	192	117	2	58.50	2-84	0	0	3.65	1	
Int		3	2	0	19	17	9.50	0	0	84	71	3	23.66	2-17	0	0	5.07	1	
Lim		9	8	1	99	23	14.14	0	0	312	278	9	30.88	2-17	0	0	5.34	3	
FC	2010	2	4	0	113	65	28.25	0	1	452	236	9	26.22	4-63	0	0	3.13	1	
Int	2010	10	8	2	59	22	9.83	0	0	414	327	12	27.25	4-33	1	0	4.73	3	
Lim	2009	22	20	5	161	23	10.73	0	0	880	787	26	30.26	4-33	1	0	5.36	5	
PETRIE, Marc John (Scotland, Scotland to England) b Dundee, Angus 2.3.1990 LHB WK																			
Lim		2	2	1	13	7*	13.00	0	0									0	
Int	2009	4	2	0	3	3	1.50	0	0									3	1
Lim	2009	7	5	1	16	7*	4.00	0	0									3	1
POONIA, Navdeep Singh (Scotland to Kenya, Scotland to United Arab Emirates) b Govan, Glasgow, Lanarkshire 11.5.1986 RHB RMF																			
FC	2006	14	22	0	557	111	25.31	1	2									5	
Int	2006	21	21	0	237	67	11.28	0	1									7	
Lim	2002	42	41	1	732	79	18.30	0	4									13	
I20T	2007/08	8	7	2	95	38*	19.00	0	0									2	
20T	2006	14	13	2	159	38*	14.45	0	0									2	
SHEIKH, Mohammad Qasim (Scotland, Scotland to Kenya, Scotland to Netherlands) b Glasgow, Lanarkshire 30.10.1984 LHB LM																			
FC		1	2	0	9	9	4.50	0	0									0	
FC	2005	16	26	1	691	108	27.64	3	3									3	
Int	2008	7	7	1	63	23	10.50	0	0									2	
Lim	2005	13	12	1	85	23	7.72	0	0									3	
SMITH, Simon James Stevenson (Scotland, Scotland to England, Scotland to Kenya, Scotland to Netherlands, Scotland to United Arab Emirates) b Ashington, Northumberland, England 8.12.1979 RHB WK																			
FC		1	2	1	39	20	39.00	0	0									4	
FC	2004	8	8	2	151	40	25.16	0	0									23	1
Lim	2004	12	8	2	103	41*	17.16	0	0									7	5
I20T	2009/10	4	4	1	21	9	7.00	0	0									0	1
20T	2009/10	6	5	2	24	9	8.00	0	0									2	2
STANDER, Jan Hendrik (Scotland to Kenya, Scotland to United Arab Emirates) b Port Elizabeth, Cape Province, South Africa 4.1.1982 RHB RMF																			
FC	2009	1	2	0	64	64	32.00	0	1	180	91	5	18.20	3-43	0	0	3.03	0	
Int	2008/09	4	4	1	36	22*	12.00	0	0	150	166	6	27.66	2-25	0	0	6.64	1	
Lim	2008/09	19	18	3	284	80*	18.93	0	1	847	808	24	33.66	4-41	1	0	5.72	4	
I20T	2009	6	6	1	53	45	10.60	0	0	57	114	1	114.00	1-28	0	0	12.00	2	
20T	2009	8	8	2	97	45	16.16	0	0	93	142	2	71.00	1-16	0	0	9.16	2	
WATSON, Ryan Robert (Scotland, Scotland to England, Scotland to Kenya, Scotland to United Arab Emirates) b Salisbury (now Harare), Zimbabwe 12.11.1976 RHB RM																			
Int		1	1	0	0	0	0.00	0	0									1	
Lim		3	3	0	72	48	24.00	0	0	24	42	0					10.50	2	
FC	2004	15	22	0	843	167	38.31	2	4	842	455	19	23.94	5-74	1	0	3.24	19	
Int	2006	35	35	4	956	123*	30.83	1	6	570	528	12	44.00	3-18	0	0	5.55	12	
Lim	2002	143	138	10	3371	123*	26.33	3	18	3527	3114	81	38.44	4-24	3	0	5.29	55	
I20T	2007/08	10	9	0	159	54	17.66	0	1	60	92	3	30.66	1-4	0	0	9.20	4	
20T	2007/08	13	12	0	197	54	16.41	0	1	96	112	7	16.00	2-10	0	0	7.00	5	
WATTS, David Fraser (Scotland, Scotland to England, Scotland to Kenya, Scotland to Netherlands, Scotland to United Arab Emirates) b King's Lynn, Norfolk, England 5.6.1979 RHB RM																			
FC		1	2	0	24	16	12.00	0	0									0	
Int		2	2	1	110	55*	110.00	0	2									0	
Lim		7	7	1	152	55*	25.33	0	2									1	

Cmp	Debut	M	I	NO	Runs	HS	Avge	100	50	Balls	Runs	Wkts	Avge	BB	5i	10m	RpO	ct	st
FC	1999	19	31	1	886	146	29.53	2	4									13	
Int	2006	32	31	1	884	101	29.46	1	8									7	
Lim	2001	121	118	10	2387	101	22.10	1	13									25	
I20T	2007/08	8	6	0	81	46	13.50	0	0									5	
20T	2007/08	11	9	0	170	73	18.88	0	1									7	

AFGHANISTAN TO SCOTLAND 2010

Cmp	Debut	M	I	NO	Runs	HS	Avge	100	50	Balls	Runs	Wkts	Avge	BB	5i	10m	RpO	ct	st
ABDULLAH																			
FC		1	1	0	2	2	2.00	0	0	108	20	2	10.00	2-6	0	0	1.11	0	
ASGHAR STANIKZAI																			
FC		1	2	0	129	93	64.50	0	1									0	
Int		2	1	0	0	0	0.00	0	0	36	33	1	33.00	1-33	0	0	5.50	0	
Lim		2	1	0	0	0	0.00	0	0	36	33	1	33.00	1-33	0	0	5.50	0	
HAMID HASSAN																			
FC		1	1	0	1	1	1.00	0	0	311	154	11	14.00	6-40	2	1	2.97	0	
Int		2	1	0	1	1	1.00	0	0	102	64	2	32.00	1-26	0	0	3.76	0	
Lim		2	1	0	1	1	1.00	0	0	102	64	2	32.00	1-26	0	0	3.76	0	
JAVED AHMADI																			
Int		2	1	0	25	25	25.00	0	0									1	
Lim		2	1	0	25	25	25.00	0	0									1	
KARIM SADIQ																			
FC		1	2	0	107	67	53.50	0	1									0	
Int		2	2	1	114	114*	114.00	1	0									0	
Lim		2	2	1	114	114*	114.00	1	0									0	
MIRWAIS ASHRAF																			
FC		1	1	0	19	19	19.00	0	0	180	73	1	73.00	1-48	0	0	2.43	1	
Int		2	1	0	7	7	7.00	0	0	108	54	2	27.00	1-27	0	0	3.00	0	
Lim		2	1	0	7	7	7.00	0	0	108	54	2	27.00	1-27	0	0	3.00	0	
MOHAMMAD NABI																			
FC		1	2	0	16	10	8.00	0	0	238	64	3	21.33	2-23	0	0	1.61	1	
Int		2	1	0	2	2	2.00	0	0	36	23	0					3.83	0	
Lim		2	1	0	2	2	2.00	0	0	36	23	0					3.83	0	
MOHAMMAD SHAHZAD																			
FC		1	2	1	159	105*	159.00	1	1									5	
Int		2	2	1	111	100*	111.00	1	0									4	1
Lim		2	2	1	111	100*	111.00	1	0									4	1
NAWROZ MANGAL																			
FC		1	2	0	47	29	23.50	0	0									1	
Int		2	1	0	6	6	6.00	0	0	5	7	0					8.40	1	
Lim		2	1	0	6	6	6.00	0	0	5	7	0					8.40	1	
NOOR ALI ZADRAN																			
FC		1	2	0	63	36	31.50	0	0									0	
Int		1	1	0	6	6	6.00	0	0									0	
Lim		1	1	0	6	6	6.00	0	0									0	
NOOR-UL-HAQ																			
Int		1	1	0	12	12	12.00	0	0									0	
Lim		1	1	0	12	12	12.00	0	0									0	
SAMIULLAH SHENWARI																			
FC		1	2	1	116	102	116.00	1	0	78	41	2	20.50	1-15	0	0	3.15	1	
Int		2	1	0	46	46	46.00	0	0	108	70	3	23.33	2-29	0	0	3.88	0	
Lim		2	1	0	46	46	46.00	0	0	108	70	3	23.33	2-29	0	0	3.88	0	
SHAPOOR ZADRAN																			
FC		1	1	1	2	2*		0	0	120	75	0					3.75	0	
Int		2	1	1	0	0*		0	0	108	82	4	20.50	3-69	0	0	4.55	0	
Lim		2	1	1	0	0*		0	0	108	82	4	20.50	3-69	0	0	4.55	0	

BANGLADESH TO SCOTLAND 2010

Cmp	Debut	M	I	NO	Runs	HS	Avge	100	50	Balls	Runs	Wkts	Avge	BB	5i	10m	RpO	ct	st
ABDUR RAZZAK																			
Int		1								36	50	0					8.33	0	
Lim		1								36	50	0					8.33	0	
IMRUL KAYES																			
Int		1	1	0	52	52	52.00	0	1									0	
Lim		1	1	0	52	52	52.00	0	1									0	
JAHURUL ISLAM																			
Int		1	1	0	41	41	41.00	0	0									0	
Lim		1	1	0	41	41	41.00	0	0									0	

Cmp	Debut	M	I	NO	Runs	HS	Avge	100	50	Balls	Runs	Wkts	Avge	BB	5i	10m	RpO	ct	st
JUNAID SIDDIQUE																			
Int		1	1	0	31	31	31.00	0	0									0	
Lim		1	1	0	31	31	31.00	0	0									0	
MAHMUDULLAH																			
Int		1	1	1	28	28*		0	0									0	
Lim		1	1	1	28	28*		0	0									0	
MASHRAFE MORTAZA																			
Int		1	1	0	18	18	18.00	0	0	36	43	0					7.16	1	
Lim		1	1	0	18	18	18.00	0	0	36	43	0					7.16	1	
MUSHFIQUR RAHIM																			
Int		1	1	0	0	0	0.00	0	0									0	
Lim		1	1	0	0	0	0.00	0	0									0	
NAZMUL HOSSAIN																			
Int		1								36	28	2	14.00	2-28	0	0	4.66	0	
Lim		1								36	28	2	14.00	2-28	0	0	4.66	0	
SHAFIUL ISLAM																			
Int		1								35	38	0					6.51	0	
Lim		1								35	38	0					6.51	0	
SHAKIB AL HASAN																			
Int		1	1	0	15	15	15.00	0	0	30	36	2	18.00	2-36	0	0	7.20	0	
Lim		1	1	0	15	15	15.00	0	0	30	36	2	18.00	2-36	0	0	7.20	0	
TAMIM IQBAL																			
Int		1	1	0	2	2	2.00	0	0									0	
Lim		1	1	0	2	2	2.00	0	0									0	

DURHAM TO SCOTLAND 2010

Cmp	Debut	M	I	NO	Runs	HS	Avge	100	50	Balls	Runs	Wkts	Avge	BB	5i	10m	RpO	ct	st
BENKENSTEIN, D.M.																			
Lim		1	1	0	34	34	34.00	0	0									0	
BLACKWELL, I.D.																			
Lim		1	1	0	11	11	11.00	0	0	36	35	3	11.66	3-35	0	0	5.83	0	
BREESE, G.R.																			
Lim		1	1	1	0	0*		0	0	36	27	0					4.50	1	
DI VENUTO, M.J.																			
Lim		1	1	0	63	63	63.00	0	1									3	
HARMISON, B.W.																			
Lim		1	1	1	12	12*		0	0	6	12	0					12.00	0	
HARMISON, S.J.																			
Lim		1								24	17	2	8.50	2-17	0	0	4.25	1	
MUCHALL, G.J.																			
Lim		1	1	0	8	8	8.00	0	0	6	7	0					7.00	0	
MUSTARD, P.																			
Lim		1	1	0	12	12	12.00	0	0									1	
PLUNKETT, L.E.																			
Lim		1	1	0	2	2	2.00	0	0	24	12	1	12.00	1-12	0	0	3.00	0	
RUSHWORTH, C.																			
Lim		1								24	14	1	14.00	1-14	0	0	3.50	2	
STOKES, B.A.																			
Lim		1	1	0	39	39	39.00	0	0	24	21	1	21.00	1-21	0	0	5.25	0	

ENGLAND TO SCOTLAND 2010

Cmp	Debut	M	I	NO	Runs	HS	Avge	100	50	Balls	Runs	Wkts	Avge	BB	5i	10m	RpO	ct	st
ANDERSON, J.M.																			
Int		1								54	43	2	21.50	2-43	0	0	4.77	0	
Lim		1								54	43	2	21.50	2-43	0	0	4.77	0	
BROAD, S.C.J.																			
Int		1								48	49	0					6.12	1	
Lim		1								48	49	0					6.12	1	
COLLINGWOOD, P.D.																			
Int		1	1	1	38	38*		0	0	18	11	1	11.00	1-11	0	0	3.66	0	
Lim		1	1	1	38	38*		0	0	18	11	1	11.00	1-11	0	0	3.66	0	
KIESWETTER, C.																			
Int		1	1	0	69	69	69.00	0	1									0	1
Lim		1	1	0	69	69	69.00	0	1									0	1
MORGAN, E.J.G.																			
Int		1	1	1	24	24*		0	0									0	
Lim		1	1	1	24	24*		0	0									0	

Cmp	Debut	M	I	NO	Runs	HS	Avge	100	50	Balls	Runs	Wkts	Avge	BB	5i	10m	RpO	ct	st
PIETERSEN, K.P.																			
Int		1	1	0	17	17	17.00	0	0									0	
Lim		1	1	0	17	17	17.00	0	0									0	
SHAHZAD, A.																			
Int		1								59	31	2	15.50	2-31	0	0	3.15	0	
Lim		1								59	31	2	15.50	2-31	0	0	3.15	0	
STRAUSS, A.J.																			
Int		1	1	0	61	61	61.00	0	1									0	
Lim		1	1	0	61	61	61.00	0	1									0	
SWANN, G.P.																			
Int		1								60	29	2	14.50	2-29	0	0	2.90	2	
Lim		1								60	29	2	14.50	2-29	0	0	2.90	2	
WRIGHT, L.J.																			
Int		1																0	
Lim		1																0	
YARDY, M.H.																			
Int		1								60	41	3	13.66	3-41	0	0	4.10	1	
Lim		1								60	41	3	13.66	3-41	0	0	4.10	1	

HAMPSHIRE TO SCOTLAND 2010

Cmp	Debut	M	I	NO	Runs	HS	Avge	100	50	Balls	Runs	Wkts	Avge	BB	5i	10m	RpO	ct	st
ADAMS, J.H.K.																			
Lim		1	1	1	74	74*		0	1									0	
BATES, A.M.																			
Lim		1																1	1
BRIGGS, D.R.																			
Lim		1								48	26	1	26.00	1-26	0	0	3.25	1	
CARBERRY, M.A.																			
Lim		1																1	
CORK, D.G.																			
Lim		1								36	16	1	16.00	1-16	0	0	2.66	0	
DAWSON, L.A.																			
Lim		1								36	29	1	29.00	1-29	0	0	4.83	1	
ERVINE, S.M.																			
Lim		1	1	0	63	63	63.00	0	1	38	39	2	19.50	2-39	0	0	6.15	1	
McKENZIE, N.D.																			
Lim		1	1	1	14	14*		0	0									0	
RIAZUDDIN, H.																			
Lim		1								30	20	1	20.00	1-20	0	0	4.00	1	
VINCE, J.M.																			
Lim		1	1	0	9	9	9.00	0	0									0	
WOOD, C.P.																			
Lim		1								48	33	4	8.25	4-33	1	0	4.12	2	

INDIA A TO SCOTLAND 2010

Cmp	Debut	M	I	NO	Runs	HS	Avge	100	50	Balls	Runs	Wkts	Avge	BB	5i	10m	RpO	ct	st
DHAWAN, S.																			
Lim		2	2	0	4	4	2.00	0	0									0	
GANAPATHY, C.																			
Lim		1	1	0	6	6	6.00	0	0	60	62	1	62.00	1-62	0	0	6.20	0	
IQBAL ABDULLA																			
Lim		1	1	0	15	15	15.00	0	0	46	21	3	7.00	3-21	0	0	2.73	0	
JASKARAN SINGH																			
Lim		2	2	0	9	8	4.50	0	0	87	56	1	56.00	1-37	0	0	3.86	0	
KULKARNI, D.S.																			
Lim		2	2	2	6	4*		0	0	114	79	8	9.87	5-29	0	1	4.15	1	
MUKUND, A.																			
Lim		1	1	0	50	50	50.00	0	1									2	
PANDEY, M.K.																			
Lim		1	1	0	32	32	32.00	0	0									0	
PUJARA, C.A.																			
Lim		2	2	1	122	122*	122.00	1	0									1	
RAHANE, A.M.																			
Lim		2	2	0	137	108	68.50	1	0									0	
SAHA, W.P.																			
Lim		2	2	0	12	9	6.00	0	0									4	
SHARMA, B.																			
Lim		1	1	0	24	24	24.00	0	0	48	52	0					6.50	0	

Cmp Debut	M	I	NO	Runs	HS	Avge	100	50	Balls	Runs	Wkts	Avge	BB	5i	10m	RpO	ct	st
TIWARY, M.K.																		
Lim	2	2	0	112	71	56.00	0	1	24	33	0					8.25	2	
TYAGI, S.																		
Lim	2								90	56	4	14.00	3-45	0	0	3.73	0	
UNADKAT, J.D.																		
Lim	1								41	28	1	28.00	1-28	0	0	4.09	0	

KENT TO SCOTLAND 2010

Cmp Debut	M	I	NO	Runs	HS	Avge	100	50	Balls	Runs	Wkts	Avge	BB	5i	10m	RpO	ct	st
AZHAR MAHMOOD																		
Lim	1								48	37	1	37.00	1-37	0	0	4.62	0	
BLAKE, A.J.																		
Lim	1																0	
COOK, S.J.																		
Lim	1								48	39	3	13.00	3-39	0	0	4.87	0	
DENLY, J.L.																		
Lim	1	1	0	38	38	38.00	0	0									0	
JONES, G.O.																		
Lim	1																1	1
KEY, R.W.T.																		
Lim	1	1	1	67	67*		0	1									1	
KHAN, A.																		
Lim	1								48	33	1	33.00	1-33	0	0	4.12	1	
NTINI, M.																		
Lim	1								48	35	1	35.00	1-35	0	0	4.37	0	
STEVENS, D.I.																		
Lim	1																0	
TREDWELL, J.C.																		
Lim	1								48	32	0					4.00	0	
VAN JAARSVELD, M.																		
Lim	1	1	1	72	72*		0	1									0	

LEICESTERSHIRE TO SCOTLAND 2010

Cmp Debut	M	I	NO	Runs	HS	Avge	100	50	Balls	Runs	Wkts	Avge	BB	5i	10m	RpO	ct	st
BENNING, J.G.E.																		
Lim	1	1	0	42	42	42.00	0	0	48	33	2	16.50	2-33	0	0	4.12	0	
BOYCE, M.A.G.																		
Lim	1	1	0	2	2	2.00	0	0									1	
DUTOIT, J.																		
Lim	1	1	0	0	0	0.00	0	0									0	
GURNEY, H.F.																		
Lim	1								48	29	2	14.50	2-29	0	0	3.62	0	
HENDERSON, C.W.																		
Lim	1	1	0	1	1	1.00	0	0	48	25	4	6.25	4-25	1	0	3.12	0	
MALIK, M.N.																		
Lim	1								48	39	1	39.00	1-39	0	0	4.87	0	
NAIK, J.K.H.																		
Lim	1	1	1	5	5*		0	0	48	34	0					4.25	0	
NEW, T.J.																		
Lim	1	1	0	7	7	7.00	0	0									0	
SMITH, G.P.																		
Lim	1	1	0	4	4	4.00	0	0									0	
TAYLOR, J.W.A.																		
Lim	1	1	0	11	11	11.00	0	0									1	
WHITE, W.A.																		
Lim	1	1	1	27	27*		0	0									0	

NETHERLANDS TO SCOTLAND 2010

Cmp Debut	M	I	NO	Runs	HS	Avge	100	50	Balls	Runs	Wkts	Avge	BB	5i	10m	RpO	ct	st
ADEEL RAJA																		
Int	1								36	46	0					7.66	0	
Lim	1								36	46	0					7.66	0	
BARRESI, W.																		
Int	1	1	1	64	64*		0	1									0	
Lim	1	1	1	64	64*		0	1									0	
BORREN, P.W.																		
Int	1	1	0	5	5	5.00	0	0	36	30	3	10.00	3-30	0	0	5.00	0	
Lim	1	1	0	5	5	5.00	0	0	36	30	3	10.00	3-30	0	0	5.00	0	

Cmp	Debut	M	I	NO	Runs	HS	Avge	100	50	Balls	Runs	Wkts	Avge	BB	5i	10m	RpO	ct	st
BUURMAN, A.F.																			
Int		1																2	
Lim		1																2	
COOPER, T.L.W.																			
Int		1	1	0	8	8	8.00	0	0	12	10	0					5.00	0	
Lim		1	1	0	8	8	8.00	0	0	12	10	0					5.00	0	
JONKMAN, M.B.S.																			
Int		1								36	52	2	26.00	2-52	0	0	8.66	0	
Lim		1								36	52	2	26.00	2-52	0	0	8.66	0	
KERVEZEE, A.N.																			
Int		1	1	0	15	15	15.00	0	0									0	
Lim		1	1	0	15	15	15.00	0	0									0	
KRUGER, B.P.																			
Int		1								24	26	0					6.50	3	
Lim		1								24	26	0					6.50	3	
MUDASSAR BUKHARI																			
Int		1								36	33	2	16.50	2-33	0	0	5.50	0	
Lim		1								36	33	2	16.50	2-33	0	0	5.50	0	
SZWARCZYNSKI, E.S.																			
Int		1	1	0	67	67	67.00	0	1									0	
Lim		1	1	0	67	67	67.00	0	1									0	
ZUIDERENT, B.																			
Int		1	1	1	35	35*		0	0									0	
Lim		1	1	1	35	35*		0	0									0	

NOTTINGHAMSHIRE TO SCOTLAND 2010

Cmp	Debut	M	I	NO	Runs	HS	Avge	100	50	Balls	Runs	Wkts	Avge	BB	5i	10m	RpO	ct	st
BROWN, A.D.																			
Lim		1	1	0	4	4	4.00	0	0									1	
CARTER, A.																			
Lim		1								24	28	1	28.00	1-28	0	0	7.00	0	
EDWARDS, N.J.																			
Lim		1	1	0	11	11	11.00	0	0									0	
FRANKS, P.J.																			
Lim		1	1	1	1	1*		0	0	42	47	1	47.00	1-47	0	0	6.71	0	
HALES, A.D.																			
Lim		1	1	0	69	69	69.00	0	1									1	
MULLANEY, S.J.																			
Lim		1	1	0	23	23	23.00	0	0	30	21	2	10.50	2-21	0	0	4.20	1	
PATEL, S.R.																			
Lim		1	1	0	61	61	61.00	0	1	36	39	0					6.50	1	
READ, C.M.W.																			
Lim		1	1	1	22	22*		0	0									1	1
SIDEBOTTOM, R.J.																			
Lim		1								42	38	1	38.00	1-38	0	0	5.42	0	
WHITE, G.G.																			
Lim		1								39	35	5	7.00	5-35	0	1	5.38	3	
WOOD, M.J.																			
Lim		1	1	0	60	60	60.00	0	1									0	

WARWICKSHIRE TO SCOTLAND 2010

Cmp	Debut	M	I	NO	Runs	HS	Avge	100	50	Balls	Runs	Wkts	Avge	BB	5i	10m	RpO	ct	st
BARKER, K.H.D.																			
Lim		1	1	0	12	12	12.00	0	0									1	
BOTHA, A.G.																			
Lim		1								42	27	2	13.50	2-27	0	0	3.85	1	
CARTER, N.M.																			
Lim		1	1	0	4	4	4.00	0	0	36	17	1	17.00	1-17	0	0	2.83	0	
CLARKE, R.																			
Lim		1																0	
IMRAN TAHIR																			
Lim		1								30	13	2	6.50	2-13	0	0	2.60	0	
JOHNSON, R.M.																			
Lim		1																2	
MADDY, D.L.																			
Lim		1	1	1	43	43*		0	0									0	
RANKIN, W.B.																			
Lim		1								28	14	2	7.00	2-14	0	0	3.00	0	

Cmp	Debut	M	I	NO	Runs	HS	Avge	100	50	Balls	Runs	Wkts	Avge	BB	5i	10m	RpO	ct	st
TROUGHTON, J.O.																			
Lim		1	1	0	28	28	28.00	0	0									0	
WESTWOOD, I.J.																			
Lim		1	1	1	7	7*		0	0									0	
WOAKES, C.R.																			
Lim		1								42	16	3	5.33	3-16	0	0	2.28	1	

SOUTH AFRICA

SuperSport Series winners 2009/10 (first-class): Cape Cobras
CSA Provincial Three-Day Competition winners 2009/10 (first-class): Eastern Province
MTN40 2009/10 (limited overs): Warriors
CSA Provincial One-Day Competition winners 2009/10 (limited overs): Northerns
Standard Bank Pro20 Series winners 2009/10 (twenty20): Warriors

2009/10 and 2010 AND CAREER RECORDS FOR SOUTH AFRICAN PLAYERS

Cmp	*Debut*	*M*	*I*	*NO*	*Runs*	*HS*	*Avge*	*100*	*50*	*Balls*	*Runs*	*Wkts*	*Avge*	*BB*	*5i*	*10m*	*RpO*	*ct*	*st*
ABBAS, Moeneeb (Western Province) b Cape Town, Cape Province 22.1.1983 RHB RM																			
FC		9	15	0	409	64	27.26	0	4									5	
Lim		8	8	1	229	111*	32.71	1	0									2	
FC	2008/09	10	17	0	460	64	27.05	0	5									6	
Lim	2008/09	9	9	1	236	111*	29.50	1	0									2	
ABBOTT, Kyle John (Dolphins, KwaZulu-Natal) b Empangeni, Natal 18.6.1987 RHB RM																			
FC		5	6	0	142	50	23.66	0	1	544	310	15	20.66	6-42	1	0	3.41	2	
Lim		8	4	2	32	22*	16.00	0	0	296	223	10	22.30	3-25	0	0	4.52	1	
FC	2008/09	9	14	2	232	50*	19.33	0	2	1222	592	32	18.50	6-42	2	0	2.90	4	
Lim	2008/09	9	5	2	39	22*	13.00	0	0	349	261	11	23.72	3-25	0	0	4.48	1	
ABDULLA, Yusuf Adam (Dolphins, South Africa, Kings XI Punjab) b Johannesburg, South Africa 17.1.1983 LHB LFM																			
FC		4	5	3	40	25	20.00	0	0	574	331	8	41.37	5-62	1	0	3.46	2	
Lim		7	1	1	1	1*		0	0	247	200	6	33.33	2-24	0	0	4.85	4	
I20T		1								24	28	1	28.00	1-28	0	0	7.00	0	
20T		1								24	28	1	28.00	1-28	0	0	7.00	0	
FC	2005/06	23	28	8	182	54	9.10	0	1	3263	1902	54	35.22	5-62	2	0	3.49	4	
Lim	2005/06	51	15	11	88	31*	22.00	0	0	2146	1729	57	30.33	4-41	2	0	4.83	9	
I20T	2008/09	2								42	44	2	22.00	1-16	0	0	6.28	0	
20T	2005/06	38	3	2	4	3	4.00	0	0	809	895	50	17.90	4-31	2	0	6.63	3	
ABRAHAMS, Umar (Eastern Province) b Port Elizabeth, Cape Province 7.2.1981 LHB RM																			
FC		4	6	0	171	50	28.50	0	1									1	
Lim		7	7	1	185	75*	30.83	0	1									3	
FC	1998/99	36	64	4	1558	134*	25.96	3	6	47	40	0					5.10	16	
Lim	2000/01	43	40	7	900	107*	27.27	1	6									9	
ACKERMAN, Hylton Deon (Dolphins, KwaZulu-Natal) b Cape Town, Cape Province 14.2.1973 RHB RM																			
Lim		4	3	0	39	39	13.00	0	0									1	
Test	1997/98	4	8	0	161	57	20.12	0	1									1	
FC	1993/94	220	369	34	14625	309*	43.65	40	75	102	57	0					3.35	183	
Lim	1993/94	230	222	25	6366	139	32.31	4	41	48	52	0					6.50	83	
20T	2003/04	55	55	7	1811	87	37.72	0	17									13	
ADAIR, Sean Robin (Eastern Province) b Johannesburg, Transvaal 26.12.1986 RHB WK																			
FC		13	21	1	492	88	24.60	0	4	102	69	1	69.00	1-37	0	0	4.05	29	1
Lim		13	13	3	210	55*	21.00	0	1									6	1
FC	2005/06	37	62	8	1508	101*	27.92	1	9	102	69	1	69.00	1-37	0	0	4.05	82	3
Lim	2005/06	34	31	5	623	72*	23.96	0	3									30	4
ADAMS, Roy Andre (Griqualand West) b Caledon, Cape Province 31.1.1989 RHB RM																			
FC		9	14	3	173	35	15.72	0	0	817	480	5	96.00	3-16	0	0	3.52	2	
Lim		10	7	1	50	14	8.33	0	0	209	182	6	30.33	2-23	0	0	5.22	2	
FC	2006/07	16	21	4	307	46	18.05	0	0	1460	821	20	41.05	5-19	1	0	3.37	6	
Lim	2006/07	19	15	4	100	36*	9.09	0	0	432	371	9	41.22	2-23	0	0	5.15	5	
ADDICOTT, Glen Neal (KwaZulu-Natal Inland, KwaZulu-Natal Inland to Namibia) b Pietermaritzburg, Natal 3.5.1985 RHB RMF																			
FC		9	17	1	675	106	42.18	3	2									5	
Lim		11	11	0	243	56	22.09	0	2									1	
FC	2006/07	19	34	2	1200	125	37.50	5	3	29	3	0					0.62	11	
Lim	2006/07	22	22	1	511	79	24.33	0	3	7	8	1	8.00	1-0	0	0	6.85	1	
AGATHAGELOU, Andrea Peter (North West) b Rustenberg, Transvaal 16.11.1989 RHB LB																			
FC		13	26	1	1076	158	43.04	4	4	358	244	6	40.66	2-62	0	0	4.08	27	
Lim		12	11	0	301	90	27.36	0	2	30	35	0					7.00	8	1
FC	2007/08	17	33	1	1232	158	38.50	4	6	358	244	6	40.66	2-62	0	0	4.08	31	
Lim	2007/08	14	13	1	341	90	28.41	0	2	30	35	0					7.00	8	1
AKOOJEE, Muhammad (North West) b Klerksdorp, Transvaal 21.11.1984 RHB LB																			
FC		6	12	0	491	142	40.91	2	1									2	
Lim		5	4	0	24	9	6.00	0	0									2	
FC	2004/05	44	81	5	2597	158*	34.17	7	9	590	457	8	57.12	1-4	0	0	4.64	22	

Cmp	Debut	M	I	NO	Runs	HS	Avge	100	50	Balls	Runs	Wkts	Avge	BB	5i	10m	RpO	ct	st
Lim	2004/05	37	35	1	958	127	28.17	1	7	174	178	3	59.33	2-28	0	0	6.13	6	
20T	2006/07	1	1	1	13	13*		0	0									0	
ALEXANDER, Craig John (Lions, North West) b Cape Town, Cape Province 5.1.1987 RHB RF																			
FC		2	3	2	23	13*	23.00	0	0	348	240	7	34.28	3-34	0	0	4.13	0	
Lim		2	2	0	11	7	5.50	0	0	84	94	0					6.71	1	
FC	2004/05	32	39	19	160	25	8.00	0	0	5162	3171	96	33.03	5-59	4	0	3.68	9	
Lim	2004/05	26	19	8	65	31*	5.90	0	0	1146	1114	28	39.78	4-27	2	0	5.83	2	
20T	2008/09	3								60	58	5	11.60	3-14	0	0	5.80	0	
ALEXANDER, Michael Gray (KwaZulu-Natal) b Cape Town, Cape Province 31.10.1990 RHB RMF																			
FC		6	9	0	76	27	8.44	0	0									1	
Lim		7	6	2	145	46*	36.25	0	0	18	14	1	14.00	1-14	0	0	4.66	0	
ALLI, Hussein (North West) b Lichtenburg, Transvaal 2.8.1990 RHB RMF																			
FC		1								60	23	0					2.30	0	
Lim		4								36	25	1	25.00	1-25	0	0	4.16	0	
ALLIE, Zahid (Western Province) b Cape Town, Cape Province 1.5.1984 RHB WK																			
FC		3	5	0	70	38	14.00	0	0									8	
Lim		7	7	0	106	39	15.14	0	0									3	1
AMLA, Ahmed Mahomed (Dolphins) b Durban, Natal 15.9.1979 RHB LB																			
FC		10	17	1	589	134	36.81	1	3	21	19	1	19.00	1-3	0	0	5.42	8	
Lim		11	11	1	367	85*	36.70	0	3	54	58	2	29.00	1-24	0	0	6.44	3	
20T		5	5	1	121	43	30.25	0	0									1	
FC	1997/98	106	179	17	5651	164*	34.88	11	31	843	547	8	68.37	2-53	0	0	3.89	60	
Lim	1999/00	109	104	13	2864	107*	31.47	2	19	198	204	6	34.00	1-8	0	0	6.18	33	
20T	2003/04	38	37	10	602	47	22.29	0	0	108	183	6	30.50	2-30	0	0	10.16	13	
AMLA, Hashim Mahomed (Dolphins, South Africa, South Africa A, Nottinghamshire, South Africa to India, South Africa to West Indies) b Durban, Natal 31.3.1983 RHB RM																			
Test		4	7	0	311	100	44.42	1	2									2	
FC		9	16	0	539	100	33.68	1	3	6	3	0					3.00	7	
Int		6	6	0	274	86	45.66	0	3									4	
Lim		11	11	0	519	86	47.18	0	6									8	
Test	2004/05	46	81	6	3383	253*	45.10	10	16	42	28	0					4.00	37	
FC	1999/00	132	219	20	9688	253*	48.68	29	48	315	224	1	224.00	1-10	0	0	4.26	100	
Int	2007/08	29	28	3	1371	140	54.84	3	8									11	
Lim	2001/02	82	80	5	2989	140	39.85	6	19	16	28	0					10.50	31	
I20T	2008/09	2	2	0	52	26	26.00	0	0									0	
20T	2003/04	26	25	0	555	57	22.20	0	2									3	
ANAND, Deepak (KwaZulu-Natal Inland) b Delhi, India 25.12.1975 RHB RMF																			
FC		4	7	0	110	35	15.71	0	0	42	39	0					5.57	2	
Lim		9	9	0	92	45	10.22	0	0									0	
APRIL, Wilfred Clayd (North West) b Oudtshoorn, Cape Province 9.6.1986 RHB RM																			
FC		4	7	2	133	51	26.60	0	2									0	
Lim		4	2	0	26	18	13.00	0	0									0	
ARENDSE, Rayno Garth (Boland) b Worcester, Cape Province 8.12.1978 RHB RM																			
FC		2	2	0	4	4	2.00	0	0									2	
Lim		1	1	0	1	1	1.00	0	0									0	
FC	1997/98	44	73	6	1533	95	22.88	0	8	6	15	0					15.00	35	
Lim	2001/02	37	30	8	651	74	29.59	0	3									11	
ARTHUR, Mario Charles (Griqualand West) b Kimberley, Cape Province 25.2.1972 RHB RM																			
FC		1	2	0	36	34	18.00	0	0									0	
FC	1998/99	9	18	1	177	34	10.41	0	0	54	50	0					5.55	5	
Lim	2004/05	4	4	0	76	63	19.00	0	1									0	
ARTHUR, Nathan Oswald (Griqualand West) b Kimberley, Cape Province 29.3.1977 RHB LB																			
FC		4	6	3	43	20*	14.33	0	0	576	296	10	29.60	4-67	0	0	3.08	0	
Lim		5	3	1	0	0*	0.00	0	0	180	136	4	34.00	2-20	0	0	4.53	1	
FC	2004/05	27	41	14	386	45	14.29	0	0	3646	2024	60	33.73	6-27	1	0	3.33	7	
Lim	2004/05	24	14	7	39	19	5.57	0	0	1017	762	22	34.63	4-19	1	0	4.49	6	
AUGUST, Clayton John (Boland, Boland to Namibia) b Vredenburg, Cape Province 16.2.1990 LHB LFM																			
FC		3	5	1	31	10*	7.75	0	0	439	236	16	14.75	9-37	1	1	3.22	1	
Lim		9	3	1	6	3	3.00	0	0	359	287	9	31.88	3-26	0	0	4.79	2	
FC	2006/07	4	5	1	31	10*	7.75	0	0	469	248	16	15.50	9-37	1	1	3.17	2	
Lim	2007/08	11	5	2	17	6	5.66	0	0	437	353	12	29.41	3-26	0	0	4.84	2	
AVONTUUR, Sammy-Joe Earl (South Western Districts) b Oudtshoorn, Cape Province 31.7.1987 RHB LB																			
FC		8	14	0	345	123	24.64	1	1	6	3	0					3.00	3	
Lim		4	4	0	22	11	5.50	0	0									0	
FC	2006/07	24	44	0	1077	123	24.47	2	5	24	30	0					7.50	9	
Lim	2006/07	22	22	2	283	51	14.15	0	1									5	
BAARTMAN, Douglas Donay George (South Western Districts, South Western Districts to Namibia) b Oudtshoorn, Cape Province 19.6.1985 RHB RMF																			
FC		12	17	7	64	25	6.40	0	0	1552	789	36	21.91	4-39	0	0	3.05	6	
Lim		10	6	3	12	6*	4.00	0	0	270	264	9	29.33	2-25	0	0	5.86	1	

Cmp	Debut	M	I	NO	Runs	HS	Avge	100	50	Balls	Runs	Wkts	Avge	BB	5i	10m	RpO	ct	st
FC	2008/09	15	22	10	76	25	6.33	0	0	1876	977	40	24.42	4-39	0	0	3.12	8	
Lim	2008/09	14	8	4	13	6*	3.25	0	0	414	403	10	40.30	2-25	0	0	5.84	3	
BAILEY, Ryan Tyrone (Eagles, Eagles to India, Khulna, South Africa A to Bangladesh, South Africa A to Sri Lanka) b Cape Town, Cape Province 8.9.1982 RHB RM																			
FC		10	17	2	548	89	36.53	0	5	916	556	12	46.33	3-46	0	0	3.64	3	
Lim		9	9	2	408	105*	58.28	1	3	36	42	2	21.00	2-27	0	0	7.00	6	
20T		5	5	2	127	73*	42.33	0	1	12	22	0					11.00	3	
FC	2003/04	69	121	12	3436	186*	31.52	4	20	2533	1473	26	56.65	3-42	0	0	3.48	33	
Lim	2003/04	77	67	13	1608	105*	29.77	1	8	527	520	12	43.33	2-27	0	0	5.92	18	
20T	2003/04	39	29	8	395	73*	18.80	0	1	162	195	10	19.50	2-25	0	0	7.22	16	
BARENDS, Brady Lee (KwaZulu-Natal Inland, KwaZulu-Natal Inland to Namibia) b Durban, Natal 21.1.1989 RHB RM																			
FC		4	7	4	39	23*	13.00	0	0	366	238	5	47.60	2-11	0	0	3.90	2	
Lim		5								72	119	3	39.66	1-13	0	0	9.91	1	
FC	2009/10	5	8	5	48	23*	16.00	0	0	510	307	9	34.11	2-11	0	0	3.61	3	
Lim	2009/10	6								90	140	4	35.00	1-13	0	0	9.33	1	
BARNES, Bradley Graeme (Dolphins, KwaZulu-Natal) b Johannesburg, Transvaal 20.10.1988 RHB WK																			
FC		14	25	2	785	157	34.13	2	5									35	1
Lim		10	10	1	185	53	20.55	0	1									7	5
FC	2008/09	20	34	2	970	157	30.31	2	7	6	6	0					6.00	46	1
Lim	2008/09	17	14	2	259	53	21.58	0	1									15	9
BARRON, Chad Arthur Haig (KwaZulu-Natal Inland, KwaZulu-Natal Inland to Namibia) b Pietermaritzburg, Natal 4.6.1988 RHB OB																			
FC		6	11	1	342	109	34.20	1	1									3	
Lim		7	6	1	185	76*	37.00	0	1									2	1
FC	2009/10	7	13	1	376	109	31.33	1	1									3	
Lim	2009/10	8	7	2	219	76*	43.80	0	1									2	1
BAVUMA, Temba (Gauteng, Gauteng to Namibia) b Cape Town, Cape Province 17.5.1990 RHB RM																			
FC		11	16	2	633	152*	45.21	1	4	36	27	0					4.50	6	
Lim		12	11	1	272	64	27.20	0	1									5	
FC	2008/09	16	23	2	756	152*	36.00	1	4	72	68	1	68.00	1-41	0	0	5.66	9	
Lim	2008/09	17	16	1	405	79	27.00	0	2	3	4	0					8.00	6	
BAXTER, Chad (Eastern Province) b East London, Cape Province 23.2.1983 RHB RM																			
FC		4	8	1	80	55*	11.42	0	1	132	80	0					3.63	1	
Lim		2	2	0	19	13	9.50	0	0									0	
FC	2003/04	36	69	5	1632	103	25.50	1	13	156	97	0					3.73	24	
Lim	2002/03	34	33	2	1048	106*	33.80	1	7									11	
BEHARDIEN, Farhaan (Titans) b Johannesburg, Transvaal 9.10.1983 RHB RMF																			
FC		11	17	0	576	106	33.88	1	5	329	168	6	28.00	3-56	0	0	3.06	5	
Lim		8	7	1	186	73*	31.00	0	2	72	98	1	98.00	1-42	0	0	8.16	4	
20T		7	3	1	52	19*	26.00	0	0									3	
FC	2004/05	44	65	5	2233	150*	37.21	4	15	1148	603	18	33.50	3-48	0	0	3.15	28	
Lim	2004/05	52	36	7	868	73*	29.93	0	8	678	597	14	42.64	3-16	0	0	5.28	17	
20T	2006/07	25	18	4	233	35	16.64	0	0									11	
BEKKER, Martin (KwaZulu-Natal) b Durban, Natal 15.5.1985 RHB RM																			
FC		5	9	3	328	81*	54.66	0	3									3	
Lim		5	5	0	250	85	50.00	0	3									1	
FC	2005/06	36	56	5	1944	138	38.11	4	12	369	240	9	26.66	3-12	0	0	3.90	26	
Lim	2005/06	33	30	6	882	85	36.75	0	7	240	190	7	27.14	2-31	0	0	4.75	11	
20T	2007/08	3	3	1	10	4*	5.00	0	0									1	
BELL, Warren Eldrid (Eastern Province) b Port Elizabeth, Cape Province 23.7.1986 LHB RMF																			
FC		11	16	4	342	100*	28.50	1	1	790	422	12	35.16	4-38	0	0	3.20	9	
Lim		12	11	5	214	40*	35.66	0	0	240	209	5	41.80	3-28	0	0	5.22	4	
FC	2004/05	34	55	9	962	100*	20.91	1	4	2303	1334	44	30.31	4-38	0	0	3.47	21	
Lim	2004/05	39	33	9	493	40*	20.54	0	0	809	634	28	22.64	4-8	1	0	4.70	13	
20T	2008/09	2								18	44	0					14.66	0	
BENKENSTEIN, Dale Martin (Dolphins, Durham, Durham to Scotland, Durham to United Arab Emirates) b Salisbury (now Harare), Zimbabwe 9.6.1974 RHB RM,OB																			
Lim		7	7	0	245	76	35.00	0	3	6	4	0					4.00	2	
20T		5	5	0	43	21	8.60	0	0	54	55	1	55.00	1-24	0	0	6.11	1	
FC	1993/94	226	343	38	13741	259	45.05	34	72	7037	3375	97	34.79	4-16	0	0	2.87	153	
Int	1998/99	23	20	3	305	69	17.94	0	1	65	44	4	11.00	3-5	0	0	4.06	3	
Lim	1992/93	279	252	58	6826	107*	35.18	1	42	3071	2572	86	29.90	4-16	3	0	5.02	104	
20T	2003/04	74	70	14	1428	57*	25.50	0	4	366	455	16	28.43	3-10	0	0	7.45	25	
BENNETT, Bevan Leon (Border, Warriors, Western Province, Border to Namibia) b East London, Cape Province 9.9.1981 RHB LB																			
FC		4	7	0	155	51	22.14	0	1									1	
Lim		7	7	1	272	136*	45.33	1	1									1	
20T		1	1	0	18	18	18.00	0	0									0	
FC	2001/02	42	78	3	2079	150	27.72	3	10	1076	738	21	35.14	5-21	1	0	4.11	25	
Lim	2004/05	31	31	1	613	136*	20.43	1	2	139	128	4	32.00	2-22	0	0	5.52	10	

Cmp	Debut	M	I	NO	Runs	HS	Avge	100	50	Balls	Runs	Wkts	Avge	BB	5i	10m	RpO	ct	st
BENNETT, Clive Neil (Griqualand West) b Kimberley, Cape Province 10.10.1979 RHB LB																			
FC		1	2	1	24	24*	24.00	0	0									0	
Lim		2	2	0	16	16	8.00	0	0									0	
FC	2005/06	16	30	2	620	64	22.14	0	1	66	42	0					3.81	9	
Lim	2005/06	16	16	0	251	67	15.68	0	1									2	
BENNETT, Kevin Dean (Border, Border to Namibia) b East London, Cape Province 9.9.1981 RHB RM																			
FC		10	18	1	436	112*	25.64	1	1									5	
Lim		10	10	2	252	65	31.50	0	2									2	
FC	2005/06	23	38	3	1029	176	29.40	2	3	121	95	1	95.00	1-47	0	0	4.71	10	
Lim	2005/06	22	22	4	428	65	23.77	0	3									4	
BEUKES, Jonathan Alan (Free State) b Kimberley, Cape Province 15.3.1979 LHB OB																			
FC		12	20	8	700	120*	58.33	1	5									14	
Lim		12	12	2	434	130*	43.40	1	2									8	
FC	1997/98	83	149	20	4596	135*	35.62	8	27	47	34	2	17.00	1-8	0	0	4.34	90	
Lim	1997/98	114	103	7	3291	130*	34.28	4	19	60	41	2	20.50	2-23	0	0	4.10	51	
20T	2003/04	12	11	0	288	57	26.18	0	1	30	24	1	24.00	1-5	0	0	4.80	3	
BHAYAT, Riyaadh (North West) b Johannesburg, Transvaal 30.12.1986 RHB RMF																			
FC		10	17	1	173	27	10.81	0	0	763	463	18	25.72	6-110	1	0	3.64	2	
Lim		10	8	1	149	79*	21.28	0	1	108	140	1	140.00	1-28	0	0	7.77	1	
FC	2004/05	31	49	5	755	107	17.15	2	0	2338	1512	54	28.00	6-110	2	0	3.88	17	
Lim	2004/05	30	25	4	682	79*	32.47	0	5	726	748	19	39.36	3-65	0	0	6.18	4	
BIRCH, Andrew Charles Ross (Eastern Province, Warriors) b East London, Cape Province 7.6.1985 RHB RMF																			
FC		10	15	2	214	47	16.46	0	0	1796	952	38	25.05	5-42	1	0	3.18	2	
Lim		10	7	1	99	45	16.50	0	0	348	283	11	25.72	4-43	1	0	4.87	3	
FC	2004/05	26	38	6	545	55	17.03	0	2	4714	2418	108	22.38	6-62	4	0	3.07	8	
Lim	2004/05	26	21	5	238	45	14.87	0	0	1121	809	45	17.97	4-34	3	0	4.33	5	
20T	2006/07	4	1	0	6	6	6.00	0	0	79	116	5	23.20	4-22	1	0	8.81	0	
BIRKENSTOCK, Uwe Karl Janko (Boland) b Pretoria, Transvaal 26.5.1989 RHB OB																			
FC		9	17	2	774	112	51.60	2	4	246	145	3	48.33	1-18	0	0	3.53	3	
Lim		11	11	2	236	53	26.22	0	1									4	
BODI, Gulam Hussain (Easterns, Titans) b Hathuran, India 4.1.1979 LHB SLC																			
FC		12	17	0	476	159	28.00	1	2	90	77	0					5.13	3	
Lim		13	13	1	373	103*	31.08	1	1									3	
20T		7	6	1	206	88*	41.20	0	1									7	
FC	1996/97	88	136	13	4018	160*	32.66	8	18	3989	2555	61	41.88	6-63	2	0	3.84	34	
Int	2007/08	2	2	0	83	51	41.50	0	1	6	8	0					8.00	1	
Lim	1999/00	119	111	8	3455	153	33.54	6	23	1464	1257	39	32.23	5-46	1	1	5.15	30	
I20T	2007/08	1	1	0	8	8	8.00	0	0									0	
20T	2003/04	47	38	2	938	88*	26.05	0	4	6	6	1	6.00	1-6	0	0	6.00	16	
BODIBE, Tumelo Mphunzi (Easterns, Titans, Easterns to Namibia) b Vosloorus, Transvaal 22.6.1987 RHB WK																			
FC		11	18	3	501	100*	33.40	1	1									14	3
Lim		13	13	1	292	88	24.33	0	2									5	4
FC	2004/05	47	79	9	1628	100*	23.25	1	7									114	12
Lim	2004/05	47	42	9	823	88	24.93	0	4									44	13
BOJE, Nico (Warriors, Northamptonshire, Northamptonshire to Netherlands) b Bloemfontein, Orange Free State 20.3.1973 LHB SLA																			
Lim		12	8	1	85	18	12.14	0	0	441	401	7	57.28	2-36	0	0	5.45	3	
20T		8	5	2	63	32	21.00	0	0	168	179	10	17.90	3-10	0	0	6.39	7	
Test	1999/00	43	62	10	1312	85	25.23	0	4	8620	4265	100	42.65	5-62	3	0	2.96	18	
FC	1990/91	212	318	55	8975	226*	34.12	8	55	42325	18756	577	32.50	8-93	22	2	2.65	123	
Int	1995/96	115	71	18	1414	129	26.67	2	4	4541	3415	96	35.57	5-21	2	1	4.51	33	
Lim	1993/94	289	207	49	4032	129	25.51	2	16	12064	8742	274	31.90	5-21	9	1	4.34	88	
I20T	2005/06	1								24	27	1	27.00	1-27	0	0	6.75	0	
20T	2003/04	58	41	12	693	58*	23.89	0	3	1062	1225	57	21.49	3-10	0	0	6.92	24	
BOOI, Siyabonga (Border) b Mdatsane 29.7.1986 RHB RMF																			
FC		3	5	0	66	35	13.20	0	0	36	25	0					4.16	1	
Lim		3	3	1	33	16*	16.50	0	0	66	80	2	40.00	1-18	0	0	7.27	0	
FC	2007/08	10	18	2	263	68	16.43	0	1	48	39	0					4.87	9	
Lim	2007/08	11	9	1	164	47	20.50	0	0	132	146	3	48.66	1-18	0	0	6.63	1	
BOOTE, Matthew William Nelson (KwaZulu-Natal) b Pietermaritzburg, Natal 7.8.1990 RHB WK																			
FC		2	4	0	96	59	24.00	0	1									3	1
Lim		1	1	0	23	23	23.00	0	0									0	
BOOYSEN, Jaco (Easterns, Easterns to Namibia) b Witbank, Transvaal 10.3.1985 RHB RM																			
FC		11	18	1	703	145	41.35	2	3	48	15	1	15.00	1-15	0	0	1.87	9	
Lim		11	11	0	361	82	32.81	0	2									3	
FC	2003/04	44	73	6	2835	207*	42.31	7	14	150	75	2	37.50	1-15	0	0	3.00	47	
Lim	2004/05	48	46	4	1257	82	29.92	0	8	42	58	0					8.28	21	1
20T	2007/08	3	3	0	6	3	2.00	0	0									2	

Cmp	*Debut*	*M*	*I*	*NO*	*Runs*	*HS*	*Avge*	*100*	*50*	*Balls*	*Runs*	*Wkts*	*Avge*	*BB*	*5i*	*10m*	*RpO*	*ct*	*st*
BOSMAN, Lungile Edgar (Dolphins, KwaZulu-Natal, South Africa, South Africa A, Derbyshire, South Africa to India, South Africa to West Indies) b Kimberley, Cape Province 14.4.1977 RHB RM																			
FC		6	11	2	373	100*	41.44	1	2	6	1	0					1.00	2	
Lim		10	10	0	191	44	19.10	0	0									0	
I20T		2	2	0	152	94	76.00	0	2									0	
20T		6	6	0	223	94	37.16	0	2									1	
FC	1997/98	94	169	12	4568	140	29.09	5	23	576	343	8	42.87	3-25	0	0	3.57	51	
Int	2006/07	14	12	0	301	88	25.08	0	2									3	
Lim	1997/98	148	143	9	3804	99*	28.38	0	22	85	77	1	77.00	1-36	0	0	5.43	36	
I20T	2005/06	10	10	1	272	94	30.22	0	3									0	
20T	2003/04	57	55	3	1570	104	30.19	1	9									8	
BOSSENGER, Wendell (Griqualand West) b Cape Town, Cape Province 23.10.1976 RHB LB WK																			
FC		13	20	5	844	168	56.26	3	2	432	244	4	61.00	2-38	0	0	3.38	36	1
Lim		11	9	4	182	55*	36.40	0	1	76	79	4	19.75	2-30	0	0	6.23	2	
FC	1996/97	116	204	33	6143	168	35.92	8	37	552	325	8	40.62	3-16	0	0	3.53	385	17
Lim	1996/97	123	102	37	2159	157*	33.21	2	7	139	154	4	38.50	2-30	0	0	6.64	129	15
BOTHA, Johan (South Africa, Warriors, South Africa to India, South Africa to West Indies) b Johannesburg, Transvaal 2.5.1982 RHB OB																			
FC		6	8	1	464	109	66.28	1	4	749	469	15	31.26	4-69	0	0	3.75	3	
Int		5	3	0	22	21	7.33	0	0	270	216	5	43.20	2-22	0	0	4.80	0	
Lim		17	11	1	233	55	23.30	0	1	823	673	21	32.04	3-29	0	0	4.90	5	
I20T		1								24	36	0					9.00	1	
20T		3	1	1	29	29*		0	0	72	68	3	22.66	2-17	0	0	5.66	1	
Test	2005/06	3	3	1	54	25	27.00	0	0	464	280	11	25.45	4-56	0	0	3.62	2	
FC	2000/01	63	105	16	3087	109	34.68	1	22	8836	4503	147	30.63	6-42	4	1	3.05	46	
Int	2005/06	57	31	10	352	46	16.76	0	0	2772	2143	52	41.21	4-19	1	0	4.63	26	
Lim	2001/02	134	90	24	1381	55*	20.92	0	3	6024	4553	121	37.62	4-19	2	0	4.53	41	
I20T	2005/06	21	13	7	113	28*	18.83	0	0	420	422	22	19.18	3-16	0	0	6.02	10	
20T	2003/04	57	40	17	388	44*	16.86	0	0	1218	1194	52	22.96	4-19	1	0	5.88	22	
BOTHA, Patrick (Free State) b Bloemfontein, Free State 23.1.1990 LHB OB																			
FC		6	9	0	202	74	22.44	0	1	444	276	7	39.42	3-69	0	0	3.73	5	
Lim		5	5	1	117	51	29.25	0	1	134	107	5	21.40	2-34	0	0	4.79	1	
BOTHA, Riaan (South Western Districts) b Port Elizabeth, Cape Province 20.11.1991 RHB RMF																			
FC		3	5	1	15	9	3.75	0	0	222	134	9	14.88	6-26	1	0	3.62	1	
Lim		3	2	0	0	0	0.00	0	0	90	72	5	14.40	3-49	0	0	4.80	0	
BOTHMA, Johannes Paulus (Boland) b Bellville, Cape Province 28.3.1988 RHB RF																			
FC		8	13	4	104	28*	11.55	0	0	1068	631	14	45.07	3-39	0	0	3.54	2	
Lim		7	4	3	19	8*	19.00	0	0	300	253	19	13.31	5-29	0	1	5.06	0	
FC	2006/07	21	34	13	377	57	17.95	0	1	3022	1717	62	27.69	6-59	2	0	3.40	8	
Lim	2006/07	20	12	7	99	47*	19.80	0	0	818	611	43	14.20	5-29	1	2	4.48	2	
BOUCHER, Mark Verdon (South Africa, Warriors, Royal Challengers Bangalore, South Africa to India, South Africa to West Indies) b East London, Cape Province 3.12.1976 RHB RM WK																			
Test		4	7	1	341	95	56.83	0	3									16	
FC		4	7	1	341	95	56.83	0	3									16	
Int		8	8	2	176	31*	29.33	0	0									8	
Lim		12	12	2	246	47	24.60	0	0									13	
I20T		1																0	
20T		2	1	1	27	27*		0	0									0	2
Test	1997/98	134	189	22	5171	125	30.96	5	33	8	6	1	6.00	1-6	0	0	4.50	482	22
FC	1995/96	196	285	40	8279	134	33.79	9	51	26	26	1	26.00	1-6	0	0	6.00	660	36
Int	1997/98	292	218	56	4664	147*	28.79	1	26									400	22
Lim	1995/96	357	281	67	6137	147*	28.67	2	35									473	30
I20T	2005/06	25	21	6	268	36*	17.86	0	0									18	1
20T	2003/04	64	51	18	871	57*	26.39	0	2									38	9
BRAND, Derek (Western Province, Cape Cobras to India) b Bellville, Cape Province 29.5.1975 RHB RM																			
Lim		2	2	0	24	16	12.00	0	0									0	
FC	1998/99	14	26	2	571	62	23.79	0	2	702	313	5	62.60	2-42	0	0	2.67	21	3
Lim	1998/99	21	20	0	621	131	31.05	1	4	18	13	2	6.50	2-8	0	0	4.33	8	
20T	2008/09	5	5	0	136	68	27.20	0	1	6	17	1	17.00	1-17	0	0	17.00	1	
BREDENKAMP, Leroi Luke (North West) b George, Cape Province 19.10.1990 RHB LM																			
FC		1																1	
Lim		4																1	
BREDENKAMP, Neil (South Western Districts, South Western Districts to Namibia) b Potchefstroom, Transvaal 22.7.1987 RHB RM																			
FC		12	24	0	619	116	25.79	1	5	602	332	12	27.66	5-41	1	0	3.30	6	
Lim		11	11	0	227	73	20.63	0	1	330	300	8	37.50	2-20	0	0	5.45	1	
FC	2006/07	27	52	1	1570	125	30.78	4	10	683	400	15	26.66	5-41	1	0	3.51	14	
Lim	2006/07	26	25	1	582	73	24.25	0	4	414	398	11	36.18	2-20	0	0	5.76	7	
BROUWERS, Nigel Grant (South Western Districts) b Port Elizabeth, Cape Province 4.9.1976 LHB SLA																			
FC		4	7	0	60	29	8.57	0	0	604	348	13	26.76	5-83	1	0	3.45	2	
Lim		3	3	0	30	17	10.00	0	0	120	100	5	20.00	3-16	0	0	5.00	1	

Cmp	Debut	M	I	NO	Runs	HS	Avge	100	50	Balls	Runs	Wkts	Avge	BB	5i	10m	RpO	ct	st
FC	1998/99	31	54	3	955	63	18.72	0	4	4095	1957	75	26.09	6-57	3	0	2.86	22	
Lim	2000/01	30	23	2	574	94	27.33	0	4	1211	947	28	33.82	3-16	0	0	4.69	10	
BROWN, Darryl Lewis (Border, Warriors, Border to Namibia) b East London, Cape Province 25.3.1983 RHB RMF																			
FC		12	20	1	309	54	16.26	0	2	894	487	8	60.87	2-57	0	0	3.26	6	
Lim		9	9	1	197	69	24.62	0	1	186	145	2	72.50	1-29	0	0	4.67	3	
FC	2005/06	37	58	9	1286	112*	26.24	1	7	3572	1949	70	27.84	4-14	0	0	3.27	19	
Lim	2004/05	35	31	6	768	76	30.72	0	5	1118	994	27	36.81	3-32	0	0	5.33	6	
BROWN, Lyndon (KwaZulu-Natal Inland) b Pietermaritzburg, Natal 11.3.1983 LHB RFM																			
FC		3	3	0	17	8	5.66	0	0	246	183	5	36.60	2-85	0	0	4.46	1	
Lim		3	2	1	45	27*	45.00	0	0	42	51	1	51.00	1-33	0	0	7.28	0	
FC	2006/07	12	18	3	338	77	22.53	0	3	654	438	10	43.80	3-45	0	0	4.01	7	
Lim	2006/07	13	12	1	289	105	26.27	1	1	102	99	2	49.50	1-21	0	0	5.82	3	
BUCKTHORP, Kyle Gareth (KwaZulu-Natal) b Durban, Natal 16.7.1989 RHB OB																			
FC		5	5	2	40	22	13.33	0	0	564	280	7	40.00	3-45	0	0	2.97	0	
Lim		6	4	1	117	51	39.00	0	1	228	200	4	50.00	2-29	0	0	5.26	1	
BULA, Thandisizwe Andrew (North West) b Whittlesea, Cape Province 1.1.1981 RHB LB WK																			
Lim		1	1	0	6	6	6.00	0	0									0	2
FC	2001/02	53	83	15	1801	102	26.48	1	11	36	17	0					2.83	151	8
Lim	2001/02	46	32	7	675	76*	27.00	0	2	0	1	0						37	7
20T	2004/05	5	4	0	28	19	7.00	0	0									2	
BURGER, Shane (Gauteng, Lions, Gauteng to Namibia) b Johannesburg, Transvaal 31.8.1982 RHB RFM																			
FC		7	11	5	447	138*	74.50	3	0	859	336	25	13.44	5-13	1	0	2.34	4	
Lim		10	10	5	198	48*	39.60	0	0	318	286	9	31.77	3-20	0	0	5.39	3	
20T		7	2	2	28	16*		0	0	155	209	4	52.25	2-24	0	0	8.09	1	
FC	2001/02	33	46	13	1227	138*	37.18	3	6	4764	2239	102	21.95	5-13	4	0	2.82	19	
Lim	2002/03	42	32	12	495	54*	24.75	0	1	1512	1230	49	25.10	5-44	0	1	4.88	22	
20T	2007/08	9	3	3	29	16*		0	0	196	248	8	31.00	2-15	0	0	7.59	1	
CAMERON, Richard (Gauteng, Lions, Gauteng to Namibia) b Johannesburg, Transvaal 17.6.1986 RHB RMF																			
FC		8	10	0	165	36	16.50	0	0	826	455	16	28.43	3-36	0	0	3.30	6	
Lim		11	11	0	460	114	41.81	2	2	330	315	9	35.00	3-30	0	0	5.72	3	
20T		4	4	0	75	36	18.75	0	0	48	61	5	12.20	4-23	1	0	7.62	0	
FC	2006/07	19	26	4	554	80	25.18	0	2	1986	1047	38	27.55	4-70	0	0	3.16	10	
Lim	2006/07	34	27	3	632	114	26.33	2	2	1212	974	36	27.05	4-35	2	0	4.82	7	
CAMPHER, Jaco Pieter (North West) b Klerksdorp, Transvaal 9.10.1985 RHB LF																			
FC		1	1	0	4	4	4.00	0	0	135	103	4	25.75	4-56	0	0	4.57	0	
Lim		2	2	1	6	5*	6.00	0	0	96	88	4	22.00	2-44	0	0	5.50	0	
FC	2005/06	15	18	5	88	17	6.76	0	0	1920	1395	41	34.02	5-69	2	0	4.35	3	
Lim	2005/06	11	8	4	58	15	14.50	0	0	412	397	20	19.85	4-28	2	0	5.78	2	
20T	2005/06	2								42	62	0					8.85	1	
CANNING, Ryan Clement Cavanagh (Cape Cobras, Western Province, Cape Cobras to India) b Cape Town, Cape Province 22.2.1984 RHB WK																			
FC		16	23	3	598	116	29.90	1	4									51	3
Lim		5	5	0	103	41	20.60	0	0									4	
20T		1	1	0	3	3	3.00	0	0									1	
FC	2004/05	59	89	10	2308	122	29.21	3	13									188	10
Lim	2004/05	44	37	7	919	67	30.63	0	5	6	2	0					2.00	62	8
20T	2007/08	11	4	1	40	20	13.33	0	0									11	2
CAROLUS, Deon Dean (Griqualand West) b Port Elizabeth, Cape Province 10.7.1978 RHB RFM																			
FC		10	7	4	32	10*	10.66	0	0	996	536	9	59.55	3-65	0	0	3.22	4	
Lim		7								100	63	4	15.75	2-16	0	0	3.78	2	
FC	2003/04	35	44	15	270	33	9.31	0	0	4736	2399	96	24.98	5-25	5	0	3.03	13	
Lim	2004/05	35	20	8	80	17*	6.66	0	0	1308	1017	43	23.65	4-27	3	0	4.66	5	
CARTER, Neil Miller (Cape Cobras, Warwickshire, Warwickshire to Scotland) b Cape Town, Cape Province 29.1.1975 LHB LMF																			
Lim		5	3	1	43	30*	21.50	0	0	180	151	3	50.33	1-13	0	0	5.03	0	
FC	1999/00	107	148	24	2872	103	23.16	1	13	17725	10258	297	34.53	6-63	13	0	3.47	24	
Lim	1999/00	167	142	15	2853	135	22.46	3	12	7187	5804	220	26.38	5-31	6	2	4.84	14	
20T	2003	79	76	2	1217	58	16.44	0	2	1606	1869	77	24.27	5-19	0	1	6.98	11	
CHETTY, Cody (KwaZulu-Natal) b Durban, Natal 28.6.1991 RHB LB																			
FC		8	12	1	192	32	17.45	0	0	6	5	0					5.00	7	
Lim		9	6	1	65	23	13.00	0	0									3	
FC	2008/09	10	15	2	268	61*	20.61	0	1	18	23	0					7.66	7	
Lim	2008/09	11	8	2	129	51*	21.50	0	1									4	
CHETTY, Kemeshin (Dolphins, KwaZulu-Natal Inland, KwaZulu-Natal Inland to Namibia) b Durban, Natal 9.1.1988 RHB RMF																			
FC		7	10	3	66	34	9.42	0	0	1019	645	19	33.94	4-38	0	0	3.79	3	
Lim		8	2	0	6	5	3.00	0	0	204	229	3	76.33	2-66	0	0	6.73	5	
FC	2009/10	8	12	3	86	34	9.55	0	0	1229	747	23	32.47	4-38	0	0	3.64	3	
Lim	2008/09	10	3	0	17	11	5.66	0	0	252	267	3	89.00	2-66	0	0	6.35	5	

Cmp	Debut	M	I	NO	Runs	HS	Avge	100	50	Balls	Runs	Wkts	Avge	BB	5i	10m	RpO	ct	st
CHILDS, Daniel Barry (Boland, Boland to Namibia) b Cape Town, Cape Province 16.11.1988 RHB RFM																			
FC		5	7	1	3	3	0.50	0	0	742	382	10	38.20	3-63	0	0	3.08	0	
Lim		4								137	137	3	45.66	2-32	0	0	6.00	1	
FC	2007/08	10	14	5	5	3	0.55	0	0	1365	721	22	32.77	4-15	0	0	3.16	1	
Lim	2007/08	9	2	2	2	2*		0	0	305	251	5	50.20	2-32	0	0	4.93	1	
CLOETE, Gihan Love (Griqualand West) b Springbok, Cape Province 4.10.1992 LHB OB																			
FC		8	14	0	480	103	34.28	1	2	12	6	0					3.00	6	
Lim		7	6	1	58	31	11.60	0	0									0	
FC	2008/09	10	18	0	586	103	32.55	1	2	12	6	0					3.00	6	
Lim	2008/09	8	7	1	85	31	14.16	0	0									0	
CLOETE, Tiaan Willam Raymond (Boland, Boland to Namibia) b Paarl, Cape Province 12.11.1989 LHB SLA																			
FC		8	15	2	145	41	11.15	0	0	449	226	9	25.11	4-23	0	0	3.02	3	
Lim		7	5	0	91	52	18.20	0	1	102	89	3	29.66	2-40	0	0	5.23	3	
FC	2009/10	9	16	2	181	41	12.92	0	0	467	233	9	25.88	4-23	0	0	2.99	4	
Lim	2009/10	8	6	1	130	52	26.00	0	1	102	89	3	29.66	2-40	0	0	5.23	3	
COETSEE, Werner Loubser (Lions, North West) b Bethlehem 16.3.1983 RHB OB																			
FC		4	8	2	202	92*	33.66	0	2	851	405	18	22.50	5-78	2	0	2.85	5	
Lim		16	13	1	243	32	20.25	0	0	669	568	19	29.89	3-41	0	0	5.09	7	
20T		4	3	1	9	4*	4.50	0	0	90	139	2	69.50	1-37	0	0	9.26	1	
FC	2003/04	61	104	13	2808	131	30.85	3	20	10525	5274	145	36.37	5-73	3	0	3.00	45	
Lim	2002/03	86	73	10	1535	130*	24.36	2	4	3661	2850	83	34.33	4-20	1	0	4.67	29	
20T	2004/05	21	17	2	158	33	10.53	0	0	431	564	14	40.28	2-20	0	0	7.85	5	
COETZEE, Jandre (Eagles, Griqualand West, Eagles to India) b Springbok, Cape Province 15.1.1984 LHB LF																			
FC		7	9	2	184	97*	26.28	0	1	966	520	16	32.50	5-64	1	0	3.23	3	
Lim		8	6	1	43	22	8.60	0	0	348	276	10	27.60	3-11	0	0	4.75	1	
20T		5	2	2	11	9*		0	0	114	137	4	34.25	2-31	0	0	7.21	0	
FC	2004/05	41	59	17	1164	97*	27.71	0	4	6720	3401	155	21.94	7-42	8	0	3.03	21	
Lim	2004/05	38	33	7	652	60*	25.07	0	1	1673	1315	57	23.07	5-15	2	1	4.71	5	
20T	2007/08	15	7	5	16	9*	8.00	0	0	342	359	22	16.31	3-15	0	0	6.29	1	
COETZEE, Martin (South Western Districts) b Johannesburg, Transvaal 12.10.1988 RHB																			
Lim		2	2	1	23	23*	23.00	0	0									1	
CONWAY, Devon Philip (Gauteng) b Johannesburg, Transvaal 8.7.1991 LHB RM																			
FC		8	10	3	417	128	59.57	2	0	151	93	4	23.25	2-14	0	0	3.69	6	
FC	2008/09	9	12	3	427	128	47.44	2	0	151	93	4	23.25	2-14	0	0	3.69	6	
Lim	2008/09	1	1	0	6	6	6.00	0	0									0	
COOK, Stephen Craig (Gauteng, Lions, South Africa A to Sri Lanka) b Johannesburg, Transvaal 29.11.1982 RHB RM																			
FC		18	30	4	1642	390	63.15	5	9	36	33	0					5.50	22	
Lim		9	9	1	322	72	40.25	0	4									1	
FC	2000/01	92	168	13	6279	390	40.50	17	28	468	274	6	45.66	3-42	0	0	3.51	51	
Lim	2001/02	83	82	8	2866	116*	38.72	2	27	98	111	3	37.00	1-2	0	0	6.79	15	
20T	2003/04	10	10	0	220	45	22.00	0	0									2	
COOKE, Christopher Barry (Western Province) b Johannesburg, Transvaal 30.5.1986 RHB WK																			
FC		6	11	1	186	44*	18.60	0	0									12	1
Lim		11	11	3	351	109*	43.87	1	1									9	2
Lim	2008/09	14	14	3	415	109*	37.72	1	1									9	2
CROWIE, Fabian Shaun (KwaZulu-Natal) b Durban, Natal 7.6.1985 RHB RM																			
FC		3	4	0	71	36	17.75	0	0									2	
Lim		5	5	1	68	28	17.00	0	0									1	
DANIELS, Dominic Lesley (Boland) b Paarl, Cape Province 8.1.1992 RHB OB																			
FC		3	5	1	37	15*	9.25	0	0									3	
Lim		5	4	2	118	53*	59.00	0	1									3	
DAS NEVES, Richard (Gauteng, Gauteng to Namibia) b Johannesburg, Transvaal 18.12.1986 RHB OB																			
FC		1	2	0	24	13	12.00	0	0	18	7	0					2.33	1	
Lim		9	6	2	88	23*	22.00	0	0	408	288	12	24.00	3-13	0	0	4.23	3	
FC	2006/07	7	8	0	92	32	11.50	0	0	594	318	15	21.20	5-52	1	0	3.21	2	
Lim	2006/07	20	13	5	146	24*	18.25	0	0	839	604	34	17.76	4-24	2	0	4.31	8	
DAVIDS, Henry (Boland, Cape Cobras, South Africa A, Boland to Namibia, Cape Cobras to India) b Stellenbosch, Cape Province 19.1.1980 RHB RMF																			
FC		7	11	0	237	56	21.54	0	2	185	142	4	35.50	3-49	0	0	4.60	7	
Lim		5	5	0	305	147	61.00	1	1	6	15	0					15.00	1	
20T		6	5	0	78	25	15.60	0	0									2	
FC	2000/01	72	130	7	3966	158	32.24	8	25	1002	635	17	37.35	3-11	0	0	3.80	55	
Lim	2000/01	92	89	7	2525	147	30.79	4	14	573	537	9	59.66	3-44	0	0	5.62	34	
20T	2003/04	45	41	5	760	112*	21.11	1	3									12	
DAVIS-TAYLOR, Terence Andrew (South Western Districts) b Uitenhage, Cape Province 2.9.1978 RHB RMF																			
FC		1	2	1	14	14*	14.00	0	0	162	131	1	131.00	1-95	0	0	4.85	0	
Lim		1								30	47	1	47.00	1-47	0	0	9.40	0	
FC	2008/09	4	6	1	24	14*	4.80	0	0	534	305	9	33.88	4-31	0	0	3.42	1	
Lim	2007/08	8	4	1	8	4	2.66	0	0	235	233	7	33.28	3-51	0	0	5.94	1	

Cmp	Debut	M	I	NO	Runs	HS	Avge	100	50	Balls	Runs	Wkts	Avge	BB	5i	10m	RpO	ct	st
DEACON, Wycliffe Andrew (Lions, North West) b Kroonstad, Orange Free State 23.6.1980 LHB LFM																			
FC		12	20	3	567	69*	33.35	0	3	2282	1263	52	24.28	6-75	2	0	3.32	7	
Lim		15	10	3	196	82*	28.00	0	2	610	622	19	32.73	5-23	0	1	6.11	3	
20T		1	1	0	5	5	5.00	0	0	18	35	1	35.00	1-35	0	0	11.66	2	
FC	2003/04	47	71	16	1842	82	33.49	0	11	8452	4416	154	28.67	6-45	5	0	3.13	25	
Lim	2000/01	88	65	18	1146	112	24.38	1	8	3936	3276	97	33.77	5-23	1	3	4.99	26	
20T	2003/04	33	21	6	163	27	10.86	0	0	730	706	42	16.80	4-15	1	0	5.80	9	
DE BRUYN, Pierre (Dolphins, KwaZulu-Natal) b Pretoria, Transvaal 31.3.1977 RHB RFM																			
FC		6	11	2	358	77	39.77	0	3	234	100	1	100.00	1-32	0	0	2.56	9	
Lim		7	7	4	199	111*	66.33	1	0	120	93	1	93.00	1-16	0	0	4.65	6	
20T		3	2	1	7	6*	7.00	0	0	24	25	1	25.00	1-11	0	0	6.25	1	
FC	1995/96	91	146	21	4637	202	37.09	10	23	6882	3201	108	29.63	6-38	3	0	2.79	87	
Lim	1999/00	108	86	26	1791	111*	29.85	1	9	2934	2287	60	38.11	4-28	1	0	4.67	54	4
20T	2004/05	28	20	9	286	44*	26.00	0	0	217	255	12	21.25	4-11	1	0	7.05	12	2
DE BRUYN, Zander (Lions, Somerset, Somerset to India) b Johannesburg, Transvaal 5.7.1975 RHB RFM																			
FC		8	12	0	468	144	39.00	1	3	1015	571	12	47.58	4-65	0	0	3.37	4	
Lim		10	10	3	212	54*	30.28	0	1	237	314	5	62.80	1-18	0	0	7.94	3	
20T		8	8	3	138	39	27.60	0	0	84	158	1	158.00	1-21	0	0	11.28	3	
Test	2004/05	3	5	1	155	83	38.75	0	1	216	92	3	30.66	2-32	0	0	2.55	0	
FC	1995/96	167	279	27	10008	266*	39.71	21	54	13123	7573	191	39.64	7-67	3	0	3.46	103	
Lim	1995/96	181	165	33	4829	122*	36.58	5	30	4471	4045	128	31.60	5-44	2	1	5.42	43	
20T	2004/05	79	72	21	1544	95*	30.27	0	6	678	995	34	29.26	4-18	1	0	8.80	17	
DEEB, Dale Robin (Gauteng) b Johannesburg, Transvaal 8.9.1990 RHB SLA																			
FC		1	2	1	6	5*	6.00	0	0	56	32	2	16.00	2-32	0	0	3.42	1	
Lim		1	1	0	0	0	0.00	0	0	48	36	2	18.00	2-36	0	0	4.50	0	
FC	2007/08	9	13	2	150	58	13.63	0	1	1237	671	24	27.95	6-50	1	0	3.25	6	
Lim	2008/09	4	4	1	24	16*	8.00	0	0	131	86	5	17.20	3-25	0	0	3.93	0	
DE KOCK, Hendrik Gabriel (Griqualand West) b Pretoria, Transvaal 12.12.1983 RHB LB																			
FC		3	6	1	142	49	28.40	0	0									1	
Lim		3	2	0	2	2	1.00	0	0									0	
FC	2004/05	27	50	3	1202	93	25.57	0	7	686	420	14	30.00	4-45	0	0	3.67	12	
Lim	2004/05	24	23	1	613	107	27.86	1	1	82	109	5	21.80	4-49	1	0	7.97	3	
DE KOCK, Quinton (Gauteng) b Johannesburg, Transvaal 17.12.1992 LHB WK																			
FC		1	2	0	15	9	7.50	0	0									4	1
Lim		3	3	0	5	5	1.66	0	0									3	1
DE KOCK, Shaun (Border, Border to Namibia) b East London, Cape Province 7.5.1985 LHB SLA																			
FC		11	20	2	541	100*	30.05	1	3	1688	977	42	23.26	8-64	3	1	3.47	9	
Lim		11	11	0	194	54	17.63	0	1	436	314	12	26.16	3-26	0	0	4.32	2	
FC	2004/05	38	62	4	1141	100*	19.67	1	5	4579	2419	91	26.58	8-64	3	1	3.17	22	
Lim	2004/05	38	34	3	532	90*	17.16	0	4	1545	1119	38	29.44	3-26	0	0	4.34	13	
DE LANGE, Con de Wet (Eagles, Free State) b Bellville, Cape Province 11.2.1981 RHB SLA																			
FC		11	15	2	256	54	19.69	0	2	2076	1027	22	46.68	3-107	0	0	2.96	4	
Lim		13	8	2	225	51	37.50	0	1	438	354	13	27.23	3-21	0	0	4.84	7	
20T		1	1	0	6	6	6.00	0	0	24	36	1	36.00	1-36	0	0	9.00	2	
FC	1997/98	80	130	12	2592	109	21.96	1	11	14329	6607	171	38.63	7-48	5	1	2.76	44	
Lim	1999/00	109	74	18	1313	66	23.44	0	6	4589	3310	113	29.29	4-8	2	0	4.32	32	
20T	2006/07	16	7	2	23	8	4.60	0	0	306	360	14	25.71	2-14	0	0	7.05	10	
DELPORT, Cameron Scott (Dolphins, KwaZulu-Natal) b Durban, Natal 12.5.1989 LHB RM																			
FC		14	24	3	588	61	28.00	0	2	258	140	1	140.00	1-55	0	0	3.25	16	
Lim		14	13	0	181	43	13.92	0	0	128	121	2	60.50	1-17	0	0	5.67	8	
20T		1	1	0	0	0	0.00	0	0									0	
FC	2008/09	22	38	3	1049	110	29.97	1	4	414	278	4	69.50	2-25	0	0	4.02	18	
Lim	2008/09	18	17	0	249	43	14.64	0	0	158	147	3	49.00	1-16	0	0	5.58	10	
DESAI, Ziyaad (Gauteng) b Lenasia, Transvaal 18.5.1980 RHB RM																			
FC		2	3	0	53	32	17.66	0	0	36	1	1	1.00	1-1	0	0	0.16	0	
Lim		3	2	2	20	17*		0	0	36	42	2	21.00	2-28	0	0	7.00	0	
FC	2004/05	8	15	1	216	49	15.42	0	0	54	7	1	7.00	1-1	0	0	0.77	4	
Lim	2008/09	4	3	2	23	17*	23.00	0	0	36	42	2	21.00	2-28	0	0	7.00	0	
DE VILLIERS, Abraham Benjamin (South Africa, Titans, Delhi Daredevils, South Africa to India, South Africa to West Indies) b Pretoria, Transvaal 17.2.1984 RHB RM																			
Test		4	7	0	276	64	39.42	0	3									5	
FC		4	7	0	276	64	39.42	0	3									5	
Int		8	8	1	331	121	47.28	1	2									5	
Lim		11	11	1	488	121	48.80	1	4									7	
I20T		2	2	1	34	24	34.00	0	0									1	
20T		3	3	1	44	24	22.00	0	0									2	
Test	2004/05	61	105	12	4232	217*	45.50	10	23	198	99	2	49.50	2-49	0	0	3.00	86	1
FC	2003/04	85	148	17	6081	217*	46.41	13	37	228	133	2	66.50	2-49	0	0	3.50	132	2
Int	2004/05	101	97	14	3616	146	43.56	7	22	12	22	0					11.00	63	
Lim	2003/04	126	121	17	4642	146	44.63	9	30	12	22	0					11.00	84	

Cmp	Debut	M	I	NO	Runs	HS	Avge	100	50	Balls	Runs	Wkts	Avge	BB	5i	10m	RpO	ct	st
I20T	2005/06	30	29	6	579	79*	25.17	0	4									32	4
20T	2003/04	69	65	12	1574	105*	29.69	1	9									62	6
DE VILLIERS, Cornelius Johannes du Preez (Eagles, Free State, South Africa A, Eagles to India, South Africa A to Sri Lanka) b Kroonstad, Orange Free State 16.3.1986 RHB RFM																			
FC		10	12	1	217	50*	19.72	0	2	1825	1059	33	32.09	4-36	0	0	3.48	3	
Lim		11	7	1	63	32	10.50	0	0	418	459	12	38.25	2-15	0	0	6.58	3	
20T		1	1	1	1	1*		0	0	18	19	2	9.50	2-19	0	0	6.33	0	
FC	2006/07	40	59	9	906	84	18.12	0	5	6888	3606	126	28.61	5-36	2	0	3.14	13	
Lim	2006/07	26	17	4	205	36	15.76	0	0	1098	1058	31	34.12	5-39	0	1	5.78	6	
20T	2008/09	14	7	4	25	7*	8.33	0	0	281	297	22	13.50	5-12	2	1	6.34	3	
DE VRIES, Morne Heinrich (Boland) b Wellington, Cape Province 7.5.1984 RHB WK																			
Lim		1	1	0	12	12	12.00	0	0	24	32	0					8.00	0	
DE WEE, Granville Ruwayne (Griqualand West) b Upington, Cape Province 9.7.1988 RHB RFM																			
FC		4	4	1	32	26	10.66	0	0	276	108	7	15.42	5-15	1	0	2.34	2	
Lim		6	3	0	11	9	3.66	0	0	144	117	6	19.50	2-14	0	0	4.87	2	
DE WET, Friedel (Lions, South Africa) b Durban, Natal 26.6.1980 RHB RFM																			
Test		2	2	0	20	20	10.00	0	0	426	186	6	31.00	4-55	0	0	2.62	1	
FC		7	7	2	79	35*	15.80	0	0	1603	816	26	31.38	4-55	0	0	3.05	2	
Lim		4								174	172	4	43.00	3-33	0	0	5.93	1	
FC	2001/02	47	65	13	812	56	15.61	0	1	9709	4576	194	23.58	7-61	10	2	2.82	19	
Lim	2001/02	52	23	14	258	56*	28.66	0	1	2348	1874	61	30.72	5-59	1	1	4.78	9	
20T	2004/05	16	7	4	43	17	14.33	0	0	322	439	17	25.82	2-18	0	0	8.18	5	
DE WET, Hennie Wouter (Boland) b Cape Town, Cape Province 17.4.1989 RHB RFM																			
FC		6	9	0	137	38	15.22	0	0	928	496	16	31.00	3-40	0	0	3.20	3	
Lim		5	3	1	43	24*	21.50	0	0	172	150	9	16.66	5-54	0	1	5.23	1	
FC	2007/08	14	23	0	249	38	10.82	0	0	2242	1107	45	24.60	5-17	2	0	2.96	5	
Lim	2007/08	16	9	1	63	24*	7.87	0	0	670	501	27	18.55	5-54	0	1	4.48	2	
DE WETT, Burton Christopher (South Western Districts, South Western Districts to Namibia) b East London, Cape Province 25.12.1980 LHB LBG																			
FC		12	24	1	642	108	27.91	1	4	648	442	13	34.00	3-32	0	0	4.09	12	
Lim		11	11	0	328	88	29.81	0	3	78	74	2	37.00	2-33	0	0	5.69	7	
FC	2000/01	59	109	5	2731	182	26.25	4	13	2699	1743	45	38.73	7-95	1	0	3.87	43	
Lim	2000/01	60	55	4	1246	88	24.43	0	8	491	393	15	26.20	3-19	0	0	4.80	24	
20T	2004/05	9	8	0	78	16	9.75	0	0									2	
DIPPENAAR, Hendrik Human (Eagles, Eagles to India) b Kimberley, Cape Province 14.6.1977 RHB OB																			
FC		9	17	3	495	112*	35.35	2	2	30	5	0					1.00	16	
Lim		10	10	0	216	76	21.60	0	1									1	
20T		5	4	1	90	36*	30.00	0	0									2	
Test	1999/00	38	62	5	1718	177*	30.14	3	7	12	1	0					0.50	27	
FC	1995/96	184	313	31	11619	250*	41.20	33	50	120	66	1	66.00	1-6	0	0	3.30	193	
Int	1999/00	107	95	14	3421	125*	42.23	4	26									36	
Lim	1995/96	245	224	31	7596	125*	39.35	8	52	18	7	1	7.00	1-5	0	0	2.33	90	
I20T	2005/06	1	1	0	1	1	1.00	0	0									0	
20T	2003/04	59	51	8	885	63	20.58	0	2									24	
DLAMINI, Melusi (Easterns) b Boksburg, Transvaal 16.5.1991 RHB RFM																			
FC		2	2	0	1	1	0.50	0	0	132	105	4	26.25	2-52	0	0	4.77	0	
DOLLEY, Corbyn Richard (Eastern Province, Warriors) b Port Elizabeth, Cape Province 26.11.1987 RHB OB																			
FC		7	11	3	101	30	12.62	0	0	1090	524	16	32.75	5-151	1	0	2.88	6	
Lim		8	5	2	12	10	4.00	0	0	338	233	11	21.18	3-29	0	0	4.13	5	
FC	2006/07	19	26	6	258	37	12.90	0	0	2300	1131	38	29.76	5-151	1	0	2.95	14	
Lim	2006/07	24	13	7	59	14*	9.83	0	0	979	671	25	26.84	3-28	0	0	4.11	11	
20T	2006/07	7	1	1	1	1*		0	0	84	130	3	43.33	2-29	0	0	9.28	2	
DORASAMY, Sashen (KwaZulu-Natal Inland) b Pietermartizburg, Natal 12.1.1981 RHB RMF																			
FC		1								50	30	0					3.60	0	
FC	2006/07	10	12	1	177	52	16.09	0	1	446	224	4	56.00	2-25	0	0	3.01	4	
Lim	2006/07	13	9	2	51	21	7.28	0	0	246	204	4	51.00	1-21	0	0	4.97	6	
DRUMMOND, Timothy James (KwaZulu-Natal Inland, KwaZulu-Natal Inland to Namibia) b Cape Town, Cape Province 5.3.1988 RHB WK																			
FC		9	17	3	440	67	31.42	0	2									16	1
Lim		11	11	0	287	59	26.09	0	1									7	5
FC	2007/08	18	31	4	641	67	23.74	0	2									43	3
Lim	2007/08	20	20	2	639	125*	35.50	1	3									15	6
DUMINY, Jean-Paul (Cape Cobras, South Africa, Cape Cobras to India, Mumbai Indians, South Africa to India, South Africa to West Indies) b Strandfontein, Cape Town, Cape Province 14.4.1984 LHB OB																			
Test		4	7	0	114	56	16.28	0	1	323	169	8	21.12	3-89	0	0	3.13	2	
FC		4	7	0	114	56	16.28	0	1	323	169	8	21.12	3-89	0	0	3.13	2	
Int		7	7	1	199	111*	33.16	1	0	84	70	3	23.33	2-25	0	0	5.00	7	
Lim		11	10	1	360	111*	40.00	2	0	228	195	6	32.50	2-25	0	0	5.13	8	
I20T		2	2	0	8	6	4.00	0	0									0	
20T		2	2	0	8	6	4.00	0	0									0	
Test	2008/09	12	20	2	518	166	28.77	1	3	671	408	11	37.09	3-89	0	0	3.64	12	

Cmp	Debut	M	I	NO	Runs	HS	Avge	100	50	Balls	Runs	Wkts	Avge	BB	5i	10m	RpO	ct	st
FC	2001/02	61	102	17	4085	169	48.05	12	21	2324	1384	35	39.54	5-108	1	0	3.57	47	
Int	2004	58	51	12	1391	111*	35.66	1	7	697	581	16	36.31	3-31	0	0	5.00	23	
Lim	2002/03	107	92	15	2709	111*	35.18	2	18	1055	880	23	38.26	3-31	0	0	5.00	33	
I20T	2007/08	25	24	5	456	78	24.00	0	2	42	52	4	13.00	1-3	0	0	7.42	12	
20T	2003/04	81	77	18	1961	99*	33.23	0	14	373	444	22	20.18	4-24	1	0	7.14	26	
DU PLESSIS, Francois (Titans) b Pretoria, Transvaal 13.7.1984 RHB LB																			
FC		7	10	1	267	73	29.66	0	2	210	103	1	103.00	1-21	0	0	2.94	9	
Lim		10	9	0	262	52	29.11	0	2	102	97	1	97.00	1-15	0	0	5.70	13	
20T		6	4	1	59	23	19.66	0	0	66	72	4	18.00	3-18	0	0	6.54	2	
FC	2003/04	68	111	10	3529	176	34.94	4	26	2012	1132	31	36.51	4-39	0	0	3.37	61	
Lim	2003/04	89	78	16	2502	114*	40.35	4	15	1435	1292	34	38.00	4-47	1	0	5.40	52	
20T	2006/07	43	38	4	692	78*	20.35	0	3	528	626	34	18.41	3-18	0	0	7.11	14	
DU PLESSIS, Johannes Jacobus (Griqualand West) b Upington, Cape Province 28.3.1986 RHB OB																			
FC		2	3	0	59	58	19.66	0	1	128	90	2	45.00	1-41	0	0	4.21	1	
Lim		2	1	0	0	0	0.00	0	0	24	28	0					7.00	0	
DU PLESSIS, Rico (Gauteng) b Johannesburg, Transvaal 7.5.1991 RHB RM																			
FC		1	2	0	14	10	7.00	0	0	36	8	1	8.00	1-3	0	0	1.33	0	
DU PLESSIS, Ruan Andre (Easterns, Easterns to Namibia) b Johannesburg, Transvaal 1.8.1989 RHB RM																			
FC		9	16	0	486	112	30.37	1	3									3	
Lim		8	8	0	130	57	16.25	0	1									0	
FC	2006/07	15	26	0	712	112	27.38	1	4	6	4	0					4.00	4	
Lim	2006/07	12	12	0	216	57	18.00	0	1									0	
DU PREEZ, Dillon (Eagles, Free State, Eagles to India) b Queenstown, Cape Province 8.11.1981 RHB RMF																			
FC		5	6	1	30	16	6.00	0	0	1101	535	26	20.57	6-31	2	1	2.91	3	
Lim		10	9	1	67	27	8.37	0	0	416	434	14	31.00	4-33	1	0	6.26	2	
20T		5	3	0	20	10	6.66	0	0	120	127	10	12.70	3-17	0	0	6.35	2	
FC	2003/04	52	73	8	1043	122	16.04	1	3	9584	4348	190	22.88	7-108	7	2	2.72	12	
Lim	2004/05	70	51	20	873	107*	28.16	1	2	3226	2721	79	34.44	4-22	2	0	5.06	11	
20T	2005/06	39	29	9	324	40*	16.20	0	0	756	928	42	22.09	3-17	0	0	7.36	11	
DU PREEZ, Johannes Hendrik (Easterns) b Kempton Park, Transvaal 21.8.1992 LHB WK																			
FC		1	1	1	20	20*		0	0									1	
Lim		1	1	0	7	7	7.00	0	0									0	
DYILI, Athenkosi Ziphozihle Madoda (Eastern Province, Warriors) b King William's Town, Cape Province 17.7.1984 LHB WK																			
FC		8	12	4	189	43	23.62	0	0									29	5
Lim		10	10	0	157	43	15.70	0	0									12	
FC	2004/05	43	72	10	1350	98	21.77	0	8									114	15
Lim	2004/05	43	41	5	859	100	23.86	1	2									39	6
20T	2005/06	14	10	0	116	28	11.60	0	0									5	4
ECCLES, Keagan Wesley (KwaZulu-Natal) b Welkom, Free State 8.12.1990 RHB LFM																			
FC		2	3	0	79	59	26.33	0	1	222	100	1	100.00	1-74	0	0	2.70	0	
Lim		1	1	0	17	17	17.00	0	0	18	18	0					6.00	1	
ELGAR, Dean (Eagles, Free State, South Africa A, Eagles to India, South Africa A to Bangladesh, South Africa A to Sri Lanka) b Welkom, Orange Free State 11.6.1987 LHB SLA																			
FC		12	22	3	1193	189*	62.78	5	4	246	179	3	59.66	1-12	0	0	4.36	8	
Lim		12	12	1	245	108	22.27	1	1	141	128	1	128.00	1-15	0	0	5.44	3	
20T		2	2	0	45	30	22.50	0	0	24	30	0					7.50	0	
FC	2005/06	49	89	8	3753	225	46.33	12	14	1216	830	15	55.33	3-68	0	0	4.09	42	
Lim	2005/06	57	56	12	1519	108	34.52	1	9	979	832	14	59.42	2-39	0	0	5.09	15	
20T	2007/08	18	15	3	359	47	29.91	0	0	153	135	9	15.00	3-10	0	0	5.29	5	
ENGELBRECHT, Rabian (Boland) b Paarl, Cape Province 4.11.1992 RHB RFM																			
Lim		1								42	56	1	56.00	1-56	0	0	8.00	0	
ENGELBRECHT, Sybrand Abraham (Cape Cobras, Western Province, Cape Cobras to India) b Johannesburg, Transvaal 15.9.1988 RHB OB																			
FC		2	2	2	13	8*		0	0	156	102	2	51.00	2-74	0	0	3.92	1	
Lim		11	6	4	135	69*	67.50	0	1	425	401	8	50.12	3-39	0	0	5.66	5	
20T		3	1	1	5	5*		0	0	18	25	0					8.33	1	
FC	2007/08	7	11	3	192	45	24.00	0	0	527	350	8	43.75	3-47	0	0	3.98	5	
Lim	2007/08	19	12	6	190	69*	31.66	0	1	698	587	16	36.68	3-35	0	0	5.04	9	
20T	2008/09	5	2	1	8	5*	8.00	0	0	48	67	0					8.37	1	
ERASMUS, Ockert Johannes (Boland, Boland to Namibia) b Ladysmith, Natal 20.1.1988 RHB OB																			
FC		2	3	0	96	67	32.00	0	1	244	157	4	39.25	2-33	0	0	3.86	0	
Lim		11	8	1	55	18	7.85	0	0	463	368	19	19.36	4-18	1	0	4.76	5	
Lim	2008/09	14	9	1	55	18	6.87	0	0	537	417	22	18.95	4-18	1	0	4.65	6	
ERLANK, Michael Nicholas (Free State) b Kimberley, Cape Province 4.7.1990 LHB OB																			
FC		12	15	0	214	32	14.26	0	0	786	428	14	30.57	4-42	0	0	3.26	6	
Lim		12	8	1	121	51*	17.28	0	1	196	157	7	22.42	2-33	0	0	4.80	4	
FC	2007/08	15	19	0	367	85	19.31	0	1	786	428	14	30.57	4-42	0	0	3.26	6	
Lim	2007/08	15	10	1	161	51*	17.88	0	1	196	157	7	22.42	2-33	0	0	4.80	6	

Cmp	Debut	M	I	NO	Runs	HS	Avge	100	50	Balls	Runs	Wkts	Avge	BB	5i	10m	RpO	ct	st
ERWEE, Sarel Johannes (KwaZulu-Natal) b Pietermaritzburg, Natal 10.11.1989 LHB OB																			
FC		1	2	0	10	10	5.00	0	0									0	
Lim		2	1	0	0	0	0.00	0	0									1	
FC	2008/09	3	4	0	41	23	10.25	0	0									0	
Lim	2007/08	4	2	0	1	1	0.50	0	0	36	40	0					6.66	1	
FERRIS, Ryan Lyle (Free State) b Kimberley, Cape Province 22.6.1989 RHB RMF																			
Lim		2	2	2	2	2*		0	0									0	
FLOWERS, Calvin Anthony (KwaZulu-Natal) b Durban, Natal 20.7.1985 RHB OB																			
FC		4	7	2	80	28	16.00	0	0	513	361	17	21.23	5-92	1	0	4.22	4	
Lim		3	2	0	25	25	12.50	0	0	114	104	3	34.66	1-30	0	0	5.47	0	
FC	2006/07	9	17	6	254	57*	23.09	0	1	974	615	25	24.60	5-92	1	0	3.78	5	
Lim	2006/07	11	7	2	118	41*	23.60	0	0	414	321	8	40.12	2-29	0	0	4.65	1	
FOJELA, Phaphama (Border, Border to Namibia) b King William's Town, Cape Province 28.8.1984 RHB RFM																			
FC		7	13	6	92	23	13.14	0	0	720	536	14	38.28	4-73	0	0	4.46	1	
Lim		11	5	2	72	27	24.00	0	0	480	521	25	20.84	5-43	1	1	6.51	3	
FC	2004/05	29	33	13	304	28	15.20	0	0	3205	1797	72	24.95	5-45	1	0	3.36	6	
Lim	2004/05	28	17	3	161	27	11.50	0	0	1142	1039	39	26.64	5-43	2	1	5.45	6	
FOTHERINGHAM, Gregory Stephen (KwaZulu-Natal) b Johannesburg, Transvaal 5.8.1986 RHB RM																			
FC		8	14	0	245	93	17.50	0	2									7	
Lim		7	6	0	235	109	39.16	1	1									3	
FC	2008/09	14	24	2	598	93	27.18	0	6	4	8	0					12.00	11	
Lim	2008/09	13	11	0	378	109	34.36	1	2									5	
FOURIE, Johan Christiaan (Easterns) b Johannesburg, Transvaal 1.11.1982 RHB RM																			
FC		3	6	3	231	113*	77.00	1	0	66	42	3	14.00	3-24	0	0	3.81	4	
Lim		3	3	1	56	36	28.00	0	0	36	26	0					4.33	2	
FC	2007/08	7	14	7	394	113*	56.28	1	0	120	65	4	16.25	3-24	0	0	3.25	6	
Lim	2007/08	10	10	1	171	36	19.00	0	0	126	98	2	49.00	1-2	0	0	4.66	3	
FRANSMAN, Bardo Llewellyn (South Western Districts) b Worcester, Cape Province 3.3.1979 RHB RMF																			
FC		8	10	2	56	19*	7.00	0	0	893	418	15	27.86	3-40	0	0	2.80	2	
Lim		7	6	3	47	16*	15.66	0	0	232	268	2	134.00	1-31	0	0	6.93	4	
FC	2003/04	31	42	12	194	40	6.46	0	0	3889	1941	83	23.38	5-31	4	0	2.99	8	
Lim	2003/04	38	19	7	120	42	10.00	0	0	1615	1354	53	25.54	6-40	2	1	5.03	11	
FRIEND, Quinton (Dolphins, KwaZulu-Natal, South Africa A to Bangladesh, South Africa A to Sri Lanka) b Bellville, Cape Town, Cape Province 16.2.1982 RHB RFM																			
FC		9	12	0	221	63	18.41	0	2	1787	847	50	16.94	6-45	3	1	2.84	6	
Lim		9	6	2	23	10	5.75	0	0	302	325	10	32.50	2-26	0	0	6.45	4	
20T		5	3	2	11	8	11.00	0	0	84	94	2	47.00	1-27	0	0	6.71	2	
FC	2002/03	60	71	15	1000	78	17.85	0	4	9218	4652	197	23.61	7-31	7	1	3.02	22	
Lim	2001/02	54	28	8	157	25*	7.85	0	0	2267	1804	67	26.92	4-38	1	0	4.77	17	
20T	2003/04	24	9	4	33	18	6.60	0	0	475	558	14	39.85	2-22	0	0	7.04	4	
FRYLINCK, Robert (Gauteng, Lions, Gauteng to Namibia) b Durban, Natal 27.9.1984 RHB RFM																			
FC		6	9	1	207	70	25.87	0	1	1044	513	19	27.00	5-78	1	0	2.94	2	
Lim		9	7	2	92	22	18.40	0	0	294	387	7	55.28	3-38	0	0	7.89	2	
20T		8	7	3	43	15	10.75	0	0	192	227	14	16.21	4-31	1	0	7.09	2	
FC	2005/06	26	38	4	846	100*	24.88	1	6	4086	2053	80	25.66	6-94	2	0	3.01	8	
Lim	2004/05	33	24	7	524	82*	30.82	0	3	1056	1032	35	29.48	5-39	0	2	5.86	8	
20T	2005/06	17	16	6	126	29	12.60	0	0	312	367	21	17.47	4-31	1	0	7.05	7	
FYNN, Warrick Francis Sinclair (Eastern Province) b Durban, Natal 19.4.1985 LHB SLA																			
FC		2	3	0	55	51	18.33	0	1	354	181	4	45.25	3-58	0	0	3.06	2	
Lim		1	1	0	17	17	17.00	0	0	18	24	1	24.00	1-24	0	0	8.00	0	
FC	2004/05	10	17	2	367	104	24.46	1	1	1325	674	24	28.08	6-59	2	0	3.05	9	
Lim	2006/07	12	10	2	182	89*	22.75	0	1	570	434	19	22.84	4-30	1	0	4.56	2	
GERBER, Etienne (Lions, North West) b Kempton Park, Johannesburg, Transvaal 6.7.1988 RHB RMF																			
FC		6	6	0	18	9	3.00	0	0	876	453	12	37.75	4-73	0	0	3.10	0	
Lim		4	2	2	5	5*		0	0	174	140	6	23.33	2-24	0	0	4.82	1	
FC	2006/07	19	19	3	123	29*	7.68	0	0	3075	1432	60	23.86	5-37	2	0	2.79	12	
Lim	2006/07	14	7	5	57	25	28.50	0	0	647	493	18	27.38	4-31	2	0	4.57	4	
GIBBS, Herschelle Herman (Cape Cobras, South Africa, South Africa A, Cape Cobras to India, Deccan Chargers, South Africa to India, South Africa to West Indies, Yorkshire) b Green Point, Cape Town, Cape Province 23.2.1974 RHB LB																			
Int		1	1	0	22	22	22.00	0	0									0	
Lim		13	12	3	542	121*	60.22	2	3									4	
20T		3	3	0	103	53	34.33	0	1									1	
Test	1996/97	90	154	7	6167	228	41.95	14	26	6	4	0					4.00	94	
FC	1990/91	193	331	13	13425	228	42.21	31	60	138	78	3	26.00	2-14	0	0	3.39	176	
Int	1996/97	248	240	16	8094	175	36.13	21	37									108	
Lim	1990/91	383	366	32	11860	175	35.50	27	62	66	57	2	28.50	1-16	0	0	5.18	169	
I20T	2005/06	23	23	1	400	90*	18.18	0	3									8	
20T	2003/04	100	98	9	2380	101*	26.74	1	16									54	
GIDANA, Siviwe (Eastern Province) b Port Elizabeth, Cape Province 7.8.1987 RHB RFM																			
FC		1								72	58	1	58.00	1-36	0	0	4.83	0	
Lim		6	1	1	2	2*		0	0	132	135	6	22.50	3-32	0	0	6.13	0	

Cmp	Debut	M	I	NO	Runs	HS	Avge	100	50	Balls	Runs	Wkts	Avge	BB	5i	10m	RpO	ct	st
FC	2008/09	3	3	2	9	4*	9.00	0	0	258	177	2	88.50	1-29	0	0	4.11	0	
Lim	2008/09	9	3	1	8	6	4.00	0	0	232	197	11	17.90	4-30	1	0	5.09	0	
GOBIND, Viyash (Dolphins, KwaZulu-Natal) b Durban, Natal 22.12.1984 LHB RFM																			
FC		8	12	3	78	32	8.66	0	0	943	590	25	23.60	4-49	0	0	3.75	2	
Lim		13	5	4	30	14*	30.00	0	0	537	522	21	24.85	4-39	1	0	5.83	2	
20T		1								19	34	1	34.00	1-34	0	0	10.73	1	
FC	2004/05	19	30	6	251	37	10.45	0	0	2402	1389	52	26.71	5-38	1	0	3.47	5	
Lim	2007/08	19	7	5	37	14*	18.50	0	0	837	796	32	24.87	4-39	2	0	5.70	4	
GOVENDER, Nashen (KwaZulu-Natal) b Durban, Natal 5.10.1989 RHB SLA																			
FC		2	4	0	36	17	9.00	0	0									0	
Lim		3	3	1	158	105*	79.00	1	0									0	
FC	2008/09	3	6	0	45	17	7.50	0	0									0	
GOVENDER, Ugasen (Gauteng, Lions) b Tongaat, Natal 17.12.1983 RHB RF																			
FC		11	8	2	32	12	5.33	0	0	1368	710	21	33.80	5-30	1	0	3.11	2	
Lim		6	1	1	0	0*		0	0	144	158	7	22.57	4-28	1	0	6.58	3	
FC	2004/05	49	50	22	150	21*	5.35	0	0	7677	3919	144	27.21	6-59	5	0	3.06	13	
Lim	2004/05	23	4	3	10	9*	10.00	0	0	749	678	20	33.90	4-28	1	0	5.43	5	
20T	2004/05	1								12	29	0					14.50	0	
GQADUSHE, Mbasa (KwaZulu-Natal Inland, KwaZulu-Natal Inland to Namibia) b East London, Cape Province 24.3.1986 LHB OB WK																			
FC		9	11	3	160	40	20.00	0	0	256	178	5	35.60	2-19	0	0	4.17	11	
Lim		12	11	3	128	36	16.00	0	0	172	145	6	24.16	2-28	0	0	5.05	6	
FC	2006/07	28	39	8	636	54*	20.51	0	1	292	201	6	33.50	2-19	0	0	4.13	44	3
Lim	2006/07	33	30	10	353	44*	17.65	0	0	172	145	6	24.16	2-28	0	0	5.05	21	3
GQAMANE, Ayabulela (Border) b King William's Town, Cape Province 31.8.1989 RHB RFM																			
FC		2	4	1	65	36*	21.66	0	0	216	148	8	18.50	3-32	0	0	4.11	0	
Lim		2	2	1	28	26*	28.00	0	0	66	65	3	21.66	2-39	0	0	5.90	0	
GRAY, Alistair John Alec (Cape Cobras, Western Province) b Johannesburg, Transvaal 8.7.1982 RHB LB																			
FC		19	32	2	1281	127	42.70	3	7	1474	905	30	30.16	4-27	0	0	3.68	28	
Lim		10	10	0	194	49	19.40	0	0	348	264	12	22.00	4-30	1	0	4.55	4	
FC	2004/05	58	104	8	3772	188*	39.29	9	17	2883	1783	54	33.01	5-31	1	0	3.71	69	
Lim	2004/05	28	28	1	841	123	31.14	1	4	522	418	19	22.00	4-30	1	0	4.80	8	
GROBLER, Stephanus Frederick (South Western Districts, South Western Districts to Namibia) b Pretoria, Transvaal 11.11.1982 RHB OB																			
FC		4	7	1	233	106	38.83	1	0	523	300	14	21.42	5-38	1	0	3.44	2	
Lim		3	3	0	27	20	9.00	0	0	84	55	3	18.33	2-41	0	0	3.92	3	
FC	2005/06	21	32	4	551	106	19.67	1	0	2910	1640	49	33.46	5-38	2	0	3.38	9	
Lim	2007/08	11	9	2	97	27	13.85	0	0	419	356	11	32.36	4-44	1	0	5.09	5	
HALL, Andrew James (Dolphins, North West, Northamptonshire, Northamptonshire to Netherlands) b Johannesburg, Transvaal 31.7.1975 RHB RFM																			
FC		6	9	1	139	48	17.37	0	0	796	377	11	34.27	4-45	0	0	2.84	9	
Lim		14	12	1	249	58*	22.63	0	2	582	612	18	34.00	3-37	0	0	6.30	5	1
20T		4	3	0	12	10	4.00	0	0	66	93	4	23.25	2-38	0	0	8.45	1	
Test	2001/02	21	33	4	760	163	26.20	1	3	3001	1617	45	35.93	3-1	0	0	3.23	16	
FC	1995/96	173	254	32	7606	163	34.26	8	47	26818	12863	490	26.25	6-77	15	1	2.87	156	
Int	1998/99	88	56	13	905	81	21.04	0	3	3341	2515	95	26.47	5-18	3	1	4.51	29	
Lim	1994/95	286	227	40	5451	129*	29.14	6	29	11547	9048	329	27.50	5-18	10	1	4.70	85	1
I20T	2005/06	2	1	0	11	11	11.00	0	0	48	60	3	20.00	3-22	0	0	7.50	0	
20T	2003	73	64	15	1204	66*	24.57	0	4	1435	1869	91	20.53	6-21	1	2	7.81	21	
HAMPSON, Garry Michael (South Western Districts) b Pietermaritzburg, Natal 18.2.1977 RHB RMF																			
Lim		2	1	1	1	1*		0	0	72	100	3	33.33	2-36	0	0	8.33	0	
FC	2002/03	15	22	1	303	60	14.42	0	1	2775	1296	50	25.92	4-59	0	0	2.80	12	
Lim	2002/03	25	20	4	273	50	17.06	0	1	1181	877	39	22.48	4-31	2	0	4.45	6	
HANTAM, William Chesney (South Western Districts, South Western Districts to Namibia) b Cape Town, Cape Province 21.9.1983 LHB LMF																			
FC		10	19	3	589	102	36.81	1	3	1929	1038	27	38.44	5-53	1	0	3.22	5	
Lim		9	8	2	386	97*	64.33	0	5	408	393	11	35.72	3-45	0	0	5.77	0	
FC	2004/05	20	36	7	920	102	31.72	1	3	3221	1746	57	30.63	6-39	2	0	3.25	20	
Lim	2004/05	33	27	8	647	97*	34.05	0	6	1460	1204	47	25.61	5-22	1	2	4.94	7	
20T	2003/04	8	3	0	25	15	8.33	0	0	132	149	4	37.25	3-25	0	0	6.77	1	
HARMER, Simon Ross (Eastern Province) b Pretoria, Transvaal 10.2.1989 RHB OB																			
FC		5	6	5	90	54*	90.00	0	1	1004	553	22	25.13	5-68	2	0	3.30	6	
Lim		5	4	0	38	25	9.50	0	0	234	147	10	14.70	3-17	0	0	3.76	3	
HARRIDAVE, Narvaar (KwaZulu-Natal Inland, KwaZulu-Natal Inland to Namibia) b Pietermartizburg, Natal 2.9.1988 RHB RM																			
FC		8	12	6	101	23*	16.83	0	0	816	436	7	62.28	3-52	0	0	3.20	1	
Lim		12	6	5	27	10*	27.00	0	0	363	304	11	27.63	4-22	1	0	5.02	2	
FC	2007/08	10	15	7	149	47	18.62	0	0	912	486	8	60.75	3-52	0	0	3.19	3	
Lim	2007/08	16	8	6	33	10*	16.50	0	0	477	382	12	31.83	4-22	1	0	4.80	3	

Cmp	Debut	M	I	NO	Runs	HS	Avge	100	50	Balls	Runs	Wkts	Avge	BB	5i	10m	RpO	ct	st
HARRIS, Paul Lee (South Africa, Titans, South Africa to India, South Africa to West Indies, South Africa A to Bangladesh) b Salisbury (now Harare), Zimbabwe 2.11.1978 RHB SLA																			
Test		3	5	1	97	38	24.25	0	0	900	444	11	40.36	5-123	1	0	2.96	0	
FC		10	14	3	197	38	17.90	0	0	2345	1102	34	32.41	6-54	3	0	2.82	3	
Lim		3								60	46	3	15.33	2-15	0	0	4.60	0	
20T		3	1	1	0	0*		0	0	72	80	7	11.42	3-32	0	0	6.66	0	
Test	2006/07	32	42	5	427	46	11.54	0	0	7387	3414	92	37.10	6-127	3	0	2.77	14	
FC	1998/99	104	126	18	1568	55	14.51	0	3	23527	10793	347	31.10	7-94	19	1	2.75	40	
Int	2007/08	3								180	83	3	27.66	2-30	0	0	2.76	2	
Lim	2002/03	46	12	3	67	15*	7.44	0	0	1968	1422	51	27.88	5-27	0	1	4.33	17	
20T	2005	18	5	4	5	3	5.00	0	0	372	445	21	21.19	3-18	0	0	7.17	3	
HARTSLIEF, Wessel (South Western Districts, South Western Districts to Namibia) b George, Cape Province 30.5.1986 RHB RMF																			
FC		4	7	1	88	31	14.66	0	0	498	276	12	23.00	3-72	0	0	3.32	2	
Lim		4	4	0	9	6	2.25	0	0	69	97	1	97.00	1-36	0	0	8.43	1	
FC	2006/07	18	32	5	392	44	14.51	0	0	2283	1250	48	26.04	6-91	2	0	3.28	7	
Lim	2006/07	18	15	4	56	30*	5.09	0	0	674	529	17	31.11	4-50	1	0	4.70	2	
HENDERSON, Claude William (Cape Cobras to India, Leicestershire, Leicestershire to Scotland) b Worcester, Cape Province 14.6.1972 RHB SLA																			
Test	2001/02	7	7	0	65	30	9.28	0	0	1962	928	22	42.18	4-116	0	0	2.83	2	
FC	1990/91	239	326	70	4775	81	18.65	0	15	57233	24413	791	30.86	7-57	30	1	2.55	82	
Int	2001/02	4								217	132	7	18.85	4-17	1	0	3.65	0	
Lim	1990/91	241	138	66	1110	45	15.41	0	0	10699	7674	304	25.24	6-29	13	2	4.30	52	
20T	2004	70	31	11	161	32	8.05	0	0	1354	1540	64	24.06	3-23	0	0	6.82	17	
HENDRICKS, Beuran Eric (Western Province) b Cape Town 8.6.1990 LHB LFM																			
FC		4	6	2	7	5*	1.75	0	0	462	276	13	21.23	5-52	1	0	3.58	3	
Lim		2								30	26	2	13.00	2-26	0	0	5.20	1	
HENDRICKS, Dominic Andrew (Gauteng, Gauteng to Namibia) b Port Elizabeth, Cape Province 7.11.1990 LHB OB																			
FC		3	4	1	155	72	51.66	0	2									3	
Lim		5	2	0	63	51	31.50	0	1									0	
Lim	2009/10	6	3	1	71	51	35.50	0	1									1	
HENDRICKS, Reeza Raphael (Eagles, Griqualand West) b Kimberley, Cape Province 14.8.1989 RHB RM																			
FC		14	24	3	974	133	46.38	3	6	48	47	0					5.87	13	
Lim		13	13	1	289	82	24.08	0	2									5	
20T		4	3	1	30	14*	15.00	0	0									1	
FC	2006/07	38	66	7	2270	151*	38.47	5	13	114	101	0					5.31	35	
Lim	2006/07	25	22	2	463	82	23.15	0	2	30	32	1	32.00	1-17	0	0	6.40	12	
20T	2008/09	11	7	2	58	14*	11.60	0	0									3	
HEWER, Nicolas David (KwaZulu-Natal) b Durban, KwaZulu-Natal 6.7.1984 RHB RMF																			
FC		3	6	1	28	13	5.60	0	0	434	231	8	28.87	4-58	0	0	3.19	2	
Lim		1	1	1	2	2*		0	0	48	33	0					4.12	0	
FC	2005/06	13	18	3	88	23*	5.86	0	0	1822	1074	38	28.26	5-45	1	0	3.53	5	
Lim	2003/04	6	5	3	44	29	22.00	0	0	252	179	7	25.57	3-24	0	0	4.26	0	
20T	2003/04	1								24	37	0					9.25	0	
HEWITT, Douglas (Northerns) b Pretoria, Transvaal 16.2.1988 RHB LB WK																			
FC		2	3	0	115	103	38.33	1	0	6	5	0					5.00	2	
HILLERMANN, Rudy Erwin (South Western Districts, South Western Districts to Namibia) b Pietermaritzburg, Natal 8.10.1985 RHB RMF																			
FC		11	22	5	484	140*	28.47	1	1	979	574	18	31.88	5-55	1	0	3.51	6	
Lim		11	11	1	221	54	22.10	0	1	327	297	7	42.42	2-38	0	0	5.45	4	
FC	2006/07	23	43	7	971	140*	26.97	2	3	1892	1095	35	31.28	5-55	1	0	3.47	10	
Lim	2006/07	25	23	3	461	54	23.05	0	1	837	730	23	31.73	4-28	1	0	5.23	9	
HLELA, Richard Thokozani (KwaZulu-Natal Inland, KwaZulu-Natal Inland to Namibia) b Pietermaritzburg, Natal 29.11.1980 RHB RFM																			
FC		10	12	0	77	19	6.41	0	0	838	527	13	40.53	4-103	0	0	3.77	2	
Lim		10	6	2	31	21*	7.75	0	0	170	171	2	85.50	1-29	0	0	6.03	1	
FC	2008/09	14	19	2	95	19	5.58	0	0	1374	838	24	34.91	5-60	1	0	3.65	2	
Lim	2008/09	17	10	3	39	21*	5.57	0	0	446	386	8	48.25	4-33	1	0	5.19	6	
HLENGANI, Israel Christopher (Easterns, Easterns to Namibia) b Johannesburg, Transvaal 28.7.1988 LHB SLA																			
FC		7	8	2	126	35	21.00	0	0	407	243	9	27.00	3-55	0	0	3.58	1	
Lim		12	6	4	20	11	10.00	0	0	363	340	11	30.90	3-30	0	0	5.62	3	
FC	2005/06	33	47	8	487	35	12.48	0	0	3381	1822	56	32.53	7-107	2	0	3.23	18	
Lim	2005/06	37	24	7	349	69	20.52	0	2	1190	978	30	32.60	3-25	0	0	4.93	12	
HOBSON, Arthur Lloyd (Eastern Province) b Jansenville, Cape Province 22.10.1985 RHB OB																			
FC		1	1	0	5	5	5.00	0	0	234	145	1	145.00	1-47	0	0	3.71	0	
Lim		3	1	1	9	9*		0	0	97	75	3	25.00	3-15	0	0	4.63	2	
Lim	2007/08	5	3	2	9	9*	9.00	0	0	205	131	5	26.20	3-15	0	0	3.83	4	
HOLMES, Muneer (Western Province) b Cape Town, Cape Province 7.8.1985 LHB OB																			
FC		1	2	0	27	27	13.50	0	0									0	
Lim		1	1	0	15	15	15.00	0	0									0	

Cmp	Debut	M	I	NO	Runs	HS	Avge	100	50	Balls	Runs	Wkts	Avge	BB	5i	10m	RpO	ct	st
HOLTZHAUSEN, Frederick Stephanus (Griqualand West) b Hartswater, Cape Province 17.4.1985 RHB RMF																			
FC		7	12	0	260	94	21.66	0	2	852	429	19	22.57	6-29	1	0	3.02	2	
Lim		6	4	1	64	28	21.33	0	0	204	162	6	27.00	3-33	0	0	4.76	0	
FC	2004/05	33	53	5	995	94	20.72	0	6	4897	2593	98	26.45	6-29	3	0	3.17	18	
Lim	2004/05	32	26	5	429	49*	20.42	0	0	1343	1144	28	40.85	3-30	0	0	5.11	13	
HOUBERT, Ryan Andrew (Northerns) b Port Elizabeth, Cape Province 28.2.1983 RHB SLA																			
FC		2	3	0	16	15	5.33	0	0	252	181	1	181.00	1-99	0	0	4.31	0	
HUGO, Roelof Petrus (South Western Districts, South Western Districts to Namibia) b Johannesburg, Transvaal 1.7.1983 RHB WK																			
FC		11	21	4	299	37*	17.58	0	0									22	5
Lim		12	12	2	167	54*	16.70	0	1									8	4
FC	2006/07	32	62	9	1221	91	23.03	0	4									80	13
Lim	2006/07	34	33	6	746	106*	27.62	1	4									28	9
HULETT, Matthew Mark (KwaZulu-Natal) b Pietermaritzburg, Natal 1.8.1991 RHB LB																			
FC		1	2	0	29	29	14.50	0	0									1	
Lim		6	6	0	59	21	9.83	0	0	120	102	2	51.00	1-15	0	0	5.10	6	
HUME, Graham Ian (Gauteng) b Johannesburg, Transvaal 23.11.1990 LHB RMF																			
FC		5	4	1	98	53*	32.66	0	1	649	253	18	14.05	5-44	1	0	2.33	6	
Lim		2	1	1	1	1*		0	0	72	64	2	32.00	1-29	0	0	5.33	0	
HUMPHRIES, Oliver Erich (KwaZulu-Natal Inland) b Pietermaritzburg, Natal 25.6.1987 RHB RFM																			
FC		6	10	0	241	85	24.10	0	2	525	359	7	51.28	2-19	0	0	4.10	0	
Lim		9	5	0	87	37	17.40	0	0	266	255	5	51.00	2-57	0	0	5.75	4	
FC	2006/07	15	24	5	471	85	24.78	0	3	1851	1142	39	29.28	6-59	1	0	3.70	3	
Lim	2006/07	13	8	0	126	37	15.75	0	0	420	403	11	36.63	2-40	0	0	5.75	4	
HYKES, Julian Allen (Border) b East London, Cape Province 6.10.1982 RHB RMF																			
Lim		2	2	0	9	9	4.50	0	0	24	40	1	40.00	1-40	0	0	10.00	0	
IMRAN TAHIR, Mohammad (Easterns, Titans, Warwickshire, Warwickshire to Scotland) b Lahore, Punjab, Pakistan 27.3.1979 RHB LBG																			
FC		12	13	2	233	55*	21.18	0	1	2620	1498	67	22.35	7-82	8	2	3.43	9	
Lim		10	7	1	111	32	18.50	0	0	361	318	8	39.75	3-29	0	0	5.28	1	
FC	1996/97	123	155	32	1794	77*	14.58	0	3	23851	12765	505	25.27	8-76	35	7	3.21	56	
Lim	1997/98	87	30	9	304	41*	14.47	0	0	3840	2920	125	23.36	5-27	4	3	4.56	19	
20T	2005/06	37	11	4	47	13	6.71	0	0	822	868	40	21.70	3-13	0	0	6.33	9	
INGRAM, Colin Alexander (Warriors, South Africa A to Bangladesh, South Africa A to Sri Lanka) b Port Elizabeth, Cape Province 3.7.1985 LHB LB																			
FC		11	19	2	536	93	31.52	0	3	30	37	0					7.40	4	
Lim		12	12	2	600	125*	60.00	1	5									8	
20T		8	8	2	283	82	47.16	0	3									5	
FC	2004/05	45	79	3	2439	190	32.09	4	11	1600	911	24	37.95	4-16	0	0	3.41	28	
Lim	2004/05	46	46	5	1788	127	43.60	3	11	306	240	8	30.00	2-13	0	0	4.70	15	
20T	2006/07	18	17	2	449	84	29.93	0	4									6	
JACOBS, Arno (Warriors) b Potchefstroom, Transvaal 13.3.1977 LHB OB																			
FC		11	18	1	476	119	28.00	1	3	18	21	0					7.00	18	
Lim		10	8	0	141	42	17.62	0	0									6	1
20T		3	3	0	65	54	21.66	0	1									4	
FC	1997/98	110	193	26	6523	218*	39.05	14	35	930	645	3	215.00	1-2	0	0	4.16	136	
Lim	1995/96	136	129	10	3898	118	32.75	6	19	370	345	9	38.33	2-22	0	0	5.59	73	3
20T	2003/04	41	37	5	514	54	16.06	0	1	151	187	13	14.38	5-26	0	1	7.43	16	
JACOBS, David Johan (Warriors) b Klerksdorp, Transvaal 4.11.1982 RHB RM WK																			
FC		7	10	0	233	80	23.30	0	1									8	1
Lim		10	9	4	211	63	42.20	0	2									7	1
20T		8	7	3	162	56	40.50	0	1									3	1
FC	2001/02	75	134	7	4625	218	36.41	12	23	34	20	0					3.52	126	4
Lim	2001/02	85	82	12	2011	101*	28.72	1	12									75	7
20T	2003/04	41	38	9	847	71*	29.20	0	3	6	14	0					14.00	20	4
JANSE VAN RENSBURG, Rhyno Adriaan (Griqualand West) b Kimberley, Cape Province 16.12.1990 RHB RMF																			
FC		2	4	0	35	18	8.75	0	0									1	
JAPPIE, Rushdi (Easterns, Easterns to Namibia) b Cape Town, Cape Province 3.9.1985 RHB OB																			
FC		12	16	3	312	81*	24.00	0	1	102	47	2	23.50	2-36	0	0	2.76	7	
Lim		12	12	3	285	109	31.66	1	0									3	
FC	2007/08	31	49	5	882	81*	20.04	0	4	150	105	3	35.00	2-36	0	0	4.20	14	
Lim	2006/07	26	26	5	588	109	28.00	1	2	48	38	1	38.00	1-6	0	0	4.75	4	
JEFTHA, Petrus Johannes Nicolas (Boland, Boland to Namibia) b Touwsrivier, Cape Province 7.4.1987 RHB RFM																			
FC		2	2	0	22	21	11.00	0	0	216	157	2	78.50	1-51	0	0	4.36	1	
Lim		6	5	1	95	43	23.75	0	0	102	112	5	22.40	2-17	0	0	6.58	1	
FC	2009/10	3	3	0	73	51	24.33	0	1	270	180	2	90.00	1-51	0	0	4.00	3	
JEGGELS, Riaan Ruche (Eastern Province) b Port Elizabeth, Cape Province 10.9.1981 RHB																			
FC		9	14	3	513	104*	46.63	1	4									12	
Lim		10	9	0	172	58	19.11	0	1									3	
FC	2004/05	40	68	9	1998	151*	33.86	2	9									31	

Cmp	Debut	M	I	NO	Runs	HS	Avge	100	50	Balls	Runs	Wkts	Avge	BB	5i	10m	RpO	ct	st
Lim	2004/05	53	47	7	801	74*	20.02	0	5									20	
20T	2007/08	2	2	0	46	43	23.00	0	0									0	
JOKO, Mark Mawande (Border) b Middledrift, Cape Province 25.11.1986 RHB WK																			
Lim		1	1	1	12	12*		0	0									0	
FC	2007/08	1	2	1	17	12*	17.00	0	0									0	
Lim	2007/08	2	1	1	12	12*		0	0									0	
JONKER, Christiaan (North West) b Rustenburg, Transvaal 24.9.1986 RHB RMF																			
FC		12	24	1	795	100*	34.56	2	5	48	17	3	5.66	3-16	0	0	2.12	5	
Lim		12	12	3	329	115*	36.55	1	1	48	40	1	40.00	1-22	0	0	5.00	3	
FC	2006/07	31	58	5	1918	143	36.18	4	12	252	162	5	32.40	3-16	0	0	3.85	16	
Lim	2005/06	32	32	5	952	115*	35.25	1	7	180	198	7	28.28	3-13	0	0	6.60	7	
JORDAAN, Hendrik Johannes (Boland to Namibia) b Pretoria, Transvaal 16.10.1988 RHB RM																			
FC	2009/10	1	1	0	10	10	10.00	0	0									0	
Lim	2009/10	1	1	0	18	18	18.00	0	0									1	
JORDAAN, Justin Jovan (South Western Districts, South Western Districts to Namibia) b Oudtshoorn, Cape Province 9.1.1992 RHB SLA																			
FC		1	1	0	4	4	4.00	0	0	138	89	1	89.00	1-63	0	0	3.87	1	
Lim		8								374	361	10	36.10	3-25	0	0	5.79	0	
Lim	2009/10	9								422	393	11	35.72	3-25	0	0	5.58	0	
JOUBERT, Pierre (Titans) b Pretoria, Transvaal 2.5.1978 RHB RFM																			
FC		9	13	1	152	56	12.66	0	1	1203	511	24	21.29	6-89	1	0	2.54	5	
Lim		8	5	4	58	38*	58.00	0	0	306	243	7	34.71	3-26	0	0	4.76	3	
20T		6								112	146	5	29.20	3-23	0	0	7.82	3	
FC	1995/96	93	130	37	2575	112*	27.68	1	16	14076	5598	247	22.66	7-32	10	2	2.38	55	
Lim	1996/97	106	61	24	937	87*	25.32	0	4	4599	3318	119	27.88	4-82	1	0	4.32	33	
20T	2007/08	18	9	5	117	26*	29.25	0	0	220	291	12	24.25	3-12	0	0	7.93	7	
JUMAT, Jeandré Ryan (Northerns) b Cape Town, Cape Province 29.1.1987 LHB RMF																			
FC		9	12	1	201	71	18.27	0	1	492	327	8	40.87	3-76	0	0	3.98	0	
Lim		11	6	2	89	33	22.25	0	0	174	149	8	18.62	2-19	0	0	5.13	5	
FC	2005/06	14	19	3	331	71	20.68	0	2	738	486	8	60.75	3-76	0	0	3.95	1	
Lim	2005/06	16	8	2	153	53	25.50	0	1	248	203	10	20.30	2-19	0	0	4.91	8	
KALLIS, Jacques Henry (South Africa, Warriors, Royal Challengers Bangalore, South Africa to India, South Africa to West Indies) b Pinelands, Cape Town, Cape Province 16.10.1975 RHB RFM																			
Test		4	7	0	363	120	51.85	2	1	330	143	2	71.50	1-27	0	0	2.60	5	
FC		4	7	0	363	120	51.85	2	1	330	143	2	71.50	1-27	0	0	2.60	5	
Int		4	4	0	170	81	42.50	0	1	108	81	1	81.00	1-14	0	0	4.50	2	
Lim		6	6	2	330	87*	82.50	0	3	108	81	1	81.00	1-14	0	0	4.50	3	
I20T		1	1	0	7	7	7.00	0	0									0	
20T		2	2	0	62	55	31.00	0	1	6	10	0					10.00	0	
Test	1995/96	140	237	35	11126	189*	55.07	35	53	17887	8403	266	31.59	6-54	5	0	2.81	159	
FC	1993/94	230	377	52	17478	200	53.77	52	91	26622	12367	401	30.84	6-54	8	0	2.78	222	
Int	1995/96	303	289	52	10838	139	45.72	17	78	10108	8142	254	32.05	5-30	2	2	4.83	115	
Lim	1994/95	397	379	63	14019	155*	44.36	23	100	12917	10148	330	30.75	5-30	3	3	4.71	144	
I20T	2005/06	16	16	1	512	73	34.13	0	4	186	229	5	45.80	2-20	0	0	7.38	6	
20T	2003/04	65	65	9	1920	89*	34.28	0	17	1064	1427	32	44.59	3-18	0	0	8.04	24	
KANNEMEYER, Quinton Kurt (Boland) b Vredenburg, Cape Province 31.5.1984 RHB RMF																			
FC		4	7	1	117	55	19.50	0	1	239	140	0					3.51	3	
Lim		5	5	0	36	25	7.20	0	0	54	46	1	46.00	1-23	0	0	5.11	3	
FC	2005/06	13	23	1	401	70	18.22	0	2	689	383	7	54.71	3-39	0	0	3.33	5	
Lim	2005/06	22	18	4	293	60	20.92	0	1	443	377	7	53.85	2-31	0	0	5.10	7	
KEMP, Justin Miles (Cape Cobras, Chennai Super Kings) b Queenstown, Cape Province 2.10.1977 RHB RFM																			
FC		5	7	0	197	93	28.14	0	1	517	207	9	23.00	4-39	0	0	2.40	11	
Lim		11	8	2	285	71	47.50	0	2	81	80	2	40.00	1-21	0	0	5.92	5	
20T		7	7	1	193	59	32.16	0	1	48	45	3	15.00	2-8	0	0	5.62	1	
Test	2000/01	4	6	0	80	55	13.33	0	1	479	222	9	24.66	3-33	0	0	2.78	3	
FC	1996/97	128	205	24	6422	188	35.48	14	30	12149	5771	203	28.42	6-56	5	0	2.85	181	
Int	2000/01	85	66	18	1512	100*	31.50	1	10	1303	1015	32	31.71	3-20	0	0	4.67	33	
Lim	1997/98	266	225	60	5934	107*	35.96	3	42	6704	5405	182	29.69	6-20	6	3	4.83	114	
I20T	2005/06	8	7	3	203	89*	50.75	0	1	6	5	0					5.00	3	
20T	2003/04	64	53	13	1079	89*	26.97	0	3	494	620	32	19.37	3-12	0	0	7.53	25	
KENNEDY, Matthew James (Eastern Province) b Port Elizabeth, Cape Province 6.3.1991 RHB RFM																			
FC		3								516	274	8	34.25	3-55	0	0	3.18	1	
Lim		4								160	106	9	11.77	4-30	1	0	3.97	0	
FC	2008/09	5	1	1	23	23*		0	0	828	418	15	27.86	4-53	0	0	3.02	2	
Lim	2008/09	5	1	1	11	11*		0	0	196	137	10	13.70	4-30	1	0	4.19	0	
KENT, Jon Carter (Dolphins, KwaZulu-Natal) b Cape Town, Cape Province 7.5.1979 RHB RMF																			
FC		13	23	6	715	158*	42.05	2	1	1184	613	20	30.65	4-73	0	0	3.10	8	
Lim		7	6	0	190	63	31.66	0	2	186	207	4	51.75	2-41	0	0	6.67	3	
FC	1997/98	94	149	18	4620	178*	35.26	9	22	9755	4728	149	31.73	6-77	1	0	2.90	66	

Cmp	Debut	M	I	NO	Runs	HS	Avge	100	50	Balls	Runs	Wkts	Avge	BB	5i	10m	RpO	ct	st
Int	2001/02	2								48	57	0					7.12	1	
Lim	1998/99	140	120	21	2835	115*	28.63	1	20	5022	4072	111	36.68	4-29	1	0	4.86	48	
20T	2003/04	30	26	7	271	46*	14.26	0	0	306	418	17	24.58	4-25	1	0	8.19	8	
KGAMADI, Liphaphang Jimmy (Lions, North West) b Klerksdorp, Transvaal 7.10.1983 RHB LB																			
FC		10	19	0	455	98	23.94	0	3	276	231	4	57.75	3-86	0	0	5.02	15	
Lim		11	10	1	244	99*	27.11	0	2									5	
FC	2004/05	45	82	4	2162	125*	27.71	2	15	697	469	13	36.07	5-74	1	0	4.03	55	
Lim	2004/05	49	45	6	727	99*	18.64	0	5	60	33	0					3.30	19	
KHAN, Imraan (Dolphins) b Durban, Natal 27.4.1984 LHB OB																			
FC		10	18	1	408	99	24.00	0	1	48	27	0					3.37	1	
Lim		11	10	0	329	72	32.90	0	4	24	19	0					4.75	3	
20T		5	5	0	110	45	22.00	0	0									0	
Test	2008/09	1	1	0	20	20	20.00	0	0									1	
FC	2003/04	76	129	12	4239	150	36.23	7	24	3279	1883	46	40.93	6-43	1	0	3.44	36	
Lim	2001/02	78	71	3	1857	110*	27.30	1	14	682	580	8	72.50	2-31	0	0	5.10	19	
20T	2003/04	29	24	0	369	50	15.37	0	1	102	156	6	26.00	2-15	0	0	9.17	14	
KLEINVELDT, Rory Keith (Cape Cobras, South Africa A, Cape Cobras to India, South Africa to West Indies, South Africa A to Sri Lanka) b Cape Town, Cape Province 15.3.1983 RHB RMF																			
FC		8	9	2	159	60	22.71	0	1	1371	605	21	28.80	3-32	0	0	2.64	1	
Lim		8	3	0	5	5	1.66	0	0	370	355	9	39.44	4-25	1	0	5.75	1	
20T		8	7	2	25	13	5.00	0	0	162	190	5	38.00	3-23	0	0	7.03	2	
FC	2002/03	59	89	10	1489	115*	18.84	1	7	9877	4743	152	31.20	8-47	5	1	2.88	28	
Lim	2002/03	68	44	7	539	54*	14.56	0	1	2960	2283	80	28.53	4-25	3	0	4.62	10	
I20T	2008/09	2	1	1	3	3*		0	0	30	68	3	22.66	2-48	0	0	13.60	0	
20T	2003/04	52	42	13	398	46	13.72	0	0	1050	1326	47	28.21	3-18	0	0	7.57	13	
KOOPMAN, Gionne Verlyn James (Border) b East London, Cape Province 28.12.1991 LHB OB																			
FC		2	4	0	97	57	24.25	0	1	273	105	6	17.50	3-17	0	0	2.30	2	
Lim		3	2	1	19	13*	19.00	0	0	90	85	2	42.50	2-38	0	0	5.66	0	
KREUSCH, Justin Peter (Warriors) b East London, Cape Province 27.9.1979 RHB RM																			
FC		8	12	0	333	130	27.75	1	0	252	152	0					3.61	5	
Lim		12	12	0	463	102	38.58	1	3	36	22	0					3.66	7	
20T		7	7	0	104	61	14.85	0	1	72	87	0					7.25	6	
FC	1999/00	54	93	2	2036	130	22.37	1	10	3267	1546	53	29.16	5-31	1	0	2.83	37	
Lim	1999/00	84	79	10	2458	119*	35.62	4	15	1553	1218	33	36.90	3-21	0	0	4.70	33	
20T	2003/04	44	41	5	658	73	18.27	0	2	230	263	12	21.91	3-23	0	0	6.86	19	
KRIEK, Emile Christiaan (Boland, Boland to Namibia) b Pretoria, Transvaal 11.12.1989 RHB RM																			
FC		9	18	1	458	149	26.94	1	2									7	
Lim		7	7	0	40	23	5.71	0	0									3	
FC	2008/09	14	27	1	562	149	21.61	1	2									8	
Lim	2008/09	13	13	1	175	39*	14.58	0	0									6	
KRUGER, Alan Kevin (Eagles, Griqualand West, Eagles to India) b Kimberley, Cape Province 16.2.1981 RHB RMF																			
FC		5	9	2	157	51	22.42	0	1	346	153	3	51.00	1-26	0	0	2.65	1	
Lim		12	9	3	64	18*	10.66	0	0	193	178	12	14.83	2-6	0	0	5.53	3	
20T		1	1	1	2	2*		0	0	6	11	0					11.00	0	
FC	2000/01	59	101	11	2380	158	26.44	4	10	6822	4214	126	33.44	6-37	5	1	3.70	23	
Lim	2001/02	63	56	6	939	86	18.78	0	4	1797	1659	59	28.11	4-20	2	0	5.53	15	
20T	2006/07	10	3	3	2	2*		0	0	54	60	2	30.00	1-14	0	0	6.66	4	
KRUGER, Bruce Thomas (KwaZulu-Natal) b Durban, Natal 25.5.1991 RHB OB																			
Lim		2	2	0	16	11	8.00	0	0									0	
KRUGER, Garnett John-Peter (Warriors) b Port Elizabeth, Cape Province 5.1.1977 RHB RMF																			
FC		4	7	1	36	24*	6.00	0	0	697	427	12	35.58	5-71	1	0	3.67	0	
Lim		6	2	2	25	24*		0	0	162	191	7	27.28	2-32	0	0	7.07	0	
20T		6	1	0	11	11	11.00	0	0	126	166	9	18.44	3-26	0	0	7.90	0	
FC	1997/98	115	142	41	1111	58	11.00	0	2	20269	11469	368	31.16	8-112	15	2	3.39	25	
Int	2005/06	3	2	1	0	0*	0.00	0	0	138	139	2	69.50	1-43	0	0	6.04	1	
Lim	1999/00	132	41	20	167	24*	7.95	0	0	5659	4664	176	26.50	6-23	2	4	4.94	20	
I20T	2005/06	1	1	0	3	3	3.00	0	0	24	29	0					7.25	0	
20T	2003/04	42	11	9	58	19*	29.00	0	0	848	1129	43	26.25	4-10	1	0	7.98	5	
KUHN, Heino Gunther (South Africa, South Africa A, Titans, South Africa A to Bangladesh, South Africa A to Sri Lanka) b Piet Retief, Mpumalanga 1.4.1984 RHB WK																			
FC		9	15	1	577	160*	41.21	1	3									28	2
Lim		9	8	1	240	55	34.28	0	2									12	2
I20T		1	1	1	5	5*		0	0									1	
20T		9	6	3	117	35*	39.00	0	0									3	1
FC	2004/05	63	108	10	4477	216	45.68	10	22									188	14
Lim	2004/05	59	50	3	1374	113*	29.23	3	7									64	13
20T	2006/07	23	19	4	304	68	20.26	0	1									9	4
LAING, Peter Charles (Western Province) b Johannesburg, Transvaal 5.10.1984 RHB RMF																			
FC		2	3	1	62	56*	31.00	0	1	132	90	1	90.00	1-51	0	0	4.09	1	
Lim		5	5	0	73	31	14.60	0	0	150	152	6	25.33	3-46	0	0	6.08	1	

Cmp	Debut	M	I	NO	Runs	HS	Avge	100	50	Balls	Runs	Wkts	Avge	BB	5i	10m	RpO	ct	st
FC	2005/06	17	25	2	643	154	27.95	1	3	1468	911	22	41.40	4-19	0	0	3.72	15	
Lim	2005/06	16	15	1	350	86*	25.00	0	2	462	452	19	23.78	4-42	2	0	5.87	6	
LANGEVELDT, Charl Kenneth (Cape Cobras, South Africa, Cape Cobras to India, Derbyshire, Kolkata Knight Riders, South Africa to India, South Africa to West Indies) b Stellenbosch, Cape Province 17.12.1974 RHB RFM																			
FC		1	1	0	6	6	6.00	0	0	204	96	5	19.20	4-45	0	0	2.82	0	
Int		4	2	2	6	6*		0	0	186	139	5	27.80	3-36	0	0	4.48	1	
Lim		11	3	3	6	6*		0	0	479	432	14	30.85	5-17	0	1	5.41	4	
I20T		1								24	39	1	39.00	1-39	0	0	9.75	0	
20T		4	1	0	1	1	1.00	0	0	90	145	4	36.25	3-18	0	0	9.66	2	
Test	2004/05	6	4	2	16	10	8.00	0	0	999	593	16	37.06	5-46	1	0	3.56	2	
FC	1997/98	93	116	39	1106	56	14.36	0	1	17559	8670	310	27.96	6-48	9	1	2.96	25	
Int	2001/02	68	20	9	69	12	6.27	0	0	3255	2728	93	29.33	5-39	1	2	5.02	10	
Lim	1997/98	195	77	31	359	33*	7.80	0	0	9121	7033	293	24.00	5-7	7	7	4.62	36	
I20T	2005/06	9	3	2	4	2*	4.00	0	0	198	241	17	14.17	4-19	1	0	7.30	1	
20T	2003/04	58	15	10	36	9*	7.20	0	0	1242	1408	86	16.37	5-16	4	1	6.80	17	
LATEGAN, Waldo (Free State) b Oudtshoorn, Cape Province 15.4.1989 LHB WK																			
FC		7	11	2	379	92	42.11	0	2									15	2
FC	2006/07	10	15	3	430	92	35.83	0	2									26	2
Lim	2006/07	3	2	1	3	3	3.00	0	0									3	
LAZENBY, Marinus (North West) b Klerksdorp, Transvaal 31.1.1988 RHB SLA																			
FC		3	5	0	102	51	20.40	0	1									2	
Lim		2	2	0	43	33	21.50	0	0									0	
FC	2006/07	13	23	3	548	71	27.40	0	6	87	79	3	26.33	2-9	0	0	5.44	7	
Lim	2006/07	9	8	2	214	37*	35.66	0	0									2	
LE CLUS, Jacobus Francois (Northerns) b Johannesburg, Transvaal 23.6.1987 LHB SLA																			
FC		9	14	1	602	103	46.30	1	5	6	9	0					9.00	10	
Lim		8	8	0	194	53	24.25	0	2									3	
LEMMETJIES, Bradley William (Griqualand West) b Kimberley, Cape Province 18.8.1977 RHB LB																			
FC		3	4	0	49	27	12.25	0	0	306	177	1	177.00	1-46	0	0	3.47	0	
Lim		4	2	0	63	62	31.50	0	1	66	88	4	22.00	3-37	0	0	8.00	0	
FC	1998/99	16	26	4	397	41*	18.04	0	0	1454	926	14	66.14	4-27	0	0	3.82	5	
Lim	2004/05	11	8	2	117	62	19.50	0	1	129	181	9	20.11	4-25	1	0	8.41	5	
LEVENSON, Neil Gavin (Easterns) b Johannesburg, Transvaal 5.1.1982 RHB OB																			
FC		1	2	1	4	4*	4.00	0	0									0	
Lim		1	1	0	4	4	4.00	0	0									0	
LEVI, Richard Ernst (Cape Cobras, Western Province) b Johannesburg, Transvaal 14.1.1988 RHB RM																			
FC		9	12	0	316	137	26.33	1	1									7	
Lim		7	5	1	110	34*	27.50	0	0									2	
20T		7	7	2	91	43*	18.20	0	0									5	
FC	2006/07	27	43	5	1455	150*	38.28	4	8									15	
Lim	2004/05	30	26	3	588	102	25.56	1	1									7	
20T	2007/08	18	16	4	286	48*	23.83	0	0									6	
LINKS, Eden Ruben (Northerns) b Hermanus, Cape Province 25.3.1989 RHB OB																			
FC		4	5	2	76	44*	25.33	0	0	470	243	6	40.50	2-29	0	0	3.10	2	
Lim		11	2	1	2	2	2.00	0	0	481	320	16	20.00	4-22	1	0	3.99	6	
LOUW, Brendon Ivan (South Western Districts) b Knysna, Cape Province 15.11.1991 LHB WK																			
FC		1	2	1	11	8	11.00	0	0									4	
Lim		1	1	0	9	9	9.00	0	0									1	
LOUW, Johann (Cape Cobras, Dolphins) b Cape Town, Cape Province 12.4.1979 RHB RMF																			
FC		10	12	3	208	41	23.11	0	0	1908	758	38	19.94	6-50	1	1	2.38	6	
Lim		10	8	3	77	26*	15.40	0	0	412	389	9	43.22	2-39	0	0	5.66	1	
20T		4	3	0	3	2	1.00	0	0	72	68	6	11.33	3-27	0	0	5.66	1	
FC	2000/01	119	170	28	3138	124	22.09	1	15	21072	10772	343	31.40	6-39	12	2	3.06	41	
Int	2008/09	3	1	0	23	23	23.00	0	0	156	148	2	74.00	1-45	0	0	5.69	0	
Lim	2000/01	135	101	24	1382	72	17.94	0	3	6170	5031	187	26.90	5-27	8	4	4.89	17	
I20T	2008/09	2	1	1	1	1*		0	0	42	54	2	27.00	2-36	0	0	7.71	0	
20T	2004	53	31	7	240	48*	10.00	0	0	1102	1354	68	19.91	4-18	2	0	7.37	12	
LWANA, Lwando Lennox (Border, Border to Namibia) b Pirie Mission, near King William's Town, Cape Province 26.12.1983 RHB RFM																			
FC		6	8	1	16	12	2.28	0	0	528	349	9	38.77	3-42	0	0	3.96	5	
Lim		8								306	281	9	31.22	3-39	0	0	5.51	1	
FC	2004/05	19	22	6	164	38	10.25	0	0	1582	991	33	30.03	4-42	0	0	3.75	9	
Lim	2004/05	24	8	0	26	10	3.25	0	0	846	753	26	28.96	5-58	1	1	5.34	2	
MABUYA, Anthony Phakamile Tebogo (Griqualand West) b Kimberley, Cape Province 15.7.1977 RHB SLA																			
FC		9	12	3	101	25	11.22	0	0	1149	611	25	24.44	4-43	0	0	3.19	4	
Lim		11	5	1	23	13	5.75	0	0	476	279	18	15.50	3-21	0	0	3.51	3	
FC	2001/02	20	29	7	242	30	11.00	0	0	2052	1156	35	33.02	4-43	0	0	3.38	11	
Lim	2005/06	19	9	1	46	17	5.75	0	0	740	494	27	18.29	5-29	0	1	4.00	7	
McKENZIE, Neil Douglas (Lions, Hampshire, Hampshire to Scotland) b Johannesburg, Transvaal 24.11.1975 RHB RM																			
FC		10	16	1	798	140	53.20	3	3									9	
Lim		10	10	0	419	125	41.90	1	3									6	

Cmp	Debut	M	I	NO	Runs	HS	Avge	100	50	Balls	Runs	Wkts	Avge	BB	5i	10m	RpO	ct	st
20T		8	8	0	185	46	23.12	0	0									4	
Test	2000	58	94	7	3253	226	37.39	5	16	90	68	0					4.53	54	
FC	1994/95	209	353	42	13563	226	43.61	35	66	864	464	9	51.55	2-13	0	0	3.22	184	
Int	1999/00	64	55	10	1688	131*	37.51	2	10	46	27	0					3.52	21	
Lim	1995/96	228	206	31	6365	131*	36.37	8	43	255	248	4	62.00	2-19	0	0	5.83	68	
I20T	2005/06	2	1	1	7	7*		0	0									0	
20T	2003/04	53	52	14	1290	85*	33.94	0	9	12	19	0					9.50	20	
McLAREN, Adrian Peter (Eagles, Griqualand West, Eagles to India) b Kimberley, Cape Province 21.4.1980 RHB RM WK																			
FC		7	11	2	514	125*	57.11	1	5	6	4	0					4.00	5	
Lim		11	11	1	388	75	38.80	0	3									7	2
20T		5	5	0	81	33	16.20	0	0									2	
FC	1998/99	68	121	8	4404	164	38.97	14	20	24	12	0					3.00	115	3
Lim	2000/01	72	69	6	2021	132	32.07	2	13									31	5
20T	2007/08	17	16	1	264	61	17.60	0	1									8	
McLAREN, Ryan (Eagles, South Africa, Eagles to India, Mumbai Indians, South Africa to West Indies) b Kimberley, Cape Province 9.2.1983 LHB RMF																			
Test		1	1	1	33	33*		0	0	78	43	1	43.00	1-30	0	0	3.30	0	
FC		2	3	1	134	86	67.00	0	1	302	160	6	26.66	3-56	0	0	3.17	1	
Int		5	4	1	11	6*	3.66	0	0	204	163	4	40.75	3-51	0	0	4.79	2	
Lim		12	10	4	96	39*	16.00	0	0	490	481	13	37.00	3-51	0	0	5.89	3	
I20T		2	1	1	1	1*		0	0	48	59	4	14.75	3-33	0	0	7.37	0	
20T		2	1	1	1	1*		0	0	48	59	4	14.75	3-33	0	0	7.37	0	
FC	2003/04	80	115	19	2711	140	28.23	2	14	12627	6361	255	24.94	8-38	10	1	3.02	40	
Int	2009/10	10	8	2	37	12	6.16	0	0	432	366	8	45.75	3-51	0	0	5.08	5	
Lim	2003/04	105	78	30	1561	82*	32.52	0	8	3919	3322	105	31.63	5-46	4	1	5.08	35	
I20T	2009/10	4	3	3	8	6*		0	0	95	107	9	11.88	5-19	0	1	6.75	1	
20T	2004/05	81	55	27	583	46*	20.82	0	0	1554	1944	68	28.58	5-19	1	1	7.50	33	
MAFA, Johnson Tumelo (Gauteng, Gauteng to Namibia) b Johannesburg, Transvaal 5.2.1978 RHB RFM																			
FC		9	4	0	33	17	8.25	0	0	1131	675	22	30.68	6-44	1	0	3.58	3	
Lim		9	2	0	19	15	9.50	0	0	246	229	5	45.80	2-35	0	0	5.58	0	
FC	1997/98	61	56	20	173	19*	4.80	0	0	8693	5180	183	28.30	7-39	8	1	3.57	19	
Lim	1999/00	70	21	9	40	15	3.33	0	0	2587	2135	74	28.85	4-34	3	0	4.95	11	
MAHARAJ, Keshav Athmanand (Dolphins, KwaZulu-Natal) b Durban, Natal 7.2.1990 RHB SLA																			
FC		12	16	1	126	45	8.40	0	0	1648	941	34	27.67	5-30	1	0	3.42	4	
Lim		11	7	1	48	15*	8.00	0	0	432	299	22	13.59	4-21	1	0	4.15	3	
20T		1								18	29	1	29.00	1-29	0	0	9.66	0	
FC	2006/07	21	28	4	328	45	13.66	0	0	2986	1755	55	31.90	5-30	1	0	3.52	6	
Lim	2006/07	21	12	3	68	15*	7.55	0	0	868	657	35	18.77	4-21	1	0	4.54	7	
MAHLOMBE, Mondli (Western Province) b Cape Town, Cape Province 11.11.1985 RHB RFM																			
FC		4	4	1	19	16	6.33	0	0	390	179	3	59.66	2-35	0	0	2.75	2	
Lim		4	1	1	5	5*		0	0	96	88	1	88.00	1-34	0	0	5.50	0	
FC	2005/06	18	20	2	164	36	9.11	0	0	1812	957	35	27.34	3-11	0	0	3.16	7	
Lim	2005/06	25	11	5	61	14*	10.16	0	0	833	617	19	32.47	3-34	0	0	4.44	8	
MAKHAPHELA, Viyusa (Border) b Alice, Cape Province 20.12.1986 RHB RM																			
FC		2	4	0	80	45	20.00	0	0									1	
Lim		1	1	0	11	11	11.00	0	0									0	
FC	2006/07	3	6	0	119	45	19.83	0	0	12	3	0					1.50	1	
MAKONGOLO, Sithembile (Border) b Middledrift, Cape Province 21.4.1985 RHB OB																			
FC		6	12	0	178	50	14.83	0	1	24	25	0					6.25	4	
Lim		2	2	1	17	16*	17.00	0	0									0	
FC	2005/06	11	22	1	365	56	17.38	0	2	186	131	3	43.66	2-37	0	0	4.22	4	
Lim	2004/05	5	5	2	58	17*	19.33	0	0	48	38	1	38.00	1-38	0	0	4.75	1	
MALAN, Heinrich (Northerns) b Pretoria, Transvaal 6.4.1981 RHB RM																			
FC		1	1	0	4	4	4.00	0	0									2	
FC	2004/05	10	13	0	296	64	22.76	0	1	100	71	1	71.00	1-21	0	0	4.26	12	
Lim	2005/06	9	8	0	164	78	20.50	0	1	48	78	0					9.75	5	
MALAN, Pieter Jacobus (Northerns, Titans) b Nelspruit, Transvaal 13.8.1989 RHB RMF																			
FC		17	30	2	1031	168	36.82	3	4	12	9	1	9.00	1-1	0	0	4.50	16	
Lim		9	9	4	685	134*	137.00	4	2									4	
20T		1	1	0	3	3	3.00	0	0									0	
FC	2006/07	29	52	6	1880	168	40.86	5	10	102	61	2	30.50	1-1	0	0	3.58	22	
Lim	2006/07	25	24	6	1268	169*	70.44	6	2	77	109	0					8.49	13	
MASEKELA, Lerutla Matheko Gershon (Northerns, Titans) b Pietersburg, Transvaal 21.7.1987 RHB RMF																			
FC		15	18	5	154	36	11.84	0	0	1578	810	41	19.75	5-69	1	0	3.08	4	
Lim		12	1	0	1	1	1.00	0	0	335	347	11	31.54	2-17	0	0	6.21	5	
FC	2006/07	32	44	14	306	36	10.20	0	0	3489	1835	91	20.16	6-30	4	0	3.15	6	
Lim	2006/07	31	14	9	67	24*	13.40	0	0	1115	962	32	30.06	3-52	0	0	5.17	12	
MASHIMBYI, Mandla Abednigo (Northerns, Titans) b Phalaborwa, Northern Province 10.11.1980 RHB RMF																			
FC		11	15	3	192	43*	16.00	0	0	1853	876	41	21.36	6-31	2	0	2.83	2	
Lim		11	7	1	123	28	20.50	0	0	390	400	15	26.66	5-35	1	1	6.15	1	
FC	2003/04	48	67	13	1153	73*	21.35	0	5	6211	3317	114	29.09	6-31	4	0	3.20	21	

Cmp	Debut	M	I	NO	Runs	HS	Avge	100	50	Balls	Runs	Wkts	Avge	BB	5i	10m	RpO	ct	st
Lim	2003/04	49	31	9	523	62*	23.77	0	1	1847	1654	58	28.51	5-35	3	1	5.37	10	
20T	2003/04	1																1	
MASIMELA, Merlin (South Western Districts) b Oudtshoorn, Cape Province 22.4.1987 RHB RMF																			
Lim		7	6	1	76	33*	15.20	0	0	223	248	8	31.00	4-55	1	0	6.67	3	
FC	2006/07	6	11	0	164	65	14.90	0	1	560	368	10	36.80	5-17	1	0	3.94	2	
Lim	2006/07	14	11	1	92	33*	9.20	0	0	301	327	8	40.87	4-55	1	0	6.51	8	
MASINGATHA, Lazola (Border) b King William's Town, Cape Province 26.2.1984 RHB RM																			
FC		4	7	0	133	52	19.00	0	1									1	
Lim		3	3	0	43	21	14.33	0	0									0	
FC	2006/07	13	22	0	478	75	21.72	0	3									7	
Lim	2006/07	12	12	1	196	52	17.81	0	1									2	
MATHEBULA, Brian Michael (Easterns, Easterns to Namibia) b Tembisa, Transvaal 26.6.1985 RHB RFM																			
FC		9	8	3	23	8	4.60	0	0	1027	724	14	51.71	4-72	0	0	4.23	3	
Lim		7								264	235	6	39.16	2-40	0	0	5.34	0	
FC	2003/04	42	43	15	237	31	8.46	0	0	5149	3525	87	40.51	5-56	1	0	4.10	8	
Lim	2004/05	26	7	2	30	16	6.00	0	0	845	760	27	28.14	6-41	0	1	5.39	2	
MATSHIKWE, Pumelela (Gauteng, Lions, Gauteng to Namibia) b Johannesburg, Transvaal 19.6.1984 RHB RFM																			
FC		8	7	3	26	9*	6.50	0	0	1199	616	24	25.66	3-22	0	0	3.08	4	
Lim		8	1	0	0	0	0.00	0	0	274	211	12	17.58	4-28	1	0	4.62	3	
FC	2008/09	10	9	4	26	9*	5.20	0	0	1379	739	26	28.42	3-22	0	0	3.21	5	
Lim	2006/07	11	3	0	3	2	1.00	0	0	370	262	14	18.71	4-28	1	0	4.24	3	
MAZIBUKO, Vusumuzi Cornelius McKenzie (North West) b Johannesburg, Transvaal 5.8.1985 RHB RMF																			
FC		12	13	4	59	15*	6.55	0	0	1437	867	24	36.12	6-108	1	0	3.62	3	
Lim		12	5	1	38	21	9.50	0	0	372	413	13	31.76	6-25	0	1	6.66	3	
FC	2005/06	21	29	6	192	22	8.34	0	0	2081	1380	34	40.58	6-108	1	0	3.97	8	
Lim	2003/04	31	13	3	166	36*	16.60	0	0	760	779	28	27.82	6-25	1	1	6.15	6	
MAZZONCINI, Alberto (Griqualand West) b Kimberley, Cape Province 14.2.1991 LHB LMF																			
FC		2	3	1	45	23*	22.50	0	0									0	
Lim		3	2	2	23	21*		0	0									4	
MBANE, Lundi (Border, Border to Namibia) b Mdantsane, Cape Province 10.10.1982 RHB RFM																			
FC		11	18	2	271	59	16.93	0	1	1254	800	17	47.05	2-44	0	0	3.82	3	
Lim		11	10	0	153	46	15.30	0	0	449	448	16	28.00	4-23	1	0	5.98	1	
FC	2004/05	41	59	8	1045	71	20.49	0	4	4650	2727	81	33.66	5-26	1	0	3.51	19	
Lim	2004/05	42	32	5	319	46	11.81	0	0	1507	1266	39	32.46	4-14	3	0	5.04	6	
MBHALATI, Nkateko Ethy (Titans) b Tzaneen, Northern Province 18.11.1981 RHB RFM																			
FC		9	11	7	46	18	11.50	0	0	1270	661	20	33.05	5-56	1	0	3.12	2	
Lim		9								360	306	16	19.12	4-41	1	0	5.10	0	
20T		7								144	169	6	28.16	4-20	1	0	7.04	2	
FC	2002/03	75	86	48	260	18	6.84	0	0	11094	5904	190	31.07	5-26	2	0	3.19	15	
Lim	2002/03	79	15	9	34	14*	5.66	0	0	3375	2645	99	26.71	4-36	3	0	4.70	9	
20T	2004/05	34	6	3	6	2*	2.00	0	0	678	797	34	23.44	4-12	2	0	7.05	5	
MEYER, Lyall (Eastern Province, Warriors) b Port Elizabeth, Cape Province 23.3.1982 LHB RF																			
FC		11	11	1	203	51	20.30	0	1	1800	890	28	31.78	5-33	2	0	2.96	5	
Lim		12	9	3	99	34*	16.50	0	0	339	332	10	33.20	2-30	0	0	5.87	5	
20T		6	2	2	4	4*		0	0	114	164	8	20.50	2-23	0	0	8.63	0	
FC	2001/02	41	58	11	1044	72*	22.21	0	5	5504	2766	86	32.16	5-33	3	0	3.01	17	
Lim	2001/02	67	47	14	459	37	13.90	0	0	2029	1772	61	29.04	5-24	1	2	5.24	22	
20T	2005/06	16	10	6	96	28	24.00	0	0	288	432	20	21.60	2-23	0	0	9.00	5	
MGENGE, Njabulo Lungelo (KwaZulu-Natal) b Tongaat, Natal 1.2.1991 RHB RMF																			
FC		2	3	1	0	0*	0.00	0	0	168	119	4	29.75	2-55	0	0	4.25	1	
Lim		4								144	114	6	19.00	3-35	0	0	4.75	2	
MGIJIMA, Aviwe (Western Province) b East London, Cape Province 10.8.1988 RHB RMF																			
FC		6	11	1	176	54*	17.60	0	1	642	309	11	28.09	5-24	1	0	2.88	4	
Lim		7	7	0	65	18	9.28	0	0	78	80	4	20.00	2-9	0	0	6.15	3	
FC	2007/08	7	12	1	177	54*	16.09	0	1	664	319	12	26.58	5-24	1	0	2.88	5	
Lim	2007/08	9	9	0	69	18	7.66	0	0	84	88	4	22.00	2-9	0	0	6.28	3	
MILLER, David Andrew (Dolphins, KwaZulu-Natal, South Africa to West Indies, South Africa A to Bangladesh, South Africa A to Sri Lanka) b Pietermaritzburg, Natal 10.6.1989 LHB OB																			
FC		9	14	3	445	108*	40.45	1	1	8	4	0					3.00	4	
Lim		12	12	2	374	86	37.40	0	3									5	
20T		5	5	2	159	90*	53.00	0	1									3	
FC	2007/08	22	34	4	910	108*	30.33	1	5	8	4	0					3.00	14	
Int	2010	4	3	2	54	26*	54.00	0	0									1	
Lim	2007/08	36	31	8	942	115*	40.95	1	5									14	
I20T	2010	1	1	0	33	33	33.00	0	0									0	
20T	2007/08	8	8	3	193	90*	38.60	0	1									4	
MLONGO, Saidi (KwaZulu-Natal) b Stanger, Natal 21.9.1983 RHB LMF																			
FC		7	9	5	55	14	13.75	0	0	761	383	15	25.53	5-35	1	0	3.02	7	
Lim		8	1	1	4	4*		0	0	276	186	10	18.60	3-14	0	0	4.04	1	
FC	2004/05	42	48	20	261	21	9.32	0	0	5611	2637	105	25.11	6-65	3	0	2.82	20	

Cmp	Debut	M	I	NO	Runs	HS	Avge	100	50	Balls	Runs	Wkts	Avge	BB	5i	10m	RpO	ct	st
Lim	2004/05	31	10	7	21	11*	7.00	0	0	1208	775	36	21.52	5-29	1	1	3.84	9	
20T	2007/08	3								54	56	3	18.66	2-20	0	0	6.22	0	
MNYANDA, Luthando Lucas (Border, Border to Namibia) b East London, Cape Province 22.10.1989 RHB OB																			
FC		8	14	0	212	44	15.14	0	0	819	429	14	30.64	4-30	0	0	3.14	3	
Lim		5	5	1	110	37	27.50	0	0	12	11	0					5.50	2	
FC	2008/09	11	18	1	246	44	14.47	0	0	1083	580	19	30.52	4-30	0	0	3.21	6	
Lim	2008/09	7	7	1	117	37	19.50	0	0	72	68	1	68.00	1-27	0	0	5.66	2	
MOFOKENG, Petros Tsepo (Easterns) b Johannesburg, Transvaal 22.5.1983 RHB LMF																			
FC		1								132	100	3	33.33	2-57	0	0	4.54	0	
Lim		7	3	1	2	2	1.00	0	0	222	180	7	25.71	4-36	1	0	4.86	2	
FC	2004/05	22	24	13	75	12*	6.81	0	0	1645	1137	25	45.48	4-47	0	0	4.14	7	
Lim	2004/05	24	9	3	35	16	5.83	0	0	786	686	24	28.58	4-36	1	0	5.23	8	
MOFOKENG, Samuel Fese (Northerns) b Bloemfontein, Free State 5.8.1991 RHB RFM																			
FC		1	1	1	6	6*		0	0	66	34	0					3.09	0	
Lim		2								12	35	0					17.50	0	
MOKOENA, Thabang Grant (Gauteng, Lions, Gauteng to Namibia) b Johannesburg, Transvaal 15.8.1987 RHB RMF																			
FC		13	19	0	475	68	25.00	0	5									4	
Lim		12	12	1	190	43	17.27	0	0									3	
FC	2008/09	16	24	0	630	71	26.25	0	6	6	4	0					4.00	7	
Lim	2008/09	15	15	1	213	43	15.21	0	0									3	
MOKONYAMA, Matsobane James (Northerns) b Mamelodi, Pretoria, Transvaal 13.2.1981 RHB OB																			
FC		13	19	0	547	74	28.78	0	4	8	6	0					4.50	14	
Lim		11	10	0	163	51	16.30	0	1									4	
FC	2002/03	35	49	5	1302	92	29.59	0	9	8	6	0					4.50	24	
Lim	2002/03	41	31	3	309	51	11.03	0	1									9	
MOOTHOSAMY, Khaalid (Gauteng) b Johannesburg, Transvaal 18.9.1984 RHB OB																			
Lim		7	6	3	64	25	21.33	0	0	54	43	0					4.77	5	
FC	2004/05	6	10	0	156	42	15.60	0	0	24	16	1	16.00	1-3	0	0	4.00	2	
Lim	2004/05	15	13	5	125	25	15.62	0	0	54	43	0					4.77	10	
MORKEL, Johannes Albertus (South Africa, Titans, Chennai Super Kings, Durham, South Africa to India, South Africa to West Indies) b Vereeniging, Transvaal 10.6.1981 LHB RMF																			
FC		5	7	1	304	102	50.66	1	1	640	336	12	28.00	4-70	0	0	3.15	3	
Int		6	6	3	135	50*	45.00	0	1	168	170	4	42.50	3-20	0	0	6.07	2	
Lim		14	14	3	336	84	30.54	0	2	366	412	12	34.33	3-20	0	0	6.75	7	
I20T		2	2	1	23	14	23.00	0	0	36	67	2	33.50	2-35	0	0	11.16	1	
20T		5	3	2	36	14	36.00	0	0	81	117	5	23.40	2-22	0	0	8.66	2	
Test	2008/09	1	1	0	58	58	58.00	0	1	192	132	1	132.00	1-44	0	0	4.12	0	
FC	1999/00	65	93	15	3296	204*	42.25	5	20	9779	5049	169	29.87	6-36	4	0	3.09	27	
Int	2003/04	47	34	8	621	97	23.88	0	2	1816	1629	48	33.93	4-29	2	0	5.38	12	
Lim	1999/00	158	121	32	2434	97	27.34	0	11	6174	5081	170	29.88	4-23	4	0	4.93	35	
I20T	2005/06	29	25	6	443	43	23.31	0	0	406	549	16	34.31	2-12	0	0	8.11	12	
20T	2003/04	127	104	31	1867	71	25.57	0	4	2137	2888	100	28.88	4-30	2	0	8.10	24	
MORKEL, Morné (South Africa, South Africa A, Titans, Rajasthan Royals, South Africa to India, South Africa to West Indies) b Vereeniging, Transvaal 6.10.1984 LHB RFM																			
Test		4	5	1	73	23	18.25	0	0	882	408	19	21.47	5-75	1	0	2.77	3	
FC		9	11	1	196	60	19.60	0	1	1664	796	38	20.94	5-75	1	0	2.87	4	
Int		2	1	0	7	7	7.00	0	0	92	58	3	19.33	3-39	0	0	3.78	0	
Lim		7	5	0	62	29	12.40	0	0	288	250	10	25.00	5-34	0	1	5.20	1	
20T		2	2	2	0	0*		0	0	36	49	0					8.16	0	
Test	2006/07	26	31	3	370	40	13.21	0	0	4855	2831	92	30.77	5-50	2	0	3.49	7	
FC	2003/04	58	72	9	1027	82*	16.30	0	4	10134	5778	212	27.25	6-43	9	2	3.42	24	
Int	2007	28	10	3	102	25	14.57	0	0	1439	1216	45	27.02	4-21	2	0	5.07	6	
Lim	2005/06	49	20	6	207	35	14.78	0	0	2336	1922	72	26.69	5-34	3	1	4.93	10	
I20T	2007/08	14	2	1	2	1*	2.00	0	0	317	346	23	15.04	4-17	2	0	6.54	1	
20T	2005	42	12	7	36	8	7.20	0	0	874	1027	44	23.34	4-17	2	0	7.05	7	
MORRIS, Christopher Henry (North West) b Pretoria, Transvaal 30.4.1987 RHB RFM																			
FC		8	12	2	437	145	43.70	1	2	1007	549	20	27.45	5-44	1	0	3.27	12	
Lim		6	3	0	60	44	20.00	0	0	208	225	7	32.14	3-42	0	0	6.49	5	
MOSEHLE, Mangaliso (Easterns, Titans) b Duduza 24.4.1990 RHB WK																			
FC		10	16	1	421	74	28.06	0	3									32	3
Lim		8	8	1	125	41	17.85	0	0									6	3
FC	2008/09	14	22	2	449	74	22.45	0	3									49	4
Lim	2008/09	12	12	2	164	41	16.40	0	0									9	3
20T	2008/09	1																0	
MOSENA, Bokang Brian (Free State) b Bloemfontein, Free State 6.2.1991 RHB RMF																			
Lim		2	1	0	0	0	0.00	0	0	24	33	0					8.25	0	
MOSENA, Lefa Nelson (Free State) b Bloemfontein, Orange Free State 18.3.1987 RHB																			
FC		3	4	0	66	44	16.50	0	0									5	
Lim		5	5	1	97	48*	24.25	0	0									1	
FC	2005/06	23	40	1	807	83	20.69	0	4									44	1
Lim	2005/06	22	19	3	384	70	24.00	0	2									16	

Cmp	Debut	M	I	NO	Runs	HS	Avge	100	50	Balls	Runs	Wkts	Avge	BB	5i	10m	RpO	ct	st
MOSES, Bradley (Dolphins, KwaZulu-Natal Inland, KwaZulu-Natal Inland to Namibia) b Durban, Natal 3.4.1983 RHB OB																			
FC		10	19	0	555	119	29.21	1	2	242	169	4	42.25	2-7	0	0	4.19	4	
Lim		11	10	0	291	73	29.10	0	2	278	235	11	21.36	4-29	1	0	5.07	0	
FC	2006/07	23	40	1	1112	119	28.51	1	6	435	280	8	35.00	2-7	0	0	3.86	16	
Lim	2006/07	23	22	1	628	79*	29.90	0	4	398	343	15	22.86	4-29	1	0	5.17	1	
MOSTERT, Johan Francois (North West) b Pretoria, Transvaal 14.3.1986 RHB OB																			
FC		11	22	3	806	163*	42.42	2	3	583	348	9	38.66	4-40	0	0	3.58	1	
Lim		5	5	1	142	73*	35.50	0	1	162	149	1	149.00	1-53	0	0	5.51	1	
FC	2005/06	27	52	9	1888	163*	43.90	4	11	1470	890	29	30.68	4-16	0	0	3.63	8	
Lim	2004/05	20	18	3	475	89*	31.66	0	3	588	498	13	38.30	3-53	0	0	5.08	4	
MOSTERT, Tianne Jacques (North West) b Klerksdorp, Transvaal 18.6.1987 RHB RM																			
FC		1	2	0	7	6	3.50	0	0	42	22	0					3.14	0	
FC	2006/07	3	6	0	68	27	11.33	0	0	84	43	0					3.07	2	
Lim	2006/07	1								18	30	0					10.00	0	
MOTSAMAI, Tello Sylvester (Free State) b Bloemfontein, Orange Free State 21.9.1982 RHB RFM																			
FC		1	1	0	5	5	5.00	0	0	60	43	0					4.30	0	
Lim		3	1	1	1	1*		0	0	12	20	1	20.00	1-20	0	0	10.00	2	
FC	2003/04	28	36	13	396	51*	17.21	0	1	2900	1623	34	47.73	3-53	0	0	3.35	5	
Lim	2003/04	27	15	4	78	18	7.09	0	0	965	890	21	42.38	3-54	0	0	5.53	6	
MPITSANG, Phenyo Victor (Eagles, Free State, Eagles to India) b Kimberley, Cape Province 28.3.1980 RHB RFM																			
FC		10	10	4	42	13	7.00	0	0	1516	763	23	33.17	5-50	1	0	3.02	1	
Lim		10	1	0	2	2	2.00	0	0	360	335	11	30.45	5-44	0	1	5.58	1	
20T		1								18	11	0					3.66	0	
FC	1997/98	94	114	49	376	23	5.78	0	0	14799	6710	227	29.55	5-24	5	0	2.72	17	
Int	1998/99	2	1	1	1	1*		0	0	60	63	2	31.50	2-49	0	0	6.30	0	
Lim	1998/99	91	25	14	59	20*	5.36	0	0	3686	2824	84	33.61	5-44	1	1	4.59	5	
20T	2005/06	16	2	1	3	3	3.00	0	0	246	306	13	23.53	3-19	0	0	7.46	3	
MURRAY, Nathan Marcel (South Western Districts, South Western Districts to Namibia) b Beaufort West, Cape Province 6.9.1983 RHB RMF																			
FC		4	6	2	78	60	19.50	0	1	342	199	4	49.75	2-27	0	0	3.49	4	
Lim		9	9	1	120	24	15.00	0	0	66	69	2	34.50	2-33	0	0	6.27	3	
FC	2006/07	22	36	13	603	60	26.21	0	4	2347	1332	43	30.97	5-29	1	0	3.40	14	
Lim	2006/07	28	23	6	264	39*	15.52	0	0	812	711	26	27.34	7-16	1	1	5.25	6	
MYBURGH, Stephanus Johannes (Northerns) b Pretoria, Transvaal 28.2.1984 LHB OB																			
FC		1	2	1	39	33	39.00	0	0	30	15	0					3.00	0	
Lim		9	9	1	119	53	14.87	0	1									3	
FC	2005/06	7	9	2	125	33	17.85	0	0	48	26	0					3.25	4	
Lim	2005/06	19	19	2	464	90*	27.29	0	4	54	30	2	15.00	2-30	0	0	3.33	5	
MYOLI, Ayavuya (Border) b King William's Town, Cape Province 8.6.1990 RHB RF																			
FC		1	2	1	0	0*	0.00	0	0	48	28	0					3.50	1	
MZEMA, Vusumzi Joseph (North West) b Parys, Orange Free State 5.6.1983 RHB RMF																			
FC		5	3	1	7	6	3.50	0	0	326	206	3	68.66	1-3	0	0	3.79	0	
Lim		4	1	1	4	4*		0	0	96	89	5	17.80	2-28	0	0	5.56	0	
FC	2006/07	10	13	5	21	6	2.62	0	0	602	361	4	90.25	1-3	0	0	3.59	3	
Lim	2006/07	8	3	3	6	4*		0	0	216	159	10	15.90	3-27	0	0	4.41	1	
NAGAN, Keegan (KwaZulu-Natal) b Durban, Natal 23.4.1984 RHB RFM																			
FC		1																0	
Lim		1								45	49	3	16.33	3-49	0	0	6.53	0	
NAICKER, Kreeson Meges (North West) b Pretoria, Transvaal 14.4.1989 LHB OB																			
FC		3	4	1	20	10*	6.66	0	0	120	95	1	95.00	1-31	0	0	4.75	1	
Lim		2								18	22	1	22.00	1-22	0	0	7.33	0	
FC	2007/08	9	8	3	21	10*	4.20	0	0	1080	768	17	45.17	5-120	1	0	4.26	5	
Lim	2007/08	6	3	1	15	10	7.50	0	0	90	93	2	46.50	1-22	0	0	6.20	0	
NAIDOO, Shershan (Northerns) b Pretoria, Transvaal 29.1.1990 RHB OB																			
Lim		1	1	1	11	11*		0	0	48	35	1	35.00	1-35	0	0	4.37	0	
NDLELA, Buntu Prince (Easterns) b Qumbu, Transvaal 24.10.1989 RHB RM																			
Lim		1	1	0	0	0	0.00	0	0									0	
NDLOVU, Abraham Lepho (Northerns) b Mamelodi, Pretoria, Transvaal 25.2.1986 RHB OB WK																			
FC		3	4	0	119	84	29.75	0	1									6	
Lim		5	3	1	24	13	12.00	0	0									6	3
FC	2006/07	25	34	7	823	84	30.48	0	5									89	7
Lim	2005/06	33	22	5	334	62*	19.64	0	2									31	7
NEL, Andre (Lions, Surrey) b Germiston, Transvaal 15.7.1977 RHB RFM																			
FC		3	4	2	84	50*	42.00	0	1	642	284	11	25.81	5-64	1	0	2.65	1	
Lim		7	2	0	5	5	2.50	0	0	272	289	7	41.28	4-49	1	0	6.37	0	
Test	2001/02	36	42	8	337	34	9.91	0	0	7630	3919	123	31.86	6-32	3	1	3.08	16	
FC	1996/97	132	153	43	1692	96	15.38	0	4	25915	12212	446	27.38	6-25	14	1	2.82	53	
Int	2000/01	79	22	12	127	30*	12.70	0	0	3801	2935	106	27.68	5-45	3	1	4.63	21	
Lim	1997/98	214	85	44	482	58	11.75	0	1	10454	7627	295	25.85	6-27	7	4	4.37	49	
I20T	2005/06	2	1	1	0	0*		0	0	48	42	2	21.00	2-19	0	0	5.25	1	
20T	2003	46	26	11	140	19	9.33	0	0	1038	1139	31	36.74	2-13	0	0	6.58	10	

Cmp	Debut	M	I	NO	Runs	HS	Avge	100	50	Balls	Runs	Wkts	Avge	BB	5i	10m	RpO	ct	st
NEL, Leon Gerhard (Northerns) b Pretoria, Transvaal 9.11.1987 RHB LMF																			
FC		3	5	0	26	17	5.20	0	0	498	215	4	53.75	2-43	0	0	2.59	1	
Lim		3	3	1	27	19*	13.50	0	0	108	93	3	31.00	3-40	0	0	5.16	0	
FC	2007/08	5	8	0	102	42	12.75	0	0	612	304	8	38.00	2-20	0	0	2.98	1	
Lim	2007/08	6	5	1	74	41	18.50	0	0	168	181	4	45.25	3-40	0	0	6.46	2	
NHLAPO, Cheslin Eric Marcus (KwaZulu-Natal Inland, KwaZulu-Natal Inland to Namibia) b Welkom, Free State 7.3.1987 RHB RM																			
FC		2	4	0	27	15	6.75	0	0									1	
Lim		3	3	1	23	18	11.50	0	0									1	
Lim	2009/10	4	3	1	23	18	11.50	0	0									1	
NIEUWOUDT, Griffin Nathan (Free State) b Welkom, Orange Free State 22.5.1987 LHB SLA																			
FC		2	4	0	135	71	33.75	0	1									0	
Lim		1	1	0	0	0	0.00	0	0									0	
FC	2007/08	14	24	3	743	83	35.38	0	6	6	3	0					3.00	0	
Lim	2007/08	11	11	1	170	60	17.00	0	1									4	
NIPPER, Kyle (Dolphins, KwaZulu-Natal Inland, KwaZulu-Natal Inland to Namibia) b Pietermartizburg, Natal 25.11.1987 LHB SLA																			
FC		8	13	2	149	32	13.54	0	0	1415	980	28	35.00	5-143	1	0	4.15	3	
Lim		11	10	4	174	43*	29.00	0	0	438	316	15	21.06	4-24	1	0	4.32	1	
20T		2	1	0	0	0	0.00	0	0	42	42	3	14.00	2-10	0	0	6.00	1	
FC	2006/07	13	21	4	246	38	14.47	0	0	2173	1375	39	35.25	5-143	1	0	3.79	6	
Lim	2006/07	21	20	4	333	54	20.81	0	1	832	621	23	27.00	4-24	1	0	4.47	11	
NOWAK, Sean Andrew (Northerns) b Pretoria, Transvaal 6.1.1987 RHB RFM																			
FC		11	12	6	87	20	14.50	0	0	1572	863	33	26.15	5-32	1	0	3.29	0	
Lim		9	4	4	7	5*		0	0	273	228	11	20.72	3-28	0	0	5.01	1	
FC	2008/09	18	20	8	129	20	10.75	0	0	2494	1474	53	27.81	5-32	1	0	3.54	2	
Lim	2008/09	14	6	4	9	5*	4.50	0	0	474	441	18	24.50	3-28	0	0	5.58	1	
NQOLO, Maphelo Jerry (Border) b Alice, Cape Province 23.7.1991 RHB RM																			
FC		1	2	0	83	58	41.50	0	1	72	31	1	31.00	1-16	0	0	2.58	0	
Lim		4	3	1	83	47*	41.50	0	0	18	24	0					8.00	0	
NTINI, Makhaya (South Africa, Warriors, Kent, Kent to Scotland) b Mdingi, nr King William's Town, Cape Province 6.7.1977 RHB RF																			
Test		2	3	3	11	6*		0	0	420	233	2	116.50	2-78	0	0	3.32	0	
FC		9	11	9	34	16*	17.00	0	0	1434	660	13	50.76	3-45	0	0	2.76	0	
Lim		9	3	1	19	10*	9.50	0	0	384	343	16	21.43	5-26	0	1	5.35	4	
20T		8	1	0	0	0	0.00	0	0	186	217	12	18.08	2-12	0	0	7.00	0	
Test	1997/98	101	116	45	699	32*	9.84	0	0	20834	11242	390	28.82	7-37	18	4	3.23	25	
FC	1995/96	186	217	82	1274	34*	9.43	0	0	34468	18586	648	28.68	7-37	27	5	3.23	40	
Int	1997/98	173	47	24	199	42*	8.65	0	0	8687	6559	266	24.65	6-22	8	4	4.53	30	
Lim	1995/96	246	73	33	284	42*	7.10	0	0	11848	8878	357	24.86	6-22	9	6	4.49	45	
I20T	2005/06	9	3	1	9	5	4.50	0	0	168	252	6	42.00	2-22	0	0	9.00	1	
20T	2003/04	34	9	4	27	11	5.40	0	0	750	910	32	28.43	4-21	1	0	7.28	2	
NTSHONA, Siyamtanda (Eastern Province) b Port Elizabeth, Cape Province 31.8.1990 RHB RMF																			
FC		1	1	0	2	2	2.00	0	0	92	52	2	26.00	2-40	0	0	3.39	1	
NYAWO, Ephrahim (Easterns) b Springs, Transvaal 4.4.1983 RHB RM																			
FC		1	1	0	13	13	13.00	0	0	132	94	2	47.00	2-77	0	0	4.27	0	
Lim		2	1	1	16	16*		0	0	30	25	0					5.00	0	
FC	2005/06	13	21	4	236	50*	13.88	0	1	132	94	2	47.00	2-77	0	0	4.27	11	
Lim	2005/06	23	13	6	141	28*	20.14	0	0	198	146	3	48.66	2-29	0	0	4.42	5	
O'CONNOR, Sean Patrick (Easterns, Easterns to Namibia) b Johannesburg, Transvaal 21.1.1977 RHB RM																			
FC		12	14	4	261	47	26.10	0	0	344	204	4	51.00	2-59	0	0	3.55	8	
Lim		12	10	4	75	39	12.50	0	0	282	286	11	26.00	3-43	0	0	6.08	5	
FC	1997/98	55	82	10	1136	58	15.77	0	1	3198	2031	49	41.44	4-61	0	0	3.81	20	
Lim	2003/04	49	36	15	521	46	24.80	0	0	1484	1325	40	33.12	4-36	1	0	5.35	17	
OLIVIER, Andre (South Western Districts) b Johannesburg, Transvaal 13.5.1985 RHB OB																			
FC		3	6	0	87	67	14.50	0	1	6	18	0					18.00	2	
Lim		3	3	1	19	15	9.50	0	0									0	
FC	2006/07	11	21	0	274	67	13.04	0	2	24	34	0					8.50	4	
Lim	2006/07	10	10	2	159	44	19.87	0	0	42	29	1	29.00	1-29	0	0	4.14	1	
OLIVIER, Mario (KwaZulu-Natal Inland, KwaZulu-Natal Inland to Namibia) b Port Elizabeth, Cape Province 16.4.1979 LHB RM																			
FC		9	17	1	487	133	30.43	2	0									1	
Lim		4	4	1	203	74*	67.66	0	2									2	
FC	2008/09	11	21	1	643	133	32.15	2	1	3	0	1	0.00	1-0	0	0	0.00	1	
Lim	2009/10	5	5	1	226	74*	56.50	0	2									2	
OLIVIER, Mario Wicus (Cape Cobras, Western Province) b Pretoria, Transvaal 3.11.1982 RHB RFM																			
FC		8	13	4	144	48	16.00	0	0	1201	843	21	40.14	6-97	1	0	4.21	4	
Lim		9	5	2	50	24	16.66	0	0	306	328	13	25.23	5-37	0	1	6.43	0	
FC	2004/05	46	69	13	574	51	10.25	0	1	6391	4143	130	31.86	10-65	6	2	3.89	10	
Lim	2004/05	23	11	4	81	24	11.57	0	0	815	874	40	21.85	5-37	0	3	6.43	1	
20T	2006/07	5	2	1	12	11*	12.00	0	0	90	114	4	28.50	2-22	0	0	7.60	0	

Cmp	Debut	M	I	NO	Runs	HS	Avge	100	50	Balls	Runs	Wkts	Avge	BB	5i	10m	RpO	ct	st
ONTONG, Justin Lee (Boland, Cape Cobras, South Africa A, Cape Cobras to India) b Paarl, Cape Province 4.1.1980 RHB OB,LB																			
FC		10	14	1	374	69	28.76	0	2	437	233	10	23.30	5-62	1	0	3.19	9	
Lim		14	11	3	307	122*	38.37	1	1	85	70	3	23.33	1-3	0	0	4.94	5	
20T		8	8	1	133	37*	19.00	0	0	72	101	6	16.83	3-27	0	0	8.41	3	
Test	2001/02	2	4	1	57	32	19.00	0	0	185	133	1	133.00	1-79	0	0	4.31	1	
FC	1997/98	120	196	10	6797	166	36.54	13	41	8612	4625	105	44.04	5-62	1	0	3.22	92	
Int	2000/01	26	15	1	167	32	11.92	0	0	538	396	9	44.00	3-30	0	0	4.41	13	
Lim	1998/99	161	136	17	3133	122*	26.32	1	22	3000	2340	55	42.54	3-29	0	0	4.68	65	
I20T	2007/08	3	2	0	20	14	10.00	0	0	12	25	1	25.00	1-25	0	0	12.50	0	
20T	2003/04	49	43	6	724	59*	19.56	0	1	426	575	21	27.38	3-27	0	0	8.09	23	
O'REILLY, Ethan (Gauteng, Lions) b Port Elizabeth, Cape Province 27.12.1985 RHB RFM																			
FC		1	1	1	0	0*		0	0	156	94	3	31.33	2-67	0	0	3.61	1	
Lim		2								42	70	0					10.00	0	
20T		8	3	1	5	3	2.50	0	0	180	245	11	22.27	3-27	0	0	8.16	0	
FC	2008/09	6	7	4	71	42*	23.66	0	0	695	408	21	19.42	5-3	1	0	3.52	5	
Lim	2008/09	7	3	0	9	5	3.00	0	0	260	248	7	35.42	3-36	0	0	5.72	1	
PANESAR, Mudhsuden Singh (England Lions, Sussex, Lions) b Luton, Bedfordshire, England 25.4.1982 LHB SLA																			
FC		6	7	0	69	37	9.85	0	0	1264	586	15	39.06	4-42	0	0	2.78	2	
Test	2005/06	39	51	17	187	26	5.50	0	0	9042	4331	126	34.37	6-37	8	1	2.87	9	
FC	2001	131	168	53	1021	46*	8.87	0	0	28767	13562	419	32.36	7-181	21	3	2.82	29	
Int	2006/07	26	8	3	26	13	5.20	0	0	1308	980	24	40.83	3-25	0	0	4.49	3	
Lim	2002	66	23	10	135	17*	10.38	0	0	2951	2226	65	34.24	5-20	0	1	4.52	10	
I20T	2006/07	1	1	0	1	1	1.00	0	0	24	40	2	20.00	2-40	0	0	10.00	0	
20T	2006	19	6	2	7	3*	1.75	0	0	366	461	12	38.41	2-22	0	0	7.55	2	
PANGABANTU, Yanda (Border, Border to Namibia) b King William's Town, Cape Province 8.4.1981 RHB RFM																			
FC		10	16	7	78	43	8.66	0	0	1284	733	21	34.90	4-89	0	0	3.42	3	
Lim		11	2	2	11	6*		0	0	432	359	11	32.63	2-13	0	0	4.98	8	
FC	2005/06	32	36	22	146	43	10.42	0	0	4312	2122	87	24.39	5-48	1	0	2.95	5	
Lim	2004/05	37	13	9	32	10	8.00	0	0	1416	1070	33	32.42	3-33	0	0	4.53	12	
PARNELL, Wayne Dillon (South Africa, Warriors, South Africa to India) b Port Elizabeth, Cape Province 30.7.1989 LHB LFM																			
Test		1								66	35	2	17.50	2-17	0	0	3.18	1	
FC		5	5	0	161	72	32.20	0	1	504	373	9	41.44	4-122	0	0	4.44	4	
Int		5	2	1	11	10*	11.00	0	0	261	274	16	17.12	5-48	0	2	6.29	0	
Lim		12	5	1	28	10*	7.00	0	0	552	554	24	23.08	5-48	0	2	6.02	0	
20T		2								42	43	1	43.00	1-10	0	0	6.14	0	
Test	2009/10	3	2	0	34	22	17.00	0	0	306	227	5	45.40	2-17	0	0	4.45	1	
FC	2006/07	23	28	3	542	90	21.68	0	3	3605	1992	56	35.57	4-7	0	0	3.31	6	
Int	2008/09	11	4	1	78	49	26.00	0	0	591	626	25	25.04	5-48	1	2	6.35	1	
Lim	2006/07	41	24	8	305	49	19.06	0	0	1906	1823	65	28.04	5-48	3	2	5.73	8	
I20T	2008/09	8								173	192	11	17.45	4-13	1	0	6.65	0	
20T	2007/08	25	7	5	32	11*	16.00	0	0	503	538	25	21.52	4-13	1	0	6.41	2	
PATEL, Mohamed Zain (KwaZulu-Natal) b Durban, Natal 30.9.1985 RHB LB																			
FC		1	2	1	2	2*	2.00	0	0	72	25	0					2.08	0	
PATERSON, Dane (Western Province) b Cape Town, Cape Province 4.4.1989 RHB RFM																			
FC		7	11	1	68	15	6.80	0	0	887	509	17	29.94	3-31	0	0	3.44	4	
Lim		4								130	99	6	16.50	4-27	1	0	4.56	0	
Lim	2008/09	5	1	0	5	5	5.00	0	0	172	131	6	21.83	4-27	1	0	4.57	0	
PAULSE, Hillroy Henrico (Boland, Cape Cobras, Boland to Namibia) b Paarl, Cape Province 6.9.1985 RHB RF																			
FC		9	12	3	112	54	12.44	0	1	779	439	11	39.90	4-50	0	0	3.38	4	
Lim		7	3	2	7	5*	7.00	0	0	211	173	7	24.71	3-17	0	0	4.91	0	
FC	2004/05	34	38	16	203	54	9.22	0	1	3714	2322	76	30.55	5-65	1	0	3.75	8	
Lim	2005/06	21	11	5	62	19	10.33	0	0	811	635	30	21.16	5-45	1	1	4.69	3	
PEDI, Kagisho (Free State) b Bloemfontein, Orange Free State 21.8.1989 RHB RMF																			
Lim		1																0	
PELSER, Brett Jonathan (North West) b Durban, Natal 23.4.1985 RHB RM																			
FC		11	20	10	1003	163*	100.30	4	4	406	228	5	45.60	2-10	0	0	3.36	8	
Lim		13	12	3	228	62	25.33	0	2	192	162	5	32.40	2-18	0	0	5.06	10	
FC	2007/08	20	32	12	1384	163*	69.20	4	7	688	419	6	69.83	2-10	0	0	3.65	14	
Lim	2007/08	21	20	5	513	66	34.20	0	5	384	328	8	41.00	2-18	0	0	5.12	15	
PETERSEN, Alviro Nathan (Lions, North West, South Africa, Khulna to Bangladesh, South Africa to India, South Africa to West Indies, South Africa A to Bangladesh) b Port Elizabeth, Cape Province 25.11.1980 RHB RM																			
FC		7	12	2	557	128	55.70	2	4	6	0	0					0.00	5	
Int		5	5	1	218	64	54.50	0	3									0	
Lim		15	15	1	379	64	27.07	0	3	42	45	0					6.42	5	
20T		2	2	0	18	13	9.00	0	0									2	
Test	2009/10	4	8	0	272	100	34.00	1	1	42	21	1	21.00	1-2	0	0	3.00	4	
FC	2000/01	97	176	10	6352	152	38.26	19	27	234	125	4	31.25	2-7	0	0	3.20	81	
Int	2006/07	14	12	1	377	80	34.27	0	4	6	7	0					7.00	2	
Lim	2001/02	116	111	7	3316	124	31.88	5	22	161	140	3	46.66	1-13	0	0	5.21	38	

Cmp	Debut	M	I	NO	Runs	HS	Avge	100	50	Balls	Runs	Wkts	Avge	BB	5i	10m	RpO	ct	st
I20T	2010	2	2	0	14	8	7.00	0	0									1	
20T	2003/04	36	32	5	748	78*	27.70	0	7	24	44	0					11.00	19	
PETERSON, Robin John (Cape Cobras, Derbyshire, Derbyshire to Netherlands) b Port Elizabeth, Cape Province 4.8.1979 LHB SLA																			
FC		8	10	1	316	100	35.11	1	2	1408	709	30	23.63	5-45	3	0	3.02	0	
Lim		11	8	1	277	78*	39.57	0	2	480	452	15	30.13	3-29	0	0	5.65	6	
20T		7	6	1	100	50*	20.00	0	1	150	179	6	29.83	2-25	0	0	7.16	1	
Test	2003	6	7	1	163	61	27.16	0	1	959	497	14	35.50	5-33	1	0	3.10	5	
FC	1998/99	114	177	22	3964	130	25.57	6	14	21038	10547	321	32.85	6-67	14	1	3.00	49	
Int	2002/03	35	15	4	147	36	13.36	0	0	1252	992	17	58.35	2-26	0	0	4.75	7	
Lim	1999/00	145	101	11	2294	101	25.48	1	14	5836	4427	152	29.12	7-24	1	4	4.55	49	
I20T	2005/06	5	2	0	42	34	21.00	0	0	65	86	6	14.33	3-30	0	0	7.93	2	
20T	2003/04	56	50	6	830	72*	18.86	0	3	1048	1202	47	25.57	3-24	0	0	6.88	10	
PHANGISO, Aaron Mpho (Gauteng, Lions, Gauteng to Namibia) b Garunkuwa, Transvaal 21.1.1984 RHB SLA																			
FC		3	3	1	48	40	24.00	0	0	557	277	5	55.40	2-74	0	0	2.98	1	
Lim		14	8	3	36	11*	7.20	0	0	609	563	17	33.11	3-40	0	0	5.54	3	
20T		8	3	0	6	3	2.00	0	0	186	202	4	50.50	3-23	0	0	6.51	2	
FC	2004/05	45	60	13	1195	71	25.42	0	5	5176	2731	70	39.01	5-60	2	0	3.16	28	1
Lim	2004/05	54	37	7	384	68	12.80	0	1	1969	1527	48	31.81	3-19	0	0	4.65	10	
20T	2005/06	27	11	1	67	25	6.70	0	0	328	385	11	35.00	3-23	0	0	7.04	7	
PHILANDER, Vernon Darryl (Cape Cobras, Western Province, Cape Cobras to India, South Africa A to Bangladesh, South Africa A to Sri Lanka) b Bellville, Cape Province 24.6.1985 RHB RMF																			
FC		11	13	3	342	102	34.20	1	0	1945	765	59	12.96	5-16	3	0	2.36	1	
Lim		8	5	2	40	23*	13.33	0	0	243	202	5	40.40	3-51	0	0	4.98	2	
20T		7	6	4	76	37*	38.00	0	0	146	158	11	14.36	5-17	0	1	6.49	1	
FC	2003/04	57	85	12	2025	168	27.73	2	6	9711	4109	200	20.54	7-64	7	0	2.53	17	
Int	2007	7	5	2	73	23	24.33	0	0	275	209	6	34.83	4-12	1	0	4.56	2	
Lim	2004	81	58	18	966	76*	24.15	0	3	3306	2588	68	38.05	4-12	1	0	4.69	7	
I20T	2007/08	7	4	0	14	6	3.50	0	0	83	114	4	28.50	2-23	0	0	8.24	1	
20T	2004/05	48	36	19	478	56*	28.11	0	1	643	868	31	28.00	5-17	0	1	8.10	15	
PIEDT, Dane Lee-Roy (Western Province) b Cape Town, Cape Province 6.3.1990 RHB OB																			
FC		3	6	0	21	7	3.50	0	0	402	265	10	26.50	3-63	0	0	3.95	0	
Lim		8	6	3	39	23	13.00	0	0	294	231	6	38.50	2-28	0	0	4.71	2	
Lim	2008/09	9	6	3	39	23	13.00	0	0	344	261	8	32.62	2-28	0	0	4.55	2	
PIENAAR, Abraham Jacobus (Free State) b Bloemfontein, Free State 12.12.1989 RHB LFM																			
FC		4	6	0	113	65	18.83	0	1	582	289	18	16.05	5-27	1	0	2.97	1	
Lim		4	4	1	114	50*	38.00	0	1	143	116	6	19.33	5-15	0	1	4.86	2	
FC	2008/09	7	10	0	189	65	18.90	0	2	1002	517	33	15.66	5-27	1	0	3.09	7	
Lim	2008/09	5	5	2	121	50*	40.33	0	1	185	152	8	19.00	5-15	0	1	4.93	4	
PIENAAR, Jacobus Johannes (Easterns, Titans, Easterns to Namibia) b Klerksdorp, Transvaal 23.10.1985 LHB RMF																			
FC		11	18	2	753	135	47.06	2	4	1203	608	24	25.33	5-40	1	0	3.03	2	
Lim		9	9	0	288	119	32.00	1	1	334	330	4	82.50	1-22	0	0	5.92	3	
FC	2004/05	30	49	2	1565	154	33.29	3	7	3286	1939	73	26.56	5-39	2	0	3.54	12	
Lim	2006/07	27	24	2	643	119	29.22	1	3	977	851	36	23.63	5-45	3	1	5.22	12	
PIETERSEN, Charl (Eagles, Griqualand West) b Kimberley, Cape Province 6.1.1983 LHB LMF																			
FC		16	23	2	886	140	42.19	1	4	2297	1294	32	40.43	5-34	2	0	3.38	8	
Lim		12	10	2	252	59	31.50	0	1	386	324	18	18.00	4-24	1	0	5.03	5	
FC	2001/02	60	91	18	2142	140	29.34	1	8	9404	5169	178	29.03	6-43	6	0	3.29	25	
Lim	2002/03	53	37	13	540	59	22.50	0	1	2028	1763	64	27.54	7-10	2	1	5.21	10	
20T	2006	2	1	1	3	3*		0	0	36	57	3	19.00	3-35	0	0	9.50	3	
PIETERSEN, Ruan (Dolphins, Griqualand West) b Kimberley, Cape Province 10.2.1988 RHB LFM																			
FC		7	7	3	36	13	9.00	0	0	974	463	28	16.53	7-41	2	1	2.85	1	
Lim		5	1	1	0	0*		0	0	216	168	4	42.00	2-36	0	0	4.66	0	
20T		1								24	39	0					9.75	0	
FC	2005/06	23	30	15	95	13	6.33	0	0	2910	1557	78	19.96	7-41	3	1	3.21	6	
Lim	2005/06	13	2	1	0	0*	0.00	0	0	558	506	11	46.00	3-51	0	0	5.44	0	
PILLAY, Myren (KwaZulu-Natal) b Durban, Natal 30.5.1982 LHB OB																			
FC		6	11	0	254	78	23.09	0	2									5	
Lim		5	5	0	76	38	15.20	0	0									1	
FC	2008/09	7	12	0	336	82	28.00	0	3									6	
Lim	2008/09	7	7	1	127	40*	21.16	0	0									1	
PILLAY, Tyron Duncan (KwaZulu-Natal) b Durban, Natal 18.11.1984 RHB LB																			
FC		2	4	0	21	11	5.25	0	0	301	155	11	14.09	4-39	0	0	3.09	5	
Lim		2	1	1	21	21*		0	0	84	46	3	15.33	2-23	0	0	3.28	1	
FC	2004/05	24	29	10	210	32	11.05	0	0	4148	2092	65	32.18	5-45	2	0	3.02	28	
Lim	2004/05	19	7	5	54	21*	27.00	0	0	714	506	21	24.09	3-30	0	0	4.25	3	
20T	2003/04	1								18	33	2	16.50	2-33	0	0	11.00	0	
PLAATJIES, Francois Chessley (Cape Cobras, Western Province, Cape Cobras to India) b Oudtshoorn, Cape Province 26.8.1986 RHB RF																			
FC		5	4	1	5	4	1.66	0	0	676	382	19	20.10	4-21	0	0	3.39	0	
Lim		10								403	412	19	21.68	4-44	1	0	6.13	2	

Cmp	Debut	M	I	NO	Runs	HS	Avge	100	50	Balls	Runs	Wkts	Avge	BB	5i	10m	RpO	ct	st
20T		1								24	33	0					8.25	0	
FC	2006/07	12	13	6	42	21*	6.00	0	0	1558	933	34	27.44	4-21	0	0	3.59	2	
Lim	2006/07	23	3	2	8	4	8.00	0	0	999	908	38	23.89	4-24	2	0	5.45	5	
20T	2009/10	2	1	1	0	0*		0	0	48	46	0					5.75	0	
PRICE, Michael Lynn (Eastern Province) b Grahamstown, Cape Province 6.10.1981 RHB OB																			
FC		12	21	1	953	179	47.65	2	4	110	68	2	34.00	1-4	0	0	3.70	12	
Lim		10	10	0	300	102	30.00	1	1	66	79	1	79.00	1-17	0	0	7.18	2	
FC	2001/02	23	41	2	1392	179	35.69	2	8	194	128	2	64.00	1-4	0	0	3.95	18	
Lim	2002/03	20	18	0	466	102	25.88	1	2	186	186	5	37.20	3-25	0	0	6.00	3	
PRINCE, Ashwell Gavin (South Africa, Warriors, Lancashire, South Africa to India, South Africa to West Indies) b Port Elizabeth, Cape Province 28.5.1977 LHB OB																			
Test		4	7	0	97	45	13.85	0	0									3	
FC		11	19	0	580	154	30.52	2	1									7	
Lim		4	4	0	186	128	46.50	1	0									2	
20T		4	4	0	112	69	28.00	0	1									2	
Test	2001/02	57	91	14	3355	162*	43.57	11	10	96	47	1	47.00	1-2	0	0	2.93	36	
FC	1995/96	189	304	41	11418	254	43.41	28	55	276	166	4	41.50	2-11	0	0	3.60	127	
Int	2002/03	52	41	12	1018	89*	35.10	0	3	12	3	0					1.50	26	
Lim	1996/97	206	180	35	4539	128	31.30	2	22	91	86	0					5.67	93	
I20T	2005/06	1	1	0	5	5	5.00	0	0									0	
20T	2003/04	22	20	3	476	69	28.00	0	1	4	5	0					7.50	7	
PUCHERT, Hendro (Free State) b Tygerberg 11.8.1986 LHB RMF																			
FC		6	9	3	196	48*	32.66	0	0	789	393	12	32.75	3-49	0	0	2.98	2	
Lim		3	3	0	34	19	11.33	0	0	96	64	1	64.00	1-14	0	0	4.00	2	
FC	2007/08	9	14	6	285	48*	35.62	0	0	1047	557	14	39.78	3-49	0	0	3.19	3	
Lim	2007/08	8	7	1	103	30*	17.16	0	0	316	252	8	31.50	2-33	0	0	4.78	3	
PUTTICK, Andrew George (Cape Cobras, South Africa A, Cape Cobras to India) b Cape Town, Cape Province 11.12.1980 LHB RM																			
FC		10	17	4	678	180	52.15	3	0									11	
Lim		12	11	1	515	122*	51.50	1	4									12	2
20T		7	7	0	76	22	10.85	0	0									2	
FC	2000/01	97	173	17	6661	250*	42.69	15	31									119	2
Int	2005/06	1	1	0	0	0	0.00	0	0									1	
Lim	1999/00	111	107	17	3061	143	34.01	7	15									80	7
20T	2003/04	44	39	4	816	104*	23.31	1	4									11	3
RABIE, Gurshwin Renier (Western Province) b Oudtshoorn, Cape Province 26.6.1983 RHB RFM																			
FC		6	5	5	34	27*		0	0	976	428	13	32.92	5-29	1	0	2.63	1	
Lim		7	3	2	7	6	7.00	0	0	288	243	11	22.09	3-31	0	0	5.06	1	
FC	2008/09	14	15	11	71	27*	17.75	0	0	2263	1012	31	32.64	6-48	2	0	2.68	3	
Lim	2008/09	16	6	4	8	6	4.00	0	0	669	540	24	22.50	3-22	0	0	4.84	2	
RAMELA, Omphile Abel (Boland, Cape Cobras, Boland to Namibia) b Soweto, Transvaal 14.3.1988 LHB SLA																			
FC		11	22	0	614	104	27.90	1	4									10	
Lim		8	8	1	183	57	26.14	0	1									4	
FC	2007/08	23	43	2	1129	104	27.53	1	6	54	32	0					3.55	22	
Lim	2007/08	22	22	2	695	79	34.75	0	6									8	
RAMOO, Romano Jude (Western Province) b East London, Cape Province 25.4.1987 RHB RM																			
FC		9	16	1	451	93	30.06	0	2	12	14	0					7.00	5	
Lim		9	9	0	290	68	32.22	0	3	6	4	0					4.00	1	
FC	2008/09	13	23	3	628	93	31.40	0	3	60	34	0					3.40	5	
Lim	2008/09	16	16	2	471	74*	33.64	0	4	78	61	2	30.50	1-16	0	0	4.69	1	
RANDALL, Darryn (Border) b King William's Town, Cape Province 2.12.1980 RHB WK																			
FC		4	7	0	133	46	19.00	0	0									6	1
Lim		4	4	1	24	14	8.00	0	0									5	
RANGER, Murray Neil (Border) b Stutterheim, Cape Province 18.4.1984 RHB RM																			
Lim		2	2	0	94	85	47.00	0	1									1	
FC	2004/05	26	39	6	1139	96	34.51	0	9	1848	858	25	34.32	6-30	1	0	2.78	25	
Lim	2004/05	24	23	4	434	85	22.84	0	3	576	412	15	27.46	4-42	1	0	4.29	7	
20T	2005/06	2	1	1	9	9*		0	0	6	11	0					11.00	0	
RAUBENHEIMER, Carl Helgaard (Boland, Boland to Namibia) b Pretoria, Transvaal 19.12.1983 RHB LB																			
FC		9	14	7	67	18	9.57	0	0	1343	817	21	38.90	4-78	0	0	3.65	3	
Lim		1																0	
FC	2009/10	10	15	8	76	18	10.85	0	0	1517	903	28	32.25	6-65	1	0	3.57	3	
Lim	2009/10	2								78	69	1	69.00	1-41	0	0	5.30	0	
REEVES, Ryan Ashley (KwaZulu-Natal) b Durban, Natal 16.6.1983 RHB RFM																			
FC		2	4	0	56	20	14.00	0	0	198	176	6	29.33	3-59	0	0	5.33	1	
Lim		1	1	0	24	24	24.00	0	0	48	45	0					5.62	1	
FC	2005/06	4	7	1	129	41	21.50	0	0	258	240	8	30.00	3-59	0	0	5.58	2	
Lim	2005/06	3	3	0	60	34	20.00	0	0	48	45	0					5.62	1	
RICHARDS, Rowan Ronaldo (Western Province) b East London, Cape Province 8.7.1984 LHB LFM																			
FC		8	10	5	89	45*	17.80	0	0	1179	601	26	23.11	4-41	0	0	3.05	3	
Lim		9	4	2	29	17	14.50	0	0	262	247	5	49.40	3-35	0	0	5.65	1	

Cmp	Debut	M	I	NO	Runs	HS	Avge	100	50	Balls	Runs	Wkts	Avge	BB	5i	10m	RpO	ct	st
FC	2005/06	15	17	7	108	45*	10.80	0	0	2303	1163	50	23.26	5-30	2	0	3.03	4	
Lim	2005/06	14	7	3	42	17	10.50	0	0	418	345	13	26.53	3-13	0	0	4.95	1	
RICHARDSON, Mathew Frank (Border) b Port Elizabeth, Cape Province 6.9.1985 RHB RMF																			
Lim		2	2	0	1	1	0.50	0	0									0	
FC	2006/07	13	25	1	609	70	25.37	0	3	6	3	0					3.00	10	
Lim	2005/06	16	16	0	438	69	27.37	0	4									2	
ROSSOUW, Rilee Roscoe (Eagles, Free State, South Africa A, Eagles to India, South Africa A to Bangladesh, South Africa A to Sri Lanka) b Bloemfontein, Orange Free State 9.10.1989 LHB OB																			
FC		13	22	0	1261	319	57.31	4	5	5	10	1	10.00	1-10	0	0	12.00	15	
Lim		15	15	0	361	104	24.06	1	1									10	
20T		4	4	0	58	23	14.50	0	0									4	
FC	2007/08	30	54	1	2541	319	47.94	8	12	5	10	1	10.00	1-10	0	0	12.00	32	
Lim	2007/08	38	37	1	1217	131	33.80	2	8									15	
20T	2007/08	15	15	0	224	65	14.93	0	1									6	
RUDOLPH, Jacobus Andries (Titans, Yorkshire, Yorkshire to Netherlands) b Springs, Transvaal 4.5.1981 LHB LBG																			
FC		10	16	1	591	192	39.40	1	3	54	38	0					4.22	9	
Lim		10	10	1	497	93	55.22	0	5	11	10	2	5.00	2-10	0	0	5.45	9	
20T		7	5	1	175	69	43.75	0	2	6	14	0					14.00	3	
Test	2003	35	63	7	2028	222*	36.21	5	8	664	432	4	108.00	1-1	0	0	3.90	22	
FC	1997/98	186	317	21	13337	228*	45.05	38	61	4451	2521	58	43.46	5-80	3	0	3.39	174	
Int	2003	45	39	6	1174	81	35.57	0	7	24	26	0					6.50	11	
Lim	2000/01	192	180	28	7280	134*	47.89	12	49	388	351	12	29.25	4-40	1	0	5.42	75	
I20T	2005/06	1	1	1	6	6*		0	0									0	
20T	2003/04	64	58	9	1384	71	28.24	0	9	163	221	10	22.10	3-16	0	0	8.13	19	
SALIWA, Mario Ngqiliyomzi (KwaZulu-Natal) b King William's Town, Cape Province 6.3.1984 RHB RFM																			
FC		4	3	1	1	1	0.50	0	0	251	173	4	43.25	2-33	0	0	4.13	1	
Lim		2								36	45	0					7.50	0	
FC	2006/07	25	31	13	146	26	8.11	0	0	2927	2141	58	36.91	5-56	1	0	4.38	5	
Lim	2006/07	16	11	4	28	9*	4.00	0	0	597	627	18	34.83	4-35	1	0	6.30	2	
SAVAGE, Calvin Peter (KwaZulu-Natal Inland to Namibia) b Durban, Natal 4.1.1993 RHB RF																			
FC	2009/10	1	2	0	11	7	5.50	0	0	204	97	4	24.25	2-36	0	0	2.85	0	
Lim	2009/10	1								48	24	2	12.00	2-24	0	0	3.00	0	
SCHOEMAN, Christiaan Frederik (Northerns) b Pretoria, Transvaal 13.8.1990 LHB SLA																			
FC		9	14	2	673	100	56.08	1	6	54	31	0					3.44	8	
Lim		9	8	1	158	66	22.57	0	2	79	91	4	22.75	3-27	0	0	6.91	1	
SCHOEMAN, Christoffel Frederick Jacobus (North West) b Bloemfontein, Otange Free State 5.8.1988 LHB SLA																			
FC		5	9	3	190	70*	31.66	0	2									13	1
Lim		5	3	0	21	11	7.00	0	0									3	1
FC	2008/09	10	14	4	302	70*	30.20	0	3									25	1
Lim	2008/09	9	6	0	53	30	8.83	0	0									6	1
SCOTT, Wayne Lionel (Northerns) b Pretoria, Transvaal 20.12.1987 RHB RFM																			
Lim		2								36	40	1	40.00	1-17	0	0	6.66	1	
SEKHOTO, Mpho Remofiloe (Easterns, Easterns to Namibia) b Johannesburg, Transvaal 2.3.1982 RHB OB																			
FC		10	12	1	306	74	27.81	0	2									6	
Lim		11	10	1	111	28	12.33	0	0									1	
FC	2001/02	32	48	6	1159	81	27.59	0	7	72	67	3	22.33	2-42	0	0	5.58	27	
Lim	2001/02	31	28	5	313	28	13.60	0	0									4	
SELEKA, Letlhogonolo Aloysius (Griqualand West) b Kimberley, Cape Province 7.8.1989 LHB OB																			
FC		7	14	0	254	72	18.14	0	1									1	
Lim		6	5	0	83	79	16.60	0	1									2	
SELOWA, Phillimon Mpho (Northerns) b Pretoria, Transvaal 3.8.1986 LHB WK																			
FC		10	13	1	298	92	24.83	0	3	6	2	0					2.00	29	
Lim		8	5	2	62	23*	20.66	0	0									6	2
FC	2005/06	15	20	2	408	92	22.66	0	3	6	2	0					2.00	35	
Lim	2005/06	16	13	2	175	42	15.90	0	0									7	3
SESELE, Lehlohonolo Letlotlo Lefa (Free State) b Bloemfontein, Free State 23.3.1988 RHB OB WK																			
FC		8	14	0	284	48	20.28	0	0									12	3
Lim		9	9	0	146	43	16.22	0	0									4	
FC	2006/07	15	26	0	550	48	21.15	0	0									24	3
Lim	2006/07	16	16	0	259	43	16.18	0	0									8	
SEYIBOKWE, Somila (Border, Border to Namibia) b Eastern Cape 31.10.1987 RHB RM																			
FC		3	5	0	153	74	30.60	0	1									0	
Lim		7	7	1	51	29	8.50	0	0									0	
FC	2008/09	6	11	0	185	74	16.81	0	1	42	31	0					4.42	1	
Lim	2008/09	9	8	2	57	29	9.50	0	0	30	37	1	37.00	1-37	0	0	7.40	0	
SHAMSI, Tabraiz (Gauteng, Lions, Gauteng to Namibia) b Johannesburg, Transvaal 18.2.1990 RHB SLC																			
FC		10	9	4	60	24	12.00	0	0	1587	936	44	21.27	6-89	2	0	3.53	0	
Lim		6	4	1	28	13*	9.33	0	0	203	155	11	14.09	3-8	0	0	4.58	1	
FC	2009/10	11	10	4	60	24	10.00	0	0	1896	1082	50	21.64	6-89	2	0	3.42	0	

Cmp	Debut	M	I	NO	Runs	HS	Avge	100	50	Balls	Runs	Wkts	Avge	BB	5i	10m	RpO	ct	st
SHANKLAND, Warren Lindsey (Gauteng) b Johannesburg, Transvaal 26.9.1987 RHB RMF WK																			
FC		2	3	1	39	17	19.50	0	0	24	7	0					1.75	0	
FC	2008/09	4	7	1	112	36	18.66	0	0	30	13	0					2.60	1	
Lim	2008/09	2	2	0	70	44	35.00	0	0									1	
SHEZI, Mthokozisi (Dolphins, KwaZulu-Natal) b Imbali, Pietermaritzburg, Natal 9.9.1987 RHB LMF																			
FC		11	15	6	144	64	16.00	0	1	1303	716	29	24.68	7-45	1	0	3.29	2	
Lim		5	3	0	32	16	10.66	0	0	102	93	4	23.25	1-19	0	0	5.47	0	
FC	2006/07	20	25	11	181	64	12.92	0	1	2209	1232	44	28.00	7-45	1	0	3.34	6	
Lim	2007/08	12	6	1	37	16	7.40	0	0	400	305	13	23.46	2-26	0	0	4.57	1	
SIBOTO, Malusi Paul (North West) b Cape Town, Cape Province 20.8.1987 LHB RMF																			
FC		8	9	5	208	46*	52.00	0	0	891	430	11	39.09	3-35	0	0	2.89	2	
Lim		10	6	3	79	50*	26.33	0	1	360	381	14	27.21	6-49	0	1	6.35	4	
FC	2007/08	18	21	9	364	46*	30.33	0	0	2435	1221	35	34.88	5-56	1	0	3.00	8	
Lim	2007/08	21	15	5	123	50*	12.30	0	1	743	777	20	38.85	6-49	0	1	6.27	7	
SIMETU, Siyabulela (Western Province) b Cape Town, Cape Province 22.8.1991 RHB SLA																			
FC		1	2	0	17	15	8.50	0	0	55	30	2	15.00	2-28	0	0	3.27	0	
SIMPSON, Shaun William (KwaZulu-Natal) b Durban, Natal 21.2.1989 RHB RM																			
FC		2	4	0	86	48	21.50	0	0	72	64	0					5.33	1	
Lim		2	2	1	6	3*	6.00	0	0	24	32	0					8.00	1	
SMIT, Daryn (Dolphins) b Durban, Natal 28.1.1984 RHB LB WK																			
FC		10	14	0	334	94	23.85	0	1	1262	654	10	65.40	4-50	0	0	3.10	28	
Lim		11	10	5	180	53*	36.00	0	1	384	341	9	37.88	2-35	0	0	5.32	7	1
20T		5	4	1	24	16	8.00	0	0	36	46	1	46.00	1-10	0	0	7.66	1	
FC	2004/05	49	69	12	1590	107*	27.89	1	8	4594	2465	61	40.40	4-50	0	0	3.21	139	4
Lim	2004/05	49	35	12	615	55*	26.73	0	3	1249	993	30	33.10	3-13	0	0	4.77	45	4
20T	2003/04	35	19	7	209	36	17.41	0	0	300	317	18	17.61	3-19	0	0	6.34	25	1
SMITH, Graeme Craig (Cape Cobras, South Africa, Rajasthan Royals, South Africa to India, South Africa to West Indies) b Johannesburg, Transvaal 1.2.1981 LHB OB																			
Test		4	7	0	427	183	61.00	2	1									7	
FC		4	7	0	427	183	61.00	2	1									7	
Int		8	8	0	362	141	45.25	1	3									5	
Lim		12	11	0	376	141	34.18	1	3									7	
I20T		2	2	0	129	88	64.50	0	1									1	
20T		2	2	0	129	88	64.50	0	1									1	
Test	2001/02	86	151	9	7170	277	50.49	21	28	1322	805	8	100.62	2-145	0	0	3.65	114	
FC	1999/00	123	213	14	10121	311	50.85	29	38	1690	1052	11	95.63	2-145	0	0	3.73	169	
Int	2001/02	154	152	9	5732	141	40.08	8	41	1026	951	18	52.83	3-30	0	0	5.56	81	
Lim	1999/00	211	207	14	7958	141	41.23	12	60	1968	1796	47	38.21	3-30	0	0	5.47	110	
I20T	2005/06	27	27	2	803	89*	32.12	0	4	24	57	0					14.25	15	
20T	2003/04	71	71	6	2061	105	31.70	1	10	96	148	4	37.00	3-23	0	0	9.25	31	
SMITH, Michael Bruce Argo (Eastern Province, Warriors) b King William's Town, Cape Province 5.5.1980 RHB OB																			
FC		17	31	2	1089	108	37.55	2	8	354	278	4	69.50	2-12	0	0	4.71	8	
Lim		11	11	0	341	76	31.00	0	3	147	143	2	71.50	1-38	0	0	5.83	11	
FC	2003/04	55	98	6	2851	179*	30.98	4	16	863	546	13	42.00	2-10	0	0	3.79	66	
Lim	2003/04	52	50	3	1288	87	27.40	0	9	465	390	6	65.00	2-12	0	0	5.03	24	
20T	2005/06	6	6	1	97	49	19.40	0	0									1	
SMITH, Stephan (Free State) b Bloemfontein, Free State 11.11.1990 RHB RFM																			
FC		1	2	0	0	0	0.00	0	0	60	42	0					4.20	0	
SMUTS, Jon-Jon Trevor (Eastern Province, Warriors) b Grahamstown, Cape Province 21.8.1988 RHB SLA																			
FC		14	26	4	1134	150*	51.54	4	4	1610	923	18	51.27	3-55	0	0	3.44	3	
Lim		12	12	2	447	101	44.70	1	4	161	154	4	38.50	1-26	0	0	5.73	0	
20T		7	7	0	121	43	17.28	0	0									2	
FC	2006/07	30	58	4	2031	150*	37.61	4	12	2217	1311	35	37.45	6-80	1	1	3.54	10	
Lim	2007/08	31	30	3	1020	104*	37.77	2	9	427	369	13	28.38	3-16	0	0	5.18	6	
20T	2007/08	10	10	0	152	43	15.20	0	0									2	
SMUTS, Kelly Royce (Eastern Province) b Grahamstown, Cape Province 22.1.1990 LHB RMF																			
FC		13	21	2	816	102	42.94	2	5									7	
Lim		13	13	0	214	46	16.46	0	0									3	
SNIJMAN, Blake Douglas (Northerns, Titans) b Krugersdorp, Transvaal 28.10.1985 RHB RM																			
FC		9	17	1	547	128	34.18	1	2	18	15	0					5.00	5	
Lim		9	9	1	417	157	52.12	1	2									3	
20T		6	5	1	185	89*	46.25	0	2									1	
FC	2003/04	59	108	7	3139	128	31.07	4	15	718	444	15	29.60	4-26	0	0	3.71	50	
Lim	2004/05	47	47	4	1533	157	35.65	1	11	204	166	5	33.20	2-22	0	0	4.88	17	
20T	2006/07	21	19	2	503	89*	29.58	0	5									9	
SODUMO, Abongile Mzimkhulu (Border, Border to Namibia) b King William's Town, Cape Province 16.6.1982 RHB WK																			
FC		7	13	3	393	73*	39.30	0	3									19	4
Lim		6	5	0	44	31	8.80	0	0									12	1
FC	2002/03	45	73	11	1449	77*	23.37	0	9									132	19
Lim	2002/03	39	27	3	240	58	10.00	0	1									51	7
20T	2004/05	9	6	2	33	12	8.25	0	0									6	1

Cmp	Debut	M	I	NO	Runs	HS	Avge	100	50	Balls	Runs	Wkts	Avge	BB	5i	10m	RpO	ct	st
STANLEY, Dylan (Northerns) b Johannesburg, Transvaal 5.8.1991 RHB LFM																			
FC		2	3	2	7	3	7.00	0	0	192	112	3	37.33	1-24	0	0	3.50	0	
Lim		1								18	13	0					4.33	0	
STEVENS, Godfrey Cyril (Boland, Boland to Namibia) b Porterville, Cape Province 24.6.1986 LHB SLA																			
FC		10	19	2	327	58	19.23	0	1	1268	680	26	26.15	4-32	0	0	3.21	6	
Lim		10	9	0	229	77	25.44	0	2	378	314	9	34.88	3-44	0	0	4.98	3	
FC	2005/06	17	31	2	555	58	19.13	0	2	2091	1093	37	29.54	4-32	0	0	3.13	8	
Lim	2005/06	23	20	1	385	77	20.26	0	2	849	610	25	24.40	3-18	0	0	4.31	12	
STEYN, Dale Willem (South Africa, Titans, Royal Challengers Bangalore, South Africa to India, South Africa to West Indies) b Phalaborwa, Northern Province 27.6.1983 RHB RF																			
Test		3	5	2	78	47	26.00	0	0	713	357	15	23.80	5-51	1	0	3.00	1	
FC		4	7	3	105	47	26.25	0	0	876	443	19	23.31	5-51	1	0	3.03	2	
Int		6	2	1	29	17*	29.00	0	0	329	295	8	36.87	3-47	0	0	5.38	0	
Lim		8	4	3	39	17*	39.00	0	0	377	331	12	27.58	4-36	1	0	5.26	0	
I20T		2								48	69	3	23.00	2-29	0	0	8.62	0	
20T		3	1	0	22	22	22.00	0	0	72	107	3	35.66	2-29	0	0	8.91	0	
Test	2004/05	41	52	12	540	76	13.50	0	1	8273	4881	211	23.13	7-51	14	4	3.54	11	
FC	2003/04	82	98	24	1044	82	14.10	0	3	15723	8875	365	24.31	8-41	22	6	3.38	17	
Int	2005/06	41	14	5	86	35	9.55	0	0	2012	1778	58	30.65	4-16	3	0	5.30	7	
Lim	2004/05	85	29	12	131	35	7.70	0	0	4072	3246	127	25.55	5-20	4	2	4.78	13	
I20T	2007/08	21	4	2	8	5	4.00	0	0	468	531	29	18.31	4-9	1	0	6.80	8	
20T	2004/05	66	16	5	51	22	4.63	0	0	1476	1670	70	23.85	4-9	1	0	6.78	17	
STRYDOM, Johannes Gerhardus (South Western Districts, South Western Districts to Namibia) b Cape Town, Cape Province 6.9.1979 LHB RM																			
FC		12	24	1	1014	134	44.08	2	8									11	
Lim		12	12	0	318	83	26.50	0	3									2	
FC	2000/01	71	132	6	4232	151	33.58	8	28	96	49	0					3.06	52	
Lim	1999/00	65	62	3	1737	135*	29.44	2	9									22	
STUURMAN, Pieter Andrew (South Western Districts, South Western Districts to Namibia) b Oudtshoorn, Cape Province 23.5.1981 RHB RM WK																			
FC		11	21	1	426	108	21.30	1	1									5	
Lim		11	11	2	350	89	38.88	0	1									3	
FC	2006/07	29	55	4	1158	108	22.70	1	5	24	12	0					3.00	14	
Lim	2006/07	29	27	3	632	89	26.33	0	2	11	13	1	13.00	1-13	0	0	7.09	14	
SULEMAN, Mohammed Faheem (KwaZulu-Natal Inland) b Pietermaritzburg, Natal 29.5.1986 LHB RFM																			
Lim		1	1	0	3	3	3.00	0	0	30	38	2	19.00	2-38	0	0	7.60	0	
SWANEPOEL, Aubrey Ryan (Eagles, Griqualand West) b Kimberley, Cape Province 18.6.1989 RHB OB																			
FC		11	15	0	374	53	24.93	0	1	390	310	6	51.66	2-66	0	0	4.76	7	
Lim		12	11	1	342	60	34.20	0	3	168	115	8	14.37	4-23	1	0	4.10	11	
20T		3	1	0	12	12	12.00	0	0	48	70	1	70.00	1-34	0	0	8.75	1	
FC	2006/07	23	30	3	674	108*	24.96	1	2	1844	1108	27	41.03	4-37	0	0	3.60	17	
Lim	2006/07	26	22	3	449	60	23.63	0	3	725	475	24	19.79	4-20	2	0	3.93	13	
20T	2008/09	5	1	0	12	12	12.00	0	0	78	109	1	109.00	1-34	0	0	8.38	1	
SWARTZ, Zandre (Griqualand West) b Kimberley, Cape Province 15.5.1991 RHB WK																			
FC		4	6	1	84	25	16.80	0	0									4	
Lim		7	6	1	136	72*	27.20	0	1									10	1
SYMES, Jean (Gauteng, Lions, Gauteng to Namibia) b Johannesburg, Transvaal 13.11.1986 LHB SLA																			
FC		9	13	2	522	147*	47.45	2	2	752	444	14	31.71	6-61	1	0	3.54	8	
Lim		11	11	0	263	66	23.90	0	1	264	216	6	36.00	3-25	0	0	4.90	2	
20T		1	1	1	30	30*		0	0	6	12	0					12.00	0	
FC	2005/06	41	68	5	2446	193	38.82	6	12	3247	1896	46	41.21	6-61	1	0	3.50	30	
Lim	2006/07	39	39	0	1261	170	32.33	2	6	1172	930	37	25.13	4-8	1	0	4.76	17	
20T	2007/08	5	5	1	58	30*	14.50	0	0	54	61	2	30.50	1-11	0	0	6.77	3	
TARR, Scott Richard (KwaZulu-Natal Inland) b Pietermaritzburg, Natal 29.1.1988 LHB RM																			
FC		2	4	1	10	6*	3.33	0	0	126	87	2	43.50	1-28	0	0	4.14	0	
Lim		1	1	0	1	1	1.00	0	0	30	24	0					4.80	0	
TELO, Filipe Dominic (Western Province) b Cape Town, Cape Province 4.3.1986 RHB RM																			
FC		1	2	0	13	13	6.50	0	0									3	
Lim		1	1	0	18	18	18.00	0	0									0	
FC	2005/06	26	47	3	1414	134*	32.13	3	6	47	48	1	48.00	1-36	0	0	6.12	11	
Lim	2005/06	24	22	2	519	90	25.95	0	4									3	
20T	2005/06	16	13	0	256	48	19.69	0	0									4	
TEMOOR, Abdul-Aziz (Western Province) b Strand, Cape Province 7.11.1982 RHB LB																			
FC		10	14	0	240	57	17.14	0	1	1714	965	31	31.12	5-31	1	0	3.37	6	
Lim		3	2	0	17	14	8.50	0	0	66	76	3	25.33	2-18	0	0	6.90	1	
FC	2007/08	16	23	1	313	57	14.22	0	1	2756	1702	47	36.21	5-31	1	0	3.70	10	
Lim	2007/08	5	4	0	41	14	10.25	0	0	156	151	4	37.75	2-18	0	0	5.80	2	
TERBLANCHE, Roman Kelvin (Free State) b Bloemfontein, Orange Free State 10.6.1986 LHB LFM																			
FC		12	15	2	280	62	21.53	0	2	1074	641	10	64.10	3-30	0	0	3.58	6	
Lim		12	10	4	149	55*	24.83	0	1	258	233	5	46.60	3-36	0	0	5.41	4	
FC	2006/07	23	29	6	530	64*	23.04	0	3	1884	1128	26	43.38	4-77	0	0	3.59	10	

Cmp	Debut	M	I	NO	Runs	HS	Avge	100	50	Balls	Runs	Wkts	Avge	BB	5i	10m	RpO	ct	st
Lim	2006/07	23	17	7	224	55*	22.40	0	1	591	523	14	37.35	3-30	0	0	5.31	7	
20T	2006/07	2																0	
THERON, Juan (South Africa A, Warriors, Kings XI Punjab, South Africa A to Sri Lanka) b Potchefstroom, Transvaal 24.7.1985 RHB RMF																			
FC		9	11	0	117	66	10.63	0	1	1269	623	24	25.95	5-27	1	0	2.94	4	
Lim		9	5	3	41	23*	20.50	0	0	365	395	21	18.80	4-33	2	0	6.49	5	
20T		9	2	1	6	3*	6.00	0	0	200	227	12	18.91	2-20	0	0	6.81	7	
FC	2005/06	40	51	10	570	66	13.90	0	2	6371	2994	131	22.85	7-46	7	0	2.82	12	
Lim	2005/06	59	33	13	371	41	18.55	0	0	2460	2052	102	20.11	4-33	7	0	5.00	17	
20T	2007/08	31	11	3	52	24*	6.50	0	0	650	746	32	23.31	3-16	0	0	6.88	13	
THOMAS, Alfonso Clive (Dolphins, Somerset, Somerset to India) b Cape Town, Cape Province 9.2.1977 RHB RFM																			
Lim		10	2	2	0	0*		0	0	432	485	10	48.50	3-43	0	0	6.73	3	
20T		3	2	1	0	0*	0.00	0	0	36	58	3	19.33	2-32	0	0	9.66	1	
FC	1998/99	112	158	33	3158	119*	25.26	2	11	20188	9655	353	27.35	7-54	16	1	2.87	31	
Lim	2000/01	134	67	33	504	28*	14.82	0	0	5798	4917	178	27.62	4-18	6	0	5.08	30	
I20T	2006/07	1								24	25	3	8.33	3-25	0	0	6.25	0	
20T	2003/04	82	27	14	153	30*	11.76	0	0	1578	1892	99	19.11	4-27	1	0	7.19	25	
THOMAS, Bryn Jerome (Border, Border to Namibia) b Durban, Natal 19.8.1979 LHB RM																			
FC		8	14	0	433	75	30.92	0	4	49	23	0					2.81	5	
Lim		8	8	2	147	82*	24.50	0	1									3	
FC	2008/09	13	24	2	594	75	27.00	0	4	49	23	0					2.81	9	
Lim	2008/09	12	12	2	312	84	31.20	0	2									3	
THOMSON, Grant Michael (Gauteng) b Kempton Park, Transvaal 18.3.1988 RHB RMF																			
FC		1	1	0	7	7	7.00	0	0	96	48	2	24.00	2-21	0	0	3.00	1	
Lim		2	1	1	7	7*		0	0	43	41	2	20.50	2-8	0	0	5.72	1	
THYSSEN, Craig Andre (Border, Warriors) b Port Elizabeth, Cape Province 25.3.1984 RHB RF																			
FC		9	16	2	443	80	31.64	0	2									6	
Lim		8	7	2	128	56*	25.60	0	1									2	
20T		8	6	2	101	27*	25.25	0	0									2	
FC	2003/04	50	88	7	2374	200	29.30	3	10	600	371	5	74.20	2-14	0	0	3.71	31	
Lim	2002/03	61	46	11	738	56*	21.08	0	3	420	384	12	32.00	4-38	1	0	5.48	9	
20T	2003/04	35	28	9	319	41*	16.78	0	0	81	83	4	20.75	2-19	0	0	6.14	14	
TOWNSEND, Travis Kim Millar (Western Province) b Cape Town, Cape Province 9.9.1985 RHB																			
FC		6	12	1	255	53	23.18	0	2									5	
Lim		4	4	0	86	37	21.50	0	0									2	
Lim	2008/09	5	5	0	93	37	18.60	0	0									4	
TRIEGAARDT, Jean-Pierre Horatio (Griqualand West) b Kimberley, Cape Province 10.3.1984 RHB WK																			
Lim		1																2	
Lim	2005/06	3	2	0	10	10	5.00	0	0									3	
TSHABALALA, Mthandeki Samson (Eagles, Free State, South Africa A, Eagles to India, South Africa A to Bangladesh, South Africa A to Sri Lanka) b Welkom, Orange Free State 19.11.1984 RHB OB																			
FC		7	7	2	90	30*	18.00	0	0	948	642	15	42.80	3-73	0	0	4.06	1	
Lim		13	4	3	13	11*	13.00	0	0	453	425	6	70.83	1-28	0	0	5.62	3	
20T		2								42	47	4	11.75	2-16	0	0	6.71	1	
FC	2003/04	59	82	16	797	55	12.07	0	2	8208	5118	118	43.37	5-68	2	0	3.74	22	
Int	2007	4	1	1	2	2*		0	0	150	151	3	50.33	1-30	0	0	6.04	0	
Lim	2003/04	97	33	16	157	17*	9.23	0	0	3917	3239	85	38.10	4-24	2	0	4.96	18	
20T	2003/04	45	9	6	62	21*	20.66	0	0	818	912	48	19.00	4-13	1	0	6.68	12	
TSOLEKILE, Thami Lungisa (Lions, South Africa A to Bangladesh, South Africa A to Sri Lanka) b Cape Town, Cape Province 9.10.1980 RHB OB WK																			
FC		10	15	5	581	141	58.10	1	3									37	2
Lim		10	9	5	223	65*	55.75	0	1									9	1
20T		8	7	2	56	20	11.20	0	0									5	2
Test	2004/05	3	5	0	47	22	9.40	0	0									6	
FC	1999	111	154	21	3668	141	27.57	4	18									356	27
Lim	1998/99	112	72	23	944	65*	19.26	0	1									161	16
20T	2003/04	26	19	9	322	52	32.20	0	1									22	5
TSOTSOBE, Lonwabo Lennox (South Africa, South Africa A, Warriors, South Africa to India, South Africa to West Indies, South Africa A to Bangladesh) b Port Elizabeth, Cape Province 7.3.1984 RHB LFM																			
FC		9	13	5	44	12*	5.50	0	0	1306	743	17	43.70	3-37	0	0	3.41	1	
Int		2								90	64	2	32.00	1-23	0	0	4.26	0	
Lim		15	1	1	5	5*		0	0	625	568	22	25.81	4-27	1	0	5.45	1	
Test	2010	2	1	1	3	3*		0	0	294	106	2	53.00	1-20	0	0	2.16	0	
FC	2004/05	48	62	26	225	27*	6.25	0	0	8020	4055	165	24.57	7-39	5	1	3.03	11	
Int	2008/09	8	1	1	4	4*		0	0	382	338	15	22.53	4-50	1	0	5.30	4	
Lim	2004/05	56	17	7	53	11*	5.30	0	0	2496	2183	77	28.35	5-28	4	1	5.24	10	
I20T	2008/09	2	1	0	1	1	1.00	0	0	36	44	1	44.00	1-16	0	0	7.33	0	
20T	2006/07	17	3	2	4	3*	4.00	0	0	338	348	14	24.85	2-23	0	0	6.17	4	
VAALTYN, Lionel Isaac (Eastern Province) b Port Elizabeth, Cape Province 20.12.1991 LHB LB																			
Lim		1	1	0	1	1	1.00	0	0	36	28	0					4.66	0	

Cmp	Debut	M	I	NO	Runs	HS	Avge	100	50	Balls	Runs	Wkts	Avge	BB	5i	10m	RpO	ct	st
VALLIE, Mohammad Yaseen (Western Province) b Cape Town, Cape Province 30.9.1989 RHB OB																			
FC		12	21	3	865	119	48.05	3	3	66	31	0					2.81	4	
Lim		11	11	1	351	89	35.10	0	2	126	114	1	114.00	1-50	0	0	5.42	4	
Lim	2008/09	12	12	1	363	89	33.00	0	2	162	150	1	150.00	1-50	0	0	5.55	4	
VAN BILJON, Petrus Johannes (Eastern Province) b Bloemfontein, Orange Free State 15.4.1986 RHB RM WK																			
FC		3	5	0	226	96	45.20	0	2									1	
Lim		3	3	0	55	43	18.33	0	0									2	
FC	2006/07	18	29	1	864	188	30.85	1	5	1	0	0					0.00	9	
Lim	2006/07	19	19	0	513	91	27.00	0	3									4	
VAN BUUREN, Graeme Lourens (Northerns, Titans) b Pretoria, Transvaal 22.8.1990 RHB SLA																			
FC		3	4	0	155	86	38.75	0	2	390	206	11	18.72	4-74	0	0	3.16	4	
Lim		4	4	1	33	16	11.00	0	0	120	104	7	14.85	4-29	1	0	5.20	1	
VAN DEN BERGH, Nicholas Jacques (North West) b Potchefstroon, Transvaal 20.6.1989 RHB WK																			
FC		1	2	1	22	17*	22.00	0	0									1	
Lim		1	1	0	0	0	0.00	0	0									0	
VAN DER DUSSEN, Hendrik Erasmus (Northerns) b Pretoria, Transvaal 7.2.1989 RHB LB																			
FC		13	22	3	904	124	47.57	3	6	30	36	0					7.20	10	
Lim		8	8	1	293	114*	41.85	1	0									4	
FC	2007/08	20	35	5	1201	124	40.03	3	8	102	91	1	91.00	1-43	0	0	5.35	12	
Lim	2008/09	13	13	1	428	114*	35.66	2	0	30	26	1	26.00	1-26	0	0	5.20	4	
VAN DER MERWE, Gert Johannes Jakobus (Northerns) b Pretoria, Transvaal 19.9.1989 RHB																			
FC		1	2	0	41	39	20.50	0	0									1	
VAN DER MERWE, Roelof Erasmus (Northerns, South Africa, Titans, Royal Challengers Bangalore, South Africa to India, South Africa to West Indies) b Johannesburg, Transvaal 31.12.1984 RHB SLA																			
FC		2	3	0	58	56	19.33	0	1	222	105	2	52.50	1-0	0	0	2.83	1	
Int		6	3	1	8	5	4.00	0	0	315	276	5	55.20	3-27	0	0	5.25	2	
Lim		16	13	5	71	26*	8.87	0	0	645	613	17	36.05	3-27	0	0	5.70	5	
I20T		2								36	56	1	56.00	1-39	0	0	9.33	1	
20T		5								78	105	2	52.50	1-15	0	0	8.07	1	
FC	2006/07	16	23	5	568	81	31.55	0	3	2273	1168	30	38.93	4-59	0	0	3.08	9	
Int	2008/09	13	7	3	39	12	9.75	0	0	705	561	17	33.00	3-27	0	0	4.77	3	
Lim	2006/07	64	53	16	905	72	24.45	0	4	2908	2278	98	23.24	5-31	6	1	4.70	24	
I20T	2008/09	13	6	3	57	48	19.00	0	0	264	305	14	21.78	2-14	0	0	6.93	6	
20T	2007/08	43	27	6	397	70*	18.90	0	2	865	1025	47	21.80	3-18	0	0	7.11	17	
VAN DER WATH, Johannes Jacobus (Eagles, Free State, South Africa A to Bangladesh) b Newcastle, Natal 10.1.1978 RHB RFM																			
FC		5	7	0	171	61	24.42	0	1	933	567	20	28.35	5-54	1	0	3.64	2	
Lim		12	12	2	146	35	14.60	0	0	492	534	10	53.40	3-36	0	0	6.51	3	
20T		4	3	1	32	23*	16.00	0	0	89	103	5	20.60	3-27	0	0	6.94	0	
FC	1996/97	100	147	23	3029	113*	24.42	2	18	16864	8606	333	25.84	7-60	16	1	3.06	31	
Int	2005/06	10	8	2	89	37*	14.83	0	0	526	551	13	42.38	2-21	0	0	6.28	3	
Lim	1995/96	143	115	33	2131	91	25.98	0	11	6195	5134	174	29.50	4-31	5	0	4.97	34	
I20T	2005/06	8	4	1	46	21	15.33	0	0	186	231	8	28.87	2-31	0	0	7.45	0	
20T	2003/04	64	45	15	526	48*	17.53	0	0	1276	1582	61	25.93	3-23	0	0	7.43	5	
VANDIAR, Jonathan David (Lions, South Africa A to Bangladesh, South Africa A to Sri Lanka) b Paarl, Cape Province 25.4.1990 LHB LB																			
FC		10	16	1	585	128*	39.00	1	3	94	81	2	40.50	2-12	0	0	5.17	7	
Lim		10	10	0	418	108	41.80	2	3									1	
20T		8	8	0	187	68	23.37	0	2									1	
FC	2007/08	25	39	3	1315	172*	36.52	2	8	526	345	5	69.00	2-12	0	0	3.93	16	
Lim	2006/07	27	26	1	692	108	27.68	2	4	66	83	3	27.66	3-42	0	0	7.54	9	
20T	2008/09	9	9	1	190	68	23.75	0	2									1	
VAN JAARSVELD, Vaughn Bernard (Gauteng, Lions, South Africa A) b Johannesburg, Transvaal 2.2.1985 LHB RM																			
FC		9	14	1	492	135	37.84	2	2	48	16	1	16.00	1-11	0	0	2.00	6	
Lim		13	13	0	430	95	33.07	0	4	12	28	0					14.00	5	
20T		9	9	0	272	72	30.22	0	1									5	
FC	2003/04	51	88	6	3132	159	38.19	7	23	66	27	1	27.00	1-11	0	0	2.45	49	
Int	2008/09	2	2	0	9	5	4.50	0	0									1	
Lim	2002/03	80	74	8	2305	106	34.92	2	17	30	45	0					9.00	33	
I20T	2008/09	3	3	0	15	12	5.00	0	0									0	
20T	2003/04	41	39	5	912	72	26.82	0	5									18	
VAN SCHALKWYK, Shadley Claude (Eagles, Free State, Eagles to India) b Cape Town, Cape Province 5.8.1988 LHB RFM																			
FC		9	12	3	220	86	24.44	0	2	1165	654	16	40.87	3-40	0	0	3.36	4	
Lim		10	9	1	138	38	17.25	0	0	314	295	12	24.58	3-8	0	0	5.63	8	
20T		5								111	138	5	27.60	2-30	0	0	7.45	3	
FC	2008/09	13	18	6	296	86	24.66	0	2	1679	885	26	34.03	4-39	0	0	3.16	6	
Lim	2007/08	16	14	3	209	38	19.00	0	0	590	531	26	20.42	5-30	0	1	5.40	8	
20T	2008/09	17	4	1	21	10	7.00	0	0	297	365	13	28.07	2-12	0	0	7.37	8	
VAN VUUREN, Morne Schumyn (KwaZulu-Natal Inland) b Pietermaritzburg, Natal 11.8.1982 RHB SLA																			
FC		2	3	1	44	36	22.00	0	0	300	181	0					3.62	2	
Lim		10	10	0	304	52	30.40	0	2	396	345	13	26.53	3-33	0	0	5.22	4	

Cmp	Debut	M	I	NO	Runs	HS	Avge	100	50	Balls	Runs	Wkts	Avge	BB	5i	10m	RpO	ct	st
FC	2006/07	20	31	3	793	101	28.32	1	4	2029	1136	29	39.17	4-63	0	0	3.35	13	
Lim	2006/07	32	28	1	632	86	23.40	0	4	1074	914	33	27.69	4-19	2	0	5.10	14	
20T	2004/05	16	11	3	107	38	13.37	0	0	240	293	13	22.53	2-13	0	0	7.32	3	
VAN WYK, Divan Jaco (Eagles, Free State) b Bloemfontein, Orange Free State 25.2.1985 RHB RM																			
FC		13	23	3	1159	153	57.95	4	4	18	22	0					7.33	15	
Lim		12	12	0	449	115	37.41	1	3									9	
FC	2004/05	35	59	4	2323	153	42.23	5	12	18	22	0					7.33	35	
Lim	2004/05	35	34	3	1380	118	44.51	3	10									25	
VAN WYK, Diaan Marinus (Gauteng) b Roodepoort, Transvaal 19.1.1981 RHB WK																			
Lim		5	4	0	158	61	39.50	0	2									5	1
FC	2005/06	19	29	6	931	122*	40.47	1	7									80	13
Lim	2005/06	21	18	4	636	83*	45.42	0	7									29	4
VAN WYK, Esmund Peter (Western Province) b Cape Town, Cape Province 19.11.1981 RHB RMF																			
FC		4	5	2	70	34	23.33	0	0	444	194	3	64.66	1-31	0	0	2.62	3	
Lim		4	3	1	10	9	5.00	0	0	158	130	8	16.25	5-33	0	1	4.93	2	
FC	2007/08	15	23	6	697	99*	41.00	0	5	1938	992	37	26.81	5-20	2	0	3.07	6	
Lim	2006/07	22	17	5	250	48	20.83	0	0	1027	774	42	18.42	5-33	1	1	4.52	3	
VAN WYK, Jandre (Eagles, Free State) b Pretoria, Transvaal 20.3.1989 RHB WK																			
FC		1	2	0	0	0	0.00	0	0									2	
Lim		6	6	1	118	37	23.60	0	0									4	
FC	2008/09	4	6	0	44	26	7.33	0	0									5	
Lim	2008/09	8	8	1	119	37	17.00	0	0									5	
VAN WYK, Lenert (Boland, Cape Cobras) b Cape Town, Cape Province 13.7.1989 RHB RMF																			
FC		5	9	1	217	63	27.12	0	2	144	85	0					3.54	2	
Lim		6	4	1	90	53*	30.00	0	1	31	21	2	10.50	1-10	0	0	4.06	1	
FC	2007/08	10	19	1	492	67	27.33	0	4	258	176	1	176.00	1-67	0	0	4.09	3	
Lim	2007/08	13	10	1	156	53*	17.33	0	1	151	105	3	35.00	1-10	0	0	4.17	4	
VAN WYK, Morne Nico (Eagles, Free State, Eagles to India, South Africa A to Bangladesh, South Africa A to Sri Lanka) b Bloemfontein, Orange Free State 20.3.1979 RHB SLA WK																			
FC		9	13	2	345	86*	31.36	0	3									36	
Lim		12	12	1	514	168*	46.72	2	1									10	1
20T		5	5	1	227	85*	56.75	0	3									3	
FC	1996/97	110	187	23	5589	200*	34.07	11	28	78	36	2	18.00	2-25	0	0	2.76	281	12
Int	2003	6	6	0	195	82	32.50	0	2									1	
Lim	1997/98	173	167	18	6164	168*	41.36	16	32	129	124	7	17.71	2-28	0	0	5.76	157	18
I20T	2006/07	2	1	0	1	1	1.00	0	0									1	
20T	2003/04	58	54	8	1462	89*	31.78	0	11									48	14
VAN ZYL, Petrus Johannes (Gauteng) b Brakpan, Transvaal 20.4.1988 RHB WK																			
FC		6	5	2	72	24	24.00	0	0									18	1
Lim		2	1	0	4	4	4.00	0	0									0	
VAN ZYL, Stiaan (Boland, Cape Cobras, Cape Cobras to India, South Africa A to Bangladesh, South Africa A to Sri Lanka) b Cape Town, Cape Province 19.9.1987 LHB RM																			
FC		12	19	3	872	167*	54.50	3	3	348	121	1	121.00	1-20	0	0	2.08	7	
Lim		14	12	2	462	114*	46.20	2	1	54	56	0					6.22	4	
20T		5	4	0	56	29	14.00	0	0									1	
FC	2006/07	42	75	15	2442	167*	40.70	5	10	1789	796	23	34.60	4-36	0	0	2.67	29	
Lim	2006/07	50	46	6	1399	114*	34.97	4	5	475	408	8	51.00	2-19	0	0	5.15	14	
20T	2007/08	16	11	1	130	30	13.00	0	0	24	27	1	27.00	1-5	0	0	6.75	7	
VAN ZYL, Willem Johannes (Free State) b Bloemfontein, Orange Free State 14.4.1988 LHB SLC																			
FC		3	2	1	27	21	27.00	0	0	354	186	4	46.50	2-23	0	0	3.15	0	
Lim		8	4	0	36	19	9.00	0	0	282	202	8	25.25	3-28	0	0	4.29	4	
FC	2007/08	13	15	2	171	40	13.15	0	0	1268	733	23	31.86	6-96	1	0	3.46	1	
Lim	2007/08	15	10	2	84	19	10.50	0	0	552	437	17	25.70	4-34	1	0	4.75	5	
VARDHAN, Kyllin Myles (North West) b Durban, Natal 31.7.1989 LHB LM																			
FC		5	8	1	113	42	16.14	0	0	232	140	7	20.00	5-25	1	0	3.62	1	
Lim		8	6	1	178	72	35.60	0	1	174	158	4	39.50	2-46	0	0	5.44	4	
VENTER, Manfred (Free State) b Pretoria, Transvaal 9.6.1987 RHB RF																			
FC		4	5	1	22	8	5.50	0	0	540	300	4	75.00	2-58	0	0	3.33	3	
FC	2006/07	5	5	1	22	8	5.50	0	0	702	390	5	78.00	2-58	0	0	3.33	3	
Lim	2006/07	1								54	34	1	34.00	1-34	0	0	3.77	1	
VILAS, Dane James (Gauteng, Lions, Gauteng to Namibia) b Johannesburg, Transvaal 10.6.1985 RHB WK																			
FC		6	9	1	394	135*	49.25	1	2									17	1
Lim		14	14	1	322	111	24.76	1	0									5	3
20T		5	5	1	123	53	30.75	0	1									1	
FC	2006/07	29	46	2	1907	203	43.34	5	11									76	4
Lim	2006/07	41	40	6	1091	120	32.08	3	4									28	9
20T	2008/09	9	9	3	238	55*	39.66	0	2									5	
VILJOEN, G C (Easterns, Titans, Easterns to Namibia) b Witbank, Transvaal 6.3.1989 RHB RF																			
FC		12	14	5	210	61	23.33	0	1	1872	1165	41	28.41	6-55	2	1	3.73	2	
Lim		9	5	1	21	14	5.25	0	0	325	313	9	34.77	3-43	0	0	5.77	4	

Cmp	Debut	M	I	NO	Runs	HS	Avge	100	50	Balls	Runs	Wkts	Avge	BB	5i	10m	RpO	ct	st
FC	2008/09	17	21	6	343	61	22.86	0	2	2726	1696	56	30.28	6-55	3	1	3.73	3	
Lim	2008/09	13	6	1	23	14	4.60	0	0	493	461	15	30.73	3-43	0	0	5.61	6	
VIRET, Vincent Brandon (Eastern Province) b Cape Town, Cape Province 4.7.1988 RHB LMF																			
FC		9	7	3	75	23*	18.75	0	0	1246	631	26	24.26	4-61	0	0	3.03	4	
Lim		10	7	4	15	4*	5.00	0	0	396	342	14	24.42	3-19	0	0	5.18	4	
VOLKWYN, Lyndon Jacobus (Free State) b Grootbrak River 7.2.1989 RHB RMF																			
FC		1	1	1	1	1*		0	0	60	45	0					4.50	0	
FC	2007/08	3	4	3	2	1*	2.00	0	0	156	100	2	50.00	1-12	0	0	3.84	0	
Lim	2008/09	2	1	0	0	0	0.00	0	0	42	35	0					5.00	3	
VON BERG, Shaun (Northerns, Titans) b Pretoria, Transvaal 16.9.1986 RHB LB																			
FC		12	16	3	296	44	22.76	0	0	1940	1144	49	23.34	6-34	4	1	3.53	13	
Lim		9	6	1	98	47*	19.60	0	0	324	222	9	24.66	4-19	1	0	4.11	3	
20T		1								18	24	1	24.00	1-24	0	0	8.00	0	
VON RAUENSTEIN, Hancke Oscar (Free State) b Johannesburg, Transvaal 27.7.1980 RHB LB																			
FC		5	8	2	230	97*	38.33	0	2	612	386	7	55.14	3-84	0	0	3.78	4	
Lim		5	5	0	25	14	5.00	0	0	73	56	6	9.33	6-21	0	1	4.60	6	
FC	2006/07	21	34	3	971	116	31.32	2	5	1204	748	13	57.53	3-84	0	0	3.72	21	
Lim	2007/08	17	17	3	428	87	30.57	0	3	331	262	13	20.15	6-21	0	1	4.74	13	
VRIES, Gino Angelo (Eagles, Free State) b Bloemfontein, Free State 14.11.1987 RHB RFM																			
FC		17	20	12	99	20	12.37	0	0	2698	1354	37	36.59	6-92	1	0	3.01	4	
Lim		11	1	1	0	0*		0	0	385	385	15	25.66	4-46	1	0	6.00	1	
FC	2007/08	28	32	16	131	20	8.18	0	0	3932	1867	58	32.18	6-92	1	0	2.84	5	
Lim	2006/07	21	6	3	19	12	6.33	0	0	823	744	29	25.65	4-40	2	0	5.42	1	
WALTERS, Basheeru-Deen (Easterns, Titans, Easterns to Namibia) b Port Elizabeth, Eastern Province 16.9.1986 RHB RF																			
FC		9	10	4	114	30*	19.00	0	0	1184	727	16	45.43	3-43	0	0	3.68	3	
Lim		12	3	1	7	6*	3.50	0	0	464	493	19	25.94	3-26	0	0	6.37	3	
20T		7								130	179	7	25.57	2-30	0	0	8.26	2	
FC	2007/08	27	32	9	349	39	15.17	0	0	3697	2114	66	32.03	5-38	1	0	3.43	9	
Lim	2007/08	31	10	4	41	12	6.83	0	0	1149	1134	42	27.00	5-39	2	1	5.92	8	
20T	2008/09	10	2	0	5	4	2.50	0	0	190	244	8	30.50	2-30	0	0	7.70	2	
WALTERS, Lee-Roy (Boland, Boland to Namibia) b Paarl, Cape Province 3.12.1986 RHB WK																			
FC		11	18	3	423	67*	28.20	0	4	6	4	1	4.00	1-4	0	0	4.00	25	3
Lim		11	8	1	149	39*	21.28	0	0									10	3
FC	2004/05	39	63	10	1441	82	27.18	0	10	6	4	1	4.00	1-4	0	0	4.00	110	12
Lim	2005/06	39	29	8	432	48	20.57	0	0									47	12
WALTERS, Martin Dennis (Western Province) b East London, Cape Province 12.3.1985 RHB RMF																			
FC		12	20	1	478	110	25.15	1	1	140	88	1	88.00	1-44	0	0	3.77	9	
Lim		12	12	2	449	98	44.90	0	4									7	
FC	2005/06	20	33	2	804	110	25.93	2	2	176	113	2	56.50	1-19	0	0	3.85	12	
Lim	2005/06	18	18	4	575	98	41.07	0	5									7	
WATSON, Douglas James (KwaZulu-Natal Inland) b Pietermaritzburg, Natal 15.5.1973 RHB RM																			
FC		4	6	4	299	103*	149.50	1	1									3	
Lim		5	5	1	110	51*	27.50	0	1									0	
FC	1993/94	139	233	24	7693	220	36.80	13	42	323	144	4	36.00	2-7	0	0	2.67	77	
Lim	1993/94	136	135	12	4353	142	35.39	7	27	85	79	2	39.50	2-22	0	0	5.57	38	
20T	2003/04	13	13	0	303	62	23.30	0	1									4	
WERNARS, Kirk Ogilvy (Western Province) b Cape Town, Cape Province 14.6.1991 LHB RFM																			
FC		1	2	1	30	22*	30.00	0	0	58	30	3	10.00	2-11	0	0	3.10	1	
Lim		2	2	1	41	28*	41.00	0	0	36	55	0					9.16	0	
WIESE, David (Easterns, Titans, Easterns to Namibia) b Roodepoort, Transvaal 18.5.1985 RHB RFM																			
FC		4	5	1	115	87	28.75	0	1	315	148	9	16.44	3-10	0	0	2.81	6	
Lim		11	10	3	336	86	48.00	0	2	336	333	9	37.00	3-36	0	0	5.94	2	
20T		3	2	2	36	26*		0	0	60	73	6	12.16	5-19	0	1	7.30	2	
FC	2005/06	32	52	6	1905	208	41.41	5	9	4678	2638	100	26.38	5-58	2	0	3.38	27	
Lim	2005/06	46	38	9	1250	108	43.10	1	8	1648	1399	41	34.12	3-7	0	0	5.09	14	
20T	2007/08	6	5	3	44	26*	22.00	0	0	66	88	6	14.66	5-19	0	1	8.00	3	
WILLIAMS, Brandon (Boland) b East London, Cape Province 20.9.1989 RHB SLA																			
FC		1	1	1	3	3*		0	0	144	49	1	49.00	1-40	0	0	2.04	0	
Lim		1								12	12	0					6.00	0	
WILLIAMS, Reece Chesray (Eastern Province) b Kimberley, Cape Province 12.1.1990 RHB RFM																			
FC		13	9	4	51	19	10.20	0	0	1897	1125	50	22.50	7-60	3	1	3.55	5	
Lim		8	1	0	4	4	4.00	0	0	322	339	18	18.83	4-46	2	0	6.31	1	
FC	2007/08	15	13	6	91	20	13.00	0	0	2128	1252	54	23.18	7-60	3	1	3.53	6	
Lim	2007/08	10	2	0	4	4	2.00	0	0	418	391	19	20.57	4-46	2	0	5.61	1	
WILLIAMSON, Myles (Western Province) b Cape Town, Cape Province 3.1.1984 RHB RM																			
FC		1	2	0	26	22	13.00	0	0									0	
Lim		2	2	0	35	34	17.50	0	0									0	
FC	2005/06	24	44	3	892	121	21.75	1	3	5	4	0					4.80	13	
Lim	2005/06	24	24	3	803	101*	38.23	1	5									14	

Cmp	Debut	M	I	NO	Runs	HS	Avge	100	50	Balls	Runs	Wkts	Avge	BB	5i	10m	RpO	ct	st
XULU, Victor Sandile (KwaZulu-Natal) b Durban, Natal 11.4.1983 RHB OB																			
FC		1	2	0	0	0	0.00	0	0									0	
Lim		1	1	0	10	10	10.00	0	0									1	
ZONDEKI, Monde (Cape Cobras, Western Province, Cape Cobras to India) b King William's Town, Cape Province 25.7.1982 RHB RF																			
FC		9	8	2	53	15	8.83	0	0	1432	711	20	35.55	4-45	0	0	2.97	2	
Lim		6	1	0	0	0	0.00	0	0	270	261	9	29.00	3-22	0	0	5.80	0	
20T		7	2	1	0	0*	0.00	0	0	126	118	4	29.50	2-21	0	0	5.61	1	
Test	2003	6	5	0	82	59	16.40	0	1	780	480	19	25.26	6-39	1	0	3.69	1	
FC	2000/01	82	109	32	702	59	9.11	0	1	13648	7211	248	29.07	6-39	9	1	3.17	24	
Int	2002/03	13	3	2	4	3*	4.00	0	0	558	504	11	45.81	2-40	0	0	5.41	3	
Lim	2001/02	84	31	13	133	23	7.38	0	0	3666	3030	97	31.23	6-37	2	2	4.95	12	
I20T	2005/06	1	1	0	0	0	0.00	0	0	18	41	1	41.00	1-41	0	0	13.66	0	
20T	2003/04	19	5	2	1	1*	0.33	0	0	352	419	12	34.91	2-19	0	0	7.14	3	
ZONDO, Khayelihle (Dolphins, KwaZulu-Natal) b Durban, Natal 7.3.1990 RHB OB																			
FC		13	20	2	558	100*	31.00	1	3	120	64	1	64.00	1-20	0	0	3.20	6	
Lim		10	9	2	255	95*	36.42	0	2	30	18	1	18.00	1-13	0	0	3.60	5	
20T		2	2	0	47	32	23.50	0	0									0	
FC	2007/08	26	42	3	1070	100*	27.43	1	6	216	141	1	141.00	1-20	0	0	3.91	12	
Lim	2007/08	20	18	2	496	95*	31.00	0	5	132	87	4	21.75	3-34	0	0	3.95	8	

AUSTRALIA TO SOUTH AFRICA 2009/10

Cmp	Debut	M	I	NO	Runs	HS	Avge	100	50	Balls	Runs	Wkts	Avge	BB	5i	10m	RpO	ct	st
FERGUSON, C.J.																			
Int		5	3	1	29	20	14.50	0	0									0	
Lim		5	3	1	29	20	14.50	0	0									0	
HAURITZ, N.M.																			
Int		5	2	2	16	9*		0	0	185	116	5	23.20	3-37	0	0	3.76	2	
Lim		5	2	2	16	9*		0	0	185	116	5	23.20	3-37	0	0	3.76	2	
HOPES, J.R.																			
Int		5	3	1	28	22*	14.00	0	0	120	105	2	52.50	1-27	0	0	5.25	2	
Lim		5	3	1	28	22*	14.00	0	0	120	105	2	52.50	1-27	0	0	5.25	2	
HUSSEY, M.E.K.																			
Int		5	4	0	148	67	37.00	0	2									2	
Lim		5	4	0	148	67	37.00	0	2									2	
JOHNSON, M.G.																			
Int		5	2	1	82	73*	82.00	0	1	240	185	4	46.25	2-45	0	0	4.62	2	
Lim		5	2	1	82	73*	82.00	0	1	240	185	4	46.25	2-45	0	0	4.62	2	
LEE, B.																			
Int		5	2	1	37	25	37.00	0	0	222	162	6	27.00	2-45	0	0	4.37	0	
Lim		5	2	1	37	25	37.00	0	0	222	162	6	27.00	2-45	0	0	4.37	0	
PAINE, T.D.																			
Int		5	5	0	123	56	24.60	0	1									8	1
Lim		5	5	0	123	56	24.60	0	1									8	1
PONTING, R.T.																			
Int		5	5	1	288	111*	72.00	1	2									2	
Lim		5	5	1	288	111*	72.00	1	2									2	
SIDDLE, P.M.																			
Int		5								198	146	6	24.33	3-55	0	0	4.42	0	
Lim		5								198	146	6	24.33	3-55	0	0	4.42	0	
WATSON, S.R.																			
Int		5	5	2	265	136*	88.33	2	0	202	151	6	25.16	2-32	0	0	4.48	0	
Lim		5	5	2	265	136*	88.33	2	0	202	151	6	25.16	2-32	0	0	4.48	0	
WHITE, C.L.																			
Int		5	4	1	106	62	35.33	0	1									1	
Lim		5	4	1	106	62	35.33	0	1									1	

ENGLAND TO SOUTH AFRICA 2009/10

Cmp	Debut	M	I	NO	Runs	HS	Avge	100	50	Balls	Runs	Wkts	Avge	BB	5i	10m	RpO	ct	st
ANDERSON, J.M.																			
Test		4	7	3	56	29	14.00	0	0	977	548	16	34.25	5-63	1	0	3.36	1	
FC		4	7	3	56	29	14.00	0	0	977	548	16	34.25	5-63	1	0	3.36	1	
Int		7	4	3	12	5*	12.00	0	0	392	301	15	20.06	5-23	0	1	4.60	0	
Lim		8	4	3	12	5*	12.00	0	0	428	319	17	18.76	5-23	0	1	4.47	0	
I20T		2								42	52	1	52.00	1-28	0	0	7.42	1	
20T		2								42	52	1	52.00	1-28	0	0	7.42	1	
BELL, I.R.																			
Test		4	7	0	313	140	44.71	1	1									3	
FC		4	7	0	313	140	44.71	1	1									3	

Cmp Debut	M	I	NO	Runs	HS	Avge	100	50	Balls	Runs	Wkts	Avge	BB	5i	10m	RpO	ct	st
BOPARA, R.S.																		
Int	2	2	0	31	30	15.50	0	0									1	
Lim	2	2	0	31	30	15.50	0	0									1	
BRESNAN, T.T.																		
Int	4	2	0	87	80	43.50	0	1	216	173	3	57.66	2-46	0	0	4.80	1	
Lim	5	3	1	87	80	43.50	0	1	276	231	4	57.75	2-46	0	0	5.02	2	
I20T	2	2	1	3	3*	3.00	0	0	36	73	0					12.16	1	
20T	3	3	1	7	4	3.50	0	0	57	89	0					9.36	1	
BROAD, S.C.J.																		
Test	4	7	0	76	25	10.85	0	0	930	435	13	33.46	4-43	0	0	2.80	2	
FC	4	7	0	76	25	10.85	0	0	930	435	13	33.46	4-43	0	0	2.80	2	
Int	5	3	0	11	10	3.66	0	0	288	256	16	16.00	4-39	2	0	5.33	0	
Lim	6	4	0	22	11	5.50	0	0	312	284	18	15.77	4-39	2	0	5.46	0	
COLLINGWOOD, P.D.																		
Test	4	7	1	344	91	57.33	0	3	120	66	0					3.30	8	
FC	4	7	1	344	91	57.33	0	3	120	66	0					3.30	8	
Int	7	7	1	395	105*	65.83	1	2	264	230	5	46.00	2-20	0	0	5.22	3	
Lim	8	8	1	403	105*	57.57	1	2	286	239	7	34.14	2-9	0	0	5.01	3	
I20T	1	1	0	57	57	57.00	0	1									1	
20T	2	2	0	75	57	37.50	0	1	12	16	0					8.00	1	
COOK, A.N.																		
Test	4	7	0	287	118	41.00	1	2									4	
FC	4	7	0	287	118	41.00	1	2									4	
I20T	2	2	0	37	26	18.50	0	0									0	
20T	3	3	0	59	26	19.66	0	0									1	
DAVIES, S.M.																		
Int	1	1	0	5	5	5.00	0	0									1	
Lim	1	1	0	5	5	5.00	0	0									1	
DENLY, J.L.																		
Int	4	4	0	67	36	16.75	0	0									2	
Lim	6	6	0	93	36	15.50	0	0	18	20	1	20.00	1-20	0	0	6.66	2	
I20T	2	2	0	14	14	7.00	0	0	6	9	1	9.00	1-9	0	0	9.00	0	
20T	3	3	0	21	14	7.00	0	0	12	24	1	24.00	1-9	0	0	12.00	2	
MAHMOOD, S.I.																		
Int	1								42	41	1	41.00	1-41	0	0	5.85	0	
Lim	3								138	120	4	30.00	2-21	0	0	5.21	1	
I20T	2	1	1	1	1*		0	0	42	92	2	46.00	1-31	0	0	13.14	1	
20T	3	2	1	2	1*	2.00	0	0	60	104	3	34.66	1-12	0	0	10.40	1	
MORGAN, E.J.G.																		
Int	7	7	3	202	67	50.50	0	2									6	
Lim	9	9	4	290	67*	58.00	0	3									6	
I20T	2	2	1	95	85*	95.00	0	1									1	
20T	3	3	1	106	85*	53.00	0	1									1	
ONIONS, G.																		
Test	3	5	5	11	4*		0	0	690	366	8	45.75	3-86	0	0	3.18	0	
FC	3	5	5	11	4*		0	0	690	366	8	45.75	3-86	0	0	3.18	0	
Int	3	1	0	1	1	1.00	0	0	150	157	3	52.33	2-58	0	0	6.28	1	
Lim	4	1	0	1	1	1.00	0	0	204	203	5	40.60	2-46	0	0	5.97	1	
PIETERSEN, K.P.																		
Test	4	7	0	177	81	25.28	0	1	54	30	0					3.33	0	
FC	4	7	0	177	81	25.28	0	1	54	30	0					3.33	0	
Int	3	3	0	52	45	17.33	0	0									0	
Lim	4	4	0	56	45	14.00	0	0									1	
I20T	1	1	0	29	29	29.00	0	0	12	27	1	27.00	1-27	0	0	13.50	0	
20T	1	1	0	29	29	29.00	0	0	12	27	1	27.00	1-27	0	0	13.50	0	
PRIOR, M.J.																		
Test	4	7	0	158	76	22.57	0	2									12	
FC	4	7	0	158	76	22.57	0	2									12	
Int	4	2	1	44	28*	44.00	0	0									7	
Lim	6	4	1	117	54	39.00	0	1									10	1
I20T	2	2	1	10	10*	10.00	0	0									0	
20T	3	3	1	11	10*	5.50	0	0									1	1
RASHID, A.U.																		
Int	1								18	27	0					9.00	0	
Lim	2								66	71	0					6.45	0	
I20T	1	1	0	1	1	1.00	0	0	6	25	0					25.00	0	
20T	2	2	1	7	6*	7.00	0	0	30	47	2	23.50	2-22	0	0	9.40	0	
SHAH, O.A.																		
Int	4	4	0	145	98	36.25	0	1	6	11	0					11.00	1	
Lim	4	4	0	145	98	36.25	0	1	6	11	0					11.00	1	

Cmp	Debut	M	I	NO	Runs	HS	Avge	100	50	Balls	Runs	Wkts	Avge	BB	5i	10m	RpO	ct	st
SIDEBOTTOM, R.J.																			
Test		1	2	0	15	15	7.50	0	0	186	98	2	49.00	2-98	0	0	3.16	0	
FC		1	2	0	15	15	7.50	0	0	186	98	2	49.00	2-98	0	0	3.16	0	
Int		1	1	0	20	20	20.00	0	0	36	32	1	32.00	1-32	0	0	5.33	0	
Lim		1	1	0	20	20	20.00	0	0	36	32	1	32.00	1-32	0	0	5.33	0	
STRAUSS, A.J.																			
Test		4	7	0	170	54	24.28	0	1									2	
FC		4	7	0	170	54	24.28	0	1									2	
Int		7	7	0	120	32	17.14	0	0									5	
Lim		9	9	0	257	72	28.55	0	2									6	
SWANN, G.P.																			
Test		4	7	1	171	85	28.50	0	1	1262	659	21	31.38	5-54	2	0	3.13	3	
FC		4	7	1	171	85	28.50	0	1	1262	659	21	31.38	5-54	2	0	3.13	3	
Int		6	4	2	43	18	21.50	0	0	156	146	1	146.00	1-43	0	0	5.61	3	
Lim		7	4	2	43	18	21.50	0	0	186	161	3	53.66	2-15	0	0	5.19	4	
I20T		1								18	30	1	30.00	1-30	0	0	10.00	0	
20T		2	1	0	1	1	1.00	0	0	42	39	3	13.00	2-9	0	0	5.57	0	
TROTT, I.J.L.																			
Test		4	7	0	190	69	27.14	0	1	66	58	0					5.27	2	
FC		4	7	0	190	69	27.14	0	1	66	58	0					5.27	2	
Int		3	3	1	148	87	74.00	0	2	48	29	0					3.62	2	
Lim		5	5	1	307	87	76.75	0	4	48	29	0					3.62	2	
I20T		2	2	0	84	51	42.00	0	1									0	
20T		3	3	0	91	51	30.33	0	1									0	
WRIGHT, L.J.																			
Int		7	4	0	84	48	21.00	0	0	204	208	4	52.00	2-66	0	0	6.11	3	
Lim		9	6	1	133	48	26.60	0	0	276	272	6	45.33	2-48	0	0	5.91	3	
I20T		2	2	0	14	12	7.00	0	0	36	57	2	28.50	1-17	0	0	9.50	1	
20T		3	3	0	16	12	5.33	0	0	36	57	2	28.50	1-17	0	0	9.50	1	

INDIA TO SOUTH AFRICA 2009/10

Cmp	Debut	M	I	NO	Runs	HS	Avge	100	50	Balls	Runs	Wkts	Avge	BB	5i	10m	RpO	ct	st
DHONI, M.S.																			
Int		3	1	0	3	3	3.00	0	0	12	14	1	14.00	1-14	0	0	7.00	5	
Lim		3	1	0	3	3	3.00	0	0	12	14	1	14.00	1-14	0	0	7.00	5	
DRAVID, R.S.																			
Int		3	2	0	80	76	40.00	0	1									2	
Lim		3	2	0	80	76	40.00	0	1									2	
GAMBHIR, G.																			
Int		3	2	0	63	57	31.50	0	1									1	
Lim		3	2	0	63	57	31.50	0	1									1	
HARBHAJAN SINGH																			
Int		3	1	0	13	13	13.00	0	0	162	139	3	46.33	2-14	0	0	5.14	3	
Lim		3	1	0	13	13	13.00	0	0	162	139	3	46.33	2-14	0	0	5.14	3	
KARTHIK, K.D.																			
Int		1	1	0	34	34	34.00	0	0									1	
Lim		1	1	0	34	34	34.00	0	0									1	
KOHLI, V.																			
Int		3	2	1	95	79*	95.00	0	1	18	21	0					7.00	1	
Lim		3	2	1	95	79*	95.00	0	1	18	21	0					7.00	1	
KUMAR, P.																			
Int		2								102	56	3	18.66	3-22	0	0	3.29	1	
Lim		2								102	56	3	18.66	3-22	0	0	3.29	1	
MISHRA, A.																			
Int		2								90	72	2	36.00	1-27	0	0	4.80	1	
Lim		2								90	72	2	36.00	1-27	0	0	4.80	1	
NAYAR, A.M.																			
Int		1	1	1	0	0*		0	0	18	17	0					5.66	0	
Lim		1	1	1	0	0*		0	0	18	17	0					5.66	0	
NEHRA, A.																			
Int		3	1	1	0	0*		0	0	156	124	8	15.50	4-55	1	0	4.76	0	
Lim		3	1	1	0	0*		0	0	156	124	8	15.50	4-55	1	0	4.76	0	
PATHAN, Y.K.																			
Int		1	1	0	5	5	5.00	0	0	60	56	1	56.00	1-56	0	0	5.60	1	
Lim		1	1	0	5	5	5.00	0	0	60	56	1	56.00	1-56	0	0	5.60	1	
RAINA, S.K.																			
Int		3	1	0	46	46	46.00	0	0	6	8	0					8.00	1	
Lim		3	1	0	46	46	46.00	0	0	6	8	0					8.00	1	

Cmp Debut	M	I	NO	Runs	HS	Avge	100	50	Balls	Runs	Wkts	Avge	BB	5i	10m	RpO	ct	st
SHARMA, I.																		
Int	2	1	0	0	0	0.00	0	0	93	92	3	30.66	2-39	0	0	5.93	0	
Lim	2	1	0	0	0	0.00	0	0	93	92	3	30.66	2-39	0	0	5.93	0	
SINGH, R.P.																		
Int	1	1	0	2	2	2.00	0	0	54	59	1	59.00	1-59	0	0	6.55	0	
Lim	1	1	0	2	2	2.00	0	0	54	59	1	59.00	1-59	0	0	6.55	0	
TENDULKAR, S.R.																		
Int	2	1	0	8	8	8.00	0	0									1	
Lim	2	1	0	8	8	8.00	0	0									1	

NAMIBIA TO SOUTH AFRICA 2009/10

Cmp Debut	M	I	NO	Runs	HS	Avge	100	50	Balls	Runs	Wkts	Avge	BB	5i	10m	RpO	ct	st
AMBAMBI, N.E.																		
FC	2	3	2	13	8	13.00	0	0	210	131	2	65.50	1-44	0	0	3.74	0	
Lim	4								66	78	2	39.00	2-23	0	0	7.09	0	
BAARD, S.J.																		
FC	1	2	0	65	45	32.50	0	0	6	5	0					5.00	1	
Lim	1	1	0	18	18	18.00	0	0									0	
BARNARD, P.J.																		
Lim	1								36	49	1	49.00	1-49	0	0	8.16	0	
BURGER, L.J.																		
FC	1	2	0	39	36	19.50	0	0	66	44	1	44.00	1-44	0	0	4.00	0	
Lim	1	1	0	20	20	20.00	0	0									0	
BURGER, S.F.																		
FC	3	6	2	198	123*	49.50	1	0	450	236	6	39.33	2-33	0	0	3.14	3	
Lim	2	2	0	24	21	12.00	0	0	72	67	2	33.50	2-21	0	0	5.58	2	
GROENEWALD, W.J.																		
FC	5	9	0	68	33	7.55	0	0	162	115	4	28.75	1-14	0	0	4.25	3	
Lim	5	4	0	68	44	17.00	0	0	130	102	1	102.00	1-18	0	0	4.70	2	
KLAZINGA, L.																		
FC	7	11	1	112	31	11.20	0	0	1041	548	27	20.29	5-50	2	0	3.15	2	
Lim	6	5	2	30	13*	10.00	0	0	228	203	4	50.75	2-42	0	0	5.34	3	
LOUW, T.																		
Lim	1	1	0	0	0	0.00	0	0									0	
MANYANDE, R.N.																		
FC	7	13	1	197	35	16.41	0	0	159	83	5	16.60	5-29	1	0	3.13	4	
Lim	5	5	0	53	31	10.60	0	0	18	25	1	25.00	1-25	0	0	8.33	3	
MYBURGH, W.																		
Lim	1	1	0	5	5	5.00	0	0									0	
PALLADINO, A.P.																		
FC	3	6	0	49	27	8.16	0	0	294	150	9	16.66	4-65	0	0	3.06	3	
Lim	3	3	0	34	26	11.33	0	0	102	93	4	23.25	3-44	0	0	5.47	0	
ROSSOUW, P.																		
FC	1	2	0	2	1	1.00	0	0	138	68	1	68.00	1-20	0	0	2.95	1	
Lim	1	1	1	11	11*		0	0	18	20	0					6.66	1	
RUDOLPH, G.J.																		
FC	7	14	0	336	98	24.00	0	2	12	16	0					8.00	9	
Lim	6	6	0	82	39	13.66	0	0									2	
SCHOLTZ, B.M.																		
FC	5	9	7	79	23	39.50	0	0	438	235	7	33.57	3-56	0	0	3.21	0	
Lim	5	3	0	29	24	9.66	0	0	120	120	1	120.00	1-42	0	0	6.00	0	
SCHOLTZ, N.R.P.																		
FC	4	7	1	143	62	23.83	0	1	210	105	1	105.00	1-10	0	0	3.00	3	
Lim	3	3	1	24	14	12.00	0	0	68	74	0					6.52	0	
SLABBER, W.																		
FC	1	2	1	0	0*	0.00	0	0	192	115	1	115.00	1-57	0	0	3.59	0	
Lim	1	1	0	4	4	4.00	0	0	12	15	0					7.50	0	
SNYMAN, G.																		
FC	1	2	0	23	17	11.50	0	0	48	36	0					4.50	1	
Lim	1	1	1	55	55*		0	1									1	
STEENKAMP, E.																		
FC	2	4	1	110	91	36.66	0	1									5	
Lim	2	2	0	60	43	30.00	0	0									2	
VAN DER WESTHUIZEN, L.P.																		
FC	2	4	0	54	41	13.50	0	0	114	57	1	57.00	1-27	0	0	3.00	0	
Lim	1	1	1	51	51*		0	1	48	33	3	11.00	3-33	0	0	4.12	2	
VAN ROOI, A.																		
FC	2	1	1	1	1*		0	0	96	45	0					2.81	0	

Cmp	Debut	M	I	NO	Runs	HS	Avge	100	50	Balls	Runs	Wkts	Avge	BB	5i	10m	RpO	ct	st
VAN SCHOOR, R.																			
FC		7	14	0	274	69	19.57	0	1	40	40	2	20.00	2-22	0	0	6.00	18	
Lim		6	6	2	185	68*	46.25	0	2	30	33	1	33.00	1-33	0	0	6.60	4	
VAN VUUREN, W.																			
FC		2	4	0	65	49	16.25	0	0									1	
Lim		4	4	0	68	26	17.00	0	0									0	
VERWEY, T.																			
FC		2	3	2	17	8*	17.00	0	0	204	140	0					4.11	1	
Lim		1	1	0	13	13	13.00	0	0	6	4	0					4.00	0	
VILJOEN, C.																			
FC		5	9	0	86	27	9.55	0	0	841	432	15	28.80	4-36	0	0	3.08	3	
Lim		5	4	0	5	3	1.25	0	0	198	185	8	23.12	3-43	0	0	5.60	1	
VORSTER, L.P.																			
FC		1	2	0	52	30	26.00	0	0									0	
WILLIAMS, C.G.																			
FC		6	11	0	480	122	43.63	1	3	636	370	12	30.83	4-30	0	0	3.49	7	
Lim		6	6	0	109	59	18.16	0	1	120	130	4	32.50	2-7	0	0	6.50	2	

NEW ZEALAND TO SOUTH AFRICA 2009/10

Cmp	Debut	M	I	NO	Runs	HS	Avge	100	50	Balls	Runs	Wkts	Avge	BB	5i	10m	RpO	ct	st
BOND, S.E.																			
Int		5	2	1	3	3*	3.00	0	0	294	242	6	40.33	3-21	0	0	4.93	0	
Lim		5	2	1	3	3*	3.00	0	0	294	242	6	40.33	3-21	0	0	4.93	0	
BROOM, N.T.																			
Int		5	5	1	73	37	18.25	0	0									2	
Lim		5	5	1	73	37	18.25	0	0									2	
BUTLER, I.G.																			
Int		3	1	0	6	6	6.00	0	0	162	128	5	25.60	4-44	1	0	4.74	0	
Lim		3	1	0	6	6	6.00	0	0	162	128	5	25.60	4-44	1	0	4.74	0	
ELLIOTT, G.D.																			
Int		5	5	1	126	75*	31.50	0	1	72	49	4	12.25	4-31	1	0	4.08	1	
Lim		5	5	1	126	75*	31.50	0	1	72	49	4	12.25	4-31	1	0	4.08	1	
FRANKLIN, J.E.C.																			
Int		4	3	2	63	33	63.00	0	0	192	146	2	73.00	2-40	0	0	4.56	0	
Lim		4	3	2	63	33	63.00	0	0	192	146	2	73.00	2-40	0	0	4.56	0	
GUPTILL, M.J.																			
Int		5	5	0	191	66	38.20	0	2	6	13	0					13.00	3	
Lim		5	5	0	191	66	38.20	0	2	6	13	0					13.00	3	
HOPKINS, G.J.																			
Int		2	2	0	15	13	7.50	0	0									0	
Lim		2	2	0	15	13	7.50	0	0									0	
McCULLUM, B.B.																			
Int		5	5	0	155	48	31.00	0	0									8	
Lim		5	5	0	155	48	31.00	0	0									8	
MILLS, K.D.																			
Int		5	3	1	30	18*	15.00	0	0	289	206	9	22.88	3-27	0	0	4.27	1	
Lim		5	3	1	30	18*	15.00	0	0	289	206	9	22.88	3-27	0	0	4.27	1	
PATEL, J.S.																			
Int		1	1	1	16	16*		0	0	38	44	0					6.94	1	
Lim		1	1	1	16	16*		0	0	38	44	0					6.94	1	
REDMOND, A.J.																			
Int		2	2	0	57	31	28.50	0	0									1	
Lim		2	2	0	57	31	28.50	0	0									1	
RYDER, J.D.																			
Int		2	2	0	82	74	41.00	0	1	12	15	0					7.50	0	
Lim		2	2	0	82	74	41.00	0	1	12	15	0					7.50	0	
TAYLOR, L.R.P.L.																			
Int		5	5	0	121	72	24.20	0	1									9	
Lim		5	5	0	121	72	24.20	0	1									9	
TUFFEY, D.R.																			
Int		2	1	0	4	4	4.00	0	0	106	91	4	22.75	2-39	0	0	5.15	0	
Lim		2	1	0	4	4	4.00	0	0	106	91	4	22.75	2-39	0	0	5.15	0	
VETTORI, D.L.																			
Int		4	4	2	100	48	50.00	0	0	187	124	7	17.71	3-43	0	0	3.97	2	
Lim		4	4	2	100	48	50.00	0	0	187	124	7	17.71	3-43	0	0	3.97	2	

PAKISTAN TO SOUTH AFRICA 2009/10

Cmp Debut	M	I	NO	Runs	HS	Avge	100	50	Balls	Runs	Wkts	Avge	BB	5i	10m	RpO	ct	st
IMRAN NAZIR																		
Int	3	3	0	53	28	17.66	0	0									1	
Lim	3	3	0	53	28	17.66	0	0									1	
KAMRAN AKMAL																		
Int	4	4	0	92	44	23.00	0	0									3	2
Lim	4	4	0	92	44	23.00	0	0									3	2
MISBAH-UL-HAQ																		
Int	2	2	0	47	41	23.50	0	0									1	
Lim	2	2	0	47	41	23.50	0	0									1	
MOHAMMAD AAMER																		
Int	3	2	1	19	19*	19.00	0	0	150	102	6	17.00	3-24	0	0	4.08	1	
Lim	3	2	1	19	19*	19.00	0	0	150	102	6	17.00	3-24	0	0	4.08	1	
MOHAMMAD ASIF																		
Int	1								48	34	2	17.00	2-34	0	0	4.25	0	
Lim	1								48	34	2	17.00	2-34	0	0	4.25	0	
MOHAMMAD YOUSUF																		
Int	4	4	0	200	87	50.00	0	1									1	
Lim	4	4	0	200	87	50.00	0	1									1	
NAVED-UL-HASAN																		
Int	4	3	2	26	11*	26.00	0	0	198	170	4	42.50	2-48	0	0	5.15	1	
Lim	4	3	2	26	11*	26.00	0	0	198	170	4	42.50	2-48	0	0	5.15	1	
SAEED AJMAL																		
Int	4	2	2	14	14*		0	0	185	117	8	14.62	2-16	0	0	3.79	1	
Lim	4	2	2	14	14*		0	0	185	117	8	14.62	2-16	0	0	3.79	1	
SHAHID AFRIDI																		
Int	4	4	1	40	17*	13.33	0	0	231	166	5	33.20	2-39	0	0	4.31	1	
Lim	4	4	1	40	17*	13.33	0	0	231	166	5	33.20	2-39	0	0	4.31	1	
SHOAIB MALIK																		
Int	4	4	0	180	128	45.00	1	0	60	50	1	50.00	1-16	0	0	5.00	1	
Lim	4	4	0	180	128	45.00	1	0	60	50	1	50.00	1-16	0	0	5.00	1	
UMAR AKMAL																		
Int	4	4	2	98	55	49.00	0	1									1	
Lim	4	4	2	98	55	49.00	0	1									1	
UMAR GUL																		
Int	4	2	0	6	6	3.00	0	0	191	169	5	33.80	3-28	0	0	5.30	2	
Lim	4	2	0	6	6	3.00	0	0	191	169	5	33.80	3-28	0	0	5.30	2	
YOUNIS KHAN																		
Int	3	3	0	53	20	17.66	0	0									1	
Lim	3	3	0	53	20	17.66	0	0									1	

SRI LANKA TO SOUTH AFRICA 2009/10

Cmp Debut	M	I	NO	Runs	HS	Avge	100	50	Balls	Runs	Wkts	Avge	BB	5i	10m	RpO	ct	st
DILSHAN, T.M.																		
Int	3	3	0	149	106	49.66	1	0									1	
Lim	3	3	0	149	106	49.66	1	0									1	
JAYASURIYA, S.T.																		
Int	3	3	0	34	24	11.33	0	0	60	39	3	13.00	3-39	0	0	3.90	0	
Lim	3	3	0	34	24	11.33	0	0	60	39	3	13.00	3-39	0	0	3.90	0	
JAYAWARDENE, D.P.M.D.																		
Int	3	3	0	163	77	54.33	0	2									3	
Lim	3	3	0	163	77	54.33	0	2									3	
KANDAMBY, S.H.T.																		
Int	3	3	0	70	53	23.33	0	1	6	2	0					2.00	1	
Lim	3	3	0	70	53	23.33	0	1	6	2	0					2.00	1	
KULASEKARA, K.M.D.N.																		
Int	3	3	2	75	57*	75.00	0	1	138	138	3	46.00	2-42	0	0	6.00	0	
Lim	3	3	2	75	57*	75.00	0	1	138	138	3	46.00	2-42	0	0	6.00	0	
MALINGA, S.L.																		
Int	3	2	0	15	15	7.50	0	0	160	171	4	42.75	2-43	0	0	6.41	0	
Lim	3	2	0	15	15	7.50	0	0	160	171	4	42.75	2-43	0	0	6.41	0	
MATHEWS, A.D.																		
Int	3	3	0	69	52	23.00	0	1	132	102	4	25.50	2-33	0	0	4.63	2	
Lim	3	3	0	69	52	23.00	0	1	132	102	4	25.50	2-33	0	0	4.63	2	
MENDIS, B.A.W.																		
Int	3	2	0	8	5	4.00	0	0	150	114	3	38.00	3-30	0	0	4.56	0	
Lim	3	2	0	8	5	4.00	0	0	150	114	3	38.00	3-30	0	0	4.56	0	

Cmp	Debut	M	I	NO	Runs	HS	Avge	100	50	Balls	Runs	Wkts	Avge	BB	5i	10m	RpO	ct	st
MIRANDO, M.T.T.																			
Int		1	1	0	11	11	11.00	0	0	42	50	0					7.14	0	
Lim		1	1	0	11	11	11.00	0	0	42	50	0					7.14	0	
MURALITHARAN, M.																			
Int		2	2	1	18	18	18.00	0	0	108	106	1	106.00	1-60	0	0	5.88	0	
Lim		2	2	1	18	18	18.00	0	0	108	106	1	106.00	1-60	0	0	5.88	0	
SAMARAWEERA, T.T.																			
Int		3	3	0	84	37	28.00	0	0									0	
Lim		3	3	0	84	37	28.00	0	0									0	
SANGAKKARA, K.C.																			
Int		3	3	0	66	54	22.00	0	1									2	
Lim		3	3	0	66	54	22.00	0	1									2	

WEST INDIES TO SOUTH AFRICA 2009/10

Cmp	Debut	M	I	NO	Runs	HS	Avge	100	50	Balls	Runs	Wkts	Avge	BB	5i	10m	RpO	ct	st
BERNARD, D.E.																			
Int		3	3	0	36	22	12.00	0	0	120	113	3	37.66	2-63	0	0	5.65	0	
Lim		3	3	0	36	22	12.00	0	0	120	113	3	37.66	2-63	0	0	5.65	0	
BEST, T.L.																			
Int		1	1	0	8	8	8.00	0	0	39	50	0					7.69	0	
Lim		1	1	0	8	8	8.00	0	0	39	50	0					7.69	0	
CRANDON, R.T.																			
Int		1	1	0	5	5	5.00	0	0									0	
Lim		1	1	0	5	5	5.00	0	0									0	
DOWLIN, T.M.																			
Int		3	3	0	69	55	23.00	0	1									1	
Lim		3	3	0	69	55	23.00	0	1									1	
FLETCHER, A.D.S.																			
Int		3	3	0	61	54	20.33	0	1									1	
Lim		3	3	0	61	54	20.33	0	1									1	
MILLER, N.O.																			
Int		3	3	1	72	51	36.00	0	1	79	44	2	22.00	2-24	0	0	3.34	0	
Lim		3	3	1	72	51	36.00	0	1	79	44	2	22.00	2-24	0	0	3.34	0	
POWELL, K.O.A.																			
Int		1	1	0	5	5	5.00	0	0									0	
Lim		1	1	0	5	5	5.00	0	0									0	
REIFER, F.L.																			
Int		3	3	0	36	28	12.00	0	0									0	
Lim		3	3	0	36	28	12.00	0	0									0	
RICHARDS, D.M.																			
Int		2	1	0	1	1	1.00	0	0									0	
Lim		2	1	0	1	1	1.00	0	0									0	
ROACH, K.A.J.																			
Int		2	2	0	7	4	3.50	0	0	96	100	3	33.33	2-73	0	0	6.25	0	
Lim		2	2	0	7	4	3.50	0	0	96	100	3	33.33	2-73	0	0	6.25	0	
SAMMY, D.J.G.																			
Int		3	3	0	68	25	22.66	0	0	162	107	1	107.00	1-53	0	0	3.96	0	
Lim		3	3	0	68	25	22.66	0	0	162	107	1	107.00	1-53	0	0	3.96	0	
SMITH, D.S.																			
Int		3	3	0	56	21	18.66	0	0									0	
Lim		3	3	0	56	21	18.66	0	0									0	
TONGE, G.C.																			
Int		3	3	2	9	5	9.00	0	0	180	116	5	23.20	4-25	1	0	3.86	0	
Lim		3	3	2	9	5	9.00	0	0	180	116	5	23.20	4-25	1	0	3.86	0	
WALTON, C.A.K.																			
Int		2	2	0	0	0	0.00	0	0									6	1
Lim		2	2	0	0	0	0.00	0	0									6	1

ZIMBABWE TO SOUTH AFRICA 2009/10

Cmp	Debut	M	I	NO	Runs	HS	Avge	100	50	Balls	Runs	Wkts	Avge	BB	5i	10m	RpO	ct	st
CHIBHABHA, C.J.																			
Int		1	1	0	21	21	21.00	0	0	54	64	1	64.00	1-64	0	0	7.11	0	
Lim		1	1	0	21	21	21.00	0	0	54	64	1	64.00	1-64	0	0	7.11	0	
CHIGUMBURA, E.																			
Int		2	2	0	8	4	4.00	0	0	24	27	0					6.75	1	
Lim		2	2	0	8	4	4.00	0	0	24	27	0					6.75	1	
COVENTRY, C.K.																			
Int		1	1	0	10	10	10.00	0	0									0	
Lim		1	1	0	10	10	10.00	0	0									0	

Cmp Debut	M	I	NO	Runs	HS	Avge	100	50	Balls	Runs	Wkts	Avge	BB	5i	10m	RpO	ct	st
CREMER, A.G.																		
Int	2	2	1	12	11	12.00	0	0	96	88	1	88.00	1-47	0	0	5.50	1	
Lim	2	2	1	12	11	12.00	0	0	96	88	1	88.00	1-47	0	0	5.50	1	
JARVIS, K.M.																		
Int	1	1	0	13	13	13.00	0	0	60	76	0					7.60	0	
Lim	1	1	0	13	13	13.00	0	0	60	76	0					7.60	0	
MASAKADZA, H.																		
Int	2	2	0	11	11	5.50	0	0									1	
Lim	2	2	0	11	11	5.50	0	0									1	
MATSIKENYERI, S.																		
Int	2	2	0	99	86	49.50	0	1	6	8	0					8.00	0	
Lim	2	2	0	99	86	49.50	0	1	6	8	0					8.00	0	
MPOFU, C.B.																		
Int	2	1	1	1	1*		0	0	120	145	0					7.25	1	
Lim	2	1	1	1	1*		0	0	120	145	0					7.25	1	
PRICE, R.W.																		
Int	2	1	0	9	9	9.00	0	0	120	99	6	16.50	3-44	0	0	4.95	0	
Lim	2	1	0	9	9	9.00	0	0	120	99	6	16.50	3-44	0	0	4.95	0	
TAIBU, T.																		
Int	2	2	1	155	103*	155.00	1	1									0	1
Lim	2	2	1	155	103*	155.00	1	1									0	1
TAYLOR, B.R.M.																		
Int	2	2	0	2	2	1.00	0	0									0	
Lim	2	2	0	2	2	1.00	0	0									0	
UTSEYA, P.																		
Int	2	1	0	1	1	1.00	0	0	120	112	2	56.00	2-53	0	0	5.60	0	
Lim	2	1	0	1	1	1.00	0	0	120	112	2	56.00	2-53	0	0	5.60	0	
VERMEULEN, M.A.																		
Int	1	1	0	8	8	8.00	0	0									3	
Lim	1	1	0	8	8	8.00	0	0									3	

SRI LANKA

Premier Championship winners 2009/10 (first-class): Chilaw Marians
Iner-Provincial Tournament winners 2009/10 (first-class); Basnahira North and Basnahira South shared
Premier Limited Overs Tournament winners 2009/10 (limited overs): Tamil Union
Inter-Provincial Limited Overs Tournament winners 2009/10 (limited overs): Kandurata
Inter-Provincial Twenty20 Tournament winners 2009/10 (twenty20): Wayamba

2009/10 AND CAREER RECORDS FOR SRI LANKAN PLAYERS

Cmp	*Debut*	*M*	*I*	*NO*	*Runs*	*HS*	*Avge*	*100*	*50*	*Balls*	*Runs*	*Wkts*	*Avge*	*BB*	*5i*	*10m*	*RpO*	*ct*	*st*
ABEYDEERA, Ruchintha Dunilkumara (Singha) b Colombo 28.9.1984 RHB SLA																			
FC		5	9	4	98	47	19.60	0	0	747	386	19	20.31	4-46	0	0	3.10	3	
Lim		2	2	1	13	9	13.00	0	0	120	80	4	20.00	2-31	0	0	4.00	1	
FC	2005/06	18	26	11	225	47	15.00	0	0	2106	1078	49	22.00	5-50	2	0	3.07	9	
Lim	2004/05	27	14	3	68	15	6.18	0	0	1098	736	38	19.36	5-20	0	1	4.02	12	
20T	2005/06	7	4	2	28	13*	14.00	0	0	132	106	13	8.15	4-19	1	0	4.81	3	
ABEYKOON, Muthukuda Walawwe Yasitha Prabodha (Burgher) b Colombo 12.5.1990 LHB LFM																			
FC		1	2	1	15	15*	15.00	0	0	114	87	1	87.00	1-26	0	0	4.57	0	
Lim		3	3	1	16	15*	8.00	0	0	126	110	2	55.00	1-50	0	0	5.23	1	
ABEYRATNE, Ganewattage Nilakshan (Saracens) b Batticaloa 3.9.1979 RHB OB																			
FC		11	17	0	381	76	22.41	0	3									8	
Lim		4	4	0	60	37	15.00	0	0									0	
FC	1999/00	55	87	2	1737	79	20.43	0	9	36	22	0					3.66	46	
Lim	1999/00	37	32	2	472	55*	15.73	0	2	7	10	0					8.57	14	
20T	2005/06	9	9	1	167	63*	20.87	0	1									0	
ABEYRATNE, Jerad Prashan Malinda (Police) b Homagama 11.10.1982 LHB LB																			
FC		4	6	0	179	47	29.83	0	0									1	
Lim		1	1	0	6	6	6.00	0	0									0	
FC	2002/03	18	29	1	582	51	20.78	0	1	90	63	2	31.50	1-3	0	0	4.20	13	
Lim	2007/08	14	12	0	306	57	25.50	0	2									0	
ABEYRATNE, Wegamuwage Thamara (Lankan) b Panadura 21.9.1978 RHB OB																			
FC		9	13	1	384	67	32.00	0	2	1384	715	35	20.42	5-47	2	0	3.10	9	
Lim		8	7	1	43	17	7.16	0	0	293	177	8	22.12	3-33	0	0	3.62	0	
FC	2000/01	73	115	19	1847	67	19.23	0	5	7018	3625	129	28.10	6-48	5	0	3.09	49	
Lim	2000/01	63	51	11	639	70	15.97	0	1	1998	1193	67	17.80	5-19	3	1	3.58	18	
20T	2004/05	4	2	0	3	3	1.50	0	0	43	25	4	6.25	3-9	0	0	3.48	3	
ABEYSINGHE, Eshan Sanija (Saracens) b Colombo 29.7.1983 LHB SLA																			
FC		2	4	0	38	21	9.50	0	0									0	
Lim		2	2	0	13	9	6.50	0	0	6	7	1	7.00	1-7	0	0	7.00	2	
FC	2001/02	23	45	5	933	83	23.32	0	6	90	37	1	37.00	1-24	0	0	2.46	9	
Lim	2003/04	17	16	1	208	35*	13.86	0	0	6	7	1	7.00	1-7	0	0	7.00	6	
20T	2006/07	1	1	0	12	12	12.00	0	0									0	
ABEYWARDENE, Sanjeewa Roshan (Sebastianites) b Panadura 4.10.1982 RHB SLA																			
FC		4	7	2	51	15*	10.20	0	0	159	68	4	17.00	2-10	0	0	2.56	4	
Lim		1								12	17	0					8.50	1	
FC	2000/01	54	85	26	858	62	14.54	0	1	4754	2647	86	30.77	5-43	2	0	3.34	32	
Lim	2002/03	34	26	7	216	23	11.36	0	0	1106	808	36	22.44	4-45	1	0	4.38	12	
20T	2004/05	6	5	1	39	24	9.75	0	0	101	143	13	11.00	6-15	0	1	8.49	2	
ALLES, Hettiarachchige Surath Hemantha (Seeduwa Raddoluwa) b Colombo 10.11.1976 RHB RM																			
FC		3	3	1	16	8	8.00	0	0	210	108	3	36.00	2-56	0	0	3.08	1	
Lim		2	2	0	19	19	9.50	0	0	90	58	4	14.50	3-42	0	0	3.86	1	
FC	1995/96	72	84	30	811	61	15.01	0	3	6393	3303	152	21.73	7-90	6	0	3.10	37	
Lim	1999/00	22	14	7	84	19	12.00	0	0	768	485	29	16.72	3-16	0	0	3.78	2	
ALWIS, Waduthantrige Geeth Rasanga Kumarasiri (Ruhuna, Saracens) b Colombo 21.2.1987 LHB SLA																			
FC		15	23	1	1016	219	46.18	3	4	1513	696	25	27.84	6-36	1	0	2.76	4	
Lim		9	9	0	231	73	25.66	0	2	286	207	8	25.87	3-32	0	0	4.34	4	
20T		1	1	1	2	2*		0	0	10	17	1	17.00	1-17	0	0	10.20	0	
FC	2007/08	33	53	3	1877	219	37.54	4	10	3104	1426	56	25.46	6-36	1	0	2.75	11	
Lim	2007/08	25	25	0	678	90	27.12	0	6	1015	653	24	27.20	3-23	0	0	3.86	6	
ALWITIGALA, Kaniksha Gihan (Colts, Kandurata) b Homagama 7.6.1986 RHB RMF																			
FC		5	4	0	73	50	18.25	0	1	661	451	11	41.00	2-39	0	0	4.09	7	
Lim		3	1	1	4	4*		0	0	90	85	1	85.00	1-23	0	0	5.66	0	
20T		1								24	35	1	35.00	1-35	0	0	8.75	0	
FC	2007/08	16	18	1	226	60	13.29	0	2	1629	963	31	31.06	3-41	0	0	3.54	14	
Lim	2008/09	9	4	1	9	5	3.00	0	0	306	280	6	46.66	2-41	0	0	5.49	2	

Cmp	Debut	M	I	NO	Runs	HS	Avge	100	50	Balls	Runs	Wkts	Avge	BB	5i	10m	RpO	ct	st
AMERASINGHE, Merenna Koralage Don Ishara (Colts) b Colombo 5.3.1978 RHB RFM																			
FC		2	3	2	24	11*	24.00	0	0	175	110	4	27.50	3-38	0	0	3.77	1	
Lim		2								84	86	2	43.00	2-55	0	0	6.14	0	
Test	2007/08	1	2	2	0	0*		0	0	150	105	1	105.00	1-62	0	0	4.20	0	
FC	1997/98	99	104	57	324	46	6.89	0	0	11755	5917	246	24.05	5-12	7	1	3.02	30	
Int	2007	8	4	4	6	5*		0	0	426	363	9	40.33	3-44	0	0	5.11	1	
Lim	1998/99	76	22	16	40	5*	6.66	0	0	3031	2300	93	24.73	5-44	2	1	4.55	10	
20T	2005/06	4	2	2	4	2*		0	0	78	83	2	41.50	1-14	0	0	6.38	1	
ANAND, Subramanian (Badureliya) b Madras (now Chennai), Tamil Nadu, India 14.1.1986 RHB LBG																			
FC		3	6	0	98	24	16.33	0	0	36	33	0					5.50	5	
Lim		4	3	0	67	56	22.33	0	1	72	71	6	11.83	4-36	1	0	5.91	4	
ANANDA, Rathabalage Lasanka Sampath (Singha) b Colombo 23.1.1983 RHB RFM																			
Lim		3	3	2	1	1	1.00	0	0	60	47	1	47.00	1-26	0	0	4.70	0	
FC	2003/04	2	2	1	1	1	1.00	0	0	42	39	0					5.57	0	
Lim	2003/04	8	7	6	11	5*	11.00	0	0	217	178	6	29.66	2-14	0	0	4.92	0	
ARAVINDA, Udage Kankanamalage Dilshan (Moratuwa) b Anamaduwa 1.7.1984 LHB WK																			
FC		9	12	0	267	79	22.25	0	1	648	240	7	34.28	2-6	0	0	2.22	2	
Lim		9	9	0	316	76	35.11	0	2	300	203	11	18.45	4-36	1	0	4.06	4	
FC	2005/06	18	27	0	536	88	19.85	0	3	750	271	8	33.87	2-6	0	0	2.16	11	3
Lim	2003/04	19	19	0	432	76	22.73	0	2	300	203	11	18.45	4-36	1	0	4.06	4	
20T	2006/07	1	1	0	0	0	0.00	0	0									0	
ARIYASINGHE, Bulatwatte Munasinghe Dewagedarage Thiina Dasun (Lankan) b Piliyandala 7.12.1985 LHB																			
FC		4	7	0	166	56	23.71	0	2	60	26	2	13.00	2-17	0	0	2.60	3	
Lim		6	6	0	57	18	9.50	0	0	24	15	0					3.75	1	
FC	2006/07	20	37	3	860	76*	25.29	0	6	366	191	6	31.83	2-17	0	0	3.13	12	1
Lim	2006/07	20	19	1	193	26	10.72	0	0	36	20	1	20.00	1-5	0	0	3.33	2	
20T	2006/07	3	3	0	41	28	13.66	0	0	18	24	0					8.00	0	
ARNOLDA, Duncan Fredrick (Badureliya) b Kandy 17.1.1975 RHB RM																			
FC		5	5	0	46	19	9.20	0	0	258	172	7	24.57	5-64	1	0	4.00	1	
Lim		6	5	1	48	25	12.00	0	0	197	142	9	15.77	2-23	0	0	4.32	2	
FC	1994/95	110	153	13	3164	129*	22.60	1	16	6291	3903	149	26.19	5-64	3	0	3.72	86	
Lim	1998/99	54	48	8	931	89	23.27	0	3	1255	1089	44	24.75	4-41	1	0	5.20	13	
20T	2004/05	8	8	3	78	18*	15.60	0	0	60	80	8	10.00	4-18	1	0	8.00	5	
ARUMATHANTHRI, Binara Yohan (Saracens) b Galle 18.11.1982 LHB OB																			
Lim		1	1	0	17	17	17.00	0	0									0	
FC	2002/03	22	42	1	1077	101	26.26	1	7	621	299	8	37.37	4-12	0	0	2.88	8	
Lim	2005/06	10	10	1	178	60	19.77	0	1	18	21	0					7.00	3	
20T	2005/06	1	1	0	0	0	0.00	0	0									0	
ASKER, Mohamed Azkar Mohamed (Burgher) b Ragama 13.12.1986 LHB SLA																			
FC		2	4	1	86	75*	28.66	0	1									1	3
Lim		5	5	0	78	61	15.60	0	1									5	
ATHUKORALA, Athukorala Arachchige Chatura Eranga (Burgher) b Akmeemana 6.7.1984 LHB RMF																			
FC		7	9	1	100	38	12.50	0	0	1015	584	33	17.69	7-78	2	1	3.45	2	
Lim		3	3	1	21	14*	10.50	0	0	136	102	2	51.00	1-25	0	0	4.50	0	
FC	2005/06	28	36	11	496	79*	19.84	0	3	3193	1792	85	21.08	7-21	4	2	3.36	13	
Lim	2004/05	25	12	4	92	23	11.50	0	0	977	695	30	23.16	5-55	1	1	4.26	5	
20T	2004/05	2	2	1	7	4*	7.00	0	0	24	40	0					10.00	1	
ATHULATHMUDALI, Don Nisitha Amal (Basnahira North, Chilaw Marians) b Colombo 21.1.1987 LHB RFM																			
FC		9	14	0	428	153	30.57	1	2	30	15	0					3.00	8	
Lim		13	13	0	372	80	28.61	0	3	36	42	0					7.00	3	
20T		3	3	0	77	38	25.66	0	0									0	
FC	2007/08	20	35	1	1023	153	30.08	1	6	30	15	0					3.00	13	
Lim	2007/08	28	28	0	758	80	27.07	0	5	48	52	0					6.50	10	
20T	2007/08	11	11	0	234	38	21.27	0	0									2	
ATTANAYAKE, Tharindu Prabashwara (Badureliya) b Colombo 29.5.1986 RHB RS																			
FC		9	13	1	432	113	36.00	1	2	42	13	0					1.85	4	
FC	2006/07	18	28	2	692	113	26.61	1	2	72	35	0					2.91	10	
Lim	2006/07	7	5	1	41	21*	10.25	0	0	6	8	0					8.00	5	
BAGAI, Ashish (Canada, Canada to Netherlands, Canada to Sri Lanka, Canada to United Arab Emirates, Canada to West Indies, Ragama) b Delhi, India 26.1.1982 RHB WK																			
FC		1	2	0	13	9	6.50	0	0									0	
Lim		2	2	0	76	75	38.00	0	1									1	1
I20T		2	2	0	95	53	47.50	0	1									0	
20T		3	3	0	120	53	40.00	0	1									0	
FC	2004	13	25	1	749	93	31.20	0	6	27	28	0					6.22	29	3
Int	2002/03	54	53	7	1736	137*	37.73	2	14									48	10
Lim	1999/00	86	84	11	2374	137*	32.52	2	18									82	20
I20T	2008	7	7	1	169	53	28.16	0	1									3	4
20T	2008	11	11	2	300	53	33.33	0	2									4	4

Cmp	Debut	M	I	NO	Runs	HS	Avge	100	50	Balls	Runs	Wkts	Avge	BB	5i	10m	RpO	ct	st
BAIDWAN, Harvir Singh (Canada, Canada to Netherlands, Canada to Sri Lanka, Canada to United Arab Emirates, Canada to West Indies, Colts) b Chandigarh, Punjab, India 31.7.1987 RHB RM																			
FC		5	1	0	0	0	0.00	0	0	368	147	6	24.50	4-16	0	0	2.39	0	
Lim		4	2	1	10	8*	10.00	0	0	219	151	5	30.20	2-20	0	0	4.13	0	
I20T		2								47	61	4	15.25	3-23	0	0	7.78	1	
20T		3								65	78	4	19.50	3-23	0	0	7.20	1	
Int	2008	19	11	5	147	33	24.50	0	0	942	759	24	31.62	3-24	0	0	4.83	4	
Lim	2008	32	18	7	233	38*	21.18	0	0	1401	1144	34	33.64	3-24	0	0	4.89	8	
I20T	2008	11	6	2	6	4*	1.50	0	0	203	245	19	12.89	4-19	1	0	7.24	5	
20T	2008	15	9	2	9	4*	1.28	0	0	276	348	20	17.40	4-19	1	0	7.56	6	
BALASOORIYA, Balasooriya Arachilage Damith (Sri Lanka Army) b Kandy 15.7.1982 RHB OB																			
FC		1	2	2	10	9*		0	0	48	35	1	35.00	1-35	0	0	4.37	0	
Lim		9	8	0	51	14	6.37	0	0	450	248	12	20.66	3-21	0	0	3.30	1	
FC	2006/07	11	19	4	283	59	18.86	0	1	811	429	17	25.23	4-49	0	0	3.17	3	
Lim	2006/07	19	18	2	142	27	8.87	0	0	816	500	18	27.77	3-21	0	0	3.67	3	
20T	2006/07	3	3	0	9	7	3.00	0	0	28	25	3	8.33	2-23	0	0	5.35	0	
BANDARA, Ambahera Mudiyanselage Charith Madushanka Kumara (Police) b Kandy 21.6.1986 LHB LMF																			
FC		4	4	1	48	30*	16.00	0	0	367	234	7	33.42	3-57	0	0	3.82	0	
FC	2007/08	7	9	3	91	32	15.16	0	0	607	385	11	35.00	3-57	0	0	3.80	3	
BANDARA, Herath Mudiyanselage Charitha Malinga (Basnahira South, Ragama, Kent, Sri Lanka to Bangladesh) b Kalutara 31.12.1979 RHB LBG																			
FC		15	21	3	407	108	22.61	1	1	1880	1029	55	18.70	7-74	3	0	3.28	2	
Lim		14	13	6	224	59*	32.00	0	1	619	517	17	30.41	4-19	1	0	5.01	2	
20T		6	3	3	27	15*		0	0	141	195	8	24.37	3-27	0	0	8.29	1	
Test	1998	8	11	3	124	43	15.50	0	0	1152	633	16	39.56	3-84	0	0	3.29	4	
FC	1996/97	150	214	45	3415	108	20.20	1	14	20992	10943	432	25.33	8-49	14	2	3.12	95	
Int	2005/06	31	17	4	160	31	12.30	0	0	1470	1232	36	34.22	4-31	2	0	5.02	9	
Lim	1998	129	87	28	1005	64	17.03	0	2	5456	4284	181	23.66	5-22	7	4	4.71	38	
I20T	2006/07	4	3	1	12	7	6.00	0	0	84	96	4	24.00	3-32	0	0	6.85	1	
20T	2005/06	36	19	8	126	31*	11.45	0	0	717	903	41	22.02	3-14	0	0	7.55	8	
BANDARATILLEKE, Mapa Rallalage Chandima Niroshan (Badureliya) b Colombo 16.5.1975 RHB SLA																			
FC		11	14	1	214	52	16.46	0	1	1139	601	20	30.05	6-65	1	0	3.16	8	
Lim		6	5	1	34	19*	8.50	0	0	257	144	6	24.00	3-35	0	0	3.36	1	
Test	1998	7	9	1	93	25	11.62	0	0	1722	698	23	30.34	5-36	1	0	2.43	0	
FC	1993/94	177	230	33	3624	80	18.39	0	17	28363	12190	573	21.27	8-78	28	2	2.57	113	
Int	1998	3	1	0	0	0	0.00	0	0	144	111	2	55.50	2-34	0	0	4.62	0	
Lim	1993/94	90	52	15	594	44*	16.05	0	0	4003	2417	95	25.44	4-13	1	0	3.62	25	
20T	2005/06	2	2	0	8	7	4.00	0	0	48	57	4	14.25	3-19	0	0	7.12	1	
BERENGER, Andri Raffaelo (Sri Lanka Cricket Combined XI) b Colombo 29.8.1991 RHB WK																			
Lim		3	3	0	39	20	13.00	0	0									5	
20T		1	1	0	0	0	0.00	0	0									0	
FC	2008/09	1	2	0	17	17	8.50	0	0									0	
Lim	2008/09	4	4	0	65	26	16.25	0	0									6	
BODHISHA, Pathiranage Kasun (Panadura) b Matara 13.9.1985 LHB SLA																			
FC		8	10	0	298	74	29.80	0	2	222	131	4	32.75	4-88	0	0	3.54	9	
Lim		8	8	1	319	87	45.57	0	3	66	38	0					3.45	2	
FC	2004/05	40	66	4	1867	226*	30.11	3	9	1835	935	29	32.24	4-88	0	0	3.05	25	
Lim	2004/05	35	33	2	865	87	27.90	0	6	1044	696	31	22.45	7-14	1	1	4.00	10	
20T	2004/05	10	8	0	48	23	6.00	0	0	199	257	7	36.71	2-21	0	0	7.74	3	
BORALESSA, Sohan Chinthaka de Silva (Basnahira North, Colombo) b Riyadh, Saudi Arabia 6.8.1985 RHB SLA																			
FC		14	16	7	136	27*	15.11	0	0	2346	1326	72	18.41	9-47	3	1	3.39	4	
Lim		3	2	1	6	4	6.00	0	0	60	43	1	43.00	1-43	0	0	4.30	1	
FC	2004/05	29	36	10	391	45*	15.03	0	0	4309	2417	117	20.65	9-47	5	1	3.36	5	
Lim	2005/06	10	6	2	31	9	7.75	0	0	268	234	11	21.27	5-35	0	1	5.23	1	
BOTEJU, Jayawardene Welathanthrige Hemantha Devapriya (Lankan) b Colombo 3.11.1977 RHB RM																			
FC		9	13	0	349	77	26.84	0	3	96	44	1	44.00	1-15	0	0	2.75	4	
Lim		8	8	1	144	43	20.57	0	0	90	53	3	17.66	2-28	0	0	3.53	5	
FC	1995/96	114	169	17	4267	108	28.07	4	27	7935	3640	172	21.16	5-18	3	0	2.75	67	
Int	1998/99	2	2	1	3	2	3.00	0	0	102	113	0					6.64	1	
Lim	1996/97	86	62	11	1272	102*	24.94	1	3	2103	1525	66	23.10	4-24	3	0	4.35	26	
20T	2004/05	9	8	1	117	32	16.71	0	0									4	
BOTEJU, Welathanthrige Kanishka Chathuranga (Sebastianites) b Colombo 11.4.1988 LHB OB																			
FC		1	2	1	11	11	11.00	0	0	66	55	1	55.00	1-16	0	0	5.00	0	
FC	2008/09	3	4	2	17	11	8.50	0	0	210	131	3	43.66	2-26	0	0	3.74	2	
Lim	2008/09	6	3	2	14	8	14.00	0	0	186	113	3	37.66	1-25	0	0	3.64	2	
BOWALA, Dhanushka Shohan Praveen Bandara (Ragama) b Colombo 25.1.1985 RHB RMF																			
FC		1	2	0	0	0	0.00	0	0	84	87	2	43.50	1-5	0	0	6.21	0	
Lim		2	2	0	2	2	1.00	0	0	54	60	0					6.66	0	
FC	2004/05	3	4	0	18	13	4.50	0	0	252	206	6	34.33	2-46	0	0	4.90	0	
Lim	2005/06	4	2	0	2	2	1.00	0	0	120	102	3	34.00	2-18	0	0	5.10	0	

Cmp	Debut	M	I	NO	Runs	HS	Avge	100	50	Balls	Runs	Wkts	Avge	BB	5i	10m	RpO	ct	st
BUDDIKA, Muthukumarana Landage Rumesh (Ragama, Sri Lanka Cricket Combined XI) b Matara 14.11.1990 LHB OB																			
Lim		7	7	0	150	94	21.42	0	1	144	114	5	22.80	2-23	0	0	4.75	4	
20T		4	4	0	62	25	15.50	0	0	22	39	0					10.63	0	
BULATHWALA, Bulathwalage Weranga Kasun Sanjeewa (Sri Lanka Air Force) b Kurunegala 2.1.1988 RHB RMF																			
FC		1	2	0	26	16	13.00	0	0									1	
CHAMARA, Delwala Bandulage Nuwan (Burgher) b Colombo 29.4.1983 LHB RM																			
Lim		1								36	35	1	35.00	1-35	0	0	5.83	1	
Lim	2008/09	2	1	1	0	0*		0	0	78	81	2	40.50	1-35	0	0	6.23	2	
CHAMARA, Palagasinghe Kodithuwakku Arachchige Tasitha (Nondescripts) b Matara 29.10.1986 RHB OB																			
FC		1	1	0	8	8	8.00	0	0	12	16	0					8.00	0	
Lim		2								36	26	2	13.00	2-26	0	0	4.33	0	
CHAMIKA, Sattambi (Sri Lanka Navy) b Galle 2.10.1985 RHB RFM																			
FC		9	13	0	139	70	10.69	0	1	705	490	18	27.22	5-58	2	0	4.17	5	
Lim		7	6	0	37	17	6.16	0	0	283	281	13	21.61	5-38	0	1	5.95	1	
CHANAKA, Payagala Udawattage Manoj (Panadura) b Panadura 17.11.1984 RHB RFM																			
FC		5	7	1	85	24	14.16	0	0	372	239	9	26.55	4-58	0	0	3.85	0	
Lim		4	3	0	36	22	12.00	0	0	90	92	0					6.13	2	
FC	2000/01	35	46	17	268	24	9.24	0	0	3354	2328	77	30.23	4-29	0	0	4.16	11	
Lim	2002/03	28	13	3	62	22	6.20	0	0	850	746	12	62.16	3-33	0	0	5.26	4	
20T	2004/05	15	5	2	12	7	4.00	0	0	288	344	20	17.20	4-35	1	0	7.16	1	
CHANDIMAL, Lokuge Dinesh (Nondescripts, Ruhuna, Sri Lanka A, Sri Lanka Board President's XI, Sri Lanka to United States of America, Sri Lanka to West Indies, Sri Lanka to Zimbabwe, Sri Lanka A to Australia) b Balapitiya 18.11.1989 RHB WK																			
FC		18	26	3	1365	244	59.34	4	5	6	1	0					1.00	34	6
Lim		21	20	2	429	90	23.83	0	4									16	
20T		7	7	1	320	75	53.33	0	3									6	1
FC	2009	22	33	3	1634	244	54.46	5	7	6	1	0					1.00	36	6
Int	2010	4	4	2	143	111	71.50	1	0									4	1
Lim	2009	30	29	4	702	111	28.08	1	5									27	1
I20T	2010	4	3	0	57	29	19.00	0	0									0	
20T	2007/08	22	21	1	586	75	29.30	0	3									13	2
CHANDRAKUMARA, Pahalage Don Gamini (Colombo) b Colombo 6.5.1983 RHB RFM																			
FC		5	5	0	63	30	12.60	0	0	282	128	4	32.00	3-49	0	0	2.72	0	
Lim		11	9	4	147	36*	29.40	0	0	290	204	10	20.40	2-21	0	0	4.22	4	
FC	2001/02	46	69	10	1115	81	18.89	0	3	3566	1933	82	23.57	5-23	1	0	3.25	15	
Lim	2003/04	43	37	7	401	39*	13.36	0	0	1431	927	38	24.39	5-25	0	1	3.88	11	
20T	2004/05	7	7	3	123	45*	30.75	0	0	118	182	4	45.50	1-21	0	0	9.25	0	
CHANDRAN, Poovathingal Shijit (Sebastianites) b Ambattur, Tamil Nadu, India 11.12.1986 RHB OB																			
FC		3	5	0	75	39	15.00	0	0	18	14	0					4.66	0	
Lim		3	3	0	49	29	16.33	0	0	6	11	0					11.00	0	
CHANDRASEKARA, Kuruppu Appuhamilage Pubudu Dharshana (Tamil Union) b Colombo 17.4.1981 LHB OB																			
Lim		1	1	0	6	6	6.00	0	0									0	
CHANDRASIRI, Hewa Kahakandage Don Vindika Nadeera (Sri Lanka Navy) b Ragama 28.1.1988 LHB RMF																			
FC		6	11	2	216	46	24.00	0	0	96	79	2	39.50	1-13	0	0	4.93	6	
Lim		4	4	0	61	31	15.25	0	0	66	69	3	23.00	2-20	0	0	6.27	0	
CHANUKA, Embulawala Walawwe Yashira (Seeduwa Raddoluwa) b Kandy 29.3.1989 LHB RMF																			
FC		1	2	1	3	3	3.00	0	0	42	34	0					4.85	0	
Lim		2	2	1	28	18	28.00	0	0	72	53	2	26.50	2-34	0	0	4.41	0	
CHATURANGA, Jasinthuliyana Umega (Moors) b Galle 3.6.1984 LHB SLA																			
FC		7	8	5	27	10*	9.00	0	0	505	339	12	28.25	5-45	1	0	4.02	0	
Lim		4	1	0	0	0	0.00	0	0	168	84	9	9.33	6-24	0	1	3.00	1	
FC	2005/06	11	15	8	37	10*	5.28	0	0	1046	646	20	32.30	5-45	1	0	3.70	2	
Lim	2006/07	5	1	0	0	0	0.00	0	0	186	103	9	11.44	6-24	0	1	3.32	1	
CHRISTOPHER, Kaburawala Withanage Gayas (Sri Lanka Navy) b Negombo 4.2.1987 RHB LB																			
FC		4	8	0	167	55	20.87	0	2									1	
Lim		1	1	0	0	0	0.00	0	0									0	
COORAY, Malith Lalitha (Sebastianites) b Galle 30.1.1990 RHB RFM																			
FC		5	7	0	124	52	17.71	0	1	228	142	5	28.40	3-16	0	0	3.73	1	
Lim		1	1	0	51	51	51.00	0	1									0	
20T	2008/09	3	3	0	5	5	1.66	0	0	29	59	0					12.20	1	
COORAY, Manampeli Mahapatabandiralalage Dinesh Ranga (Panadura) b Kalutara 1.3.1987 RHB RM																			
FC		6	7	0	192	51	27.42	0	1	162	52	2	26.00	2-1	0	0	1.92	4	
Lim		10	10	1	211	56	23.44	0	1	276	169	9	18.77	4-12	1	0	3.67	6	
FC	2008/09	10	13	0	448	92	34.46	0	3	288	128	3	42.66	2-1	0	0	2.66	5	
Lim	2008/09	19	19	1	466	67	25.88	0	3	402	282	16	17.62	4-12	2	0	4.20	8	
COORAY, Muthuthantrige Nilantha Rohana (Panadura) b Moratuwa 20.11.1978 RHB LB																			
FC		9	11	0	202	56	18.36	0	1	1059	504	20	25.20	5-65	1	0	2.85	4	
Lim		6	5	2	135	40*	45.00	0	0	240	186	13	14.30	5-31	0	1	4.65	2	
FC	1998/99	85	133	12	2529	139	20.90	1	13	7163	3469	167	20.77	6-34	5	0	2.90	51	
Lim	1999/00	64	56	11	1149	107*	25.53	1	5	1426	1038	55	18.87	5-31	2	2	4.36	25	
20T	2005/06	5	3	0	57	37	19.00	0	0	54	79	2	39.50	1-14	0	0	8.77	1	

Cmp	Debut	M	I	NO	Runs	HS	Avge	100	50	Balls	Runs	Wkts	Avge	BB	5i	10m	RpO	ct	st
COORAY, Nawalage Harsha Gihan (Chilaw Marians, Ruhuna) b Colombo 23.11.1983 RHB OB WK																			
FC		14	20	3	648	89	38.11	0	6	30	24	0					4.80	13	5
Lim		1	1	1	4	4*		0	0									2	1
FC	2005/06	49	83	10	1995	114	27.32	3	9	480	333	7	47.57	3-17	0	0	4.16	48	8
Lim	2005/06	10	10	2	95	27*	11.87	0	0	48	33	3	11.00	3-33	0	0	4.12	6	1
20T	2005/06	4	3	0	64	38	21.33	0	0	24	55	0					13.75	4	
COORAY, Pestheruweliyanralalage Dilhan Mario Anthony (Burgher) b Colombo 10.3.1987 RHB LB																			
FC		4	7	1	177	60	29.50	0	2	12	9	0					4.50	2	
Lim		3	3	0	64	38	21.33	0	0	30	19	1	19.00	1-19	0	0	3.80	0	
FC	2006/07	18	31	3	578	67	20.64	0	5	43	42	2	21.00	1-9	0	0	5.86	13	
Lim	2006/07	11	10	1	128	38	14.22	0	0	55	56	2	28.00	1-19	0	0	6.10	3	
DAHANAYAKE, Demintha Harshan (Saracens, Sri Lanka Cricket Combined XI) b Kandy 19.9.1986 RHB OB																			
FC		8	11	1	149	66*	14.90	0	1	18	21	0					7.00	5	
Lim		11	11	1	328	76	32.80	0	2	222	167	9	18.55	4-31	1	0	4.51	3	
20T		4	3	0	63	25	21.00	0	0	90	90	5	18.00	2-12	0	0	6.00	0	
FC	2006/07	10	15	1	156	66*	11.14	0	1	96	102	1	102.00	1-52	0	0	6.37	5	
Lim	2008/09	13	13	1	354	76	29.50	0	2	222	167	9	18.55	4-31	1	0	4.51	3	
20T	2006/07	5	4	1	64	25	21.33	0	0	105	112	6	18.66	2-12	0	0	6.40	0	
DANANJAYA, Rankoth Gedara Krishan Dinidu (Panadura) b Panadura 3.6.1990 RHB RFM																			
FC		2	3	1	33	17*	16.50	0	0									1	
Lim		2	2	1	52	33	52.00	0	0									0	
DANIEL, Gerald Ian (Ragama, Ruhuna) b Colombo 17.8.1981 RHB RM																			
FC		12	19	2	415	52	24.41	0	3	93	49	2	24.50	2-25	0	0	3.16	3	
Lim		5	5	0	129	55	25.80	0	1	24	30	1	30.00	1-12	0	0	7.50	0	
FC	1999/00	136	232	14	6854	165	31.44	14	31	1783	830	38	21.84	5-19	2	0	2.79	83	
Lim	1999/00	76	75	8	1859	82*	27.74	0	13	257	196	5	39.20	2-13	0	0	4.57	24	
20T	2004/05	6	5	1	21	10	5.25	0	0									3	
DARSHANAPRIYA, Thawalampolage Dinesh Daminda (Basnahira North, Ragama, Sri Lanka A to Australia) b Ragama 23.10.1983 RHB RMF																			
FC		11	10	1	99	56*	11.00	0	1	1180	699	32	21.84	6-71	2	0	3.55	9	
Lim		7	5	0	18	12	3.60	0	0	288	240	9	26.66	3-41	0	0	5.00	1	
20T		3								66	73	3	24.33	2-19	0	0	6.63	0	
FC	2004/05	40	47	14	438	64*	13.27	0	2	5048	2869	126	22.76	8-51	7	1	3.41	15	
Lim	2004/05	27	19	4	89	28*	5.93	0	0	1090	891	35	25.45	4-31	1	0	4.90	4	
20T	2004/05	11	4	0	18	7	4.50	0	0	210	284	13	21.84	2-17	0	0	8.11	3	
DAWOOD, Mohamed Farhan Hussain (Burgher) b Colombo 30.3.1987 RHB WK																			
FC		2	4	0	81	34	20.25	0	0									0	
Lim		1	1	0	8	8	8.00	0	0									0	
FC	2007/08	7	13	0	281	43	21.61	0	0									8	
Lim	2007/08	7	7	3	119	62	29.75	0	1									10	
DE ALWIS, Wathuthantrige Buddika (Sri Lanka Navy) b Colombo 21.12.1990 LHB LBG																			
Lim		1	1	0	1	1	1.00	0	0									0	
DE MEL, Widanalage Pathum Dhanushka (Moratuwa) b Colombo 23.8.1985 RHB RM																			
FC		8	9	1	95	19*	11.87	0	0	670	330	13	25.38	3-35	0	0	2.95	2	
Lim		9	8	1	69	32	9.85	0	0	363	286	11	26.00	3-23	0	0	4.72	2	
FC	2007/08	17	23	4	241	38*	12.68	0	0	1477	828	26	31.84	3-35	0	0	3.36	4	
Lim	2007/08	19	18	2	164	32	10.25	0	0	699	605	15	40.33	3-23	0	0	5.19	2	
20T	2005/06	1	1	0	26	26	26.00	0	0	18	16	2	8.00	2-16	0	0	5.33	1	
DE SARAM, Siriwardene Dhanushka (Lankan) b Colombo 22.5.1985 LHB RFM																			
FC		1	2	0	27	27	13.50	0	0	12	9	0					4.50	0	
Lim		4	4	0	76	28	19.00	0	0	54	33	0					3.66	1	
FC	2006/07	9	15	1	208	99	14.85	0	1	558	418	9	46.44	4-74	0	0	4.49	0	
Lim	2007/08	15	14	0	298	65	21.28	0	1	462	335	12	27.91	3-38	0	0	4.35	3	
20T	2006/07	2	2	0	1	1	0.50	0	0	42	69	1	69.00	1-31	0	0	9.85	1	
DE SARAM, Samantha Indika (Ragama, Ruhuna, Sylhet) b Matara 2.9.1973 RHB OB																			
FC		9	16	3	691	119*	53.15	2	4	438	242	4	60.50	2-92	0	0	3.31	14	
Lim		15	14	0	442	76	31.57	0	4	204	116	4	29.00	1-3	0	0	3.41	6	
20T		7	6	1	62	19	12.40	0	0									2	
Test	1999/00	4	5	0	117	39	23.40	0	0									1	
FC	1990/91	182	292	21	10585	237	39.05	22	60	913	528	8	66.00	2-92	0	0	3.47	189	8
Int	1999	15	13	2	183	38	16.63	0	0									9	
Lim	1993/94	149	137	9	3704	138	28.93	3	24	436	304	9	33.77	2-5	0	0	4.18	50	1
I20T	2008/09	1																1	
20T	2004/05	30	27	6	631	94	30.04	0	3	30	50	4	12.50	4-34	1	0	10.00	17	2
DE SILVA, Batuwatta Gamage Yahampath Maduranga (Police) b Colombo 23.4.1981 LHB LB																			
FC		2	3	1	14	12	7.00	0	0	257	163	3	54.33	2-67	0	0	3.80	1	
DE SILVA, Chethan Dulara (Bloomfield) b Colombo 25.9.1989 LHB WK																			
FC		4	6	0	60	23	10.00	0	0									13	
FC	2006/07	5	8	1	69	23	9.85	0	0									15	

Cmp	Debut	M	I	NO	Runs	HS	Avge	100	50	Balls	Runs	Wkts	Avge	BB	5i	10m	RpO	ct	st
DE SILVA, Ellawala Kankanamalage Yasith Aravinda (Sri Lanka Air Force) b Colombo 15.6.1987 LHB OB																			
FC		2	3	0	14	8	4.66	0	0	36	27	1	27.00	1-20	0	0	4.50	1	
Lim		5	4	0	22	11	5.50	0	0	162	112	2	56.00	2-20	0	0	4.14	1	
FC	2008/09	9	15	2	217	64	16.69	0	1	867	510	21	24.28	3-23	0	0	3.52	2	
Lim	2008/09	13	11	0	90	24	8.18	0	0	308	220	9	24.44	3-20	0	0	4.28	4	
DE SILVA, Geemuni Sajith Kalumpriya (Tamil Union) b Galle 20.5.1990 RHB WK																			
FC		3	5	0	66	35	13.20	0	0									2	
Lim		2	2	0	26	26	13.00	0	0									0	
DE SILVA, Gihan Trevor (Ruhuna, Tamil Union) b Colombo 25.7.1985 LHB WK																			
FC		13	17	4	345	66	26.53	0	2									23	3
Lim		17	15	4	215	42	19.54	0	0									24	8
FC	2001/02	59	91	12	1751	117*	22.16	1	10									133	19
Lim	2004/05	61	50	10	920	110	23.00	1	2									81	23
20T	2004/05	18	8	1	79	36	11.28	0	0									8	8
DE SILVA, Hathurusingha Danuja Nandana (Panadura) b Kalutara 17.3.1981 LHB RFM																			
FC		8	8	4	34	16*	8.50	0	0	569	270	17	15.88	7-33	1	0	2.84	3	
Lim		8	5	1	6	3	1.50	0	0	247	184	9	20.44	2-18	0	0	4.47	0	
FC	2005/06	33	38	20	224	17	12.44	0	0	2613	1458	56	26.03	7-33	1	0	3.34	9	
Lim	2005/06	26	15	4	33	10	3.00	0	0	793	599	21	28.52	3-35	0	0	4.53	4	
20T	2006/07	2	1	1	1	1*		0	0	12	21	0					10.50	1	
DE SILVA, Jayamuni Dinesh Manjula (Seeduwa Raddoluwa) b Colombo 6.9.1984 RHB RM																			
FC		5	6	2	106	76	26.50	0	1	294	140	5	28.00	2-24	0	0	2.85	3	
Lim		7	3	2	31	17*	31.00	0	0	233	157	6	26.16	2-27	0	0	4.04	3	
FC	2004/05	34	54	18	640	76	17.77	0	1	3295	1834	68	26.97	6-72	3	1	3.34	15	
Lim	2004/05	33	23	15	242	44	30.25	0	0	1217	847	32	26.46	5-14	1	1	4.17	10	
20T	2004/05	5	3	1	4	2*	2.00	0	0	90	125	5	25.00	2-26	0	0	8.33	3	
DE SILVA, Kananke Kankanamalage Harsha Udaya Kumara (Badureliya, Police) b Colombo 16.12.1984 LHB RMF																			
FC		8	12	1	386	81	35.09	0	2									4	
Lim		3	3	0	24	11	8.00	0	0									0	
FC	2007/08	26	44	3	1360	135	33.17	2	8	72	50	0					4.16	30	
Lim	2007/08	20	20	0	466	90	23.30	0	3	101	78	0					4.63	5	
DE SILVA, Koggala Marakkalage Pradeep Chirantha (Singha) b Colombo 1.4.1988 LHB WK																			
Lim		1	1	0	25	25	25.00	0	0									2	
FC	2008/09	8	14	0	168	32	12.00	0	0									19	2
Lim	2008/09	9	7	1	142	57*	23.66	0	1									11	3
DE SILVA, Kalumith Madura Sanjaya (Sri Lanka Air Force) b Polwatta 12.3.1983 RHB OB																			
FC		8	14	1	181	35*	13.92	0	0	763	456	13	35.07	4-73	0	0	3.58	3	
Lim		3	2	0	36	20	18.00	0	0	162	106	9	11.77	5-42	0	1	3.92	2	
FC	2004/05	25	44	2	606	53	14.42	0	1	1697	984	27	36.44	4-73	0	0	3.47	8	
Lim	2005/06	16	14	0	181	31	12.92	0	0	358	277	12	23.08	5-42	0	1	4.64	4	
20T	2005/06	2	1	0	3	3	3.00	0	0									0	
DE SILVA, Kaluperuma Shanika Hasitha (Ragama) b Colombo 29.6.1987 RHB RFM																			
Lim		2	2	1	1	1*	1.00	0	0	54	69	2	34.50	1-31	0	0	7.66	0	
FC	2007/08	6	10	3	111	35	15.85	0	0	624	362	17	21.29	5-41	1	0	3.48	2	
Lim	2006/07	11	10	2	62	18	7.75	0	0	378	364	6	60.66	3-42	0	0	5.77	4	
DE SILVA, Kaluarachchige Yohan (Basnahira South, Nondescripts) b Anuradapura 14.10.1985 LHB OB																			
FC		14	21	0	728	164	34.66	1	4	30	17	1	17.00	1-17	0	0	3.40	11	
Lim		10	10	0	296	56	29.60	0	1									2	
20T		2	2	0	15	15	7.50	0	0									0	
FC	2005/06	45	76	1	2421	164*	32.28	4	15	33	21	1	21.00	1-17	0	0	3.81	40	
Lim	2004/05	30	29	0	667	69	23.00	0	3									9	
20T	2004/05	15	14	3	177	42	16.09	0	0									6	
DE SILVA, Liyanage Asanka Heshan (Sri Lanka Air Force) b Matale 3.10.1985 RHB OB																			
FC		5	9	0	125	33	13.88	0	0	372	250	8	31.25	2-26	0	0	4.03	4	
Lim		7	6	1	59	16*	11.80	0	0	374	205	10	20.50	3-55	0	0	3.28	2	
FC	2007/08	10	19	0	284	63	14.94	0	1	810	533	16	33.31	3-79	0	0	3.94	7	
Lim	2007/08	20	19	2	320	38	18.82	0	0	576	389	16	24.31	3-55	0	0	4.05	7	
20T	2006/07	1																0	
DE SILVA, Manimeldura Nimesha Chathuranga (Colts) b Galle 10.3.1987 RHB RMF																			
FC		1								54	26	1	26.00	1-15	0	0	2.88	1	
DE SILVA, Muthumuni Raween Lakshitha (Seeduwa Raddoluwa) b Chilaw 30.4.1990 RHB RMF																			
FC		1	2	1	20	14*	20.00	0	0	60	53	0					5.30	0	
Lim		3	3	0	83	46	27.66	0	0	24	22	0					5.50	0	
DE SILVA, Nishshanka Asiri Hemalal (Sri Lanka Navy) b Panadura 10.6.1983 RHB RFM																			
FC		3	5	0	86	53	17.20	0	1									0	
Lim		2	2	0	28	21	14.00	0	0									1	
DE SILVA, Pinnaduwage Chaturanga (Moors) b Galle 17.1.1990 LHB SLA																			
FC		5	7	2	82	38	16.40	0	0	12	6	0					3.00	2	
Lim		6	6	0	130	70	21.66	0	1	78	69	1	69.00	1-13	0	0	5.30	1	
20T	2007/08	9	9	0	110	26	12.22	0	0	54	71	3	23.66	2-34	0	0	7.88	4	

Cmp	Debut	M	I	NO	Runs	HS	Avge	100	50	Balls	Runs	Wkts	Avge	BB	5i	10m	RpO	ct	st
DE SILVA, Seekkuarachchige Jeewan Chamikara (Seeduwa Raddoluwa) b Panadura 10.8.1984 RHB OB																			
FC		1	1	1	3	3*		0	0	24	22	0					5.50	0	
Lim		1	1	0	1	1	1.00	0	0	42	33	0					4.71	0	
FC	2004/05	11	13	4	191	41*	21.22	0	0	1171	784	24	32.66	5-74	1	0	4.01	8	
Lim	2007/08	4	3	0	43	21	14.33	0	0	108	93	0					5.16	2	
DE SILVA, Thakurathi Devadithya Gardiyawasam Lindamulage Tharanga Anthony (Moratuwa) b Colombo 21.6.1987 LHB RMF																			
FC		9	11	1	427	127	42.70	1	2	30	7	0					1.40	1	
Lim		7	6	1	100	36	20.00	0	0	12	7	0					3.50	2	
FC	2007/08	26	40	4	1136	127	31.55	2	6	126	62	0					2.95	8	
Lim	2007/08	22	21	2	483	94	25.42	0	4	173	141	7	20.14	3-12	0	0	4.89	7	
DE SILVA, Warshamannada Pradeep (Singha) b Galle 30.9.1989 RHB RMF																			
Lim		3	3	0	42	29	14.00	0	0	12	24	0					12.00	0	
DE SILVA, Weddikkara Ruwan Sujeewa (Colombo, Ruhuna) b Beruwala 7.10.1979 RHB LMF																			
FC		6	8	2	30	13	5.00	0	0	546	370	5	74.00	2-57	0	0	4.06	4	
Lim		9	4	2	8	6	4.00	0	0	357	287	11	26.09	3-35	0	0	4.82	2	
Test	2002	3	2	1	10	5*	10.00	0	0	432	209	11	19.00	4-35	0	0	2.90	1	
FC	1999/00	97	122	31	856	47	9.40	0	0	11778	7163	301	23.79	7-49	10	0	3.64	32	
Lim	1999/00	69	36	12	148	21*	6.16	0	0	2871	2267	103	22.00	7-25	4	2	4.73	13	
20T	2004/05	16	5	4	4	2*	4.00	0	0	297	347	25	13.88	4-16	2	0	7.01	4	
DE SILVA, Yakupiti Gayan Asanka (Colombo) b Balapitiya 1.12.1988 RHB																			
Lim		4	4	0	26	13	6.50	0	0									1	
Lim	2008/09	6	5	0	27	13	5.40	0	0									1	
DE ZOYSA, Handamuni Hareendra Manjula (Sri Lanka Army) b Beruwala 11.7.1983 RHB RM WK																			
FC		10	15	1	380	73	27.14	0	2	300	218	4	54.50	2-16	0	0	4.36	7	
Lim		4	4	0	31	14	7.75	0	0	78	57	1	57.00	1-46	0	0	4.38	2	
FC	2003/04	50	86	6	1965	140*	24.56	2	9	1565	856	30	28.53	3-6	0	0	3.28	61	1
Lim	2005/06	32	32	4	576	64*	20.57	0	1	670	420	17	24.70	3-27	0	0	3.76	12	
20T	2005/06	6	5	1	67	39*	16.75	0	0	18	47	2	23.50	2-47	0	0	15.66	2	
DE ZOYSA, Runmuni Sudheera Randeera (Moratuwa) b Colombo 8.10.1984 LHB LB																			
FC		9	12	3	220	111*	24.44	1	0	1074	621	19	32.68	4-118	0	0	3.46	3	
Lim		9	8	2	70	24	11.66	0	0	440	266	20	13.30	3-25	0	0	3.62	3	
FC	2002/03	29	49	10	776	111*	19.89	1	1	3561	1872	81	23.11	7-43	5	0	3.15	11	
Lim	2004/05	38	29	5	390	36	16.25	0	0	1582	1069	51	20.96	4-19	1	0	4.05	12	
20T	2004/05	2	2	1	4	3	4.00	0	0	36	40	2	20.00	1-11	0	0	6.66	1	
DE ZOYSA, Ranulu Sameera Sadarange Saman (Ragama, Wayamba, Wayamba to India) b Kurunegala 31.1.1987 LHB WK																			
FC		10	14	2	475	86	39.58	0	4									21	1
Lim		10	9	3	139	36	23.16	0	0									10	4
FC	2004/05	36	56	3	1308	104	24.67	1	8									71	5
Lim	2003/04	31	28	4	570	80	23.75	0	1									27	10
20T	2004/05	12	11	1	162	36	16.20	0	0									5	8
DHAMMIKA, Dunusinghe Gedera Ranil (Seeduwa Raddoluwa) b Colombo 27.12.1980 LHB SLA																			
FC		9	12	0	307	72	25.58	0	2	1269	631	34	18.55	6-41	1	0	2.98	4	
Lim		7	6	2	102	37	25.50	0	0	322	180	10	18.00	3-20	0	0	3.35	4	
FC	1999/00	63	82	13	1478	100	21.42	1	9	8921	4468	217	20.58	9-83	9	2	3.00	27	
Lim	1999/00	67	46	13	656	61	19.87	0	1	3203	1958	112	17.48	6-39	3	1	3.66	25	
20T	2004/05	4	2	1	14	13	14.00	0	0	60	47	6	7.83	3-16	0	0	4.70	1	
DIAS, Alahapperuma Arachchige Anura Prasad (Colombo) b Colombo 21.8.1988 RHB WK																			
FC		4	4	0	17	12	4.25	0	0									0	
Lim		5	5	0	118	67	23.60	0	1									6	1
FC	2008/09	6	8	1	57	15*	8.14	0	0									0	
Lim	2008/09	10	10	1	195	67	21.66	0	1									7	1
DIAS, Kalupahena Liyanage Sajeewa Lassana (Badureliya) b Galle 9.12.1979 LHB SLA																			
FC		2	1	0	5	5	5.00	0	0	144	80	1	80.00	1-28	0	0	3.33	1	
Lim		6	3	1	3	2	1.50	0	0	282	164	5	32.80	3-29	0	0	3.48	2	
FC	2000/01	68	99	43	488	38	8.71	0	0	9386	4407	217	20.30	7-37	14	4	2.81	33	
Lim	2001/02	49	29	19	124	22	12.40	0	0	1985	1176	54	21.77	4-29	2	0	3.55	14	
20T	2004/05	9	5	3	23	11*	11.50	0	0	205	182	12	15.16	3-27	0	0	5.32	0	
DIAS, Wadugemudalige Manuel Milinda Sandun (Nondescripts, Sri Lanka Air Force) b Kandy 29.7.1985 RHB RFM																			
FC		3	4	0	111	58	27.75	0	1	24	26	0					6.50	4	
Lim		1	1	0	5	5	5.00	0	0									0	
FC	2003/04	27	47	1	832	76	18.08	0	4	246	207	3	69.00	1-25	0	0	5.04	18	
Lim	2004/05	31	29	2	473	48	17.51	0	0	156	158	3	52.66	1-15	0	0	6.07	11	
20T	2004/05	10	10	0	158	35	15.80	0	0									5	
DILANTHA, Ramanayake Suduweli Kandage Anushka Priya (Police) b Akuressa 27.7.1979 RHB RM																			
FC		1								12	4	0					2.00	0	
Lim		8	6	1	60	34	12.00	0	0	194	143	6	23.83	3-26	0	0	4.42	1	
FC	1999/00	15	20	7	68	12	5.23	0	0	1233	888	18	49.33	3-76	0	0	4.32	2	
Lim	1999/00	35	26	11	141	34	9.40	0	0	1010	916	27	33.92	3-23	0	0	5.44	4	

Cmp	Debut	M	I	NO	Runs	HS	Avge	100	50	Balls	Runs	Wkts	Avge	BB	5i	10m	RpO	ct	st
DILHARA, Loku Hettige Danushka (Moors, Ruhuna) b Colombo 3.7.1980 RHB RFM																			
FC		8	12	1	211	47	19.18	0	0	477	322	12	26.83	3-11	0	0	4.05	4	
Lim		15	14	2	305	52	25.41	0	2	389	262	7	37.42	3-32	0	0	4.04	3	
20T		7	5	1	57	22*	14.25	0	0	72	114	2	57.00	1-11	0	0	9.50	2	
FC	2000/01	99	155	12	3474	211	24.29	3	11	11359	6057	233	25.99	7-64	7	0	3.19	57	
Int	2005	8	8	0	77	29	9.62	0	0	282	221	6	36.83	2-30	0	0	4.70	3	
Lim	2000/01	101	93	10	1724	93	20.77	0	6	3269	2418	76	31.81	4-65	1	0	4.43	37	
I20T	2008/09	2	1	1	18	18*		0	0	30	30	2	15.00	2-6	0	0	6.00	0	
20T	2004/05	28	23	3	262	53	13.10	0	1	345	465	12	38.75	2-6	0	0	8.08	9	
DILRUK, Wijeweera Kankanamge <u>Gihan</u> (Seeduwa Raddoluwa) b Colombo 8.10.1986 RHB OB																			
FC		9	13	4	296	57*	32.88	0	1	823	356	15	23.73	5-34	1	0	2.59	7	
Lim		9	6	2	110	33	27.50	0	0	398	265	11	24.09	3-12	0	0	3.99	3	
FC	2008/09	17	27	9	504	57*	28.00	0	1	1519	680	32	21.25	5-34	1	0	2.68	13	
Lim	2008/09	13	8	3	128	33	25.60	0	0	530	325	16	20.31	3-12	0	0	3.67	4	
DILSHAN, Tillakaratne Mudiyanselage (Basnahira South, Bloomfield, Sri Lanka, Delhi Daredevils, Northern Districts, Sri Lanka to Bangladesh, Sri Lanka to India, Sri Lanka to South Africa, Sri Lanka to United States of America, Sri Lanka to West Indies, Sri Lanka to Zimbabwe) b Kalutara 14.10.1976 RHB OB																			
Test		3	6	1	215	68*	43.00	0	2	258	119	3	39.66	3-56	0	0	2.76	3	
FC		3	6	1	215	68*	43.00	0	2	258	119	3	39.66	3-56	0	0	2.76	3	
Int		9	9	0	352	110	39.11	1	1	90	67	3	22.33	3-37	0	0	4.46	2	
Lim		10	10	1	419	110	46.55	1	2	132	101	5	20.20	3-37	0	0	4.59	4	
20T		1	1	0	0	0	0.00	0	0	6	5	0					5.00	0	
Test	1999/00	63	101	11	3906	168	43.40	11	15	1184	590	16	36.87	4-10	0	0	2.99	73	
FC	1993/94	198	320	22	11572	200*	38.83	30	48	3796	1844	59	31.25	5-49	1	0	2.91	334	27
Int	1999/00	188	165	29	4860	160	35.73	8	20	2881	2281	54	42.24	4-29	2	0	4.75	80	1
Lim	1996/97	272	243	41	7654	188	37.89	13	36	3972	3084	83	37.15	4-17	3	0	4.65	154	8
I20T	2006	31	30	5	717	96*	28.68	0	5	120	151	4	37.75	2-4	0	0	7.55	13	2
20T	2004/05	77	74	9	1606	96*	24.70	0	11	433	491	17	28.88	3-23	0	0	6.80	37	3
DILUKSHAN, Induruwa Arachchige <u>Yaditha</u> (Sebastianites) b Panadura 4.4.1983 LHB LFM																			
FC		2	3	3	2	1*		0	0	174	100	2	50.00	2-34	0	0	3.44	0	
Lim		4	3	1	5	4	2.50	0	0	192	106	3	35.33	2-25	0	0	3.31	0	
FC	2005/06	14	21	11	39	15*	3.90	0	0	1158	795	24	33.12	5-91	1	0	4.11	2	
Lim	2005/06	16	9	5	13	5	3.25	0	0	594	444	17	26.11	3-31	0	0	4.48	1	
20T	2005/06	2	2	2	6	5*		0	0	36	33	0					5.50	0	
DISSANAYAKE, Dissanayake Mudiyanselage Gimhan <u>Shanuka</u> (Basnahira North, Bloomfield) b Ragama 10.5.1977 RHB SLA																			
FC		10	14	2	502	205	41.83	1	2	1519	727	18	40.38	5-29	1	0	2.87	6	
Lim		12	9	2	205	69	29.28	0	1	581	349	28	12.46	5-45	2	1	3.60	7	
20T		5	4	3	37	23*	37.00	0	0	108	130	3	43.33	1-12	0	0	7.22	6	
FC	1995/96	109	152	19	3430	205	25.78	3	18	11451	5294	240	22.05	6-63	9	1	2.77	84	
Lim	1997/98	86	63	12	1303	110	25.54	1	4	3186	1918	94	20.40	5-45	3	1	3.61	54	
20T	2005/06	20	16	7	131	33*	14.55	0	0	392	397	25	15.88	5-15	0	2	6.07	8	
DISSANAYAKE, Maddumage Weranga <u>Buddike</u> (Burgher) b Negombo 22.9.1985 RHB RMF																			
FC		1	2	0	17	17	8.50	0	0									1	
Lim		4	4	0	65	49	16.25	0	0	103	50	2	25.00	1-16	0	0	2.91	1	
FC	2007/08	10	17	2	237	50	15.80	0	1	20	12	0					3.60	6	
Lim	2007/08	11	10	0	127	49	12.70	0	0	175	112	3	37.33	1-16	0	0	3.84	2	
DISSANAYAKE, Ruwan Dilruk (Ragama) b Colombo 25.12.1978 RHB OB																			
FC		2	1	0	1	1	1.00	0	0	276	189	2	94.50	1-48	0	0	4.10	1	
Lim		4	4	3	15	13*	15.00	0	0	185	124	2	62.00	1-41	0	0	4.02	1	
FC	2001	70	98	26	679	44*	9.43	0	0	8411	4334	162	26.75	6-71	5	0	3.09	44	
Lim	2001/02	49	37	13	245	33	10.20	0	0	2066	1368	43	31.81	4-22	1	0	3.97	20	
20T	2004/05	10	4	1	14	8*	4.66	0	0	138	136	11	12.36	4-14	1	0	5.91	2	
DUSHYANTHA, Makavita Gamachchilage <u>Tharaka</u> (Sebastianites) b Matara 3.11.1988 RHB WK																			
FC		5	9	0	215	59	23.88	0	1									3	
Lim		6	6	0	131	88	21.83	0	1									1	
EDIRIWEERA, Prince <u>Bradman</u> (Lankan) b Colombo 19.9.1975 LHB RM																			
FC		8	10	0	298	125	29.80	1	1									9	
Lim		5	4	0	129	38	32.25	0	0									1	
FC	1995/96	113	170	8	5348	154	33.01	12	25	1368	861	30	28.70	3-28	0	0	3.77	93	
Lim	1996/97	58	54	8	1294	118*	28.13	1	5	229	163	7	23.28	3-24	0	0	4.27	20	
20T	2005/06	1	1	0	7	7	7.00	0	0	18	30	1	30.00	1-30	0	0	10.00	0	
EKANAYAKE, Buwaneka Milinda Bandara (Moors) b Colombo 18.9.1989 RHB WK																			
FC		1	2	0	48	36	24.00	0	0									2	
20T	2008/09	3	3	0	39	38	13.00	0	0									0	
ERANGA, Galkandage Don <u>Romesh</u> (Burgher) b Ragama 16.6.1985 LHB LFM																			
FC		7	12	2	111	54	11.10	0	1	802	509	16	31.81	4-67	0	0	3.80	2	
FC	2007/08	24	40	6	549	54	16.14	0	1	2947	1884	77	24.46	6-82	3	0	3.83	10	
Lim	2007/08	11	7	3	59	19	14.75	0	0	488	393	23	17.08	8-30	0	1	4.83	3	

Cmp	Debut	M	I	NO	Runs	HS	Avge	100	50	Balls	Runs	Wkts	Avge	BB	5i	10m	RpO	ct	st
ERANGA, Ranaweera Mudiyanselage Shaminda (Chilaw Marians, Ruhuna, Sri Lanka A) b Chilaw 23.6.1986 RHB RMF																			
FC		13	11	7	59	19	14.75	0	0	916	694	16	43.37	2-11	0	0	4.54	8	
Lim		12	4	4	5	3*		0	0	492	396	9	44.00	4-38	1	0	4.82	7	
20T		1	1	1	0	0*		0	0	12	15	0					7.50	0	
FC	2006/07	23	29	14	145	21	9.66	0	0	1975	1397	34	41.08	3-22	0	0	4.24	14	
Lim	2006/07	17	6	4	27	16	13.50	0	0	726	557	14	39.78	4-38	1	0	4.60	9	
ERANGA, Walgamakankanamge Achira (Sri Lanka Air Force, Sri Lanka Cricket Combined XI) b Galle 9.6.1987 RHB OB																			
FC		9	16	0	427	65	26.68	0	2	48	29	0					3.62	3	
Lim		9	9	0	209	47	23.22	0	0	12	9	0					4.50	1	
20T		5	5	0	78	23	15.60	0	0									1	
FC	2007/08	22	41	0	1005	65	24.51	0	3	84	53	0					3.78	10	
Lim	2007/08	18	17	0	367	47	21.58	0	0	24	23	0					5.75	2	
FAUX, Denver Anthony (Singha) b Colombo 18.5.1983 RHB																			
FC		7	12	0	244	49	20.33	0	0									2	
Lim		3	3	0	50	29	16.66	0	0									0	
FC	2007/08	25	47	1	1204	77	26.17	0	7									15	
Lim	2007/08	11	11	0	378	128	34.36	1	2									1	
FERNANDO, Aththachchi Nuwan Pradeep Roshan (Basnahira North, Bloomfield, Sri Lanka A, Sri Lanka A to Australia) b Negombo 19.10.1986 RHB RFM																			
FC		10	12	6	33	16	5.50	0	0	603	421	10	42.10	3-46	0	0	4.18	5	
Lim		7	2	0	3	3	1.50	0	0	307	263	13	20.23	4-58	1	0	5.14	3	
20T		4	1	0	5	5	5.00	0	0	72	86	3	28.66	1-6	0	0	7.16	0	
FC	2007/08	29	37	18	72	16	3.78	0	0	2434	1593	43	37.04	5-36	1	0	3.92	11	
Lim	2007/08	19	8	3	17	5*	3.40	0	0	724	627	27	23.22	4-38	2	0	5.19	3	
20T	2008/09	7	3	1	5	5	2.50	0	0	144	177	6	29.50	2-40	0	0	7.37	1	
FERNANDO, Biyagamage Manoj Prasanna Deshapriya (Burgher) b Colombo 15.2.1981 RHB RFM																			
FC		3	5	1	59	30*	14.75	0	0									1	
Lim		3	3	0	79	47	26.33	0	0									0	
FC	2000/01	30	54	5	939	82	19.16	0	4	156	129	1	129.00	1-35	0	0	4.96	25	
Lim	2003/04	8	8	0	164	53	20.50	0	1									0	
FERNANDO, Congenige Randhi Dilhara (Kandurata, Sinhalese, Sri Lanka, Sri Lanka Board President's XI, Mumbai Indians, Sri Lanka to India, Sri Lanka to Zimbabwe) b Colombo 19.7.1979 RHB RFM																			
Test		1								188	116	1	116.00	1-116	0	0	3.70	0	
FC		7	1	0	0	0	0.00	0	0	655	379	6	63.16	2-70	0	0	3.47	1	
Int		1	1	1	6	6*		0	0	48	33	2	16.50	2-33	0	0	4.12	0	
Lim		11	4	3	7	6*	7.00	0	0	516	365	20	18.25	4-29	1	0	4.24	4	
20T		5	2	1	3	3	3.00	0	0	96	142	7	20.28	3-44	0	0	8.87	0	
Test	2000	34	40	13	198	36*	7.33	0	0	5314	3188	89	35.82	5-42	3	0	3.60	10	
FC	1997	100	98	28	505	42	7.21	0	0	13440	7979	269	29.66	6-29	6	0	3.56	38	
Int	2000/01	139	56	32	237	20	9.87	0	0	6080	5270	176	29.94	6-27	3	1	5.20	26	
Lim	1998/99	197	82	43	320	21*	8.20	0	0	8764	7287	272	26.79	6-27	5	2	4.98	41	
I20T	2006	15	5	2	24	21	8.00	0	0	318	392	16	24.50	3-19	0	0	7.39	2	
20T	2004/05	38	13	7	36	21	6.00	0	0	834	1024	49	20.89	4-14	2	0	7.36	9	
FERNANDO, Charith Sylvester (Colombo) b Badulla 30.12.1982 LHB WK																			
FC		3	5	1	122	44	30.50	0	0									5	1
Lim		7	7	0	50	15	7.14	0	0									3	1
FC	2001	84	144	18	3589	111	28.48	3	16									190	28
Lim	2001/02	69	62	5	808	68	14.17	0	1									80	23
20T	2004/05	18	16	2	164	44	11.71	0	0									6	9
FERNANDO, Edirippulige Felician Mahinda Upul (Lankan) b Ragama 8.6.1973 RHB RM WK																			
FC		9	13	3	440	94	44.00	0	3									17	4
Lim		6	6	1	129	32*	25.80	0	0									4	1
FC	1992	139	228	19	6492	164	31.06	10	32	126	78	2	39.00	1-16	0	0	3.71	247	33
Lim	1995	65	62	7	1337	93*	24.30	0	8	12	12	0					6.00	51	13
20T	2004/05	6	6	2	229	61*	57.25	0	3									11	2
FERNANDO, Gallage Chaminda Lakruwan (Moratuwa) b Colombo 3.4.1980 RHB WK																			
Lim		1	1	0	27	27	27.00	0	0									0	
FC	2005/06	3	5	0	34	12	6.80	0	0	6	2	0					2.00	1	
Lim	2005/06	4	4	0	47	27	11.75	0	0									2	
20T	2005/06	1	1	1	1	1*		0	0									1	
FERNANDO, Gumge Suresh Umayanga (Panadura) b Panadura 31.3.1987 LHB SLA																			
FC		8	11	2	330	62*	36.66	0	2	318	128	6	21.33	2-24	0	0	2.41	6	
Lim		7	6	0	191	86	31.83	0	1	76	39	3	13.00	3-20	0	0	3.07	3	
FC	2005/06	37	64	4	1605	155	26.75	2	6	989	513	23	22.30	4-42	0	0	3.11	30	
Lim	2005/06	33	31	2	848	86	29.24	0	3	244	135	7	19.28	3-20	0	0	3.32	7	
20T	2005/06	4	4	0	46	33	11.50	0	0	25	39	0					9.36	1	
FERNANDO, Hewadewage Buddika Dananjaya (Sebastianites) b Moratuwa 13.2.1983 RHB OB																			
FC		7	10	2	151	41*	18.87	0	0	877	389	22	17.68	5-60	1	0	2.66	2	
Lim		8	7	1	140	51	23.33	0	1	229	185	7	26.42	2-12	0	0	4.84	4	
FC	2003/04	20	32	6	446	51*	17.15	0	1	2348	1277	54	23.64	6-74	2	0	3.26	12	

Cmp	Debut	M	I	NO	Runs	HS	Avge	100	50	Balls	Runs	Wkts	Avge	BB	5i	10m	RpO	ct	st
Lim	2004/05	13	11	2	253	69*	28.11	0	2	313	276	9	30.66	2-12	0	0	5.29	6	
20T	2005/06	1	1	0	34	34	34.00	0	0	12	20	0					10.00	0	
FERNANDO, Horanage Manjula Prabath (Sri Lanka Air Force) b Moratuwa 17.9.1978 RHB RM																			
FC		1	2	0	11	8	5.50	0	0									0	
FC	1998/99	46	77	3	1231	102*	16.63	1	5	6	7	0					7.00	40	
Lim	1999/00	22	21	0	308	42	14.66	0	0									6	
20T	2005/06	5	5	2	20	10	6.66	0	0									0	
FERNANDO, Kandana Arachchige Dinusha Manoj (Nondescripts) b Panadura 10.8.1979 RHB RFM																			
FC		1	1	0	12	12	12.00	0	0	114	80	2	40.00	2-63	0	0	4.21	0	
Lim		5	2	0	21	15	10.50	0	0	195	124	11	11.27	4-28	1	0	3.81	0	
Test	2003/04	2	3	1	56	51*	28.00	0	1	126	107	1	107.00	1-29	0	0	5.09	0	
FC	1998/99	119	170	25	3903	138	26.91	2	24	14307	8284	335	24.72	8-34	19	3	3.47	74	
Int	2003/04	1								42	13	2	6.50	2-13	0	0	1.85	1	
Lim	1998/99	75	63	18	1161	77*	25.80	0	4	3163	2134	118	18.08	6-28	4	4	4.04	16	
20T	2004/05	6	6	0	122	70	20.33	0	1	108	116	7	16.57	2-17	0	0	6.44	3	
FERNANDO, Koralagamage Gayan Dinusha (Lankan) b Colombo 27.12.1985 RHB RMF																			
FC		3	4	2	13	7	6.50	0	0	186	133	4	33.25	2-33	0	0	4.29	2	
Lim		1	1	0	13	13	13.00	0	0	30	44	0					8.80	1	
FC	2005/06	14	19	9	184	55	18.40	0	1	1195	859	28	30.67	5-57	1	0	4.31	6	
Lim	2005/06	14	8	6	51	18*	25.50	0	0	554	442	15	29.46	4-28	1	0	4.78	4	
20T	2005/06	3	2	2	5	5*		0	0	66	69	1	69.00	1-23	0	0	6.27	0	
FERNANDO, Kandage Hasantha Ruwan Kumara (Basnahira South, Moors) b Panadura 14.10.1979 RHB RMF																			
FC		9	14	1	645	115	49.61	1	4	90	59	1	59.00	1-11	0	0	3.93	5	
Lim		13	13	1	348	60*	29.00	0	2	293	265	8	33.12	2-29	0	0	5.42	6	
20T		5	4	0	23	13	5.75	0	0	20	34	1	34.00	1-14	0	0	10.20	4	
Test	2002/03	2	4	0	38	24	9.50	0	0	234	108	4	27.00	3-63	0	0	2.76	1	
FC	2001/02	109	174	10	5390	186	32.86	7	33	9680	5015	215	23.32	6-38	8	0	3.10	97	1
Int	2002	7	5	3	43	23*	21.50	0	0	234	159	6	26.50	3-12	0	0	4.07	2	
Lim	2001/02	79	76	12	1958	117*	30.59	1	13	2623	2095	64	32.73	4-14	1	0	4.79	31	
20T	2004/05	33	30	0	499	58	16.63	0	1	421	519	20	25.95	3-22	0	0	7.39	17	
FERNANDO, Kurukulasuriya Mervan (Seeduwa Raddoluwa) b Negombo 16.3.1981 RHB SLA																			
FC		9	12	3	489	121	54.33	1	4	54	16	0					1.77	4	
Lim		6	6	2	115	28	28.75	0	0									2	
FC	2002/03	49	79	15	1940	164*	30.31	3	7	498	282	10	28.20	3-17	0	0	3.39	37	
Lim	2002/03	42	34	9	541	64	21.64	0	2	374	267	10	26.70	2-27	0	0	4.28	13	
20T	2004/05	8	5	2	84	38*	28.00	0	0	66	90	4	22.50	1-4	0	0	8.18	0	
FERNANDO, Kaludura Nadisha Chathuranga (Saracens) b Colombo 18.2.1983 RHB OB																			
FC		1	2	0	35	27	17.50	0	0									3	
Lim		4	4	0	21	16	5.25	0	0	18	23	0					7.66	1	
FC	2003/04	16	29	1	334	55	11.92	0	2	73	66	1	66.00	1-20	0	0	5.42	21	
Lim	2004/05	24	24	0	317	88	13.20	0	1	86	59	2	29.50	1-9	0	0	4.11	4	
20T	2005/06	7	7	0	140	52	20.00	0	2	6	8	0					8.00	3	
FERNANDO, Merennage Akshu Prihan (Panadura) b Panadura 11.3.1991 RHB OB																			
Lim		2	2	0	9	5	4.50	0	0									0	
FERNANDO, Muthuthanthri Basthiyange Milindu Pramesh Kumarasiri (Moratuwa) b Panadura 7.11.1986 RHB LB																			
FC		4	4	4	34	24*		0	0	162	95	4	23.75	3-65	0	0	3.51	1	
Lim		5	3	0	12	6	4.00	0	0	199	117	6	19.50	2-32	0	0	3.52	2	
FERNANDO, Maddumage Lilan Anuruddha (Sinhalese) b Ratnapura 27.7.1989 RHB RFM																			
FC		1																0	
Lim		2	2	1	0	0*	0.00	0	0	18	22	0					7.33	0	
Lim	2008/09	3	3	1	6	6	3.00	0	0	42	43	0					6.14	0	
FERNANDO, Mandadege Rasika (Sebastianites) b Panadura 25.1.1984 RHB LB																			
Lim		5	5	0	88	61	17.60	0	1									3	
FC	2003/04	13	21	2	324	64	17.05	0	1	444	232	14	16.57	5-34	1	0	3.13	11	
Lim	2003/04	18	18	2	288	61	18.00	0	1	18	27	0					9.00	8	
20T	2004/05	4	3	0	45	45	15.00	0	0									0	
FERNANDO, Moratuwage Sanjaya Devapriya (Sinhalese, Sri Lanka Cricket Combined XI) b Colombo 25.12.1988 RHB OB																			
FC		1																0	
Lim		3	1	0	1	1	1.00	0	0	30	23	1	23.00	1-23	0	0	4.60	0	
20T		1								18	36	0					12.00	0	
FC	2008/09	9	12	3	141	46	15.66	0	0	799	420	19	22.10	3-11	0	0	3.15	2	
Lim	2008/09	9	6	2	40	24	10.00	0	0	258	152	9	16.88	3-16	0	0	3.53	3	
FERNANDO, Mandadige Tharanga Priyadharshana (Sebastianites) b Panadura 20.11.1981 RHB OB																			
FC		8	13	0	161	31	12.38	0	0	949	447	14	31.92	5-70	1	0	2.82	7	
Lim		8	7	0	102	39	14.57	0	0	408	232	19	12.21	4-8	1	0	3.41	4	
FC	2000/01	50	75	10	1103	79	16.96	0	3	2344	1295	55	23.54	5-55	2	0	3.31	27	
Lim	1998/99	44	37	4	526	41	15.93	0	0	1178	823	51	16.13	4-8	3	0	4.19	15	
20T	2004/05	7	4	0	33	12	8.25	0	0	87	87	2	43.50	1-10	0	0	6.00	2	
FERNANDO, Maddumage Tharinda Thushara (Panadura) b Panadura 9.10.1989 LHB OB WK																			
FC		6	8	0	156	68	19.50	0	1	12	2	0					1.00	8	4
Lim		10	10	0	235	65	23.50	0	1									9	4

Cmp	Debut	M	I	NO	Runs	HS	Avge	100	50	Balls	Runs	Wkts	Avge	BB	5i	10m	RpO	ct	st
FC	2007/08	17	28	1	701	126*	25.96	2	3	12	2	0					1.00	27	6
Lim	2007/08	23	23	0	503	65	21.86	0	3									16	5
20T	2006/07	7	7	1	117	55	19.50	0	1									1	
FERNANDO, Payagalage Charith Miharan (Moratuwa) b Colombo 7.10.1987 RHB RMF																			
FC		8	9	3	96	36*	16.00	0	0	636	413	12	34.41	3-30	0	0	3.89	4	
Lim		8	4	3	18	15*	18.00	0	0	359	277	11	25.18	2-22	0	0	4.63	1	
FC	2007/08	25	33	10	363	67*	15.78	0	1	3054	1796	70	25.65	5-44	1	0	3.52	11	
Lim	2007/08	23	16	8	70	15*	8.75	0	0	1055	881	28	31.46	2-22	0	0	5.01	9	
FERNANDO, Pallidora Hewage Muditha Gayan (Burgher) b Dehiwala 9.9.1980 RHB																			
FC		6	10	0	212	80	21.20	0	1									9	2
Lim		3	3	0	32	26	10.66	0	0									1	1
FC	2000/01	53	84	7	1762	91*	22.88	0	9	30	27	0					5.40	75	12
Lim	2001/02	33	31	5	438	55	16.84	0	1									26	4
20T	2004/05	4	4	0	87	55	21.75	0	1									2	2
FERNANDO, Palliya Madinage Sumith Marlon (Sri Lanka Air Force) b Colombo 12.2.1988 d Maharagama 9.7.2010 RHB WK																			
FC		8	15	1	412	94	29.42	0	2									20	13
Lim		8	8	1	173	44	24.71	0	0									10	2
FC	2008/09	16	29	1	740	94	26.42	0	3									39	22
Lim	2008/09	17	17	2	472	100*	31.46	1	1									18	7
FERNANDO, Palamandadige Nayana Priyanjana (Moratuwa) b Panadura 14.10.1988 RHB RAB																			
FC		4	6	0	156	58	26.00	0	2									7	4
Lim		3	3	0	29	26	9.66	0	0									1	
FERNANDO, Sham Eran Chathuranga (Seeduwa Raddoluwa) b Kandana 20.1.1987 RHB WK																			
FC		3	4	0	35	17	8.75	0	0									6	
Lim		2	2	0	36	24	18.00	0	0									3	1
FC	2006/07	4	6	0	63	17	10.50	0	0									9	
Lim	2006/07	4	3	0	36	24	12.00	0	0									4	1
FERNANDO, Sehan Hans (Sinhalese, Sri Lanka Cricket Combined XI) b Colombo 4.12.1986 RHB RM																			
FC		10	14	1	489	103	37.61	2	1									1	
Lim		13	13	3	377	67	37.70	0	2	72	60	0					5.00	4	
20T		5	5	0	141	66	28.20	0	2									0	
FC	2006/07	23	35	4	888	103	28.64	3	2	36	13	0					2.16	7	
Lim	2006/07	24	24	3	638	69	30.38	0	4	72	60	0					5.00	9	
20T	2006/07	8	7	0	176	66	25.14	0	2									1	
FERNANDO, Sajith Ian (Tamil Union) b Kandy 27.9.1972 LHB OB																			
FC		11	15	0	515	67	34.33	0	3	8	3	1	3.00	1-3	0	0	2.25	5	
Lim		9	7	0	113	36	16.14	0	0	180	118	3	39.33	3-36	0	0	3.93	3	
FC	1993/94	190	300	26	10594	178*	38.66	16	53	14757	6392	269	23.76	7-37	8	2	2.59	118	
Lim	1992/93	108	101	7	2920	118	31.06	4	15	3465	2286	83	27.54	4-15	2	0	3.95	29	
20T	2005/06	6	6	0	152	41	25.33	0	0	126	147	4	36.75	2-15	0	0	7.00	1	
FERNANDO, Thudellage Charitha Buddhika (Bloomfield) b Panadura 22.8.1980 RHB RFM																			
FC		4	3	1	25	19*	12.50	0	0	228	132	7	18.85	2-21	0	0	3.47	2	
Test	2001/02	9	8	3	132	45	26.40	0	0	1270	792	18	44.00	4-27	0	0	3.74	4	
FC	1999/00	74	102	23	1708	81	21.62	0	5	8997	4951	190	26.05	6-19	5	1	3.30	19	
Int	2001/02	17	10	6	29	14*	7.25	0	0	700	586	15	39.06	5-67	0	1	5.02	3	
Lim	1999/00	69	49	18	637	49*	20.54	0	0	2920	2100	68	30.88	5-67	1	1	4.31	10	
20T	2004/05	4	4	0	28	18	7.00	0	0	30	36	1	36.00	1-25	0	0	7.20	1	
FERNANDO, Uswatta Liyanage Kalum Deshapriya (Sebastianites) b Dehiwala 28.5.1979 RHB RMF																			
FC		5	7	0	162	56	23.14	0	1	114	83	1	83.00	1-15	0	0	4.36	3	
Lim		3	3	1	28	10	14.00	0	0	42	27	0					3.85	2	
FC	2000/01	46	69	1	1271	101	18.69	1	4	1204	800	24	33.33	4-41	0	0	3.98	64	4
Lim	2000/01	49	45	5	635	50*	15.87	0	1	635	417	10	41.70	2-22	0	0	3.94	21	1
20T	2005/06	5	5	0	55	18	11.00	0	0	36	48	1	48.00	1-27	0	0	8.00	0	1
FERNANDO, Ungamandadige Savinda Milan (Sinhalese) b Colombo 27.8.1988 LHB SLA																			
FC		2	3	2	1	1*	1.00	0	0	306	175	7	25.00	3-42	0	0	3.43	1	
Lim	2008/09	1								54	37	1	37.00	1-37	0	0	4.11	0	
FERNANDO, Weerahannadige Lasith Priyamal (Ruhuna, Sinhalese) b Colombo 8.4.1983 RHB OB																			
FC		15	22	3	592	102	31.15	1	2	210	109	0					3.11	8	
Lim		11	9	3	247	55	41.16	0	2	186	160	3	53.33	1-20	0	0	5.16	4	
FC	2002/03	65	105	10	3012	142	31.70	7	9	1827	936	24	39.00	4-68	0	0	3.07	35	
Lim	2002/03	45	41	6	774	82*	22.11	0	5	659	461	15	30.73	3-12	0	0	4.19	7	
20T	2005/06	6	6	0	61	22	10.16	0	0	42	50	4	12.50	3-31	0	0	7.14	2	
FERNANDO, Weerahannadige Niroshan Lakmal (Moratuwa) b Colombo 28.11.1987 RHB WK																			
Lim		1	1	0	2	2	2.00	0	0									2	1
FC	2008/09	6	8	0	71	26	8.87	0	0									16	1
Lim	2007/08	10	5	1	14	7	3.50	0	0									12	5
FERNANDO, Wesley Rasika (Moors) b Colombo 3.2.1977 RHB WK																			
FC		4	6	1	132	36*	26.40	0	0									12	2
Lim		6	6	2	105	41*	26.25	0	0									4	
FC	1998/99	71	109	16	2420	150	26.02	2	11	12	13	0					6.50	168	17

Cmp	Debut	M	I	NO	Runs	HS	Avge	100	50	Balls	Runs	Wkts	Avge	BB	5i	10m	RpO	ct	st
Lim	1999/00	45	37	10	464	50	17.18	0	1									42	13
20T	2004/05	6	5	2	30	10	10.00	0	0									2	4
FERNANDO, Weerapurage Samith Dushantha (Saracens) b Aluthgama 30.11.1984 RHB																			
FC		11	17	2	446	77*	29.73	0	2									9	
Lim		10	10	1	259	74*	28.77	0	3									3	
FC	2006/07	33	54	3	1210	82	23.72	0	5	12	8	1	8.00	1-2	0	0	4.00	24	
Lim	2005/06	36	34	1	812	74*	24.60	0	6	20	19	0					5.70	8	
20T	2005/06	8	7	0	130	29	18.57	0	0									5	
FERNANDO, Wannakuwatta Waduge Chamesh Sanka (Moratuwa) b Colombo 1.3.1989 RHB OB																			
Lim		3	3	1	37	22*	18.50	0	0	78	45	2	22.50	2-25	0	0	3.46	1	
Lim	2008/09	4	4	1	57	22*	19.00	0	0	78	45	2	22.50	2-25	0	0	3.46	1	
FERNANDO, Wannakuwatta Waduge Suresh Tharaka (Sri Lanka Army) b Kalutara 7.6.1986 RHB OB																			
FC		1	1	0	10	10	10.00	0	0									0	
Lim		2	2	0	34	34	17.00	0	0									0	
FERNANDO, Yohan Shanaka (Saracens) b Colombo 29.8.1988 RHB																			
FC		4	6	1	99	58	19.80	0	1									2	
Lim		3	3	0	19	9	6.33	0	0									2	
Lim	2008/09	5	5	0	26	9	5.20	0	0									3	
FONSEKA, Hewage Mohan Fonseka (Panadura) b Panadura 5.6.1987 LHB OB																			
FC		6	7	2	20	11	4.00	0	0	630	395	11	35.90	3-45	0	0	3.76	2	
Lim		3	2	0	30	16	15.00	0	0	99	47	5	9.40	3-20	0	0	2.84	0	
FC	2006/07	23	31	12	264	30	13.89	0	0	1537	860	31	27.74	4-22	0	0	3.35	11	
Lim	2007/08	12	7	1	76	27	12.66	0	0	344	254	11	23.09	3-20	0	0	4.43	2	
20T	2006/07	1	1	1	10	10*		0	0									0	
GAJANAYAKE, Malintha Krishantha (Bloomfield) b Colombo 5.10.1980 RHB OB																			
FC		5	8	1	123	26	17.57	0	0	78	45	2	22.50	2-22	0	0	3.46	2	
Lim		6	6	2	36	19	9.00	0	0	45	43	0					5.73	1	1
FC	2000/01	99	166	8	3435	105	21.74	2	20	2838	1553	62	25.04	4-57	0	0	3.28	97	1
Lim	2000/01	87	78	18	1710	105*	28.50	2	10	652	469	13	36.07	2-10	0	0	4.31	34	4
20T	2004/05	21	19	1	359	76	19.94	0	1	113	120	9	13.33	2-4	0	0	6.37	2	
GALLAGE, Saminda (Singha) b Colombo 3.1.1984 RHB OB																			
FC		3	5	1	114	36	28.50	0	0	216	106	7	15.14	3-8	0	0	2.94	2	
Lim		6	5	0	35	20	7.00	0	0	214	145	3	48.33	2-22	0	0	4.06	1	
FC	2003/04	6	9	1	124	36	15.50	0	0	364	170	8	21.25	3-8	0	0	2.80	3	
Lim	2003/04	11	8	2	74	20*	12.33	0	0	316	223	4	55.75	2-22	0	0	4.23	3	
20T	2006/07	4	4	1	33	15	11.00	0	0	21	32	2	16.00	2-14	0	0	9.14	1	
GAMAGE, Panagamuwa Lihuru Sampath (Nondescripts, Sri Lanka Cricket Combined XI) b Maradana 5.4.1988 RHB RM																			
FC		1	1	0	2	2	2.00	0	0	66	57	2	28.50	2-57	0	0	5.18	0	
Lim		2	1	0	0	0	0.00	0	0	48	43	1	43.00	1-17	0	0	5.37	1	
20T		1	1	0	2	2	2.00	0	0	12	29	1	29.00	1-29	0	0	14.50	1	
FC	2006/07	15	22	9	155	26	11.92	0	0	1350	968	40	24.20	5-61	1	0	4.30	5	
Lim	2006/07	4	2	0	0	0	0.00	0	0	138	134	3	44.66	2-46	0	0	5.82	1	
GAMAGE, Tyron Prabath (Bloomfield, Kandurata) b Colombo 14.3.1979 RHB RFM																			
FC		10	9	4	53	23*	10.60	0	0	786	426	15	28.40	3-40	0	0	3.25	3	
Lim		5								164	158	6	26.33	3-32	0	0	5.78	3	
FC	2001	67	91	32	332	25	5.62	0	0	7244	4549	207	21.97	8-32	7	0	3.76	16	
Lim	2001/02	42	22	11	73	10	6.63	0	0	1481	1214	46	26.39	3-19	0	0	4.91	9	
20T	2006/07	2	1	0	0	0	0.00	0	0	12	25	0					12.50	1	
GANEGAMA, Withanaarchchige Chamara Akalanka (Kandurata, Nondescripts) b Colombo 29.3.1981 RHB RFM																			
FC		11	12	2	251	93	25.10	0	2	793	528	17	31.05	4-35	0	0	3.99	6	
Lim		10	6	1	19	7	3.80	0	0	357	268	6	44.66	3-33	0	0	4.50	2	
FC	2000/01	95	122	23	1621	93	16.37	0	4	10659	6118	237	25.81	7-25	11	0	3.44	42	
Int	2000/01	4	2	0	7	7	3.50	0	0	66	88	2	44.00	2-27	0	0	8.00	1	
Lim	2000/01	102	53	16	450	31	12.16	0	0	4119	2937	129	22.76	5-20	4	2	4.27	27	
20T	2004/05	12	9	3	77	38	12.83	0	0	196	219	16	13.68	4-13	1	0	6.70	4	
GANGODA, Weeratunga Mudiyanselage Muhandiram Walawwe Eranga Vishvanath (Saracens) b Kandy 22.8.1986 RHB OB																			
FC		11	16	2	323	72	23.07	0	1	1443	895	26	34.42	5-65	3	0	3.72	6	
Lim		6	5	2	72	31	24.00	0	0	138	134	2	67.00	1-21	0	0	5.82	0	
FC	2006/07	22	34	4	793	116	26.43	1	2	1985	1216	36	33.77	5-65	3	0	3.67	10	
Lim	2006/07	9	8	2	90	31	15.00	0	0	210	173	6	28.83	4-22	1	0	4.94	1	
GANGODAWILA, Gangodawila Appuhamilage Sanjaya Kumara (Bloomfield, Kandurata) b Colombo 20.6.1984 LHB RF																			
FC		12	17	4	565	103*	43.46	1	5	66	50	2	25.00	1-7	0	0	4.54	3	
Lim		12	10	3	174	35	24.85	0	0	24	22	1	22.00	1-14	0	0	5.50	8	
20T		1	1	0	1	1	1.00	0	0									0	
FC	2005/06	27	40	6	1223	113	35.97	2	9	450	300	12	25.00	5-64	1	0	4.00	17	
Lim	2004/05	37	30	8	580	70*	26.36	0	1	230	210	10	21.00	5-25	0	1	5.47	18	
20T	2005/06	8	8	1	39	14	5.57	0	0	18	20	1	20.00	1-12	0	0	6.66	3	
GHOUSE, Mohamed Isham (Moors) b Colombo 24.3.1990 RHB OB																			
FC		2	4	0	64	32	16.00	0	0									1	
Lim		3	3	0	85	69	28.33	0	1									0	

Cmp	Debut	M	I	NO	Runs	HS	Avge	100	50	Balls	Runs	Wkts	Avge	BB	5i	10m	RpO	ct	st
GUNARATNE, Downdegedara Asela Sampath (Sri Lanka Army) b Kegalle 8.1.1986 RHB RMF																			
FC		7	10	0	197	48	19.70	0	0	67	25	1	25.00	1-11	0	0	2.23	3	
Lim		6	6	0	84	49	14.00	0	0	186	120	2	60.00	1-21	0	0	3.87	1	
FC	2008/09	11	18	0	385	58	21.38	0	1	259	139	4	34.75	2-36	0	0	3.22	7	
Lim	2008/09	10	10	0	164	49	16.40	0	0	210	146	2	73.00	1-21	0	0	4.17	2	
GUNARATNE, Gunarathna Kulasekara Dilesh Buddika (Colombo) b Embilipitya 2.4.1989 LHB LFM																			
Lim		2	1	0	0	0	0.00	0	0	69	53	0					4.60	0	
GUNARATNE, Liyanabadlge Janaka Prabath (Basnahira South, Chilaw Marians, Sri Lanka A) b Panadura 14.3.1981 RHB OB																			
FC		19	23	2	1062	130	50.57	2	8	1687	1006	35	28.74	4-93	0	0	3.57	15	
Lim		18	16	0	426	77	26.62	0	2	503	418	18	23.22	5-25	0	1	4.98	12	
20T		6	5	2	85	29	28.33	0	0	114	130	12	10.83	4-21	1	0	6.84	1	
FC	2001	108	168	17	5250	143	34.76	10	27	9475	5219	191	27.32	8-133	6	1	3.30	78	
Lim	2001/02	72	65	5	1082	77	18.03	0	5	2276	1680	78	21.53	5-25	2	1	4.42	28	
20T	2004/05	25	20	6	247	29	17.64	0	0	382	379	32	11.84	4-21	2	0	5.95	8	
GUNARATNE, Milan Tharaka (Bloomfield) b Kandy 11.2.1978 LHB RM																			
FC		8	11	0	318	126	28.90	1	2	135	51	5	10.20	4-37	0	0	2.26	7	
FC	1997/98	63	104	8	2022	126	21.06	3	7	1589	785	23	34.13	4-37	0	0	2.96	54	
Lim	1998/99	17	12	3	129	29*	14.33	0	0	378	288	11	26.18	3-19	0	0	4.57	6	
20T	2005/06	5	4	0	38	20	9.50	0	0	15	17	2	8.50	2-17	0	0	6.80	2	
GUNASEKERA, Hadunnetti Rannulu Malith Chathuranga (Panadura) b Nagoda 17.10.1990 RHB RMF																			
Lim		3	2	1	27	27	27.00	0	0	156	87	6	14.50	2-15	0	0	3.34	0	
GUNASENA, Yaddehige Isuru Sahanshika (Moors) b Colombo 2.4.1987 RHB RM																			
FC		3	4	0	77	44	19.25	0	0	102	66	3	22.00	3-41	0	0	3.88	0	
Lim		5	3	2	38	14*	38.00	0	0	222	134	5	26.80	2-27	0	0	3.62	0	
FC	2007/08	9	14	2	165	44	13.75	0	0	606	402	15	26.80	5-52	1	0	3.98	5	
Lim	2007/08	17	12	6	112	21*	18.66	0	0	813	597	27	22.11	4-43	2	0	4.40	1	
GUNASINGHE, Chathupama (Sinhalese) b Galle 5.5.1987 RHB RMF																			
FC		5	7	0	45	19	6.42	0	0	402	267	7	38.14	4-72	0	0	3.98	2	
FC	2007/08	12	14	4	57	19	5.70	0	0	913	578	15	38.53	4-72	0	0	3.79	3	
Lim	2008/09	5	2	1	17	17	17.00	0	0	216	173	6	28.83	3-39	0	0	4.80	2	
GUNASINGHE, Malshan Nimesh (Sri Lanka Navy) b Colombo 15.6.1991 LHB OB																			
Lim		4	4	1	21	14	7.00	0	0	102	98	2	49.00	1-8	0	0	5.76	1	
GUNATHILAKE, Dushan Malith (Chilaw Marians) b Colombo 29.3.1987 RHB LB																			
FC		3	3	0	7	7	2.33	0	0	30	25	0					5.00	2	
Lim		1	1	0	22	22	22.00	0	0									0	
FC	2007/08	12	19	2	312	62	18.35	0	1	480	286	6	47.66	2-26	0	0	3.57	7	
Lim	2008/09	8	6	1	106	36	21.20	0	0	60	51	2	25.50	2-22	0	0	5.10	3	
GUNATHILAKE, GK Pathiranalage Senaka Madushan (Sri Lanka Navy) b Polpithigama 5.4.1989 LHB WK																			
Lim		1	1	1	10	10*		0	0									1	
GUNATHILLEKE, Mashtayage Dhanushka (Colombo, Sri Lanka Cricket Combined XI) b Panadura 17.3.1991 LHB RMF																			
Lim		5	2	0	9	8	4.50	0	0									2	
20T		4	4	1	59	32	19.66	0	0	6	20	0					20.00	0	
20T	2007/08	6	6	1	65	32	13.00	0	0	24	35	2	17.50	2-15	0	0	8.75	0	
GUNATHILLEKE, Metrige Don Hashan Dananjaya (Seeduwa Raddoluwa) b Colombo 17.4.1986 RHB OB																			
FC		2	3	0	62	32	20.66	0	0	6	4	0					4.00	2	
Lim		8	8	0	198	62	24.75	0	2									3	
GUNAWARDENE, Dihan Avishka (Sinhalese) b Colombo 26.5.1977 LHB																			
FC		2	1	1	20	20*		0	0									0	
Lim		1	1	0	7	7	7.00	0	0									0	
Test	1998/99	6	11	0	181	43	16.45	0	0									2	
FC	1996/97	129	199	11	6680	209	35.53	12	40	18	28	0					9.33	64	
Int	1997/98	61	61	1	1708	132	28.46	1	12									13	
Lim	1996/97	184	183	4	5362	132	29.95	6	35									46	
20T	2004/05	6	6	1	85	29*	17.00	0	0									2	
GUNAWARDENE, Kanchana Deshsapriya (Kandurata, Tamil Union) b Colombo 9.10.1984 LHB OB																			
FC		15	23	1	753	130	34.22	1	4	6	2	0					2.00	12	
Lim		12	11	1	257	51	25.70	0	1	12	13	0					6.50	3	
20T		1	1	0	21	21	21.00	0	0									0	
FC	2000/01	71	116	5	3696	185	33.29	7	16	404	203	8	25.37	4-28	0	0	3.01	55	
Lim	2001/02	59	57	5	1252	96	24.07	0	4	30	29	0					5.80	16	
20T	2004/05	12	12	0	186	45	15.50	0	0									4	
GUNAWARDENE, Nuwan Radiv Pujitha (Saracens) b Negombo 17.4.1984 LHB RM																			
Lim		1	1	0	3	3	3.00	0	0	11	22	0					12.00	0	
FC	2006/07	4	6	0	59	29	9.83	0	0	444	219	6	36.50	3-19	0	0	2.95	3	
Lim	2006/07	10	7	2	55	25*	11.00	0	0	178	195	6	32.50	3-32	0	0	6.57	2	
HERATH, Herath Mudiyanselage Rangana Keerthi Bandara (Moors, Sri Lanka, Wayamba, Hampshire, Sri Lanka to India, Wayamba to India) b Kurunegala 19.3.1978 LHB SLA																			
Test		1	1	1	80	80*		0	1	270	122	1	122.00	1-62	0	0	2.71	0	
FC		6	10	1	183	80*	20.33	0	2	1504	788	32	24.62	5-68	3	0	3.14	4	
Int		3	1	0	2	2	2.00	0	0	102	66	4	16.50	2-31	0	0	3.88	1	
Lim		10	6	3	29	10*	9.66	0	0	377	232	11	21.09	2-18	0	0	3.69	1	

Cmp	Debut	M	I	NO	Runs	HS	Avge	100	50	Balls	Runs	Wkts	Avge	BB	5i	10m	RpO	ct	st
20T		2								42	46	3	15.33	2-29	0	0	6.57	0	
Test	1999	22	28	5	287	80*	12.47	0	1	5383	2690	71	37.88	5-99	4	0	2.99	4	
FC	1996/97	184	262	60	3304	80*	16.35	0	12	36475	16602	668	24.85	8-43	38	5	2.73	84	
Int	2004	9	2	1	2	2	2.00	0	0	336	215	9	23.88	3-28	0	0	3.83	4	
Lim	1998/99	112	72	32	802	88*	20.05	0	1	4566	3051	141	21.63	4-19	3	0	4.00	28	
20T	2004/05	20	12	4	44	9	5.50	0	0	397	375	27	13.88	3-14	0	0	5.66	4	
HETTIARACHCHI, Dinuka (Basnahira South, Chilaw Marians) b Colombo 15.7.1976 RHB SLA																			
FC		13	12	5	95	25	13.57	0	0	2608	1498	69	21.71	8-66	6	3	3.44	3	
Lim		8	6	3	13	5*	4.33	0	0	378	271	17	15.94	4-12	2	0	4.30	2	
Test	2000/01	1	2	1	0	0*	0.00	0	0	162	41	2	20.50	2-36	0	0	1.51	0	
FC	1994/95	170	203	75	1148	48*	8.96	0	0	30514	14701	677	21.71	8-26	48	13	2.89	39	
Lim	1997/98	100	55	21	260	23	7.64	0	0	4388	2836	160	17.72	6-43	7	3	3.87	9	
20T	2004/05	14	8	3	41	25	8.20	0	0	221	186	19	9.78	3-0	0	0	5.05	1	
HETTIARACHCHI, Dimuth Indeewara (Sri Lanka Air Force) b Colombo 23.4.1990 RHB OB																			
Lim		1	1	0	8	8	8.00	0	0	30	10	1	10.00	1-10	0	0	2.00	0	
HETTIARACHCHI, Gardhige Darshana Sandakalum Hettiarachchi (Badureliya) b Colombo 1.8.1986 RHB																			
FC		2	4	0	25	13	6.25	0	0									6	
Lim		2	2	0	27	17	13.50	0	0									0	
HETTIARACHCHI, Milan Dilricksha (Lankan) b Colombo 30.3.1986 RHB LB																			
FC		1	1	1	9	9*		0	0	72	42	1	42.00	1-35	0	0	3.50	0	
Lim		2								96	60	3	20.00	3-34	0	0	3.75	1	
Lim	2007/08	3	1	0	3	3	3.00	0	0	114	79	3	26.33	3-34	0	0	4.15	1	
20T	2006/07	1																0	
HEWAGE, Pishan Chathuska (Moors) b Colombo 6.6.1987 RHB OB																			
Lim		2	1	1	18	18*		0	0	81	77	2	38.50	1-35	0	0	5.70	0	
FC	2007/08	9	15	4	236	51	21.45	0	1	1260	533	27	19.74	5-60	1	0	2.53	13	
Lim	2008/09	12	8	4	90	20	22.50	0	0	381	254	11	23.09	3-8	0	0	4.00	4	
HITTATIYA, Hittatiya Lokugamage Don Indunil Priyanga (Burgher) b Colombo 14.12.1978 RHB OB																			
Lim		1	1	0	8	8	8.00	0	0									0	
FC	1998/99	20	32	4	499	83	17.82	0	3	84	62	0					4.42	24	
Lim	2000/01	8	7	0	102	21	14.57	0	0	18	29	0					9.66	3	
HUNUKUMBURA, Damitha Nayanagith (Moors, Wayamba) b Kurunegala 7.11.1977 LHB																			
FC		15	24	1	761	116	33.08	1	4									4	
Lim		5	5	0	72	31	14.40	0	0									1	1
20T		2	1	0	18	18	18.00	0	0									0	
FC	1996/97	121	200	11	5953	119	31.49	8	35									107	12
Lim	1998/99	71	71	3	1625	75	23.89	0	9									19	5
20T	2004/05	15	14	0	354	87	25.28	0	2									3	1
ILLEPERUMA, Illeperuma Arachchige Roshan Laksiri (Nondescripts) b Colombo 4.10.1987 LHB SLA																			
Lim		7	2	0	16	10	8.00	0	0	246	153	7	21.85	3-24	0	0	3.73	5	
Lim	2008/09	15	8	2	84	19	14.00	0	0	574	429	17	25.23	3-24	0	0	4.48	6	
INDIKA, Ginimala Dewage Damith (Sri Lanka Army) b Kotahena 9.1.1984 RHB LB																			
FC		9	14	3	357	74*	32.45	0	4	120	80	0					4.00	4	
Lim		5	5	1	121	45*	30.25	0	0									2	
FC	2002/03	41	66	8	1533	85	26.43	0	11	480	340	6	56.66	3-16	0	0	4.25	29	
Lim	2004/05	31	25	3	446	61	20.27	0	1	83	85	3	28.33	3-21	0	0	6.14	10	
20T	2005/06	5	2	0	43	29	21.50	0	0									3	
INDIKA, Tharanga (Police) b Galle 4.3.1975 LHB RM																			
Lim		1	1	0	7	7	7.00	0	0									0	
FC	1995/96	5	9	1	53	14	6.62	0	0	96	71	0					4.43	2	
INDRASIRI, Singakutti Achige Don Upul (Ragama) b Colombo 2.11.1982 LHB SLA																			
FC		9	10	2	153	41	19.12	0	0	1037	601	16	37.56	5-103	1	0	3.47	4	
Lim		7	3	1	16	15	8.00	0	0	225	170	6	28.33	3-20	0	0	4.53	0	
FC	2001/02	55	76	17	748	52	12.67	0	1	7147	3419	169	20.23	8-29	9	2	2.87	29	
Lim	2003/04	50	37	10	235	38	8.70	0	0	1989	1269	58	21.87	5-33	2	1	3.82	11	
20T	2004/05	8	6	1	13	6	2.60	0	0	127	128	6	21.33	2-31	0	0	6.04	2	
ISANKA, Daramura Hettige Akila (Sri Lanka Air Force) b Colombo 15.1.1989 LHB SLA																			
FC		9	14	3	136	27	12.36	0	0	1500	874	32	27.31	6-51	2	0	3.49	7	
Lim		8	7	2	91	41	18.20	0	0	374	236	13	18.15	4-49	1	0	3.78	4	
ISHANKA, Mathra Chamindu (Singha) b Galle 10.4.1988 RHB OB																			
FC		6	10	0	172	34	17.20	0	0	18	8	0					2.66	5	
Lim		6	5	0	72	43	14.40	0	0	96	73	4	18.25	2-40	0	0	4.56	3	
JANITH, Padigamage Buddika (Sebastianites) b Colombo 3.2.1989 RHB SLA																			
FC		1	2	0	18	15	9.00	0	0	24	25	0					6.25	2	
JANODA, Jamburathu Godagamage Arosh (Basnahira North, Chilaw Marians, Sri Lanka Cricket Combined XI) b Colombo 11.9.1987 RHB RMF																			
FC		6	4	0	56	31	14.00	0	0	404	232	9	25.77	3-30	0	0	3.44	3	
Lim		11	11	2	95	28	10.55	0	0	440	402	14	28.71	4-72	1	0	5.48	2	
20T		5	3	1	3	3*	1.50	0	0	89	152	1	152.00	1-31	0	0	10.24	0	
FC	2007/08	14	14	2	221	53	18.41	0	1	1028	595	21	28.33	3-30	0	0	3.47	8	
Lim	2006/07	18	17	2	181	56	12.06	0	1	662	568	25	22.72	6-42	1	1	5.14	3	

Cmp	Debut	M	I	NO	Runs	HS	Avge	100	50	Balls	Runs	Wkts	Avge	BB	5i	10m	RpO	ct	st
JANSZE, Ansley Prajeev (Chilaw Marians) b Chilaw 12.2.1986 RHB																			
Lim		3	3	1	45	21*	22.50	0	0									0	
FC	2007/08	4	8	0	166	49	20.75	0	0									3	
Lim	2007/08	7	7	1	67	21*	11.16	0	0									2	
JAYAMAHA, Jayamaha Mudalige Don Nalin Vimukthi (Ragama) b Kattiyawa-Talawa 28.2.1988 LHB WK																			
FC		5	9	0	158	57	17.55	0	1									3	1
Lim		4	1	0	12	12	12.00	0	0									1	
JAYAMPATHI, Wijesinghe Mudiyanselage Charith (Basnahira South, Sri Lanka Cricket Combined XI) b Mathale 1.2.1991 LHB LMF																			
FC		1	2	1	100	96	100.00	0	1	78	64	0					4.92	1	
Lim		3	3	0	52	39	17.33	0	0	72	60	1	60.00	1-18	0	0	5.00	0	
20T		5	5	2	68	36	22.66	0	0	54	71	2	35.50	2-28	0	0	7.88	0	
FC	2008/09	2	4	2	111	96	55.50	0	1	150	108	1	108.00	1-44	0	0	4.32	1	
20T	2007/08	10	9	3	83	36	13.83	0	0	153	233	6	38.83	2-28	0	0	9.13	2	
JAYANTHA, Warushavithana Saman (Bloomfield) b Ambalangoda 26.1.1974 RHB OB																			
FC		6	9	1	171	53*	21.37	0	1	108	49	0					2.72	0	
Lim		8	8	2	263	74	43.83	0	1	297	190	8	23.75	2-14	0	0	3.83	1	
FC	1992/93	148	251	14	8175	212*	34.49	15	40	7931	3330	118	28.22	5-54	2	0	2.51	105	
Int	2003/04	17	17	2	400	74*	26.66	0	2	55	46	0					5.01	5	
Lim	1994/95	129	127	13	3459	147*	30.34	3	20	1766	1211	45	26.91	3-5	0	0	4.11	41	2
20T	2004/05	10	10	4	264	84*	44.00	0	2	54	61	2	30.50	1-10	0	0	6.77	6	
JAYAPRAKASHDARAN, Pradeep Sri (Tamil Union) b Colombo 13.1.1984 RHB RFM																			
FC		2	2	1	7	7	7.00	0	0	162	117	1	117.00	1-34	0	0	4.33	1	
FC	2003/04	41	60	23	578	50*	15.62	0	1	3710	2521	71	35.50	6-46	3	0	4.07	13	
Int	2005	1								36	21	1	21.00	1-21	0	0	3.50	0	
Lim	2003/04	26	10	6	29	10	7.25	0	0	925	701	37	18.94	4-16	2	0	4.54	4	
20T	2004/05	5	2	0	15	15	7.50	0	0	108	150	8	18.75	3-15	0	0	8.33	2	
JAYARATHNE, Pallepolagedera Lahiru Madushan (Ragama) b Matale 12.10.1991 RHB RMF																			
Lim		1	1	0	1	1	1.00	0	0	42	61	0					8.71	1	
20T	2007/08	5	1	0	2	2	2.00	0	0	78	103	4	25.75	2-26	0	0	7.92	1	
JAYASINGHE, Chinthaka Umesh (Bloomfield, Kandurata, Sri Lanka A, Sri Lanka to India, Sri Lanka to United States of America, Sri Lanka to West Indies) b Kalutara 19.5.1978 RHB RM																			
FC		7	9	1	138	35	17.25	0	0	30	8	1	8.00	1-7	0	0	1.60	3	
Lim		15	11	2	287	69*	31.88	0	2	510	344	9	38.22	3-13	0	0	4.04	4	
20T		8	7	2	83	41*	16.60	0	0	132	188	9	20.88	2-15	0	0	8.54	1	
FC	1996/97	123	191	19	4953	142	28.79	6	27	5246	2517	103	24.43	5-39	1	0	2.87	98	
Lim	1998/99	115	95	22	1931	86*	26.45	0	11	3914	2378	106	22.43	5-44	3	1	3.64	43	
I20T	2009/10	5	3	2	49	38	49.00	0	0									0	
20T	2004/05	35	31	9	644	67	29.27	0	1	438	535	28	19.10	4-17	1	0	7.32	10	
JAYASINGHE, Kalurachchige Asela Sudarsha (Colts) b Ragama 23.8.1974 LHB RM																			
FC		4	4	1	125	40*	41.66	0	0	48	27	0					3.37	2	
Lim		1	1	0	40	40	40.00	0	0									0	
FC	1994/95	88	142	10	4068	183	30.81	5	24	2280	1176	43	27.34	4-43	0	0	3.09	60	
Lim	1996/97	28	27	3	568	70	23.66	0	2	180	120	5	24.00	2-23	0	0	4.00	7	
20T	2005/06	6	5	0	140	70	28.00	0	1									1	
JAYASUNDERA, Jayasundera Mudiyanselage Praneeth Chamara (Lankan) b Colombo 6.8.1980 RHB LB																			
FC		5	6	1	90	27	18.00	0	0	376	250	11	22.72	3-77	0	0	3.98	2	
Lim		5	5	1	41	27	10.25	0	0	150	105	3	35.00	2-29	0	0	4.20	3	
FC	2001	72	105	14	2453	112*	26.95	2	13	6447	3355	132	25.41	5-23	3	0	3.12	46	
Lim	2001/02	50	38	6	370	39	11.56	0	0	1555	1093	41	26.65	5-41	1	1	4.21	18	
20T	2004/05	13	12	3	165	40	18.33	0	0	137	141	8	17.62	3-11	0	0	6.17	4	
JAYASUNDERA, Madurawelage Don Udara Supeksha (Sri Lanka Navy) b Minuwangoda 3.1.1991 LHB LB																			
FC		3	6	0	179	102	29.83	1	0	124	54	5	10.80	3-30	0	0	2.61	0	
Lim		2	2	0	166	148	83.00	1	0	36	49	3	16.33	3-49	0	0	8.16	0	
20T	2007/08	6	6	0	75	36	12.50	0	0	65	79	5	15.80	3-14	0	0	7.29	2	
JAYASURIYA, Dampalage Shehan Naveendra Fonseka Gunawardene (Police) b Colombo 12.9.1991 LHB OB																			
FC		1	1	0	10	10	10.00	0	0									0	
Lim		6	5	0	166	61	33.20	0	2	240	128	3	42.66	1-25	0	0	3.20	3	
JAYASURIYA, Sanath Teran (Bloomfield, Ruhuna, Mumbai Indians, Sri Lanka to India, Sri Lanka to South Africa, Sri Lanka to United States of America, Sri Lanka to West Indies, Worcestershire) b Matara 30.6.1969 LHB SLA																			
FC		2	2	0	40	32	20.00	0	0									0	
Lim		12	12	0	257	87	21.41	0	1	402	260	8	32.50	4-26	1	0	3.88	1	
20T		6	6	0	133	53	22.16	0	1	127	189	6	31.50	3-44	0	0	8.92	1	
Test	1990/91	110	188	14	6973	340	40.07	14	31	8188	3366	98	34.34	5-34	2	0	2.46	78	
FC	1988/89	263	417	33	14782	340	38.49	29	70	15113	6719	205	32.77	5-34	2	0	2.66	162	
Int	1989/90	444	432	18	13428	189	32.43	28	68	14838	11825	322	36.72	6-29	8	4	4.78	123	
Lim	1989/90	545	530	25	15734	189	31.15	31	78	17730	14069	399	35.26	6-29	12	5	4.76	149	
I20T	2006	30	29	3	621	88	23.88	0	4	353	438	17	25.76	3-21	0	0	7.44	4	
20T	2004/05	92	91	6	2052	114*	24.14	1	11	1263	1634	62	26.35	4-24	1	0	7.76	16	

Cmp	Debut	M	I	NO	Runs	HS	Avge	100	50	Balls	Runs	Wkts	Avge	BB	5i	10m	RpO	ct	st
JAYATHILAKE, Sanguge Dinidu (Seeduwa Raddoluwa) b Colombo 8.5.1988 RHB RM																			
FC		7	11	1	257	87	25.70	0	1									7	1
Lim		8	8	0	165	44	20.62	0	0									11	7
JAYATISSA, Dooliwala Kandiyagedera Roshan Chanaka (Sri Lanka Army) b Kandy 5.6.1989 RHB OB																			
FC		1	1	1	4	4*		0	0	24	34	0					8.50	0	
JAYAWARDENE, Denagamage Proboth Mahela de Silva (Sinhalese, Sri Lanka, Wayamba, Kings XI Punjab, Sri Lanka to Bangladesh, Sri Lanka to India, Sri Lanka to South Africa, Sri Lanka to United States of America, Sri Lanka to West Indies, Wayamba to India) b Colombo 27.5.1977 RHB RM																			
Test		3	5	0	288	174	57.60	1	1									9	
FC		4	7	0	343	174	49.00	1	1	12	16	0					8.00	11	
Int		9	9	2	301	59*	43.00	0	3									3	
Lim		16	16	2	398	59*	28.42	0	3	6	8	0					8.00	6	
20T		6	6	0	293	91	48.83	0	4	18	21	1	21.00	1-21	0	0	7.00	4	
Test	1997	113	187	13	9408	374	54.06	28	36	547	292	6	48.66	2-32	0	0	3.20	161	
FC	1995	195	310	22	15177	374	52.69	45	64	2959	1611	52	30.98	5-72	1	0	3.26	256	
Int	1997/98	326	307	32	9003	128	32.73	12	55	582	558	7	79.71	2-56	0	0	5.75	168	
Lim	1995	401	375	41	10787	128	32.29	12	67	1239	1094	23	47.56	3-25	0	0	5.29	202	
I20T	2006	31	31	4	760	100	28.14	1	4	6	8	0					8.00	9	
20T	2004/05	84	81	16	2049	110*	31.52	2	11	69	82	3	27.33	2-22	0	0	7.13	38	
JAYAWARDENE, Hewasandatchige Asiri Prasanna Wishvanath (Basnahira South, Bloomfield, Sri Lanka, Sri Lanka Board President's XI, Sri Lanka to India) b Colombo 9.10.1979 RHB WK																			
Test		3	3	0	36	27	12.00	0	0									5	2
FC		14	21	1	680	155	34.00	2	2									26	6
Lim		13	11	0	192	35	17.45	0	0									13	7
20T		6	4	2	68	29*	34.00	0	0									4	2
Test	2000	33	43	6	1080	154*	29.18	2	2									66	22
FC	1997/98	180	277	31	6679	166*	27.15	9	29	18	9	0					3.00	417	82
Int	2002/03	6	5	0	27	20	5.40	0	0									4	1
Lim	1998	117	98	9	1884	62	21.16	0	7									124	52
20T	2004/05	13	11	3	131	29*	16.37	0	0	12	8	1	8.00	1-8	0	0	4.00	9	4
JAYAWARDENE, Hewamanalage Manjula (Police) b Kegalle 24.3.1983 RHB OB																			
FC		5	7	2	125	33	25.00	0	0	408	207	5	41.40	2-53	0	0	3.04	2	
Lim		7	5	4	60	19*	60.00	0	0	145	112	2	56.00	2-22	0	0	4.63	3	
FC	2002/03	48	74	19	915	77	16.63	0	2	5521	2963	96	30.86	6-52	3	0	3.22	30	
Lim	2003/04	45	30	13	253	66	14.88	0	1	1520	1037	39	26.58	3-6	0	0	4.09	16	
20T	2005/06	3	2	1	7	5*	7.00	0	0	72	56	2	28.00	1-12	0	0	4.66	2	
JAYAWARDENE, Sulan Lahiru (Sri Lanka Army) b Hambanthota 20.10.1985 RHB RMF																			
FC		2	3	0	42	18	14.00	0	0									0	
Lim		4	4	0	40	24	10.00	0	0									3	
FC	2008/09	5	9	0	105	18	11.66	0	0	18	15	1	15.00	1-15	0	0	5.00	5	
Lim	2008/09	8	8	0	154	42	19.25	0	0									7	
JEEWANTHA, Pithigala Arachchi Saliya Saman (Ragama) b Balapitiya 25.11.1985 RHB RFM																			
FC		2	4	2	34	17*	17.00	0	0	102	57	1	57.00	1-35	0	0	3.35	0	
Lim		5	3	2	36	22*	36.00	0	0	162	146	4	36.50	2-46	0	0	5.40	0	
FC	2004/05	25	34	7	627	107*	23.22	1	2	2330	1363	64	21.29	5-18	2	0	3.51	8	
Lim	2004/05	23	18	6	159	46*	13.25	0	0	713	594	16	37.12	3-9	0	0	4.99	4	
20T	2004/05	8	7	1	59	17*	9.83	0	0	72	85	4	21.25	2-17	0	0	7.08	3	
KAHAGALLA, Kahagallage Sajan Charuka (Sebastianites) b Diwulapitiya 9.6.1988 LHB OB																			
FC		4	6	0	61	20	10.16	0	0	6	6	0					6.00	2	
Lim		5	4	1	64	27	21.33	0	0									3	
KAHINGALA, Sumudu Saranga (Saracens) b Kalutara 12.2.1981 RHB OB																			
FC		3	5	2	91	51*	30.33	0	1	138	83	0					3.60	1	
Lim		8	7	0	79	53	11.28	0	1	292	207	4	51.75	2-27	0	0	4.25	2	
KALAVITIGODA, Shantha (Moors) b Colombo 23.12.1977 RHB LB																			
FC		6	11	0	424	124	38.54	1	2									3	
Lim		5	5	0	126	66	25.20	0	1									4	
Test	2004/05	1	2	0	8	7	4.00	0	0									2	
FC	1997/98	144	238	14	6907	169	30.83	13	31	84	39	0					2.78	118	
Lim	1997/98	90	87	9	2047	121	26.24	1	12									25	
20T	2004/05	5	5	1	145	50*	36.25	0	1									3	
KALUARACHCHI, Kaluarachchige Romesh Malaka Deepal (Saracens) b Habarana 27.5.1985 LHB RFM																			
FC		6	6	3	37	17	12.33	0	0	488	337	8	42.12	2-44	0	0	4.14	0	
Lim		7	6	1	59	21	11.80	0	0	230	201	8	25.12	3-34	0	0	5.24	0	
Lim	2006/07	8	6	1	59	21	11.80	0	0	290	235	9	26.11	3-34	0	0	4.86	0	
20T	2006/07	3	2	1	21	13*	21.00	0	0	42	53	3	17.66	2-23	0	0	7.57	2	
KALUARACHCHI, Prasad Nalaka (Sri Lanka Army) b Galle 19.5.1981 RHB WK																			
Lim		4	4	0	30	13	7.50	0	0									3	
FC	2003/04	14	24	0	485	113	20.20	1	0	12	10	0					5.00	14	3
Lim	2003/04	22	22	0	338	61	15.36	0	1	2	4	0					12.00	14	2
20T	2005/06	3	3	0	31	17	10.33	0	0									2	

Cmp	Debut	M	I	NO	Runs	HS	Avge	100	50	Balls	Runs	Wkts	Avge	BB	5i	10m	RpO	ct	st
KALUHALAMULLA, Hewa Kaluhalmullage Suraj Randiv (Bloomfield, Kandurata, Sri Lanka, Sri Lanka to Bangladesh, Sri Lanka to India, Sri Lanka to United States of America, Sri Lanka to West Indies, Sri Lanka to Zimbabwe) b Matara 30.1.1985 RHB OB																			
Test		2	2	0	14	8	7.00	0	0	763	384	11	34.90	5-82	1	0	3.02	0	
FC		14	17	2	486	112	32.40	1	2	3048	1768	78	22.66	9-109	8	2	3.48	9	
Int		4	2	0	47	43	23.50	0	0	158	118	3	39.33	3-40	0	0	4.48	1	
Lim		22	11	3	127	43	15.87	0	0	994	671	38	17.65	5-15	2	1	4.05	9	
20T		5	2	0	1	1	0.50	0	0	106	144	7	20.57	2-24	0	0	8.15	5	
FC	2002/03	68	91	13	1331	112	17.06	1	5	12267	6875	272	25.27	9-62	18	4	3.36	51	
Int	2009/10	18	9	1	139	56	17.37	0	1	842	638	19	33.57	3-23	0	0	4.54	5	
Lim	2004	72	37	7	342	56	11.40	0	1	2937	2228	96	23.20	5-15	3	2	4.55	29	
I20T	2010	5	2	0	8	6	4.00	0	0	78	90	4	22.50	3-20	0	0	6.92	0	
20T	2005/06	18	7	1	41	20	6.83	0	0	298	358	16	22.37	3-20	0	0	7.20	7	
KALUM, Kamburugamuwa Gam Acharige Sathpath (Saracens) b Matara 26.2.1980 RHB RM																			
FC		1	1	1	1	1*		0	0	120	77	0					3.85	0	
Lim		4	4	2	37	20	18.50	0	0	114	106	1	106.00	1-41	0	0	5.57	0	
FC	1998/99	55	87	26	558	28	9.14	0	0	5559	3452	103	33.51	8-76	3	1	3.72	28	
Lim	1998/99	33	20	8	117	20	9.75	0	0	1127	855	36	23.75	3-39	0	0	4.55	3	
20T	2006/07	2	1	1	3	3*		0	0	30	28	2	14.00	2-23	0	0	5.60	0	
KANDAMBY, Sahan Hewa Thilina (Basnahira North, Sinhalese, Sri Lanka, Sri Lanka A, Sri Lanka Board President's XI, Dhaka, Sri Lanka to Bangladesh, Sri Lanka to India, Sri Lanka to South Africa) b Colombo 4.6.1982 LHB LB																			
FC		11	16	4	638	102	53.16	3	2	302	208	5	41.60	2-22	0	0	4.13	3	
Int		2	2	1	38	31	38.00	0	0	60	51	2	25.50	2-37	0	0	5.10	0	
Lim		16	12	2	202	63	20.20	0	1	330	248	8	31.00	3-25	0	0	4.50	2	
20T		5	4	0	108	44	27.00	0	0									1	
FC	2000/01	107	163	10	5659	202	36.98	12	24	1815	1356	36	37.66	4-36	0	0	4.48	61	
Int	2004	33	31	6	814	93*	32.56	0	5	168	164	2	82.00	2-37	0	0	5.85	5	
Lim	2001/02	148	129	19	3516	128*	31.96	2	24	879	786	23	34.17	4-68	1	0	5.36	37	
I20T	2008/09	4	4	0	13	10	3.25	0	0									3	
20T	2004/05	29	28	3	470	47*	18.80	0	0	93	101	5	20.20	3-21	0	0	6.51	13	
KAPUGEDERA, Chamara Kantha (Colombo, Kandurata, Sri Lanka, Sri Lanka A, Sri Lanka to India, Sri Lanka to United States of America, Sri Lanka to West Indies, Sri Lanka to Zimbabwe, Sri Lanka A to Australia) b Kandy 24.2.1987 RHB RM																			
FC		8	8	0	309	96	38.62	0	4	126	69	1	69.00	1-37	0	0	3.28	3	1
Int		9	6	3	125	55*	41.66	0	1									2	
Lim		22	17	4	384	88	29.53	0	3	54	38	1	38.00	1-35	0	0	4.22	7	
20T		9	7	0	118	31	16.85	0	0									1	
Test	2006	8	15	3	418	96	34.83	0	4	12	9	0					4.50	6	
FC	2005/06	41	65	10	2048	150*	37.23	3	15	425	242	4	60.50	1-1	0	0	3.41	27	1
Int	2005/06	82	69	7	1423	95	22.95	0	7	240	200	2	100.00	1-24	0	0	5.00	26	
Lim	2005	141	121	12	2700	101	24.77	1	16	403	341	5	68.20	1-23	0	0	5.07	46	
I20T	2006	19	17	3	276	47	19.71	0	0									7	
20T	2005/06	50	44	5	769	96*	19.71	0	2	29	74	0					15.31	20	
KARUNADASA, Kothalawalage Sudeera Nihal (Sri Lanka Navy) b Kegalle 28.6.1982 RHB OB																			
FC		9	13	12	14	4*	14.00	0	0	1220	686	44	15.59	7-111	4	2	3.37	10	
KARUNANAYAKE, Karunanayake Pathiranalage Nipun Madusanka (Bloomfield) b Ragama 11.1.1991 LHB LB																			
Lim		2	1	1	29	29*		0	0	12	20	0					10.00	0	
20T	2007/08	5	5	2	31	16	10.33	0	0	51	66	0					7.76	0	
KARUNANAYAKE, Karunanayake Pathiranalage Shalika Piyamal (Sinhalese, Wayamba) b Kurunegala 14.2.1987 RHB RFM																			
FC		10	15	2	570	172	43.84	1	3	336	227	3	75.66	1-29	0	0	4.05	3	
Lim		5	1	1	6	6*		0	0	162	158	5	31.60	2-30	0	0	5.85	1	
20T		7	6	3	57	30*	19.00	0	0	54	71	2	35.50	1-14	0	0	7.88	1	
FC	2004/05	46	63	9	1648	172	30.51	2	7	3383	2192	71	30.87	4-32	0	0	3.88	21	
Lim	2003/04	37	23	6	276	35*	16.23	0	0	1401	1089	53	20.54	5-25	1	2	4.66	12	
20T	2004/05	20	14	5	101	30*	11.22	0	0	180	226	8	28.25	3-20	0	0	7.53	5	
KARUNARATNE, Dissanayaka Mudiyanselage Asiri Deepal (Sri Lanka Air Force) b Dambulla 18.9.1986 RHB LMF																			
FC		4	6	5	18	11*	18.00	0	0	471	268	15	17.86	6-33	1	0	3.41	0	
Lim		1	1	1	9	9*		0	0	30	20	2	10.00	2-20	0	0	4.00	0	
FC	2008/09	10	13	9	23	11*	5.75	0	0	1171	739	35	21.11	6-33	2	0	3.78	2	
Lim	2008/09	9	7	7	21	9*		0	0	326	293	15	19.53	5-39	0	1	5.39	3	
KARUNARATNE, Frank Dimuth Madushanka (Basnahira North, Sinhalese, Sri Lanka A, Sri Lanka A to Australia) b Colombo 28.4.1988 LHB RM																			
FC		17	28	1	1493	185	55.29	3	11	24	21	0					5.25	18	
Lim		18	17	0	488	106	28.70	1	2	12	21	2	10.50	2-13	0	0	10.50	11	
20T		6	6	0	98	50	16.33	0	1									1	1
FC	2008/09	26	39	1	1711	185	45.02	3	13	48	36	0					4.50	23	
Lim	2008/09	25	22	0	583	106	26.50	1	3	12	21	2	10.50	2-13	0	0	10.50	12	
20T	2009/10	7	7	0	108	50	15.42	0	1									1	1
KARUNARATNE, Mudunkothge Lakpriya Ravindra (Chilaw Marians) b Kandy 31.3.1987 RHB RM																			
FC		5	5	0	45	22	9.00	0	0	293	158	6	26.33	2-6	0	0	3.23	4	
Lim		9	7	4	83	42	27.66	0	0	300	206	10	20.60	3-29	0	0	4.12	3	

Cmp	Debut	M	I	NO	Runs	HS	Avge	100	50	Balls	Runs	Wkts	Avge	BB	5i	10m	RpO	ct	st
FC	2007/08	12	15	3	308	69*	25.66	0	3	1208	658	23	28.60	4-74	0	0	3.26	5	
Lim	2007/08	10	8	4	89	42	22.25	0	0	300	206	10	20.60	3-29	0	0	4.12	3	
KARUNARATNE, Thennakoon Mudiyanselage Umesh Samantha (Seeduwa Raddoluwa) b Sri Jayawardenepura 19.1.1989 RHB OB																			
FC		9	13	2	466	92	42.36	0	5	1493	845	50	16.90	7-146	5	1	3.39	19	
Lim		10	10	2	280	70*	35.00	0	2	252	207	8	25.87	3-38	0	0	4.92	6	
FC	2008/09	18	28	3	840	92	33.60	0	8	2676	1505	86	17.50	7-146	8	1	3.37	30	
Lim	2008/09	18	17	3	429	70*	30.64	0	3	590	385	16	24.06	3-38	0	0	3.91	10	
KARUNATILLEKE, Randeerage Don Indika Aruna (Sri Lanka Army) b Kandy 13.10.1983 RHB RMF																			
FC		10	14	0	174	48	12.42	0	0	703	413	14	29.50	4-69	0	0	3.52	4	
Lim		9	9	0	188	56	20.88	0	1	378	289	6	48.16	2-32	0	0	4.58	2	
FC	2006/07	32	54	2	807	66	15.51	0	3	2154	1099	45	24.42	6-43	1	0	3.06	16	
Lim	2006/07	28	28	0	605	75	21.60	0	4	1159	808	29	27.86	4-19	1	0	4.18	8	
20T	2006/07	3	3	0	40	28	13.33	0	0	66	67	4	16.75	2-18	0	0	6.09	0	
KATIPIARACHCHI, Anoj Udayanga (Bloomfield) b Colombo 12.7.1987 LHB RMF																			
FC		2	3	2	25	15*	25.00	0	0	84	52	3	17.33	2-26	0	0	3.71	1	
Lim		8	6	0	46	18	7.66	0	0	96	86	2	43.00	2-46	0	0	5.37	3	
FC	2006/07	12	22	5	298	44	17.52	0	0	450	322	10	32.20	2-23	0	0	4.29	5	
Lim	2006/07	14	11	0	165	64	15.00	0	1	108	94	2	47.00	2-46	0	0	5.22	6	
KAVINGA, Hetti Hewa Rishan (Singha) b Borakanda 13.1.1988 LHB WK																			
FC		9	15	0	343	129	22.86	1	1									16	6
Lim		8	8	0	226	84	28.25	0	1									9	2
FC	2006/07	30	52	3	1296	129	26.44	2	7									57	13
Lim	2006/07	31	30	3	586	84	21.70	0	3	40	26	1	26.00	1-24	0	0	3.90	23	9
KEERTHIRATNE, Kaluwadewa Lakmal (Sri Lanka Navy) b Galle 21.3.1989 RHB LB																			
FC		7	11	1	193	45	19.30	0	0	198	159	5	31.80	3-51	0	0	4.81	2	
Lim		3	3	0	23	21	7.66	0	0	12	10	0					5.00	0	
FC	2008/09	8	12	2	198	45	19.80	0	0	324	227	6	37.83	3-51	0	0	4.20	2	
Lim	2008/09	5	5	2	29	21	9.66	0	0	71	69	1	69.00	1-42	0	0	5.83	1	
KEERTHISINGHE, Deegala Charith Buddika (Burgher) b Panadura 21.9.1985 LHB SLA																			
FC		4	6	3	22	9	7.33	0	0	312	150	5	30.00	2-44	0	0	2.88	2	
Lim		3	3	3	2	2*		0	0	114	94	2	47.00	2-36	0	0	4.94	0	
FC	2006/07	15	22	9	60	14	4.61	0	0	1106	568	25	22.72	4-44	0	0	3.08	12	
Lim	2006/07	5	5	3	10	7	5.00	0	0	144	120	2	60.00	2-36	0	0	5.00	4	
KOMASARU, Nishan Chanaka (Nondescripts, Ruhuna) b Matara 10.9.1983 LHB SLA																			
FC		14	13	8	28	6	5.60	0	0	2316	1166	50	23.32	5-52	3	0	3.02	3	
Lim		8	2	1	9	7*	9.00	0	0	399	210	10	21.00	4-30	1	0	3.15	3	
FC	2000/01	83	104	54	456	42	9.12	0	0	14477	6540	294	22.24	7-28	14	0	2.71	33	
Lim	2001/02	55	22	13	71	22*	7.88	0	0	2229	1367	69	19.81	5-29	3	1	3.68	9	
20T	2004/05	5	3	2	1	1*	1.00	0	0	96	84	10	8.40	4-16	1	0	5.25	2	
KOSALA, Mudliyarge Hasantha (Sri Lanka Navy) b Colombo 5.12.1979 RHB WK																			
FC		1	2	0	14	7	7.00	0	0									0	
KOTTEHEWA, Dasun Tharaka (Nondescripts) b Colombo 27.6.1985 RHB RFM																			
FC		8	8	1	181	63*	25.85	0	1	553	323	14	23.07	4-66	0	0	3.50	2	
Lim		6	4	1	26	13	8.66	0	0	175	157	6	26.16	2-34	0	0	5.38	2	
FC	2006/07	34	49	9	567	63*	14.17	0	2	4098	2129	84	25.34	4-33	0	0	3.11	10	
Lim	2005/06	31	17	8	225	36*	25.00	0	0	1167	916	48	19.08	8-20	2	2	4.71	4	
20T	2007/08	3	3	1	8	4	4.00	0	0	42	79	2	39.50	1-30	0	0	11.28	1	
KULASEKARA, Chamith Kosala Bandara (Nondescripts, Ruhuna, Sri Lanka A, Sri Lanka A to Australia) b Mavanalle 15.7.1985 RHB RFM																			
FC		15	19	1	315	50*	17.50	0	1	1617	1056	44	24.00	5-50	1	0	3.91	7	
Lim		20	17	3	341	74	24.35	0	1	560	506	14	36.14	3-37	0	0	5.42	5	
20T		8	5	0	81	42	16.20	0	0	159	257	8	32.12	4-26	1	0	9.69	1	
FC	2004/05	58	90	4	2332	129	27.11	2	13	4932	2843	113	25.15	6-13	2	0	3.45	29	
Lim	2004/05	65	57	11	1107	74	24.06	0	3	2139	1617	58	27.87	4-27	1	0	4.53	20	
20T	2005/06	27	20	3	259	98	15.23	0	1	447	581	26	22.34	4-26	1	0	7.79	8	
KULASEKARA, Kulasekara Mudiyanselage Dinesh Nuwan (Basnahira North, Colts, Sri Lanka, Sri Lanka to Bangladesh, Sri Lanka to India, Sri Lanka to South Africa, Sri Lanka to United States of America, Sri Lanka to West Indies, Sri Lanka to Zimbabwe) b Nittambuwa 22.7.1982 RHB RFM																			
FC		2	2	0	66	58	33.00	0	1	246	113	1	113.00	1-44	0	0	2.75	0	
Int		8	5	1	63	22	15.75	0	0	331	244	5	48.80	2-31	0	0	4.42	3	
Lim		12	8	2	90	22	15.00	0	0	539	435	14	31.07	4-39	1	0	4.84	5	
20T		4	4	2	54	30*	27.00	0	0	96	118	7	16.85	3-13	0	0	7.37	3	
Test	2004/05	11	16	1	245	64	16.33	0	1	1612	862	25	34.48	4-21	0	0	3.20	4	
FC	2002/03	73	97	21	1417	95	18.64	0	4	10092	5469	242	22.59	7-27	9	1	3.25	26	
Int	2003/04	79	50	23	475	57*	17.59	0	1	3605	2719	94	28.92	4-40	2	0	4.52	20	
Lim	2002/03	147	91	39	900	84	17.30	0	2	6580	4705	197	23.88	5-29	8	1	4.29	35	
I20T	2008/09	12	9	2	52	19*	7.42	0	0	269	373	11	33.90	3-4	0	0	8.32	5	
20T	2004/05	28	21	7	153	30*	10.92	0	0	632	818	30	27.26	3-4	0	0	7.76	12	

Cmp	Debut	M	I	NO	Runs	HS	Avge	100	50	Balls	Runs	Wkts	Avge	BB	5i	10m	RpO	ct	st
KULATUNGA, Hettiarachchi Gamage Jeevantha Mahesh (Colts, Wayamba, Barisal, Wayamba to India) b Kurunegala 2.11.1973 RHB RM																			
FC		12	16	1	725	158	48.33	3	3	429	191	10	19.10	4-13	0	0	2.67	6	
Lim		13	13	0	445	132	34.23	1	3	24	32	0					8.00	5	
20T		6	6	2	277	104*	69.25	1	1	12	17	0					8.50	0	
FC	1990/91	186	272	15	8315	234	32.35	13	50	5219	2358	81	29.11	5-67	1	0	2.71	187	
Lim	1993/94	102	92	11	2345	132	28.95	1	14	725	516	22	23.45	5-21	2	1	4.27	54	
I20T	2008/09	2	2	0	19	11	9.50	0	0									2	
20T	2004/05	36	34	5	761	104*	26.24	1	2	210	244	15	16.26	4-28	1	0	6.97	12	
KUMAR, Shanmugan Ramesh (Tamil Union) b Kandy 16.7.1986 RHB RFM																			
FC		1	1	0	13	13	13.00	0	0	60	29	0					2.90	1	
Lim		8	7	2	83	28	16.60	0	0									3	
FC	2007/08	12	22	0	433	82	19.68	0	3	210	146	2	73.00	2-31	0	0	4.17	12	
Lim	2006/07	20	18	2	348	106	21.75	1	1	132	95	5	19.00	2-31	0	0	4.31	10	
KUMARA, Hallawa Arachchilage Indika Dinesh (Police) b Kebithigollewa 13.1.1987 LHB RFM																			
Lim		1	1	0	0	0	0.00	0	0	12	18	0					9.00	0	
KUMARA, Hiramutungodage Geeth (Seeduwa Raddoluwa) b Colombo 15.5.1988 RHB LB																			
FC		9	13	1	467	93	38.91	0	4	128	78	2	39.00	2-14	0	0	3.65	9	
Lim		9	7	2	179	72*	35.80	0	2	192	159	7	22.71	3-49	0	0	4.96	5	
FC	2008/09	18	29	1	890	93	31.78	0	7	584	301	10	30.10	3-21	0	0	3.09	13	
Lim	2008/09	18	16	3	338	72*	26.00	0	2	390	277	10	27.70	3-49	0	0	4.26	13	
KUMARA, Henda Witharana Mahesh (Singha) b Ambalangoda 6.9.1980 LHB OB																			
FC		8	13	0	194	69	14.92	0	2	765	340	14	24.28	5-34	1	0	2.66	6	
Lim		5	5	1	69	28*	17.25	0	0	178	128	7	18.28	4-32	1	0	4.31	1	
FC	1999/00	42	77	5	1814	164*	25.19	2	6	1092	519	19	27.31	5-34	1	0	2.85	34	
Lim	1999/00	17	17	1	235	46	14.68	0	0	179	132	7	18.85	4-32	1	0	4.42	6	
KUMARA, Kosgodage Ajith (Sri Lanka Air Force) b Colombo 27.11.1977 RHB RMF																			
FC		9	16	1	287	51	19.13	0	1	196	184	8	23.00	3-13	0	0	5.63	4	
Lim		9	9	0	177	64	19.66	0	1	94	94	5	18.80	2-2	0	0	6.00	2	
FC	2000/01	71	120	6	2567	122*	22.51	2	12	1078	781	21	37.19	3-13	0	0	4.34	36	
Lim	2001/02	51	50	2	839	72	17.47	0	3	284	289	13	22.23	2-2	0	0	6.10	15	
20T	2004/05	5	5	1	65	24	16.25	0	0	24	50	0					12.50	0	
KUMARA, Kuruwalagamage Mangala Pradeep (Seeduwa Raddoluwa) b Padukka 12.1.1987 RHB SLA																			
FC		7	6	1	76	33	15.20	0	0	883	292	14	20.85	4-43	0	0	1.98	3	
Lim		10	5	0	24	8	4.80	0	0	439	244	18	13.55	4-19	1	0	3.33	2	
FC	2008/09	13	15	6	160	51*	17.77	0	1	2001	728	34	21.41	4-43	0	0	2.18	7	
Lim	2008/09	14	7	1	29	8	4.83	0	0	604	325	26	12.50	4-19	1	0	3.22	4	
KUMARA, Kalugala Yoshan (Moratuwa) b Galle 8.6.1990 RHB RM																			
FC		1	1	0	1	1	1.00	0	0	48	15	0					1.87	1	
Lim		1	1	1	1	1*		0	0	42	44	0					6.28	0	
KUMARA, Thirimanna Hettige Don Chandika Charitha (Burgher) b Kegalle 30.8.1985 LHB RFM																			
FC		1	2	0	4	4	2.00	0	0	72	35	4	8.75	3-21	0	0	2.91	1	
Lim		4	4	1	55	23*	18.33	0	0	18	33	0					11.00	2	
FC	2007/08	4	8	0	121	45	15.12	0	0	222	162	6	27.00	3-21	0	0	4.37	4	
Lim	2008/09	10	9	1	133	45	16.62	0	0	87	115	1	115.00	1-4	0	0	7.93	4	
LAKMAL, Madduma Wellalage Lahiru Sri (Bloomfield) b 5.5.1989 RHB RMF																			
FC		1	1	0	0	0	0.00	0	0	62	38	0					3.67	2	
Lim		2	1	1	1	1*		0	0	60	38	0					3.80	1	
LAKMAL, Ranasinghe Arachchige Suranga (Basnahira South, Sri Lanka A, Tamil Union, Sri Lanka to Bangladesh, Sri Lanka to India) b Matara 10.3.1987 RHB RMF																			
FC		10	9	1	39	24*	4.87	0	0	1021	700	22	31.81	4-33	0	0	4.11	1	
Lim		18	9	7	12	5*	6.00	0	0	744	658	30	21.93	5-47	1	1	5.30	5	
20T		4	1	0	1	1	1.00	0	0	72	86	2	43.00	1-24	0	0	7.16	0	
FC	2007/08	26	29	7	160	25*	7.27	0	0	3407	2370	79	30.00	5-78	1	0	4.17	7	
Int	2009/10	6	1	1	0	0*		0	0	270	298	4	74.50	2-55	0	0	6.62	2	
Lim	2007/08	45	18	13	26	10*	5.20	0	0	2040	1821	64	28.45	5-31	1	2	5.35	14	
20T	2007/08	13	5	4	7	3*	7.00	0	0	277	328	15	21.86	3-30	0	0	7.10	2	
LAKMAL, Rajapakse Kankanamalage Udara (Sri Lanka Navy) b Colombo 12.4.1987 RHB RMF																			
FC		7	11	1	204	51	20.40	0	1	597	375	19	19.73	4-49	0	0	3.76	3	
Lim		8	7	2	49	22	9.80	0	0	369	230	11	20.90	3-34	0	0	3.74	1	
FC	2007/08	8	13	1	241	51	20.08	0	1	723	420	20	21.00	4-49	0	0	3.48	3	
LAKSHITHA, Ahangama Baduge Tharanga (Bloomfield, Ruhuna, Sri Lanka A) b Matara 30.4.1982 RHB RFM																			
FC		13	19	5	217	36	15.50	0	0	1459	840	25	33.60	4-60	0	0	3.45	3	
Lim		12	6	2	27	8	6.75	0	0	419	334	17	19.64	3-50	0	0	4.78	1	
20T		6	2	1	2	2*	2.00	0	0	72	112	3	37.33	2-29	0	0	9.33	2	
FC	1999/00	90	125	35	926	36	10.28	0	0	10397	6337	214	29.61	7-59	9	0	3.65	36	
Lim	2000/01	71	37	16	248	57*	11.80	0	1	2899	2188	97	22.55	5-17	2	3	4.52	13	
20T	2004/05	18	7	3	18	8	4.50	0	0	243	339	19	17.84	5-16	2	1	8.37	3	

Cmp	Debut	M	I	NO	Runs	HS	Avge	100	50	Balls	Runs	Wkts	Avge	BB	5i	10m	RpO	ct	st
LAKSHITHA, Materba Kanatha Gamage Chamila Premanath (Sri Lanka Air Force) b Unawatuna 4.1.1979 RHB RFM																			
FC		9	15	1	252	79	18.00	0	1	999	545	18	30.27	4-33	0	0	3.27	4	
Lim		7	5	0	102	35	20.40	0	0	348	243	9	27.00	4-18	1	0	4.19	1	
Test	2002	2	3	0	42	40	14.00	0	0	288	158	5	31.60	2-33	0	0	3.29	1	
FC	2000/01	98	152	26	1841	79	14.61	0	1	14481	7407	374	19.80	7-23	21	2	3.06	33	
Int	2002	7	2	1	7	4	7.00	0	0	300	254	8	31.75	2-34	0	0	5.08	0	
Lim	2001/02	52	44	8	461	52*	12.80	0	1	2606	1721	78	22.06	4-18	3	0	3.96	8	
20T	2004/05	3	2	1	9	5*	9.00	0	0	60	59	4	14.75	2-25	0	0	5.90	0	
LEELARATNE, Supunsara (Sri Lanka Navy) b Colombo 27.5.1981 RHB OB																			
FC		9	17	2	667	84*	44.46	0	8	268	186	5	37.20	1-11	0	0	4.16	13	
Lim		9	9	0	303	126	33.66	1	1	42	35	1	35.00	1-27	0	0	5.00	1	
LIVERA, Anton Nelendra Madushanka (Tamil Union) b Colombo 8.6.1988 RHB RMF																			
Lim		1	1	0	8	8	8.00	0	0									1	
FC	2006/07	4	6	1	21	9	4.20	0	0	300	171	6	28.50	3-43	0	0	3.42	0	
Lim	2006/07	8	5	1	67	24	16.75	0	0	84	66	2	33.00	1-19	0	0	4.71	3	
LIYANAGE, Chamara Hawpe (Sebastianites) b Colombo 20.12.1977 RHB OB																			
Lim		2	2	0	14	13	7.00	0	0	60	44	1	44.00	1-44	0	0	4.40	0	
FC	1997/98	34	49	6	571	81	13.27	0	2	3709	1588	74	21.45	6-93	1	0	2.56	22	
Lim	1998/99	9	6	2	59	30*	14.75	0	0	216	172	6	28.66	2-13	0	0	4.77	1	
20T	2006/07	3	2	0	10	5	5.00	0	0	68	56	1	56.00	1-13	0	0	4.94	0	
LIYANAGE, Don Peduru Manjula Liyanage (Seeduwa Raddoluwa) b Kolonna 20.2.1980 RHB LMF																			
FC		4	3	1	12	7*	6.00	0	0	202	129	3	43.00	3-51	0	0	3.83	1	
Lim		2	1	1	1	1*		0	0	90	45	6	7.50	4-27	1	0	3.00	1	
FC	2007/08	7	7	2	12	7*	2.40	0	0	483	330	11	30.00	4-55	0	0	4.09	1	
Lim	2008/09	6	4	1	10	8	3.33	0	0	169	119	12	9.91	5-31	1	1	4.22	3	
20T	2005/06	1	1	0	7	7	7.00	0	0	12	24	0					12.00	0	
LIYANAGE, Darshina Saminda (Sebastianites) b Colombo 17.11.1980 RHB RFM																			
Lim		1	1	1	1	1*		0	0	24	30	0					7.50	0	
FC	2002/03	12	18	6	20	12	1.66	0	0	1109	739	30	24.63	5-51	1	0	3.99	5	
Lim	2004/05	2	2	1	1	1*	1.00	0	0	54	62	0					6.88	0	
LIYANAGE, Nevil Cristy Kumara (Singha) b Matugama 9.10.1975 RHB LMF																			
FC		9	15	2	164	39*	12.61	0	0	1115	583	39	14.94	6-29	4	1	3.13	8	
Lim		9	8	0	105	31	13.12	0	0	378	362	13	27.84	5-48	0	1	5.74	5	
FC	2005/06	36	54	5	573	58*	11.69	0	1	4425	2890	137	21.09	7-36	10	1	3.91	18	
Lim	2005/06	35	25	5	230	31	11.50	0	0	1195	1116	37	30.16	5-48	1	1	5.60	13	
20T	2005/06	1	1	0	3	3	3.00	0	0	18	25	1	25.00	1-25	0	0	8.33	0	
LIYANAGE, Pramuka Sudesh (Panadura) b Kaluthara 4.10.1982 LHB LFM																			
FC		9	12	2	294	69	29.40	0	3	444	210	1	210.00	1-26	0	0	2.83	1	
Lim		7	6	1	84	27	16.80	0	0	240	186	9	20.66	5-21	0	1	4.65	2	
FC	2002/03	62	85	15	1408	90	20.11	0	10	4200	2450	91	26.92	7-33	1	0	3.50	22	
Lim	2002/03	42	35	4	359	70	11.58	0	1	1400	1045	44	23.75	5-21	0	3	4.47	11	
20T	2004/05	10	8	2	39	18	6.50	0	0	157	289	9	32.11	3-29	0	0	11.04	4	
LIYANAGUNAWARDENE, Sanjaya Chathuranga (Tamil Union) b Matara 3.5.1986 RHB SLA																			
FC		5	6	1	21	12	4.20	0	0	559	417	20	20.85	5-63	2	0	4.47	2	
FC	2006/07	19	26	3	141	20	6.13	0	0	2570	1749	56	31.23	6-94	4	0	4.08	11	
Lim	2006/07	2	1	0	10	10	10.00	0	0	48	32	0					4.00	0	
20T	2006/07	4	3	1	44	24*	22.00	0	0	48	46	5	9.20	3-21	0	0	5.75	0	
LIYANAJAYAWARDENE, Mathsahan (Sri Lanka Air Force) b Mahamodara 25.7.1990 LHB LMF																			
Lim		2	2	0	10	8	5.00	0	0	84	73	2	36.50	2-51	0	0	5.21	0	
LIYANAPATHIRANA, Nuwan Kumara (Sri Lanka Army) b Matale 22.5.1987 RHB RFM																			
FC		3	4	2	16	8	8.00	0	0	180	128	3	42.66	2-26	0	0	4.26	1	
FC	2008/09	4	5	2	16	8	5.33	0	0	288	190	3	63.33	2-26	0	0	3.95	1	
Lim	2007/08	8	5	2	33	22	11.00	0	0	216	197	4	49.25	1-23	0	0	5.47	1	
LIYANAPATHIRANAGE, Maduka Ayeshmantha (Chilaw Marians, Sri Lanka Cricket Combined XI) b Colombo 1.4.1992 RHB OB																			
Lim		6	5	1	21	13	5.25	0	0	317	244	7	34.85	2-50	0	0	4.61	1	
20T		5	2	2	3	2*		0	0	98	129	0					7.89	1	
LOKUARACHCHI, Kaushal Samaraweera (Sinhalese, Wayamba, Rajshahi to Bangladesh, Wayamba to India) b Colombo 20.5.1982 RHB LB																			
FC		10	14	0	241	65	17.21	0	1	1241	630	18	35.00	4-15	0	0	3.04	3	
Lim		10	8	2	189	70	31.50	0	1	456	245	14	17.50	2-22	0	0	3.22	4	
20T		6	4	1	54	29	18.00	0	0	54	60	5	12.00	2-18	0	0	6.66	6	
Test	2003	4	5	1	94	28*	23.50	0	0	594	295	5	59.00	2-47	0	0	2.98	1	
FC	2000/01	104	143	13	3405	101*	26.19	2	15	14984	6730	273	24.65	7-17	7	1	2.69	54	
Int	2002/03	21	18	3	210	69	14.00	0	1	1011	725	31	23.38	4-44	1	0	4.30	5	
Lim	2001/02	118	85	14	1529	77*	21.53	0	7	5399	3810	165	23.09	5-27	5	1	4.23	44	
20T	2004/05	25	19	1	255	42	14.16	0	0	380	420	23	18.26	3-16	0	0	6.63	12	
LOKUGE, Isuru (Sri Lanka Navy) b Matara 5.7.1982 RHB WK																			
Lim		1	1	0	7	7	7.00	0	0									0	
Lim	2000/01	3	3	0	44	33	14.66	0	0									0	

Cmp	Debut	M	I	NO	Runs	HS	Avge	100	50	Balls	Runs	Wkts	Avge	BB	5i	10m	RpO	ct	st
MADANAYAKE, Suwanji (Sebastianites) b Kandy 28.8.1975 LHB SLA																			
FC		9	14	1	188	33	14.46	0	0	1619	722	37	19.51	5-32	1	0	2.67	5	
Lim		5	4	0	51	20	12.75	0	0	233	94	10	9.40	5-15	0	1	2.42	4	
FC	1991/92	103	155	15	2829	110	20.20	1	13	12034	5771	272	21.21	7-15	13	2	2.87	63	
Lim	1998/99	63	53	5	893	52	18.60	0	1	2619	1597	84	19.01	5-15	4	1	3.65	18	
20T	2005/06	2	1	0	4	4	4.00	0	0	22	34	2	17.00	2-18	0	0	9.27	0	
MADANAYAKE, Thushara Jayananda (Singha) b Kandy 10.8.1981 LHB OB																			
FC		5	9	1	142	45	17.75	0	0	18	16	0					5.33	1	
Lim		7	6	0	54	15	9.00	0	0	208	155	4	38.75	2-22	0	0	4.47	2	
FC	2000/01	40	71	6	1404	115	21.60	1	5	1132	658	11	59.81	3-60	0	0	3.48	18	
Lim	2005/06	31	26	1	344	40	13.76	0	0	519	382	13	29.38	3-44	0	0	4.41	8	
20T	2004/05	4	3	0	32	30	10.66	0	0									0	
MADUSANKA, Candauda Arachchige Marlan (Burgher) b Matara 31.1.1988 RHB SLA																			
FC		9	12	2	126	25	12.60	0	0	1291	783	42	18.64	5-39	4	1	3.63	8	
Lim		6	5	2	14	5*	4.66	0	0	318	162	12	13.50	3-21	0	0	3.05	1	
FC	2007/08	26	41	9	478	51	14.93	0	1	4011	2178	110	19.80	8-76	7	2	3.25	13	
Lim	2007/08	17	11	7	42	11*	10.50	0	0	810	422	27	15.62	3-21	0	0	3.12	4	
MAGAGE, Krishal (Moratuwa) b Ragama 22.3.1987 LHB RMF																			
FC		4	5	0	113	45	22.60	0	0	90	43	2	21.50	1-5	0	0	2.86	2	
Lim		2	2	0	9	8	4.50	0	0	90	47	2	23.50	1-16	0	0	3.13	0	
FC	2007/08	9	12	0	258	76	21.50	0	1	102	55	2	27.50	1-5	0	0	3.23	3	
Lim	2008/09	7	6	2	45	24	11.25	0	0	90	47	2	23.50	1-16	0	0	3.13	4	
MAHAROOF, Mohamed Farveez (Nondescripts, Sri Lanka, Sri Lanka A, Wayamba, Delhi Daredevils, Wayamba to India) b Colombo 7.9.1984 RHB RFM																			
FC		5	8	1	236	115*	33.71	1	0	517	273	6	45.50	2-32	0	0	3.16	4	
Int		3	2	0	11	10	5.50	0	0	144	136	5	27.20	5-42	0	1	5.66	1	
Lim		18	14	3	358	70*	32.54	0	3	756	652	19	34.31	5-42	0	1	5.17	3	
20T		6	3	1	16	6*	8.00	0	0	108	126	3	42.00	1-4	0	0	7.00	5	
Test	2004	20	31	4	538	72	19.92	0	3	2628	1458	24	60.75	4-52	0	0	3.32	6	
FC	2001/02	49	72	7	1442	115*	22.18	2	4	5958	3234	99	32.66	7-73	1	0	3.25	25	
Int	2004	94	64	15	984	69*	20.08	0	2	3932	3133	121	25.89	6-14	4	2	4.78	20	
Lim	2002/03	149	110	23	1866	70*	21.44	0	6	6072	4875	173	28.17	6-14	6	2	4.81	34	
I20T	2006	7	4	1	23	13*	7.66	0	0	144	173	7	24.71	2-18	0	0	7.20	2	
20T	2004/05	44	29	11	288	39	16.00	0	0	900	1101	45	24.46	3-21	0	0	7.34	13	
MALIGASPE, Nemesh Malinga (Burgher) b Colombo 20.6.1986 LHB WK																			
FC		2	3	0	17	9	5.66	0	0									3	
Lim		3	3	0	46	28	15.33	0	0									2	1
FC	2008/09	7	12	1	145	47	13.18	0	0									14	
Lim	2008/09	8	8	1	134	52*	19.14	0	1									10	2
20T	2006/07	1	1	1	0	0*		0	0									0	
MALINGA, Surappulige Dilan Chamikara (Tamil Union) b Colombo 8.8.1983 RHB RFM																			
FC		5	6	2	23	10*	5.75	0	0	372	253	7	36.14	3-42	0	0	4.08	2	
Lim		3	2	1	1	1*	1.00	0	0	90	59	2	29.50	2-13	0	0	3.93	0	
FC	2001/02	54	81	23	600	59*	10.34	0	2	6945	3939	175	22.50	7-29	6	1	3.40	25	
Lim	2002/03	37	26	7	120	20	6.31	0	0	1405	1151	37	31.10	4-40	1	0	4.91	6	
20T	2004/05	5	5	3	45	29*	22.50	0	0	113	136	10	13.60	5-20	0	1	7.22	2	
MALINGA, Separamadu Lasith Swarnajith (Nondescripts, Ruhuna, Sri Lanka, Mumbai Indians, Sri Lanka to India, Sri Lanka to South Africa, Sri Lanka to United States of America, Sri Lanka to West Indies) b Galle 4.9.1983 RHB RF																			
Test		2	3	0	83	64	27.66	0	1	432	273	10	27.30	5-50	1	0	3.79	0	
FC		3	3	0	83	64	27.66	0	1	540	335	13	25.76	5-50	1	0	3.72	1	
Int		8	3	0	28	16	9.33	0	0	380	265	16	16.56	5-34	0	1	4.18	1	
Lim		13	7	2	42	16	8.40	0	0	610	479	26	18.42	5-34	1	1	4.71	1	
Test	2004	30	37	13	275	64	11.45	0	1	5209	3349	101	33.15	5-50	3	0	3.85	7	
FC	2001/02	83	100	41	584	64	9.89	0	1	11885	7755	255	30.41	6-17	7	0	3.91	23	
Int	2004	72	34	12	152	16	6.90	0	0	3494	2896	106	27.32	5-34	5	1	4.97	12	
Lim	2001/02	115	61	20	276	23*	6.73	0	0	5519	4600	182	25.27	5-34	8	2	5.00	20	
I20T	2006	28	12	7	63	27	12.60	0	0	564	702	34	20.64	3-12	0	0	7.46	12	
20T	2004/05	66	20	11	68	27	7.55	0	0	1363	1577	77	20.48	4-22	1	0	6.94	19	
MANOHARA, Petta Yaddehi Ushan (Sinhalese) b Galle 26.8.1989 RHB RFM																			
FC		5	4	3	7	6*	7.00	0	0	223	158	3	52.66	2-57	0	0	4.25	0	
Lim		3								140	113	5	22.60	2-37	0	0	4.84	0	
MANOJ, Waduge Lasantha (Colombo) b Peradeniya 24.1.1988 LHB RMF																			
FC		4	3	1	4	4	2.00	0	0	327	257	6	42.83	3-43	0	0	4.71	2	
FC	2008/09	16	20	12	28	9	3.50	0	0	1747	1112	40	27.80	5-35	1	0	3.81	6	
Lim	2008/09	4	1	1	5	5*		0	0	186	136	5	27.20	3-34	0	0	4.38	0	
MAPA BANDARA, Mapa Ralalage Damith Gunaratne (Colts) b Kurunegala 20.5.1986 RHB WK																			
FC		9	9	4	202	104*	40.40	1	0									16	8
Lim		4	2	0	25	21	12.50	0	0									2	1
FC	2001/02	34	52	12	755	104*	18.87	1	2									84	15
Lim	2005/06	25	19	1	327	50	18.16	0	1									28	6
20T	2005/06	5	4	2	34	18*	17.00	0	0									1	5

Cmp	Debut	M	I	NO	Runs	HS	Avge	100	50	Balls	Runs	Wkts	Avge	BB	5i	10m	RpO	ct	st
MAPATUNA, Carman Prabath (Panadura) b Colombo 10.9.1972 RHB LBG																			
FC		9	11	2	255	52	28.33	0	1	192	119	8	14.87	4-26	0	0	3.71	10	
Lim		9	8	1	273	127	39.00	1	0	24	15	2	7.50	2-15	0	0	3.75	3	
FC	1990/91	89	127	14	3048	129*	26.97	5	11	2026	1091	45	24.24	5-31	2	0	3.23	76	
Lim	1992/93	46	38	7	869	127	28.03	1	3	156	98	5	19.60	2-15	0	0	3.76	21	
20T	2006/07	3	3	0	29	12	9.66	0	0									1	
MASMULLA, Thilina Sachinda (Bloomfield, Sri Lanka Army) b Colombo 28.6.1985 LHB OB																			
FC		6	12	0	168	33	14.00	0	0	12	29	0					14.50	3	
Lim		7	7	0	96	28	13.71	0	0	12	14	0					7.00	0	
FC	2005/06	37	67	3	1665	132	26.01	2	6	352	310	6	51.66	3-17	0	0	5.28	33	
Lim	2003/04	23	22	0	399	84	18.13	0	2	18	17	0					5.66	5	
20T	2005/06	6	6	2	110	40	27.50	0	0	48	65	3	21.66	2-16	0	0	8.12	2	
MASSALAGE, Indika (Seeduwa Raddoluwa) b Colombo 11.2.1990 LHB RMF																			
FC		2	3	0	30	13	10.00	0	0									0	
Lim		7	7	0	126	57	18.00	0	1	30	21	0					4.20	3	
Lim	2008/09	10	10	0	181	57	18.10	0	1	30	21	0					4.20	3	
MATHEWS, Angelo Davis (Basnahira North, Colts, Sri Lanka, Kolkata Knight Riders, Sri Lanka to India, Sri Lanka to South Africa, Sri Lanka to United States of America, Sri Lanka to West Indies, Sri Lanka to Zimbabwe) b Colombo 2.6.1987 RHB RFM																			
Test		3	3	0	91	45	30.33	0	0	162	74	1	74.00	1-13	0	0	2.74	0	
FC		4	4	0	188	97	47.00	0	1	222	104	1	104.00	1-13	0	0	2.81	2	
Int		9	6	2	113	55*	28.25	0	1	324	227	10	22.70	3-36	0	0	4.20	3	
Lim		14	11	3	318	58	39.75	0	4	324	227	10	22.70	3-36	0	0	4.20	7	
20T		5	5	1	146	60*	36.50	0	1	6	8	1	8.00	1-8	0	0	8.00	3	
Test	2009	10	14	1	470	99	36.15	0	2	696	376	6	62.66	1-13	0	0	3.24	2	
FC	2006/07	40	60	6	2770	270	51.29	8	11	3159	1503	36	41.75	5-47	1	0	2.85	24	
Int	2008/09	29	23	4	563	75	29.63	0	5	1002	765	27	28.33	6-20	0	1	4.58	9	
Lim	2005/06	55	45	10	1065	75	30.42	0	10	1533	1149	44	26.11	6-20	1	1	4.49	19	
I20T	2009	20	18	8	293	58	29.30	0	1	283	346	15	23.06	3-16	0	0	7.33	7	
20T	2006/07	52	46	13	857	65*	25.96	0	3	673	894	32	27.93	4-19	1	0	7.97	19	
MAZAHIR, Mohamed Nisham (Ragama) b Colombo 24.3.1989 LHB RFM																			
FC		6	8	0	213	104	26.62	1	1									1	
Lim		6	6	1	127	65*	25.40	0	1									1	
FC	2008/09	10	14	0	394	104	28.14	1	4	20	25	0					7.50	2	
Lim	2007/08	14	14	1	323	67	24.84	0	2	66	68	1	68.00	1-19	0	0	6.18	1	
MENDIS, Balapuwaduge Ajantha Winslo (Sri Lanka, Sri Lanka Army, Sri Lanka Board President's XI, Wayamba, Kolkata Knight Riders, Sri Lanka to India, Sri Lanka to South Africa, Sri Lanka to United States of America, Sri Lanka to West Indies, Sri Lanka to Zimbabwe, Wayamba to India) b Moratuwa 11.3.1985 RHB RS																			
Test		2	2	0	81	78	40.50	0	1	642	346	6	57.66	4-172	0	0	3.23	1	
FC		4	5	0	110	78	22.00	0	1	1005	519	20	25.95	6-64	2	0	3.09	1	
Int		2								60	42	1	42.00	1-42	0	0	4.20	0	
Lim		8	3	0	32	28	10.66	0	0	343	251	9	27.88	3-28	0	0	4.39	1	
20T		6	1	1	0	0*		0	0	134	138	8	17.25	4-9	1	0	6.17	2	
Test	2008	12	13	4	145	78	16.11	0	1	3228	1644	50	32.88	6-117	2	1	3.05	2	
FC	2006/07	35	47	4	572	78	13.30	0	1	7545	3597	185	19.44	7-37	11	2	2.86	11	
Int	2007/08	44	21	9	91	15*	7.58	0	0	2073	1511	78	19.37	6-13	3	3	4.37	5	
Lim	2006/07	69	39	12	450	71*	16.66	0	2	3150	2144	123	17.43	6-13	5	3	4.08	10	
I20T	2008/09	19	4	2	7	4*	3.50	0	0	432	409	33	12.39	4-15	2	0	5.68	2	
20T	2006/07	46	15	8	25	9	3.57	0	0	1020	1043	64	16.29	4-9	3	0	6.13	12	
MENDIS, Balapuwaduge Manukulasuriya Amith Jeewan (Kandurata, Sri Lanka A, Tamil Union, Dhaka, Sri Lanka to Zimbabwe, Sri Lanka A to Australia) b Colombo 15.1.1983 LHB LB																			
FC		18	24	6	896	153*	49.77	3	3	2039	1153	47	24.53	5-32	2	0	3.39	17	
Lim		26	20	6	698	94	49.85	0	5	868	636	25	25.44	4-28	2	0	4.39	9	
20T		7	6	1	101	36	20.20	0	0	54	71	0					7.88	1	
FC	2000/01	94	150	20	4021	153*	30.93	7	21	4574	2565	85	30.17	5-32	2	0	3.36	89	
Int	2010	4	2	1	42	35*	42.00	0	0	162	119	4	29.75	2-12	0	0	4.40	2	
Lim	2002/03	91	79	11	1700	94	25.00	0	9	1802	1365	51	26.76	5-26	3	1	4.54	37	1
20T	2004/05	31	27	4	553	48	24.04	0	0	114	133	3	44.33	2-20	0	0	7.00	11	
MENDIS, Balapuwaduge Manukulasuriya Dulanjana Kalhara (Sri Lanka Navy) b Colombo 20.5.1990 RHB LB																			
FC		5	7	0	26	11	3.71	0	0	676	375	18	20.83	5-42	2	0	3.32	1	
Lim		7	6	3	7	6*	2.33	0	0	331	234	13	18.00	6-66	1	1	4.24	1	
MENDIS, Balapuwaduge Manukulasuriya Thiwantha Tharindu (Colombo) b Colombo 21.4.1981 RHB OB																			
FC		8	10	2	144	39	18.00	0	0	110	64	7	9.14	3-13	0	0	3.49	11	
Lim		9	9	3	156	47*	26.00	0	0									2	
FC	2000/01	71	107	9	2387	92	24.35	0	13	1099	528	23	22.95	3-13	0	0	2.88	89	
Lim	2001/02	51	46	8	753	83*	19.81	0	3	197	135	5	27.00	2-6	0	0	4.11	19	
20T	2005/06	5	3	0	33	19	11.00	0	0	12	24	0					12.00	3	
MENDIS, Balpuwaduge Rajitha Prageeth (Sri Lanka Air Force) b Colombo 6.7.1988 LHB OB WK																			
Lim		4	4	0	55	25	13.75	0	0									0	
Lim	2008/09	9	9	0	160	82	17.77	0	1									0	

Cmp	Debut	M	I	NO	Runs	HS	Avge	100	50	Balls	Runs	Wkts	Avge	BB	5i	10m	RpO	ct	st
MENDIS, Balpuwaduge Rajitha Suren (Panadura) b Colombo 14.3.1987 LHB RM																			
FC		1	1	0	1	1	1.00	0	0	66	43	0					3.90	1	
Lim		3	2	2	0	0*		0	0	120	65	1	65.00	1-18	0	0	3.25	0	
FC	2007/08	4	5	1	8	5*	2.00	0	0	384	231	9	25.66	6-48	1	0	3.60	1	
Lim	2007/08	7	6	4	34	19*	17.00	0	0	180	135	2	67.50	1-18	0	0	4.50	0	
MENDIS, Rashimal Madurank (Sebastianites) b Moratuwa 24.2.1985 RHB RAB																			
FC		9	14	1	230	39	17.69	0	0									18	6
Lim		7	6	1	131	61	26.20	0	1									3	5
FC	2007/08	18	31	4	543	89	20.11	0	1	12	5	0					2.50	28	6
Lim	2007/08	17	16	1	325	95	21.66	0	2									7	5
MENDIS, Thirimadura Romesh Danushka (Sri Lanka Army) b Balapitiya 19.7.1980 RHB RFM																			
Lim		4	4	0	61	39	15.25	0	0									1	
FC	1998/99	43	73	7	1179	81*	17.86	0	3	1541	645	15	43.00	3-31	0	0	2.51	26	
Lim	1998/99	30	28	4	317	39	13.20	0	0	666	382	15	25.46	3-27	0	0	3.44	7	
20T	2005/06	6	5	1	31	13	7.75	0	0	66	65	3	21.66	1-16	0	0	5.90	3	
MENDIS, Yagamuni Amila Nuwan (Police) b Matara 9.6.1982 LHB SLA																			
FC		7	8	0	147	59	18.37	0	1	1037	465	22	21.13	5-106	1	0	2.69	2	
Lim		8	7	2	56	34*	11.20	0	0	295	204	8	25.50	3-8	0	0	4.14	2	
FC	1998/99	38	55	13	613	59	14.59	0	2	4149	2165	87	24.88	5-47	3	0	3.13	35	
Lim	2003/04	30	18	4	166	34*	11.85	0	0	1076	771	35	22.02	4-31	1	0	4.29	13	
20T	2004/05	4	2	1	9	9	9.00	0	0	66	69	4	17.25	2-19	0	0	6.27	3	
MENDIS, Yagamuni Suminda Sampath (Bloomfield) b Matara 31.10.1979 RHB WK																			
FC		3	3	0	18	10	6.00	0	0									2	
Lim		2	1	1	0	0*		0	0									1	2
FC	1997/98	45	67	1	880	86	13.33	0	3	54	34	1	34.00	1-34	0	0	3.77	102	11
Lim	2004/05	26	20	2	191	50*	10.61	0	1	6	7	0					7.00	23	5
20T	2005/06	6	4	0	21	11	5.25	0	0									2	6
MIRANDO, Magina Thilan Thushara (Kandurata, Sinhalese, Sri Lanka A, Chennai Super Kings, Sri Lanka to Bangladesh, Sri Lanka to South Africa, Sri Lanka to West Indies, Sri Lanka to Zimbabwe) b Balapitiya 1.3.1981 LHB LFM																			
FC		1	2	0	64	59	32.00	0	1	12	5	0					2.50	0	
Lim		10	5	3	43	21	21.50	0	0	476	455	15	30.33	5-39	0	1	5.73	5	
20T		4	2	1	25	17*	25.00	0	0	78	102	1	102.00	1-25	0	0	7.84	2	
Test	2003	9	13	2	90	15*	8.18	0	0	1542	961	28	34.32	5-83	1	0	3.73	3	
FC	1998/99	99	146	15	2032	103*	15.51	1	6	12698	7536	256	29.43	6-50	8	1	3.56	38	
Int	2007/08	38	27	6	392	54*	18.66	0	1	1676	1393	50	27.86	5-47	0	1	4.98	4	
Lim	1999/00	124	84	20	1139	75*	17.79	0	3	4841	3916	147	26.63	6-28	1	4	4.85	18	
I20T	2008/09	6	2	0	4	3	2.00	0	0	132	179	7	25.57	2-37	0	0	8.13	2	
20T	2004/05	33	21	7	134	33*	9.57	0	0	687	824	38	21.68	3-23	0	0	7.19	12	
MUBARAK, Jehan (Colombo, Wayamba, Wayamba to India) b Washington, United States of America 10.1.1981 LHB OB																			
FC		10	16	0	518	110	32.37	1	4	858	402	7	57.42	2-28	0	0	2.81	19	
Lim		12	11	0	295	79	26.81	0	2	180	153	3	51.00	1-14	0	0	5.10	8	
20T		7	6	2	174	62*	43.50	0	1	36	55	2	27.50	2-23	0	0	9.16	2	
Test	2002	10	17	1	254	48	15.87	0	0	84	50	0					3.57	13	
FC	1999/00	123	214	16	6399	169	32.31	9	37	5429	2853	69	41.34	6-11	1	0	3.15	128	
Int	2002/03	38	36	6	696	72	23.20	0	4	111	76	2	38.00	1-10	0	0	4.10	12	
Lim	1999/00	149	143	17	3734	113	29.63	2	20	1619	1328	41	32.39	5-50	0	2	4.92	65	
I20T	2007/08	16	15	4	238	46*	21.63	0	0	8	17	1	17.00	1-9	0	0	12.75	9	
20T	2004/05	45	40	8	925	94*	28.90	0	5	162	230	12	19.16	4-29	1	0	8.51	24	
MUDALIGE, Chamikara Ravinda Bentota (Nondescripts) b Galle 5.7.1976 RHB OB																			
FC		5	6	2	12	6*	3.00	0	0	307	184	7	26.28	4-46	0	0	3.59	4	
Lim		3	2	2	4	4*		0	0	90	75	0					5.00	0	
FC	1995/96	122	158	44	1022	56	8.96	0	2	16604	8699	329	26.44	9-111	10	2	3.14	70	
Lim	1998/99	62	33	17	145	18*	9.06	0	0	2619	1855	68	27.27	4-16	1	0	4.25	22	
20T	2004/05	6	2	1	12	10*	12.00	0	0	90	118	5	23.60	2-30	0	0	7.86	2	
MUNAWEERA, Eldeniya Meda Gedara Dilshan Yasika (Basnahira North, Bloomfield, Sri Lanka A to Australia) b Colombo 24.4.1989 RHB OB																			
FC		12	20	0	768	153	38.40	2	5	84	55	0					3.92	8	
Lim		12	12	0	358	107	29.83	1	2	103	72	4	18.00	2-5	0	0	4.19	6	
20T		3	3	0	33	16	11.00	0	0	6	15	0					15.00	1	
FC	2008/09	17	29	0	839	153	28.93	2	5	452	235	8	29.37	3-27	0	0	3.11	10	
Lim	2008/09	19	18	0	469	107	26.05	1	3	337	212	9	23.55	3-37	0	0	3.77	9	
20T	2009/10	4	4	0	39	16	9.75	0	0	6	15	0					15.00	1	
MURALITHARAN, Muttiah (Kandurata, Sri Lanka, Tamil Union, Chennai Super Kings, Sri Lanka to India, Sri Lanka to South Africa, Sri Lanka to West Indies) b Kandy 17.4.1972 RHB OB																			
Test		1	1	1	5	5*		0	0	370	191	8	23.87	5-63	1	0	3.09	0	
FC		1	1	1	5	5*		0	0	370	191	8	23.87	5-63	1	0	3.09	0	
Int		3	2	1	3	2	3.00	0	0	168	143	3	47.66	2-38	0	0	5.10	0	
Lim		11	5	1	33	27	8.25	0	0	533	398	15	26.53	3-29	0	0	4.48	5	
20T		4	2	0	0	0	0.00	0	0	83	89	7	12.71	2-12	0	0	6.43	1	
Test	1992	133	164	56	1261	67	11.67	0	1	44039	18180	800	22.72	9-51	67	22	2.47	72	
FC	1990	232	276	83	2192	67	11.35	0	1	66933	26997	1374	19.64	9-51	119	34	2.42	123	

Cmp	Debut	M	I	NO	Runs	HS	Avge	100	50	Balls	Runs	Wkts	Avge	BB	5i	10m	RpO	ct	st
Int	1993	337	159	61	663	33*	6.76	0	0	18169	11885	515	23.07	7-30	14	10	3.92	128	
Lim	1991/92	434	200	73	924	33*	7.27	0	0	22802	14637	654	22.38	7-30	16	12	3.85	155	
I20T	2006/07	11	2	0	1	1	0.50	0	0	258	266	13	20.46	3-29	0	0	6.18	0	
20T	2005	66	15	3	38	11	3.16	0	0	1523	1569	83	18.90	4-16	3	0	6.18	16	
MUTALIPH, Tuan Mohamed Ishan (Colts, Kandurata) b Colombo 8.2.1983 RHB WK																			
FC		12	15	1	530	125	37.85	1	2									9	
Lim		4	3	0	33	30	11.00	0	0									2	
FC	2001/02	72	118	6	3072	142*	27.42	3	13	42	22	1	22.00	1-22	0	0	3.14	86	14
Lim	2001/02	42	41	2	942	107	24.15	1	4									28	7
20T	2004/05	17	17	1	296	60	18.50	0	1									1	7
NAMAL, Jagodage Raju Gayashan (Burgher, Sri Lanka Cricket Combined XI) b Panadura 23.6.1988 LHB OB																			
FC		9	15	2	628	154	48.30	2	1	102	75	1	75.00	1-27	0	0	4.41	8	
Lim		10	10	0	320	67	32.00	0	3	107	74	4	18.50	2-31	0	0	4.15	8	1
FC	2006/07	30	53	4	1578	154	32.20	4	7	576	345	5	69.00	1-6	0	0	3.59	18	1
Lim	2006/07	31	28	3	682	67	27.28	0	5	255	173	9	19.22	2-16	0	0	4.07	16	1
20T	2006/07	3	3	0	84	34	28.00	0	0									0	
NAWELA, Nawela Mahagamaralalage Nadeera Prabath (Kandurata, Moors, Sri Lanka A, Sri Lanka A to Australia) b Maharagama 4.10.1984 RHB RFM																			
FC		16	26	1	1020	115	40.80	2	7									8	
Lim		6	6	0	54	25	9.00	0	0									2	
FC	2002/03	75	122	7	3250	148*	28.26	7	13	655	476	14	34.00	5-52	1	0	4.36	50	
Lim	2003/04	45	45	3	843	69	20.07	0	3	138	150	2	75.00	1-33	0	0	6.52	14	
20T	2005/06	6	4	1	22	12*	7.33	0	0									6	
NAYANAKANTHA, Hewawasam Gamage Dharshana (Ragama) b Colombo 2.3.1979 RHB RFM																			
FC		6	7	0	32	15	4.57	0	0	381	235	9	26.11	5-37	1	0	3.70	1	
Lim		3	2	0	4	2	2.00	0	0	102	81	6	13.50	3-31	0	0	4.76	0	
FC	1998/99	101	123	35	660	40	7.50	0	0	11216	6590	248	26.57	5-37	6	0	3.52	27	
Int	2003	3	2	1	3	2*	3.00	0	0	95	83	2	41.50	1-26	0	0	5.24	2	
Lim	1999/00	73	36	9	153	28	5.66	0	0	2894	2158	91	23.71	4-14	2	0	4.47	17	
20T	2004/05	10	7	4	49	17*	16.33	0	0	192	225	8	28.12	2-16	0	0	7.03	1	
NIKETHANA, Artigala Vidanalage Sujith (Seeduwa Raddoluwa) b Colombo 26.4.1986 LHB RSM																			
FC		7	10	0	278	81	27.80	0	1	36	18	1	18.00	1-14	0	0	3.00	5	
Lim		3	2	0	44	34	22.00	0	0	78	36	3	12.00	3-27	0	0	2.76	1	
FC	2007/08	13	19	2	416	81	24.47	0	2	101	56	4	14.00	3-21	0	0	3.32	8	
Lim	2007/08	11	10	8	98	34	49.00	0	0	346	220	8	27.50	3-27	0	0	3.81	3	
NIRMAL, Pratapasinghe Ravin (Police) b Galle 17.8.1982 RHB OB																			
FC		8	12	0	274	74	22.83	0	2	258	103	2	51.50	1-5	0	0	2.39	12	
Lim		9	9	1	353	100	44.12	1	2	202	142	3	47.33	1-15	0	0	4.21	2	
FC	2003/04	45	75	5	1562	202	22.31	1	9	444	176	6	29.33	2-17	0	0	2.37	61	
Lim	2000/01	46	43	8	1134	103	32.40	2	4	680	415	17	24.41	4-20	1	0	3.66	18	
20T	2005/06	3	3	0	36	32	12.00	0	0									0	
NIRMALA, Punchi Hewa Kankanamage Supun (Police) b Anuradhapura 25.12.1982 LHB WK																			
FC		8	11	4	213	104*	30.42	1	0									10	2
Lim		9	9	0	236	44	26.22	0	0									6	1
FC	2002/03	53	94	9	1958	116	23.03	2	7	18	14	0					4.66	113	19
Lim	2003/04	42	40	5	845	105*	24.14	1	3									29	12
20T	2005/06	3	3	0	61	27	20.33	0	0									1	5
NIROSHAN, Weeratunga Arachchilage Suresh (Chilaw Marians, Kandurata) b Colombo 29.11.1985 RHB WK																			
FC		7	11	2	128	32	14.22	0	0	18	11	0					3.66	14	5
Lim		10	9	0	212	67	23.55	0	1									8	8
20T		1	1	1	10	10*		0	0									0	
FC	2004/05	24	38	3	857	138	24.48	2	3	30	16	1	16.00	1-2	0	0	3.20	37	16
Lim	2007/08	28	26	1	426	67	17.04	0	1									26	18
NISHANTHA, Kumarage Don Janaka (Burgher) b Colombo 17.7.1978 LHB OB																			
FC		4	5	0	84	33	16.80	0	0	126	71	1	71.00	1-16	0	0	3.38	1	
Lim		6	5	1	72	21	18.00	0	0	253	133	9	14.77	6-20	0	1	3.15	1	
FC	1998/99	12	21	2	363	62*	19.10	0	1	696	430	14	30.71	4-61	0	0	3.70	8	
Lim	2007/08	18	16	1	263	51	17.53	0	1	593	361	23	15.69	6-20	0	1	3.65	3	
NISHANTHA, Liyanaarchchige Don Pradeep (Saracens) b Colombo 23.2.1984 RHB OB																			
FC		1	1	0	0	0	0.00	0	0	54	43	1	43.00	1-43	0	0	4.77	1	
Lim		3	3	0	31	29	10.33	0	0	138	90	3	30.00	2-29	0	0	3.91	0	
FC	2005/06	28	43	7	466	57*	12.94	0	1	5737	2611	102	25.59	6-53	3	0	2.73	9	
Lim	2005/06	24	21	7	151	29	10.78	0	0	1113	606	26	23.30	3-12	0	0	3.26	5	
20T	2005/06	9	6	1	39	37	7.80	0	0	198	172	14	12.28	3-15	0	0	5.21	2	
NONIS, Paththini Kuttige Jude Ruwantha Nilushan (Bloomfield) b Colombo 3.9.1987 RHB RMF																			
FC		4	6	0	60	17	10.00	0	0	24	9	0					2.25	5	
Lim		4	4	0	50	26	12.50	0	0									0	
FC	2007/08	9	15	3	206	73	17.16	0	1	102	52	1	52.00	1-15	0	0	3.05	12	
Lim	2007/08	12	12	3	265	77*	29.44	0	2	120	86	2	43.00	2-47	0	0	4.30	1	

Cmp	Debut	M	I	NO	Runs	HS	Avge	100	50	Balls	Runs	Wkts	Avge	BB	5i	10m	RpO	ct	st
OSINDE, Henry (Canada, Canada to Sri Lanka, Canada to West Indies, Tamil Union) b Uganda 17.10.1978 RHB RMF																			
FC		5	5	1	17	9*	4.25	0	0	324	186	6	31.00	3-33	0	0	3.44	0	
Lim		4	3	3	10	9*		0	0	66	70	3	23.33	2-30	0	0	6.36	1	
I20T		1								6	13	0					13.00	1	
20T		2								24	37	0					9.25	1	
FC	2005	20	31	9	231	60*	10.50	0	1	3150	1650	62	26.61	7-53	2	0	3.14	4	
Int	2006	34	22	10	54	21*	4.50	0	0	1359	1133	35	32.37	4-33	1	0	5.00	9	
Lim	2005	48	28	13	66	21*	4.40	0	0	1803	1481	49	30.22	4-33	2	0	4.92	13	
I20T	2008	6	2	1	3	2	3.00	0	0	120	112	6	18.66	2-12	0	0	5.60	6	
20T	2008	9	2	1	3	2	3.00	0	0	156	162	6	27.00	2-12	0	0	6.23	6	
PALIHAKKARA, Sahan Praneeth (Saracens) b Kandy 14.10.1989 RHB LB																			
FC		2	3	1	32	16*	16.00	0	0	250	126	3	42.00	3-103	0	0	3.02	0	
Lim		5	3	2	8	8	8.00	0	0	162	121	4	30.25	3-37	0	0	4.48	0	
PALLEGURUGE, Waligama Ravindra (Sri Lanka Army, Wayamba) b Galle 6.4.1985 LHB SLA																			
FC		9	12	4	166	41	20.75	0	0	1153	604	29	20.82	5-44	1	0	3.14	4	
Lim		7	5	3	14	8	7.00	0	0	258	146	7	20.85	3-30	0	0	3.39	0	
FC	2006/07	29	39	14	431	41	17.24	0	0	2853	1430	65	22.00	5-44	1	0	3.00	14	
Lim	2006/07	27	16	8	81	20	10.12	0	0	1043	607	34	17.85	4-34	2	0	3.49	6	
PARANAVITANA, Nishad Tharanga (Kandurata, Sinhalese, Sri Lanka, Sri Lanka A, Sri Lanka to India, Sri Lanka A to Australia) b Kegalle 15.4.1982 LHB OB																			
Test		3	6	1	292	111	58.40	2	0									2	
FC		12	19	1	853	111	47.38	3	4	66	25	0					2.27	9	
Lim		19	19	2	926	116*	54.47	3	5	119	108	0					5.44	9	
20T		7	7	0	217	67	31.00	0	3	36	43	1	43.00	1-5	0	0	7.16	4	
Test	2008/09	13	24	1	822	111	35.73	2	4	90	76	1	76.00	1-26	0	0	5.06	6	
FC	2001/02	103	170	16	6345	236	41.20	17	26	1388	703	20	35.15	4-39	0	0	3.03	102	
Lim	2001/02	79	78	11	2833	116*	42.28	5	18	751	566	11	51.45	4-25	1	0	4.52	44	
20T	2005/06	22	22	1	532	67*	25.33	0	5	96	117	4	29.25	1-3	0	0	7.31	10	
PARANAVITANA, Pramod Eranga (Badureliya) b Kegalle 25.4.1985 RHB OB																			
Lim		1	1	0	0	0	0.00	0	0									0	
PARANAVITANA, Prasad Suranga (Sri Lanka Navy) b Galigamuwa 17.7.1977 RHB OB																			
FC		1	1	0	5	5	5.00	0	0	24	13	0					3.25	0	
Lim		4	4	0	30	16	7.50	0	0	12	9	0					4.50	0	
PATHIRANA, Dhanuka Nadun (Colts) b Colombo 26.5.1982 RHB OB																			
FC		11	12	1	293	78	26.63	0	2	114	87	3	29.00	2-19	0	0	4.57	8	
Lim		5	5	1	152	77*	38.00	0	1	3	2	0					4.00	0	
FC	2001/02	77	118	8	2933	150	26.66	5	15	1206	659	24	27.45	2-2	0	0	3.27	69	
Lim	2001/02	57	55	7	1347	126*	28.06	2	9	190	168	5	33.60	2-7	0	0	5.30	11	
20T	2004/05	14	14	2	247	63*	20.58	0	1	78	100	5	20.00	3-29	0	0	7.69	4	
PATHIRANA, Sachith Shanaka (Colombo, Kandurata) b Kandy 21.3.1989 LHB SLA																			
FC		8	11	0	327	85	29.72	0	3	1015	673	24	28.04	5-57	1	0	3.97	4	
Lim		9	8	2	219	47	36.50	0	0	231	167	6	27.83	2-23	0	0	4.33	1	
20T		3	2	1	25	16	25.00	0	0	24	39	1	39.00	1-18	0	0	9.75	1	
FC	2008/09	20	28	1	767	85	28.40	0	6	2501	1659	53	31.30	6-90	4	0	3.98	12	
Lim	2008/09	18	15	3	341	66	28.41	0	1	524	377	17	22.17	2-9	0	0	4.31	2	
20T	2007/08	8	6	4	43	16	21.50	0	0	84	89	5	17.80	3-16	0	0	6.35	1	
PEIRIS, B H Amal Chinthaka (Sebastianites) b Ratnapura 7.6.1985 LHB LB																			
Lim		1	1	0	20	20	20.00	0	0	38	37	4	9.25	4-37	1	0	5.84	1	
PEIRIS, Jayalajjage Sunendra Kumara (Panadura) b Panadura 8.4.1973 RHB OB																			
FC		7	9	1	117	39	14.62	0	0	144	54	2	27.00	1-6	0	0	2.25	6	
Lim		8	7	0	112	53	16.00	0	1	29	38	3	12.66	3-38	0	0	7.86	6	
FC	1991/92	149	246	25	6558	142	29.67	8	32	6583	2971	98	30.31	4-35	0	0	2.70	124	
Lim	1992/93	73	69	6	1485	74*	23.57	0	9	1801	1200	49	24.48	4-17	1	0	3.99	26	
20T	2004/05	8	7	1	221	63*	36.83	0	2	104	171	7	24.42	3-37	0	0	9.86	4	
PEIRIS, Kalutara Patabedige Chathura Madushanka (Sri Lanka Cricket Combined XI, Wayamba) b Panadura 23.9.1990 LHB LFM																			
FC		1	1	1	32	32*		0	0	174	94	1	94.00	1-79	0	0	3.24	0	
Lim		4	4	0	96	60	24.00	0	1	202	197	6	32.83	3-49	0	0	5.85	1	
20T		1								12	35	0					17.50	0	
20T	2007/08	9	8	3	56	21*	11.20	0	0	162	194	8	24.25	3-18	0	0	7.18	1	
PEIRIS, Mahathelge Amal Buddika (Sebastianites) b Moratuwa 14.5.1983 RHB OB																			
FC		2	3	0	22	13	7.33	0	0	66	30	0					2.72	0	
Lim		1	1	0	2	2	2.00	0	0	48	63	1	63.00	1-63	0	0	7.87	0	
FC	2002/03	15	25	1	556	88	23.16	0	4	835	479	18	26.61	5-41	1	0	3.44	9	
Lim	2005/06	14	12	1	143	34*	13.00	0	0	423	299	13	23.00	3-30	0	0	4.24	2	
20T	2005/06	1	1	1	0	0*		0	0									0	
PEIRIS, Mahathelge Janaka Rukmal (Sri Lanka Air Force) b Kalutara 29.8.1987 RHB OB																			
FC		1	2	0	4	4	2.00	0	0	12	9	0					4.50	1	
PEIRIS, Malwattage Sukitha Priyadarhsana (Burgher) b Colombo 12.10.1982 RHB LB																			
Lim		2	2	0	17	15	8.50	0	0									0	
FC	2002/03	9	15	1	172	35	12.28	0	0									12	

Cmp	Debut	M	I	NO	Runs	HS	Avge	100	50	Balls	Runs	Wkts	Avge	BB	5i	10m	RpO	ct	st
Lim	2001/02	13	11	0	148	43	13.45	0	0									2	
20T	2005/06	2	2	0	8	7	4.00	0	0									3	
PEIRIS, Prangige Pubudu Mahasen (Sri Lanka Army) b Ratnapura 12.5.1984 RHB RMF																			
FC		3	4	0	47	16	11.75	0	0	186	141	4	35.25	3-69	0	0	4.54	2	
Lim		7	7	2	117	57	23.40	0	1	216	192	6	32.00	2-19	0	0	5.33	1	
FC	2007/08	12	14	6	72	16	9.00	0	0	684	520	13	40.00	4-64	0	0	4.56	6	
Lim	2007/08	11	10	5	149	57	29.80	0	1	327	273	10	27.30	3-47	0	0	5.00	1	
PEIRIS, Thelge Lahiru Thushara (Ragama) b Colombo 1.6.1987 RHB																			
Lim		2	2	0	8	8	4.00	0	0									0	
FC	2007/08	8	14	0	306	104	21.85	1	1									5	
Lim	2007/08	5	4	0	21	9	5.25	0	0									0	
PEIRIS, Thelge Sanka Vimukthi (Moratuwa) b Ratnapura 2.5.1988 RHB LB																			
FC		9	12	1	342	76	31.09	0	4	54	24	0					2.66	4	
Lim		5	5	0	90	27	18.00	0	0									3	
PEIRIS, Udara (Tamil Union) b Colombo 10.5.1988 LHB OB																			
FC		3	2	0	32	28	16.00	0	0	75	50	2	25.00	2-15	0	0	4.00	2	
Lim		4	2	1	9	9*	9.00	0	0	60	32	2	16.00	2-12	0	0	3.20	0	
FC	2008/09	5	6	1	75	28	15.00	0	0	435	218	9	24.22	2-15	0	0	3.00	2	
Lim	2008/09	8	5	3	113	75*	56.50	0	1	198	117	6	19.50	3-19	0	0	3.54	1	
PERERA, Angelo Kanishka (Basnahira North, Nondescripts) b Moratuwa 23.2.1990 RHB SLA																			
FC		12	15	1	626	178	44.71	1	3	138	94	0					4.08	9	
Lim		14	11	4	146	36	20.85	0	0	251	184	12	15.33	5-20	0	1	4.39	2	
20T		2	2	0	4	3	2.00	0	0	24	36	1	36.00	1-23	0	0	9.00	0	
20T	2007/08	10	10	1	193	47	21.44	0	0	24	36	1	36.00	1-23	0	0	9.00	9	
PERERA, Aganpodi Madura Lakmal (Sinhalese, Sri Lanka A, Wayamba) b Kalutara 21.7.1985 RHB RMF																			
FC		6	6	2	33	23	8.25	0	0	438	298	7	42.57	3-45	0	0	4.08	3	
Lim		5	2	1	23	20*	23.00	0	0	177	191	3	63.66	3-57	0	0	6.47	3	
FC	2003/04	39	44	9	396	49	11.31	0	0	3443	2301	77	29.88	5-27	2	0	4.01	13	
Lim	2004/05	34	20	6	134	23*	9.57	0	0	1283	1125	42	26.78	4-39	1	0	5.26	14	
20T	2004/05	9	5	1	35	18*	8.75	0	0	141	218	5	43.60	1-24	0	0	9.27	2	
PERERA, Anhettige Suresh Asanka (Moors) b Colombo 16.2.1978 RHB RFM																			
Lim		6	6	0	66	33	11.00	0	0									1	
Test	1998	3	4	1	77	43*	25.66	0	0	408	180	1	180.00	1-104	0	0	2.64	1	
FC	1995/96	88	120	19	2431	78	24.06	0	7	6914	3661	147	24.90	7-73	2	0	3.17	44	
Int	1998	20	13	2	195	56*	17.72	0	1	579	522	13	40.15	2-25	0	0	5.40	4	
Lim	1997/98	105	82	14	1622	90	23.85	0	7	1805	1714	60	28.56	4-20	1	0	5.69	26	
20T	2004/05	21	19	3	206	58*	12.87	0	1	12	13	3	4.33	3-13	0	0	6.50	1	
PERERA, Bulathwaduge Manukulasuriya Suranga (Sri Lanka Navy) b Colombo 22.1.1987 RHB LB																			
FC		8	15	0	349	89	23.26	0	2	24	8	0					2.00	5	
Lim		4	4	1	42	24	14.00	0	0	19	20	1	20.00	1-20	0	0	6.31	3	
FC	2007/08	11	19	0	433	89	22.78	0	2	120	86	2	43.00	2-21	0	0	4.30	9	
PERERA, Dingirimudiyanselage Charith Gayan (Sri Lanka Air Force) b Colombo 13.5.1988 RHB RM																			
Lim		2	2	0	24	19	12.00	0	0	24	15	0					3.75	0	
FC	2008/09	3	6	0	88	44	14.66	0	0	14	16	0					6.85	4	
Lim	2008/09	11	10	3	103	31*	14.71	0	0	24	15	0					3.75	3	
PERERA, Dehiwaduge Rasika Sampath (Singha) b Galle 22.7.1982 RHB RFM																			
FC		5	8	1	85	24	12.14	0	0	378	209	7	29.85	3-56	0	0	3.31	3	
Lim		8	7	1	44	21	7.33	0	0	336	301	10	30.10	2-34	0	0	5.37	2	
FC	2008/09	11	17	2	217	31	14.46	0	0	972	581	22	26.40	5-64	1	0	3.58	4	
Lim	2007/08	19	15	3	80	21	6.66	0	0	672	557	21	26.52	3-11	0	0	4.97	3	
PERERA, Gagabada Arachchige Chinthaka Rasanga (Basnahira South, Chilaw Marians) b Colombo 14.2.1985 RHB RFM																			
FC		9	10	2	127	31	15.87	0	0	774	510	18	28.33	4-39	0	0	3.95	2	
Lim		11	9	3	86	28*	14.33	0	0	394	366	12	30.50	3-47	0	0	5.57	3	
20T		4	4	1	34	22	11.33	0	0	66	90	5	18.00	3-27	0	0	8.18	1	
FC	2002/03	37	53	9	663	57	15.06	0	1	3875	2643	73	36.20	4-39	0	0	4.09	10	
Lim	2005/06	27	21	7	184	45	13.14	0	0	1012	894	33	27.09	4-22	1	0	5.30	9	
20T	2005/06	14	11	3	72	22	9.00	0	0	270	379	17	22.29	4-19	1	0	8.42	1	
PERERA, Gamage Amila Shiral (Panadura) b Panadura 2.4.1979 LHB SLA																			
FC		9	9	0	161	56	17.88	0	1	1447	530	30	17.66	6-29	3	0	2.19	6	
Lim		8	6	1	58	33*	11.60	0	0	359	182	12	15.16	3-36	0	0	3.04	4	
FC	1998/99	106	161	24	3272	115*	23.88	1	15	15637	7210	312	23.10	7-45	14	0	2.76	70	
Lim	1998/99	69	57	11	876	57	19.04	0	2	2715	1656	78	21.23	4-19	3	0	3.66	21	
20T	2005/06	3	3	0	7	4	2.33	0	0	54	62	6	10.33	3-9	0	0	6.88	1	
PERERA, Gihan Ranjith (Burgher) b Wellawatta 28.4.1981 RHB OB																			
FC		9	15	0	334	101	22.26	1	0	12	13	0					6.50	8	
Lim		2	2	0	5	5	2.50	0	0									2	
FC	2000/01	42	69	8	1642	122	26.91	3	6	225	187	3	62.33	2-21	0	0	4.98	30	
Lim	2003/04	15	14	6	158	39*	19.75	0	0	48	71	3	23.66	3-2	0	0	8.87	6	
20T	2005/06	3	3	0	38	28	12.66	0	0	66	73	3	24.33	2-21	0	0	6.63	1	

Cmp	Debut	M	I	NO	Runs	HS	Avge	100	50	Balls	Runs	Wkts	Avge	BB	5i	10m	RpO	ct	st
PERERA, Gumgamuya Yakdhehige Sammika Ruwan (Panadura) b Kalutara 14.5.1985 LHB WK																			
FC		4	5	0	88	32	17.60	0	0	12	6	0					3.00	3	5
Lim		5	5	0	32	19	6.40	0	0									4	3
FC	2004/05	41	71	4	1243	94	18.55	0	4	18	14	1	14.00	1-8	0	0	4.66	65	13
Lim	2004/05	39	38	0	753	78	19.81	0	2									31	12
20T	2004/05	10	10	0	103	26	10.30	0	0									9	5
PERERA, Henarath Mohottige Deshadi (Lankan) b Colombo 7.8.1988 RHB OB																			
FC		1	1	0	0	0	0.00	0	0	6	3	0					3.00	0	
PERERA, Hettiarchchige Prabuddha Geetharach (Burgher) b Colombo 11.2.1987 RHB OB																			
FC		1	2	0	4	4	2.00	0	0									0	
Lim		4	4	0	67	25	16.75	0	0									0	
FC	2006/07	13	24	0	362	65	15.08	0	1									6	
Lim	2006/07	14	12	1	149	25	13.54	0	0									5	
20T	2006/07	3	3	0	16	8	5.33	0	0									1	
PERERA, Hewamannage Sithara Kasun (Sri Lanka Navy) b Colombo 3.4.1989 RHB OB																			
FC		1	2	0	10	10	5.00	0	0	108	49	2	24.50	2-18	0	0	2.72	1	
Lim		5	5	0	74	32	14.80	0	0	96	72	0					4.50	2	
PERERA, Induruwalage Chamil Duminda (Burgher) b Colombo 31.10.1979 RHB RFM																			
FC		6	9	1	175	113*	21.87	1	0	3	0	1	0.00	1-0	0	0	0.00	4	
Lim		7	7	1	166	32	27.66	0	0	1	4	0					24.00	2	
FC	2000/01	78	129	5	3171	153	25.57	4	16	489	278	8	34.75	3-62	0	0	3.41	66	
Lim	2000/01	46	43	4	877	124	22.48	1	3	109	90	3	30.00	2-1	0	0	4.95	9	
20T	2004/05	5	5	1	52	19	13.00	0	0	72	74	9	8.22	4-25	1	0	6.16	0	
PERERA, Jayasundera Mudalige Sameera (Ragama) b Kegalle 20.8.1988 RHB SLA																			
Lim		2	1	0	0	0	0.00	0	0	78	55	4	13.75	3-37	0	0	4.23	3	
PERERA, Janaka Sampath (Sri Lanka Army) b Bandaragama 25.12.1987 RHB LB																			
FC		4	6	2	74	24*	18.50	0	0	378	239	3	79.66	2-27	0	0	3.79	0	
Lim		9	8	7	30	15*	30.00	0	0	425	282	8	35.25	4-37	1	0	3.98	3	
FC	2008/09	5	7	3	78	24*	19.50	0	0	516	323	5	64.60	2-27	0	0	3.75	1	
Lim	2007/08	13	11	7	39	15*	9.75	0	0	631	424	13	32.61	4-37	1	0	4.03	5	
20T	2006/07	3	3	1	17	16*	8.50	0	0	69	73	5	14.60	3-20	0	0	6.34	1	
PERERA, Kodikara Arachchige Kashshapa Wimanga (Sri Lanka Air Force) b Kandy 5.2.1990 RHB RM																			
FC		1	1	0	2	2	2.00	0	0	42	47	1	47.00	1-47	0	0	6.71	0	
Lim		1	1	0	1	1	1.00	0	0	30	14	1	14.00	1-14	0	0	2.80	1	
PERERA, Kaluarachchige Primosh Asitha (Nondescripts) b Colombo 17.5.1989 LHB LB																			
FC		1	1	0	6	6	6.00	0	0									0	
FC	2008/09	4	5	0	61	32	12.20	0	0	30	28	0					5.60	0	
Lim	2008/09	2	2	0	23	23	11.50	0	0									0	
PERERA, Karunage Ranesh Nishan Uddipana (Badureliya, Sri Lanka Cricket Combined XI) b Colombo 11.10.1985 RHB LB																			
FC		8	9	4	280	123*	56.00	1	1	607	509	17	29.94	5-103	1	0	5.03	7	
Lim		11	9	0	105	28	11.66	0	0	276	230	7	32.85	3-39	0	0	5.00	4	
20T		4	2	1	5	3*	5.00	0	0	53	69	0					7.81	1	
FC	2005/06	30	46	9	795	123*	21.48	1	3	1841	1264	41	30.82	5-103	1	0	4.12	22	
Lim	2004/05	30	25	5	277	38*	13.85	0	0	768	574	28	20.50	5-37	1	1	4.48	6	
20T	2004/05	16	9	3	72	39*	12.00	0	0	110	135	3	45.00	1-9	0	0	7.36	6	
PERERA, Kurugamage Ruwan Sanjeewa (Burgher) b Ragama 23.1.1988 RHB RMF																			
FC		3	4	1	12	8	4.00	0	0	270	162	5	32.40	2-45	0	0	3.60	1	
Lim		2	1	1	0	0*		0	0	74	52	1	52.00	1-32	0	0	4.21	0	
Lim	2008/09	6	3	2	10	9	10.00	0	0	258	208	6	34.66	3-43	0	0	4.83	2	
PERERA, Kandanearachchige Sameen Tharindu (Sri Lanka Air Force) b Colombo 24.3.1988 RHB OB																			
FC		5	8	1	149	72	21.28	0	1	114	89	2	44.50	1-17	0	0	4.68	3	
Lim		7	7	2	82	21	16.40	0	0	18	21	0					7.00	0	
FC	2008/09	13	23	2	493	72	23.47	0	4	162	122	3	40.66	1-17	0	0	4.51	11	
Lim	2008/09	14	14	4	193	27	19.30	0	0	18	21	0					7.00	2	
PERERA, Liiyana Andarage Heshitha Navin (Sinhalese) b Colombo 17.4.1986 LHB																			
FC		5	6	1	228	153*	45.60	1	0									3	
Lim		5	5	1	163	62	40.75	0	1									2	
FC	2006/07	21	32	4	867	153*	30.96	1	6									18	
Lim	2006/07	15	15	1	344	62	24.57	0	2									4	
PERERA, Liyanage Dammika Indrajith (Lankan) b Colombo 27.6.1979 RHB RM																			
FC		8	8	2	118	38	19.66	0	0	582	454	9	50.44	2-31	0	0	4.68	3	
Lim		6	4	1	15	8	5.00	0	0	249	189	20	9.45	6-18	1	1	4.55	1	
FC	2001	63	76	21	829	58	15.07	0	1	6438	3812	161	23.67	6-40	6	0	3.55	28	
Lim	2001/02	44	25	7	206	35	11.44	0	0	1702	1276	69	18.49	6-18	4	1	4.49	6	
20T	2004/05	2	1	0	6	6	6.00	0	0	36	42	0					7.00	1	
PERERA, Liyanage Don Shehan Abisheka (Seeduwa Raddoluwa) b Colombo 11.2.1987 RHB LB																			
FC		1	2	1	15	10*	15.00	0	0	18	11	1	11.00	1-11	0	0	3.66	0	
Lim		4	4	1	24	10*	8.00	0	0	24	25	1	25.00	1-25	0	0	6.25	1	
Lim	2007/08	5	5	1	31	10*	7.75	0	0	24	25	1	25.00	1-25	0	0	6.25	1	
20T	2006/07	1	1	1	14	14*		0	0	24	24	3	8.00	3-24	0	0	6.00	0	

Cmp	Debut	M	I	NO	Runs	HS	Avge	100	50	Balls	Runs	Wkts	Avge	BB	5i	10m	RpO	ct	st
PERERA, Mahawaduge Dilruwan Kamalaneth (Basnahira South, Colts) b Panadura 22.7.1982 RHB OB																			
FC		11	13	0	282	72	21.69	0	3	1791	1005	34	29.55	6-78	1	0	3.36	6	
Lim		16	15	2	215	30*	16.53	0	0	742	486	13	37.38	4-47	1	0	3.93	5	
20T		5	5	0	91	40	18.20	0	0	78	95	1	95.00	1-16	0	0	7.30	1	
FC	2000/01	107	177	10	4021	134	24.07	3	17	16382	8127	302	26.91	7-71	12	0	2.97	87	
Int	2007/08	4	4	0	44	30	11.00	0	0	42	28	1	28.00	1-17	0	0	4.00	0	
Lim	2000/01	102	99	2	1775	74	18.29	0	5	3878	2568	80	32.10	5-26	1	1	3.97	30	
20T	2004/05	24	24	1	335	40	14.56	0	0	414	436	15	29.06	2-19	0	0	6.31	5	
PERERA, Mathurage Don Kushal Janith (Colts, Wayamba) b Kalubovila 17.8.1990 LHB WK																			
FC		8	11	0	216	51	19.63	0	1									9	2
Lim		9	8	1	257	66	36.71	0	2									1	4
20T		7	5	3	51	34	25.50	0	0									3	5
20T	2007/08	16	14	3	167	56	15.18	0	1									4	5
PERERA, Maddumage Don Selvin (Lankan) b Moratuwa 16.12.1976 RHB LB																			
Lim		2	1	0	10	10	10.00	0	0									2	
FC	2005/06	19	31	2	424	68	14.62	0	2	2174	1424	41	34.73	6-54	2	0	3.93	16	
Lim	2005/06	28	23	4	342	53*	18.00	0	1	848	578	23	25.13	4-32	2	0	4.09	12	
20T	2005/06	4	3	2	11	8	11.00	0	0	51	83	6	13.83	3-33	0	0	9.76	0	
PERERA, Mukundadura Mahesh (Sri Lanka Navy) b Balapitiya 13.4.1978 LHB LM																			
FC		4	8	2	200	71	33.33	0	1	198	117	5	23.40	4-30	0	0	3.54	1	
Lim		8	8	0	132	79	16.50	0	1	276	216	8	27.00	2-18	0	0	4.69	4	
FC	2000/01	21	41	2	734	72	18.82	0	4	2109	1100	66	16.66	6-40	1	0	3.12	18	
PERERA, Modara Muthugalage Don Nimesh Randika Gayan (Chilaw Marians) b Colombo 5.9.1977 LHB LB																			
FC		9	13	3	461	102*	46.10	1	3	72	56	2	28.00	2-23	0	0	4.66	10	
Lim		10	10	3	184	58	26.28	0	1	18	24	0					8.00	8	
FC	1995	132	203	20	5225	152	28.55	8	26	10969	7006	257	27.26	8-24	12	2	3.83	98	
Lim	1995	79	77	16	1506	89	24.68	0	6	1208	1010	33	30.60	4-28	1	0	5.01	37	
20T	2004/05	21	18	2	270	50	16.87	0	1	33	53	4	13.25	3-21	0	0	9.63	10	
PERERA, Modara Mehellage Don Pasanna Viraj (Badureliya) b Galle 9.6.1978 LHB OB																			
FC		7	13	0	182	74	14.00	0	1									9	
Lim		6	6	1	170	83	34.00	0	2	12	7	0					3.50	4	
FC	1998/99	69	118	10	2348	109	21.74	2	11	4047	2337	104	22.47	6-25	4	1	3.46	70	
Lim	1999/00	50	46	8	639	83	16.81	0	2	1155	904	36	25.11	4-27	3	0	4.69	16	
20T	2004/05	4	4	0	36	22	9.00	0	0	54	84	1	84.00	1-33	0	0	9.33	0	
PERERA, Mahamarakkala Patabandige Nuwan Laknath (Colombo) b Colombo 29.6.1984 RHB RM																			
FC		6	6	2	61	37*	15.25	0	0	427	262	5	52.40	3-31	0	0	3.68	1	
Lim		11	7	2	45	15	9.00	0	0	390	260	12	21.66	3-14	0	0	4.00	2	
FC	2003/04	25	34	5	438	50	15.10	0	1	2963	1555	58	26.81	8-63	2	1	3.14	20	
Lim	2003/04	33	24	8	280	38	17.50	0	0	1169	711	35	20.31	4-29	2	0	3.64	8	
20T	2006/07	3	3	0	1	1	0.33	0	0	66	89	5	17.80	2-27	0	0	8.09	0	
PERERA, Nanumee Arachchige Chanaka Thushantha (Singha) b Colombo 2.5.1982 RHB RFM																			
FC		6	8	6	35	24*	17.50	0	0	577	339	16	21.18	5-51	1	0	3.52	4	
Lim		4	2	0	2	1	1.00	0	0	130	111	6	18.50	2-27	0	0	5.12	0	
FC	2007/08	20	27	14	68	24*	5.23	0	0	2743	1778	65	27.35	5-51	2	0	3.88	9	
Lim	2007/08	8	5	1	19	12	4.75	0	0	278	239	9	26.55	3-23	0	0	5.15	0	
PERERA, Nettasinghe Appuhamilage Nimesh Nuwan (Burgher) b Colombo 9.1.1982 RHB RSM WK																			
FC		8	15	1	818	211	58.42	2	6	138	73	1	73.00	1-20	0	0	3.17	9	
Lim		3	3	0	59	34	19.66	0	0	156	79	3	26.33	3-23	0	0	3.03	3	
FC	2001	53	98	3	2544	211	26.77	3	16	378	214	4	53.50	1-17	0	0	3.39	54	2
Lim	2001/02	47	44	1	944	114*	21.95	2	4	558	318	15	21.20	3-19	0	0	3.41	23	
20T	2004/05	10	10	1	312	78*	34.66	0	4	189	248	16	15.50	4-30	1	0	7.87	6	
PERERA, Nawalage Kasun Madura (Tamil Union, Wayamba) b Colombo 7.3.1987 LHB RMF																			
FC		6	6	0	40	11	6.66	0	0	400	294	7	42.00	2-25	0	0	4.41	1	
Lim		6	1	1	7	7*		0	0	180	178	8	22.25	2-30	0	0	5.93	0	
FC	2005/06	16	15	3	84	16	7.00	0	0	1030	806	18	44.77	3-31	0	0	4.69	6	
Lim	2005/06	18	6	4	39	18*	19.50	0	0	593	519	29	17.89	4-24	2	0	5.25	2	
20T	2005/06	1	1	0	0	0	0.00	0	0	12	20	0					10.00	0	
PERERA, Narangoda Liyanaarachchilage Tissara Chirantha (Colts, Sri Lanka, Wayamba, Chennai Super Kings, Sri Lanka to Bangladesh, Sri Lanka to India, Sri Lanka to United States of America, Sri Lanka to West Indies, Sri Lanka to Zimbabwe, Sri Lanka A to Australia, Wayamba to India) b Colombo 3.4.1989 LHB RMF																			
FC		4	7	2	261	113*	52.20	1	1	461	322	10	32.20	5-69	1	0	4.19	1	
Int		2	1	0	6	6	6.00	0	0	100	64	8	8.00	5-28	0	1	3.84	1	
Lim		13	7	1	101	25*	16.83	0	0	412	374	17	22.00	5-28	0	1	5.44	6	
20T		7	5	1	18	11	4.50	0	0	102	118	9	13.11	3-18	0	0	6.94	2	
FC	2008/09	14	24	6	745	113*	41.38	1	5	1373	818	24	34.08	5-69	1	0	3.57	10	
Int	2009/10	12	7	2	130	36*	26.00	0	0	414	378	15	25.20	5-28	0	1	5.47	5	
Lim	2008/09	38	26	7	449	50	23.63	0	1	1356	1264	49	25.79	5-28	1	2	5.59	15	
I20T	2010	6	5	2	57	24	19.00	0	0	78	80	3	26.66	2-19	0	0	6.15	0	
20T	2007/08	30	23	8	142	24	9.46	0	0	512	592	32	18.50	3-17	0	0	6.93	11	

Cmp	Debut	M	I	NO	Runs	HS	Avge	100	50	Balls	Runs	Wkts	Avge	BB	5i	10m	RpO	ct	st
PERERA, Nawagamuwage Vimukthi Ramesh (Moors) b Colombo 14.11.1989 LHB LFM																			
FC		7	9	3	49	20*	8.16	0	0	461	333	10	33.30	3-48	0	0	4.33	2	
Lim		1	1	1	0	0*		0	0	30	26	1	26.00	1-26	0	0	5.20	0	
20T	2008/09	2	2	2	3	2*		0	0	42	37	4	9.25	3-21	0	0	5.28	0	
PERERA, Panagodage Don Ruchira Laksiri (Basnahira South, Colts) b Colombo 6.4.1977 LHB LMF																			
FC		6	7	1	59	19	9.83	0	0	795	608	19	32.00	5-102	1	0	4.58	1	
Lim		11	6	4	53	13*	26.50	0	0	450	352	13	27.07	4-33	1	0	4.69	5	
20T		1								12	23	0					11.50	1	
Test	1998/99	8	9	6	33	11*	11.00	0	0	1130	661	17	38.88	3-40	0	0	3.51	2	
FC	1996/97	108	121	52	637	33*	9.23	0	0	14062	8629	349	24.72	7-40	12	1	3.68	46	
Int	1998/99	19	7	2	8	4*	1.60	0	0	888	820	19	43.15	3-23	0	0	5.54	2	
Lim	1998	99	44	21	193	21*	8.39	0	0	4211	3374	135	24.99	5-16	8	1	4.80	21	
I20T	2006	2	2	2	0	0*		0	0	42	77	0					11.00	0	
20T	2006	4	3	2	1	1	1.00	0	0	60	115	0					11.50	1	
PERERA, Rigama Acharige Asanka Indrajith (Moratuwa) b Colombo 29.12.1979 LHB SLA																			
FC		7	10	1	254	74	28.22	0	2	24	13	0					3.25	3	
Lim		4	4	0	40	27	10.00	0	0	6	11	1	11.00	1-11	0	0	11.00	1	
FC	2002/03	22	39	2	788	74	21.29	0	4	121	82	0					4.06	8	
Lim	2002/03	15	13	0	203	64	15.61	0	2	278	231	8	28.87	2-31	0	0	4.98	1	
PERERA, Ranasinghe Hettige Thushan Anjula (Sebastianites) b Panadura 19.12.1979 LHB LSM																			
FC		3	5	0	63	35	12.60	0	0									0	
Lim		6	6	0	80	30	13.33	0	0									3	
FC	1998/99	79	138	5	2197	95	16.51	0	11	55	40	2	20.00	1-0	0	0	4.36	43	1
Lim	1999/00	61	58	3	1058	74	19.23	0	6	42	52	1	52.00	1-29	0	0	7.42	20	
20T	2004/05	7	6	1	135	53	27.00	0	1									4	
PERERA, Undugodage Ramitha Praveen (Badureliya, Sri Lanka Air Force) b Kotte 18.12.1985 RHB OB																			
FC		4	6	1	57	50	11.40	0	1	84	20	0					1.42	0	
Lim		1	1	0	0	0	0.00	0	0									0	
FC	2007/08	9	16	3	207	71*	15.92	0	2	294	224	3	74.66	1-35	0	0	4.57	2	
Lim	2007/08	4	4	1	40	28	13.33	0	0									0	
PERERA, Weerakondabaduge Chanaka Milinda (Sri Lanka Air Force) b Kalutara 26.11.1987 RHB LMF																			
Lim		1	1	0	16	16	16.00	0	0	36	32	2	16.00	2-32	0	0	5.33	1	
FC	2007/08	3	4	1	48	18	16.00	0	0	96	61	4	15.25	2-13	0	0	3.81	2	
PERERA, Weerasekera Diyalatotage Duminda Sanjeewa (Ragama) b Colombo 29.10.1979 RHB RFM																			
FC		11	15	2	177	41	13.61	0	0	90	54	1	54.00	1-18	0	0	3.60	5	
Lim		8	7	0	120	35	17.14	0	0	132	101	4	25.25	4-38	1	0	4.59	4	
FC	1998/99	121	179	14	4667	135	28.28	9	17	3277	1476	66	22.36	5-37	1	0	2.70	112	
Lim	1998/99	79	68	12	1239	73*	22.12	0	4	1623	1075	35	30.71	4-38	1	0	3.97	41	
20T	2004/05	10	8	1	112	61*	16.00	0	1	115	144	6	24.00	2-19	0	0	7.51	2	
PERERA, Warnakulasuriya Joe Sudeepa Delantha (Lankan) b Colombo 28.12.1978 LHB RFM																			
FC		9	14	1	167	42	12.84	0	0	445	256	11	23.27	5-35	1	0	3.45	3	
Lim		7	7	1	178	79	29.66	0	2	230	205	6	34.16	2-41	0	0	5.34	2	
FC	2001/02	63	105	9	2427	175	25.28	3	13	4827	3009	105	28.65	6-59	2	0	3.74	18	1
Lim	1999/00	54	49	6	909	79	21.13	0	6	1521	1227	50	24.54	4-35	1	0	4.84	13	
20T	2004/05	3	3	0	19	15	6.33	0	0	60	101	2	50.50	1-25	0	0	10.10	1	
PERERA, Wagawattage Maithree Bathiya (Basnahira North, Colombo) b Colombo 28.4.1977 RHB LB																			
FC		14	18	0	542	123	30.11	1	3	36	21	0					3.50	16	
Lim		7	6	0	149	65	24.83	0	1	24	21	1	21.00	1-21	0	0	5.25	2	
FC	1996/97	149	230	29	6950	220*	34.57	10	40	5628	3661	103	35.54	6-51	1	0	3.90	156	
Lim	1997	92	82	8	2029	102	27.41	1	12	869	626	29	21.58	4-30	1	0	4.32	48	
20T	2004/05	11	11	2	361	96*	40.11	0	2	12	21	2	10.50	2-21	0	0	10.50	6	
PERUMPULI, Shanaka Gayan (Sebastianites) b Colombo 1.2.1984 RHB WK																			
FC		1	2	1	71	57*	71.00	0	1	2	6	0					18.00	1	
Lim		1	1	0	15	15	15.00	0	0									0	1
FC	2003/04	16	25	4	531	71	25.28	0	4	2	6	0					18.00	20	
Lim	2003/04	18	15	1	165	34	11.78	0	0									15	11
20T	2005/06	1																1	2
PRABATH, Mapatunage Don Roshan (Moratuwa) b Colombo 28.3.1978 RHB OB																			
FC		2	2	0	6	5	3.00	0	0	207	94	3	31.33	1-3	0	0	2.72	3	
Lim		1	1	1	9	9*		0	0	36	16	1	16.00	1-16	0	0	2.66	0	
FC	1999/00	37	55	5	847	56	16.94	0	1	2011	1063	38	27.97	4-38	0	0	3.17	31	
Lim	2005/06	22	21	4	387	59	22.76	0	2	611	506	16	31.62	3-33	0	0	4.96	7	
20T	2005/06	3	3	0	1	1	0.33	0	0	18	20	1	20.00	1-18	0	0	6.66	0	
PRADEEP, Damunu Hewage Susantha (Nondescripts) b Kalutara 5.9.1980 RHB LB																			
FC		8	11	0	307	104	27.90	1	1	234	139	4	34.75	1-7	0	0	3.56	4	
Lim		5	4	1	99	59	33.00	0	1	90	88	2	44.00	2-51	0	0	5.86	3	
FC	1996/97	52	72	6	1306	104	19.78	1	5	3482	1691	68	24.86	6-41	3	0	2.91	27	
Lim	1999/00	40	30	8	352	59	16.00	0	2	1276	817	32	25.53	3-16	0	0	3.84	12	
PRASAD, Kaluwahande Chandima (Sri Lanka Army) b Galle 22.9.1984 RHB RFM																			
FC		11	17	2	318	68*	21.20	0	2	100	122	3	40.66	2-49	0	0	7.32	14	
Lim		11	11	0	175	69	15.90	0	1	18	25	1	25.00	1-25	0	0	8.33	3	

Cmp	Debut	M	I	NO	Runs	HS	Avge	100	50	Balls	Runs	Wkts	Avge	BB	5i	10m	RpO	ct	st
FC	2006/07	35	58	7	1289	153*	25.27	2	5	100	122	3	40.66	2-49	0	0	7.32	25	
Lim	2006/07	32	30	1	611	81	21.06	0	3	18	25	1	25.00	1-25	0	0	8.33	15	
PRASAD, Kariyawasam Tirana Gamage Dammika (Basnahira North, Sinhalese, Sri Lanka, Sri Lanka A, Sri Lanka to India, Sri Lanka A to Australia) b Ragama 30.5.1983 RHB RFM																			
Test		1								132	101	0					4.59	0	
FC		10	10	2	283	103*	35.37	1	0	1023	738	25	29.52	6-74	2	0	4.32	3	
Lim		5	4	0	29	15	7.25	0	0	226	242	5	48.40	3-63	0	0	6.42	2	
Test	2008	5	4	0	66	36	16.50	0	0	866	668	13	51.38	3-82	0	0	4.62	1	
FC	2001/02	61	67	9	1203	103*	20.74	1	6	7924	5017	182	27.56	6-25	4	1	3.79	15	
Int	2005/06	5	3	0	17	8	5.66	0	0	216	217	5	43.40	2-29	0	0	6.02	0	
Lim	2002/03	56	30	7	291	31	12.65	0	0	2245	1803	63	28.61	4-39	1	0	4.81	11	
20T	2006/07	4	4	1	14	9	4.66	0	0	42	49	3	16.33	2-18	0	0	7.00	1	
PRASAD, Uyangoda Manage Amila (Badureliya, Basnahira South) b Matara 11.6.1983 RHB RM																			
FC		13	17	1	177	72	11.06	0	1	1464	1087	33	32.93	4-60	0	0	4.45	1	
Lim		10	8	2	38	18*	6.33	0	0	434	331	15	22.06	4-42	1	0	4.57	0	
FC	2004/05	36	49	13	318	72	8.83	0	1	4058	2792	87	32.09	5-30	1	0	4.12	7	
Lim	2004/05	33	20	7	62	18*	4.76	0	0	1335	1039	41	25.34	6-32	2	1	4.67	3	
20T	2005/06	6	2	2	9	9*		0	0	103	110	5	22.00	2-10	0	0	6.40	1	
PRASANNA, Seekkuge (Kandurata, Sri Lanka A, Sri Lanka Army, Sri Lanka A to Australia) b Balapitiya 27.6.1985 RHB LB																			
FC		15	19	0	246	38	12.94	0	0	3067	1725	64	26.95	8-123	3	1	3.37	6	
Lim		15	13	0	176	62	13.53	0	1	717	500	21	23.80	4-24	1	0	4.18	6	
20T		4	1	1	13	13*		0	0	96	108	5	21.60	3-13	0	0	6.75	0	
FC	2006/07	46	72	4	1077	70	15.83	0	3	8313	4410	210	21.00	8-59	12	2	3.18	24	
Lim	2006/07	39	34	2	411	92*	12.84	0	2	1688	1062	54	19.66	4-13	3	0	3.77	13	
20T	2008/09	6	2	2	14	13*		0	0	144	159	6	26.50	3-13	0	0	6.62	1	
PREMAKUMARA, Kande Dinesh Asanka (Moors) b Galle 21.7.1983 RHB RMF																			
FC		3	5	3	6	5*	3.00	0	0	126	99	1	99.00	1-43	0	0	4.71	2	
FC	2004/05	20	30	10	304	61	15.20	0	1	1440	986	29	34.00	4-24	0	0	4.10	6	
Lim	2004/05	7	5	4	41	20*	41.00	0	0	162	152	5	30.40	2-26	0	0	5.63	2	
20T	2005/06	2								30	35	2	17.50	1-7	0	0	7.00	0	
PREMARATNE, Weda Gedara Heeran Nilanka (Ragama, Sri Lanka Cricket Combined XI) b Kandy 17.6.1988 RHB LMF																			
FC		8	7	6	3	2*	3.00	0	0	801	537	20	26.85	5-58	1	0	4.02	1	
Lim		3	2	2	0	0*		0	0	82	113	0					8.26	0	
PRIYADARSHANA, Batepola Arachchige Rasika Suranga (Lankan) b Matara 23.11.1975 RHB RFM																			
FC		8	11	2	512	123	56.88	1	3	204	154	2	77.00	1-5	0	0	4.52	5	
Lim		4	4	0	197	105	49.25	1	1	71	74	0					6.25	0	
FC	1993/94	127	199	14	4902	140	26.49	4	28	14091	8268	317	26.08	8-85	12	0	3.52	57	
Lim	1998/99	54	52	5	1100	105	23.40	2	4	1841	1209	54	22.38	5-43	0	1	3.94	16	
20T	2005/06	2	2	0	20	14	10.00	0	0	24	40	1	40.00	1-29	0	0	10.00	0	
PRIYADARSHANA, Kariyawasam Patuwatha Withanage Mahesh (Police) b Galle 24.10.1981 RHB RM																			
FC		5	7	1	149	38	24.83	0	0	486	298	4	74.50	2-64	0	0	3.67	6	
Lim		4	4	0	91	35	22.75	0	0	66	56	0					5.09	1	
FC	2004/05	26	39	4	503	53	14.37	0	1	2572	1534	63	24.34	6-41	3	0	3.57	26	
Lim	2004/05	23	16	5	201	35	18.27	0	0	483	412	9	45.77	2-25	0	0	5.11	6	
20T	2005/06	3	2	1	19	14*	19.00	0	0	42	59	5	11.80	3-19	0	0	8.42	0	
PRIYANJAN, Subasinghe Mudiyanselage Ashan (Ruhuna, Tamil Union) b Colombo 14.8.1989 RHB RMF																			
FC		11	18	1	541	75	31.82	0	6	264	113	3	37.66	2-43	0	0	2.56	7	
Lim		12	11	1	191	54	19.10	0	1									4	
20T		7	6	1	68	28	13.60	0	0									4	
FC	2008/09	24	40	2	1308	99	34.42	0	13	282	118	3	39.33	2-43	0	0	2.51	20	
Lim	2007/08	25	23	2	522	87	24.85	0	4	18	21	0					7.00	8	
20T	2007/08	10	8	1	96	28	13.71	0	0									5	
PRIYANKARA, Gulawitage Sidath (Sri Lanka Air Force) b Unawatuna 20.9.1983 RHB LM																			
FC		1	1	1	0	0*		0	0	78	33	2	16.50	2-29	0	0	2.53	0	
Lim		6	4	3	11	11*	11.00	0	0	276	186	8	23.25	3-31	0	0	4.04	5	
FC	2007/08	3	4	2	2	2	1.00	0	0	198	129	2	64.50	2-29	0	0	3.90	0	
Lim	2004/05	19	14	6	38	11*	4.75	0	0	849	697	23	30.30	3-30	0	0	4.92	7	
PRIYANKARA, Ranaweera Koralage Prabath (Nondescripts) b Panadura 28.5.1988 LHB LMF																			
Lim		1	1	1	6	6*		0	0	24	49	1	49.00	1-49	0	0	12.25	1	
FC	2008/09	9	10	3	34	17	4.85	0	0	984	687	29	23.68	6-71	2	0	4.18	6	
Lim	2008/09	2	2	1	6	6*	6.00	0	0	54	93	1	93.00	1-49	0	0	10.33	1	
PRIYANTHA, Hewa Pathinige Aruna (Police) b Colombo 4.2.1973 RHB LM																			
FC		9	11	1	249	57	24.90	0	2	84	26	2	13.00	2-13	0	0	1.85	2	
Lim		9	8	1	151	46	21.57	0	0									3	
FC	1995/96	124	202	6	4094	93	20.88	0	22	10478	4652	200	23.26	7-77	6	0	2.66	52	
Lim	1998/99	66	58	6	999	80*	19.21	0	4	1776	1212	38	31.89	3-21	0	0	4.09	17	
20T	2004/05	1	1	0	2	2	2.00	0	0	18	23	2	11.50	2-23	0	0	7.66	0	
PRIYANTHA, Panawannage Manjula (Seeduwa Raddoluwa) b Colombo 15.10.1980 RHB LB																			
FC		1	2	0	16	15	8.00	0	0									2	
Lim		3	3	1	72	45	36.00	0	0									0	
FC	2000/01	13	22	2	326	69	16.30	0	1	6	13	0					13.00	13	

Cmp	Debut	M	I	NO	Runs	HS	Avge	100	50	Balls	Runs	Wkts	Avge	BB	5i	10m	RpO	ct	st
Lim	2001/02	19	18	3	244	50	16.26	0	1	17	15	1	15.00	1-15	0	0	5.29	5	
20T	2006/07	4	4	0	65	33	16.25	0	0									1	
PUSHPAKUMARA, Muthumudalige (Basnahira North, Tamil Union, Sri Lanka to Bangladesh, Sri Lanka to India) b Colombo 26.9.1981 LHB OB																			
FC		9	12	2	286	85	28.60	0	2	1200	631	23	27.43	5-79	1	0	3.15	11	
Lim		11	9	1	219	55	27.37	0	2	369	242	11	22.00	3-41	0	0	3.93	7	
20T		4	3	0	31	20	10.33	0	0	36	63	1	63.00	1-16	0	0	10.50	1	
FC	1999/00	104	154	16	3976	114	28.81	4	25	12147	6386	249	25.64	6-62	5	0	3.15	112	
Int	2009/10	3	1	1	7	7*		0	0	30	21	0					4.20	0	
Lim	1999/00	94	71	15	1176	55	21.00	0	4	3415	2355	88	26.76	3-10	0	0	4.13	44	
I20T	2009/10	1								18	27	1	27.00	1-27	0	0	9.00	1	
20T	2004/05	23	19	2	272	31	16.00	0	0	375	417	28	14.89	4-18	2	0	6.67	6	
PUSHPAKUMARA, Paulage Malinda (Chilaw Marians) b Colombo 24.3.1987 RHB SLA																			
FC		3	1	0	4	4	4.00	0	0	344	177	10	17.70	4-63	0	0	3.08	2	
Lim		5	3	0	23	15	7.66	0	0	222	169	12	14.08	5-42	1	1	4.56	1	
FC	2006/07	25	28	8	303	80*	15.15	0	1	4498	2087	108	19.32	6-65	5	1	2.78	18	
Lim	2006/07	17	10	2	62	15	7.75	0	0	742	546	30	18.20	5-42	1	1	4.41	7	
PUSHPALAL, Kankanige Don Chandana (Burgher) b Panadura 28.2.1982 LHB RFM																			
Lim		3	3	1	27	15	13.50	0	0	132	99	2	49.50	1-31	0	0	4.50	0	
FC	2001/02	17	24	6	225	51	12.50	0	1	1585	940	24	39.16	5-64	1	0	3.55	9	
Lim	2001/02	21	14	5	102	21	11.33	0	0	852	546	23	23.73	4-29	1	0	3.84	4	
20T	2005/06	2	1	0	3	3	3.00	0	0	48	37	3	12.33	3-17	0	0	4.62	0	
PUSSEGOLLA, Chandima Shashrika (Nondescripts) b Colombo 14.7.1987 RHB RMF																			
FC		4	5	1	94	54	23.50	0	1									3	
Lim		6	5	1	99	53*	24.75	0	1									2	
FC	2008/09	13	20	4	513	98	32.06	0	4	305	185	8	23.12	2-8	0	0	3.63	9	
Lim	2008/09	14	13	1	205	53*	17.08	0	1	172	146	4	36.50	2-26	0	0	5.09	2	
RABEL, Amira Keshawa (Burgher) b Colombo 28.2.1989 RHB OB																			
Lim		1	1	0	1	1	1.00	0	0									0	
RAJAKARUNA, Dadodallage Thilina Maduranga (Singha) b Galle 10.11.1985 RHB OB																			
FC		6	10	1	204	71	22.66	0	2	42	7	1	7.00	1-7	0	0	1.00	3	
Lim		6	6	1	139	78*	27.80	0	1									5	
FC	2008/09	15	27	2	565	71	22.60	0	3	78	42	1	42.00	1-7	0	0	3.23	7	
Lim	2008/09	14	14	2	199	78*	16.58	0	1	1	6	0					36.00	10	
RAJAPAKSA, Pramod Bhanuka Bandara (Sinhalese, Sri Lanka Cricket Combined XI, Barisal) b Colombo 24.10.1991 LHB RMF																			
Lim		6	6	0	116	59	19.33	0	1									2	
20T		4	4	0	99	58	24.75	0	1									1	
20T	2008/09	11	11	1	242	58	24.20	0	2									2	
RAJITHA, Bopagamage Suranjana (Sebastianites) b Colombo 4.11.1981 RHB SLA																			
Lim		2	2	1	9	9*	9.00	0	0	96	82	3	27.33	2-43	0	0	5.12	2	
FC	2006/07	7	10	6	52	12	13.00	0	0	816	353	18	19.61	5-34	1	0	2.59	3	
Lim	2004/05	10	5	3	13	9*	6.50	0	0	263	237	9	26.33	4-13	1	0	5.40	5	
20T	2005/06	1								18	17	2	8.50	2-17	0	0	5.66	0	
RAMANAYAKE, Waruna Chandra Kumara (Police) b Matara 25.3.1977 RHB RFM																			
FC		3	3	0	4	4	1.33	0	0	231	127	6	21.16	5-53	1	0	3.29	2	
FC	2007/08	6	6	1	18	14	3.60	0	0	501	241	9	26.77	5-53	1	0	2.88	2	
Lim	2007/08	2								90	61	1	61.00	1-34	0	0	4.06	0	
RAMYAKUMARA, Wijekoon Mudiyanselage Gayan (Basnahira North, Chilaw Marians) b Gampaha 21.12.1976 LHB LM																			
FC		10	12	3	366	89	40.66	0	1	626	227	12	18.91	4-35	0	0	2.17	2	
Lim		12	11	0	290	63	26.36	0	2	306	204	4	51.00	1-18	0	0	4.00	2	
20T		2	1	1	4	4*		0	0	24	27	2	13.50	1-4	0	0	6.75	0	
Test	2005	2	3	0	38	14	12.66	0	0	114	66	2	33.00	2-49	0	0	3.47	0	
FC	1996/97	149	236	30	7783	150*	37.78	15	40	11996	6320	251	25.17	7-25	3	1	3.16	56	
Lim	1996/97	129	113	10	2672	116	25.94	1	12	4993	3225	132	24.43	6-33	2	3	3.87	29	
I20T	2007/08	3	2	1	1	1*	1.00	0	0	66	101	2	50.50	1-12	0	0	9.18	0	
20T	2004/05	23	20	5	205	36*	13.66	0	0	362	446	17	26.23	4-24	1	0	7.39	3	
RANASINGHE, Matheesha Pasan (Saracens) b Kalaniya 16.7.1983 RHB RFM																			
FC		3	4	1	27	13*	9.00	0	0	306	190	6	31.66	2-19	0	0	3.72	0	
FC	2002/03	24	38	3	454	58	12.97	0	1	2618	1602	68	23.55	5-56	1	0	3.67	8	
Lim	2004/05	24	19	4	256	50	17.06	0	1	755	513	19	27.00	3-18	0	0	4.07	5	
20T	2005/06	7	6	3	40	13	13.33	0	0	96	137	2	68.50	1-26	0	0	8.56	2	
RANASINGHE, Nalinda (Singha) b Galle 20.7.1989 RHB RMF																			
FC		1	2	0	10	10	5.00	0	0									1	
Lim		3	3	0	45	26	15.00	0	0									1	
RANASINGHE, Ranasinghe Arachchige Nipuna Madawa (Sri Lanka Navy) b Panadura 17.6.1989 RHB LB																			
FC		2	3	0	76	47	25.33	0	0	27	21	1	21.00	1-7	0	0	4.66	1	
Lim		4	4	0	39	25	9.75	0	0									1	
RANASURIYA, Shivanga Anthony Prashan (Singha) b Colombo 17.1.1990 RHB OB																			
FC		9	16	1	373	87	24.86	0	1	6	5	0					5.00	7	
Lim		6	6	0	184	61	30.66	0	1									1	

Cmp	Debut	M	I	NO	Runs	HS	Avge	100	50	Balls	Runs	Wkts	Avge	BB	5i	10m	RpO	ct	st
RANATUNGA, Chandika (Singha) b Galle 12.6.1985 RHB SLA																			
FC		4	5	1	12	5	3.00	0	0	290	209	9	23.22	3-40	0	0	4.32	5	
Lim		3	3	3	4	2*		0	0	78	61	3	20.33	2-18	0	0	4.69	0	
FC	2003/04	8	13	5	19	5	2.37	0	0	722	545	18	30.27	3-40	0	0	4.52	7	
RANATUNGA, Dhushantha Anjana (Ragama) b Negombo 8.11.1981 RHB LB																			
FC		7	10	2	188	81	23.50	0	1									6	
Lim		2	2	0	51	36	25.50	0	0									0	
FC	2001/02	69	121	10	2801	133	25.23	3	13									78	
Lim	2001/02	47	46	0	620	69	13.47	0	2									19	
20T	2004/05	15	14	1	253	64*	19.46	0	1									7	
RANAWEERA, Balage Don Ashan Priyanka (Moors) b Horana 1.12.1973 RHB RM																			
Lim		3	3	1	26	15	13.00	0	0	39	19	1	19.00	1-4	0	0	2.92	0	
FC	1996/97	58	100	11	1825	70	20.50	0	8	4660	2101	83	25.31	3-17	0	0	2.70	37	
Lim	1998/99	29	26	3	330	44	14.34	0	0	464	361	18	20.05	5-27	0	1	4.66	3	
20T	2004/05	4	4	0	45	28	11.25	0	0	54	64	3	21.33	2-15	0	0	7.11	1	
RANAWEERA, Daminda Kumara (Colombo) b Kandy 29.2.1980 LHB RFM WK																			
FC		8	10	0	189	79	18.90	0	1									7	2
Lim		4	4	0	84	33	21.00	0	0									2	1
FC	1999/00	85	147	7	3261	99	23.29	0	20									171	19
Lim	1999/00	49	45	3	732	81	17.42	0	3									40	15
20T	2005/06	4	3	1	25	24	12.50	0	0									2	3
RANAWEERA, Horadugoda Gamage Pubudu (Moratuwa) b Colombo 29.12.1980 LHB SLA																			
FC		7	8	0	158	70	19.75	0	1	826	410	20	20.50	6-52	2	0	2.97	2	
Lim		8	7	0	85	50	12.14	0	1	426	245	9	27.22	3-46	0	0	3.45	4	
FC	2000/01	50	74	5	1320	105*	19.13	1	3	2200	1077	48	22.43	6-52	3	0	2.93	21	
Lim	2001/02	40	36	5	524	50	16.90	0	1	1023	625	30	20.83	4-25	2	0	3.66	14	
20T	2006/07	2	2	0	1	1	0.50	0	0	7	15	1	15.00	1-11	0	0	12.85	1	
RANAWEERA, Wekade Gedara Chanaka Dhanushka (Sebastianites) b Kandy 13.8.1987 LHB LFM																			
FC		4	8	2	29	18*	4.83	0	0	444	216	13	16.61	5-37	1	0	2.91	3	
Lim		2	2	2	14	14*		0	0	60	43	2	21.50	1-17	0	0	4.30	0	
RANDIKA, Kankana Gamage Nisal (Colombo) b Colombo 30.7.1982 LHB SLC																			
FC		9	13	2	297	65	27.00	0	1	56	40	1	40.00	1-25	0	0	4.28	11	
Lim		6	6	0	41	16	6.83	0	0	51	46	3	15.33	3-30	0	0	5.41	1	
FC	2001/02	62	106	11	2676	97	28.16	0	17	1994	1029	48	21.43	6-18	3	0	3.09	60	
Lim	2003/04	45	42	10	600	37	18.75	0	0	835	655	27	24.25	3-16	0	0	4.70	11	
20T	2004/05	8	6	1	135	48	27.00	0	0	112	111	10	11.10	4-9	1	0	5.94	1	
RANDIKA, Mabogodage Dasun (Saracens) b Colombo 15.1.1986 RHB WK																			
FC		11	16	2	393	84	28.07	0	3									16	8
Lim		10	10	3	128	26*	18.28	0	0									4	2
FC	2006/07	19	30	4	562	84	21.61	0	3									40	10
Lim	2006/07	30	29	5	395	43	16.45	0	0									26	9
RANDUNU, Sayakkara Kankanamge Chatura (Singha) b Colombo 1.4.1984 LHB SLA																			
FC		5	8	1	73	23	10.42	0	0	634	276	14	19.71	6-60	1	0	2.61	3	
Lim		8	7	0	113	29	16.14	0	0	408	267	13	20.53	5-20	0	1	3.92	3	
FC	2007/08	13	21	3	266	34	14.77	0	0	2211	931	44	21.15	6-60	2	0	2.52	11	
Lim	2007/08	17	16	0	291	34	18.18	0	0	890	558	25	22.32	5-20	0	1	3.76	4	
RANGANA, Dasanayaka Aluthge Asela (Sinhalese) b Colombo 22.6.1987 LHB RMF																			
FC		1	2	0	15	15	7.50	0	0	6	11	0					11.00	1	
RANJITH, Paragodagamage Nandika (Moors) b Colombo 6.12.1972 LHB LFM																			
FC		4	4	2	41	20*	20.50	0	0	247	142	3	47.33	3-55	0	0	3.44	1	
FC	1997/98	95	127	33	1181	72	12.56	0	4	11950	6608	320	20.65	8-48	19	1	3.31	38	
Lim	2001/02	60	38	12	296	42	11.38	0	0	2680	1956	84	23.28	6-17	2	3	4.37	12	
20T	2004/05	13	7	3	112	56*	28.00	0	1	288	368	9	40.88	3-18	0	0	7.66	3	
RASANGA, Tantirige Ranil (Sri Lanka Navy) b Matara 24.4.1986 RHB WK																			
FC		9	14	0	360	81	25.71	0	2									13	5
Lim		8	8	0	213	93	26.62	0	1									7	6
FC	2006/07	13	22	0	420	81	19.09	0	2									16	5
Lim	2008/09	11	11	1	273	93	27.30	0	1									8	6
RASMIJINAN, Mohamed Marzook (Police) b Matara 6.12.1981 LHB LFM																			
FC		4	6	1	151	99*	30.20	0	1	432	275	5	55.00	3-86	0	0	3.81	1	
Lim		9	8	0	77	23	9.62	0	0	302	203	13	15.61	3-22	0	0	4.03	1	
FC	2000/01	46	73	13	1451	99*	24.18	0	10	5890	3437	118	29.12	8-48	4	1	3.50	27	
Lim	2003/04	40	30	1	361	35	12.44	0	0	1603	1270	55	23.09	7-19	1	1	4.75	10	1
20T	2004/05	1	1	1	18	18*		0	0	18	31	1	31.00	1-31	0	0	10.33	0	
RATHIKA, Rajkumar (Saracens) b Colombo 23.8.1985 RHB RM																			
FC		10	16	0	337	51	21.06	0	1	195	137	4	34.25	3-44	0	0	4.21	8	
Lim		4	4	0	40	24	10.00	0	0	24	28	0					7.00	2	
FC	2004/05	15	23	0	413	51	17.95	0	1	195	137	4	34.25	3-44	0	0	4.21	13	
Lim	2004/05	12	9	1	144	45	18.00	0	0	114	106	3	35.33	3-43	0	0	5.57	3	

Cmp	Debut	M	I	NO	Runs	HS	Avge	100	50	Balls	Runs	Wkts	Avge	BB	5i	10m	RpO	ct	st
RATHNAYAKE, Pahala Kapuralalage Navantha Mahesh Kumara (Sri Lanka Army) b Gokarella 9.2.1979 RHB RFM																			
Lim		1	1	1	1	1*		0	0	60	67	2	33.50	2-67	0	0	6.70	0	
FC	2006/07	28	43	9	389	52	11.44	0	1	3356	1969	96	20.51	6-64	6	1	3.52	16	
Lim	2006/07	19	14	6	70	13	8.75	0	0	818	574	22	26.09	4-41	1	0	4.21	2	
20T	2006/07	3	2	1	13	9	13.00	0	0	60	53	2	26.50	1-16	0	0	5.30	3	
RATNAYAKE, Bammanna Mudiyanselage Rajitha Nuwan Bandara (Sri Lanka Air Force) b Kurunegala 11.5.1987 RHB WK																			
FC		8	13	0	349	71	26.84	0	3	5	10	0					12.00	2	
Lim		5	4	0	60	29	15.00	0	0									2	
RATNAYAKE, Michel Ishan (Saracens) b Colombo 23.2.1982 RHB RFM																			
FC		7	9	0	156	51	17.33	0	1	615	402	10	40.20	3-55	0	0	3.92	5	
Lim		3	2	0	10	9	5.00	0	0	96	132	3	44.00	2-24	0	0	8.25	2	
FC	2001/02	48	61	32	332	51	11.44	0	1	5222	2984	109	27.37	5-28	4	0	3.42	23	
Lim	2002/03	22	12	10	53	24*	26.50	0	0	798	654	22	29.72	5-54	0	1	4.91	9	
20T	2005/06	3	1	1	3	3*		0	0	60	85	4	21.25	2-32	0	0	8.50	1	
RIDEEGAMMANAGEDERA, Anil (Moors) b Galle 23.6.1976 RHB LB																			
FC		9	14	0	254	61	18.14	0	1	549	271	5	54.20	2-23	0	0	2.96	2	
Lim		7	7	0	129	58	18.42	0	1	246	216	4	54.00	1-6	0	0	5.26	0	
FC	1995/96	147	240	25	6020	125*	28.00	6	33	18572	7485	282	26.54	5-8	5	0	2.41	85	
Lim	1997/98	87	79	7	1830	88	25.41	0	9	3422	2366	97	24.39	5-17	1	2	4.14	21	
20T	2005/06	16	14	2	159	43	13.25	0	0	180	266	8	33.25	1-10	0	0	8.86	4	
RIZAN, Abuthahir (Sri Lanka Air Force) b Kurunegala 24.12.1973 RHB OB																			
FC		5	9	3	73	22*	12.16	0	0	713	501	19	26.36	4-49	0	0	4.21	5	
Lim		4	4	1	31	16	10.33	0	0	132	97	2	48.50	1-19	0	0	4.40	4	
FC	2000/01	80	134	18	2254	80	19.43	0	7	7011	4322	175	24.69	7-44	8	1	3.69	91	1
Lim	2001/02	57	56	9	846	100	18.00	1	2	1212	1019	29	35.13	4-26	3	0	5.04	20	1
20T	2004/05	5	5	0	79	29	15.80	0	0	49	66	3	22.00	2-19	0	0	8.08	1	
RODRIGO, Aluth Baduge Lakshan Dinuka (Moratuwa) b Panadura 19.5.1987 RHB LB																			
FC		4	4	1	106	67*	35.33	0	1	258	148	6	24.66	3-47	0	0	3.44	4	
Lim		5	5	1	50	21*	12.50	0	0	24	21	0					5.25	1	
FC	2006/07	23	37	6	706	67*	22.77	0	3	1722	1125	42	26.78	4-12	0	0	3.92	16	
Lim	2007/08	16	15	5	280	67*	28.00	0	3	318	205	9	22.77	3-38	0	0	3.86	4	
RUKMAL, Lokugamarachchilage Dinuka (Sri Lanka Navy) b Colombo 22.8.1988 RHB LFM																			
Lim		1	1	0	0	0	0.00	0	0	18	19	0					6.33	1	
RUPASINGHE, Rushantha Chamil (Moratuwa) b Balapitiya 18.11.1977 RHB RM																			
Lim		3	3	0	28	14	9.33	0	0									2	
FC	2001/02	22	43	1	1175	121	27.97	1	8	1083	611	21	29.09	5-34	1	0	3.38	16	
Lim	2007/08	13	12	0	165	39	13.75	0	0									4	
RUPASINGHE, Rupasinghe Jayawardene Mudiyanselage Gihan Madushanka (Basnahira South, Sri Lanka A, Tamil Union) b Watupitiwala 5.3.1986 LHB LB																			
FC		6	6	1	89	40	17.80	0	0	129	57	1	57.00	1-46	0	0	2.65	1	
Lim		11	11	2	275	74*	30.55	0	2	66	48	2	24.00	1-15	0	0	4.36	8	
20T		6	5	0	68	28	13.60	0	0									0	
FC	2006/07	35	59	5	1918	154*	35.51	5	9	1165	674	22	30.63	2-14	0	0	3.47	16	
Lim	2006/07	34	32	6	739	102*	28.42	1	3	328	258	13	19.84	3-9	0	0	4.72	11	
I20T	2009	2	2	0	33	18	16.50	0	0									1	
20T	2006/07	22	21	2	278	46	14.63	0	0	40	51	4	12.75	2-32	0	0	7.65	4	
RUWANSIRI, Lokukuruppu Arichchilage Chanaka (Sri Lanka Navy) b Colombo 14.10.1989 RHB LB																			
Lim		4	4	0	32	17	8.00	0	0									1	
SAMARAWEERA, Thilan Thusara (Kandurata, Sinhalese, Sri Lanka, Sri Lanka Board President's XI, Sri Lanka to Bangladesh, Sri Lanka to India, Sri Lanka to South Africa, Sri Lanka to Zimbabwe) b Colombo 22.9.1976 RHB OB																			
Test		3	5	3	306	137*	153.00	1	2									0	
FC		9	15	3	873	214	72.75	4	2									4	
Int		4	3	1	60	36*	30.00	0	0									1	
Lim		11	9	3	293	55	48.83	0	2	6	7	0					7.00	4	
20T		5	4	1	99	67	33.00	0	1									2	
Test	2001	60	95	16	4244	231	53.72	12	23	1291	679	14	48.50	4-49	0	0	3.15	36	
FC	1995	219	305	55	12257	231	49.02	33	60	17458	8132	347	23.43	6-55	15	2	2.79	175	
Int	1998/99	41	34	7	748	105*	27.70	2	0	690	538	10	53.80	3-34	0	0	4.67	11	
Lim	1995	151	112	30	2459	105*	29.98	2	10	4648	3097	108	28.67	7-30	0	2	3.99	49	
20T	2004/05	13	12	2	288	70	28.80	0	2	44	37	3	12.33	3-17	0	0	5.04	2	
SAMARAWICKRAME, Wedagedera Buddi Heshan (Seeduwa Raddoluwa) b Colombo 13.11.1988 RHB OB																			
FC		7	9	0	166	58	18.44	0	1	36	10	0					1.66	4	
Lim		7	5	0	44	26	8.80	0	0	264	118	9	13.11	4-20	1	0	2.68	3	
FC	2008/09	15	22	2	505	113	25.25	1	2	36	10	0					1.66	7	
Lim	2008/09	12	10	0	89	26	8.90	0	0	276	132	10	13.20	4-20	1	0	2.87	5	
SAMEERA, Kohumulla Arachchige Nuwan (Saracens) b Panadura 13.2.1985 RHB RM																			
Lim		1								24	28	0					7.00	0	
SAMPATH, Tillakaratne Mudiyanselage Nishan (Badureliya, Ruhuna) b Jaffna 23.6.1982 RHB RM																			
FC		9	14	0	517	158	36.92	2	2	582	464	9	51.55	4-50	0	0	4.78	8	
Lim		17	16	1	310	91*	20.66	0	3	390	310	11	28.18	3-22	0	0	4.76	5	
20T		7	5	2	50	24	16.66	0	0	78	120	3	40.00	1-15	0	0	9.23	5	

Cmp	Debut	M	I	NO	Runs	HS	Avge	100	50	Balls	Runs	Wkts	Avge	BB	5i	10m	RpO	ct	st
FC	2004/05	42	71	2	1610	158	23.33	3	7	2146	1377	37	37.21	4-50	0	0	3.85	60	3
Lim	2004/05	56	54	1	1056	91*	19.92	0	9	1675	1274	41	31.07	5-21	0	1	4.56	16	
20T	2004/05	26	19	3	330	92*	20.62	0	2	240	320	12	26.66	3-27	0	0	8.00	13	
SAMSUDEEN, Mohamed Umhar (Singha) b Colombo 16.9.1987 RHB RFM																			
Lim		1	1	0	1	1	1.00	0	0	6	9	0					9.00	0	
Lim	2008/09	2	1	0	1	1	1.00	0	0	30	39	1	39.00	1-30	0	0	7.80	0	
SANDAGIRIGODA, Dilan Harshana (Burgher) b Colombo 12.6.1986 LHB OB																			
FC		1	2	0	39	39	19.50	0	0									0	
Lim		6	6	0	65	26	10.83	0	0	30	21	1	21.00	1-21	0	0	4.20	3	
FC	2007/08	14	27	0	546	104	20.22	1	1	6	2	0					2.00	7	
Lim	2007/08	19	19	0	570	91	30.00	0	4	66	47	2	23.50	1-21	0	0	4.27	6	
SANDARUWAN, Mananadevage Amila (Moors) b Colombo 25.12.1984 RHB																			
FC		2	4	0	57	36	14.25	0	0									1	
Lim		1	1	0	28	28	28.00	0	0	30	15	0					3.00	0	
FC	2004/05	31	57	2	1371	136	24.92	1	6	60	37	0					3.70	22	1
Lim	2003/04	33	33	2	648	90	20.90	0	3	96	76	1	76.00	1-19	0	0	4.75	4	1
20T	2004/05	7	7	1	164	60	27.33	0	1									3	
SANDARUWAN, Pethiyangaha Wattage Buddika (Sri Lanka Air Force) b Galle 11.7.1989 RHB LB																			
Lim		1	1	0	6	6	6.00	0	0	6	8	0					8.00	0	
SANGAKKARA, Kumar Chokshanada (Kandurata, Nondescripts, Sri Lanka, Kings XI Punjab, Sri Lanka to Bangladesh, Sri Lanka to India, Sri Lanka to South Africa, Sri Lanka to United States of America, Sri Lanka to West Indies) b Matale 27.10.1977 LHB OB WK																			
Test		3	5	1	467	219	116.75	2	1									6	
FC		3	5	1	467	219	116.75	2	1									6	
Int		9	9	1	358	73	44.75	0	3									17	3
Lim		20	20	2	830	116	46.11	2	4									27	7
20T		5	5	1	114	51*	28.50	0	1									3	3
Test	2000	91	152	11	8016	287	56.85	23	33	66	38	0					3.45	163	20
FC	1997/98	176	281	21	12400	287	47.69	31	57	192	108	1	108.00	1-13	0	0	3.37	324	33
Int	2000	276	259	28	8510	138*	36.83	10	58									272	68
Lim	1997/98	359	338	37	11672	156*	38.77	16	76									355	91
I20T	2006	28	27	2	733	78	29.32	0	6									12	8
20T	2004/05	79	75	5	2138	94	30.54	0	16									40	21
SANJEEV, Kishore Martin (Sebastianites) b Madras (now Chennai), Tamil Nadu, India 1.5.1988 RHB RMF																			
FC		1	2	0	48	48	24.00	0	0	126	74	2	37.00	2-63	0	0	3.52	1	
Lim		2	2	0	16	14	8.00	0	0	90	54	1	54.00	1-29	0	0	3.60	1	
SANJEEWA, Bopitiyage Buddika (Badureliya) b Panadura 23.3.1987 RHB RFM																			
Lim		2	2	1	5	5*	5.00	0	0	60	33	2	16.50	1-9	0	0	3.30	0	
FC	2007/08	1	2	2	6	6*		0	0	84	65	1	65.00	1-65	0	0	4.64	0	
Lim	2007/08	4	2	1	5	5*	5.00	0	0	108	104	3	34.66	1-9	0	0	5.77	0	
SANJEEWA, Rajapakse Gamage Dammika (Police) b Dehiwala 15.5.1971 RHB OB																			
FC		9	13	0	442	124	34.00	1	3	600	299	20	14.95	6-36	2	0	2.99	8	
Lim		9	9	0	244	74	27.11	0	2	282	203	4	50.75	1-9	0	0	4.31	2	
FC	1989/90	128	203	9	4942	157	25.47	6	21	8506	3930	148	26.55	6-36	2	0	2.77	90	
Lim	1995/96	74	67	11	1810	85	32.32	0	14	2021	1415	45	31.44	3-13	0	0	4.20	20	
20T	2004/05	4	4	0	58	22	14.50	0	0	52	61	4	15.25	3-24	0	0	7.03	0	
SANJEEWA, Sriyam Obinimuni (Sri Lanka Army) b Ambalangoda 25.4.1979 RHB OB																			
Lim		3	3	0	25	12	8.33	0	0	42	25	2	12.50	2-25	0	0	3.57	1	
FC	1999/00	43	75	4	1530	81*	21.54	0	6	600	307	5	61.40	3-33	0	0	3.07	33	
Lim	1999/00	32	31	1	500	66	16.66	0	3	431	330	11	30.00	3-67	0	0	4.59	6	
20T	2005/06	1	1	0	5	5	5.00	0	0									0	
SARAVANAN, Sathiamoorty Vasanth (Badureliya) b Namakkal, Tamil Nadu, India 22.9.1978 RHB RM																			
FC		3	5	0	43	27	8.60	0	0	132	74	3	24.66	2-19	0	0	3.36	2	
Lim		3	3	1	55	32*	27.50	0	0	36	38	2	19.00	2-38	0	0	6.33	1	
FC	1998/99	43	68	6	2143	126	34.56	5	13	1129	463	17	27.23	5-24	1	0	2.46	23	
Lim	1997/98	44	36	8	885	95	31.60	0	5	636	561	7	80.14	2-38	0	0	5.29	16	
SENANAYAKE, Arambewelage Dilan Lasantha (Saracens) b Kandy 28.4.1987 RHB SLA																			
FC		1	2	1	0	0*	0.00	0	0	6	8	0					8.00	0	
Lim		1	1	0	6	6	6.00	0	0	18	14	0					4.66	0	
SENANAYAKE, Senanayake Mudiyanselage Sachithra Madhushanka (Ruhuna, Sinhalese, Sri Lanka A, Sri Lanka Board President's XI, Sri Lanka A to Australia) b Colombo 9.2.1985 RHB OB																			
FC		19	24	9	386	89	25.73	0	1	4324	2172	94	23.10	8-117	9	0	3.01	18	
Lim		23	12	7	175	51*	35.00	0	1	1129	669	42	15.92	4-20	3	0	3.55	14	
20T		9	4	0	20	12	5.00	0	0	210	188	17	11.05	3-25	0	0	5.37	2	
FC	2006/07	48	61	17	818	89	18.59	0	2	10462	5000	237	21.09	8-70	18	3	2.86	37	
Lim	2006/07	50	25	12	278	51*	21.38	0	1	2185	1430	78	18.33	5-59	4	1	3.92	28	
20T	2006/07	16	6	0	33	12	5.50	0	0	354	341	26	13.11	3-16	0	0	5.78	5	
SENARATNE, Makulupagodagedara Indika Gihan (Ragama) b Gampola 15.2.1986 RHB OB																			
FC		2	3	0	51	36	17.00	0	0									1	
Lim		5	4	0	79	42	19.75	0	0									2	
FC	2006/07	11	20	0	437	61	21.85	0	3									6	

Cmp	Debut	M	I	NO	Runs	HS	Avge	100	50	Balls	Runs	Wkts	Avge	BB	5i	10m	RpO	ct	st
Lim	2006/07	26	25	1	463	52	19.29	0	1									6	
20T	2006/07	10	10	0	109	26	10.90	0	0									3	
SENAVIRATNE, Praboda Ireshan (Tamil Union) b Colombo 12.3.1990 RHB OB																			
FC		3	6	0	140	39	23.33	0	0	30	14	0					2.80	1	
SENDANAYAKE, Tharaka Chandima (Sri Lanka Army) b Panadura 19.7.1985 RHB LB																			
Lim		2	2	0	43	43	21.50	0	0									0	
FC	2008/09	2	4	0	16	12	4.00	0	0									1	
Lim	2007/08	5	5	0	66	43	13.20	0	0									0	
SENEVIRATNE, Kankanmala Pubudu Prasad Bandara (Burgher) b Kegalle 9.1.1980 RHB OB																			
Lim		1	1	0	10	10	10.00	0	0									0	
FC	1999/00	53	87	7	1640	91	20.50	0	9	1550	703	21	33.47	5-81	1	0	2.72	27	
Lim	2001/02	47	43	4	652	69	16.71	0	2	576	454	11	41.27	2-20	0	0	4.72	4	
20T	2004/05	6	6	0	107	43	17.83	0	0	84	78	2	39.00	1-15	0	0	5.57	2	
SEPALA, Nanayakkara Mahanamage Samitha Milinda (Moratuwa) b Colombo 8.11.1983 LHB LB																			
FC		5	7	1	181	63	30.16	0	1									7	
Lim		8	8	0	159	101	19.87	1	0									15	6
FC	2005/06	22	38	3	819	104*	23.40	1	3									23	3
Lim	2005/06	23	22	0	477	101	21.68	1	3									19	6
SERASINGHE, Sachithra Chaturanga (Basnahira North, Sri Lanka A, Tamil Union) b Colombo 13.4.1987 RHB OB																			
FC		14	22	5	837	126	49.23	2	4	951	500	16	31.25	4-23	0	0	3.15	5	
Lim		19	17	4	582	97	44.76	0	5	847	501	23	21.78	5-28	0	1	3.54	8	
20T		5	4	0	48	37	12.00	0	0	84	104	6	17.33	2-17	0	0	7.42	2	
FC	2006/07	32	51	9	1713	126	40.78	4	7	2747	1449	54	26.83	4-23	0	0	3.16	17	
Lim	2006/07	36	34	6	841	97	30.03	0	7	1287	798	29	27.51	5-28	0	1	3.72	13	
SHANTHA, Gagabadawatta Arachilage Lakpriya Waruna (Lankan) b Boralla 16.12.1980 RHB RFM																			
Lim		4	3	1	38	21*	19.00	0	0									4	1
FC	2007/08	7	12	0	151	60	12.58	0	1									8	1
20T	2005/06	4	4	0	55	34	13.75	0	0									3	1
SHIROMAN, Polwatta Samaraweera Arachchige Nuwan (Sebastianites) b Galle 14.9.1974 RHB RM																			
FC		9	15	2	322	78*	24.76	0	2	25	13	0					3.12	15	
Lim		3	3	1	103	58*	51.50	0	1	24	24	0					6.00	0	
FC	1995/96	122	206	11	4751	115	24.36	5	23	2985	1580	56	28.21	4-46	0	0	3.17	115	
Lim	1997/98	73	71	3	1849	103*	27.19	1	12	1186	830	28	29.64	3-23	0	0	4.19	22	
20T	2004/05	6	6	0	89	32	14.83	0	0	24	43	2	21.50	2-28	0	0	10.75	3	
SHIROSH, Palliya Madinage Uddika (Police) b Panadura 11.7.1985 LHB WK																			
FC		3	5	0	83	29	16.60	0	0									4	1
Lim		3	3	0	19	12	6.33	0	0									1	
FC	2006/07	9	16	0	240	32	15.00	0	0									17	5
Lim	2006/07	15	14	2	177	28	14.75	0	0	12	15	0					7.50	9	2
SILVA, Alankara Asanka Sriyan (Badureliya, Kandurata) b Kalutara 4.4.1985 RHB OB																			
FC		12	15	3	328	66	27.33	0	3	1324	942	31	30.38	7-73	1	1	4.26	12	
Lim		7	6	1	82	20*	16.40	0	0	204	166	5	33.20	1-12	0	0	4.88	0	
FC	2005/06	36	56	9	736	75*	15.65	0	5	4079	2585	93	27.79	7-73	2	1	3.80	27	
Lim	2005/06	22	19	5	272	43*	19.42	0	0	651	514	13	39.53	2-50	0	0	4.73	6	
20T	2006/07	3	2	1	9	9*	9.00	0	0	60	71	4	17.75	2-23	0	0	7.10	2	
SILVA, Ambawalage Dilan Chandima (Sri Lanka Navy) b Ragama 12.2.1990 RHB LB																			
FC		9	16	1	279	53	18.60	0	1	359	226	9	25.11	3-42	0	0	3.77	11	
Lim		4	4	0	40	21	10.00	0	0	84	69	3	23.00	2-17	0	0	4.92	1	
20T	2008/09	1	1	0	6	6	6.00	0	0									0	
SILVA, Athege Roshen Shivanka (Basnahira North, Colts) b Colombo 17.11.1988 RHB OB																			
FC		11	15	2	654	155	50.30	1	3	66	38	0					3.45	13	
Lim		11	10	4	347	54	57.83	0	3	34	35	1	35.00	1-1	0	0	6.17	7	
FC	2006/07	25	36	4	1152	155	36.00	2	5	114	79	2	39.50	2-22	0	0	4.15	20	
Lim	2006/07	26	24	7	671	71*	39.47	0	5	94	91	4	22.75	2-18	0	0	5.80	13	
SILVA, Anuk Shehantha (Nondescripts) b Colombo 3.3.1988 RHB RMF																			
Lim		2	2	0	6	6	3.00	0	0									0	
SILVA, Dadimuni Geeth Chaturanga (Sebastianites) b Colombo 17.9.1984 RHB RM																			
FC		5	5	0	21	13	4.20	0	0	288	160	4	40.00	1-17	0	0	3.33	3	
Lim		6	3	0	26	18	8.66	0	0	264	173	9	19.22	3-54	0	0	3.93	0	
FC	2007/08	14	22	4	229	59*	12.72	0	1	1156	829	18	46.05	3-103	0	0	4.30	8	
Lim	2004/05	19	11	1	171	32	17.10	0	0	859	599	30	19.96	6-13	0	1	4.18	5	
20T	2004/05	2	2	0	8	7	4.00	0	0	42	53	3	17.66	2-25	0	0	7.57	0	
SILVA, Disenthuwahandi Oshan Lasantha (Burgher) b Balapitiya 21.12.1984 RHB RM																			
FC		3	5	1	32	21	8.00	0	0	278	142	5	28.40	4-39	0	0	3.06	3	
Lim		2	1	0	19	19	19.00	0	0	105	75	5	15.00	3-47	0	0	4.28	0	
FC	2005/06	20	33	6	291	48	10.77	0	0	1436	916	30	30.53	4-35	0	0	3.82	17	
Lim	2005/06	15	13	0	138	36	10.61	0	0	534	441	21	21.00	3-33	0	0	4.95	2	
20T	2005/06	4	2	1	20	15*	20.00	0	0	78	91	3	30.33	2-39	0	0	7.00	2	

Cmp	Debut	M	I	NO	Runs	HS	Avge	100	50	Balls	Runs	Wkts	Avge	BB	5i	10m	RpO	ct	st
SILVA, Galgamuge Namal Chaturanga Dharmasena (Sri Lanka Air Force) b Negombo 21.11.1984 RHB RM																			
Lim		1	1	0	28	28	28.00	0	0									1	
Lim	2005/06	7	7	0	107	28	15.28	0	0									1	
20T	2005/06	4	4	0	69	27	17.25	0	0	6	14	0					14.00	1	
SILVA, Heema Hewage Malith Kumara (Police) b Panadura 14.11.1989 RHB LB																			
FC		8	7	4	49	13*	16.33	0	0	775	500	22	22.72	4-36	0	0	3.87	5	
Lim		4	4	2	17	13*	8.50	0	0	192	151	7	21.57	2-29	0	0	4.71	0	
SILVA, Jayan Kaushal (Basnahira North, Sinhalese, Sri Lanka A, Sri Lanka Board President's XI, Sri Lanka A to Australia) b Colombo 27.5.1986 RHB WK																			
FC		15	23	7	1062	158	66.37	3	6									37	5
Lim		14	13	2	350	71*	31.81	0	1									16	4
20T		5	4	1	113	47	37.66	0	0									2	3
FC	2002/03	85	136	23	5043	158	44.62	12	23	12	7	0					3.50	226	31
Lim	2002/03	83	67	17	1809	126	36.18	1	9									97	17
20T	2005/06	19	15	4	333	60*	30.27	0	2									11	11
SILVA, Kumbo Roy Prasanga (Colts) b Balapitiya 9.5.1980 RHB RFM																			
FC		9	10	0	223	92	22.30	0	2	372	251	4	62.75	1-11	0	0	4.04	16	
Lim		8	6	3	47	17	15.66	0	0	234	130	7	18.57	2-14	0	0	3.33	2	
FC	2000/01	71	112	7	2490	171	23.71	3	11	3721	2364	83	28.48	7-41	3	0	3.81	72	
Lim	2001/02	47	43	8	411	40	11.74	0	0	961	692	32	21.62	4-40	1	0	4.32	11	
20T	2004/05	4	4	0	83	37	20.75	0	0	18	12	1	12.00	1-12	0	0	4.00	0	
SILVA, Lokubahithige Chanaka Eranga (Sri Lanka Army) b Kandy 13.8.1988 RHB LB																			
FC		4	4	0	42	18	10.50	0	0	168	70	3	23.33	3-18	0	0	2.50	2	
Lim		2	2	0	34	31	17.00	0	0	90	58	2	29.00	1-20	0	0	3.86	0	
FC	2008/09	10	14	0	177	35	12.64	0	0	450	258	9	28.66	3-18	0	0	3.44	4	
Lim	2008/09	8	8	0	62	31	7.75	0	0	216	147	7	21.00	2-29	0	0	4.08	1	
SILVA, Lindamlilage Prageeth Chamara (Basnahira South, Bloomfield, Sri Lanka, Sri Lanka to Bangladesh, Sri Lanka to Zimbabwe, Sri Lanka A to Australia) b Panadura 14.12.1979 RHB LB																			
FC		15	25	1	1035	145	43.12	3	4	204	150	5	30.00	4-32	0	0	4.41	19	
Int		3	2	2	67	41*		0	0									1	
Lim		15	14	3	373	74*	33.90	0	2									8	
20T		6	6	0	108	45	18.00	0	0									2	
Test	2006/07	11	17	1	537	152*	33.56	1	2	102	65	1	65.00	1-57	0	0	3.82	7	
FC	1996/97	145	244	14	8657	152*	37.63	19	50	2163	1506	46	32.73	4-24	0	0	4.17	132	
Int	1999	61	52	7	1400	107*	31.11	1	11	24	21	1	21.00	1-21	0	0	5.25	18	
Lim	1998/99	188	172	27	4514	107*	31.13	2	32	287	267	6	44.50	1-1	0	0	5.58	73	
I20T	2006/07	15	14	2	171	38	14.25	0	0	18	15	1	15.00	1-4	0	0	5.00	5	
20T	2004/05	35	34	6	704	56	25.14	0	1	24	36	1	36.00	1-4	0	0	9.00	15	
SILVA, Patiharamada Juwan Hewage Sanath Ranjan (Sri Lanka Army) b Kalutara 18.11.1988 RHB OB																			
FC		1	1	0	1	1	1.00	0	0									0	
FC	2008/09	2	3	0	1	1	0.33	0	0	12	13	1	13.00	1-13	0	0	6.50	3	
Lim	2008/09	2	2	0	49	30	24.50	0	0									1	
SILVA, Rupage Chasun Randeera Priyankara (Badureliya) b Kalutara 27.7.1976 RHB RFM																			
FC		2	2	1	3	3*	3.00	0	0	156	124	2	62.00	1-17	0	0	4.76	0	
Lim		4	2	1	1	1	1.00	0	0	156	100	7	14.28	3-19	0	0	3.84	1	
FC	1996/97	79	105	32	366	27	5.01	0	0	10183	6582	225	29.25	6-65	7	0	3.87	23	
Lim	1996/97	36	17	10	47	11*	6.71	0	0	1526	1100	58	18.96	4-17	3	0	4.32	4	
20T	2004/05	8	3	3	6	6*		0	0	174	233	9	25.88	3-24	0	0	8.03	3	
SILVA, Sandaradur Himesh Madushanka (Badureliya) b Kuwait 6.2.1985 RHB RMF																			
FC		9	12	6	114	48	19.00	0	0	806	531	15	35.40	2-30	0	0	3.95	0	
Lim		7	4	3	11	7*	11.00	0	0	226	196	6	32.66	3-36	0	0	5.20	1	
FC	2005/06	39	53	30	255	48	11.08	0	0	4226	2609	87	29.98	5-43	3	0	3.70	6	
Lim	2005/06	35	14	8	35	13	5.83	0	0	1422	1050	53	19.81	5-22	2	2	4.43	8	
20T	2005/06	10	7	3	25	13	6.25	0	0	186	216	9	24.00	2-16	0	0	6.96	3	
SILVA, Sella Hannadige Suranjith Mudushan Kanchana (Lankan) b Colombo 4.3.1975 RHB LB																			
FC		8	8	2	144	51	24.00	0	1	582	315	13	24.23	7-52	1	0	3.24	3	
Lim		6	4	1	136	58	45.33	0	2	186	119	5	23.80	2-39	0	0	3.83	2	
FC	1993/94	127	149	28	2488	92	20.56	0	7	17618	9077	378	24.01	8-130	15	2	3.09	53	
Lim	1993/94	66	37	11	449	58	17.26	0	2	2346	1513	78	19.39	4-30	4	0	3.87	25	
20T	2004/05	5	3	2	20	9	20.00	0	0	84	114	5	22.80	2-23	0	0	8.14	1	
SILVA, Thewahettige Kapila Mark Yohan (Sri Lanka Air Force) b Colombo 9.10.1988 LHB LB																			
Lim		1	1	0	6	6	6.00	0	0	24	20	1	20.00	1-20	0	0	5.00	0	
SILVA, Weerasinghage Manuka Umesh (Panadura) b Panadura 30.8.1987 RHB OB																			
FC		2	2	0	34	24	17.00	0	0	222	107	4	26.75	2-40	0	0	2.89	0	
Lim		7	5	3	35	25*	17.50	0	0	241	130	12	10.83	4-9	1	0	3.23	1	
FC	2004/05	4	4	0	38	24	9.50	0	0	222	107	4	26.75	2-40	0	0	2.89	2	
20T	2005/06	1	1	1	5	5*		0	0									0	
SIRISOMA, Rajpakse Manikkunambi Gayan Kavinda (Lankan) b Ambalangoda 22.9.1981 RHB SLA																			
FC		9	8	3	43	23	8.60	0	0	1894	790	52	15.19	7-53	5	2	2.50	5	
Lim		8	4	2	24	16*	12.00	0	0	394	231	14	16.50	4-65	1	0	3.51	0	
FC	2002/03	39	54	16	269	31	7.07	0	0	6965	3152	177	17.80	8-96	13	5	2.71	21	

Cmp	Debut	M	I	NO	Runs	HS	Avge	100	50	Balls	Runs	Wkts	Avge	BB	5i	10m	RpO	ct	st
Lim	2004/05	40	19	4	127	26	8.46	0	0	1828	1199	53	22.62	4-33	2	0	3.93	7	
20T	2005/06	4	3	3	28	21*		0	0	79	106	6	17.66	4-25	1	0	8.05	0	
SIRIWARDENE, Lekamwasam Sisira Prathapa (Singha) b Galle 2.7.1989 RHB RMF																			
Lim		2	2	1	8	7	8.00	0	0	12	19	0					9.50	1	
SIRIWARDENE, Tissa Appuhamilage Milinda (Basnahira South, Chilaw Marians, Sri Lanka A, Dhaka) b Nagoda 4.12.1985 LHB SLA																			
FC		12	19	3	703	151*	43.93	1	5	748	491	19	25.84	4-102	0	0	3.93	11	
Lim		21	18	1	358	44	21.05	0	0	526	387	11	35.18	3-20	0	0	4.41	13	
20T		9	9	2	144	54*	20.57	0	1	95	120	8	15.00	3-5	0	0	7.57	6	
FC	2005/06	45	75	7	2094	151*	30.79	2	14	2457	1616	53	30.49	5-26	2	0	3.94	33	
Lim	2005/06	62	53	10	902	76	20.97	0	2	1302	948	41	23.12	6-40	0	1	4.36	30	
20T	2005/06	28	27	4	340	54*	14.78	0	1	260	324	17	19.05	4-22	1	0	7.47	18	
SOLOMONS, Andy Dextor (Burgher) b Colombo 18.9.1987 RHB RFM																			
Lim		5	4	0	34	20	8.50	0	0	228	188	7	26.85	2-35	0	0	4.94	0	
FC	2006/07	4	4	0	4	4	1.00	0	0	108	62	1	62.00	1-20	0	0	3.44	4	
Lim	2006/07	15	13	0	212	42	16.30	0	0	354	289	8	36.12	2-35	0	0	4.89	2	
20T	2006/07	2	2	0	8	4	4.00	0	0	30	45	2	22.50	2-25	0	0	9.00	1	
SOYSA, Iddadura Chamara (Saracens) b Galle 12.10.1978 RHB RM																			
FC		1	1	0	10	10	10.00	0	0									0	
Lim		5	4	0	33	14	8.25	0	0	48	37	0					4.62	2	
FC	1994/95	89	130	20	2921	121*	26.55	3	14	5822	3424	119	28.77	5-50	1	0	3.52	46	
Lim	1998/99	39	35	3	661	66	20.65	0	4	792	690	16	43.12	3-50	0	0	5.22	12	
20T	2005/06	6	5	1	112	52*	28.00	0	1	42	63	3	21.00	2-10	0	0	9.00	1	
SOYSA, Thilakamuni Dilan Thilina (Sri Lanka Army) b Ragama 8.3.1986 RHB WK																			
FC		11	16	2	320	42	22.85	0	0									21	10
Lim		11	11	0	204	58	18.54	0	1									11	6
FC	2006/07	38	58	7	993	62	19.47	0	3									75	22
Lim	2006/07	29	27	2	398	58	15.92	0	1									29	14
20T	2006/07	3	2	0	2	2	1.00	0	0									1	
SRIYAPALA, Endeerage Don Janudika (Sinhalese) b Colombo 23.8.1985 RHB OB																			
FC		5	7	0	126	46	18.00	0	0									15	
Lim		4	2	1	84	62*	84.00	0	1									3	2
FC	2007/08	12	19	4	289	62*	19.26	0	1									21	
Lim	2007/08	11	7	2	155	62*	31.00	0	1									9	2
SUBRAMANIA SIVA, V (Tamil Nadu, Badureliya) b Surandai, Tamil Nadu, India 3.3.1984 RHB RM																			
FC		8	12	0	328	64	27.33	0	2	54	36	0					4.00	5	
Lim		4	4	0	152	57	38.00	0	1									2	
20T	2009/10	1	1	0	12	12	12.00	0	0									0	
SUMATHIPALA, Chamil Navindra (Tamil Union) b Colombo 15.11.1980 RHB RM																			
FC		2	2	2	1	1*		0	0	72	63	4	15.75	2-23	0	0	5.25	0	
FC	2000/01	8	9	3	29	13*	4.83	0	0	408	255	10	25.50	3-39	0	0	3.75	1	
Lim	2006/07	3	1	1	0	0*		0	0	84	71	3	23.66	2-19	0	0	5.07	0	
20T	2005/06	2								36	52	0					8.66	0	
TARAKA, Watta Waduge Pubudu (Sri Lanka Army) b Colombo 27.2.1986 RHB RM																			
FC		2	4	0	61	29	15.25	0	0									0	
FC	2006/07	13	21	1	404	127	20.20	1	0	342	133	2	66.50	1-7	0	0	2.33	8	
Lim	2006/07	14	13	0	267	71	20.53	0	2	252	161	5	32.20	2-29	0	0	3.83	5	
THARANGA, Warushavithana Upul (Nondescripts, Ruhuna, Sri Lanka, Sri Lanka Board President's XI, Sri Lanka to Bangladesh, Sri Lanka to India, Sri Lanka to Zimbabwe) b Balapitiya 2.2.1985 LHB																			
FC		13	18	0	687	155	38.16	2	2									5	
Int		9	9	1	219	70	27.37	0	2									2	
Lim		22	22	1	704	106	33.52	1	4									10	
20T		7	7	1	162	83*	27.00	0	1									2	
Test	2005/06	15	26	1	713	165	28.52	1	3									11	
FC	2000/01	82	137	4	4720	265*	35.48	10	19	18	4	0					1.33	61	1
Int	2005	106	102	3	3246	120	32.78	8	17									19	
Lim	2003/04	169	163	5	5170	173*	32.72	11	28									42	2
I20T	2006	8	8	0	114	37	14.25	0	0									1	
20T	2006	25	25	2	485	83*	21.08	0	3									6	
THIRIMANNE, Hettige Don Rumesh Lahiru (Basnahira South, Ragama, Sri Lanka A, Sri Lanka Board President's XI, Sri Lanka to Bangladesh, Sri Lanka to Zimbabwe, Sri Lanka A to Australia) b Moratuwa 8.9.1989 LHB RMF																			
FC		16	28	2	1287	148	49.50	4	8									10	
Lim		16	14	0	316	70	22.57	0	1									2	
20T		6	6	1	138	42	27.60	0	0									4	
FC	2008/09	30	53	3	2105	148	42.10	5	13	18	19	0					6.33	26	
Int	2009/10	3	2	0	37	22	18.50	0	0									1	
Lim	2008/09	28	24	2	558	70	25.36	0	3	10	10	1	10.00	1-5	0	0	6.00	8	
20T	2008/09	12	12	1	247	70	22.45	0	1									7	
TILLAKARATNE, Hetti Arachchilage Heshan Udara (Badureliya) b Colombo 16.12.1976 RHB RFM																			
FC		1	2	0	44	39	22.00	0	0									0	
Lim		4	4	0	37	11	9.25	0	0									1	

Cmp	Debut	M	I	NO	Runs	HS	Avge	100	50	Balls	Runs	Wkts	Avge	BB	5i	10m	RpO	ct	st
FC	1998/99	72	129	2	3050	164	24.01	4	11	182	88	1	88.00	1-4	0	0	2.90	53	
Lim	1998/99	60	60	1	1024	71	17.35	0	2	89	91	2	45.50	2-49	0	0	6.13	15	
20T	2004/05	6	6	0	81	38	13.50	0	0									0	
TILLAKARATNE, Yasas Nilantha (Lankan) b Colombo 15.9.1972 LHB LB																			
FC		7	9	1	232	48	29.00	0	0	36	23	0					3.83	12	
Lim		6	6	2	133	45*	33.25	0	0	102	80	2	40.00	1-25	0	0	4.70	5	
FC	1992/93	70	104	7	3003	153	30.95	4	11	2329	1287	46	27.97	6-47	2	0	3.31	70	
Lim	1989/90	13	12	4	227	45*	28.37	0	0	212	155	9	17.22	4-32	1	0	4.38	6	
UDANA, Isuru Tillakaratna (Sri Lanka A, Tamil Union, Wayamba, Sri Lanka A to Australia, Wayamba to India) b Balangoda 17.2.1988 RHB LMF																			
FC		11	14	3	206	61*	18.72	0	1	1092	661	18	36.72	4-60	0	0	3.63	4	
Lim		14	11	2	130	38	14.44	0	0	575	436	15	29.06	4-36	1	0	4.55	3	
20T		10	1	1	9	9*		0	0	198	233	10	23.30	2-21	0	0	7.06	5	
FC	2008/09	23	30	5	558	88	22.32	0	3	2637	1585	47	33.72	4-60	0	0	3.60	9	
Lim	2008/09	33	22	8	299	49*	21.35	0	0	1436	1218	49	24.85	4-36	1	0	5.08	19	
I20T	2009	5	1	0	1	1	1.00	0	0	108	164	5	32.80	2-17	0	0	9.11	1	
20T	2008/09	24	4	2	31	11*	15.50	0	0	482	599	32	18.71	4-31	1	0	7.45	8	
UDAWATTE, Mahela Lakmal (Chilaw Marians, Sri Lanka A, Wayamba, Khulna to Bangladesh, Sri Lanka A to Australia, Wayamba to India) b Colombo 19.7.1986 LHB OB																			
FC		13	21	3	533	90	29.61	0	4	18	20	0					6.66	10	
Lim		19	19	0	549	107	28.89	1	2									6	
20T		6	6	1	174	103*	34.80	1	0									5	
FC	2005/06	65	116	8	3345	168	30.97	3	22	228	164	5	32.80	2-31	0	0	4.31	36	
Int	2007/08	9	9	0	257	73	28.55	0	2									0	
Lim	2004/05	87	86	2	2607	161	31.03	3	14	42	31	1	31.00	1-24	0	0	4.42	21	
I20T	2008/09	5	5	0	77	25	15.40	0	0									0	
20T	2005	41	39	2	765	103*	20.67	1	2	37	39	2	19.50	2-17	0	0	6.32	14	
UDAYANGA, Rajapaksha Jasanthunambi Imesh (Moors, Sri Lanka Cricket Combined XI) b Balapitiya 14.1.1990 RHB OB																			
FC		11	16	4	234	52*	19.50	0	1	1039	658	24	27.41	4-31	0	0	3.80	6	
Lim		7	6	0	101	80	16.83	0	1	192	155	4	38.75	3-28	0	0	4.84	3	
20T		2	1	0	0	0	0.00	0	0	42	52	2	26.00	1-17	0	0	7.42	0	
FC	2008/09	12	17	4	234	52*	18.00	0	1	1045	662	24	27.58	4-31	0	0	3.80	6	
Lim	2008/09	12	8	0	111	80	13.87	0	1	192	155	4	38.75	3-28	0	0	4.84	4	
20T	2007/08	11	10	3	36	15*	5.14	0	0	174	206	12	17.16	2-12	0	0	7.10	3	
VAAS, Warnakulasuriya Patabendige Ushantha Joseph Chaminda (Basnahira North, Colts, Deccan Chargers, Northamptonshire) b Mattumagala 27.1.1974 LHB LFM																			
FC		6	7	1	136	35	22.66	0	0	363	218	10	21.80	2-18	0	0	3.60	2	
Lim		10	8	2	272	76*	45.33	0	3	246	184	2	92.00	1-21	0	0	4.48	5	
20T		4	4	2	64	27*	32.00	0	0	90	98	6	16.33	3-22	0	0	6.53	1	
Test	1994	111	162	35	3089	100*	24.32	1	13	23438	10501	355	29.58	7-71	12	2	2.68	31	
FC	1990/91	202	272	57	5525	134	25.69	4	24	37222	17068	683	24.98	7-54	27	3	2.75	57	
Int	1993/94	322	220	72	2025	50*	13.68	0	1	15775	11014	400	27.53	8-19	9	4	4.18	60	
Lim	1992/93	392	268	88	2903	76*	16.12	0	6	18664	12947	480	26.97	8-19	11	4	4.16	79	
I20T	2006/07	6	2	1	33	21	33.00	0	0	132	128	6	21.33	2-14	0	0	5.81	0	
20T	2005/06	45	39	8	622	73	20.06	0	4	927	1059	55	19.25	3-16	0	0	6.85	7	
VANDORT, Michael Graydon (Colombo, Wayamba, Wayamba to India) b Colombo 19.1.1980 LHB RM																			
FC		10	16	0	489	100	30.56	1	3									7	
Lim		5	5	0	185	62	37.00	0	2									1	
Test	2001/02	20	33	2	1144	140	36.90	4	4									6	
FC	1998/99	148	248	15	7756	226	33.28	18	35	67	62	1	62.00	1-46	0	0	5.55	109	
Int	2005/06	1	1	0	48	48	48.00	0	0									0	
Lim	1999/00	78	76	10	2562	118	38.81	4	16									24	
20T	2004/05	13	13	1	202	42	16.83	0	0									5	
VARUNA, Hewa Wellalage Udara (Saracens) b Colombo 11.3.1984 LHB RMF																			
FC		4	5	0	40	18	8.00	0	0	444	354	6	59.00	2-68	0	0	4.78	2	
Lim		1								24	36	0					9.00	0	
FC	2002/03	29	38	7	503	42	16.22	0	0	2442	1555	41	37.92	3-34	0	0	3.82	8	
Lim	2002/03	34	14	2	161	48	13.41	0	0	843	710	25	28.40	5-24	0	1	5.05	10	
20T	2004/05	9	5	1	74	36	18.50	0	0	109	104	8	13.00	3-25	0	0	5.72	2	
VIDANAPATHIRANA, Chaminda Wijayakumara (Colombo, Kandurata, Sri Lanka A, Sri Lanka A to Australia) b Morawake 25.1.1983 RHB RFM																			
FC		17	17	4	168	34*	12.92	0	0	2193	1251	33	37.90	3-28	0	0	3.42	11	
Lim		16	7	3	28	16*	7.00	0	0	569	469	23	20.39	4-26	1	0	4.94	2	
20T		2								48	51	3	17.00	2-25	0	0	6.37	0	
FC	2002/03	72	82	23	678	42*	11.49	0	0	9379	5108	197	25.92	6-53	2	0	3.26	28	
Lim	2002/03	59	25	10	171	27	11.40	0	0	2333	1725	63	27.38	4-26	1	0	4.43	10	
20T	2005/06	14	5	1	14	6*	3.50	0	0	282	323	20	16.15	4-25	1	0	6.87	0	
VISHWARANGA, Liyanaarachchi Appuhamilage Sameera (Moors) b Colombo 11.11.1982 RHB RFM																			
FC		6	8	1	54	12	7.71	0	0	464	376	8	47.00	3-86	0	0	4.86	3	
Lim		4	3	1	8	4*	4.00	0	0	179	148	4	37.00	2-52	0	0	4.96	0	

Cmp	Debut	M	I	NO	Runs	HS	Avge	100	50	Balls	Runs	Wkts	Avge	BB	5i	10m	RpO	ct	st
FC	2007/08	16	20	7	119	26	9.15	0	0	1366	1058	29	36.48	3-23	0	0	4.64	6	
Lim	2007/08	12	9	4	10	4*	2.00	0	0	437	366	11	33.27	2-30	0	0	5.02	0	
VITHANA, Harsha Eranga (Ragama) b Galle 15.8.1985 RHB OB																			
Lim		4	4	1	28	10*	9.33	0	0									1	
FC	2003/04	50	79	6	1832	120	25.09	3	5	1386	665	27	24.62	6-60	1	0	2.87	30	
Lim	2003/04	44	42	3	798	105	20.46	1	4	498	360	12	30.00	3-24	0	0	4.33	12	
20T	2004/05	6	6	2	51	17	12.75	0	0	37	48	2	24.00	2-18	0	0	7.78	2	
VITHANA, Sameera Irantha (Burgher) b Galle 7.7.1983 RHB OB																			
FC		6	9	2	220	45	31.42	0	0	713	439	11	39.90	3-31	0	0	3.69	4	
Lim		5	5	0	7	4	1.40	0	0	162	124	2	62.00	1-35	0	0	4.59	0	
FC	2003/04	30	46	11	845	68*	24.14	0	2	3864	2061	102	20.20	6-52	4	1	3.20	17	
Lim	2003/04	36	30	8	305	44*	13.86	0	0	1237	842	33	25.51	5-16	1	1	4.08	6	
20T	2005/06	3	2	0	21	21	10.50	0	0	16	27	1	27.00	1-4	0	0	10.12	0	
VITHANAGE, Kasun Disi Kithuruwan (Sri Lanka Cricket Combined XI) b Colombo 26.2.1991 LHB LB																			
Lim		5	5	0	114	53	22.80	0	1									0	
20T		4	4	1	89	62*	29.66	0	1									1	
VITHARANA, Dorake Witharanage Ashana Niroshan Dilshan (Badureliya) b Kandy 13.5.1978 LHB WK																			
FC		8	11	1	368	67	36.80	0	2	26	39	0					9.00	11	1
Lim		7	7	1	63	35*	10.50	0	0									12	1
FC	1997/98	94	146	4	3429	114	24.14	2	16	68	86	0					7.58	180	44
Lim	1999/00	61	60	5	1232	87*	22.40	0	5									58	19
20T	2005/06	11	11	3	157	49*	19.62	0	0									7	3
WANASINGHE, Wasala Mudiyanselage Pasan Nirmitha (Sebastianites) b Colombo 30.9.1970 RHB RFM																			
FC		9	14	1	294	108	22.61	1	1	1154	531	28	18.96	5-42	1	0	2.76	4	
Lim		5	5	1	98	28	24.50	0	0	168	112	5	22.40	2-30	0	0	4.00	1	
FC	1990/91	133	217	17	5377	136	26.88	8	29	14363	7368	295	24.97	6-36	10	0	3.07	53	
Lim	1996/97	65	57	6	1350	93*	26.47	0	8	2220	1444	74	19.51	3-15	0	0	3.90	18	
20T	2005/06	4	4	1	184	74*	61.33	0	2	43	70	3	23.33	2-11	0	0	9.76	1	
WANIGARATNE, Manampeli Mahapata Bandhi Ralalage Supun Tharanga Coory (Sri Lanka Air Force) b Kaluthara 22.3.1986 RHB RM																			
Lim		2	2	0	27	21	13.50	0	0	24	30	0					7.50	1	
FC	2006/07	3	6	0	81	57	13.50	0	1	299	201	5	40.20	3-101	0	0	4.03	3	
Lim	2006/07	3	3	0	31	21	10.33	0	0	24	30	0					7.50	2	
20T	2006/07	5	5	2	40	27*	13.33	0	0	30	45	1	45.00	1-31	0	0	9.00	1	
WARNAPURA, Basnayake Shalith Malinda (Basnahira South, Colts) b Colombo 26.5.1979 LHB OB																			
FC		10	13	0	275	56	21.15	0	1	122	62	2	31.00	1-7	0	0	3.04	5	
Lim		16	16	1	442	73	29.46	0	2	174	122	2	61.00	1-23	0	0	4.20	12	
Test	2007	14	24	1	821	120	35.69	2	7	54	40	0					4.44	14	
FC	1998	153	232	22	7373	242	35.10	16	37	6918	3272	118	27.72	6-22	4	0	2.83	103	
Int	2007	3	3	0	35	30	11.66	0	0									3	
Lim	1998	117	102	15	2451	104*	28.17	3	8	2246	1609	69	23.31	5-33	2	1	4.29	51	
20T	2005/06	12	12	1	139	53	12.63	0	1	79	93	5	18.60	3-19	0	0	7.06	4	
WARNAPURA, Madawa Sachinthana (Seeduwa Raddoluwa) b Colombo 4.6.1988 RHB RM																			
FC		2	3	0	38	27	12.66	0	0	24	20	1	20.00	1-14	0	0	5.00	4	
FC	2008/09	10	18	2	388	72	24.25	0	3	36	33	1	33.00	1-14	0	0	5.50	15	
Lim	2008/09	7	7	1	74	19*	12.33	0	0									1	
WEERAKOON, Sajeewa (Colts, Ruhuna) b Galle 17.2.1978 LHB SLA																			
FC		11	9	3	36	9	6.00	0	0	2318	1193	42	28.40	5-54	4	1	3.08	5	
Lim		17	8	2	26	11*	4.33	0	0	843	557	26	21.42	5-24	0	1	3.96	6	
20T		7	3	1	4	2	2.00	0	0	138	134	9	14.88	2-16	0	0	5.82	1	
FC	1995/96	142	168	49	1763	90	14.81	0	4	27466	11991	586	20.46	7-40	35	10	2.61	89	
Lim	1997/98	104	51	22	375	53*	12.93	0	1	4643	2796	140	19.97	5-24	1	2	3.61	37	
20T	2004/05	23	10	2	81	28	10.12	0	0	411	371	27	13.74	3-14	0	0	5.41	6	
WEERAKOON, Weerakoon Mudiyanselage Vishvashantha (Sri Lanka Army) b Panadura 21.7.1987 LHB LMF																			
FC		5	5	2	9	5	3.00	0	0	396	252	7	36.00	3-55	0	0	3.81	5	
FC	2008/09	6	7	3	10	5	2.50	0	0	570	374	9	41.55	3-55	0	0	3.93	6	
Lim	2007/08	2	2	1	9	7	9.00	0	0	36	40	1	40.00	1-22	0	0	6.66	0	
WEERARATNE, Kaushalya (Kandurata, Ragama, Sri Lanka to India, Sylhet) b Gampola 29.1.1981 LHB RMF																			
FC		10	10	0	407	86	40.70	0	4	727	442	15	29.46	4-57	0	0	3.64	3	
Lim		15	13	3	474	143	47.40	1	3	396	327	15	21.80	4-42	1	0	4.95	7	
20T		6	6	2	151	60	37.75	0	1	36	82	0					13.66	3	
FC	1999/00	89	129	10	3125	135	26.26	2	16	9400	5827	232	25.11	6-47	5	0	3.71	41	
Int	2000	15	9	1	160	41	20.00	0	0	480	385	6	64.16	3-46	0	0	4.81	3	
Lim	1999/00	107	81	21	1497	143	24.95	1	7	3628	2718	110	24.70	5-19	2	2	4.49	31	
I20T	2008/09	5	5	2	49	20*	16.33	0	0	90	126	4	31.50	4-19	1	0	8.40	4	
20T	2005/06	34	31	7	603	76*	25.12	0	2	437	581	15	38.73	4-19	1	0	7.97	11	
WEERASINGHE, Don Rajeeva Frank (Colts) b Colombo 28.7.1987 RHB OB																			
FC		1	2	1	0	0*	0.00	0	0	102	37	4	9.25	3-18	0	0	2.17	1	
Lim		4	3	0	15	15	5.00	0	0	126	79	3	26.33	2-23	0	0	3.76	1	
FC	2006/07	14	25	9	292	60	18.25	0	1	1618	896	28	32.00	5-59	1	0	3.32	9	
Lim	2006/07	12	9	1	96	45*	12.00	0	0	319	207	10	20.70	2-13	0	0	3.89	4	

Cmp	Debut	M	I	NO	Runs	HS	Avge	100	50	Balls	Runs	Wkts	Avge	BB	5i	10m	RpO	ct	st
WEERASINGHE, Don Shameera Dane (Moors) b Colombo 25.9.1989 RHB LB																			
FC		3	3	1	37	17*	18.50	0	0	36	53	1	53.00	1-27	0	0	8.83	0	
Lim		3	3	2	40	21*	40.00	0	0	96	85	0					5.31	1	
FC	2008/09	5	7	2	92	30	18.40	0	0	270	201	6	33.50	2-46	0	0	4.46	4	
Lim	2008/09	6	5	4	47	21*	47.00	0	0	210	160	2	80.00	2-13	0	0	4.57	3	
20T	2008/09	2	1	1	0	0*		0	0	42	51	3	17.00	2-30	0	0	7.28	2	
WEERASINGHE, Roshan Nawaz (Singha) b Colombo 20.8.1976 LHB RM																			
FC		2	4	0	101	46	25.25	0	0	48	13	2	6.50	2-6	0	0	1.62	0	
Lim		1	1	0	7	7	7.00	0	0	36	14	0					2.33	1	
FC	1998/99	22	36	2	759	86	22.32	0	4	1019	572	20	28.60	5-41	1	0	3.36	7	
Lim	1999/00	10	8	2	66	19*	11.00	0	0	186	121	6	20.16	2-5	0	0	3.90	1	
20T	2004/05	5	4	1	16	8*	5.33	0	0	72	106	3	35.33	1-15	0	0	8.83	2	
WEERASINGHE, Tharindu Amila Nuwan (Police) b Galle 29.4.1983 RHB RM																			
FC		8	11	0	371	87	33.72	0	3	528	265	9	29.44	4-74	0	0	3.01	7	
Lim		7	7	1	58	28	9.66	0	0	156	107	5	21.40	4-31	1	0	4.11	2	
FC	2003/04	27	39	4	775	87	22.14	0	4	2067	1107	37	29.91	4-74	0	0	3.21	22	
Lim	2003/04	31	23	1	288	54	13.09	0	1	636	444	15	29.60	4-31	1	0	4.18	6	
20T	2005/06	3	3	1	16	9*	8.00	0	0									1	
WEGODAPOLA, Senevirathne Panditha Abeykoon Bandaranayaka Wasala Mudiyense Ralahamilage Anura Bandara (Sri Lanka Navy) b Polgolla 23.3.1981 LHB OB																			
Lim		5	5	1	62	22	15.50	0	0	168	92	2	46.00	1-20	0	0	3.28	2	
WELAGEDARA, Uda Walawwe Mahim Bandaralage Chanaka Asanka (Moors, Sri Lanka, Sri Lanka Board President's XI, Wayamba, Sri Lanka to Bangladesh, Sri Lanka to India, Sri Lanka to West Indies, Wayamba to India) b Matale 20.3.1981 RHB LFM																			
Test		2	2	1	8	4*	8.00	0	0	267	234	2	117.00	1-43	0	0	5.25	1	
FC		5	6	1	88	76	17.60	0	1	633	502	11	45.63	4-37	0	0	4.75	2	
Int		2								93	73	2	36.50	2-31	0	0	4.71	0	
Lim		13	5	4	28	18*	28.00	0	0	569	470	15	31.33	3-24	0	0	4.95	1	
20T		6								117	120	8	15.00	3-19	0	0	6.15	0	
Test	2007/08	6	6	2	27	8	6.75	0	0	993	707	12	58.91	4-87	0	0	4.27	2	
FC	2002/03	69	86	30	552	76	9.85	0	1	9465	5586	189	29.55	5-34	6	1	3.54	14	
Int	2009/10	10	3	2	4	2*	4.00	0	0	457	433	15	28.86	5-66	0	1	5.68	2	
Lim	2002/03	68	32	16	84	18*	5.25	0	0	2977	2432	93	26.15	5-16	2	3	4.90	15	
I20T	2010	2	1	1	2	2*		0	0	36	61	1	61.00	1-21	0	0	10.16	0	
20T	2004/05	23	10	6	42	12*	10.50	0	0	501	537	33	16.27	3-18	0	0	6.43	2	
WERAGALA, Lahiru Anirudda (Chilaw Marians) b Colombo 12.3.1989 RHB SLA																			
FC		4	6	0	106	30	17.66	0	0									3	
Lim		4	4	1	169	115*	56.33	1	0									2	
WETHATHASINGHE, Amila Chathuranga (Colombo) b Kaluthara 3.10.1982 RHB RMF																			
FC		10	12	1	240	67	21.81	0	2	162	109	0					4.03	6	
Lim		8	7	1	161	60	26.83	0	1	24	21	1	21.00	1-21	0	0	5.25	2	
FC	2002/03	57	87	11	2097	136*	27.59	3	9	3873	2034	66	30.81	4-24	0	0	3.15	43	
Lim	2002/03	46	41	3	560	75	14.73	0	2	1006	721	29	24.86	5-14	1	1	4.30	20	
20T	2004/05	7	5	1	92	60*	23.00	0	1	96	131	6	21.83	3-26	0	0	8.18	2	
WEWALWALA, Asela Sampath (Singha) b Galle 11.5.1975 RHB RFM																			
FC		9	15	0	403	75	26.86	0	3	81	32	1	32.00	1-12	0	0	2.37	5	
Lim		4	4	0	100	35	25.00	0	0	18	18	0					6.00	3	
FC	1994/95	109	184	13	4297	125	25.12	1	22	3884	2320	65	35.69	5-40	2	0	3.58	58	
Lim	1998/99	45	41	4	588	56*	15.89	0	1	650	474	21	22.57	3-22	0	0	4.37	13	
20T	2004/05	4	4	0	150	90	37.50	0	1	24	37	0					9.25	2	
WICKRAMARACHCHI, Rajitha Sameera (Moors) b Kandy 21.12.1987 LHB WK																			
FC		6	9	0	236	76	26.22	0	2									5	
Lim		2	2	1	53	36*	53.00	0	0									2	
FC	2008/09	15	23	1	422	80	19.18	0	3									26	10
Lim	2008/09	8	8	1	92	36*	13.14	0	0									8	1
WICKRAMARATNE, Dushan Dinushri Nirmal (Colts) b Colombo 23.3.1983 RHB RFM																			
FC		1	1	0	3	3	3.00	0	0	30	25	0					5.00	1	
FC	2003/04	22	31	5	474	59	18.23	0	2	665	398	12	33.16	3-12	0	0	3.59	16	
Lim	2003/04	15	8	3	130	62*	26.00	0	1	276	204	11	18.54	4-23	1	0	4.43	3	
20T	2004/05	7	7	3	63	23	15.75	0	0	60	97	4	24.25	2-18	0	0	9.70	1	
WICKRAMARATNE, Ranasinghe Pattikirikoralalage Aruna Hemantha (Badureliya) b Colombo 21.2.1971 LHB SLA																			
FC		6	9	0	164	62	18.22	0	2	36	27	1	27.00	1-27	0	0	4.50	3	
Lim		7	6	0	121	36	20.16	0	0	18	10	0					3.33	3	
FC	1990/91	195	279	28	10284	209	40.97	21	65	1406	868	22	39.45	3-62	0	0	3.70	204	
Int	1993	3	2	0	4	3	2.00	0	0									0	
Lim	1990/91	98	85	12	1768	82	24.21	0	5	64	43	0					4.03	38	1
20T	2004/05	13	12	0	169	33	14.08	0	0									2	
WICKRAMASINGHE, Dadallege Chaminda Mohan (Colts, Sri Lanka Air Force) b Colombo 24.1.1981 LHB SLA																			
FC		4	6	0	223	91	37.16	0	2	42	35	0					5.00	1	
Lim		1	1	0	34	34	34.00	0	0									0	
FC	2000/01	7	10	0	285	91	28.50	0	2	78	42	0					3.23	2	

Cmp	Debut	M	I	NO	Runs	HS	Avge	100	50	Balls	Runs	Wkts	Avge	BB	5i	10m	RpO	ct	st
Lim	2004/05	7	5	0	91	35	18.20	0	0	27	33	0					7.33	0	
20T	2004/05	9	8	0	98	42	12.25	0	0	84	108	5	21.60	4-19	1	0	7.71	3	
WIJENAYAKE, Wijenayake Gamaarachchige Roshan Lakmal (Nondescripts) b Galle 2.1.1989 RHB SLA																			
FC		5	5	2	27	8*	9.00	0	0	520	345	16	21.56	5-37	2	1	3.98	3	
WIJERATNE, Mahamandige Sahan Rangana (Badureliya) b Colombo 27.8.1984 RHB OB																			
FC		9	13	3	281	50*	28.10	0	1	48	41	0					5.12	4	
Lim		5	4	1	75	66*	25.00	0	1									1	
FC	2001/02	50	83	11	1641	123	22.79	2	6	548	275	9	30.55	2-4	0	0	3.01	27	
Lim	2002/03	33	26	2	660	85	27.50	0	5	66	60	0					5.45	10	
20T	2005/06	3	2	2	55	46*		0	0									1	
WIJERATNE, Saman Asiri (Police) b Kalubowila 31.1.1978 RHB OB																			
FC		2	2	0	16	12	8.00	0	0	12	18	1	18.00	1-18	0	0	9.00	1	
Lim		3	3	0	19	12	6.33	0	0	12	6	0					3.00	2	
FC	1997/98	68	117	5	2087	107	18.63	1	6	3706	1910	53	36.03	4-32	0	0	3.09	53	
Lim	1999/00	37	34	1	459	64	13.90	0	2	585	442	29	15.24	6-29	0	1	4.53	24	
20T	2004/05	4	4	0	133	43	33.25	0	0	33	30	2	15.00	2-10	0	0	5.45	3	
WIJESINGHE, Chanaka Gimhana (Nondescripts, Wayamba) b Kandy 4.2.1982 RHB OB																			
FC		12	17	5	487	81*	40.58	0	3	96	76	1	76.00	1-19	0	0	4.75	12	
Lim		8	7	2	153	43*	30.60	0	0	78	84	0					6.46	4	
FC	2002/03	71	123	12	3552	250	32.00	5	13	1935	1111	33	33.66	4-21	0	0	3.44	56	
Lim	2003/04	52	50	9	1142	100*	27.85	1	6	484	434	17	25.52	5-52	0	1	5.38	16	
20T	2004/05	5	4	0	22	19	5.50	0	0	23	24	3	8.00	3-24	0	0	6.26	0	
WIJESINGHE, Samantha Nalin (Moratuwa) b Colombo 27.10.1979 RHB RM																			
FC		9	12	1	281	55*	25.54	0	3									8	
Lim		7	7	1	96	33	16.00	0	0									6	
FC	1998/99	80	132	16	2813	114	24.25	2	16	486	236	3	78.66	1-12	0	0	2.91	48	
Lim	1998/99	56	55	2	908	79	17.13	0	5	36	22	0					3.66	15	
20T	2004/05	3	3	0	39	29	13.00	0	0									1	
WIJESIRI, Mudiyanselage Sahan Manjitha (Tamil Union) b Colombo 9.1.1988 RHB WK																			
Lim		1																0	
FC	2008/09	2	3	2	45	28*	45.00	0	0									6	
Lim	2008/09	2	1	1	1	1*		0	0									0	
WIJESIRI, Rankatige Upesh Assaji (Sinhalese) b Kandy 12.4.1987 LHB RMF																			
FC		2	2	0	30	16	15.00	0	0									0	
WIJETHILAKE, Gayan Malinga (Saracens) b Galgamuwa 23.1.1985 RHB LB																			
FC		2	2	1	27	26	27.00	0	0	125	92	2	46.00	2-14	0	0	4.41	0	
Lim		3	3	0	1	1	0.33	0	0	66	64	3	21.33	2-2	0	0	5.81	0	
FC	2007/08	5	7	1	32	26	5.33	0	0	399	232	10	23.20	3-33	0	0	3.48	1	
Lim	2008/09	11	11	3	111	34*	13.87	0	0	236	221	10	22.10	2-2	0	0	5.61	1	
WIJEWEERA, Hewa Hakuru Duminda Chathuranga (Sri Lanka Navy) b Galle 9.12.1986 RHB RFM																			
FC		2	3	0	2	2	0.66	0	0	24	8	0					2.00	2	
Lim		2	2	1	29	25*	29.00	0	0	48	42	1	42.00	1-16	0	0	5.25	1	
WILLE, Mark Stephen (Sri Lanka Air Force) b Wellawatta 24.1.1987 RHB WK																			
FC		2	3	0	33	12	11.00	0	0									1	
Lim		4	3	0	87	62	29.00	0	1									1	
WIMALADARMA, Weliwitagoda Rakitha Dilshan (Saracens, Wayamba) b Colombo 20.11.1984 RHB OB																			
FC		11	13	1	149	40	12.41	0	0	2326	1507	53	28.43	8-68	6	3	3.88	9	
Lim		7	6	4	78	25*	39.00	0	0	282	229	6	38.16	2-37	0	0	4.87	2	
FC	2004/05	21	29	7	321	40	14.59	0	0	3291	2063	73	28.26	8-68	7	4	3.76	12	
Lim	2004/05	12	10	5	186	71	37.20	0	1	480	407	15	27.13	3-38	0	0	5.08	3	
20T	2005/06	4	1	1	3	3*		0	0	71	81	5	16.20	2-20	0	0	6.84	1	
WITHANAGE, Chanaka Mawalle (Sri Lanka Army) b Galle 26.6.1976 LHB RM																			
FC		10	16	1	335	57	22.33	0	2									7	
Lim		6	6	0	90	53	15.00	0	1	24	10	0					2.50	2	
FC	1996/97	91	160	7	3666	166	23.96	2	19	787	510	14	36.42	3-15	0	0	3.88	52	1
Lim	1999/00	42	41	0	731	93	17.82	0	4	109	67	1	67.00	1-4	0	0	3.68	11	
20T	2004/05	4	4	0	24	14	6.00	0	0	24	20	3	6.66	3-20	0	0	5.00	1	
WITHARANA, Amila Eranga (Sebastianites) b Matara 23.9.1986 RHB LB																			
FC		2	2	0	10	6	5.00	0	0									1	
FC	2008/09	3	4	0	27	15	6.75	0	0									1	
ZOYSA, Demuni Nuwan Tharanga (Basnahira South, Sinhalese, Khulna) b Colombo 13.5.1978 LHB LFM																			
FC		5	5	0	94	42	18.80	0	0	382	238	7	34.00	2-58	0	0	3.73	1	
Lim		14	14	0	234	53	16.71	0	1	614	438	15	29.20	4-46	1	0	4.28	2	
20T		5	4	0	86	41	21.50	0	0	66	103	3	34.33	2-20	0	0	9.36	0	
Test	1996/97	30	40	6	288	28*	8.47	0	0	4422	2157	64	33.70	5-20	1	0	2.92	4	
FC	1996/97	118	142	25	2062	114	17.62	1	8	14905	7155	301	23.77	7-58	7	0	2.88	20	
Int	1996/97	95	47	21	343	47*	13.19	0	0	4259	3213	108	29.75	5-26	2	1	4.52	13	
Lim	1996/97	185	108	27	1320	53	16.29	0	3	8311	6004	239	25.12	6-14	5	2	4.33	25	
20T	2004/05	17	14	4	203	41	20.30	0	0	324	376	21	17.90	4-10	2	0	6.96	1	

Cmp	Debut	M	I	NO	Runs	HS	Avge	100	50	Balls	Runs	Wkts	Avge	BB	5i	10m	RpO	ct	st
ZOYSA, Hannadige Somasiri Maduranga (Saracens) b Moratuwa 27.9.1984 RHB LB																			
Lim		2	2	0	17	17	8.50	0	0									0	
FC	2005/06	15	26	1	455	73	18.20	0	2	78	77	1	77.00	1-10	0	0	5.92	21	
Lim	2005/06	23	22	4	457	63	25.38	0	2	181	171	11	15.54	4-25	2	0	5.66	6	

AFGHANISTAN TO SRI LANKA 2009/10

Cmp	Debut	M	I	NO	Runs	HS	Avge	100	50	Balls	Runs	Wkts	Avge	BB	5i	10m	RpO	ct	st
ASGHAR STANIKZAI																			
FC		1	1	0	39	39	39.00	0	0									0	
I20T		1	1	0	1	1	1.00	0	0									0	
20T		1	1	0	1	1	1.00	0	0									0	
DAWLAT AHMADZAI																			
FC		1	1	1	7	7*		0	0	156	84	5	16.80	5-52	1	0	3.23	0	
Lim		1	1	0	4	4	4.00	0	0	54	66	0					7.33	0	
I20T		1	1	1	2	2*		0	0	12	25	1	25.00	1-25	0	0	12.50	0	
20T		1	1	1	2	2*		0	0	12	25	1	25.00	1-25	0	0	12.50	0	
HAMID HASSAN																			
FC		1	1	0	7	7	7.00	0	0	210	118	4	29.50	3-91	0	0	3.37	2	
I20T		2	1	0	2	2	2.00	0	0	42	41	3	13.66	2-27	0	0	5.85	0	
20T		3	1	0	2	2	2.00	0	0	66	67	6	11.16	3-26	0	0	6.09	0	
KARIM SADIQ																			
FC		1	2	0	20	19	10.00	0	0	102	36	1	36.00	1-31	0	0	2.11	1	
Lim		1	1	0	69	69	69.00	0	1	60	46	1	46.00	1-46	0	0	4.60	0	
I20T		2	2	0	45	42	22.50	0	0	36	37	2	18.50	2-17	0	0	6.16	0	
20T		3	3	0	45	42	15.00	0	0	48	55	2	27.50	2-17	0	0	6.87	0	
MIRWAIS ASHRAF																			
Lim		1	1	1	15	15*		0	0	54	34	1	34.00	1-34	0	0	3.77	0	
I20T		1								24	23	0					5.75	0	
20T		2	1	1	25	25*		0	0	42	46	0					6.57	0	
MOHAMMAD NABI																			
FC		1	1	0	64	64	64.00	0	1	297	135	5	27.00	4-33	0	0	2.72	0	
Lim		1	1	0	32	32	32.00	0	0	48	46	1	46.00	1-46	0	0	5.75	0	
I20T		2	2	0	25	23	12.50	0	0	42	44	2	22.00	1-19	0	0	6.28	1	
20T		3	3	0	28	23	9.33	0	0	66	71	3	23.66	1-19	0	0	6.45	2	
MOHAMMAD SHAHZAD																			
FC		1	2	1	130	88	130.00	0	1									6	1
Lim		1	1	0	80	80	80.00	0	1									1	
I20T		2	2	0	28	18	14.00	0	0									2	
20T		3	3	0	84	56	28.00	0	1									2	
NAWROZ MANGAL																			
FC		1	2	1	100	84	100.00	0	1	12	7	0					3.50	0	
Lim		1	1	0	13	13	13.00	0	0									0	
I20T		2	2	1	34	27	34.00	0	0	1	4	0					24.00	0	
20T		3	3	1	38	27	19.00	0	0	1	4	0					24.00	0	
NOOR ALI ZADRAN																			
FC		1	2	0	110	57	55.00	0	2	12	21	0					10.50	0	
Lim		1	1	0	26	26	26.00	0	0									0	
I20T		1	1	0	31	31	31.00	0	0									0	
20T		2	2	0	41	31	20.50	0	0									0	
RAEES AHMADZAI																			
Lim		1	1	0	6	6	6.00	0	0									0	
I20T		2	1	1	33	33*		0	0									0	
20T		3	2	1	36	33*	36.00	0	0									0	
SAMIULLAH SHENWARI																			
FC		1	1	0	19	19	19.00	0	0	240	107	4	26.75	4-75	0	0	2.67	1	
Lim		1	1	0	13	13	13.00	0	0	24	21	0					5.25	0	
I20T		2	2	1	22	14	22.00	0	0	42	45	1	45.00	1-26	0	0	6.42	1	
20T		3	3	1	23	14	11.50	0	0	66	89	1	89.00	1-26	0	0	8.09	1	
SHABIR NOORI																			
FC		1	2	0	106	85	53.00	0	1									0	
SHAFIQULLAH																			
Lim		1	1	0	0	0	0.00	0	0									1	
I20T		2	2	0	32	23	16.00	0	0									0	
20T		3	3	0	33	23	11.00	0	0									0	
SHAPOOR ZADRAN																			
FC		1	1	0	2	2	2.00	0	0	132	74	1	74.00	1-33	0	0	3.36	0	
Lim		1	1	1	0	0*		0	0	60	88	1	88.00	1-88	0	0	8.80	0	
I20T		2	1	0	0	0	0.00	0	0	30	34	0					6.80	0	
20T		3	1	0	0	0	0.00	0	0	48	69	1	69.00	1-35	0	0	8.62	0	

BANGLADESH TO SRI LANKA 2010

Cmp	Debut	M	I	NO	Runs	HS	Avge	100	50	Balls	Runs	Wkts	Avge	BB	5i	10m	RpO	ct	st
ABDUR RAZZAK																			
Int		1								60	48	1	48.00	1-48	0	0	4.80	0	
Lim		1								60	48	1	48.00	1-48	0	0	4.80	0	
IMRUL KAYES																			
Int		3	3	0	106	66	35.33	0	1									0	
Lim		3	3	0	106	66	35.33	0	1									0	
JAHURUL ISLAM																			
Int		1	1	1	11	11*		0	0									0	
Lim		1	1	1	11	11*		0	0									0	
JUNAID SIDDIQUE																			
Int		2	2	0	135	97	67.50	0	1									0	
Lim		2	2	0	135	97	67.50	0	1									0	
MAHMUDULLAH																			
Int		3	3	1	32	23	16.00	0	0	84	80	1	80.00	1-28	0	0	5.71	0	
Lim		3	3	1	32	23	16.00	0	0	84	80	1	80.00	1-28	0	0	5.71	0	
MASHRAFE MORTAZA																			
Int		3	2	1	15	15	15.00	0	0	112	154	2	77.00	2-37	0	0	8.25	0	
Lim		3	2	1	15	15	15.00	0	0	112	154	2	77.00	2-37	0	0	8.25	0	
MOHAMMAD ASHRAFUL																			
Int		2	2	0	29	20	14.50	0	0	24	19	0					4.75	0	
Lim		2	2	0	29	20	14.50	0	0	24	19	0					4.75	0	
MUSHFIQUR RAHIM																			
Int		3	3	0	37	30	12.33	0	0									2	2
Lim		3	3	0	37	30	12.33	0	0									2	2
NAEEM ISLAM																			
Int		2	2	0	18	15	9.00	0	0	18	21	0					7.00	0	
Lim		2	2	0	18	15	9.00	0	0	18	21	0					7.00	0	
SHAFIUL ISLAM																			
Int		3	2	0	2	2	1.00	0	0	156	180	5	36.00	3-95	0	0	6.92	0	
Lim		3	2	0	2	2	1.00	0	0	156	180	5	36.00	3-95	0	0	6.92	0	
SHAKIB AL HASAN																			
Int		3	3	0	52	25	17.33	0	0	180	171	5	34.20	2-49	0	0	5.70	3	
Lim		3	3	0	52	25	17.33	0	0	180	171	5	34.20	2-49	0	0	5.70	3	
SUHRAWADI SHUVO																			
Int		2	1	0	4	4	4.00	0	0	72	86	0					7.16	1	
Lim		2	1	0	4	4	4.00	0	0	72	86	0					7.16	1	
SYED RASEL																			
Int		2	2	1	0	0*	0.00	0	0	78	86	0					6.61	0	
Lim		2	2	1	0	0*	0.00	0	0	78	86	0					6.61	0	
TAMIM IQBAL																			
Int		3	3	0	107	51	35.66	0	1									1	
Lim		3	3	0	107	51	35.66	0	1									1	

CANADA TO SRI LANKA 2009/10

Cmp	Debut	M	I	NO	Runs	HS	Avge	100	50	Balls	Runs	Wkts	Avge	BB	5i	10m	RpO	ct	st
BAGAI, A.																			
Lim		1	1	0	75	75	75.00	0	1									0	
I20T		2	2	0	95	53	47.50	0	1									0	
20T		3	3	0	120	53	40.00	0	1									0	
BAIDWAN, H.S.																			
Lim		2	2	1	10	8*	10.00	0	0	100	103	1	103.00	1-59	0	0	6.18	0	
I20T		2								47	61	4	15.25	3-23	0	0	7.78	1	
20T		3								65	78	4	19.50	3-23	0	0	7.20	1	
BASTIAMPILLAI, T.C.																			
Lim		2	2	0	47	33	23.50	0	0									2	
I20T		2																0	
20T		3	1	0	16	16	16.00	0	0									0	
DHANIRAM, S.																			
Lim		1	1	0	4	4	4.00	0	0									0	
I20T		2	1	0	18	18	18.00	0	0	36	41	0					6.83	0	
20T		3	2	0	19	18	9.50	0	0	48	53	0					6.62	0	
JYOTI, S.																			
Lim		2	2	0	21	20	10.50	0	0	48	44	1	44.00	1-40	0	0	5.50	1	
20T		1	1	0	5	5	5.00	0	0									0	
KESHVANI, S.																			
Lim		2	2	0	21	18	10.50	0	0	72	54	1	54.00	1-31	0	0	4.50	1	
I20T		2	1	1	0	0*		0	0									1	
20T		3	2	2	11	11*		0	0	6	10	0					10.00	1	

Cmp Debut	M	I	NO	Runs	HS	Avge	100	50	Balls	Runs	Wkts	Avge	BB	5i	10m	RpO	ct	st
KHURRAM CHAUHAN																		
Lim	2	2	2	32	28*		0	0	96	106	4	26.50	3-57	0	0	6.62	1	
I20T	2	2	1	8	8	8.00	0	0	48	59	1	59.00	1-24	0	0	7.37	0	
20T	3	2	1	8	8	8.00	0	0	60	73	2	36.50	1-14	0	0	7.30	0	
OSINDE, H.																		
Lim	2	1	1	1	1*		0	0	36	40	1	40.00	1-23	0	0	6.66	0	
I20T	1								6	13	0					13.00	1	
20T	2								24	37	0					9.25	1	
PATEL, H.																		
I20T	2	2	1	99	88*	99.00	0	1	6	6	0					6.00	0	
20T	2	2	1	99	88*	99.00	0	1	6	6	0					6.00	0	
RIZWAN CHEEMA																		
Lim	2	2	0	39	29	19.50	0	0	90	80	0					5.33	1	
I20T	2	2	0	48	34	24.00	0	0	48	79	1	79.00	1-38	0	0	9.87	2	
20T	3	3	0	49	34	16.33	0	0	54	87	1	87.00	1-38	0	0	9.66	2	
SAAD BIN ZAFAR																		
Lim	2	2	0	32	23	16.00	0	0									1	
SAMAD, A.M.																		
Lim	2	2	0	15	15	7.50	0	0									1	
I20T	1	1	0	26	26	26.00	0	0									0	
20T	2	2	0	50	26	25.00	0	0									1	
UMAR BHATTI																		
Lim	2	2	0	85	51	42.50	0	1	54	38	4	9.50	3-22	0	0	4.22	0	
I20T	2	2	1	10	6	10.00	0	0	48	45	4	11.25	3-26	0	0	5.62	0	
20T	3	3	2	14	6	14.00	0	0	54	54	4	13.50	3-26	0	0	6.00	0	
USMAN LIMBADA																		
I20T	2																1	
20T	2																1	

INDIA TO SRI LANKA 2010

Cmp Debut	M	I	NO	Runs	HS	Avge	100	50	Balls	Runs	Wkts	Avge	BB	5i	10m	RpO	ct	st
DHONI, M.S.																		
Test	3	4	0	128	76	32.00	0	1									6	
FC	4	5	0	138	76	27.60	0	1									7	3
Int	9	9	2	313	67	44.71	0	2									16	3
Lim	9	9	2	313	67	44.71	0	2									16	3
DINDA, A.B.																		
Int	1	1	0	2	2	2.00	0	0	30	39	0					7.80	0	
Lim	1	1	0	2	2	2.00	0	0	30	39	0					7.80	0	
DRAVID, R.S.																		
Test	3	5	0	95	44	19.00	0	0									3	
FC	4	6	0	106	44	17.66	0	0									3	
GAMBHIR, G.																		
Test	1	2	0	2	2	1.00	0	0									0	
FC	2	3	0	91	89	30.33	0	1									2	
Int	4	4	0	203	83	50.75	0	2									0	
Lim	4	4	0	203	83	50.75	0	2									0	
HARBHAJAN SINGH																		
Test	2	3	0	10	8	3.33	0	0	527	304	2	152.00	1-35	0	0	3.46	1	
FC	2	3	0	10	8	3.33	0	0	527	304	2	152.00	1-35	0	0	3.46	1	
Int	3	2	2	22	15*		0	0	144	109	3	36.33	2-47	0	0	4.54	1	
Lim	3	2	2	22	15*		0	0	144	109	3	36.33	2-47	0	0	4.54	1	
JADEJA, R.A.																		
Int	8	6	1	68	25*	13.60	0	0	319	246	7	35.14	2-29	0	0	4.62	4	
Lim	8	6	1	68	25*	13.60	0	0	319	246	7	35.14	2-29	0	0	4.62	4	
KARTHIK, K.D.																		
Int	7	7	0	139	66	19.85	0	1									4	
Lim	7	7	0	139	66	19.85	0	1									4	
KHAN, Z.																		
Int	4	1	0	0	0	0.00	0	0	177	148	6	24.66	2-36	0	0	5.01	2	
Lim	4	1	0	0	0	0.00	0	0	177	148	6	24.66	2-36	0	0	5.01	2	
KOHLI, V.																		
Int	7	7	0	112	37	16.00	0	0	18	16	0					5.33	1	
Lim	7	7	0	112	37	16.00	0	0	18	16	0					5.33	1	
KUMAR, P.																		
Int	9	6	1	24	14	4.80	0	0	456	363	15	24.20	3-34	0	0	4.77	3	
Lim	9	6	1	24	14	4.80	0	0	456	363	15	24.20	3-34	0	0	4.77	3	
LAXMAN, V.V.S.																		
Test	3	5	1	279	103*	69.75	1	2									3	
FC	4	6	1	285	103*	57.00	1	2	6	0	0					0.00	6	

Cmp Debut	M	I	NO	Runs	HS	Avge	100	50	Balls	Runs	Wkts	Avge	BB	5i	10m	RpO	ct	st
MISHRA, A.																		
Test	1	1	0	40	40	40.00	0	0	356	187	4	46.75	3-47	0	0	3.15	1	
FC	2	2	0	41	40	20.50	0	0	579	367	7	52.42	3-47	0	0	3.80	1	
MITHUN, A.																		
Test	3	4	0	120	46	30.00	0	0	552	372	6	62.00	4-105	0	0	4.04	0	
FC	4	5	1	129	46	32.25	0	0	738	513	7	73.28	4-105	0	0	4.17	0	
Int	1	1	0	4	4	4.00	0	0	24	24	0					6.00	0	
Lim	1	1	0	4	4	4.00	0	0	24	24	0					6.00	0	
NEHRA, A.																		
Int	8	4	0	8	4	2.00	0	0	372	321	14	22.92	4-40	2	0	5.17	2	
Lim	8	4	0	8	4	2.00	0	0	372	321	14	22.92	4-40	2	0	5.17	2	
OJHA, P.P.																		
Test	3	4	2	35	18*	17.50	0	0	984	515	8	64.37	4-115	0	0	3.14	0	
FC	4	5	2	39	18*	13.00	0	0	1281	753	16	47.06	5-153	1	0	3.52	0	
Int	4	3	3	2	2*		0	0	175	143	4	35.75	3-36	0	0	4.90	2	
Lim	4	3	3	2	2*		0	0	175	143	4	35.75	3-36	0	0	4.90	2	
PATEL, M.M.																		
Int	2	2	1	7	7	7.00	0	0	96	64	5	12.80	3-21	0	0	4.00	0	
Lim	2	2	1	7	7	7.00	0	0	96	64	5	12.80	3-21	0	0	4.00	0	
RAINA, S.K.																		
Test	2	3	1	223	120	111.50	1	1	30	21	0					4.20	4	
FC	2	3	1	223	120	111.50	1	1	30	21	0					4.20	4	
Int	9	9	1	147	34	18.37	0	0									3	
Lim	9	9	1	147	34	18.37	0	0									3	
SEHWAG, V.																		
Test	3	5	0	348	109	69.60	2	1	354	193	7	27.57	3-51	0	0	3.27	1	
FC	4	6	0	366	109	61.00	2	1	462	260	8	32.50	3-51	0	0	3.37	1	
Int	7	7	1	289	110	48.16	1	1	89	68	4	17.00	4-6	1	0	4.58	2	
Lim	7	7	1	289	110	48.16	1	1	89	68	4	17.00	4-6	1	0	4.58	2	
SHARMA, I.																		
Test	3	5	2	75	31*	25.00	0	0	594	432	7	61.71	3-72	0	0	4.36	1	
FC	4	6	2	80	31*	20.00	0	0	762	562	9	62.44	3-72	0	0	4.42	2	
Int	4	3	1	11	8*	5.50	0	0	157	128	7	18.28	2-15	0	0	4.89	1	
Lim	4	3	1	11	8*	5.50	0	0	157	128	7	18.28	2-15	0	0	4.89	1	
SHARMA, R.G.																		
Int	8	8	0	152	69	19.00	0	1	12	14	1	14.00	1-5	0	0	7.00	3	
Lim	8	8	0	152	69	19.00	0	1	12	14	1	14.00	1-5	0	0	7.00	3	
TENDULKAR, S.R.																		
Test	3	5	0	390	203	78.00	1	2									2	
FC	4	6	0	394	203	65.66	1	2									2	
VIJAY, M.																		
Test	2	3	0	99	58	33.00	0	1									1	
FC	2	3	0	99	58	33.00	0	1									1	
YUVRAJ SINGH																		
Test	1	2	0	57	52	28.50	0	1									0	
FC	2	3	0	175	118	58.33	1	1	6	11	0					11.00	0	
Int	4	4	0	75	38	18.75	0	0	72	60	2	30.00	1-23	0	0	5.00	0	
Lim	4	4	0	75	38	18.75	0	0	72	60	2	30.00	1-23	0	0	5.00	0	

IRELAND TO SRI LANKA 2009/10

Cmp Debut	M	I	NO	Runs	HS	Avge	100	50	Balls	Runs	Wkts	Avge	BB	5i	10m	RpO	ct	st
BOTHA, A.C.																		
FC	1	2	0	27	27	13.50	0	0	174	64	3	21.33	3-44	0	0	2.20	0	
I20T	2	2	0	16	11	8.00	0	0	48	49	6	8.16	3-14	0	0	6.12	1	
20T	2	2	0	16	11	8.00	0	0	48	49	6	8.16	3-14	0	0	6.12	1	
CONNELL, P.																		
FC	1	2	0	28	18	14.00	0	0	138	64	1	64.00	1-52	0	0	2.78	0	
20T	1								18	31	0					10.33	0	
CUSACK, A.R.																		
FC	1	2	0	43	39	21.50	0	0	87	81	1	81.00	1-25	0	0	5.58	0	
I20T	1								24	38	0					9.50	1	
20T	2	1	0	11	11	11.00	0	0	44	81	2	40.50	2-43	0	0	11.04	1	
DOCKRELL, G.H.																		
I20T	1								24	11	2	5.50	2-11	0	0	2.75	0	
20T	2								36	33	3	11.00	2-11	0	0	5.50	0	
EAGLESTONE, P.S.																		
I20T	1								12	16	0					8.00	0	
20T	1								12	16	0					8.00	0	

Cmp	Debut	M	I	NO	Runs	HS	Avge	100	50	Balls	Runs	Wkts	Avge	BB	5i	10m	RpO	ct	st
JOHNSTON, D.T.																			
FC		1	2	1	65	63*	65.00	0	1	180	101	2	50.50	1-13	0	0	3.36	0	
I20T		2	1	0	2	2	2.00	0	0	48	48	4	12.00	4-22	1	0	6.00	0	
20T		2	1	0	2	2	2.00	0	0	48	48	4	12.00	4-22	1	0	6.00	0	
JONES, N.G.																			
20T		1	1	0	2	2	2.00	0	0	24	22	1	22.00	1-22	0	0	5.50	0	
KIDD, G.E.																			
FC		1	2	0	4	4	2.00	0	0	192	104	2	52.00	1-36	0	0	3.25	0	
I20T		1	1	1	1	1*		0	0	18	32	0					10.66	0	
20T		2	1	1	1	1*		0	0	30	56	0					11.20	1	
MOONEY, J.F.																			
FC		1	2	1	76	58*	76.00	0	1	24	22	0					5.50	1	
I20T		2	2	1	17	9	17.00	0	0	12	16	0					8.00	0	
20T		3	3	1	26	9	13.00	0	0	24	35	1	35.00	1-19	0	0	8.75	0	
O'BRIEN, K.J.																			
FC		1	2	0	19	16	9.50	0	0	114	57	0					3.00	1	
I20T		2	2	0	6	5	3.00	0	0	48	72	0					9.00	2	
20T		3	3	0	17	11	5.66	0	0	60	87	0					8.70	2	
O'BRIEN, N.J.																			
FC		1	2	0	75	66	37.50	0	1									6	
I20T		2	2	0	68	50	34.00	0	1									0	2
20T		3	3	0	127	59	42.33	0	2									1	2
PORTERFIELD, W.T.S.																			
FC		1	2	0	92	78	46.00	0	1									0	
I20T		2	2	0	65	46	32.50	0	0									0	
20T		2	2	0	65	46	32.50	0	0									0	
STIRLING, P.R.																			
I20T		2	2	0	39	22	19.50	0	0	6	10	0					10.00	0	
20T		3	3	0	82	43	27.33	0	0	6	10	0					10.00	1	
WHITE, A.R.																			
FC		1	2	0	47	43	23.50	0	0	200	114	4	28.50	4-99	0	0	3.42	0	
I20T		2	1	1	18	18*		0	0									1	
20T		3	2	2	19	18*		0	0									1	
WILSON, G.C.																			
FC		1	2	0	80	53	40.00	0	1									0	
I20T		2	2	1	42	26	42.00	0	0									2	
20T		3	3	2	67	26	67.00	0	0									2	

NEW ZEALAND TO SRI LANKA 2010

Cmp	Debut	M	I	NO	Runs	HS	Avge	100	50	Balls	Runs	Wkts	Avge	BB	5i	10m	RpO	ct	st
ELLIOTT, G.D.																			
Int		3	2	0	18	11	9.00	0	0									0	
Lim		3	2	0	18	11	9.00	0	0									0	
GUPTILL, M.J.																			
Int		3	3	0	11	11	3.66	0	0									1	
Lim		3	3	0	11	11	3.66	0	0									1	
HOPKINS, G.J.																			
Int		4	3	0	21	11	7.00	0	0									6	
Lim		4	3	0	21	11	7.00	0	0									6	
INGRAM, P.J.																			
Int		2	1	0	12	12	12.00	0	0									0	
Lim		2	1	0	12	12	12.00	0	0									0	
McCULLUM, N.L.																			
Int		3	2	0	41	36	20.50	0	0	136	98	4	24.50	3-35	0	0	4.32	2	
Lim		3	2	0	41	36	20.50	0	0	136	98	4	24.50	3-35	0	0	4.32	2	
McKAY, A.J.																			
Int		3	3	3	7	4*		0	0	108	68	2	34.00	1-11	0	0	3.77	1	
Lim		3	3	3	7	4*		0	0	108	68	2	34.00	1-11	0	0	3.77	1	
MILLS, K.D.																			
Int		4	3	0	72	52	24.00	0	1	179	139	8	17.37	4-41	1	0	4.65	3	
Lim		4	3	0	72	52	24.00	0	1	179	139	8	17.37	4-41	1	0	4.65	3	
ORAM, J.D.P.																			
Int		2	1	0	14	14	14.00	0	0	90	41	2	20.50	2-15	0	0	2.73	1	
Lim		2	1	0	14	14	14.00	0	0	90	41	2	20.50	2-15	0	0	2.73	1	
SOUTHEE, T.G.																			
Int		2	2	0	23	13	11.50	0	0	96	90	5	18.00	4-49	1	0	5.62	0	
Lim		2	2	0	23	13	11.50	0	0	96	90	5	18.00	4-49	1	0	5.62	0	
STYRIS, S.B.																			
Int		4	3	0	114	89	38.00	0	1	144	95	3	31.66	2-36	0	0	3.95	2	
Lim		4	3	0	114	89	38.00	0	1	144	95	3	31.66	2-36	0	0	3.95	2	

Cmp Debut	M	I	NO	Runs	HS	Avge	100	50	Balls	Runs	Wkts	Avge	BB	5i	10m	RpO	ct	st
TAYLOR, L.R.P.L.																		
Int	4	3	0	119	95	39.66	0	1									8	
Lim	4	3	0	119	95	39.66	0	1									8	
TUFFEY, D.R.																		
Int	3	2	0	19	19	9.50	0	0	126	116	4	29.00	3-34	0	0	5.52	0	
Lim	3	2	0	19	19	9.50	0	0	126	116	4	29.00	3-34	0	0	5.52	0	
WATLING, B.J.																		
Int	3	2	0	57	55	28.50	0	1									2	
Lim	3	2	0	57	55	28.50	0	1									2	
WILLIAMSON, K.S.																		
Int	4	3	0	13	13	4.33	0	0	84	48	1	48.00	1-2	0	0	3.42	1	
Lim	4	3	0	13	13	4.33	0	0	84	48	1	48.00	1-2	0	0	3.42	1	

PAKISTAN TO SRI LANKA 2010

Cmp Debut	M	I	NO	Runs	HS	Avge	100	50	Balls	Runs	Wkts	Avge	BB	5i	10m	RpO	ct	st
ABDUL RAZZAQ																		
Int	3	3	2	50	26*	50.00	0	0	120	92	2	46.00	1-18	0	0	4.60	0	
Lim	3	3	2	50	26*	50.00	0	0	120	92	2	46.00	1-18	0	0	4.60	0	
ABDUR REHMAN																		
Int	1	1	1	1	1*		0	0	60	37	0					3.70	0	
Lim	1	1	1	1	1*		0	0	60	37	0					3.70	0	
ASAD SHAFIQ																		
Int	1	1	0	17	17	17.00	0	0									0	
Lim	5	5	1	244	109*	61.00	1	1	60	57	0					5.70	4	
IMRAN FARHAT																		
Int	2	2	0	91	66	45.50	0	1	30	21	1	21.00	1-21	0	0	4.20	1	
Lim	2	2	0	91	66	45.50	0	1	30	21	1	21.00	1-21	0	0	4.20	1	
KAMRAN AKMAL																		
Int	3	3	0	88	51	29.33	0	1									3	
Lim	3	3	0	88	51	29.33	0	1									3	
MOHAMMAD AAMER																		
Int	2	2	0	8	5	4.00	0	0	119	113	2	56.50	2-57	0	0	5.69	0	
Lim	2	2	0	8	5	4.00	0	0	119	113	2	56.50	2-57	0	0	5.69	0	
MOHAMMAD ASIF																		
Int	2	1	0	0	0	0.00	0	0	114	115	2	57.50	1-55	0	0	6.05	0	
Lim	2	1	0	0	0	0.00	0	0	114	115	2	57.50	1-55	0	0	6.05	0	
SAEED AJMAL																		
Int	1	1	0	0	0	0.00	0	0	60	56	3	18.66	3-56	0	0	5.60	0	
Lim	1	1	0	0	0	0.00	0	0	60	56	3	18.66	3-56	0	0	5.60	0	
SALMAN BUTT																		
Int	2	2	0	74	74	37.00	0	1									1	
Lim	2	2	0	74	74	37.00	0	1									1	
SHAHID AFRIDI																		
Int	3	3	0	265	124	88.33	2	0	180	138	3	46.00	1-41	0	0	4.60	0	
Lim	3	3	0	265	124	88.33	2	0	180	138	3	46.00	1-41	0	0	4.60	0	
SHAHZAIB HASAN																		
Int	2	2	0	61	50	30.50	0	1									0	
Lim	2	2	0	61	50	30.50	0	1									0	
SHOAIB AKHTAR																		
Int	3	2	1	4	3*	4.00	0	0	168	120	4	30.00	3-41	0	0	4.28	1	
Lim	3	2	1	4	3*	4.00	0	0	168	120	4	30.00	3-41	0	0	4.28	1	
SHOAIB MALIK																		
Int	2	2	0	47	39	23.50	0	0	48	42	2	21.00	1-14	0	0	5.25	0	
Lim	2	2	0	47	39	23.50	0	0	48	42	2	21.00	1-14	0	0	5.25	0	
UMAR AKMAL																		
Int	3	3	0	101	50	33.66	0	1									3	
Lim	3	3	0	101	50	33.66	0	1									3	
UMAR AMIN																		
Int	3	3	0	34	22	11.33	0	0									1	
Lim	3	3	0	34	22	11.33	0	0									1	

PAKISTAN A TO SRI LANKA 2010

Cmp Debut	M	I	NO	Runs	HS	Avge	100	50	Balls	Runs	Wkts	Avge	BB	5i	10m	RpO	ct	st
AAMER SAJJAD																		
FC	2	3	1	71	51*	35.50	0	1	30	20	0					4.00	2	
Lim	4	4	0	146	77	36.50	0	1	6	2	0					2.00	0	
ABID ALI																		
FC	2	3	0	39	20	13.00	0	0									3	

Cmp	Debut	M	I	NO	Runs	HS	Avge	100	50	Balls	Runs	Wkts	Avge	BB	5i	10m	RpO	ct	st
ASAD SHAFIQ																			
Int		1	1	0	17	17	17.00	0	0									0	
Lim		5	5	1	244	109*	61.00	1	1	60	57	0					5.70	4	
AZEEM GHUMMAN																			
FC		2	3	0	54	42	18.00	0	0	6	5	0					5.00	0	
Lim		4	4	0	51	28	12.75	0	0	12	18	0					9.00	1	
HAMMAD AZAM																			
FC		1	2	0	53	40	26.50	0	0	85	34	4	8.50	4-19	0	0	2.40	2	
Lim		4	4	1	106	63*	35.33	0	1	138	110	2	55.00	1-26	0	0	4.78	0	
JUNAID KHAN																			
FC		2	2	1	8	4*	8.00	0	0	280	150	10	15.00	5-50	1	0	3.21	0	
Lim		3	1	0	32	32	32.00	0	0	174	117	4	29.25	3-41	0	0	4.03	0	
KHURRAM MANZOOR																			
FC		2	3	0	56	45	18.66	0	0									0	
Lim		4	4	0	47	19	11.75	0	0									2	
MOHAMMAD IRFAN																			
Lim		4	2	1	2	1*	2.00	0	0	226	144	7	20.57	3-30	0	0	3.82	0	
MOHAMMAD RAMEEZ																			
FC		1	2	1	29	16	29.00	0	0	96	42	1	42.00	1-16	0	0	2.62	0	
MOHAMMAD TALHA																			
FC		2	2	0	2	2	1.00	0	0	270	146	2	73.00	1-41	0	0	3.24	0	
Lim		4	3	1	26	17*	13.00	0	0	208	198	5	39.60	2-32	0	0	5.71	1	
NAEEM ANJUM																			
FC		2	3	1	80	53*	40.00	0	1									6	1
Lim		4	4	0	39	17	9.75	0	0									3	
NAVED YASIN																			
FC		2	3	0	28	16	9.33	0	0									0	
Lim		1	1	0	11	11	11.00	0	0									0	
SHEHARYAR GHANI																			
FC		1	1	0	6	6	6.00	0	0									0	
Lim		3	3	0	71	36	23.66	0	0									0	
TABISH KHAN																			
FC		1								120	68	1	68.00	1-68	0	0	3.40	0	
YASIR SHAH																			
FC		1								120	62	0					3.10	0	
Lim		4	4	2	56	39*	28.00	0	0	222	164	6	27.33	3-29	0	0	4.43	2	
ZULFIQAR BABAR																			
FC		1	2	0	0	0	0.00	0	0	114	43	4	10.75	4-38	0	0	2.26	0	
Lim		1	1	1	1	1*		0	0	42	34	0					4.85	0	

SOUTH AFRICA A TO SRI LANKA 2010

Cmp	Debut	M	I	NO	Runs	HS	Avge	100	50	Balls	Runs	Wkts	Avge	BB	5i	10m	RpO	ct	st
BAILEY, R.T.																			
Lim		3	1	1	9	9*		0	0	18	33	0					11.00	0	
COOK, S.C.																			
FC		2	4	0	116	52	29.00	0	1									0	
DE VILLIERS, C.J.D.																			
Lim		2								90	79	2	39.50	1-28	0	0	5.26	1	
ELGAR, D.																			
FC		2	4	0	431	174	107.75	2	2	264	158	0					3.59	3	
Lim		5	5	3	245	79*	122.50	0	2	150	122	2	61.00	2-50	0	0	4.88	1	
FRIEND, Q.																			
FC		2	2	2	0	0*		0	0	258	197	5	39.40	4-68	0	0	4.58	0	
INGRAM, C.A.																			
Lim		5	5	1	170	85	42.50	0	1									0	
KLEINVELDT, R.K.																			
FC		1	2	0	1	1	0.50	0	0	138	78	2	39.00	2-63	0	0	3.39	1	
Lim		4								144	78	2	39.00	1-30	0	0	3.25	0	
KUHN, H.G.																			
FC		2	4	2	182	87	91.00	0	2									0	
Lim		3	1	0	101	101	101.00	1	0									3	
MILLER, D.A.																			
Lim		5	3	3	112	82*		0	1									4	
PHILANDER, V.D.																			
FC		2	3	1	68	34	34.00	0	0	257	118	2	59.00	2-31	0	0	2.75	0	
Lim		5								228	163	7	23.28	3-39	0	0	4.28	0	
ROSSOUW, R.R.																			
FC		2	4	0	172	131	43.00	1	0									0	
Lim		4	3	0	43	22	14.33	0	0									1	

Cmp Debut	M	I	NO	Runs	HS	Avge	100	50	Balls	Runs	Wkts	Avge	BB	5i	10m	RpO	ct	st
THERON, J.																		
FC	1	1	0	23	23	23.00	0	0	120	49	1	49.00	1-49	0	0	2.45	0	
Lim	4								174	130	8	16.25	4-47	1	0	4.48	0	
TSHABALALA, M.S.																		
FC	2	2	0	4	4	2.00	0	0	462	351	2	175.50	1-89	0	0	4.55	0	
Lim	5								240	169	4	42.25	3-38	0	0	4.22	0	
TSOLEKILE, T.L.																		
FC	2	3	0	20	13	6.66	0	0									3	
Lim	2																0	
VANDIAR, J.D.																		
FC	2	3	0	90	68	30.00	0	1	6	5	1	5.00	1-5	0	0	5.00	1	
VAN WYK, M.N.																		
Lim	4	4	2	269	136*	134.50	2	0									2	
VAN ZYL, S.																		
FC	2	4	0	98	81	24.50	0	1	210	81	1	81.00	1-28	0	0	2.31	0	
Lim	4	4	0	67	39	16.75	0	0	138	125	1	125.00	1-48	0	0	5.43	2	

UGANDA

CAREER RECORDS FOR UGANDA PLAYERS

Cmp	Debut	M	I	NO	Runs	HS	Avge	100	50	Balls	Runs	Wkts	Avge	BB	5i	10m	RpO	ct	st
ARINAITWE, Davis Karashani (Uganda to Kenya, Uganda to United Arab Emirates) b Mbarara 20.4.1987 RHB RM																			
FC	2009	2	3	1	54	30*	27.00	0	0	374	121	9	13.44	4-34	0	0	1.94	4	
Lim	2007/08	13	8	4	21	7	5.25	0	0	515	444	13	34.15	4-53	1	0	5.17	3	
20T	2009/10	5	5	3	28	16*	14.00	0	0	90	84	4	21.00	2-18	0	0	5.60	1	
BAIG, Akbar Mirza (Uganda to Kenya, Uganda to United Arab Emirates) b India 5.5.1974 RHB RM																			
FC	2003/04	6	12	0	171	51	14.25	0	1	325	190	8	23.75	3-23	0	0	3.50	5	
Lim	2008/09	9	7	1	68	28*	11.33	0	0	294	245	8	30.62	2-33	0	0	5.00	3	
20T	2009/10	5	5	0	90	38	18.00	0	0	60	80	0					8.00	1	
ISABIRYE, Fred (Uganda to Kenya) b Jinja 22.9.1984 RHB WK																			
FC	2009	1	1	0	0	0	0.00	0	0									5	
20T	2009/10	1	1	0	2	2	2.00	0	0									0	
KYOBE, Arthur Solomon (Uganda to Kenya, Uganda to United Arab Emirates) b Jinja 29.11.1988 LHB																			
FC	2009/10	1	2	0	57	49	28.50	0	0									0	
Lim	2007/08	13	13	0	239	50	18.38	0	1									1	
20T	2009/10	6	6	1	113	51*	22.60	0	1									1	
MUHUMZA, Deusdedit (Uganda to Kenya, Uganda to United Arab Emirates) b Kakira 30.9.1989 RHB RM																			
Lim	2009/10	1	1	0	3	3	3.00	0	0	12	23	1	23.00	1-23	0	0	11.50	0	
20T	2009/10	3	3	1	39	17	19.50	0	0	68	71	2	35.50	1-14	0	0	6.26	1	
MUKASA, Roger Galwanao (Uganda to Kenya, Uganda to United Arab Emirates) b 22.8.1989 RHB RM																			
FC	2009	2	4	0	66	46	16.50	0	0	6	0	0					0.00	0	
Lim	2008/09	9	9	0	329	117	36.55	1	1	12	23	1	23.00	1-23	0	0	11.50	1	2
20T	2009/10	6	6	0	130	66	21.66	0	1	12	24	0					12.00	4	2
MUSOKE, Benjamin (Uganda to Kenya, Uganda to United Arab Emirates) b Rubaga, Kampala 23.10.1976 RHB RM																			
FC	2003/04	6	12	1	226	72	20.54	0	1	18	7	0					2.33	8	
Lim	2005	18	16	2	211	44*	15.07	0	0									8	
20T	2009/10	4	4	0	54	31	13.50	0	0									0	
NSUBUGA, Franco (Uganda to Kenya, Uganda to United Arab Emirates) b Nsambia 28.8.1980 RHB OB																			
FC	2003/04	6	11	1	334	64	33.40	0	2	977	467	19	24.57	4-20	0	0	2.86	10	
Lim	2005	22	20	2	477	98	26.50	0	2	1110	708	26	27.23	4-39	1	0	3.82	10	
20T	2009/10	6	6	0	74	22	12.33	0	0	113	128	6	21.33	3-9	0	0	6.79	0	
OTIM, Raymond (Uganda to Kenya) b Kampala 21.10.1986 RHB LB																			
Lim	2005	3	3	0	11	8	3.66	0	0									1	
20T	2009/10	2	2	0	34	25	17.00	0	0									1	
SEBANJA, Jonathan (Uganda to Kenya, Uganda to United Arab Emirates) b Nasguru 10.9.1988 RHB RMF																			
FC	2009	1	1	0	3	3	3.00	0	0	48	17	0					2.12	0	
Lim	2009	2	2	0	1	1	0.50	0	0	12	21	0					10.50	2	
20T	2009/10	3	3	1	3	2*	1.50	0	0	42	67	0					9.57	0	
SEIGA, Asadu (Uganda to Kenya) b Kampala 28.9.1986 RHB RM																			
Lim	2008/09	5	2	1	12	8*	12.00	0	0	192	208	6	34.66	3-79	0	0	6.50	2	
20T	2009/10	2	2	1	1	1*	1.00	0	0	36	50	1	50.00	1-34	0	0	8.33	1	
SEMATIMBA, Laurence (Uganda to Kenya, Uganda to United Arab Emirates) b Kampala 28.6.1982 RHB OB WK																			
FC	2003/04	5	9	0	214	89	23.77	0	2									14	1
Lim	2005	13	10	0	156	48	15.60	0	0									10	
20T	2009/10	4	4	0	32	12	8.00	0	0									1	1
SENYONDO, Henry (Uganda to Kenya, Uganda to United Arab Emirates) b Nsambya 12.8.1993 RHB SLA																			
Lim	2009/10	1	1	1	5	5*		0	0									0	
20T	2009/10	4	3	1	6	2*	3.00	0	0	72	81	3	27.00	3-20	0	0	6.75	0	
SSEMANDA, Ronald (Uganda to Kenya, Uganda to United Arab Emirates) b 15.12.1988 RHB RM																			
FC	2009	2	3	1	69	41	34.50	0	0	198	99	2	49.50	2-66	0	0	3.00	2	
Lim	2007/08	12	10	2	134	72	16.75	0	1	516	316	7	45.14	3-29	0	0	3.67	5	
20T	2009/10	3	3	0	23	14	7.66	0	0	66	80	3	26.66	2-18	0	0	7.27	1	
TABBY, Dennis (Uganda to Kenya, Uganda to United Arab Emirates) b Jinja 24.9.1989 RHB RFM																			
FC	2009	2	2	2	7	4*		0	0	378	164	6	27.33	2-23	0	0	2.60	4	
Lim	2009	2	2	0	1	1	0.50	0	0	48	30	1	30.00	1-14	0	0	3.75	0	
20T	2009/10	4	2	1	0	0*	0.00	0	0	66	72	5	14.40	2-10	0	0	6.54	1	
THAWITHEMWIRA, Ivan (Uganda to Kenya) b Kampala 10.5.1982 RHB RM																			
20T	2009/10	3	3	0	18	17	6.00	0	0									2	
WAISWA, Charles (Uganda to Kenya, Uganda to United Arab Emirates) b Jinja 29.12.1987 LHB LMF																			
FC	2005	4	6	3	28	11	9.33	0	0	522	277	12	23.08	4-58	0	0	3.18	3	
Lim	2005	11	7	7	14	5*		0	0	459	348	7	49.71	2-32	0	0	4.54	0	
20T	2009/10	3	3	0	21	12	7.00	0	0	54	61	2	30.50	1-24	0	0	6.77	3	
ZIRABA, Arthur (Uganda to Kenya, Uganda to United Arab Emirates) b Mengo, Kampala 8.8.1989 RHB WK																			
FC	2009/10	1	2	0	11	10	5.50	0	0									1	
20T	2009/10	2	2	0	15	8	7.50	0	0									1	

UNITED ARAB EMIRATES

2009/10 and 2010 AND CAREER RECORDS FOR UNITED ARAB EMIRATES PLAYERS

Cmp	*Debut*	*M*	*I*	*NO*	*Runs*	*HS*	*Avge*	*100*	*50*	*Balls*	*Runs*	*Wkts*	*Avge*	*BB*	*5i*	*10m*	*RpO*	*ct*	*st*
ABDUL REHMAN (United Arab Emirates, United Arab Emirates to Bermuda, United Arab Emirates to Namibia) b Ajman 2.1.1987 RHB WK																			
FC		1	2	0	7	6	3.50	0	0									2	
Lim		1																3	
20T		7	6	0	76	20	12.66	0	0									3	3
FC	2006/07	5	10	1	181	65	20.11	0	1									11	
Int	2004	1	1	0	1	1	1.00	0	0									0	
Lim	2004	16	12	4	255	71	31.87	0	2									17	10
20T	2009/10	9	8	0	85	20	10.62	0	0									3	4
AHMED RAZA (United Arab Emirates, United Arab Emirates to Bermuda, United Arab Emirates to Namibia) b Pakistan 10.10.1988 LHB SLA																			
Lim		1								28	2	2	1.00	2-2	0	0	0.42	0	
20T		7	3	2	14	10*	14.00	0	0	137	118	7	16.85	2-17	0	0	5.16	1	
FC	2006/07	7	11	1	180	46	18.00	0	0	1171	480	19	25.26	4-55	0	0	2.45	6	
Lim	2006	6	4	1	46	21*	15.33	0	0	247	169	13	13.00	5-29	0	1	4.10	0	
20T	2009/10	9	3	2	14	10*	14.00	0	0	179	147	9	16.33	2-10	0	0	4.92	2	
AMJAD ALI Chaudhry (United Arab Emirates to Bermuda, United Arab Emirates to Namibia) b Lahore, Punjab, Pakistan 25.9.1979 LHB RM																			
FC	2001/02	8	15	3	312	55	26.00	0	3									19	2
Int	2008	2	2	0	96	77	48.00	0	1									4	1
Lim	2008	8	8	0	203	77	25.37	0	1									9	2
20T	2010	2	2	0	158	105	79.00	1	1									2	
AMJAD JAVED (United Arab Emirates, United Arab Emirates to Bermuda, United Arab Emirates to Namibia) b Dubai 5.7.1980 RHB RM																			
FC		1	2	0	15	13	7.50	0	0	196	71	5	14.20	4-48	0	0	2.17	1	
Lim		1								42	23	2	11.50	2-23	0	0	3.28	0	
FC	2006/07	6	10	0	93	35	9.30	0	0	574	251	9	27.88	4-48	0	0	2.62	1	
Int	2008	1	1	0	10	10	10.00	0	0	12	24	0					12.00	0	
Lim	2006	26	24	2	698	164	31.72	2	2	797	645	22	29.31	3-60	0	0	4.85	4	
20T	2010	2	2	0	16	9	8.00	0	0	12	16	0					8.00	0	
ARFAN HAIDER (United Arab Emirates, United Arab Emirates to Namibia) b Pakistan 28.10.1980 LHB SLA																			
FC		1	2	0	10	9	5.00	0	0	24	8	0					2.00	2	
Lim		1	1	1	29	29*		0	0									0	
20T		7	7	0	161	59	23.00	0	1									2	
FC	2009/10	2	4	0	101	84	25.25	0	1	42	13	1	13.00	1-5	0	0	1.85	2	
ARSHAD ALI (United Arab Emirates, United Arab Emirates to Bermuda, United Arab Emirates to Namibia) b Sialkot, Punjab, Pakistan 6.4.1976 RHB RM																			
FC		1	2	0	163	130	81.50	1	0	114	43	2	21.50	2-43	0	0	2.26	0	
Lim		1	1	1	7	7*		0	0									0	
FC	2003/04	18	35	2	1490	185	45.15	4	6	1406	693	26	26.65	5-43	1	0	2.95	9	
Int	2004	4	4	0	54	41	13.50	0	0	102	105	1	105.00	1-5	0	0	6.17	1	
Lim	2003/04	40	40	2	1137	139	29.92	2	5	1192	914	44	20.77	7-41	1	1	4.60	13	
20T	2010	2	2	0	31	16	15.50	0	0	42	34	3	11.33	2-22	0	0	4.85	0	
AWAIS ALAM (United Arab Emirates) b Faisalabad, Punjab, Pakistan 3.7.1977 RHB RFM																			
20T		1	1	1	3	3*		0	0	12	30	1	30.00	1-30	0	0	15.00	0	
FAHAD Afdhal ALHASHMI (United Arab Emirates to Namibia) b Dubai 31.7.1982 RHB RFM																			
FC	2005/06	7	13	4	65	21	7.22	0	0	636	411	11	37.36	3-40	0	0	3.87	4	
Int	2008	2	2	0	0	0	0.00	0	0	60	60	2	30.00	2-39	0	0	6.00	0	
Lim	2008	6	3	0	4	4	1.33	0	0	150	158	2	79.00	2-39	0	0	6.32	2	
FAYYAZ AHMED (United Arab Emirates, United Arab Emirates to Namibia) b Gujrat, Punjab, Pakistan 12.5.1983 LHB SLA																			
FC		1	2	0	29	18	14.50	0	0	228	83	3	27.66	3-74	0	0	2.18	1	
Lim		1								30	5	1	5.00	1-5	0	0	1.00	0	
20T		7	4	0	25	9	6.25	0	0	90	92	6	15.33	3-18	0	0	6.13	1	
FC	2009/10	2	4	0	87	52	21.75	0	1	595	235	10	23.50	4-75	0	0	2.37	2	
Lim	2000/01	16	13	6	277	63	39.57	0	3	828	528	26	20.30	6-24	1	1	3.82	9	
KHURRAM KHAN (United Arab Emirates, United Arab Emirates to Bermuda, United Arab Emirates to Namibia) b Multan, Punjab, Pakistan 21.6.1971 LHB SLA																			
FC		1	2	0	88	87	44.00	0	1	42	17	0					2.42	1	
Lim		1																0	
20T		7	7	2	154	52*	30.80	0	1	108	119	1	119.00	1-15	0	0	6.61	2	
FC	2003/04	15	28	1	1017	109	37.66	1	8	2428	956	31	30.83	6-98	1	0	2.36	15	
Int	2004	4	4	0	93	78	23.25	0	1	240	213	7	30.42	4-32	1	0	5.32	3	
Lim	2003/04	40	38	9	1262	124	43.51	3	10	1566	1225	46	26.63	4-32	2	0	4.69	13	
20T	2009/10	8	8	3	160	52*	32.00	0	1	108	119	1	119.00	1-15	0	0	6.61	2	

Cmp	Debut	M	I	NO	Runs	HS	Avge	100	50	Balls	Runs	Wkts	Avge	BB	5i	10m	RpO	ct	st
MOHAMMAD IQBAL (United Arab Emirates, United Arab Emirates to Namibia) b Dubai 29.3.1977 RHB RMF																			
Lim		1	1	0	12	12	12.00	0	0									1	
20T		7	7	0	68	20	9.71	0	0									3	
FC	2006/07	2	4	0	58	43	14.50	0	0									0	
Lim	2007/08	9	9	0	365	111	40.55	1	1									2	
MOHAMMAD TAUQIR Khan (United Arab Emirates to Namibia) b Dubai 14.1.1972 RHB OB																			
FC	2003/04	9	15	3	209	64	17.41	0	1	1381	652	25	26.08	6-17	2	1	2.83	5	
Int	2004	4	4	0	87	55	21.75	0	1	198	133	3	44.33	2-47	0	0	4.03	2	
Lim	2003/04	22	17	4	163	55	12.53	0	1	1008	651	20	32.55	3-19	0	0	3.87	7	
MOIZ SHAHID (United Arab Emirates, United Arab Emirates to Bermuda, United Arab Emirates to Namibia) b 27.4.1988 RHB LMF																			
FC		1	2	1	15	13*	15.00	0	0	96	54	0					3.37	0	
20T		1	1	1	2	2*		0	0	12	21	2	10.50	2-21	0	0	10.50	0	
FC	2009/10	2	3	2	23	13*	23.00	0	0	132	79	0					3.59	1	
Lim	2009/10	2	2	2	17	17*		0	0	78	46	2	23.00	2-25	0	0	3.53	0	
20T	2009/10	3	1	1	2	2*		0	0	24	52	3	17.33	2-21	0	0	13.00	1	
NAEEMUDDIN ASLAM (United Arab Emirates) b Dubai 31.5.1982 RHB																			
FC		1	2	0	161	152	80.50	1	0									0	
Lim		1																0	
20T		6	5	2	111	60*	37.00	0	1									0	
FC	2003/04	8	14	1	380	152	29.23	1	0									2	
Int	2004	2	2	0	12	12	6.00	0	0									1	
Lim	2003/04	26	22	3	399	76	21.00	0	2									14	1
PATIL, Swapnil Prakash (United Arab Emirates to Bermuda) b Darpale, Maharashtra, India 15.4.1985 RHB WK																			
FC	2010	1	1	0	37	37	37.00	0	0									1	1
Lim	2010	1	1	0	26	26	26.00	0	0									3	
20T	2010	2	2	0	43	37	21.50	0	0									1	
QADAR NAWAZ (United Arab Emirates) b Pakistan 13.10.1974 RHB																			
Lim		1								60	16	4	4.00	4-16	1	0	1.60	0	
20T		7	4	1	11	5*	3.66	0	0	132	150	9	16.66	3-23	0	0	6.81	2	
QASIM ZUBAIR (United Arab Emirates, United Arab Emirates to Bermuda, United Arab Emirates to Namibia) b Dubai 31.8.1987 RHB RMF																			
FC		1	2	2	35	18*		0	0	144	69	3	23.00	3-16	0	0	2.87	0	
20T		7	3	2	11	6*	11.00	0	0	129	161	8	20.12	5-24	0	1	7.48	1	
FC	2006/07	6	8	3	96	28*	19.20	0	0	728	405	11	36.81	3-16	0	0	3.33	3	
Lim	2008/09	7	4	2	35	25*	17.50	0	0	194	173	5	34.60	3-62	0	0	5.35	1	
SAQIB ALI (United Arab Emirates, United Arab Emirates to Bermuda, United Arab Emirates to Namibia) b Multan, Punjab, Pakistan 14.4.1978 RHB OB																			
FC		1	2	0	82	77	41.00	0	1	42	20	0					2.85	0	
Lim		1								18	2	0					0.66	0	
20T		7	7	1	211	63	35.16	0	1	78	73	4	18.25	2-9	0	0	5.61	2	
FC	2006/07	13	24	2	1078	195	49.00	4	4	657	315	9	35.00	3-84	0	0	2.87	6	
Int	2008	2	2	0	29	19	14.50	0	0	60	57	1	57.00	1-44	0	0	5.70	0	
Lim	1994/95	28	27	3	775	91	32.29	0	4	444	365	12	30.41	3-20	0	0	4.93	9	
20T	2009/10	9	9	1	237	63	29.62	0	1	114	109	6	18.16	2-9	0	0	5.73	2	
SAQIB Hussain SHAH (United Arab Emirates to Bermuda) b Attock, Punjab, Pakistan 1.9.1979 RHB																			
Lim	2010	2	2	0	43	35	21.50	0	0									1	
20T	2010	1	1	0	37	37	37.00	0	0									0	
SHOAIB SARWAR (United Arab Emirates, United Arab Emirates to Bermuda, United Arab Emirates to Namibia) b Sharjah 15.10.1986 RHB RMF																			
FC		1	2	0	25	20	12.50	0	0	138	76	3	25.33	2-20	0	0	3.30	0	
20T		1								12	18	0					9.00	1	
FC	2008	5	9	1	159	61	19.87	0	2	618	385	7	55.00	2-20	0	0	3.73	1	
Lim	2006	4	2	1	21	13*	21.00	0	0	102	96	3	32.00	2-16	0	0	5.64	0	
20T	2009/10	2	1	0	5	5	5.00	0	0	24	34	1	34.00	1-16	0	0	8.50	1	
SILVA, Elle Hennadige Shadeep Nadeeja (United Arab Emirates to Bermuda, United Arab Emirates) b Galle, Sri Lanka 18.8.1978 LHB SLA																			
20T		5	4	1	28	12	9.33	0	0	102	91	8	11.37	2-7	0	0	5.35	1	
FC	2000/01	12	18	3	162	43	10.80	0	0	1187	553	20	27.65	3-4	0	0	2.79	1	
Int	2008	1	1	0	7	7	7.00	0	0	42	33	0					4.71	0	
Lim	2000/01	13	4	1	26	9	8.66	0	0	487	390	14	27.85	2-13	0	0	4.80	1	
20T	2009/10	7	6	3	30	12	10.00	0	0	150	140	12	11.66	3-19	0	0	5.60	3	
TAHIR BUTT (United Arab Emirates to Bermuda) b Lahore, Punjab, Pakistan 24.4.1982 RHB RFM																			
FC	2010	1								135	88	1	88.00	1-25	0	0	3.91	1	
Lim	2010	1								24	25	0					6.25	0	
20T	2010	1								18	15	0					5.00	0	

AFGHANISTAN TO UNITED ARAB EMIRATES 2009/10

Cmp	Debut	M	I	NO	Runs	HS	Avge	100	50	Balls	Runs	Wkts	Avge	BB	5i	10m	RpO	ct	st
AFTAB ALAM																			
Int		2	1	1	6	6*		0	0	72	84	1	84.00	1-49	0	0	7.00	0	
Lim		2	1	1	6	6*		0	0	72	84	1	84.00	1-49	0	0	7.00	0	
ASGHAR STANIKZAI																			
FC		1	2	1	47	24	47.00	0	0	42	15	0					2.14	0	
Int		2	2	0	39	33	19.50	0	0	2	0	0					0.00	0	
Lim		2	2	0	39	33	19.50	0	0	2	0	0					0.00	0	
I20T		1																0	
20T		2	1	0	26	26	26.00	0	0									0	
DAWLAT AHMADZAI																			
Int		1								16	28	0					10.50	0	
Lim		1								16	28	0					10.50	0	
HAMID HASSAN																			
I20T		4	2	2	3	2*		0	0	91	100	7	14.28	3-32	0	0	6.59	1	
20T		6	2	2	3	2*		0	0	139	137	12	11.41	3-14	0	0	5.91	2	
KARIM SADIQ																			
FC		1	2	0	74	42	37.00	0	0	78	46	0					3.53	0	
Int		2	2	0	4	4	2.00	0	0	92	63	2	31.50	2-28	0	0	4.10	0	
Lim		2	2	0	4	4	2.00	0	0	92	63	2	31.50	2-28	0	0	4.10	0	
I20T		4	4	0	59	34	14.75	0	0	72	69	4	17.25	3-17	0	0	5.75	0	
20T		6	6	0	86	34	14.33	0	0	102	103	4	25.75	3-17	0	0	6.05	0	
MIRWAIS ASHRAF																			
FC		1	1	0	8	8	8.00	0	0	233	129	4	32.25	3-103	0	0	3.32	1	
I20T		4	3	1	28	19	14.00	0	0	72	60	1	60.00	1-13	0	0	5.00	2	
20T		6	3	1	28	19	14.00	0	0	120	89	4	22.25	2-15	0	0	4.45	2	
MOHAMMAD NABI																			
FC		1	2	1	128	80	128.00	0	1	258	179	2	89.50	2-144	0	0	4.16	0	
Int		2	2	0	70	62	35.00	0	1	108	68	4	17.00	2-23	0	0	3.77	2	
Lim		2	2	0	70	62	35.00	0	1	108	68	4	17.00	2-23	0	0	3.77	2	
I20T		4	3	1	44	43*	22.00	0	0	84	98	8	12.25	3-23	0	0	7.00	1	
20T		6	5	2	70	43*	23.33	0	0	126	137	13	10.53	3-17	0	0	6.52	2	
MOHAMMAD SHAHZAD																			
FC		1	2	1	237	214*	237.00	1	0									4	
Int		2	2	0	118	118	59.00	1	0									1	
Lim		2	2	0	118	118	59.00	1	0									1	
I20T		4	4	1	118	65*	39.33	0	1									1	2
20T		6	6	1	127	65*	25.40	0	1									2	3
NAWROZ MANGAL																			
FC		1	2	0	87	70	43.50	0	1	48	41	1	41.00	1-34	0	0	5.12	0	
Int		2	2	0	47	32	23.50	0	0	18	26	0					8.66	0	
Lim		2	2	0	47	32	23.50	0	0	18	26	0					8.66	0	
I20T		4	4	1	62	21*	20.66	0	0	24	23	3	7.66	3-23	0	0	5.75	3	
20T		6	6	1	106	30	21.20	0	0	24	23	3	7.66	3-23	0	0	5.75	5	
NOOR ALI ZADRAN																			
FC		1	2	0	68	52	34.00	0	1									1	
Int		1	1	0	114	114	114.00	1	0									0	
Lim		1	1	0	114	114	114.00	1	0									0	
I20T		4	4	0	118	42	29.50	0	0									1	
20T		6	6	1	182	42	36.40	0	0									2	
RAEES AHMADZAI																			
FC		1	1	0	24	24	24.00	0	0	24	22	0					5.50	0	
Int		2	2	1	43	37	43.00	0	0	24	16	0					4.00	0	
Lim		2	2	1	43	37	43.00	0	0	24	16	0					4.00	0	
I20T		4	3	1	49	23	24.50	0	0									2	
20T		6	5	3	75	26*	37.50	0	0									2	
SAMIULLAH SHENWARI																			
FC		1	1	0	8	8	8.00	0	0	222	128	4	32.00	4-118	0	0	3.45	3	
Int		2	1	0	4	4	4.00	0	0	114	67	4	16.75	4-31	1	0	3.52	0	
Lim		2	1	0	4	4	4.00	0	0	114	67	4	16.75	4-31	1	0	3.52	0	
I20T		4	3	0	22	19	7.33	0	0	54	56	2	28.00	1-9	0	0	6.22	1	
20T		6	4	0	26	19	6.50	0	0	78	84	3	28.00	1-9	0	0	6.46	1	
SHABIR NOORI																			
FC		1	1	0	60	60	60.00	0	1									0	
Int		1	1	0	9	9	9.00	0	0									0	
Lim		1	1	0	9	9	9.00	0	0									0	
SHAFIQULLAH																			
Int		1	1	0	0	0	0.00	0	0									0	
Lim		1	1	0	0	0	0.00	0	0									0	

Cmp Debut	M	I	NO	Runs	HS	Avge	100	50	Balls	Runs	Wkts	Avge	BB	5i	10m	RpO	ct	st
I20T	3	3	0	5	3	1.66	0	0									1	
20T	4	3	0	5	3	1.66	0	0									1	
SHAPOOR ZADRAN																		
FC	1	1	0	0	0	0.00	0	0	246	175	3	58.33	2-85	0	0	4.26	0	
Int	2	1	0	0	0	0.00	0	0	90	98	1	98.00	1-39	0	0	6.53	0	
Lim	2	1	0	0	0	0.00	0	0	90	98	1	98.00	1-39	0	0	6.53	0	
I20T	4								72	84	3	28.00	1-8	0	0	7.00	1	
20T	6								120	115	4	28.75	1-8	0	0	5.75	1	

CANADA TO UNITED ARAB EMIRATES 2009/10

Cmp Debut	M	I	NO	Runs	HS	Avge	100	50	Balls	Runs	Wkts	Avge	BB	5i	10m	RpO	ct	st
ARSALAN QADIR																		
I20T	1								6	12	0					12.00	0	
20T	1								6	12	0					12.00	0	
BAGAI, A.																		
FC	1	2	1	95	93	95.00	0	1									3	
Int	2	2	1	143	91*	143.00	0	2									2	
Lim	2	2	1	143	91*	143.00	0	2									2	
I20T	2	2	0	50	36	25.00	0	0									1	1
20T	3	3	0	71	36	23.66	0	0									1	1
BAIDWAN, H.S.																		
Int	2								114	109	3	36.33	2-55	0	0	5.73	0	
Lim	2								114	109	3	36.33	2-55	0	0	5.73	0	
I20T	2	2	2	4	4*		0	0	30	40	1	40.00	1-27	0	0	8.00	0	
20T	3	3	2	6	4*	6.00	0	0	54	67	2	33.50	1-27	0	0	7.44	0	
BARNETT, G.E.F.																		
I20T	2	2	0	66	36	33.00	0	0	6	11	0					11.00	0	
20T	3	3	0	85	36	28.33	0	0	6	11	0					11.00	1	
BASTIAMPILLAI, T.C.																		
FC	1	2	0	128	73	64.00	0	2									1	
Int	2	2	0	51	33	25.50	0	0									0	
Lim	2	2	0	51	33	25.50	0	0									0	
BILLCLIFF, I.S.																		
I20T	2	2	0	51	37	25.50	0	0									0	
20T	3	3	0	51	37	17.00	0	0									0	
DAVID, R.R.																		
FC	1	2	1	55	28*	55.00	0	0	114	78	2	39.00	1-8	0	0	4.10	1	
Int	1								12	15	0					7.50	0	
Lim	1								12	15	0					7.50	0	
DAVISON, J.M.																		
I20T	2	2	0	0	0	0.00	0	0	36	43	1	43.00	1-24	0	0	7.16	0	
20T	3	3	0	8	8	2.66	0	0	60	72	2	36.00	1-24	0	0	7.20	0	
DAWOOD, J.J.																		
Int	1	1	1	25	25*		0	0									0	
Lim	1	1	1	25	25*		0	0									0	
DHANIRAM, S.																		
FC	1	2	0	134	130	67.00	1	0	84	38	1	38.00	1-30	0	0	2.71	1	
Int	2	2	0	64	56	32.00	0	1	66	42	0					3.81	0	
Lim	2	2	0	64	56	32.00	0	1	66	42	0					3.81	0	
I20T	2	2	0	5	4	2.50	0	0	36	31	1	31.00	1-17	0	0	5.16	0	
20T	3	3	0	5	4	1.66	0	0	60	48	2	24.00	1-17	0	0	4.80	1	
HANSRA, A.S.																		
FC	1	1	0	7	7	7.00	0	0									2	
JYOTI, S.																		
FC	1	2	1	67	35*	67.00	0	0	210	150	2	75.00	2-45	0	0	4.28	0	
Int	2	2	0	39	38	19.50	0	0	48	38	0					4.75	2	
Lim	2	2	0	39	38	19.50	0	0	48	38	0					4.75	2	
KESHVANI, S.																		
20T	1	1	0	1	1	1.00	0	0	6	13	0					13.00	0	
KHURRAM CHAUHAN																		
FC	1	1	1	26	26*		0	0	186	101	0					3.25	0	
Int	2	1	0	8	8	8.00	0	0	120	82	8	10.25	4-39	2	0	4.10	0	
Lim	2	1	0	8	8	8.00	0	0	120	82	8	10.25	4-39	2	0	4.10	0	
I20T	2	2	1	10	7*	10.00	0	0	25	47	0					11.28	1	
20T	3	3	2	18	8*	18.00	0	0	43	67	3	22.33	3-20	0	0	9.34	3	
KUMAR, N.R.																		
FC	1	1	0	74	74	74.00	0	1	130	101	3	33.66	3-58	0	0	4.66	1	
Int	1																0	
Lim	1																0	

Cmp Debut	M	I	NO	Runs	HS	Avge	100	50	Balls	Runs	Wkts	Avge	BB	5i	10m	RpO	ct	st
PATEL, H.																		
FC	1	2	0	55	36	27.50	0	0	78	68	1	68.00	1-47	0	0	5.23	0	
Int	1	1	0	3	3	3.00	0	0	12	19	0					9.50	1	
Lim	1	1	0	3	3	3.00	0	0	12	19	0					9.50	1	
I20T	2	2	0	29	25	14.50	0	0	23	41	0					10.69	0	
20T	2	2	0	29	25	14.50	0	0	23	41	0					10.69	0	
RIZWAN CHEEMA																		
FC	1	2	0	48	27	24.00	0	0	217	152	2	76.00	1-33	0	0	4.20	0	
Int	2	2	0	69	61	34.50	0	1	114	90	2	45.00	2-24	0	0	4.73	3	
Lim	2	2	0	69	61	34.50	0	1	114	90	2	45.00	2-24	0	0	4.73	3	
I20T	2	2	1	35	32	35.00	0	0	12	16	0					8.00	0	
20T	3	3	1	39	32	19.50	0	0	30	37	1	37.00	1-21	0	0	7.40	0	
SAAD BIN ZAFAR																		
20T	1	1	0	18	18	18.00	0	0									0	
UMAR BHATTI																		
FC	1	1	0	31	31	31.00	0	0	95	61	2	30.50	2-61	0	0	3.85	0	
Int	2	2	0	3	3	1.50	0	0	73	66	2	33.00	2-28	0	0	5.42	1	
Lim	2	2	0	3	3	1.50	0	0	73	66	2	33.00	2-28	0	0	5.42	1	
I20T	2	2	0	19	12	9.50	0	0	30	39	1	39.00	1-26	0	0	7.80	0	
20T	3	3	0	36	17	12.00	0	0	36	52	1	52.00	1-26	0	0	8.66	0	
USMAN LIMBADA																		
Int	2	2	1	26	14*	26.00	0	0									2	
Lim	2	2	1	26	14*	26.00	0	0									2	
I20T	1																0	
20T	1																0	

DURHAM TO UNITED ARAB EMIRATES 2010

Cmp Debut	M	I	NO	Runs	HS	Avge	100	50	Balls	Runs	Wkts	Avge	BB	5i	10m	RpO	ct	st
BENKENSTEIN, D.M.																		
FC	1	2	0	41	41	20.50	0	0									1	
BLACKWELL, I.D.																		
FC	1	2	0	39	26	19.50	0	0	198	86	4	21.50	4-70	0	0	2.60	0	
BORTHWICK, S.G.																		
FC	1	2	0	0	0	0.00	0	0	101	84	8	10.50	4-27	0	0	4.99	1	
CLAYDON, M.E.																		
FC	1	1	0	0	0	0.00	0	0	96	53	0					3.31	0	
COETZER, K.J.																		
FC	1	2	1	224	172	224.00	1	1									1	
DIVENUTO, M.J.																		
FC	1	1	0	131	131	131.00	1	0									1	
HARMISON, S.J.																		
FC	1								120	76	4	19.00	2-37	0	0	3.80	0	
MUSTARD, P.																		
FC	1	2	1	73	50	73.00	0	1									3	
SMITH, W.R.																		
FC	1	2	0	24	13	12.00	0	0									1	
STOKES, B.A.																		
FC	1	2	0	58	51	29.00	0	1	54	37	1	37.00	1-14	0	0	4.11	0	
THORP, C.D.																		
FC	1	2	1	79	79*	79.00	0	1	60	25	3	8.33	3-25	0	0	2.50	1	

ENGLAND TO UNITED ARAB EMIRATES 2009/10

Cmp Debut	M	I	NO	Runs	HS	Avge	100	50	Balls	Runs	Wkts	Avge	BB	5i	10m	RpO	ct	st
BRESNAN, T.T.																		
I20T	2	1	0	0	0	0.00	0	0	42	55	2	27.50	2-30	0	0	7.85	1	
20T	3	2	1	14	14*	14.00	0	0	66	84	2	42.00	2-30	0	0	7.63	1	
BROAD, S.C.J.																		
I20T	2								48	47	3	15.66	2-23	0	0	5.87	4	
20T	3								72	65	4	16.25	2-23	0	0	5.41	4	
COLLINGWOOD, P.D.																		
I20T	2	2	1	11	11*	11.00	0	0	18	29	0					9.66	1	
20T	3	3	1	12	11*	6.00	0	0	18	29	0					9.66	1	
DENLY, J.L.																		
I20T	2	2	0	6	5	3.00	0	0									1	
20T	3	3	0	10	5	3.33	0	0	6	8	0					8.00	2	
MORGAN, E.J.G.																		
I20T	2	2	1	76	67*	76.00	0	1									3	
20T	3	3	1	79	67*	39.50	0	1									3	

Cmp Debut	M	I	NO	Runs	HS	Avge	100	50	Balls	Runs	Wkts	Avge	BB	5i	10m	RpO	ct	st
PIETERSEN, K.P.																		
I20T	2	2	1	105	62	105.00	0	1									0	
20T	3	3	1	131	62	65.50	0	1									0	
PRIOR, M.J.																		
I20T	2	1	1	1	1*		0	0									2	1
20T	3	2	1	34	33	34.00	0	0									3	1
SHAHZAD, A.																		
I20T	1								24	38	2	19.00	2-38	0	0	9.50	0	
20T	1								24	38	2	19.00	2-38	0	0	9.50	0	
SIDEBOTTOM, R.J.																		
I20T	1								24	21	0					5.25	0	
20T	2								48	51	2	25.50	2-30	0	0	6.37	0	
SWANN, G.P.																		
I20T	2								42	32	5	6.40	3-14	0	0	4.57	0	
20T	3								60	62	5	12.40	3-14	0	0	6.20	1	
TROTT, I.J.L.																		
I20T	2	2	0	43	39	21.50	0	0									0	
20T	3	3	0	67	39	22.33	0	0									1	
WRIGHT, L.J.																		
I20T	2	1	0	13	13	13.00	0	0	36	48	1	48.00	1-27	0	0	8.00	0	
20T	3	2	1	55	42*	55.00	0	0	60	89	3	29.66	2-41	0	0	8.90	0	

ENGLAND LIONS TO UNITED ARAB EMIRATES 2009/10

Cmp Debut	M	I	NO	Runs	HS	Avge	100	50	Balls	Runs	Wkts	Avge	BB	5i	10m	RpO	ct	st
BELL, I.R.																		
Lim	3	3	1	76	46*	38.00	0	0									3	
20T	4	4	1	98	48	32.66	0	0									1	
CARBERRY, M.A.																		
Lim	1	1	0	0	0	0.00	0	0									0	
20T	1	1	0	8	8	8.00	0	0									0	
DAVIES, S.M.																		
Lim	3	3	0	67	24	22.33	0	0									5	1
20T	3	3	0	48	17	16.00	0	0									1	
FINN, S.T.																		
Lim	3	2	0	2	1	1.00	0	0	174	112	5	22.40	2-30	0	0	3.86	0	
20T	2								48	50	3	16.66	2-25	0	0	6.25	0	
GALE, A.W.																		
Lim	3	3	0	55	21	18.33	0	0									0	
20T	4	3	2	42	36*	42.00	0	0									2	
KIESWETTER, C.																		
20T	4	4	2	248	81	124.00	0	3									4	2
KIRBY, S.P.																		
20T	4								72	99	5	19.80	3-33	0	0	8.25	0	
LUMB, M.J.																		
Lim	3	3	0	145	110	48.33	1	0									1	
20T	4	4	1	77	58*	25.66	0	1									4	
MAHMOOD, S.I.																		
Lim	3	2	1	0	0*	0.00	0	0	132	103	4	25.75	2-38	0	0	4.68	0	
20T	3								59	84	3	28.00	2-22	0	0	8.54	0	
RASHID, A.U.																		
Lim	3	3	1	11	11	5.50	0	0	162	109	2	54.50	1-30	0	0	4.03	2	
20T	4								96	91	9	10.11	3-13	0	0	5.68	2	
TAYLOR, J.W.A.																		
Lim	3	3	0	64	61	21.33	0	1									1	
TREDWELL, J.C.																		
20T	4	1	1	0	0*		0	0	90	75	1	75.00	1-12	0	0	5.00	0	
TREGO, P.D.																		
Lim	2	2	0	11	7	5.50	0	0	90	71	1	71.00	1-24	0	0	4.73	0	
20T	4	2	1	14	14*	14.00	0	0	42	81	2	40.50	2-38	0	0	11.57	1	
WAINWRIGHT, D.J.																		
Lim	3	3	1	3	3	1.50	0	0	180	107	5	21.40	3-26	0	0	3.56	0	
WOAKES, C.R.																		
Lim	3	3	0	10	6	3.33	0	0	149	104	6	17.33	4-38	1	0	4.18	0	
20T	3								71	75	3	25.00	2-23	0	0	6.33	4	

IRELAND TO UNITED ARAB EMIRATES 2009/10

Cmp Debut	M	I	NO	Runs	HS	Avge	100	50	Balls	Runs	Wkts	Avge	BB	5i	10m	RpO	ct	st
BOTHA, A.C.																		
I20T	3	2	0	13	13	6.50	0	0	60	57	4	14.25	2-15	0	0	5.70	2	
20T	5	3	0	16	13	5.33	0	0	103	103	6	17.16	2-15	0	0	6.00	3	

Cmp	Debut	M	I	NO	Runs	HS	Avge	100	50	Balls	Runs	Wkts	Avge	BB	5i	10m	RpO	ct	st
CONNELL, P.																			
I20T		4	2	1	3	3*	3.00	0	0	87	106	4	26.50	2-17	0	0	7.31	1	
20T		6	2	1	3	3*	3.00	0	0	129	150	10	15.00	4-14	1	0	6.97	1	
CUSACK, A.R.																			
I20T		4	4	0	110	65	27.50	0	1	66	75	1	75.00	1-21	0	0	6.81	1	
20T		6	6	0	166	65	27.66	0	1	90	94	4	23.50	3-19	0	0	6.26	4	
DOCKRELL, G.H.																			
I20T		4	1	1	0	0*		0	0	75	86	7	12.28	4-20	1	0	6.88	0	
20T		6	1	1	0	0*		0	0	111	140	8	17.50	4-20	1	0	7.56	0	
JOHNSTON, D.T.																			
I20T		4	4	1	45	18	15.00	0	0	96	80	8	10.00	3-20	0	0	5.00	1	
20T		6	6	2	76	19	19.00	0	0	144	121	10	12.10	3-20	0	0	5.04	1	
JONES, N.G.																			
I20T		1	1	0	14	14	14.00	0	0	6	8	0					8.00	0	
20T		1	1	0	14	14	14.00	0	0	6	8	0					8.00	0	
MOONEY, J.F.																			
I20T		4	4	1	41	17*	13.66	0	0									2	
20T		6	5	2	53	17*	17.66	0	0									3	
O'BRIEN, K.J.																			
I20T		4	4	1	19	10*	6.33	0	0	39	47	2	23.50	1-11	0	0	7.23	2	
20T		6	6	1	35	13	7.00	0	0	57	70	3	23.33	1-11	0	0	7.36	2	
O'BRIEN, N.J.																			
I20T		4	4	0	58	28	14.50	0	0									1	3
20T		6	6	0	188	84	31.33	0	1									2	3
PORTERFIELD, W.T.S.																			
I20T		4	4	0	79	35	19.75	0	0									1	
20T		6	6	0	146	45	24.33	0	0									3	
STIRLING, P.R.																			
I20T		1	1	0	21	21	21.00	0	0									1	
20T		1	1	0	21	21	21.00	0	0									1	
WHITE, A.R.																			
I20T		3	3	2	40	19	40.00	0	0									1	
20T		5	4	3	44	19	44.00	0	0	24	23	0					5.75	1	
WILSON, G.C.																			
I20T		4	4	0	61	29	15.25	0	0									2	
20T		6	6	1	85	29	17.00	0	0									4	

KENYA TO UNITED ARAB EMIRATES 2009/10

Cmp	Debut	M	I	NO	Runs	HS	Avge	100	50	Balls	Runs	Wkts	Avge	BB	5i	10m	RpO	ct	st
KAMANDE, J.K.																			
I20T		2	1	0	42	42	42.00	0	0	42	37	2	18.50	2-18	0	0	5.28	1	
20T		3	2	1	64	42	64.00	0	0	66	71	2	35.50	2-18	0	0	6.45	1	
NGOCHE, S.O.																			
I20T		2	1	0	0	0	0.00	0	0	24	32	1	32.00	1-15	0	0	8.00	0	
20T		2	1	0	0	0	0.00	0	0	24	32	1	32.00	1-15	0	0	8.00	0	
OBANDA, A.A.																			
I20T		2	2	0	84	79	42.00	0	1									0	
20T		3	3	0	97	79	32.33	0	1									1	
OBUYA, C.O.																			
I20T		2	2	1	39	33	39.00	0	0									1	
20T		3	3	2	81	42*	81.00	0	0									2	
OBUYA, D.O.																			
20T		1	1	0	2	2	2.00	0	0									0	
ODHIAMBO, N.M.																			
20T		1								24	33	2	16.50	2-33	0	0	8.25	0	
ODHIAMBO, N.N.																			
I20T		2	1	0	18	18	18.00	0	0	31	41	3	13.66	3-16	0	0	7.93	2	
20T		3	1	0	18	18	18.00	0	0	55	75	4	18.75	3-16	0	0	8.18	2	
ONYANGO, L.N.																			
I20T		2	1	0	5	5	5.00	0	0	24	27	3	9.00	2-17	0	0	6.75	0	
20T		3	1	0	5	5	5.00	0	0	48	59	5	11.80	2-17	0	0	7.37	0	
OUMA, M.A.																			
I20T		2	1	0	12	12	12.00	0	0									2	
20T		3	2	0	51	39	25.50	0	0									2	
PATEL, R.R.																			
I20T		2	1	0	7	7	7.00	0	0									2	
20T		3	2	0	7	7	3.50	0	0									2	
SUJI, A.O.																			
I20T		2	1	0	1	1	1.00	0	0	24	37	0					9.25	0	
20T		2	1	0	1	1	1.00	0	0	24	37	0					9.25	0	

Cmp Debut	M	I	NO	Runs	HS	Avge	100	50	Balls	Runs	Wkts	Avge	BB	5i	10m	RpO	ct	st
TIKOLO, S.O.																		
I20T	2	2	1	50	50*	50.00	0	1	48	56	1	56.00	1-32	0	0	7.00	1	
20T	3	3	1	75	50*	37.50	0	1	60	66	1	66.00	1-32	0	0	6.60	1	
VARAIYA, H.A.																		
I20T	2	1	1	0	0*		0	0	42	38	1	38.00	1-18	0	0	5.42	0	
20T	3	1	1	0	0*		0	0	54	55	1	55.00	1-18	0	0	6.11	3	

MCC TO UNITED ARAB EMIRATES 2010

Cmp Debut	M	I	NO	Runs	HS	Avge	100	50	Balls	Runs	Wkts	Avge	BB	5i	10m	RpO	ct	st
COSKER, D.A.																		
FC	1	2	0	15	14	7.50	0	0	228	96	2	48.00	1-19	0	0	2.52	0	
FOSTER, J.S.																		
FC	1	2	0	32	26	16.00	0	0									1	1
GIDMAN, A.P.R.																		
FC	1	2	0	46	29	23.00	0	0	90	54	1	54.00	1-18	0	0	3.60	1	
KIRBY, S.P.																		
FC	1	2	0	29	16	14.50	0	0	156	58	3	19.33	2-10	0	0	2.23	0	
LEWIS, J.																		
FC	1	2	0	32	32	16.00	0	0	96	53	1	53.00	1-19	0	0	3.31	0	
MALAN, D.J.																		
FC	1	2	0	54	41	27.00	0	0	108	88	4	22.00	4-20	0	0	4.88	2	
MIDDLEBROOK, J.D.																		
FC	1	2	1	20	11*	20.00	0	0	258	140	4	35.00	3-118	0	0	3.25	0	
MURTAGH, T.J.																		
FC	1	2	1	76	55*	76.00	0	1	162	119	0					4.40	0	
NEWMAN, S.A.																		
FC	1	2	0	5	5	2.50	0	0									2	
SALES, D.J.G.																		
FC	1	2	0	7	4	3.50	0	0									2	
TAYLOR, J.W.A.																		
FC	1	2	0	39	39	19.50	0	0	78	63	0					4.84	1	

NETHERLANDS TO UNITED ARAB EMIRATES 2009/10

Cmp Debut	M	I	NO	Runs	HS	Avge	100	50	Balls	Runs	Wkts	Avge	BB	5i	10m	RpO	ct	st
BORREN, P.W.																		
I20T	4	3	0	21	12	7.00	0	0	90	96	0					6.40	2	
20T	5	4	1	53	32*	17.66	0	0	108	126	0					7.00	2	
BUURMAN, A.F.																		
I20T	4	2	0	0	0	0.00	0	0									1	1
20T	5	3	0	3	3	1.00	0	0									3	1
DEGROOTH, T.N.																		
I20T	1																2	
20T	2	1	0	0	0	0.00	0	0									2	
JONKMAN, M.B.S.																		
I20T	3	1	0	1	1	1.00	0	0	48	47	4	11.75	2-21	0	0	5.87	2	
20T	3	1	0	1	1	1.00	0	0	48	47	4	11.75	2-21	0	0	5.87	2	
KERVEZEE, A.N.																		
I20T	4	4	0	113	39	28.25	0	0									3	
20T	5	5	0	122	39	24.40	0	0									3	
MOHAMMAD KASHIF																		
I20T	3	1	1	0	0*		0	0	42	55	4	13.75	2-28	0	0	7.85	1	
20T	4	1	1	0	0*		0	0	66	81	4	20.25	2-28	0	0	7.36	1	
MUDASSAR BUKHARI																		
I20T	4	2	1	3	3*	3.00	0	0	94	113	6	18.83	4-33	1	0	7.21	0	
20T	5	3	1	3	3*	1.50	0	0	117	151	7	21.57	4-33	1	0	7.74	0	
SCHIFERLI, E.																		
I20T	1								18	27	1	27.00	1-27	0	0	9.00	0	
20T	1								18	27	1	27.00	1-27	0	0	9.00	0	
SEELAAR, P.M.																		
I20T	4	1	0	1	1	1.00	0	0	90	87	8	10.87	4-19	1	0	5.80	2	
20T	5	2	1	1	1	1.00	0	0	114	123	8	15.37	4-19	1	0	6.47	2	
SZWARCZYNSKI, E.S.																		
I20T	4	4	0	108	45	27.00	0	0									1	
20T	5	5	0	114	45	22.80	0	0									1	
TENDOESCHATE, R.N.																		
I20T	4	4	2	94	32	47.00	0	0	84	97	3	32.33	1-15	0	0	6.92	2	
20T	5	5	2	94	32	31.33	0	0	102	126	4	31.50	1-15	0	0	7.41	2	

Cmp Debut	M	I	NO	Runs	HS	Avge	100	50	Balls	Runs	Wkts	Avge	BB	5i	10m	RpO	ct	st
VANBUNGE, D.L.S.																		
I20T	4	4	2	26	24	13.00	0	0	12	14	1	14.00	1-14	0	0	7.00	2	
20T	5	5	2	102	76	34.00	0	1	18	21	1	21.00	1-14	0	0	7.00	2	
ZUIDERENT, B.																		
I20T	4	4	1	83	43*	27.66	0	0									1	
20T	5	5	1	107	43*	26.75	0	0									1	

NEW ZEALAND TO UNITED ARAB EMIRATES 2009/10

Cmp Debut	M	I	NO	Runs	HS	Avge	100	50	Balls	Runs	Wkts	Avge	BB	5i	10m	RpO	ct	st
BOND, S.E.																		
Int	3	3	3	25	11*		0	0	176	150	4	37.50	2-61	0	0	5.11	0	
Lim	3	3	3	25	11*		0	0	176	150	4	37.50	2-61	0	0	5.11	0	
I20T	2	1	1	1	1*		0	0	48	50	2	25.00	2-17	0	0	6.25	2	
20T	2	1	1	1	1*		0	0	48	50	2	25.00	2-17	0	0	6.25	2	
BROOM, N.T.																		
Int	2	2	0	0	0	0.00	0	0									0	
Lim	2	2	0	0	0	0.00	0	0									0	
I20T	2	1	0	14	14	14.00	0	0									0	
20T	2	1	0	14	14	14.00	0	0									0	
BUTLER, I.G.																		
Int	1	1	0	4	4	4.00	0	0	42	54	1	54.00	1-54	0	0	7.71	1	
Lim	1	1	0	4	4	4.00	0	0	42	54	1	54.00	1-54	0	0	7.71	1	
I20T	2	1	0	1	1	1.00	0	0	42	70	3	23.33	3-28	0	0	10.00	1	
20T	2	1	0	1	1	1.00	0	0	42	70	3	23.33	3-28	0	0	10.00	1	
FRANKLIN, J.E.C.																		
I20T	1	1	1	5	5*		0	0	18	26	1	26.00	1-26	0	0	8.66	0	
20T	1	1	1	5	5*		0	0	18	26	1	26.00	1-26	0	0	8.66	0	
GUPTILL, M.J.																		
Int	3	3	0	74	62	24.66	0	1									3	
Lim	3	3	0	74	62	24.66	0	1									3	
I20T	2	2	0	25	17	12.50	0	0									0	
20T	2	2	0	25	17	12.50	0	0									0	
MCCULLUM, B.B.																		
Int	3	3	0	228	131	76.00	1	1									5	
Lim	3	3	0	228	131	76.00	1	1									5	
I20T	2	2	0	66	47	33.00	0	0									0	
20T	2	2	0	66	47	33.00	0	0									0	
MCCULLUM, N.L.																		
Int	1	1	0	0	0	0.00	0	0	18	29	0					9.66	0	
Lim	1	1	0	0	0	0.00	0	0	18	29	0					9.66	0	
I20T	2	1	0	22	22	22.00	0	0	31	34	1	34.00	1-16	0	0	6.58	1	
20T	2	1	0	22	22	22.00	0	0	31	34	1	34.00	1-16	0	0	6.58	1	
MILLS, K.D.																		
Int	2	2	0	8	4	4.00	0	0	120	119	3	39.66	2-57	0	0	5.95	1	
Lim	2	2	0	8	4	4.00	0	0	120	119	3	39.66	2-57	0	0	5.95	1	
ORAM, J.D.P.																		
Int	3	3	1	44	33*	22.00	0	0	151	93	4	23.25	3-20	0	0	3.69	1	
Lim	3	3	1	44	33*	22.00	0	0	151	93	4	23.25	3-20	0	0	3.69	1	
REDMOND, A.J.																		
Int	3	3	0	79	52	26.33	0	1									1	
Lim	3	3	0	79	52	26.33	0	1									1	
I20T	1								17	24	2	12.00	2-24	0	0	8.47	2	
20T	1								17	24	2	12.00	2-24	0	0	8.47	2	
SOUTHEE, T.G.																		
Int	3	2	0	5	4	2.50	0	0	168	128	4	32.00	2-26	0	0	4.57	1	
Lim	3	2	0	5	4	2.50	0	0	168	128	4	32.00	2-26	0	0	4.57	1	
I20T	2	1	0	6	6	6.00	0	0	48	59	3	19.66	3-28	0	0	7.37	1	
20T	2	1	0	6	6	6.00	0	0	48	59	3	19.66	3-28	0	0	7.37	1	
STYRIS, S.B.																		
Int	3	3	0	28	14	9.33	0	0	24	23	3	7.66	3-23	0	0	5.75	2	
Lim	3	3	0	28	14	9.33	0	0	24	23	3	7.66	3-23	0	0	5.75	2	
I20T	2	2	0	47	43	23.50	0	0	36	51	1	51.00	1-32	0	0	8.50	1	
20T	2	2	0	47	43	23.50	0	0	36	51	1	51.00	1-32	0	0	8.50	1	
TAYLOR, L.R.P.L.																		
Int	3	3	0	44	44	14.66	0	0									3	
Lim	3	3	0	44	44	14.66	0	0									3	
I20T	2	2	0	18	13	9.00	0	0									0	
20T	2	2	0	18	13	9.00	0	0									0	

Cmp Debut	M	I	NO	Runs	HS	Avge	100	50	Balls	Runs	Wkts	Avge	BB	5i	10m	RpO	ct	st
VETTORI, D.L.																		
Int	3	3	0	83	38	27.66	0	0	180	113	5	22.60	2-34	0	0	3.76	1	
Lim	3	3	0	83	38	27.66	0	0	180	113	5	22.60	2-34	0	0	3.76	1	
WATLING, B.J.																		
I20T	2	2	0	29	22	14.50	0	0									2	
20T	2	2	0	29	22	14.50	0	0									2	

PAKISTAN TO UNITED ARAB EMIRATES 2009/10

Cmp Debut	M	I	NO	Runs	HS	Avge	100	50	Balls	Runs	Wkts	Avge	BB	5i	10m	RpO	ct	st
ABDUL RAZZAQ																		
Int	3	3	0	61	35	20.33	0	0	132	117	4	29.25	2-38	0	0	5.31	1	
Lim	3	3	0	61	35	20.33	0	0	132	117	4	29.25	2-38	0	0	5.31	1	
I20T	4	4	2	94	46*	47.00	0	0	66	50	3	16.66	2-9	0	0	4.54	0	
20T	4	4	2	94	46*	47.00	0	0	66	50	3	16.66	2-9	0	0	4.54	0	
FAWAD ALAM																		
I20T	4	4	1	83	28	27.66	0	0									1	
20T	4	4	1	83	28	27.66	0	0									1	
IMRAN FARHAT																		
I20T	2	2	0	14	14	7.00	0	0									1	
20T	2	2	0	14	14	7.00	0	0									1	
IMRAN NAZIR																		
I20T	4	4	0	83	58	20.75	0	1									1	
20T	4	4	0	83	58	20.75	0	1									1	
KAMRAN AKMAL																		
Int	3	3	1	75	67*	37.50	0	1									2	
Lim	3	3	1	75	67*	37.50	0	1									2	
I20T	2	2	0	39	26	19.50	0	0									3	1
20T	2	2	0	39	26	19.50	0	0									3	1
KHALID LATIF																		
Int	3	3	0	128	64	42.66	0	1									1	
Lim	3	3	0	128	64	42.66	0	1									1	
I20T	1	1	0	4	4	4.00	0	0									0	
20T	1	1	0	4	4	4.00	0	0									0	
MOHAMMAD AAMER																		
Int	3	3	1	85	73*	42.50	0	1	153	120	4	30.00	2-41	0	0	4.70	2	
Lim	3	3	1	85	73*	42.50	0	1	153	120	4	30.00	2-41	0	0	4.70	2	
I20T	2	1	0	2	2	2.00	0	0	42	54	2	27.00	2-21	0	0	7.71	0	
20T	2	1	0	2	2	2.00	0	0	42	54	2	27.00	2-21	0	0	7.71	0	
MOHAMMAD YOUSUF																		
Int	2	2	0	48	30	24.00	0	0									0	
Lim	2	2	0	48	30	24.00	0	0									0	
SAEED AJMAL																		
Int	3	3	2	36	33	36.00	0	0	164	110	6	18.33	4-33	1	0	4.02	1	
Lim	3	3	2	36	33	36.00	0	0	164	110	6	18.33	4-33	1	0	4.02	1	
I20T	4								90	89	4	22.25	2-18	0	0	5.93	0	
20T	4								90	89	4	22.25	2-18	0	0	5.93	0	
SALMAN BUTT																		
Int	3	3	0	84	59	28.00	0	1									0	
Lim	3	3	0	84	59	28.00	0	1									0	
SARFRAZ AHMED																		
I20T	2	1	0	5	5	5.00	0	0									0	
20T	2	1	0	5	5	5.00	0	0									0	
SHAHID AFRIDI																		
Int	3	3	0	75	70	25.00	0	1	180	128	5	25.60	2-46	0	0	4.26	0	
Lim	3	3	0	75	70	25.00	0	1	180	128	5	25.60	2-46	0	0	4.26	0	
I20T	3	3	0	54	24	18.00	0	0	63	69	3	23.00	2-21	0	0	6.57	1	
20T	3	3	0	54	24	18.00	0	0	63	69	3	23.00	2-21	0	0	6.57	1	
SHOAIB MALIK																		
Int	2	2	0	37	26	18.50	0	0	42	32	1	32.00	1-32	0	0	4.57	1	
Lim	2	2	0	37	26	18.50	0	0	42	32	1	32.00	1-32	0	0	4.57	1	
I20T	4	4	0	59	33	14.75	0	0	30	47	0					9.40	4	
20T	4	4	0	59	33	14.75	0	0	30	47	0					9.40	4	
SOHAIL TANVIR																		
I20T	2	1	0	12	12	12.00	0	0	42	36	2	18.00	1-14	0	0	5.14	0	
20T	2	1	0	12	12	12.00	0	0	42	36	2	18.00	1-14	0	0	5.14	0	
UMAR AKMAL																		
Int	2	2	0	21	12	10.50	0	0									0	
Lim	2	2	0	21	12	10.50	0	0									0	
I20T	4	4	1	108	56*	36.00	0	1									1	
20T	4	4	1	108	56*	36.00	0	1									1	

Cmp Debut	M	I	NO	Runs	HS	Avge	100	50	Balls	Runs	Wkts	Avge	BB	5i	10m	RpO	ct	st
UMAR GUL																		
Int	3	3	0	10	6	3.33	0	0	144	130	5	26.00	2-24	0	0	5.41	0	
Lim	3	3	0	10	6	3.33	0	0	144	130	5	26.00	2-24	0	0	5.41	0	
I20T	4	1	1	1	1*		0	0	81	121	3	40.33	2-29	0	0	8.96	2	
20T	4	1	1	1	1*		0	0	81	121	3	40.33	2-29	0	0	8.96	2	
YASIR ARAFAT																		
I20T	2	2	2	14	9*		0	0	48	50	4	12.50	3-32	0	0	6.25	0	
20T	2	2	2	14	9*		0	0	48	50	4	12.50	3-32	0	0	6.25	0	
YOUNIS KHAN																		
Int	3	3	0	22	19	7.33	0	0									2	
Lim	3	3	0	22	19	7.33	0	0									2	

PAKISTAN A TO UNITED ARAB EMIRATES 2009/10

Cmp Debut	M	I	NO	Runs	HS	Avge	100	50	Balls	Runs	Wkts	Avge	BB	5i	10m	RpO	ct	st
AAMER SAJJAD																		
Lim	3	3	0	76	39	25.33	0	0									1	
20T	3	3	0	44	23	14.66	0	0									0	
ABDUR REHMAN																		
Lim	3	3	1	27	20	13.50	0	0	169	101	7	14.42	4-25	1	0	3.58	1	
20T	3	1	0	4	4	4.00	0	0	72	71	3	23.66	2-21	0	0	5.91	1	
ASAD SHAFIQ																		
Lim	3	3	0	86	52	28.66	0	1									4	
20T	3	3	0	41	31	13.66	0	0									0	
HAMMAD AZAM																		
Lim	3	3	0	46	22	15.33	0	0	48	35	1	35.00	1-11	0	0	4.37	0	
KASHIF SIDDIQ																		
20T	3	3	1	13	11	6.50	0	0	18	18	0					6.00	0	
MOHAMMAD HAFEEZ																		
Lim	3	3	0	63	51	21.00	0	1	144	65	3	21.66	2-8	0	0	2.70	2	
20T	3	3	0	23	11	7.66	0	0	60	62	1	62.00	1-20	0	0	6.20	1	
MOHAMMAD TALHA																		
Lim	2	2	1	4	4	4.00	0	0	72	55	1	55.00	1-30	0	0	4.58	0	
20T	1								24	46	0					11.50	0	
NAEEM ANJUM																		
Lim	3	3	0	53	24	17.66	0	0									0	
20T	3	3	1	43	27*	21.50	0	0									0	1
NAVED YASIN																		
Lim	2	2	0	78	46	39.00	0	0									1	
RAZA HASAN																		
Lim	3	1	1	3	3*		0	0	141	74	9	8.22	3-13	0	0	3.14	0	
SHAHZAIB HASAN																		
Lim	1	1	0	8	8	8.00	0	0									0	
20T	3	3	0	88	57	29.33	0	1									1	
TABISH KHAN																		
20T	1								24	36	1	36.00	1-36	0	0	9.00	0	
TANVIR AHMED																		
20T	3	3	2	37	21*	37.00	0	0	49	70	0					8.57	0	
UMAIR KHAN																		
Lim	3	3	0	66	61	22.00	0	1									1	
20T	3	3	0	56	49	18.66	0	0									0	
UZAIR-UL-HAQ																		
20T	1								12	25	0					12.50	0	
WAHAB RIAZ																		
Lim	3	3	1	31	22	15.50	0	0	108	92	3	30.66	3-52	0	0	5.11	0	
20T	2	2	1	33	28*	33.00	0	0	40	51	4	12.75	3-34	0	0	7.65	0	
YASIR SHAH																		
Lim	1	1	0	51	51	51.00	0	1	60	33	2	16.50	2-33	0	0	3.30	1	
20T	1	1	0	4	4	4.00	0	0	24	25	0					6.25	1	

SCOTLAND TO UNITED ARAB EMIRATES 2009/10

Cmp Debut	M	I	NO	Runs	HS	Avge	100	50	Balls	Runs	Wkts	Avge	BB	5i	10m	RpO	ct	st
BERRINGTON, R.D.																		
I20T	2	2	1	19	19*	19.00	0	0	30	31	0					6.20	0	
20T	3	3	1	27	19*	13.50	0	0	42	42	0					6.00	1	
COETZER, K.J.																		
I20T	2	2	0	45	43	22.50	0	0	42	39	5	7.80	3-25	0	0	5.57	0	
20T	3	3	0	45	43	15.00	0	0	54	53	5	10.60	3-25	0	0	5.88	0	
DRUMMOND, G.D.																		
I20T	2	2	0	40	35	20.00	0	0	42	42	3	14.00	2-14	0	0	6.00	0	
20T	3	3	0	46	35	15.33	0	0	60	53	3	17.66	2-14	0	0	5.30	0	

Cmp Debut	M	I	NO	Runs	HS	Avge	100	50	Balls	Runs	Wkts	Avge	BB	5i	10m	RpO	ct	st
HAMILTON, G.M.																		
I20T	2	2	0	37	32	18.50	0	0									2	
20T	3	3	0	78	41	26.00	0	0									2	
HAQ, R.M.																		
I20T	2	2	1	2	1*	2.00	0	0	42	40	2	20.00	2-16	0	0	5.71	0	
20T	3	2	1	2	1*	2.00	0	0	66	69	2	34.50	2-16	0	0	6.27	0	
LYONS, R.T.																		
I20T	1	1	0	0	0	0.00	0	0	24	26	1	26.00	1-26	0	0	6.50	0	
20T	1	1	0	0	0	0.00	0	0	24	26	1	26.00	1-26	0	0	6.50	0	
MCCALLUM, N.F.I.																		
I20T	2	2	0	38	38	19.00	0	0									0	
20T	2	2	0	38	38	19.00	0	0									0	
NEL, J.D.																		
I20T	2	1	0	0	0	0.00	0	0	42	47	1	47.00	1-23	0	0	6.71	1	
20T	3	1	0	0	0	0.00	0	0	61	68	2	34.00	1-21	0	0	6.68	1	
POONIA, N.S.																		
I20T	1	1	0	0	0	0.00	0	0									0	
20T	2	2	0	12	12	6.00	0	0									0	
SMITH, S.J.S.																		
I20T	2	2	0	8	8	4.00	0	0									0	1
20T	3	3	1	11	8	5.50	0	0									0	1
STANDER, J.H.																		
I20T	2	2	0	6	4	3.00	0	0	18	28	1	28.00	1-28	0	0	9.33	1	
20T	3	3	1	25	19*	12.50	0	0	36	44	2	22.00	1-16	0	0	7.33	1	
WATSON, R.R.																		
20T	1	1	0	14	14	14.00	0	0	12	10	2	5.00	2-10	0	0	5.00	0	
WATTS, D.F.																		
I20T	2	2	0	12	12	6.00	0	0									3	
20T	3	3	0	18	12	6.00	0	0									4	

UGANDA TO UNITED ARAB EMIRATES 2009/10

Cmp Debut	M	I	NO	Runs	HS	Avge	100	50	Balls	Runs	Wkts	Avge	BB	5i	10m	RpO	ct	st
ARINAITWE, D.K.																		
FC	1	1	0	1	1	1.00	0	0	200	80	3	26.66	2-45	0	0	2.40	0	
20T	1	1	1	1	1*		0	0	6	12	0					12.00	0	
BAIG, A.M.																		
FC	1	2	0	61	51	30.50	0	1	96	53	1	53.00	1-42	0	0	3.31	0	
Lim	1	1	0	0	0	0.00	0	0									0	
20T	2	2	0	15	12	7.50	0	0	42	59	0					8.42	0	
KYOBE, A.S.																		
FC	1	2	0	57	49	28.50	0	0									0	
Lim	1	1	0	6	6	6.00	0	0									0	
20T	2	2	0	42	31	21.00	0	0									1	
MUHUMZA, D.																		
Lim	1	1	0	3	3	3.00	0	0	12	23	1	23.00	1-23	0	0	11.50	0	
MUKASA, R.G.																		
FC	1	2	0	62	46	31.00	0	0	6	0	0					0.00	0	
Lim	1	1	0	9	9	9.00	0	0									0	
20T	2	2	0	34	29	17.00	0	0									2	
MUSOKE, B.																		
FC	1	2	0	40	40	20.00	0	0									0	
Lim	1	1	0	12	12	12.00	0	0									0	
20T	2	2	0	53	31	26.50	0	0									0	
NSUBUGA, F.																		
FC	1	2	1	42	37	42.00	0	0	324	176	6	29.33	3-76	0	0	3.25	3	
Lim	1	1	0	0	0	0.00	0	0									0	
20T	2	2	0	18	12	9.00	0	0	41	36	3	12.00	3-9	0	0	5.26	0	
SEBANJA, J.																		
Lim	1	1	0	1	1	1.00	0	0	6	10	0					10.00	1	
20T	1	1	1	2	2*		0	0									0	
SEMATIMBA, L.																		
FC	1	2	0	89	89	44.50	0	1									3	
Lim	1	1	0	6	6	6.00	0	0									0	
20T	2	2	0	18	9	9.00	0	0									1	
SENYONDO, H.																		
Lim	1	1	1	5	5*		0	0									0	
20T	2	1	0	2	2	2.00	0	0	24	24	0					6.00	0	

Cmp	Debut	M	I	NO	Runs	HS	Avge	100	50	Balls	Runs	Wkts	Avge	BB	5i	10m	RpO	ct	st
SSEMANDA, R.																			
FC		1	2	1	63	41	63.00	0	0	168	90	2	45.00	2-66	0	0	3.21	1	
Lim		1	1	0	0	0	0.00	0	0									0	
20T		2	2	0	9	8	4.50	0	0	42	40	2	20.00	2-18	0	0	5.71	1	
TABBY, D.																			
FC		1	1	1	4	4*		0	0	240	121	3	40.33	2-72	0	0	3.02	2	
Lim		1	1	0	1	1	1.00	0	0	18	16	0					5.33	0	
20T		2	1	1	0	0*		0	0	36	30	3	10.00	2-10	0	0	5.00	0	
WAISWA, C.																			
FC		1	1	0	2	2	2.00	0	0	192	111	1	111.00	1-51	0	0	3.46	0	
20T		1	1	0	12	12	12.00	0	0	24	24	1	24.00	1-24	0	0	6.00	2	
ZIRABA, A.																			
FC		1	2	0	11	10	5.50	0	0									1	
20T		1	1	0	8	8	8.00	0	0									1	

UNITED STATES OF AMERICA TO UNITED ARAB EMIRATES 2009/10

Cmp	Debut	M	I	NO	Runs	HS	Avge	100	50	Balls	Runs	Wkts	Avge	BB	5i	10m	RpO	ct	st
ALLEN, T.P.																			
20T		3	3	0	15	9	5.00	0	0	42	61	4	15.25	2-29	0	0	8.71	0	
BAKER, O.M.																			
20T		3	2	2	28	28*		0	0	36	51	1	51.00	1-18	0	0	8.50	0	
CUSH, L.J.																			
20T		3	3	0	50	41	16.66	0	0	72	83	2	41.50	1-18	0	0	6.91	0	
DARLINGTON, K.G.																			
20T		3								72	90	2	45.00	2-19	0	0	7.50	0	
DHANIRAM, S.																			
20T		3	3	1	6	4	3.00	0	0	72	62	1	62.00	1-12	0	0	5.16	1	
IMRAN AWAN																			
20T		1								18	25	0					8.33	0	
MARSHALL, R.A.																			
20T		3	2	0	19	19	9.50	0	0									0	
MASSIAH, S.J.																			
20T		3	3	2	8	5*	8.00	0	0									0	
NADKARNI, S.S.																			
20T		2	2	0	13	12	6.50	0	0									2	
THYAGARAJAN, A.																			
20T		2	2	1	86	72*	86.00	0	1									1	
USMAN SHUJA																			
20T		2								36	43	1	43.00	1-26	0	0	7.16	1	
VERMA, S.																			
20T		2								12	23	1	23.00	1-23	0	0	11.50	0	
WRIGHT, C.D.																			
20T		3	3	0	92	62	30.66	0	1									3	1

UNITED STATES OF AMERICA

2009/10 AND CAREER RECORDS FOR UNITED STATES OF AMERICA PLAYERS

Cmp	*Debut*	*M*	*I*	*NO*	*Runs*	*HS*	*Avge*	*100*	*50*	*Balls*	*Runs*	*Wkts*	*Avge*	*BB*	*5i*	*10m*	*RpO*	*ct*	*st*
ALLEN, Timroy Patrick (United States of America to United Arab Emirates) b Westmoreland, Jamaica 22.1.1987 RHB RFM																			
Lim	2008/09	3	3	2	33	15*	33.00	0	0	84	58	1	58.00	1-26	0	0	4.14	0	
20T	2009/10	3	3	0	15	9	5.00	0	0	42	61	4	15.25	2-29	0	0	8.71	0	
BAKER, Orlando M (United States of America to United Arab Emirates) b St Catherine, Jamaica 15.9.1979 RHB RM																			
FC	2000/01	1	2	0	5	5	2.50	0	0									0	
Lim	2008/09	3	3	0	32	13	10.66	0	0	63	61	4	15.25	4-46	1	0	5.81	0	
20T	2009/10	3	2	2	28	28*		0	0	36	51	1	51.00	1-18	0	0	8.50	0	
CUSH, Lennox Joseph (Guyana, United States of America to United Arab Emirates) b Georgetown, Demerara, Guyana 12.12.1974 RHB OB																			
FC	1995/96	38	63	3	1249	154	20.81	2	2	2640	1100	26	42.30	4-57	0	0	2.50	12	
Lim	1998/99	28	27	4	488	70	21.21	0	2	1209	775	25	31.00	4-33	2	0	3.84	7	
20T	2006	15	10	1	122	49	13.55	0	0	348	381	23	16.56	4-25	2	0	6.56	2	
DARLINGTON, Kevin Godfrey (United States of America to United Arab Emirates) b New Amsterdam, West Bank, Berbice, Guyana 26.4.1972 RHB RFM																			
FC	1994/95	30	41	17	154	18	6.41	0	0	4508	2275	79	28.79	6-25	3	0	3.02	7	
Lim	1995/96	22	3	2	3	3*	3.00	0	0	840	455	18	25.27	2-14	0	0	3.25	2	
20T	2009/10	3								72	90	2	45.00	2-19	0	0	7.50	0	
DHANIRAM, Sudesh (United States of America to United Arab Emirates) b Port Mourant, Berbice, Guyana 14.1.1967 RHB OB																			
FC	1986/87	46	72	2	2040	131	29.14	4	10	398	243	4	60.75	2-55	0	0	3.66	22	
Lim	1986/87	37	35	1	667	63*	19.61	0	2	233	175	8	21.87	3-29	0	0	4.50	7	
20T	2009/10	3	3	1	6	4	3.00	0	0	72	62	1	62.00	1-12	0	0	5.16	1	
IMRAN Pervez AWAN (United States of America to United Arab Emirates) b Sialkot, Punjab, Pakistan 2.6.1979 RHB RMF																			
Lim	2005	8	5	0	48	30	9.60	0	0	300	303	10	30.30	4-46	1	0	6.06	3	
20T	2009/10	1								18	25	0					8.33	0	
MARSHALL, Rashard Antonio (United States of America to United Arab Emirates) b 30.8.1982 RHB																			
20T	2009/10	3	2	0	19	19	9.50	0	0									0	
MASSIAH, Steven J (United States of America to United Arab Emirates) b Georgetown, Guyana 21.6.1979 RHB OB																			
FC	2004	2	4	0	160	104	40.00	1	0	66	35	1	35.00	1-10	0	0	3.18	1	
Int	2004	2	2	0	23	23	11.50	0	0									0	
Lim	2000/01	17	17	4	503	108*	38.69	1	3	157	163	8	20.37	2-20	0	0	6.22	4	
20T	2009/10	3	3	2	8	5*	8.00	0	0									0	
NADKARNI, Sushilkumar Suhas (United States of America to United Arab Emirates) b India 31.5.1976 LHB OB																			
FC	1995/96	3	3	0	47	43	15.66	0	0									1	
Lim	1995/96	3	3	0	91	53	30.33	0	1									0	
20T	2009/10	2	2	0	13	12	6.50	0	0									2	
THYAGARAJAN, Aditya (United States of America to United Arab Emirates) b Bangalore, Karnataka, India 7.11.1978 RHB LB																			
Lim	2008/09	3	3	0	58	42	19.33	0	0	78	58	5	11.60	3-30	0	0	4.46	1	
20T	2009/10	2	2	1	86	72*	86.00	0	1									1	
USMAN SHUJA (United States of America to United Arab Emirates) b Karachi, Sind, Pakistan 29.11.1978 RHB RFM																			
20T	2009/10	2								36	43	1	43.00	1-26	0	0	7.16	1	
VERMA, Saurabh (United States of America to United Arab Emirates) b Bhopal, Madhya Pradesh, India 4.11.1981 RHB LBG																			
20T	2009/10	2								12	23	1	23.00	1-23	0	0	11.50	0	
WRIGHT, Carl Da Costa (United States of America to United Arab Emirates) b St Elizabeth, Jamaica 17.9.1977 RHB																			
FC	1997/98	11	21	1	379	95*	18.95	0	2									14	
Lim	2008/09	3	3	0	112	90	37.33	0	1	36	37	0					6.16	0	
20T	2009/10	3	3	0	92	62	30.66	0	1									3	1

NEW ZEALAND TO UNITED STATES OF AMERICA 2010

Cmp	Debut	M	I	NO	Runs	HS	Avge	100	50	Balls	Runs	Wkts	Avge	BB	5i	10m	RpO	ct	st
GUPTILL, M.J.																			
I20T		1	1	0	10	10	10.00	0	0									0	
20T		1	1	0	10	10	10.00	0	0									0	
HOPKINS, G.J.																			
I20T		1	1	0	1	1	1.00	0	0									0	1
20T		1	1	0	1	1	1.00	0	0									0	1
McCULLUM, B.B.																			
I20T		2	2	0	19	18	9.50	0	0									3	
20T		2	2	0	19	18	9.50	0	0									3	
McCULLUM, N.L.																			
I20T		2	2	1	45	36*	45.00	0	0	36	34	2	17.00	2-15	0	0	5.66	1	
20T		2	2	1	45	36*	45.00	0	0	36	34	2	17.00	2-15	0	0	5.66	1	

Cmp	Debut	M	I	NO	Runs	HS	Avge	100	50	Balls	Runs	Wkts	Avge	BB	5i	10m	RpO	ct	st
McKAY, A.J.																			
I20T		2	1	0	0	0	0.00	0	0	34	31	2	15.50	2-20	0	0	5.47	0	
20T		2	1	0	0	0	0.00	0	0	34	31	2	15.50	2-20	0	0	5.47	0	
MILLS, K.D.																			
I20T		2	2	1	2	2*	2.00	0	0	42	35	2	17.50	2-17	0	0	5.00	0	
20T		2	2	1	2	2*	2.00	0	0	42	35	2	17.50	2-17	0	0	5.00	0	
NICOL, R.J.																			
I20T		2	2	0	10	10	5.00	0	0	9	9	0					6.00	1	
20T		2	2	0	10	10	5.00	0	0	9	9	0					6.00	1	
ORAM, J.D.P.																			
I20T		1	1	0	3	3	3.00	0	0	12	3	1	3.00	1-3	0	0	1.50	0	
20T		1	1	0	3	3	3.00	0	0	12	3	1	3.00	1-3	0	0	1.50	0	
REDMOND, A.J.																			
I20T		2	2	0	9	8	4.50	0	0									1	
20T		2	2	0	9	8	4.50	0	0									1	
SOUTHEE, T.G.																			
I20T		2	1	0	4	4	4.00	0	0	24	25	0					6.25	0	
20T		2	1	0	4	4	4.00	0	0	24	25	0					6.25	0	
STYRIS, S.B.																			
I20T		1	1	0	10	10	10.00	0	0	18	10	3	3.33	3-10	0	0	3.33	1	
20T		1	1	0	10	10	10.00	0	0	18	10	3	3.33	3-10	0	0	3.33	1	
TAYLOR, L.R.P.L.																			
I20T		2	2	0	32	27	16.00	0	0									0	
20T		2	2	0	32	27	16.00	0	0									0	
VETTORI, D.L.																			
I20T		2	2	1	48	27	48.00	0	0	36	21	1	21.00	1-11	0	0	3.50	0	
20T		2	2	1	48	27	48.00	0	0	36	21	1	21.00	1-11	0	0	3.50	0	

SRI LANKA TO UNITED STATES OF AMERICA 2010

Cmp	Debut	M	I	NO	Runs	HS	Avge	100	50	Balls	Runs	Wkts	Avge	BB	5i	10m	RpO	ct	st
CHANDIMAL, L.D.																			
I20T		1																0	
20T		1																0	
DILSHAN, T.M.																			
I20T		2	2	1	39	33*	39.00	0	0	6	4	0					4.00	0	
20T		2	2	1	39	33*	39.00	0	0	6	4	0					4.00	0	
JAYASINGHE, C.U.																			
I20T		1	1	1	9	9*		0	0									0	
20T		1	1	1	9	9*		0	0									0	
JAYASURIYA, S.T.																			
I20T		1								6	12	0					12.00	0	
20T		1								6	12	0					12.00	0	
JAYAWARDENE, D.P.M.D.																			
I20T		2	2	0	17	17	8.50	0	0									1	
20T		2	2	0	17	17	8.50	0	0									1	
KALUHALAMULLA, H.K.S.R.																			
I20T		1	1	0	6	6	6.00	0	0	12	12	1	12.00	1-12	0	0	6.00	0	
20T		1	1	0	6	6	6.00	0	0	12	12	1	12.00	1-12	0	0	6.00	0	
KAPUGEDERA, C.K.																			
I20T		2	1	0	7	7	7.00	0	0									1	
20T		2	1	0	7	7	7.00	0	0									1	
KULASEKARA, K.M.D.N.																			
I20T		2	1	0	6	6	6.00	0	0	36	26	4	6.50	3-4	0	0	4.33	0	
20T		2	1	0	6	6	6.00	0	0	36	26	4	6.50	3-4	0	0	4.33	0	
MALINGA, S.L.																			
I20T		2	1	0	0	0	0.00	0	0	39	37	4	9.25	3-12	0	0	5.69	1	
20T		2	1	0	0	0	0.00	0	0	39	37	4	9.25	3-12	0	0	5.69	1	
MATHEWS, A.D.																			
I20T		2	2	1	27	27	27.00	0	0	42	39	2	19.50	1-17	0	0	5.57	1	
20T		2	2	1	27	27	27.00	0	0	42	39	2	19.50	1-17	0	0	5.57	1	
MENDIS, B.A.W.																			
I20T		2	1	0	2	2	2.00	0	0	48	37	4	9.25	2-18	0	0	4.62	0	
20T		2	1	0	2	2	2.00	0	0	48	37	4	9.25	2-18	0	0	4.62	0	
PERERA, N.L.T.C.																			
I20T		2	2	0	27	24	13.50	0	0	36	33	0					5.50	0	
20T		2	2	0	27	24	13.50	0	0	36	33	0					5.50	0	
SANGAKKARA, K.C.																			
I20T		2	2	0	22	17	11.00	0	0									1	
20T		2	2	0	22	17	11.00	0	0									1	

WEST INDIES

Regional Four-Day Competition winners 2009/10 (first-class): Jamaica
West Indies Cricket Board Cup 2009/10 (first-class): Trinidad and Tobago
Caribbean T20 2010 (twenty20): Guyana

2009/10 and 2010 AND CAREER RECORDS FOR WEST INDIAN PLAYERS

Cmp	*Debut*	*M*	*I*	*NO*	*Runs*	*HS*	*Avge*	*100*	*50*	*Balls*	*Runs*	*Wkts*	*Avge*	*BB*	*5i*	*10m*	*RpO*	*ct*	*st*
ATHANAZE, Justin Jason (Leeward Islands) b Antigua 29.1.1988 RHB OB																			
FC		5	10	0	113	31	11.30	0	0	726	253	6	42.16	2-40	0	0	2.09	6	
Lim		2	1	0	0	0	0.00	0	0	60	36	3	12.00	3-36	0	0	3.60	0	
20T		2	2	1	18	10	18.00	0	0	48	47	1	47.00	1-28	0	0	5.87	0	
FC	2006/07	12	19	1	233	35	12.94	0	0	1821	791	17	46.52	3-68	0	0	2.60	12	
Lim	2006/07	12	10	4	178	43*	29.66	0	0	504	329	12	27.41	3-36	0	0	3.91	2	
20T	2007/08	4	4	1	39	21	13.00	0	0	96	89	3	29.66	2-30	0	0	5.56	1	
AUSTIN, Ryan Anthony (Combined Campuses and Colleges) b Arima, Trinidad 15.11.1981 RHB OB																			
FC		6	10	2	83	24	10.37	0	0	1273	529	27	19.59	7-42	2	1	2.49	2	
Lim		3	1	1	5	5*		0	0	114	62	3	20.66	2-42	0	0	3.26	1	
20T		1								24	31	2	15.50	2-31	0	0	7.75	1	
Test	2009	2	4	0	39	19	9.75	0	0	326	155	3	51.66	1-29	0	0	2.85	3	
FC	2000/01	48	73	12	691	56*	11.32	0	1	9891	4615	182	25.35	7-42	10	1	2.80	20	
BABB, Larry La-Vere (Barbados) b Harrison Tenantry, St Lucy, Barbados 6.5.1983 RHB LMF																			
20T		2	1	1	12	12*		0	0	10	17	2	8.50	2-17	0	0	10.20	0	
BADREE, Samuel (Trinidad and Tobago, Trinidad and Tobago to India) b Barrackpore, Trinidad 8.3.1981 RHB LB																			
Lim		3	3	1	24	22	12.00	0	0	141	62	1	62.00	1-26	0	0	2.63	0	
20T		2								30	18	0					3.60	1	
FC	2001/02	12	19	1	323	55	17.94	0	1	1256	525	14	37.50	2-9	0	0	2.50	7	
Lim	2002/03	22	17	3	138	29	9.85	0	0	985	625	23	27.17	3-14	0	0	3.80	10	
20T	2006	17	8	5	21	7*	7.00	0	0	316	256	15	17.06	3-6	0	0	4.86	5	
BAKER, Lionel Sionne (Leeward Islands, West Indies XI, West Indies A to Bangladesh, West Indies A to England) b Montserrat 6.9.1984 LHB RFM																			
FC		5	9	3	73	32	12.16	0	0	740	347	23	15.08	8-31	2	1	2.81	5	
Lim		2	1	1	2	2*		0	0	60	32	2	16.00	2-32	0	0	3.20	0	
20T		4	2	1	1	1	1.00	0	0	50	55	3	18.33	2-9	0	0	6.60	0	
Test	2008/09	4	6	4	23	17	11.50	0	0	660	395	5	79.00	2-39	0	0	3.59	1	
FC	2002/03	29	41	14	268	32	9.92	0	0	4051	2344	78	30.05	8-31	3	1	3.47	11	
Int	2008/09	10	4	2	13	11*	6.50	0	0	426	355	11	32.27	3-47	0	0	5.00	1	
Lim	2003/04	30	14	7	81	18*	11.57	0	0	1349	1187	33	35.96	4-32	1	0	5.27	9	
I20T	2008/09	3								48	58	2	29.00	1-12	0	0	7.25	0	
20T	2006	10	5	2	31	17	10.33	0	0	170	201	8	25.12	2-8	0	0	7.09	1	
BANKS, Omari Ahmed Clemente (Leeward Islands, Somerset to India) b Road Bay, Anguilla 17.7.1982 RHB OB																			
FC		6	11	0	319	60	29.00	0	2	926	467	24	19.45	7-41	2	1	3.02	3	
20T		1	1	0	3	3	3.00	0	0	6	19	0					19.00	0	
Test	2002/03	10	16	4	318	50*	26.50	0	1	2401	1367	28	48.82	4-87	0	0	3.41	6	
FC	2000/01	78	122	18	2717	108	26.12	2	16	14321	7444	203	36.66	7-41	8	2	3.11	43	
Int	2002/03	5	5	0	83	33	16.60	0	0	270	189	7	27.00	2-24	0	0	4.20	0	
Lim	2001/02	71	58	17	1187	77*	28.95	0	9	3037	2241	81	27.66	4-23	2	0	4.42	16	
20T	2007/08	9	7	2	153	50*	30.60	0	1	144	217	6	36.16	1-14	0	0	9.04	1	
BARATH, Adrian Boris (Trinidad and Tobago, West Indies, Kings XI Punjab, Trinidad and Tobago to India, West Indies to Australia) b Chaguanas, Trinidad 14.4.1990 RHB OB																			
FC		1	2	0	138	79	69.00	0	2									2	
Int		5	5	0	131	50	26.20	0	1									1	
Lim		8	8	0	178	50	22.25	0	1	6	0	0					0.00	2	
I20T		1	1	0	8	8	8.00	0	0									1	
20T		6	6	2	181	66*	45.25	0	2									1	
Test	2009/10	2	4	0	139	104	34.75	1	0	6	3	0					3.00	2	
FC	2006/07	26	46	3	1963	192	45.65	6	10	12	3	0					1.50	17	
Lim	2006/07	17	17	0	463	72	27.23	0	3	6	0	0					0.00	5	
20T	2009/10	12	12	3	329	66*	36.55	0	3									2	
BARNWELL, Christopher Dion (Guyana) b Mackenzie, Linden, Demerara, Guyana 6.1.1987 RHB RMF																			
FC		2	4	0	52	27	13.00	0	0	234	142	4	35.50	2-83	0	0	3.64	0	
Lim		4	3	0	5	5	1.66	0	0	180	171	2	85.50	2-42	0	0	5.70	0	
20T		4	4	0	62	27	15.50	0	0	90	113	4	28.25	2-26	0	0	7.53	3	
FC	2008/09	11	20	0	446	57	22.30	0	2	1218	734	18	40.77	5-77	1	0	3.61	10	

Cmp	Debut	M	I	NO	Runs	HS	Avge	100	50	Balls	Runs	Wkts	Avge	BB	5i	10m	RpO	ct	st
Lim	2008/09	8	7	0	94	51	13.42	0	1	252	258	5	51.60	3-21	0	0	6.14	4	
20T	2007/08	7	6	0	114	27	19.00	0	0	120	146	6	24.33	2-19	0	0	7.30	3	
BASCOMBE, Miles Cameron (Combined Campuses and Colleges, Windward Islands) b St Vincent 12.1.1986 RHB																			
FC		2	3	0	20	9	6.66	0	0	12	17	0					8.50	1	
Lim		1	1	0	2	2	2.00	0	0									0	
20T		2	2	0	84	48	42.00	0	0									0	
FC	2006/07	16	29	1	607	54	21.67	0	2	15	24	0					9.60	6	
Lim	2006/07	12	11	0	78	27	7.09	0	0									1	
20T	2006	6	6	0	146	48	24.33	0	0									0	
BAUGH, Carlton Seymour (Jamaica) b Kingston, Jamaica 23.6.1982 RHB LBG WK																			
FC		7	10	1	315	124	35.00	1	1									11	1
Lim		4	3	1	46	24*	23.00	0	0									2	1
20T		7	5	0	96	40	19.20	0	0									1	6
Test	2002/03	5	10	0	196	68	19.60	0	1									4	1
FC	2000/01	74	125	16	3936	158*	36.11	11	17									142	17
Int	2002/03	30	22	7	223	29	14.86	0	0									19	4
Lim	2002/03	71	52	13	770	71	19.74	0	2									64	15
I20T	2008/09	1	1	0	2	2	2.00	0	0									0	
20T	2006	14	10	2	141	40	17.62	0	0									6	8
BENN, Sulieman Jamaal (Barbados, West Indies, West Indies XI, West Indies to Australia) b Haynesville, St James, Barbados 22.7.1981 LHB SLA																			
Test		3	5	0	101	42	20.20	0	0	1060	460	15	30.66	6-81	2	0	2.60	1	
FC		5	8	0	170	54	21.25	0	1	1540	660	24	27.50	6-81	2	0	2.57	3	
Int		7	2	0	17	17	8.50	0	0	366	219	7	31.28	2-24	0	0	3.59	0	
Lim		10	5	1	83	39	20.75	0	0	498	345	9	38.33	2-24	0	0	4.15	3	
I20T		7	3	1	19	9	9.50	0	0	132	130	7	18.57	4-6	1	0	5.90	1	
20T		15	3	1	19	9	9.50	0	0	318	323	19	17.00	4-6	1	0	6.09	1	
Test	2007/08	15	25	2	352	42	15.30	0	0	4256	2046	50	40.92	6-81	3	0	2.88	7	
FC	1999/00	62	95	13	1645	79	20.06	0	7	14513	6646	208	31.95	6-81	8	0	2.74	41	
Int	2007/08	18	10	1	87	31	9.66	0	0	900	648	13	49.84	2-23	0	0	4.32	1	
Lim	2001/02	61	33	9	321	39	13.37	0	0	2940	1993	61	32.67	5-18	0	1	4.06	23	
I20T	2008	17	7	4	37	13*	12.33	0	0	354	414	15	27.60	4-6	1	0	7.01	7	
20T	2006	33	10	5	46	13*	9.20	0	0	707	719	40	17.97	4-6	1	0	6.10	10	
BENNETT, Jason Peterson (Combined Campuses and Colleges) b Mount Standfast, St James, Barbados 8.10.1982 RHB RFM																			
FC		4	6	2	32	9	8.00	0	0	315	202	10	20.20	5-86	1	0	3.84	0	
FC	2002/03	27	47	10	270	39	7.29	0	0	4306	2270	106	21.41	6-46	9	2	3.16	5	
Lim	2003	8	6	2	16	9	4.00	0	0	397	344	12	28.66	3-44	0	0	5.19	0	
BERNARD, David Eddison (Jamaica, West Indies, West Indies XI, West Indies to South Africa, West Indies A to England, West Indies A to Ireland) b Kingston, Jamaica 19.7.1981 RHB RMF																			
FC		6	8	0	260	102	32.50	1	1	736	341	15	22.73	6-40	1	0	2.78	6	
Int		6	3	2	18	13*	18.00	0	0	192	141	4	35.25	3-32	0	0	4.40	3	
Lim		10	6	3	96	52*	32.00	0	1	325	228	8	28.50	3-32	0	0	4.20	3	
20T		8	6	3	51	36*	17.00	0	0	161	143	8	17.87	3-13	0	0	5.32	4	
Test	2002/03	3	6	1	202	69	40.40	0	3	258	185	4	46.25	2-30	0	0	4.30	0	
FC	2000/01	82	137	10	3616	120	28.47	4	19	8479	4343	144	30.15	6-40	3	0	3.07	67	
Int	2002/03	20	12	2	141	38	14.10	0	0	624	526	14	37.57	3-32	0	0	5.05	7	
Lim	2000	60	42	5	765	66	20.67	0	3	1863	1419	41	34.60	3-17	0	0	4.57	16	
I20T	2009	1	1	1	1	1*		0	0	24	17	0					4.25	0	
20T	2007/08	12	10	5	60	36*	12.00	0	0	233	205	10	20.50	3-13	0	0	5.27	5	
BESS, Brandon Jeremy (Guyana, West Indies, West Indies A) b Rosignol, West Bank, Berbice, Guyana 13.12.1987 RHB RFM																			
Test		1	2	1	11	11*	11.00	0	0	78	92	1	92.00	1-65	0	0	7.07	0	
FC		7	11	4	61	20	8.71	0	0	774	585	15	39.00	4-107	0	0	4.53	3	
20T		1								24	24	1	24.00	1-24	0	0	6.00	1	
FC	2007/08	19	27	11	102	20	6.37	0	0	1956	1556	31	50.19	4-107	0	0	4.77	7	
Lim	2008/09	2	1	1	0	0*		0	0	54	50	2	25.00	1-20	0	0	5.55	0	
BEST, Tino la Bertram (Barbados, West Indies to South Africa, Yorkshire) b 3rd Avenue, Richmond Gap, St Michael, Barbados 26.8.1981 RHB RF																			
FC		5	8	1	106	28	15.14	0	0	672	477	17	28.05	6-65	2	0	4.25	2	
Lim		2	1	1	11	11*		0	0	84	75	1	75.00	1-44	0	0	5.35	0	
Test	2002/03	14	23	3	196	27	9.80	0	0	2187	1363	28	48.67	4-46	0	0	3.73	1	
FC	2001/02	81	107	19	1102	51	12.52	0	1	10923	6756	239	28.26	7-33	10	2	3.71	23	
Int	2004	12	8	3	52	24	10.40	0	0	545	477	13	36.69	4-35	1	0	5.25	3	
Lim	2002	43	25	13	144	24	12.00	0	0	1753	1507	52	28.98	4-35	2	0	5.15	13	
20T	2007/08	11	4	2	12	10*	6.00	0	0	230	289	7	41.28	2-26	0	0	7.53	4	
BISHOO, Devendra (Guyana) b New Amsterdam, Berbice, Guyana 6.11.1985 LHB LB																			
FC		6	11	3	43	18	5.37	0	0	1291	656	24	27.33	5-45	2	1	3.04	6	
Lim		4	1	1	10	10*		0	0	192	110	8	13.75	3-24	0	0	3.43	1	
20T		4	1	1	2	2*		0	0	96	82	10	8.20	3-23	0	0	5.12	1	
FC	2007/08	18	32	7	241	39	9.64	0	0	4096	2038	71	28.70	6-64	4	1	2.98	13	
BLACKWOOD, Jermaine (West Indies Under-19s) b St Elizabeth, Jamaica 20.11.1991 RHB OB																			
Lim		1	1	1	2	2*		0	0	48	38	1	38.00	1-38	0	0	4.75	0	

Cmp	Debut	M	I	NO	Runs	HS	Avge	100	50	Balls	Runs	Wkts	Avge	BB	5i	10m	RpO	ct	st
BOLAN, Nelson Amos (West Indies Under-19s) b Tortola, British Virgin Islands 29.11.1990 RHB RFM																			
Lim		1								18	20	1	20.00	1-20	0	0	6.66	0	
20T	2007/08	1																0	
BONNER, Nkruma Eljego (Jamaica) b St Catherine, Jamaica 23.1.1989 RHB LB																			
FC		2	4	0	16	8	4.00	0	0	78	28	2	14.00	2-28	0	0	2.15	0	
Lim	2007/08	2	2	0	17	10	8.50	0	0	42	24	1	24.00	1-24	0	0	3.42	0	
BOUCHER, Rashidi Hasani (Barbados) b Gibbons Boggs, Christchurch, Barbados 17.7.1990 RHB																			
Lim		1	1	0	2	2	2.00	0	0									0	
FC	2008/09	4	7	0	95	48	13.57	0	0									3	
Lim	2007/08	2	2	0	2	2	1.00	0	0									0	
BRATHWAITE, Kraigg Clairmonte (Barbados, West Indies A, West Indies Under-19s, West Indies A to England, West Indies A to Ireland) b Belfield, Black Rock, St Michael, Barbados 1.12.1992 RHB																			
FC		3	6	1	199	62	39.80	0	1									3	
Lim		1	1	0	48	48	48.00	0	0									0	
FC	2008/09	7	13	1	353	73	29.41	0	2	6	3	1	3.00	1-3	0	0	3.00	4	
Lim	2009/10	2	2	0	63	48	31.50	0	0									0	
BRATHWAITE, Ruel Marlon Ricardo (Combined Campuses and Colleges, Durham) b Bridgetown, St Michael, Barbados 6.9.1985 RHB RFM																			
20T		1	1	0	0	0	0.00	0	0	18	33	1	33.00	1-33	0	0	11.00	0	
FC	2006	13	14	4	144	76*	14.40	0	1	2163	1294	30	43.13	5-54	1	0	3.58	0	
Lim	2007	1								18	19	1	19.00	1-19	0	0	6.33	0	
BRAVO, Dwayne John (Trinidad and Tobago, West Indies, Essex, Mumbai Indians, Trinidad and Tobago to India, Victoria, West Indies to Australia) b Santa Cruz, Trinidad 7.10.1983 RHB RFM																			
Test		3	5	0	166	61	33.20	0	2	460	180	2	90.00	1-33	0	0	2.34	4	
FC		3	5	0	166	61	33.20	0	2	460	180	2	90.00	1-33	0	0	2.34	4	
Int		8	8	0	204	74	25.50	0	1	428	339	15	22.60	4-21	1	0	4.75	1	
Lim		11	11	0	248	74	22.54	0	1	601	464	24	19.33	6-46	1	1	4.63	2	
I20T		7	6	0	108	40	18.00	0	0	114	150	5	30.00	2-5	0	0	7.89	2	
20T		12	9	1	224	55	28.00	0	1	223	258	11	23.45	2-5	0	0	6.94	8	
Test	2004	37	68	1	2175	113	32.46	3	13	6164	3270	83	39.39	6-55	2	0	3.18	39	
FC	2001/02	94	173	7	5193	197	31.28	8	29	10461	5621	168	33.45	6-11	7	0	3.22	81	
Int	2003/04	107	87	16	1715	112*	24.15	1	5	4260	3721	129	28.84	4-19	4	0	5.24	44	
Lim	2002	144	121	20	2312	112*	22.89	1	7	5489	4677	172	27.19	6-46	6	1	5.11	60	
I20T	2005/06	22	20	5	344	66*	22.93	0	2	338	491	19	25.84	4-38	1	0	8.71	5	
20T	2005/06	74	64	15	1208	70*	24.65	0	8	1315	1811	70	25.87	4-23	2	0	8.26	32	
BRAVO, Darren Michael (Trinidad and Tobago, West Indies, West Indies XI, Trinidad and Tobago to India, West Indies A to Bangladesh, West Indies A to England) b Santa Cruz, Trinidad 6.2.1989 LHB LM																			
FC		1	2	0	78	42	39.00	0	0									2	
Int		6	6	2	179	74	44.75	0	1									2	
Lim		9	9	2	299	76	42.71	0	2									2	
I20T		1	1	0	0	0	0.00	0	0									0	
20T		6	5	0	98	65	19.60	0	1									2	
FC	2006/07	17	26	1	918	111	36.72	3	2	22	9	1	9.00	1-9	0	0	2.45	21	
Int	2009	10	8	2	219	74	36.50	0	1									3	
Lim	2006/07	29	26	4	961	107*	43.68	1	7									9	
20T	2008/09	11	10	1	190	65	21.11	0	1									4	
BROOKS, Sharmarh Shaqad Joshua (Barbados) b St John's Land, Whitehall, St Michael, Barbados 1.10.1988 RHB LB																			
FC		3	5	2	112	33	37.33	0	0	144	96	2	48.00	1-22	0	0	4.00	1	
FC	2006/07	10	17	3	326	39	23.28	0	0	276	211	2	105.50	1-22	0	0	4.58	7	
Lim	2006/07	5	3	0	63	36	21.00	0	0	36	30	2	15.00	2-30	0	0	5.00	1	
BROWN, Bevon Mark (Jamaica) b Kingston, Jamaica 2.9.1979 RHB OB																			
FC		3	5	1	39	16	9.75	0	0	384	143	5	28.60	3-28	0	0	2.23	0	
Lim		2								102	65	3	21.66	2-35	0	0	3.82	0	
20T		2	1	0	10	10	10.00	0	0	48	46	5	9.20	3-26	0	0	5.75	0	
FC	2004/05	10	15	2	116	30*	8.92	0	0	1519	564	21	26.85	5-59	1	0	2.22	2	
Lim	2004/05	8	4	1	69	37*	23.00	0	0	450	269	14	19.21	4-41	1	0	3.58	1	
BROWN, Odean Vernon (Jamaica, West Indies A to Bangladesh, West Indies A to England) b Westmoreland, Jamaica 8.2.1982 RHB LB																			
FC		6	7	3	68	33	17.00	0	0	1492	668	30	22.26	8-54	3	1	2.68	3	
Lim		4	1	1	3	3*		0	0	174	107	6	17.83	4-33	1	0	3.69	1	
20T		3	1	0	20	20	20.00	0	0	66	50	3	16.66	1-14	0	0	4.54	1	
FC	2003/04	38	51	15	361	33	10.02	0	0	7054	3335	148	22.53	8-54	10	3	2.83	23	
Lim	2004/05	10	4	2	37	17	18.50	0	0	366	263	7	37.57	4-33	1	0	4.31	3	
20T	2006	6	1	0	20	20	20.00	0	0	126	96	6	16.00	2-16	0	0	4.57	1	
BROWNE, Daynason Junior (Leeward Islands) b Nevis 6.5.1986 RHB RM																			
FC		1	2	0	7	6	3.50	0	0	6	11	0					11.00	2	
20T	2006	3	3	0	73	26	24.33	0	0	18	44	0					14.66	2	
BROWNE, Patrick Anderson (Barbados) b Bayfield, St Philip, Barbados 26.1.1982 RHB WK																			
FC		4	7	1	58	25	9.66	0	0									20	1
FC	2001/02	62	106	6	2131	83	21.31	0	13	6	0	0					0.00	163	6
Int	2007/08	5	5	1	134	49*	33.50	0	0									2	

Cmp	Debut	M	I	NO	Runs	HS	Avge	100	50	Balls	Runs	Wkts	Avge	BB	5i	10m	RpO	ct	st
Lim	2005/06	26	21	1	402	52	20.10	0	1									32	5
20T	2007/08	2	2	0	62	55	31.00	0	1									3	1
BUTLER, Deighton Kelvin (Windward Islands) b South Rivers, St Vincent 17.7.1974 LHB LFM																			
FC		3	6	3	70	24*	23.33	0	0	384	213	4	53.25	1-28	0	0	3.32	5	
Lim		1	1	0	15	15	15.00	0	0	36	14	0					2.33	0	
20T		2	2	2	12	12*		0	0	30	43	0					8.60	1	
FC	2000	64	108	26	1225	66	14.93	0	4	9676	4612	176	26.20	5-29	2	0	2.86	42	
Int	2005	5	4	3	25	13*	25.00	0	0	246	188	3	62.66	1-25	0	0	4.58	0	
Lim	2001/02	32	23	8	135	15*	9.00	0	0	1326	946	27	35.03	4-30	1	0	4.28	9	
I20T	2005/06	1								18	22	0					7.33	1	
20T	2005/06	7	3	3	45	33*		0	0	132	154	2	77.00	1-21	0	0	7.00	2	
CAMPBELL, Jon-Ross Charles (Jamaica) b Kingston, Jamaica 9.7.1990 RHB OB																			
FC		1	2	0	5	5	2.50	0	0									0	
20T		2	2	0	34	28	17.00	0	0									1	
CARIAH, Yannic (West Indies Under-19s) b Trinidad 21.6.1992 LHB LB																			
Lim		2	1	0	1	1	1.00	0	0	34	23	1	23.00	1-23	0	0	4.05	0	
CARTER, Jonathan Lyndon (Barbados) b Belleplaine, Barbados 16.11.1987 LHB RM																			
Lim		3	3	0	51	27	17.00	0	0	30	39	0					7.80	0	
20T		4	4	1	156	57*	52.00	0	2									5	
FC	2007/08	8	12	1	213	52	19.36	0	1	78	38	0					2.92	6	
Lim	2007/08	12	11	1	241	71	24.10	0	1	60	58	0					5.80	3	
20T	2007/08	7	7	1	248	61	41.33	0	3									6	
CATLIN, Khismar (Combined Campuses and Colleges) b Shop Hill, St Thomas, Barbados 15.10.1985 RHB RFM																			
FC		3	4	0	25	25	6.25	0	0	270	178	5	35.60	3-47	0	0	3.95	0	
Lim		1	1	0	1	1	1.00	0	0	44	49	0					6.68	0	
FC	2008/09	10	16	2	90	40	6.42	0	0	1067	670	26	25.76	4-56	0	0	3.76	2	
Lim	2007/08	5	5	0	2	1	0.40	0	0	212	197	7	28.14	4-48	1	0	5.57	1	
CHANDERPAUL, Shivnarine (Guyana, West Indies, West Indies XI, Lancashire, West Indies to Australia) b Unity Village, East Coast, Demerara, Guyana 16.8.1974 LHB LB																			
Test		3	5	1	300	166	75.00	1	1									2	
FC		5	9	3	537	166	89.50	2	2									3	
Int		9	9	0	398	101	44.22	1	4									4	
Lim		13	13	2	508	101	46.18	1	5									6	
I20T		7	7	1	136	29	22.66	0	0									1	
20T		11	11	1	211	64	21.10	0	1									3	
Test	1993/94	126	215	33	8969	203*	49.28	22	54	1680	845	8	105.62	1-2	0	0	3.01	52	
FC	1991/92	261	424	75	19007	303*	54.46	55	97	4634	2453	56	43.80	4-48	0	0	3.17	146	
Int	1994/95	261	245	38	8648	150	41.77	11	59	740	636	14	45.42	3-18	0	0	5.15	73	
Lim	1991/92	374	348	60	12110	150	42.04	12	88	1681	1388	56	24.78	4-22	2	0	4.95	109	
I20T	2005/06	22	22	5	343	41	20.17	0	0									7	
20T	2005/06	35	34	5	534	64	18.41	0	1									13	
CHANDRIKA, Rajindra (Guyana) b Enterprise, East Coast, Demerara, Guyana 8.8.1989 RHB OB																			
FC		6	12	1	280	65	25.45	0	1									2	
Lim	2007/08	5	5	0	94	39	18.80	0	0									2	
CHARLES, Johnson (Windward Islands) b St Lucia 14.1.1989 RHB																			
20T		2	2	0	70	55	35.00	0	1									1	
FC	2008/09	8	16	1	292	55	19.46	0	1	48	41	1	41.00	1-27	0	0	5.12	14	
Lim	2008/09	4	4	0	66	27	16.50	0	0									2	1
20T	2007/08	4	4	0	93	55	23.25	0	1									1	
CHARLES, Nikolai Gabriel Ramon (Barbados) b Wildey, St Michael, Barbados 1.10.1986 RHB LB																			
FC		4	7	3	67	20	16.75	0	0	555	325	10	32.50	4-46	0	0	3.51	2	
Lim		1	1	0	0	0	0.00	0	0	60	37	2	18.50	2-37	0	0	3.70	0	
FC	2008/09	11	18	6	179	54*	14.91	0	1	1533	925	29	31.89	5-99	1	0	3.62	3	
Lim	2008/09	4	4	2	5	4*	2.50	0	0	168	124	8	15.50	4-39	1	0	4.42	0	
CHATTERGOON, Sewnarine (Guyana) b Fyrish, West Bank, Berbice, Guyana 3.4.1981 LHB LB																			
FC		6	12	0	213	73	17.75	0	1	172	44	2	22.00	2-35	0	0	1.53	5	
Lim		4	4	0	31	13	7.75	0	0									1	
20T		4	4	0	80	36	20.00	0	0									1	
Test	2007/08	4	7	0	127	46	18.14	0	0									4	
FC	2000	69	118	3	3692	143	32.10	5	21	617	256	10	25.60	4-9	0	0	2.48	51	
Int	2006	18	17	2	370	54*	24.66	0	2	80	48	1	48.00	1-1	0	0	3.60	6	
Lim	2001/02	65	64	4	1660	119	27.66	2	8	297	198	9	22.00	2-17	0	0	4.00	15	
20T	2007/08	7	7	1	134	36	22.33	0	0									2	
CHRISTIAN, Derwin O'Neil (Guyana) b Kilen, Pouderoyen, Guyana 9.5.1983 RHB WK																			
FC		6	10	0	205	45	20.50	0	0									13	3
20T		4	3	2	19	9*	19.00	0	0									0	
FC	2005/06	34	54	4	907	113	18.14	1	2									62	12
Lim	2004/05	28	23	4	291	39	15.31	0	0									38	5
20T	2007/08	7	5	3	40	13*	20.00	0	0									3	1

Cmp	Debut	M	I	NO	Runs	HS	Avge	100	50	Balls	Runs	Wkts	Avge	BB	5i	10m	RpO	ct	st
COLLINS, Pedro Tyrone (Barbados, Middlesex, Middlesex to Netherlands) b Boscobelle, St Peter, Barbados 12.8.1976 RHB LFM																			
FC		6	7	4	34	17	11.33	0	0	1050	456	26	17.53	5-32	2	0	2.60	1	
Test	1998/99	32	47	7	235	24	5.87	0	0	6964	3671	106	34.63	6-53	3	0	3.16	7	
FC	1996/97	141	178	51	837	25	6.59	0	0	24193	12523	478	26.19	6-24	13	0	3.10	30	
Int	1999/00	30	12	5	30	10*	4.28	0	0	1577	1212	39	31.07	5-43	0	1	4.61	8	
Lim	1997/98	98	39	12	166	55*	6.14	0	1	4717	3444	149	23.11	7-11	3	2	4.38	17	
20T	2006	29	5	3	3	1*	1.50	0	0	598	777	26	29.88	3-13	0	0	7.79	3	
COOPER, Kevon (Trinidad and Tobago) b Trinidad 2.2.1989 RHB RM																			
20T		2								36	38	3	12.66	2-8	0	0	6.33	0	
20T	2008/09	3	1	0	6	6	6.00	0	0	48	56	3	18.66	2-8	0	0	7.00	0	
CORBIN, Kyle Anthony McDonald (Combined Campuses and Colleges) b Newbury, St George, Barbados 15.5.1990 RHB																			
FC		4	8	0	239	74	29.87	0	1									1	
FC	2008/09	11	22	1	578	74	27.52	0	3									8	
CORNWALL, Wilden Winston (Leeward Islands) b Liberta, Antigua 29.4.1973 RHB RM																			
FC		4	7	0	147	46	21.00	0	0	654	246	14	17.57	5-27	1	0	2.25	1	
Lim		2	1	0	22	22	22.00	0	0	25	14	0					3.36	1	
20T		2	2	0	22	22	11.00	0	0	36	54	1	54.00	1-35	0	0	9.00	1	
FC	1998/99	53	84	2	1959	111	23.89	3	7	6168	3250	106	30.66	6-53	4	0	3.16	29	
Lim	1998/99	49	47	2	1026	126	22.80	2	5	1499	1191	46	25.89	5-36	3	1	4.76	11	
20T	2007/08	4	4	0	52	30	13.00	0	0	42	66	1	66.00	1-35	0	0	9.42	2	
CRANDON, Esuan Asqui (Guyana) b Rose Hall, Berbice, Guyana 17.12.1981 LHB RF																			
FC		5	7	2	164	51*	32.80	0	1	807	393	15	26.20	5-39	1	0	2.92	2	
Lim		4	2	1	17	17*	17.00	0	0	198	120	3	40.00	2-34	0	0	3.63	2	
20T		4	2	0	36	30	18.00	0	0	78	90	1	90.00	1-16	0	0	6.92	2	
FC	2000/01	36	52	8	693	51*	15.75	0	1	5098	2757	87	31.68	7-125	3	0	3.24	11	
Lim	2003/04	25	14	3	110	31*	10.00	0	0	1001	693	24	28.87	3-28	0	0	4.15	6	
20T	2006	11	7	1	126	71	21.00	0	1	216	246	7	35.14	2-20	0	0	6.83	4	
CRANDON, Royston Tycho (Guyana, West Indies to South Africa) b Courtland, Berbice, Guyana 31.5.1983 RHB OB																			
FC		4	7	0	157	94	22.42	0	1	288	122	1	122.00	1-29	0	0	2.54	2	
Lim		4	2	1	70	46	70.00	0	0	227	192	9	21.33	4-25	1	0	5.07	1	
20T		4	4	1	32	15	10.66	0	0	77	122	5	24.40	4-37	1	0	9.50	3	
FC	2006/07	17	32	3	830	136*	28.62	1	5	744	378	8	47.25	3-39	0	0	3.04	6	
Int	2009/10	1	1	0	5	5	5.00	0	0									0	
Lim	2006/07	19	16	1	373	101	24.86	1	1	749	533	20	26.65	4-25	1	0	4.27	4	
20T	2007/08	7	6	1	73	35	14.60	0	0	119	187	9	20.77	4-33	2	0	9.42	4	
CRUICKSHANK, Daron Alfred (Trinidad and Tobago) b Port of Spain, Trinidad 17.6.1988 RHB RM																			
FC		1	2	0	51	35	25.50	0	0	54	45	0					5.00	0	
FC	2008/09	2	4	1	84	35	28.00	0	0	84	58	0					4.14	2	
20T	2008/09	1	1	0	6	6	6.00	0	0									0	
CURRENCY, Romel Kwesi (Combined Campuses and Colleges) b Mesopotamia, St Vincent 7.5.1982 RHB OB																			
FC		4	8	1	195	80	27.85	0	1									3	
Lim		3	3	1	29	14	14.50	0	0	60	37	2	18.50	2-30	0	0	3.70	0	
20T		2	2	0	42	34	21.00	0	0									1	
FC	2000	43	80	4	1708	121*	22.47	1	6	227	105	3	35.00	2-22	0	0	2.77	24	
Lim	2000/01	27	26	4	824	102*	37.45	1	6	126	105	7	15.00	3-20	0	0	5.00	9	
20T	2006	6	6	0	114	34	19.00	0	0	6	18	0					18.00	2	
CUSH, Lennox Joseph (Guyana, United States of America to United Arab Emirates) b Georgetown, Demerara, Guyana 12.12.1974 RHB OB																			
20T		4	1	0	2	2	2.00	0	0	90	137	11	12.45	4-25	2	0	9.13	1	
FC	1995/96	38	63	3	1249	154	20.81	2	2	2640	1100	26	42.30	4-57	0	0	2.50	12	
Lim	1998/99	28	27	4	488	70	21.21	0	2	1209	775	25	31.00	4-33	2	0	3.84	7	
20T	2006	15	10	1	122	49	13.55	0	0	348	381	23	16.56	4-25	2	0	6.56	2	
DAWES, Jason O'Brian (Jamaica) b Westmoreland, Jamaica 27.12.1988 RHB RF																			
FC		3	5	3	16	9*	8.00	0	0	180	114	3	38.00	1-20	0	0	3.80	1	
FC	2008/09	4	7	5	17	9*	8.50	0	0	312	181	5	36.20	2-40	0	0	3.48	1	
Lim	2007/08	2	2	1	2	2*	2.00	0	0	60	49	5	9.80	3-42	0	0	4.90	0	
DEFREITAS, Bront Arson (Leeward Islands) b St Vincent 12.11.1978 RHB RFM																			
FC		2	3	1	4	4*	2.00	0	0	192	121	4	30.25	2-28	0	0	3.78	0	
FC	2007/08	9	14	5	62	19	6.88	0	0	771	566	18	31.44	5-88	1	0	4.40	2	
Lim	2002/03	2	2	0	6	6	3.00	0	0	84	91	1	91.00	1-70	0	0	6.50	0	
20T	2006	2	2	0	10	7	5.00	0	0	45	66	3	22.00	2-40	0	0	8.80	0	
DEONARINE, Narsingh (Guyana, West Indies, West Indies XI, West Indies to Australia) b Chesney Estate, Albion, Berbice, Guyana 16.8.1983 LHB OB																			
Test		3	5	0	163	65	32.60	0	1	18	20	0					6.66	1	
FC		5	9	1	347	104*	43.37	1	1	425	182	6	30.33	3-41	0	0	2.56	2	
Int		10	10	3	312	65*	44.57	0	3	120	100	1	100.00	1-18	0	0	5.00	2	
Lim		14	14	4	498	102*	49.80	1	4	282	198	3	66.00	1-15	0	0	4.21	3	
I20T		5	4	0	13	10	3.25	0	0	12	15	0					7.50	0	
20T		13	11	1	136	40	13.60	0	0	126	152	5	30.40	4-14	1	0	7.23	1	
Test	2004/05	8	13	1	370	82	30.83	0	2	503	246	4	61.50	2-74	0	0	2.93	5	

Cmp	Debut	M	I	NO	Runs	HS	Avge	100	50	Balls	Runs	Wkts	Avge	BB	5i	10m	RpO	ct	st
FC	1999/00	83	143	18	4724	198	37.79	7	30	6235	2946	86	34.25	5-94	1	0	2.83	52	
Int	2005	20	19	3	510	65*	31.87	0	4	321	312	6	52.00	2-18	0	0	5.83	6	
Lim	1999/00	79	75	9	1713	102*	25.95	1	12	1558	1282	29	44.20	2-18	0	0	4.93	25	
I20T	2009/10	7	6	1	49	36*	9.80	0	0	36	50	0					8.33	0	
20T	2006	20	17	5	240	40	20.00	0	0	252	307	13	23.61	4-14	1	0	7.31	4	
DEWAR, Akeem Mark Anthony (Jamaica, West Indies Under-19s) b Kingston, Jamaica 30.8.1991 RHB LB																			
FC		1	2	0	9	9	4.50	0	0	138	81	4	20.25	4-81	0	0	3.52	2	
Lim		1	1	0	0	0	0.00	0	0	48	25	3	8.33	3-25	0	0	3.12	1	
DOWLIN, Travis Montague (Guyana, West Indies, West Indies A, West Indies to Australia, West Indies to South Africa, West Indies A to Bangladesh) b Guyhock Gardens, Georgetown, Demerara, Guyana 24.2.1977 RHB OB																			
Test		2	3	0	15	10	5.00	0	0	6	3	0					3.00	1	
FC		5	9	0	215	84	23.88	0	1	6	3	0					3.00	5	
Lim		4	4	0	100	41	25.00	0	0									3	
20T		6	6	1	183	60	36.60	0	2									2	
Test	2009	6	11	0	343	95	31.18	0	3	6	3	0					3.00	5	
FC	1996/97	85	143	10	4013	176*	30.17	4	25	966	402	15	26.80	4-59	0	0	2.49	77	
Int	2009	11	11	2	228	100*	25.33	1	1									2	
Lim	1999/00	54	49	3	1132	119	24.60	2	5	372	282	3	94.00	1-25	0	0	4.54	16	
I20T	2009	2	2	1	68	37*	68.00	0	0									0	
20T	2006	16	16	4	529	80*	44.08	0	5									3	
DOWRICH, Shane Omari (Barbados, West Indies A, West Indies Under-19s) b West Terrace, Gardens, St James, Barbados 30.10.1991 RHB WK																			
FC		3	5	1	85	33*	21.25	0	0									12	
Lim		2	1	0	6	6	6.00	0	0									1	
20T		2	2	0	15	14	7.50	0	0									1	
EDWARDS, Corey Raymond (Barbados) b Bridgetown, St Michael, Barbados 2.9.1983 RHB RMF																			
FC		3	3	1	7	5	3.50	0	0	343	206	10	20.60	6-41	1	0	3.60	3	
EDWARDS, Kirk Anton (Barbados, West Indies A, West Indies A to Bangladesh, West Indies A to England, West Indies A to Ireland) b Mile and a Quarter, St Peter, Barbados 3.11.1984 RHB OB																			
FC		7	13	1	566	90	47.16	0	5									6	
Lim		3	3	0	105	41	35.00	0	0									0	
20T		5	5	0	82	45	16.40	0	0									2	
FC	2005/06	22	41	3	1361	107	35.81	1	11									13	
Lim	2003/04	25	23	3	527	147	26.35	1	1									4	
EMMANUEL, Craig Walt (Windward Islands) b Mon Repos, St Lucia 5.5.1986 RHB RMF																			
FC		2	3	0	37	19	12.33	0	0	96	70	0					4.37	1	
Lim		1	1	0	0	0	0.00	0	0	18	12	0					4.00	0	
20T		1	1	0	14	14	14.00	0	0	18	14	3	4.66	3-14	0	0	4.66	0	
FC	2003/04	24	41	0	809	73	19.73	0	5	354	270	1	270.00	1-37	0	0	4.57	15	
Lim	2003/04	23	23	2	265	43	12.61	0	0	277	227	5	45.40	2-47	0	0	4.91	6	
20T	2006	3	3	0	31	14	10.33	0	0	18	14	3	4.66	3-14	0	0	4.66	0	
EMRIT, Rayad Ryan (Trinidad and Tobago) b Mount Hope, St Joseph, Trinidad 8.3.1981 RHB RFM																			
FC		3	6	2	80	20*	20.00	0	0	282	140	1	140.00	1-18	0	0	2.97	4	
FC	2003/04	38	60	6	881	112	16.31	1	2	4605	2088	73	28.60	5-12	3	0	2.72	20	
Int	2006/07	2	2	1	13	13	13.00	0	0	84	99	0					7.07	1	
Lim	2003/04	29	18	6	185	33*	15.41	0	0	1108	834	29	28.75	4-27	2	0	4.51	7	
20T	2006	10	3	1	10	6*	5.00	0	0	166	158	14	11.28	3-18	0	0	5.71	1	
FINDLAY, Shawn Eli (Jamaica) b Mandeville, Jamaica 3.3.1984 LHB RFM																			
FC		1	2	0	14	11	7.00	0	0	114	37	1	37.00	1-16	0	0	1.94	2	
Lim		1																0	
FC	2003/04	11	21	1	295	70*	14.75	0	1	228	104	1	104.00	1-16	0	0	2.73	8	
Int	2008	9	8	1	146	59*	20.85	0	1									5	
Lim	2007/08	15	13	3	303	64*	30.30	0	2									8	
I20T	2008/09	2	2	0	32	19	16.00	0	0									1	
20T	2006	8	6	1	62	20	12.40	0	0									5	
FLETCHER, Andre David Stephon (West Indies, West Indies XI, Windward Islands, West Indies to South Africa, West Indies A to England, West Indies A to Ireland) b La Tante, Grenada 28.11.1987 RHB RMF WK																			
FC		5	10	1	431	80	47.88	0	5	6	8	0					8.00	3	
Int		5	5	0	58	48	11.60	0	0									2	3
Lim		6	6	0	76	48	12.66	0	0									2	4
I20T		6	6	1	51	19	10.20	0	0									5	1
20T		12	12	1	184	33	16.72	0	0									11	3
FC	2003/04	30	55	4	1595	123	31.27	2	10	121	68	0					3.37	30	1
Int	2008	15	15	0	256	54	17.06	0	2									5	3
Lim	2006/07	32	31	1	708	88	23.60	0	5									16	5
I20T	2008	14	14	2	137	53	11.41	0	1									11	1
20T	2006	28	28	5	603	90*	26.21	0	4									18	4
FOO, Jonathan Alexander (Guyana) b Guyana 11.9.1990 RHB OB																			
20T		4	4	3	103	42*	103.00	0	0									5	

Cmp	Debut	M	I	NO	Runs	HS	Avge	100	50	Balls	Runs	Wkts	Avge	BB	5i	10m	RpO	ct	st
FUDADIN, Assad Badyr (Guyana, West Indies A, West Indies A to England, West Indies A to Ireland) b Rose Hall, Berbice, Guyana 1.8.1985 LHB RMF																			
FC		5	9	0	301	78	33.44	0	2	126	58	3	19.33	2-34	0	0	2.76	6	
20T		2	2	0	35	29	17.50	0	0									1	
FC	2003/04	33	54	4	1500	93	30.00	0	7	474	248	5	49.60	2-34	0	0	3.13	24	
Lim	2003/04	25	22	4	445	57*	24.72	0	4	60	61	2	30.50	2-28	0	0	6.10	11	
GABRIEL, Shannon Terry (Trinidad and Tobago, West Indies A) b Trinidad 28.4.1988 RHB RF																			
FC		4	6	3	25	11	8.33	0	0	441	244	7	34.85	2-59	0	0	3.32	0	
20T		1								24	21	1	21.00	1-21	0	0	5.25	0	
GANGA, Daren (Trinidad and Tobago, Trinidad and Tobago to India) b Barrackpore, Trinidad 14.1.1979 RHB OB																			
FC		6	12	0	268	65	22.33	0	2									3	
Lim		3	3	1	144	79*	72.00	0	1	12	2	0					1.00	3	
20T		5	3	0	41	17	13.66	0	0									3	
Test	1998/99	48	86	2	2160	135	25.71	3	9	186	106	1	106.00	1-20	0	0	3.41	30	
FC	1996/97	164	288	25	9512	265	36.16	20	46	622	334	4	83.50	1-7	0	0	3.22	106	
Int	1998/99	35	34	1	843	71	25.54	0	9	1	4	0					24.00	11	
Lim	1996/97	101	100	11	2691	101*	30.23	2	20	301	193	5	38.60	2-20	0	0	3.84	35	
I20T	2005/06	1	1	0	26	26	26.00	0	0									0	
20T	2005/06	24	20	4	391	62*	24.43	0	1	6	18	0					18.00	7	
GANGA, Sherwin (Trinidad and Tobago, Trinidad and Tobago to India) b Barrackpore, Trinidad 13.2.1982 LHB OB																			
FC		6	12	1	275	99	25.00	0	1	564	240	6	40.00	2-21	0	0	2.55	9	
Lim		3	2	0	29	18	14.50	0	0	90	74	1	74.00	1-13	0	0	4.93	1	
20T		5	2	2	6	6*		0	0	78	94	5	18.80	2-19	0	0	7.23	2	
FC	2003/04	33	53	3	1076	99	21.52	0	5	3084	1188	40	29.70	5-40	1	0	2.31	31	
Lim	2004/05	31	27	4	540	64	23.47	0	3	1446	893	29	30.79	3-28	0	0	3.70	14	
20T	2007/08	18	11	7	74	18*	18.50	0	0	318	357	22	16.22	4-23	1	0	6.73	8	
GAYLE, Christopher Henry (Jamaica, West Indies, Kolkata Knight Riders, West Indies to Australia, Western Australia) b Kingston, Jamaica 21.9.1979 LHB OB																			
Test		3	5	0	159	73	31.80	0	2	18	4	1	4.00	1-2	0	0	1.33	2	
FC		3	5	0	159	73	31.80	0	2	18	4	1	4.00	1-2	0	0	1.33	2	
Int		10	10	0	401	88	40.10	0	3	253	191	4	47.75	2-38	0	0	4.53	5	
Lim		11	10	0	401	88	40.10	0	3	253	191	4	47.75	2-38	0	0	4.53	5	
I20T		6	6	0	146	98	24.33	0	1	26	50	3	16.66	1-5	0	0	11.53	1	
20T		9	9	0	168	98	18.66	0	1	68	93	5	18.60	2-19	0	0	8.20	1	
Test	1999/00	88	155	6	6007	317	40.31	12	33	6851	2992	72	41.55	5-34	2	0	2.62	84	
FC	1998/99	162	288	21	11761	317	44.04	28	59	12127	5012	129	38.85	5-34	2	0	2.48	142	
Int	1999	220	215	15	7885	153*	39.42	19	42	6816	5395	156	34.58	5-46	3	1	4.74	95	
Lim	1998/99	278	272	22	9957	153*	39.82	21	56	8810	6667	209	31.89	5-46	4	1	4.54	115	
I20T	2005/06	20	20	1	617	117	32.47	1	5	209	254	12	21.16	2-15	0	0	7.29	5	
20T	2005	51	50	5	1357	117	30.15	1	8	634	775	30	25.83	3-13	0	0	7.33	17	
GORDON, Nicholson Anthony (West Indies Under-19s) b Westmoreland, Jamaica 22.10.1991 RHB RMF																			
Lim		1								36	34	1	34.00	1-34	0	0	5.66	1	
GRIFFITH, Trevon (West Indies Under-19s) b Guyana 15.4.1991 LHB																			
Lim		1																0	
GUILLEN, Justin Christopher (Trinidad and Tobago, West Indies A, West Indies A to Bangladesh, West Indies A to England) b Port of Spain, Trinidad 2.1.1986 LHB OB																			
FC		7	14	0	464	134	33.14	1	1									12	
20T		1	1	0	1	1	1.00	0	0									0	
FC	2008/09	14	27	0	667	134	24.70	1	1	12	1	0					0.50	17	
Lim	2010	2	2	0	11	11	5.50	0	0									3	
20T	2008/09	3	3	0	33	31	11.00	0	0									0	
HAMILTON, Jahmar Neville (Leeward Islands) b St Thomas, Anguilla 22.9.1990 RHB WK																			
FC		3	5	1	182	98	45.50	0	1									8	1
Lim		2	1	0	34	34	34.00	0	0									2	
FC	2007/08	6	10	1	250	98	27.77	0	1									12	1
20T	2007/08	1	1	1	0	0*		0	0									0	2
HARTY, Patrick Marlon (West Indies Under-19s) b Jamaica 29.1.1991 LHB SLA																			
Lim		1								42	28	1	28.00	1-28	0	0	4.00	1	
HAYNES, Jason Adrian McCarthy (Barbados, West Indies A) b Jackman Main Road, St Michael, Barbados 3.7.1981 LHB SLA																			
FC		7	13	0	479	83	36.84	0	5									6	
20T		1	1	0	6	6	6.00	0	0									0	
FC	2002/03	31	55	1	1495	111	27.68	2	8									26	
Lim	2002/03	11	11	1	258	72	25.80	0	1									0	
20T	2006	4	3	0	69	38	23.00	0	0									0	
HECTOR, Donwell Banister (Windward Islands) b St Vincent 31.10.1988 RHB OB																			
FC		3	5	0	58	31	11.60	0	0									4	
Lim		1	1	0	2	2	2.00	0	0									0	
20T		1	1	0	11	11	11.00	0	0									1	
FC	2007/08	17	30	1	629	99	21.68	0	3	6	1	0					1.00	29	

Cmp	Debut	M	I	NO	Runs	HS	Avge	100	50	Balls	Runs	Wkts	Avge	BB	5i	10m	RpO	ct	st
Lim	2007/08	4	4	0	77	37	19.25	0	0									3	
20T	2007/08	3	3	0	17	11	5.66	0	0									1	
HICKS, Delbert (Guyana) b New Amsterdam, Berbice, Guyana 11.11.1983 LHB WK																			
Lim		4	2	0	9	8	4.50	0	0									4	2
FC	2008/09	1	2	0	33	27	16.50	0	0									0	
HINDS, Jason Omar (Barbados) b Holder's Hill, St James, Barbados 15.2.1984 RHB OB																			
20T		1	1	0	10	10	10.00	0	0	24	25	0					6.25	0	
HINDS, Ryan O'Neal (Barbados) b Holders Hill, St James, Barbados 17.2.1981 LHB SLA																			
FC		6	11	1	446	139	44.60	1	2	1146	409	16	25.56	5-59	1	0	2.14	5	
Lim		3	3	0	98	44	32.66	0	0	156	86	2	43.00	1-25	0	0	3.30	1	
20T		4	3	2	32	17*	32.00	0	0	84	79	6	13.16	2-24	0	0	5.64	0	
Test	2001/02	15	25	1	505	84	21.04	0	2	1743	870	13	66.92	2-45	0	0	2.99	7	
FC	1998/99	110	179	19	6270	240	39.18	11	32	13351	5644	211	26.74	9-68	5	1	2.53	85	
Int	2001/02	14	9	3	101	18*	16.83	0	0	407	350	6	58.33	2-19	0	0	5.16	2	
Lim	1998/99	86	75	13	1846	84	29.77	0	12	3255	2169	78	27.80	6-46	3	1	3.99	29	
20T	2007/08	7	6	4	129	45*	64.50	0	0	114	120	8	15.00	2-8	0	0	6.31	2	
HINDS, Wavell Wayne (Jamaica, West Indies, West Indies XI, West Indies to Australia) b Kingston, Jamaica 7.9.1976 LHB RM																			
FC		3	4	1	330	151	110.00	1	2									2	
Int		2	2	1	20	20	20.00	0	0									0	
Lim		4	3	1	21	20	10.50	0	0									0	
I20T		2	2	1	5	5	5.00	0	0									1	
20T		11	9	1	141	45	17.62	0	0	6	19	0					19.00	1	
Test	1999/00	45	80	1	2608	213	33.01	5	14	1123	590	16	36.87	3-79	0	0	3.15	32	
FC	1995/96	166	281	14	9476	213	35.49	21	48	3664	1736	48	36.16	3-9	0	0	2.84	76	
Int	1999	119	111	10	2880	127*	28.51	5	14	945	837	28	29.89	3-24	0	0	5.31	29	
Lim	1997/98	211	198	15	5093	127*	27.83	6	29	1508	1353	49	27.61	4-35	1	0	5.38	47	
I20T	2005/06	5	5	1	30	14	7.50	0	0									1	
20T	2005/06	40	36	7	825	72*	28.44	0	3	144	182	4	45.50	2-14	0	0	7.58	4	
HODGE, Montcin Verniel (Leeward Islands) b Anguilla 29.9.1987 RHB OB																			
FC		6	12	2	288	61	28.80	0	3									9	
FC	2007/08	21	36	3	926	78	28.06	0	8	6	7	0					7.00	15	
20T	2006	2	2	1	90	75*	90.00	0	1	12	23	2	11.50	2-23	0	0	11.50	1	
HOLDER, Alcindo Rennae (Barbados) b Barbados 24.9.1982 RHB OB																			
Lim		3	3	0	37	23	12.33	0	0	1	6	0					36.00	0	
20T		4	4	1	85	46*	28.33	0	0	6	5	0					5.00	1	
FC	2005/06	15	24	3	619	84	29.47	0	6	18	5	0					1.66	14	
Lim	2005/06	18	17	3	284	38*	20.28	0	0	25	23	0					5.52	3	
20T	2007/08	7	7	3	125	46*	31.25	0	0	6	5	0					5.00	4	
HOLDER, Jason Omar (West Indies A, West Indies Under-19s) b Rouens Village, St George, Barbados 5.11.1991 RHB RMF																			
Lim		1																0	
20T		2	1	1	7	7*		0	0	48	50	3	16.66	2-24	0	0	6.25	0	
FC	2008/09	1	1	0	7	7	7.00	0	0	96	43	2	21.50	1-19	0	0	2.68	0	
HOPE, Kyle Antonio (Barbados) b Field Place, Bayville, St Michael, Barbados 20.11.1988 RHB OB																			
FC		1	2	0	41	22	20.50	0	0									0	
HUGHES, Chesney Francis (Leeward Islands, Derbyshire, Derbyshire to Netherlands) b Anguilla 20.1.1991 LHB SLA																			
Lim		2	2	1	5	3*	5.00	0	0									0	
FC	2010	12	21	2	784	156	41.26	2	4	66	81	1	81.00	1-9	0	0	7.36	12	
Lim	2007/08	20	19	1	492	72	27.33	0	5	186	162	2	81.00	1-17	0	0	5.22	6	
20T	2006	14	12	0	192	65	16.00	0	1	12	19	0					9.50	3	
HYATT, Danza Pacino (Jamaica) b St Catherine, Jamaica 17.3.1983 RHB RM																			
FC		5	8	0	321	104	40.12	1	3									4	
Lim		3	3	0	118	102	39.33	1	0									1	
20T		7	5	0	169	89	33.80	0	1	54	52	1	52.00	1-19	0	0	5.77	1	
FC	2003/04	29	52	2	1353	104	27.06	1	10	132	63	1	63.00	1-25	0	0	2.86	27	
Lim	2004/05	19	17	4	435	102	33.46	1	0	84	48	1	48.00	1-32	0	0	3.42	9	
20T	2007/08	11	9	1	330	89	41.25	0	3	54	52	1	52.00	1-19	0	0	5.77	2	
JACKSON, Simon (Combined Campuses and Colleges) b Jamaica 18.5.1985 LHB LB																			
FC		3	6	0	79	22	13.16	0	0									4	
Lim		2	2	0	4	4	2.00	0	0									0	
FC	2007/08	17	33	1	897	83	28.03	0	4	42	29	1	29.00	1-0	0	0	4.14	16	
Lim	2007/08	8	7	0	93	34	13.28	0	0									1	
JAGGERNAUTH, Amit Sheldon (Trinidad and Tobago) b Lennard Street, Bank, Carapichaima, Trinidad 16.11.1983 LHB OB																			
FC		6	10	2	86	18	10.75	0	0	1501	668	27	24.74	5-47	1	0	2.67	3	
Test	2008	1	2	1	0	0*	0.00	0	0	138	96	1	96.00	1-74	0	0	4.17	0	
FC	2002/03	56	82	30	596	47	11.46	0	0	12077	5309	223	23.80	7-45	13	2	2.63	42	
Lim	2006/07	4	1	1	0	0*		0	0	180	100	1	100.00	1-23	0	0	3.33	1	
20T	2008/09	2								42	60	0					8.57	2	
JAMES, Lindon Omrick Dinsley (Windward Islands) b South Rivers, St Vincent 30.12.1984 RHB WK																			
FC		5	8	1	166	70*	23.71	0	1									16	1
FC	2003/04	30	49	3	860	70*	18.69	0	5									86	8

Cmp	Debut	M	I	NO	Runs	HS	Avge	100	50	Balls	Runs	Wkts	Avge	BB	5i	10m	RpO	ct	st
Lim	2006/07	10	8	0	96	23	12.00	0	0									6	5
20T	2006	5	5	2	88	73*	29.33	0	1									3	1
JEFFERS, Shane Melvon (Leeward Islands) b Sandy Point, St Kitts 12.9.1981 LHB RM																			
20T		1	1	0	5	5	5.00	0	0									0	
FC	2001/02	46	82	2	2169	128	27.11	1	14	354	229	3	76.33	2-30	0	0	3.88	43	
Lim	2001/02	15	13	0	207	100	15.92	1	0	122	123	2	61.50	2-38	0	0	6.04	2	
20T	2006	3	3	0	10	5	3.33	0	0									1	
JOHNSON, Delorn Edison (Windward Islands) b St Vincent 15.9.1988 LHB																			
FC		1	1	0	7	7	7.00	0	0	168	62	1	62.00	1-56	0	0	2.21	0	
Lim	2007/08	2	2	1	16	16	16.00	0	0	30	34	0					6.80	0	
JOSEPH, Keon (Guyana, West Indies Under-19s) b Guyana 25.11.1991 RHB RFM																			
FC		1	1	0	0	0	0.00	0	0	96	92	0					5.75	0	
Lim		1								18	21	0					7.00	0	
KANTASINGH, Kavesh (Combined Campuses and Colleges) b Trinidad 30.9.1986 LHB SLA																			
FC		6	10	1	55	34	6.11	0	0	1246	525	29	18.10	6-29	3	1	2.52	3	
Lim		3	1	0	11	11	11.00	0	0	114	33	4	8.25	3-22	0	0	1.73	2	
20T		2	1	1	1	1*		0	0	44	54	1	54.00	1-33	0	0	7.36	0	
FC	2007/08	22	35	5	216	34	7.20	0	0	4514	1868	69	27.07	6-29	3	1	2.48	10	
Lim	2007/08	10	4	2	34	11	17.00	0	0	396	194	15	12.93	4-15	1	0	2.93	5	
KELLY, Richard Alexander (Trinidad and Tobago) b Trinidad 19.2.1984 LHB RFM																			
FC		2	4	0	30	19	7.50	0	0	108	43	1	43.00	1-13	0	0	2.38	0	
FC	2004/05	43	63	7	1284	93	22.92	0	8	4996	2683	96	27.94	6-31	2	0	3.22	22	
Lim	2004/05	30	23	5	271	42*	15.05	0	0	1166	904	33	27.39	4-38	3	0	4.65	12	
20T	2007/08	4	2	1	8	8	8.00	0	0	30	29	1	29.00	1-18	0	0	5.80	0	
KHAN, Imran (Trinidad and Tobago, West Indies A, West Indies A to Bangladesh, West Indies A to England, West Indies A to Ireland) b Port of Spain, Trinidad 6.12.1984 RHB SLA																			
FC		7	13	1	230	63	19.16	0	2	1546	788	44	17.90	7-71	3	1	3.05	5	
20T		3	2	2	68	60*		0	1	48	47	1	47.00	1-29	0	0	5.87	2	
FC	2004/05	25	42	3	959	125	24.58	1	5	3680	1847	85	21.72	7-71	5	1	3.01	21	
Lim	2010	10	9	4	127	74	25.40	0	1	510	432	11	39.27	3-44	0	0	5.08	1	
LAMBERT, Tamar Lansford (Jamaica) b St Catherine, Jamaica 15.7.1981 RHB OB																			
FC		7	11	0	271	68	24.63	0	2	520	176	16	11.00	8-42	1	1	2.03	4	
Lim		2	2	0	18	18	9.00	0	0	18	10	2	5.00	2-10	0	0	3.33	0	
20T		7	4	1	14	11	4.66	0	0	85	97	5	19.40	2-7	0	0	6.84	2	
FC	2003/04	55	95	3	2794	143	30.36	2	20	1773	759	38	19.97	8-42	1	1	2.56	42	
Lim	2000	25	21	5	544	76	34.00	0	4	246	172	11	15.63	3-9	0	0	4.19	8	
20T	2007/08	8	4	1	14	11	4.66	0	0	103	108	5	21.60	2-7	0	0	6.29	2	
LESPORIS, Keddy (Windward Islands) b St Lucia 27.12.1988 RHB OB																			
FC		3	5	0	77	31	15.40	0	0									1	
FC	2008/09	7	13	0	265	50	20.38	0	1									4	
20T	2007/08	2	2	0	62	45	31.00	0	0									1	
LEWIS, Evin (West Indies Under-19s) b Trinidad 27.12.1991 LHB RM																			
Lim		2	1	0	53	53	53.00	0	1									0	
LEWIS, Rawl Nicholas (Windward Islands) b Union Village, Grenada 5.9.1974 RHB LBG																			
FC		6	10	2	308	82*	38.50	0	4	1184	567	27	21.00	5-81	1	0	2.87	3	
Lim		1	1	0	18	18	18.00	0	0	54	33	1	33.00	1-33	0	0	3.66	0	
20T		2	2	0	31	30	15.50	0	0	30	45	0					9.00	0	
Test	1997/98	5	10	0	89	40	8.90	0	0	883	456	4	114.00	2-42	0	0	3.09	0	
FC	1991/92	131	224	29	4694	117*	24.07	2	24	21168	10254	325	31.55	7-66	12	0	2.90	90	
Int	1997/98	28	21	5	291	49	18.18	0	0	1150	983	22	44.68	3-43	0	0	5.12	7	
Lim	1992/93	102	83	17	1298	67	19.66	0	5	4202	3162	109	29.00	4-13	1	0	4.51	35	
I20T	2007/08	1	1	0	0	0	0.00	0	0	6	9	0					9.00	1	
20T	2006	7	7	1	98	36	16.33	0	0	108	129	5	25.80	3-18	0	0	7.16	3	
LIBURD, Javier Springteen (Leeward Islands) b Rawlins, Nevis 9.2.1987 RHB OB																			
20T		2	2	0	64	39	32.00	0	0									0	
FC	2006/07	6	9	0	212	43	23.55	0	0									3	
Lim	2006/07	4	4	0	75	30	18.75	0	0									1	
20T	2006	7	6	1	102	39	20.40	0	0	12	25	0					12.50	1	
LIBURD, Steve Stuart Wayne (Leeward Islands) b Basseterre, St Kitts 26.2.1985 RHB OB																			
FC		6	11	0	165	48	15.00	0	0	56	17	2	8.50	2-13	0	0	1.82	8	
Lim		2	1	0	38	38	38.00	0	0									0	
20T		1	1	0	12	12	12.00	0	0									0	
FC	2005/06	25	41	3	967	116*	25.44	1	3	293	179	7	25.57	3-46	0	0	3.66	35	1
Lim	2003/04	9	7	1	171	38	28.50	0	0	34	51	1	51.00	1-20	0	0	9.00	2	
20T	2006	3	3	0	68	55	22.66	0	1									0	
MCCLEAN, Kevin Ramon (Combined Campuses and Colleges) b Castle, St Peter, Barbados 24.1.1988 LHB RF																			
FC		6	11	3	129	24*	16.12	0	0	563	352	9	39.11	3-61	0	0	3.75	4	
Lim		3	2	1	44	23	44.00	0	0	49	39	3	13.00	2-7	0	0	4.77	0	
FC	2007/08	19	31	9	420	50*	19.09	0	1	2122	1211	48	25.22	5-49	1	0	3.42	6	
MARSHALL, Kemar (Jamaica) b Jamaica 9.10.1991 RHB OB WK																			
Lim		2	2	0	24	16	12.00	0	0									0	2

Cmp	Debut	M	I	NO	Runs	HS	Avge	100	50	Balls	Runs	Wkts	Avge	BB	5i	10m	RpO	ct	st
MARSHALL, Xavier Melbourne (Jamaica) b St Ann, Jamaica 27.3.1986 RHB OB																			
FC		2	4	0	25	13	6.25	0	0									3	
Lim		2	1	0	5	5	5.00	0	0									0	
20T		5	5	1	149	62*	37.25	0	2									4	
Test	2005	7	12	0	243	85	20.25	0	2	12	0	0					0.00	7	
FC	2003/04	30	53	2	1238	85	24.27	0	8	36	14	0					2.33	32	
Int	2004/05	24	24	3	375	157*	17.85	1	0	9	6	0					4.00	9	
Lim	2003/04	41	40	5	801	157*	22.88	2	3	15	10	0					4.00	17	
I20T	2008	6	6	0	96	36	16.00	0	0									3	
20T	2006	17	16	1	339	62*	22.60	0	2									7	
MARTIN, Anthony (Leeward Islands, West Indies A to England, West Indies A to Ireland) b Bethesda, Antigua 18.11.1982 RHB LB																			
FC		6	11	5	20	8	3.33	0	0	1399	488	21	23.23	4-55	0	0	2.09	5	
Lim		2	1	0	0	0	0.00	0	0	18	20	0					6.66	0	
20T		2								46	36	1	36.00	1-21	0	0	4.69	0	
FC	2007/08	23	35	15	118	14*	5.90	0	0	4485	1905	78	24.42	7-81	3	1	2.54	13	
Lim	2008/09	13	7	3	15	10	3.75	0	0	596	439	12	36.58	3-25	0	0	4.41	5	
20T	2007/08	4	1	1	0	0*		0	0	88	82	4	20.50	2-25	0	0	5.59	0	
MATHURIN, Garey Earl (Windward Islands) b St Lucia 23.9.1983 LHB SLA																			
FC		2	3	0	47	31	15.66	0	0	321	130	2	65.00	2-34	0	0	2.43	2	
20T		2	2	1	17	12	17.00	0	0	36	47	0					7.83	0	
FC	2006/07	3	5	0	90	31	18.00	0	0	459	170	3	56.66	2-34	0	0	2.22	2	
Lim	2006/07	5	3	2	40	29*	40.00	0	0	177	130	2	65.00	1-23	0	0	4.40	1	
20T	2006	6	6	2	60	28*	15.00	0	0	126	129	6	21.50	4-25	1	0	6.14	3	
MENTORE, Kerry Hanse (Leeward Islands) b All Saints, Antigua 19.9.1984 RHB WK																			
20T		2	2	1	63	48*	63.00	0	0									1	
MILLER, Horace (Jamaica) b Jamaica 26.10.1989 LHB WK																			
FC		2	3	0	70	66	23.33	0	1									5	
Lim	2008/09	4	4	0	98	42	24.50	0	0									2	
MILLER, Nikita O'Neil (Jamaica, West Indies, West Indies XI, West Indies to Australia, West Indies to South Africa) b St Elizabeth, Jamaica 16.5.1982 RHB SLA																			
FC		3	3	1	31	15*	15.50	0	0	971	283	22	12.86	7-28	2	0	1.74	2	
Int		8	4	2	25	13*	12.50	0	0	360	250	12	20.83	4-43	1	0	4.16	6	
Lim		10	5	2	30	13*	10.00	0	0	414	278	14	19.85	4-43	1	0	4.02	7	
I20T		4	3	2	17	10*	17.00	0	0	84	76	3	25.33	1-13	0	0	5.42	0	
20T		12	5	2	19	10*	6.33	0	0	228	237	6	39.50	1-13	0	0	6.23	3	
Test	2009	1	2	0	5	5	2.50	0	0	132	67	0					3.04	0	
FC	2004/05	38	57	11	785	86	17.06	0	1	9236	3073	163	18.85	8-41	6	2	1.99	22	
Int	2008	33	20	9	223	51	20.27	0	1	1435	1088	30	36.26	4-43	1	0	4.54	12	
Lim	2004/05	56	32	11	272	51	12.95	0	1	2347	1682	48	35.04	4-43	1	0	4.30	20	
I20T	2009	7	4	3	28	11*	28.00	0	0	154	174	9	19.33	2-20	0	0	6.77	1	
20T	2007/08	19	7	3	30	11*	7.50	0	0	370	402	13	30.92	2-20	0	0	6.51	5	
MOHAMED, Zaheer Shadir (Guyana) b Georgetown, Demerara, Guyana 10.10.1985 RHB OB																			
FC		2	3	1	61	58*	30.50	0	1	318	119	3	39.66	2-60	0	0	2.24	0	
FC	2003/04	12	16	2	211	58*	15.07	0	1	1723	859	28	30.67	4-40	0	0	2.99	8	
Lim	2007/08	2	2	2	18	17*		0	0	114	77	2	38.50	1-35	0	0	4.05	0	
MOHAMMED, Dave (Trinidad and Tobago, Trinidad and Tobago to India) b Knolly Street, Princes Town, Trinidad 8.10.1979 LHB SLC																			
FC		3	6	0	102	37	17.00	0	0	318	158	2	79.00	1-11	0	0	2.98	1	
Lim		3	2	2	21	18*		0	0	174	93	5	18.60	3-25	0	0	3.20	0	
20T		5	1	0	0	0	0.00	0	0	90	88	7	12.57	2-10	0	0	5.86	0	
Test	2003/04	5	8	1	225	52	32.14	0	1	1065	668	13	51.38	3-98	0	0	3.76	1	
FC	2000/01	70	105	15	1527	74*	16.96	0	5	12675	6083	227	26.79	7-48	6	2	2.88	37	
Int	2006	7	1	1	0	0*		0	0	353	235	10	23.50	3-37	0	0	3.99	1	
Lim	2001/02	31	16	7	172	43	19.11	0	0	1439	867	45	19.26	4-23	2	0	3.61	8	
20T	2007/08	18	6	2	13	8*	3.25	0	0	327	315	27	11.66	5-8	1	1	5.78	4	
MOHAMMED, Gibran (Trinidad and Tobago) b Barrackpore, Trinidad 31.7.1983 LHB WK																			
FC		3	5	1	62	26*	15.50	0	0									7	2
FC	2003/04	27	41	5	677	60	18.80	0	3	6	10	0					10.00	65	7
Lim	2003/04	6	4	0	75	35	18.75	0	0									7	1
MOHAMMED, Jason Nazimuddin (Trinidad and Tobago) b Barrackpore, Trinidad 23.9.1986 RHB OB																			
FC		5	10	0	236	87	23.60	0	1	12	1	0					0.50	10	
FC	2005/06	19	33	2	743	124*	23.96	1	2	48	10	0					1.25	30	
Lim	2006/07	7	5	2	82	39	27.33	0	0	18	16	0					5.33	1	
20T	2007/08	1																0	
MOORE, Gilford (Combined Campuses and Colleges) b Henrietta, Essequibo, Guyana 26.2.1982 RHB RMF																			
FC		1	2	0	4	4	2.00	0	0	96	59	2	29.50	2-45	0	0	3.68	0	
20T		2	1	1	1	1*		0	0	48	55	4	13.75	3-18	0	0	6.87	1	
FC	2007/08	3	5	3	19	10*	9.50	0	0	348	193	3	64.33	2-45	0	0	3.32	1	
Lim	2008/09	1								24	24	0					6.00	0	

Cmp	Debut	M	I	NO	Runs	HS	Avge	100	50	Balls	Runs	Wkts	Avge	BB	5i	10m	RpO	ct	st
MORGAN, Dean Lloyd (Jamaica) b St Catherine, Jamaica 14.10.1981 RHB OB																			
20T		1								6	4	0					4.00	0	
MORRIS, Carlo Antoine (Barbados) b Westmorland, St James, Barbados 13.1.1980 RHB WK																			
Lim		3	3	0	49	23	16.33	0	0									2	1
20T		4	3	1	49	42*	24.50	0	0									1	
FC	2006/07	6	8	1	138	70	19.71	0	1									24	1
Lim	2006/07	5	4	0	57	23	14.25	0	0									5	2
20T	2006	8	6	1	60	42*	12.00	0	0									5	2
MORTON, Runako Shakur (Leeward Islands, West Indies to Australia) b Rawlins, Gingerland, Nevis 22.7.1978 RHB OB																			
FC		2	4	0	287	108	71.75	1	2									1	
Lim		2	1	0	7	7	7.00	0	0									0	
20T		1	1	0	22	22	22.00	0	0									0	
Test	2005	15	27	1	573	70*	22.03	0	4	66	50	0					4.54	20	
FC	1996/97	90	151	8	5791	231	40.49	14	35	473	290	8	36.25	3-17	0	0	3.67	100	
Int	2001/02	56	51	6	1519	110*	33.75	2	10	6	2	0					2.00	20	
Lim	1997/98	120	113	17	3642	126	37.93	5	24	210	254	8	31.75	2-35	0	0	7.25	48	
I20T	2005/06	7	7	1	96	40	16.00	0	0									2	
20T	2005/06	11	11	1	164	40	16.40	0	0	6	4	0					4.00	2	
NARINE, Sunil Philip (Trinidad and Tobago) b Trinidad 26.5.1988 LHB OB																			
FC		1	2	0	2	2	1.00	0	0	66	19	1	19.00	1-9	0	0	1.72	4	
FC	2008/09	2	3	1	2	2	1.00	0	0	144	44	1	44.00	1-9	0	0	1.83	4	
NASH, Brendan Paul (Jamaica, West Indies, West Indies to Australia, West Indies A to Bangladesh) b Attadale, Western Australia, Australia 14.12.1977 LHB LM																			
Test		3	5	0	142	114	28.40	1	0	78	18	0					1.38	1	
FC		6	10	2	291	114	36.37	1	0	90	19	0					1.26	2	
Lim		2	1	0	12	12	12.00	0	0	18	23	0					7.66	0	
Test	2008/09	15	24	0	889	114	37.04	2	6	408	196	1	196.00	1-34	0	0	2.88	5	
FC	2000/01	66	113	13	3358	176	33.58	7	13	936	403	10	40.30	2-7	0	0	2.58	29	
Int	2008	9	7	3	104	39*	26.00	0	0	294	224	5	44.80	3-56	0	0	4.57	1	
Lim	2000/01	58	41	9	842	71	26.31	0	3	660	448	13	34.46	4-20	1	0	4.07	19	
20T	2007/08	1								6	8	0					8.00	0	
NURSE, Ashley Renaldo (Barbados) b Gibbons, Christ Church, Barbados 22.12.1988 RHB OB																			
20T		4	2	1	6	4	6.00	0	0	92	110	10	11.00	5-35	0	1	7.17	2	
Lim	2007/08	1	1	0	16	16	16.00	0	0	12	16	0					8.00	0	
NURSE, Martin Andre (Barbados) b Durants, Christ Church, Barbados 11.6.1985 LHB RM																			
Lim		3	3	0	86	46	28.66	0	0									0	
FC	2001/02	20	38	0	695	77	18.28	0	4	234	150	7	21.42	4-66	0	0	3.84	6	
Lim	2004/05	17	17	0	519	70	30.52	0	3	73	76	2	38.00	2-40	0	0	6.24	1	
20T	2006	3	2	0	39	35	19.50	0	0									0	
OTTLEY, Kjorn Yohance (Combined Campuses and Colleges) b Trinidad 9.12.1989 LHB SLC																			
FC		3	6	0	156	66	26.00	0	1									2	
Lim		2	2	0	65	39	32.50	0	0									1	
OTTLEY, Khesan Yannick Gabriel (West Indies Under-19s) b Trinidad 7.9.1991 RHB SLA																			
Lim		2	1	1	35	35*		0	0	6	7	0					7.00	0	
PAGON, Donovan Jomo (Jamaica) b Kingston, Jamaica 13.9.1982 RHB OB																			
FC		7	12	1	346	80	31.45	0	4									3	
Lim		1	1	0	1	1	1.00	0	0									0	
20T		2	2	1	42	33*	42.00	0	0									1	
Test	2004/05	2	3	0	37	35	12.33	0	0									0	
FC	2001/02	48	80	2	2271	110	29.11	3	12	6	0	0					0.00	23	
Lim	2002	4	4	0	35	16	8.75	0	0									0	
20T	2006	4	3	1	55	33*	27.50	0	0									4	
PARCHMENT, Brenton Anthony (Jamaica) b St Elizabeth, Jamaica 24.6.1982 RHB OB																			
FC		6	10	0	323	109	32.30	1	1	24	16	0					4.00	7	
Lim		3	3	1	105	72*	52.50	0	1									3	
20T		3	3	0	27	22	9.00	0	0									0	
Test	2007/08	2	4	0	55	20	13.75	0	0									1	
FC	1999/00	58	102	2	2672	168*	26.72	4	11	169	92	3	30.66	2-1	0	0	3.26	57	
Int	2007/08	7	7	0	122	48	17.42	0	0									0	
Lim	2000	42	42	4	1147	75	30.18	0	9	54	36	1	36.00	1-13	0	0	4.00	13	
I20T	2007/08	1	1	0	10	10	10.00	0	0									0	
20T	2007/08	5	5	0	47	22	9.40	0	0									1	
PARRIS, Nekoli (Combined Campuses and Colleges) b Lowland Park, Christ Church, Barbados 6.6.1987 RHB																			
FC		4	8	0	145	47	18.12	0	0	6	3	0					3.00	5	
Lim		3	3	1	69	40	34.50	0	0	64	46	1	46.00	1-11	0	0	4.31	0	
20T		2	2	0	29	17	14.50	0	0	48	54	2	27.00	1-23	0	0	6.75	3	
FC	2007/08	22	44	4	1027	105	25.67	1	6	60	41	0					4.10	22	
PASCAL, Nelon Troy (West Indies, West Indies A, Windward Islands, West Indies A to Bangladesh) b St David's, Grenada 25.4.1987 RHB RF																			
Test		1	2	0	12	10	6.00	0	0	102	59	0					3.47	1	
FC		8	13	3	49	12	4.90	0	0	1204	727	19	38.26	4-40	0	0	3.62	5	

Cmp	Debut	M	I	NO	Runs	HS	Avge	100	50	Balls	Runs	Wkts	Avge	BB	5i	10m	RpO	ct	st
Lim		1	1	1	0	0*		0	0	48	32	3	10.66	3-32	0	0	4.00	0	
20T		4	1	1	5	5*		0	0	90	104	7	14.85	3-21	0	0	6.93	1	
FC	2007/08	26	40	13	116	19	4.29	0	0	3495	2264	68	33.29	5-57	1	0	3.88	13	
Int	2009	1	1	0	0	0	0.00	0	0	24	29	0					7.25	0	
Lim	2007/08	11	7	2	22	9	4.40	0	0	509	464	25	18.56	4-33	2	0	5.47	0	
20T	2006	9	2	2	8	5*		0	0	192	200	10	20.00	3-21	0	0	6.25	2	

PERKINS, William Keith Donald (Trinidad and Tobago, Trinidad and Tobago to India) b Lodge Road, Christ Church, Barbados 8.10.1986 RHB OB WK

Cmp	Debut	M	I	NO	Runs	HS	Avge	100	50	Balls	Runs	Wkts	Avge	BB	5i	10m	RpO	ct	st
FC		2	4	0	44	29	11.00	0	0									2	
20T		4	4	0	40	18	10.00	0	0									2	
FC	2006/07	7	14	0	287	52	20.50	0	1									5	
Lim	2006/07	5	5	0	52	26	10.40	0	0									3	1
I20T	2008	1	1	0	9	9	9.00	0	0									1	
20T	2006	22	22	2	506	56	25.30	0	3									6	

PERMAUL, Veerasammy (Guyana) b Belvedere, Berbice, Guyana 11.8.1989 RHB OB

Cmp	Debut	M	I	NO	Runs	HS	Avge	100	50	Balls	Runs	Wkts	Avge	BB	5i	10m	RpO	ct	st
FC		6	9	1	145	47	18.12	0	0	1093	533	17	31.35	5-91	1	0	2.92	2	
Lim		4	1	0	28	28	28.00	0	0	225	144	6	24.00	3-54	0	0	3.84	2	
FC	2006/07	24	35	5	264	47	8.80	0	0	4339	1952	71	27.49	5-91	1	0	2.69	16	
Lim	2006/07	16	8	1	50	28	7.14	0	0	748	480	21	22.85	5-26	0	1	3.85	4	

PETERS, Keon Kenroy (Windward Islands) b Mesopotamia, St Vincent 24.2.1982 RHB LM

Cmp	Debut	M	I	NO	Runs	HS	Avge	100	50	Balls	Runs	Wkts	Avge	BB	5i	10m	RpO	ct	st
FC		5	9	1	128	52	16.00	0	1	648	314	11	28.54	3-31	0	0	2.90	2	
FC	2000	39	63	23	543	52	13.57	0	1	5851	2401	97	24.75	5-60	1	0	2.46	15	
Lim	2000/01	25	13	9	172	38*	43.00	0	0	1015	663	27	24.55	3-24	0	0	3.91	4	
20T	2007/08	2	1	1	1	1*		0	0	48	43	3	14.33	2-27	0	0	5.37	0	

PHILLIP, Kadeem Idaree Travon (Leeward Islands) b Antigua 25.11.1989 LHB SLA

Cmp	Debut	M	I	NO	Runs	HS	Avge	100	50	Balls	Runs	Wkts	Avge	BB	5i	10m	RpO	ct	st
20T		1	1	0	20	20	20.00	0	0									0	

PHILLIPS, Omar Jamel (Combined Campuses and Colleges, West Indies A to Bangladesh, West Indies A to England, West Indies A to Ireland) b Boscobel, St Peter, Barbados 12.10.1986 LHB RM

Cmp	Debut	M	I	NO	Runs	HS	Avge	100	50	Balls	Runs	Wkts	Avge	BB	5i	10m	RpO	ct	st
FC		6	12	1	309	88	28.09	0	2									8	
Lim		3	3	0	22	22	7.33	0	0									3	
20T		2	1	0	5	5	5.00	0	0									2	
Test	2009	2	4	0	160	94	40.00	0	1									1	
FC	2007/08	22	43	3	1236	204	30.90	1	5									23	
Lim	2007/08	11	11	0	157	34	14.27	0	0									4	

POLIUS, Dalton (West Indies Under-19s) b St Lucia 12.9.1990 LHB SLA

Cmp	Debut	M	I	NO	Runs	HS	Avge	100	50	Balls	Runs	Wkts	Avge	BB	5i	10m	RpO	ct	st
Lim		1																0	

POLLARD, Kieron Adrian (Trinidad and Tobago, West Indies, Mumbai Indians, Somerset, South Australia, Trinidad and Tobago to India, West Indies to Australia) b Cacariqua, Trinidad 12.5.1987 RHB RM

Cmp	Debut	M	I	NO	Runs	HS	Avge	100	50	Balls	Runs	Wkts	Avge	BB	5i	10m	RpO	ct	st
Int		10	10	0	221	44	22.10	0	0	346	294	11	26.72	3-27	0	0	5.09	1	
Lim		13	13	0	295	57	22.69	0	1	412	340	16	21.25	3-27	0	0	4.95	2	
I20T		8	8	0	87	27	10.87	0	0	96	137	3	45.66	2-22	0	0	8.56	4	
20T		13	11	1	160	53*	16.00	0	1	192	265	11	24.09	4-31	1	0	8.28	5	
FC	2006/07	20	33	1	1199	174	37.46	3	5	571	313	6	52.16	2-29	0	0	3.28	32	
Int	2006/07	30	27	0	538	62	19.92	0	1	936	833	30	27.76	3-27	0	0	5.34	10	
Lim	2006/07	48	43	3	1109	87	27.72	0	7	1410	1214	57	21.29	4-32	1	0	5.16	22	
I20T	2008	20	17	2	190	38	12.66	0	0	258	360	11	32.72	2-22	0	0	8.37	11	
20T	2006	80	69	13	1391	89*	24.83	0	6	1178	1514	81	18.69	4-15	2	0	7.71	35	

POWELL, Daren Brent Lyle (Jamaica, Lancashire) b Malvenn, St Elizabeth, Jamaica 15.4.1978 RHB RFM

Cmp	Debut	M	I	NO	Runs	HS	Avge	100	50	Balls	Runs	Wkts	Avge	BB	5i	10m	RpO	ct	st
FC		2	2	0	19	15	9.50	0	0	240	146	2	73.00	1-34	0	0	3.65	0	
Lim		2	1	0	6	6	6.00	0	0	78	63	1	63.00	1-43	0	0	4.84	1	
Test	2002	37	57	5	407	36*	7.82	0	0	7077	4068	85	47.85	5-25	1	0	3.44	8	
FC	2000/01	102	144	23	1525	69	12.60	0	4	16806	9318	276	33.76	6-49	6	0	3.32	31	
Int	2002/03	55	25	3	118	48*	5.36	0	0	2850	2239	71	31.53	4-27	2	0	4.71	13	
Lim	2002	108	48	11	274	48*	7.40	0	0	5212	4179	148	28.23	5-23	6	1	4.81	29	
I20T	2007	5	1	1	1	1*		0	0	102	131	2	65.50	1-6	0	0	7.70	2	
20T	2007	16	3	3	2	1*		0	0	307	373	7	53.28	2-15	0	0	7.29	3	

POWELL, Elsroy Junior (Leeward Islands) b St Kitts 9.11.1981 RHB RFM

Cmp	Debut	M	I	NO	Runs	HS	Avge	100	50	Balls	Runs	Wkts	Avge	BB	5i	10m	RpO	ct	st
FC		1	2	0	16	12	8.00	0	0	54	30	0					3.33	0	
FC	2001/02	6	11	3	164	61*	20.50	0	1	873	471	11	42.81	4-71	0	0	3.23	1	
Lim	2001/02	12	7	2	37	12	7.40	0	0	514	390	13	30.00	3-18	0	0	4.55	1	
20T	2006	2	2	0	8	7	4.00	0	0	30	44	3	14.66	2-27	0	0	8.80	1	

POWELL, Kieran Omar Akeem (Leeward Islands, West Indies to South Africa) b Government Road, Charlestown, Nevis 6.3.1990 LHB RM

Cmp	Debut	M	I	NO	Runs	HS	Avge	100	50	Balls	Runs	Wkts	Avge	BB	5i	10m	RpO	ct	st
FC		6	12	1	272	48	24.72	0	0	12	5	0					2.50	6	
Lim		2	2	1	69	38	69.00	0	0									1	
FC	2007/08	19	33	3	1043	99	34.76	0	6	25	19	0					4.56	12	
Int	2009	2	2	0	5	5	2.50	0	0									1	
Lim	2007/08	11	11	1	156	38	15.60	0	0									3	
20T	2006	3	3	0	47	26	15.66	0	0									0	

Cmp	Debut	M	I	NO	Runs	HS	Avge	100	50	Balls	Runs	Wkts	Avge	BB	5i	10m	RpO	ct	st

RAMDIN, Denesh (Trinidad and Tobago, West Indies, West Indies XI, Trinidad and Tobago to India, West Indies to Australia) b Mission Road, Freeport, Couva, Trinidad 13.3.1985 RHB WK

Cmp	Debut	M	I	NO	Runs	HS	Avge	100	50	Balls	Runs	Wkts	Avge	BB	5i	10m	RpO	ct	st
Test		3	5	1	63	27	15.75	0	0									3	1
FC		6	11	4	403	166*	57.57	2	0									9	2
Int		9	7	2	94	21*	18.80	0	0									9	
Lim		12	10	3	183	44*	26.14	0	0									14	2
I20T		4	4	2	29	23*	14.50	0	0									7	
20T		11	8	3	61	23*	12.20	0	0									11	3
Test	2005	42	73	8	1482	166	22.80	1	8									119	3
FC	2003/04	81	137	19	3346	166*	28.35	7	14									214	21
Int	2005	81	62	16	899	74*	19.54	0	2									109	5
Lim	2003/04	110	90	21	1615	84	23.40	0	5									144	14
I20T	2005/06	22	17	4	219	44	16.84	0	0									19	2
20T	2005/06	46	34	6	504	44	18.00	0	0									38	9

RAMPAUL, Ravindranath (Trinidad and Tobago, West Indies, West Indies XI, Trinidad and Tobago to India, West Indies to Australia) b Preysal, Trinidad 15.10.1984 LHB RFM

Cmp	Debut	M	I	NO	Runs	HS	Avge	100	50	Balls	Runs	Wkts	Avge	BB	5i	10m	RpO	ct	st
Test		2	3	1	49	31	24.50	0	0	270	149	0					3.31	1	
FC		5	7	2	52	31	10.40	0	0	578	342	4	85.50	2-75	0	0	3.55	3	
Int		9	4	0	29	14	7.25	0	0	450	344	10	34.40	2-21	0	0	4.58	1	
Lim		12	5	1	35	14	8.75	0	0	588	445	15	29.66	3-50	0	0	4.54	1	
I20T		3	2	1	11	8	11.00	0	0	60	97	4	24.25	3-17	0	0	9.70	0	
20T		6	4	3	23	8*	23.00	0	0	120	152	10	15.20	3-17	0	0	7.60	2	
Test	2009/10	5	9	3	114	40*	19.00	0	0	732	439	4	109.75	1-21	0	0	3.59	1	
FC	2001/02	42	59	9	713	64*	14.26	0	2	6127	3652	118	30.94	7-51	6	1	3.57	15	
Int	2003/04	50	19	2	165	26*	9.70	0	0	1990	1673	49	34.14	4-37	3	0	5.04	6	
Lim	2003/04	87	39	8	360	40*	11.61	0	0	3851	3040	107	28.41	4-26	5	0	4.73	15	
I20T	2007	8	3	2	11	8	11.00	0	0	180	274	9	30.44	3-17	0	0	9.13	0	
20T	2007	21	10	6	31	8*	7.75	0	0	450	568	24	23.66	4-25	1	0	7.57	4	

REIFER, Floyd Lamonte (Combined Campuses and Colleges, West Indies to South Africa) b Parish Land, Christ Church, Barbados 23.7.1972 LHB RM

Cmp	Debut	M	I	NO	Runs	HS	Avge	100	50	Balls	Runs	Wkts	Avge	BB	5i	10m	RpO	ct	st
FC		6	12	0	235	71	19.58	0	2									9	
Lim		3	2	1	58	45*	58.00	0	0									0	
20T		2	2	1	75	49	75.00	0	0									0	
Test	1996/97	6	12	0	111	29	9.25	0	0									6	
FC	1991/92	131	226	19	6971	200	33.67	13	39	252	156	1	156.00	1-19	0	0	3.71	139	
Int	1996/97	8	8	0	117	40	14.62	0	0									3	
Lim	1991/92	117	110	15	2958	130	31.13	3	15	251	217	3	72.33	1-6	0	0	5.18	36	
I20T	2009	1	1	0	22	22	22.00	0	0									1	
20T	2006	6	5	1	124	49	31.00	0	0									2	

RICHARDS, Dale Maurice (Barbados, West Indies, West Indies to South Africa) b Isolation Road, Belleplaine, St Andrew, Barbados 16.7.1976 RHB

Cmp	Debut	M	I	NO	Runs	HS	Avge	100	50	Balls	Runs	Wkts	Avge	BB	5i	10m	RpO	ct	st
Test		1	2	0	17	17	8.50	0	0									1	
FC		7	14	2	474	67	39.50	0	6									15	
Int		4	4	0	157	59	39.25	0	2									3	
Lim		4	4	0	157	59	39.25	0	2									3	
20T		4	4	0	105	40	26.25	0	0									1	
Test	2009	3	6	0	125	69	20.83	0	1									4	
FC	2000	48	87	3	3182	159	37.88	4	23									55	
Int	2009	8	7	0	179	59	25.57	0	2									5	
Lim	2000/01	48	47	1	1370	121*	29.78	1	9									14	
I20T	2009	1	1	0	0	0	0.00	0	0									0	
20T	2006	10	9	0	136	40	15.11	0	0									2	

RICHARDS, Mali Alexander (Leeward Islands) b Taunton, Somerset, England 2.9.1983 LHB RM

Cmp	Debut	M	I	NO	Runs	HS	Avge	100	50	Balls	Runs	Wkts	Avge	BB	5i	10m	RpO	ct	st
FC		3	5	0	49	20	9.80	0	0									3	
FC	2004	15	23	2	275	43	13.09	0	0	1332	847	15	56.46	3-62	0	0	3.81	12	
Lim	2002/03	2	1	0	1	1	1.00	0	0									0	
20T	2007/08	1	1	0	5	5	5.00	0	0									0	

RICHARDSON, Andrew Peter (Jamaica) b Kingston, Jamaica 6.9.1981 LHB RFM

Cmp	Debut	M	I	NO	Runs	HS	Avge	100	50	Balls	Runs	Wkts	Avge	BB	5i	10m	RpO	ct	st
FC		5	8	2	79	23*	13.16	0	0	426	287	5	57.40	2-35	0	0	4.04	3	
Lim		2	1	1	14	14*		0	0	72	65	1	65.00	1-34	0	0	5.41	1	
20T		1	1	1	0	0*		0	0	12	9	1	9.00	1-9	0	0	4.50	0	
FC	2002/03	49	69	20	463	31*	9.44	0	0	6388	3588	138	26.00	5-32	4	0	3.37	16	
Lim	2002/03	25	13	9	70	23*	17.50	0	0	1002	887	18	49.27	4-36	1	0	5.31	5	

ROACH, Kemar Andre Jamal (Barbados, West Indies, Deccan Chargers, West Indies to Australia, West Indies to South Africa) b Checker Hall, St Lucy, Barbados 30.6.1988 RHB RF

Cmp	Debut	M	I	NO	Runs	HS	Avge	100	50	Balls	Runs	Wkts	Avge	BB	5i	10m	RpO	ct	st
Test		2	3	1	11	8	5.50	0	0	388	186	6	31.00	3-22	0	0	2.87	1	
FC		5	7	2	19	8	3.80	0	0	933	421	15	28.06	7-23	1	0	2.70	2	
Int		4	2	2	3	2*		0	0	211	129	8	16.12	3-28	0	0	3.66	0	
Lim		6	4	4	23	13*		0	0	295	194	8	24.25	3-28	0	0	3.94	0	
I20T		6	1	1	3	3*		0	0	144	141	7	20.14	2-25	0	0	5.87	0	
20T		8	1	1	3	3*		0	0	174	188	7	26.85	2-25	0	0	6.48	0	

Cmp	Debut	M	I	NO	Runs	HS	Avge	100	50	Balls	Runs	Wkts	Avge	BB	5i	10m	RpO	ct	st
Test	2009	7	13	4	57	17	6.33	0	0	1472	772	26	29.69	6-48	1	0	3.14	4	
FC	2007/08	26	35	8	266	52*	9.85	0	1	4007	2365	73	32.39	7-23	3	0	3.54	14	
Int	2008	13	8	4	20	10	5.00	0	0	677	554	26	21.30	5-44	1	1	4.91	1	
Lim	2006/07	18	10	6	40	13*	10.00	0	0	843	706	29	24.34	5-44	1	1	5.02	1	
I20T	2008	10	1	1	3	3*		0	0	210	248	9	27.55	2-25	0	0	7.08	1	
20T	2008	14	2	1	13	10	13.00	0	0	288	375	9	41.66	2-25	0	0	7.81	2	
ROGERS, Codville Leon (Leeward Islands) b Sinletts, Nevis 4.7.1976 LHB																			
FC		1	2	0	7	5	3.50	0	0									2	
FC	2003/04	9	15	0	286	49	19.06	0	0									6	
Lim	2006/07	2	2	0	54	50	27.00	0	1									3	
20T	2007/08	1	1	0	13	13	13.00	0	0									0	
RUSSELL, Andre Dwayne (Jamaica, West Indies A to England, West Indies A to Ireland) b Jamaica 29.4.1988 RHB RF																			
FC		2	3	1	138	108*	69.00	1	0	201	93	7	13.28	4-41	0	0	2.77	1	
Lim		2	1	1	19	19*		0	0	99	66	6	11.00	5-42	0	1	4.00	1	
20T		7	5	1	55	16	13.75	0	0	102	166	2	83.00	1-23	0	0	9.76	3	
FC	2006/07	10	14	1	294	108*	22.61	1	0	1149	607	23	26.39	5-68	2	0	3.17	4	
Lim	2008/09	10	8	2	208	64	34.66	0	1	469	443	21	21.09	6-42	0	2	5.66	3	
SAMMY, Darren Julius Garvey (West Indies, West Indies XI, Windward Islands, West Indies to Australia, West Indies to South Africa) b Micoud, St Lucia 20.12.1983 RHB RM																			
FC		2	3	0	43	24	14.33	0	0	288	93	5	18.60	2-22	0	0	1.93	1	
Int		11	8	5	110	58*	36.66	0	1	432	286	10	28.60	4-26	1	0	3.97	9	
Lim		12	9	5	175	65	43.75	0	2	474	320	10	32.00	4-26	1	0	4.05	9	
I20T		8	7	1	82	30	13.66	0	0	141	125	13	9.61	5-26	0	1	5.31	6	
20T		14	13	4	168	30	18.66	0	0	221	244	17	14.35	5-26	0	1	6.62	10	
Test	2007	8	15	0	291	48	19.40	0	0	1462	749	27	27.74	7-66	3	0	3.07	8	
FC	2002/03	61	102	7	2382	121	25.07	1	16	8467	3804	147	25.87	7-66	9	0	2.69	76	
Int	2004	43	32	11	508	58*	24.19	0	2	1790	1335	31	43.06	4-26	1	0	4.47	23	
Lim	2001/02	96	78	17	1491	65	24.44	0	5	4140	3078	93	33.09	4-16	4	0	4.46	53	
I20T	2007	19	14	5	140	30	15.55	0	0	345	359	24	14.95	5-26	0	1	6.24	9	
20T	2006	30	22	8	248	30	17.71	0	0	509	544	35	15.54	5-26	0	1	6.41	18	
SAMUELS, Marlon Nathaniel (Jamaica) b Kingston, Jamaica 5.1.1981 RHB OB																			
20T		5	5	2	60	18*	20.00	0	0									1	
Test	2000/01	29	53	4	1408	105	28.73	2	9	1596	889	7	127.00	2-49	0	0	3.34	13	
FC	1996/97	67	115	8	3724	257	34.80	6	22	4540	2290	37	61.89	5-87	1	0	3.02	39	
Int	2000/01	107	99	16	2513	108*	30.27	2	18	3079	2465	57	43.24	3-25	0	0	4.80	29	
Lim	2000	160	149	24	4032	108*	32.25	4	30	4827	3650	99	36.86	4-21	2	0	4.53	44	
I20T	2007	6	6	0	131	51	21.83	0	1	72	128	2	64.00	1-24	0	0	10.66	0	
20T	2006	17	17	3	347	51	24.78	0	1	188	241	8	30.12	2-19	0	0	7.69	1	
SANTOKIE, Krishmar (Jamaica) b Jamaica 20.12.1984 LHB LM																			
Lim		2								102	60	3	20.00	2-34	0	0	3.52	2	
20T		7	3	2	9	8*	9.00	0	0	150	131	15	8.73	5-24	0	1	5.24	1	
Lim	2007/08	5	1	0	0	0	0.00	0	0	210	138	4	34.50	2-34	0	0	3.94	2	
SARWAN, Ramnaresh Ronnie (Guyana, West Indies, West Indies XI, West Indies to Australia) b Wakenaam Island, Essequibo, Guyana 23.6.1980 RHB LB																			
FC		1	1	0	116	116	116.00	1	0	18	16	0					5.33	0	
Int		4	4	2	191	100*	95.50	1	0									4	
Lim		8	8	3	361	100*	72.20	1	1									5	
I20T		7	6	0	97	28	16.16	0	0									3	
20T		15	14	0	245	52	17.50	0	1									7	
Test	1999/00	83	146	8	5759	291	41.73	15	31	2022	1163	23	50.56	4-37	0	0	3.45	50	
FC	1995/96	187	314	22	11739	291	40.20	31	62	4193	2224	54	41.18	6-62	1	0	3.18	134	
Int	2000	156	146	30	5098	115*	43.94	4	33	581	586	16	36.62	3-31	0	0	6.05	43	
Lim	1996/97	222	210	38	7214	118*	41.94	8	42	1112	980	35	28.00	5-10	0	1	5.28	64	
I20T	2007/08	18	16	3	298	59	22.92	0	2	12	10	2	5.00	2-10	0	0	5.00	7	
20T	2006	40	37	5	648	59	20.25	0	3	18	22	2	11.00	2-10	0	0	7.33	15	
SCANTLEBURY-SEARLES, Javon Philip Ramon (Barbados) b Durants Village, St James, Barbados 21.12.1986 RHB RFM																			
20T		3								65	80	5	16.00	4-19	1	0	7.38	2	
FC	2008/09	2	4	0	8	5	2.00	0	0	156	169	2	84.50	1-42	0	0	6.50	2	
Lim	2006/07	1								126	110	4	27.50	3-51	0	0	5.23	0	
SEBASTIEN, Liam Andrew Shannon (Windward Islands) b Roseau, Dominica 9.9.1984 LHB OB																			
FC		5	9	0	247	143	27.44	1	0	226	112	0					2.97	2	
Lim		1	1	0	15	15	15.00	0	0	12	21	0					10.50	1	
20T		2	2	0	8	7	4.00	0	0	30	40	0					8.00	2	
FC	2002/03	30	51	4	1020	143	21.70	2	4	2141	1010	32	31.56	5-47	1	0	2.83	19	
Lim	2001/02	31	29	7	475	72*	21.59	0	1	1081	761	31	24.54	5-28	0	1	4.22	13	
20T	2006	5	5	0	23	8	4.60	0	0	90	82	6	13.66	5-20	0	1	5.46	2	
SHILLINGFORD, Shane (West Indies, West Indies A, Windward Islands, West Indies A to Bangladesh) b Dominica 22.2.1983 RHB OB																			
Test		3	5	0	59	27	11.80	0	0	978	520	9	57.77	3-96	0	0	3.19	1	
FC		10	16	1	197	52	13.13	0	1	2999	1417	45	31.48	6-98	1	0	2.83	5	
Lim		1	1	0	22	22	22.00	0	0	54	20	2	10.00	2-20	0	0	2.22	1	

Cmp	Debut	M	I	NO	Runs	HS	Avge	100	50	Balls	Runs	Wkts	Avge	BB	5i	10m	RpO	ct	st
20T		4	2	0	0	0	0.00	0	0	84	77	9	8.55	4-16	1	0	5.50	1	
FC	2000/01	61	102	18	1136	63	13.52	0	4	13703	5966	225	26.51	7-66	8	0	2.61	31	
Lim	2000/01	26	17	6	119	22	10.81	0	0	1240	732	31	23.61	4-22	1	0	3.54	7	
20T	2006	7	5	1	1	1*	0.25	0	0	137	112	12	9.33	4-16	1	0	4.90	3	

SIMMONS, Lendl Mark Platter (Trinidad and Tobago, Trinidad and Tobago to India, West Indies to Australia) b Port of Spain, Trinidad 25.1.1985 RHB RMF WK

Cmp	Debut	M	I	NO	Runs	HS	Avge	100	50	Balls	Runs	Wkts	Avge	BB	5i	10m	RpO	ct	st
FC		3	6	0	164	107	27.33	1	0	192	85	2	42.50	1-12	0	0	2.65	1	
Lim		3	3	0	86	44	28.66	0	0	36	28	1	28.00	1-28	0	0	4.66	2	
20T		5	5	2	79	36*	26.33	0	0	36	55	3	18.33	1-4	0	0	9.16	2	
Test	2008/09	3	6	0	87	24	14.50	0	0	180	139	1	139.00	1-60	0	0	4.63	3	
FC	2001/02	65	114	9	3536	282	33.67	8	15	678	398	12	33.16	3-6	0	0	3.52	76	4
Int	2006/07	19	18	2	308	70	19.25	0	2	6	9	0					9.00	4	
Lim	2002	66	64	6	1515	112*	26.12	2	8	108	101	2	50.50	1-20	0	0	5.61	28	2
I20T	2007	8	8	1	187	77	26.71	0	1	36	55	6	9.16	4-19	1	0	9.16	4	
20T	2007	27	27	4	477	77	20.73	0	1	180	251	14	17.92	4-19	1	0	8.36	17	

SINGH, Gajanand (Guyana) b Cumberland, East Canjie, Berbice, Guyana 3.10.1987 LHB LM

Cmp	Debut	M	I	NO	Runs	HS	Avge	100	50	Balls	Runs	Wkts	Avge	BB	5i	10m	RpO	ct	st
FC		3	6	1	213	66	42.60	0	2	6	1	0					1.00	1	
FC	2007/08	8	14	2	350	66	29.16	0	2	59	23	1	23.00	1-22	0	0	2.33	2	
Lim	2008/09	2	2	1	30	21*	30.00	0	0									0	

SINGH, Vishaul Anthony (Guyana) b Georgetown, Demerara, Guyana 12.1.1989 LHB SLA

Cmp	Debut	M	I	NO	Runs	HS	Avge	100	50	Balls	Runs	Wkts	Avge	BB	5i	10m	RpO	ct	st
FC		2	4	0	69	31	17.25	0	0	6	14	0					14.00	4	
FC	2008/09	3	6	0	107	34	17.83	0	0	12	17	0					8.50	4	

SMITH, Dwayne Romel (Barbados, West Indies, Deccan Chargers, New South Wales, Sussex, Sussex to India, West Indies to Australia) b Storey Gap, Codrington Hill, St Michael, Barbados 12.4.1983 RHB RM

Cmp	Debut	M	I	NO	Runs	HS	Avge	100	50	Balls	Runs	Wkts	Avge	BB	5i	10m	RpO	ct	st
FC		1	2	0	23	12	11.50	0	0	256	147	3	49.00	2-97	0	0	3.44	1	
Int		1	1	0	4	4	4.00	0	0	18	18	0					6.00	0	
Lim		4	4	0	14	6	3.50	0	0	146	123	4	30.75	2-27	0	0	5.05	1	
I20T		1	1	0	12	12	12.00	0	0									0	
20T		5	5	1	63	24	15.75	0	0	60	71	1	71.00	1-20	0	0	7.10	3	
Test	2003/04	10	14	1	320	105*	24.61	1	0	651	344	7	49.14	3-71	0	0	3.17	9	
FC	2001/02	81	134	9	3679	155	29.43	7	14	8096	4054	124	32.69	4-22	0	0	3.00	78	
Int	2003/04	77	61	4	925	68	16.22	0	3	2510	2060	56	36.78	5-45	3	1	4.92	26	
Lim	2003/04	133	113	9	2274	96	21.86	0	14	3871	3123	94	33.22	6-29	3	2	4.84	44	
I20T	2005/06	8	8	0	73	29	9.12	0	0	104	155	7	22.14	3-24	0	0	8.94	1	
20T	2005/06	74	70	7	1220	72*	19.36	0	4	1084	1411	55	25.65	4-9	1	0	7.81	28	

SMITH, Devon Sheldon (West Indies A, Windward Islands, West Indies to South Africa, West Indies A to Bangladesh, West Indies A to England, West Indies A to Ireland) b Hermitage, Sauters, St Patrick, Grenada 21.10.1981 LHB OB

Cmp	Debut	M	I	NO	Runs	HS	Avge	100	50	Balls	Runs	Wkts	Avge	BB	5i	10m	RpO	ct	st
FC		6	11	0	546	193	49.63	2	1	12	2	0					1.00	13	
Lim		1	1	0	0	0	0.00	0	0									1	
20T		4	4	0	38	31	9.50	0	0									3	
Test	2002/03	31	55	2	1315	108	24.81	1	4	6	3	0					3.00	27	
FC	1998/99	129	229	9	8138	212	36.99	18	36	444	218	2	109.00	1-2	0	0	2.94	122	
Int	2002/03	32	30	2	681	91	24.32	0	3									10	
Lim	1999/00	94	91	4	2548	135	29.28	4	13	60	44	1	44.00	1-18	0	0	4.40	39	
I20T	2007	6	6	0	203	61	33.83	0	2									1	
20T	2007	11	11	0	258	61	23.45	0	2									4	

SMITH, Jamal (Combined Campuses and Colleges) b Deacon Road, St Michael, Barbados 16.10.1984 RHB OB

Cmp	Debut	M	I	NO	Runs	HS	Avge	100	50	Balls	Runs	Wkts	Avge	BB	5i	10m	RpO	ct	st
FC		2	4	0	30	24	7.50	0	0									2	
FC	2007/08	9	17	1	235	56	14.68	0	1	60	42	1	42.00	1-13	0	0	4.20	10	

SPRINGER, Khalid Kevin (Barbados) b Pie Corner, St Lucy, Barbados 3.7.1982 RHB RMF

Cmp	Debut	M	I	NO	Runs	HS	Avge	100	50	Balls	Runs	Wkts	Avge	BB	5i	10m	RpO	ct	st
Lim		2	2	1	41	35	41.00	0	0	90	54	1	54.00	1-31	0	0	3.60	1	
20T	2007/08	3								66	60	6	10.00	4-20	1	0	5.45	0	

STEWART, Navin Derrick (Trinidad and Tobago, Trinidad and Tobago to India) b Roxborough, Tobago 13.6.1983 RHB RFM

Cmp	Debut	M	I	NO	Runs	HS	Avge	100	50	Balls	Runs	Wkts	Avge	BB	5i	10m	RpO	ct	st
FC		2	4	0	23	16	5.75	0	0	216	110	2	55.00	1-33	0	0	3.05	0	
20T		3	1	0	1	1	1.00	0	0	66	110	1	110.00	1-25	0	0	10.00	1	
FC	2008/09	4	6	0	27	16	4.50	0	0	534	317	7	45.28	2-74	0	0	3.56	1	
20T	2008/09	8	4	1	64	33*	21.33	0	0	144	215	5	43.00	2-26	0	0	8.95	2	

STOUTE, Kevin Andre (Barbados, West Indies A to England, West Indies A to Ireland) b Black Rock, St Michael, Barbados 12.11.1985 RHB RMF

Cmp	Debut	M	I	NO	Runs	HS	Avge	100	50	Balls	Runs	Wkts	Avge	BB	5i	10m	RpO	ct	st
FC		6	10	0	264	74	26.40	0	1	557	194	13	14.92	3-14	0	0	2.09	2	
Lim		1	1	0	2	2	2.00	0	0	24	36	2	18.00	2-36	0	0	9.00	0	
20T		1								12	32	0					16.00	0	
FC	2006/07	22	37	1	1049	186	29.13	2	5	1745	878	43	20.41	6-64	1	0	3.01	6	
Lim	2006/07	16	14	4	446	73	44.60	0	4	302	308	14	22.00	8-52	0	1	6.11	6	

TAYLOR, Jacques David Chesney (Leeward Islands) b St Kitts 19.4.1988 RHB OB

Cmp	Debut	M	I	NO	Runs	HS	Avge	100	50	Balls	Runs	Wkts	Avge	BB	5i	10m	RpO	ct	st
20T		1																1	
20T	2006	3	2	0	61	41	30.50	0	0	36	55	2	27.50	1-26	0	0	9.16	1	

TAYLOR, Jerome Everton (Jamaica, West Indies, West Indies XI, West Indies to Australia) b St Elizabeth, Jamaica 22.6.1984 RHB RF

Cmp	Debut	M	I	NO	Runs	HS	Avge	100	50	Balls	Runs	Wkts	Avge	BB	5i	10m	RpO	ct	st
Int		4	3	0	6	6	2.00	0	0	210	187	6	31.16	2-50	0	0	5.34	1	
Lim		5	3	0	6	6	2.00	0	0	240	201	8	25.12	2-14	0	0	5.02	1	

Cmp	Debut	M	I	NO	Runs	HS	Avge	100	50	Balls	Runs	Wkts	Avge	BB	5i	10m	RpO	ct	st
I20T		5	4	2	27	16*	13.50	0	0	108	129	6	21.50	3-14	0	0	7.16	2	
20T		6	5	3	37	16*	18.50	0	0	132	159	7	22.71	3-14	0	0	7.22	2	
Test	2003	29	46	6	629	106	15.72	1	1	4935	2923	82	35.64	5-11	3	0	3.55	5	
FC	2002/03	64	97	17	1085	106	13.56	1	1	9995	5421	203	26.70	8-59	11	2	3.25	15	
Int	2003	66	30	7	204	43*	8.86	0	0	3280	2629	98	26.82	5-48	3	1	4.80	17	
Lim	2003	85	39	11	285	43*	10.17	0	0	4171	3299	129	25.57	5-48	4	1	4.74	21	
I20T	2005/06	17	9	5	47	16*	11.75	0	0	360	473	23	20.56	3-6	0	0	7.88	5	
20T	2005/06	25	11	6	57	16*	11.40	0	0	538	679	39	17.41	5-10	0	1	7.57	7	
THEOPHILE, Tyrone (Windward Islands) b Dominica 12.8.1989 RHB WK																			
FC		4	7	1	106	46	17.66	0	0	6	0	0					0.00	1	
THOMAS, Devon Cuthbert (Leeward Islands) b Bethesda, Antigua 12.11.1989 RHB RM																			
FC		2	4	0	95	52	23.75	0	1									4	
FC	2007/08	19	28	0	712	105	25.42	1	3									47	1
Int	2009	2	1	1	29	29*		0	0	7	11	2	5.50	2-11	0	0	9.42	3	
Lim	2007/08	10	8	1	103	35	14.71	0	0	7	11	2	5.50	2-11	0	0	9.42	6	1
I20T	2009	1																0	
20T	2009	1																0	
TONGE, Gavin Courtney (Leeward Islands, West Indies to Australia, West Indies to South Africa, West Indies A to Bangladesh, West Indies A to England, West Indies A to Ireland) b St John's, Antigua 13.2.1983 RHB RFM																			
FC		2	4	0	40	32	10.00	0	0	264	172	6	28.66	3-95	0	0	3.90	0	
Lim		2	1	0	28	28	28.00	0	0	54	36	1	36.00	1-36	0	0	4.00	0	
20T		2	1	1	0	0*		0	0	36	48	2	24.00	2-22	0	0	8.00	0	
Test	2009/10	1	2	1	25	23*	25.00	0	0	168	113	1	113.00	1-28	0	0	4.03	0	
FC	2002/03	34	54	9	541	57	12.02	0	2	4728	2794	95	29.41	7-58	4	0	3.54	17	
Int	2009	5	4	2	10	5	5.00	0	0	300	224	5	44.80	4-25	1	0	4.48	0	
Lim	2005/06	36	22	6	153	28	9.56	0	0	1753	1492	54	27.62	4-25	4	0	5.10	4	
I20T	2009	1								24	25	1	25.00	1-25	0	0	6.25	1	
20T	2006	6	4	4	14	10*		0	0	132	151	6	25.16	2-16	0	0	6.86	1	
TYSON, Kejel Karim (West Indies Under-19s) b Nevis 26.10.1990 RHB OB																			
Lim		2	1	0	14	14	14.00	0	0									0	
WALLACE, Gavin (Combined Campuses and Colleges) b Jamaica 22.12.1984 RHB LB																			
FC		3	6	2	16	5*	4.00	0	0	241	146	8	18.25	3-16	0	0	3.63	4	
Lim		2								48	34	0					4.25	0	
FC	2007/08	17	24	7	113	25*	6.64	0	0	2165	1275	53	24.05	8-20	2	1	3.53	8	
Lim	2008/09	5	1	0	0	0	0.00	0	0	203	107	5	21.40	2-14	0	0	3.16	1	
WALTERS, Kelbert Orlando (West Indies Under-19s) b Anguilla 4.12.1990 RHB RM																			
Lim		1								18	14	0					4.66	0	
Lim	2007/08	3	2	1	3	3	3.00	0	0	102	96	0					5.64	0	
20T	2006	2								48	52	2	26.00	1-22	0	0	6.50	0	
WALTON, Chadwick Antonio Kirkpatrick (Combined Campuses and Colleges, West Indies to South Africa, West Indies A to Bangladesh, West Indies A to England, West Indies A to Ireland) b Jamaica 3.7.1985 RHB WK																			
FC		5	10	1	237	43	26.33	0	0									11	2
Lim		3	2	0	4	2	2.00	0	0									3	
20T		2	2	0	1	1	0.50	0	0									1	1
Test	2009	2	4	0	13	10	3.25	0	0									10	
FC	2007/08	30	52	3	1160	87	23.67	0	6	30	23	0					4.60	83	6
Int	2009/10	2	2	0	0	0	0.00	0	0									6	1
Lim	2007/08	22	19	1	316	64	17.55	0	1									31	4
WARRICAN, Jomel (West Indies Under-19s) b St Vincent 20.5.1992 RHB SLA																			
Lim		1																0	
WIGGINS, Ryan Alexander (Combined Campuses and Colleges) b Howell's Cross Road, St Michael, Barbados 30.1.1984 RHB OB																			
20T		2	2	1	47	39*	47.00	0	0	24	40	1	40.00	1-27	0	0	10.00	1	
Lim	2006/07	4	2	0	60	39	30.00	0	0	114	97	1	97.00	1-30	0	0	5.10	1	
WILKINSON, Kurt Jason (Combined Campuses and Colleges) b Applethwaites, Barbados 14.8.1981 RHB RM																			
Lim		2	1	0	1	1	1.00	0	0	12	21	0					10.50	0	
FC	2000	49	86	5	2022	135	24.96	3	7	1353	702	21	33.42	4-45	0	0	3.11	52	
Lim	2001/02	27	22	1	468	76	22.28	0	3	302	238	12	19.83	3-24	0	0	4.72	9	
WILLETT, Tonito Akanni (Leeward Islands) b Government Road, Charlestown, Nevis 6.2.1983 RHB RM																			
FC		2	4	0	36	14	9.00	0	0	111	67	1	67.00	1-12	0	0	3.62	0	
Lim		2	1	0	10	10	10.00	0	0	60	50	0					5.00	0	
20T		2	2	0	39	37	19.50	0	0	18	42	0					14.00	0	
FC	2000/01	57	97	6	2337	93	25.68	0	15	3291	1749	54	32.38	5-31	2	0	3.18	28	
Lim	2001/02	33	29	2	487	61*	18.03	0	3	844	708	21	33.71	5-19	0	1	5.03	10	
20T	2006	7	7	1	177	86*	29.50	0	1	114	151	5	30.20	2-20	0	0	7.94	0	
WILLIAMS, Gavin Anjez (Leeward Islands) b Bolans, Antigua 18.11.1984 RHB RM																			
FC		3	5	0	101	44	20.20	0	0									0	
20T	2007/08	1	1	0	11	11	11.00	0	0									0	

Cmp	Debut	M	I	NO	Runs	HS	Avge	100	50	Balls	Runs	Wkts	Avge	BB	5i	10m	RpO	ct	st
YEARWOOD, Barrington Bjorn Beckenbauer (Combined Campuses and Colleges) b Castle, St Peter, Barbados 18.8.1986 LHB RFM																			
20T		2	2	0	9	7	4.50	0	0	30	51	1	51.00	1-27	0	0	10.20	1	
FC	2008/09	2	4	0	69	32	17.25	0	0	114	58	0					3.05	0	
Lim	2003/04	2	1	0	0	0	0.00	0	0	31	29	1	29.00	1-25	0	0	5.61	0	

AFGHANISTAN TO WEST INDIES 2010

Cmp	Debut	M	I	NO	Runs	HS	Avge	100	50	Balls	Runs	Wkts	Avge	BB	5i	10m	RpO	ct	st
ASGHAR STANIKZAI																			
I20T		2	2	0	33	30	16.50	0	0									0	
20T		2	2	0	33	30	16.50	0	0									0	
DAWLAT AHMADZAI																			
I20T		1								12	21	1	21.00	1-21	0	0	10.50	0	
20T		1								12	21	1	21.00	1-21	0	0	10.50	0	
HAMID HASSAN																			
I20T		2	2	0	28	22	14.00	0	0	42	29	4	7.25	3-21	0	0	4.14	0	
20T		2	2	0	28	22	14.00	0	0	42	29	4	7.25	3-21	0	0	4.14	0	
KARIM SADIQ																			
I20T		2	2	0	2	2	1.00	0	0	12	22	0					11.00	0	
20T		2	2	0	2	2	1.00	0	0	12	22	0					11.00	0	
MIRWAIS ASHRAF																			
I20T		1	1	0	23	23	23.00	0	0	12	18	0					9.00	0	
20T		1	1	0	23	23	23.00	0	0	12	18	0					9.00	0	
MOHAMMAD NABI																			
I20T		2	2	0	0	0	0.00	0	0	42	66	1	66.00	1-33	0	0	9.42	1	
20T		2	2	0	0	0	0.00	0	0	42	66	1	66.00	1-33	0	0	9.42	1	
MOHAMMAD SHAHZAD																			
I20T		2	2	0	8	6	4.00	0	0									1	1
20T		2	2	0	8	6	4.00	0	0									1	1
NAWROZ MANGAL																			
I20T		2	2	0	6	5	3.00	0	0	23	34	1	34.00	1-20	0	0	8.87	3	
20T		2	2	0	6	5	3.00	0	0	23	34	1	34.00	1-20	0	0	8.87	3	
NOOR ALI ZADRAN																			
I20T		2	2	0	50	50	25.00	0	1									0	
20T		2	2	0	50	50	25.00	0	1									0	
RAEES AHMADZAI																			
I20T		2	2	1	9	5*	9.00	0	0									0	
20T		2	2	1	9	5*	9.00	0	0									0	
SAMIULLAH SHENWARI																			
I20T		2	2	0	18	11	9.00	0	0	36	25	1	25.00	1-11	0	0	4.16	0	
20T		2	2	0	18	11	9.00	0	0	36	25	1	25.00	1-11	0	0	4.16	0	
SHAPOOR ZADRAN																			
I20T		2	2	2	1	1*		0	0	30	35	1	35.00	1-29	0	0	7.00	1	
20T		2	2	2	1	1*		0	0	30	35	1	35.00	1-29	0	0	7.00	1	

AUSTRALIA TO WEST INDIES 2010

Cmp	Debut	M	I	NO	Runs	HS	Avge	100	50	Balls	Runs	Wkts	Avge	BB	5i	10m	RpO	ct	st
CLARKE, M.J.																			
I20T		7	6	0	92	27	15.33	0	0	36	53	1	53.00	1-2	0	0	8.83	5	
20T		7	6	0	92	27	15.33	0	0	36	53	1	53.00	1-2	0	0	8.83	5	
HADDIN, B.J.																			
I20T		7	7	0	98	42	14.00	0	0									3	2
20T		7	7	0	98	42	14.00	0	0									3	2
HARRIS, R.J.																			
I20T		1	1	1	2	2*		0	0	22	28	1	28.00	1-28	0	0	7.63	0	
20T		1	1	1	2	2*		0	0	22	28	1	28.00	1-28	0	0	7.63	0	
HUSSEY, D.J.																			
I20T		7	7	1	179	59	29.83	0	2	48	47	6	7.83	2-3	0	0	5.87	6	
20T		7	7	1	179	59	29.83	0	2	48	47	6	7.83	2-3	0	0	5.87	6	
HUSSEY, M.E.K.																			
I20T		7	6	4	188	60*	94.00	0	1									8	
20T		7	6	4	188	60*	94.00	0	1									8	
JOHNSON, M.G.																			
I20T		6	2	1	5	5*	5.00	0	0	134	145	10	14.50	3-15	0	0	6.49	1	
20T		6	2	1	5	5*	5.00	0	0	134	145	10	14.50	3-15	0	0	6.49	1	
NANNES, D.P.																			
I20T		7	1	1	0	0*		0	0	156	183	14	13.07	4-18	1	0	7.03	0	
20T		7	1	1	0	0*		0	0	156	183	14	13.07	4-18	1	0	7.03	0	

Cmp	Debut	M	I	NO	Runs	HS	Avge	100	50	Balls	Runs	Wkts	Avge	BB	5i	10m	RpO	ct	st
SMITH, S.P.D.																			
I20T		7	5	2	34	27	11.33	0	0	138	163	11	14.81	3-20	0	0	7.08	6	
20T		7	5	2	34	27	11.33	0	0	138	163	11	14.81	3-20	0	0	7.08	6	
TAIT, S.W.																			
I20T		7	1	0	0	0	0.00	0	0	142	131	9	14.55	3-20	0	0	5.53	1	
20T		7	1	0	0	0	0.00	0	0	142	131	9	14.55	3-20	0	0	5.53	1	
WARNER, D.A.																			
I20T		7	7	0	150	72	21.42	0	1									8	
20T		7	7	0	150	72	21.42	0	1									8	
WATSON, S.R.																			
I20T		7	7	0	163	81	23.28	0	2	96	163	2	81.50	1-13	0	0	10.18	0	
20T		7	7	0	163	81	23.28	0	2	96	163	2	81.50	1-13	0	0	10.18	0	
WHITE, C.L.																			
I20T		7	7	3	180	85*	45.00	0	1									2	
20T		7	7	3	180	85*	45.00	0	1									2	

BANGLADESH TO WEST INDIES 2010

Cmp	Debut	M	I	NO	Runs	HS	Avge	100	50	Balls	Runs	Wkts	Avge	BB	5i	10m	RpO	ct	st
ABDUR RAZZAK																			
I20T		2	1	1	3	3*		0	0	48	70	1	70.00	1-29	0	0	8.75	1	
20T		2	1	1	3	3*		0	0	48	70	1	70.00	1-29	0	0	8.75	1	
AFTAB AHMED																			
I20T		1	1	0	1	1	1.00	0	0									2	
20T		1	1	0	1	1	1.00	0	0									2	
IMRUL KAYES																			
I20T		2	2	0	0	0	0.00	0	0									0	
20T		2	2	0	0	0	0.00	0	0									0	
JAHURUL ISLAM																			
I20T		1	1	0	18	18	18.00	0	0									1	
20T		1	1	0	18	18	18.00	0	0									1	
MAHMUDULLAH																			
I20T		2	2	0	2	2	1.00	0	0									1	
20T		2	2	0	2	2	1.00	0	0									1	
MASHRAFE MORTAZA																			
I20T		2	2	0	7	6	3.50	0	0	48	67	2	33.50	2-28	0	0	8.37	0	
20T		2	2	0	7	6	3.50	0	0	48	67	2	33.50	2-28	0	0	8.37	0	
MOHAMMAD ASHRAFUL																			
I20T		2	2	0	65	65	32.50	0	1	30	32	1	32.00	1-24	0	0	6.40	0	
20T		2	2	0	65	65	32.50	0	1	30	32	1	32.00	1-24	0	0	6.40	0	
MUSHFIQUR RAHIM																			
I20T		2	2	0	28	24	14.00	0	0									1	
20T		2	2	0	28	24	14.00	0	0									1	
NAEEM ISLAM																			
I20T		2	2	1	17	10*	17.00	0	0	12	18	0					9.00	0	
20T		2	2	1	17	10*	17.00	0	0	12	18	0					9.00	0	
SHAFIUL ISLAM																			
I20T		2	1	0	16	16	16.00	0	0	48	59	1	59.00	1-25	0	0	7.37	1	
20T		2	1	0	16	16	16.00	0	0	48	59	1	59.00	1-25	0	0	7.37	1	
SHAKIB AL HASAN																			
I20T		2	2	0	75	47	37.50	0	0	48	51	4	12.75	2-24	0	0	6.37	0	
20T		2	2	0	75	47	37.50	0	0	48	51	4	12.75	2-24	0	0	6.37	0	
SUHRAWADI SHUVO																			
I20T		1	1	1	1	1*		0	0	6	12	0					12.00	0	
20T		1	1	1	1	1*		0	0	6	12	0					12.00	0	
TAMIM IQBAL																			
I20T		1	1	0	19	19	19.00	0	0									0	
20T		1	1	0	19	19	19.00	0	0									0	

CANADA TO WEST INDIES 2009/10

Cmp	Debut	M	I	NO	Runs	HS	Avge	100	50	Balls	Runs	Wkts	Avge	BB	5i	10m	RpO	ct	st
BAGAI, A.																			
Int		1	1	0	4	4	4.00	0	0									0	
Lim		2	2	0	57	53	28.50	0	1									2	
20T		2	2	1	85	51*	85.00	0	1									1	
BAIDWAN, H.S.																			
Lim		1	1	0	8	8	8.00	0	0	24	24	1	24.00	1-24	0	0	6.00	1	
20T		2	2	0	1	1	0.50	0	0	31	59	0					11.41	1	
BARNETT, G.E.F.																			
20T		2	2	0	45	37	22.50	0	0									1	

Cmp Debut	M	I	NO	Runs	HS	Avge	100	50	Balls	Runs	Wkts	Avge	BB	5i	10m	RpO	ct	st
BASTIAMPILLAI, T.C.																		
Int	1	1	0	2	2	2.00	0	0	12	11	0					5.50	0	
Lim	2	2	0	11	9	5.50	0	0	12	11	0					5.50	0	
20T	4	4	1	44	24	14.66	0	0	6	3	1	3.00	1-3	0	0	3.00	0	
DAWOOD, J.J.																		
Lim	1	1	0	7	7	7.00	0	0									0	
20T	2	2	0	6	6	3.00	0	0									0	
DESAI, P.A.																		
Int	1	1	0	2	2	2.00	0	0	54	60	1	60.00	1-60	0	0	6.66	0	
Lim	2	2	1	2	2	2.00	0	0	92	79	1	79.00	1-60	0	0	5.15	0	
20T	4	1	1	0	0*		0	0	96	73	3	24.33	3-21	0	0	4.56	0	
DHANIRAM, S.																		
Int	1	1	0	8	8	8.00	0	0	18	15	0					5.00	0	
Lim	2	2	0	23	15	11.50	0	0	18	15	0					5.00	0	
20T	1	1	0	2	2	2.00	0	0	24	35	1	35.00	1-35	0	0	8.75	0	
GORDON, T.G.																		
20T	2	2	0	26	25	13.00	0	0	6	12	0					12.00	0	
HAMZA TARIQ																		
20T	2	2	1	16	11*	16.00	0	0									0	
KHURRAM CHAUHAN																		
Int	1	1	0	3	3	3.00	0	0	60	47	0					4.70	0	
Lim	2	2	0	9	6	4.50	0	0	78	60	1	60.00	1-13	0	0	4.61	0	
20T	2	2	1	2	2*	2.00	0	0	36	43	0					7.16	1	
OSINDE, H.																		
Int	1	1	0	7	7	7.00	0	0	30	26	0					5.20	0	
Lim	2	2	0	8	7	4.00	0	0	78	85	3	28.33	3-59	0	0	6.53	1	
20T	2								18	26	0					8.66	0	
PATEL, H.																		
Int	1	1	0	6	6	6.00	0	0	24	28	1	28.00	1-28	0	0	7.00	0	
Lim	2	2	0	11	6	5.50	0	0	24	28	1	28.00	1-28	0	0	7.00	0	
20T	4	4	0	19	9	4.75	0	0	72	96	3	32.00	2-11	0	0	8.00	1	
RIZWAN CHEEMA																		
Int	1	1	0	10	10	10.00	0	0	42	63	1	63.00	1-63	0	0	9.00	1	
Lim	2	2	0	17	10	8.50	0	0	84	89	2	44.50	1-26	0	0	6.35	2	
20T	4	4	0	37	24	9.25	0	0	48	62	3	20.66	3-19	0	0	7.75	1	
SURKARI, Z.E.																		
Int	1	1	0	19	19	19.00	0	0									1	
Lim	1	1	0	19	19	19.00	0	0									1	
20T	4	4	0	47	26	11.75	0	0									2	
UMAR BHATTI																		
Int	1	1	1	32	32*		0	0	60	61	1	61.00	1-61	0	0	6.10	0	
Lim	1	1	1	32	32*		0	0	60	61	1	61.00	1-61	0	0	6.10	0	
20T	4	4	1	24	17*	8.00	0	0	66	90	2	45.00	2-28	0	0	8.18	1	
USMAN LIMBADA																		
Int	1	1	0	5	5	5.00	0	0									1	
Lim	2	2	0	29	24	14.50	0	0									1	
20T	3	3	0	21	19	7.00	0	0									0	

ENGLAND TO WEST INDIES 2010

Cmp Debut	M	I	NO	Runs	HS	Avge	100	50	Balls	Runs	Wkts	Avge	BB	5i	10m	RpO	ct	st
BOPARA, R.S.																		
I20T	1	1	0	9	9	9.00	0	0									0	
20T	1	1	0	9	9	9.00	0	0									0	
BRESNAN, T.T.																		
I20T	7	4	2	41	23*	20.50	0	0	132	158	3	52.66	1-20	0	0	7.18	3	
20T	7	4	2	41	23*	20.50	0	0	132	158	3	52.66	1-20	0	0	7.18	3	
BROAD, S.C.J.																		
I20T	7	1	1	0	0*		0	0	125	140	8	17.50	2-21	0	0	6.72	3	
20T	7	1	1	0	0*		0	0	125	140	8	17.50	2-21	0	0	6.72	3	
COLLINGWOOD, P.D.																		
I20T	7	7	1	61	16	10.16	0	0	6	10	0					10.00	4	
20T	7	7	1	61	16	10.16	0	0	6	10	0					10.00	4	
KIESWETTER, C.																		
I20T	7	7	0	222	63	31.71	0	1									4	1
20T	7	7	0	222	63	31.71	0	1									4	1
LUMB, M.J.																		
I20T	7	7	0	137	33	19.57	0	0									3	
20T	7	7	0	137	33	19.57	0	0									3	

Cmp Debut	M	I	NO	Runs	HS	Avge	100	50	Balls	Runs	Wkts	Avge	BB	5i	10m	RpO	ct	st
MORGAN, E.J.G.																		
I20T	7	7	2	183	55	36.60	0	1									2	
20T	7	7	2	183	55	36.60	0	1									2	
PIETERSEN, K.P.																		
I20T	6	6	2	248	73*	62.00	0	2									3	
20T	6	6	2	248	73*	62.00	0	2									3	
SIDEBOTTOM, R.J.																		
I20T	7								129	160	10	16.00	3-23	0	0	7.44	2	
20T	7								129	160	10	16.00	3-23	0	0	7.44	2	
SWANN, G.P.																		
I20T	7	3	3	9	7*		0	0	132	144	10	14.40	3-24	0	0	6.54	1	
20T	7	3	3	9	7*		0	0	132	144	10	14.40	3-24	0	0	6.54	1	
WRIGHT, L.J.																		
I20T	7	5	2	90	45*	30.00	0	0	6	5	1	5.00	1-5	0	0	5.00	2	
20T	7	5	2	90	45*	30.00	0	0	6	5	1	5.00	1-5	0	0	5.00	2	
YARDY, M.H.																		
I20T	7	3	1	8	8*	4.00	0	0	120	136	4	34.00	2-19	0	0	6.80	3	
20T	7	3	1	8	8*	4.00	0	0	120	136	4	34.00	2-19	0	0	6.80	3	

INDIA TO WEST INDIES 2010

Cmp Debut	M	I	NO	Runs	HS	Avge	100	50	Balls	Runs	Wkts	Avge	BB	5i	10m	RpO	ct	st
CHAWLA, P.P.																		
I20T	2								42	55	1	55.00	1-27	0	0	7.85	2	
20T	2								42	55	1	55.00	1-27	0	0	7.85	2	
DHONI, M.S.																		
I20T	5	5	3	85	29	42.50	0	0									6	1
20T	5	5	3	85	29	42.50	0	0									6	1
GAMBHIR, G.																		
I20T	4	4	0	69	41	17.25	0	0									1	
20T	4	4	0	69	41	17.25	0	0									1	
HARBHAJAN SINGH																		
I20T	5	3	1	27	14	13.50	0	0	120	123	0					6.15	1	
20T	5	3	1	27	14	13.50	0	0	120	123	0					6.15	1	
JADEJA, R.A.																		
I20T	4	2	1	9	5*	9.00	0	0	72	117	2	58.50	1-15	0	0	9.75	1	
20T	4	2	1	9	5*	9.00	0	0	72	117	2	58.50	1-15	0	0	9.75	1	
KARTHIK, K.D.																		
I20T	2	2	0	29	16	14.50	0	0									1	
20T	2	2	0	29	16	14.50	0	0									1	
KHAN, Z.																		
I20T	3	2	1	9	9	9.00	0	0	66	105	2	52.50	1-24	0	0	9.54	1	
20T	3	2	1	9	9	9.00	0	0	66	105	2	52.50	1-24	0	0	9.54	1	
KUMAR, P.																		
I20T	2								24	17	2	8.50	2-14	0	0	4.25	0	
20T	2								24	17	2	8.50	2-14	0	0	4.25	0	
NEHRA, A.																		
I20T	5	2	0	0	0	0.00	0	0	120	156	10	15.60	3-19	0	0	7.80	1	
20T	5	2	0	0	0	0.00	0	0	120	156	10	15.60	3-19	0	0	7.80	1	
PATHAN, Y.K.																		
I20T	5	4	0	42	17	10.50	0	0	96	140	4	35.00	2-42	0	0	8.75	2	
20T	5	4	0	42	17	10.50	0	0	96	140	4	35.00	2-42	0	0	8.75	2	
RAINA, S.K.																		
I20T	5	5	0	219	101	43.80	1	1	12	23	0					11.50	0	
20T	5	5	0	219	101	43.80	1	1	12	23	0					11.50	0	
SHARMA, R.G.																		
I20T	3	2	1	84	79*	84.00	0	1									2	
20T	3	2	1	84	79*	84.00	0	1									2	
VIJAY, M.																		
I20T	4	4	0	57	48	14.25	0	0									2	
20T	4	4	0	57	48	14.25	0	0									2	
VINAY KUMAR, R.																		
I20T	1								24	30	2	15.00	2-30	0	0	7.50	0	
20T	1								24	30	2	15.00	2-30	0	0	7.50	0	
YUVRAJ SINGH																		
I20T	5	5	1	74	37	18.50	0	0	24	30	2	15.00	2-20	0	0	7.50	1	
20T	5	5	1	74	37	18.50	0	0	24	30	2	15.00	2-20	0	0	7.50	1	

Cmp	Debut	M	I	NO	Runs	HS	Avge	100	50	Balls	Runs	Wkts	Avge	BB	5i	10m	RpO	ct	st

IRELAND TO WEST INDIES 2009/10

Cmp	Debut	M	I	NO	Runs	HS	Avge	100	50	Balls	Runs	Wkts	Avge	BB	5i	10m	RpO	ct	st
BOTHA, A.C.																			
FC		1	1	0	15	15	15.00	0	0	66	33	2	16.50	1-14	0	0	3.00	0	
Int		1	1	0	9	9	9.00	0	0	42	38	0					5.42	1	
Lim		2	2	0	22	13	11.00	0	0	42	38	0					5.42	1	
I20T		2	1	1	4	4*		0	0	36	36	3	12.00	2-7	0	0	6.00	3	
20T		4	3	2	18	10	18.00	0	0	84	94	5	18.80	2-7	0	0	6.71	3	
CONNELL, P.																			
FC		1	1	0	0	0	0.00	0	0	113	114	4	28.50	4-77	0	0	6.05	1	
Int		1	1	1	2	2*		0	0	48	25	1	25.00	1-25	0	0	3.12	0	
Lim		2	2	2	13	11*		0	0	98	73	2	36.50	1-25	0	0	4.46	0	
20T		3	1	1	6	6*		0	0	60	79	4	19.75	2-34	0	0	7.90	0	
CUSACK, A.R.																			
FC		1	1	0	53	53	53.00	0	1	78	29	0					2.23	0	
Int		1	1	0	1	1	1.00	0	0	30	24	0					4.80	1	
Lim		2	2	0	5	4	2.50	0	0	30	24	0					4.80	1	
I20T		2	1	0	2	2	2.00	0	0	24	26	2	13.00	2-19	0	0	6.50	1	
20T		6	5	1	33	15	8.25	0	0	90	125	7	17.85	3-19	0	0	8.33	3	
DOCKRELL, G.H.																			
Int		1	1	0	0	0	0.00	0	0	30	34	1	34.00	1-34	0	0	6.80	1	
Lim		2	2	0	1	1	0.50	0	0	90	73	1	73.00	1-34	0	0	4.86	1	
I20T		2	1	0	0	0	0.00	0	0	48	35	3	11.66	3-16	0	0	4.37	0	
20T		3	1	0	0	0	0.00	0	0	72	59	4	14.75	3-16	0	0	4.91	0	
JOHNSTON, D.T.																			
FC		1	1	1	12	12*		0	0	108	54	1	54.00	1-42	0	0	3.00	3	
Int		1	1	0	5	5	5.00	0	0	54	43	1	43.00	1-43	0	0	4.77	0	
Lim		1	1	0	5	5	5.00	0	0	54	43	1	43.00	1-43	0	0	4.77	0	
I20T		2	1	0	5	5	5.00	0	0	48	50	1	50.00	1-14	0	0	6.25	0	
20T		5	4	1	84	39	28.00	0	0	114	112	5	22.40	2-19	0	0	5.89	2	
JONES, N.G.																			
Lim		1	1	0	30	30	30.00	0	0	60	49	1	49.00	1-49	0	0	4.90	2	
20T		2	2	0	21	21	10.50	0	0	12	26	0					13.00	0	
KIDD, G.E.																			
FC		1	1	0	1	1	1.00	0	0	156	146	4	36.50	3-102	0	0	5.61	3	
20T		3	1	0	1	1	1.00	0	0	48	59	3	19.66	2-13	0	0	7.37	0	
MOONEY, J.F.																			
Lim		1	1	0	6	6	6.00	0	0	36	23	0					3.83	0	
I20T		2	1	0	1	1	1.00	0	0									2	
20T		6	5	2	42	15	14.00	0	0									5	
O'BRIEN, K.J.																			
FC		1	1	0	23	23	23.00	0	0	90	50	1	50.00	1-29	0	0	3.33	0	
Int		1	1	0	54	54	54.00	0	1	30	17	0					3.40	0	
Lim		2	2	0	80	54	40.00	0	1	78	50	1	50.00	1-33	0	0	3.84	0	
I20T		2	1	0	9	9	9.00	0	0	24	30	2	15.00	2-22	0	0	7.50	1	
20T		5	4	1	33	13	11.00	0	0	78	108	5	21.60	2-22	0	0	8.30	2	
O'BRIEN, N.J.																			
FC		1	1	0	62	62	62.00	0	1	9	12	1	12.00	1-12	0	0	8.00	2	
Int		1	1	0	49	49	49.00	0	0									0	
Lim		1	1	0	49	49	49.00	0	0									0	
I20T		2	2	1	15	9*	15.00	0	0									2	
20T		6	6	1	97	62	19.40	0	1									3	1
PORTERFIELD, W.T.S.																			
FC		1	1	0	1	1	1.00	0	0	36	29	1	29.00	1-29	0	0	4.83	1	
Int		1	1	0	10	10	10.00	0	0									0	
Lim		2	2	0	54	44	27.00	0	0									0	
I20T		2	2	1	8	4*	8.00	0	0									2	
20T		6	6	1	64	25	12.80	0	0									4	
RANKIN, W.B.																			
I20T		2	1	0	1	1	1.00	0	0	48	60	4	15.00	2-25	0	0	7.50	1	
20T		2	1	0	1	1	1.00	0	0	48	60	4	15.00	2-25	0	0	7.50	1	
STIRLING, P.R.																			
FC		1	1	0	65	65	65.00	0	1	171	92	3	30.66	2-45	0	0	3.22	0	
Int		1	1	0	51	51	51.00	0	1	30	30	1	30.00	1-30	0	0	6.00	1	
Lim		2	2	0	51	51	25.50	0	1	42	46	1	46.00	1-30	0	0	6.57	1	
I20T		2	2	0	0	0	0.00	0	0	12	15	0					7.50	0	
20T		6	6	0	80	33	13.33	0	0	78	84	1	84.00	1-13	0	0	6.46	1	
WHITE, A.R.																			
FC		1	1	0	22	22	22.00	0	0	102	75	0					4.41	1	
Int		1	1	0	19	19	19.00	0	0									0	

Cmp Debut	M	I	NO	Runs	HS	Avge	100	50	Balls	Runs	Wkts	Avge	BB	5i	10m	RpO	ct	st
Lim	2	2	0	20	19	10.00	0	0	18	19	0					6.33	0	
20T	3	2	0	25	16	12.50	0	0	6	17	1	17.00	1-17	0	0	17.00	0	
WILSON, G.C.																		
FC	1	1	0	6	6	6.00	0	0	12	2	0					1.00	1	
Int	1	1	0	4	4	4.00	0	0									0	
Lim	2	2	0	57	53	28.50	0	1									0	
I20T	2	1	0	17	17	17.00	0	0									3	
20T	6	5	0	47	17	9.40	0	0									7	

NEW ZEALAND TO WEST INDIES 2010

Cmp Debut	M	I	NO	Runs	HS	Avge	100	50	Balls	Runs	Wkts	Avge	BB	5i	10m	RpO	ct	st
BOND, S.E.																		
I20T	5								114	145	5	29.00	2-29	0	0	7.63	0	
20T	5								114	145	5	29.00	2-29	0	0	7.63	0	
BUTLER, I.G.																		
I20T	2	1	1	0	0*		0	0	30	29	3	9.66	3-19	0	0	5.80	1	
20T	2	1	1	0	0*		0	0	30	29	3	9.66	3-19	0	0	5.80	1	
GUPTILL, M.J.																		
I20T	4	4	1	45	19	15.00	0	0									4	
20T	4	4	1	45	19	15.00	0	0									4	
HOPKINS, G.J.																		
I20T	5	4	0	22	18	5.50	0	0									2	1
20T	5	4	0	22	18	5.50	0	0									2	1
McCULLUM, B.B.																		
I20T	5	5	1	94	33	23.50	0	0									2	
20T	5	5	1	94	33	23.50	0	0									2	
McCULLUM, N.L.																		
I20T	5	4	4	57	26*		0	0	114	124	7	17.71	3-16	0	0	6.52	6	
20T	5	4	4	57	26*		0	0	114	124	7	17.71	3-16	0	0	6.52	6	
MILLS, K.D.																		
I20T	2								43	65	3	21.66	2-33	0	0	9.07	1	
20T	2								43	65	3	21.66	2-33	0	0	9.07	1	
ORAM, J.D.P.																		
I20T	3	2	0	15	15	7.50	0	0	42	58	2	29.00	1-22	0	0	8.28	1	
20T	3	2	0	15	15	7.50	0	0	42	58	2	29.00	1-22	0	0	8.28	1	
REDMOND, A.J.																		
I20T	1	1	0	16	16	16.00	0	0									0	
20T	1	1	0	16	16	16.00	0	0									0	
RYDER, J.D.																		
I20T	5	5	0	93	42	18.60	0	0									0	
20T	5	5	0	93	42	18.60	0	0									0	
SOUTHEE, T.G.																		
I20T	3	1	1	0	0*		0	0	54	78	3	26.00	1-18	0	0	8.66	1	
20T	3	1	1	0	0*		0	0	54	78	3	26.00	1-18	0	0	8.66	1	
STYRIS, S.B.																		
I20T	5	4	0	82	31	20.50	0	0	54	48	6	8.00	3-5	0	0	5.33	0	
20T	5	4	0	82	31	20.50	0	0	54	48	6	8.00	3-5	0	0	5.33	0	
TAYLOR, L.R.P.L.																		
I20T	5	4	0	75	44	18.75	0	0									3	
20T	5	4	0	75	44	18.75	0	0									3	
VETTORI, D.L.																		
I20T	5	4	2	69	38	34.50	0	0	115	109	3	36.33	2-10	0	0	5.68	1	
20T	5	4	2	69	38	34.50	0	0	115	109	3	36.33	2-10	0	0	5.68	1	

PAKISTAN TO WEST INDIES 2010

Cmp Debut	M	I	NO	Runs	HS	Avge	100	50	Balls	Runs	Wkts	Avge	BB	5i	10m	RpO	ct	st
ABDUL RAZZAQ																		
I20T	6	6	2	69	29	17.25	0	0	60	83	2	41.50	1-16	0	0	8.30	0	
20T	6	6	2	69	29	17.25	0	0	60	83	2	41.50	1-16	0	0	8.30	0	
ABDUR REHMAN																		
I20T	3	2	1	4	2*	4.00	0	0	66	87	6	14.50	2-19	0	0	7.90	4	
20T	3	2	1	4	2*	4.00	0	0	66	87	6	14.50	2-19	0	0	7.90	4	
FAWAD ALAM																		
I20T	3	2	0	17	16	8.50	0	0									2	
20T	3	2	0	17	16	8.50	0	0									2	
KAMRAN AKMAL																		
I20T	6	6	0	180	73	30.00	0	2									3	6
20T	6	6	0	180	73	30.00	0	2									3	6

Cmp Debut	M	I	NO	Runs	HS	Avge	100	50	Balls	Runs	Wkts	Avge	BB	5i	10m	RpO	ct	st
KHALID LATIF																		
I20T	2	2	0	20	13	10.00	0	0									1	
20T	2	2	0	20	13	10.00	0	0									1	
MISBAH-UL-HAQ																		
I20T	6	6	1	68	41	13.60	0	0									2	
20T	6	6	1	68	41	13.60	0	0									2	
MOHAMMAD AAMER																		
I20T	6	2	0	5	3	2.50	0	0	138	152	8	19.00	3-23	0	0	6.60	1	
20T	6	2	0	5	3	2.50	0	0	138	152	8	19.00	3-23	0	0	6.60	1	
MOHAMMAD ASIF																		
I20T	1	1	1	0	0*		0	0	24	43	0					10.75	0	
20T	1	1	1	0	0*		0	0	24	43	0					10.75	0	
MOHAMMAD HAFEEZ																		
I20T	6	4	0	39	18	9.75	0	0	84	123	2	61.50	1-28	0	0	8.78	2	
20T	6	4	0	39	18	9.75	0	0	84	123	2	61.50	1-28	0	0	8.78	2	
MOHAMMAD SAMI																		
I20T	3	1	1	5	5*		0	0	66	108	6	18.00	3-29	0	0	9.81	2	
20T	3	1	1	5	5*		0	0	66	108	6	18.00	3-29	0	0	9.81	2	
SAEED AJMAL																		
I20T	6	2	1	17	13*	17.00	0	0	134	169	11	15.36	4-26	1	0	7.56	1	
20T	6	2	1	17	13*	17.00	0	0	134	169	11	15.36	4-26	1	0	7.56	1	
SALMAN BUTT																		
I20T	6	6	1	223	73	44.60	0	2									0	
20T	6	6	1	223	73	44.60	0	2									0	
SHAHID AFRIDI																		
I20T	6	6	0	91	33	15.16	0	0	144	182	4	45.50	2-29	0	0	7.58	1	
20T	6	6	0	91	33	15.16	0	0	144	182	4	45.50	2-29	0	0	7.58	1	
UMAR AKMAL																		
I20T	6	5	1	155	56*	38.75	0	2									7	
20T	6	5	1	155	56*	38.75	0	2									7	

SOUTH AFRICA TO WEST INDIES 2010

Cmp Debut	M	I	NO	Runs	HS	Avge	100	50	Balls	Runs	Wkts	Avge	BB	5i	10m	RpO	ct	st
AMLA, H.M.																		
Test	3	6	0	122	44	20.33	0	0									1	
FC	3	6	0	122	44	20.33	0	0									1	
Int	5	5	0	402	129	80.40	2	1									0	
Lim	5	5	0	402	129	80.40	2	1									0	
BOSMAN, L.E.																		
I20T	4	4	0	15	8	3.75	0	0									0	
20T	4	4	0	15	8	3.75	0	0									0	
BOTHA, J.																		
Test	1	1	0	9	9	9.00	0	0	239	102	7	14.57	4-56	0	0	2.56	1	
FC	1	1	0	9	9	9.00	0	0	239	102	7	14.57	4-56	0	0	2.56	1	
Int	5	3	0	45	24	15.00	0	0	276	232	4	58.00	2-47	0	0	5.04	3	
Lim	5	3	0	45	24	15.00	0	0	276	232	4	58.00	2-47	0	0	5.04	3	
I20T	5	4	0	54	23	13.50	0	0	102	92	9	10.22	3-22	0	0	5.41	1	
20T	5	4	0	54	23	13.50	0	0	102	92	9	10.22	3-22	0	0	5.41	1	
BOUCHER, M.V.																		
Test	3	3	0	103	69	34.33	0	1									10	
FC	3	3	0	103	69	34.33	0	1									10	
Int	1	1	0	6	6	6.00	0	0									1	
Lim	1	1	0	6	6	6.00	0	0									1	
I20T	5	5	2	29	12	9.66	0	0									5	
20T	5	5	2	29	12	9.66	0	0									5	
DE VILLIERS, A.B.																		
Test	3	6	4	330	135*	165.00	1	2									4	
FC	3	6	4	330	135*	165.00	1	2									4	
Int	5	5	1	283	102	70.75	1	2									5	
Lim	5	5	1	283	102	70.75	1	2									5	
I20T	7	7	1	183	53	30.50	0	1									9	2
20T	7	7	1	183	53	30.50	0	1									9	2
DUMINY, J.P.																		
Int	3	3	1	98	51	49.00	0	1	18	19	0					6.33	1	
Lim	3	3	1	98	51	49.00	0	1	18	19	0					6.33	1	
I20T	7	6	1	84	39	16.80	0	0	6	11	1	11.00	1-11	0	0	11.00	1	
20T	7	6	1	84	39	16.80	0	0	6	11	1	11.00	1-11	0	0	11.00	1	
GIBBS, H.H.																		
I20T	3	3	0	41	30	13.66	0	0									5	
20T	3	3	0	41	30	13.66	0	0									5	

Cmp Debut	M	I	NO	Runs	HS	Avge	100	50	Balls	Runs	Wkts	Avge	BB	5i	10m	RpO	ct	st
HARRIS, P.L.																		
Test	3	2	0	21	11	10.50	0	0	777	358	5	71.60	2-91	0	0	2.76	1	
FC	3	2	0	21	11	10.50	0	0	777	358	5	71.60	2-91	0	0	2.76	1	
KALLIS, J.H.																		
Test	3	6	2	283	110	70.75	1	1	337	166	5	33.20	2-36	0	0	2.95	4	
FC	3	6	2	283	110	70.75	1	1	337	166	5	33.20	2-36	0	0	2.95	4	
Int	5	5	0	225	85	45.00	0	3	138	107	3	35.66	1-7	0	0	4.65	7	
Lim	5	5	0	225	85	45.00	0	3	138	107	3	35.66	1-7	0	0	4.65	7	
I20T	6	6	0	224	73	37.33	0	2	102	109	2	54.50	1-28	0	0	6.41	2	
20T	6	6	0	224	73	37.33	0	2	102	109	2	54.50	1-28	0	0	6.41	2	
KLEINVELDT, R.K.																		
I20T	1								24	48	2	24.00	2-48	0	0	12.00	0	
20T	1								24	48	2	24.00	2-48	0	0	12.00	0	
LANGEVELDT, C.K.																		
Int	3	2	1	6	6	6.00	0	0	138	137	5	27.40	3-30	0	0	5.95	0	
Lim	3	2	1	6	6	6.00	0	0	138	137	5	27.40	3-30	0	0	5.95	0	
I20T	5	1	1	2	2*		0	0	114	135	12	11.25	4-19	1	0	7.10	0	
20T	5	1	1	2	2*		0	0	114	135	12	11.25	4-19	1	0	7.10	0	
McLAREN, R.																		
Int	5	4	1	26	12	8.66	0	0	228	203	4	50.75	2-37	0	0	5.34	3	
Lim	5	4	1	26	12	8.66	0	0	228	203	4	50.75	2-37	0	0	5.34	3	
I20T	2	2	2	7	6*		0	0	47	48	5	9.60	5-19	0	1	6.12	1	
20T	2	2	2	7	6*		0	0	47	48	5	9.60	5-19	0	1	6.12	1	
MILLER, D.A.																		
Int	4	3	2	54	26*	54.00	0	0									1	
Lim	4	3	2	54	26*	54.00	0	0									1	
I20T	1	1	0	33	33	33.00	0	0									0	
20T	1	1	0	33	33	33.00	0	0									0	
MORKEL, J.A.																		
I20T	5	5	1	82	40	20.50	0	0	60	100	1	100.00	1-39	0	0	10.00	1	
20T	5	5	1	82	40	20.50	0	0	60	100	1	100.00	1-39	0	0	10.00	1	
MORKEL, M.																		
Test	3	2	0	11	9	5.50	0	0	500	265	14	18.92	4-19	0	0	3.18	0	
FC	3	2	0	11	9	5.50	0	0	500	265	14	18.92	4-19	0	0	3.18	0	
Int	4	1	0	14	14	14.00	0	0	193	175	11	15.90	4-21	1	0	5.44	0	
Lim	4	1	0	14	14	14.00	0	0	193	175	11	15.90	4-21	1	0	5.44	0	
I20T	5	1	0	1	1	1.00	0	0	114	134	10	13.40	4-20	1	0	7.05	0	
20T	5	1	0	1	1	1.00	0	0	114	134	10	13.40	4-20	1	0	7.05	0	
PETERSEN, A.N.																		
Test	3	6	0	151	52	25.16	0	1	42	21	1	21.00	1-2	0	0	3.00	4	
FC	3	6	0	151	52	25.16	0	1	42	21	1	21.00	1-2	0	0	3.00	4	
Int	2	2	0	17	16	8.50	0	0									1	
Lim	2	2	0	17	16	8.50	0	0									1	
I20T	2	2	0	14	8	7.00	0	0									1	
20T	2	2	0	14	8	7.00	0	0									1	
PRINCE, A.G.																		
Test	3	4	2	160	78*	80.00	0	2									2	
FC	3	4	2	160	78*	80.00	0	2									2	
SMITH, G.C.																		
Test	3	6	0	371	132	61.83	1	2	3	4	0					8.00	2	
FC	3	6	0	371	132	61.83	1	2	3	4	0					8.00	2	
Int	5	5	0	119	37	23.80	0	0									4	
Lim	5	5	0	119	37	23.80	0	0									4	
I20T	7	7	0	161	37	23.00	0	0									5	
20T	7	7	0	161	37	23.00	0	0									5	
STEYN, D.W.																		
Test	3	3	1	63	39	31.50	0	0	495	272	15	18.13	5-29	1	0	3.29	1	
FC	3	3	1	63	39	31.50	0	0	495	272	15	18.13	5-29	1	0	3.29	1	
Int	3	2	1	2	2*	2.00	0	0	150	115	4	28.75	2-37	0	0	4.60	0	
Lim	3	2	1	2	2*	2.00	0	0	150	115	4	28.75	2-37	0	0	4.60	0	
I20T	7	2	1	6	5	6.00	0	0	162	172	6	28.66	2-6	0	0	6.37	5	
20T	7	2	1	6	5	6.00	0	0	162	172	6	28.66	2-6	0	0	6.37	5	
TSOTSOBE, L.L.																		
Test	2	1	1	3	3*		0	0	294	106	2	53.00	1-20	0	0	2.16	0	
FC	2	1	1	3	3*		0	0	294	106	2	53.00	1-20	0	0	2.16	0	
Int	4	1	1	4	4*		0	0	181	166	6	27.66	2-31	0	0	5.50	1	
Lim	4	1	1	4	4*		0	0	181	166	6	27.66	2-31	0	0	5.50	1	
I20T	1								24	28	0					7.00	0	
20T	1								24	28	0					7.00	0	

Cmp	Debut	M	I	NO	Runs	HS	Avge	100	50	Balls	Runs	Wkts	Avge	BB	5i	10m	RpO	ct	st
VAN DER MERWE, R.E.																			
Int		1	1	1	10	10*		0	0	60	27	1	27.00	1-27	0	0	2.70	0	
Lim		1	1	1	10	10*		0	0	60	27	1	27.00	1-27	0	0	2.70	0	
I20T		4	3	3	8	4*		0	0	60	84	2	42.00	1-17	0	0	8.40	1	
20T		4	3	3	8	4*		0	0	60	84	2	42.00	1-17	0	0	8.40	1	

SRI LANKA TO WEST INDIES 2010

Cmp	Debut	M	I	NO	Runs	HS	Avge	100	50	Balls	Runs	Wkts	Avge	BB	5i	10m	RpO	ct	st
CHANDIMAL, L.D.																			
I20T		3	3	0	57	29	19.00	0	0									0	
20T		3	3	0	57	29	19.00	0	0									0	
DILSHAN, T.M.																			
I20T		6	6	1	71	33	14.20	0	0	18	19	0					6.33	0	
20T		6	6	1	71	33	14.20	0	0	18	19	0					6.33	0	
JAYASINGHE, C.U.																			
I20T		2	1	1	2	2*		0	0									0	
20T		2	1	1	2	2*		0	0									0	
JAYASURIYA, S.T.																			
I20T		6	6	2	15	6	3.75	0	0	42	52	1	52.00	1-17	0	0	7.42	1	
20T		6	6	2	15	6	3.75	0	0	42	52	1	52.00	1-17	0	0	7.42	1	
JAYAWARDENE, D.P.M.D.																			
I20T		6	6	1	302	100	60.40	1	2									3	
20T		6	6	1	302	100	60.40	1	2									3	
KALUHALAMULLA, H.K.S.R.																			
I20T		4	1	0	2	2	2.00	0	0	66	78	3	26.00	3-20	0	0	7.09	0	
20T		4	1	0	2	2	2.00	0	0	66	78	3	26.00	3-20	0	0	7.09	0	
KAPUGEDERA, C.K.																			
I20T		6	6	1	95	37*	19.00	0	0									3	
20T		6	6	1	95	37*	19.00	0	0									3	
KULASEKARA, K.M.D.N.																			
I20T		1								24	27	1	27.00	1-27	0	0	6.75	0	
20T		1								24	27	1	27.00	1-27	0	0	6.75	0	
MALINGA, S.L.																			
I20T		6	2	1	3	2*	3.00	0	0	125	165	6	27.50	3-28	0	0	7.92	2	
20T		6	2	1	3	2*	3.00	0	0	125	165	6	27.50	3-28	0	0	7.92	2	
MATHEWS, A.D.																			
I20T		6	5	0	119	58	23.80	0	1	72	83	4	20.75	2-24	0	0	6.91	3	
20T		6	5	0	119	58	23.80	0	1	72	83	4	20.75	2-24	0	0	6.91	3	
MENDIS, B.A.W.																			
I20T		5	1	0	1	1	1.00	0	0	108	128	4	32.00	3-24	0	0	7.11	1	
20T		5	1	0	1	1	1.00	0	0	108	128	4	32.00	3-24	0	0	7.11	1	
MIRANDO, M.T.T.																			
I20T		1								24	41	2	20.50	2-41	0	0	10.25	0	
20T		1								24	41	2	20.50	2-41	0	0	10.25	0	
MURALITHARAN, M.																			
I20T		2								48	51	2	25.50	2-25	0	0	6.37	0	
20T		2								48	51	2	25.50	2-25	0	0	6.37	0	
PERERA, N.L.T.C.																			
I20T		4	3	2	30	23	30.00	0	0	42	47	3	15.66	2-19	0	0	6.71	0	
20T		4	3	2	30	23	30.00	0	0	42	47	3	15.66	2-19	0	0	6.71	0	
SANGAKKARA, K.C.																			
I20T		6	6	0	139	68	23.16	0	1									2	1
20T		6	6	0	139	68	23.16	0	1									2	1
WELAGEDARA, U.W.M.B.C.A.																			
I20T		2	1	1	2	2*		0	0	36	61	1	61.00	1-21	0	0	10.16	0	
20T		2	1	1	2	2*		0	0	36	61	1	61.00	1-21	0	0	10.16	0	

ZIMBABWE TO WEST INDIES 2010

Cmp	Debut	M	I	NO	Runs	HS	Avge	100	50	Balls	Runs	Wkts	Avge	BB	5i	10m	RpO	ct	st
BLIGNAUT, A.M.																			
FC		1	2	0	72	72	36.00	0	1	60	43	0					4.30	2	
I20T		1	1	0	8	8	8.00	0	0									0	
20T		2	2	0	8	8	4.00	0	0	6	12	1	12.00	1-12	0	0	12.00	0	
CHATARA, T.L.																			
FC		1	2	1	1	1*	1.00	0	0	171	110	1	110.00	1-79	0	0	3.86	1	
CHIBHABHA, C.J.																			
FC		1	2	0	57	40	28.50	0	0	150	50	1	50.00	1-26	0	0	2.00	0	
20T		2	2	0	43	33	21.50	0	0	21	33	1	33.00	1-20	0	0	9.42	1	

Cmp Debut	M	I	NO	Runs	HS	Avge	100	50	Balls	Runs	Wkts	Avge	BB	5i	10m	RpO	ct	st
CHIGUMBURA, E.																		
Int	5	5	0	148	50	29.60	0	1	138	145	6	24.16	2-32	0	0	6.30	3	
Lim	5	5	0	148	50	29.60	0	1	138	145	6	24.16	2-32	0	0	6.30	3	
I20T	3	2	0	37	34	18.50	0	0	18	28	1	28.00	1-21	0	0	9.33	1	
20T	3	2	0	37	34	18.50	0	0	18	28	1	28.00	1-21	0	0	9.33	1	
COVENTRY, C.K.																		
FC	1	2	0	13	11	6.50	0	0									0	
Int	1	1	0	56	56	56.00	0	1									0	
Lim	1	1	0	56	56	56.00	0	1									0	
I20T	2	1	0	0	0	0.00	0	0									0	
20T	3	2	0	0	0	0.00	0	0									0	
CREMER, A.G.																		
FC	1	2	0	51	47	25.50	0	0	306	132	2	66.00	1-59	0	0	2.58	1	
Int	5	4	1	57	19*	19.00	0	0	240	186	7	26.57	3-34	0	0	4.65	2	
Lim	5	4	1	57	19*	19.00	0	0	240	186	7	26.57	3-34	0	0	4.65	2	
I20T	3	2	0	2	2	1.00	0	0	42	34	4	8.50	3-11	0	0	4.85	1	
20T	4	3	1	11	9*	5.50	0	0	66	64	5	12.80	3-11	0	0	5.81	1	
ERVINE, C.R.																		
FC	1	2	0	80	58	40.00	0	1									1	
I20T	2	1	0	1	1	1.00	0	0									1	
20T	3	2	0	26	25	13.00	0	0									2	
LAMB, G.A.																		
Int	5	5	1	60	23	15.00	0	0	234	138	5	27.60	1-16	0	0	3.53	0	
Lim	5	5	1	60	23	15.00	0	0	234	138	5	27.60	1-16	0	0	3.53	0	
I20T	3	2	1	25	14*	25.00	0	0	49	49	4	12.25	2-14	0	0	6.00	0	
20T	4	3	1	36	14*	18.00	0	0	73	61	5	12.20	2-14	0	0	5.01	0	
MARUMA, T.																		
FC	1	2	0	22	18	11.00	0	0	174	96	2	48.00	1-41	0	0	3.31	2	
Int	3	3	0	12	9	4.00	0	0	58	54	2	27.00	1-16	0	0	5.58	2	
Lim	3	3	0	12	9	4.00	0	0	58	54	2	27.00	1-16	0	0	5.58	2	
I20T	1	1	0	4	4	4.00	0	0									0	
20T	3	3	0	4	4	1.33	0	0	40	43	1	43.00	1-18	0	0	6.45	2	
MASAKADZA, H.																		
FC	1	2	0	30	30	15.00	0	0	18	6	0					2.00	0	
Int	5	5	0	90	41	18.00	0	0									2	
Lim	5	5	0	90	41	18.00	0	0									2	
I20T	3	3	0	68	44	22.66	0	0									1	
20T	5	5	0	105	44	21.00	0	0	6	12	0					12.00	2	
MASAKADZA, S.W.																		
Int	1								18	36	3	12.00	3-36	0	0	12.00	0	
Lim	1								18	36	3	12.00	3-36	0	0	12.00	0	
I20T	1	1	0	0	0	0.00	0	0	6	6	0					6.00	1	
20T	1	1	0	0	0	0.00	0	0	6	6	0					6.00	1	
MATSIKENYERI, S.																		
Int	4	4	1	19	16*	6.33	0	0	12	8	0					4.00	1	
Lim	4	4	1	19	16*	6.33	0	0	12	8	0					4.00	1	
I20T	1	1	0	0	0	0.00	0	0	6	10	0					10.00	0	
20T	1	1	0	0	0	0.00	0	0	6	10	0					10.00	0	
MPOFU, C.B.																		
FC	1	2	0	14	9	7.00	0	0	269	83	8	10.37	7-37	1	0	1.85	0	
Int	1	1	0	0	0	0.00	0	0	24	30	0					7.50	0	
Lim	1	1	0	0	0	0.00	0	0	24	30	0					7.50	0	
I20T	1								18	27	0					9.00	2	
20T	2	1	1	5	5*		0	0	30	38	0					7.60	2	
PRICE, R.W.																		
Int	5	4	0	13	5	3.25	0	0	266	161	3	53.66	2-31	0	0	3.63	1	
Lim	5	4	0	13	5	3.25	0	0	266	161	3	53.66	2-31	0	0	3.63	1	
I20T	3	2	1	2	2	2.00	0	0	72	63	3	21.00	2-31	0	0	5.25	1	
20T	5	2	1	2	2	2.00	0	0	120	106	6	17.66	2-16	0	0	5.30	2	
SIBANDA, V.																		
Int	5	5	0	119	95	23.80	0	1									1	
Lim	5	5	0	119	95	23.80	0	1									1	
I20T	1	1	0	0	0	0.00	0	0									0	
20T	3	3	0	17	11	5.66	0	0									0	
TAIBU, T.																		
FC	1	2	1	145	86*	145.00	0	2									3	
Int	5	5	0	102	56	20.40	0	1									1	5
Lim	5	5	0	102	56	20.40	0	1									1	5
I20T	3	3	1	33	21	16.50	0	0									1	
20T	5	5	1	56	21	14.00	0	0									4	1

Cmp Debut	M	I	NO	Runs	HS	Avge	100	50	Balls	Runs	Wkts	Avge	BB	5i	10m	RpO	ct	st
TAYLOR, B.R.M.																		
FC	1	2	0	9	5	4.50	0	0									2	
Int	5	5	0	75	47	15.00	0	0	18	20	1	20.00	1-6	0	0	6.66	2	
Lim	5	5	0	75	47	15.00	0	0	18	20	1	20.00	1-6	0	0	6.66	2	
I20T	2	2	1	11	11*	11.00	0	0	6	1	0					1.00	0	
20T	4	4	1	49	37	16.33	0	0	6	1	0					1.00	0	
UTSEYA, P.																		
Int	5	4	3	31	13*	31.00	0	0	252	203	5	40.60	2-41	0	0	4.83	1	
Lim	5	4	3	31	13*	31.00	0	0	252	203	5	40.60	2-41	0	0	4.83	1	
I20T	3	2	0	0	0	0.00	0	0	72	65	3	21.66	1-12	0	0	5.41	1	
20T	5	4	2	16	15*	8.00	0	0	120	111	5	22.20	1-12	0	0	5.55	1	

ZIMBABWE

Logan Cup winners 2009/10 (first-class): Mashonaland Eagles
Faithwear Metbank One-Day Competition winners 2009/10 (limited overs): Mountaineers
Stanbic Bank Twenty20 winners 2009/10 (twenty20): Mountaineers

2009/10 AND CAREER RECORDS FOR ZIMBABWE PLAYERS

Cmp	*Debut*	*M*	*I*	*NO*	*Runs*	*HS*	*Avge*	*100*	*50*	*Balls*	*Runs*	*Wkts*	*Avge*	*BB*	*5i*	*10m*	*RpO*	*ct*	*st*
ALISENI, Gerald Tendaishe (Matabeleland Tuskers) b Makonde 29.2.1988 RHB RMF																			
FC		2	1	0	0	0	0.00	0	0	168	98	3	32.66	2-29	0	0	3.50	0	
Lim		1	1	1	1	1*		0	0	18	14	0					4.66	0	
Lim	2008	3	2	2	1	1*		0	0	66	56	0					5.09	0	
20T	2007/08	1								12	12	0					6.00	0	
BLIGNAUT, Arnoldus Mauritius (Matabeleland Tuskers, Zimbabwe, Zimbabwe to West Indies) b Salisbury (now Harare) 1.8.1978 LHB RMF																			
Int		3	1	0	1	1	1.00	0	0	78	42	1	42.00	1-22	0	0	3.23	0	
Lim		3	1	0	1	1	1.00	0	0	78	42	1	42.00	1-22	0	0	3.23	0	
20T		5	4	1	111	63*	37.00	0	1	6	15	0					15.00	2	
Test	2000/01	19	36	3	886	92	26.84	0	6	3173	1964	53	37.05	5-73	3	0	3.71	13	
FC	1997/98	57	91	5	2375	194	27.61	2	15	8112	4862	133	36.55	5-73	3	0	3.59	40	
Int	1999	54	41	8	626	63*	18.96	0	5	2348	2063	50	41.26	4-43	2	0	5.27	11	
Lim	1997/98	80	61	9	915	63*	17.59	0	6	3341	2973	70	42.47	4-43	2	0	5.33	17	
I20T	2010	1	1	0	8	8	8.00	0	0									0	
20T	2005/06	13	11	4	264	63*	37.71	0	2	88	138	6	23.00	2-31	0	0	9.40	5	
BUTTERWORTH, Ryan Eric (Mashonaland Eagles) b Harare 14.4.1981 RHB RM																			
FC		12	21	1	608	109	30.40	2	1	150	74	4	18.50	2-27	0	0	2.96	6	
Lim		8	7	1	113	44	18.83	0	0	42	31	1	31.00	1-31	0	0	4.42	2	
20T		2	2	0	10	9	5.00	0	0									1	
FC	2000/01	27	49	4	1202	113	26.71	3	1	234	151	5	30.20	2-27	0	0	3.87	22	
Lim	2000/01	21	18	2	192	44	12.00	0	0	114	65	3	21.66	2-11	0	0	3.42	10	
CHAKABVA, Regis Wiriranai (Mashonaland Eagles, Zimbabwe XI, Zimbabwe XI to Canada, Zimbabwe XI to Netherlands) b Harare 20.9.1987 RHB OB WK																			
FC		14	22	0	739	111	33.59	1	5	12	6	0					3.00	36	4
Lim		6	3	0	83	62	27.66	0	1									3	2
20T		6	5	2	51	24	17.00	0	0									3	
FC	2006/07	36	62	3	1950	131	33.05	3	10	18	19	0					6.33	83	8
Int	2008/09	1	1	0	41	41	41.00	0	0									2	
Lim	2006/07	38	35	3	779	71*	24.34	0	3									29	13
I20T	2008/09	1	1	0	1	1	1.00	0	0									0	
20T	2007/08	18	15	3	196	39*	16.33	0	0									5	
CHAPUNGU, Bothwell Madaufipo (Mid West Rhinos) b Kwekwe 22.11.1987 LHB OB																			
FC		10	17	0	344	75	20.23	0	2	150	108	3	36.00	3-74	0	0	4.32	10	
Lim		7	7	0	81	27	11.57	0	0									7	
20T		2	2	0	17	15	8.50	0	0									0	
FC	2003/04	24	45	0	894	85	19.86	0	5	156	109	3	36.33	3-74	0	0	4.19	13	
Lim	2005/06	24	24	0	276	60	11.50	0	1	42	34	2	17.00	2-18	0	0	4.85	13	1
20T	2007/08	11	10	0	212	75	21.20	0	1									2	
CHARUMBIRA, Patient (Southern Rocks) b Gweru 11.11.1987 RHB RFM																			
FC		1	2	0	1	1	0.50	0	0	90	51	1	51.00	1-31	0	0	3.40	0	
Lim		1	1	1	18	18*		0	0	24	18	0					4.50	0	
FC	2006	12	22	5	197	38	11.58	0	0	1390	760	13	58.46	3-39	0	0	3.28	9	
Lim	2005/06	15	12	4	47	18*	5.87	0	0	543	430	16	26.87	3-12	0	0	4.75	6	
20T	2007/08	9	5	3	40	17*	20.00	0	0	159	231	9	25.66	3-12	0	0	8.71	2	
CHATARA, Tendai Larry (Mountaineers, Zimbabwe, Zimbabwe to West Indies, Zimbabwe XI to Canada) b Chimaniamani 28.2.1991 RHB RFM																			
FC		3	4	1	22	14	7.33	0	0	306	160	6	26.66	5-42	1	0	3.13	1	
Lim		4								168	126	5	25.20	2-39	0	0	4.50	0	
I20T		1								24	27	1	27.00	1-27	0	0	6.75	1	
20T		7	2	2	1	1*		0	0	132	175	5	35.00	1-20	0	0	7.95	2	
FC	2009/10	5	7	3	28	14	7.00	0	0	617	309	13	23.76	5-42	1	0	3.00	2	
CHATORA, Paxton (Mountaineers) b Mutare 9.7.1985 LHB																			
FC		1	2	0	21	21	10.50	0	0									0	
Lim	2006/07	1	1	0	1	1	1.00	0	0									0	
CHAULUKA, Erick (Southern Rocks) b Harare 3.9.1983 RHB RM																			
FC		8	14	2	321	113*	26.75	1	1	30	7	0					1.40	1	
Lim		7	7	1	120	44	20.00	0	0									0	

Cmp	Debut	M	I	NO	Runs	HS	Avge	100	50	Balls	Runs	Wkts	Avge	BB	5i	10m	RpO	ct	st
20T		1																0	
FC	2002/03	38	73	6	1514	113*	22.59	2	5	186	100	2	50.00	1-5	0	0	3.22	23	
Lim	2003/04	26	25	2	477	70	20.73	0	3	84	73	2	36.50	1-30	0	0	5.21	7	
20T	2007/08	6	4	0	45	28	11.25	0	0	24	53	1	53.00	1-53	0	0	13.25	1	
CHIBHABHA, Chamunorwa Justice (Southern Rocks, Zimbabwe, Zimbabwe XI, Zimbabwe to Bangladesh, Zimbabwe to South Africa, Zimbabwe to West Indies, Zimbabwe XI to Netherlands) b Masvingo 6.9.1986 RHB RM																			
FC		10	19	0	445	99	23.42	0	4	805	510	10	51.00	2-27	0	0	3.80	4	
Int		1	1	0	58	58	58.00	0	1	24	40	0					10.00	0	
Lim		6	6	0	128	58	21.33	0	1	162	179	4	44.75	2-30	0	0	6.63	0	
I20T		2	2	0	47	40	23.50	0	0	18	19	1	19.00	1-19	0	0	6.33	0	
20T		7	7	1	277	82*	46.16	0	3	120	161	2	80.50	1-19	0	0	8.05	3	
FC	2003/04	53	101	2	2487	103	25.12	1	15	4441	2649	91	29.10	5-96	1	0	3.57	24	
Int	2005/06	50	50	0	1092	73	21.84	0	8	816	981	20	49.05	2-28	0	0	7.21	22	
Lim	2003/04	102	101	5	2295	121*	23.90	1	15	2030	2035	56	36.33	3-29	0	0	6.01	35	
I20T	2006/07	9	9	0	147	40	16.33	0	0	65	74	3	24.66	1-14	0	0	6.83	3	
20T	2006/07	34	34	2	858	86*	26.81	0	6	421	566	18	31.44	3-29	0	0	8.06	11	
CHIFAMBA, Maxwell (Mashonaland Eagles) b Harare 26.3.1991 RHB RM																			
FC		1	2	0	6	6	3.00	0	0	30	31	0					6.20	1	
CHIGUMBURA, Elton (Mashonaland Eagles, Zimbabwe, Northamptonshire, Northamptonshire to Netherlands, Zimbabwe to Bangladesh, Zimbabwe to South Africa, Zimbabwe to West Indies) b Kwekwe, Midlands 14.3.1986 RHB RM																			
FC		10	16	1	756	105	50.40	1	6	1882	949	41	23.14	4-49	0	0	3.02	8	
Int		8	7	2	100	25	20.00	0	0	192	248	1	248.00	1-50	0	0	7.75	3	
Lim		16	13	5	311	90*	38.87	0	1	422	463	10	46.30	3-40	0	0	6.58	4	
I20T		2	2	0	21	18	10.50	0	0	12	22	0					11.00	1	
20T		8	8	1	205	53	29.28	0	1	128	168	4	42.00	2-27	0	0	7.87	1	
Test	2004	6	12	0	187	71	15.58	0	1	829	498	9	55.33	5-54	1	0	3.60	2	
FC	2001/02	70	122	7	4014	186	34.90	3	28	8580	4709	167	28.19	5-33	4	0	3.29	29	
Int	2004	113	105	11	2292	79	24.38	0	13	2971	2953	79	37.37	4-28	1	0	5.96	36	
Lim	2002/03	166	152	21	3447	97*	26.31	0	20	4413	4283	119	35.99	4-23	2	0	5.82	50	
I20T	2006/07	12	11	1	138	34	13.80	0	0	156	212	12	17.66	4-31	1	0	8.15	5	
20T	2006/07	46	45	11	834	103*	24.52	1	3	698	864	42	20.57	5-13	4	1	7.42	17	
CHIKUNYA, Innocent (Mid West Rhinos) b Mutare 16.7.1985 RHB RM																			
FC		7	14	1	363	75	27.92	0	3									7	1
Lim		7	7	0	84	41	12.00	0	0									4	
FC	2004/05	17	33	2	650	75	20.96	0	3	54	29	0					3.22	28	1
Lim	2004/05	18	17	0	180	41	10.58	0	0									7	
20T	2007/08	1	1	0	5	5	5.00	0	0									0	
CHIMHAMHIWA, Stephen (Matabeleland Tuskers) b Gokwe 5.3.1991 RHB RMF																			
Lim		1	1	1	3	3*		0	0	32	41	0					7.68	0	
CHINOUYA, Michael Tawanda (Mid West Rhinos) b Kwekwe 9.6.1986 RHB RM																			
FC		9	10	6	10	4	2.50	0	0	1048	564	14	40.28	3-35	0	0	3.22	4	
Lim		8	5	3	14	6*	7.00	0	0	324	218	9	24.22	3-20	0	0	4.03	2	
20T		5	1	1	5	5*		0	0	96	111	2	55.50	1-21	0	0	6.93	0	
FC	2003/04	21	30	13	67	23	3.94	0	0	2616	1311	46	28.50	5-30	1	0	3.00	6	
Lim	2005/06	22	15	6	47	13	5.22	0	0	915	627	21	29.85	3-20	0	0	4.11	7	
20T	2007/08	13	5	3	26	17*	13.00	0	0	288	365	15	24.33	4-17	1	0	7.60	1	
CHINYENGETERE, Robertson (Southern Rocks) b Masvingo 30.6.1982 RHB RMF																			
FC		6	9	0	181	59	20.11	0	2	58	43	1	43.00	1-19	0	0	4.44	6	
Lim		4	2	1	23	16	23.00	0	0	18	25	0					8.33	1	
FC	2006	17	28	2	592	94	22.76	0	5	58	43	1	43.00	1-19	0	0	4.44	17	
Lim	2005/06	17	14	3	251	72*	22.81	0	1	72	68	2	34.00	2-30	0	0	5.66	4	
20T	2007/08	4	3	1	26	25	13.00	0	0	6	9	0					9.00	3	
CHINYOKA, Innocent Murambiwa (Mashonaland Eagles) b Harare 21.6.1982 RHB RM																			
FC		1	2	0	4	4	2.00	0	0	152	106	4	26.50	4-83	0	0	4.18	0	
FC	2001/02	24	45	4	674	62	16.43	0	2	2305	1569	36	43.58	4-83	0	0	4.08	20	
Lim	2003/04	18	12	0	132	34	11.00	0	0	624	472	20	23.60	4-36	1	0	4.53	2	
CHISORO, Tendai Sam (Southern Rocks, Zimbabwe XI) b Masvingo 12.2.1988 LHB LFM																			
FC		8	15	3	197	35	16.41	0	0	733	495	10	49.50	3-79	0	0	4.05	4	
Lim		6	4	0	64	31	16.00	0	0	192	152	6	25.33	3-45	0	0	4.75	4	
20T		5	3	0	4	3	1.33	0	0									2	
FC	2006	16	29	5	430	48*	17.91	0	0	1489	948	18	52.66	3-79	0	0	3.82	6	
Lim	2005/06	20	17	1	216	31	13.50	0	0	659	501	26	19.26	3-45	0	0	4.56	8	
20T	2007/08	14	11	2	176	85	19.55	0	1	144	231	4	57.75	2-18	0	0	9.62	4	
CHITONGO, Tendai (Southern Rocks) b Kadoma, Mashonaland 6.9.1989 RHB LB																			
FC		6	10	1	153	66	17.00	0	1	497	358	6	59.66	4-53	0	0	4.32	3	
Lim		8	7	2	123	36	24.60	0	0	78	93	3	31.00	3-47	0	0	7.15	1	
FC	2007/08	10	18	2	297	66	18.56	0	1	869	594	7	84.85	4-53	0	0	4.10	5	
Lim	2008/09	14	12	5	159	36	22.71	0	0	340	264	10	26.40	3-47	0	0	4.65	3	
20T	2009	7	5	1	51	41	12.75	0	0	102	112	4	28.00	2-20	0	0	6.58	3	

Cmp	Debut	M	I	NO	Runs	HS	Avge	100	50	Balls	Runs	Wkts	Avge	BB	5i	10m	RpO	ct	st
COVENTRY, Charles Kevin (Matabeleland Tuskers, Zimbabwe, Zimbabwe to Bangladesh, Zimbabwe to South Africa, Zimbabwe to West Indies, Zimbabwe XI to Netherlands) b Kwekwe, Midlands 8.3.1983 RHB LB																			
FC		9	15	2	437	100*	33.61	2	0									23	
Int		10	8	0	143	32	17.87	0	0									6	
Lim		16	14	0	268	46	19.14	0	0									9	
I20T		1	1	0	28	28	28.00	0	0									0	
20T		7	7	1	90	28	15.00	0	0									2	1
Test	2005/06	2	4	0	88	37	22.00	0	0									3	
FC	1998/99	51	93	3	2365	106	26.27	3	10	210	155	2	77.50	1-26	0	0	4.42	78	2
Int	2003	32	29	1	766	194*	27.35	1	3									16	1
Lim	2001/02	85	80	6	2217	194*	29.95	2	13	24	30	0					7.50	42	2
I20T	2010	3	2	0	28	28	14.00	0	0									0	
20T	2009	17	16	3	256	49*	19.69	0	0									8	1
CREMER, Alexander Graeme (Mid West Rhinos, Zimbabwe, Zimbabwe to Bangladesh, Zimbabwe to South Africa, Zimbabwe to West Indies) b Harare 19.9.1986 RHB LBG																			
FC		11	18	4	738	94	52.71	0	8	3286	1668	59	28.27	8-92	5	1	3.04	10	
Int		10	4	1	47	31*	15.66	0	0	469	366	13	28.15	6-46	0	1	4.68	0	
Lim		18	11	3	188	39	23.50	0	0	913	654	25	26.16	6-46	0	1	4.29	2	
I20T		1								6	9	0					9.00	1	
20T		6	3	1	43	35*	21.50	0	0	126	128	3	42.66	2-14	0	0	6.09	1	
Test	2004/05	6	12	1	29	12	2.63	0	0	870	595	13	45.76	3-86	0	0	4.10	3	
FC	2004	60	104	19	1878	171*	22.09	1	9	11984	6381	227	28.11	8-92	11	2	3.19	48	
Int	2008/09	29	17	5	159	31*	13.25	0	0	1371	1048	43	24.37	6-46	2	1	4.58	8	
Lim	2004/05	70	51	15	812	55*	22.55	0	2	3453	2469	104	23.74	6-46	4	1	4.29	20	
I20T	2008/09	5	2	0	2	2	1.00	0	0	66	53	6	8.83	3-11	0	0	4.81	2	
20T	2007/08	23	14	4	164	35*	16.40	0	0	465	406	18	22.55	3-11	0	0	5.23	5	
DABENGWA, Keith Mbusi (Matabeleland Tuskers, Zimbabwe XI to Canada) b Bulawayo 17.8.1980 LHB SLA																			
FC		9	14	0	646	158	46.14	2	3	1056	529	15	35.26	4-33	0	0	3.00	3	
Lim		5	5	0	52	25	10.40	0	0	234	172	7	24.57	2-18	0	0	4.41	3	
20T		6	4	0	33	19	8.25	0	0	120	115	4	28.75	2-13	0	0	5.75	0	
Test	2005/06	3	6	0	90	35	15.00	0	0	438	249	5	49.80	3-127	0	0	3.41	1	
FC	1999/00	65	114	8	2724	161	25.69	3	13	7815	4158	107	38.85	7-1	5	1	3.19	65	
Int	2005/06	32	29	7	433	45	19.68	0	0	941	790	21	37.61	3-15	0	0	5.03	10	
Lim	2000/01	79	69	13	1148	71*	20.50	0	2	2270	1774	64	27.71	5-19	2	1	4.68	34	
I20T	2006/07	6	5	2	38	16*	12.66	0	0	54	80	2	40.00	1-1	0	0	8.88	2	
20T	2006/07	29	26	3	383	74*	16.65	0	1	444	472	24	19.66	3-13	0	0	6.37	6	
DUFFIN, Terrence (Matabeleland Tuskers) b Kwekwe, Midlands 20.3.1982 LHB RM																			
FC		7	12	0	254	144	21.16	1	0									4	
Lim		3	3	0	140	68	46.66	0	2									1	
Test	2005/06	2	4	0	80	56	20.00	0	1									1	
FC	2000/01	51	96	4	2522	144	27.41	2	17	36	19	0					3.16	33	
Int	2005/06	23	23	0	546	88	23.73	0	3									6	
Lim	2000/01	58	56	5	1323	88	25.94	0	8									27	
20T	2006/07	5	5	0	105	40	21.00	0	0									0	
EBRAHIM, Dion Digby (Matabeleland Tuskers) b Bulawayo 7.8.1980 RHB RM																			
FC		10	16	0	746	114	46.62	1	6	210	86	4	21.50	2-14	0	0	2.45	7	
Lim		7	7	0	266	67	38.00	0	4	78	56	5	11.20	5-45	0	1	4.30	4	
20T		4	3	0	24	19	8.00	0	0	12	10	0					5.00	0	
Test	2000/01	29	55	1	1226	94	22.70	0	10									16	
FC	1999/00	88	155	8	4439	188	30.19	5	28	442	236	8	29.50	2-14	0	0	3.20	65	
Int	2000/01	82	76	6	1443	121	20.61	1	4	5	11	0					13.20	23	
Lim	1999/00	130	122	7	2405	121	20.91	1	12	230	165	8	20.62	5-45	0	1	4.30	44	
ERVINE, Craig Richard (Southern Rocks, Zimbabwe, Zimbabwe to West Indies, Zimbabwe XI to Canada, Zimbabwe XI to Netherlands) b Harare 19.8.1985 LHB OB																			
FC		10	17	0	575	108	33.82	1	5									9	
Int		5	3	1	83	67*	41.50	0	1									0	
Lim		11	8	3	328	111*	65.60	1	2									2	
I20T		1	1	0	30	30	30.00	0	0									0	
20T		6	4	1	98	62*	32.66	0	1									1	
FC	2003/04	23	40	1	1688	177	43.28	4	12	204	140	3	46.66	2-44	0	0	4.11	26	
Lim	2003/04	25	18	6	577	111*	48.08	1	4	158	125	1	125.00	1-25	0	0	4.74	10	
I20T	2010	3	2	0	31	30	15.50	0	0									1	
20T	2009/10	9	6	1	124	62*	24.80	0	1									3	
ERVINE, Ryan (Southern Rocks) b Chinhoyi 19.7.1988 RHB RM																			
Lim		2	2	0	5	4	2.50	0	0	96	83	1	83.00	1-51	0	0	5.18	0	
20T		3	1	0	21	21	21.00	0	0	6	16	0					16.00	0	
ERVINE, Sean Michael (Southern Rocks, Hampshire, Hampshire to Scotland) b Harare 6.12.1982 LHB RM																			
FC		2	4	0	393	208	98.25	2	0	221	202	4	50.50	2-63	0	0	5.48	1	
20T		5	5	0	41	23	8.20	0	0	80	115	4	28.75	3-19	0	0	8.62	0	
Test	2003	5	8	0	261	86	32.62	0	3	570	388	9	43.11	4-146	0	0	4.08	7	
FC	2000/01	117	185	19	5863	237*	35.31	11	30	13145	7838	181	43.30	6-82	5	0	3.57	96	

Cmp	Debut	M	I	NO	Runs	HS	Avge	100	50	Balls	Runs	Wkts	Avge	BB	5i	10m	RpO	ct	st
Int	2001/02	42	34	7	698	100	25.85	1	2	1649	1561	41	38.07	3-29	0	0	5.68	5	
Lim	2000/01	169	151	24	4035	167*	31.77	6	17	5994	5578	166	33.60	5-50	5	2	5.58	46	
20T	2005	66	63	14	1229	74*	25.08	0	6	770	1103	47	23.46	4-12	2	0	8.59	24	
EWING, Gavin Mackie (Matabeleland Tuskers) b Harare 21.1.1981 RHB OB																			
FC		7	10	3	335	71	47.85	0	4	186	88	1	88.00	1-10	0	0	2.83	7	
Lim		6	6	1	168	48*	33.60	0	0	156	126	0					4.84	1	
20T		6	6	0	55	40	9.16	0	0	102	102	3	34.00	2-13	0	0	6.00	2	
Test	2003/04	3	6	0	108	71	18.00	0	1	426	260	2	130.00	1-27	0	0	3.66	1	
FC	2001/02	38	66	7	2295	212	38.89	4	16	6817	3184	97	32.82	7-64	4	0	2.80	21	
Int	2004/05	7	7	0	97	46	13.85	0	0	312	236	5	47.20	3-31	0	0	4.53	3	
Lim	2002/03	43	36	6	699	56*	23.30	0	3	1918	1366	33	41.39	3-18	0	0	4.27	13	
GARWE, Trevor Nyasha (Mashonaland Eagles, Zimbabwe, Zimbabwe XI) b Harare 7.1.1986 LHB RFM																			
FC		12	17	3	472	117	33.71	1	2	1607	848	33	25.69	5-43	1	0	3.16	8	
Int		1								36	50	1	50.00	1-50	0	0	8.33	1	
Lim		9	4	1	49	27*	16.33	0	0	270	267	8	33.37	3-51	0	0	5.93	6	
20T		6	3	1	20	15*	10.00	0	0	36	52	1	52.00	1-12	0	0	8.66	1	
FC	2004/05	39	60	20	895	117	22.37	1	3	4932	2662	98	27.16	6-65	2	0	3.23	23	
Lim	2004/05	35	21	6	229	42*	15.26	0	0	1207	1116	30	37.20	3-16	0	0	5.54	14	
20T	2007/08	16	11	3	132	39*	16.50	0	0	192	214	16	13.37	5-20	1	1	6.68	3	
GUMUNYU-MANATSA, Lovemore Tatenda (Mashonaland Eagles) b Harare 17.5.1990 LHB RMF																			
Lim		1								18	21	0					7.00	1	
FC	2008/09	1	1	1	0	0*		0	0	48	18	0					2.25	0	
GUPO, Simbarashe Prince (Mashonaland Eagles) b Kadoma 7.7.1989 RHB OB																			
FC		1	2	0	2	2	1.00	0	0									0	
Lim		3	3	0	54	21	18.00	0	0									2	
FC	2006/07	9	18	0	249	35	13.83	0	0									6	
Lim	2006/07	10	10	0	134	23	13.40	0	0									4	
HARVEY, Ian Joseph (Southern Rocks) b Wonthaggi, Victoria, Australia 10.4.1972 RHB RM																			
Lim		1	1	0	4	4	4.00	0	0	6	3	0					3.00	0	
20T		3	2	1	1	1*	1.00	0	0	48	63	0					7.87	0	
FC	1993/94	165	272	29	8409	209*	34.60	15	46	24274	11693	425	27.51	8-101	15	2	2.89	114	
Int	1997/98	73	51	11	715	48*	17.87	0	0	3279	2577	85	30.31	4-16	4	0	4.71	17	
Lim	1993/94	305	268	27	5977	112	24.80	2	28	13607	9952	445	22.36	5-19	21	9	4.38	83	
20T	2003	54	52	5	1470	109	31.27	3	5	965	1234	52	23.73	4-18	1	0	7.67	18	
HIGGINS, Dylon Robert (Matabeleland Tuskers, Mid West Rhinos) b Harare 5.4.1991 RHB LB																			
FC		2	3	0	17	14	5.66	0	0	339	151	11	13.72	6-93	2	1	2.67	1	
Lim		3	2	1	16	16*	16.00	0	0	138	88	2	44.00	2-33	0	0	3.82	2	
20T		4	3	2	20	11	20.00	0	0	36	45	2	22.50	1-7	0	0	7.50	1	
HONDO, Douglas Tafadzwa (Mashonaland Eagles) b Bulawayo 7.7.1979 RHB RFM																			
FC		7	8	3	52	18	10.40	0	0	1132	554	19	29.15	3-20	0	0	2.93	4	
Lim		5	1	0	12	12	12.00	0	0	224	194	3	64.66	2-28	0	0	5.19	0	
20T		6	3	1	8	4*	4.00	0	0	108	114	3	38.00	2-13	0	0	6.33	1	
Test	2001/02	9	15	6	83	19	9.22	0	0	1486	774	21	36.85	6-59	1	0	3.12	5	
FC	1999/00	42	60	21	544	85*	13.94	0	2	6558	3207	122	26.28	6-59	3	0	2.93	23	
Int	2001/02	56	29	12	127	17	7.47	0	0	2381	2171	61	35.59	4-37	3	0	5.47	15	
Lim	1999/00	92	49	24	286	39*	11.44	0	0	3965	3413	114	29.93	4-32	4	0	5.16	22	
20T	2009	11	5	2	25	10	8.33	0	0	190	240	6	40.00	2-13	0	0	7.57	4	
IRELAND, Anthony John (Southern Rocks, Gloucestershire) b Masvingo 30.8.1984 RHB RM																			
20T		5	1	1	6	6*		0	0	107	135	5	27.00	3-25	0	0	7.57	0	
FC	2002/03	36	53	16	135	16*	3.64	0	0	5313	3271	113	28.94	7-36	4	1	3.69	9	
Int	2005/06	26	13	5	30	8*	3.75	0	0	1326	1115	38	29.34	3-41	0	0	5.04	2	
Lim	2004/05	65	31	15	90	17	5.62	0	0	2805	2520	88	28.63	4-16	2	0	5.39	9	
I20T	2006/07	1	1	1	2	2*		0	0	18	33	1	33.00	1-33	0	0	11.00	0	
20T	2006/07	31	10	4	32	8*	5.33	0	0	569	845	35	24.14	3-10	0	0	8.91	9	
JARVIS, Kyle Malcolm (Mashonaland Eagles, Zimbabwe, Zimbabwe XI, Zimbabwe to Bangladesh, Zimbabwe to South Africa) b Harare 16.2.1989 RHB RFM																			
FC		5	6	2	36	10*	9.00	0	0	676	403	15	26.86	6-60	1	0	3.57	1	
Int		4	1	1	6	6*		0	0	192	185	5	37.00	3-36	0	0	5.78	1	
Lim		6	1	1	6	6*		0	0	222	220	5	44.00	3-36	0	0	5.94	2	
Int	2009/10	9	5	2	19	13	6.33	0	0	413	422	10	42.20	3-36	0	0	6.13	1	
Lim	2009/10	12	6	3	20	13	6.66	0	0	497	504	11	45.81	3-36	0	0	6.08	2	
KAMUNGOZI, Tafadzwa (Southern Rocks, Zimbabwe XI) b Harare 8.6.1987 RHB LB																			
FC		9	17	1	227	71*	14.18	0	1	2037	1166	26	44.84	4-86	0	0	3.43	9	
Lim		5	3	0	24	10	8.00	0	0	238	236	4	59.00	2-59	0	0	5.95	0	
20T		4	1	0	7	7	7.00	0	0	54	77	3	25.66	1-11	0	0	8.55	2	
FC	2006/07	25	44	7	504	71*	13.62	0	1	5141	2539	78	32.55	8-125	4	0	2.96	16	
Int	2006/07	4	3	2	0	0*	0.00	0	0	180	163	5	32.60	2-55	0	0	5.43	2	
Lim	2005/06	34	24	5	158	20	8.31	0	0	1608	1087	36	30.19	4-8	1	0	4.05	6	
20T	2006/07	15	6	0	12	7	2.00	0	0	300	360	12	30.00	2-10	0	0	7.20	6	

Cmp	Debut	M	I	NO	Runs	HS	Avge	100	50	Balls	Runs	Wkts	Avge	BB	5i	10m	RpO	ct	st
KASTENI, Friday (Mid West Rhinos, Zimbabwe XI) b Kadoma 25.3.1988 LHB SLA																			
FC		14	25	2	632	101*	27.47	2	1	99	66	4	16.50	1-8	0	0	4.00	13	
Lim		10	9	0	280	80	31.11	0	1	24	28	0					7.00	4	
20T		4	2	2	20	14*		0	0	12	8	1	8.00	1-8	0	0	4.00	3	
FC	2004/05	25	47	3	1207	101*	27.43	3	4	141	108	4	27.00	1-8	0	0	4.59	23	
Int	2006/07	3	3	0	18	9	6.00	0	0									0	
Lim	2006	29	26	0	597	80	22.96	0	2	66	77	0					7.00	8	
20T	2007/08	13	10	2	172	58	21.50	0	1	30	36	1	36.00	1-8	0	0	7.20	5	
KATSANDE, Benjamin (Mountaineers) b Harare 7.6.1985 RHB WK																			
FC		2	3	1	73	47	36.50	0	0									2	1
Lim		1																2	
KONDO, Keith (Southern Rocks) b Harare 5.11.1988 RHB RM																			
FC		1	2	0	11	11	5.50	0	0									0	
FC	2007/08	6	9	0	78	30	8.66	0	0									3	
Lim	2005/06	6	6	1	82	58	16.40	0	1	120	89	5	17.80	3-15	0	0	4.45	1	
KULINGA, Keith (Southern Rocks) b Salisbury (now Harare) 14.4.1979 RHB OB																			
FC		1	2	2	0	0*		0	0	60	39	0					3.90	0	
Lim		1								60	37	1	37.00	1-37	0	0	3.70	0	
FC	2002/03	2	3	3	0	0*		0	0	96	72	0					4.50	2	
Lim	2003/04	7	3	1	3	2	1.50	0	0	204	103	3	34.33	2-3	0	0	3.02	2	
LAMB, Gregory Arthur (Mashonaland Eagles, Zimbabwe, Zimbabwe to West Indies) b Harare 4.3.1980 RHB RM,OB																			
FC		12	19	2	1050	171	61.76	3	4	1240	612	10	61.20	4-38	0	0	2.96	8	
Int		4	3	0	74	37	24.66	0	0	168	129	3	43.00	3-45	0	0	4.60	0	
Lim		13	10	2	335	88*	41.87	0	2	528	373	10	37.30	3-45	0	0	4.23	1	
I20T		2	2	1	7	7*	7.00	0	0	24	31	0					7.75	0	
20T		8	8	1	126	40	18.00	0	0	102	127	0					7.47	1	
FC	1998/99	50	78	9	2225	171	32.24	4	10	3544	2037	49	41.57	7-73	1	0	3.44	39	
Int	2009/10	9	8	1	134	37	19.14	0	0	402	267	8	33.37	3-45	0	0	3.98	0	
Lim	1998/99	74	62	10	1349	100*	25.94	1	7	1715	1380	41	33.65	4-38	2	0	4.82	30	
I20T	2009/10	5	4	2	32	14*	16.00	0	0	73	80	4	20.00	2-14	0	0	6.57	0	
20T	2004	50	42	6	624	67	17.33	0	2	542	711	24	29.62	4-28	1	0	7.87	12	
LEWIS, Justin Morley (Mid West Rhinos) b Redcliffe, Midlands 30.12.1982 RHB LM																			
FC		4	6	4	45	32	22.50	0	0	480	249	2	124.50	1-24	0	0	3.11	2	
Lim		4	3	1	33	29	16.50	0	0	138	125	3	41.66	1-21	0	0	5.43	1	
FC	1999/00	18	31	18	156	32	12.00	0	0	1720	1015	25	40.60	4-40	0	0	3.54	7	
Lim	2001	8	5	2	39	29	13.00	0	0	211	211	6	35.16	2-21	0	0	6.00	1	
MABUZA, Mbekezele Mark (Matabeleland Tuskers) b Bulawayo 6.1.1985 RHB RM,OB																			
FC		2	3	0	16	11	5.33	0	0	70	72	1	72.00	1-72	0	0	6.17	2	
Lim		1	1	0	24	24	24.00	0	0	7	10	0					8.57	0	
FC	2003/04	20	38	1	562	106	15.18	1	1	576	408	8	51.00	2-60	0	0	4.25	19	
Lim	2004/05	17	16	2	261	61*	18.64	0	1	389	361	9	40.11	2-1	0	0	5.56	7	
20T	2007/08	12	11	0	137	42	12.45	0	0	66	75	6	12.50	5-14	0	1	6.81	6	
MACHIRI, Tendai (Southern Rocks) b Harare 2.4.1985 RHB OB																			
FC		5	9	1	178	79	22.25	0	1	30	31	0					6.20	4	
Lim		3	3	1	27	12	13.50	0	0	20	14	2	7.00	1-6	0	0	4.20	1	
FC	2006/07	11	21	2	375	79	19.73	0	2	264	167	5	33.40	3-23	0	0	3.79	13	
Lim	2006/07	9	9	1	147	56	18.37	0	2	127	70	9	7.77	4-21	1	0	3.30	2	
MADHIRI, Taurai (Matabeleland Tuskers) b Bindura 11.10.1985 LHB LM																			
FC		2	4	0	31	15	7.75	0	0	204	157	3	52.33	2-64	0	0	4.61	0	
FC	2007/08	9	18	0	176	41	9.77	0	0	258	201	4	50.25	2-64	0	0	4.67	6	
Lim	2008	2	2	0	18	16	9.00	0	0									1	
MAHWIRE, Ngonidzashe Blessing (Southern Rocks) b Bikita, Masvingo 31.7.1982 RHB RFM																			
FC		10	16	6	197	61	19.70	0	1	1537	811	21	38.61	5-92	1	0	3.16	3	
Lim		9	6	2	20	11*	5.00	0	0	384	307	6	51.16	2-31	0	0	4.79	3	
20T		5	1	0	8	8	8.00	0	0	72	92	4	23.00	2-21	0	0	7.66	3	
Test	2002/03	10	17	6	147	50*	13.36	0	1	1287	915	18	50.83	4-92	0	0	4.26	1	
FC	2000/01	69	115	20	1544	115	16.25	1	3	9865	5442	182	29.90	7-64	5	0	3.31	26	
Int	2003/04	23	19	8	117	22*	10.63	0	0	885	775	21	36.90	3-29	0	0	5.25	6	
Lim	2000/01	75	55	15	625	85	15.62	0	3	3094	2476	77	32.15	4-23	1	0	4.80	14	
20T	2007/08	9	4	0	58	22	14.50	0	0	119	155	7	22.14	2-9	0	0	7.81	3	
MANYUMWA, Admire Marvellous (Mashonaland Eagles, Zimbabwe XI) b Chitungwiza, Mashonaland 28.12.1987 RHB RM																			
FC		8	10	3	151	61	21.57	0	1	1155	580	16	36.25	5-41	1	0	3.01	6	
Lim		4	3	3	36	19*		0	0	128	110	5	22.00	3-40	0	0	5.15	1	
20T		6	3	0	12	8	4.00	0	0	72	77	3	25.66	2-15	0	0	6.41	1	
FC	2006	29	42	12	490	61	16.33	0	2	3797	1800	84	21.42	5-15	6	0	2.84	15	
Lim	2005/06	29	20	6	143	25*	10.21	0	0	1132	878	26	33.76	3-32	0	0	4.65	5	
20T	2007/08	13	6	0	26	11	4.33	0	0	174	187	11	17.00	2-15	0	0	6.44	5	
MAREGWEDE, Alester (Southern Rocks) b Harare 5.8.1981 RHB WK																			
FC		10	20	2	389	82*	21.61	0	2									14	2
Lim		7	7	1	224	91*	37.33	0	1									9	1
20T		5	5	4	115	48*	115.00	0	0									1	1

Cmp	Debut	M	I	NO	Runs	HS	Avge	100	50	Balls	Runs	Wkts	Avge	BB	5i	10m	RpO	ct	st
Test	2004	2	4	0	74	28	18.50	0	0									1	
FC	1997/98	65	121	7	2628	107	23.05	2	17	6	9	0					9.00	125	9
Int	2003/04	11	11	1	124	37	12.40	0	0									2	
Lim	1997/98	72	66	4	1224	91*	19.74	0	5									58	6
MARILLIER, Douglas Anthony (Mashonaland Eagles) b Salisbury (now Harare) 24.4.1978 RHB OB																			
20T		6	6	0	109	74	18.16	0	1	42	40	2	20.00	2-11	0	0	5.71	0	
Test	2000/01	5	7	1	185	73	30.83	0	2	616	322	11	29.27	4-57	0	0	3.13	2	
FC	1998/99	41	71	4	2611	202	38.97	7	14	3407	2131	56	38.05	4-44	0	0	3.75	39	
Int	2000/01	48	41	4	672	100	18.16	1	3	1574	1235	30	41.16	4-38	1	0	4.70	12	
Lim	1998/99	93	84	7	1895	117	24.61	3	9	2910	2297	56	41.01	4-38	1	0	4.73	27	
MARILLIER, Stephan James (Southern Rocks) b Harare 25.9.1984 RHB OB																			
FC		6	11	0	294	57	26.72	0	2									4	
Lim		4	4	0	24	21	6.00	0	0									0	
MARUMA, Timycen (Mountaineers, Zimbabwe XI, Zimbabwe to West Indies, Zimbabwe XI to Canada, Zimbabwe XI to Netherlands) b Harare 19.4.1988 RHB LBG																			
FC		12	20	0	573	76	28.65	0	5	2176	1260	64	19.68	6-40	7	2	3.47	8	
Lim		9	6	2	310	104*	77.50	1	2	342	283	10	28.30	2-17	0	0	4.96	5	
20T		6	3	0	41	25	13.66	0	0	72	74	6	12.33	3-24	0	0	6.16	3	
FC	2006	41	69	5	1394	76	21.78	0	9	7037	3639	153	23.78	7-82	9	2	3.10	45	
Int	2007/08	8	7	0	53	32	7.57	0	0	207	204	4	51.00	2-50	0	0	5.91	3	
Lim	2005/06	43	33	3	601	104*	20.03	1	3	1550	1105	45	24.55	5-17	1	1	4.27	15	
I20T	2008/09	4	4	0	18	7	4.50	0	0	18	20	1	20.00	1-8	0	0	6.66	2	
20T	2006/07	28	20	0	186	72	9.30	0	1	454	489	26	18.80	3-23	0	0	6.46	12	
MARUMISA, Johnson (Mountaineers) b Harare 1.3.1983 RHB LB																			
FC		4	7	1	200	64	33.33	0	3									3	
Lim		5	2	1	20	18	20.00	0	0									0	
FC	2003/04	24	41	3	1241	101	32.65	1	8	12	7	0					3.50	26	
Lim	2004/05	25	20	3	296	66	17.41	0	1									8	
20T	2007/08	10	8	0	46	17	5.75	0	0									4	
MASAKADZA, Hamilton (Mountaineers, Zimbabwe, Zimbabwe to Bangladesh, Zimbabwe to South Africa, Zimbabwe to West Indies) b Harare 9.8.1983 RHB LBG,RM																			
FC		11	18	3	1111	188	74.06	4	3	312	150	7	21.42	2-4	0	0	2.88	6	
Int		10	10	1	648	178*	72.00	2	3	150	119	4	29.75	2-22	0	0	4.76	4	
Lim		18	17	4	940	178*	72.30	2	6	204	163	5	32.60	2-22	0	0	4.79	7	
I20T		2	2	0	3	2	1.50	0	0									1	
20T		8	8	1	320	102	45.71	1	3	36	38	2	19.00	1-8	0	0	6.33	3	
Test	2001	15	30	1	785	119	27.06	1	3	126	39	2	19.50	1-9	0	0	1.85	8	
FC	1999/00	78	137	6	5215	188	39.80	12	26	2625	1190	39	30.51	4-11	0	0	2.72	56	
Int	2001/02	95	95	4	2601	178*	28.58	3	16	901	840	24	35.00	3-39	0	0	5.59	40	
Lim	2001	152	151	11	4419	178*	31.56	4	30	1627	1358	47	28.89	4-36	1	0	5.00	68	
I20T	2006/07	12	12	0	329	79	27.41	0	2	18	25	1	25.00	1-9	0	0	8.33	5	
20T	2006/07	37	36	6	1146	102	38.20	2	8	246	246	15	16.40	2-6	0	0	6.00	13	
MASAKADZA, Shingirai Winston (Mountaineers, Zimbabwe XI, Zimbabwe to West Indies, Zimbabwe XI to Canada, Zimbabwe XI to Netherlands) b Harare 4.9.1986 RHB RM																			
FC		14	21	3	394	100*	21.88	1	1	2192	1225	45	27.22	6-54	1	0	3.35	8	
Lim		9	3	3	114	57*		0	1	351	286	8	35.75	3-20	0	0	4.88	1	
20T		6	3	0	16	9	5.33	0	0	102	147	3	49.00	1-28	0	0	8.64	5	
FC	2007/08	26	38	9	598	100*	20.62	1	2	4240	2260	98	23.06	6-54	3	0	3.19	9	
Int	2009/10	1								18	36	3	12.00	3-36	0	0	12.00	0	
Lim	2008	20	9	5	194	57*	48.50	0	1	852	661	26	25.42	4-21	1	0	4.65	4	
I20T	2009/10	1	1	0	0	0	0.00	0	0	6	6	0					6.00	1	
20T	2007/08	16	10	2	89	33*	11.12	0	0	257	379	5	75.80	1-26	0	0	8.84	7	
MASVAURE, Prince Spencer (Mashonaland Eagles) b Bulawayo 7.10.1988 LHB LFM																			
FC		8	14	0	394	101	28.14	1	1	702	372	7	53.14	3-49	0	0	3.17	2	
Lim		8	7	1	225	60	37.50	0	1	156	154	5	30.80	2-18	0	0	5.92	3	
20T		6	6	0	60	24	10.00	0	0	84	91	2	45.50	1-6	0	0	6.50	3	
FC	2006/07	20	33	2	826	101	26.64	1	4	1374	745	17	43.82	3-49	0	0	3.25	10	
Lim	2006/07	16	14	2	316	60	26.33	0	1	448	378	16	23.62	3-22	0	0	5.06	4	
20T	2007/08	17	15	1	170	26*	12.14	0	0	138	183	3	61.00	1-6	0	0	7.95	7	
MATAMBANADZO, Darlington Rutendo (Southern Rocks) b Salisbury (now Harare) 13.4.1976 RHB RMF																			
FC		3	5	0	122	82	24.40	0	1	18	14	0					4.66	2	
Lim		3	3	0	41	28	13.66	0	0									0	
FC	1993/94	28	42	3	765	82	19.61	0	4	1799	1180	34	34.70	4-52	0	0	3.93	12	
Lim	1999/00	7	7	0	144	62	20.57	0	1	30	30	0					6.00	2	
MATANGA, Hilary (Southern Rocks) b Marondera 9.7.1984 LHB OB																			
FC		11	16	5	176	38	16.00	0	0	2191	1253	33	37.96	5-98	1	0	3.43	8	
Lim		6	3	1	4	2	2.00	0	0	252	179	7	25.57	2-33	0	0	4.26	1	
FC	2004/05	24	40	11	322	45	11.10	0	0	4398	2490	65	38.30	6-90	2	0	3.39	16	
Lim	2004/05	22	17	6	82	19	7.45	0	0	864	597	27	22.11	3-10	0	0	4.14	3	
20T	2007/08	4	2	1	0	0*	0.00	0	0	90	96	3	32.00	1-14	0	0	6.40	3	

Cmp	Debut	M	I	NO	Runs	HS	Avge	100	50	Balls	Runs	Wkts	Avge	BB	5i	10m	RpO	ct	st
MATSIKENYERI, Stuart (Mountaineers, Zimbabwe, Zimbabwe to Bangladesh, Zimbabwe to South Africa, Zimbabwe to West Indies, Zimbabwe XI to Canada, Zimbabwe XI to Netherlands) b Harare 3.5.1983 RHB OB																			
FC		11	17	1	710	110	44.37	1	5	231	115	5	23.00	2-46	0	0	2.98	4	
Int		5	4	2	167	71*	83.50	0	2	18	15	0					5.00	3	
Lim		14	10	4	385	78*	64.16	0	4	185	150	3	50.00	1-24	0	0	4.86	7	
20T		6	4	2	78	35	39.00	0	0									1	
Test	2003/04	8	16	1	351	57	23.40	0	2	483	345	2	172.50	1-58	0	0	4.28	7	
FC	1999/00	97	171	12	4955	201	31.16	8	26	3702	2527	59	42.83	5-41	1	0	4.09	69	
Int	2002/03	109	106	9	2196	90	22.63	0	13	920	778	16	48.62	2-25	0	0	5.07	36	
Lim	2001	192	184	18	4066	96	24.49	0	27	1787	1463	29	50.44	2-2	0	0	4.91	63	
I20T	2006/07	8	8	0	33	15	4.12	0	0	12	20	0					10.00	5	
20T	2006/07	33	31	4	486	65	18.00	0	3	73	104	3	34.66	1-3	0	0	8.54	12	
MAUNZE, Kudzai Oliver (Southern Rocks) b Harare 10.4.1991 RHB OB																			
FC		2	4	1	18	13	6.00	0	0									0	
FC	2008/09	3	6	2	25	13	6.25	0	0									1	
MAWOYO, Tinotenda Mbiri Kanayi (Mountaineers) b Umtali (now Mutare), Manicaland 8.1.1986 RHB RMF																			
FC		12	20	2	474	86*	26.33	0	3	6	10	0					10.00	2	
Lim		10	9	2	424	97	60.57	0	4									1	
FC	2001/02	54	96	7	2347	124	26.37	1	11	72	44	2	22.00	1-0	0	0	3.66	38	
Int	2006/07	2	2	0	24	14	12.00	0	0									0	
Lim	2003/04	36	32	3	956	97	32.96	0	7									9	1
20T	2007/08	12	11	1	197	64*	19.70	0	1									1	
MAWUDZI, Jethro (Mountaineers) b Mutare 10.3.1991 RHB LB																			
FC		4	7	0	223	105	31.85	1	1	6	6	0					6.00	1	
Lim		2	1	0	7	7	7.00	0	0									0	
MBOFANA, Mark Ramon Henry (Mashonaland Eagles) b Harare 25.3.1988 RHB RM																			
FC		3	5	2	51	29	17.00	0	0	392	188	6	31.33	2-16	0	0	2.87	0	
Lim		3	3	1	62	30	31.00	0	0	42	20	4	5.00	4-20	1	0	2.85	2	
MBOYI, Thabo Mkhululi (Matabeleland Tuskers) b Bulawayo 17.5.1985 RHB RM																			
FC		5	9	3	186	60	31.00	0	2	483	237	8	29.62	2-34	0	0	2.94	4	
Lim		1	1	1	8	8*		0	0	6	14	0					14.00	0	
FC	2003/04	17	27	8	346	60	18.21	0	3	1059	676	15	45.06	2-34	0	0	3.83	12	
Lim	2003/04	18	16	5	195	53	17.72	0	1	300	257	7	36.71	5-39	0	1	5.14	3	
20T	2007/08	11	9	2	58	17*	8.28	0	0	114	149	6	24.83	3-20	0	0	7.84	7	
METH, Keagan Orry (Matabeleland Tuskers) b Bulawayo 8.2.1988 RHB RM																			
FC		9	13	1	405	70	33.75	0	3	1341	561	29	19.34	5-26	1	0	2.51	4	
Lim		6	6	1	85	51	17.00	0	1	318	228	3	76.00	2-32	0	0	4.30	0	
20T		6	4	2	49	30*	24.50	0	0	108	144	6	24.00	2-27	0	0	8.00	3	
FC	2006	12	17	1	495	70	30.93	0	3	1703	702	32	21.93	5-26	1	0	2.47	7	
Int	2005/06	5	3	0	73	53	24.33	0	1	108	96	1	96.00	1-6	0	0	5.33	0	
Lim	2005/06	20	16	2	200	53	14.28	0	2	732	484	16	30.25	3-12	0	0	3.96	2	
MIRE, Solomon Farai (Mid West Rhinos) b Harare 21.8.1989 RHB RMF																			
FC		4	7	0	147	66	21.00	0	1	360	236	2	118.00	1-44	0	0	3.93	3	
Lim		4	4	1	180	69*	60.00	0	2	180	195	4	48.75	2-40	0	0	6.50	1	
FC	2006/07	9	16	1	333	66	22.20	0	1	606	390	5	78.00	1-10	0	0	3.86	4	
Lim	2006/07	12	12	3	452	94	50.22	0	5	516	397	11	36.09	4-22	1	0	4.61	2	
20T	2007/08	3	3	1	45	22*	22.50	0	0	60	80	4	20.00	3-24	0	0	8.00	2	
MLAMBO, Bernard (Mountaineers) b Mbare, Harare 2.12.1985 LHB LB WK																			
FC		9	15	1	309	57	22.07	0	2									7	
Lim		6	4	1	108	81*	36.00	0	1									2	
20T		5	5	0	53	24	10.60	0	0									2	
FC	2004/05	30	53	1	1256	158	24.15	1	4	6	11	0					11.00	19	
Lim	2004/05	29	26	3	592	81*	25.73	0	4									8	
20T	2009	10	10	0	162	45	16.20	0	0									3	
MPOFU, Christopher Bobby (Matabeleland Tuskers, Zimbabwe, Zimbabwe XI, Zimbabwe to Bangladesh, Zimbabwe to South Africa, Zimbabwe to West Indies) b Plumtree, Matabeleland 27.11.1985 RHB RFM																			
FC		11	15	4	194	34	17.63	0	0	2176	1156	41	28.19	5-52	2	0	3.18	4	
Int		5	2	1	6	6	6.00	0	0	200	192	7	27.42	3-44	0	0	5.76	1	
Lim		11	7	2	55	29*	11.00	0	0	494	431	16	26.93	3-27	0	0	5.23	2	
I20T		2	1	1	3	3*		0	0	42	60	2	30.00	2-31	0	0	8.57	0	
20T		8	3	2	6	3*	6.00	0	0	177	214	11	19.45	4-17	1	0	7.25	3	
Test	2004/05	6	12	6	17	7	2.83	0	0	830	556	8	69.50	4-109	0	0	4.01	0	
FC	2003/04	60	100	32	612	36	9.00	0	0	9709	5093	156	32.64	7-37	3	0	3.14	13	
Int	2004/05	42	25	13	29	6	2.41	0	0	1945	1702	44	38.68	6-52	1	1	5.25	5	
Lim	2003/04	78	47	20	196	29*	7.25	0	0	3615	2923	92	31.77	6-8	1	3	4.85	11	
I20T	2008/09	6	1	1	3	3*		0	0	108	135	6	22.50	3-16	0	0	7.50	2	
20T	2007/08	25	11	7	77	27*	19.25	0	0	520	598	27	22.14	4-17	1	0	6.90	6	
MUFAMBISI, Tafadzwa Vintlane (Mashonaland Eagles) b Glen View, Harare 17.12.1986 RHB OB WK																			
FC		4	7	0	188	58	26.85	0	2									6	
Lim		4	2	0	39	38	19.50	0	0									0	
FC	2003/04	23	40	2	1169	101*	30.76	1	7									46	2

Cmp	Debut	M	I	NO	Runs	HS	Avge	100	50	Balls	Runs	Wkts	Avge	BB	5i	10m	RpO	ct	st
Int	2006	6	6	0	55	21	9.16	0	0									1	
Lim	2004/05	18	16	3	186	38	14.30	0	0									5	4
20T	2009	6	5	0	48	20	9.60	0	0	1	4	0					24.00	0	
MUGAVA, Simon Munyaradzi (Mid West Rhinos) b Harare 29.11.1990 RHB OB																			
FC		2	2	0	7	4	3.50	0	0	198	99	2	49.50	2-30	0	0	3.00	0	
Lim		2	2	1	7	5	7.00	0	0	66	57	0					5.18	0	
MUGOCHI, Brighton (Mid West Rhinos) b Harare 23.7.1988 LHB SLA																			
FC		3	4	2	48	33*	24.00	0	0	384	188	4	47.00	2-29	0	0	2.93	3	
FC	2006/07	16	25	9	214	33*	13.37	0	0	3221	1502	61	24.62	5-48	5	0	2.79	10	
Lim	2006/07	5	5	2	39	22	13.00	0	0	248	122	8	15.25	3-17	0	0	2.95	1	
20T	2007/08	10	4	2	9	7	4.50	0	0	186	229	7	32.71	2-20	0	0	7.38	2	
MUJAJI, Silent (Mountaineers) b Mutare 24.9.1985 RHB RFM																			
FC		4	5	1	30	23	7.50	0	0	451	307	5	61.40	2-28	0	0	4.08	0	
Lim		1								30	26	0					5.20	0	
FC	2006/07	12	17	7	58	23	5.80	0	0	1281	754	24	31.41	3-28	0	0	3.53	4	
Lim	2005/06	10	3	1	22	21*	11.00	0	0	330	335	11	30.45	3-41	0	0	6.09	2	
20T	2007/08	2								12	32	2	16.00	2-32	0	0	16.00	2	
MUJURU, Bornaparte (Matabeleland Tuskers) b Chitungwiza 10.4.1987 RHB LB																			
FC		9	15	1	507	74	36.21	0	4	78	63	1	63.00	1-17	0	0	4.84	4	
Lim		6	6	0	163	89	27.16	0	2									1	
FC	2006/07	22	38	1	1059	90	28.62	0	8	78	63	1	63.00	1-17	0	0	4.84	9	
Lim	2005/06	21	19	1	520	89	28.88	0	5	126	98	2	49.00	2-22	0	0	4.66	7	
20T	2007/08	3	3	0	32	25	10.66	0	0									1	
MUNYARADZI, Tanyaradzwa (Southern Rocks) b Harare 20.6.1988 RHB RM																			
FC		3	6	2	30	20	7.50	0	0	223	166	7	23.71	4-58	0	0	4.46	0	
Lim	2008/09	1								6	18	0					18.00	0	
MUNYEDE, Kudakwashe (Mashonaland Eagles) b Harare 30.4.1991 RHB SLA																			
FC		1	2	1	2	2*	2.00	0	0	94	64	2	32.00	1-14	0	0	4.08	1	
MUPARIWA, Tawanda (Matabeleland Tuskers) b Bulawayo 16.4.1985 RHB RFM																			
FC		12	18	2	239	39	14.93	0	0	2263	1049	30	34.96	6-52	1	0	2.78	5	
Lim		8	8	1	111	26	15.85	0	0	338	304	6	50.66	2-19	0	0	5.39	1	
20T		6	3	0	62	31	20.66	0	0	96	135	2	67.50	1-16	0	0	8.43	0	
Test	2004	1	2	1	15	14	15.00	0	0	204	136	0					4.00	0	
FC	2001/02	51	87	15	1213	64*	16.84	0	3	8517	4252	145	29.32	6-52	3	0	2.99	21	
Int	2004	35	28	9	165	33	8.68	0	0	1773	1446	55	26.29	4-39	3	0	4.89	8	
Lim	2003/04	80	60	18	501	49	11.92	0	0	3733	3079	102	30.18	4-22	5	0	4.94	16	
I20T	2007/08	4	2	2	5	3*		0	0	78	94	1	94.00	1-22	0	0	7.23	0	
20T	2007/08	27	18	7	203	37*	18.45	0	0	525	627	17	36.88	2-11	0	0	7.16	2	
MUSHANGWE, Natsai (Mountaineers, Zimbabwe XI to Netherlands) b Mhangura 9.2.1991 RHB LB																			
FC		4	7	1	96	53	16.00	0	1	546	278	10	27.80	3-45	0	0	3.05	0	
Lim		6	2	1	1	1	1.00	0	0	282	160	14	11.42	4-40	1	0	3.40	0	
20T		6	2	1	10	9*	10.00	0	0	126	129	4	32.25	2-23	0	0	6.14	0	
FC	2008/09	10	15	1	136	53	9.71	0	1	1475	759	28	27.10	4-40	0	0	3.08	1	
Lim	2008/09	13	4	1	10	7	3.33	0	0	615	359	20	17.95	4-40	1	0	3.50	0	
20T	2009	12	3	2	32	22*	32.00	0	0	234	255	7	36.42	2-23	0	0	6.53	0	
MUSOSO, Steady (Mountaineers) b Mutare 24.9.1986 RHB RFM																			
FC		1	1	1	1	1*		0	0	150	83	0					3.32	0	
Lim		5								192	162	5	32.40	2-33	0	0	5.06	1	
FC	2006/07	9	12	6	65	18*	10.83	0	0	1115	684	23	29.73	5-43	1	0	3.68	3	
Lim	2005/06	15	4	2	1	1*	0.50	0	0	523	424	16	26.50	3-14	0	0	4.86	2	
20T	2007/08	7	2	1	5	4	5.00	0	0	72	100	7	14.28	2-6	0	0	8.33	2	
MUTIZWA, Forster (Mashonaland Eagles, Zimbabwe, Zimbabwe XI, Zimbabwe to Bangladesh, Zimbabwe XI to Canada, Zimbabwe XI to Netherlands) b Harare 24.8.1985 RHB OB WK																			
FC		14	25	5	1149	190	57.45	3	5	83	42	2	21.00	2-18	0	0	3.03	18	2
Int		2	2	0	134	79	67.00	0	2									0	
Lim		10	9	1	381	79	47.62	0	3	54	44	1	44.00	1-9	0	0	4.88	5	
20T		6	6	2	72	17	18.00	0	0									2	1
FC	2004/05	32	53	7	2030	190	44.13	6	10	83	42	2	21.00	2-18	0	0	3.03	83	8
Int	2008/09	9	8	1	263	79	37.57	0	3									5	2
Lim	2003/04	42	37	8	977	79	33.68	0	6	96	90	1	90.00	1-9	0	0	5.62	35	7
20T	2007/08	18	15	2	183	28	14.07	0	0									16	8
MUTOMBODZI, Confidence Tinotenda (Mashonaland Eagles) b Harare 21.12.1990 RHB LBG																			
FC		6	7	2	106	34	21.20	0	0	1044	553	16	34.56	7-84	1	0	3.17	4	
Lim		4	2	1	24	13	24.00	0	0	171	132	3	44.00	2-47	0	0	4.63	5	
FC	2008/09	7	9	3	109	34	18.16	0	0	1074	576	16	36.00	7-84	1	0	3.21	5	
Lim	2008/09	9	5	2	51	19	17.00	0	0	411	292	8	36.50	2-23	0	0	4.26	5	
20T	2009	7	2	2	1	1*		0	0	144	143	7	20.42	2-20	0	0	5.95	1	
MUTUMBAMI, Richmond (Southern Rocks) b Masvingo 11.6.1989 RHB OB WK																			
FC		7	10	0	197	100	19.70	1	0									13	2
Lim		5	4	1	46	43	15.33	0	0									1	
FC	2006/07	19	30	1	589	100	20.31	1	2									48	5

Cmp	Debut	M	I	NO	Runs	HS	Avge	100	50	Balls	Runs	Wkts	Avge	BB	5i	10m	RpO	ct	st
Lim	2005/06	20	19	2	238	53	14.00	0	1									20	
20T	2007/08	8	8	0	171	58	21.37	0	1									1	1
MUTYAMBIZI, Luther Kurauone (Mid West Rhinos) b Gwelo (now Gweru), Midlands 26.6.1978 RHB RM																			
FC		1	2	0	12	6	6.00	0	0									0	
Lim		1	1	0	1	1	1.00	0	0									0	
FC	1999/00	11	20	1	126	27*	6.63	0	0									2	
Lim	2003/04	6	5	0	40	21	8.00	0	0									3	
MUZARABANI, Taurai (Mid West Rhinos) b Centenary, Mashonaland 27.3.1987 RHB RMF																			
FC		12	15	4	152	51*	13.81	0	1	1607	865	26	33.26	3-29	0	0	3.23	3	
Lim		9	5	1	57	29	14.25	0	0	384	301	13	23.15	2-19	0	0	4.70	2	
20T		5	1	0	1	1	1.00	0	0	96	149	5	29.80	2-24	0	0	9.31	1	
FC	2006/07	29	42	9	303	51*	9.18	0	1	4160	2133	60	35.55	4-13	0	0	3.07	10	
Lim	2006/07	25	13	6	113	29	16.14	0	0	1140	827	34	24.32	4-12	1	0	4.35	4	
20T	2007/08	13	4	1	13	6	4.33	0	0	270	421	9	46.77	2-15	0	0	9.35	1	
MUZHANGE, Richard (Mid West Rhinos) b Kadoma 30.1.1991 RHB RM																			
FC		1	1	1	3	3*		0	0	180	86	4	21.50	3-58	0	0	2.86	0	
MWAKAYENI, Samuel (Mashonaland Eagles) b Harare 17.8.1988 RHB OB																			
FC		9	15	1	358	76	25.57	0	2	36	35	0					5.83	6	
Lim		2	2	0	40	40	20.00	0	0									1	
FC	2006/07	23	39	1	725	76	19.07	0	2	774	423	12	35.25	5-42	1	0	3.27	16	
Lim	2005/06	16	15	1	136	40	9.71	0	0	204	135	4	33.75	2-21	0	0	3.97	10	
20T	2007/08	9	6	0	40	20	6.66	0	0	33	38	1	38.00	1-6	0	0	6.90	4	
NCUBE, Njabulo (Mountaineers) b Bulawayo 14.10.1989 RHB RFM																			
FC		12	11	8	73	22	24.33	0	0	1620	722	21	34.38	3-41	0	0	2.67	6	
Lim		7								318	193	5	38.60	2-27	0	0	3.64	3	
20T		3								66	100	3	33.33	2-15	0	0	9.09	1	
FC	2008/09	18	22	13	91	22	10.11	0	0	2274	1127	29	38.86	3-41	0	0	2.97	9	
Lim	2008/09	11	3	2	20	15*	20.00	0	0	462	307	10	30.70	3-56	0	0	3.98	5	
20T	2007/08	12	2	0	11	10	5.50	0	0	198	227	13	17.46	2-15	0	0	6.87	3	
NGULUBE, Tafadzwa (Matabeleland Tuskers) b Bulawayo 3.5.1988 RHB WK																			
FC		6	11	0	168	44	15.27	0	0									17	3
Lim		4	4	1	60	33	20.00	0	0									3	2
FC	2007/08	16	31	3	697	112	24.89	1	2									38	5
Lim	2005/06	18	15	2	195	35	15.00	0	0									16	3
20T	2007/08	10	9	0	81	21	9.00	0	0									2	1
NKALA, Mluleki Luke (Mid West Rhinos) b Bulawayo 1.4.1981 RHB RFM																			
FC		3	6	0	186	57	31.00	0	2	237	119	2	59.50	1-21	0	0	3.01	0	
Lim		1								30	16	2	8.00	2-16	0	0	3.20	0	
20T		2	1	0	0	0	0.00	0	0	18	20	0					6.66	1	
Test	2000	10	15	2	187	47	14.38	0	0	1452	727	11	66.09	3-82	0	0	3.00	4	
FC	1999/00	49	78	9	1826	168	26.46	2	10	6083	3437	84	40.91	4-33	0	0	3.39	22	
Int	1998/99	50	35	5	324	47	10.80	0	0	1582	1570	22	71.36	3-12	0	0	5.95	6	
Lim	1997/98	87	61	12	696	54*	14.20	0	2	2893	2649	66	40.13	4-24	2	0	5.49	17	
I20T	2006/07	1	1	0	1	1	1.00	0	0									0	
20T	2006/07	3	2	0	1	1	0.50	0	0	18	20	0					6.66	1	
NTULI, Khawulani (Matabeleland Tuskers) b Bulawayo 20.8.1986 RHB RFM																			
FC		1	2	1	0	0*	0.00	0	0	120	79	2	39.50	2-68	0	0	3.95	0	
FC	2007/08	2	4	3	14	10*	14.00	0	0	186	117	4	29.25	2-38	0	0	3.77	0	
Lim	2006/07	2	2	1	37	32	37.00	0	0	48	62	1	62.00	1-21	0	0	7.75	0	
NYAMUZINGA, Steven Kudzai (Mountaineers) b Marondera 30.11.1986 RHB RM																			
FC		4	5	1	34	18	8.50	0	0	12	6	0					3.00	2	
Lim		5	4	1	11	7	3.66	0	0	12	15	0					7.50	0	
20T		3	1	0	3	3	3.00	0	0									1	
FC	2006/07	22	38	6	889	120	27.78	2	4	939	464	16	29.00	3-2	0	0	2.96	13	
Lim	2006/07	23	18	5	240	58	18.46	0	1	338	299	10	29.90	3-45	0	0	5.30	7	
20T	2007/08	16	12	5	129	33	18.42	0	0	60	80	2	40.00	2-24	0	0	8.00	1	
NYATHI, Remembrance (Mid West Rhinos) b Bulawayo 10.12.1986 RHB OB																			
FC		8	14	2	235	61	19.58	0	2	180	89	4	22.25	3-44	0	0	2.96	6	
Lim		6	5	1	31	15	7.75	0	0	18	20	0					6.66	2	
FC	2006/07	16	28	3	517	100	20.68	1	3	1382	727	22	33.04	3-44	0	0	3.15	10	
Lim	2005/06	20	18	4	159	48*	11.35	0	0	528	353	12	29.41	3-34	0	0	4.01	7	
20T	2007/08	10	6	1	55	18	11.00	0	0	60	72	2	36.00	1-16	0	0	7.20	5	
NYUMBU, John (Matabeleland Tuskers, Zimbabwe XI) b Harare 1.3.1983 RHB OB																			
FC		13	16	7	144	45	16.00	0	0	2398	1108	34	32.58	4-29	0	0	2.77	12	
Lim		8	6	2	15	7	3.75	0	0	432	302	10	30.20	3-27	0	0	4.19	8	
20T		2	1	1	1	1*		0	0	18	34	1	34.00	1-12	0	0	11.33	0	
FC	2003/04	26	38	13	304	45	12.16	0	0	4284	2117	65	32.56	5-42	2	0	2.96	29	
Lim	2005/06	19	13	8	32	7	6.40	0	0	984	655	22	29.77	3-27	0	0	3.99	12	
20T	2007/08	14	8	7	18	5*	18.00	0	0	192	225	4	56.25	1-12	0	0	7.03	4	

Cmp	Debut	M	I	NO	Runs	HS	Avge	100	50	Balls	Runs	Wkts	Avge	BB	5i	10m	RpO	ct	st
ODOYO, Thomas Migai (Kenya to Netherlands, Kenya, Southern Rocks) b Nairobi, Kenya 12.5.1978 RHB RMF																			
FC		8	13	1	218	47	18.16	0	0	957	432	14	30.85	3-39	0	0	2.70	1	
Int		3	3	0	82	30	27.33	0	0	150	145	3	48.33	2-54	0	0	5.80	0	
Lim		9	8	1	215	55*	30.71	0	1	370	335	6	55.83	2-44	0	0	5.43	1	
FC	1997	40	63	7	1476	137	26.35	2	8	4367	2138	86	24.86	5-21	3	0	2.93	13	
Int	1995/96	126	110	16	2307	111*	24.54	1	7	5262	4016	133	30.19	4-25	5	0	4.57	25	
Lim	1995/96	186	165	27	3574	111*	25.89	1	16	7478	5603	200	28.01	5-27	6	1	4.49	41	
I20T	2007/08	8	7	0	85	22	12.14	0	0	150	122	6	20.33	2-13	0	0	4.88	4	
20T	2007/08	8	7	0	85	22	12.14	0	0	150	122	6	20.33	2-13	0	0	4.88	4	
PRICE, Raymond William (Mashonaland Eagles, Zimbabwe, Zimbabwe to Bangladesh, Zimbabwe to South Africa, Zimbabwe to West Indies) b Salisbury (now Harare) 12.6.1976 RHB SLA																			
FC		10	13	3	159	41	15.90	0	0	2622	838	35	23.94	5-57	1	0	1.91	12	
Int		10	3	0	9	9	3.00	0	0	509	341	10	34.10	2-15	0	0	4.02	1	
Lim		16	6	1	70	34*	14.00	0	0	806	489	15	32.60	2-15	0	0	3.64	3	
I20T		2	1	0	2	2	2.00	0	0	42	49	3	16.33	2-24	0	0	7.00	0	
20T		8	4	2	19	11*	9.50	0	0	161	150	8	18.75	5-12	0	1	5.59	1	
Test	1999/00	18	30	7	224	36	9.73	0	0	5135	2475	69	35.86	6-73	5	1	2.89	3	
FC	1995/96	105	164	29	2303	117*	17.05	1	11	25158	10999	373	29.48	8-35	20	3	2.62	54	
Int	2002/03	79	44	11	296	46	8.96	0	0	4084	2658	74	35.91	4-22	1	0	3.90	14	
Lim	1997/98	192	107	29	854	49	10.94	0	0	9320	6045	199	30.37	4-21	5	0	3.89	45	
I20T	2008/09	9	5	2	5	2	1.66	0	0	210	164	11	14.90	2-6	0	0	4.68	2	
20T	2005	41	17	8	60	14	6.66	0	0	851	880	38	23.15	5-12	0	1	6.20	11	
RAINSFORD, Edward Charles (Mid West Rhinos, Zimbabwe, Zimbabwe XI, Zimbabwe XI to Canada, Zimbabwe XI to Netherlands) b Kadoma, Mashonaland 14.12.1984 RHB RFM																			
FC		12	14	0	206	30	14.71	0	0	1916	871	40	21.77	6-66	3	0	2.72	4	
Lim		8	4	2	55	31*	27.50	0	0	371	310	10	31.00	4-48	1	0	5.01	2	
I20T		1	1	1	1	1*		0	0	18	25	0					8.33	0	
20T		3	2	2	3	2*		0	0	40	73	2	36.50	1-22	0	0	10.95	1	
FC	2001/02	52	75	17	672	51	11.58	0	2	7401	3553	173	20.53	6-20	9	1	2.88	26	
Int	2004	36	21	12	40	9*	4.44	0	0	1757	1286	35	36.74	3-16	0	0	4.39	8	
Lim	2002/03	65	41	19	147	31*	6.68	0	0	3044	2256	69	32.69	4-32	2	0	4.44	14	
20T	2006/07	12	7	3	36	12	9.00	0	0	224	351	6	58.50	3-48	0	0	9.40	3	
RAYNER, Oliver Philip (Sussex, Mid West Rhinos) b Fallingbostel, Germany 1.11.1985 RHB OB																			
20T		5	3	0	30	24	10.00	0	0	90	109	3	36.33	1-19	0	0	7.26	1	
FC	2006	38	45	9	782	101	21.72	1	3	6034	3086	89	34.67	5-49	3	0	3.06	42	
Lim	2006	20	17	9	213	61	26.62	0	1	672	670	14	47.85	2-31	0	0	5.98	7	
20T	2006	17	9	2	115	41*	16.42	0	0	235	307	9	34.11	1-16	0	0	7.83	1	
ROBERTSON, Duncan (Mid West Rhinos) b Harare 11.7.1990 RHB RM																			
FC		1	2	0	3	3	1.50	0	0									0	
Lim		1	1	0	2	2	2.00	0	0									0	
ROGERS, Barney Guy (Mashonaland Eagles) b Harare 20.8.1982 LHB OB																			
Lim		3	3	0	52	41	17.33	0	0	12	20	0					10.00	1	
Test	2004/05	4	8	0	90	29	11.25	0	0	18	17	0					5.66	1	
FC	2000/01	36	62	2	1980	141	33.00	3	12	1924	1219	33	36.93	4-34	0	0	3.80	23	
Int	2002/03	15	15	0	478	84	31.86	0	5	324	321	6	53.50	2-55	0	0	5.94	7	
Lim	2000/01	47	45	4	1097	84*	26.75	0	8	859	822	21	39.14	3-36	0	0	5.74	15	
SAURAMBA, Kudzai (Mountaineers) b Mutare 24.1.1992 RHB WK																			
FC		1	2	0	10	10	5.00	0	0									4	
Lim		1																0	
SENZERE, Ishmael (Mashonaland Eagles) b Shamva 31.8.1981 RHB RM																			
FC		3	5	0	44	28	8.80	0	0									1	
FC	2006/07	8	14	0	240	131	17.14	1	0	12	9	0					4.50	2	
Lim	2005/06	8	8	1	100	36	14.28	0	0									5	
SIBANDA, Vusimuzi (Mid West Rhinos, Zimbabwe XI, Zimbabwe to West Indies, Zimbabwe XI to Canada, Zimbabwe XI to Netherlands) b Highfields, Harare 10.10.1983 RHB RM																			
FC		14	26	4	1612	215	73.27	9	2	777	477	4	119.25	2-44	0	0	3.68	15	
Lim		10	10	1	266	82	29.55	0	2	141	123	3	41.00	2-50	0	0	5.23	6	
20T		5	5	0	117	61	23.40	0	1	12	27	0					13.50	1	
Test	2003/04	3	6	0	48	18	8.00	0	0									4	
FC	2001/02	67	128	6	3808	215	31.21	10	16	1485	993	15	66.20	4-30	0	0	4.01	60	
Int	2003/04	84	83	2	1796	116	22.17	1	12	138	148	2	74.00	1-12	0	0	6.43	27	
Lim	2002/03	150	146	6	3129	116	22.35	1	20	393	408	5	81.60	2-50	0	0	6.22	51	
I20T	2007/08	3	3	0	52	29	17.33	0	0									1	
20T	2006/07	11	11	0	196	61	17.81	0	1	12	27	0					13.50	2	
SIKANDAR RAZA Butt (Southern Rocks) b Sialkot, Punjab, Pakistan 24.4.1986 RHB RM																			
Lim		1	1	0	7	7	7.00	0	0	5	5	1	5.00	1-5	0	0	6.00	0	
20T		5	5	0	111	53	22.20	0	1	48	54	2	27.00	1-20	0	0	6.75	1	
FC	2006/07	5	9	0	201	84	22.33	0	1	204	86	3	28.66	3-26	0	0	2.52	8	
Lim	2006/07	5	5	0	76	36	15.20	0	0	5	5	1	5.00	1-5	0	0	6.00	3	

Cmp	Debut	M	I	NO	Runs	HS	Avge	100	50	Balls	Runs	Wkts	Avge	BB	5i	10m	RpO	ct	st
SILVERWOOD, Christopher Eric Wilfred (Mashonaland Eagles) b Pontefract, Yorkshire, England 5.3.1975 RHB RFM																			
FC		1	1	1	0	0*		0	0	144	70	3	23.33	3-47	0	0	2.91	0	
Lim		1								48	42	0					5.25	1	
Test	1996/97	6	7	3	29	10	7.25	0	0	828	444	11	40.36	5-91	1	0	3.21	2	
FC	1993	184	243	49	3075	80	15.85	0	9	29917	15819	577	27.41	7-93	25	1	3.17	43	
Int	1996/97	7	4	0	17	12	4.25	0	0	306	244	6	40.66	3-43	0	0	4.78	0	
Lim	1993	202	114	37	1046	61	13.58	0	4	9040	6488	259	25.05	5-28	6	1	4.30	32	
20T	2003	20	12	7	69	18*	13.80	0	0	438	550	14	39.28	2-22	0	0	7.53	4	
SMITH, Gregory Marc (Derbyshire, Derbyshire to Netherlands, Mountaineers) b Johannesburg, Transvaal, South Africa 20.4.1983 RHB RMF																			
20T		4	3	0	17	10	5.66	0	0	52	48	9	5.33	5-27	0	1	5.53	0	
FC	2003/04	71	122	10	3308	165*	29.53	3	22	7334	4090	113	36.19	5-54	2	0	3.34	19	
Lim	2003/04	62	62	5	1346	88	23.61	0	5	1723	1653	49	33.73	4-53	1	0	5.75	24	
20T	2007	44	42	2	900	100*	22.50	1	4	454	594	25	23.76	5-27	0	1	7.85	18	
STEVENS, Darren Ian (England Lions, Kent, Kent to Scotland, Mid West Rhinos) b Leicester, England 30.4.1976 RHB RM																			
20T		5	5	2	102	43*	34.00	0	0	108	139	8	17.37	4-26	1	0	7.72	1	
FC	1997	170	276	20	8836	208	34.51	21	42	6786	3407	94	36.24	4-36	0	0	3.01	128	
Lim	1997	218	204	24	5454	133	30.30	4	36	2183	1806	51	35.41	5-32	0	1	4.96	84	
20T	2003	84	78	19	1746	77	29.59	0	8	690	839	39	21.51	4-14	2	0	7.29	27	
STRYDOM, Gregory Mark (Matabeleland Tuskers, Zimbabwe XI) b Pretoria, Transvaal, South Africa 26.3.1984 RHB RM																			
FC		12	18	0	651	89	36.16	0	6	654	356	9	39.55	3-38	0	0	3.26	6	
Lim		8	8	0	147	53	18.37	0	1	96	128	0					8.00	0	
20T		6	5	1	71	29*	17.75	0	0	6	7	0					7.00	1	
FC	2000/01	39	68	4	2423	216	37.85	4	15	2961	1835	42	43.69	4-48	0	0	3.71	27	
Int	2005/06	12	10	0	147	58	14.70	0	1	66	61	1	61.00	1-28	0	0	5.54	4	
Lim	2002/03	55	46	1	965	69	21.44	0	6	776	652	20	32.60	4-20	1	0	5.04	18	
20T	2007/08	11	10	1	176	38	19.55	0	0	36	40	0					6.66	4	
TAIBU, Tatenda (Mountaineers, Zimbabwe, Zimbabwe XI, Zimbabwe to Bangladesh, Zimbabwe to South Africa, Zimbabwe to West Indies) b Harare 14.5.1983 RHB RM WK																			
FC		10	17	0	899	172	52.88	2	6									30	2
Int		3	3	2	126	71	126.00	0	1									2	2
Lim		11	9	2	203	71	29.00	0	2	30	26	0					5.20	15	7
I20T		2	2	1	49	45*	49.00	0	0									1	1
20T		8	8	4	254	71*	63.50	0	2									7	2
Test	2001	24	46	3	1273	153	29.60	1	9	48	27	1	27.00	1-27	0	0	3.37	48	4
FC	1999/00	106	182	18	6198	175*	37.79	11	34	924	431	22	19.59	8-43	1	0	2.79	282	29
Int	2001	120	107	20	2466	107*	28.34	2	13	84	61	2	30.50	2-42	0	0	4.35	102	22
Lim	2001	197	179	35	4292	121*	29.80	4	25	569	430	14	30.71	4-25	1	0	4.53	182	43
I20T	2007/08	11	11	4	173	45*	24.71	0	0	24	41	0					10.25	4	5
20T	2007/08	36	35	8	631	89	23.37	0	3	24	41	0					10.25	23	12
TAYLOR, Brendan Ross Murray (Mid West Rhinos, Zimbabwe, Zimbabwe to Bangladesh, Zimbabwe to South Africa, Zimbabwe to West Indies) b Harare 6.2.1986 RHB OB WK																			
FC		10	18	2	1058	217	66.12	5	1	72	38	1	38.00	1-9	0	0	3.16	13	
Int		10	10	3	549	119*	78.42	1	5									11	3
Lim		18	18	5	965	119*	74.23	2	8									20	4
I20T		2	2	0	42	27	21.00	0	0									0	
20T		7	7	1	141	45*	23.50	0	0									2	
Test	2004	10	20	0	422	78	21.10	0	3	42	38	0					5.42	7	
FC	2001/02	60	112	6	3856	217	36.37	10	14	330	199	4	49.75	2-36	0	0	3.61	65	4
Int	2004	102	101	10	2889	119*	31.74	2	19	228	244	9	27.11	3-54	0	0	6.42	57	18
Lim	2003/04	147	145	13	4137	139	31.34	4	25	336	331	15	22.06	5-28	0	1	5.91	84	26
I20T	2006/07	7	7	2	165	60*	33.00	0	1	6	1	0					1.00	2	1
20T	2006/07	25	25	5	623	85*	31.15	0	4	6	1	0					1.00	8	1
TICHANA, Alois (Mashonaland Eagles) b Harare 5.12.1984 RHB OB																			
FC		4	7	0	63	33	9.00	0	0	6	9	0					9.00	1	
Lim		1	1	0	10	10	10.00	0	0									0	
FC	2006/07	17	29	0	600	106	20.68	1	3	565	202	8	25.25	3-20	0	0	2.14	5	
Lim	2005/06	13	13	0	102	26	7.84	0	0	382	238	10	23.80	2-17	0	0	3.73	1	
TIKOLO, Stephen Ogonji (Kenya, Kenya to United Arab Emirates, Southern Rocks) b Nairobi, Kenya 25.6.1971 RHB RM																			
FC		8	13	0	376	61	28.92	0	3	828	430	12	35.83	3-23	0	0	3.11	12	
Int		4	4	0	74	49	18.50	0	0	216	167	2	83.50	2-38	0	0	4.63	2	
Lim		11	10	0	396	91	39.60	0	3	432	349	6	58.16	2-38	0	0	4.84	4	
20T		4	4	0	123	65	30.75	0	1	72	104	1	104.00	1-33	0	0	8.66	2	
FC	1995/96	56	92	5	4276	220	49.14	11	21	5464	2879	78	36.91	6-80	1	0	3.16	57	
Int	1995/96	126	121	10	3304	111	29.76	3	23	3794	3010	90	33.44	4-41	2	0	4.76	64	
Lim	1995/96	192	184	13	5541	133	32.40	9	34	5903	4560	143	31.88	4-41	4	0	4.63	92	
I20T	2007/08	11	11	3	260	56*	32.50	0	2	102	121	3	40.33	1-10	0	0	7.11	5	
20T	2007/08	17	17	3	471	65	33.64	0	4	204	252	4	63.00	1-10	0	0	7.41	8	

Cmp	Debut	M	I	NO	Runs	HS	Avge	100	50	Balls	Runs	Wkts	Avge	BB	5i	10m	RpO	ct	st
TIRIPANO, Donald Tatenda (Mountaineers) b Mutare 17.3.1988 RHB RM																			
FC		8	12	3	229	61	25.44	0	1	603	334	7	47.71	2-33	0	0	3.32	2	
Lim		7	1	0	9	9	9.00	0	0	267	200	8	25.00	4-27	1	0	4.49	2	
20T		3	2	0	3	2	1.50	0	0	18	28	1	28.00	1-28	0	0	9.33	1	
FC	2008/09	10	15	3	258	61	21.50	0	1	717	386	7	55.14	2-33	0	0	3.23	2	
Lim	2008/09	9	3	1	12	9	6.00	0	0	283	207	10	20.70	4-27	1	0	4.38	2	
20T	2009	6	3	1	33	30*	16.50	0	0	36	74	1	74.00	1-28	0	0	12.33	1	
UTSEYA, Prosper (Mountaineers, Zimbabwe, Zimbabwe to Bangladesh, Zimbabwe to South Africa, Zimbabwe to West Indies) b Harare 26.3.1985 RHB OB																			
FC		10	13	1	314	58	26.16	0	2	2213	801	30	26.70	5-28	1	0	2.17	2	
Int		10	4	1	21	10*	7.00	0	0	503	359	15	23.93	4-46	1	0	4.28	3	
Lim		17	8	3	78	30*	15.60	0	0	861	534	24	22.25	4-46	1	0	3.72	5	
I20T		1	1	0	6	6	6.00	0	0	12	12	0					6.00	1	
20T		7	4	0	19	8	4.75	0	0	144	145	7	20.71	3-24	0	0	6.04	1	
Test	2004	1	2	0	45	45	22.50	0	0	72	55	0					4.58	2	
FC	2001/02	63	108	7	2097	115*	20.76	1	11	11449	5194	180	28.85	7-56	8	2	2.72	26	
Int	2004	111	86	31	749	68*	13.61	0	2	5583	3863	84	45.98	4-46	1	0	4.15	33	
Lim	2003/04	162	128	41	1225	68*	14.08	0	2	7986	5430	132	41.13	4-16	2	0	4.08	51	
I20T	2006/07	11	8	3	36	13*	7.20	0	0	246	220	12	18.33	3-25	0	0	5.36	4	
20T	2006/07	36	29	11	243	41*	13.50	0	0	799	753	37	20.35	4-12	1	0	5.65	10	
VERMEULEN, Mark Andrew (Matabeleland Tuskers, Zimbabwe, Zimbabwe to Bangladesh, Zimbabwe to South Africa) b Salisbury (now Harare) 2.3.1979 RHB OB																			
FC		3	5	0	144	73	28.80	0	1	12	10	0					5.00	4	
Int		4	4	0	143	56	35.75	0	1	5	5	1	5.00	1-5	0	0	6.00	3	
Lim		7	7	0	253	73	36.14	0	2	5	5	1	5.00	1-5	0	0	6.00	4	
20T		3	3	0	23	14	7.66	0	0									2	
Test	2002/03	8	16	0	414	118	25.87	1	2	6	5	0					5.00	6	
FC	1997/98	71	134	4	4822	198	37.09	11	19	905	479	15	31.93	3-26	0	0	3.17	72	
Int	2000/01	43	43	4	868	92	22.25	0	6	5	5	1	5.00	1-5	0	0	6.00	19	
Lim	1998/99	97	96	6	2270	105	25.22	1	15	71	66	1	66.00	1-5	0	0	5.57	34	
20T	2009	10	10	0	334	108	33.40	1	2									2	
VITORI, Brian Vitalis (Southern Rocks) b Masvingo 22.2.1990 LHB LM																			
FC		2	2	1	1	1	1.00	0	0	162	143	2	71.50	2-56	0	0	5.29	0	
Lim		2								12	22	0					11.00	0	
FC	2007/08	7	10	5	38	16*	7.60	0	0	492	325	8	40.62	2-37	0	0	3.96	1	
Lim	2005/06	5	1	1	0	0*		0	0	102	58	3	19.33	2-18	0	0	3.41	1	
20T	2007/08	1	1	0	3	3	3.00	0	0	12	14	1	14.00	1-14	0	0	7.00	0	
WALLER, Malcolm Noel (Mid West Rhinos, Zimbabwe, Zimbabwe to Bangladesh) b Harare 28.9.1984 RHB LBG																			
FC		11	18	1	582	124	34.23	2	2	472	279	5	55.80	1-0	0	0	3.54	7	
Int		2	1	1	1	1*		0	0	18	15	0					5.00	1	
Lim		10	8	1	84	29	12.00	0	0	275	228	10	22.80	3-35	0	0	4.97	8	
20T		5	3	0	104	55	34.66	0	1									2	
FC	2007/08	20	35	3	1183	124	36.96	2	8	790	432	10	43.20	1-0	0	0	3.28	16	
Int	2008/09	14	13	1	189	63	15.75	0	1	96	109	0					6.81	4	
Lim	2004/05	39	35	3	575	72	17.96	0	3	576	502	20	25.10	3-35	0	0	5.22	20	
20T	2007/08	15	13	3	358	73	35.80	0	2	12	19	0					9.50	4	
WALLER, Nathan (Zimbabwe XI to Netherlands) b Harare 19.11.1991 RHB RFM																			
FC	2010	1	1	0	0	0	0.00	0	0	126	45	2	22.50	2-16	0	0	2.14	0	
Lim	2008/09	3	3	0	31	21	10.33	0	0	60	24	2	12.00	2-24	0	0	2.40	0	
WESSELS, Mattheus Hendrik (Mid West Rhinos) b Marogudoore, Queensland, Australia 12.11.1985 RHB WK																			
FC		8	14	2	448	114	37.33	2	1	60	29	2	14.50	1-10	0	0	2.90	19	1
Lim		5	5	1	229	74*	57.25	0	3	49	48	1	48.00	1-0	0	0	5.87	2	
20T		5	5	1	168	86*	42.00	0	1									6	
FC	2004	74	122	9	3485	114	30.84	6	21	78	42	2	21.00	1-10	0	0	3.23	146	12
Lim	2005	74	70	8	1794	100	28.93	1	11	49	48	1	48.00	1-0	0	0	5.87	55	
20T	2005	51	42	9	836	86*	25.33	0	3									17	12
WILLIAMS, Matthew Lee (Matabeleland Tuskers) b Bulawayo 28.6.1990 RHB RM																			
FC		2	3	1	86	49*	43.00	0	0	120	46	1	46.00	1-14	0	0	2.30	1	
Lim		3	2	0	8	8	4.00	0	0	24	44	1	44.00	1-26	0	0	11.00	1	
FC	2006/07	4	7	1	130	49*	21.66	0	0	120	46	1	46.00	1-14	0	0	2.30	2	
WILLIAMS, Sean Colin (Matabeleland Tuskers, Zimbabwe, Zimbabwe XI to Canada, Zimbabwe XI to Netherlands) b Bulawayo 26.9.1986 LHB SLA																			
FC		4	7	0	230	76	32.85	0	2	80	54	1	54.00	1-3	0	0	4.05	3	
Int		3	2	1	35	33	35.00	0	0	30	14	0					2.80	1	
Lim		8	7	1	189	58	31.50	0	1	204	182	3	60.66	2-42	0	0	5.35	1	
20T		6	6	2	106	44*	26.50	0	0	66	76	4	19.00	2-16	0	0	6.90	2	
FC	2004/05	25	47	5	1635	129	38.92	3	11	1019	454	11	41.27	3-60	0	0	2.67	25	
Int	2004/05	41	40	7	983	75	29.78	0	10	669	574	9	63.77	3-23	0	0	5.14	14	
Lim	2003/04	70	65	7	1629	102	28.08	1	13	1568	1253	28	44.75	3-19	0	0	4.79	22	
I20T	2006/07	1	1	0	38	38	38.00	0	0	24	28	1	28.00	1-28	0	0	7.00	0	
20T	2006/07	13	13	5	185	44*	23.12	0	0	186	223	9	24.77	2-16	0	0	7.19	5	

Cmp	Debut	M	I	NO	Runs	HS	Avge	100	50	Balls	Runs	Wkts	Avge	BB	5i	10m	RpO	ct	st
ZHUWAO, Cephas (Mashonaland Eagles, Zimbabwe XI) b Harare 15.12.1984 LHB LB																			
FC		4	7	0	93	40	13.28	0	0	162	86	2	43.00	1-3	0	0	3.18	2	
Lim		5	5	0	89	27	17.80	0	0	18	20	0					6.66	1	
20T		4	4	1	104	81*	34.66	0	1									2	
FC	2006/07	11	19	1	298	51	16.55	0	1	576	225	5	45.00	2-39	0	0	2.34	2	
Int	2008/09	1	1	0	16	16	16.00	0	0	18	15	0					5.00	0	
Lim	2005/06	24	21	2	375	42*	19.73	0	0	251	186	4	46.50	1-9	0	0	4.44	7	
I20T	2008/09	3	3	0	12	12	4.00	0	0	2	1	1	1.00	1-1	0	0	3.00	1	
20T	2007/08	16	15	3	225	81*	18.75	0	2	112	130	8	16.25	3-8	0	0	6.96	4	

AFGHANISTAN TO ZIMBABWE 2010

Cmp	Debut	M	I	NO	Runs	HS	Avge	100	50	Balls	Runs	Wkts	Avge	BB	5i	10m	RpO	ct	st
AHMED SHAH																			
FC		1	2	0	77	40	38.50	0	0	84	56	0					4.00	1	
ASGHAR STANIKZAI																			
FC		1	2	0	19	14	9.50	0	0									1	
DAWLAT AHMADZAI																			
FC		1	1	0	6	6	6.00	0	0	88	54	4	13.50	2-14	0	0	3.68	0	
HAMID HASSAN																			
FC		1	1	1	0	0*		0	0	288	220	4	55.00	2-100	0	0	4.58	1	
MOHAMMAD NABI																			
FC		1	1	0	102	102	102.00	1	0	340	144	5	28.80	3-90	0	0	2.54	1	
MOHAMMAD SHAHZAD																			
FC		1	2	0	120	79	60.00	0	1									1	
NAWROZ MANGAL																			
FC		1	1	0	25	25	25.00	0	0	78	48	0					3.69	1	
NOOR ALI ZADRAN																			
FC		1	2	1	230	130	230.00	2	0	2	4	0					12.00	0	
RAEES AHMADZAI																			
FC		1	2	0	13	8	6.50	0	0	12	13	0					6.50	0	
SAMIULLAH SHENWARI																			
FC		1	1	0	10	10	10.00	0	0	84	82	1	82.00	1-36	0	0	5.85	1	
SHAPOOR ZADRAN																			
FC		1	1	0	0	0	0.00	0	0	198	145	2	72.50	2-64	0	0	4.39	1	

INDIA TO ZIMBABWE 2010

Cmp	Debut	M	I	NO	Runs	HS	Avge	100	50	Balls	Runs	Wkts	Avge	BB	5i	10m	RpO	ct	st
ASHWIN, R.																			
Int		1	1	0	38	38	38.00	0	0	60	50	2	25.00	2-50	0	0	5.00	0	
Lim		1	1	0	38	38	38.00	0	0	60	50	2	25.00	2-50	0	0	5.00	0	
I20T		2								48	70	2	35.00	1-22	0	0	8.75	0	
20T		2								48	70	2	35.00	1-22	0	0	8.75	0	
CHAWLA, P.P.																			
I20T		1								24	14	1	14.00	1-14	0	0	3.50	0	
20T		1								24	14	1	14.00	1-14	0	0	3.50	0	
DINDA, A.B.																			
Int		4	2	0	16	16	8.00	0	0	197	189	3	63.00	2-44	0	0	5.75	0	
Lim		4	2	0	16	16	8.00	0	0	197	189	3	63.00	2-44	0	0	5.75	0	
I20T		2								42	42	4	10.50	2-15	0	0	6.00	0	
20T		2								42	42	4	10.50	2-15	0	0	6.00	0	
JADEJA, R.A.																			
Int		4	3	1	131	61*	65.50	0	2	222	181	5	36.20	2-27	0	0	4.89	0	
Lim		4	3	1	131	61*	65.50	0	2	222	181	5	36.20	2-27	0	0	4.89	0	
KARTHIK, K.D.																			
Int		4	4	0	100	33	25.00	0	0									0	1
Lim		4	4	0	100	33	25.00	0	0									0	1
KOHLI, V.																			
Int		4	4	0	168	82	42.00	0	2									2	
Lim		4	4	0	168	82	42.00	0	2									2	
I20T		2	1	1	26	26*		0	0									0	
20T		2	1	1	26	26*		0	0									0	
MISHRA, A.																			
Int		3	1	0	0	0	0.00	0	0	174	143	1	143.00	1-47	0	0	4.93	0	
Lim		3	1	0	0	0	0.00	0	0	174	143	1	143.00	1-47	0	0	4.93	0	
I20T		1								24	21	1	21.00	1-21	0	0	5.25	0	
20T		1								24	21	1	21.00	1-21	0	0	5.25	0	
OJHA, N.V.																			
Int		1	1	0	1	1	1.00	0	0									0	1
Lim		1	1	0	1	1	1.00	0	0									0	1

Cmp Debut	M	I	NO	Runs	HS	Avge	100	50	Balls	Runs	Wkts	Avge	BB	5i	10m	RpO	ct	st
I20T	2	2	0	12	10	6.00	0	0									0	
20T	2	2	0	12	10	6.00	0	0									0	
OJHA, P.P.																		
Int	3	2	2	12	7*		0	0	180	122	4	30.50	2-44	0	0	4.06	0	
Lim	3	2	2	12	7*		0	0	180	122	4	30.50	2-44	0	0	4.06	0	
I20T	2								48	37	3	12.33	2-11	0	0	4.62	0	
20T	2								48	37	3	12.33	2-11	0	0	4.62	0	
PANKAJ SINGH																		
Int	1	1	1	3	3*		0	0	42	45	0					6.42	1	
Lim	1	1	1	3	3*		0	0	42	45	0					6.42	1	
PATHAN, Y.K.																		
Int	4	3	1	70	44	35.00	0	0	48	60	0					7.50	2	
Lim	4	3	1	70	44	35.00	0	0	48	60	0					7.50	2	
I20T	2	2	1	41	37*	41.00	0	0	12	10	0					5.00	1	
20T	2	2	1	41	37*	41.00	0	0	12	10	0					5.00	1	
RAINA, S.K.																		
Int	4	4	1	83	37	27.66	0	0									1	
Lim	4	4	1	83	37	27.66	0	0									1	
I20T	2	2	1	100	72*	100.00	0	1									2	
20T	2	2	1	100	72*	100.00	0	1									2	
SHARMA, R.G.																		
Int	4	4	1	260	114	86.66	2	0	6	5	0					5.00	0	
Lim	4	4	1	260	114	86.66	2	0	6	5	0					5.00	0	
I20T	2	2	1	10	10	10.00	0	0									2	
20T	2	2	1	10	10	10.00	0	0									2	
VIJAY, M.																		
Int	3	3	0	46	21	15.33	0	0									2	
Lim	3	3	0	46	21	15.33	0	0									2	
I20T	2	2	0	51	46	25.50	0	0									1	
20T	2	2	0	51	46	25.50	0	0									1	
VINAY KUMAR, R.																		
Int	1								48	51	2	25.50	2-51	0	0	6.37	0	
Lim	1								48	51	2	25.50	2-51	0	0	6.37	0	
I20T	2								42	52	3	17.33	3-24	0	0	7.42	0	
20T	2								42	52	3	17.33	3-24	0	0	7.42	0	
YADAV, U.T.																		
Int	3	1	1	3	3*		0	0	132	129	1	129.00	1-61	0	0	5.86	1	
Lim	3	1	1	3	3*		0	0	132	129	1	129.00	1-61	0	0	5.86	1	

KENYA TO ZIMBABWE 2010

Cmp Debut	M	I	NO	Runs	HS	Avge	100	50	Balls	Runs	Wkts	Avge	BB	5i	10m	RpO	ct	st
AGA, R.G.																		
FC	1	2	0	38	29	19.00	0	0	144	102	2	51.00	1-43	0	0	4.25	0	
KAMANDE, J.K.																		
FC	1	2	0	15	9	7.50	0	0	174	79	2	39.50	1-23	0	0	2.72	0	
Int	4	4	0	68	37	17.00	0	0	198	172	2	86.00	1-37	0	0	5.21	1	
Lim	4	4	0	68	37	17.00	0	0	198	172	2	86.00	1-37	0	0	5.21	1	
LUSENO, A.S.																		
Int	1	1	0	1	1	1.00	0	0	30	41	0					8.20	0	
Lim	1	1	0	1	1	1.00	0	0	30	41	0					8.20	0	
OBANDA, A.A.																		
FC	1	2	0	85	51	42.50	0	1									3	
Int	5	5	0	127	65	25.40	0	1									2	
Lim	5	5	0	127	65	25.40	0	1									2	
OBUYA, C.O.																		
FC	1	2	0	38	21	19.00	0	0									1	
Int	5	5	0	113	52	22.60	0	1									1	
Lim	5	5	0	113	52	22.60	0	1									1	
OBUYA, D.O.																		
FC	1	2	0	74	37	37.00	0	0									2	
Int	5	5	0	197	56	39.40	0	1									2	1
Lim	5	5	0	197	56	39.40	0	1									2	1
ODHIAMBO, N.N.																		
FC	1	2	1	41	26*	41.00	0	0	208	177	4	44.25	3-105	0	0	5.10	0	
Int	5	5	1	50	27	12.50	0	0	269	269	12	22.41	4-61	1	0	6.00	1	
Lim	5	5	1	50	27	12.50	0	0	269	269	12	22.41	4-61	1	0	6.00	1	
ODOYO, T.M.																		
FC	8	13	1	218	47	18.16	0	0	957	432	14	30.85	3-39	0	0	2.70	1	
Int	3	3	0	82	30	27.33	0	0	150	145	3	48.33	2-54	0	0	5.80	0	
Lim	9	8	1	215	55*	30.71	0	1	370	335	6	55.83	2-44	0	0	5.43	1	

Cmp Debut	M	I	NO	Runs	HS	Avge	100	50	Balls	Runs	Wkts	Avge	BB	5i	10m	RpO	ct	st
ONGONDO, P.J.																		
Int	2	2	0	13	12	6.50	0	0	102	94	0					5.52	0	
Lim	2	2	0	13	12	6.50	0	0	102	94	0					5.52	0	
ONYANGO, L.N.																		
Int	5	5	2	45	17	15.00	0	0	204	234	1	234.00	1-44	0	0	6.88	0	
Lim	5	5	2	45	17	15.00	0	0	204	234	1	234.00	1-44	0	0	6.88	0	
OTIENO, E.																		
Int	2	2	1	8	8*	8.00	0	0	48	69	0					8.62	0	
Lim	2	2	1	8	8*	8.00	0	0	48	69	0					8.62	0	
OUMA, M.A.																		
FC	1	2	0	92	54	46.00	0	1									0	
Int	5	5	0	127	58	25.40	0	1									0	
Lim	5	5	0	127	58	25.40	0	1									0	
PATEL, R.R.																		
FC	1	2	0	22	14	11.00	0	0									0	
Int	5	5	0	116	47	23.20	0	0	60	47	0					4.70	4	
Lim	5	5	0	116	47	23.20	0	0	60	47	0					4.70	4	
TIKOLO, S.O.																		
FC	8	13	0	376	61	28.92	0	3	828	430	12	35.83	3-23	0	0	3.11	12	
Int	4	4	0	74	49	18.50	0	0	216	167	2	83.50	2-38	0	0	4.63	2	
Lim	11	10	0	396	91	39.60	0	3	432	349	6	58.16	2-38	0	0	4.84	4	
20T	4	4	0	123	65	30.75	0	1	72	104	1	104.00	1-33	0	0	8.66	2	
VARAIYA, H.A.																		
FC	1	2	1	11	7	11.00	0	0	234	102	3	34.00	2-64	0	0	2.61	0	
Int	4	2	2	23	21*		0	0	210	167	5	33.40	3-38	0	0	4.77	0	
Lim	4	2	2	23	21*		0	0	210	167	5	33.40	3-38	0	0	4.77	0	

NAMIBIA TO ZIMBABWE 2009/10

Cmp Debut	M	I	NO	Runs	HS	Avge	100	50	Balls	Runs	Wkts	Avge	BB	5i	10m	RpO	ct	st
GROENEWALD, W.J.																		
20T	5	1	1	2	2*		0	0	36	50	0					8.33	1	
KLAZINGA, L.																		
20T	6	3	2	25	22*	25.00	0	0	121	116	7	16.57	3-41	0	0	5.75	3	
LOUW, T.																		
20T	1	1	0	19	19	19.00	0	0									2	
MANYANDE, R.N.																		
20T	6	5	0	79	51	15.80	0	1									2	
PALLADINO, A.P.																		
20T	6	3	2	19	8*	19.00	0	0	107	116	12	9.66	4-21	1	0	6.50	1	
PRETORIUS, D.																		
20T	6	6	1	193	48*	38.60	0	0	54	67	3	22.33	1-13	0	0	7.44	4	
RUDOLPH, G.J.																		
20T	6	6	0	45	19	7.50	0	0									1	
SCHOLTZ, B.M.																		
20T	6	1	0	7	7	7.00	0	0	30	47	2	23.50	2-15	0	0	9.40	0	
VAN SCHOOR, R.																		
20T	6	6	0	139	46	23.16	0	0	24	24	2	12.00	2-24	0	0	6.00	4	
VERWEY, T.																		
20T	6	6	2	91	22*	22.75	0	0	18	28	0					9.33	3	
VILJOEN, C.																		
20T	6	3	1	61	41	30.50	0	0	120	101	6	16.83	2-14	0	0	5.05	0	
WILLIAMS, C.G.																		
20T	6	6	0	132	50	22.00	0	1	93	96	6	16.00	3-28	0	0	6.19	2	

SRI LANKA TO ZIMBABWE 2010

Cmp Debut	M	I	NO	Runs	HS	Avge	100	50	Balls	Runs	Wkts	Avge	BB	5i	10m	RpO	ct	st
CHANDIMAL, L.D.																		
Int	4	4	2	143	111	71.50	1	0									4	1
Lim	4	4	2	143	111	71.50	1	0									4	1
DILSHAN, T.M.																		
Int	5	5	2	328	108*	109.33	1	3	72	54	2	27.00	1-5	0	0	4.50	3	
Lim	5	5	2	328	108*	109.33	1	3	72	54	2	27.00	1-5	0	0	4.50	3	
FERNANDO, C.R.D.																		
Int	4	2	1	0	0*	0.00	0	0	188	157	5	31.40	3-36	0	0	5.01	1	
Lim	4	2	1	0	0*	0.00	0	0	188	157	5	31.40	3-36	0	0	5.01	1	
KALUHALAMULLA, H.K.S.R.																		
Int	5	2	1	10	9*	10.00	0	0	246	186	6	31.00	3-23	0	0	4.53	0	
Lim	5	2	1	10	9*	10.00	0	0	246	186	6	31.00	3-23	0	0	4.53	0	

Cmp Debut	M	I	NO	Runs	HS	Avge	100	50	Balls	Runs	Wkts	Avge	BB	5i	10m	RpO	ct	st
KAPUGEDERA, C.K.																		
Int	5	3	0	74	42	24.66	0	0	12	8	0					4.00	3	
Lim	5	3	0	74	42	24.66	0	0	12	8	0					4.00	3	
KULASEKARA, K.M.D.N.																		
Int	4	1	0	19	19	19.00	0	0	174	110	3	36.66	1-17	0	0	3.79	1	
Lim	4	1	0	19	19	19.00	0	0	174	110	3	36.66	1-17	0	0	3.79	1	
MATHEWS, A.D.																		
Int	2	1	0	75	75	75.00	0	1	24	14	0					3.50	0	
Lim	2	1	0	75	75	75.00	0	1	24	14	0					3.50	0	
MENDIS, B.A.W.																		
Int	4	1	0	2	2	2.00	0	0	216	183	5	36.60	2-21	0	0	5.08	0	
Lim	4	1	0	2	2	2.00	0	0	216	183	5	36.60	2-21	0	0	5.08	0	
MENDIS, B.M.A.J.																		
Int	4	2	1	42	35*	42.00	0	0	162	119	4	29.75	2-12	0	0	4.40	2	
Lim	4	2	1	42	35*	42.00	0	0	162	119	4	29.75	2-12	0	0	4.40	2	
MIRANDO, M.T.T.																		
Int	2	1	0	7	7	7.00	0	0	113	107	4	26.75	3-57	0	0	5.68	1	
Lim	2	1	0	7	7	7.00	0	0	113	107	4	26.75	3-57	0	0	5.68	1	
PERERA, N.L.T.C.																		
Int	4	2	0	40	32	20.00	0	0	84	108	1	108.00	1-33	0	0	7.71	3	
Lim	4	2	0	40	32	20.00	0	0	84	108	1	108.00	1-33	0	0	7.71	3	
SAMARAWEERA, T.T.																		
Int	4	3	1	63	28*	31.50	0	0									1	
Lim	4	3	1	63	28*	31.50	0	0									1	
SILVA, L.P.C.																		
Int	2	1	0	5	5	5.00	0	0									0	
Lim	2	1	0	5	5	5.00	0	0									0	
THARANGA, W.U.																		
Int	5	5	0	209	72	41.80	0	2									1	
Lim	5	5	0	209	72	41.80	0	2									1	
THIRIMANNE, H.D.R.L.																		
Int	1	1	0	15	15	15.00	0	0									0	
Lim	1	1	0	15	15	15.00	0	0									0	

INTERNATIONAL WOMEN PLAYERS

The lines of statistics after the players' biographical details in this section are:

WT Appearances in Women's Test Cricket in 2009/10 and 2010

WInt Appearances in Women's One-Day Internationals in 2009/10 and 2010

W20T Appearances in Women's Twenty20 Internationals in 2009/10 and 2010

2009/10 and 2010 AND CAREER RECORDS FOR AUSTRALIA WOMEN PLAYERS

Cmp	*Debut*	*M*	*I*	*NO*	*Runs*	*HS*	*Avge*	*100*	*50*	*Balls*	*Runs*	*Wkts*	*Avge*	*BB*	*5i*	*10m*	*RpO*	*ct*	*st*
ANDREWS, Sarah Joy b Moruya, New South Wales 26.12.1981 RHB RFM																			
WInt		7	1	0	0	0	0.00	0	0	306	193	10	19.30	2-18	0	0	3.78	1	
W20T		4	1	1	1	1*		0	0	90	97	1	97.00	1-27	0	0	6.46	1	
WT	2005/06	3	5	2	33	11	11.00	0	0	447	135	4	33.75	2-29	0	0	1.81	3	
WInt	2005/06	39	15	5	102	21*	10.20	0	0	1666	1142	54	21.14	4-50	1	0	4.11	10	
W20T	2006/07	16	3	3	12	10*		0	0	327	368	10	36.80	3-16	0	0	6.75	3	
BLACKWELL, Alexandra Joy b Wagga Wagga, New South Wales 31.8.1983 RHB RM																			
WInt		8	7	0	235	92	33.57	0	2									4	
W20T		10	10	0	199	61	19.90	0	1									5	
WT	2002/03	7	13	1	225	68	18.75	0	2	72	10	0					0.83	3	
WInt	2002/03	76	68	14	1724	106*	31.92	2	11	132	63	6	10.50	2-8	0	0	2.86	26	
W20T	2005	23	19	2	341	61	20.05	0	1	6	14	0					14.00	12	
CAMERON, Jessica Evelyn b Williamstown, Victoria 27.6.1989 RHB LB																			
WInt		4	2	0	101	68	50.50	0	1									6	
W20T		8	8	1	101	27	14.42	0	0									4	
WInt	2008/09	16	13	3	238	68	23.80	0	1									16	
W20T	2008/09	13	10	1	117	27	13.00	0	0									6	
EBSARY, Lauren Kaye b Snowtown, South Australia 15.3.1983 RHB RM																			
WInt		4	3	1	31	19	15.50	0	0									1	
W20T		4	4	0	39	16	9.75	0	0									1	
WT	2009	1	2	0	24	21	12.00	0	0	96	43	2	21.50	2-35	0	0	2.68	0	
WInt	2008/09	19	17	3	402	86	28.71	0	2	126	85	3	28.33	1-13	0	0	4.04	6	
W20T	2008/09	13	11	3	111	24*	13.87	0	0									4	
EDWARDS, Sarah Jane b Melbourne, Victoria 4.1.1982 RHB LBG																			
WInt		8	7	1	221	62	36.83	0	3	66	43	2	21.50	2-14	0	0	3.90	3	
W20T		7	6	1	47	19*	9.40	0	0	24	34	1	34.00	1-2	0	0	8.50	2	
WInt	2005	22	16	3	416	96	32.00	0	4	78	56	2	28.00	2-14	0	0	4.30	8	
W20T	2005	11	8	1	52	19*	7.42	0	0	24	34	1	34.00	1-2	0	0	8.50	3	
FARRELL, Rene Michelle b Kogarah, Sydney, New South Wales 13.1.1987 RHB RM																			
WInt		5	2	0	0	0	0.00	0	0	199	108	5	21.60	1-16	0	0	3.25	3	
W20T		9	6	1	24	13	4.80	0	0	198	205	8	25.62	2-25	0	0	6.21	3	
WT	2009	1	2	0	12	8	6.00	0	0	222	36	3	12.00	3-32	0	0	0.97	0	
WInt	2007	20	12	6	122	39*	20.33	0	0	772	482	21	22.95	3-26	0	0	3.74	6	
W20T	2009	17	10	5	81	31*	16.20	0	0	366	386	16	24.12	3-13	0	0	6.32	3	
HAYNES, Rachael Louise b Carlton, Melbourne, Victoria 26.12.1986 LHB LM																			
WInt		8	7	2	204	75*	40.80	0	2									0	
W20T		5	5	1	53	16	13.25	0	0	12	19	3	6.33	3-19	0	0	9.50	4	
WT	2009	1	2	0	114	98	57.00	0	1	54	13	1	13.00	1-0	0	0	1.44	0	
WInt	2009	9	8	2	230	75*	38.33	0	2									0	
HEALY, Alyssa Jean b Gold Coast, Queensland 24.3.1990 RHB WK																			
WInt		5	4	0	25	21	6.25	0	0									5	1
W20T		10	9	2	62	15	8.85	0	0									4	1
HUNTER, Julie Lauren b Box Hill, Melbourne, Victoria 5.3.1984 RHB RM																			
WInt		4	1	1	6	6*		0	0	186	133	7	19.00	3-40	0	0	4.29	2	
W20T		2	2	0	6	6	3.00	0	0	48	52	2	26.00	1-23	0	0	6.50	0	
NITSCHKE, Shelley b Adelaide, South Australia 3.12.1976 LHB SLA																			
WInt		8	8	2	342	113*	57.00	1	1	318	159	12	13.25	4-24	1	0	3.00	3	
W20T		10	10	0	265	56	26.50	0	1	210	209	10	20.90	2-14	0	0	5.97	3	
WT	2005	5	9	2	273	88*	39.00	0	2	952	284	11	25.81	3-59	0	0	1.79	0	
WInt	2004/05	71	60	9	1718	113*	33.68	1	11	3106	1838	83	22.14	7-24	2	1	3.55	28	
W20T	2005	23	22	1	582	56	27.71	0	3	474	452	25	18.08	4-21	1	0	5.72	5	
OSBORNE, Erin Alyce b Taree, New South Wales 27.6.1989 RHB OB																			
WInt		6	2	2	15	13*		0	0	234	161	5	32.20	2-29	0	0	4.12	1	
W20T		2	1	0	1	1	1.00	0	0	24	33	1	33.00	1-13	0	0	8.25	1	
WInt	2008/09	18	8	6	44	13*	22.00	0	0	870	508	19	26.73	3-32	0	0	3.50	5	
W20T	2008/09	5	1	0	1	1	1.00	0	0	90	91	4	22.75	2-24	0	0	6.06	2	

Cmp	Debut	M	I	NO	Runs	HS	Avge	100	50	Balls	Runs	Wkts	Avge	BB	5i	10m	RpO	ct	st
PERRY, Ellyse Alexandra b Wahroonga, New South Wales 3.11.1990 RHB RFM																			
WInt		8	5	2	90	30	30.00	0	0	391	282	18	15.66	5-31	0	1	4.32	5	
W20T		10	4	0	27	15	6.75	0	0	219	175	15	11.66	3-14	0	0	4.79	3	
WT	2007/08	2	4	1	51	21	17.00	0	0	336	129	5	25.80	2-49	0	0	2.30	2	
WInt	2007	39	28	8	401	51	20.05	0	1	1703	1234	54	22.85	5-31	0	1	4.34	12	
W20T	2007/08	19	7	2	63	29*	12.60	0	0	387	354	24	14.75	4-20	1	0	5.48	4	
POULTON, Leah Joy b Newcastle, New South Wales 27.2.1984 RHB LBG																			
WInt		6	6	1	196	104*	39.20	1	0									3	
W20T		9	9	1	153	39	19.12	0	0									1	
WT	2009	1	2	0	24	23	12.00	0	0	24	15	0					3.75	1	
WInt	2006/07	32	30	1	716	104*	24.68	2	2	150	109	3	36.33	2-9	0	0	4.36	7	
W20T	2006/07	20	20	1	335	39	17.63	0	0	18	20	2	10.00	2-20	0	0	6.66	4	
SMITH, Clea Rosemary b Melbourne, Victoria 6.1.1979 RHB RM																			
W20T		5	2	2	2	1*		0	0	108	109	4	27.25	1-19	0	0	6.05	0	
WT	2005	1	2	0	46	42	23.00	0	0	72	25	1	25.00	1-25	0	0	2.08	0	
WInt	1999/00	42	10	5	56	11*	11.20	0	0	1869	939	36	26.08	3-17	0	0	3.01	8	
W20T	2007	6	3	2	3	1*	3.00	0	0	132	119	5	23.80	1-10	0	0	5.40	0	
STHALEKAR, Lisa Caprini b Poona (now Pune), Maharashtra, India 13.8.1979 RHB OB																			
WInt		7	6	2	51	21*	12.75	0	0	348	231	12	19.25	5-35	0	1	3.98	3	
W20T		10	9	2	74	23*	10.57	0	0	233	219	11	19.90	3-29	0	0	5.63	3	
WT	2002/03	7	13	1	406	120*	33.83	1	2	1469	425	21	20.23	5-30	1	0	1.73	3	
WInt	2001	100	92	20	2397	104*	33.29	2	15	4566	2822	112	25.19	5-35	1	1	3.70	33	
W20T	2005	24	23	5	306	46	17.00	0	0	535	502	29	17.31	3-11	0	0	5.63	7	
VILLANI, Elyse Jayne b Melbourne, Victoria 6.10.1989 RHB RFM																			
W20T		5	5	0	28	13	5.60	0	0									0	
W20T	2009	6	6	0	39	13	6.50	0	0									0	

2009/10 and 2010 AND CAREER RECORDS FOR ENGLAND WOMEN PLAYERS

Cmp	Debut	M	I	NO	Runs	HS	Avge	100	50	Balls	Runs	Wkts	Avge	BB	5i	10m	RpO	ct	st
ATKINS, Caroline Mary Ghislaine b Brighton, Sussex 13.1.1981 RHB RM																			
WInt		7	7	1	135	44*	22.50	0	0									1	
W20T		5	4	1	13	13*	4.33	0	0									0	
WT	2001	8	15	0	348	90	23.20	0	3	72	39	1	39.00	1-9	0	0	3.25	4	
WInt	2001	58	49	6	1291	145	30.02	1	6	6	4	0					4.00	14	
W20T	2006	17	11	3	54	20*	6.75	0	0									2	
BEAUMONT, Tamsin Tilley b Dover, Kent 11.3.1991 RHB WK																			
WInt		7	5	3	35	19*	17.50	0	0									4	3
W20T		6	3	1	13	7	6.50	0	0									2	4
BRUNT, Katherine Helen b Barnsley, Yorkshire 2.7.1985 RHB RMF																			
WInt		14	11	4	77	21*	11.00	0	0	810	485	23	21.08	5-22	0	1	3.59	9	
W20T		12	10	4	45	15*	7.50	0	0	282	252	12	21.00	2-21	0	0	5.36	0	
WT	2004	6	6	3	93	52	31.00	0	1	1205	521	27	19.29	6-69	2	0	2.59	2	
WInt	2004/05	52	20	7	124	21*	9.53	0	0	2493	1369	59	23.20	5-22	0	2	3.29	11	
W20T	2005	20	13	7	51	15*	8.50	0	0	462	370	23	16.08	3-6	0	0	4.80	3	
COLVIN, Holly Louise b Chichester, Sussex 7.9.1989 RHB SLA																			
WInt		9	6	3	44	19*	14.66	0	0	502	320	14	22.85	4-24	1	0	3.82	4	
W20T		7	4	2	30	17*	15.00	0	0	168	155	7	22.14	2-22	0	0	5.53	3	
WT	2005	4	5	3	23	17*	11.50	0	0	649	337	13	25.92	3-42	0	0	3.11	1	
WInt	2006	51	18	10	95	19*	11.87	0	0	2560	1465	71	20.63	4-20	2	0	3.43	14	
W20T	2007	19	6	2	38	17*	9.50	0	0	432	382	24	15.91	3-18	0	0	5.30	6	
EDWARDS, Charlotte Marie b Huntingdon 17.12.1979 RHB LB																			
WInt		13	12	1	374	72	34.00	0	4	245	173	7	24.71	2-17	0	0	4.23	1	
W20T		12	12	0	281	46	23.41	0	0	82	93	1	93.00	1-20	0	0	6.80	4	
WT	1996	18	33	3	1380	117	46.00	3	8	1112	570	12	47.50	2-28	0	0	3.07	9	
WInt	1997	140	130	17	4101	173*	36.29	4	33	1453	1020	46	22.17	4-37	1	0	4.21	31	
W20T	2004	28	27	3	796	76*	33.16	0	4	222	244	5	48.80	2-7	0	0	6.59	8	
GREENWAY, Lydia Sophie b Farnborough, Kent 6.8.1985 LHB OB																			
WInt		12	11	1	363	65	36.30	0	2									7	
W20T		9	9	4	157	34*	31.40	0	0									8	
WT	2002/03	9	15	1	269	70	19.21	0	2									11	
WInt	2003	79	68	19	1260	65	25.71	0	5									31	
W20T	2004	25	23	6	353	34*	20.76	0	0									15	
GUHA, Isa Tara b High Wycombe, Buckinghamshire 21.5.1985 RHB RF																			
WInt		9	7	6	15	7*	15.00	0	0	402	290	4	72.50	2-39	0	0	4.32	3	
W20T		3	2	1	14	13*	14.00	0	0	72	53	3	17.66	3-21	0	0	4.41	0	
WT	2002	7	8	3	83	31*	16.60	0	0	1309	483	25	19.32	5-40	1	0	2.21	3	
WInt	2001	77	30	17	117	26	9.00	0	0	3467	2132	95	22.44	5-14	2	2	3.69	24	
W20T	2004	13	4	1	23	13*	7.66	0	0	264	252	8	31.50	3-21	0	0	5.72	3	

Cmp	Debut	M	I	NO	Runs	HS	Avge	100	50	Balls	Runs	Wkts	Avge	BB	5i	10m	RpO	ct	st
GUNN, Jennifer Louise b Nottingham 9.5.1986 RHB RMF																			
WInt		13	12	1	248	64	22.54	0	2	481	283	18	15.72	5-31	0	1	3.53	2	
W20T		12	12	0	178	35	14.83	0	0	30	31	2	15.50	2-10	0	0	6.20	14	
WT	2004	7	12	0	209	41	17.41	0	0	1397	457	17	26.88	3-40	0	0	1.96	3	
WInt	2003/04	84	67	15	1144	73	22.00	0	4	3507	2166	78	27.76	5-31	2	1	3.70	20	
W20T	2004	28	25	1	331	38	13.79	0	0	293	332	18	18.44	4-9	1	0	6.79	20	
HAZELL, Danielle b Durham 13.5.1988 RHB OB																			
WInt		8	6	1	83	24*	16.60	0	0	379	255	5	51.00	2-38	0	0	4.03	1	
W20T		10	8	0	57	18	7.12	0	0	228	201	15	13.40	3-16	0	0	5.28	1	
KNIGHT, Heather Clare b Rochdale, Lancashire 26.12.1990 RHB RM																			
WInt		7	7	0	207	49	29.57	0	0									0	
MARSH, Laura Alexandra b Pembury, Kent 5.12.1986 RHB OB,RFM																			
WInt		14	11	1	186	67	18.60	0	1	777	483	9	53.66	3-34	0	0	3.73	0	
W20T		11	11	2	136	46*	15.11	0	0	228	220	10	22.00	3-17	0	0	5.78	1	
WT	2006	4	5	0	48	38	9.60	0	0	797	276	10	27.60	3-44	0	0	2.07	4	
WInt	2006	42	23	5	276	67	15.33	0	1	2165	1349	58	23.25	5-15	1	1	3.73	5	
W20T	2007	23	18	4	155	46*	11.07	0	0	493	422	24	17.58	3-17	0	0	5.13	2	
MORGAN, Beth Louisa b Harrow, Middlesex 27.9.1981 RHB RM																			
WInt		10	9	0	74	24	8.22	0	0	24	15	1	15.00	1-8	0	0	3.75	4	
W20T		9	9	0	104	28	11.55	0	0									5	
WT	2005	7	12	2	244	58	24.40	0	1	1025	374	6	62.33	1-17	0	0	2.18	1	
WInt	1999	70	48	6	588	77	14.00	0	1	1360	960	27	35.55	3-19	0	0	4.23	25	
W20T	2005	25	22	2	300	46*	15.00	0	0	82	104	5	20.80	2-8	0	0	7.61	8	
RAINFORD-BRENT, Ebony-Jewel Cora-Lee Rosamond Camellia b Lambeth, Surrey 31.12.1983 RHB RMF																			
WInt		8	8	0	222	72	27.75	0	2									0	
W20T		3	3	0	30	19	10.00	0	0									0	
WInt	2001	22	19	3	377	72	23.56	0	2	96	90	2	45.00	1-8	0	0	5.62	4	
W20T	2008	7	7	1	53	23*	8.83	0	0									0	
SHAW, Nicola Jayne b Nuneaton, Warwickshire 30.12.1981 RHB RFM																			
WInt		6	6	0	54	27	9.00	0	0	281	150	4	37.50	3-34	0	0	3.20	3	
W20T		8	5	3	24	8*	12.00	0	0	168	179	11	16.27	3-17	0	0	6.39	2	
WT	2001	5	7	0	48	27	6.85	0	0	795	357	11	32.45	3-67	0	0	2.69	1	
WInt	1999	70	43	6	353	35	9.54	0	0	2394	1353	46	29.41	4-34	1	0	3.39	15	
W20T	2004	22	15	8	83	12*	11.85	0	0	456	433	19	22.78	3-17	0	0	5.69	5	
SHRUBSOLE, Anya b Bath, Somerset 7.12.1991 RHB RM																			
WInt		3	1	0	0	0	0.00	0	0	114	61	1	61.00	1-12	0	0	3.21	0	
W20T		6	1	0	1	1	1.00	0	0	102	139	8	17.37	2-16	0	0	8.17	3	
WInt	2008	5	1	0	0	0	0.00	0	0	207	114	2	57.00	1-12	0	0	3.30	1	
W20T	2008	7	1	0	1	1	1.00	0	0	126	158	11	14.36	3-19	0	0	7.52	3	
TAYLOR, Samantha Claire b Amersham, Buckinghamshire 25.9.1975 RHB																			
WInt		6	6	1	193	66	38.60	0	2									0	
W20T		6	6	0	72	34	12.00	0	0									1	
WT	1999	15	27	2	1030	177	41.20	4	2									18	
WInt	1998	120	114	17	3883	156*	40.03	8	21									39	5
W20T	2004	20	19	4	514	76*	34.26	0	2									7	
TAYLOR, Sarah Jane b Whitechapel, Middlesex 20.5.1989 RHB WK																			
WInt		7	7	1	168	64	28.00	0	1									4	3
W20T		6	6	0	170	73	28.33	0	1									1	5
WT	2006	4	7	0	124	28	17.71	0	0									7	1
WInt	2006	56	50	5	1693	129	37.62	3	8									35	23
W20T	2006	20	20	2	470	73	26.11	0	3									6	11
WYATT, Danielle Nicole b Stoke-on-Trent, Staffordshire 22.4.1991 RHB OB																			
WInt		1	1	1	28	28*		0	0	24	24	0					6.00	0	
W20T		7	6	2	27	16	6.75	0	0	47	44	7	6.28	4-11	1	0	5.61	1	

2009/10 and 2010 AND CAREER RECORDS FOR INDIA WOMEN PLAYERS

Cmp	Debut	M	I	NO	Runs	HS	Avge	100	50	Balls	Runs	Wkts	Avge	BB	5i	10m	RpO	ct	st
AL KHADER, Nooshin b Tehran, Iran 13.2.1981 RHB OB																			
WInt		2	1	0	1	1	1.00	0	0	60	56	0					5.60	0	
WT	2003/04	5	7	2	46	16*	9.20	0	0	1239	373	14	26.64	3-30	0	0	1.80	0	
WInt	2001/02	77	26	8	137	21	7.61	0	0	3978	2360	99	23.83	5-14	4	1	3.56	17	
W20T	2006	2								42	41	1	41.00	1-28	0	0	5.85	0	
CHOPRA, Anjum b Delhi 20.5.1977 LHB RM																			
WInt		5	5	1	71	61*	17.75	0	1									0	
W20T		3	3	0	42	22	14.00	0	0									1	
WT	1995/96	12	20	2	548	98	30.44	0	4	258	88	2	44.00	1-9	0	0	2.04	13	
WInt	1994/95	121	106	21	2777	100	32.67	1	18	601	414	9	46.00	2-9	0	0	4.13	31	
W20T	2006	8	7	1	122	37*	20.33	0	0									3	

Cmp	Debut	M	I	NO	Runs	HS	Avge	100	50	Balls	Runs	Wkts	Avge	BB	5i	10m	RpO	ct	st
DABIR, Soniya b Pune, Maharashtra 17.7.1980 RHB RM																			
WInt		2	1	1	31	31*		0	0	48	37	2	18.50	2-37	0	0	4.62	0	
W20T		3	2	1	12	12	12.00	0	0	54	70	3	23.33	3-23	0	0	7.77	1	
DAVID, Diana b Prakasham, Andhra Pradesh 2.3.1985 RHB OB																			
WInt		1	1	0	9	9	9.00	0	0	48	31	0					3.87	0	
W20T		6	2	1	1	1*	1.00	0	0	144	106	12	8.83	4-12	2	0	4.41	1	
WInt	2003/04	6	3	0	12	9	4.00	0	0	296	151	8	18.87	2-15	0	0	3.06	1	
DESHPANDE, Anagha Arun b Solapur, Maharashtra 19.11.1985 RHB RAB WK																			
WInt		3	3	0	15	14	5.00	0	0									1	5
WInt	2008	12	12	1	257	45	23.36	0	0									5	9
DHAR, Rumeli b Calcutta (now Kolkata), Bengal 9.12.1983 RHB RM																			
WInt		5	5	1	28	13	7.00	0	0	282	137	9	15.22	4-19	1	0	2.91	5	
W20T		7	3	3	36	18*		0	0	114	102	4	25.50	1-8	0	0	5.36	5	
WT	2005/06	4	8	0	236	57	29.50	0	1	552	174	8	21.75	2-16	0	0	1.89	0	
WInt	2002/03	71	53	10	894	92*	20.79	0	6	2709	1510	55	27.45	4-19	1	0	3.34	33	
W20T	2006	13	9	4	112	66*	22.40	0	1	222	198	10	19.80	3-13	0	0	5.35	5	
DIMRI, Preeti b Agra, Uttar Pradesh 18.10.1986 LHB SLC																			
WInt		4	1	0	0	0	0.00	0	0	210	96	7	13.71	3-18	0	0	2.74	1	
WT	2006	2	3	2	19	19	19.00	0	0	468	182	5	36.40	3-75	0	0	2.33	0	
WInt	2006	23	5	3	23	12*	11.50	0	0	1217	650	28	23.21	3-14	0	0	3.20	4	
W20T	2006	1								24	19	1	19.00	1-19	0	0	4.75	0	
GOSWAMI, Jhulan b Kalyani, Calcutta (now Kolkata), Bengal 25.11.1982 RHB RM																			
WInt		5	2	0	19	19	9.50	0	0	276	129	11	11.72	3-16	0	0	2.80	2	
W20T		5	3	0	16	10	5.33	0	0	84	81	1	81.00	1-19	0	0	5.78	4	
WT	2001/02	8	11	2	263	69	29.22	0	2	1618	540	33	16.36	5-25	3	1	2.00	5	
WInt	2001/02	105	56	19	439	46	11.86	0	0	5011	2600	120	21.66	5-16	3	1	3.11	40	
W20T	2006	11	6	3	59	27*	19.66	0	0	216	202	3	67.33	2-14	0	0	5.61	6	
KAUR, Harmanpreet Singh b Moga, Punjab 8.3.1989 RHB RM																			
WInt		2	1	0	84	84	84.00	0	1	12	14	0					7.00	0	
W20T		7	5	1	102	33	25.50	0	0									3	
WInt	2008/09	8	4	1	124	84	41.33	0	1	60	46	0					4.60	2	
W20T	2009	11	7	1	110	33	18.33	0	0	18	17	0					5.66	5	
MALHOTRA, Reema b Delhi 17.10.1980 RHB LB																			
W20T		4	1	0	7	7	7.00	0	0	60	56	3	18.66	2-25	0	0	5.60	2	
WT	2006	1	2	1	23	12*	23.00	0	0	18	17	0					5.66	0	
WInt	2002/03	30	22	9	269	59*	20.69	0	1	569	421	16	26.31	3-31	0	0	4.43	1	
W20T	2006	10	5	2	30	12	10.00	0	0	84	87	4	21.75	2-25	0	0	6.21	2	
MANDLIK, Babita b Indore, Madhya Pradesh 16.7.1981 RHB RM																			
W20T		2	1	0	3	3	3.00	0	0									0	
WInt	2002/03	3	3	1	6	5*	3.00	0	0									0	
NAIK, Sulakshana b Bombay (now Mumbai), Maharashtra 10.11.1978 RHB WK																			
WInt		2	2	0	14	13	7.00	0	0									1	3
W20T		7	7	0	163	59	23.28	0	1									3	12
WT	2002	2	3	0	62	25	20.66	0	0									1	2
WInt	2002	33	29	3	481	79*	18.50	0	2									17	21
W20T	2006	13	13	0	232	59	17.84	0	1									5	14
RAJ, Mithali b Jodhpur, Rajasthan 3.12.1982 RHB LB																			
WInt		5	4	2	287	91*	143.50	0	4									0	
W20T		7	7	2	205	52*	41.00	0	1									0	
WT	2001/02	8	13	2	572	214	52.00	1	3	72	32	0					2.66	7	
WInt	1999	120	107	30	3836	114*	49.81	2	32	171	91	8	11.37	3-4	0	0	3.19	25	
W20T	2006	13	13	4	375	52*	41.66	0	2	6	6	0					6.00	0	
RAUT, Punam Ganesh b Bombay (now Mumbai), Maharashtra 14.10.1989 LHB SLA																			
WInt		3	3	0	59	44	19.66	0	0									1	
W20T		6	5	1	136	54*	34.00	0	1	24	12	3	4.00	3-12	0	0	3.00	0	
WInt	2008/09	4	4	0	59	44	14.75	0	0	30	4	1	4.00	1-4	0	0	0.80	2	
W20T	2009	9	8	1	171	54*	24.42	0	1	42	29	3	9.66	3-12	0	0	4.14	2	
ROY, Priyanka b Calcutta (now Kolkata), Bengal 2.3.1988 RHB LB																			
WInt		4	4	1	75	69*	25.00	0	1	78	55	0					4.23	2	
W20T		6	2	0	23	21	11.50	0	0	120	119	6	19.83	3-19	0	0	5.95	0	
WInt	2008	21	17	1	257	69*	16.06	0	1	410	277	12	23.08	4-14	1	0	4.05	6	
W20T	2009	10	5	0	43	21	8.60	0	0	167	166	12	13.83	5-16	0	1	5.96	3	
SHARMA, Amita b Delhi 12.9.1982 RHB RMF																			
WInt		5	4	2	67	40	33.50	0	0	180	113	1	113.00	1-26	0	0	3.76	1	
W20T		7	6	5	73	28*	73.00	0	0	62	63	1	63.00	1-11	0	0	6.09	0	
WT	2003/04	5	7	1	82	50	13.66	0	1	748	252	5	50.40	2-19	0	0	2.02	0	
WInt	2002	92	53	14	608	45*	15.58	0	0	3740	2301	75	30.68	4-16	1	0	3.69	29	
W20T	2006	13	9	6	103	28*	34.33	0	0	176	167	5	33.40	2-21	0	0	5.69	1	
SULTANA, Gouhar b Hyderabad, Andhra Pradesh 31.3.1988 RHB SLA																			
WInt		5	2	1	3	2*	3.00	0	0	271	139	12	11.58	4-30	1	0	3.07	1	
W20T		7								163	168	9	18.66	3-26	0	0	6.18	2	

Cmp Debut	M	I	NO	Runs	HS	Avge	100	50	Balls	Runs	Wkts	Avge	BB	5i	10m	RpO	ct	st
WInt 2008	23	8	5	25	10*	8.33	0	0	977	493	30	16.43	4-30	1	0	3.02	8	
W20T 2008/09	12	1	1	2	2*		0	0	275	282	14	20.14	3-26	0	0	6.15	3	
THIRUSH KAMINI, Murugesan Dickeshvashankar b Madras (now Chennai), Tamil Nadu 30.7.1990 LHB LBG																		
WInt	2	2	1	30	28	30.00	0	0									0	
WInt 2006/07	21	19	3	282	60*	17.62	0	1	378	268	9	29.77	3-19	0	0	4.25	4	
W20T 2008/09	1	1	0	11	11	11.00	0	0									0	

2009/10 and 2010 AND CAREER RECORDS FOR IRELAND WOMEN PLAYERS

Cmp Debut	M	I	NO	Runs	HS	Avge	100	50	Balls	Runs	Wkts	Avge	BB	5i	10m	RpO	ct	st
BEAMISH, Emma Anne b Merrion, Leinster 29.11.1982 RHB RM																		
WInt	1	1	0	18	18	18.00	0	0									0	
WInt 2003	18	16	0	131	40	8.18	0	0									4	
W20T 2008	6	5	1	33	14	8.25	0	0									0	
DELANY, Laura b 23.12.1992 RHB RM																		
WInt	3	3	0	44	43	14.66	0	0	126	116	2	58.00	1-29	0	0	5.52	1	
GARTH, Kimberley Jennifer b Dublin 25.4.1996 RHB RAB																		
WInt	3	3	0	14	7	4.66	0	0									1	
JOYCE, Cecelia Nora Isobel Mary b Wicklow 25.7.1983 RHB LB																		
WInt	2	2	0	43	27	21.50	0	0									2	
WInt 2001	30	27	2	561	77	22.44	0	2	112	104	1	104.00	1-12	0	0	5.57	4	
W20T 2008	6	5	2	80	41	26.66	0	0	18	31	1	31.00	1-31	0	0	10.33	0	
JOYCE, Isobel Mary Helen Cecilia b Wicklow 25.7.1983 RHB LM																		
WInt	3	3	1	45	36*	22.50	0	0	144	130	5	26.00	2-45	0	0	5.41	1	
WT 2000	1								67	21	6	3.50	6-21	1	0	1.88	1	
WInt 1999	48	35	4	409	67*	13.19	0	1	1952	1243	46	27.02	4-20	2	0	3.82	11	
W20T 2008	6	6	1	126	56*	25.20	0	1	137	135	3	45.00	2-27	0	0	5.91	2	
KENEALY, Suzanne Elizabeth b Dublin 27.11.1981 RHB RM																		
WInt	1	1	1	1	1*		0	0	30	33	0					6.60	0	
WInt 2008	3	3	1	5	4	2.50	0	0	72	70	0					5.83	0	
W20T 2009	2	1	0	2	2	2.00	0	0	18	29	0					9.66	0	
McCARTHY, Louise Noreen b Dublin 18.10.1993 RHB RM																		
WInt	2	2	1	12	7*	12.00	0	0	66	45	3	15.00	2-6	0	0	4.09	0	
METCALFE, Ciara Johanna b Dublin 29.9.1979 LHB SLA																		
WInt	3	2	0	1	1	0.50	0	0	174	121	5	24.20	3-54	0	0	4.17	1	
WT 2000	1								120	42	4	10.50	4-26	0	0	2.10	0	
WInt 1999	35	28	5	75	12*	3.26	0	0	1512	986	41	24.04	5-18	2	1	3.91	9	
W20T 2009	1								24	16	0					4.00	0	
RICHARDSON, Eimear Ann Jermyn b Dublin 14.9.1986 RHB OB																		
WInt	1	1	0	21	21	21.00	0	0	30	10	0					2.00	0	
WInt 2005	14	14	2	189	50*	15.75	0	1	394	221	10	22.10	5-13	0	1	3.36	3	
W20T 2008	6	4	0	51	23	12.75	0	0	102	93	5	18.60	2-20	0	0	5.47	1	
SCOTT-HAYWARD, Melissa Erica Maria O'Carroll b Dublin 10.8.1990 RHB RM																		
WInt	3	3	0	52	23	17.33	0	0									2	
WInt 2008	8	7	0	79	23	11.28	0	0	66	53	1	53.00	1-27	0	0	4.81	6	
W20T 2008	5	3	1	7	6	3.50	0	0	37	47	1	47.00	1-30	0	0	7.62	0	
SHILLINGTON, Clare Mary Alice b Belfast 8.1.1981 RHB OB																		
WInt	2	2	1	28	23	28.00	0	0									2	
WT 2000	1																1	
WInt 1997	57	48	6	653	95*	15.54	0	3	746	412	20	20.60	3-34	0	0	3.31	20	
W20T 2008	6	6	1	154	58*	30.80	0	1									0	
WALDRON, Mary Veronica b Dublin 5.5.1984 RHB WK																		
WInt	3	2	1	0	0*	0.00	0	0									1	
WHELAN, Heather Elizabeth b Dublin 8.10.1977 RHB RMF																		
WInt	3	3	0	14	13	4.66	0	0	168	110	2	55.00	1-12	0	0	3.92	0	
WInt 1997/98	39	27	9	102	13	5.66	0	0	1847	1197	31	38.61	3-14	0	0	3.88	5	
W20T 2009	4	1	0	1	1	1.00	0	0	78	40	6	6.66	3-11	0	0	3.07	0	
WHELAN, Jill Amy b Dublin 28.12.1986 RHB RM																		
WInt	3	3	0	40	36	13.33	0	0	162	124	5	24.80	2-29	0	0	4.59	1	
WInt 2004	22	18	4	211	39*	15.07	0	0	932	588	22	26.72	3-7	0	0	3.78	7	
W20T 2008	5	3	1	11	7	5.50	0	0	108	98	3	32.66	2-26	0	0	5.44	1	

2009/10 and 2010 AND CAREER RECORDS FOR NETHERLANDS WOMEN PLAYERS

Cmp Debut	M	I	NO	Runs	HS	Avge	100	50	Balls	Runs	Wkts	Avge	BB	5i	10m	RpO	ct	st
BRAAT, Danielle Marloes b Vlaardingen 6.4.1990 RHB RM																		
WInt	1	1	1	9	9*		0	0	60	30	2	15.00	2-30	0	0	3.00	0	
WT 2007	1	2	1	6	4	6.00	0	0	15	11	2	5.50	2-11	0	0	4.40	0	
WInt 2006	13	13	4	56	14*	6.22	0	0	577	381	11	34.63	3-39	0	0	3.96	0	
W20T 2008	3	2	1	12	10*	12.00	0	0	51	54	3	18.00	2-21	0	0	6.35	0	

Cmp	Debut	M	I	NO	Runs	HS	Avge	100	50	Balls	Runs	Wkts	Avge	BB	5i	10m	RpO	ct	st
DE GROOT, Carlijn Marjolijn b Schiedam 10.9.1986 RHB RM																			
WInt		1	1	0	6	6	6.00	0	0									0	
WInt	2007	6	6	0	53	21	8.83	0	0									1	
W20T	2008	1	1	0	0	0	0.00	0	0									0	
DE LANGE, Esther Laura Talitha b Amsterdam 18.2.1984 RHB OB																			
WInt		1	1	0	0	0	0.00	0	0	42	21	1	21.00	1-21	0	0	3.00	0	
WInt	2005	2	2	1	7	7*	7.00	0	0	66	41	1	41.00	1-21	0	0	3.72	0	
HANNEMA, Denise b Amsterdam 9.12.1990 RHB RM																			
WInt		1	1	0	12	12	12.00	0	0									0	
WInt	2008	5	4	1	13	12	4.33	0	0	86	60	1	60.00	1-7	0	0	4.18	1	
W20T	2008	2	1	1	1	1*		0	0	24	28	0					7.00	0	
KORNET, Mariska b Rotterdam 4.3.1988 RHB RMF																			
WInt		1	1	1	1	1*		0	0	49	25	1	25.00	1-25	0	0	3.06	0	
LANSER, Esther b Masterton, New Zealand 6.1.1984 RHB OB																			
WInt		1	1	0	16	16	16.00	0	0	60	23	1	23.00	1-23	0	0	2.30	1	
NIJMAN, Marijn Elise b Gronigen 27.8.1985 RHB RM																			
WInt		1	1	0	11	11	11.00	0	0									0	
WT	2007	1	2	0	5	5	2.50	0	0	90	36	0					2.40	0	
WInt	2005	9	9	2	133	35	19.00	0	0	348	284	5	56.80	1-24	0	0	4.89	3	
W20T	2009	1	1	1	29	29*		0	0									0	
RAMBALDO, Helmien Willie b The Hague 13.11.1980 RHB OB																			
WInt		1	1	0	22	22	22.00	0	0									1	
WT	2007	1	2	0	18	17	9.00	0	0									1	
WInt	1998	33	33	0	434	46	13.15	0	0	320	265	4	66.25	2-13	0	0	4.96	10	
W20T	2008	2	2	1	45	28*	45.00	0	0									1	
SALOMONS, Carolien Aimee b Amsterdam 20.7.1974 RHB OB																			
WInt		1	1	0	4	4	4.00	0	0									0	
WInt	1995	50	47	4	882	89	20.51	0	5	1432	691	37	18.67	3-11	0	0	2.89	23	1
W20T	2008	2	2	0	43	27	21.50	0	0									2	
TANKE, Annemarie Suzanne b Velsen 27.2.1978 RHB LB																			
WInt		1	1	0	3	3	3.00	0	0	24	25	0					6.25	0	
WT	2007	1	2	0	0	0	0.00	0	0	60	39	1	39.00	1-39	0	0	3.90	0	
WInt	1997	34	33	2	381	61	12.29	0	1	587	498	15	33.20	5-40	0	1	5.09	4	
W20T	2008	3	3	0	20	20	6.66	0	0	42	62	1	62.00	1-18	0	0	8.85	1	
WATTENBERG, Violet Cornelia Elizabeth b Goa, India 5.12.1978 RHB WK																			
WInt		1	1	0	7	7	7.00	0	0									0	
WT	2007	1	2	0	52	49	26.00	0	0									1	2
WInt	2007	12	12	0	120	34	10.00	0	0									4	1
W20T	2008	3	3	0	34	16	11.33	0	0									1	

2009/10 AND 2010 AND CAREER RECORDS FOR NEW ZEALAND WOMEN PLAYERS

Cmp	Debut	M	I	NO	Runs	HS	Avge	100	50	Balls	Runs	Wkts	Avge	BB	5i	10m	RpO	ct	st
BATES, Suzannah Wilson b Dunedin, Otago 16.9.1987 RHB RM																			
WInt		8	8	1	185	75*	26.42	0	2	205	174	5	34.80	3-27	0	0	5.09	2	
W20T		13	13	0	264	68	20.30	0	2	132	120	9	13.33	3-24	0	0	5.45	3	
WInt	2005/06	34	32	2	956	168	31.86	2	4	953	753	29	25.96	4-7	1	0	4.74	9	
W20T	2007	26	26	1	608	68	24.32	0	4	301	319	13	24.53	3-24	0	0	6.35	7	
BERMINGHAM, Erin Margaret b Greymouth, Canterbury 18.4.1988 RHB LB																			
WInt		3	1	0	1	1	1.00	0	0	180	103	6	17.16	4-35	1	0	3.43	1	
W20T		5	3	1	9	8*	4.50	0	0	72	66	3	22.00	2-15	0	0	5.50	0	
BROADMORE, Kate Ellen b New Plymouth, Taranaki 11.11.1991 RHB RM																			
WInt		4	4	4	17	8*		0	0	204	104	2	52.00	1-21	0	0	3.05	0	
W20T		11	3	2	7	4*	7.00	0	0	168	171	4	42.75	1-10	0	0	6.10	3	
BROWNE, Nicola Jane b Matamata, Waikato 14.9.1983 RHB RM																			
WInt		13	12	1	167	37	15.18	0	0	568	367	9	40.77	3-31	0	0	3.87	3	
W20T		12	10	1	147	24	16.33	0	0	258	213	16	13.31	4-15	1	0	4.95	9	
WT	2003/04	2	2	0	24	23	12.00	0	0	210	83	1	83.00	1-43	0	0	2.37	2	
WInt	2001/02	102	83	24	1623	61	27.50	0	8	3744	2381	69	34.50	4-20	1	0	3.81	25	
W20T	2004	26	23	6	269	32	15.82	0	0	438	403	25	16.12	4-15	1	0	5.52	13	
BULLEN, Saskia Mary b Auckland 20.7.1983 RHB SLA																			
W20T		1								12	18	1	18.00	1-18	0	0	9.00	0	
W20T	2009	3								54	57	3	19.00	2-20	0	0	6.33	0	
BURROWS, Abby Kirstyn b Whakatane, Bay of Plenty 29.1.1977 LHB RM																			
WInt		4	3	3	1	1*		0	0	162	143	3	47.66	3-27	0	0	5.29	0	
WInt	2008/09	9	5	5	5	3*		0	0	337	267	7	38.14	3-27	0	0	4.75	2	
CAMPBELL, Emma Maree b Timaru, Canterbury 18.2.1982 RHB LB																			
WInt		2	2	1	14	8*	14.00	0	0	84	69	2	34.50	1-19	0	0	4.92	2	
DEVINE, Sophie Frances Monique b Wellington 1.9.1989 RHB RM																			
WInt		13	12	1	268	74*	24.36	0	2	530	429	9	47.66	2-34	0	0	4.85	7	
W20T		13	13	1	262	48	21.83	0	0	258	260	16	16.25	3-24	0	0	6.04	6	

Cmp	Debut	M	I	NO	Runs	HS	Avge	100	50	Balls	Runs	Wkts	Avge	BB	5i	10m	RpO	ct	st
WInt	2006/07	43	36	7	505	74*	17.41	0	2	1931	1421	36	39.47	3-38	0	0	4.41	17	
W20T	2006/07	23	21	3	335	48	18.61	0	0	456	436	24	18.16	3-24	0	0	5.73	11	
DODD, Natalie Claire b Hamilton, Waikato 22.11.1992 RHB OB																			
WInt		5	5	0	50	22	10.00	0	0									2	
DOOLAN, Lucy Rose b Lower Hutt, Wellington 11.12.1987 LHB OB																			
WInt		6	6	1	144	34	28.80	0	0	162	101	6	16.83	3-7	0	0	3.74	2	
W20T		8	4	1	20	8	6.66	0	0	180	167	12	13.91	3-26	0	0	5.56	2	
WInt	2007/08	22	18	5	371	48	28.53	0	0	753	486	23	21.13	3-7	0	0	3.87	7	
W20T	2007/08	17	12	2	122	41	12.20	0	0	324	313	17	18.41	3-16	0	0	5.79	2	
FAHEY, Maria Frances b Timaru, Canterbury 5.3.1984 LHB OB																			
WInt		9	9	0	186	61	20.66	0	2									3	
W20T		6	5	1	74	42	18.50	0	0									1	
WT	2003/04	2	4	1	125	60*	41.66	0	1									1	
WInt	2003/04	54	53	2	1403	91	27.50	0	14									15	
W20T	2006/07	8	7	1	134	43	22.33	0	0									1	
LIND, Victoria Jayne b Auckland 15.5.1985 RHB WK																			
WInt		8	8	0	178	68	22.25	0	1									5	
W20T	2009	2	2	0	29	20	14.50	0	0									0	
McGLASHAN, Sara Jade b Napier, Hawke's Bay 28.3.1982 RHB WK																			
WInt		14	14	1	255	65*	19.61	0	1									3	
W20T		13	13	1	294	84	24.50	0	1									8	
WT	2003/04	2	2	0	20	14	10.00	0	0									0	
WInt	2002	94	90	14	1710	97*	22.50	0	6									20	
W20T	2004	29	28	2	456	84	17.53	0	1									12	
MARTIN, Katey Jane b Dunedin, Otago 7.2.1985 RHB WK																			
WInt		8	8	0	121	35	15.12	0	0									2	
W20T		5	5	0	21	9	4.20	0	0									2	
WT	2003/04	1	2	0	49	46	24.50	0	0									0	
WInt	2003/04	26	26	2	423	79	17.62	0	1									8	3
W20T	2007/08	11	9	0	39	15	4.33	0	0									2	
NIELSEN, Morna Jessie Godwin b Tauranga, Bay of Plenty 24.2.1990 RHB LM																			
WInt		3	3	0	9	8	3.00	0	0	78	69	0					5.30	0	
PERRY, Elizabeth Cecilia b Taumarunui, Wanganui 22.11.1987 RHB RM																			
WInt		3	3	0	98	70	32.66	0	1	42	35	0					5.00	2	
W20T		7	6	2	56	21	14.00	0	0									0	
PRIEST, Rachel Holly b New Plymouth, Taranaki 13.6.1985 RHB WK																			
WInt		8	5	4	83	36*	83.00	0	0									5	1
W20T		13	11	5	56	20	9.33	0	0									9	8
WInt	2007	28	21	10	315	42	28.63	0	0									19	9
W20T	2007	26	19	7	110	20	9.16	0	0									13	13
PULFORD, Katherine Louise b Nelson 27.8.1980 RHB RM																			
WInt		7	6	0	69	19	11.50	0	0	284	198	8	24.75	2-33	0	0	4.18	1	
W20T		3	3	1	17	9	8.50	0	0	66	54	4	13.50	2-21	0	0	4.90	0	
WT	2003/04	1	2	0	0	0	0.00	0	0	78	15	2	7.50	2-15	0	0	1.15	1	
WInt	1998/99	46	40	0	743	95	18.57	0	3	1197	782	30	26.06	4-5	1	0	3.92	10	
W20T	2008/09	12	8	2	66	29	11.00	0	0	234	186	11	16.90	2-21	0	0	4.76	1	
RUCK, Sian Elizabeth Ansley b Auckland 8.12.1983 RHB LM																			
WInt		9	3	2	26	12*	26.00	0	0	372	226	5	45.20	2-32	0	0	3.64	0	
W20T		9	1	1	1	1*		0	0	174	149	9	16.55	3-15	0	0	5.13	1	
W20T	2009	16	3	2	2	1*	2.00	0	0	318	262	18	14.55	3-12	0	0	4.94	1	
SATTERTHWAITE, Amy Ella b Christchurch, Canterbury 7.10.1986 LHB RM																			
WInt		13	13	0	265	81	20.38	0	2	332	287	12	23.91	3-18	0	0	5.18	2	
W20T		11	7	2	72	42	14.40	0	0	30	38	2	19.00	2-17	0	0	7.60	3	
WInt	2007	38	36	2	790	81	23.23	0	4	506	414	13	31.84	3-18	0	0	4.90	6	
W20T	2007	24	18	4	187	42	13.35	0	0	90	95	10	9.50	6-17	0	1	6.33	5	
WATKINS, Aimee Louise b New Plymouth, Taranaki 11.10.1982 LHB OB																			
WInt		14	14	2	222	68	18.50	0	1	568	404	12	33.66	4-60	1	0	4.26	4	
W20T		13	13	0	229	44	17.61	0	0	183	189	11	17.18	3-8	0	0	6.19	8	
WT	2003/04	2	2	0	15	14	7.50	0	0	249	105	3	35.00	2-68	0	0	2.53	2	
WInt	2001/02	98	89	7	1733	111	21.13	2	5	4242	2757	88	31.32	4-2	5	0	3.90	33	
W20T	2004	28	28	3	620	89*	24.80	0	3	363	369	18	20.50	3-8	0	0	6.09	12	

2009/10 and 2010 AND CAREER RECORDS FOR PAKISTAN WOMEN PLAYERS

Cmp	Debut	M	I	NO	Runs	HS	Avge	100	50	Balls	Runs	Wkts	Avge	BB	5i	10m	RpO	ct	st
ARMAAN KHAN b Chagi, Baluchistan 4.4.1980 RHB WK																			
W20T		1	1	0	1	1	1.00	0	0									0	
WInt	2005/06	12	12	1	114	43*	10.36	0	0									8	2
W20T	2009	5	5	0	4	2	0.80	0	0									0	

Cmp	Debut	M	I	NO	Runs	HS	Avge	100	50	Balls	Runs	Wkts	Avge	BB	5i	10m	RpO	ct	st
ASMAVIA IQBAL Khokhar b Multan, Punjab 1.1.1988 RHB RFM																			
W20T		2	1	1	5	5*		0	0	12	22	0					11.00	1	
WInt	2005/06	30	27	7	230	38	11.50	0	0	1032	772	18	42.88	2-20	0	0	4.48	5	
W20T	2009	8	5	3	38	12*	19.00	0	0	102	84	2	42.00	1-12	0	0	4.94	2	
BATOOL FATIMA Naqvi, Syeda b Karachi, Sind 14.8.1982 RHB RMF WK																			
W20T		3	2	1	4	4*	4.00	0	0									0	2
WT	2003/04	1	1	0	0	0	0.00	0	0									3	2
WInt	2000/01	50	45	7	376	36	9.89	0	0	90	61	1	61.00	1-33	0	0	4.06	26	20
W20T	2009	9	4	2	12	8*	6.00	0	0									1	4
BISMAH MAROOF b Lahore, Punjab 18.7.1991 LHB																			
W20T		3	3	0	43	42	14.33	0	0									0	
WInt	2006/07	26	26	1	351	45	14.04	0	0									5	
W20T	2009	7	7	1	117	50*	19.50	0	1									1	
JAVERIA KHAN Wadood b Karachi, Sind 14.5.1988 RHB OB																			
W20T		3	3	0	30	14	10.00	0	0	50	61	2	30.50	2-24	0	0	7.32	0	
WInt	2008	13	11	0	107	23	9.72	0	0	523	335	9	37.22	3-22	0	0	3.84	4	
W20T	2009	9	7	1	53	16*	8.83	0	0	168	149	6	24.83	2-24	0	0	5.32	1	
NAIN Fatima ABIDI, Syeda b Karachi, Sind 23.5.1985 RHB																			
W20T		3	3	0	36	20	12.00	0	0									0	
WInt	2006/07	22	21	1	268	52	13.40	0	1									4	
W20T	2009	9	9	0	125	55	13.88	0	1									2	
NIDA Rasheed DAR b Sialkot, Punjab 2.1.1987 RHB OB																			
W20T		3	3	0	11	9	3.66	0	0	12	10	2	5.00	2-10	0	0	5.00	0	
QANITA JALIL b Abbottabad, North-West Frontier Province 21.3.1978 RHB RFM																			
W20T		3	2	0	1	1	0.50	0	0	28	35	0					7.50	0	
WInt	2005/06	30	29	6	146	20*	6.34	0	0	1068	826	22	37.54	5-62	0	1	4.64	3	
W20T	2009	9	6	0	6	4	1.00	0	0	136	152	3	50.66	1-12	0	0	6.70	1	
RABIYA SHAH b Karachi, Sind 27.4.1992 LHB OB																			
W20T		1	1	0	2	2	2.00	0	0									0	
SADIA YOUSUF b 4.11.1989 RHB SLA																			
W20T		1	1	1	0	0*		0	0	12	9	2	4.50	2-9	0	0	4.50	0	
WInt	2007/08	4	4	2	0	0*	0.00	0	0	120	69	3	23.00	2-20	0	0	3.45	1	
SAJJIDA SHAH, Syed b Hyderabad, Sind 3.2.1988 RHB OB																			
W20T		2	2	0	14	12	7.00	0	0	36	32	1	32.00	1-17	0	0	5.33	1	
WT	2000	2	3	0	100	98	33.33	0	1	6	0	0					0.00	0	
WInt	2000	60	59	5	863	52	15.98	0	1	2724	1473	51	28.88	7-4	1	1	3.24	8	
W20T	2009	8	8	1	86	27*	12.28	0	0	72	72	3	24.00	1-11	0	0	6.00	3	
SANA MIR b Abbottabad, North-West Frontier Province 5.1.1986 RHB RMF																			
W20T		3	3	0	42	35	14.00	0	0	48	41	3	13.66	2-12	0	0	5.12	2	
WInt	2005/06	31	30	6	325	35	13.54	0	0	1400	821	31	26.48	4-10	1	0	3.51	9	
W20T	2009	9	7	2	82	35	16.40	0	0	173	133	12	11.08	4-13	1	0	4.61	2	
SANIA Iqbal KHAN b Multan, Punjab 23.3.1985 RHB RMF																			
W20T		2	2	1	17	15	17.00	0	0	18	32	1	32.00	1-21	0	0	10.66	1	
WInt	2008/09	3	3	1	7	4	3.50	0	0	42	53	0					7.57	0	
UROOJ MUMTAZ Khan b Karachi, Sind 1.10.1985 RHB LB																			
W20T		3	3	1	41	26*	20.50	0	0	51	39	1	39.00	1-19	0	0	4.58	2	
WT	2003/04	1	1	0	0	0	0.00	0	0	198	97	2	48.50	1-24	0	0	2.93	3	
WInt	2003/04	38	37	2	502	57	14.34	0	1	1085	878	36	24.38	5-33	1	2	4.85	13	
W20T	2009	9	9	2	87	26*	12.42	0	0	177	127	6	21.16	2-14	0	0	4.30	3	

2009/10 AND 2010 AND CAREER RECORDS FOR SOUTH AFRICA WOMEN PLAYERS

Cmp	Debut	M	I	NO	Runs	HS	Avge	100	50	Balls	Runs	Wkts	Avge	BB	5i	10m	RpO	ct	st
BENADE, Susanna Maria b Lichtenburg, Transvaal 16.2.1982 RHB RMF																			
W20T		2	2	0	24	14	12.00	0	0	12	17	0					8.50	1	
WT	2007	1	2	0	51	51	25.50	0	1	24	1	2	0.50	2-1	0	0	0.25	1	
WInt	2004/05	19	19	2	291	58	17.11	0	1	472	308	10	30.80	2-11	0	0	3.91	7	
W20T	2007	11	11	1	134	44	13.40	0	0	138	163	6	27.16	2-21	0	0	7.08	3	
BRITS, Crizelda b Rustenburg, Transvaal 20.11.1983 RHB RMF																			
WInt		4	4	1	150	60*	50.00	0	1									3	
W20T		3	3	0	74	43	24.66	0	0									0	
WT	2001/02	4	8	1	150	61	21.42	0	1	507	255	6	42.50	2-68	0	0	3.01	2	
WInt	2001/02	46	41	6	1097	107*	31.34	1	7	811	576	22	26.18	4-37	1	0	4.26	14	
W20T	2007	12	12	2	226	57*	22.60	0	1									2	
CHETTY, Trisha b Durban, Natal 26.6.1988 RHB WK																			
WInt		4	4	0	97	42	24.25	0	0									2	3
W20T		6	6	0	87	31	14.50	0	0									3	2
WT	2007	1	1	0	2	2	2.00	0	0									1	1
WInt	2006/07	24	19	7	415	58	34.58	0	1									24	10
W20T	2007	14	14	2	170	36	14.16	0	0									4	4

Cmp	*Debut*	*M*	*I*	*NO*	*Runs*	*HS*	*Avge*	*100*	*50*	*Balls*	*Runs*	*Wkts*	*Avge*	*BB*	*5i*	*10m*	*RpO*	*ct*	*st*
DU PREEZ, Mignon b Pretoria, Transvaal 13.6.1989 RHB																			
WInt		4	4	2	175	70*	87.50	0	2									0	
W20T		6	6	2	100	53*	25.00	0	1									1	
WInt	2006/07	14	13	5	426	81*	53.25	0	4									0	
W20T	2007	11	11	2	146	53*	16.22	0	1									2	
FRITZ, Shandre Alvida b Cape Town, Cape Province 21.7.1985 RHB RM																			
WInt		3	3	1	52	31	26.00	0	0	67	30	5	6.00	3-11	0	0	2.68	1	
W20T		5	5	0	120	58	24.00	0	1	12	18	0					9.00	2	
WInt	2003	30	24	3	348	48	16.57	0	0	742	506	22	23.00	4-36	1	0	4.09	9	
W20T	2008	10	9	0	183	58	20.33	0	1	42	60	1	60.00	1-12	0	0	8.57	4	
ISMAIL, Shabnim b Cape Town, Cape Province 5.10.1988 LHB RFM																			
WInt		4								132	101	1	101.00	1-31	0	0	4.59	2	
W20T		5	2	2	0	0*		0	0	93	121	4	30.25	3-30	0	0	7.80	1	
WT	2007	1	1	0	1	1	1.00	0	0	150	20	3	6.66	2-5	0	0	0.80	0	
WInt	2006/07	15	4	1	12	7	4.00	0	0	660	405	10	40.50	2-7	0	0	3.68	3	
W20T	2007	9	4	3	2	1*	2.00	0	0	189	237	11	21.54	3-27	0	0	7.52	2	
KAPP, Marizanne b Port Elizabeth, Cape Province 4.1.1990 RHB RM																			
W20T		2	2	0	11	8	5.50	0	0									0	
WInt	2008/09	2	2	0	7	7	3.50	0	0	18	25	0					8.33	0	
W20T	2009	3	3	1	29	18*	14.50	0	0	12	21	0					10.50	0	
KILOWAN, Ashlyn Petro Carlyle b Paarl, Cape Province 19.12.1982 LHB LM																			
WInt		1								18	25	0					8.33	0	
W20T		3	2	1	4	2*	4.00	0	0	44	55	5	11.00	3-20	0	0	7.50	2	
WT	2007	1	1	1	28	28*		0	0	66	2	0					0.18	0	
WInt	2003	32	16	4	124	21	10.33	0	0	1347	778	33	23.57	4-23	1	0	3.46	7	
W20T	2007	11	6	2	33	22	8.25	0	0	218	236	10	23.60	3-20	0	0	6.49	3	
LETSOALO, Matshipi Marcia b Phalaborwa, Northern Province 11.4.1984 RHB RM																			
WInt		3								150	73	2	36.50	1-22	0	0	2.92	1	
W20T		3	1	0	0	0	0.00	0	0	60	53	2	26.50	2-16	0	0	5.30	2	
WT	2007	1	1	0	3	3	3.00	0	0	90	15	0					1.00	1	
WInt	2006/07	15	4	1	11	4*	3.66	0	0	624	300	9	33.33	3-27	0	0	2.88	3	
W20T	2007	7	4	1	12	10	4.00	0	0	102	114	3	38.00	2-16	0	0	6.70	3	
LOUBSER, Sunette b Paarl, Cape Province 26.9.1982 RHB OB																			
WInt		4	2	2	8	7*		0	0	228	125	6	20.83	2-35	0	0	3.28	3	
W20T		3	2	1	10	7	10.00	0	0	54	55	4	13.75	3-22	0	0	6.11	1	
WT	2007	1	1	0	3	3	3.00	0	0	327	59	8	7.37	5-37	1	0	1.08	0	
WInt	2006/07	21	12	3	100	22	11.11	0	0	1051	537	24	22.37	2-10	0	0	3.06	12	
W20T	2007	12	9	1	55	19	6.87	0	0	258	272	13	20.92	3-22	0	0	6.32	5	
SMITH, Alicia Esther b Cape Town, Cape Province 13.3.1984 RHB RFM																			
WInt		4	3	1	80	35*	40.00	0	0	99	67	4	16.75	2-13	0	0	4.06	2	
W20T		6	5	1	71	44	17.75	0	0	42	52	3	17.33	2-23	0	0	7.42	5	
WT	2003	3	5	2	86	24*	28.66	0	0	336	136	4	34.00	2-4	0	0	2.42	1	
WInt	2003	37	30	3	557	68	20.62	0	1	1699	1059	50	21.18	5-7	1	1	3.74	6	
W20T	2007	14	13	3	156	44	15.60	0	0	156	182	7	26.00	2-23	0	0	7.00	8	
TAAI, Angelique Samantha b King William's Town, Cape Province 31.3.1987 RHB RMF																			
WInt		1								6	10	0					10.00	0	
W20T		5	5	1	21	11	5.25	0	0	66	94	3	31.33	1-9	0	0	8.54	1	
WInt	2004/05	8	6	2	38	22*	9.50	0	0	124	83	1	83.00	1-22	0	0	4.01	0	
THOMSON, Kirstie b Johannesburg, Transvaal 21.10.1988 RHB RM																			
WInt		4	4	0	87	27	21.75	0	0	36	28	0					4.66	2	
W20T		3	3	0	48	32	16.00	0	0									1	
TRYON, Chloe-Lesleigh b Kingsway, Durban, Natal 25.1.1994 LHB LMF																			
W20T		3	2	0	23	13	11.50	0	0	66	76	4	19.00	2-28	0	0	6.90	1	
VAN DER WESTHUIZEN, Charlize b Pretoria, Transvaal 17.2.1984 RHB SLA																			
WInt		4								228	128	3	42.66	2-31	0	0	3.36	2	
W20T		5	3	0	9	4	3.00	0	0	120	110	6	18.33	2-27	0	0	5.50	3	
WT	2003	2	4	0	159	83	39.75	0	1	240	116	3	38.66	2-49	0	0	2.90	0	
WInt	2003	33	23	7	165	25*	10.31	0	0	1519	814	26	31.30	4-30	1	0	3.21	7	
W20T	2008	12	6	1	37	14*	7.40	0	0	271	268	10	26.80	2-27	0	0	5.93	4	
VAN NIEKERK, Dane b Pretoria, Transvaal 14.5.1993 RHB LB																			
WInt		4	2	0	8	5	4.00	0	0	180	98	7	14.00	3-25	0	0	3.26	2	
W20T		6	4	0	21	8	5.25	0	0	99	108	2	54.00	1-19	0	0	6.54	2	
WInt	2008/09	6	3	0	9	5	3.00	0	0	270	133	11	12.09	3-11	0	0	2.95	2	
W20T	2009	9	6	0	29	8	4.83	0	0	159	181	5	36.20	2-26	0	0	6.83	3	

2009/10 and 2010 AND CAREER RECORDS FOR SRI LANKA WOMEN PLAYERS

Cmp	Debut	M	I	NO	Runs	HS	Avge	100	50	Balls	Runs	Wkts	Avge	BB	5i	10m	RpO	ct	st
DE ALWIS, Suwini Priyanga b Kandy 17.5.1975 LHB SLA																			
WInt		2	2	0	20	10	10.00	0	0	78	46	3	15.33	3-33	0	0	3.53	1	
W20T		6	6	0	70	26	11.66	0	0	117	122	5	24.40	2-10	0	0	6.25	2	
WInt	2004/05	37	35	3	423	37	13.21	0	0	1595	956	46	20.78	4-24	2	0	3.59	11	
DOLAWATTE, Sadamali Kumuduni b Colombo 10.2.1983 RHB LB																			
W20T		4	4	1	42	17*	14.00	0	0									0	
WInt	2001/02	27	19	3	67	13	4.18	0	0	486	308	16	19.25	5-16	1	1	3.80	7	
W20T	2009	6	5	1	48	17*	12.00	0	0									0	
FERNANDO, Wannakawattawadune Hiruka Dilani b Moratuwa 30.9.1976 LHB SLA																			
WInt		1	1	0	3	3	3.00	0	0									0	
W20T		1	1	0	4	4	4.00	0	0									0	
WInt	1997/98	55	54	10	961	78*	21.84	0	3	396	257	8	32.12	3-14	0	0	3.89	9	
W20T	2009	4	4	0	12	6	3.00	0	0									0	
GALAGEDARA, Sanjeewani Inoka b Colombo 17.7.1977 RHB RFM																			
WInt		1	1	0	5	5	5.00	0	0									0	
W20T		5	5	0	59	25	11.80	0	0									1	
WInt	2001/02	33	28	1	146	25	5.40	0	0	39	30	2	15.00	1-2	0	0	4.61	8	
W20T	2009	8	8	0	117	37	14.62	0	0									1	
JAYANGANI, Atapattumudiyanselage Chamari b Gokarella 9.2.1990 LHB RM																			
WInt		2	2	0	38	38	19.00	0	0									0	
W20T		5	5	0	67	27	13.40	0	0	24	18	1	18.00	1-13	0	0	4.50	2	
W20T	2009	6	6	0	83	27	13.83	0	0	24	18	1	18.00	1-13	0	0	4.50	2	
KAUSHALYA, Lokusuriyage Eshani b Panadura 1.6.1984 RHB RM																			
WInt		2	2	0	33	32	16.50	0	0	66	46	3	15.33	2-24	0	0	4.18	2	
W20T		6	6	0	35	11	5.83	0	0	108	109	4	27.25	2-30	0	0	6.05	1	
WInt	2004/05	33	31	4	391	57	14.48	0	1	846	580	21	27.61	3-25	0	0	4.11	5	
W20T	2009	9	9	0	69	23	7.66	0	0	174	164	12	13.66	4-18	1	0	5.65	2	
KUMARIHAMI, Polgampola Ralalage Chamari Sarojika b Warakapola 20.3.1981 LHB RMF																			
W20T		1	1	0	2	2	2.00	0	0	24	29	0					7.25	0	
WInt	2003/04	37	37	0	490	58	13.24	0	2	1171	684	24	28.50	4-26	1	0	3.50	13	
W20T	2009	4	4	0	9	4	2.25	0	0	90	97	2	48.50	1-24	0	0	6.46	1	
PRABODHANI, Kaluwa Dewage Udeshika b Darga Town 20.9.1985 RHB LM																			
WInt		2	1	0	8	8	8.00	0	0	99	57	2	28.50	2-21	0	0	3.45	1	
W20T		6	4	3	6	4*	6.00	0	0	126	104	3	34.66	2-18	0	0	4.95	0	
WInt	2008/09	7	4	1	9	8	3.00	0	0	297	158	5	31.60	2-20	0	0	3.19	2	
W20T	2009	9	4	3	6	4*	6.00	0	0	198	161	8	20.12	2-18	0	0	4.87	0	
RASANGIKA, Herath Mudiyanselage Deepika b Colombo 13.12.1983 LHB MF																			
WInt		2	2	1	8	6	8.00	0	0									0	
W20T		6	6	2	68	31*	17.00	0	0	24	34	2	17.00	2-34	0	0	8.50	1	
WInt	2008	9	8	2	36	16*	6.00	0	0									2	
W20T	2009	9	9	3	114	31*	19.00	0	0	24	34	2	17.00	2-34	0	0	8.50	1	
SENEVIRATNE, Chamani Roshini b Anuradhapura 14.11.1978 RHB RM																			
WInt		2	2	0	50	33	25.00	0	0	102	49	2	24.50	1-22	0	0	2.88	0	
W20T		6	6	0	23	11	3.83	0	0	102	112	5	22.40	4-21	1	0	6.58	5	
WT	1997/98	1	2	1	148	105*	148.00	1	0	210	59	7	8.42	5-31	1	0	1.68	0	
WInt	1997/98	49	43	7	537	56	14.91	0	1	1909	1031	42	24.54	4-23	1	0	3.24	17	
SILVA, Lidamulage Dedunu Vindya Vijayanthi b Colombo 12.2.1978 RHB RM																			
WInt		2	2	0	39	20	19.50	0	0									0	
W20T		6	6	0	95	36	15.83	0	0									3	1
WInt	2000/01	42	42	0	884	78	21.04	0	6									8	
SIRIWARDENE, Hettimulla Appuhamilage Shashikala Dedunu b Colombo 14.2.1985 RHB RMF																			
WInt		2	2	0	20	20	10.00	0	0	87	42	1	42.00	1-16	0	0	2.89	1	
W20T		3	3	0	11	7	3.66	0	0	51	66	5	13.20	3-20	0	0	7.76	1	
WInt	2002/03	46	43	1	848	66	20.19	0	4	2033	1155	48	24.06	4-11	3	0	3.40	21	
SURANGIKA, Manodara Acharige Don Dilani b Kandy 8.12.1982 RHB WK																			
WInt		2	2	1	34	26*	34.00	0	0									1	
W20T		5	5	1	32	12	8.00	0	0									2	1
WInt	2006/07	23	18	6	173	33*	14.41	0	0									14	9
W20T	2009	8	8	3	71	22*	14.20	0	0									2	2
WEERAKKODY, Sripali Shiromala b Kiridiwela 7.1.1986 LHB RM																			
WInt		2	2	1	16	11*	16.00	0	0	48	40	1	40.00	1-25	0	0	5.00	0	
W20T		6	6	2	30	9*	7.50	0	0	132	135	7	19.28	3-31	0	0	6.13	0	
WInt	2006/07	24	17	7	108	17	10.80	0	0	882	491	15	32.73	3-26	0	0	3.34	4	
W20T	2009	9	9	4	50	12*	10.00	0	0	197	204	7	29.14	3-31	0	0	6.21	0	

2009/10 and 2010 AND CAREER RECORDS FOR WEST INDIES WOMEN PLAYERS

Cmp Debut	M	I	NO	Runs	HS	Avge	100	50	Balls	Runs	Wkts	Avge	BB	5i	10m	RpO	ct	st
AGUILLEIRA, Merissa Ria b Trinidad 14.12.1985 RHB WK																		
WInt	8	7	0	135	44	19.28	0	0									2	4
W20T	12	10	2	96	26	12.00	0	0									2	1
WInt 2008	23	21	1	238	44	11.90	0	0									18	4
W20T 2009	15	12	3	115	26	12.77	0	0									4	1
ALEXANDER, Kirbyina Nasie b Trinidad 6.7.1987 RHB RF																		
WInt	1	1	0	0	0	0.00	0	0	30	18	0					3.60	0	
W20T	1	1	1	0	0*		0	0	12	14	0					7.00	0	
WInt 2004/05	20	14	3	70	16	6.36	0	0	582	332	17	19.52	3-6	0	0	3.42	3	
W20T 2008	6	4	2	15	11	7.50	0	0	78	85	3	28.33	3-20	0	0	6.53	0	
CAMPBELLE, Shemaine Altia b Berbice, Guyana 14.10.1992 RHB RMF																		
WInt	7	5	1	20	6	5.00	0	0	180	104	2	52.00	2-22	0	0	3.46	3	1
W20T	13	5	3	14	9*	7.00	0	0	192	164	8	20.50	3-7	0	0	5.12	3	7
COOPER, Britney b Trinidad 23.8.1989 RHB RFM																		
WInt	4	4	1	56	16	18.66	0	0									3	
W20T	12	10	2	106	27	13.25	0	0									4	
DALEY, Shanel Francine b Jamaica 25.12.1988 LHB LM																		
WInt	7	6	2	104	38*	26.00	0	0	226	146	4	36.50	1-20	0	0	3.87	2	
W20T	13	11	3	97	19	12.12	0	0	247	240	13	18.46	3-13	0	0	5.83	5	
WInt 2008/09	14	12	3	184	38*	20.44	0	0	472	311	13	23.92	4-29	1	0	3.95	3	
W20T 2009	14	12	4	106	19	13.25	0	0	271	259	14	18.50	3-13	0	0	5.73	5	
DOTTIN, Deandra Jalisa Shakira b Barbados 21.6.1991 RHB RF																		
WInt	7	7	1	136	41	22.66	0	0	102	85	0					5.00	0	
W20T	13	13	2	248	112*	22.54	1	1	174	177	5	35.40	2-31	0	0	6.10	6	
WInt 2008	26	25	2	484	66	21.04	0	2	273	219	5	43.80	2-0	0	0	4.81	3	
W20T 2008	19	19	4	330	112*	22.00	1	2	222	216	6	36.00	2-31	0	0	5.83	10	
JACK, Cordel Patricia b St Vincent 22.2.1982 RHB OB																		
WInt	9	9	1	183	81*	22.87	0	1	210	143	3	47.66	1-22	0	0	4.08	2	
W20T	10	10	0	133	41	13.30	0	0	84	91	2	45.50	1-12	0	0	6.50	7	
WInt 2004/05	17	16	1	239	81*	15.93	0	1	252	172	4	43.00	1-12	0	0	4.09	3	
W20T 2009	11	11	0	157	41	14.27	0	0	108	120	3	40.00	1-12	0	0	6.66	7	
KING, Stacy-Ann Camille-Ann b Trinidad 17.7.1983 LHB LM																		
WInt	9	9	0	135	40	15.00	0	0	108	66	3	22.00	2-26	0	0	3.66	2	
W20T	13	13	4	108	25	12.00	0	0	84	90	2	45.00	1-10	0	0	6.42	7	
WInt 2008	27	24	1	377	70	16.39	0	1	243	181	9	20.11	3-33	0	0	4.46	8	
W20T 2008	19	19	5	290	79*	20.71	0	2	102	115	2	57.50	1-10	0	0	6.76	7	
LAVINE, Pamela Yvonne b Barbados 12.3.1969 RHB RF																		
WInt	9	9	0	211	57	23.44	0	1	335	208	13	16.00	4-17	1	0	3.72	3	
W20T	12	11	1	161	61	16.10	0	1	138	142	5	28.40	4-21	1	0	6.17	1	
WInt 2004/05	24	24	4	548	66*	27.40	0	3	836	536	19	28.21	4-17	1	0	3.84	5	
W20T 2009	15	14	1	202	61	15.53	0	1	190	209	7	29.85	4-21	1	0	6.60	2	
MOHAMMED, Anisa b Trinidad 7.8.1988 RHB OB																		
WInt	9	7	4	63	23*	21.00	0	0	315	209	4	52.25	2-33	0	0	3.98	1	
W20T	12	3	1	11	5	5.50	0	0	230	194	24	8.08	5-10	2	1	5.06	2	
WInt 2003	30	20	8	134	23*	11.16	0	0	1264	663	25	26.52	3-24	0	0	3.14	10	
W20T 2008	17	4	2	13	5	6.50	0	0	314	285	31	9.19	5-10	3	1	5.44	2	
NATION, Chedean Natasha b Jamaica 31.10.1986 RHB																		
WInt	5	5	1	26	17	6.50	0	0	192	133	5	26.60	3-22	0	0	4.15	2	
W20T	2	2	0	11	6	5.50	0	0	36	31	3	10.33	2-14	0	0	5.16	0	
WInt 2008	12	10	1	71	21	7.88	0	0	241	177	5	35.40	3-22	0	0	4.40	4	
W20T 2008	5	4	1	13	6	4.33	0	0	78	56	5	11.20	2-14	0	0	4.30	0	
NERO, Juliana Barbara b St Vincent 14.7.1979 RHB RM																		
WInt	1	1	0	3	3	3.00	0	0									1	
W20T	4	4	0	90	32	22.50	0	0									0	
WT 2003/04	1	2	0	33	32	16.50	0	0	12	13	0					6.50	0	
WInt 2002/03	44	41	4	639	71*	17.27	0	2	78	67	4	16.75	3-25	0	0	5.15	16	
W20T 2008	10	10	0	159	32	15.90	0	0									1	
SAMAROO, Amanda Mindy b Trinidad 2.11.1992 RHB RM																		
WInt	3	3	0	25	16	8.33	0	0	12	13	0					6.50	1	
W20T	2	2	0	8	6	4.00	0	0									0	
SELMAN, Shakera Casandra b Barbados 1.9.1989 RHB RM																		
WInt	6	3	2	6	5*	6.00	0	0	162	121	3	40.33	2-24	0	0	4.48	2	
W20T	6	2	2	2	1*		0	0	66	70	4	17.50	2-27	0	0	6.36	1	
WInt 2008	19	8	6	27	12*	13.50	0	0	660	357	16	22.31	4-11	1	0	3.24	4	
W20T 2008	11	3	2	2	1*	2.00	0	0	144	131	6	21.83	2-27	0	0	5.45	3	
SMALL, Danielle Gloria Kamesha b Barbados 16.3.1989 RHB RF																		
WInt	1	1	0	2	2	2.00	0	0	30	18	2	9.00	2-18	0	0	3.60	0	
W20T	2	1	1	4	4*		0	0	36	31	0					5.16	0	

Cmp Debut	M	I	NO	Runs	HS	Avge	100	50	Balls	Runs	Wkts	Avge	BB	5i	10m	RpO	ct	st
WInt 2008	12	10	3	82	37*	11.71	0	0	389	215	8	26.87	3-27	0	0	3.31	1	
W20T 2008	5	2	1	11	7	11.00	0	0	78	70	2	35.00	2-20	0	0	5.38	1	
SMARTT, Tremayne b Guyana 17.9.1985 RHB																		
WInt	3	2	0	18	9	9.00	0	0	48	58	0					7.25	0	
W20T	5	3	0	11	7	3.66	0	0	30	26	1	26.00	1-16	0	0	5.20	0	
TAITT, Charlene Olivia b Barbados 2.9.1984 RHB OB																		
WInt	1	1	0	11	11	11.00	0	0	18	14	1	14.00	1-14	0	0	4.66	0	
WInt 2008	16	14	1	173	47	13.30	0	0	390	222	6	37.00	1-9	0	0	3.41	3	
W20T 2008	1	1	0	4	4	4.00	0	0	18	7	2	3.50	2-7	0	0	2.33	1	
TAYLOR, Stafanie Roxann b Jamaica 11.6.1991 RHB OB																		
WInt	9	9	1	332	108*	41.50	1	1	504	276	11	25.09	3-29	0	0	3.28	3	
W20T	11	11	2	329	58*	36.55	0	4	204	209	11	19.00	3-16	0	0	6.14	7	
WInt 2008	26	26	3	803	108*	34.91	1	4	1148	573	30	19.10	4-17	1	0	2.99	13	
W20T 2008	16	15	3	540	90	45.00	0	7	276	281	14	20.07	3-16	0	0	6.10	9	

FIRST-CLASS MATCHES PLAYED IN 2009/10 and 2010

2009/10

AUSTRALIA (39)

South Australia v Tasmania	Adelaide[1]	Oct 13-16
Western Australia v Queensland	Perth	Oct 13-16
South Australia v Victoria	Adelaide[1]	Oct 30-Nov 2
Queensland v Tasmania	Brisbane[2]	Nov 1-4
New South Wales v Western Australia	Sydney[3]	Nov 3-6
South Australia v Queensland	Adelaide[1]	Nov 8-11
New South Wales v Tasmania	Sydney[3]	Nov 17-20
Victoria v Western Australia	Melbourne[2]	Nov 17-20
Queensland v West Indians	Brisbane[3]	Nov 18-21
Tasmania v South Australia	Hobart[3]	Nov 24-27
AUSTRALIA v WEST INDIES	Brisbane[2]	Nov 26-28
Victoria v Queensland	Melbourne[2]	Nov 27-29
Western Australia v New South Wales	Perth	Nov 27-29
AUSTRALIA v WEST INDIES	Adelaide[1]	Dec 4-8
Tasmania v Western Australia	Hobart[3]	Dec 8-11
Victoria v South Australia	Melbourne[2]	Dec 10-13
Queensland v New South Wales	Brisbane[2]	Dec 11-14
AUSTRALIA v WEST INDIES	Perth	Dec 16-20
New South Wales v Victoria	Newcastle	Dec 18-21
South Australia v Western Australia	Adelaide[1]	Dec 18-21
Tasmania v Pakistanis	Hobart[3]	Dec 19-21
AUSTRALIA v PAKISTAN	Melbourne[2]	Dec 26-30
AUSTRALIA v PAKISTAN	Sydney[3]	Jan 3-6
AUSTRALIA v PAKISTAN	Hobart[3]	Jan 14-18
New South Wales v Queensland	Sydney[3]	Jan 29-Feb 1
Tasmania v Victoria	Hobart[3]	Jan 29-Feb 1
Tasmania v Queensland	Hobart[3]	Feb 8-11
Western Australia v South Australia	Perth	Feb 8-11
Victoria v New South Wales	Melbourne[2]	Feb 12-15
South Australia v New South Wales	Adelaide[1]	Feb 19-22
Western Australia v Tasmania	Perth	Feb 19-22
Queensland v Victoria	Brisbane[2]	Feb 22-25
Queensland v South Australia	Brisbane[2]	Mar 3-6
Tasmania v New South Wales	Hobart[3]	Mar 3-6
Western Australia v Victoria	Perth	Mar 3-6
New South Wales v South Australia	Sydney[3]	Mar 10-12
Queensland v Western Australia	Brisbane[2]	Mar 10-12
Victoria v Tasmania	Melbourne[2]	Mar 10-12
Victoria v Queensland	Melbourne[2]	Mar 17-21

BANGLADESH (26)

The format of the National League was changed so that after the teams had played each other once the bottom two teams dropped out and the rest played each other again with all their points from the first stage also to count. The top two teams at the end of the second stage played in the final.

Barisal v Chittagong	Khulna	Jan 14-17
Dhaka v Khulna	Rajshahi	Jan 14-16
Rajshahi v Sylhet	Fatullah	Jan 14-16
BANGLADESH v INDIA	Chittagong[2]	Jan 17-21
Barisal v Dhaka	Khulna	Jan 20-22
Chittagong v Rajshahi	Savar[1]	Jan 20-22
Khulna v Sylhet	Bogra	Jan 20-23
BANGLADESH v INDIA	Mirpur	Jan 24-27
Barisal v Khulna	Fatullah	Jan 26-29
Chittagong v Sylhet	Rajshahi	Jan 26-28
Dhaka v Rajshahi	Chittagong[2]	Jan 26-29
Barisal v Sylhet	Khulna	Feb 2-3
Chittagong v Dhaka	Bogra	Feb 2-5
Khulna v Rajshahi	Chittagong[2]	Feb 2-5
Barisal v Rajshahi	Khulna	Feb 8-11
Chittagong v Khulna	Rajshahi	Feb 8-11
Dhaka v Sylhet	Bogra	Feb 8-10
Chittagong v Rajshahi	Bogra	Feb 15-17
Dhaka v Khulna	Chittagong[2]	Feb 15-18
Chittagong v Dhaka	Khulna	Feb 22-25
Khulna v Rajshahi	Savar[2]	Feb 22-25
Chittagong v Khulna	Bogra	Feb 28-Mar 3
Dhaka v Rajshahi	Khulna	Feb 28-Mar 3
Chittagong v Rajshahi	Mirpur	Mar 6-10
BANGLADESH v ENGLAND	Chittagong[2]	Mar 12-16
BANGLADESH v ENGLAND	Mirpur	Mar 20-24

INDIA (93)

Rest of India v Mumbai	Nagpur[3]	Oct 1-5
Assam v Rajasthan	Guwahati[3]	Nov 3-6
Baroda v Delhi	Vadodara[5]	Nov 3-6
Gujarat v Orissa	Ahmedabad[3]	Nov 3-6
Hyderabad v Himachal Pradesh	Secunderabad[1]	Nov 3-6
Jharkhand v Tripura	Ranchi[1]	Nov 3-6
Kerala v Andhra	Thalassery[2]	Nov 3-6
Madhya Pradesh v Haryana	Indore[7]	Nov 3-6
Maharashtra v Bengal	Poona[3]	Nov 3-6
Punjab v Mumbai	Chandigarh	Nov 3-6
Railways v Tamil Nadu	Delhi[6]	Nov 3-6
Uttar Pradesh v Karnataka	Meerut[3]	Nov 3-6
Vidarbha v Goa	Nagpur[3]	Nov 3-6
Bengal v Baroda	Kolkata[1]	Nov 10-13
Delhi v Karnataka	Delhi[2]	Nov 10-13
Goa v Assam	Margao[1]	Nov 10-13
Gujarat v Tamil Nadu	Ahmedabad[3]	Nov 10-13
Jammu and Kashmir v Haryana	Srinagar[2]	Nov 10-13
Jharkhand v Vidarbha	Ranchi[1]	Nov 10-13
Madhya Pradesh v Kerala	Indore[6]	Nov 10-13
Mumbai v Orissa	Mumbai[4]	Nov 10-13
Punjab v Hyderabad	Mohali	Nov 10-13
Railways v Himachal Pradesh	Delhi[6]	Nov 10-13
Saurashtra v Uttar Pradesh	Rajkot[2]	Nov 10-13
Tripura v Rajasthan	Agartala[2]	Nov 10-13
INDIA v SRI LANKA	Ahmedabad[4]	Nov 16-20
Andhra v Madhya Pradesh	Vijayawada[2]	Nov 17-20
Assam v Jharkhand	Guwahati[2]	Nov 17-20
Goa v Rajasthan	Margao[1]	Nov 17-20
Hyderabad v Gujarat	Hyderabad[2]	Nov 17-20
Jammu and Kashmir v Kerala	Jammu[2]	Nov 17-19
Karnataka v Bengal	Mysore[4]	Nov 17-20
Mumbai v Himachal Pradesh	Mumbai[8]	Nov 17-20
Orissa v Railways	Bhubaneswar	Nov 17-20
Punjab v Tamil Nadu	Amritsar	Nov 17-20
Saurashtra v Maharashtra	Rajkot[2]	Nov 17-20
Uttar Pradesh v Baroda	Mohan Nagar	Nov 17-20
Vidarbha v Tripura	Nagpur[3]	Nov 17-20
Bengal v Saurashtra	Kolkata[1]	Nov 24-27
Himachal Pradesh v Tamil Nadu	Dharmasala[2]	Nov 24-27
Hyderabad v Orissa	Hyderabad[2]	Nov 24-27
INDIA v SRI LANKA	Kanpur[1]	Nov 24-27
Maharashtra v Karnataka	Poona[3]	Nov 24-27
Punjab v Gujarat	Mohali	Nov 24-27
Railways v Mumbai	Delhi[6]	Nov 24-27
Uttar Pradesh v Delhi	Lucknow[7]	Nov 24-27
Andhra v Haryana	Anantapur[3]	Dec 1-4
Assam v Tripura	Guwahati[2]	Dec 1-3
Baroda v Karnataka	Vadodara[5]	Dec 1-3
Delhi v Saurashtra	Delhi[2]	Dec 1-4
Gujarat v Railways	Valsad[3]	Dec 1-4
Hyderabad v Mumbai	Hyderabad[2]	Dec 1-4
Jharkhand v Goa	Dhanbad	Dec 1-4
Madhya Pradesh v Jammu and Kashmir	Indore[6]	Dec 1-4
Maharashtra v Uttar Pradesh	Poona[3]	Dec 1-4
Orissa v Tamil Nadu	Sambalpur	Dec 1-4
Punjab v Himachal Pradesh	Mohali	Dec 1-3
Rajasthan v Vidarbha	Jaipur[4]	Dec 1-4
INDIA v SRI LANKA	Mumbai[4]	Dec 2-6
Andhra v Jammu and Kashmir	Anantapur[3]	Dec 8-10
Assam v Vidarbha	Guwahati[2]	Dec 8-11
Baroda v Saurashtra	Vadodara[5]	Dec 8-9
Delhi v Maharashtra	Delhi[2]	Dec 8-11
Gujarat v Himachal Pradesh	Surat[7]	Dec 8-10
Haryana v Kerala	Rohtak[3]	Dec 8-10
Hyderabad v Railways	Hyderabad[2]	Dec 8-11
Jharkhand v Rajasthan	Dhanbad	Dec 8-11
Mumbai v Tamil Nadu	Mumbai[8]	Dec 8-11
Punjab v Orissa	Chandigarh	Dec 8-11
Tripura v Goa	Agartala[2]	Dec 8-11
Uttar Pradesh v Bengal	Kanpur[1]	Dec 8-10

Assam v Andhra	Guwahati[2]	Dec 15-18
Bengal v Delhi	Kolkata[5]	Dec 15-18
Haryana v Tripura	Rohtak[3]	Dec 15-18
Himachal Pradesh v Orissa	Dharmasala[2]	Dec 15-18
Hyderabad v Tamil Nadu	Hyderabad[2]	Dec 15-18
Maharashtra v Baroda	Poona[3]	Dec 15-18
Mumbai v Gujarat	Mumbai[4]	Dec 15-18
Railways v Punjab	Delhi[6]	Dec 15-18
Saurashtra v Karnataka	Rajkot[6]	Dec 15-18
Assam v Uttar Pradesh	Guwahati[3]	Dec 24-27
Delhi v Tamil Nadu	Delhi[5]	Dec 24-27
Haryana v Mumbai	Rohtak[3]	Dec 24-27
Karnataka v Punjab	Mysore[4]	Dec 24-27
Karnataka v Uttar Pradesh	Bangalore[4]	Jan 3-6
Mumbai v Delhi	Mumbai[4]	Jan 3-6
Karnataka v Mumbai	Mysore[4]	Jan 11-14
Central Zone v East Zone	Amritsar	Jan 19-22
Central Zone v South Zone	Indore[6]	Jan 26-29
West Zone v North Zone	Rajkot[2]	Jan 26-29
South Zone v West Zone	Hyderabad[2]	Feb 2-6
INDIA v SOUTH AFRICA	Nagpur[3]	Feb 6-9
INDIA v SOUTH AFRICA	Kolkata[1]	Feb 14-18

KENYA (3)

Kenya v Scotland	Nairobi[1]	Jan 25-28
Kenya v Netherlands	Nairobi[1]	Feb 20-23

NAMIBIA (8)

Namibia played in the South African Airways competition.

Namibia v Easterns	Windhoek[2]	Oct 22-24
Namibia v Boland	Windhoek[2]	Oct 29-30
Namibia v Gauteng	Windhoek[2]	Nov 12-14
Namibia v United Arab Emirates	Windhoek[2]	Dec 5-8
Namibia v Border	Windhoek[2]	Jan 7-9
Namibia v KwaZulu-Natal Inland	Windhoek[2]	Mar 4-6
Namibia v South Western Districts	Windhoek[2]	Mar 11-13
Namibia v Bermuda	Windhoek[2]	Apr 3-5

NEW ZEALAND (36)

Following the end of the previous sponsorship deal the domestic competition reverted to the Plunket Shield.

Central Districts v Auckland	Napier[3]	Nov 10-13
Otago v Northern Districts	Dunedin[5]	Nov 10-12
Wellington v Canterbury	Wellington[1]	Nov 10-13
Canterbury v Otago	Rangiora[2]	Nov 17-20
Northern Districts v Central Districts	Whangarei[2]	Nov 17-19
Wellington v Auckland	Wellington[1]	Nov 17-20
Canterbury v Auckland	Christchurch[5]	Nov 24-27
Central Districts v Otago	Napier[3]	Nov 24-27
NEW ZEALAND v PAKISTAN	Dunedin[5]	Nov 24-28
Northern Districts v Wellington	Hamilton	Nov 24-27
Auckland v Northern Districts	Auckland[6]	Dec 3-6
Canterbury v Central Districts	Rangiora[2]	Dec 3-5
NEW ZEALAND v PAKISTAN	Wellington[1]	Dec 3-6
Otago v Wellington	Queenstown	Dec 3-6
NEW ZEALAND v PAKISTAN	Napier[4]	Dec 11-15
Auckland v Otago	Auckland[6]	Dec 12-15
Northern Districts v Canterbury	Hamilton	Dec 12-14
Wellington v Central Districts	Wellington[1]	Dec 12-15
NEW ZEALAND v BANGLADESH	Hamilton	Feb 15-19
Auckland v Wellington	Auckland[6]	Feb 25-28
Canterbury v Northern Districts	Rangiora[2]	Feb 25-28
Otago v Central Districts	Invercargill[2]	Feb 25-28
Central Districts v Canterbury	New Plymouth	Mar 4-7
Otago v Auckland	Dunedin[5]	Mar 4-7
Wellington v Northern Districts	Wellington[1]	Mar 4-6
Central Districts v Wellington	Napier[4]	Mar 12-15
Northern Districts v Auckland	Whangarei[2]	Mar 12-14
Otago v Canterbury	Queenstown	Mar 12-15
NEW ZEALAND v AUSTRALIA	Wellington[1]	Mar 19-23
Auckland v Central Districts	Auckland[6]	Mar 20-23
Canterbury v Wellington	Rangiora[2]	Mar 20-23
Northern Districts v Otago	Whangarei[2]	Mar 20-23
NEW ZEALAND v AUSTRALIA	Hamilton	Mar 27-31
Auckland v Canterbury	Auckland[6]	Mar 29-Apr 1
Central Districts v Northern Districts	Napier[4]	Mar 29-Apr 1
Wellington v Otago	Wellington[1]	Mar 29-Apr 1

PAKISTAN (122)

Abbottabad v Quetta	Abbottabad	Oct 10-13
Islamabad v Hyderabad	Islamabad[5]	Oct 10-13
Karachi Whites v Habib Bank	Karachi[16]	Oct 10-12
KRL v PIA	Karachi[5]	Oct 10-13
Lahore Ravi v Multan	Lahore[11]	Oct 10-12
Lahore Shalimar v National Bank	Lahore[8]	Oct 10-13
Customs v Sui Southern Gas	Karachi[12]	Oct 10-13
Sialkot v Faisalabad	Sialkot[1]	Oct 10-12
Sui Northern Gas v WAPDA	Faisalabad[4]	Oct 10-13
Karachi Blues v Peshawar	Rawalpindi[4]	Oct 11-13
Abbottabad v Karachi Blues	Abbottabad	Oct 16-19
Faisalabad v Multan	Faisalabad[4]	Oct 16-19
Habib Bank v KRL	Karachi[5]	Oct 16-19
Hyderabad v Rawalpindi	Islamabad[5]	Oct 16-18
Karachi Whites v Customs	Karachi[11]	Oct 16-18
Lahore Ravi v Sialkot	Muridke	Oct 16-19
Lahore Shalimar v ZTBL	Lahore[11]	Oct 16-19
National Bank v WAPDA	Lahore[8]	Oct 16-19
PIA v Sui Southern Gas	Karachi[12]	Oct 16-19
Peshawar v Quetta	Islamabad[6]	Oct 16-18
Abbottabad v Hyderabad	Abbottabad	Oct 22-25
Faisalabad v Peshawar	Sargodha[1]	Oct 22-25
Habib Bank v WAPDA	Lahore[8]	Oct 22-25
Islamabad v Karachi Blues	Islamabad[5]	Oct 22-25
Karachi Whites v KRL	Karachi[5]	Oct 22-24
Lahore Shalimar v Sui Northern Gas	Lahore[11]	Oct 22-25
National Bank v ZTBL	Faisalabad[4]	Oct 22-23
Customs v PIA	Karachi[16]	Oct 22-25
Rawalpindi v Quetta	Islamabad[6]	Oct 22-24
Sialkot v Multan	Sialkot[1]	Oct 22-25
Abbottabad v Sialkot	Abbottabad	Oct 28-30
Faisalabad v Lahore Ravi	Faisalabad[4]	Oct 28-31
Habib Bank v National Bank	Lahore[8]	Oct 28-31
Hyderabad v Peshawar	Muridke	Oct 28-31
Islamabad v Quetta	Islamabad[5]	Oct 28-31
Karachi Blues v Rawalpindi	Islamabad[6]	Oct 28-30
Karachi Whites v PIA	Karachi[5]	Oct 28-31
KRL v ZTBL	Rawalpindi[4]	Oct 28-31
Lahore Shalimar v WAPDA	Lahore[11]	Oct 28-30
Sui Northern Gas v Sui Southern Gas	Sheikhupura	Oct 28-30
Habib Bank v ZTBL	Islamabad[1]	Nov 3-6
Islamabad v Faisalabad	Islamabad[5]	Nov 3-6
Karachi Blues v Multan	Karachi[5]	Nov 3-6
KRL v Sui Northern Gas	Rawalpindi[4]	Nov 3-6
Lahore Ravi v Hyderabad	Lahore[11]	Nov 3-6
Lahore Shalimar v Customs	Muridke	Nov 3-5
National Bank v Sui Southern Gas	Faisalabad[4]	Nov 3-6
PIA v WAPDA	Lahore[8]	Nov 3-6
Peshawar v Rawalpindi	Islamabad[6]	Nov 3-5
Sialkot v Quetta	Sialkot[1]	Nov 3-5
Abbottabad v Peshawar	Abbottabad	Nov 9-12
Faisalabad v Quetta	Sargodha[1]	Nov 9-12
Habib Bank v Sui Southern Gas	Rawalpindi[4]	Nov 9-12
Hyderabad v Multan	Hyderabad[2]	Nov 9-11
Islamabad v Rawalpindi	Islamabad[5]	Nov 9-12
Karachi Blues v Lahore Ravi	Karachi[5]	Nov 9-12
Lahore Shalimar v Karachi Whites	Lahore[8]	Nov 9-12
National Bank v PIA	Faisalabad[4]	Nov 9-12
Customs v Sui Northern Gas	Islamabad[1]	Nov 9-12
WAPDA v ZTBL	Gujranwala[1]	Nov 9-12
Habib Bank v Sui Northern Gas	Islamabad[5]	Nov 15-18
Islamabad v Peshawar	Islamabad[6]	Nov 15-18
Karachi Whites v WAPDA	Karachi[16]	Nov 15-18
KRL v National Bank	Rawalpindi[4]	Nov 15-18
Lahore Ravi v Quetta	Lahore[11]	Nov 15-17
Lahore Shalimar v Sui Southern Gas	Lahore[8]	Nov 15-18
Multan v Abbottabad	Okara	Nov 15-18
Customs v ZTBL	Islamabad[1]	Nov 15-18
Sialkot v Rawalpindi	Sialkot[1]	Nov 15-18
Karachi Blues v Faisalabad	Karachi[5]	Nov 16-19
Habib Bank v PIA	Islamabad[1]	Nov 21-23
Hyderabad v Faisalabad	Hyderabad[2]	Nov 21-24
Islamabad v Abbottabad	Islamabad[5]	Nov 21-23
Karachi Whites v Sui Northern Gas	Karachi[5]	Nov 21-24
Lahore Ravi v Rawalpindi	Lahore[11]	Nov 21-24
Multan v Quetta	Okara	Nov 21-23

National Bank v Customs	Islamabad[6]	Nov 21-23
Sialkot v Peshawar	Sialkot[1]	Nov 21-24
Sui Southern Gas v ZTBL	Lahore[8]	Nov 21-24
KRL v WAPDA	Rawalpindi[4]	Nov 22-25
Faisalabad v Rawalpindi	Faisalabad[4]	Dec 3-6
Habib Bank v Customs	Islamabad[5]	Dec 3-6
Hyderabad v Karachi Blues	Mirpur Khas[2]	Dec 3-5
Karachi Whites v ZTBL	Karachi[12]	Dec 3-6
Lahore Ravi v Abbottabad	Muridke	Dec 3-6
Lahore Shalimar v KRL	Lahore[8]	Dec 3-6
Multan v Peshawar	Multan[5]	Dec 3-6
PIA v Sui Northern Gas	Gujranwala[1]	Dec 3-6
Sialkot v Islamabad	Sialkot[1]	Dec 3-6
Sui Southern Gas v WAPDA	Sheikhupura	Dec 3-6
Abbottabad v Rawalpindi	Islamabad[6]	Dec 9-12
Hyderabad v Sialkot	Hyderabad[2]	Dec 9-12
Karachi Blues v Quetta	Karachi[5]	Dec 9-12
Karachi Whites v National Bank	Karachi[16]	Dec 9-12
KRL v Sui Southern Gas	Rawalpindi[4]	Dec 9-12
Lahore Ravi v Peshawar	Lahore[11]	Dec 9-12
Lahore Shalimar v PIA	Lahore[8]	Dec 9-12
Multan v Islamabad	Multan[5]	Dec 9-12
Customs v WAPDA	Islamabad[5]	Dec 9-12
Sui Northern Gas v ZTBL	Gujranwala[1]	Dec 9-12
Faisalabad v Abbottabad	Sargodha[1]	Dec 15-18
Hyderabad v Quetta	Mirpur Khas[2]	Dec 15-18
Karachi Blues v Sialkot	Karachi[5]	Dec 15-18
Karachi Whites v Sui Southern Gas	Karachi[11]	Dec 15-18
KRL v Customs	Rawalpindi[4]	Dec 15-17
Lahore Ravi v Islamabad	Lahore[11]	Dec 15-18
Lahore Shalimar v Habib Bank	Lahore[8]	Dec 15-17
Multan v Rawalpindi	Multan[5]	Dec 15-17
National Bank v Sui Northern Gas	Faisalabad[4]	Dec 15-18
PIA v ZTBL	Islamabad[5]	Dec 15-18
Karachi Blues v Habib Bank	Karachi[5]	Dec 21-23
Habib Bank v Sui Northern Gas	Karachi[16]	Jan 2-5
Karachi Blues v Sialkot	Karachi[5]	Jan 2-5
Karachi Blues v Sui Northern Gas	Karachi[16]	Jan 7-10
Sialkot v The Rest	Karachi[5]	Jan 7-10
Habib Bank v The Rest	Karachi[16]	Jan 13-16
Sialkot v Sui Northern Gas	Hyderabad[2]	Jan 13-15
Habib Bank v Sialkot	Karachi[5]	Jan 19-22
Karachi Blues v The Rest	Hyderabad[2]	Jan 19-21
Karachi Blues v Habib Bank	Karachi[5]	Jan 25-27
Sui Northern Gas v The Rest	Karachi[16]	Jan 25-28
Habib Bank v Sui Northern Gas	Karachi[5]	Jan 31-Feb 4

SOUTH AFRICA (117)

The amateur competition was played as one league all-play-all instead of in two groups.

Eagles v Cape Cobras	Bloemfontein[5]	Sep 17-20
Eagles v Lions	Kimberley[5]	Sep 24-27
Titans v Cape Cobras	Benoni[1]	Sep 24-27
Dolphins v Titans	Durban[5]	Oct 1-4
Free State v North West	Bloemfontein[5]	Oct 1-3
KwaZulu-Natal Inland v Western Province	Pietermaritzburg[1]	Oct 1-3
Lions v Warriors	Randjesfontein	Oct 1-4
Boland v Griqualand West	Paarl[1]	Oct 8-10
Border v Northerns	East London[3]	Oct 8-10
Free State v Namibia	Bloemfontein[5]	Oct 8-10
Gauteng v Eastern Province	Johannesburg[18]	Oct 8-10
KwaZulu-Natal Inland v KwaZulu-Natal	Pietermaritzburg[1]	Oct 8-10
Titans v Warriors	Benoni[1]	Oct 8-8
Griqualand West v Namibia	Kimberley[5]	Oct 15-17
Warriors v Dolphins	Port Elizabeth[1]	Oct 15-18
Western Province v South Western Districts	Cape Town[7]	Oct 15-17
Eastern Province v North West	Port Elizabeth[5]	Oct 22-24
Free State v Boland	Bloemfontein[5]	Oct 22-24
Gauteng v Border	Johannesburg[6]	Oct 22-24
KwaZulu-Natal v Northerns	Durban[5]	Oct 22-24
KwaZulu-Natal Inland v Griqualand West	Pietermaritzburg[1]	Oct 22-24
Titans v Dolphins	Centurion	Oct 22-25
Warriors v Lions	East London[3]	Oct 22-25
Border v Western Province	East London[5]	Oct 29-31
Eastern Province v Free State	Port Elizabeth[1]	Oct 29-31
North West v KwaZulu-Natal Inland	Potchefstroom[3]	Oct 29-31
South Western Districts v Easterns	Oudtshoorn	Oct 29-31
Eastern Province v Griqualand West	Port Elizabeth[5]	Nov 5-7
KwaZulu-Natal v Boland	Chatsworth	Nov 5-7
North West v Western Province	Potchefstroom[4]	Nov 5-7
Northerns v Free State	Pretoria[7]	Nov 5-7
South Western Districts v Gauteng	Oudtshoorn	Nov 5-6
Border v Griqualand West	East London[5]	Nov 12-14
Cape Cobras v Lions	Cape Town[1]	Nov 12-15
Dolphins v Eagles	Pietermaritzburg[1]	Nov 12-15
Eastern Province v South Western Districts	Port Elizabeth[5]	Nov 12-14
Easterns v North West	Benoni[1]	Nov 12-13
Warriors v Titans	Port Elizabeth[1]	Nov 12-14
Dolphins v Cape Cobras	Durban[5]	Nov 19-22
Easterns v KwaZulu-Natal	Benoni[1]	Nov 19-21
Griqualand West v Western Province	Kimberley[5]	Nov 19-21
South Western Districts v Northerns	Oudtshoorn	Nov 19-21
Warriors v Eagles	East London[3]	Nov 19-22
Cape Cobras v Warriors	Paarl[1]	Nov 26-28
Eagles v Titans	Bloemfontein[5]	Nov 26-29
Lions v Dolphins	Johannesburg[9]	Nov 26-29
Cape Cobras v Eagles	Cape Town[1]	Dec 3-5
Lions v Titans	Potchefstroom[4]	Dec 3-6
Cape Cobras v Titans	Paarl[1]	Dec 10-12
Dolphins v Warriors	Durban[5]	Dec 10-13
Lions v Eagles	Johannesburg[9]	Dec 10-13
Eagles v Dolphins	Kimberley[5]	Dec 16-19
Lions v Cape Cobras	Johannesburg[9]	Dec 16-19
SOUTH AFRICA v ENGLAND	Centurion	Dec 16-20
Warriors v Titans	Port Elizabeth[1]	Dec 16-19
North West v South Western Districts	Potchefstroom[4]	Dec 17-19
Easterns v Boland	Benoni[1]	Dec 20-22
Gauteng v KwaZulu-Natal	Johannesburg[6]	Dec 20-22
SOUTH AFRICA v ENGLAND	Durban[5]	Dec 26-30
SOUTH AFRICA v ENGLAND	Cape Town[1]	Jan 3-7
Boland v Eastern Province	Paarl[1]	Jan 7-9
KwaZulu-Natal Inland v Easterns	Pietermaritzburg[1]	Jan 7-9
North West v Griqualand West	Potchefstroom[4]	Jan 7-9
South Western Districts v KwaZulu-Natal	Oudtshoorn	Jan 7-9
Boland v Northerns	Stellenbosch[3]	Jan 14-16
Border v Eastern Province	East London[3]	Jan 14-16
Easterns v Gauteng	Benoni[1]	Jan 14-16
KwaZulu-Natal v Western Province	Chatsworth	Jan 14-16
SOUTH AFRICA v ENGLAND	Johannesburg[9]	Jan 14-17
Free State v KwaZulu-Natal Inland	Bloemfontein[5]	Jan 21-23
Griqualand West v South Western Districts	Kimberley[5]	Jan 21-23
KwaZulu-Natal v Namibia	Durban[5]	Jan 21-23
Northerns v North West	Pretoria[7]	Jan 21-23
Western Province v Gauteng	Cape Town[7]	Jan 21-23
Boland v South Western Districts	Paarl[1]	Jan 28-30
Border v Free State	East London[5]	Jan 28-30

Eastern Province v Namibia	Port Elizabeth[1]	Jan 28-30
Northerns v Easterns	Pretoria[7]	Jan 28-30
Eastern Province v Easterns	Port Elizabeth[1]	Feb 4-5
Gauteng v North West	Johannesburg[9]	Feb 4-6
Griqualand West v Free State	Kimberley[5]	Feb 4-6
Northerns v Namibia	Pretoria[7]	Feb 4-6
Easterns v Border	Benoni[1]	Feb 11-13
North West v KwaZulu-Natal	Potchefstroom[4]	Feb 11-13
South Western Districts v KwaZulu-Natal Inland	Oudtshoorn	Feb 11-12
Western Province v Northerns	Cape Town[22]	Feb 11-13
Griqualand West v Gauteng	Kimberley[5]	Feb 18-19
South Western Districts v Border	Oudtshoorn	Feb 18-20
Western Province v Free State	Cape Town[1]	Feb 18-20
Border v Boland	East London[3]	Feb 25-27
Free State v South Western Districts	Bloemfontein[5]	Feb 25-27
KwaZulu-Natal v Griqualand West	Durban[5]	Feb 25-27
KwaZulu-Natal Inland v Gauteng	Pietermaritzburg[1]	Feb 25-27
Northerns v Eastern Province	Pretoria[7]	Feb 25-27
Western Province v Namibia	Cape Town[22]	Feb 25-27
Boland v North West	Paarl[1]	Mar 4-6
Easterns v Free State	Benoni[1]	Mar 4-6
Griqualand West v Northerns	Kimberley[5]	Mar 4-6
Western Province v Eastern Province	Cape Town[1]	Mar 4-6
Easterns v Western Province	Benoni[1]	Mar 11-12
Gauteng v Boland	Johannesburg[9]	Mar 11-13
KwaZulu-Natal v Eastern Province	Durban[5]	Mar 11-13
North West v Border	Potchefstroom[4]	Mar 11-13
Border v KwaZulu-Natal	East London[5]	Mar 18-19
Cape Cobras v Dolphins	Cape Town[1]	Mar 18-21
Eagles v Warriors	Bloemfontein[5]	Mar 18-21
Eastern Province v KwaZulu-Natal Inland	Port Elizabeth[1]	Mar 18-20
Northerns v Gauteng	Pretoria[7]	Mar 18-20
Titans v Lions	Benoni[1]	Mar 18-21
Dolphins v Lions	Durban[5]	Mar 25-27
Free State v KwaZulu-Natal	Bloemfontein[5]	Mar 25-27
Griqualand West v Easterns	Kimberley[5]	Mar 25-27
KwaZulu-Natal Inland v Northerns	Pietermaritzburg[1]	Mar 25-27
North West v Namibia	Potchefstroom[4]	Mar 25-27
Titans v Eagles	Centurion	Mar 25-28
Warriors v Cape Cobras	Port Elizabeth[1]	Mar 25-27
Western Province v Boland	Cape Town[1]	Mar 25-26

SRI LANKA (122)

The Inter-Provincial Tournament was shared when rain prevented any play in the final.

Bloomfield v Saracens	Colombo[10]	Oct 2-4
Burgher v Sebastianites	Colombo[7]	Oct 2-4
Colombo v Sinhalese	Colombo[2]	Oct 2-4
Colts v Ragama	Colombo[9]	Oct 2-4
Lankan v Singha	Katunayake	Oct 2-4
Moors v Tamil Union	Colombo[8]	Oct 2-4
Moratuwa v Police	Moratuwa[1]	Oct 2-4
Nondescripts v Badureliya	Colombo[1]	Oct 2-4
Sri Lanka Air Force v Panadura	Colombo[14]	Oct 2-4
Sri Lanka Army v Chilaw Marians	Panagoda	Oct 2-4
Sri Lanka Navy v Seeduwa Raddoluwa	Welisara	Oct 2-4
Chilaw Marians v Ragama	Katunayake	Oct 9-11
Colombo v Saracens	Colombo[2]	Oct 9-11
Colts v Sinhalese	Colombo[9]	Oct 9-11
Moors v Bloomfield	Colombo[8]	Oct 9-11
Nondescripts v Sri Lanka Army	Colombo[1]	Oct 9-11
Panadura v Moratuwa	Panadura	Oct 9-11
Seeduwa Raddoluwa v Burgher	Colombo[15]	Oct 9-11
Sri Lanka Air Force v Lankan	Colombo[14]	Oct 9-11
Tamil Union v Badureliya	Colombo[3]	Oct 9-11
Bloomfield v Badureliya	Colombo[10]	Oct 16-18
Colombo v Moors	Colombo[2]	Oct 16-18
Colts v Chilaw Marians	Colombo[9]	Oct 16-18
Moratuwa v Lankan	Moratuwa[1]	Oct 16-18
Nondescripts v Ragama	Colombo[1]	Oct 16-18
Panadura v Sebastianites	Panadura	Oct 16-18
Police v Burgher	Colombo[6]	Oct 16-18
Sinhalese v Saracens	Colombo[4]	Oct 16-18
Sri Lanka Air Force v Sri Lanka Navy	Colombo[14]	Oct 16-18
Tamil Union v Sri Lanka Army	Colombo[3]	Oct 16-18
Badureliya v Saracens	Panadura	Oct 23-25
Bloomfield v Sri Lanka Army	Colombo[10]	Oct 23-25
Burgher v Panadura	Colombo[7]	Oct 23-25
Colombo v Chilaw Marians	Colombo[2]	Oct 23-25
Colts v Nondescripts	Colombo[9]	Oct 23-25
Police v Seeduwa Raddoluwa	Colombo[6]	Oct 23-25
Ragama v Tamil Union	Colombo[1]	Oct 23-25
Sebastianites v Lankan	Moratuwa[1]	Oct 23-25
Sinhalese v Moors	Colombo[4]	Oct 23-25
Sri Lanka Air Force v Singha	Colombo[14]	Oct 23-25
Sri Lanka Navy v Moratuwa	Welisara	Oct 23-25
Bloomfield v Ragama	Colombo[15]	Oct 30-Nov 1
Burgher v Lankan	Katunayake	Oct 30-Nov 1
Moors v Badureliya	Colombo[8]	Oct 30-Nov 1
Nondescripts v Colombo	Colombo[1]	Oct 30-Nov 1
Panadura v Police	Panadura	Oct 30-Nov 1
Sebastianites v Sri Lanka Navy	Moratuwa[1]	Oct 30-Nov 1
Sinhalese v Chilaw Marians	Colombo[4]	Oct 30-Nov 1
Sri Lanka Air Force v Seeduwa Raddoluwa	Colombo[14]	Oct 30-Nov 1
Sri Lanka Army v Saracens	Panagoda	Oct 30-Nov 1
Tamil Union v Colts	Colombo[3]	Oct 30-Nov 1
Badureliya v Ragama	Colombo[3]	Nov 6-8
Bloomfield v Colts	Colombo[10]	Nov 6-8
Burgher v Singha	Colombo[7]	Nov 6-8
Chilaw Marians v Saracens	Colombo[9]	Nov 6-8
Colombo v Tamil Union	Colombo[2]	Nov 6-8
Moors v Sri Lanka Army	Colombo[8]	Nov 6-8
Nondescripts v Sinhalese	Colombo[1]	Nov 6-8
Panadura v Lankan	Panadura	Nov 6-8
Sebastianites v Sri Lanka Air Force	Moratuwa[1]	Nov 6-8
Seeduwa Raddoluwa v Moratuwa	Colombo[15]	Nov 6-8
Sri Lanka Navy v Police	Welisara	Nov 6-8
Colombo v Bloomfield	Colombo[2]	Nov 13-15
Moors v Ragama	Colombo[8]	Nov 13-15
Moratuwa v Sebastianites	Moratuwa[1]	Nov 13-15
Nondescripts v Chilaw Marians	Colombo[1]	Nov 13-15
Police v Singha	Colombo[6]	Nov 13-15
Seeduwa Raddoluwa v Lankan	Colombo[15]	Nov 13-15
Sri Lanka Army v Colts	Panagoda	Nov 13-15
Sri Lanka Navy v Panadura	Welisara	Nov 13-15
Tamil Union v Sinhalese	Colombo[3]	Nov 13-15
Moratuwa v Singha	Moratuwa[1]	Nov 20-22
Burgher v Moratuwa	Colombo[7]	Nov 27-29
Colombo v Badureliya	Colombo[2]	Nov 27-29
Colts v Saracens	Colombo[9]	Nov 27-29
Moors v Nondescripts	Colombo[8]	Nov 27-29
Panadura v Singha	Panadura	Nov 27-29
Police v Sri Lanka Air Force	Colombo[6]	Nov 27-29
Sebastianites v Seeduwa Raddoluwa	Moratuwa[1]	Nov 27-29
Sinhalese v Bloomfield	Colombo[4]	Nov 27-29
Sri Lanka Army v Ragama	Panagoda	Nov 27-29
Sri Lanka Navy v Lankan	Welisara	Nov 27-29
Tamil Union v Chilaw Marians	Colombo[3]	Nov 27-29
Bloomfield v Chilaw Marians	Katunayake	Dec 4-6B
Burgher v Sri Lanka Navy	Colombo[7]	Dec 4-6
Colts v Colombo	Colombo[9]	Dec 4-6
Moors v Saracens	Colombo[8]	Dec 4-6
Nondescripts v Tamil Union	Colombo[1]	Dec 4-6
Police v Lankan	Colombo[6]	Dec 4-6
Sebastianites v Singha	Colombo[10]	Dec 4-6
Seeduwa Raddoluwa v Panadura	Colombo[15]	Dec 4-6
Sinhalese v Ragama	Colombo[4]	Dec 4-6
Sri Lanka Army v Badureliya	Panagoda	Dec 4-6
Moratuwa v Sri Lanka Air Force	Moratuwa[1]	Dec 6-8
Badureliya v Chilaw Marians	Katunayake	Dec 11-13
Bloomfield v Nondescripts	Colombo[10]	Dec 11-13
Colombo v Ragama	Colombo[1]	Dec 11-13
Colts v Moors	Colombo[9]	Dec 11-13
Police v Sebastianites	Colombo[6]	Dec 11-13

Sinhalese v Sri Lanka Army	Colombo[4]	Dec 11-13
Sri Lanka Air Force v Burgher	Colombo[14]	Dec 11-13
Tamil Union v Saracens	Colombo[3]	Dec 11-13
Sri Lanka Navy v Singha	Welisara	Dec 14-16
Bloomfield v Tamil Union	Colombo[10]	Dec 18-20
Nondescripts v Saracens	Colombo[1]	Dec 18-20
Seeduwa Raddoluwa v Singha	Colombo[17]	Dec 18-20
Sinhalese v Badureliya	Colombo[4]	Dec 18-20
Sri Lanka Army v Colombo	Panagoda	Dec 18-20
Colts v Badureliya	Colombo[9]	Dec 26-28
Moors v Chilaw Marians	Colombo[8]	Dec 26-28
Ragama v Saracens	Colombo[1]	Dec 26-28
Afghanistan v Ireland	Dambulla	Jan 21-24
Basnahira North v Kandurata	Colombo[8]	Mar 18-21
Wayamba v Basnahira South	Pallekele	Mar 18-20
Basnahira South v Kandurata	Colombo[10]	Mar 25-28
Ruhuna v Basnahira North	Galle	Mar 25-28
Basnahira North v Basnahira South	Moratuwa[1]	Apr 3-6
uhuna v Wayamba	Colombo[9]	Apr 3-6
Basnahira North v Wayamba	Moratuwa[1]	Apr 22-25
Kandurata v Ruhuna	Colombo[3]	Apr 22-25
Basnahira South v Ruhuna	Colombo[9]	May 6-9
Kandurata v Wayamba	Kandy[2]	May 6-9

UNITED ARAB EMIRATES (2)

United Arab Emirates v Uganda	Abu Dhabi	Jan 20-23
Afghanistan v Canada	Sharjah	Feb 20-23

WEST INDIES (22)

The four day competition changed so that the teams played each other once with all three matches in each round being played in the same country, the teams each having one round at home with CCC's round being played in Barbados. The Jamaica v Ireland match was part of the Jamaica Festival of Cricket which also included Canada and featured mostly limited overs matches.

Barbados v Leeward Islands	Kingston[2]	Jan 8-11
Combined Campuses and Colleges v Trinidad and Tobago	Montego Bay	Jan 8-11
Jamaica v Windward Islands	Spanish Town	Jan 8-11
Barbados v Combined Campuses and Colleges	Charlestown	Jan 15-18
Guyana v Trinidad and Tobago	North Sound	Jan 15-18
Leeward Islands v Jamaica	Basseterre	Jan 15-18
Barbados v Trinidad and Tobago	Bridgetown[3]	Jan 22-25
Combined Campuses and Colleges v Windward Islands	Bridgetown[4]	Jan 22-24
Guyana v Jamaica	St Philip	Jan 22-25
Barbados v Windward Islands	Bridgetown[3]	Jan 29-Feb 1
Combined Campuses and Colleges v Guyana	Bridgetown[4]	Jan 29-31
Leeward Islands v Trinidad and Tobago	St Philip	Jan 29-Feb 1
Combined Campuses and Colleges v Jamaica	Providence	Feb 12-15
Guyana v Barbados	Albion	Feb 12-15
Leeward Islands v Windward Islands	Georgetown[2]	Feb 12-15
Barbados v Jamaica	St Augustine	Feb 19-21
Guyana v Leeward Islands	Couva	Feb 19-22
Trinidad and Tobago v Windward Islands	Port of Spain[2]	Feb 19-22
Combined Campuses and Colleges v Leeward Islands	Gros Islet	Feb 26-28
Jamaica v Trinidad and Tobago	St Andrew's	Feb 26-28
Windward Islands v Guyana	St George's[3]	Feb 26-Mar 1
Jamaica v Ireland	Spanish Town	Apr 3-5

ZIMBABWE (33)

The teams for the Logan Cup were given new names with Southerns returning. The teams played each other three times before the top two played in the final, the original intention to play home and away twice being curtailed because of international commitments.

Zimbabwe XI v Afghanistan	Mutare	Aug 16-19
Mashonaland Eagles v Mountaineers	Harare[1]	Sep 14-17
Mid West Rhinos v Matabeleland Tuskers	Kwekwe	Sep 14-17
Mid West Rhinos v Mashonaland Eagles	Kwekwe	Sep 22-25
Mountaineers v Southern Rocks	Mutare	Sep 22-25
Mashonaland Eagles v Southern Rocks	Harare[10]	Sep 30-Oct 3
Matabeleland Tuskers v Mountaineers	Bulawayo[1]	Sep 30-Oct 3
Zimbabwe XI v Kenya	Kwekwe	Oct 7-10
Matabeleland Tuskers v Mashonaland Eagles	Bulawayo[1]	Oct 14-17
Southern Rocks v Mid West Rhinos	Masvingo	Oct 14-17
Mountaineers v Mid West Rhinos	Mutare	Oct 22-25
Southern Rocks v Matabeleland Tuskers	Masvingo	Oct 22-25
Matabeleland Tuskers v Mid West Rhinos	Bulawayo[1]	Nov 16-19
Mountaineers v Mashonaland Eagles	Mutare	Nov 16-19
Mashonaland Eagles v Mid West Rhinos	Harare[1]	Nov 24-27
Southern Rocks v Mountaineers	Masvingo	Nov 24-27
Mountaineers v Matabeleland Tuskers	Mutare	Dec 2-5
Southern Rocks v Mashonaland Eagles	Masvingo	Dec 2-5
Mashonaland Eagles v Matabeleland Tuskers	Harare[1]	Dec 10-13
Mid West Rhinos v Southern Rocks	Kwekwe	Dec 10-13
Matabeleland Tuskers v Southern Rocks	Bulawayo[1]	Jan 4-6
Mid West Rhinos v Mountaineers	Kwekwe	Jan 4-7
Mashonaland Eagles v Mountaineers	Harare[1]	Jan 13-16
Mid West Rhinos v Matabeleland Tuskers	Kwekwe	Jan 13-16
Mid West Rhinos v Mashonaland Eagles	Kwekwe	Jan 20-23
Mountaineers v Southern Rocks	Mutare	Jan 20-23
Mashonaland Eagles v Southern Rocks	Harare[1]	Jan 27-30
Matabeleland Tuskers v Mountaineers	Bulawayo[1]	Jan 27-30
Matabeleland Tuskers v Mashonaland Eagles	Bulawayo[1]	Feb 3-6
Southern Rocks v Mid West Rhinos	Masvingo	Feb 3-6
Mountaineers v Mid West Rhinos	Mutare	Mar 23-25
Southern Rocks v Matabeleland Tuskers	Masvingo	Mar 23-26
Mashonaland Eagles v Mid West Rhinos	Harare[1]	Mar 30-Apr 3

2010

AUSTRALIA (2)

Australia A v Sri Lanka A	Brisbane[3]	Jun 18-21
Australia A v Sri Lanka A	Townsville[2]	Jun 25-27

BANGLADESH (4)

Bangladesh A v South Africa A	Mirpur	Apr 23-26
Bangladesh A v South Africa A	Savar[2]	Apr 29-May 2
Bangladesh A v West Indies A	Mirpur	May 17-20
Bangladesh A v West Indies A	Savar[2]	May 23-26

BERMUDA (1)

Bermuda v United Arab Emirates	Hamilton	July 5-7

CANADA (2)

Canada v Zimbabwe XI	King City[1]	Aug 2-4
Canada v Ireland	Toronto[2]	Aug 31-Sep 3

ENGLAND (171)

The traditional MCC v county champions fixture was staged by MCC for the first time outside of England in the UAE and so is counted as part of the UAE season.

Cambridge MCCU v Surrey	Cambridge[2]	Apr 3-5
Oxford MCCU v Northamptonshire	Oxford[4]	Apr 3-5
Essex v Hampshire	Chelmsford[1]	Apr 9-12
Glamorgan v Sussex	Cardiff[2]	Apr 9-12
Leicestershire v Northamptonshire	Leicester[3]	Apr 9-12
Surrey v Derbyshire	Kennington	Apr 9-12
Warwickshire v Yorkshire	Birmingham[3]	Apr 9-12
Worcestershire v Middlesex	Worcester	Apr 9-11
Durham MCCU v Nottinghamshire	Durham	Apr 10-12
Kent v Loughborough MCCU	Canterbury[2]	Apr 10-12
Derbyshire v Leicestershire	Derby	Apr 15-18
Durham v Essex	Chester-le-Street[2]	Apr 15-18
Gloucestershire v Northamptonshire	Bristol[1]	Apr 15-17
Lancashire v Warwickshire	Manchester[3]	Apr 15-18
Middlesex v Glamorgan	Lord's[3]	Apr 15-18
Nottinghamshire v Kent	Nottingham[2]	Apr 15-17
Oxford MCCU v Hampshire	Oxford[4]	Apr 15-17
Sussex v Surrey	Hove[2]	Apr 15-18
Yorkshire v Somerset	Leeds[1]	Apr 15-18
Cambridge MCCU v Leicestershire	Cambridge[2]	Apr 21-23
Derbyshire v Glamorgan	Derby	Apr 21-24

Durham v Hampshire	Chester-le-Street[2]	Apr 21-24
Essex v Lancashire	Chelmsford[1]	Apr 21-23
Gloucestershire v Sussex	Bristol[1]	Apr 21-23
Kent v Yorkshire	Canterbury[2]	Apr 21-24
Northamptonshire v Middlesex	Northampton[2]	Apr 21-24
Nottinghamshire v Somerset	Nottingham[2]	Apr 21-23
Surrey v Worcestershire	Croydon	Apr 21-24
Lancashire v Kent	Manchester[3]	Apr 27-30
Middlesex v Gloucestershire	Lord's[3]	Apr 27-30
Northamptonshire v Derbyshire	Northampton[2]	Apr 27-30
Somerset v Essex	Taunton	Apr 27-30
Sussex v Leicestershire	Hove[2]	Apr 27-29
Warwickshire v Hampshire	Birmingham[3]	Apr 27-30
Worcestershire v Glamorgan	Worcester	Apr 27-28
Yorkshire v Durham	Leeds[1]	Apr 27-30
Hampshire v Nottinghamshire	Southampton[4]	May 4-7
Kent v Warwickshire	Canterbury[2]	May 4-7
Lancashire v Somerset	Manchester[3]	May 4-7
Leicestershire v Worcestershire	Leicester[3]	May 4-7
Surrey v Gloucestershire	Kennington	May 4-6
Yorkshire v Essex	Scarborough	May 4-6
Durham MCCU v Durham	Durham	May 5-7
Sussex v Middlesex	Hove[2]	May 5-8
Surrey v Bangladeshis	Kennington	May 9-11
Essex v Kent	Chelmsford[1]	May 10-13
Glamorgan v Northamptonshire	Cardiff[2]	May 10-13
Gloucestershire v Leicestershire	Bristol[1]	May 10-13
Hampshire v Somerset	Southampton[4]	May 10-13
Middlesex v Derbyshire	Lord's[3]	May 10-12
Nottinghamshire v Durham	Nottingham[2]	May 10-13
Yorkshire v Loughborough MCCU	Leeds[1]	May 10-12
Cambridge MCCU v Sussex	Cambridge[2]	May 12-14
Essex v Bangladeshis	Chelmsford[1]	May 14-16
Glamorgan v Gloucestershire	Cardiff[2]	May 17-20
Kent v Durham	Canterbury[2]	May 17-20
Nottinghamshire v Hampshire	Nottingham[2]	May 17-20
Somerset v Yorkshire	Taunton	May 17-20
Surrey v Middlesex	Kennington	May 17-20
Warwickshire v Lancashire	Birmingham[3]	May 17-20
Worcestershire v Derbyshire	Worcester	May 17-20
Northamptonshire v Sussex	Northampton[2]	May 18-20
England Lions v Bangladeshis	Derby	May 19-21
Derbyshire v Gloucestershire	Derby	May 24-27
Durham v Kent	Chester-le-Street[2]	May 24-25
Hampshire v Yorkshire	Southampton[4]	May 24-27
Lancashire v Essex	Manchester[3]	May 24-27
Leicestershire v Glamorgan	Leicester[3]	May 24-26
Northamptonshire v Surrey	Northampton[2]	May 24-27
Somerset v Warwickshire	Taunton	May 24-26
Sussex v Worcestershire	Hove[2]	May 24-27
Oxford MCCU v Middlesex	Oxford[4]	May 25-27
ENGLAND v BANGLADESH	Lord's[3]	May 27-31
Glamorgan v Surrey	Cardiff[2]	May 29-Jun 1
Leicestershire v Middlesex	Leicester[3]	May 29-Jun 1
Nottinghamshire v Essex	Nottingham[2]	May 29-Jun 1
Warwickshire v Durham	Birmingham[3]	May 29-Jun 1
Worcestershire v Gloucestershire	Worcester	May 29-Jun 1
Yorkshire v Lancashire	Leeds[1]	May 29-Jun 1
ENGLAND v BANGLADESH	Manchester[3]	Jun 4-6
Hampshire v Essex	Southampton[4]	Jun 4-7
Kent v Nottinghamshire	Tunbridge Wells[2]	Jun 4-7
Middlesex v Northamptonshire	Lord's[3]	Jun 4-7
Surrey v Leicestershire	Kennington	Jun 4-6
Warwickshire v Somerset	Birmingham[3]	Jun 4-6
Derbyshire v Sussex	Derby	Jun 5-8
Glamorgan v West Indies A	Cardiff[2]	Jun 5-7
Yorkshire v India A	Leeds[1]	Jun 5-7
India A v West Indies A	Leicester[3]	Jun 10-13
India A v West Indies A	Croydon	Jun 17-20
Derbyshire v Surrey	Chesterfield[2]	Jun 28-July 1
Durham v Warwickshire	Chester-le-Street[2]	Jun 28-July 1
Gloucestershire v Middlesex	Bristol[1]	Jun 28-30
Kent v Pakistanis	Canterbury[2]	Jun 28-30
Lancashire v Yorkshire	Manchester[3]	Jun 28-July 1
Worcestershire v Leicestershire	Worcester	Jun 28-30
Essex v Nottinghamshire	Chelmsford[1]	July 5-7
Hampshire v Kent	Southampton[4]	July 5-7
Northamptonshire v Glamorgan	Northampton[2]	July 5-7
Yorkshire v Warwickshire	Leeds[1]	July 5-8
Oxford University v Cambridge University	Oxford[4]	July 6-9
Sussex v Gloucestershire	Arundel	July 7-9
AUSTRALIA v PAKISTAN	Lord's[3]	July 13-16
Durham v Lancashire	Chester-le-Street[2]	July 20-23
Essex v Yorkshire	Chelmsford[1]	July 20-23
Somerset v Kent	Taunton	July 20-23
Surrey v Northamptonshire	Kennington	July 20-22
Warwickshire v Nottinghamshire	Birmingham[3]	July 20-22
AUSTRALIA v PAKISTAN	Leeds[1]	July 21-24
Derbyshire v Worcestershire	Derby	July 21-24
Glamorgan v Leicestershire	Swansea	July 21-24
Middlesex v Sussex	Uxbridge[2]	July 21-24
ENGLAND v PAKISTAN	Nottingham[2]	July 29-Aug 1
Hampshire v Lancashire	Southampton[4]	July 29-Aug 1
Kent v Essex	Canterbury[2]	July 29-Aug 1
Leicestershire v Sussex	Leicester[3]	July 29-31
Middlesex v Surrey	Lord's[3]	July 29-31
Somerset v Nottinghamshire	Taunton	July 29-31
Worcestershire v Northamptonshire	Worcester	July 29-31
Gloucestershire v Glamorgan	Cheltenham[1]	July 30-Aug 1
Hampshire v Durham	Basingstoke	Aug 3-6
Kent v Somerset	Canterbury[2]	Aug 3-6
Leicestershire v Derbyshire	Leicester[3]	Aug 3-6
Yorkshire v Nottinghamshire	Leeds[1]	Aug 3-6
Essex v Warwickshire	Southend-on-Sea[2]	Aug 4-6
Gloucestershire v Worcestershire	Cheltenham[1]	Aug 4-7
ENGLAND v PAKISTAN	Birmingham[3]	Aug 6-9
Derbyshire v Northamptonshire	Chesterfield[2]	Aug 9-12
Glamorgan v Worcestershire	Colwyn Bay[1]	Aug 9-12
Lancashire v Durham	Manchester[3]	Aug 9-12
Middlesex v Leicestershire	Lord's[3]	Aug 9-12
Somerset v Hampshire	Taunton	Aug 9-12
Surrey v Sussex	Guildford	Aug 9-12
Durham v Yorkshire	Chester-le-Street[2]	Aug 16-19
Glamorgan v Middlesex	Cardiff[2]	Aug 16-19
Northamptonshire v Gloucestershire	Northampton[3]	Aug 16-18
Nottinghamshire v Warwickshire	Nottingham[2]	Aug 16-17
Worcestershire v Surrey	Worcester	Aug 16-19
ENGLAND v PAKISTAN	Kennington	Aug 18-21
Essex v Somerset	Colchester[1]	Aug 18-20
Kent v Lancashire	Canterbury[2]	Aug 18-21
Sussex v Derbyshire	Horsham[2]	Aug 18-20
Yorkshire v Hampshire	Scarborough	Aug 23-26
Leicestershire v Surrey	Leicester[3]	Aug 24-27
Nottinghamshire v Lancashire	Nottingham[2]	Aug 24-27
Somerset v Durham	Taunton	Aug 24-27
Derbyshire v Middlesex	Derby	Aug 25-28
Northamptonshire v Worcestershire	Northampton[2]	Aug 25-28
Warwickshire v Essex	Birmingham[3]	Aug 25-28
ENGLAND v PAKISTAN	Lord's[3]	Aug 26-29
Sussex v Glamorgan	Hove[2]	Aug 27-30
Durham v Nottinghamshire	Chester-le-Street[2]	Aug 31-Sep 3
Gloucestershire v Derbyshire	Bristol[1]	Aug 31-Sep 1
Lancashire v Hampshire	Liverpool[2]	Aug 31-Sep 3
Warwickshire v Kent	Birmingham[3]	Aug 31-Sep 2
Essex v Durham	Chelmsford[1]	Sep 7-10
Kent v Hampshire	Canterbury[2]	Sep 7-10
Leicestershire v Gloucestershire	Leicester[3]	Sep 7-10
Middlesex v Worcestershire	Lord's[3]	Sep 7-10
Nottinghamshire v Yorkshire	Nottingham[2]	Sep 7-9

Somerset v Lancashire	Taunton	Sep 7-9
Surrey v Glamorgan	Kennington	Sep 7-10
Sussex v Northamptonshire	Hove[2]	Sep 7-9
Durham v Somerset	Chester-le-Street[2]	Sep 13-16
Glamorgan v Derbyshire	Cardiff[2]	Sep 13-16
Gloucestershire v Surrey	Bristol[1]	Sep 13-16
Hampshire v Warwickshire	Southampton[4]	Sep 13-16
Lancashire v Nottinghamshire	Manchester[3]	Sep 13-16
Northamptonshire v Leicestershire	Northampton[2]	Sep 13-16
Worcestershire v Sussex	Worcester	Sep 13-16
Yorkshire v Kent	Leeds[1]	Sep 13-16

IRELAND (1)

Ireland v Netherlands	Dublin[2]	Aug 11-13

NETHERLANDS (2)

Netherlands v Scotland	Deventer	Jun 10-13
Netherlands v Zimbabwe XI	Amstelveen	July 25-28

SCOTLAND (1)

Scotland v Afghanistan	Ayr[2]	Aug 11-14

SRI LANKA (9)

Sri Lanka Board President's XI v Indians	Colombo[9]	July 13-15
SRI LANKA v INDIA	Galle	July 18-22
SRI LANKA v INDIA	Colombo[4]	July 26-30
SRI LANKA v INDIA	Colombo[3]	Aug 3-7
Sri Lanka A v South Africa A	Pallekele	Aug 10-13
Sri Lanka A v South Africa A	Colombo[4]	Aug 16-19
Sri Lanka A v Pakistan A	Galle	Sep 9-12
Sri Lanka A v Pakistan A	Hambantota	Sep 15-17

UNITED ARAB EMIRATES (1)

MCC v Durham	Abu Dhabi	Mar 29-Apr 1

WEST INDIES (4)

West Indies A v Zimbabweans	St George's[3]	Apr 16-19
WEST INDIES v SOUTH AFRICA	Port of Spain[2]	Jun 10-13
WEST INDIES v SOUTH AFRICA	Basseterre	Jun 18-22
WEST INDIES v SOUTH AFRICA	Bridgetown[3]	Jun 26-29

A total of 52,567 first-class matches had been played by the end of the 2019 season. This total excludes matches already played in seasons designated 2010/11.

This total includes 237 matches from the 18th century which the ACS now include in the enumeration of matches.

MATCHES ABANDONED WITHOUT A BALL BEING BOWLED

The following matches would have been first-class had any play taken place. Unless otherwise indicated, the abandonment was due to bad weather. These matches are not counted in the enumeration of first-class matches, nor in first-class career records.

INDIA

2009/10	Nov 3-6	Jammu and Kashmir v Services (Services did not turn up for this match and were expelled from the Ranji Trophy by the BCCI and so their other matches were cancelled)	Srinagar (2)
	Nov 10-13	Andhra v Services	Visakhapatnam (5)
	Nov 11-13	Indian Board President's XI v Sri Lankans	Mumbai (8)
	Nov 17-20	Haryana v Services	Sirsa
	Dec 1-4	Services v Kerala	Delhi (6)
	Dec 8-11	Madhya Pradesh v Services	Indore (7)

SOUTH AFRICA

2009/10	Nov 12-14	Boland v KwaZulu-Natal Inland	Paarl (1)
	Nov 19-21	Gauteng v Free State (As this match was abandoned Lindique Oval, Alberton has yet to stage a first-class match)	Alberton
	Nov 19-21	KwaZulu-Natal Inland v Border	Pietermaritzburg (1)

SRI LANKA

2010	May 13-16	Basnahira North v Basnahira South	Colombo (4)

ENGLAND

2010	Apr 3-5	Derbyshire v Loughborough MCCU	Derby
	Apr 3-5	Durham MCCU v Lancashire	Durham

GROUNDS ON WHICH FIRST-CLASS MATCHES WERE PLAYED IN 2009/10 and 2010

Australia First-Class Grounds

Place	Ground Name	Home Team	First Match	Last Match	No of Matches
Adelaide (1)	Adelaide Oval	South Australia	1877/78	2009/10	578
Brisbane (2)	Brisbane Cricket Ground, Woolloongabba	Queensland	1897/98	2009/10	458
Brisbane (3)	Allan Border Field		1999/00	2010	11
Hobart (3)	Bellerive Oval	Tasmania	1987/88	2009/10	129
Melbourne (2)	Melbourne Cricket Ground	Victoria	1855/56	2009/10	638
Newcastle	No 1 Sports Ground	New South Wales	1981/82	2009/10	20
Perth	Western Australia Cricket Association Ground	Western Australia	1898/99	2009/10	420
Sydney (3)	Sydney Cricket Ground	New South Wales	1877/78	2009/10	651
Townsville (2)	Riverway Stadium	New South Wales	2009	2010	3
					3255

Bangladesh First-Class Grounds

Place	Ground Name	Home Team	First Match	Last Match	No of Matches
Bogra	Shaheed Chandu Stadium		2003/04	2009/10	21
Chittagong (2)	Chittagong Divisional Stadium	Chittagong Division	2004/05	2009/10	36
Fatullah	Fatullah Khan Saheb Osmani Stadium	Rajshahi Division	2002/03	2009/10	30
Khulna	Khulna Divisional Stadium	Khulna Division	2004/05	2009/10	28
Mirpur	Shere Bangla National Stadium	Dhaka Division	2005/06	2010	20
Rajshahi	Rajshahi Stadium	Rajshahi Division	2000/01	2009/10	36
Savar (1)	Bangladesh Krira Shikkha Protisthan Ground	Sylhet Division	2000/01	2009/10	10
Savar (2)	Bangladesh Krira Shikkha Protisthan No 2 Ground		2005/06	2010	4
					336

Bermuda First-Class Grounds

Place	Ground Name	Home Team	First Match	Last Match	No of Matches
Hamilton	National Stadium		1971/72	2010	6
					6

Canada First-Class Grounds

Place	Ground Name	Home Team	First Match	Last Match	No of Matches
King City (1)	Maple Leaf North-West Ground		2006	2010	3
Toronto (2)	Toronto Cricket, Skating and Curling Club		1951	2010	5
					15

England and Wales First-Class Grounds

Place	Ground Name	Home Team	First Match	Last Match	No of Matches
Arundel	Arundel Castle	Sussex	1990	2010	27
Basingstoke	May's Bounty	Hampshire	1906	2010	46
Birmingham (3)	Edgbaston	Warwickshire	1886	2010	1280
Bristol (1)	County Ground	Gloucestershire	1889	2010	782
Cambridge (2)	F.P.Fenner's Ground	Cambridge Univ	1848	2010	887
Canterbury (2)	St. Lawrence Ground	Kent	1847	2010	564
Cardiff (2)	Sophia Gardens	Glamorgan	1967	2010	249
Chelmsford (1)	County Ground,	Essex	1925	2010	319
Cheltenham (1)	College Ground	Gloucestershire	1872	2010	320
Chesterfield (2)	Queen's Park	Derbyshire	1898	2010	399
Chester-le-Street (2)	Riverside Ground	Durham	1995	2010	131
Colchester (1)	Castle Park Cricket Ground	Essex	1914	2010	117
Colwyn Bay (1)	Rhos Ground	Glamorgan	1930	2010	27
Croydon	Whitgift School	Surrey	2003	2010	9
Derby	County Ground	Derbyshire	1871	2010	731
Durham	The Racecourse, Durham University	Durham MCCU	1992	2010	25
Guildford	Woodbridge Road	Surrey	1938	2010	89
Horsham (2)	Cricket Field Road Ground	Sussex	1908	2010	99
Hove (2)	County Ground	Sussex	1872	2010	1156
Kennington	Kennington Oval	Surrey	1846	2010	2035
Leeds (1)	Headingley	Yorkshire	1890	2010	483
Leicester (3)	Grace Road	Leicestershire	1894	2010	772
Liverpool (2)	Aigburth	Lancashire	1881	2010	184
Lord's (3)	Lord's Cricket Ground	MCC / Middlesex	1814	2010	2736
Manchester (3)	Old Trafford	Lancashire	1860	2010	1373
Northampton (2)	County Ground	Northamptonshire	1905	2010	987
Nottingham (2)	Trent Bridge	Nottinghamshire	1840	2010	1519
Oxford (4)	The University Parks	Oxford University	1881	2010	775
Scarborough	North Marine Road Ground	Yorkshire	1874	2010	408
Southampton (4)	The Rose Bowl	Hampshire	2001	2010	82
Southend-on-Sea (2)	Garon Park	Essex	2005	2010	6
Swansea	St Helen's	Glamorgan	1912	2010	412
Taunton	County Ground	Somerset	1882	2010	812
Tunbridge Wells (2)	Nevill Ground	Kent	1901	2010	182
Uxbridge (2)	Uxbridge Cricket Club Ground, Park Road	Middlesex	1980	2010	39
Worcester	County Ground, New Road	Worcestershire	1899	2010	1083
					30061

India First-Class Grounds

	Place	Ground Name	Home Team	First Match	Last Match	No of Matches
	Agartala (2)	Maharaja Bir Bikram College Stadium	Tripura	1998/99	2009/10	26
	Ahmedabad (3)	Sardar Vallabhbhai Patel Stadium	Gujarat	1960/61	2009/10	25
	Ahmedabad (4)	Sardar Patel Stadium	Gujarat	1983/84	2009/10	44
	Amritsar	Gandhi Sports Complex Ground	Punjab	1933/34	2009/10	54
	Anantapur (3)	Rural Development Trust Stadium	Andhra	2004/05	2009/10	9
	Bangalore (4)	M.Chinnaswamy Stadium	Karnataka	1972/73	2009/10	128
	Bhubaneswar	East Coast Railway Sports Association Ground	Orissa	2008/09	2009/10	3
	Chandigarh	Sector 16 Stadium	Haryana	1965/66	2009/10	32
	Delhi (2)	Roshanara Club Ground	Delhi	1926/27	2009/10	15
	Delhi (5)	Palam A Ground, Model Sports Complex	Services	1958/59	2009/10	97
	Delhi (6)	Karnail Singh Stadium	Railways	1958/59	2009/10	127
NEW	Dhanbad	Railway Stadium	Jharkhand	2009/10	2009/10	2
	Dharmasala (2)	Himachal Pradesh Cricket Association Stadium	Himachel Pradesh	2003/04	2009/10	24
	Guwahati (2)	Nehru Stadium	Assam	1964/65	2009/10	39
	Guwahati (3)	North East Frontier Railway Stadium, Maligaon	Assam	1976/77	2009/10	33
	Hyderabad (2)	Rajiv Gandhi International Stadium, Uppal	Hyderabad	2004/05	2009/10	22
	Indore (6)	Maharani Usharaje Trust Cricket Ground	Madhya Pradesh	1996/97	2009/10	31
	Indore (7)	Emerald High School Ground	Madhya Pradesh	2008/09	2009/10	3
	Jaipur (4)	K.L.Saini Groud	Rajasthan	1991/92	2009/10	37
	Jammu (2)	Gandhi Memorial Science College Ground	Jammu and Kashmir	1976/77	2009/10	7
	Kanpur (1)	Modi Stadium	Uttar Pradesh	1945/46	2009/10	59
	Kolkata (1)	Eden Gardens	Bengal	1917/18	2009/10	268
	Kolkata (5)	Jadavpur University Complex	Bengal	2004/05	2009/10	3
	Lucknow (7)	Dr Akhilesh Das Stadium	Uttar Pradesh	2007/08	2009/10	2
	Margao (1)	Dr Rajendra Prasad Stadium	Goa	1967/68	2009/10	21
	Meerut (3)	Bhamashah Stadium	Uttar Pradesh	2003/04	2009/10	2
	Mohali	Punjab Cricket Association Stadium	Punjab	1993/94	2009/10	61
	Mohan Nagar	Narendra Mohan Sports Stadium	Uttar Pradesh	1976/77	2009/10	8
	Mumbai (4)	Brabourne Stadium	Mumbai	1937/38	2009/10	220
	Mumbai (8)	Bandra Kurla Complex	Mumbai	2008/09	2009/10	3
	Mysore (4)	Gangothri Glades Cricket Ground	Karnataka	2006/07	2009/10	6
	Nagpur (3)	Vidarbha Cricket Association Stadium, Namtha	Vidarbha	2008/09	2009/10	6
	Poona (3)	Pune Club Ground	Maharashtra	1935/36	2009/10	39
	Rajkot (2)	Madhavrao Scindia Cricket Ground	Saurashtra	1935/36	2009/10	97
	Rajkot (6)	Khanderi Cricket Stadium	Saurashtra	2008/09	2009/10	2
	Ranchi (1)	Metallurgical and Engineering Consultant Limited Sail Stadium	Bihar	1984/85	2009/10	18
	Rohtak (3)	Chaudhary Bansi Lal Cricket Stadium	Haryana	2006/07	2009/10	12
	Sambalpur	Veer Surendra Sai Stadium	Orissa	1973/74	2009/10	11
	Secunderabad (1)	Gymkhana Ground	Hyderabad	1930/31	2009/10	109

India First-Class Grounds						
	Place	Ground Name	Home Team	First Match	Last Match	No of Matches
	Srinagar (2)	Sher-i-Kashmir Stadium	Jammu and Kashmir	1985/85	2009/10	17
	Surat (7)	Lalabhai Contractor Stadium	Gujarat	1993/94	2009/10	11
NEW	Thalassery (2)	Conor Vyal Stadium	Kerala	2009/10	2009/10	1
	Vadodara (5)	Moti Bagh Stadium	Baroda	1957/58	2009/10	109
	Valsad (3)	Sardar Vallabhai Patel Stadium	Gujarat	1979/80	2009/10	21
	Vijawada (2)	Indira Gandhi Municipal Corporation Stadium	Andhra	1969/70	2009/10	24
						5085

Ireland First-Class Grounds						
	Place	Ground Name	Home Team	First Match	Last Match	No of Matches
	Dublin (2)	Rathmines		1998	2010	2
						13

Kenya First-Class Grounds						
	Place	Ground Name	Home Team	First Match	Last Match	No of Matches
	Nairobi (1)	Gymkhana Club Ground		1974/74	2009/10	11
						26

Namibia First-Class Grounds						
	Place	Ground Name	Home Team	First Match	Last Match	No of Matches
	Windhoek (2)	Wanderers Cricket Ground		2004	2009/10	28
						29

Netherlands First-Class Grounds						
	Place	Ground Name	Home Team	First Match	Last Match	No of Matches
	Amstelveen	VRA Ground		2007	2010	4
	Deventer	Sportpark Het Schootsveld		2004	2010	2
						9

New Zealand First-Class Grounds

	Place	Ground Name	Home Team	First Match	Last Match	No of Matches
	Auckland (6)	Colin Maiden Park	Auckland	1998/99	2009/10	11
	Christchurch (5)	Village Green	Canterbury	1998/99	2009/10	30
	Dunedin (5)	University Oval	Otago	1978/79	2009/10	24
	Hamilton	Seddon Park	Northern Districts	1956/57	2009/10	159
	Invercargill (2)	Queen's Park	Otago	1975/76	2009/10	15
	Napier (3)	Nelson Park	Central Districts	1919/20	2009/10	8
	Napier (4)	McLean Park	Central Districts	1951/52	2009/10	70
	New Plymouth	Pukekura Park	Central Districts	1950/51	2009/10	53
	Queenstown	Queenstown Events Centre	Otago	2001/02	2009/10	11
	Rangiora (2)	Recreation Ground	Canterbury	2003/04	2009/10	9
	Wellington (1)	Basin Reserve	Wellington	1873/74	2009/10	401
	Whangarei (2)	Cobham Oval (New)	Northern Districts	2008/09	2009/10	5
						2140

Pakistan First-Class Grounds

	Place	Ground Name	Home Team	First Match	Last Match	No of Matches
	Abbottabad	Abbottabad Cricket Stadium	Abbottabad	2003/04	2009/10	12
	Faisalabad (4)	Iqbal Stadium	Faisalabad	1966/67	2009/10	203
	Gujranwala (1)	Jinnah Stadium	Sialkot	1983/84	2009/10	58
	Hyderabad (2)	Niaz Stadium	Hyderabad	1961/62	2009/10	128
	Islamabad (1)	Marghzar Cricket Ground	Islamabad	1992/93	2009/10	23
	Islamabad (5)	Diamond Club Ground	Islamabad	2005/06	2009/10	41
NEW	Islamabad (6)	National Ground	Islamabad	2009/10	2009.10	7
	Karachi (5)	National Stadium	Karachi	1954/55	2009/10	490
	Karachi (11)	Defence Housing Authority Stadium	Karachi	1990/91	2009/10	23
	Karachi (12)	United Bank Limited Sports Complex	United Bank	1993/94	2009/10	109
	Karachi (16)	National Bank of Pakistan Sports Complex	National Bank	1998/99	2009/10	41
	Lahore (8)	Gaddafi Stadium	Lahore	1959/60	2009/10	350
	Lahore (11)	Lahore City Cricket Association Ground	Lahore	1979/80	2009/10	241
	Mirpur Khas (2)	Municipal Sports Stadium	Hyderabad	2008/09	2009/10	3
	Multan (5)	Multan Cricket Stadium	Multan	2001/02	2009/10	45
	Muridke	Lahore Country Club	Lahore	2001/02	2009/10	21
	Okara	Gymkhana Ground	Multan	2001/02	2009/10	12
	Rawalpindi (4)	Khan Research Laboratory Ground	KRL	1988/89	2009/10	131
	Sargodha (1)	Sargodha Stadium	Faisalabad	1955/56	2009/10	92
	Sheikhupura	Sheikhupura Stadium	Sheikhupura	1996/97	2009/10	76
	Sialkot (1)	Jinnah Stadium	Sialkot	1951/52	2009/10	91
						3595

Scotland First-Class Grounds

	Place	Ground Name	Home Team	First Match	Last Match	No of Matches
	Ayr(2)	Cambusdoon New Ground		2000	2010	3
						14

South Africa First-Class Grounds

	Place	Ground Name	Home Team	First Match	Last Match	No of Matches
	Benoni (1)	Willowmoore Park Main Oval	Easterns	1923/24	2009/10	108
	Bloemfontein (5)	Goodyear Park	Free State/Eagles	1989/90	2009/10	128
	Cape Town (1)	Newlands	Western Province/ Cape Cobras	1888/89	2009/10	417
	Cape Town (7)	Northerns-Goodwood Cricket Club Oval	Western Province B	1993/94	2009/10	5
NEW	Cape Town (22)	Durbanville Cricket Club Ground	Western Province B	2009/10	2009/10	2
	Centurion	Centurion Park	Northerns/Titans	1986//87	2009/10	134
	Chatsworth	Chatsworth Stadium	KwaZulu-Natal	1979/80	2009/10	18
	Durban (5)	Kingsmead	KwaZulu-Natal/ Dolphins	1922/23	2009/10	349
	East London (3)	Buffalo Park	Border/Warriors	1988/89	2009/10	113
	East London (5)	Schoeman Sports Ground, Buffalo Flats	Border	2008/09	2009/10	5
	Johannesburg (6)	Old Edwardians Cricket Club A Ground	Gauteng	1931/32	2009/10	4
	Johannnesburg (9)	New Wanderers Stadium	Gauteng/Lions	1956/57	2009/10	340
	Johannesburg (18)	Orban Park	Gauteng	2005/06	2009/10	3
	Kimberley (5)	De Beers Diamond Oval	Griqualand West	1973/74	2009/10	148
	Oudtshoorn	Recreation Ground	South Western Districts	2006/07	2009/10	16
	Paarl (1)	Boland Bank Park	Boland	1994/95	2009/10	75
	Pietermaritzburg (1)	City Oval	KwaZulu-Natal	1894/95	2009/10	65
	Port Elizabeth (1)	St George's Park	Eastern Province/ Warriors	1888/89	2009/10	339
	Port Elizabeth (5)	University of Port Elizabeth No 1 Oval	Eastern Province	1982/83	2009/10	15
	Potchefstroom (3)	Witrand Cricket Field	North West	1991/92	2009/10	13
	Potchefstroom (4)	North West Cricket Stadium	North West/Lions	1999/00	2009/10	67
	Pretoria (7)	L.C.de Villiers Oval	Northerns	1997/98	2009/10	25
	Randjesfontein	N.F.Oppenheimer Ground	Gauteng	1994/95	2009/10	4
NEW	Stellenbosch (3)	Van der Stel Cricket Club Ground	Boland	2009/10	2009/10	1
						3891

Sri Lanka First-Class Grounds

	Place	Ground Name	Home Team	First Match	Last Match	No of Matches
	Colombo (1)	Nondescripts Cricket Club Ground	Nondescripts	1925/26	2009/10	162
	Colombo (2)	Colombo Cricket Club Ground	Colombo	1926/27	2009/10	149
	Colombo (3)	P.Saravanamuttu Stadium	Tamil Union	1944/45	2010	212
	Colombo (4)	Sinhalese Sports Club Ground	Sinhalese	1971/72	2010	196
	Colombo (6)	Police Park Ground	Police	1974/74	2009/10	90
	Colombo (7)	Burgher Recreation Club Ground	Burgher	1988/89	2009/10	113
	Colombo (8)	Moors Sports Club Ground	Moors	1988/89	2009/10	142
	Colombo (9)	Colts Cricket Club Ground	Colts	1988/89	2010	141
	Colombo (10)	Bloomfield Cricket and Athletic Club Ground	Bloomfield	1991/92	2009/10	123
	Colombo (14)	Air Force Ground	Sri Lanka Air Force	2003/04	2009/10	32
	Colombo (15)	Thurstan College Ground	Seeduwa Raddoluwa	2005/06	2009/10	12
NEW	Colombo (17)	Ananda College Ground		2009/10	2009/10	1
	Dambulla	Rangiri Dambulla International Stadium		2001	2009.10	18
	Galle	Galle International Stadium		1983/84	2010	81
NEW	Hambantota	Mahinda Rajapaksha International Cricket Stadium		2010	2010	1
	Kandy (2)	Asgiriya Stadium		1975/76	2009/10	41
	Katunayake	FTZ Sports Complex (Board of Investment)		2000/01	2009/10	54
	Moratuwa (1)	Tyronne Fernando Stadium	Moratuwa / Sebastianites	1982/83	2009/19	142
NEW	Pallekele	Pallekele Cricket Stadium		2009/10	2010	2
	Panadura	Panadura Esplanade	Panadura	1988/89	2009/10	114
	Panagoda	Army Ground	Sri Lanka Army	2007/08	2009/10	15
	Welisara	Navy Ground	Sri Lanka Navy	2005/06	2009/10	14
						2093

United Arab Emirates First-Class Grounds

Place	Ground Name	Home Team	First Match	Last Match	No of Matches
Abu Dhabi	Sheikh Zayed Stadium		2004/05	2010	6
Sharjah	Sharjah Cricket Association Stadium		2001/02	2009/10	14
					20

West Indies First-Class Grounds

Place	Ground Name	Home Team	First Match	Last Match	No of Matches
Albion	Albion Spors Complex	Guyana	1978/79	2009/10	28
Basseterre, St Kitts	Warner Park	Leeward Islands	1961/62	2009/10	41
Bridgetown (3)	Kensington Oval	Barbados	1894/95	2010	268
Bridgetown (4)	Three Ws Oval	Barbados	2002/03	2009/10	14

West Indies First-Class Grounds

	Place	Ground Name	Home Team	First Match	Last Match	No of Matches
	Charlestown, Nevis	Grove Park	Leeward Islands	1976/77	2009/10	21
	Couva	National Cricket Centre	Trinidad and Tobago	2002/03	2009/10	6
	Georgetown (2)	Bourda	Guyana	1887/88	2009/10	187
	Gros Islet, St Lucia	Beausejour Stadium	Windward Islands	2001/02	2009/10	13
	Kingston (2)	Kensington Park	Jamaica	1908/09	2009/10	7
	Kingstown, St Vincent	Arnos Vale Ground	Windward Islands	1971/72	2009	42
	Montego Bay	Jarrett Park	Jamaica	1964/65	2009/10	18
	North Sound, Antigua	Sir Vivian Richards Stadium		2008	2009/10	3
	Port of Spain (2)	Queen's Park Oval	Trinidad and Tobago	1896/97	2010	237
	Providence	Providence Stadium	Guyana	2007/08	2009/10	8
	Spanish Town	Chedwin Park	Jamaica	1980/81	2009/10	22
	St Andrews, Grenada	Progress Park	Windward Islands	2008/09	2009/10	2
	St Augustine	Sir Frank Worrell Memorial Ground	Trinidad and Tobago	1973/74	2009/10	6
	St George's, Grenada (3)	Queen's Park (New)	Windward Islands	1999/00	2010	18
NEW	St Philip	Foursquare Park	Barbados	2009/10	2009/10	2
						1545

Zimbabwe First-Class Grounds

Place	Ground Name	Home Team	First Match	Last Match	No of Matches
Bulawayo (1)	Queens Sports Club	Matabeleland Tuskers	1980/81	2009/10	56
Harare (1)	Harare Sports Club	Mashonaland Eagles	1980/81	2009/10	130
Harare (10)	Harare Country Club		1999/00	2009/10	17
Kewkwe	Kwekwe Sports Club	Mid West Rhinos	1998/99	2009/10	36
Masvingo	Masvingo Sports Club	Southern Rocks	2006/07	2009/10	10
Mutare	Mutare Sports Club	Mountaineers	1999/00	2009/10	31
					358

GROUNDS USED IN MORE THAN ONE SECTION

Matches in Scotland and Ireland up to 1996 are included in the British Isles (now given as England and Wales) totals; once the ICC admitted them as Associate Members their matches are recorded separately.
Matches in Bermuda, Canada and USA were all grouped together in the totals in volume 5 of the ACS First-Class Match List but are now shown separately.
Matches in East Africa were all grouped together in the totals in volume 5 of the ACS First-Class Match List but matches in Kenya are now shown separately.
Matches in Zimbabwe prior to 1980/81 season (when Rhodesia) are included in the South Africa totals.
A match in 1988/89 played in what is now Namibia is included in the South Africa total.
Matches in what is now Pakistan played prior to partition in 1947/48 are included in the India total.
Matches in what is now Bangladesh played prior to independence in 1971 are included in the Pakistan total.

The following grounds which were used in 2009/10 or 2010 have totals included in more than one country:

Bulawayo	Queens Sports Club	South Africa/Zimbabwe	1909/10	2009/19	107
Dublin (2)	Rathmines	British Isles/Ireland	1912	2010	11
Harare	Harare Sports Club	South Africa/Zimbabwe	1909/10	2009/10	152

A total of 1,308 different grounds have been used for first-class cricket world-wide. This total includes the 18th century grounds now included by the ACS in the enumeration of matches.